THE NAVY LIST 2000

Corrected to 12th April 2000
(See Notes on page iii)

LONDON; The
Stationery Office

Published with the permission of the Ministry of Defence on behalf of the Controller of Her Majesty's Stationery Office.

First Published 2000

ISBN 0 11 772944 2

The Navy List is compiled and published by order of the Defence Council for the convenience of the Naval Service, but as errors may occasionally occur the Council must expressly reserve the right to determine the status of an Officer according to the actual circumstances of the case, independently of any entry in the Navy List

By Command of the Defence Council,

KEVIN TEBBIT

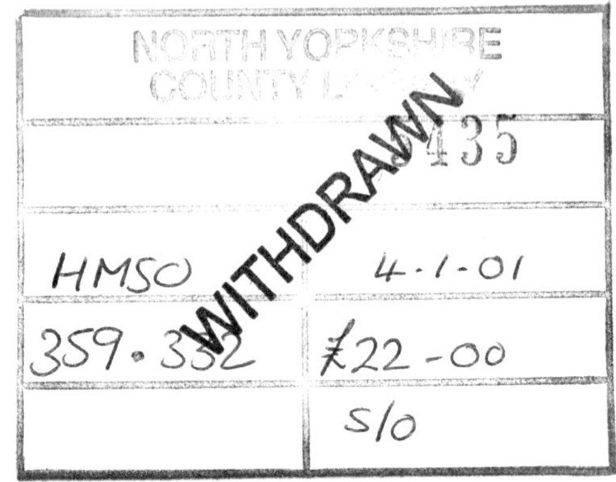

Printed in the United Kingdom by The Stationery Office Limited
TJ 002355 C25 10/00 544748

PREFACE

The Navy List is on sale to the public and is published annually in July or as soon as possible thereafter. The Navy List of Retired Officers, also on sale to the public, is published separately and biennially in August.

This edition of the Navy List has been produced largely from the information held in the Naval Manpower Management Information System and is corrected to include those promotions, appointments etc. promulgated on or before 12 April 2000 as becoming effective on or before 30 June 2000. Section 1 is corrected as far as possible, up to the date of going to press.

Serving officers who notice errors or omissions in Sections 2 and 3 of the List should advise their Appointer. Other errors or omissions should be brought to the attention of the Editor of the Navy List. Any other reader who notices errors or omissions is invited to write to:

MRS Tracy Ballinger
The Editor of the Navy List
2SL/CNH
Room 115
Victory Building
Portsmouth Naval Base
Portsmouth
Hampshire
PO1 3LS

quoting the page(s) in question. Every effort will be made to include corrections and omissions received by the Editor before 28 March. Regrettably, letters cannot be acknowledged.

Sections ten and eleven of this edition of the Navy List contain largely static data which was last published in the 1995 edition, and will next be published in the 2005 edition.

Officers who succeed to peerages, baronetcies or courtesy titles should notify their appointer so that their computer records can be updated and the changes reflected in the Navy List. The degrees shown after Active Service Officers' names are not necessarily a complete list of those held, but are generally confined to degrees of an honorary nature conferred specially upon an Officer, and those that are so related to the professional duties of an Officer as to give some indication of his professional qualifications.

The master Allowance List for the free distribution of the Navy List is controlled by the Editor. DSDC(L) at Llangennech is responsible for the issue of this publication strictly according to the Allowance List. Units are asked to ensure that the Editor and DSDC(L) are informed of any reduction in requirement. Requests for additional copies and amendment to the master Allowance List should be addressed to DSDC(L) at Llangennech (using RN Form 53001(Demand for Naval Books)). Firmly attached to this demand should be a letter addressed to the Editor with a clear supporting case.

THE THREE TIER COMMISSION

1. On 1 April 1999 a new career structure for the officer corps of the Royal Navy will be introduced, representing the most significant change in career management since the formation of the General List. It will not apply to Medical, Dental or Nursing Officers.

2. The Three Tier Commission (3TC) structure will enable more efficient management and provide more equitable career opportunities for the individual Officer and reflects both the expectation for shorter periods of individual commitment and the growing importance of flexible human resource management.

3. Due to the scale and complexity of the change from the present list based structure and the need for an evolutionary period before full implementation, the Defence Council Instruction which authorised the introduction of the 3TC is included in this Navy List in order to inform all readers. The 3TC nomenclature will be applied in the 1999 edition of the Navy List.

Introduction of the Three Tier Commission

Introduction

1. The Navy Board has endorsed proposals for the implementation and integration of the List-free Three Tier Commission (3TC) structure from 1 Apr 99. The new structure will encompass the X, E, S, RM, Chaplaincy and Medical Services branches and Female Non-Specialist officers, up to and including One-Star rank (Commodore RN, Brigadier RM and Principal Chaplain). All new entrants joining the officer corps of these branches on or after 1 Apr 99 will do so under the terms and conditions of service of the 3TC. Officers entered prior to 1 Apr 99 will be integrated into the 3TC, but will retain reserved rights to the terms and conditions of service of their existing rank and commission. The 3TC does not include Medical, Dental or Nursing Officers whose career structure is subject to separate work, or the very small Careers and Family Services branches which will continue to be governed by separate arrangements.

Background

2. In 1995 the Independent Review (IR) recommended, *inter alia*, that the Armed Forces should adopt a 3TC structure for officers with a Retirement Age of 55 years (RA55) for those serving on the final tier. The Ministry of Defence Information Document "The Armed Forces of the Future - A Personnel Strategy" translates these principles into policy for each of the three Services. The proposal to adopt a 3TC structure reflects both the unwillingness of recruits to commit themselves to one organisation for very long periods of time and the employer's need to be flexible in managing people. Introduction of the 3TC is a natural extension of the practice of awarding an increasing number of shorter commissions that has been evident for several years.

Linkage Of The 3TC With A Revised Mechanism For Officer Promotion

3. This DCI establishes the officer career structure from 1 Apr 99. Parallel work to establish revised promotion arrangements is expected to be complete by early 1998. Both areas will then be summarised in a pamphlet which will be distributed to all officers and potential officers to allow individuals to understand fully the impact of revised regulations and procedures at least 12 months before the introduction of change.

OUTLINE OF THE THREE TIER COMMISSION STRUCTURE

General

4. This section describes the framework of the new structure and should be read in conjunction with the schematic diagrams of the 3TC for the RN, RM and Chaplains at Annexes A to C. *Note*. The existing regulations governing resignation, return of service, voluntary retirement, and extensions of service (BR 8373) are unaffected by the introduction of the 3TC.

Initial Commission (IC)

5. *Length of Commission.* From 1 Apr 99 all officers will enter the Naval Service on an IC of:entrants to the officer corps, whether recruited from the civil sector or from the ranks, will join on an IC as follows:

a. RN officers: 12 years (but subject to retirement at age 55 years).
b. RM officers: 8 years (but subject to retirement at age 55 years).
c. Chaplains: 6 years.

6. *Opportunity For Transfer To a Longer Commission.* All officers serving on an IC will be eligible for competitive selection (based on requirement) to a Career Commission (CC) in the zone:

a. RN Officers: 5-11 years' officer service.
b. RM Officers: 3-7 years' officer service.
c. Chaplains: 3-5 years' service.

Officers wishing to be considered for transfer should ensure that Section 7b - the "Volunteer" box of the (new) S206 is ticked on every occasion a report is written, including the period prior to zone entry. Should a S206 report not be coincident either with an initial wish to volunteer for transfer, or a change of career intention, officers may indicate this in writing at any time to the Naval Secretary through their Second Reporting Officer.

7. *Pension Arrangements.* All officers serving on an IC will be offered membership of the Armed Forces Pension Scheme (with a statutory right to opt out). Gratuity Earning Terms of Service will not be available to officers entering on or after 1 Apr 99.

Career Commission (CC)

8. *Length of Commission.* The CC is the middle tier of officer employment. It will extend a career through to 16 years' officer service from age 21, or from the date of entry as an officer, whichever is the later. Service on the CC will be subject to RA55.

9. *Opportunity For Transfer To a Longer Commission.* All officers serving on a CC will be eligible for competitive selection (based on requirement) to a Full Term Commission (FTC) in the zone:

a. RN Officers: 8 years' officer service -1 year before expiry of the CC.
b. RM Officers: 6 years' officer service -1 year before expiry of the CC.
c. Chaplains: 10 years' service -1 year before expiry of the CC.

Officers wishing to be considered for transfer to the FTC should follow the procedure outlined at Paragraph 6, commencing with their first report on the CC.

10. *Pension Arrangements.* All officers serving on a CC will have the opportunity to complete 16 years' reckonable service from the age of 21 or age on entry, whichever is the later, and thus qualify for payment of an Immediate Pension (IP).

Notes. (1) Reckonable service for an officer's pension commences at age 21 and may include any rating/other rank service from this age.
(2) The current requirement of a minimum retirement age of 38 years for officers serving on an MCC to qualify for an IP, will not apply to officers joining on or after 1 Apr 99.

Full Term Commission (FTC)

11. *Length of Commission.* The FTC is the final tier of commissioned service through to RA55 for those joining the Naval Service on or after 1 Apr 99.

12. *Pension Arrangements.* Current pension arrangements and terminal benefits are unaffected by the introduction of the FTC.

PROMOTION FROM THE RANKS

Special Duties (SD) - Introduction of New Nomenclature

13. The SD List will be abolished on 1 Apr 99 and all serving SD officers will be integrated into the common structure of the 3TC. However, there will be a continuing requirement to describe the former SD candidate during the officer selection and training process. From 1 Apr 99 the appropriate term will be: "Senior Upper Yardman" (SUY) in the RN and "Senior Corps Commission" (SCC) in the RM.

Age Bracket for Commissioning Via the SUY/SCC Scheme

14. With effect from 1 Apr 99, the normal age range for promotion to the officer corps via the SUY/SCC scheme will be standardised across the Naval Service from a minimum age of 26 years, to under 46 years of age on the first day of the month that officer training commences. With immediate effect, Forms S205CW, S206CW and RM CR1 may be raised and applications made to attend the AIB by candidates currently precluded by age who will fulfil the revised criteria from 1 Apr 99. All elements of the selection process may be completed before 1 Apr 99, but officer training for this group may not commence until after the new rules become effective.

Retirement Age for Officers Commissioned Under the SUY/SCC Scheme

15. To maintain an equitable career opportunity for all officers serving before 1 Apr 99, personnel promoted to the officer corps via the SUY/SCC scheme who joined the Naval Service as a rating/other rank before 1 Apr 99 will serve to the existing rank related retirement age unless this is specifically extended for a particular rank. In this event, individuals affected will retain the right to leave at the existing rank-related retirement age if they so wish.

Provision of Pension Benefits for Officers Commissioned Under the SUY/SCC Scheme

16. All officers commissioned via the SUY/SCC scheme will qualify for the award of an IP. This will be achieved by combining officer/other rank reckonable service from the age of 21 years; should this fall short of achieving the requisite 16 years' reckonable service, an extension of service will be offered to ensure that the minimum qualifying period is served.

AWARD OF ANTE-DATED SENIORITY ON JOINING THE OFFICER CORPS

General

17. The revised arrangements (detailed below) for the award of ante-dated seniority are applicable to all branches included within the 3TC structure, apart from the E(TM) specialisation and the Chaplaincy Service which will continue to be governed by existing rules. The rules governing seniority for previous service (BR8373) are unaffected by the introduction of the 3TC.

Seniority

18. In order to create a common baseline on which to build an equitable structure, the 3TC will recognise previous experience and skills gained by all officer entrants, rather than only those of the graduate and SD officer as at present. Seniority awards will be linked to an upper age of 21 years. Therefore, with effect from 1 Apr 99:

a. Officers recruited via the SUY route will be aligned with the current RM SD officer scheme and awarded 3 years' seniority (ie, join as a Sub Lieutenant with 1 year's seniority).
b. All direct entry and Upper Yardman/Corps Commission (UY/CC) recruited officers who join at age 21 years or over will be awarded 3 years' seniority (ie, join as a Sub Lieutenant with 1 year's seniority); those at age 20 will be awarded 2 years' seniority (ie, join as a Sub Lieutenant), and those at age 19, one year's seniority (ie, join as a Midshipman with 1 year's seniority).

Note. Although the RM will grant identical levels of seniority, this will continue to be awarded on completion of Phase 2 Training.

19. To avoid disadvantaging non-graduates and former UY/CC promoted officers awarded no seniority prior to 1 Apr 99, ante-dated seniority will be awarded as follows:

a. Two years' to those joining over the age of 21 between 1 Apr 98 and 31 Mar 99.
b. One year to those joining over the age of 21 between 1 Apr 97 and 31 Mar 98.
c. One year to those joining at age 20 between 1 Apr 98 and 31 Mar 99.

The Naval Secretary and AFPAA (Centurion) will take retrospective action to adjust the service records and pay of those who gained seniority in the year beginning 1 Apr 97.

INTEGRATION OF THE EXISTING CAREER STRUCTURE INTO THE 3TC

General

20. The final transfer Boards convened under existing rules will sit at the end of 1998 (results published in early 1999). Officers who are selected for transfer by these Boards will move to the appropriate stage of the 3TC (as detailed below) on 1 Apr 99 when all officers of One Star rank and below will be integrated into the new career structure. In practice this will involve little more than the adoption of the 3TC commission titles due to the impact of an individual's reserved rights to the terms and conditions of service in being on 31 Mar 99. The correlation between current commission titles and the 3TC is:

SCC = IC (with the opportunity to transfer to a CC and then to a FTC).
MCC = CC (with the opportunity to transfer to a FTC).
EMCC = FTC.
FCC = FTC.
SD = FTC.

Retirement Age and the 3TC

21. Integration of the existing structure into the 3TC is set against the key perspective that there is no practical mechanism that would allow all officers serving before 1 Apr 99 to serve to RA55 without creating an unmanageable surplus of manpower. This restriction will also apply to ratings/other ranks who joined the Naval Service before this date and who are subsequently commissioned under the SUY/SCC scheme. Selective extensions of service will continue to be available and manpower planners will keep the retirement policy under review.

SCC/IC

22. IC nomenclature will apply to all those previously serving on a SCC (eg, an officer serving on a SCC of 8 years will be known as IC(8) and an aircrew officer serving on a SCC of 12 years will be known as IC(12)).

23. Selection for longer service will be to the terms and conditions of the CC.

24. Reserved rights for selection to a longer commission mean that those serving on a SCC before 1 Apr 99 will be considered for transfer to the CC after 3 years' service (the zone will end 1 year before the expiry of the SCC). All applications for transfer to a MCC which remain extant on 31 Mar 99 will automatically be considered for a CC.

25. There will no longer be an opportunity to transfer directly to the FTC along the lines of the current SL/GL transfer scheme from 1 Apr 99; the route to the FTC is via the CC. All applications for transfer to a FCC which remain unfulfilled on 31 Mar 99 will automatically be considered for a CC.

MCC/CC

26. CC nomenclature will apply to all previously serving on a MCC.

27. Former MCC officers whose terms of service include automatic promotion to Lieutenant Commander after 12 years as a Lieutenant (if not promoted before) will retain this reserved right.

28. From 1 Apr 99 all applications in the pipeline for longer service, ie, to EMCC or FCC, will automatically be considered for a FTC.

EMCC/FTC

29. FTC nomenclature will apply to all previously serving on an EMCC.

30. To maintain an equitable structure, including subsequent promotion opportunity, former EMCC Commanders transferring to the FTC on 1 Apr 99 (who currently retire at age 50) will be offered alignment with their former GL/SD counterparts. Therefore, all former EMCC Commanders serving on 1 Apr 99 will be offered an opportunity to extend to RA53 (these officers will be contacted individually by the appropriate appointing section).

FCC/SD/FTC

31. FTC nomenclature will apply to all previously serving on a FCC or on the SD List.

32. Former FCC and SD officers will retain reserved rights to terms and conditions of service extant prior to 1 Apr 99, in particular:

a. Automatic (and early selective) promotion to Lieutenant Commander and Captain (RM) for GL FCC officers.

b. Selective promotion to Lieutenant Commander and Captain (RM) for officers on the SD List before 1 Apr 99.

c. Rank related retirement at age 50 for Lieutenant Commanders and Captains/Majors (RM) (eg, FTC (50)), 51 for Lieutenant Colonels/Colonels/Brigadiers (RM), 53 for Commanders, 55 for substantive Captains (RN) with a seniority date after 1 Jul 97, and an aggregate of 9 years Captain/Commodore service for all RN One Star officers and those substantive Captains with a seniority date on, or before, 30 Jun 97.

Alignment of RN and RM Retirement Ages

33. RM officers joining after 1 Apr 99 will align with the RN policy for RA55; transition arrangements to align RM officers serving before this date with the retirement ages of their RN counterparts (in the medium term) will be promulgated separately.

Publications

34. BR8373 (Officer's Career Regulations), BR8748 (Terms of Service for RN, QARNNS and WRNS Ratings and RM Ranks), Queen's Regulations for the Royal Navy and other publications will be amended to reflect this Instruction. In the meantime, a copy of this DCI is to be kept within the covers of BR 8373 and BR8748.

Annex A
Three Tier Commission Structure (3TC) - Royal Navy

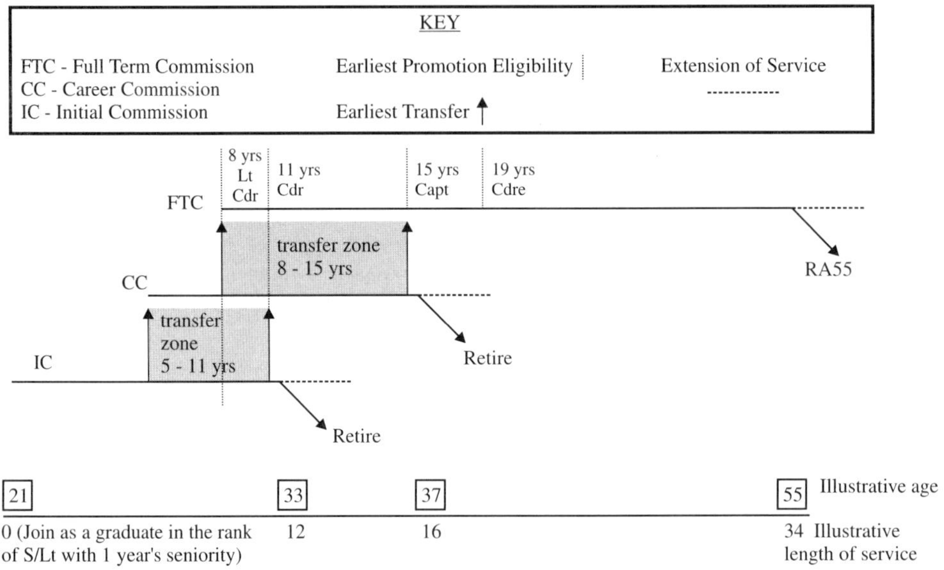

Annex B
Three Tier Commission Structure (3TC) - Royal Marines

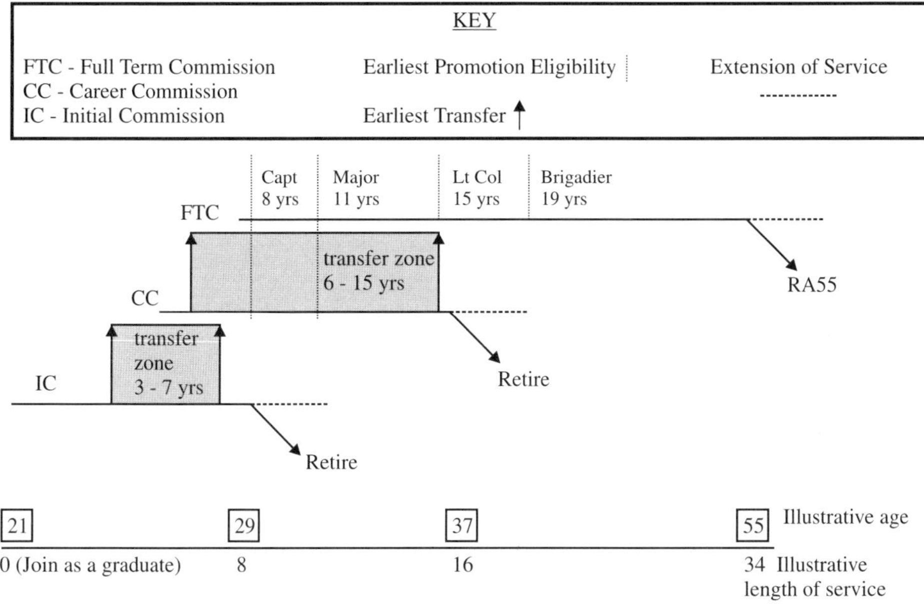

Annex C
Three Tier Commission Structure (3TC) - Royal Navy Chaplaincy Service

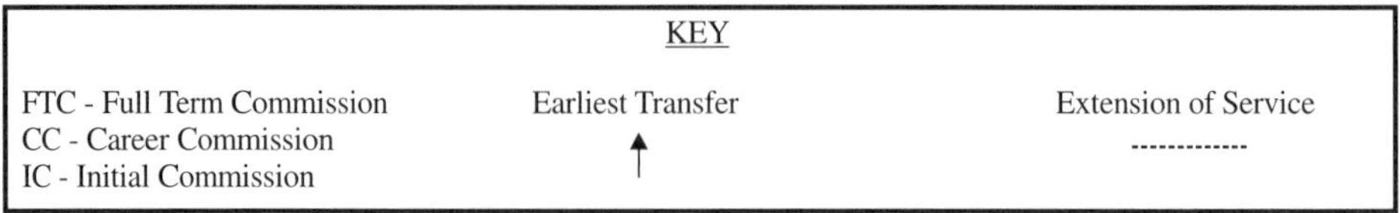

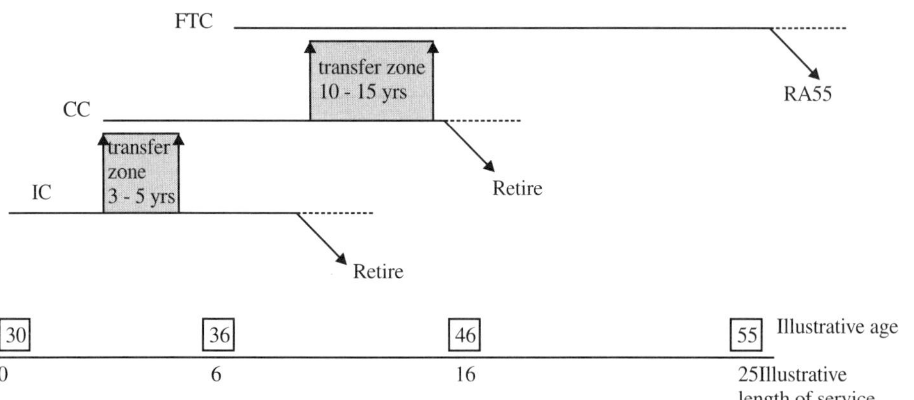

CONTENTS

Page

Section 1

Section 2

Section 3

Section 4

Section 5

Section 6

Section 7

CONTENTS

Page

Section 8

Section 9

Section 10

Section 11

Index

Her Majesty The Queen

LORD HIGH ADMIRAL OF THE UNITED KINGDOM 1964

MEMBERS OF THE ROYAL FAMILY

HIS ROYAL HIGHNESS PRINCE PHILIP THE DUKE OF EDINBURGH KG, KT, OM, GBE, AC, QSO

Admiral of the Fleet .... 15 Jan 53
Captain General Royal Marines .... 1 Jun 53
Admiral of the Fleet Royal Australian Navy .... 1 Apr 54
Admiral of the Fleet Royal New Zealand Navy .... 15 Jan 53
Admiral of the Royal Canadian Sea Cadets .... 15 Jan 53

HER MAJESTY QUEEN ELIZABETH THE QUEEN MOTHER

Commandant in Chief for Women in the Royal Navy .... 1 Nov 93

HIS ROYAL HIGHNESS THE PRINCE OF WALES KG, KT, GCB, AK, QSO, ADC

Rear Admiral .... 14 Nov 98

HIS ROYAL HIGHNESS THE DUKE OF YORK CVO, ADC

Admiral of the Sea Cadet Corps .... 11 May 92

Commander Royal Navy .... 27 Apr 99

HER ROYAL HIGHNESS THE PRINCESS ROYAL KG, GCVO, QSO

Rear Admiral Chief Commandant for Women in the Royal Navy .... 1 Nov 93

HIS ROYAL HIGHNESS PRINCE MICHAEL OF KENT KCVO

Honorary Commodore Royal Naval Reserve .... 1 Apr 94

HER ROYAL HIGHNESS PRINCESS ALEXANDRA THE HON LADY OGILVY GCVO

Patron, Queen Alexandra's Royal Naval Nursing Service .... 12 Nov 55

VICE ADMIRAL OF THE UNITED KINGDOM AND LIEUTENANT OF THE ADMIRALTY

Admiral Sir Nicholas Hunt GCB, LVO

REAR ADMIRAL OF THE UNITED KINGDOM

Admiral Sir Jeremy Black GBE, KCB, DSO

PERSONAL AIDES-DE-CAMP TO THE QUEEN

Rear Admiral His Royal Highness The Prince of Wales KG, KT, GCB, AK, QSO, ADC

Commander His Royal Highness The Duke of York CVO, ADC

FIRST AND PRINCIPAL NAVAL AIDE-DE-CAMP TO THE QUEEN

Admiral Sir Michael Boyce GCB, OBE, ADC .... 08 Oct 98

FLAG AIDE-DE-CAMP TO THE QUEEN

Vice Admiral P Spencer ADC .... 19 Jan 00

NAVAL AND MARINE AIDES-DE-CAMP TO THE QUEEN

Captain S.R.J.Goodall (Commodore)	Appointed	10 Jan 00	Seniority	31 Dec 93
Captain M.W.G.Kerr (Commodore)	Appointed	12 Oct 99	Seniority	31 Dec 93
Captain A.M.Willmett (Commodore)	Appointed	24 May 00	Seniority	31 Dec 93
Captain A.L.Chilton OBE (Commodore)	Appointed	16 Sep 98	Seniority	31 Dec 91
Captain R.F.Cheadle (Commodore)	Appointed	25 May 00	Seniority	30 Jun 93
Captain P.D.Greenish (Commodore)	Appointed	01 Apr 98	Seniority	31 Dec 91
Captain J.C.Rapp (Commodore)	Appointed	17 Jan 00	Seniority	31 Dec 92
Captain D.A.H.M.Smith (Commodore)	Appointed	28 Apr 99	Seniority	31 Dec 92
Colonel A.R.Pillar OBE (Brigadier)	Appointed	12 Apr 99	Seniority	30 Jun 98

EXTRA NAVAL AND MARINE EQUERRIES TO THE QUEEN

Vice Admiral Sir Peter Ashmore KCB, KCVO, DSC
Lieutenant General Sir John Richards KCB, KCVO
Rear Admiral Sir Richard Trowbridge KCVO
Rear Admiral Sir Paul Greening GCVO
Rear Admiral Sir John Garnier KCVO, CBE
Rear Admiral Sir Robert Woodard KCVO
Commodore A.J.C.Morrow CVO Royal Navy

NAVAL AND MARINE RESERVE AIDES-DE-CAMP TO THE QUEEN

Commodore G.N.Wood JP, RD*, ADC	Appointed	28 Oct 99	Seniority	28 Oct 99
Colonel A.C.L.Smith RD*, ADC	Appointed	29 Mar 99	Seniority	29 Mar 99
Captain A.C.Adams RD, ADC	Appointed	30 Sept 99	Seniority	30 Sep 99

HONORARY CHAPLAINS TO THE QUEEN

The Reverend A.T.Maze BSc
The Venerable S.J.Golding QHC
The Reverend Monsignor T.M.Burns SM, VG, BA, BD, MBIM
The Reverend B.K.Hammett MA

HONORARY PHYSICIANS TO THE QUEEN

Surgeon Commodore G.H.G.McMillan OStJ, MB BCH, FFOM, FRCP, FICSH, MRCP(UK) MD, QHP
Surgeon Commodore N.E.Baldock MB BS, FFOM, Dip Av Med, FRCP, QHP
Surgeon Commodore C. W. Evans, MB BS, MRCS LRCP, MFOM, MPH, DIH, DTMH, RCDS, QHP

HONORARY SURGEONS TO THE QUEEN

Surgeon Rear Admiral I.L.Jenkins CVO, OStJ, MB BCH, FRCS, QHS
Surgeon Captain M.A.Farquharson-Roberts MB BS, OStJ, FRCS, QHS

HONORARY DENTAL SURGEON TO THE QUEEN

Surgeon Commodore (D) J. Hargraves MSc, BDS, DGDP(UK), LDS RCS(Eng)

NAVAL RESERVE HONORARY PHYSICIAN TO THE QUEEN

Surgeon Captain N.R.J.Hooper RD*, QHP

HONORARY NURSING SISTER TO THE QUEEN

Captain J.C.Brown ARRC, QHNS, QARNNS

HONORARY OFFICERS IN HER MAJESTY'S FLEET

ADMIRAL

His Majesty The King of Sweden KG .... 25 Jun 75

His Royal Highness Don Juan of Bourbon and Battenberg, Count of Barcelona .... 31 July 87

HONORARY OFFICERS IN HER MAJESTY'S ROYAL MARINES

COLONEL

His Majesty The King of Norway GCVO .... 18 Mar 81

THE DEFENCE COUNCIL

Chairman

THE RIGHT HONOURABLE GEOFF HOON MP

(Secretary of State for Defence)

MR JOHN F SPELLAR MP

(Minister of State for the Armed Forces)

BARONESS ELIZABETH CONWAY SYMONS OF VERNHAM DEAN

(Minister of State for Defence Procurement)

DOCTOR LEWIS MOONIE MP

(Parliamentary Under-Secretary of State for Defence)

GENERAL SIR CHARLES GUTHRIE GCB, LVO, OBE, ADC Gen

(Chief of Defence Staff)

MR KEVIN TEBBIT

(Permanent Under-Secretary of State)

ADMIRAL SIR MICHAEL BOYCE GCB, OBE, ADC

(Chief of the Naval Staff and First Sea Lord)

GENERAL SIR MICHAEL WALKER GCB, CMG, CBE, ADC Gen

(Chief of the General Staff)

AIR CHIEF MARSHAL SIR PETER SQUIRE KCB, DFC, AFC, ADC, FRAes, RAF

(Chief of the Air Staff)

ADMIRAL SIR PETER ABBOTT GBE, KCB

(Vice Chief of the Defence Staff)

SIR ROBERT WALMSLEY KCB, FREng

(Chief of Defence Procurement)

PROFESSOR SIR KEITH O'NIONS FRS

(Chief Scientific Adviser)

MR ROGER T JACKLING CB, CBE

(Second Permanent Under-Secretary of State)

GENERAL SIR SAM COWAN KCB, CBE

(Chief of Defence Logistics)

THE ADMIRALTY BOARD

Chairman

THE RIGHT HONOURABLE GEOFF HOON MP

(Secretary of State for Defence)

(Chairman of the Defence Council and Chairman of the

Admiralty Board of the Defence Council)

MR JOHN F SPELLAR MP

(Minister of State for the Armed Forces)

BARONESS ELIZABETH CONWAY SYMONS OF VERNHAM DEAN

(Minister of State for Defence Procurement)

DOCTOR LEWIS MOONIE MP

(Parliamentary Under-Secretary of State for Defence)

ADMIRAL SIR MICHAEL BOYCE GCB, OBE, ADC

(Chief of the Naval Staff and First Sea Lord)

ADMIRAL SIR NIGEL ESSENHIGH KCB

(Commander in Chief Fleet)

VICE ADMIRAL PETER SPENCER ADC

(Second Sea Lord and Commander in Chief Naval Home Command)

REAR ADMIRAL BRIAN B PEROWNE

(Chief of Fleet Support)

REAR ADMIRAL JAMES M BURNELL-NUGENT CBE

(Assistant Chief of Naval Staff)

REAR ADMIRAL NIGEL C F GUILD

(Controller of the Navy)

MR ROGER T JACKLING CB, CBE

(Second Permanent Under-Secretary of State and Secretary of the Admiralty Board)

OFFICERS ON THE ACTIVE LIST OF THE ROYAL NAVY, THE ROYAL MARINES, THE QUEEN ALEXANDRA'S ROYAL NAVAL NURSING SERVICE; AND RETIRED AND EMERGENCY OFFICERS SERVING AND LIST OF RFA OFFICERS' NAMES

A

Name	Rank	Branch	Spec	Seniority	Where Serving
Abbey, Michael Keith , *MSc, CEng, MIMarE*	LT CDR(FTC)	E	MESM	16.05.92	CSST SEA
Abbey, Michael Peter , *MBE, pcea*	LT CDR(FTC)	X	P	01.10.88	CHFHQ
Abbott, Charles Peregrine George , *OBE, psc*	CDR(FTC)	S		30.06.84	NMA PORTSMOUTH
Abbott, David Anthony , *BTech*	LT(FTC)	E	WE	24.02.95	CFM PORTSMOUTH
Abbott, *Sir* Peter (Charles) , *GBE, KCB, MA, rcds, pce*	ADM	-	C	03.10.95	MOD (LONDON)
Abbott, Robert James	SLT(IC)	X	ATCU/T	01.09.98	RAF SHAWBURY
Abbott, Simon Saintclair	LT CDR(FTC)	X	PWO(U)	01.06.92	LN DERA CDA HLS
Abel, Nigel Philip	LT(CC)	X	P	16.08.96	RAF SHAWBURY
Abernethy, James Richard Gordon , *pce*	LT CDR(FTC)	X	PWO(N)	01.08.96	SANDOWN
Abernethy, Lee John Francis	LT CDR(FTC)	X	PWO(C)	11.07.94	FOST SEA
Ablett, Simon David , *BEng*	LT(FTC)	E	WE	01.01.98	EDINBURGH
Abraham, Paul , *pce(sm)*	CDR(FTC)	X	SM	31.12.96	CSST SEA
Abson, Ian Tyas	LT(CC)	X	O	01.06.91	702 SQN HERON
Ackerley, Richard St John	LT(IC)	X	SM	01.11.99	SCEPTRE
Ackland, Heber Kemble , *BA*	LT CDR(FTC)	S		01.11.99	SOUTHAMPTON
Acland, David Daniel , *pce, pcea*	LT CDR(FTC)	X	P	01.10.93	801 SQN
Adair, Allan Alexander Shafto , *pce, psc(a)*	CAPT(FTC)	X	PWO	30.06.98	SA PARIS
Adam, Ian Kennedy , *pce*	LT CDR(FTC)	X	PWO(A)	01.01.97	DRYAD
Adams, Alistair John , *BA, BSc, pce*	CDR(FTC)	X	PWO(C)	31.12.98	RICHMOND
Adams, Andrew Mark , *BEng, MIMarE*	LT CDR(FTC)	E	MESM	01.08.96	FOSM NWOOD HQ
Adams, Benjamin Mark	LT(CC)	X	P	16.05.91	RNAS YEOVILTON
Adams, Edwin Smyth , *BEng*	LT(IC)	X	P U/T	01.04.00	FONA LINTON/OUSE
Adams, George	LT(CC)	E	ME	01.05.97	FEARLESS
Adams, Geoffrey Hugh , *BEng, MSc*	LT(FTC)	E	ME	01.04.93	PORTLAND
Adams, Ian , *BA*	LT(CC)	X	P	01.11.90	RAF CRANWELL EFS
Adams, Peter , *BSc, PGCE*	LT CDR(FTC)	E	TM	01.01.94	NMA PORTSMOUTH
Adams, Peter Nigel Elliott , *n*	LT(FTC)	X		01.07.96	BLAZER
Adams, Richard Anthony Skelton , *BSc*	CDR(FTC)	E	MESM	30.06.92	CNSA BRISTOL
Adams, Raymond John , *MA, pce*	LT CDR(FTC)	X	PWO(C)	01.08.88	FOSF
Adams, Richard Joseph , *BEng*	LT(FTC)	E	MESM	01.03.95	NEPTUNE DSQ
Adamson, Daniel Dunbar , *BSc*	LT(IC)	X		01.04.98	ARGYLL
Adcock, Graham Edward	LT RM(FTC)	RM		01.01.98	45 CDO RM
Adlam, Gail Margaret , *BA*	LT(FTC)	S		01.10.92	RALEIGH
Ager, Robin Gordon , *BSc, CEng, MIMarE, MIMechE, psc*	LT CDR(FTC)	E	ME	01.08.82	DRAKE NBC
Agnew, Robert Le Page , *BA, MPhil*	SLT(IC)	X		01.09.98	DARTMOUTH BRNC
Ahern, Henrietta , *BSc*	LT(IC)	E	TM	01.09.96	DARTMOUTH BRNC
Ahlgren, Edward Graham	LT(FTC)	X	SM	01.09.94	EXPLORER
Ahling-Smith, Helena Edith Maria , *BM, BS*	SURG LT	-		01.08.95	NELSON (PAY)
Aiken, Stephen Ronald , *pce, pce(sm)*	LT CDR(FTC)	X	SM	01.07.93	TORBAY
Ainsley, Andrew Malcolm James	SLT(CC)	X		01.04.98	BANGOR
Ainsley, Roger Stewart , *MA, jsdc, pce, hcsc (COMMODORE)*	CAPT(FTC)	X	AWO(A)	31.12.94	COMUKTG/CASWSF
Ainslie, Arthur Andrew , *MBA, FIMgt (Act Capt)*	CDR(FTC)	S	SM	30.06.89	DA PEKING
Airey, Simon Edward , *MA, jsdc*	CDR(FTC)	S		31.12.94	DEF SCH OF LANG
Aitken, Andrew John , *BA, SM(n)*	LT(FTC)	X	SM	01.09.94	RALEIGH
Aitken, Frederick James , *BSc, PGCE, FRMS, jsdc*	CDR(FTC)	X	METOC	31.12.92	2SL/CNH

Name	Rank	Branch	Spec	Seniority	Where Serving
Aitken, Kenneth Matthew	LT CDR(FTC)	S	(S)	01.10.96	FEARLESS
Aitken, Steven Robert, *BSc, MSc*	SLT(CC)	X	P U/T	01.01.98	RNAS YEOVILTON
Ajala, Ahmedrufai Abiodun, *BEng*	LT(CC)	E	WE	01.09.94	MOD (LONDON)
Alabaster, Martin Brian, *MA, MSc, psc*	CAPT(FTC)	E	WE	30.06.98	MOD (LONDON)
Alberts, Paul William	SLT(FTC)	E	WE	01.04.98	COLLINGWOOD
Albon, Mark, *Cert Ed, PGDip*	LT CDR(FTC)	X	H2	12.08.98	ILLUSTRIOUS
Albon, Ross, *BSc (BARRISTER)*	CDR(FTC)	S	BAR	30.06.93	MOD (LONDON)
Alcindor, David John, *BSc*	LT(IC)	X	NO-S/S	01.04.98	CATTISTOCK
Alcock, Christopher, *pce, pcea, psc*	CDR(FTC)	X	O	30.06.98	2SL/CNH
Alderson, Richard James, *BSc*	CAPT RM(CC)	RM	P U/T	01.05.98	40 CDO RM
Alderwick, Jason Royston Claude, *BA*	LT(IC)	X		01.12.99	RNSOMO
Aldous, Benjamin Walker, *LLB*	SLT(FTC)	X		01.09.97	DRYAD
Aldridge, Dean	SLT(IC)	X	P U/T	01.05.98	RAF CRANWELL EFS
Aldwinckle, Terence William	LT	Q	IC	23.06.91	RN GIBRALTAR
Alexander, Amy, *BA*	LT(IC)	E	TM	01.09.99	COLLINGWOOD
Alexander, Giles David, *BSc*	CAPT RM(FTC)	RM		01.05.99	45 CDO RM
Alexander, Geofrey Ernest	LT CDR(FTC)	X	C	15.02.86	RN GIBRALTAR
Alexander, Oliver Douglas Dudley	LT(CC)	X	MCD	01.11.97	ATHERSTONE
Alexander, Phillip Michael Duncan, *MEng*	SLT(FTC)	E	ME	01.01.98	EXCELLENT
Alexander, Robert Stuart, *MA, pce, pcea, psc*	CDR(FTC)	X	P	30.06.99	FONA NORTHWOOD
Alexander, Stephen James	CDR(FTC)	E	WESM	01.10.93	NEPTUNE SWS
Alison, Lynn Alexander	LT CDR(FTC)	E	WE	01.10.94	COLLINGWOOD
Allan, Chris Ruthven, *BSc*	LT(FTC)	X		01.09.98	WALNEY
Allcock, Edward	SURG SLT	-		24.07.98	DARTMOUTH BRNC
Allen, Anthony David, *PGDIPAN, pce*	LT CDR(FTC)	X	PWO(N)	01.02.98	FOST MPV(SEA)
Allen, Douglas James Keith, *BEng*	LT(CC)	X	P	16.01.94	846 SQN
Allen, David Peter	LT(FTC)	E	WE	15.06.90	SUP SHIPS PTSMTH
Allen, David Robert, *BEng, AMIEE*	LT CDR(FTC)	E	WE	01.11.95	NELSON (PAY)
Allen, Leslie Bernard	LT(CC)	X	MW	01.10.92	CAMBRIDGE
Allen, Michael John, *pce, psc*	LT CDR(FTC)	X	MCD	01.12.87	FDG
Allen, Patrick Lyons, *pcea*	LT CDR(FTC)	X	O	01.06.99	SUTHERLAND
Allen, Paul Miles	LT(CC)	X	O	01.05.91	815 FLT 202
Allen, Richard	LT CDR(FTC)	X	SM	20.07.99	CSST SHORE DEVPT
Allen, Robert John	MAJ(FTC)	RM		01.09.93	DCTA
Allen, Richard Mark, *pce(sm)*	CDR(FTC)	X	SM	30.06.99	VICTORIOUS(PORT)
Allen, Stephen Michael, *pce*	LT CDR(FTC)	X	O	01.12.97	FOST SEA
Allfree, Joseph, *BA*	LT(FTC)	X		01.01.95	LIVERPOOL
Allibon, Mark Christopher, *pce*	CDR(FTC)	X	PWO(A)	30.06.00	QUORN
Allison, Aubrey Stuart Crawford, *MB, BS, LRCP, MRCGP, MRCS, AFOM, psc, MSc*	SURG CDR	-	GMPP	30.06.91	NELSON (PAY)
Allison, Glenn	LT(CC)	X	P	16.11.94	702 SQN HERON
Allison, Guy John	LT(FTC)	X		01.03.98	NORTHUMBERLAND
Allison, Kenneth Richard, *MBE*	MAJ(FTC)	RM		25.04.96	RM Poole
Allkins, Helen Louise, *BSc*	LT CDR	Q	ACC/EM	31.12.97	MODHU DERRIFORD
Allsford, Karen Marie, *BA*	LT(IC)	S		01.12.97	FEARLESS
Allsop, Alistair, *MB, BA, BCh*	SURG LT	-		05.08.98	CDO LOG REGT RM
Allwood, Christopher, *BSc, PGCE, adp (Act Capt)*	CDR(FTC)	E	IS	31.12.93	DITMTC SHRIVNHAM
Almond, David Edwin Magor, *BA, psc*	LT CDR(FTC)	S		01.07.89	CSSG (SEA)
Alsop, Sweyn Hamish	LT(CC)	X	P	01.02.99	819 SQN
Ambler, Kerry Kirston	LT(CC)	W	C	04.04.91	RN GIBRALTAR
Ambrose, Rachel	SURG SLT	-		20.02.00	DARTMOUTH BRNC
Ames, Jeremy Peter, *BD, AKC*	CHAPLAIN	CE		19.06.75	RH HASLAR
Ames, Karen Margaret Mary, *LLB*	LT(IC)	S		01.12.99	RALEIGH
Amey, John Miles, *BA*	LT(IC)	X		01.09.98	SHEFFIELD
Ameye, Christopher Robin, *pce*	CDR(FTC)	X	MCD	31.12.97	DEF DIVING SCHL
Amorosi, Riccardo Guy Filippo Luigi	MID(UCE)(IC)	E	ME	01.09.99	YORK
Amos, Julian Harvey James	MAJ(FTC)	RM		01.09.98	42 CDO RM
Amphlett, Nigel Gavin, *BSc, pce, pcea*	LT CDR(FTC)	X	PWO(A)	01.05.95	FOST SEA
Ancona, Simon James, *MA, pce, pcea, psc*	CDR(FTC)	X	O	30.06.98	NEWCASTLE
Anderson, Fraser Boyd, *BSc*	LT CDR(FTC)	X	O	01.10.93	700M MERLIN IFTU
Anderson, Garry Stephen, *SM(n)*	LT(IC)	X	SM	01.10.98	SCEPTRE
Anderson, Hugh Alastair, *LLB*	LT CDR(FTC)	S	BAR	16.12.97	FOST DPORT SHORE
Anderson, Jeremy John, *BA, IEng, MIEEIE*	LT CDR(FTC)	E	WE	01.10.96	SHERWOOD
Anderson, Lindsy Claire	MID(UCE)(FTC)	E	WE	01.09.98	DARTMOUTH BRNC

Name	Rank	Branch	Spec	Seniority	Where Serving
Anderson, Mark, *BSc,pce,pce(sm)*	CAPT(FTC)	X	SM	31.12.99	DLO LONDON
Anderson, Mark Edgar John, *BSc*	LT(FTC)	X		01.12.97	LEDBURY
Anderson, Melvin John	CDR(FTC)	S	(S)	01.10.96	RN GIBRALTAR
Anderson, Robert Gordon, *BSc, MSc, AMIEE, psc*	CDR(FTC)	E	WE	31.12.95	ILLUSTRIOUS
Anderson, Stuart Christopher, *pcea*	LT CDR(CC)	X	P	01.10.99	819 SQN
Anderson, Stephen Ronald	SLT(IC)	X	O U/T	01.04.98	702 SQN HERON
Anderson, Steven Thomas	MAJ(FTC)	RM	SO(LE)	01.10.96	CDO LOG REGT RM
Anderton, Simon William, *BDS*	SG LT(D)	-		06.09.99	DRAKE CBP(CNH)
Andrew, Peter	LT(CC)	E	MESM	01.01.00	DARTMOUTH BRNC
Andrew, William George, *psc,pce*	CDR(FTC)	X	PWO(A)	30.06.93	CNSA BRISTOL
Andrews, Christopher, *BSc*	SLT(IC)	E	TM	01.05.97	SULTAN
Andrews, Charles John, *BSc*	SLT(CC)	X	P U/T	01.05.97	RAF CRANWELL EFS
Andrews, Ian	LT CDR(FTC)	E	MESM	01.10.95	SPARTAN
Andrews, Iain Stuart, *DipEd*	SLT(IC)	X		01.09.98	DARTMOUTH BRNC
Andrews, James Paul, *BSc*	SLT(IC)	X	O U/T	01.09.98	DARTMOUTH BRNC
Andrews, Paul Nicholas, *pce*	LT CDR(FTC)	X	PWO(A)	01.06.94	ILLUSTRIOUS
Andrews, Stephen Gary	LT CDR(FTC)	S		28.03.95	EXCHANGE USA
Aniyi, Christopher Bamidele Jost, *BEng, MSc*	LT(FTC)	E	ME	01.06.93	RALEIGH
Ankah, Gregory Kofi Esiaw	LT(FTC)	E	ME	01.12.96	SULTAN
Annett, Ian Gordon, *BEng, MSc, CEng, MIEE*	LT CDR(FTC)	E	WE	01.05.97	MOD (LONDON)
Ansell, Christopher Neil, *BA*	LT(CC)	X		01.01.99	SUPERB
Anstey, Robert James, *pce*	LT CDR(FTC)	X	SM	01.05.98	VICTORIOUS(STBD)
Antcliffe, Graham Albert, *BSc, CEng, MIEE*	CDR(FTC)	E	WESM	31.12.89	DRAKE NBSD
Anthony, Derek James, *MBE, jsdc, pce, pce(sm), hcsc (COMMODORE)*	CAPT(FTC)	X	SM	30.06.91	BDS WASHINGTON
Anthony, Nicholas Mark Kenwood, *MBE, psc(j), MA*	MAJ(FTC)	RM	LC	01.09.94	EXCHANGE ARMY UK
Aplin, Adrian Trevor	LT CDR(FTC)	S		01.11.98	2SL/CNH
Appelquist, Paul	LT CDR(FTC)	E	WESM	01.10.99	FOSM FASLANE
Appleyard, Timothy Paul, *MA, MNI, MRIN, psc*	LT CDR(FTC)	X	FC	05.06.88	RNAS YEOVILTON
Archdale, Peter Mervyn	LT CDR(FTC)	X	PWO(U)	16.03.85	DPA BRISTOL
Archer, Graham William, *BEng*	LT CDR(FTC)	E	AE	01.04.94	JHCHQ
Archibald, Brian Robert, *BSc, pce, jsdc*	CDR(FTC)	X	PWO(A)	30.06.94	MOD (LONDON)
Arden, Victoria Grace	LT(FTC)	X	P U/T	01.07.97	RAF CRANWELL EFS
Arding, Nicholas Miles Bennett, *BSc, psc*	LT COL(FTC)	RM		30.06.98	FEARLESS
Arend, Faye Marie, *BA*	LT(FTC)	S		01.01.99	NEPTUNE
Argent-Hall, Dominic, *BSc, psc*	CDR(FTC)	E	WE	30.06.00	SSA BRISTOL
Arkle, Nicholas James, *BA*	LT(IC)	X	P	01.04.99	FONA VALLEY
Armour, Graeme Alexander	MAJ(FTC)	RM		01.05.99	CINCFLEET
Armstrong, Charles Albert, *pce, psc(a)*	CDR(FTC)	X	PWO(U)	31.12.91	FOSNNI OPS CFS
Armstrong, Colin David	SLT(IC)	X		01.04.98	DUMBARTON CASTLE
Armstrong, Euan McAlpine, *MB, ChB*	SURG LT	-		05.02.97	MODHU DERRIFORD
Armstrong, Maxine Anne	LT	Q	REGM	28.04.97	RN GIBRALTAR
Armstrong, Nicholas Peter Bruce, *pcea*	LT CDR(FTC)	X	O	01.10.96	MERLIN IPT
Armstrong, Neil Stanley	LT(IC)	X	P	01.07.96	819 SQN
Armstrong, Philip William	LT(CS)	-		13.12.88	DNR RCHQ NORTH
Armstrong, Roger Ian, *psc(m)*	LT COL(FTC)	RM		31.12.92	MWC SOUTHWICK
Armstrong, Stuart McAlpine, *BSc*	SLT(FTC)	X		01.09.97	RALEIGH
Armstrong, Scott Thomas	LT(CC)	X	P	16.08.95	845 SQN
Arnall-Culliford, Nigel David, *AFC, MRAeS, psc,*	CDR(FTC)	X	P	01.10.92	LOAN DERA BSC DN *tp*
Arnell, Stephen John	LT CDR(FTC)	E	WE	01.10.98	NOTTINGHAM
Arnold, Andrew Stewart	LT(FTC)	S	(W)	17.12.93	UKNMR SHAPE
Arnold, Bruce William Henry, *MEng, MSc, CEng, MIMechE*	CDR(FTC)	E	MESM	31.12.92	SACLANT USA
Arnold, Mark Edward, *MBE, TEng, MITE (Act Lt Cdr)*	LT(FTC)	E	WESM	03.11.83	MOD DGSWS BARROW
Arrow, John William, *BSc, MNI, pce*	CDR(FTC)	X	MCD	31.12.92	HQRM
Arthur, Andrew Warren, *BSc, CEng, MIMarE, MIMechE*	LT(CC)	E	ME	15.03.90	CAPT IST STAFF
Arthur, Iain Davidson, *pce(sm)*	CDR(FTC)	X	SM	30.06.94	MOD (LONDON)
Arthur, John Christopher White	CDR(FTC)	E	MESM	30.06.90	NP DERBY
Asbridge, Jonathan Ian, *MILT*	LT CDR(FTC)	S	SM	16.11.97	COLLINGWOOD
Ash, Timothy	LT CDR(FTC)	X	MW	01.10.99	ILLUSTRIOUS
Ashby, Keith John, *BEng*	LT(CC)	E	WE	01.09.97	CORNWALL
Ashby, Maxine Kim	LT(CC)	S		01.12.97	RALEIGH
Ashby, Philip James Conyers, *BSc*	MAJ(FTC)	RM	MLDR	01.09.99	NP 1066
Ashcroft, Adam Charles, *MA, pce, pcea, psc(j)*	LT CDR(FTC)	X	P	01.12.94	PJHQ
Ashcroft, Christopher, *pce*	LT CDR(FTC)	X	MW	01.08.93	PJHQ

Name	Rank	Branch	Spec	Seniority	Where Serving
Ashley, Paul David	SLT(IC)	S		01.04.98	DARTMOUTH BRNC
Ashlin, James Matthew, *BSc*	LT(IC)	X	P	01.04.99	RNAS YEOVILTON
Ashman, Rodney Guy, *AIMgt*	LT CDR(FTC)	S	CMA	28.02.00	RALEIGH
Ashton, Christopher Nicholas, *BA*	CAPT RM(FTC)	RM		01.09.96	RMR LONDON
Ashton, Roy David	LT CDR(FTC)	E	WE	01.10.96	EXETER
Ashton, Richard Eric, *MA, MB, BCh, MD, FRCP*	SURG CDR	-	(CK)	31.12.85	RH HASLAR
Ashton Jones, Geraint, *BSc, PGCE*	LT CDR(FTC)	E	IS	01.10.96	RMC OF SCIENCE
Ashworth, Helen Joanne, *BEng*	LT(FTC)	E	ME	01.12.96	WESTMINSTER
Aspden, Andrew Mark, *BA, pce, pcea, psc(j)*	LT CDR(FTC)	X	O	01.12.95	MONMOUTH
Aspden, Mark Charles, *n*	LT(FTC)	X		01.10.95	NEWCASTLE
Asquith, Simon Phillip, *SM(n)*	LT(FTC)	X	SM	01.06.95	RALEIGH
Astle, Dawn Sandra	LT(CC)	X	FC	01.12.98	SOUTHAMPTON
Aston, James, *BEng*	LT(IC)	E	TM	01.01.00	SULTAN
Aston, Mark William, *BDS, MSc, MGDS RCS*	SGCDR(D)	-		30.06.97	ILLUSTRIOUS
Athayde Banazol, Claire Victoria, *ACIS*	LT CDR(FTC)	S		04.04.99	CHATHAM
Atherton, Bruce William	CAPT RM(IC)	RM	P	01.09.97	847 SQN
Atherton, Gary, *BA(OU)*	LT CDR(FTC)	E	WESM	01.10.99	SSA BRISTOL
Atherton, Jason Ratcliffe	CAPT RM(IC)	RM	P	01.09.98	HQRM
Atherton, Martin John, *MA, psc(j)*	CDR(FTC)	S		31.12.97	INVINCIBLE
Atkins, Ian, *BEng, MSc*	LT(FTC)	E	ME	01.01.93	MOD (BATH)
Atkinson, Adrian Nicholas Charles	SLT(CC)	X	ATCU/T	01.04.98	RNAS CULDROSE
Atkinson, Charlotte Penelope, *BSc*	LT(CC)	X	H2	01.04.95	ENDURANCE
Atkinson, Garth Carson, *BSc*	LT(CC)	X	MW	01.02.92	FOST MPV(SEA)
Atkinson, Ian Neville	LT(CC)	S		01.04.91	CALEDONIA CFS
Atkinson, John Clarke	MAJ(FTC)	RM	SO(LE)	01.10.95	RMB STONEHOUSE
Atkinson, Mark, *pce*	LT CDR(FTC)	X	MCD	01.02.96	MCM2 SEA
Atkinson, Neil Craig	2LT(GRAD)(FTC)	RM		29.04.98	42 CDO RM
Atkinson, Penelope Ann, *MB, ChB*	SURG LT	-		01.08.96	MODHU DERRIFORD
Atkinson, Richard Jonathan	LT(FTC)	X	FC	01.07.96	FOST SEA
Atkinson, Simon Reay, *QCVS, Eur Ing, BSc, CEng, MIEE, MRIN*	CDR(FTC)	E	WE	30.06.00	OCEAN
Attrill, Alexander Anthony	LT CDR(CC)	X	P	01.10.96	899 SQN HERON
Aubrey-Rees, Adam William, *BSc*	LT CDR(FTC)	E	WE	16.04.84	LOAN BRUNEI
Auld, Douglas Martin, *BEng*	LT(CC)	E	MESM	01.02.98	SULTAN
Austen, Richard Mark	LT(FTC)	S	(W)	08.04.94	DRAKE CFM
Austin, Christopher John	LT(FTC)	E	ME	19.06.98	EXCELLENT
Austin, Ian	LT(TC)	X	H CH	18.06.93	NP 1016 IN SURV
Austin, John Damien, *BTech*	LT CDR(FTC)	X		01.10.92	FOSF NORTHWOOD
Austin, Peter Nigel	SLT(FTC)	E	WESM	09.01.98	VANGUARD(PORT)
Austin, Stewart John, *MBE, MA, psc*	LT CDR(FTC)	S	CMA	16.12.82	UKSU IBERLANT
Austin, Stephen Timothy, *BSc*	SLT(FTC)	E	ME	02.05.97	NORFOLK
Auty, Stephen John, *BSc, FRMS, MinstP, ARCS, rcds, jsdc, psc (COMMODORE)*	CAPT(FTC)	X	METOC	30.06.95	MOD (LONDON)
Avery, Malcolm Byrne, *BSc, MRINA, pce, pce(sm), psc*	CAPT(FTC)	X	SM	31.12.97	CSST SHORE FSLN
Avison, Matthew James	LT CDR(FTC)	X	O	01.10.99	MWC PORTSDOWN
Axon, David Brian, *pce*	LT CDR(FTC)	X	PWO(A)	01.07.98	RAMSEY
Ayers, Dominic Edwin Bodkin, *MB, BA, BS*	SURG LT	-		03.08.95	MODHU DERRIFORD
Ayers, Richard Peter Beedom, *BSc, CEng, MIEE, psc*	CDR(FTC)	E	WE	31.12.92	MOD (LONDON)
Ayers, Timothy Paul, *BA, n*	LT(FTC)	X		01.04.95	ARGYLL
Aylott, Peter Richard Frank Dobson, *MA, n*	LT CDR(FTC)	X	PWO(A)	29.01.00	FOST SEA
Ayres, Christopher Paul, *BSc, pce, psc*	CDR(FTC)	X	PWO(U)	30.06.96	JSCSC

B

Name	Rank	Branch	Spec	Seniority	Where Serving
Babbington, Peter Murray, *MC, nadc, psc, (act Col)*	LT COL(FTC)	RM		07.05.85	NP 1066
Backhouse, Anthony Wynter, *BSc, psc, odc(Aus)*	CDR(FTC)	S	SM	31.12.90	JHQ SOUTHCENT
Backhouse, Jonathan Roland, *BA, pce, pcea*	LT CDR(FTC)	X	O	01.03.91	RNAS YEOVILTON
Backus, Alexander Kirkwood, *OBE, jsdc, pce*	RADM	-	AWO(A)	07.09.99	FOST SEA
Backus, Robert Ian Kirkwood, *BEng*	LT(FTC)	X	P U/T	01.03.96	RNAS YEOVILTON
Baden, James, *MB, BS, BDS, BMS, FDS RCPSGlas (Act Surg Lt)*	SURG SLT	-		04.11.97	DARTMOUTH BRNC
Badrock, Bruce, *n*	LT CDR(FTC)	X	H1	05.07.98	BEAGLE
Baggaley, Jason Antony Lloyd, *BSc*	LT(FTC)	E	WE	01.01.94	EXETER
Bagnall, Sally Anne Elizabeth, *BSc*	LT	Q		28.05.96	RDMC BLOCKHOUSE
Bagshaw, Edward Frank, *BSc*	SLT(IC)	X		01.01.97	DRYAD
Bagshaw, James Richard William, *BA*	LT(CC)	X		01.09.98	YORK

Name	Rank	Branch	Spec	Seniority	Where Serving
Bagwell, Peter, *AMIEE, BEng*	LT(CC)	E	WESM	01.08.95	SSA/CWTA PORTS
Bagworth, Joanna Frances, *BSc*	LT(FTC)	S		01.07.96	NBC PORTSMOUTH
Baileff, Roger Ian, *pce*	LT CDR(FTC)	X	PWO(U)	01.12.89	2SL/CNH FOTR
Bailes, Kenneth Peter, *BA*	SLT(IC)	X		01.01.98	GRAFTON
Bailey, Anthony Mark Savile, *psc(m)*	MAJ(FTC)	RM		01.08.82	ATTURM
Bailey, Daniel Standfast	CAPT RM(FTC)	RM		01.09.96	DNR PRES TEAMS
Bailey, Ian John	MID(UCE)(FTC)	E	WE	01.09.98	SHEFFIELD
Bailey, John, *pce*	CDR(FTC)	X	PWO(U)	30.06.89	RHQ SOUTHLANT
Bailey, Jeremy James, *BEng*	LT(FTC)	E	ME	01.01.96	SOMERSET
Bailey, Jonathan James, *BEng*	CAPT RM(FTC)	RM		01.09.94	CTCRM
Bailey, James Walter, *CEng, FIMarE, MIMarE*	CDR(FTC)	E	ME	31.12.91	MOD (BATH)
Bailey, Sian, *BSc, PGCE*	LT(IC)	E	TM	01.08.99	COLLINGWOOD
Bailie, Dennis James, *MSc, CEng, MRAeS, jsdc, gw*	CDR(FTC)	E	AE	31.12.87	SACLANT USA
Baillie, Robbie William, *BSc*	SLT(IC)	E	TM	01.05.97	SULTAN
Bain, David Iain	CAPT RM(FTC)	RM	SO(LE)	01.01.93	COMACCHIO GP RM
Bainbridge, Stuart Darryl	LT(CC)	X	P	01.03.95	820 SQN
Baines, Andrew Richard, *BSc*	LT(IC)	X	P	01.01.98	845 SQN
Baines, David Michael Llewellyn, *BSc*	LT(CC)	E	IS	01.01.92	AGRIPPA AFSOUTH
Baines, Gary Anthony	LT RM(FTC)	RM	SO(LE)	01.01.98	40 CDO RM
Baines, Mark Derek, *BSc, MA, pcea, psc*	LT CDR(FTC)	X	P	01.02.93	848 SQN HERON
Bains, Baldeep *(Act Surg Lt)*	SURG SLT	-		23.07.99	DARTMOUTH BRNC
Baker, Adrian Bruce, *MB, BCh, ChB, DipAvMed*	SURG CDR	-	GMPP	30.06.94	RNAS CULDROSE
Baker, Allan Peter	LT CDR(FTC)	E	ME	26.04.86	EXCELLENT
Baker, Adrian Paul, *BEng*	LT CDR(FTC)	X	O	01.11.99	702 SQN HERON
Baker, Grant Charles, *BEng*	LT CDR(FTC)	E	AE	01.12.97	ES AIR BRISTOL
Baker, Graham Reginald	LT CDR(FTC)	E	ME	15.01.88	CFM PORTSMOUTH
Baker, Kenneth, *MSc*	CDR(FTC)	MS	(RGN)	01.10.97	RDMC BLOCKHOUSE
Baker, Michael Benson, *BA*	CAPT RM(IC)	RM	P U/T	01.09.98	RAF CRANWELL EFS
Baker, Michael John	LT CDR(FTC)	E	WE	01.06.98	JSCSC
Baker, Nicholas James *(Act Lt)*	SLT(FTC)	S	(W)	20.09.96	DRAKE DPL
Baker, Peter Guest, *Eur Ing, BSc, CEng, MIEE*	CDR(FTC)	E	WE	30.06.00	MOD (LONDON)
Bakewell, Timothy *(Act Maj)*	CAPT RM(FTC)	RM		01.09.94	CTCRM
Balchin, David	LT CDR(LC)	X		30.11.99	MOD (LONDON)
Balcombe, Jeremy Stephen, *BEng*	LT(CC)	E	AE	01.09.94	SULTAN
Baldie, Steven Anthony Hamilton, *BEng*	LT(IC)	X	P U/T	01.05.99	RNAS YEOVILTON
Baldock, Nicolas Edwin, *MB, ChB, DipAvMed, FRCP, FFOM, MRCS, QHP* *(COMMODORE)*	SURG CAPT	-	CPDATE	31.12.92	INM ALVERSTOKE
Baldwin, Christopher Martin, *BA*	LT CDR(FTC)	X	PWO(A)	01.03.95	MARLBOROUGH
Baldwin, Simon Frederic, *BSc, psc*	CAPT(FTC)	E	AE	31.12.99	MOD (LONDON)
Balhetchet, Adrian Stephen, *BEng*	LT CDR(FTC)	E	AE	01.03.00	MOD DHSA
Ball, Andrew David, *SM(n)*	LT(IC)	X	SM	01.01.99	TALENT
Ball, Michael Peter, *BSc, MIEE*	LT CDR(FTC)	E	WESM	01.09.91	CNSA BRISTOL
Ball, Matthew Peter, *BEng*	LT(CC)	E	MESM	01.12.99	SULTAN
Ball, Stephen James	LT(FTC)	E	ME	13.02.92	HERALD
Ballantyne, Malcolm Charles, *IEng*	LT CDR(FTC)	E	AE(L)	01.10.91	ES AIR BRISTOL
Ballard, Adam Paul Vence	MID(NE)(IC)	X		01.09.99	DARTMOUTH BRNC
Ballard, Mark Lewis, *BEng, AMIEE*	LT(FTC)	E	WESM	01.12.92	SSA/CWTA PORTS
Ballard, Stephen Alexis	CAPT RM(FTC)	RM		01.09.96	UNTAT WARMINSTER
Baller, Charles Rupert, *BSc*	LT(FTC)	E	ME	01.06.93	SULTAN
Balletta, Rene James, *n*	LT(FTC)	X		01.11.96	SOUTHAMPTON
Balm, Stephen Victor, *psc(a)*	LT COL(FTC)	RM	LC	30.06.92	COMATG SEA
Balmain, Stephen Service, *MA*	LT(IC)	X		01.07.94	NEPTUNE
Balmer, Anthony Victor, *MB, BSc, BS, DA, DipAvMed, MRCGP*	SURG CDR	-	GMPP	31.12.93	RNAS YEOVILTON
Balmer, Guy Austin	CAPT RM(FTC)	RM		24.04.96	CTCRM
Balston, David Charles William, *BA, pce, pce(sm),*	CDR(FTC)	X	SM	30.06.97	PJHQ*psc*
Bamforth, Christian John Milton, *BEng*	LT(FTC)	E	WESM	01.09.98	RALEIGH
Bance, Nicholas David, *BSc*	LT(CC)	X	P	16.02.89	815 SQN HQ
Band, Jonathon, *BA, jsdc, pce, hcsc*	VADM	-	PWO	11.01.00	MOD (LONDON)
Band, James Wright, *BEng*	LT CDR(FTC)	E	AE	01.09.98	ES AIR BRISTOL
Bane, Nicholas St John, *BEng*	SLT(IC)	X	P U/T	01.01.98	RNAS YEOVILTON
Banham, Alexander William Debower, *BEng*	LT(CC)	E	AE	01.12.97	820 SQN
Bankier, Stewart	LT CDR(FTC)	X		19.02.96	CAPTPORT CLYDE
Banks, Matthew Charles, *BSc*	SLT(IC)	X		01.01.98	BULLDOG

Name	Rank	Branch	Spec	Seniority	Where Serving
Banks, Richard George , *IEng, FIEEIE*	CDR(FTC)	E	AE	30.06.90	NMA GOSPORT
Bannister, Andrew Neil	LT(FTC)	E	WE	19.02.93	SSA BRISTOL
Bannister, Jonathan	SLT(IC)	X		01.04.00	DARTMOUTH BRNC
Banting, Quentin Charles Lindsay , *pce, pcea, psc*	CDR(FTC)	X	O	30.06.88	LOAN DERA KYLE
Barber, Andrew Stephen , *pcea*	LT CDR(FTC)	X	O	01.12.97	ALDERNEY
Barber, Christopher James Harrison	LT(CC)	X	O	01.02.95	750 SQN OBS SCH
Barber, Ralph Warwick , *BA*	LT(FTC)	S		01.04.96	YORK
Barclay, John Harrison Buchanan , *BSc, CEng*	LT CDR(FTC)	E	AE	01.05.91	RNAS CULDROSE
Barge, Michael Anthony , *BA, jsdc*	CDR(FTC)	S		30.06.87	2SL/CNH FOTR
Bark, Alexander Martyn , *BSc, n*	LT CDR(FTC)	X	PWO(C)	01.11.98	CUMBERLAND
Bark, James Spencer , *pce(sm)*	LT CDR(FTC)	X	SM	01.09.96	EXCHANGE USA
Barker, Charles Philip Geoffrey , *MB, BS, MCh, DipTh, FRCS, GB, FICS*	SURG CDR	-	(CGS)	31.12.89	INVINCIBLE
Barker, David Charles Kingston , *pce, pcea*	LT CDR(FTC)	X	O	28.02.96	IRON DUKE
Barker, John Edward	CAPT(CS)RM	-		01.05.98	DNR E MIDLANDS
Barker, John Wilson , *MBE*	LT CDR(FTC)	X	O	01.10.99	JSCSC
Barker, Nicholas James , *MA, pce, pcea, psc*	LT CDR(FTC)	X	P	01.05.90	FONA
Barker, Paul David , *BEng*	SLT(FTC)	E	AE	01.09.97	SULTAN
Barker, Piers Thomas , *BSc, pce(sm)*	LT CDR(FTC)	X	SM	01.04.97	FOSM NWOOD HQ
Barker, *R J D* (Richard Demetrious John) , *OBE, pce, pce(sm), psc(j)*	CDR(FTC)	X	*SM*	30.06.97	SPLENDID
Barker, Timothy John	LT(IC)	X	O	16.10.99	820 SQN
Barker, Victoria	SURG SLT	-		24.12.98	DARTMOUTH BRNC
Barling, Nicholas Reid	LT CDR(FTC)	X	ATC	01.10.97	RNAS YEOVILTON
Barlow, Bruce Michael	SLT(IC)	X		01.04.98	DRYAD
Barlow, David , *BA*	CHAPLAIN	CE		04.04.78	COLLINGWOOD
Barlow, Martin John	LT(CC)	X	O	01.03.97	849 SQN HQ
Barltrop, John Anthony , *MA, MSc, CEng, MIEE*	CDR(FTC)	E	WE	31.12.86	SA CAIRO
Barnacle, Christopher Allan , *BSc, psc (Act Capt)*	CDR(FTC)	E	WE	30.06.88	SHAPE BELGIUM
Barnard, Toby James , *BEng*	SLT(IC)	X		01.01.99	DARTMOUTH BRNC
Barnbrook, Jeremy Charles	LT CDR(FTC)	X	P	16.12.96	810 SQN SEAHAWK
Barnden, Michael John	LT CDR(FTC)	E	WE	01.10.94	MOD (BATH)
Barnes, Adam William Gordon	SLT(IC)	X		01.08.98	DARTMOUTH BRNC
Barnes, James Charles	MID(NE)(IC)	X		01.01.00	DARTMOUTH BRNC
Barnes, James Richard	LT CDR(FTC)	X	PWO(A)	01.08.99	MANCHESTER
Barnes, Patrick Alan Lambeth , *BSc*	LT(CC)	X	P U/T	01.04.94	846 SQN
Barnes, Paul Illingworth	SLT(CC)	X		01.05.98	DRYAD
Barnes, Rex Warwick , *psc*	MAJ(FTC)	RM	LC	01.05.92	40 CDO RM
Barnes-Yallowley, Jonathan James Hugh , *pce, pcea*	LT CDR(FTC)	X	P	16.07.92	PJHQ
Barnett, Alan Clive , *BA, MSc*	LT(FTC)	E	AE	01.02.94	LN DERA FARN
Barnwell, Keith Leigh	LT CDR(FTC)	S		23.04.91	2SL/CNH
Barr, Christopher John Gordon , *BEng*	LT(CC)	E	MESM	01.02.99	SULTAN
Barr, Derek Desmond	SLT(IC)	X		01.04.98	OCEAN
Barr, Simon Peter , *BSc*	LT(IC)	X	P U/T	01.09.99	DHFS
Barraclough, Carole Denise	LT(FTC)	X	REG	24.07.97	2SL/CNH
Barrand, Stuart Martin , *pce*	LT CDR(FTC)	X	PWO(A)	01.02.94	EXETER
Barratt, Stephen Mitchell	LT(FTC)	S	(W)	03.04.97	JSCSC
Barrett, David Leonard	LT(FTC)	E	AE(M)	15.10.93	ES AIR MASU
Barrett, Stephen James	LT CDR(FTC)	E	WE	01.10.99	FOREST MOOR
Barrick, Paul Vincent	LT CDR(FTC)	X	EW	01.10.98	CINCFLEET
Barritt, Michael Kenneth , *MA, FNI, FRGS, rcds, jsdc*	CAPT(FTC)	X	HCH	30.06.96	CAPT(H) DEVPT
Barritt, Oliver David , *BA*	LT(IC)	X		01.04.00	ORWELL
Barron, Jeremy Mark	SLT(IC)	X		01.05.98	DARTMOUTH BRNC
Barron, Patrick Joseph	LT(FTC)	X	C	02.04.93	FOST SEA
Barron, Philip Robert	MID(IC)	X		01.01.99	DARTMOUTH BRNC
Barrow, Charles Michael , *BSc*	SLT(IC)	X		01.01.99	DARTMOUTH BRNC
Barrows, David Malcolm , *BEng*	LT(FTC)	E	WE	01.06.95	SSA BRISTOL
Barrs, Hugh Alexander , *BSc, BEng, CEng, MIMarE*	LT CDR(FTC)	E	MESM	01.10.97	FOSM NWOOD HQ
Barry, John Peter	LT(FTC)	X	MW	11.10.94	QUORN
Bartholomew, Ian Munro , *ARICS, psc*	CDR(FTC)	X	H CH	31.12.92	CAPT(H) DEVPT
Bartlett, David Stephen George , *BSc*	LT CDR(FTC)	E	AE(P)	01.03.97	849 SQN HQ
Bartlett, Ian David , *BEng, MSc*	LT CDR(FTC)	E	MESM	01.01.98	TURBULENT
Bartlett, Mark John , *BEng*	LT(FTC)	E	WE	01.05.98	CHATHAM
Barton, Anne Jennifer , *BSc*	LT(IC)	S		01.06.92	CDRE MFP
Barton, Jane Emmeline , *BSc*	LT(CC)	X		01.03.99	RN HYDROG SCHL

Name	Rank	Branch	Spec	Seniority	Where Serving
Barton, Keith Jeffrey Atkinson , *BEng, MSc*	LT(CC)	E	AE	01.03.99	SULTAN
Barton, Mark Alfred , *BEng, CEng, MIMechE, MRINA*	LT(FTC)	E	ME	01.07.92	ILLUSTRIOUS
Barton, Peter Glenn , *BSc, MSc*	CDR(FTC)	E	WE	30.06.99	JSU NORTHWOOD
Barton, Sarah Jane , *MB, BS*	SURG LT	-		04.08.99	CFLT MED(SEA)
Barton, Timothy John , *pce, psc*	CAPT(FTC)	X	AWO(U)	30.06.94	CAPTAIN RNP TEAM
Bartram, Richard James	SLT(CC)	X	P U/T	01.04.98	RAF CRANWELL EFS
Bassett, Dean Anthony , *n*	LT(FTC)	X		01.11.95	DASHER
Bassett, Neil Edward	LT CDR(FTC)	E	WE	01.10.99	MOD (LONDON)
Basson, Andrew Paul , *BSc, MSc, psc*	CDR(FTC)	E	TM	30.06.00	SULTAN
Bate, Christopher	LT CDR(FTC)	X	PT	01.10.93	TEMERAIRE
Bate, David Ian George	LT CDR(FTC)	X	MCD	01.10.95	FEARLESS
Bateman, Graham , *pce, psc(a)*	CDR(FTC)	X	AWO(A)	31.12.86	SA STOCKHOLM
Bateman, Robert Dudley , *BA, MSc, MIMechE*	CDR(FTC)	E	AE	30.06.93	NMA PORTSMOUTH
Bateman, Richard , *MB, ChB, DMcc*	SURG LT	-		02.08.95	NELSON (PAY)
Bateman, Stephen John Francis	CDR(FTC)	X	PWO(A)	30.06.93	LOAN OMAN
Bates, Andrew James , *BSc*	LT(CC)	X	P	16.08.98	RNAS CULDROSE
Bates, Nicholas Stuart , *BSc*	SLT(IC)	X	O U/T	01.09.97	750 SQN OBS SCH
Bath, Edward George	LT CDR(FTC)	X	PWO(A)	27.12.95	DRYAD
Bath, Michael Anthony William , *BSc*	CDR(FTC)	S	SM	30.06.00	FEARLESS
Batho, William Nicholas Pakenham , *pce, psc*	CAPT(FTC)	X	AWO(A)	31.12.95	JSU NORTHWOOD
Batten, Andrew John , *BEng*	LT(FTC)	E	WE	19.02.93	FOSF
Battrick, Richard Robert	LT(FTC)	X	MCD	01.04.96	CATTISTOCK
Batty, Michael John , *MA, psc*	LT CDR(FTC)	S		01.11.93	LIVERPOOL
Baudains, David Percival , *pce, psc, psc(j)*	CDR(FTC)	X	O	30.06.87	FONA
Baudains, Terence John , *BSc, pce*	LT CDR(FTC)	X	P	01.04.89	FOSF
Baum, Stuart Richard , *BSc, pce, pce(sm)*	CDR(FTC)	X	*SM*	30.06.97	ASTUTE IPT
Baxendale, Rodney Douglas , *BA, DipTh*	CHAPLAIN	CE		14.07.83	DRAKE CBP(CNH)
Baxendale, Robert Fred , *BSc*	MAJ(FTC)	RM		01.09.99	NEPTUNE
Baxter, Frederick Joseph	SLT(FTC)	E	AE(L)	01.04.98	819 SQN
Baxter, Graham Francis , *nadc, pce*	CAPT(FTC)	X	PWO(A)	31.12.96	CNSA BRISTOL
Baxter, Iain Menzies , *BEng*	LT CDR(FTC)	E	AE	01.01.00	ES AIR YEO
Baxter, John Charles	LT(FTC)	X	*SM*	27.09.95	CSST SHORE FSLN
Baxter, Julian Simon , *psc*	LT COL(FTC)	RM	LC	30.06.92	AST(W)
Baxter, Kevin Christopher	LT CDR(FTC)	E	MESM	01.10.95	MOD (BATH)
Bazley, John Charles , *pce*	LT CDR(FTC)	X	PWO(N)	01.09.97	DRYAD
Beach, James Michael , *MA*	MAJ(FTC)	RM		01.09.99	PJHQ
Beacham, Philip Robert , *BA*	LT(FTC)	X	P	01.07.95	814 SQN
Beadle, John Thomas	CHAPLAIN	SF		30.03.95	EXCHANGE USA
Beadling, David	SLT(IC)	E	MESM	19.09.98	SULTAN
Beadnell, Robert M , *BSc, MSc*	LT(CC)	E	TM	01.01.92	SULTAN
Beadon, Colin John Alexander , *MBE, psc(a)*	LT COL(FTC)	RM		30.06.94	*BDS* WASHINGTON
Beadsmoore, Emma Jane , *MB, BS*	SURG LT	-		06.08.97	RNAS YEOVILTON
Beadsmoore, Jonathan Edgar , *pce, n*	LT CDR(FTC)	X	PWO(A)	01.02.98	LIVERPOOL
Beale, Michael Dean	LT(FTC)	X	MCD	23.07.98	BICESTER
Beanland, Peter Louis , *BSc*	SLT(CC)	X		01.09.97	DRYAD
Beard, David	SURG SLT	-		11.10.98	DARTMOUTH BRNC
Beard, Graham Thomas Charles , *BA, psc*	CDR(FTC)	S		31.12.98	CINCFLEET
Beard, Hugh Dominic	LT CDR(FTC)	X	*SM*	01.09.99	VENGEANCE(PORT)
Beard, Richard Geoffrey	LT(FTC)	X	C	10.12.98	MONTROSE
Beardall, John , *MA, psc*	CDR(FTC)	X	REG	01.10.97	NMA PORTSMOUTH
Beardall, Michael John Doodson , *pce*	LT CDR(FTC)	X	PWO(A)	01.09.95	LIVERPOOL
Beare, Amanda Louise	LT	Q	IC	10.10.97	CTCRM
Bearne, Jeremy Peter , *psc*	CDR(FTC)	X	PWO(U)	31.12.90	DRAKE DPL
Beats, Kevan Ashley , *pce*	LT CDR(FTC)	X	PWO(U)	16.02.90	RALEIGH
Beattie, Paul Spencer , *n*	LT(FTC)	X	PWO(A)	01.10.93	YORK
Beaumont, Ian Hirst , *pce, pcea*	CDR(FTC)	X	O	31.12.95	FEARLESS
Beaumont, Steven John	LT(FTC)	X	C	16.12.94	DCSA COMMCEN FSK
Beautyman, Andrew John	LT(CC)	E	MESM	01.09.94	NEPTUNE FD
Beaver, Robert Mark Steven , *BSc*	LT(IC)	E	ME	01.05.98	INVINCIBLE
Beavis, John Alexander , *BSc*	LT(IC)	X		01.04.99	EDINBURGH
Beazley, Phillip	MAJ(FTC)	RM	SO(LE)	01.10.99	HQRM
Bebbington, Simon Peter , *pce(sm)*	LT CDR(FTC)	X	SM	01.05.85	PJHQ
Beck, Simon Kingsley	LT CDR(FTC)	X	PWO(A)	01.04.99	EDINBURGH

Name	Rank	Branch	Spec	Seniority	Where Serving
Beckett, Keith Andrew, BSc MDA	CDR(FTC)	E	MESM	31.12.97	NP BRISTOL
Bedding, Darren, BA	SLT(IC)	X	P U/T	01.09.97	RAF CRANWELL EFS
Bedding, Simon William Edward, BEng, CEng, MIEE	LT CDR(FTC)	E	WE	01.04.00	JSU NORTHWOOD
Bedelle, Stephen James	LT(FTC)	E	WE	19.02.93	SSA/CWTA PORTS
Bee, Mark Thomas, BA, MSc, Cert Ed	LT(CC)	E	TM	01.09.92	2SL/CNH FOTR
Beech, Christopher Martin, pce	LT CDR(FTC)	X	PWO(C)	01.07.98	CHATHAM
Beech, Daymion John, BSc	LT(IC)	X	P	16.08.98	RNAS CULDROSE
Beegan, Clive	SLT(IC)	X		27.01.99	DARTMOUTH BRNC
Beeley, William Tyas, BA (Act Maj)	CAPT RM(FTC)	RM		01.09.96	CTCRM
Beirne, Stephen	LT(CC)	X	O	01.06.91	750 SQN OBS SCH
Bell, Andrew Dawson, BSc, CEng, MRAeS	CDR(FTC)	E	AE(P)	31.12.89	HQ NORTH
Bell, Adrian Scott, pce, psc	CDR(FTC)	X	PWO(U)	30.06.97	COMUKTG/CASWSF
Bell, Catriona Mary, BSc	LT(IC)	X		01.02.99	COVENTRY
Bell, Darrel Patrick	LT(FTC)	E	AE(L)	15.10.93	FONA
Bell, Douglas William Alexander	MAJ(FTC)	RM	MLDR	26.04.97	LOAN ARMY
Bell, Fiona Jean	MID(UCE)(IC)	E	ME	01.09.99	NORTHUMBERLAND
Bell, Jeffrey Mark, BEng	LT(FTC)	E	AE	01.05.96	HARRIER IPT
Bell, Mark	LT(FTC)	S	SM	01.10.92	UKNSE AFNORTH NY
Bell, Robert Douglas, pce	LT CDR(FTC)	X	PWO(U)	01.03.97	FOST SEA
Bell, Reginald Paul William	LT CDR(FTC)	X	PWO(A)	01.10.90	DRYAD
Bell, Scott William	SLT(FTC)	S	(W)	01.04.98	800 SQN
Bell-Davies, Richard William, BSc, pce, psc	CDR(FTC)	X	PWO(U)	30.06.93	DRYAD
Bellfield, Robert James Astley, pce	LT CDR(FTC)	X	PWO(U)	01.07.96	DARTMOUTH BRNC
Bellis, Brendan Martin, BSc	LT(FTC)	X	H2	01.03.95	FOSM NWOOD OPS
Bembridge, Simon Richard, BSc	LT(CC)	X	SM	01.11.98	TURBULENT
Benarr, Christopher Michael	MID(UCE)(FTC)	X		01.09.98	DARTMOUTH BRNC
Benbow, Warren Kenneth, pce, psc	CAPT(FTC)	X	P	30.06.93	SULTAN AIB
Bence, David Elliott	LT CDR(FTC)	X	PWO(C)	01.02.98	CORNWALL
Benfell, Niall Andrew (Act Lt)	SLT(FTC)	S	(S)	02.05.97	OCEAN
Benn, John, MSc, MIMechIE	LT(TC)	E	MESM	02.09.99	NEPTUNE NT
Benn, Stephen William, BEng, MSc	LT(FTC)	E	AE	01.01.95	LN DERA FARN
Bennett, Anthony John	LT CDR(FTC)	S	(W)	01.10.97	EXCELLENT
Bennett, Alan Reginald Courtenay, DSC, jsdc, pce, pcea, psc	CAPT(FTC)	X	P	30.06.98	JHCHQ
Bennett, Christopher David, BSc	SLT(IC)	X	P U/T	01.09.97	RAF CRANWELL EFS
Bennett, Douglas Prasad, BEng	LT(IC)	E	TM	01.05.97	SULTAN
Bennett, Graham Lingley Nepean, pce	LT CDR(FTC)	X	PWO(U)	01.07.93	FOSF
Bennett, Michael John	LT CDR(FTC)	E	ME	01.10.98	NBC PORTSMOUTH
Bennett, Neil Malcolm, BA	MAJ(FTC)	RM	C	01.09.96	BDLS CANADA
Bennett, Paul Martin, BA, pce	CDR(FTC)	X	PWO(A)	30.06.98	CINCFLEET
Bennett, Robert Webster	CAPT RM(IC)	RM		25.04.95	HQ 3 CDO BDE RM
Bennett, Stuart Albin Frances James	SURG SLT	-		01.09.97	DARTMOUTH BRNC
Bennett, Stephen Harry Guy, psc	CDR(FTC)	X	H CH	31.12.86	RNLO GULF
Bennett, William Dean	LT(FTC)	X	SM	25.07.91	DGCIS BRISTOL
Bennett, William Ellis	SLT(IC)	E	ME	01.09.97	ARGYLL
Bennetts, Michael	LT(CS)	-		16.04.89	DNR SOUTH WEST
Bennetts, Neil	LT(FTC)	X	C	03.04.97	ELANT/NAVNORTH
Benson, Richard Austin, BEng	LT(IC)	X		01.02.99	PEMBROKE
Benstead, Neil William John, BEng	LT(FTC)	E	ME	01.09.98	NEWCASTLE
Bent, George Robert, pce, psc (Act Cdr)	LT CDR(FTC)	X	PWO(C)	01.11.82	IMS BRUSSELS
Bentham-Green, Nicholas Richard Heriot, psc	MAJ(FTC)	RM	LC	01.09.92	HQRM
Bentley, David Alan (Act Lt Cdr)	LT(FTC)	X	g	06.09.85	DRYAD
Benton, Angus Michael, BSc	LT CDR(FTC)	X	MCD	01.09.96	CNOCS GROUP
Benton, Peter John, MB, BCh, FFOM, AFOM	SURG CDR		(CO/M)	31.12.93	INM ALVERSTOKE
Benzie, Nichol James Emslie, BSc	LT(IC)	X	P	01.04.99	RNAS YEOVILTON
Beresford-Green, Paul Maxwell	LT(FTC)	S		16.12.92	RALEIGH
Berisford, Andrew William, LLB	LT(FTC)	S		01.06.97	VIGILANT(PORT)
Bernard, Alain Raymond, BA	LT(IC)	X	H2	01.04.97	SCOTT
Bernau, Jeremy Charles, pce, pce(sm)	LT CDR(FTC)	X	SM	01.11.91	FOSNNI OPS CFS
Berry, Paul	LT(FTC)	E	ME	15.06.95	1 PBS SEA
Berry, Steven Mark	SLT(IC)	E	WE	27.01.99	COLLINGWOOD
Berry, Timothy James, BSc	LT(IC)	X		01.09.98	NEWCASTLE
Berryman, Charles Bliss, BEng, CEng, MIMarE	LT CDR(FTC)	E	MESM	01.08.96	SULTAN
Bessell, David Alexander, BA	LT(FTC)	X	SM	01.06.93	VICTORIOUS(STBD)

Name	Rank	Branch	Spec	Seniority	Where Serving
Best, Peter	CAPT RM(FTC)	MA, LRAM,BS		01.01.98	RM BAND SCOTLAND
Best, Russell Richard , *BA, pce, psc*	CDR(FTC)	X	PWO(U)	31.12.95	MOD (LONDON)
Bestwick, Michael Charles	CAPT RM(FTC)	RM		25.04.95	HQ 3 CDO BDE RM
Beswick, Simon David	SLT(IC)	X		01.01.99	DARTMOUTH BRNC
Betteridge, Jeremy Trevor , *MIMgt, pce, pcea, psc*	CDR(FTC)	X	P	30.06.96	SULTAN AIB
Betton, Andrew , *BA*	LT CDR(FTC)	X	O	01.02.99	GRAFTON
Bevan, Jeffrey Richard	LT(IC)	X	P	16.02.00	RNAS CULDROSE
Bevan, Noel Stuart , *MB, BS, LRCP, MRCGP, MRCS*	SURG CAPT	-	GMPP	31.12.99	DRAKE CBP(DLO)
Bevan, Simon , *BSc, MBA, jsdc*	CDR(FTC)	X	METOC	31.12.93	JSCSC
Beveridge, Graham , *BSc*	LT(CC)	X	O U/T	01.04.00	RNAS CULDROSE
Beveridge, Simon	CHAPLAIN	CE		28.04.93	42 CDO RM
Beverstock, Mark Alistair , *BSc, CEng, MIEE*	CDR(FTC)	E	WESM	30.06.96	MOD (LONDON)
Bevis, Timothy John , *psc*	LT COL(FTC)	RM		31.12.98	HQRM
Bewick, David John , *pce*	LT CDR(FTC)	X	PWO(U)	01.07.97	BRIDPORT
Bewley, Nicholas John	LT(FTC)	X	FC	01.08.99	CARDIFF
Bhattacharya, Debdash , *BSc*	LT(CC)	X	P	16.06.90	810 SQN SEAHAWK
Bibbey, Mark William , *BA, psc(m)*	LT COL(FTC)	RM		30.06.92	HQ 3 CDO BDE RM
Bickerton, Richard Edward , *BSc, gdas*	LT CDR(CC)	X	O	01.10.96	LOAN DERA BSC DN
Biggs, Colin Richard	LT CDR(FTC)	E	MESM	01.10.98	SULTAN
Biggs, David Michael , *pcea*	LT CDR(FTC)	X	O	01.10.96	849 SQN HQ
Biggs, William Patrick Lowther , *BEng, MSc, MIEE*	LT CDR(FTC)	E	WE	01.04.98	MONTROSE
Bignell, Stephen , *BEng*	LT CDR(FTC)	E	WE	01.04.00	COLLINGWOOD
Billcliff, Niels , *BSc*	LT(IC)	X	O	16.05.94	819 SQN
Billington, Nigel Stephen , *BA, psc*	LT CDR(FTC)	S	SM	01.02.88	FOSF
Billington, Sam , *BEng*	SLT(IC)	E	ME	01.09.98	INVINCIBLE
Billington, Tony John *(Act Lt Cdr)*	LT(FTC)	X	EW	02.04.93	PJHQ
Bilson, John Michael Frederick , *pce*	LT CDR(FTC)	X	PWO(A)	01.01.93	MOD (LONDON)
Bing, Neil Adrian , *BSc*	LT(CC)	X	P	16.12.93	800 SQN
Bingham, David Spencer	LT CDR(FTC)	X	PWO(A)	01.03.99	FEARLESS
Binns, Jonathan Brian , *MSc, CEng, MIMarE*	CDR(FTC)	E	MESM	30.06.87	ASTUTE IPT
Binns, John Brendon Harold , *OBE, MSc, FIMarE, MINucE, jsdc (Act Capt)*	CDR(FTC)	E	MESM	31.12.88	DRAKE CBS
Binns, Jon Frank , *BA*	SLT(IC)	X		01.05.98	CARDIFF
Binns, John	SLT(IC)	E	WE	27.01.99	COLLINGWOOD
Binstead, Kenneth Nigel	LT(CC)	X	P	01.02.93	DHFS
Birbeck, Keith	LT CDR(FTC)	E	WESM	01.10.98	RALEIGH
Birchall, James Charles , *BSc*	LT(CC)	X	P	01.09.98	845 SQN
Birchall, Stephen John , *BSc, CEng, MIMarE*	LT CDR(FTC)	E	MESM	21.10.91	MOD (BATH)
Birchfield, Gary Malcolm , *BSc*	LT(CC)	X	P U/T	01.12.99	DHFS
Bird, David Edward , *pcea*	LT CDR(FTC)	X	P	01.10.93	EXCHANGE ITALY
Bird, Gary Michael , *BA*	CAPT RM(IC)	RM		01.09.99	CTCRM
Bird, Jonathan Michael , *BEng*	LT(CC)	X	O	01.05.92	810 SQN SEAHAWK
Bird, Matthew Graham James , *BEng*	LT(FTC)	E	AE	01.11.94	SULTAN
Bird, Richard Alexander James , *n*	LT CDR(FTC)	X	H1	01.07.98	SCOTT
Bird, Toby Samuel Varnam , *BA*	LT(IC)	E	TM	01.09.98	FEARLESS
Birkett, Claire Louise , *BSc*	LT(FTC)	X		01.05.97	CAPTAIN RNP TEAM
Birleson, Paul Denzil , *BSc*	LT(FTC)	X		01.09.99	HERALD
Birley, Jonathan Hugh , *pce*	LT CDR(FTC)	X	PWO(U)	01.05.95	DRYAD
Birmingham, Tony Clarence	LT(IC)	X	P	16.09.94	846 SQN
Birrell, Gavin Craig , *BSc*	LT(FTC)	X		01.07.97	RICHMOND
Birrell, Stuart Martin , *BA, mdtc*	MAJ(FTC)	RM		01.09.96	JSCSC
Birse, Bronwen Louise	LT(CC)	S		01.12.94	NELSON
Birse, Gregor James , *BA, MSc, PGDip*	LT(FTC)	X	METOC	01.05.92	CINCFLEET
Birt, David Jonathan , *MB, BS, FRCA*	SURG LTCDR	-	(CA)	25.08.94	MODHU DERRIFORD
Bishop, David John , *BA*	LT(IC)	X		01.01.95	LOAN DARA
Bishop, George Charles	LT(FTC)	X	AV	27.07.95	PJHQ
Bishop, Paul Richard , *BSc, MIMechE, AMRAeS (Act Capt)*	CDR(FTC)	E	AE	30.06.93	LOAN DARA
Bishop, Robert Johnstone , *MNI, pce, psc*	CDR(FTC)	X	PWO(U)	31.12.91	CINCFLEET
Bishop, Roger St John Stanley , *rcds, pce, pcea*	CAPT(FTC)	X	P	31.12.91	SA THE HAGUE
Bissett, Ian Michael	LT(FTC)	E	AE(L)	17.10.91	ES AIR YEO
Bissett, Phillip Keith , *BSc*	LT(FTC)	E	AE(L)	17.10.91	ES AIR BRISTOL
Bissett, Roger William	LT(FTC)	E	AE(L)	17.10.91	ILLUSTRIOUS
Bisson, Ian Jean Paul , *BSc, MSc, CEng, MIEE, psc, gw*	CDR(FTC)	E	WE	30.06.99	MOD (LONDON)

Name	Rank	Branch	Spec	Seniority	Where Serving
Bithell, Ian Stephen	LT(FTC)	X	ATC	01.11.89	RNAS YEOVILTON
Black, Edward, *BA, BSc (Com 2lt)*	SLT(IC)	X		01.05.97	RE ENTRY(RN)
Black, Jeremy James McLaren, *BA*	LT(FTC)	X	P	01.02.93	845 SQN
Black, Simon Andrew	LT(FTC)	X		01.11.96	NEPTUNE
Blackburn, Andrew Roland James, *BEng*	LT(CC)	E	AE	01.12.98	846 SQN
Blackburn, Lee Richard, *BEng*	SLT(FTC)	E	ME	01.09.97	SULTAN
Blackburn, Paul Reza	LT(CC)	X	P	01.12.93	899 SQN HERON
Blackburn, Stephen Anthony, *BSc, CEng, MIMarE*	LT CDR(FTC)	E	ME	01.03.98	GLASGOW
Blackburn, Stuart James, *SM(n)*	LT(FTC)	X	SM	01.05.94	TALENT
Blackett, Jeffrey *(BARRISTER)*	CAPT(FTC)	S	BAR	30.06.98	2SL/CNH
Blackham, *Sir* Jeremy (Joe), *KCB, BA, rcds, pce, psc*	VADM	-	D	24.06.97	MOD (LONDON)
Blacklock, James Francis	LT(FTC)	X	MW	26.04.99	ATHERSTONE
Blackman, Nicholas Trevor, *BSc, MA, CEng, MIEE, psc(j)*	LT CDR(FTC)	E	AE	01.01.94	SULTAN
Blackmore, James, *BSc*	LT(CC)	X	P	01.07.98	FONA VALLEY
Blackmore, Mark Stuart, *pce, pcea*	LT CDR(FTC)	X	O	01.11.97	JSCSC
Blackwell, Jason Mark	LT(IC)	X	ATC	16.01.98	CHFHQ
Blackwell, Richard Edward	LT CDR(FTC)	S	SM	01.12.96	FOSM NWOOD HQ
Blacow, Carl, *BEng*	LT(FTC)	E	ME	24.04.94	ARK ROYAL
Blain, Roderick Graham, *BA (BARRISTER)*	LT CDR(FTC)	S	BAR	01.04.92	2SL/CNH FOTR
Blair, Duncan Guy Sanderman, *MB, BCh, Dip FFP*	SURG LTCDR	-		01.08.97	NELSON (PAY)
Blair, Graeme John Livingston, *BEng*	LT(FTC)	E	MESM	01.05.96	VANGUARD(PORT)
Blair, Lee David	MID(IC)	X		01.01.99	DARTMOUTH BRNC
Blair, Samuel Raymond, *BSc, pce*	LT CDR(FTC)	X	N	01.05.86	NBC PORTSMOUTH
Blake, Gary Edmund, *BSc*	CDR(FTC)	E	WESM	30.06.00	CAPTAIN SM2
Blake, Keven Barry	LT CDR(FTC)	X	REG	01.10.94	2SL/CNH
Blake, Robert Michael, *BSc, CEng, MIEE*	CDR(FTC)	E	WE	30.06.84	DRYAD
Blakeley, Anne	LT	Q	CC	17.11.98	MODHU DERRIFORD
Blakey, Adrian Lawrence	LT CDR(FTC)	X	MCD	01.03.92	MWC PORTSDOWN
Blanchford, Daniel, *BEng*	CAPT RM(FTC)	RM		01.09.96	RM Poole
Bland, Christopher David, *MEng*	SLT(IC)	E	WE	01.09.98	CAMPBELTOWN
Bland, Steven, *MB, ChB*	SURG LT	-		07.08.96	RH HASLAR
Blazeby, Nigel James, *BSc, pce*	CDR(FTC)	X	PWO(U)	31.12.97	1 PBS SEA
Block, Andrew William George, *AMIEE, MA*	LT(FTC)	E	PWO(A)	01.07.94	EXCHANGE AUSTLIA
Blocke, Andrew David	LT(FTC)	MS	(AD)	04.04.96	HQ 3 CDO BDE RM
Blois, Simon Dudley, *BSc, IEng*	SLT(FTC)	E	WE	01.04.98	COLLINGWOOD
Bloska, Robert Max	LT(FTC)	X	EW	01.01.00	PJHQ
Blount, Derek Raymond, *BSc, CEng, MIMechE*	LT CDR(FTC)	E	MESM	01.04.94	CSST SEA
Blount, Keith Edward, *pce*	LT CDR(FTC)	X	P	01.02.97	820 SQN
Blow, Philip Thomas, *BSc*	LT(CC)	E	MESM	01.09.95	VICTORIOUS(STBD)
Blowers, Michael David, *pce, pcea, psc(a)*	LT CDR(FTC)	X	O	01.09.92	MOD (LONDON)
Blunden, Jeremy Jonathan Frank, *LVO, BSc, pce*	CDR(FTC)	X	PWO(N)	30.06.96	MOD (LONDON)
Blyth, Michael	CAPT RM(IC)	RM		28.04.99	OCLC BIRM
Blythe, James	SLT(CC)	X		01.04.99	DRYAD
Blythe, Paul Christipher, *pce, pce(sm)*	LT CDR(FTC)	X	SM	01.10.99	TRIUMPH
Blythe, Tom Stewart	CAPT RM(FTC)	RM	LC	01.09.94	CDO LOG REGT RM
Boardman, Sarah Jane, *BA*	SLT(IC)	S		01.01.99	DARTMOUTH BRNC
Boast, Mark Thomas, *MBE, pcea, tp (Act Cdr)*	LT CDR(FTC)	X	P	01.09.89	MOD (LONDON)
Boddington, Jeremy Denis Leonard, *BSc, pcea*	LT CDR(FTC)	X	P	16.12.95	LOAN DERA BSC DN
Bodman, Simon Alexander, *BA, BEng*	SLT(CC)	X		01.01.98	QUORN
Body, Howard Joseph, *BA, ODC(SWISS)*	LT CDR(FTC)	E	TM	01.12.91	FOSF
Boeckx, Thomas Julius Francis, *MSc*	SLT(FTC)	X		01.01.98	DULVERTON
Boissier, Robin Paul, *MA, pce, pce(sm), psc (COMMODORE)*	CAPT(FTC)	X	PWO(N)	30.06.94	NELSON
Bolam, Andrew Guy, *BSc, CEng, MIMarE*	LT CDR(FTC)	E	ME	01.06.94	MARLBOROUGH
Bollen, Johanna Michelle	LT(CC)	S		01.01.96	DARTMOUTH BRNC
Bolton, Jonathan Praed, *BEng, CEng, MIMarE*	LT CDR(FTC)	E	ME	01.09.99	MOD (BATH)
Bolton, Matthew Thomas William, *BEng, MSc, CEng, MIMarE, MIMechE*	LT CDR(FTC)	E	ME	06.02.00	SULTAN
Bolton, Stephen Jack	LT(CC)	X	P	16.10.93	EXCHANGE USA
Bommert, Jon Karl, *BSc*	SLT(FTC)	S		01.01.98	ILLUSTRIOUS
Bond, Alan James, *BEng*	LT(FTC)	E	AE	09.06.92	FONA SEAGOING
Bond, Nigel David	LT CDR(FTC)	S		01.05.93	INVINCIBLE
Bond, Robert Douglas Acton	MID(NE)(IC)	X	P U/T	01.09.99	DARTMOUTH BRNC
Bone, Christopher John	LT CDR(FTC)	E	AE	01.05.92	2SL/CNH FOTR
Bone, Darren Nigel, *pce, psc(j)*	CDR(FTC)	X	PWO(A)	31.12.99	NELSON (PAY)

Name	Rank	Branch	Spec	Seniority	Where Serving
Bone, James	LT(FTC)	X		01.03.97	CARDIFF
Bone, Richard Charles , *BSc*	LT CDR(FTC)	E	TMSM	01.05.98	DRYAD
Bonnar, John Andrew , *BEng, AMIEE*	LT(FTC)	E	WE	01.06.93	DGSS BRISTOL
Bonnar, Susan Mary	LT(CC)	X	ATC	01.11.96	RAF WEST DRAYTON
Bonner, Neil	LT(FTC)	E	WESM	01.08.94	SSA BRISTOL
Bonner, Timothy	SURG SLT	-		09.10.97	DARTMOUTH BRNC
Bonney, James Edward , *BSc*	2LT(GRAD)(IC)	RM		01.09.99	CTCRM LYMPSTONE
Booker, Glenn Raymond	LT CDR(FTC)	X	ATC	01.10.89	FONA
Booker, Scott Richard	LT(CC)	X	P	16.06.90	810 SQN SEAHAWK
Boon, Gareth John	SLT(FTC)	X	HM	19.09.97	820 SQN
Boorman, Josephine Catherine , *BA*	LT(FTC)	X	H2	01.09.96	HERALD
Booth, Michael Dennison , *DSC, pce, psc*	CAPT(FTC)	X	P	30.06.95	NELSON
Booth, William Norman	LT(FTC)	E	ME	02.09.99	DRAKE CFM
Bootland, Erich Gustav , *psc*	CDR(FTC)	MS	(AD)	01.10.95	MODHU DERRIFORD
Boraston, Peter John , *BSc, CEng, MIEE*	LT CDR(FTC)	E	WE	01.04.90	NELSON
Borbone, Nicholas	LT(FTC)	X		06.02.95	DRYAD
Borland, Stuart Andrew , *BSc, CEng, MIEE*	LT CDR(FTC)	E	WE	01.07.94	FOST SEA
Borley, Kim John , *MA, CEng, MIEE, rcds, jsdc*	CAPT(FTC)	E	WESM	31.12.95	DPA BRISTOL
Boschi, Paul Hamilton , *BA*	CAPT RM()	RM		01.09.99	HQ 3 CDO BDE RM
Bosshardt, Robert George , *BSc, pce,* jsdc	CDR(FTC)	X	PWO(A)	31.12.93	DRYAD
Bostock, Colin Edward	LT CDR(FTC)	S		09.09.90	AGRIPPA NAVSOUTH
Boston, Justin , *BA*	LT(CC)	E	TM	01.01.93	2SL/CNH FOTR
Bosustow, Antony Michael , *CEng, MIEE*	LT CDR(FTC)	E	WE	01.06.98	ARGYLL
Bosustow, Benjamin Francis , *BEng*	LT(CC)	E	WESM	01.02.91	DCSA RADIO HQ
Boswell, Daniel John , *BEd*	LT(IC)	X		01.03.99	BICESTER
Bottomley, Steven	LT(FTC)	E	AE(L)	06.09.96	JHCHQ
Boughton, Timothy Frederick	LT(CC)	X	P	24.01.98	JSCSC
Bougourd, Mark Anthony , *BEng*	LT CDR(FTC)	E	AE	01.10.99	SULTAN
Boulind, Matthew Angus , *LLB*	SLT(IC)	X		01.01.99	DARTMOUTH BRNC
Boullin, John Paul , *BEng*	SLT(IC)	X		01.09.98	DARTMOUTH BRNC
Boulton, Neil Andrew , *BSc*	LT CDR(CC)	E	TM	20.11.98	2SL/CNH FOTR
Bourn, Kelvin Edward , *BSc, psc(a)*	LT CDR(FTC)	X	PWO(N)	09.05.85	CNOCS GROUP
Bourne, Christopher Michael , *pce*	LT CDR(FTC)	X	O	16.08.97	815 SQN HQ
Bourne, Donald Sidney	LT CDR(FTC)	E	AE(L)	01.10.98	771 SK5 SAR
Bourne, Philip John	CAPT RM(FTC)	RM	SO(LE)	01.01.96	539 ASLT SQN RM
Bouyac, David Roger Louis	SLT(IC)	X	P U/T	01.04.98	RAF CRANWELL EFS
Bowbrick, Richard Charles , *pce*	LT CDR(FTC)	X	PWO(A)	01.04.97	BERKELEY
Bowden, Matthew Neil , *BSc, PGDip*	LT CDR(CC)	E	TM	01.10.98	JSCSC
Bowden, Matthew Thomas Edward , *BEng*	LT(FTC)	E	WE	01.02.95	DRYAD
Bowen, Christopher Nicholas , *BSc, PGCE*	LT(IC)	X		01.12.99	DRYAD
Bowen, Geoffrey Philip	CDR(FTC)	X	PWO(A)	01.10.96	CNOCS GROUP
Bowen, Michael , *ARRC, BA, MSc*	CDR	Q	RNT	31.12.98	2SL/CNH
Bowen, Nigel Timothy , *pce, pcea*	LT CDR(FTC)	X	PWO(U)	01.11.96	SHEFFIELD
Bowen, Richard James	MID(UCE)(IC)	E	WE	01.09.99	NEWCASTLE
Bower, Andrew John , *BSc*	LT(FTC)	X	SM	01.08.93	SOVEREIGN
Bower, John William	LT(FTC)	S	(S)	24.07.97	ILLUSTRIOUS
Bower, Nigel Scott , *pce(sm)*	LT CDR(FTC)	X	SM	01.04.97	SUPERB
Bowers, John	LT(CC)	X	O	01.03.91	815 FLT 219
Bowhay, Simon , *BSc*	LT CDR(FTC)	E	WESM	01.05.99	FOSM NWOOD HQ
Bowie, Alan Niven , *MB, BCh*	SURG LTCDR	-		11.03.99	FEARLESS
Bowker, Eric Arthur , *psc*	CDR(FTC)	E	ME	31.12.91	SSA DEVONPORT
Bowker, Geoffrey Neil	LT CDR(FTC)	X	ATC	01.10.93	RNAS CULDROSE
Bowker, Iain Cameron , *BEng*	LT(FTC)	E	MESM	13.02.93	VICTORIOUS(PORT)
Bowker, Michael Andrew , *BSc, MSc, MIMarE, MIMechE, jsdc*	CAPT(FTC)	E	MESM	30.06.97	NP BRISTOL
Bowkett, Robert Murray , *BSc, psc(m), hcsc*	COL(FTC)	RM		31.12.96	HQRM
Bowman, Robert James , *BEng*	LT(FTC)	E	AE	01.04.95	JSCSC
Bowness, Paul	LT(FTC)	E	AE(M)	15.10.93	SULTAN
Bowra, Mark Andrew	CAPT RM(IC)	RM	MLDR	01.09.97	45 CDO RM
Bowser, Nicholas John *(Act Lt)*	SLT(FTC)	E	AE	02.05.97	849 SQN B FLT
Bowyer, Richard John	LT RM(IC)	RM	MLDR	01.05.00	MOD (LONDON)
Boxall, Pauline , *BEng*	LT(FTC)	E	ME	01.04.97	CUMBERLAND
Boxall-Hunt, Brian Paul , *OBE, AMNI, pce*	CDR(FTC)	X	PWO(A)	30.06.91	DRYAD
Boyce, *Sir* Michael (Cecil) , *GCB, OBE, ADC, rcds, psc*	ADM	-	SM	25.05.95	MOD (LONDON)

Name	Rank	Branch	Spec	Seniority	Where Serving
Boyd, James Alexander ,*jsdc,pce(sm)*	CAPT(FTC)	X	SM	30.06.96	SA TOKYO
Boyd, Nicholas ,*BSc, MSc, CEng, MIMechE*	LT CDR(FTC)	E	ME	01.03.95	MOD (BATH)
Boyes, Gareth Angus ,*BA(OU), MEng*	LT(FTC)	E	ME	01.07.97	IRON DUKE
Boyes, Martyn Richard ,*BEng*	LT(FTC)	E	MESM	01.02.95	SOVEREIGN
Boyes, Norman	LT CDR(FTC)	E	ME	11.08.88	HQRM
Boyes, Richard Austen	LT(FTC)	X	P	01.03.89	700M MERLIN IFTU
Boyle, Jonathan Bartley ,*BEng*	LT(FTC)	E	MESM	01.10.94	MOD (BATH)
Boynton, Stephen Justin ,*BSc*	LT CDR(FTC)	X	O	01.12.99	750 SQN OBS SCH
Bracher, Hugh	LT CDR(FTC)	E	WESM	01.10.96	DRAKE CBS
Bradburn, James Anthony ,*BSc*	LT(CC)	X		01.01.99	VENGEANCE(PORT)
Bradburn, Stephen Joseph ,*pcea*	LT CDR(FTC)	X	P	01.10.93	824 NAS
Bradbury, James Edward David ,*BSc, MSc*	SLT(CC)	X		01.01.98	ANGLESEY
Bradbury, Simon	CHAPLAIN	RC		18.09.96	COLLINGWOOD
Bradford, Terrance Horace Colin	LT(FTC)	MS	(AD)	04.04.96	INM ALVERSTOKE
Brading, Roland David	2LT(IC)	RM		02.09.98	CTCRM LYMPSTONE
Bradley, Matthew Thomas ,*n*	LT(FTC)	X		01.05.94	SOMERSET
Bradley, Patrick Martin ,*BEng*	LT(FTC)	E	WE	01.06.92	DGSS BRISTOL
Bradley, Rupert Litherland ,*LLB*	LT(IC)	X	P	01.11.96	820 SQN
Bradley, Trevor Adrian ,*BEng*	SLT(IC)	E	WE	01.01.99	DARTMOUTH BRNC
Brads, Wayne ,*BSc*	LT CDR(FTC)	E	TMSM	14.01.94	RALEIGH
Bradshaw, Kevin Thomas ,*BSc*	LT(FTC)	E	WE	18.02.94	CFM PORTSMOUTH
Bradshaw, Robert Julian ,*MA,pce(sm) (COMMODORE)*	CAPT(FTC)	X	SM	31.12.89	MOD (LONDON) (
Brady, Mark Rowland ,*BSc,pce*	LT CDR(FTC)	X		16.01.81	CDRE MFP
Brady, Sean Edward ,*pce*	LT CDR(FTC)	X	PWO(U)	01.09.96	EXCHANGE USA
Brady, Sean ,*BSc*	CAPT RM(IC)	RM		01.09.97	PSYOPS TEAM
Brady, Thomas William	SLT(FTC)	S	(W)	01.04.98	CHFHQ
Braham, Stephen Wyn ,*BSc, MSc, CEng, FIMarE, psc*	CDR(FTC)	E	ME	30.06.97	BDS WASHINGTON
Brailey, Ian Stewart Fordyce	LT(FTC)	X	AV	04.04.96	INVINCIBLE
Brain, William James ,*FHCIMA*	2LT(GRAD)(IC)	RM		02.09.98	45 CDO RM
Braithwaite, Geoffrey	SLT(IC)	X		01.04.00	COVENTRY
Braithwaite, Jeremy Sean	LT(FTC)	X	HM	01.01.95	RFANSU
Bramall, Kieron Scott ,*BA*	LT(CC)	X	SM	01.10.97	VIGILANT(STBD)
Bramley, Stephen ,*pce,pcea,psc*	CDR(FTC)	X	P	31.12.91	ILLUSTRIOUS
Bramwell, John Gerald	LT(CC)	X	O	01.04.93	771 SK5 SAR
Branch-Evans, Simon Jonathon ,*MBE, BSc, MDA, CEng, MRAeS*	CAPT(FTC)	E	AE	30.06.98	MOD (LONDON)
Brand, Simon Martin ,*BSc,pce,pcea*	CDR(FTC)	X	P	30.06.97	JSCSC
Bratby, Simon Paul	LT(CC)	X	P	16.11.94	815 FLT 210
Bratt, Adrian Richard ,*BSc,n*	LT(FTC)	X		01.01.96	CAMPBELTOWN
Bravery, Martin Anthony Edward	LT CDR(FTC)	X	P	01.05.99	CARDIFF
Bray, Katherine	SURG SLT	-		12.02.98	DARTMOUTH BRNC
Bray, Matthew Robert *(Act Maj)*	CAPT RM(FTC)	RM		25.04.95	NMA PORTSMOUTH
Bray, Nigel Godfrey Hensman ,*pce*	CAPT(FTC)	X	AWO(C)	30.06.95	SACLANT USA
Brayson, Mark	LT(CC)	X	P	16.10.94	702 SQN HERON
Brazendale, Colin ,*MBE*	LT CDR(FTC)	E	AE(L)	01.10.95	MOD DHSA
Brazier, Francis William Thomas ,*IEng, FIEIE*	CDR(FTC)	E	WE	01.10.97	2SL/CNH FOTR
Brazier, Lars Frank ,*MA*	LT(IC)	X	P	01.04.99	RNAS YEOVILTON
Brearley, Rosalind Lydia ,*BSc*	SLT(IC)	X		01.01.98	SHETLAND
Breckenridge, Iain Galloway ,*pce,pce(sm)*	LT CDR(FTC)	X	SM	01.07.97	CSST SEA
Bree, Stephen Edward Peter ,*MB, BCh, FRCA*	SURG CDR	-	(CA)	30.06.00	INVINCIBLE
Breen, John Edward ,*MEng*	SLT(IC)	E	AE	01.09.98	CARDIFF
Brember, Peter Bruce	LT(FTC)	X	AV	25.07.96	INVINCIBLE
Brenchley, Nigel Gerard	LT(FTC)	S		01.07.92	SUTHERLAND
Brennan, Andrew John	LT(CC)	X	SM	01.09.95	VIGILANT(STBD)
Brennan, Paul Anthony	LT(FTC)	E	MESM	02.09.99	TRENCHANT
Breslin, Michael John ,*BEM*	LT(CS)	-		07.01.90	DNR NE ENGLAND
Brewer, Christopher Edward ,*BSc*	LT(FTC)	X		01.08.99	TRAFALGAR
Brewin, David John ,*BSc*	LT(IC)	X	PU/T	01.09.99	DHFS
Brian, Neil ,*pcea*	LT(CC)	X	O	01.08.92	824 NAS
Bridgeman, Jeffrey William Treverton	LT CDR(FTC)	S	(W)	01.10.96	2SL/CNH
Bridger, David William ,*MSc, HND*	CDR(FTC)	E	TM	30.06.96	NELSON
Bridger, Richard John ,*pcea*	LT CDR(FTC)	X	O	01.06.92	820 SQN
Brier, Christopher Anthony Clive ,*AMIAM*	LT CDR(FTC)	S	(W)	01.10.97	JSU NORTHWOOD
Briers, Matthew Peter ,*pcea*	LT CDR(FTC)	X	P	01.11.96	ARGYLL

Name	Rank	Branch	Spec	Seniority	Where Serving
Briggs, Helen Claire	SLT(IC)	X	ATCU/T	01.01.99	DARTMOUTH BRNC
Briggs, Mark David, *BEng*	LT(CC)	E	WE	01.06.97	INVINCIBLE
Brighouse, Neil George	CAPT RM(FTC)	RM	P U/T	24.04.96	846 SQN
Bright, David Alan, *BSc, MSc, MCGI*	LT CDR(CC)	E	TM	01.10.92	RALEIGH
Brimacombe, Louise Marie, *BSc*	LT(IC)	S		01.04.00	RALEIGH
Brimley, Keith Stuart, *BSc, pce*	LT CDR(FTC)	X	AWO(C)†	01.12.80	DRYAD
Brims, Fraser, *MB, ChB*	SURG LT	-		05.08.98	VENGEANCE(PORT)
Brinsden, Mark Dudley, *MB, BS, MRCS*	SURG LTCDR	-		01.08.99	MODHU DERRIFORD
Brint, Ian	SLT(IC)	S	(W)	29.04.98	RALEIGH
Bristow, Geoffrey David	LT CDR(FTC)	X	SM	01.10.88	2SL/CNH FOTR
Bristowe, Paul Andrew, *BSc*	LT(FTC)	X	P U/T	01.03.93	849 SQN B FLT
Britton, Nicholas John, *MBE, BSc*	LT CDR(FTC)	X		01.04.90	MOD (LONDON)
Broad, Robert Oliver, *BSc, CEng, MIMechE, psc*	CDR(FTC)	E	ME	30.06.90	MOD (BATH)
Broadbent, Anthony, *BSc*	LT CDR(FTC)	E	WE	29.11.81	HQ DCSA
Broadbent, Andrew Craig, *BEng*	LT(FTC)	E	WESM	01.08.93	JSCSC
Broadbent, Peter Stephen, *BSc, BA(OU)*	LT(FTC)	E	WE	01.03.94	COLLINGWOOD
Broadhurst, Michael John, *BSc, psc, ocds(Can)*	CAPT(FTC)	E	ME	31.12.92	NELSON
Broadhurst, Michael Robert, *BA*	LT(FTC)	X	FC	01.12.92	DRYAD
Broadley, Kevin James, *BSc, MA, pce, pcea, psc*	CDR(FTC)	X	P	30.06.00	NEPTUNE
Brock, Mathew Jonathan	SLT(IC)	X		01.01.99	DARTMOUTH BRNC
Brock, Raymond Frederick	LT(FTC)	S		01.03.94	MONTROSE
Brockington, Gordon Colin, *BSc*	LT(FTC)	X		01.11.97	DRYAD
Brocklebank, Guy Philip, *BSc, FRSA, pce, MIMgt*	CDR(FTC)	X	PWO(C)	31.12.92	NEPTUNE CFS
Brockwell, Paul Edward Norman, *MBE, BSc, CEng, MIMarE*	CDR(FTC)	E	MESM	30.06.94	CAPTAIN SM2
Brodie, Duncan John, *BEng*	SLT(IC)	E	AE	01.01.99	DARTMOUTH BRNC
Brodie, Ross William James, *n*	LT(FTC)	X		01.12.94	DRYAD
Brodier, Mark Ian	LT(FTC)	E	AE(L)	04.09.98	ES AIR YEO
Brodribb, Timothy John	SURG LT	-		04.08.99	CTCRM
Brokenshire, Laurence Phillip, *BA, BSc, Cert Ed, MBCS, MIMA, AFIMA, jsdc*	CAPT(FTC)	E	TM	30.06.94	MOD (LONDON)
Bromage, Kenneth Charles	CHAPLAIN	CE		02.08.92	AFCC
Bromige, Timothy Robert James, *pce*	LT CDR(FTC)	X	PWO(A)	19.05.92	EXCHANGE CANADA
Brook, John Gordon, *BSc, CEng, MIEE, psc*	LT CDR(FTC)	E	WE	21.03.87	SCU LEYDENE ACNS
Brooks, Adella Maree, *BA*	SLT(CC)	X		01.01.98	GUERNSEY
Brooks, Alan Steven, *MBE, BSc, BTech, pce, pcea,*	CAPT(FTC)	X	O	31.12.98	NELSON *psc*
Brooks, Barry Philip Stewart, *BSc, ACGI, psc (COMMODORE)*	CAPT(FTC)	E	WESM	31.12.92	MOD (BATH)
Brooks, Graeme Christian Gibbon	LT(FTC)	X	MCD	01.04.97	QUORN
Brooks, Gary Lee	LT CDR(FTC)	X	H1	01.04.99	HERALD
Brooks, Mervyn Leigh	LT CDR(FTC)	X	AV	01.10.97	STG BRISTOL
Brooks, Nicholas Robert, *BEng*	SLT(IC)	E		01.09.98	SOUTHAMPTON
Brooksbank, Richard	MID(NE)(IC)	S		01.01.00	DARTMOUTH BRNC
Brooksbank, Richard James, *BSc, pce, pcea*	CDR(FTC)	X	P	31.12.97	RALEIGH
Broom, Neil John, *MBE*	LT CDR	Q	OTSPEC	01.10.99	RN GIBRALTAR
Brooman, Martin John	LT(CC)	X	P	16.08.95	771 SK5 SAR
Brosnan, Mark Anthony	LT(CC)	X	O	16.07.93	810 SQN SEAHAWK
Broster, Mark, *BA*	SLT(IC)	X		01.05.98	ILLUSTRIOUS
Broster, Patrick Thomas, *BA*	LT CDR(FTC)	X	O	01.10.97	CMSA UK
Brothers, Anthony Herbert George	LT(FTC)	E	WE	18.02.94	CAPT(H) DEVPT
Brotherton, John Darren, *QCBA*	LT(FTC)	X	P	16.04.90	810 SQN SEAHAWK
Brotherton, Michael, *MBE, BD*	CHAPLAIN	CE		04.09.84	RNAS CULDROSE
Brotton, Peter James, *BSc*	LT(FTC)	X		01.04.98	SHETLAND
Brougham, Michael John Douglas, *MBE, BSc, CEng, MRAeS, rcds, jsdc (COMMODORE)*	CAPT(FTC)	E	AE(P)	31.12.92	MOD DHSA
Brown, Andrew, *BM, BCh, BA*	SURG LT	-		05.08.98	42 CDO RM
Brown, Andrew Martyn, *BEng*	LT(FTC)	E	WE	01.12.96	GLASGOW
Brown, Andrew Paul	LT(FTC)	X	ATC	01.02.92	OCEAN
Brown, Aaron Richard Andrew	LT(IC)	X	O U/T	01.03.00	750 SQN OBS SCH
Brown, Andrew Scott, *BSc, MSc*	SLT(IC)	X		01.09.98	DARTMOUTH BRNC
Brown, Bernard Craig	SLT	Q		11.06.96	RN GIBRALTAR
Brown, Christopher Dennis, *pcea*	LT CDR(FTC)	X	P	01.09.87	LOAN DERA BSC DN
Brown, Clare Lucy, *BSc*	LT(IC)	X		01.12.95	GLASGOW
Brown, David Campbell, *MB, BCh, ChB, MSc, LRCP, FFOM, MRCS, MSRP*	SURG CDR	-	CPDATE	31.12.91	INM ALVERSTOKE
Brown, David John, *BSc*	LT CDR(FTC)	X	SM	01.04.85	PJHQ
Brown, Howard Spencer, *MBE, pce, pcea*	CDR(FTC)	X	P	31.12.99	HQ3GP HQSTC

Name	Rank	Branch	Spec	Seniority	Where Serving
Brown, James Alexander , *BSc*	SLT(IC)	X		01.01.98	ANGLESEY
Brown, Judith Claire , *ARRC, psc, QHNS*	CAPT	Q	OTSPEC	31.12.99	DMTO HQ
Brown, Jeffery Ryan , *BSc*	2LT(GRAD)(IC)	RM		01.09.99	CTCRM LYMPSTONE
Brown, Leonard Anthony , *BA*	CAPT RM(FTC)	RM	P	01.09.97	EXCHANGE USA
Brown, Michael Eric	LT CDR(FTC)	E	WE	01.10.91	NC3 AGENCY
Brown, Malcolm Keith , *MBE, BSc, pce*	CDR(FTC)	X	PWO(A)	20.09.94	SACLANT USA
Brown, Neil Logan , *LLB (BARRISTER)*	CDR(FTC)	S	BAR	31.12.98	ILLUSTRIOUS
Brown, Nigel Peter , *BSc, MA, psc(m)*	LT COL(FTC)	RM	C	30.06.98	MOD (LONDON)
Brown, Paul Angus	LT(FTC)	E	AE(M)	07.09.95	ES AIR YEO
Brown, Paul Alexander Everett , *BA, pce, n*	LT CDR(FTC)	X	PWO(A)	01.08.99	MANCHESTER
Brown, Peter Richard , *pce, psc*	LT CDR(FTC)	X	PWO(A)	16.03.85	SHAPE BELGIUM
Brown, Peter St John , *BEng, MIMarE*	LT CDR(FTC)	E	MESM	01.06.95	DRAKE CFM
Brown, Robert Andrew Mark , *OBE, pce*	CDR(FTC)	X	PWO(A)	31.12.94	MANCHESTER
Brown, Robert John	MAJ(FTC)	RM	SO(LE)	01.10.92	HQRM
Brown, Simon David , *n*	LT(FTC)	X		01.11.94	DRYAD
Brown, Stephen Glynn	SLT(CC)	X	P	04.08.97	845 SQN
Brown, Stephen	LT(FTC)	X	MCD	15.01.93	DRYAD
Brown, Spencer James	LT(CC)	X	MW	01.10.95	BRECON
Brown, Scott	CHAPLAIN	SF		20.04.93	SULTAN
Brown, William Clarke , *pce*	LT CDR(FTC)	X	PWO(A)	01.01.94	COVENTRY
Browning, Martin Lawrence Corbet	LT CDR(FTC)	X	SM	21.09.86	NEPTUNE
Browning, Rowan Susannah , *BSc, AIS*	LT(CC)	E	IS	01.01.90	PJHQ
Bruce, Steven Leonard , *BA(OU), MA, psc*	LT COL(FTC)	RM		30.06.96	IMS BRUSSELS
Bruce-Jones, Nicholas William , *BA, psc(a)*	MAJ(FTC)	RM		01.09.92	HQRM
Bruford, Robert Michael Charles	LT CDR(FTC)	X	PWO(A)	01.04.00	SOUTHAMPTON
Brundle, Paul Robert , *MBE*	LT CDR(FTC)	X	ATC	01.10.95	FONA
Brunell, Paul Jonathan	LT(FTC)	E	AE(M)	02.09.99	FONA
Brunink, James William	LT CDR(FTC)	E	WE	01.10.92	SAUDI AFPS SAUDI
Brunsdon-Brown, Sebastian Edward	LT(CC)	X	P	16.05.92	824 NAS
Brunskill, John Edmund Tanner	LT(CC)	X	P	01.06.91	EXCHANGE GERMANY
Brunton, Steven Buchanan , *MSc, CEng, MIEE, MCGI, mdtc*	CDR(FTC)	E	WESM	31.12.95	DGCIS BRISTOL
Brutton, Joseph Henry , *BEng*	LT(IC)	E	MESM	01.07.97	VENGEANCE(PORT)
Bryan, Rory John Lockton , *BA*	LT CDR(FTC)	X	PWO(U)	01.01.00	IRON DUKE
Bryant, Barry William , *pce, pcea, psc (COMMODORE)*	CAPT(FTC)	X	PWO	31.12.92	2SL/CNH
Bryant, David John	LT CDR(FTC)	X	PWO(U)	01.10.94	1 PBS SEA
Bryant, Daniel John Grenfell	LT(FTC)	S	SM	01.10.94	TURBULENT
Bryant, Graham David	LT CDR(FTC)	S	CA	01.10.99	NELSON
Bryant, Peter	LT(FTC)	E	ME	15.02.85	DRAKE CFM
Bryce, Colin Gerard , *BSc, PGCE, MBCS, adp*	LT CDR(CC)	E	IS	01.10.94	2SL/CNH FOTR
Bryce, Fiona , *MA*	SLT	Q		16.07.97	RH HASLAR
Bryce, Graeme	SG SLT(D)	-		01.01.99	DARTMOUTH BRNC
Bryce, Neville Anthony	LT(FTC)	E	MESM	14.10.94	DRAKE CFM
Bryson, Susan Ainee , *BA, n*	LT(CC)	X		01.03.94	SHEFFIELD
Bubb, Jonathan David	CAPT RM(FTC)	RM		01.05.99	CTCRM
Buchan, John Alan , *MA*	LT(IC)	X		01.09.99	DEF DIVING SCHL
Buchan-Steele, Mark Anthony , *BSc*	LT CDR(FTC)	S	SM	05.01.94	JSCSC
Buchanan, Alison Jane , *MA*	LT CDR(CC)	W	S	01.10.95	JACIG
Buchanan, Robert Michael , *BEng*	SLT(IC)	E	ME	01.05.98	ILLUSTRIOUS
Buck, James Edward , *n*	LT CDR(FTC)	X	PWO(U)	01.04.00	CDRE MFP
Buck, Sarah Rachael , *BSc*	LT(IC)	E		01.05.98	SULTAN
Buckenham, Peter James	LT(CC)	E	ME	01.10.99	DARTMOUTH BRNC
Buckett, Edward Joseph	LT CDR(FTC)	X	P	01.10.90	OCLC BRISTOL
Buckingham, Guy	LT(FTC)	X	SM	01.12.93	TURBULENT
Buckland, Richard John Francis , *pce, pcea*	CDR(FTC)	X	O	31.12.99	LANCASTER
Buckle, Iain Lawrence , *BEng, MBA, CEng, MIMarE*	LT CDR(FTC)	E	WE	01.07.96	GRAFTON
Buckley, Dominic David George , *BA*	LT(CC)	X	HM	01.02.94	RFANSU
Buckley, Martin John , *BA, pce*	LT CDR(FTC)	X	SM	16.05.85	FEARLESS
Buckley, Noel Christopher	LT(FS)	FS		19.09.97	NEPTUNE 2SL/CNH
Buckley, Paul , *pce*	LT CDR(FTC)	X	PWO(A)	01.05.84	EXCELLENT
Buckley, Phillip James Anthony , *jsdc, pce(sm), pce*	CDR(FTC)	X	PWO(U)	31.12.96	TRIUMPH
Bucklow, Stephen Paul	LT(IC)	X	P	01.06.91	819 SQN
Bucknall, Robin James Woolcott *(Act Maj)*	CAPT RM(FTC)	RM		26.04.94	HQRM
Bucknell, David Ian	LT CDR(FTC)	X	PWO(U)	01.07.96	CAPT F4 (SEA)

Name	Rank	Branch	Spec	Seniority	Where Serving
Budd, Philip Richard , *BA, pce*	LT CDR(FTC)	X	AWO(A)	16.12.80	FOSF
Budge, Russell George , *BSc, psc*	LT CDR(FTC)	E	WE	01.11.81	DGCIS BRISTOL
Bugg, Kevin John	LT(FTC)	E	AE(M)	01.03.94	EXCHANGE ARMY UK
Bukhory, Hamesh , *BEng*	SLT(IC)	E	AE	01.01.99	DARTMOUTH BRNC
Bulcock, Lindsay , *BSc, MSc*	LT(CC)	E	TM	01.11.89	SULTAN
Bulcock, Michael , *BEng (Act Lt Cdr)*	LT(FTC)	E	MESM	28.07.92	FOSNNI/NBC CLYDE
Bull, Andrew John , *pcea, psc*	CDR(FTC)	X	O	01.10.95	SA LISBON
Bull, Christopher Martin Sefton , *MA, CEng, MIEE*	LT CDR(FTC)	E	WESM	01.03.97	SCEPTRE
Bull, Charlotte Vivienne Rachel , *BA*	LT(FTC)	S		01.11.97	INVINCIBLE
Bull, Geoffrey Charles , *BEng, MSc, AMIMechE*	LT CDR(FTC)	E	MESM	01.11.94	SCEPTRE
Bull, Louis Paul , *BA*	SLT(IC)	X		01.01.98	ATHERSTONE
Bull, Michael Antony John , *BSc*	LT(CC)	X	SM	11.09.99	RALEIGH
Bullen, Michael Peter , *BA, pcea*	LT(CC)	X	P	16.08.91	DHFS
Bullock, James Richard	SLT(CC)	X	P U/T	01.01.00	RNAS YEOVILTON
Bullock, Michael Peter , *MBE*	CDR(FTC)	S	SM	31.12.95	NMA PORTSMOUTH
Bullock, Robert Arthur , *BSc*	SLT(CC)	X	O U/T	01.01.98	BANGOR
Bulmer, Renny John	CAPT RM(FTC)	RM	SO(LE)	01.01.94	RMR MERSEYSIDE
Bulter, Danielle Barbara , *BEng*	SLT(IC)	E		01.09.98	FEARLESS
Bunn, Malcolm Edward	LT CDR(FTC)	X	P	01.10.91	750 SQN (HERON)
Bunney, Graham John , *BSc*	LT(IC)	X	P	01.08.94	819 SQN
Bunt, Kevin John	LT(FTC)	S	(S)	06.04.95	MOD (LONDON)
Burbidge, Kay	LT(CC)	X	O	01.09.98	820 SQN
Burbridge, Dominic James , *BEng*	LT(FTC)	E	WESM	01.12.94	HQ DCSA
Burchell, Hannah Eve , *BA*	LT(FTC)	S		01.01.00	FOSM NWOOD HQ
Burden, John Charles	LT CDR(FTC)	X	MCD	01.11.91	EXCHANGE USA
Burdett, Richard Wyndham , *BSc, CEng, MIMechE*	LT CDR(FTC)	E	MESM	01.06.92	DSQ ROSYTH
Burdett, Richard Wyndham , *BSc*	LT(IC)	X		01.01.99	GRIMSBY
Burge, Roger George	LT(FTC)	E	WESM	19.02.93	SSA/CWTA PORTS
Burgess, Andrew James , *MB, BSc, BCh, ChB, FFARCS,*	SURG CDR	-	(CA)	30.06.96	NP 1067 KOSOVO *FRCA*
Burgess, Gary Thomas Myles , *BEng, MSc*	LT CDR(FTC)	E	MESM	01.02.00	NP BRISTOL
Burgess, Jonathan David Allen , *BSc, pcea*	LT CDR(FTC)	X	P	01.10.93	OCEAN
Burgess, Stanley , *pcea*	LT CDR(FTC)	X	P	01.10.90	DHFS
Burgess, William Charles , *BSc*	CDR(FTC)	E	AE	01.10.96	NEPTUNE CFS
Burghall, Rebecca Clare , *BSc*	SLT(IC)	X		01.05.98	LIVERPOOL
Burgon, Ross , *BSc*	SLT(IC)	X		01.01.99	DARTMOUTH BRNC
Burke, David Edward , *MA, SM(n)*	LT(FTC)	X	SM	01.07.96	SUPERB
Burke, Michael Christopher , *BSc*	LT CDR(FTC)	X	SM	01.09.95	FOSM NWOOD HQ
Burke, Paul Dominic , *BA, pce(sm)*	LT CDR(FTC)	X	SM	01.03.96	CSST SHORE FSLN
Burley, Matthew Richard , *BEng*	LT(FTC)	E	MESM	01.08.97	TALENT
Burlingham, Brett Limmer , *BSc, CEng, MIMarE*	LT CDR(FTC)	E	ME	01.11.95	JSCSC
Burnell, Jeremy Richard Jenner , *fsc*	MAJ(FTC)	RM		01.09.91	COMACCHIO GP RM
Burnell-Nugent, James Michael , *CBE, MA, jsdc, pce, pce(sm)*	RADM	-	SM	06.12.99	MOD (LONDON)
Burnett, Gilbert Arthur	LT CDR(FTC)	E	ME	01.10.99	SULTAN
Burnham, James Alistair Irby , *MA*	LT(IC)	S		01.08.97	DRYAD
Burningham, Michael Robert , *BA*	LT CDR(FTC)	S	SM	01.01.98	EXCHANGE USA
Burnip, John Matthew , *BSc*	LT CDR(FTC)	E	ME	01.08.93	SSA BRISTOL
Burns, Adrian Conleth	LT(FTC)	S	SM	04.03.94	JSCSC
Burns, Andrew Paul , *BA*	LT CDR(FTC)	X	FC	01.04.00	JSCSC
Burns, Bryan , *CBE (COMMODORE)*	CAPT(FTC)	X	C	30.06.83	NMA PORTSMOUTH
Burns, David Ian , *BSc, ARCS*	LT CDR(FTC)	X	PWO(C)	01.05.98	MOD (LONDON)
Burns, Euan Paterson , *BEng*	LT(FTC)	E	WE	01.08.98	CAMPBELTOWN
Burns, James Edward	LT(FTC)	E	WE	01.01.99	COLLINGWOOD
Burns, Rachel Charlotte , *MA*	LT(FTC)	S		01.06.92	JSCSC
Burns, Robin Douglas James , *BSc, PGDip*	LT CDR(FTC)	X	METOC	01.03.99	DRYAD
Burns, Royston John *(Act Lt)*	SLT(FTC)	S	CA	20.09.96	RNAS CULDROSE
Burns, Thomas Matthew , *QHC*	PR CHAPLAIN	RC		04.01.94	2SL/CNH
Burrell, Aleck Michael George	CAPT RM(FTC)	RM		28.04.98	COMACCHIO GP RM
Burrell, Philip Mark , *BSc, psc*	CDR(FTC)	E	TM	30.06.95	DITMTC SHRIVNHAM
Burrows, John Anthony	LT CDR(FTC)	E	WE	01.10.93	LOAN OMAN
Burrows, John Campbell	LT(FTC)	E	MESM	15.10.93	TRENCHANT
Burrows, Michael John	LT CDR(FTC)	X	P	01.10.94	EXCHANGE USA
Burrows, Michael John , *pce, jsdc*	CDR(FTC)	X	PWO(A)	31.12.94	DRYAD
Burston, Richard , *pce(sm)*	CDR(FTC)	X	SM	30.06.92	DPA BRISTOL

Name	Rank	Branch	Spec	Seniority	Where Serving
Burstow, Richard Stanley	LT CDR(FTC)	X	PWO(U)	01.05.99	CHATHAM
Burt, Paul Ronald , *BA*	LT CDR(FTC)	S	(S)	01.10.93	NELSON
Burton, Alex	SLT(FTC)	X		01.09.98	DARTMOUTH BRNC
Burton, Alexander James , *BSc, pce*	LT CDR(FTC)	X	PWO(U)	01.09.95	INVERNESS
Burton, David Stephen , *BSc, MSc*	CDR(FTC)	E	IS	31.12.95	AFPAA(CENTURION)
Burton, Nicholas Jeremy , *MBE, MSc*	LT CDR(FTC)	S		16.06.89	LARO WYTON
Burton, Paul Richard	SLT(FTC)	E	ME	02.05.97	SHEFFIELD
Burton, Tanya Jane , *BDS*	SG LT(D)	-		05.07.99	COLLINGWOOD
Burvill, Justin Paul , *BEng, CEng*	LT(FTC)	E	MESM	01.03.95	SULTAN
Burwin, Harvey Lee , *BEng*	LT CDR(FTC)	E	WE	01.11.96	CNSA BRISTOL
Bush, Alexander John Taylor	LT CDR(FTC)	X	PWO(U)	01.06.99	COVENTRY
Bush, Natalie	SLT(CC)	X		01.09.99	OCEAN
Bush, Stephen John Duyland , *OBE, psc*	LT COL(FTC)	RM		31.12.86	NMA PORTSMOUTH
Bushell, Gary Robert	LT CDR(FTC)	X	PT	09.07.99	TEMERAIRE
Bussell, Susan Lesley , *BEd*	SLT(IC)	S		01.05.98	LIVERPOOL
Bussey, Emma Louise , *BA*	LT(FTC)	X		01.10.98	NORTHUMBERLAND
Butcher, Linda Joan , *ARRC, MA(Ed), Cert Ed (Act Cdr)*	LT CDR	Q	RNT	08.01.88	MOD (LONDON)
Butcher, Martin Charles , *pce*	LT CDR(FTC)	X	PWO(C)	16.11.85	RNU RAF DIGBY
Butcher, Martin William , *MBE, pce, psc*	CDR(FTC)	X	P	30.06.91	CFPS SHORE
Butler, Ian Anthony	LT(FTC)	E	AE(L)	12.09.97	RNAS YEOVILTON
Butler, Lee Peter , *IEng, AMRAeS*	LT(FTC)	E	AE(L)	15.10.93	LOAN DERA BSC DN
Butler, Nicholas Abraham Marsh , *pce, pcea*	CAPT(FTC)	X	P	31.12.97	NELSON
Butler, Philip Michael , *BSc*	SLT(IC)	X	P U/T	01.01.98	RNAS YEOVILTON
Butler, Rachel , *BSc*	LT(IC)	X		01.01.00	RNSOMO
Butler, Robert John , *BSc, (Eur Ing), CEng, MRAeS, jsdc*	CDR(FTC)	E	AE	31.12.88	SHAPE BELGIUM
Butterfield, Neil Philip , *MB, BS, DA, DipAvMed*	SURG CDR	-	GMPP	31.12.92	PJHQ
Butterworth, Leslie	LT(FS)	FS		27.01.99	DARTMOUTH BRNC
Butterworth, Nigel Gregory , *MA*	LT(FTC)	S		01.04.93	CINCFLEET
Butterworth, Paul Gerard , *LLB*	LT(FTC)	X		01.03.97	ARGYLL
Buxton, David Adrian , *BA, BEng*	SLT(IC)	E		01.09.98	GLOUCESTER
Buxton, Peter John , *BM, BA, BCh, FRCR*	SURG CDR	-	CPDATE	31.12.95	RH HASLAR
Bye, Marc David , *BEng, CEng*	LT(FTC)	E	ME	01.05.92	AGRIPPA AFSOUTH
Byrne, Adrian Charles , *IEng, MIPlantE*	LT(FTC)	E	ME	18.06.93	539 ASLT SQN RM
Byrne, Thomas Frederick , *BEng, SM(n)*	LT(FTC)	X	SM	01.10.96	TRAFALGAR
Byrne, Terence Michael *(Act Lt Cdr)*	LT(FTC)	X	REG	13.12.95	DRAKE CBP(CNH)
Byron, James David	LT(FTC)	X	MW	01.05.95	DARTMOUTH BRNC
Bywater, Richard Lewis , *BEng, CEng, MIEE*	LT CDR(FTC)	E	WE	01.03.99	SSA BRISTOL

C

Name	Rank	Branch	Spec	Seniority	Where Serving
Cable, Phillip Mark , *LLB*	LT(CC)	X		01.11.99	DRYAD
Cahill, Karen Ann , *BA*	LT(FTC)	X		01.08.95	DRYAD
Cailes, Michael John	MAJ(FTC)	RM		10.02.81	HQRM
Cain, Christopher William	LT(FTC)	E	WESM	07.02.97	CSST RNSSS
Caldicott-Barr, Victoria Anne	LT(IC)	X		01.02.97	OCLC BRISTOL
Calhaem, Richard Tahi , *BEng*	LT(CC)	X	P	01.09.98	846 SQN
Callaghan, Paul Fraser , *MBE, BSc*	LT CDR(FTC)	X	P	01.10.99	700M MERLIN IFTU
Callister, David Roy , *pcea*	LT CDR(FTC)	X	O	01.10.95	RNAS YEOVILTON
Callon, Andrew	CHAPLAIN	CE		05.06.90	DRYAD
Calter, Mark	LT(FTC)	X	EW	26.04.99	PJHQ OSISOSEAS
Calver, Barry James , *BEng*	SLT(IC)	E	AE	01.01.99	DARTMOUTH BRNC
Cambridge, Grant Andrew , *BA*	CAPT RM(IC)	RM		01.09.99	EXCHANGE ARMY UK
Cameron, Andrew John Brunt , *pce*	CAPT(FTC)	X	PWO(U)	30.06.98	2SL/CNH FOTR
Cameron, Iain	LT CDR(FTC)	X	P	01.09.99	848 SQN HERON
Cameron, Mark John , *BEng, CEng, MIEE*	LT CDR(FTC)	E	WE	01.04.00	SSA BRISTOL
Cameron, Peter Stuart , *BA, psc(j)*	MAJ(FTC)	RM		01.09.95	HQ 3 CDO BDE RM
Campbell, David John , *MB, BS*	SURG LTCDR	-	GMPP	01.05.90	FOSM GOSPORT
Campbell, Iain Angus	LT(CC)	X	P	16.04.96	849 SQN B FLT
Campbell, James Colin , *Cert Ed, HNC*	LT(CC)	E	IS	01.09.89	CINCFLEET FIMU
Campbell, James Kininmonth , *MB, BS, LRCP, FRCS, FRCSEd, MRCS*	SURG CDR	-	(CGS)	30.06.92	MODHU DERRIFORD
Campbell, Katrina Louise	LT CDR(CC)	W	X	01.10.97	CAPTAIN RNP TEAM
Campbell, Lawrie Gordon , *BA*	CAPT RM(FTC)	RM		01.09.96	45 CDO RM
Campbell, Leslie Michael , *BA*	LT(FTC)	X	MW	01.07.92	OCLC ROSYTH

Name	Rank	Branch	Spec	Seniority	Where Serving
Campbell, Malcolm Alexander, *BEd*	LT CDR(CC)	E	IS	01.01.00	CINCFLEET FIMU
Campbell, Mark Alan McMillian, *BEng*	LT(CC)	X	P U/T	01.04.97	846 SQN
Campbell, Peter Robert	LT(IC)	X	O	01.01.94	702 SQN HERON
Campbell, Robin David Hastings, *BSc, BEng*	LT CDR(FTC)	E	WESM	01.02.95	CAPTAIN SM2
Campbell, Timothy Ross, *BSc*	SLT(IC)	X		01.09.97	GRIMSBY
Campbell-Balcombe, Andre Alexander, *AMIEE*	LT(CC)	E	WE	01.07.94	JSU NORTHWOOD
Canale, Andrew James, *BA*	LT(FTC)	X		01.07.97	EXCHANGE BELGIUM
Cannell, Graham Martin, *BSc*	SLT(IC)	X	P U/T	01.05.97	FONA LINTON/OUSE
Canning, Christopher Paul, *BSc*	LT(CC)	X	O	01.03.92	824 NAS
Canning, William Andrew, *psc(m)*	LT COL(FTC)	RM		30.06.93	PJHQ
Cannon, Leslie Brian, *MB, BSc, BS, FRCS*	SURG LTCDR	-		01.08.97	NELSON (PAY)
Cantellow, Stuart John, *BEng*	SLT(IC)	E		01.09.98	SHEFFIELD
Cantrill, Richard John, *BSc*	CAPT RM(FTC)	RM		01.09.98	42 CDO RM
Canty, Nigel Robert, *BSc*	LT CDR(FTC)	E	MESM	01.09.91	NEPTUNE SM1
Capes, Stuart George, *SM(n)*	LT(FTC)	X	SM	01.04.96	VANGUARD(PORT)
Capewell, David Andrew, *psc(m), fsc*	COL(FTC)	RM		31.12.99	40 CDO RM
Caple, Jonathan Neil	LT(CC)	S		01.07.99	CUMBERLAND
Carbery, Stephen James	SLT(IC)	E	WE	27.01.99	COLLINGWOOD
Carcone, Paul Nicholas, *BSc*	LT(IC)	S		01.01.00	RALEIGH
Carden, Peter David, *pce, pcea*	CDR(FTC)	X	O	30.06.99	JSCSC
Cargen, Malcolm Robert, *BSc, psc*	LT CDR(FTC)	E	AE	01.02.93	CHF AED
Carlisle, Christopher Richard, *BEng*	LT(FTC)	E	ME	01.03.95	STG BRISTOL
Carlton, Ian Philip	LT CDR(FTC)	X	g	01.10.89	MOD (LONDON)
Carne, John Richard Camin, *MB, BA, BCh, BAO*	SURG CAPT	-	GMPP	30.06.93	NELSON
Carne, Richard James Power, *pcea*	LT(CC)	X	O	16.05.87	824 NAS
Carnell, Gregory James, *pcea*	LT(CC)	X	O	01.09.91	702 SQN HERON
Carnell, Richard Paul, *BA(Hon)*	LT	Q		06.11.98	NP 1067 KOSOVO
Carnie, Manson John, *BA*	LT(FTC)	X		01.09.99	HURWORTH
Carolan, Kevin Stuart, *BEng*	LT(IC)	X		01.08.98	GLASGOW
Carpenter, Bryony Helen, *BSc, PGCE*	LT(IC)	E	TM	01.01.95	NP 1061
Carpenter, Christopher John, *BSc*	LT CDR(FTC)	E	WESM	01.09.90	MOD (BATH)
Carpenter, George Edward	SLT(UCE)(FTC)	X		01.09.99	DARTMOUTH BRNC
Carpenter, Philip John, *BA*	LT(CC)	X	P	01.02.94	EXCHANGE RAF UK
Carr, David Leslie, *pcea*	LT CDR(FTC)	X	O	01.10.89	FONA
Carr, Geoffrey, *BSc, MSc, Eur Ing, CEng, FIMarE, MIMech*	LT CDR(FTC)	E	ME	06.03.86	MOD (BATH)
Carr, Martin Paul	LT CDR(FTC)	E	WE	01.10.98	MOD (BATH)
Carr, Robert Alexander	LT(CC)	X	P	13.04.91	845 SQN
Carr, Robert Grenville, *BEng, MAPM, CEng, MIEE*	LT(FTC)	E	WESM	01.10.92	FOSM FASLANE
Carretta, Mark Vincent, *BSc*	LT CDR(FTC)	X	P	01.10.95	LOAN DERA BSC DN
Carrick, James Paul, *BSc*	LT(FTC)	X	SM	01.12.97	VIGILANT(STBD)
Carrick, Richard James, *MSc, BEng, CEng, MIMechE*	LT CDR(FTC)	E	MESM	01.05.97	TRAFALGAR
Carrigan, Jonathan Andrew	LT(FTC)	S		01.01.98	FOSF
Carrington, Victoria Louise, *BA*	LT(IC)	X		01.01.99	CORNWALL
Carrington-Wood, Clive Gordon, *pce*	LT CDR(FTC)	X	PWO(A)	01.10.91	MOD (LONDON)
Carroll, Benjamin John, *BA, n*	LT CDR(FTC)	X	PWO(U)	01.02.98	GRAFTON
Carroll, Paul Christopher, *BEng, MSc*	LT(FTC)	E	ME	01.03.94	KENT
Carroll, Philip John, *BSc*	LT CDR(CC)	X	H1	01.01.98	ACE SRGN TURKEY
Carroll, Peter William Mark, *pce, pce(sm) (Act Cdr)*	LT CDR(FTC)	X	SM	01.10.89	FOSM NWOOD HQ
Carroll, Stephen Laurence, *BEng, MSc*	LT(CC)	E	AE	01.01.99	SULTAN
Carson, Neil Douglas Ernest, *BSc*	LT CDR(FTC)	X	SM	01.01.97	VIGILANT(STBD)
Carter, Ashley Francis Rees, *BSc, CEng, MIEE*	CDR(FTC)	E	WE	31.12.97	INVINCIBLE
Carter, Graham Richard	SLT(IC)	S		01.05.97	RALEIGH
Carter, Ian Paul, *pce*	CDR(FTC)	X	PWO(A)	30.06.00	MOD (LONDON)
Carter, Jonathon Mark, *BSc*	LT CDR(FTC)	E	WESM	01.06.96	VIGILANT(STBD)
Carter, Kendall, *BSc, pce*	CDR(FTC)	X	PWO(N)	30.06.95	AGRIPPA NAVSOUTH
Carter, Kevin Stanley	LT(FTC)	X	PT	29.07.94	RALEIGH
Carter, Nigel	SLT(IC)	X	AV	29.04.98	RNAS CULDROSE
Carter, Paul	SLT(FTC)	E	WESM	01.04.98	DARTMOUTH BRNC
Carter, Robert Ian	LT CDR(FTC)	X	ATC	01.10.95	FONA SEA YEOVLTN
Carter, Stephen Frank, *FFA, psc*	CDR(FTC)	S	SM	31.12.89	NMA GOSPORT
Carter, Simon Neil	LT CDR(FTC)	S	SM	01.02.96	RALEIGH
Carter, Simon Peter	LT(FTC)	S	CA	04.04.96	CNH(R)
Carthew, Richard James, *BA*	SLT(IC)	S		01.05.98	YORK

Name	Rank	Branch	Spec	Seniority	Where Serving
Cartwright, Darren	LT CDR(FTC)	X	O	01.09.98	819 SQN
Cartwright, James Andrew, *BEng*	LT(FTC)	E	MESM	01.01.99	SULTAN
Carty, Jonathan, *MB, ChB*	SURG LT	-		05.08.98	CFLT MED(SEA)
Carver, Anthony Graham, *BSc*	LT CDR(FTC)	E	WESM	01.05.89	LN DERA WNFRITH
Case, Anthony	LT(FTC)	S	CA	26.04.99	RALEIGH
Case, Alexander Charles, *BSc*	MAJ(FTC)	RM		24.04.99	JSCSC
Case, Paul, *MILog*	LT CDR(FTC)	S	(S)	01.10.98	NEWCASTLE
Cass, Paul Stuart	LT CDR(FTC)	S		11.02.89	SULTAN
Cassar, Adrian Peter Felix, *BA, MA, pce, psc(j)*	CDR(FTC)	X	MCD	30.06.98	MOD (LONDON)
Casson, Neil Philip, *BSc*	LT CDR(FTC)	E	TMSM	01.03.99	SULTAN
Casson, Paul Richard, *BEng, MBA, psc(j)*	LT CDR(FTC)	E	ME	01.02.96	MOD (LONDON)
Casson, Roy Frederick	SLT(CC)	E	ME	01.05.98	DARTMOUTH BRNC
Castle, Alastair Stuart, *BSc*	LT(CC)	X	P	01.12.89	UKMILREP BRUSS
Castle, Colin David	SLT(FTC)	X	EW	19.09.97	DRYAD
Catherall, Mark Leslie	CHAPLAIN	CE		01.09.98	CDO LOG REGT RM
Cattroll, David	LT(FTC)	E	MESM	13.06.97	RENOWN(PORT)
Cattroll, Iain Murdo, *BSc*	LT CDR(FTC)	E	WE	01.03.94	CNSA BRISTOL
Cave, Joseph Henry James, *MA*	SLT(IC)	X	P U/T	01.05.98	DARTMOUTH BRNC
Cavill, Niki	2LT(GRAD)(IC)	RM		28.04.99	CTCRM LYMPSTONE
Cawthorne, Matthew William Southworth, *MA, psc(m)*	LT COL(FTC)	RM	MLDR	30.06.00	RM WARMINSTER
Cessford, Richard Ian, *BEng*	LT(IC)	E	WE	01.12.99	COLLINGWOOD
Chacksfield, Edward Nicholas, *BA*	LT(IC)	X		01.11.98	RN HYDROG SCHL
Chadfield, Laurence James, *BA*	LT(CC)	X		01.03.94	ORWELL
Chadwick, Geoffrey Edward, *BSc*	LT CDR(FTC)	E	WESM	01.04.82	JPS UK
Chadwick, John, *CEng, FIEE, MIEE, jsdc*	RADM	-	WESM	23.07.98	2SL/CNH FOTR
Chadwick, Kara, *BA*	SLT(IC)	S		01.01.99	DARTMOUTH BRNC
Challands, Guy David, *BSc, MPhil, CEng, FIEE, MIEE (COMMODORE)*	CAPT(FTC)	E	WESM	30.06.92	MOD (LONDON)
Challis, Sarah Elizabeth	SLT(IC)	S		01.04.98	DARTMOUTH BRNC
Chalmers, Donald Peter, *pce*	CDR(FTC)	X	PWO(U)	31.12.99	JSCSC
Chalmers, Paul, *BSc*	LT CDR(FTC)	X	FC	01.10.99	899 SQN HERON
Chaloner, Andrew Clifford	LT(IC)	X	P	01.07.94	820 SQN
Chamberlain, Nicholas Richard Lawrence	LT(FTC)	E	WE	01.11.93	SSA BRISTOL
Chamberlain, Trevor Ian	LT CDR(FTC)	E	ME	01.10.96	NEPTUNE NT
Chambers, Christopher Paul, *BSc*	LT(IC)	X	P U/T	01.12.99	FONA LINTON/OUSE
Chambers, Ian Richard, *BEng, CEng, MIEE, AMIEE*	LT(FTC)	E	WESM	01.05.92	NEPTUNE NT
Chambers, Nigel Maurice Christopher, *BSc, pce*	CDR(FTC)	X	PWO(U)	30.06.91	MOD (LONDON)
Chambers, Paul	LT(FTC)	E	WE	18.02.94	HQ DCSA
Chambers, Paul David, *BEng*	LT(CC)	E	WE	01.09.98	COLLINGWOOD
Chambers, Richard, *BSc*	SLT(IC)	X		01.09.97	ARGYLL
Chambers, Thomas George	LT CDR(FTC)	X	MCD	01.10.88	DRYAD
Chambers, William John, *pce*	CDR(FTC)	X	PWO(A)	30.06.93	LOAN BMATT(EC)
Chan-A-Sue, Stephen Sangster	LT(CC)	X	P	16.01.92	848 SQN HERON
Chandler, George Edward	SLT(IC)	X		01.05.98	DARTMOUTH BRNC
Chandler, Michael, FISM	CDR(FTC)	MS	(AD)	01.10.96	NELSON (PAY)
Chandler, Marcus Ffrench Hamilton	MAJ(CC)	RM	P	01.05.98	846 SQN
Chandler, Nigel James, *pce*	LT CDR(FTC)	X	PWO(C)	01.03.97	COMATG SEA
Chandler, Philip John, *BEng*	SLT(IC)	X		01.01.99	DARTMOUTH BRNC
Chandler, Stephen Arthur	LT CDR(FTC)	X	PWO(U)	01.01.87	VIVID
Chapell, Andrew, *BA*	LT CDR(FTC)	S	SM	01.03.97	FOSM NWOOD HQ
Chapman, Charles Leslie	LT CDR(FTC)	E	WESM	29.11.99	DCS *SM* BRISTOL
Chapman, Darren Andrew	LT CDR(CC)	X	P	01.10.98	JSCSC
Chapman, Geoffrey John Douglas, *BSc, MSc*	LT CDR(CC)	E	TM	01.10.95	NELSON RNSETT
Chapman, James Lawrence John, *BSc*	SLT(IC)	X		01.01.99	DARTMOUTH BRNC
Chapman, Martin	SLT(IC)	S		01.09.98	DARTMOUTH BRNC
Chapman, Nicholas John, *BA, pce(sm)*	LT CDR(FTC)	X	*SM*	01.05.90	PJHQ OSISOSEAS
Chapman, Nolan Phillip	LT CDR(FTC)	S	(W)	01.10.92	MOD (LONDON)
Chapman, Peter, *BEng*	LT(FTC)	E	WE	01.09.93	RMC OF SCIENCE
Chapman, Simon, *BA*	MAJ(FTC)	RM		01.09.98	DARTMOUTH BRNC
Chapman, Simon John, *pce*	LT CDR(FTC)	X	PWO(A)	01.04.98	GLASGOW
Chapman, Simon James	SLT(FTC)	X		01.04.98	DRYAD
Chapman-Andrews, Peter Charles, *LVO, pce, psc*	CDR(FTC)	X	PWO(N)†	30.06.89	NBC PORTSMOUTH
Chapple, Colin Peter, *BSc, PGCE*	LT CDR(FTC)	X	METOC	01.05.90	RNSOMO
Charlesworth, Graham Keith, *BSc, MSc, CEng, MIEE, MCGI*	LT CDR(FTC)	E	WESM	01.02.94	NMA PORTSMOUTH

Name	Rank	Branch	Spec	Seniority	Where Serving
Charlier, Simon Boyce , *pce, pcea, psc*	CAPT(FTC)	X	P	30.06.00	MOD (LONDON)
Charlton, Christopher Robin Arthur MacGaw , *BA*	CDR(FTC)	S		31.12.97	RNAS CULDROSE
Chaston, Stephen Paul	LT(FTC)	X	SM	01.03.93	VIGILANT(STBD)
Chattin, Antony Paul , *BEng (Act Maj)*	CAPT RM(FTC)	RM	MLDR	29.04.94	CTCRM
Chatwin, Nicholas John , *BSc, pce, pcea*	LT CDR(FTC)	X	P	01.07.90	PJHQ
Chaudhary, Rahul	MID(UCE)(IC)	E		01.01.00	DARTMOUTH BRNC
Chawira, Denis Nyarono , *BSc*	LT(IC)	X		01.08.97	BANGOR
Cheadle, Richard Frank , *MSc, CEng, FIMgt, MIMechE, jsdc (COMMODORE)*	CAPT(FTC)	E	MESM	30.06.93	DRAKE NBC
Cheesman, Christopher John , *BEng, MSc (Act Cdr)*	LT CDR(FTC)	E	AE	28.06.92	MOD (LONDON)
Cheesman, Daniel James Edward , *BSc*	CAPT RM(FTC)	RM		01.09.98	CDO LOG REGT RM
Chelton, Simon Roger Lewis , *BA, MIL, CDipAF, (JAP)*	CDR(FTC)	S	SM	30.06.94	JSCSC *OCDS*
Cheseldine, David	LT(FTC)	E	AE(M)	16.10.92	RALEIGH
Cheshire, Thomas Edward , *BEng, CEng, MIMechE*	LT(IC)	E	MESM	01.02.94	NP BRISTOL
Chester, Adam David Mark , *BA*	SLT(IC)	X	O U/T	01.09.97	750 SQN OBS SCH
Chesterman, Graham John , *pce, pcea*	LT CDR(FTC)	X	O	01.02.93	NORTHUMBERLAND
Chesters, David Martin Brandon	SLT(FTC)	S		01.09.98	DARTMOUTH BRNC
Chestnutt, James Muir , *BEng*	LT(FTC)	E	P U/T	01.01.98	RAF CRANWELL EFS
Cheyne, Roger Duncan , *BEng*	SLT(IC)	E		01.09.98	CORNWALL
Chichester, Mark Arlington Raleigh , *BSc, pce, pce(sm)*	LT CDR(FTC)	X	SM	01.10.90	MOD (LONDON)
Chick, Nicholas Stevens	LT(CC)	X	P	16.11.95	819 SQN
Chick, Stephen John , *BSc, pce*	CDR(FTC)	X	PWO(A)	30.06.96	FOSF
Chicken, Simon Timothy , *MBE, MA, psc*	LT COL(FTC)	RM	LC	31.12.95	COMATG SEA
Chidley, Timothy James , *BEng, CEng, MIMarE, psc(j)*	CDR(FTC)	E	ME	31.12.98	MOD (BATH)
Chilcott, Peter Leslie Herbert , *MISM*	LT(FTC)	MS	SM	02.04.93	INM ALVERSTOKE
Childs, David Geoffrey , *BSc*	LT CDR(FTC)	E	AE(P)	01.05.96	845 SQN
Childs, John Richard	LT(FTC)	X	FC	01.04.94	899 SQN HERON
Chilman, Peter William Howard	LT CDR(FTC)	S	SM	01.03.93	CINCFLEET
Chilton, Antony Lovel , *LVO, OBE, ADC, FIMgt, jsdc, pce, psc, psc(j) (COMMODORE)*	CAPT(FTC)	X	N	31.12.91	2SL/CNH FOTR
Chilton, Jerard , *BEng*	LT(CC)	E	WE	01.09.98	COLLINGWOOD
Chilvers, Leah	LT	Q		14.11.99	RH HASLAR
Chilvers, Martyn Iain	CAPT RM(IC)	RM		01.09.97	RMR MERSEYSIDE
Chittenden, Timothy Clive , *MA, MSc, CEng, MIMechE, MINucE, jsdc (COMMODORE)*	CAPT(FTC)	E	MESM	31.12.94	MOD (BATH)
Chittick, William Brian Oliver , *BDS*	SG LT(D)	-		10.07.97	CALEDONIA CFS
Chivers, Paul Austin , *pce, pcea*	CDR(FTC)	X	O	30.06.00	JSCSC
Choat, Jeffery Hugh	LT(CC)	X	O	16.08.93	810 SQN SEAHAWK
Choules, Barrie , *MEng*	LT(IC)	E	TMSM	01.09.90	SULTAN
Chrishop, Timothy Ian , *pce, pcea*	LT CDR(FTC)	X	O	01.04.96	CINCFLEET
Christian, David	LT CDR(FTC)	E	ME	01.05.98	ARGYLL
Christie, Andrew	SLT(IC)	S	(S)	29.04.98	MOD (LONDON)
Christie, Campbell Stuart , *BEd, psc, psc(j)*	CDR(FTC)	E	TM	30.06.94	FOSF
Christie, David William , *BSc*	SLT(IC)	X		01.09.98	DARTMOUTH BRNC
Christmas, Stephen Peter	LT(CC)	X	P	16.08.91	824 NAS
Chubb, John James , *BEng, MSc, CEng, MIEE, gw*	LT CDR(FTC)	E	WE	01.07.96	SOMERSET
Church, Alan David	CDR(FTC)	S		31.12.96	*BDS* WASHINGTON
Church, Carl Robert	LT(CC)	S	SM	01.09.90	2SL/CNH
Church, Stephen Cofield	LT(CC)	X	P	16.07.96	815 FLT 216
Churcher, Jeremy Edward , *n*	LT CDR(FTC)	X	H1	01.08.99	CAPT(H)DEVPT SEA
Churcher-Brown, Christopher John , *DPM, LRCP, FRC.Psych, MRCPsych, MRCS*	SURG CAPT	-	CPDATE	31.12.97	RH HASLAR
Churchill, Timothy Charles , *BA, pce*	CDR(FTC)	X	PWO(N)	31.12.93	MOD (LONDON)
Churchill, William John	LT CDR(FTC)	E	HULL	01.10.86	CNH(R)
Churchward, Matthew James	CAPT RM(IC)	RM		01.05.98	RM POOLE
Cirin, Wladislaw Roman Joseph , *BSc, psc*	CDR(FTC)	E	MESM	30.06.88	MOD (BATH)
Clague, John Joseph , *BEng, MEng*	LT(IC)	X	O U/T	01.03.97	750 SQN OBS SCH
Clapham, Grantley Thom , *BEng*	SLT(IC)	X	P U/T	01.09.98	DARTMOUTH BRNC
Clapp, Richard Julian , *BSc, jsdc, pce, pcea (COMMODORE)*	CAPT(FTC)	X	P	30.06.95	RNAS YEOVILTON
Clapson, Keith , *osc*	MAJ(FTC)	RM		01.07.85	CTCRM
Clare, Jonathan Francis	CAPT RM(FTC)	RM	SO(LE)	01.01.99	HQ 3 CDO BDE RM
Clare, Katharine , *BSc, PhD*	LT(IC)	E	TM	01.06.96	CINCFLEET CIS
Clare, Roy Alexander George , *rcds, pce, psc*	RADM	-	AWO(A)	23.08.99	RHQ AFNORTH
Clark, Angela Catherine , *BSc, PGDip, MIPD*	LT(CC)	W		06.10.92	2SL/CNH FOTR

Name	Rank	Branch	Spec	Seniority	Where Serving
Clark, Anthony Ivo Harvey , *BSc, CEng, MIEE, psc* *(COMMODORE)*	CAPT(FTC)	E	WE	31.12.94	NC3 AGENCY
Clark, Andrew Nelham , *BSc*	LT CDR(FTC)	E	MESM	01.09.91	FOSM NWOOD HQ
Clark, Alan Sutherland	LT(FTC)	X	SM	03.04.97	DCSA COMMCEN FAS
Clark, Alastair William Charles , *pce, pcea, psc(j)*	CDR(FTC)	X	O	31.12.98	MOD (LONDON)
Clark, Caroline Louise	SLT(IC)	S		01.04.98	CFM PORTSMOUTH
Clark, Donald Kennedy , *BSc, CEng, AMIMarE*	CDR(FTC)	E	MESM	30.06.98	FEARLESS
Clark, Dennis Michael James , *MA, psc*	LT COL(FTC)	RM	SO(LE)	31.12.99	CTCRM
Clark, Ian David , *BSc, MSc, MIMarE*	LT CDR(FTC)	E	MESM	01.11.94	SCEPTRE
Clark, James Lea , *n*	LT(FTC)	X		01.06.94	CINCFLEET
Clark, Jessica Margaret , *BEng*	LT(IC)	X		01.06.97	CUMBERLAND
Clark, Kevin Charles , *BEng, MSc, CEng, MIMarE, MCGI*	LT CDR(FTC)	E	ME	01.11.94	SULTAN
Clark, Kenneth Ian MacDonald , *pce(sm)*	CDR(FTC)	X	SM	31.12.94	NEPTUNE SM1
Clark, Michael Alwyn Stephen	LT CDR(FTC)	X	O	01.10.88	CHFHQ
Clark, Michael Howard , *n*	LT(FTC)	X		01.03.96	CARDIFF
Clark, Matthew Thomas	LT CDR(FTC)	S	SM	01.11.98	COVENTRY
Clark, Paul Anthony	CAPT RM(FTC)	RM	SO(LE)	01.01.97	HQRM
Clark, Paul Michael Colin	LT CDR(FTC)	X	ATC	01.10.93	RNAS CULDROSE
Clark, Russell Anthony	LT(FTC)	X		01.08.99	MANCHESTER
Clark, Robert William	LT CDR(FTC)	S		01.07.88	MOD (BATH)
Clark, Simon Mansfield	LT CDR(FTC)	S	CMA	01.12.98	MOD (LONDON)
Clark, Simon Richard , *BEng, adp*	LT CDR(FTC)	E	WESM	01.05.97	PJHQ
Clark, Stephen , *BSc*	LT(IC)	E	TM	01.09.97	COLLINGWOOD
Clark, Timothy Hubert Vian , *MA, pce, psc*	CDR(FTC)	X	AWO(U)	30.06.91	MOD (LONDON)
Clarke, Adam Gregory , *BSc*	SLT(IC)	S		01.09.97	RALEIGH
Clarke, Andrew Patrick	LT(FTC)	X	P	16.05.90	848 SQN HERON
Clarke, Andrew Richard , *BEng*	LT(FTC)	E	AE	03.01.93	ES AIR NAML
Clarke, Bernard Ronald	CHAPLAIN	CE		30.06.81	NELSON
Clarke, Charles Maxwell Lorne , *pce*	CDR(FTC)	X	PWO(U)	30.06.95	MCM3 SEA
Clarke, Daniel	LT(CC)	X	O	16.03.94	815 FLT 227
Clarke, Daniel	LT(FTC)	X	SM	01.01.99	VIGILANT(PORT)
Clarke, Ian Bruce , *n*	LT(FTC)	X		01.07.95	ORWELL
Clarke, James	LT CDR(FTC)	E	WE	01.10.98	COLLINGWOOD
Clarke, John , *MB, BS, DObstRCOG, Dip FFP, MRCGP*	SURG LTCDR	-	GMPP	01.08.94	DARTMOUTH BRNC
Clarke, John Patrick , *CB, LVO, MBE, pce*	RADM	-	SM(N)	14.03.94	LOAN HYDROG
Clarke, Mark	SLT(FTC)	X	SM	01.04.98	VICTORIOUS(PORT)
Clarke, Matthew	SLT(IC)	X		01.01.99	DARTMOUTH BRNC
Clarke, Matthew Dickon , *MB, BS, MRCS*	SURG LTCDR	-		04.08.99	NELSON (PAY)
Clarke, Matthew David , *BSc*	LT(IC)	E	TM	01.05.98	SULTAN
Clarke, Nicholas John , *pce, pcea*	CDR(FTC)	X	P	30.06.99	FONA
Clarke, Peter Martin	LT RM(IC)	RM		24.01.00	702 SQN HERON
Clarke, Richard , *BA, MBA*	LT CDR(FTC)	E	TM	01.10.96	CINCFLEET
Clarke, Roger Donald , *BSc*	LT CDR(FTC)	E	WE	27.05.92	RMC OF SCIENCE
Clarke, Robert	LT(CC)	X	P	16.08.96	819 SQN
Clarke, Richard William , *BEng*	LT(FTC)	E	AE	01.03.94	849 SQN A FLT
Clarkson, Suzanne Jane , *MB, BCh*	SURG LT	-		01.08.96	RH HASLAR
Claxton, Martin Geoffrey	LT CDR(FTC)	E	MESM	18.02.93	NEPTUNE SM1
Clay, Jason Christopher , *BSc, SM(n)*	LT(FTC)	X	SM	01.03.96	TRIUMPH
Clay, Toby Charles De Candole , *BSc*	LT(CC)	X	P	01.05.98	DHFS
Clayden, John William Anthony , *ADC, BSc, CEng, MIMechE, jsdc* *(COMMODORE)*	CAPT(FTC)	E	MESM	31.12.91	NELSON
Clayton, Christopher Hugh Trevor , *pce, psc (COMMODORE)*	CAPT(FTC)	X	P	31.12.95	FONA
Clayton, Michael James , *BA (LOC Maj)*	CAPT RM(IC)	RM		01.09.97	LOAN BALBAT
Clayton, Steven	LT CDR(IC)	X	P	01.07.96	899 SQN HERON
Clear, Nichola Jane , *BEng*	LT(IC)	E	ME	01.11.99	SULTAN
Cleary, Christopher	SLT(IC)	S		27.01.99	DARTMOUTH BRNC
Cleary, Stephen Peter , *pce*	CAPT(FTC)	X	PWO(A)	30.06.00	MOD (LONDON)
Cleaver, James Patrick , *BSc*	CAPT RM(IC)	RM		24.04.99	RM WARMINSTER
Clegg, Martin Leslie , *BSc, FRGS*	LT CDR(FTC)	X	H CH	01.06.90	NP 1008 OFS SVY
Clelland, Graham	LT(FTC)	X	REG	23.07.98	CINCFLEET
Clement, Colin James , *BSc*	LT CDR(FTC)	E	ME	01.10.89	INVINCIBLE
Clements, Elizabeth Joanne	LT(IC)	S		01.05.99	RNAS YEOVILTON
Clements, Stephen James	LT(FTC)	X	g	02.04.93	FOSF

Name	Rank	Branch	Spec	Seniority	Where Serving
Cleminson, Mark David , *BEng*	LT(CC)	E	MESM	01.02.93	SUPERB
Clemson, Anthony James , *BSc*	LT(IC)	X		01.08.97	MANCHESTER
Clifford, Clive	LT(FTC)	X	EW	25.09.96	EXCELLENT
Clifford, Timothy John , *BEng, MSc, CEng, MRAeS*	LT CDR(FTC)	E	AE	01.10.95	FONA NORTHWOOD
Clink, Adam Duncan , *BSc*	LT(CC)	X	P	16.06.94	800 SQN
Clink, John Robert Hamilton , *pce*	CDR(FTC)	X	PWO(N)	30.06.99	KENT
Clough, Christopher Ralph , *MSc, CEng, MIEE, gw*	LT CDR(FTC)	E	WE	28.04.96	MOD (LONDON)
Clucas, Malcolm Richard , *pcea*	LT CDR(FTC)	X	P	01.10.97	INVINCIBLE
Clucas, Paul Richard	LT(FTC)	X	PT	04.04.91	LOAN SAUDI ARAB
Cluett-Green, Stephen Mark , *pce*	LT CDR(FTC)	X	P	01.02.94	JHCHQ
Coackley, Jane , *MA*	LT(IC)	X		01.01.99	LEEDS CASTLE
Coaker, Stewart Andrew	LT(IC)	S		01.12.96	CNH(R)
Coates, Philip James Barton , *MB, BS*	SURG LT	-		04.08.99	CFLT MED(SEA)
Coats, Daniel Simon , *LLB*	CAPT RM(IC)	RM		01.09.98	CTCRM
Cobb, David Robert	LT CDR(FTC)	X	PWO(A)	01.11.93	T45 IPT
Cobb, Jill Elizabeth	LT CDR(FTC)	W	S	01.10.97	SULTAN
Cobban, Michael James , *BSc*	LT(IC)	X		01.03.00	RALEIGH
Cobbett, James Frank , *pcea*	LT(CC)	X	P	16.05.90	FEARLESS
Cochrane, *The Hon Micael*(Michael Charles Nicholas), *OBE, pce*	CDR(FTC)	X	PWO(N)	31.12.96	MOD (LONDON)
Cochrane, Malcolm David	LT CDR(FTC)	E	AE	09.08.91	MOD DHSA
Cockton, Peter George , *QGM*	CAPT RM(FTC)	RM	SO(LE)	01.01.98	847 SQN
Codd, Justin Sandall , *BSc, SM(n)*	LT(IC)	X	SM	01.02.97	SUPERB
Cogan, Robert Edward Charles , *BSc*	LT(CC)	S		01.11.92	KENT
Cogdell, Phillip Charles , *HND*	LT(CC)	E	TM	01.01.89	SSA BRISTOL
Coldrick, Simon Alexander	MAJ(FTC)	RM	C	01.05.97	BDMT
Cole, Alan Charles , *BA*	LT CDR(FTC)	S	SM	01.02.00	SSA BRISTOL
Cole, Benjamin Barry , *LLB*	SLT(IC)	S		01.09.98	DARTMOUTH BRNC
Cole, Christopher Michael , *psc*	CDR(FTC)	S		31.12.88	MOD (BATH)
Cole, David John , *BA*	LT(CC)	X	O	01.04.97	819 SQN
Cole, Simon Philip	LT CDR(FTC)	E	WE	01.10.97	CFM PORTSMOUTH
Cole, Simon Richard	CAPT RM(IC)	RM		01.05.97	45 CDO RM
Coles, Andrew Laurence , *pce, pce(sm)*	LT CDR(FTC)	X	SM	01.08.96	JSCSC
Coles, Christopher John , *BEng*	LT CDR(FTC)	E	MESM	01.09.96	TRIUMPH
Coles, Christopher Paul , *BEng*	SLT(FTC)	E	AE	01.09.97	SULTAN
Coles, Gordon John Victor , *IEng, FIEEIE, AMIAM*	LT CDR(FTC)	E	WESM	01.10.90	COLLINGWOOD
Coles, Geoffrey William Grenville , *BSc, MSc*	CDR(FTC)	E	ME	30.06.90	MOD (BATH)
Coles, Stuart Charles , *BA, MEng*	LT(FTC)	X	SM	01.09.97	FOSNNI OPS CFS
Coley, Anthony Richard , *MRIN, pce, psc*	LT CDR(FTC)	X	PWO(A)	16.04.84	MWC PORTSDOWN
Coley, Jennifer Marian , *BA*	LT(IC)	S		01.01.97	FOSNNI/NBC CLYDE
Colin-Thome, Nicola Jill , *BA*	LT(FTC)	X		01.09.98	NORTHUMBERLAND
Collacott, Jonathan Steven , *BSc*	LT(IC)	S		01.03.99	TORBAY
Collen, Sara Jean , *BEng*	LT(CC)	E	ME	01.12.97	INVINCIBLE
Collett, Stuart	SURG LT	-		05.08.98	RM Poole
Colley, Ian Paul	MID(UCE)(IC)	E		01.09.99	MANCHESTER
Colley, Robert	SLT(IC)	X		19.09.98	DRYAD
Collicutt, John Michael	LT(CC)	X	P	16.06.94	815 FLT 201
Collier, Andrew Sheldon , *BA, FRGS*	LT CDR(FTC)	X		01.06.93	MOD (LONDON)
Collighan, Giles Thomas	LT CDR(FTC)	X	PWO(A)	01.04.99	NOTTINGHAM
Collin, Martin	CAPT RM(FTC)	RM		28.04.98	EXCHANGE ARMY UK
Collins, Andrew Charles	SLT(CC)	X	O	01.09.98	815 FLT 209
Collins, Darren	SLT(FTC)	E	WE	09.01.98	GLOUCESTER
Collins, David Anthony , *BSc, PGCE*	LT CDR(FTC)	X	METOC	01.10.95	FOST SEA
Collins, David Andrew	SLT(FTC)	E	MESM	02.05.97	SUPERB
Collins, David , *BSc, PhD*	LT(IC)	E		01.01.97	DARTMOUTH BRNC
Collins, Graham John Simon , *pce*	LT CDR(FTC)	X	MCD	07.04.96	COMUKTG/CASWSF
Collins, John	LT RM(FTC)	RM	SO(LE)	01.01.98	CDO LOG REGT RM
Collins, Mark Andrew	SLT(FTC)	E	WE	09.01.98	WESTMINSTER
Collins, Mark	LT(FTC)	X	tas	24.07.97	ARK ROYAL
Collins, Paul Nicholas , *pce, pcea, psc*	CDR(FTC)	X	P	31.12.92	MOD (LONDON)
Collins, Paul Reginald , *BSc*	LT CDR(FTC)	E	WESM	01.09.95	VICTORIOUS(PORT)
Collins, Peter Ronald	MAJ(FTC)	RM	SO(LE)	01.10.96	RM POOLE
Collins, Peter	LT(FTC)	X	EW	24.09.97	MWC PORTSDOWN
Collins, Richard John , *CEng, MRAeS*	CDR(FTC)	E	AE(M)	01.10.98	ES AIR MASU

Name	Rank	Branch	Spec	Seniority	Where Serving
Collins, Stephen Anthony	LT(FTC)	E	WESM	07.02.97	SUPERB
Collins, Sarah Jane, *BSc*	LT(CC)	E	TM	27.06.88	SULTAN
Collins, Simon Jonathan Peter, *BA*	SLT(IC)	X	O U/T	01.09.98	DARTMOUTH BRNC
Collins, Tamar Louise, *BEng, MSc, PhD*	LT(IC)	E	TM	01.01.96	NMA GOSPORT
Collis, Martin John, *BEng*	LT CDR(FTC)	E	ME	01.08.99	SULTAN
Coltman, Timothy Patrick, *MB, BS*	SURG LT	-		01.08.95	NELSON (PAY)
Combe, Gavin Robert	LT(FTC)	E	WE	01.08.94	SSA BRISTOL
Combe, Stephen Anthony Nicholson, *BA*	CAPT RM(IC)	RM	P U/T	01.09.97	AACC MIDWALLOP
Concarr, David Terry	LT(CS)	-		19.09.99	RNSR BOVINGTON
Congreve, Steven Chistopher, *BSc (Act Maj)*	CAPT RM(FTC)	RM		29.04.94	CTCRM
Conley, Daniel, *OBE, MBA, pce(sm)*	CAPT(FTC)	X	SM	31.12.90	LOAN HYDROG
Conlin, John Anthony, *BA*	LT(IC)	X		01.01.99	SHEFFIELD
Conneely, Steven Andrew	SLT(FTC)	E	WE	09.01.98	LIVERPOOL
Connell, John Andrew, *MBE, psc*	CDR(FTC)	X	EW	01.10.93	MOD (LONDON)
Connell, Martin John	LT CDR(FTC)	X	PWO(U)	01.01.00	LANCASTER
Connolly, Christopher John, *BSc, pce*	LT CDR(FTC)	X	PWO(A)	01.03.92	JSCSC
Connolly, Michael Henry	LT(CS)	-		19.09.97	DNR WEST & WALES
Connor, Daniel James, *BM, BS, BMS, FRCA*	SURG LTCDR	-		01.08.97	NELSON (PAY)
Connor, Michael	LT(FTC)	E	WESM	09.04.98	SSA BRISTOL
Considine, Keith John	SLT(IC)	X	P U/T	01.09.97	RAF CRANWELL EFS
Conway, Julian John	LT CDR(FTC)	X	PWO(C)	01.11.93	HQ NORTH
Conway, Michael John	LT(FTC)	X	EW	03.04.97	EXCHANGE USA
Conway, Stephen Andrew, *jsdc*	LT COL(FTC)	RM	C	30.06.97	COMACCHIO GP RM
Conway, Timothy Alexander, *BSc, pcea*	LT CDR(CC)	X	O	01.10.96	MERLIN IPT
Conyers, Wendy Lee	SLT(CC)	X		01.01.98	DRYAD
Cook, Christopher Buchan, *BSc, MSc*	LT(FTC)	E	IS	01.05.91	CINCFLEET CIS
Cook, David John	LT CDR(FTC)	X	O	01.10.97	MWC PORTSDOWN
Cook, Gordon Edward	LT(FTC)	X	O	16.09.89	815 SQN HQ
Cook, Harry, *MBE*	LT CDR(FTC)	X	PWO(N)	10.08.83	DRYAD
Cook, Michael, *BEng*	LT(IC)	E	TM	01.07.90	COLLINGWOOD
Cook, Myles Fitzpatrick, *BA*	CAPT RM(FTC)	RM	C	29.04.94	HQ 3 CDO BDE RM
Cook, Paul Roger, *pce*	CDR(FTC)	X	PWO(A)	31.12.98	GLOUCESTER
Cook, Peter William John	MAJ(FTC)	RM		01.05.92	RHQ SOUTHLANT
Cook, Timothy Arnold, *BA*	MAJ(FTC)	RM	C	01.09.97	HQ 3 CDO BDE RM
Cooke, David John, *MBE, pce, pce(sm)*	CAPT(FTC)	X	SM	31.12.95	CUMBERLAND
Cooke, Graham John	LT CDR(FTC)	X	PT	01.10.99	SULTAN
Cooke, Graham Spencer, *BSc*	LT(FTC)	X	O	01.10.93	815 FLT 211
Cooke, Jonathan Edward, *n*	LT(FTC)	X		18.02.95	JSCSC
Cooke, Joanne, *MB, ChB (Act Surg Lt)*	SURG SLT	-		07.07.96	DARTMOUTH BRNC
Cooke, Michael John	LT(FTC)	E	AE(M)	16.10.92	FONA
Cooke, Martin Yeats, *BA(OU), psc(m), osc*	LT COL(FTC)	RM	C	30.06.91	RMR TYNE
Cooke, Richard Glanville, *IEng, AMIMarE*	LT CDR(FTC)	E	ME	01.10.88	2SL/CNH FOTR
Cooke, Robert Neale	SLT(IC)	E	AE	29.04.98	SULTAN
Cooke, Stephen Neil, *BEng*	SLT(IC)	X		01.01.99	DARTMOUTH BRNC
Cooke-Priest, Nicholas Charles Richard	LT(CC)	X	O	01.05.95	702 SQN HERON
Cooling, Robert George, *BA, jsdc, pce*	CAPT(FTC)	X	PWO(U)	30.06.98	MONTROSE
Coomber, Jonathan Martin, *BA*	CAPT RM(FTC)	RM	MLDR	01.09.95	DRYAD
Coomber, Mark Andrew	LT CDR(FTC)	X	FC	18.07.95	RNAS YEOVILTON
Coombes, Derek	CDR(FTC)	E	WE	31.12.93	CFM PORTSMOUTH
Coope, Philip James, *BEng*	LT(FTC)	E	WE	01.03.95	MOD (LONDON)
Cooper, Andrew, *BEng, AMIMechE*	LT(IC)	E	ME	01.01.95	MOD (BATH)
Cooper, Adam, *BA*	LT(IC)	S		01.08.98	NEPTUNE 2SL/CNH
Cooper, Christopher John, *PGDip*	LT CDR(FTC)	X	H2	01.10.98	BULLDOG
Cooper, John Arnold, *BSc, CEng, MIMarE, MINucE*	CDR(FTC)	E	MESM	31.12.92	DRAKE CFM
Cooper, John Anthony, *MBE*	LT CDR(FTC)	X	PWO(A)	01.10.88	NEW IPT
Cooper, Kevin Philip, *BSc*	LT CDR(FTC)	E	WE	01.10.96	COVENTRY
Cooper, Mark Andrew, *pce, pce(sm)*	LT CDR(FTC)	X	SM	01.04.96	FOSM NWOOD HQ
Cooper, Neil	CAPT RM(FTC)	RM	SO(LE)	01.01.00	JSCSC
Cooper, Neil Philip	LT CDR(FTC)	E	ME	01.10.97	LOAN OMAN
Cooper, Peter Frank, *MSc, CEng, MIMechE*	LT CDR(FTC)	E	MESM	21.04.89	RN GIBRALTAR
Cooper, Robert Terence, *MBE*	MAJ(FTC)	RM	SO(LE)	01.10.96	RM Poole
Cooper, Simon John, *pcea, psc*	LT CDR(FTC)	X	O	01.12.93	EXCHANGE AUSTLIA
Cooper, Simon Nicholas, *LLB (BARRISTER)*	CDR(FTC)	S	BAR	30.06.94	2SL/CNH

Name	Rank	Branch	Spec	Seniority	Where Serving
Cooper, Simon Stanway , *BEng, CEng, MIEE*	LT CDR(FTC)	E	WESM	01.05.99	TLAM IPT
Cooper-Simpson, Roger John	CAPT RM(FTC)	RM	C	26.04.94	HQ 3 CDO BDE RM
Cooter, Mark Pierson , *BA, BSc, MSc*	LT CDR(FTC)	S		16.03.93	AFPAA(CENTURION)
Cope, Marcus Adrian	SLT(FTC)	E	WESM	09.01.98	VIGILANT(PORT)
Copeland, Stephen Nicholas , *BEng*	LT CDR(FTC)	E	AE	01.02.99	ES AIR BRISTOL
Copinger-Symes, Rory Sandham , *psc(j)*	MAJ(FTC)	RM		01.09.94	CTCRM
Coppin, Paul David	LT CDR(FTC)	E	AE(L)	01.10.92	SULTAN
Corbett, Andrew Scott , *pce, pce(sm)*	LT CDR(FTC)	X	SM	01.06.96	CINCFLEET
Corbett, Gerard John	LT CDR(FTC)	X	ATC	01.10.96	HQMATO UXBRIDGE
Corbett, Mark Thomas	SLT(IC)	X		01.05.98	QUORN
Corbett, Thomas James	LT(CC)	X	FC	01.04.94	EXCHANGE RAF UK
Corbett, William Roger , *BSc, FRMS, psc(m)*	LT CDR(FTC)	X	METOC	01.10.91	RNSOMO
Corbidge, Stephen John	MAJ(FTC)	RM	SO(LE)	01.10.97	CAMBRIDGE
Corden, Matthew	LT(IC)	X		01.03.99	DRYAD
Corder, Ian Fergus , *MA, jsdc, pce, pce(sm)*	CAPT(FTC)	X	SM	30.06.99	MOD (LONDON)
Corderoy, John Roger , *MSc, BEng*	LT CDR(FTC)	E	MESM	01.07.97	TIRELESS
Corderoy, Richard Ian , *BA, AMIEE*	SLT(FTC)	E	WESM	01.09.96	DOLPHIN SM SCHL
Cordner, Kenneth , *MIMgt, psc*	CDR(FTC)	S	SM	31.12.87	NMA PORTSMOUTH
Cordner, Michael , *BMS*	SURG SLT	-		20.05.99	DARTMOUTH BRNC
Corkett, Kerry	LT(FTC)	X	REG	24.07.97	MCTC
Cormack, Andrew James Ross , *MB, BSc, ChB*	SURG LT	-		05.08.98	40 CDO RM
Corn, Russell Andrew Foster , *MA*	MAJ(FTC)	RM		01.09.99	CINCFLEET
Cornberg, Malcolm Arthur , *MBA, FCMA, CDipAF (Act Capt)*	CDR(FTC)	S	CMA	30.06.92	FOSM NWOOD HQ
Corner, Gordon Charles , *pce (Act Cdr)*	LT CDR(FTC)	X	PWO(C)	01.12.90	CINCFLEET CIS
Corner, Ian Lindsey Ferguson , *fsc, osc (Act Lt Col)*	MAJ(FTC)	RM	P	01.11.83	CTCRM
Corney, Adam David	LT(FTC)	X	SM	01.09.93	RALEIGH
Cornford, Marc , *BEng*	LT(CC)	X	P U/T	01.04.00	RNAS YEOVILTON
Cornick, Robin Michael	LT CDR(FTC)	X	MCD	01.10.97	MOD (LONDON)
Cornish, Michael Christopher , *pce*	LT CDR(FTC)	X	PWO(A)	01.07.95	GLOUCESTER
Corps, Stephen David	LT(FTC)	E	WE	01.03.94	SSA/CWTA PORTS
Corrigan, Niall Richard , *BSc, pce*	CDR(FTC)	X	PWO(A)	30.06.96	2SL/CNH
Corrin, Colby St John , *LLB, jsdc*	MAJ(FTC)	RM	MLDR	01.09.92	42 CDO RM
Corry, Simon Myles , *MA, BSc, AMIEE, psc(j)*	LT CDR(FTC)	E	WE	01.02.94	FOSF
Cosby, *R A* (Richard Ashworth De Sausmarez) , *LVO, jsdc, pce*	CAPT(FTC)	X	PWO	30.06.94	NATO MEWSG VL
Costello, Gerard Thomas , *BSc,* MDA	CDR(FTC)	E	WESM	31.12.93	DSWS BRISTOL
Cottee, Benjamin Richard John	LT(CC)	X	ATC	01.09.94	EXCHANGE RAF UK
Cotterill, Bruce Maxwell , *BEng*	LT CDR(FTC)	E	WESM	01.03.00	RALEIGH
Cottingham, Neil Peter Stephen	LT CDR(FTC)	X	AV	01.10.98	RNAS CULDROSE
Cottis, Mathew Charles	LT(CC)	S	SM	16.11.90	TRIUMPH
Cotton, Emma Louise	SLT(FTC)	S	(W)	01.04.98	FOSF
Couch, Paul	CHAPLAIN	RC		05.05.92	RNAS YEOVILTON
Couch, Paul Jonathan , *MSc, CEng, MRAeS*	CDR(FTC)	E	AE	31.12.94	MOD (LONDON)
Coulson, Jeremy Richard , *BEng, PGCE*	LT CDR(FTC)	E	IS	08.12.85	NMA PORTSMOUTH
Coulson, Peter , *BEng, CEng, MIEE, MSc*	LT CDR(FTC)	E	WE	01.12.97	CUMBERLAND
Coulthard, Adrian , *BSc, MinstP*	LT(IC)	E	TM	11.05.91	DARTMOUTH BRNC
Coulthard, John Kinnear , *MSc, MIMechE, jsdc*	CDR(FTC)	E	MESM	31.12.93	MOD (LONDON)
Coulton, Ian Christopher , *MA, MBA, psc(j)*	LT CDR(FTC)	MS		01.10.96	CINCFLEET
Coulton, Julie Ann , *BA*	LT(CC)	W	S	14.07.92	FONA
Coulton, Jamie Robert Spencer	LT(CC)	X	P	16.06.95	815 FLT 235
Counter, Paul Richard , *MB, BS, MRCS*	SURG LTCDR	-		01.08.99	NELSON (PAY)
Coupland, Mark Barry	LT(CC)	X	P	01.03.89	771 SK5 SAR
Course, Andrew James , *MBE, MSc, AMIEE, gw*	LT CDR(FTC)	E	WE	01.02.97	RICHMOND
Coverdale, Anthony , *MSc, CEng, psc*	CDR(FTC)	E	MESM	31.12.93	CNNRP BRISTOL
Coverdale, Paul , *BSc*	SLT(IC)	X		01.05.97	DRYAD
Covington, William MacArtney , *pce, pcea, psc*	CAPT(FTC)	X	P	31.12.96	HQ3GP HQSTC
Cowan, Aidan Roland	SLT(FTC)	X	C	19.09.97	COLLINGWOOD
Cowan, Christopher John , *LLB*	LT(FTC)	S		01.07.95	CINCFLEET
Cowan, Kenneth Gordon	CAPT RM(IC)	RM		23.04.99	OCLC ROSYTH
Cowdrey, Mervyn Charles	CDR(FTC)	S		30.06.93	MWC SOUTHWICK
Cowie, Andrew David , *BSc*	SLT(IC)	X		01.01.99	DARTMOUTH BRNC
Cowie, Kevin Michael	LT CDR(FTC)	X	C	01.10.99	MOD (LONDON)
Cowin, Timothy James , *BSc*	LT(IC)	X	P U/T	01.04.99	RNAS YEOVILTON
Cowley, Nigel Jonathan , *pcea, psc*	CDR(FTC)	X	P	31.12.89	2SL/CNH FOTR

Name	Rank	Branch	Spec	Seniority	Where Serving
Cowley, Richard Merlin, *BSc*	LT CDR(FTC)	X	MCD	01.04.97	DEF DIVING SCHL
Cowper, Ian Robert	LT(FTC)	E	ME	10.06.94	FOSTSEA NBCDDVPT
Cowton, Elliott Neil, *BEd, adp*	LT CDR(FTC)	E	IS	01.10.91	AFPAA(CENTURION)
Cox, David John, *BEng, CEng, MIEE*	LT(FTC)	E	WE	01.06.94	LN DERA PRTSDWN
Cox, Gillian Fay, *BSc*	LT(IC)	S		01.04.98	GANNET
Cox, Jonathan Peter	LT CDR(FTC)	X	MCD	01.10.95	SSA BRISTOL
Cox, Mark Bamber	LT(FTC)	S		03.07.97	SACLANT USA
Cox, Matthew James, *BA*	LT(IC)	X		01.08.99	BEAGLE
Cox, Pieter William Studley, *BSc, CEng, MIEE*	CDR(FTC)	E	WESM	30.06.93	CSST SHORE FSLN
Cox, Rex John	LT(FTC)	X	PWO(A)	01.03.93	SHEFFIELD
Cox, Sean Adrian Joel	LT(CC)	X	P	16.08.93	848 SQN HERON
Cox, Stephen John, *psc(m)*	COL(FTC)	RM	MOR	30.06.99	JSCSC
Coyle, Gavin James, *BSc, n*	LT(FTC)	X		01.08.93	DRYAD
Coyle, Phillip John, *BSc*	LT(IC)	S		01.05.99	NEPTUNE SM1
Coyne, John Derek	LT(FTC)	X	AV	17.12.93	CHFHQ
Crabb, Antony John, *MSc*	LT(CC)	X		01.04.96	EXCHANGE SPAIN
Crabbe, Robert James, *BSc*	LT(IC)	X		01.12.98	SUTHERLAND
Crabtree, Ian Michael, *BSc, pce*	CDR(FTC)	X	PWO(A)	31.12.90	NMA PORTSMOUTH
Crabtree, Peter Dixon, *OBE, BA, ACIS (BARRISTER) (Act Capt)*	CDR(FTC)	S	BAR	31.12.93	MOD (BATH)
Cragg, Richard Darryl, *BEng*	LT(CC)	E	MESM	01.01.95	TRIUMPH
Craggs, Stuart, *BEng, CEng, MIMechE*	LT(FTC)	E	AE	01.12.94	RNAS CULDROSE
Crago, Philip Thomas, *BSc, CEng, MIMarE*	LT CDR(FTC)	E	ME	01.04.93	LPD(R) IPT
Craib, Alfred George	LT(FTC)	E	WE	05.06.92	ACE SRGN GIBLTAR
Craig, Douglas Murray	CDR(FTC)	E	AE	31.12.90	DARA
Craig, John Antony	LT(FTC)	X	MCD	01.05.94	FOST MPV(SEA)
Craig, Kenneth Mitchell, *BSc*	CAPT RM(FTC)	RM		28.04.95	JSCSC
Craig, Peter Daniel, *BEng, pce*	LT CDR(FTC)	X	PWO(N)	01.02.96	ILLUSTRIOUS
Craig, Rodney William Wilson, *MNI, jsdc, pce*	CDR(FTC)	X	PWO(A)	30.06.90	MOD (LONDON)
Cramp, Anthony Michael, *pcea*	LT CDR(FTC)	X	P	01.01.96	PJHQ
Cran, Barrie Charles, *BEng, CEng, MIMechE*	LT CDR(FTC)	E	MESM	01.12.96	SUPERB
Crane, Oliver Richard, *BSc*	LT(IC)	X	P	16.12.98	RNAS YEOVILTON
Craner, Matthew John, *MB, BCh, MRCP*	SURG LTCDR	-		01.08.98	MODHU DERRIFORD
Crascall, Stephen John	LT(FTC)	X	AV	23.07.93	RNAS YEOVILTON
Craven, John Arthur Graham, *MIL, MIMgt*	LT CDR(FTC)	S		01.09.85	2SL/CNH FOTR
Craven, Martin William, *BEng*	LT(CC)	X	P	16.12.98	702 SQN HERON
Craven-Phillips, Thomas Charles Dale	MAJ(FTC)	RM		01.02.79	RM NORTON MANOR
Crawford, Adam Timothy Stephen, *BSc*	CAPT RM(FTC)	RM		01.05.98	MOD (LONDON)
Crawford, Keith	SLT(IC)	X	P U/T	01.09.98	DARTMOUTH BRNC
Crawford, Leslie	LT(FTC)	E	WE	05.12.93	COLLINGWOOD
Crawford, Paul Ian, *MB, BS*	SURG CDR	-	SM	31.12.98	LOAN BRUNEI
Crawford, Ronald Lindsay, *psc*	LT COL(FTC)	RM	P	30.06.91	SULTAN AIB
Crawford, Valerie Elizabeth, *LLB*	SLT(IC)	X		01.01.99	DARTMOUTH BRNC
Crawley, David Anthony	SLT(FTC)	E	ME	01.04.98	FOSF
Creates, Keith Ian, *BA, pce*	LT CDR(FTC)	X	PWO(U)	01.04.87	TCM IPT
Cree, Andrew Martin, *BEng*	LT CDR(FTC)	E	TM	01.09.97	FOSF
Cree, Malcolm Charles, *BA, pce, fsc*	CDR(FTC)	X	PWO(A)	30.06.98	MOD (LONDON)
Creech, Richard David, *gdas*	LT CDR(FTC)	X	O	01.10.96	LOAN DERA BSC DN
Creek, Stephen Brain	SLT(IC)	E	WESM	27.01.99	COLLINGWOOD
Crew, Julian Maynard, *BA*	LT(IC)	X	P U/T	01.01.00	DHFS
Criddle, Gary	LT(CC)	X	O	01.06.96	702 SQN HERON
Crimmen, David John	LT(CC)	X	P	01.03.91	814 SQN
Cripps, Neil Philip James, *MB, BCh, MCh, FRCS, FRCSEd, GB*	SURG CDR	-	(CGS)	31.12.94	RH HASLAR
Crispin, Toby Alexander Baldwin, *BSc, pcea*	LT CDR(FTC)	X	O	01.04.94	HQBF CYPRUS
Critchley, Matthew Stephen, *BSc*	LT(IC)	E	TM	01.09.90	DRYAD
Crockatt, Stephen Richard James	LT(CC)	X	P	01.09.90	702 SQN HERON
Croft, David Francis, *MA*	LT(IC)	X		01.09.99	MONMOUTH
Croft, Martin, *psc*	LT CDR(FTC)	X	SM	01.10.93	FOSM NWOOD HQ
Crofts, David Jeffrey, *BEng, AMIEE*	LT CDR(FTC)	E	WE	01.02.99	JSSU OAKLEY
Croke, Anthony, *pce, pcea, psc, ocds(Can)*	CAPT(FTC)	X	P	30.06.99	DEF SCH OF LANG
Cromie, John Martin, *BSc, MSc*	SLT(CC)	X		01.01.98	SOUTHAMPTON
Crompton, Philip John	SLT(IC)	X	P	01.04.98	RNAS CULDROSE
Crook, Andrea Susan, *BA, jsdc*	CDR(FTC)	S		30.06.97	FOSF
Crookes, Waveney Alan	LT(FTC)	X	MCD	01.07.97	PEMBROKE

Name	Rank	Branch	Spec	Seniority	Where Serving
Croome-Carroll, Michael Patrick John , *MBE*	LT CDR(FTC)	X	MCD	27.01.90	ELANT/NAVNORTH
Cropley, Andrew , *BSc, MA(Ed), MIPD, psc(j)*	LT CDR(FTC)	E	TM	01.09.94	CINCFLEET
Cropper, Fraser Brunel Nicholas , *BEng*	LT(FTC)	E	AE	24.06.93	RMC OF SCIENCE
Cropper, Martin Andrew Keith , *BA*	LT CDR(FTC)	S	SM	16.05.90	CAPTAIN SM2
Crosbie, Donald Ernest Frederick	LT CDR(FTC)	X	PWO(U)	01.02.00	SOUTHAMPTON
Crosby, John Paul , *psc*	LT COL(FTC)	RM		30.06.93	SACLANT USA
Crosby, Michael , *BA*	SLT(IC)	X		01.05.98	CAMPBELTOWN
Cross, Alexander Leigh , *BEng*	LT(FTC)	E	WESM	01.01.99	VENGEANCE(PORT)
Cross, Eric John	LT RM(IC)	RM		24.01.00	847 SQN
Cross, Martin George , *BSc, psc*	LT CDR(FTC)	E	MESM	01.04.88	ASTUTE IPT
Crossley, Charles Crispin , *BSc, CEng, MIMarE, MIMechE*	CDR(FTC)	E	ME	31.12.99	RMCS SHRIVENHAM
Crossley, Guy Antony	LT(CC)	X	P	16.05.93	RAF CRANWELL EFS
Crouch, Matthew , *BSc*	SLT(IC)	X		01.05.98	CHATHAM
Crouden, Stephen Frederick	MAJ(FTC)	RM	SO(LE)	01.10.98	45 CDO RM
Crowe, David Michael	LT(FTC)	X		01.08.99	ARGYLL
Crowther, Kevin Wayne , *BSc, pce*	LT CDR(FTC)	X	PWO(A)	29.03.91	DRYAD
Crozier, Stuart Ross McDonald , *BA (BARRISTER)*	LT CDR(FTC)	S	BAR	01.04.94	2SL/CNH
Crudgington, Paul , *AFC, pcea*	LT CDR(FTC)	X	F	01.09.87	700M MERLIN IFTU
Crumplin, Carolyn Anne	LT CDR(FTC)	W	C	01.10.92	SHEFFIELD
Crundell, Richard John , *BEng*	LT(FTC)	E	WE	01.07.92	LN DERA FARN
Cryar, Timothy Martin Craven , *n*	LT CDR(FTC)	X	PWO(A)	01.08.98	YORK
Cubbage, Jamie , *BEng*	LT(FTC)	E	WE	01.04.94	2SL/CNH FOTR
Cull, Iain , *n*	LT(FTC)	X	PWO(A)	01.05.94	NEWCASTLE
Cullen, Nicola Leonie , *BSc*	LT(IC)	X		01.09.95	NEPTUNE
Cullen-Jones, Haydn , *FNI, pce*	LT CDR(FTC)	X	AWO(U)	01.09.79	JSU NORTHWOOD
Cullis, Christopher John	MAJ(FTC)	RM	LC	25.04.96	CTCRM
Culwick, Peter Francis , *BDS, MSc, MGDS, RCS*	SGCDR(D)	-		31.12.96	JSU NORTHWOOD
Cuming, Brian Hugh Douglas , *MBE, pce, psc(m)*	LT CDR(FTC)	X	PWO(U)	16.03.81	DGSS BRISTOL
Cummin, Michael Antony , *BSc, CEng, MIMarE*	CDR(FTC)	E	MESM	31.12.95	MOD (BATH)
Cumming, Robert Angus , *BEng*	LT(CC)	E	MESM	01.04.97	TRIUMPH
Cummings, Alan Thomas , *pce, pcea*	LT CDR(FTC)	X	O	01.03.97	EXCHANGE USA
Cummings, David John , *BEng*	LT(FTC)	E	WE	01.11.94	JSCSC
Cunane, John Richard	LT CDR(FTC)	S	SM	01.10.98	RNAS CULDROSE
Cundy, Robert Graham	MAJ(FTC)	RM		01.09.96	RM Poole
Cunnane, Keith John	LT(FTC)	E	WESM	01.03.94	RMC OF SCIENCE
Cunningham, Andrew Nicholas , *BA*	CAPT RM(FTC)	RM		01.09.96	HQ BAND SERVICE
Cunningham, Craig , *HND*	LT CDR(CC)	E	TMSM	01.10.95	NEPTUNE 2SL/CNH
Cunningham, David Andrew , *MB, BS, LRCP, MRCS*	SURG CAPT	-	GMPP	30.06.94	UKSU AFSOUTH
Cunningham, David Andrew , *pcea*	LT CDR(FTC)	X	O	15.12.95	RNAS CULDROSE
Cunningham, David	SLT(IC)	E	MESM	19.09.98	SULTAN
Cunningham, John Gavin , *BA, pce, pcea*	LT CDR(FTC)	X	O	01.12.93	WESTMINSTER
Cunningham, John Stewart	MAJ(FTC)	RM	SO(LE)	01.10.98	40 CDO RM
Cunningham, Justin Thomas	MAJ(FTC)	RM		01.05.99	RMCS SHRIVENHAM
Cunningham, Nigel John Whitworth	LT(FTC)	X	O	27.07.95	815 FLT 203
Cunningham, Paul	CDR(FTC)	S		31.12.97	RALEIGH
Cunningham, Richard Alister , *MBE, pce, pcea,*	CDR(FTC)	X	P	30.06.00	819 SQN *psc*
Cunningham, Thomas Anthony , *pce, pcea, psc*	CDR(FTC)	X	O	30.06.95	CV(F) IPT
Curd, Timothy Allan , *pce, psc*	CDR(FTC)	X	PWO(U)	31.12.93	SHAPE BELGIUM
Curlewis, Andrew John , *BEng*	LT CDR(FTC)	E	ME	01.04.00	MOD (BATH)
Curnow, Michael David , *BSc, CEng, MIMechE, psc*	CDR(FTC)	E	ME	31.12.98	MOD (BATH)
Curr, Ralph Donaldson , *MB, BS, LRCP, DObstRCOG, MRCGP, AKC (COMMODORE)*	SURG CAPT	-	GMPP	30.06.92	CINCFLEET
Curran, Michael Geoffrey Saxon , *BSc, CEng, MIMarE*	CDR(FTC)	E	ME	31.12.84	MOD (BATH)
Currass, Timothy David , *BEng, MSc*	LT CDR(FTC)	E	WE	01.03.99	LN DERA PRTSDWN
Currie, Duncan Gordon	LT(FTC)	X	P	16.12.89	FONA
Currie, David William , *BSc, pce*	LT CDR(FTC)	X	PWO(A)	01.04.90	LN DERA CDA HLS
Currie, Michael John , *BSc*	LT(CC)	X	O U/T	16.11.99	810 SQN SEAHAWK
Currie, Stuart McGregor	LT CDR(FTC)	E	MESM	01.08.99	FOSM FASLANE
Curry, Alexander Harold , *BA*	LT(FTC)	S	SM	01.09.95	TRAFALGAR
Curry, Benedict Rodney , *psc*	MAJ(FTC)	RM	C	25.04.96	PJHQ
Curry, Jamie Hunter , *BA*	LT(IC)	X		01.02.98	DUMBARTON CASTLE
Curry, Robert Edward , *BSc, n*	LT(FTC)	X		01.11.93	DEF SCH OF LANG
Curtis, Baden , *MBE*	MAJ(LC)	RM		01.10.88	CAPTPORT CLYDE

Name	Rank	Branch	Spec	Seniority	Where Serving
Curtis, David	LT(FTC)	E	WESM	04.09.98	CSST SHORE FSLN
Curtis, Paul Anthony *(Act Lt Cdr)*	LT(FTC)	E	WE	18.10.85	HQRM
Curtis, Robert John *(Act Lt Cdr)*	LT(FTC)	X	PWO(A)	19.10.92	LOAN OMAN
Curtis, Suzannah Elizabeth Hayton, *BMus*	SLT(IC)	S		01.09.97	RALEIGH
Curwood, Jenny Elizabeth, *BSc*	LT(IC)	S		01.09.99	COVENTRY
Cusack, Nicholas James, *MSc, jsdc*	LT COL(FTC)	RM	C	30.06.99	CTCRM
Cust, David Robert, *jsdc, pce(sm)*	CAPT(FTC)	X	SM	30.06.94	NATO DEF COL
Cust, Sally Anne	SLT(IC)	X		01.04.98	CHATHAM
Cutler, Andrew Rodney, *BSc*	LT(FTC)	X	SM	01.02.97	VICTORIOUS(PORT)
Cutler, Tristan Paul, *BSc*	LT(IC)	S		01.11.99	RALEIGH
Cutt, John James Douglas, *pce(sm), psc*	CDR(FTC)	X	SM	30.06.94	VIGILANT(PORT)

D

Name	Rank	Branch	Spec	Seniority	Where Serving
D'Arcy, Paul Andrew	LT(CC)	X	O	16.08.90	FONA
D'Silva, Daniel Mark, *BEng*	LT(CC)	E	WE	01.02.98	COVENTRY
Da Gama, Joseph Anthony Jude, *BSc, CEng, MIEE, MRAeS, psc*	CDR(FTC)	E	AE	30.06.96	NMA PORTSMOUTH
Dabell, Guy Lester, *BSc*	LT CDR(FTC)	E	MESM	01.07.94	DLO DGOBD
Dacombe, Carl Andrew	MID(UCE)(IC)	X		01.09.99	COVENTRY
Dadwal, Rajesh Kimle, *BA*	SLT(IC)	X		01.01.99	DARTMOUTH BRNC
Daglish, Hugh Blyth, *LVO, pce, psc*	CAPT(FTC)	X	PWO(A)	31.12.96	JSCSC
Dailey, Paul George Johnson, *BSc, MSc, CEng, MIEE, MIMgt, Eur Ing*	LT CDR(FTC)	E	WESM	01.04.97	VANGUARD(PORT)
Dainton, Steven, *n*	LT CDR(FTC)	X	PWO(C)	01.03.98	FOSF SEA PTSMTH
Dainty, Robin	SLT(IC)	X	SM	29.04.98	DRYAD
Dale, Alistair	LT(CC)	X	ATC	23.02.92	EXCHANGE RAF UK
Dale, Michael John, *pce, psc*	CDR(FTC)	X	PWO(C)	30.06.93	EXCHANGE USA
Dale, Nathan Andrew	MID(NE)(IC)	X	P U/T	01.09.99	DARTMOUTH BRNC
Dale, Nigel	LT(FTC)	X	SM	25.07.96	AGRIPPA NAVSOUTH
Dale, Richard Foley, *MB, BS, FRCS, FRCSEd (Act Surg Capt)*	SURG CDR	-	(CGS)	31.12.91	MOD (LONDON)
Dale, William David John, *BSc*	LT(IC)	X		01.08.98	CHATHAM
Dale-Smith, Guy, *BA, pce*	LT CDR(FTC)	X	PWO(U)	01.12.97	EXCHANGE CANADA
Dalglish, Kenneth Michael	MID(UCE)(IC)	E		01.09.99	SOUTHAMPTON
Dallamore, Rebecca Ann	SLT(IC)	X		01.04.98	DRYAD
Dalton, David John	LT CDR(FTC)	E	AE(L)	01.10.92	MOD DHSA
Dalton, Feargal John, *BEng*	LT(IC)	E	WESM	01.07.95	VANGUARD(PORT)
Daly, Andrew, *BEng, AMIEE*	LT(FTC)	E	WE	01.12.92	SSA BRISTOL
Daly, Julie Margaret, *BEd*	LT(CC)	W	TM	04.01.93	NELSON
Daly, Paul	LT(CC)	X		01.05.99	SUTHERLAND
Danbury, Ian Gerald, *BSc, AMIEE*	CDR(FTC)	E	WE	30.06.98	KENT
Dando, Jonathon Neil, *n*	LT(FTC)	X		01.08.92	DRYAD
Dane, Richard Martin Henry	LT CDR(FTC)	X	P	01.10.94	EXCHANGE USA
Daniel, Andrew Gordon	LT CDR(FTC)	X	SM	01.10.95	2SL/CNH FOTR
Daniel, Ian Robert	CAPT RM(FTC)	RM	SO(LE)	01.01.98	CTCRM
Daniell, Christopher John, *pcea*	LT CDR(FTC)	X	O	01.10.95	RNAS CULDROSE
Daniels, Ian James Russel, *BSc, pcea*	LT CDR(FTC)	X	O	01.10.95	RNAS YEOVILTON
Daniels, Stephen Anthony, *pcea, psc, tp*	CDR(FTC)	X	P	30.06.00	MOD (LONDON)
Daniels, Stuart Paul	SLT(FTC)	X	PT	18.09.98	RAMSEY
Daniels, Timothy Nicholas, *BA, psc(j)*	MAJ(FTC)	RM	C	01.09.93	MOD (LONDON)
Dann, Ace, *BA*	LT(FTC)	X		01.04.99	CARDIFF
Dann, Adrian Stuart	LT CDR(FTC)	X	MCD	01.10.98	SUPT OF DIVING
Dannatt, Timothy Mark, *BSc, MSc, CEng, MIMarE, jsdc*	CDR(FTC)	E	ME	30.06.93	MOD (LONDON)
Darch, Brian Nicholas, *BSc, CEng, MIMechE, MDA, CDipAF, psc*	CDR(FTC)	E	ME	31.12.83	MOD (BATH)
Darkins, Colin Richard, *BSc*	LT(IC)	E	TM	01.01.98	CTCRM
Darley, Matthew Edward, *BSc*	2LT(GRAD)(IC)	RM		01.09.99	CTCRM LYMPSTONE
Darling, James Ian	LT CDR(FTC)	E	WE	01.10.98	SSA/CWTA PORTS
Darling, Robert James Cyprian	CAPT RM(IC)	RM		01.09.98	RM Poole
Darlington, Mark Robinson, *BSc, pce*	CDR(FTC)	X	PWO(A)	30.06.98	MOD (LONDON)
Darlow, Paul Raymond	LT(FTC)	S	CA	03.04.97	INVINCIBLE
Dart, Duncan James	MID(NE)(IC)	E	P U/T	01.09.99	DARTMOUTH BRNC
Darwent, Andrew, *BSc, MDA*	CDR(FTC)	E	WE	30.06.99	SSA BRISTOL
Darwent, Sean Anthony, *BSc*	LT(CC)	X	O	01.03.93	810 SQN SEAHAWK
Dashfield, Adrian Kenneth, *MB, BCh, FRCA*	SURG CDR	-	(CA)	30.06.00	MODHU DERRIFORD
Dathan, Timothy James, *BEng, MSc*	LT CDR(FTC)	E	ME	01.03.95	MONMOUTH

Name	Rank	Branch	Spec	Seniority	Where Serving
Daukes, Nicholas Michael, *BSc*	CAPT RM(FTC)	RM		01.09.95	RM POOLE
Daulby, Darron James, *BEng*	SLT(IC)	X		01.01.98	BROCKLESBY
Daveney, David Alan, *BA, BSc*	LT(FTC)	X	SM	01.10.97	TIRELESS
Davenport, Nigel Jefferson, *BDS*	SGLTCDR(D)	-		16.01.97	DRAKE CBP(CNH)
Davey, Gary Stuart, *BEng*	LT CDR(FTC)	E	AE	01.11.98	FCBA IPT
Davey, Paul John, *BSc, CEng, FIMarE*	LT CDR(FTC)	E	ME	01.06.89	CNSA BRISTOL
Davey, Timothy James, *BSc*	LT(IC)	X		01.10.97	DRYAD
David, Simon Evan James, *MA, psc(j)*	LT CDR(FTC)	S		16.10.94	CINCFLEET
Davidson, Allan Miller	LT CDR(FTC)	X	P	01.06.98	819 SQN
Davidson, Martin, *BEng*	LT(FTC)	E	WESM	01.11.94	VICTORIOUS(STBD)
Davidson, Neil Richard	LT(CC)	X	P	01.04.91	848 SQN HERON
Davies, Andrew James Albert, *gdas*	LT(CC)	X	O	01.08.90	750 SQN OBS SCH
Davies, Anthony Robin, *BA, pce, psc*	CDR(FTC)	X	PWO(A)	31.12.94	NELSON
Davies, Christopher John, *pce*	LT CDR(FTC)	X	MCD	01.10.93	NMA PORTSMOUTH
Davies, Christopher Ronald	CAPT RM(IC)	RM		01.05.99	42 CDO RM
Davies, Christopher Stanley, *MA*	LT CDR(FTC)	X	METOC	01.09.90	MOD (LONDON)
Davies, Geraint William Tudor	LT(CC)	X	FC	01.12.97	ILLUSTRIOUS
Davies, Huan Charles Ayrton, *BA*	CAPT RM(FTC)	RM	MLDR	01.09.94	CTCRM
Davies, Henry George Alexander	LT(IC)	X	P	01.07.96	EXCHANGE CANADA
Davies, Ian Ellis, *n*	LT CDR(FTC)	X	H1	01.12.98	CAPT(H) DEVPT
Davies, Ian Hugh, *BSc*	LT CDR(FTC)	X	SM	16.10.83	FOST DPORT SHORE
Davies, John Huw, *BA, psc(j)*	LT CDR(FTC)	X	METOC	01.09.93	MOD (LONDON)
Davies, Jason	SLT(CAS)	MS		19.09.98	INM ALVERSTOKE
Davies, Jonathan Peter, *BA, BSc, psc(j)*	LT CDR(FTC)	S		01.10.92	ILLUSTRIOUS
Davies, John Robert, *osc(us)*	LT COL(FTC)	RM		31.12.98	MOD (LONDON)
Davies, Justin Wayne, *BEng*	LT(FTC)	E	ME	11.05.93	SSA BRISTOL
Davies, Lee, *BEng*	LT(FTC)	E	AE(P)	01.01.94	815 FLT 219
Davies, Lyndon James	LT CDR(FTC)	E	ME	01.10.98	CHATHAM
Davies, Mark Bryan, *pce, pcea*	LT CDR(FTC)	X	O	24.01.97	MWC PORTSDOWN
Davies, Michael Charles, *BSc*	SLT(IC)	X		01.01.98	SANDOWN
Davies, Nicholas Mark Samuel, *BSc*	LT(IC)	X		01.09.98	RFANSU (ARGUS)
Davies, Paul Nicholas Michael, *pce, psc(m)*	CAPT(FTC)	X	PWO(A)	31.12.98	NEPTUNE CFS
Davies, Peter Roland, *CBE, MSc, CEng, FIEE, nadc, gw (COMMODORE)*	CAPT(FTC)	E	WESM	30.06.93	COLLINGWOOD
Davies, Stephen Philip	LT(FTC)	E	WESM	05.06.92	CSST SHORE DEVPT
Davies, Susan, *MB, BS*	SURG LT	-		08.08.96	RH HASLAR
Davies, Timothy Christopher, *BSc*	SLT(IC)	X	P U/T	01.05.97	RAF CRANWELL EFS
Davies, Timothy Gordon, *BSc, MRAeS, odc(Fr)*	CDR(FTC)	E	AE(P)	31.12.98	JHCHQ
Davies, Trevor Martin, *BEng, MSc, MIExpE*	LT CDR(FTC)	E	WE	01.10.97	NORTHUMBERLAND
Davis, Andrew Richard	LT CDR(CC)	X	P	01.10.94	FONA
Davis, Bernard James, *LLB (BARRISTER)*	CDR(FTC)	S	BAR	31.12.90	NMA PORTSMOUTH
Davis, Christopher John, *BA(Hons), MMus, LRAM*	MAJ(FTC)	BS		01.10.98	RM SCHOOL MUSIC
Davis, Edward Grant Martin, *MBE, MA, psc(m)*	LT COL(FTC)	RM		31.12.98	CINCFLEET
Davis, Gary *(Act Lt)*	SLT(IC)	X		27.01.99	RNU RAF DIGBY
Davis, Martin Philip, *BSc, pce, pcea, psc*	LT CDR(FTC)	X	O	01.07.88	LOAN OMAN
Davis, Paul Barry	LT CDR(FTC)	X	P	01.10.94	EXCHANGE USA
Davis, Richard	LT(CC)	X		01.01.99	ATHERSTONE
Davis, Sarah Barbara	LT CDR(CC)	W	S	01.10.95	2SL/CNH
Davis, Stephen Rickard, *BEng*	LT(FTC)	E	WESM	01.11.96	VIGILANT(PORT)
Davis-Marks, Michael Leigh, *BSc, MA, pce, pce(sm), psc*	CDR(FTC)	X	SM	31.12.95	BDS WASHINGTON
Davison, Andrew Paul, *BSc, PGCE*	LT CDR(FTC)	X	METOC	01.10.94	CINCFLEET
Davison, Gregory James	LT(CC)	X	P	01.04.91	EXCHANGE USA
Davison, James Charles	LT CDR(FTC)	X	PWO(N)	01.11.98	DRYAD
Davison, Jeffrey Edward, *pce*	LT CDR(FTC)	X	PWO(A)	06.04.97	RANGER
Davison, Terence John	LT(FTC)	E	WE	13.06.86	SCU LEYDENE ACNS
Daw, Simon James	LT CDR(CC)	X	O	01.10.97	750 SQN OBS SCH
Dawkins, Martin William, *BSc, MRAeS*	LT CDR(CC)	X	P	01.10.97	846 SQN
Daws, Richard Patrick Anthony, *BSc, MIEE*	CDR(FTC)	E	WESM	30.06.99	RMC OF SCIENCE
Dawson, Alan James, *BTech*	LT(FTC)	E	WESM	24.02.95	RALEIGH
Dawson, Edward William, *MSc, CEng, MIEE, jsdc, gw*	CAPT(FTC)	E	AE	31.12.95	ES AIR BRISTOL
Dawson, Graham Alexander Edward, *BSc, BEng*	SLT(IC)	X	P U/T	01.09.97	RAF CRANWELL EFS
Dawson, Nigel Julian Frederick, *BSc*	LT(CC)	E	TM	01.09.94	MOD (LONDON)
Dawson, Paul	SLT(FTC)	E	MESM	01.04.98	VANGUARD(PORT)
Dawson, Peter John	LT CDR(FTC)	X	ATC	01.10.89	RNAS YEOVILTON

Name	Rank	Branch	Spec	Seniority	Where Serving
Dawson, Phillip Mark David	SLT(IC)	X		01.01.99	DARTMOUTH BRNC
Dawson, Stephen Lee, *MA, PGCE, psc*	LT CDR(FTC)	E	TM	12.09.90	2SL/CNH
Dawson, Stewart Neville, *BEng*	LT CDR(FTC)	E	WE	01.10.98	DGCIS BRISTOL
Dawson, William	LT CDR(FTC)	X	PWO(A)	01.11.98	DRYAD
Day, Benjamin Thomas, *BA*	SLT(IC)	X		01.01.99	DARTMOUTH BRNC
Day, Christopher Philip, *BSc*	SLT(IC)	X		01.05.98	NEWCASTLE
Day, Kenneth John Coryton, CEng, FIEE, FINucE,	Capt(FTC)	E	MESM	30.06.91	NELSON
Day, Michael Kershaw, *BSc*	LT(CC)	X	P	15.06.95	846 SQN
Day, Nigel Richard, *psc, psc(j)*	CDR(FTC)	S		31.12.91	RHQ AFNORTH
Day, Simon Nicholas, *BEng*	LT(FTC)	E	ME	01.10.96	CAPT F4 (SEA)
Day, Timothy Mark, *BSc, MSc*	LT CDR(CC)	E	TM	01.10.94	COLLINGWOOD
Day, Trevor Steven	LT CDR(FTC)	E	WE	01.10.95	MONTROSE
Daykin, Paul Martin	LT CDR(FTC)	X	PWO(C)	09.09.86	AGRIPPA NAVSOUTH
de Halpert, Jeremy Michael, *MRIN, jsdc, pce*	RADM	-	PWO(N)†	09.12.98	NMA PORTSMOUTH
de Jager, Hendrikus, *psc*	LT COL(FTC)	RM		31.12.91	EXCHANGE USA
De Jonghe, Paul Trevor, *IEng*	LT CDR(FTC)	E	WE	01.10.94	MOD (LONDON)
De La Mare, Richard Michael	LT CDR(FTC)	S		01.10.94	EXCHANGE AUSTLIA
De La Rue, Andrew Nicholas, *BA*	SLT(IC)	S		01.09.98	DARTMOUTH BRNC
De Reya, Anthony Luciano *(Act Maj)*	CAPT RM(FTC)	RM		01.09.95	CTCRM
De Sa, Philip John, *pce, psc*	CDR(FTC)	X	PWO(A)	31.12.91	SACLANT USA
de Val, Kevin Leslie, *rcds, psc*	LT COL(FTC)	RM		31.12.86	HQRM
Deacon, Phillip Reginald	MID(IC)	S		01.09.99	DARTMOUTH BRNC
Deacon, Stephen	LT CDR(FTC)	X	O	01.06.98	GLOUCESTER
Deakin, David John, *BSc*	LT(IC)	X	P U/T	01.01.00	DHFS
Deakin, Johanna, *BEng*	LT(CC)	E	AE	01.01.95	815 SQN HQ
Deal, Charlotte, *BEng*	LT(IC)	E	WE	01.06.99	COLLINGWOOD
Deam, Paul Andrew Victor	LT(FTC)	X	SM	23.07.98	FOSM NWOOD OPS
Dean, James Robert	LT(FTC)	S		01.10.95	MARLBOROUGH
Dean, Lea Jeffrey	SLT(IC)	X	ATCU/T	01.05.98	RAF SHAWBURY
Dean, Mark Christopher, *BSc*	2LT(GRAD)(IC)	RM		01.09.99	CTCRM LYMPSTONE
Dean, Michael Robin, *MB, BCh, DObstRCOG, MRCGP, MFOM*	SURG CDR	-	(CO/M)	30.06.93	CNNRP BRISTOL
Dean, Timothy Charles, *BDS*	SG LT(D)	-		22.07.97	CDO LOG REGT RM
Dean, William Michael Henry, *BSc*	LT CDR(FTC)	X	P	01.10.95	800 SQN
Deaney, Mark Nicholas, *BSc, CEng, MRAeS (Act Cdr)*	LT CDR(FTC)	E	AE	01.05.92	HARRIER IPT
Dearden, Steven Roy, *BSc MSc, CEng, FIMechE*	CDR(FTC)	E	MESM	31.12.96	MOD (BATH)
Dearling, Peter Charles	LT(FTC)	X	MW	29.07.88	CDRE MFP
Deavin, Matthew James	LT(IC)	X	O	01.07.95	849 SQN B FLT
Debenham, Leslie Allen, *BEng, CEng, MRAeS, CGIA, mdtc*	LT CDR(FTC)	E	AE	20.10.82	MOD (BATH)
Dechow, William Ernest, *BSc, jsdc*	LT COL(FTC)	RM		30.06.99	CINCFLEET
Dedman, Nigel John Keith, *pce, pcea, fsc*	CDR(FTC)	X	O	31.12.90	2SL/CNH
Deeks, Peter James, *BEng*	LT(IC)	E	MESM	01.12.95	VIGILANT(STBD)
Deeney, Stephen Jude	LT CDR(FTC)	X	ATC	01.10.99	PRESTWICK
Deighton, Alastair William Greenway, *BA*	LT(FTC)	X		01.09.99	BRIDPORT
Deighton, Derek Simpson, *pce*	LT CDR(FTC)	X	PWO(A)	01.05.92	MOD (LONDON)
Dekker, Barrie James, *MB, BS*	SURG LTCDR	-		01.08.99	NELSON (PAY)
Dell, Iain Martin	LT(FTC)	MS	(AD)	23.07.93	INM ALVERSTOKE
Deller, Mark Gareth, *pcea, psc*	LT CDR(FTC)	X	P	01.03.94	SOUTHAMPTON
Dembrey, Mark Nicholas Scott, *BSc*	LT(IC)	X	O	16.12.94	815 FLT 228
Dempsey, Sean Patrick	LT(FTC)	X		01.02.99	COVENTRY
Denham, Daniel John	LT(CC)	X	P	01.06.98	847 SQN
Denham, Nigel John	LT CDR(FTC)	X	SM	01.10.94	DGCIS BRISTOL
Denholm, Iain Glenwright, *pce*	LT CDR(FTC)	X	PWO(A)	13.08.94	RAF BENTLEY PRIY
Denholm, James Lovell, *MB, ChB*	SURG LT	-		07.08.96	MODHU DERRIFORD
Denison, Alan Rae Van Tiel, *BSc, MSc, CEng, MIMechE*	LT CDR(FTC)	E	ME	01.02.89	EXCHANGE NLANDS
Denney, James Robert, *BA*	LT(IC)	X		01.09.99	ALDERNEY
Denning, Paul Richard, *MA, psc(m)*	LT COL(FTC)	RM	P	31.12.96	45 CDO RM
Dennis, James Alexander, *BSc*	CAPT RM(IC)	RM		01.09.99	CTCRM
Dennis, Matthew John	LT(FTC)	X	SM	01.10.93	VIGILANT(PORT)
Dennis, Mark John, *BSc, PGCE*	LT(IC)	E	TM	01.01.97	2SL/CNH
Dennis, Philip Edward, *BSc*	LT(FTC)	X	FC	01.07.96	NEWCASTLE
Dennis-Jones, Michael, *BA, CEng, FIEE, psc*	CDR(FTC)	E	WE	30.06.87	HQ DCSA
Denny, Andrew Martin, *BDS, MGDS RCS, DGDP(UK)*	SGLTCDR(D)	-		05.01.98	DRYAD
Denovan, Paul Andrew, *BSc, CEng, MIEE*	LT CDR(FTC)	E	WESM	01.01.94	MOD (BATH)

Name	Rank	Branch	Spec	Seniority	Where Serving
Densham, Martin Philip John, *BA, BSc*	LT(IC)	X		01.10.98	CAPT F2(SEA)
Denton, Adrian Matthew, *BSc*	LT(IC)	X		01.05.98	CAMPBELTOWN
Depledge, Ian George, *BSc, MSc, CEng, MIEE*	LT CDR(FTC)	E	WE	01.04.94	FOSF
Derby, Byron Dylan, *BEng*	LT(FTC)	E	WE	01.04.94	SSA PORTSMOUTH
Derby, Peter John, *MAPM*	LT CDR(FTC)	MS	(PD)	01.10.98	MOD (LONDON)
Dermody, Ryan Thomas	SLT(IC)	X		01.04.98	LINDISFARNE
Derrick, Gareth Gwyn James, *BSc, CEng, MIEE*	CDR(FTC)	E	WESM	30.06.97	LN BANGLADESH
Derrick, Matthew John George, *BEng*	LT(IC)	E	TM	01.09.99	COLLINGWOOD
Devereux, Michael Edwin, *BA*	CAPT RM(FTC)	RM	P U/T	01.09.97	RAF SHAWBURY
Deverson, Richard Timothy Mark, *pcea*	LT(FTC)	X	P	01.10.90	702 SQN HERON
Devlin, Hugh Francis Gerard	CAPT RM(FTC)	RM	SO(LE)	01.01.93	CTCRM
Dew, Anthony, *MB, BCh (Act Surg Lt)*	SURG SLT	-		21.07.97	DARTMOUTH BRNC
Dewar, Duncan Andrew, *BSc, psc(j)*	MAJ(FTC)	RM		01.03.99	PJHQ
Dewsnap, Michael David	LT(FTC)	E	WE	18.02.94	MCM2 SEA
Dible, James Hunter	LT CDR(FTC)	X	P	16.11.96	EXCHANGE FRANCE
Dick, Colin Michael, *BEng*	LT(IC)	E	TM	01.01.97	SULTAN
Dickens, David James Rees, *pce, psc*	CDR(FTC)	X	PWO(U)	31.12.92	NMA PORTSMOUTH
Dickens, David Stephen, *BEng*	LT(CC)	E	WE	01.11.92	PORTLAND
Dickens, Mark Gerald Charles, *pce(sm)*	LT CDR(FTC)	X	SM	01.02.87	CMSA UK
Dickins, Benjamin Russell, *BA*	LT(FTC)	X		01.11.96	COMUKTG/CASWSF
Dickinson, Pamela Hepple, *BEng*	SLT(IC)	E	ME	01.09.97	SULTAN
Dickinson, Philip Neville, *BA*	LT CDR(FTC)	X	O	01.05.82	MWC PORTSDOWN
Dickinson, Richard John, *BSc, MA, psc*	LT CDR(FTC)	E	AE	01.04.90	ES AIR USA
Dickson, Andrew Peat, *pce*	CAPT(FTC)	X	PWO(A)	30.06.96	ENDURANCE
Dickson, James Ian, *BSc*	LT(FTC)	S	SM	01.08.94	SOVEREIGN
Dickson, James Peter Edward, *BSc, MSc*	LT CDR(FTC)	X	METOC	01.10.96	INVINCIBLE
Dickson, Stuart James, *MB, ChB*	SURG LT	-		02.08.95	MODHU DERRIFORD
Diggle, Wadham Nicholas Neston, *BA*	LT(FTC)	X		01.07.92	FOSM NWOOD OPS
Dilloway, Philip John, *BA(Hons)*	LT	Q	RMN	07.12.92	DRAKE CBP(CNH)
Dineen, John Micheal George, *MA*	LT(FTC)	X		01.04.94	DRYAD
Dingley, Paul Alexander	SLT(FTC)	X	O U/T	01.04.98	810 SQN SEAHAWK
Dinham, Alan Colin, *BSc, PHD*	LT CDR(FTC)	E	TM	01.10.88	COLLINGWOOD
Dinsdale, Andrew Malcolm, *BEng*	LT CDR(FTC)	E	WESM	01.02.00	FASM IPT
Disbury, Brian Nicholas	MAJ(FTC)	RM	SO(LE)	01.10.97	HQRM
Disney, Peter William, *pcea*	LT CDR(FTC)	X	O	01.10.94	824 NAS
Diver, Paul Harry, *HND*	LT(CC)	E	TM	01.01.91	RALEIGH
Dixon, Arthur Kenneth, *BEng*	SLT(IC)	E		01.09.98	MANCHESTER
Dixon, Richard Andrew	SLT(IC)	X	P	01.04.98	RNAS YEOVILTON
Dixon, Raymond Francis, *MITE, psc*	LT CDR(FTC)	E	WE	08.06.84	MOD (BATH)
Dobbin, Vincent William	LT CDR(FTC)	E	WESM	01.10.96	ACDS(POL) USA
Dobbins, Stuart James, *BA*	LT(IC)	S		01.06.97	CINCFLEET
Dobie, Fiona Elizabeth	LT(CC)	W	X	01.09.96	DISC
Dobson, Amy Clare	SLT(IC)	S		01.04.00	DARTMOUTH BRNC
Dobson, Brian John	LT CDR(FTC)	S	SM	01.10.95	RNAS YEOVILTON
Dobson, Michael Francis, *BSc, pce*	LT CDR(FTC)	X	PWO(U)	01.01.87	MWC PORTSDOWN
Dobson, Richard Andrew, *BSc*	LT CDR(FTC)	X	H CH	01.04.91	EXCHANGE USA
Docherty, Paul Thomas, *BA, MNI, pce, psc*	CAPT(FTC)	X	PWO(A)	31.12.98	LN DERA CDA HLS
Dodd, James Scott Crossley, *BSc, CEng, MIEE*	CDR(FTC)	E	WE	30.06.91	MOD (BATH)
Dodd, Kevin Michael, *QCBA, pcea*	LT CDR(FTC)	X	O	01.04.99	820 SQN
Dodd, Laura, *BA, BEng*	SLT(IC)	E		01.09.98	MONTROSE
Dodd, Nicholas Charles	LT CDR(FTC)	S	SM	01.04.99	SHEFFIELD
Dodd, Stuart Eric	SLT(IC)	X	SM	01.05.98	SUPERB
Dodds, Malcolm, *jsdc, pce*	CDR(FTC)	X	PWO(N)†	31.12.90	DA BAHRAIN
Dodds, Matthew Lewis, *BSc*	LT(FTC)	X		01.11.98	BROCKLESBY
Dodds, Ralph Scott, *pce, pcea*	LT CDR(FTC)	X	O	01.05.93	DRYAD
Dodgson, Stephen John, *BA, MSc*	CDR(FTC)	E	WESM	31.12.98	FOSM NWOOD HQ
Doggett, Raymond Arthur, *pcea*	CDR(FTC)	X	O	01.10.96	MOD (LONDON)
Doherty, Kenneth	LT CDR(FTC)	X	P	01.10.93	RAF SHAWBURY
Doig, Barry John, *BSc*	LT(CC)	X		01.12.97	CHATHAM
Dolby, Michael John	LT CDR(FTC)	E	WE	01.10.99	2SL/CNH FOTR
Dolton, Antony, *BSc, MSc, CEng, MIEE*	CDR(FTC)	E	WESM	30.06.97	MOD (LONDON)
Dominy, David John Douglas, *n*	LT CDR(FTC)	X	PWO(A)	01.03.00	RICHMOND
Donaldson, Andrew Michael	SLT(FTC)	E	WE	09.01.98	LANCASTER

Name	Rank	Branch	Spec	Seniority	Where Serving
Donaldson, James , *MIMgt, jsdc, pce*	CDR(FTC)	X	PWO(A)	30.06.92	CAMBRIDGE
Donaldson, Stuart Bruce , *pce(sm)*	LT CDR(FTC)	X	SM	01.09.91	RHQ AFNORTH
Donegan, Claire Louise , *LLB*	LT(CC)	X	P	01.10.96	820 SQN
Donnan, Hugh Martin	LT(CC)	X	O	01.04.96	810 SQN SEAHAWK
Donnelly, James Stephen , *BEng*	LT CDR(FTC)	E	AE	22.11.98	ES AIR BRISTOL
Donnelly, Samantha , *BSc, HND*	LT(IC)	E	TM	17.09.96	EXCHANGE RAF UK
Donovan, Mark Christopher , *BEng, CEng, MIMarE*	LT(FTC)	E	MESM	01.08.92	NP BRISTOL
Donovan, Patrick , *BEng*	LT(FTC)	E	MESM	01.11.91	DRAKE CBS
Donovan, Paul Anthony	CHAPLAIN	RC		22.04.85	RALEIGH
Donovan, Robin John , *BA*	LT(FTC)	S	SM	01.01.93	AGRIPPA NAVSOUTH
Donovan, Sally Jane	LT(CC)	X	ATC	01.07.97	FOST DPORT SHORE
Donworth, Desmond Maurice Joseph	LT(CC)	X		01.12.96	GRAFTON
Doolan, Martin , *BA, pce*	LT CDR(FTC)	X	PWO(U)	01.02.94	JSCSC
Doran, Iain Arthur Gustav	LT(FTC)	X		01.07.95	IRON DUKE
Doran, Katie Elizabeth , *BSc*	SLT(IC)	X		01.09.98	DARTMOUTH BRNC
Doran, Shane Edmund , *BEng*	LT(FTC)	E	ME	01.07.94	SSA BRISTOL
Dorricott, Alan Joseph	LT CDR(FTC)	E	ME	01.10.95	SUP SHIPS PTSMTH
Dorset, William , *IEng, MIEEIE*	LT(FTC)	E	WE	03.11.83	DRAKE CBP(DLO)
Doubleday, Steven	LT(CC)	X	P	16.10.98	848 SQN HERON
Douglas, Andrew Malcolm , *BSc*	CAPT RM(IC)	RM		01.05.97	CDO LOG REGT RM
Douglas, Francis Robin , *BSc, CEng, MIEE, MIMarE*	CDR(FTC)	E	MESM	31.12.89	DRAKE CBS
Douglas, Paul Gordon	LT(FTC)	X	SM	03.12.92	SPLENDID
Douglas, Patrick John	LT(FTC)	X	P	01.06.93	URNU BIRMINGHAM
Douglas-Riley, Timothy Roger , *MB, BS, LRCP, MRCS, MRCGP, jsdc*	SURG CAPT	-	GMPP	31.12.96	CINCFLEET *DA*
Douglass, Martin Colin Marc , *BEng*	LT CDR(FTC)	E	ME	01.03.99	SOUTHAMPTON
Doull, Donald James Murray , *BEng, CEng*	LT(FTC)	E	MESM	01.11.94	SULTAN
Dow, Clive Stewart	LT(FTC)	S		01.01.97	2SL/CNH
Dow, William Allister McGowan , *MB, ChB*	SURG LT	-		06.08.97	RFANSU (ARGUS)
Dowd, Jonathan Wyn , *BSc*	CAPT RM(FTC)	RM		01.09.95	HQ 3 CDO BDE RM
Dowdell, Robert Edmund John , *BSc*	LT CDR(FTC)	X	P	01.10.94	LOAN DERA BSC DN
Dowdeswell, Karen Ann , *BM, MRCP*	SURG LTCDR	-		01.08.98	NELSON (PAY)
Dowell, Paul Henry Neil , *BSc, MA, psc(j)*	LT CDR(FTC)	E	WE	01.08.94	OCEAN
Dowie, Matthew Edwin , *BSc*	SLT(IC)	X		01.01.99	DARTMOUTH BRNC
Dowling, Andrew Jonathan	SLT(IC)	X	O U/T	01.09.98	RNAS CULDROSE
Downer, Mark John , *MEng*	LT(IC)	E	ME	01.08.93	SULTAN
Downes, Colin Henry , *BSc*	LT(FTC)	X	MW	01.09.93	PEMBROKE
Downey, Karen	LT	Q	REGM	03.02.98	RN GIBRALTAR
Downie, Alan John	LT CDR(FTC)	E	WE	01.10.97	EXETER
Downing, Iain Michael	LT(CC)	X	P	16.09.94	849 SQN HQ
Downing, Phaedra Louise , *BSc*	LT(FTC)	X		01.02.99	MONTROSE
Downing, Stephen Jamie , *BSc*	LT(CC)	X		01.11.98	SOMERSET
Downing-Waite, Jeanette Ann , *LLB*	LT(FTC)	S		01.01.00	DRAKE NBC
Dowsett, Patrick Giles , *n*	LT(FTC)	X		01.09.93	DRYAD
Downton, John Gerald Murray , MA, jsdc, psc(m), ssc	COL(FTC)	RM	C	31.12.93	RM POOLE
Doxsey, Roland Arthur , *MSc, CEng, MIMechE, jsdc*	CDR(FTC)	E	ME	30.06.89	MOD (BATH)
Doyle, Andrew Bernard , *BA, MSc*	LT(IC)	X	P U/T	01.12.99	DHFS
Doyle, Gareth Brian , *BA*	LT(IC)	X	SM	01.09.97	RALEIGH
Doyle, Gary Lawrence , *pce, pcea*	CDR(FTC)	X	O	31.12.99	JSCSC
Doyle, Nicholas Patrick	LT(FTC)	X	q	17.12.93	GUERNSEY
Doyne-Ditmas, Philip Simon , *MBE, pce, pcea, psc, psc(j)*	CDR(FTC)	X	P	31.12.95	DA SINGAPORE
Drabble, Raymond Charles , *BSc*	LT CDR(FTC)	S		16.04.93	CARDIFF
Drake, Charlotte Louise , *BMus*	LT(FTC)	S		01.02.98	2SL/CNH FOTR
Drake, Edwin Denis	CDR(FTC)	E	WESM	30.06.96	JSU NORTHWOOD
Drake, Raymond , *MA, IEng, AMIEE*	LT CDR(RETL)	E	WE	16.11.90	MOD (BATH)
Drake-Wilkes, Nicholas James , *BA*	LT(FTC)	X		01.01.95	NORFOLK
Dransfield, Joseph Asa James , *BSc*	LT(CC)	X	O U/T	01.12.99	702 SQN HERON
Draper, Stephen Perry , *pce*	LT CDR(FTC)	X	PWO(A)	26.02.96	DRYAD
Dreelan, Michael Joseph	LT CDR(FTC)	X	PWO(U)	01.08.99	MONMOUTH
Dresner, Rupert James	CAPT RM(FTC)	RM	P	24.04.96	847 SQN
Drewett, Colin Edward , *BEM*	LT(CS)	-		19.09.99	DNR EAST ANGLIA
Drewett, Robin Edward , *MBE, pce, pcea*	CDR(FTC)	X	O	30.06.99	RAF AWC
Driscoll, Robert , *BSc*	LT(CC)	E	TM	22.07.97	RMB STONEHOUSE
Drodge, Andrew Paul Frank	LT(FTC)	X	O	01.10.94	810 SQN B FLIGHT

Name	Rank	Branch	Spec	Seniority	Where Serving
Drodge, Kevin Nigel, *BSc*	LT(IC)	X	P U/T	01.04.99	ILLUSTRIOUS
Drummond, Karl Bruce, *BDS*	SG LT(D)	-		13.07.98	45 CDO RM
Drury, Martin Herbert	LT CDR(FTC)	X	PT	01.10.93	KING ALFRED
Dry, Ian, *BSc*	LT()	E	TM	31.01.99	SULTAN
Drylie, Andrew John, *BSc*	LT CDR(FTC)	X	SM	01.02.92	MOD (LONDON)
Drysdale, Steven Ronald, *pce(sm)*	LT CDR(FTC)	X	SM	01.02.97	VIGILANT(PORT)
Drywood, Tobias, *BEng, MSc*	LT(FTC)	E	ME	01.04.93	LEEDS CASTLE
Du Port, Antony Neil, *pce, psc (COMMODORE)*	CAPT(FTC)	X	PWO(N)†	31.12.92	2SL/CNH
Duce, Matthew	SLT(IC)	X		01.05.98	DARTMOUTH BRNC
Dudley, Stephen Mark Terence, *MA*	LT CDR(FTC)	S		01.01.99	ARK ROYAL
Duesbury, Clive Lawrence, *BSc*	LT(CC)	E	ME	01.06.97	ILLUSTRIOUS
Duff, Andrew Patrick	LT(FTC)	X	SM	01.09.92	TURBULENT
Duff, Euan Tait, *BSc*	LT(FTC)	X	SM	01.10.97	RALEIGH
Duffy, Henry	LT CDR(FTC)	X	PWO(C)	01.05.99	INVINCIBLE
Duffy, John Bernard	LT(IC)	X	P	01.07.91	819 SQN
Dufosee, Sean William	LT(CC)	X	P	06.08.94	845 SQN
Duke, Ronald Michael	LT CDR	Q	CPN	31.12.96	MODHU DERRIFORD
Dullage, Bryan, *BSc, MSc, CEng, MIMarE, MCGI, psc(j)*	LT CDR(FTC)	E	ME	01.03.92	MOD (BATH)
Dumbell, Phillip, *BSc, MA, psc*	LT CDR(FTC)	E	WESM	01.09.91	MWC PORTSDOWN
Dumbleton, David William	SLT(FTC)	E	WE	01.04.98	COLLINGWOOD
Duncan, Colin John	LT(CC)	X	P	01.09.93	820 SQN
Duncan, Giles Stuart	LT(IC)	X	P	16.01.95	814 SQN
Duncan, Giles Spencer, *BSc*	CAPT RM(FTC)	RM		01.05.98	DNR DISP TEAM
Duncan, Ian Stewart, *BSc*	LT CDR(FTC)	E	MESM	01.06.94	CINCFLEET
Duncan, Jeremy	LT(FTC)	X	P	01.04.91	824 NAS
Duncan, Kathryn Claire, *BSc*	SLT(CC)	X		01.09.97	DRYAD
Dunham, Mark William, *BSc, psc(m)*	LT COL(FTC)	RM		31.12.96	HQRM
Dunkley, Simon Charles	LT(FTC)	X	AV	26.04.99	RNAS CULDROSE
Dunlop, Peter Francis, *BSc, pce*	LT CDR(FTC)	X	PWO(U)	01.04.91	DRYAD
Dunn, Anthony	SLT(FTC)	X	AV	01.04.98	RFANSU
Dunn, Andrew James Patrick	LT(FTC)	E	AE(M)	16.10.92	SULTAN
Dunn, Gary Russell, *BEng, CEng, Eur Ing*	LT CDR(FTC)	E	WESM	01.05.98	MOD (LONDON)
Dunn, Ian Laurence	MAJ(FTC)	RM	MLDR	01.09.86	EXCHANGE AUSTLIA
Dunn, Nicholas Geoffrey, *BSc, pcea*	LT CDR(FTC)	X	P	01.10.92	700M MERLIN IFTU
Dunn, Paul Ernest	LT(FTC)	X	PT	12.12.91	CALEDONIA CFS
Dunn, Paul Edward	LT(FTC)	X	SM	01.07.93	SUPERB
Dunn, Robert Alexander Phillip, *BEng*	LT(IC)	X	P U/T	01.12.99	DHFS
Dunn, Robert Paul	LT CDR(FTC)	X	SM	02.01.98	TURBULENT
Dunne, Michaelgerard, *BEM (Act Lt Cdr)*	LT(FTC)	X	AV	03.04.97	FONA SUPPORT
Dunningham, Stephen	LT(FTC)	E	ME	10.06.94	CFM PORTSMOUTH
Dunsby, Nicholas Byron	LT(FTC)	E	MESM	15.06.95	CAPTAIN SM2
Dunt, Peter Arthur, *rcds*	RADM	-	(S)	05.01.98	2SL/CNH
Dunthorne, Julie Agnes	LT CDR(FTC)	S		04.01.00	EXETER
Durham, Paul Christopher Langton, *BEng, n*	LT(FTC)	X		01.06.93	800 SQN
Durkin, Mark Thomas Gilchrist, *BSc, pce*	LT CDR(FTC)	X	MCD	01.06.93	ATHERSTONE
Durning, William Munro	LT CDR(FTC)	MS		01.10.99	NMA GOSPORT
Durston, David Howard, *pce, pcea, psc, psc(j)*	CDR(FTC)	X	P	30.06.92	COLLINGWOOD
Durup, Jason Michael Stanley	2LT(GRAD)(IC)	RM		02.09.98	CDO LOG REGT RM
Dustan, Andrew John	LT CDR(FTC)	E	AE	19.02.93	MOD DHSA
Dutton, Andrew Colin	LT(FTC)	S		01.02.95	TALENT
Dutton, David, *pce*	LT CDR(FTC)	X	PWO(C)	01.06.97	JSCSC
Dutton, James Benjamin, *BSc, psc(m) (BRIGADIER)*	COL(OF6)(FTC)	RM	C	31.12.98	MOD (LONDON)
Dutton, Philip John	LT CDR(FTC)	E	WESM	01.10.99	SSIP IPT
Dwane, Christopher Malcolm Robin, *BSc*	LT CDR(FTC)	S		01.01.89	DRAKE CBP(DLO)
Dyche, Trevor	LT(FTC)	E	MESM	18.10.85	SSA DEVONPORT
Dyer, Graham Richard	LT(FTC)	E	WE	05.06.92	CFPS SEA
Dyer, Jonathan David Thomas, *BSc, BTech, MSc*	LT CDR(CC)	E	IS	01.09.99	DITMTC SHRIVNHAM
Dyer, Michael David James, *BEng, MSc, CEng, MIEE*	CDR(FTC)	E	WESM	30.06.00	CSST SEA
Dyer, Simon John, *BSc, psc*	CDR(FTC)	E	WE	30.06.92	MOD (BATH)
Dyke, Christopher Leonard, *BA, pce*	LT CDR(FTC)	X	PWO(C)	01.02.96	JMOTS NORTHWOOD
Dyke, Kenneth Andrew, *BEng*	LT(FTC)	E	MESM	01.10.92	DSQ ROSYTH
Dymock, Anthony Knox, *BA, pce, psc*	RADM	-	AWO(C)	19.01.00	COMSTRIKFORSTH
Dymond, Nicholaus Robert John	LT(FTC)	E	WE	18.02.94	JSCSC

Name	Rank	Branch	Spec	Seniority	Where Serving
Dyter, Ross Courtney	SLT(UCE)(FTC)	E	ME	01.09.99	DARTMOUTH BRNC

E

Name	Rank	Branch	Spec	Seniority	Where Serving
Eagles, Anthony James, *AFC, MA, pcea, psc*	LT CDR(FTC)	X	P	01.03.84	FONA
Eardley, John Mark	LT(FTC)	E	WE	07.02.97	DRAKE CFM
Earl, Nicholas Julian Christopher, *BEng*	LT(IC)	E	AE	01.10.94	SULTAN
Eastaugh, Andrew Charles, *BSc, MSc, adp (Act Cdr)*	LT CDR(FTC)	E	IS	01.10.89	DITMTC SHRIVNHAM
Eastaugh, Timothy Colin, *pcea*	LT CDR(FTC)	X	P	01.10.93	800 SQN
Easterbrook, Kevin Ivor Edgar, *BEng*	LT CDR(FTC)	E	WE	01.12.99	FOSF ENG DEVPT
Eastlake, Amanda Clare	LT CDR(CC)	W	X	01.10.98	DISC
Eastley, Barry Roger, *BSc, CEng, MIMechE, MRAeS, jsdc*	CAPT(FTC)	E	AE	30.06.96	MOD (BATH)
Easton, Derek William	LT(FTC)	X	PT	04.04.96	COLLINGWOOD
Easton, Robert Nicoll	LT CDR(FTC)	X	PWO(A)	16.11.84	NEPTUNE FD
Easton, Richard William	CDR(FTC)	X	PWO(C)	01.10.96	ROCLANT PORTUGAL
Eastwood, Louise, *BEng*	LT(CC)	E	ME	01.06.95	SULTAN
Eastwood, Richard Noah, *MEng*	LT(IC)	X	P	01.09.98	846 SQN
Eaton, David Charles, *BA*	SLT(IC)	X	ATCU/T	01.01.99	DARTMOUTH BRNC
Eaton, Paul Graham, *BSc*	LT CDR(FTC)	X	METOC	01.06.94	CINCFLEET
Eatwell, Russell Andrew	LT(CC)	X	P	01.08.89	899 SQN HERON
Ebbens, Andrew John	MAJ(FTC)	RM		01.09.87	HQ NORTH
Eberle, Peter James Fuller, *pce, psc* *(COMMODORE)*	CAPT(FTC)	X	PWO(C)	30.06.97	MOD (LONDON)
Eccleston, Jamie Mark, *BEng*	LT(FTC)	E	ME	01.02.95	OCLC BIRM
Eddie, Alan George Watt, *BTech*	LT(FTC)	E	WE	24.02.95	RALEIGH
Edey, Michael John, *BSc, n*	LT(FTC)	X		01.12.93	ILLUSTRIOUS
Edge, John Howard, *MILT*	LT CDR(FTC)	S	SM	01.06.97	JSCSC
Edge, James Michael, *BA*	SLT(IC)	X		01.05.98	CUMBERLAND
Edge, Karla Louise	LT(FTC)	X	HM	01.10.96	CAPT(H) DEVPT
Edge, Philippa Anne, *BA*	LT CDR(CC)	W	X	01.10.99	SULTAN AIB
Edgell, John Nicholas, *OBE, pce, pce(sm), psc*	CDR(FTC)	X	SM	31.12.93	JDCC
Edgington, Simon Paul, *BSc*	SLT(FTC)	X		01.09.97	RAF SHAWBURY
Edgley, Andrew David, *BA*	LT CDR(FTC)	X	METOC	15.10.96	JACIG
Edleston, Hugh Anthony Harold Greswell, *MNI, AMBIM, jsdc, pce* *(COMMODORE)*	CAPT(FTC)	X	AWO(A)	31.12.93	MOD (LONDON)
Edmonds, Gerald	LT CDR(FTC)	X	C	02.08.85	HQAF NORTHWEST
Edmonds, Graham John Leslie, *pce, psc*	CDR(FTC)	X	AWO(A)	31.12.87	RN GIBRALTAR
Edmonds, Louisa Ann, *BSc*	LT(FTC)	X	H2	01.09.94	DARTMOUTH BRNC
Edmonds, Rebecca Mary, *BEng*	LT CDR(FTC)	E	TM	01.11.99	EXCELLENT
Edmondson, James Andrew	SLT(FTC)	X		01.04.98	CROMER
Edmondson, Simon Peter, *BA*	CAPT RM(IC)	RM		01.05.99	DHFS
Edmondstone, William Mark, *MB, BS, DIH, AFOM, FRCP*	SURG CAPT	-	(CM)	30.06.96	RH HASLAR
Edney, Andrew Ralph, *MBE, BEng, pce, pcea, psc*	CDR(FTC)	X	P	31.12.96	FONA CRANWELL
Edson, Mark Andrew	LT(FTC)	E	WE	22.02.96	COLLINGWOOD
Edward, Amanda	SURG SLT	-		03.10.98	DARTMOUTH BRNC
Edward, Gavin James, *BEng, AMIEE*	LT(FTC)	E	WE	01.07.95	SSA BRISTOL
Edwardes, Geoffrey, *pce*	CAPT(LC)	X		31.12.91	NELSON
Edwards, Andrew Donald Pryce, *MBE, BSc, MIMechE*	LT CDR(FTC)	E	MESM	01.02.88	DRAKE CFM
Edwards, Andrew George, *BEng*	LT(FTC)	E	AE(L)	01.09.95	824 NAS
Edwards, Alexander William, *BSc*	LT(IC)	X	P U/T	01.08.99	DHFS
Edwards, Carlos Carew, *BSc*	LT CDR(FTC)	S		01.07.85	DARTMOUTH BRNC
Edwards, Charles John Albert, *MB, BS, FRCA*	SURG CDR	-	(CA)	31.12.97	ILLUSTRIOUS
Edwards, David	SLT(IC)	MS		27.01.99	DARTMOUTH BRNC
Edwards, Eric George	LT CDR(FTC)	X	AV	01.10.92	RNAS CULDROSE
Edwards, Ian, *CEng, MIMechE*	CDR(FTC)	E	IS	30.06.87	2SL/CNH
Edwards, John, *BEng*	LT(CC)	E	AE	01.08.97	846 SQN
Edwards, James, *BSc*	LT(IC)	E	TM	01.09.96	SOUTHAMPTON
Edwards, James Eustice, *BEng*	LT(IC)	E		01.06.97	ILLUSTRIOUS
Edwards, Janice Mary	LT CDR(FTC)	S		01.04.86	AFPAA(CENTURION)
Edwards, John Paul Thomas, *BSc, pcea*	LT CDR(FTC)	X	P	01.10.97	LOAN DERA BSC DN
Edwards, Philip Douglas, *BChir, MA, FRCSEd*	SURG LTCDR	-	(X) UT	21.12.95	NELSON (PAY)
Edwards, Philip John, *BSc*	LT CDR(FTC)	X	METOC	01.05.91	MWC PORTSDOWN
Edwards, Richard	LT CDR(FTC)	X	EW	01.10.99	FOST SEA

Name	Rank	Branch	Spec	Seniority	Where Serving
Edwards, Richmond Arthur	LT CDR(FTC)	E	WE	01.10.95	DISC
Edwins, Mark Richard	SLT(FTC)	E	ME	02.05.97	GRAFTON
Edye, Robin Francis	2LT(GRAD)(IC)	RM		29.04.98	40 CDO RM
Eedle, Richard John, *BA*	LT CDR(FTC)	X	SM	01.03.91	2SL/CNH
Egeland-Jensen, Finn Adam	LT CDR(FTC)	X	PWO(N)	01.04.95	FEARLESS
Egerton, Paul Michael, *BSc, CEng, MIMarE, MIMechE*	CDR(FTC)	E	ME	31.12.88	DRAKE NBC
Egerton, Stephen Brian	LT(FTC)	X	C	10.12.98	DCSA NORTHWOOD
Eglin, Caroline Anne	CHAPLAIN	SF		10.09.90	DRAKE CBP(CNH)
Eglin, Ian	CHAPLAIN	CE		27.01.87	DRAKE CBP(CNH)
Eitzen, Ruari Paul, *BSc, MSc, CEng, MRAeS*	LT CDR(FTC)	E	AE	01.11.76	FAAIT MAN ORG VL
Elborn, Teresa Kathleen, *MHCIMA*	LT(FTC)	W	S	11.12.92	RALEIGH
Eldridge, Timothy John	LT(CC)	X	P	01.04.91	DHFS
Elford, David Graham, *BSc, MSc, CEng, MRAeS, AMIEE, psc(j)*	CDR(FTC)	E	AE	30.06.98	AGRIPPA AFSOUTH
Ellerton, Paul	LT(CC)	X	P	16.10.94	815 FLT 206
Ellett, Keith Geoffrey	LT(CC)	X	ATC	01.06.84	FOST DPORT SHORE
Elliman, Simon Mark	LT CDR(FTC)	X	PWO(U)	01.10.94	FOST MPV(SEA)
Ellins, Stuart John, *BSc, CEng, FIMechE, psc*	CAPT(FTC)	E	ME	31.12.99	NMA PORTSMOUTH
Elliott, James Alistair	SLT(CC)	E	AE	01.05.98	DARTMOUTH BRNC
Elliott, Stephen, *BEng*	LT(FTC)	E	WE	01.07.92	MOD (BATH)
Elliott, Steven, *BEng, AMIEE*	LT(FTC)	E	WESM	01.07.93	CSST SHORE FSLN
Elliott, Timothy Douglas	MID(UCE)(IC)	X		01.09.99	GLOUCESTER
Elliott, Thomas Fitzgerald, *MBE, TEng, IEng, AMIMarE*	LT CDR(FTC)	E	ME	01.10.90	MOD (BATH)
Ellis, Andrew Christopher, *BA*	LT(CC)	X	P U/T	01.05.99	RNAS YEOVILTON
Ellis, Charles Richard, *BEng*	SLT(FTC)	E	WESM	01.09.97	COLLINGWOOD
Ellis, James Paul, *BEng*	LT(CC)	E	ME	01.09.93	LANCASTER
Ellis, Mark Alexandar Harcourt, *BSc, ocds(No)*	MAJ(FTC)	RM		01.09.85	RMR LONDON
Ellis, Michael Philip, *psc(a)*	LT COL(FTC)	RM	P	31.12.98	MOD (BATH)
Ellis, Neil James, *BA*	LT(IC)	X		01.08.98	PENZANCE
Ellis, Nicholas Mark	LT CDR(CC)	X		18.07.97	2SL/CNH FOTR
Ellis, Peter John, *pce(sm)*	CAPT(FTC)	X	SM	30.06.92	SA SANTIAGO
Ellis, Richard William, *BSc*	CDR(FTC)	E	AE	30.06.99	ES AIR BRISTOL
Ellison, Christopher Vaughan, *pce, psc(a)*	CAPT(FTC)	X	PWO(N)†	30.06.92	SA BERLIN
Ellison, Toby George	LT(FTC)	X		01.06.97	FOSF SEA PTSMTH
Ellwood, Peter George	LT(FTC)	X	SM	29.07.94	FOSM NWOOD OPS
Elmer, Timothy Brendan, *BDS*	SGLTCDR(D)	-		15.12.94	INVINCIBLE
Elmore, Graeme Martin	CHAPLAIN	CE		30.09.86	RN GIBRALTAR
Elsey, David John, *BSc*	LT(IC)	E	TM	01.09.97	NELSON RNSETT
Elsom, Geoffrey Keith	LT(FTC)	X	C	27.07.95	CDRE MFP
Elston, Adrian John	LT(FTC)	X	REG	16.12.94	SULTAN
Eltringham, Timothy John, *OBE, jsdc, pce, pcea*	CDR(FTC)	X	P	30.06.90	NS OBERAMMERGAU
Elvin, Andrew James	LT CDR(FTC)	X	MCD	06.11.93	MCM3 SEA
Elwell-Deighton, Dean Carl	LT(CC)	X	P	16.09.93	ILLUSTRIOUS
Emerton, Mark Simon, *MA, MIMgt (BARRISTER)*	LT CDR(FTC)	S	BAR	01.02.92	2SL/CNH
Emmerson, Graham John, *pce*	LT CDR(FTC)	X	PWO(A)	01.06.92	RNLO JTF4
Emms, Stuart Michael	SLT(FTC)	E	WE	09.01.98	MONMOUTH
Endersby, Roger James Stewart, *MInstAM, MInsD*	CDR(FTC)	S		31.12.86	CDRE MFP
Enever, Shaun Andrew	LT(CC)	X	O	01.09.96	RNAS YEOVILTON
Engeham, Paul Richard, *MA, pce*	LT CDR(FTC)	X	AWO(C)	16.01.81	MOD (LONDON)
England, Lorraine	LT	Q	REGM	11.01.91	NELSON (PAY)
England, Philip Morgan, *BSc, MSc*	SLT(IC)	X		01.01.98	MIDDLETON
English, Colin Richard, *MSc, CEng, FIMarE, jsdc*	CDR(FTC)	E	ME	30.06.88	MOD (BATH)
Enticknap, Kenneth, *QGM*	CDR(FTC)	E	ME	30.06.98	PORTLAND
Entwisle, William Nicholas, *BA, psc(j)*	LT CDR(FTC)	X	P	01.02.96	MOD (LONDON)
Entwistle, Camilla, *BSc, MA*	LT(IC)	E	TM	01.09.94	SULTAN
Entwistle, Stephen Charles, *pce*	CDR(FTC)	X	PWO(A)	30.06.00	ELANT/NAVNORTH
Epps, Matthew Paul, *BSc*	SLT(IC)	S		01.05.98	GLASGOW
Erskine, Peter Anthony, *BA, MSc, MIMechE, psc*	CDR(FTC)	E	ME	30.06.96	ILLUSTRIOUS
Erskine, Robert Noel	LT CDR(FTC)	S		16.12.86	*BDS* WASHINGTON
Essenhigh, Angus Nigel Patrick, *BA*	LT(FTC)	X		01.11.96	EXCHANGE USA
Essenhigh, *Sir* Nigel (Richard), *KCB, rcds, pce, psc, hcsc*	ADM	-	PWO(N)†	11.09.98	CINCFLEET
Etchells, Stephen Barrie, *BEng*	LT(FTC)	E	WESM	03.07.92	SSA BRISTOL
Ethell, David Ross, *BEng (Act Maj)*	CAPT RM(CC)	RM	LC	28.04.95	NP 1002 DIEGOGA
Euden, Christopher Peter, *BA, n*	LT(FTC)	X		01.06.95	SOMERSET

Name	Rank	Branch	Spec	Seniority	Where Serving
Evans, Antony John , *BEng*	LT(CC)	E	AE	01.02.94	ES AIR BRISTOL
Evans, Andrew William	LT CDR(CC)	X	SM	01.10.95	MWC PORTSDOWN
Evans, Barry David (*Act Lt*)	SLT(FTC)	X	REG	02.05.97	EXCELLENT
Evans, Charles Alexander , *BA*	LT(FTC)	S	SM	01.06.96	SPLENDID
Evans, Craig Hamilton , *BSc, MSc*	LT(CC)	E	IS	01.11.88	DITMTC SHRIVNHAM
Evans, Charles William , *MB, BS, MPH, DIH, DTM&H, LRCP, MFOM, MRCS, AFOM, rcds, MPH,* (*COMMODORE*)	SURG CAPT	-	(CO/M)	30.06.89	DRAKE CBS
Evans, David Anthony	LT(CC)	X	ATC	20.12.95	ILLUSTRIOUS
Evans, David John , *BSc, CEng, MIEE, MRAeS, psc*	CDR(FTC)	E	AE(P)	30.06.95	NMA PORTSMOUTH
Evans, Desmond John	LT CDR(FTC)	X	AV	01.10.96	CAPTAIN RNP TEAM
Evans, David John	SLT(IC)	X	P	01.01.98	RNAS CULDROSE
Evans, David Melville , *BSc, pce*	CDR(FTC)	X	PWO(A)	30.06.94	MOD (LONDON)
Evans, David Mark Mortimer , *psc(m)*	MAJ(FTC)	RM	C	01.09.93	42 CDO RM
Evans, Edward Michael	LT CDR(FTC)	S	SM	16.08.97	DARTMOUTH BRNC
Evans, Geraint , *AMIEE, BEng*	LT CDR(FTC)	E	WE	01.06.98	NORFOLK
Evans, Gareth Charles	SURG LT	-		05.08.98	VICTORIOUS(PORT)
Evans, Graham Roy , *BSc, pce*	LT CDR(FTC)	X	PWO(U)	01.12.90	MWC PORTSDOWN
Evans, Ivan	SLT(IC)	X		27.01.99	LINDISFARNE
Evans, John Walter	LT CDR(FTC)	X	PWO(C)	06.05.86	NBC PORTSMOUTH
Evans, Karl Nicholas Meredith , *pce, pce(sm), psc(j)*	CDR(FTC)	X	SM	31.12.98	VANGUARD(PORT)
Evans, Laura-Jane , *BSc*	SLT(IC)	X		01.09.99	DARTMOUTH BRNC
Evans, Lee Stewart	SLT(IC)	X	P U/T	01.05.98	RAF CRANWELL EFS
Evans, Malcolm , *BSc, MSc*	LT CDR(CC)	E	TM	01.05.97	NELSON RNSETT
Evans, Martyn Alun , *BA*	MAJ(FTC)	RM		01.09.93	2SL/CNH
Evans, Michael Clive , *BSc, MA, MNI, MIMgt, pce, pcea, psc*	CDR(FTC)	X	P	31.12.94	MOD (LONDON)
Evans, Marc David , *MILDM, AMIAM*	LT CDR(FTC)	S		16.05.98	2SL/CNH
Evans, Michael Edward , *BEng*	LT(CC)	E	MESM	01.10.97	TRAFALGAR
Evans, Michael John , *BSc, FFA, MInstAM, MIMgt, jsdc*	CDR(FTC)	S		31.12.85	MOD (LONDON)
Evans, Martin Joseph , *BSc, pce*	LT CDR(FTC)	X	PWO(U)	01.09.95	DRYAD
Evans, Marius John Gunning , *psc*	LT CDR(FTC)	X	FC	01.03.86	RNAS YEOVILTON
Evans, Martin	CHAPLAIN	CE		01.09.98	45 CDO RM
Evans, Peter Colin , *BSc, MSc*	LT(IC)	E	TM	01.05.96	RNEAWC
Evans, Peter John , *BSc, mdtc*	MAJ(FTC)	RM	LC	01.09.99	JSCSC
Evans, Stephen , *BTech*	LT(FTC)	E	WESM	24.02.95	VENGEANCE(PORT)
Evans, Sarah Jane , *BSc*	LT CDR(CC)	E	IS	01.10.97	AFPAA(CENTURION)
Evans, Thomas	SURG SLT	-		01.10.98	DARTMOUTH BRNC
Evans, William Quennell Frankis , *pce*	LT CDR(FTC)	X	PWO(N)	20.10.94	GLOUCESTER
Everett, Edward Jason	CAPT RM(FTC)	RM		24.04.96	DRYAD
Everitt, Claire Julia , *BDS, LDS RCS(Eng)*	SGLTCDR(D)	-		11.03.97	RN GIBRALTAR
Everitt, Tobyn	LT(CC)	X	P	19.08.96	RNAS YEOVILTON
Everritt, Richard , *BSc*	MAJ(FTC)	RM	SO(LE)	01.10.98	42 CDO RM
Evershed, Marcus Charles , *MB, BCh, Dip FFP, MRCGP*	SURG LTCDR	-	GMPP	31.10.95	COLLINGWOOD
Every, Mark , *BM, BSc, Dip FFP, MRCGP*	SURG LTCDR	-	GMPP	03.02.98	NEPTUNE CFS
Ewen, Andrew Philip , *BEng*	LT(FTC)	E	AE	01.01.93	JSCSC
Ewen, Raymond John	LT CDR(FTC)	S	(W)	01.10.96	AFPAA WTHY DOWN
Ewence, Martin William , *BA, pce, psc(j), MA*	CDR(FTC)	X	PWO(A)	30.06.98	PJHQ
Ewer, Jonathan Edward	SLT(IC)	X	P U/T	01.04.00	RNAS YEOVILTON
Ewers, Alan Martin , *BSc*	LT CDR(FTC)	X	METOC	20.08.88	RNAS YEOVILTON
Ewing, Andrew David , *pce, psc*	CDR(FTC)	X	AWO(U)	30.06.91	MWC SOUTHWICK
Ewins, Graeme Power , *pce*	CDR(FTC)	X	AWO(C)	30.06.89	LPD(R) IPT
Exworthy, Damian Andrew Giles , *BSc, MA*	LT(FTC)	S		01.06.97	CHATHAM

F

Name	Rank	Branch	Spec	Seniority	Where Serving
Fabik, Andre Nicholas , *BA*	SLT(IC)	X		01.05.98	OCEAN
Fagan, Jamie Stefan	SLT(IC)	X	ATCU/T	01.04.98	SULTAN
Fairbairn, William David Murray , *MA, jsdc*	CAPT(FTC)	E	WE	30.06.95	FOSF
Fairbank, Brian	CHAPLAIN	CE		03.09.91	CAPT(H)DEVPT SEA
Fairbrass, John Emilio , *BEng, CEng, MIMarE*	LT CDR(FTC)	E	ME	28.04.97	JSCSC
Fairnie, David William (*Act Lt*)	SLT(FTC)	X	PR	02.05.97	RALEIGH
Falk, Benedict Hakan Geoffrey , *MNI, pce*	LT CDR(FTC)	X	PWO(A)	01.04.94	GLASGOW
Fallowfield, Jonathan Paul , *BTech*	LT(FTC)	E	WE	24.02.95	2SL/CNH
Fancy, Robert , *pce(sm)*	LT CDR(FTC)	X	SM	01.08.96	NMA PORTSMOUTH

Name	Rank	Branch	Spec	Seniority	Where Serving
Fanshawe, James Rupert , *jsdc, pce, hcsc, I(2)Fr (COMMODORE)*	CAPT(FTC)	X	PWO(U)	30.06.96	PJHQ
Farmer, John Robert	LT CDR(FTC)	X	AWO(A)	16.08.82	DRYAD
Farmer, Paul Adrian	SLT(CC)	X	P U/T	01.04.00	RNAS YEOVILTON
Farquhar, John William , *FRGS, jsdc*	CDR(FTC)	S		30.06.87	NATO DEF COL
Farquharson-Roberts, Michael Atholl M, A, *QHS, MB, BS, FRCS, LRCP, OStJ*	SURG CAPT	-	(CO/S)	30.06.93	RH HASLAR
Farr, Ian Raymond	SLT(CC)	X	P U/T	01.04.98	RNAS YEOVILTON
Farrage, Michael Edward , *BSc, psc*	CDR(FTC)	E	TM	31.12.96	HQRM
Farrant, James Derek	MID(UCE)(FTC)	S		01.09.98	DARTMOUTH BRNC
Farrell, Jamie Andrew	SLT(CC)	X		01.09.99	RALEIGH
Farrington, John Lewis , *BEng, AMIEE*	LT(FTC)	E	WESM	01.01.94	MOD (LONDON)
Farrington, Richard , *BA, jsdc, pce*	CDR(FTC)	X	PWO(C)	30.06.96	DRYAD
Farrington, Stephen Paul , *QGM, MPhil, IEng, FIMarE, FRINA, psc*	CDR(FTC)	E	ME	30.06.96	MOD (LONDON)
Faulconbridge, David , *MSc, CEng, MIMarE, AMIEE, psc*	CDR(FTC)	E	MESM	31.12.94	MOD (BATH)
Faulkner, Daniel William , *BEng, CEng, MRAeS*	LT CDR(FTC)	E	AE	29.11.97	INVINCIBLE
Faulkner, Jeffrey James , *ARICS*	LT CDR(FTC)	X	H CH	05.07.91	SCOTT
Faulkner, Richard Ian , *BSc*	LT CDR(FTC)	E	ME	01.08.89	NMA GOSPORT
Faulkner, Stuart Glen	MID(UCE)(FTC)	E	AE	01.09.98	DARTMOUTH BRNC
Faulks, David John	LT CDR(FTC)	S		01.03.91	PJHQ
Fawcett, Fiona Patricia , *BA*	LT CDR(FTC)	E	TM	01.05.98	DRYAD
Fear, Richard Keith , *BSc*	CDR(FTC)	E	WESM	30.06.99	RMC OF SCIENCE
Fearnley, Andrew Thomas	LT(FTC)	S	(S)	13.12.95	NELSON
Feasey, Ian David	SLT(UCE)(CC)	X		01.09.99	DARTMOUTH BRNC
Febbrarro, Nicholas Robert	CDR(FTC)	E	MESM	30.06.93	SSA DEVONPORT
Fedorowicz, Richard	LT(CC)	X	ATC	16.10.88	RNAS CULDROSE
Feeney, Matthew Blake	SLT(FTC)	X		01.09.97	DARTMOUTH BRNC
Feeney, Michael Leonard , *BEng, CEng, MIMarE*	LT CDR(FTC)	E	ME	01.05.97	CARDIFF
Felgate, Howard , *BSc*	LT CDR(FTC)	X		01.05.83	MOD (LONDON)
Felters, Adam William , *BSc*	LT(CC)	X	P U/T	01.05.99	RAF CRANWELL EFS
Fennell, Charles Benjamin	SLT(IC)	X		01.01.97	BRECON
Fenwick, John , *OBE, BEng*	CDR(FTC)	E	WESM	30.06.83	TORPEDO IPT
Fenwick, Julie Cheryl , *BDS*	SGLTCDR(D)	-		03.09.95	RNAS CULDROSE
Fenwick, Robin John , *BSc*	CAPT RM(IC)	RM	P U/T	01.05.97	DHFS
Ferguson, Gordon Henry , *MIEE*	LT CDR(FTC)	E	MESM	01.10.98	TRENCHANT
Ferguson, Julian Norman , *BA, BSc, pce, pce(sm)*	CDR(FTC)	X	SM	30.06.91	CSST SEA
Ferguson, Robert Grant	LT CDR(FTC)	X	C	12.12.90	HQ DCSA
Ferguson, Vikki Sara	LT	Q	CC	21.01.95	TEMERAIRE
Fergusson, Andrew Christopher , *BSc*	MAJ(FTC)	RM		01.05.99	MWC PORTSDOWN
Fergusson, Duncan Campbell McGregor , *jsdc, pce, pcea, psc*	CAPT(FTC)	X	P	30.06.97	NELSON
Fergusson, Houston James	CDR(FTC)	S	SM	30.06.00	CINCFLEET
Fergusson, Iain Buchan	SLT(IC)	X		01.05.99	DARTMOUTH BRNC
Fergusson, Nigel Andrew , *BSc, MIEE*	LT CDR(FTC)	E	WE	01.02.99	MOD (LONDON)
Fergusson, Richard Routledge , *MA, adp*	LT CDR(FTC)	E	IS	01.05.85	DRYAD
Fernihough, Michael Robert , *BSc, MIMechE*	LT CDR(FTC)	E	AE	08.12.82	RNAS YEOVILTON
Ferns, Timothy David , *LLB*	LT CDR(FTC)	S		01.06.99	ENDURANCE
Ferris, Daniel Peter Sefton , *BEng, MSc, CEng, MIEE*	LT CDR(FTC)	E	WE	01.04.98	CAMPBELTOWN
Fewtrell, Malcolm , *psc*	LT CDR(FTC)	X	PWO(U)	01.09.84	CINCFLEET
Ffrench, David John , *pcea*	LT CDR(FTC)	X	P	01.10.98	DHFS
Fiander, Peter John , *BSc, MIMechE*	LT CDR(FTC)	E	MESM	01.02.87	EAGLET
Field, Charles Richard Howard , *BEng*	LT(FTC)	E	ME	01.01.96	EDINBURGH
Field, John Dobson , *pce*	LT CDR(FTC)	X	PWO(A)	16.04.87	CAMBRIDGE
Field, Johnathan Samuel , *BA*	LT(CC)	X	SM	01.02.97	TORBAY
Field, Stephen Nigel Crawford	LT CDR(FTC)	X	MCD	01.09.86	EXCHANGE USA
Fields, David Graham , *pce*	LT CDR(FTC)	X	PWO(A)	01.06.94	SUTHERLAND
Fieldsend, Mark Andrew , *BEng, fsc*	LT CDR(FTC)	E	ME	01.03.96	RICHMOND
Fifield, David James , *jsdc, pce, ocds(Can)*	CAPT(FTC)	X	P	30.06.96	MOD (BATH)
Fillmore, Raymond Jeffrey	SLT(IC)	X		01.05.98	DRYAD
Filshie, Sarah Jane , *BA*	SLT(IC)	X		01.01.99	DARTMOUTH BRNC
Filtness, David Mark , *BSc*	SLT(IC)	X		01.09.98	KENT
Finch, Bruce Andrew , *BA, MIL*	LT(FTC)	S		01.08.93	AGRIPPA NAVSOUTH
Finch, Craig Richard	LT(CC)	X	P	16.11.91	RAF SHAWBURY
Finch, Iain Robert	LT(IC)	X		01.11.99	MIDDLETON
Finch, Robert Leonard , *BEng, MSc, CEng, MIMarE, AMIMechE*	LT CDR(FTC)	E	ME	01.05.97	EXCELLENT
Finch, Steven	SLT(IC)	E	AE	29.04.98	SULTAN

Name	Rank	Branch	Spec	Seniority	Where Serving
Finch, Timothy Stuart Aubrey	LT CDR(FTC)	S	CA	01.10.97	YORK
Fincher, Kevin John, *pce*	LT CDR(FTC)	X	PWO(C)	01.10.95	DRYAD
Finlay, Marcus Stephen, *BA*	SLT(CC)	X		01.09.97	DRYAD
Finlayson, Alasdair Grant, *MA, fsc*	CDR(FTC)	S		30.06.96	MOD (LONDON)
Finlayson, Ronald Didrik, *MA, MBA, CEng, FIEE, rcds, psc (COMMODORE)*	CAPT(FTC)	E	WE	31.12.94	MOD (LONDON)
Finley, Paul Michael, *MEng*	SLT(IC)	E		01.09.98	INVINCIBLE
Finley, Robert William, *BA (Act Maj)*	CAPT RM(FTC)	RM		29.04.93	HQ 3 CDO BDE RM
Finn, David William	LT(FTC)	MS	(AD)	03.04.97	CINCFLEET
Finn, Emma Jane	LT(IC)	S		01.04.99	FOSF
Finn, Graham John, *pcea*	LT(CC)	X	P	01.07.92	COMSTRIKFORSTH
Finn, Ivan Richard, *BEng*	LT(FTC)	E	AE	01.03.94	DARTMOUTH BRNC
Finn, James Sutherland, *BSc*	SLT(IC)	X	P U/T	01.01.98	RNAS YEOVILTON
Finn, Stuart Andrew, *BSc*	SLT(IC)	X		01.09.98	CHATHAM
Finnemore, Richard Andrew, *AMBIM, pce*	LT CDR(FTC)	X	PWO(U)	09.07.90	CAPT IST STAFF
Finney, Michael Edwin, *pce, pce(sm)*	CDR(FTC)	X	SM	30.06.94	MOD (LONDON)
Finnie, Harry Morrison	LT(FTC)	E	ME	13.06.97	RALEIGH
Firth, John Simon, *BSc*	SLT(IC)	X		01.05.97	DRYAD
Firth, Nigel Richard, *pce, pce(sm)*	LT CDR(FTC)	X	SM	01.03.95	FOSM NWOOD OPS
Firth, Rachel Jane Gardner	LT CDR(FTC)	X	ATC	08.04.00	RAF SHAWBURY
Firth, Stephen Kenneth, *MSc, CEng, MIEE*	CDR(FTC)	E	MESM	31.12.90	SSA DEVONPORT
Fisher, Aaron George, *BSc*	CAPT RM(IC)	RM		01.09.98	45 CDO RM
Fisher, Alan	SLT(IC)	X		01.09.98	RAF SHAWBURY
Fisher, Clayton Richard Allan	LT CDR(FTC)	S		06.10.98	RNAS YEOVILTON
Fisher, Giles Edmund Mortimer, *BA*	LT(CC)	X	P U/T	01.01.00	DHFS
Fisher, Morleymor Alfred Leslie, *MBE, BSc, CEng, FIMarE, MIMechE, MIMgt*	CDR(FTC)	E	MESM	30.06.94	ARK ROYAL
Fisher, Nicholas Douglas	MID(UCE)(IC)	E	WE	01.09.99	NORFOLK
Fisher, Nicholas Gorden, *MB, BS, MRCP*	SURG LTCDR	-		01.08.97	NELSON (PAY)
Fisher, Pamela Clare, *BEng*	LT(FTC)	E	AE	01.03.95	MOD (LONDON)
Fisher, Robert	LT(FTC)	E	WE	10.06.88	AGRIPPA AFSOUTH
Fisher, Robert James	LT(IC)	X	P	01.06.96	845 SQN
Fisher, Stephen John, *BA*	LT(IC)	X	P U/T	01.09.99	DHFS
Fishlock, Geoffrey Norman	LT CDR(FTC)	S		16.04.86	NEPTUNE CFS
Fitter, Ian Stuart Thain, *BSc, pcea*	LT CDR(FTC)	X	O	01.05.93	INVINCIBLE
Fitzgerald, Brian	MAJ(FTC)	RM	SO(LE)	01.10.98	RM Poole
Fitzgerald, Colin	LT(FTC)	E	AE(M)	12.09.97	FONA
Fitzgerald, Graham David, *BSc*	LT(CC)	X		01.05.98	MONMOUTH
Fitzgerald, Gary	SLT(IC)	E	WE	27.01.99	COLLINGWOOD
FitzGerald, Marcus Peter, *OBE, BSc, CEng, MIEE*	CAPT(FTC)	E	WESM	30.06.95	DSWS BRISTOL
Fitzgerald, Nicholas John	LT(CC)	X	P	01.12.92	RAF CRANWELL EFS
Fitzjohn, David, *BEng, MSc, CEng, MIEE*	LT CDR(FTC)	E	AE	01.05.96	810 SQN SEAHAWK
Fitzpatrick, John Aloysius Joseph	LT(FTC)	X	O U/T	01.07.97	750 SQN OBS SCH
Fitzpatrick, Paul	LT RM(FTC)	RM	SO(LE)	01.01.98	COMACCHIO GP RM
Fitzsimmons, Mark Brown	LT CDR(FTC)	X	PWO(A)	01.09.95	PJHQ
Fitzsimmons, Susan Mary, *BEng*	LT(FTC)	E	WE	01.04.96	SSA BRISTOL
Fitzsimons, Diane Elizabeth	SURG LT	-		05.08.98	RALEIGH
Flanagan, John, *BA (BARRISTER)*	CDR(FTC)	S	BAR	30.06.98	CINCFLEET
Flanagan, Martin Eric Anthony, *BSc, pce, pcea*	LT CDR(FTC)	X	O	01.02.92	849 SQN A FLT
Flatman, Timothy David, *BSc*	LT(IC)	X	P U/T	01.08.99	FONA LINTON/OUSE
Flatt, Leslie Declan	LT(FTC)	E	WE	02.09.99	CARDIFF
Flegg, Matthew James, *BEng*	SLT(IC)	E	AE	01.09.98	SHEFFIELD
Fleisher, Simon Matthew, *MEng, CEng, MIMechE*	LT(FTC)	E	ME	01.06.92	MOD (BATH)
Fleming, Kevin Patrick, *BSc*	LT CDR(FTC)	X	O	01.10.97	702 SQN HERON
Fleming, Ruth Ernestine, *BSc*	SLT(IC)	S		01.01.98	INVINCIBLE
Fleming, Stephen Anthony	LT CDR(FTC)	X		30.09.94	MOD (LONDON)
Fletcher, Ian James, *BSc*	LT(IC)	X		01.10.98	SCOTT
Fletcher, Nicholas Edgar, *pce, psc*	CDR(FTC)	X	PWO(A)	31.12.94	NMA PORTSMOUTH
Fletcher, Richard John, *BA*	LT CDR(FTC)	S		16.03.00	NELSON
Fletcher, Robert James	MAJ(FTC)	RM		01.03.78	RM BICKLEIGH
Flint, Helen Anne, *BSc*	LT(CC)	E	TM	01.05.90	DARTMOUTH BRNC
Flintham, Jason	LT(CC)	X	P	16.03.96	FONA LINTON/OUSE
Float, Roger Andrew, *BSc, MA, MSc, MCGI, AMIEE, psc(j)*	LT CDR(FTC)	E	WE	01.05.94	NMA PORTSMOUTH
Float, Susanne Marion	LT	Q	ACC/EM	18.01.94	NELSON (PAY)
Flockhart, David Neil, *BSc, CEng, MIEE*	LT CDR(FTC)	E	WESM	01.01.83	DRAKE CFM

Name	Rank	Branch	Spec	Seniority	Where Serving
Flynn, Andrew	LT(FTC)	E	AE(L)	01.05.96	899 SQN HERON
Flynn, Liam Peter , *BEng*	LT(IC)	X	P	01.09.92	810 SQN SEAHAWK
Flynn, Michael Thomas	LT CDR(FTC)	S		01.11.93	NELSON WF
Flynn, Patrick Joseph	LT CDR(FTC)	X	PWO(A)	31.10.81	MOD DGS PORTSMOUTH
Flynn, Simon John	SLT(FTC)	X	O	09.01.98	849 SQN B FLT
Foale, Simon John , *BA, pce*	LT CDR(FTC)	X	O	01.04.89	LN DERA FARN
Fogell, Andrew David	LT(CC)	S	SM	01.11.92	NEPTUNE CFS
Fogg, Duncan Stuart , *MA, MSc, CEng, MIEE, gw*	LT CDR(FTC)	E	WE	01.04.93	MOD (LONDON)
Follington, Daniel Charles	LT(FTC)	MS		23.07.98	MSA
Folwell, Mark William	LT CDR(FTC)	E	WE	20.08.97	COLLINGWOOD
Fomes, Christopher John Henry	LT RM(IC)	RM		23.04.97	CTCRM
Foote, Andrew Steven	SLT(CC)	E	ME	01.05.98	DARTMOUTH BRNC
Forbes, Duncan Graham , *LLB*	2LT(GRAD)(IC)	RM		01.09.99	CTCRM LYMPSTONE
Forbes, Ian Andrew , *CBE, rcds, pce, psc(a)*	RADM	-	AWO(A)	04.12.96	FOSF SEA PTSMTH
Forbes, Paul Thomas	LT(CC)	X	P	16.07.96	771 SK5 SAR
Ford, Anthony , *AMIMarE*	LT CDR(FTC)	E	ME	01.10.99	EDINBURGH
Ford, Anthony John	LT(FTC)	X	SM	04.04.96	NEPTUNE SM1
Ford, David	MAJ(FTC)	RM	SO(LE)	01.10.98	COMACCHIO GP RM
Ford, Gordon Howard	LT CDR(FTC)	X	AV	01.10.97	FONA
Ford, Graham Ronald , *BSc*	LT(FTC)	E	MESM	14.10.94	SULTAN
Ford, James Anthony , *pcea*	LT(FTC)	X	P	01.07.90	849 SQN A FLT
Ford, Jonathan Douglas	LT(FTC)	E	WE	01.12.93	SSA BRISTOL
Ford, Joanna Sophie , *BEng*	LT(CC)	E	ME	01.07.99	SULTAN
Ford, Martin John	LT CDR(FTC)	X	O	05.08.98	824 NAS
Ford, Nicholas Paul , *MBE, TEng*	LT CDR(FTC)	E	MESM	01.10.93	RALEIGH
Foreman, John Lewis Rutland , *MA, pce, psc(j)*	LT CDR(FTC)	X	PWO(C)	01.07.95	DUMBARTON CASTLE
Foreman, Susan Louise , *BSc*	LT(FTC)	X		01.05.92	NMA PORTSMOUTH
Foreman, Simon Michael , *BEng*	LT(FTC)	E	WE	01.04.97	MARLBOROUGH
Foreman, Timothy Peter	LT(CC)	X	P	01.05.94	845 SQN
Forer, Duncan Anthony , *BSc, PGCE*	LT CDR(FTC)	E	TM	01.10.98	SULTAN
Forer, Timothy John , *BA*	LT CDR(FTC)	S	BAR	01.12.93	FOSF
Forester-Bennett, Rupert Michael William	LT CDR(FTC)	X	H1	24.07.97	LOAN HYDROG
Forge, Stephen Mieczsyeaw , *BSc*	SLT(FTC)	X		01.05.97	DRYAD
Forrester, Timothy Rae , *pcea*	LT CDR(FTC)	X	O	01.12.86	PRESTWICK
Forsey, Christopher Roy , *BSc, MSc, AMIEE*	CDR(FTC)	E	WE	31.12.95	CAPT F4 (SEA)
Forshaw, David Roy	LT(FTC)	E	ME	02.09.99	SULTAN
Forster, Raymond Adrian	LT(FTC)	X	ATC	16.04.91	RNAS YEOVILTON
Forster, Robin Makepeace , *MA, psc(j)*	MAJ(FTC)	RM		01.09.94	JSCSC
Forster, Steven	CHAPLAIN	RC		08.08.94	DARTMOUTH BRNC
Forster, Timothy John Alleyne , *pce, psc*	CDR(FTC)	X	AWO(A)	31.12.88	EXCELLENT
Forsyth, Andrew Richard , *BSc*	CDR(FTC)	S		30.06.94	MOD (LONDON)
Forsyth, Andrew Westwood , *pce, psc*	CDR(FTC)	X	PWO(N)†	31.12.87	SHAPE BELGIUM
Forsyth, David Charles	LT CDR(FTC)	X	SM	01.10.98	CNOCS GROUP
Fortescue, Paul Wyatt , *BSc*	CDR(FTC)	X	METOC	31.12.91	SHAPE BELGIUM
Fortescue, Robert Christopher , *pce, pcea, psc(j)*	LT CDR(FTC)	X	O	01.03.93	MARLBOROUGH
Forward, David James	LT(FTC)	E	AE(L)	19.10.90	FOST FLT TGT GRP
Foster, Benjamin	2LT(GRAD)(IC)	RM		08.05.98	45 CDO RM
Foster, Bruce Michael Trevor , *BSc, MIProdE*	LT CDR(FTC)	E	TM	07.12.98	RN GIBRALTAR
Foster, Crawford Richard Muir , *MB, BCh, ChB, Dip FFP, MRCGP*	SURG LTCDR	-	GMPP	19.09.93	NELSON (PAY)
Foster, Duncan Graeme Scott , *BSc, pce*	LT CDR(FTC)	X	PWO(N)	01.07.95	FOST SEA
Foster, David Hugh	LT CDR(FTC)	X	MCD	01.05.99	SDG PLYMOUTH
Foster, Graham James , *BSc, AMIMechE*	LT CDR(FTC)	E	MESM	01.10.96	TURBULENT
Foster, Graeme Russell , *BSc, psc(m)*	LT COL(FTC)	RM	LC	31.12.97	HQRM
Foster, Geoffrey Russell Nicholas , *psc*	CDR(FTC)	X	P	30.06.91	MOD (LONDON)
Foster, Jeremy Stephen , *MBE, BA*	LT CDR(CC)	E	IS	01.10.98	RMC OF SCIENCE
Foster, Mark Andrew , *BSc, MA, CEng, MIMarE, psc*	CDR(FTC)	E	TM	30.06.97	SULTAN
Foster, Nicholas Paul , *BSc, MA*	LT(IC)	X	H2	01.02.97	FEARLESS
Foster, Nicholas Paul	2LT(GRAD)(FTC)	RM		29.04.98	42 CDO RM
Foster, Peter James	LT(CC)	E	MESM	01.09.95	TALENT
Foster, Stephen	CDR(FTC)	E	ME	01.10.97	NMA GOSPORT
Foster, Simon James Harry , *BEng, MSc, CEng, MIMarE, MIMechE*	LT CDR(FTC)	E	MESM	01.04.99	VENGEANCE(PORT)
Foster, Toby George , *BSc*	LT(FTC)	X	HM	01.04.95	FEARLESS
Foubister, Robert , *FIEIE*	LT(FTC)	E	WESM	18.06.87	NEPTUNE NT

Name	Rank	Branch	Spec	Seniority	Where Serving
Foulger, Thomas Edward, *BDS*	SG LT(D)	-		11.06.99	SULTAN
Foulis, Niall David Alexander, *BSc*	LT(FTC)	X	H2	01.03.95	RFANSU
Fowler, Peter James Shakespeare, *BSc, MSc*	LT CDR(FTC)	E	MESM	01.04.90	NEPTUNE FD
Fox, Kevin Andrew, *BSc, MIEE*	CDR(FTC)	E	AE(P)	30.06.94	SULTAN
Fox, Richard George	LT CDR(FTC)	X	P	01.10.92	FONA
Fox, Trefor Morgan	LT(CC)	X	SM	01.07.96	VANGUARD(PORT)
France, Sean Charles, *BSc(Hons)*	LT	Q		25.08.99	RN GIBRALTAR
Francis, Derek Edward	LT(FTC)	X	tas	10.01.00	DRYAD
Francis, John	LT CDR(FTC)	X	AV	01.10.94	FOSF
Francis, Joanne Marie, *BDS*	SGLTCDR(D)	-		09.01.99	JSU NORTHWOOD
Francis, Steven John, *BA, psc(j)*	MAJ(FTC)	RM		25.04.96	COMACCHIO GP RM
Francis, Thomas Dewolfe Hamlin, *BA*	2LT(GRAD)(IC)	RM		01.09.99	CTCRM LYMPSTONE
Frankham, Peter James, *BEng, CEng, MIMarE*	LT CDR(FTC)	E	WE	01.01.96	SSA PORTSMOUTH
Franklin, Benjamin James	LT CDR(FTC)	X	O	01.10.98	700M MERLIN IFTU
Franklin, George Durnford, *BEng*	LT(FTC)	X	FC	01.02.95	DRYAD
Franklin, William Henry, *MA*	CHAPLAIN	CE		10.01.89	CINCFLEET
Franks, Christopher Stephen, *BSc*	LT CDR(FTC)	E	WESM	01.02.98	MOD DIS SEA
Franks, Donald Ian, *adp*	LT CDR(FTC)	S		01.10.94	MOD (LONDON)
Franks, Jason Alexander, *BA*	CAPT RM(IC)	RM	P	01.09.95	847 SQN
Franks, Jeremy Peter, *BSc, MIEE, MRAeS*	LT CDR(FTC)	E	AE	01.12.85	ES AIR YEO
Franks, Kevin Brian, *BSc*	LT CDR(FTC)	X	SM	01.12.87	MWC PORTSDOWN
Franks, Peter Dennis, *BSc, MSc*	LT CDR(FTC)	E	IS	01.10.93	HQAFNORTHWEST
Fraser, Alasdair Graham	SLT(IC)	X		01.05.99	RNAS YEOVILTON
Fraser, Donald Kennedy	LT CDR(FTC)	X	PWO(U)	01.07.84	CINCFLEET
Fraser, Eric, *BSc, pce, psc*	CDR(FTC)	X	PWO(C)	31.12.94	*BDS* WASHINGTON
Fraser, Graeme William, *MA*	CAPT RM(CC)	RM	LC	01.09.95	CDO LOG REGT RM
Fraser, Heather Lee, *BEng*	LT(FTC)	E	WE	01.07.96	CAPT IST STAFF
Fraser, Ian David, *BSc, MSc*	LT(CC)	E	AE	01.08.90	810 SQN C FLIGHT
Fraser, Ian	LT(CC)	X	P	16.04.96	819 SQN
Fraser, John Anthony	LT CDR(FTC)	X	AV	01.10.99	RNAS YEOVILTON
Fraser, Michael John Simon, *BSc, MSc*	SLT(IC)	X		01.09.98	DARTMOUTH BRNC
Fraser, Patrick	LT(FTC)	E	AE(L)	01.05.96	OCLC BRISTOL
Fraser, Peter Timothy, *pcea*	LT CDR(CC)	X	O	01.10.94	750 SQN OBS SCH
Fraser, Robert William, *MVO, LLB (BARRISTER)*	CAPT(FTC)	S	BAR	31.12.99	AGRIPPA NAVSOUTH
Fraser, Timothy Peter, *pce*	CDR(FTC)	X	PWO(N)	31.12.96	MOD (LONDON)
Fraser, Wilson Cameron	LT CDR(FTC)	E	WESM	01.10.96	VICTORIOUS(STBD)
Frazer, Hamish Forbes	LT(CC)	X		01.08.99	EDINBURGH
Frean, James Peter, *BA*	LT(IC)	X	P	01.12.97	846 SQN
Freegard, Ian Paul	LT CDR(FTC)	S	(W)	01.10.99	RHQ SOUTHLANT
Freeman, David Andrew Kenneth, *LVO, pce*	CAPT(FTC)	X	PWO(N)†	30.06.99	UKNMR SHAPE
Freeman, David Russel	LT CDR(FTC)	X	O	01.06.96	CINCFLEET
Freeman, Mark Edward	MAJ(FTC)	RM		01.09.96	42 CDO RM
Freeman, Martin John, *AMIMechE*	SLT(FTC)	E	MESM	01.04.98	TIRELESS
French, Jeremy Hugh, *BEng*	SLT(IC)	X		01.01.99	DARTMOUTH BRNC
French, James Thomas	LT CDR(FTC)	E	ME	29.04.95	SULTAN
French, Kevin Lawrence, *pce*	LT CDR(FTC)	X	PWO(A)	09.07.93	FOSF
French, Stephen Amos, *BEng, MSc*	CDR(FTC)	E	MESM	31.12.99	JSCSC
Freshwater, Dennis Andrew, *MB, BS*	SURG LTCDR	-		09.08.98	RH HASLAR
Friendship, Paul Gary	CAPT RM(IC)	RM		28.04.98	OCLC ROSYTH
Frost, Mark Adrian, *BSc*	LT(CC)	E	TM	01.01.91	NELSON RNSETT
Frost, Michael John	LT RM(IC)	RM		24.01.00	847 SQN
Fry, Jonathan Mark Stewart, *BSc, MSc, CEng, MIMarE, MCGI, psc*	CDR(FTC)	E	ME	31.12.98	DGSS BRISTOL
Fry, Robert Allan, *MBE, BSc, MA, psc(m) (BRIGADIER)*	COL(OF6)(FTC)	RM		31.12.97	HQ 3 CDO BDE RM
Fry, Timothy Graham	SLT(IC)	E	WESM	27.01.99	COLLINGWOOD
Fryer, Adrian Clifford, *BSc*	LT(FTC)	X		01.02.94	EXETER
Fulford, John Philip Henry, *BSc, psc(m)*	CDR(FTC)	E	WESM	31.12.95	MOD (LONDON)
Fulford, Mark Kenneth, *BSc, pcea*	LT CDR(FTC)	X	P	01.10.95	849 SQN HQ
Fulford, Nicholas James Douglas, *BSc*	CDR(FTC)	E	WESM	30.06.83	NC3 AGENCY
Fulford, Robin Nicholas	LT(FTC)	E	WE	07.02.97	EXCELLENT
Full, Richard	LT(CC)	X	O	01.06.98	849 SQN A FLT
Fuller, Charles Edward	LT(CC)	X	P	16.08.97	819 SQN
Fuller, James Bruce, *BSc*	CAPT RM(IC)	RM		01.09.99	40 CDO RM
Fuller, James Edward	SLT(IC)	X		01.04.99	PEMBROKE

Name	Rank	Branch	Spec	Seniority	Where Serving
Fuller, Jonathan Peter , *BA*	LT(IC)	X	H2	01.06.94	ENDURANCE
Fuller, Simon Rowland *(Act Maj)*	CAPT RM(FTC)	RM		01.09.95	TRAINTEAM BRUNEI
Fulton, Craig Robert , *pce, pce(sm)*	LT CDR(FTC)	X	SM	01.03.95	CHIDDINGFOLD
Fulton, Robert Henry Gervase , *BA, rcds, psc(m), HCSC*	MAJ GEN	RM	C	23.10.98	HQRM *hcsc*
Funnell, Nicholas Charles , *pce, pcea, psc(m)*	CDR(FTC)	X	O	30.06.96	MOD (LONDON)
Furlong, Keith	LT CDR(FTC)	X	PWO(A)	01.03.96	ILLUSTRIOUS
Furness, Stuart Brian , *BSc, MSc, AFIMA, pce,*	CDR(FTC)	X	O	30.06.96	MWC SOUTHWICK *pcea*
Fyfe, Karen Sabrina	SLT(IC)	X		01.04.98	RN HYDROG SCHL
Fyfe, Peter Matthew , *MNI, psc*	CDR(FTC)	X	AWO(U)	31.12.86	SACLANT USA

G

Name	Rank	Branch	Spec	Seniority	Where Serving
Gabb, John Harry , *MB, BS*	SURG CDR	-	GMPP	31.12.87	NMA PORTSMOUTH
Gabriel, Colin James , *BSc*	LT CDR(FTC)	E	WE	01.12.88	MOD (LONDON)
Gadie, Philip Anthony	MAJ(FTC)	RM		01.05.97	MOD (LONDON)
Gadsden, Andrew Christopher , *BA*	SLT(IC)	X		01.09.97	DRYAD
Gair, Simon David Henley , *BEng, AMIEE*	LT(FTC)	E	WE	01.02.95	OCLC MANCH
Gaitley, Ian , *BEng, AMIEE*	LT CDR(FTC)	E	WESM	01.09.97	MOD (LONDON)
Gale, Crystal	LT(FTC)	S		24.12.92	MOD (BATH)
Gale, Henry Nelson , *pce*	CDR(FTC)	X	PWO(U)	30.06.88	WEU
Gale, Mark Andrew , *MA, MSc*	LT CDR(FTC)	E	MESM	01.02.00	SULTAN
Gale, Sandra Lilian	LT(CC)	W	X	25.04.93	MOD (LONDON)
Gale, Simon Philip , *pce*	LT CDR(FTC)	X	PWO(U)	01.11.96	DRYAD
Gall, Michael Robert Carnegie , *BDS, MSc, MGDS RCS*	SGCDR(D)	-		30.06.95	EXCHANGE USA
Gallimore, John Martin *(Act Lt)*	SLT(FTC)	X	EW	18.09.98	DRYAD
Gallimore, Richard	SLT(IC)	X	P U/T	01.05.98	DHFS
Galloway, Peter , *pcea, psc*	CDR(FTC)	X	O	31.12.86	AST(N)
Galvin, David	LT CDR(FTC)	E	WE	01.10.96	FEARLESS
Gamble, John *(Act Lt Cdr)*	LT(FTC)	E	AE(L)	02.11.84	SULTAN
Gamble, Mark	SLT(IC)	X		01.04.98	DARTMOUTH BRNC
Gamble, Neil	LT(CC)	X	P	01.11.93	DHFS
Gamble, Richard	LT(FTC)	E	WE	10.06.88	MOD (LONDON)
Gamble, Stephen Boston , *BA, BEng*	LT(IC)	X	P	01.12.97	702 SQN HERON
Game, Philip Gordon , *BEng*	LT(FTC)	E	WE	01.02.94	SSA BRISTOL
Garbutt, Helen Jane , *LLB*	SLT(IC)	S		01.01.99	DARTMOUTH BRNC
Gardiner, David Anthony	LT CDR(FTC)	E	ME	13.12.94	YORK
Gardiner, Dermott	SURG SLT	-		24.06.99	DARTMOUTH BRNC
Gardiner, Ian Ritchie , *rcds, psc, psc(m) (BRIGADIER)*	COL(OF6)(FTC)	RM		30.06.97	IMS BRUSSELS
Gardiner, Peter Fredrick David	LT(FTC)	X	ATC	01.09.90	RAF SHAWBURY
Gardner, Callum *(Act Surg Lt)*	SURG SLT	-		03.08.96	DARTMOUTH BRNC
Gardner, Christopher Reginald Summers , *BA, LLB, psc*	CDR(FTC)	S	SM	31.12.99	FOST DPORT SHORE
Gardner, John Edward , *BA*	LT(FTC)	X	PWO(A)	01.07.92	CARDIFF
Gardner, Malcolm Edward Francis , *BEng*	LT(FTC)	E	WE	01.03.96	HQ DCSA
Gardner, Michael Peter , *BSc*	SLT(IC)	X		01.05.97	BERKELEY
Gardner, Suzanne Lorraine	LT	Q		05.11.98	RN GIBRALTAR
Gare, Christopher James	SLT(CC)	X		01.09.97	DEF SCH OF LANG
Garland, Andrew Neil	CAPT RM(FTC)	RM	SO(LE)	01.01.00	CDO LOG REGT RM
Garland, Darren Stephen , *BEng*	T(FTC)	E	WESM	01.07.94	FOSM NWOOD HQ
Garland, John Michael Roy , *BSc*	CDR(FTC)	E	WESM	31.12.87	MOD (BATH)
Garland, Nicholas , *BSc*	LT CDR(FTC)	S	CMA	01.11.95	OCEAN
Garlick, Edward Christian	LT(FTC)	X	AV	25.07.91	INVINCIBLE
Garner, Michael Edward	SLT(IC)	X		01.09.99	DARTMOUTH BRNC
Garner, Sean Martin , *BA*	LT(CC)	X	ATC	01.08.94	RNAS CULDROSE
Garnett, *Sir* Ian (David Graham) , *KCB, psc*	VADM	-	P	24.08.95	PJHQ
Garnham, Simon William , *BA*	CAPT RM(IC)	RM		01.05.99	45 CDO RM
Garratt, John Kenneth , *BA, n*	LT CDR(FTC)	X	PWO(A)	01.05.99	COVENTRY
Garratt, Mark David , *pce, pcea*	CDR(FTC)	X	P	30.06.97	RNAS YEOVILTON
Garreta, Carlos Eduardo , *BSc*	SLT(IC)	X		01.05.98	EXETER
Garrett, Stephen Walter , *pce(sm)*	CDR(FTC)	X	SM	31.12.97	TURBULENT
Gascoyne, David John , *BSc, CEng, MIMarE*	LT CDR(FTC)	E	ME	01.04.91	DRAKE CFM
Gaskell, Harvey David , *BEng*	LT(IC)	X	P	16.12.98	RNAS YEOVILTON
Gaskin, Simon Edward , *pce*	LT CDR(FTC)	X	PWO(N)	01.11.87	FLYING FOX
Gass, Colin Joseph , *BSc, FRMS, psc, pce*	CAPT(FTC)	X	PWO(A)	30.06.97	DRYAD

Name	Rank	Branch	Spec	Seniority	Where Serving
Gasson, Nicholas Simon Charles , *pce, ocds(US)*	CDR(FTC)	X	PWO(U)	30.06.95	OCEAN
Gatenby, Christopher David , *BA*	LT(FTC)	X		01.10.97	LINDISFARNE
Gates, Daniel Alexander , *BSc*	LT(FTC)	X		01.12.99	VANGUARD(PORT)
Gates, Nigel Sinclair , *BEng*	LT(CC)	X	P	16.03.93	845 SQN
Gauld, Moray Grant Robertson , *MBA*	SLT(IC)	X	O U/T	01.01.98	DARTMOUTH BRNC
Gaunt, Neville Raymond , *pce, pcea, psc, psc(j)*	CDR(FTC)	X	O	30.06.98	JSCSC
Gay, David , *MB, BS (Act Surg Ltcdr)*	SURG LT	-		05.08.98	CAPTAIN SM2
Gayfer, Mark Ewan , *MA, AMIEE*	LT CDR(FTC)	E	WESM	01.12.99	COLLINGWOOD
Gaytano, Ronald Troy McDonald , *BEng, MSc*	SLT(IC)	E	AE	01.01.00	DARTMOUTH BRNC
Gazard, Philip Neil , *BEng*	LT CDR(FTC)	E	WE	01.10.99	SSA/CWTA PORTS
Gazzard, Julian Henry , *pce*	LT CDR(FTC)	X	PWO(N)	01.06.96	DRYAD
Geary, Michael , *BSc*	LT(CC)	X	O	01.07.93	702 SQN HERON
Geary, Timothy William , *BEng*	LT CDR(FTC)	E	ME	01.08.96	OCEAN
Geddes, William Bruce , jssc	CDR(FTC)	E	AE	30.06.90	ES AIR USA
Geddis, Richard Duncan , *BEng*	LT CDR(FTC)	E	WESM	01.09.96	UPHLDER TRG TEAM
Geldard, Michael Andrew *(Act Maj)*	CAPT RM(FTC)	RM		25.04.95	HQRM
Gelder, George Arthur , *psc*	LT COL(FTC)	RM		31.12.93	RHQ AFNORTH
Gennard, Anthony , *BA*	LT(FTC)	S		01.03.95	FOST DPORT SHORE
Gent, Richard Peter St John , *MB, BCh, MA, MRCGP*	SURG CDR	-	GMPP	31.12.99	RN GIBRALTAR
Gent, Stephanie Jean	LT CDR(CC)	W		01.10.97	2SL/CNH FOTR
George, Alan Peter , *pcea*	LT CDR(FTC)	X	O	16.01.95	FOSF SEA PTSMTH
George, David Mark	LT(FTC)	X	FC	13.03.93	DRYAD
George, Jacqueline Ellen , *BSc*	SLT(IC)	X		01.05.98	SUTHERLAND
George, Jonathan Mark , *BEng (Act Lt Cdr)*	LT(CC)	E	WE	01.11.89	CINCFLEET
George, Patrick David , *OBE, BA, psc(m)*	LT COL(FTC)	RM		30.06.89	CTCRM
George, Stephen Augustine , *BSc, MSc, CEng, MRAeS*	CDR(FTC)	E	AE	31.12.93	JF HARROLE OFF
George, Seth Duncan , *BSc*	LT(IC)	E		01.03.00	EXETER
Gerrell, Frederick John *(Act Lt Cdr)*	LT(FTC)	MS		08.04.94	RN GIBRALTAR
Getgood, James Ashley , *BSc, psc(m)*	LT COL(FTC)	RM		30.06.95	MWC SOUTHWICK
Gething, Jonathan Blair , *pce(sm)*	LT CDR(FTC)	X	SM	06.03.94	FOSM NWOOD OPS
Gibb, Roger Walter , *BSc*	CDR(FTC)	E	WESM	31.12.91	FOSM NWOOD HQ
Gibbon, Lynne	LT CDR	Q	ONC	05.10.88	MOD (LONDON)
Gibbons, Nicholas Philip	LT(CC)	X	O	01.10.92	810 SQN C FLIGHT
Gibbs, Anthony Maurice	LT(IC)	X	P	16.04.99	814 SQN
Gibbs, David John Edward , *BEng*	LT(IC)	X	P	01.08.98	846 SQN
Gibbs, Neil David , *BSc*	LT CDR(FTC)	E	ME	01.07.95	MOD (LONDON)
Gibbs, Philip Norman Charles , *BSc*	LT CDR(FTC)	X	PWO(U)	01.02.89	CNOCS GROUP
Gibson, Andrew	LT CDR(FTC)	E	AE	08.06.91	FONA
Gibson, Alastair David , *MA*	LT CDR(FTC)	S		16.11.97	GLOUCESTER
Gibson, Alexander James , *BSc*	CAPT RM(FTC)	RM		01.05.99	40 CDO RM
Gibson, Andrew Richard , *MB, BS*	SURG LTCDR	-		01.08.99	NELSON (PAY)
Gibson, David Thomas , *BSc*	LT CDR(FTC)	E	AE	01.06.91	819 SQN
Gibson, Ian Alexander , *pce*	CDR(FTC)	X	PWO(A)	31.12.92	HQ NORTH
Gibson, Jennifer Blair , *BSc*	LT(IC)	X	MCD	01.01.96	PENZANCE
Gibson, Martin Jonathan Stuart	SLT(FTC)	E	AE(M)	01.04.98	771 SK5 SAR
Gibson, Sarah Jane , *BA, MSc*	LT(IC)	E	TM	01.01.99	DARTMOUTH BRNC
Gibson, Timothy Andrew , *MBE, pce*	LT CDR(FTC)	X	N	16.03.87	EXC BRISTOL
Gibson, Terence Anthony	SLT(IC)	E	WE	27.01.99	COLLINGWOOD
Gidney, Nigel , *osc*	MAJ(FTC)	RM		01.09.88	RM WARMINSTER
Gilbert, Lee Graham , *BSc, MBA, FRSA, AMIMechE*	LT CDR(FTC)	E	AE	01.10.94	702 SQN HERON
Gilbert, Peter David , *BEng, MSc, CEng, MIMarE, MIMechE, MCGI, AMIEE*	LT CDR(FTC)	E	ME	01.03.96	JSCSC
Gilbert, Ross Grant , *LLB*	LT(FTC)	S		01.06.98	BULLDOG
Gilbert, Stephen Anthony , *BEng, psc(j)*	CDR(FTC)	E	ME	30.06.00	SSA ROSYTH
Gilbert, Stephen Kenneth	LT CDR(FTC)	S	(W)	01.10.98	CDRE MFP
Gilbert, Sarah Louise	SLT(IC)	S		01.01.99	DARTMOUTH BRNC
Gilding, Douglas Robert , *BSc*	MAJ(FTC)	RM		01.09.98	HQRM
Giles, Andrew Robert	LT CDR(FTC)	S	(S)	21.07.92	COLLINGWOOD
Giles, David William , *MBE, BSc, MIEE*	LT CDR(FTC)	E	WE	01.07.93	RMCS SHRIVENHAM
Giles, Gary John	LT RM(FTC)	RM	SO(LE)	01.01.98	45 CDO RM
Giles, Kevin David Lindsay , *BSc, pce*	LT CDR(FTC)	X	MCD	01.05.92	NELSON
Giles, Robert Keith , *BEng*	LT(FTC)	X	MCD	01.03.93	URNU LIVERPOOL
Gill, Christopher David , *BA*	SLT(FTC)	X		01.09.97	DRYAD
Gill, Christopher Michael	LT CDR(CC)	X	METOC	01.10.89	NORTHWOOD

Name	Rank	Branch	Spec	Seniority	Where Serving
Gill, Michael	CDR(FTC)	S		31.12.88	MOD (BATH)
Gill, Mark Hansen , *BEng*	LT(FTC)	X	O	01.07.94	849 SQN B FLT
Gill, Martin Robert , *BEng, MSc, psc(j)*	LT CDR(FTC)	E	MESM	01.04.95	TRIUMPH
Gill, Steven Clark	LT(FTC)	S	(S)	12.12.91	ES AIR YEO
Gillam, Richard Leslie , *BSc*	LT CDR(FTC)	E	ME	01.12.88	MOD (BATH)
Gillan, Gordon Maxwell , *BEng, MSc, gw*	LT CDR(FTC)	E	WE	01.04.95	AFPAA WTHY DOWN
Gillanders, Fergus Graeme Roy , *pce*	CDR(FTC)	X	PWO(A)	31.12.94	JDCC
Gillard, Victoria Anne	LT(FTC)	X	HM	01.07.99	DRYAD
Gillespie, Callum David	LT(FTC)	X	SM	01.08.92	CSST SHORE FSLN
Gillett, David Alexander	LT(FTC)	X		01.11.98	DULVERTON
Gillham, Paul Robert	LT(FTC)	E	WE	01.07.92	MOD (BATH)
Gillies, Elizabeth Mary , *BSc*	LT(IC)	S		01.01.98	ENDURANCE
Gillies, Robert Ross , *BEng, MIMarE*	LT CDR(FTC)	E	MESM	01.02.97	SULTAN
Gilliland, Samuel Saunderson	LT(FTC)	E	WE	13.06.91	STG BRISTOL
Gillson, Dennis Malcolm	MAJ(FTC)	RM		01.11.78	CTCRM
Gilmartin, Kieran	SURG SLT	-		04.10.99	DARTMOUTH BRNC
Gilmore, Jeremy Edward	MID(IC)	X	P U/T	01.09.98	DARTMOUTH BRNC
Gilmore, Martin Paul	LT(IC)	X	P	01.06.96	815 FLT 226
Gilmore, Steven John , *BSc*	LT(CC)	E	WE	01.04.00	COLLINGWOOD
Gilmour, Craig James Murray , *pce*	LT CDR(FTC)	X	PWO(A)	01.12.97	MOD (LONDON)
Ginn, Robert Nigel *(Act Maj)*	CAPT RM(FTC)	RM	SO(LE)	01.01.95	RM Poole
Ginnever, Mark Stuart Matthew , *BSc*	CAPT RM(IC)	RM		01.09.95	RMR BRISTOL
Gisborne, Walter Charles	LT(FTC)	E	WE	19.02.93	SSA/CWTA PORTS
Gittoes, Mark Anthony Warren	MAJ(FTC)	RM		01.09.90	RMCS SHRIVENHAM
Gladston, Stephen Anderson	LT(CC)	X	P	01.07.91	849 SQN B FLT
Gladwell, Trevor John	LT CDR(FTC)	X	SM	01.12.93	AGRIPPA NAVSOUTH
Gladwin, Michael David , *BSc*	SLT(CC)	X	ATCU/T	01.01.98	RAF SHAWBURY
Glass, Jonathan Eric , *BSc*	LT CDR(FTC)	X		01.09.94	JHQ NORTHEAST
Glaze, John William , *BSc, psc (Act Lt Col)*	MAJ(FTC)	RM	SO(LE)	01.10.92	SEA CADET CORPS
Glennie, Andrew Michael Gordon , *BSc, CEng, MIMarE*	LT CDR(FTC)	E	ME	01.01.94	NMA PORTSMOUTH
Glennie, Brian William , *MBA*	LT CDR(FTC)	E	WE	01.10.99	ARK ROYAL
Glover, Mark Alec , *BM, BA, BCh, MRCGP, AFOM*	SURG LTCDR	-	GMPP	01.08.93	FONA
Gobey, Christopher Graham	LT CDR(CC)	X	SM	01.10.95	RHQ SOUTHLANT
Goble, Ian John	LT CDR(FTC)	E	WE	01.10.95	MOD (BATH)
Goddard, Andrew Stephen Nigel , *MA, AMIEE*	LT(FTC)	E	WESM	01.02.94	TURBULENT
Goddard, David Jonathan Sinclair , *BSc, pce*	LT CDR(FTC)	X	PWO(N)	01.10.87	DRYAD
Goddard, Ian Aleksis , *BSc*	SLT(IC)	X		01.09.98	EXETER
Goddard, Ian Kenneth , *pce, psc*	CAPT(FTC)	X	PWO(U)	31.12.97	NATO DEF COL
Godfrey, Kim Richard , *BSc, pce*	LT CDR(FTC)	X	MCD	01.09.93	RN GIBRALTAR
Godfrey, Simeon David William	SLT(FTC)	X	SM	18.09.98	VIGILANT(PORT)
Godley, David	SLT(IC)	E	WE	27.01.99	COLLINGWOOD
Godwin, Christopher Anthony , *pcea*	LT CDR(FTC)	X	P	01.02.99	DRYAD
Godwin, Jeffrey Clive	LT CDR(FTC)	E	AE(M)	01.10.90	ES AIR YEO
Gold, John William	LT(FTC)	X	EW	06.04.95	FOSF
Golden, Charles Alexander	MID(UCE)(IC)	E	ME	01.09.99	CAMPBELTOWN
Golden, Dominic St Clair	LT CDR(FTC)	X	FC	01.06.99	INVINCIBLE
Golding, Simon Jefferies , *QHC*	PR CHAPLAIN	CE		03.05.77	2SL/CNH
Goldman, Barry Andrew Louis , *MNI, pce, psc (COMMODORE)*	CAPT(FTC)	X	PWO(N)†	30.06.92	CDRE MFP
Goldman, Paul Henry Louis , *BEng, MSc*	LT CDR(FTC)	E	WE	01.04.99	MOD (BATH)
Goldsmith, Darran , *pcea*	LT CDR(FTC)	X	O	01.10.99	824 NAS
Goldsmith, David Thomas , *BEng*	LT(FTC)	E	WE	01.01.94	DARTMOUTH BRNC
Goldsmith, Simon Victor William , *BSc, pce*	LT CDR(FTC)	X	PWO(C)	01.05.95	EXCHANGE CANADA
Goldstone, Richard Samuel , *BA, n*	LT(FTC)	X		01.08.94	CHATHAM
Goldsworthy, Elaine Tania	LT(CC)	S		01.08.95	RALEIGH
Goldsworthy, Peter Jarvie , *BEng*	LT(FTC)	S		01.09.94	2SL/CNH
Goldthorpe, Michael	LT CDR(FTC)	S		06.06.96	ARGYLL
Gomm, Kevin , *BSc, pce(sm)*	LT CDR(FTC)	X	SM	01.06.91	RALEIGH
Goodacre, Ian Royston	LT CDR(FTC)	X	PWO(U)	01.05.98	GLASGOW
Goodall, David Charles , *pce, pcea, psc*	CAPT(FTC)	X	P	31.12.98	CJPS
Goodall, Michael Antony , *BEng*	LT(FTC)	E		01.01.99	ILLUSTRIOUS
Goodall, Simon Richard James , *ADC, BA, psc(m) (COMMODORE)*	CAPT(FTC)	E	TM	31.12.93	2SL/CNH FOTR
Goode, Alun Nicholas	LT CDR(FTC)	X	PWO(A)	01.09.99	ILLUSTRIOUS
Gooder, Simon Philip , *MNI*	LT CDR(FTC)	X	N†	01.05.83	DRAKE DPL

Name	Rank	Branch	Spec	Seniority	Where Serving
Goodings, George James	LT CDR(FTC)	E	MESM	01.10.96	NEPTUNE NT
Goodman, Andrew Theodore, *BSc, pce, n*	LT CDR(FTC)	X	PWO(U)	01.03.98	DRYAD
Goodman, David Frederick	SLT(FTC)	X	SM	09.01.98	SOVEREIGN
Goodman, Peter Robert	LT(CC)	S		01.10.94	OCLC MANCH
Goodrich, David Leslie	LT CDR(FTC)	E	WE	01.10.93	MOD (BATH)
Goodridge, Terence James *(Act Maj)*	CAPT RM(FTC)	RM	SO(LE)	01.01.93	MOD (LONDON)
Goodrum, Simon	SLT(FTC)	MS		19.09.96	INM ALVERSTOKE
Goodsell, Christopher David, *pce*	LT CDR(FTC)	X	SM	01.02.99	SOVEREIGN
Goodship, Mark Thomas	LT(CC)	E	ME	01.09.98	SULTAN
Goodwin, David Robert, *pce*	CDR(FTC)	X	PWO(U)	31.12.93	2SL/CNH FOTR
Goodwin, Lincoln Bryan	LT(FTC)	S	(S)	03.04.98	RNAS YEOVILTON
Gopsill, Brian Richard, *MIL*	LT CDR(FTC)	S	SM	01.07.85	AGRIPPA NAVSOUTH
Goram, Malcolm	LT(CC)	X	ATC	01.05.87	RNAS CULDROSE
Gordon, Andrew Jon	MID(UCE)(IC)	E	ME	01.09.98	CHATHAM
Gordon, David, *BA, BSc, psc*	LT CDR(FTC)	E	TM	09.01.92	FOSM NWOOD HQ
Gordon, David Iain, *BSc, BEng*	SLT(IC)	X		01.05.98	MONMOUTH
Gordon, Joseph Patrick Mark, *osc, osc(us) (LOC Lt Col)*	MAJ(FTC)	RM		13.12.81	LOAN BMATT GHANA
Gordon, Mark Winston, *MA*	CAPT RM(FTC)	RM		01.09.97	CTCRM
Gordon, Neil Leslie, *BSc*	LT(CC)	E	ME	01.11.92	CLYDE MIXMAN1
Gordon, Stuart Ross, *MA, pce, pcea, psc*	LT CDR(FTC)	X	P	01.02.94	845 SQN
Gordon-Lennox, Andrew Charles, *pce, psc*	CDR(FTC)	X	AWO(U)	30.06.85	SA COPENHAGEN
Gorrod, Peter Charles Alfred	LT(FTC)	X	PR	06.09.85	FOST DPORT SHORE
Gorsuch, Paul George, *BA*	LT CDR(FTC)	S	SM	16.04.90	MOD (LONDON)
Gosden, Daniel Richard	MID(UCE)(FTC)	E	ME	01.09.98	DARTMOUTH BRNC
Gosden, Stephen Richard, *MSc, CEng, MIMarE, psc*	CDR(FTC)	E	ME	30.06.94	SULTAN
Gosling, Darren John	SLT(IC)	S		01.05.98	DARTMOUTH BRNC
Gosney, Christopher	CAPT RM(FTC)	RM	SO(LE)	01.01.99	HQ 3 CDO BDE RM
Gothard, Andrew Mark	LT(CC)	E	ME	01.11.96	ARK ROYAL
Gotke, Christopher Torben, *BEng*	LT(CC)	X	P	16.01.94	800 SQN
Goudge, Simon David Philip, *BA*	LT(FTC)	S		01.04.94	COMUKTG/CASWSF
Gough, Martyn	CHAPLAIN	CE		01.09.98	CAPT F2(SEA)
Gough, Steven Roy	LT(FTC)	X	PT	03.04.92	TEMERAIRE
Gould, James David	LT(FTC)	X		01.10.98	GUERNSEY
Goulder, Jonathan David, *BEng*	LT(IC)	X		01.11.97	BRECON
Goulding, Jonathan Paul, *n*	LT(FTC)	X		01.03.95	DRYAD
Gourlay, James Stewart, *BSc, psc*	CDR(FTC)	E	AE	30.06.96	ES AIR YEO
Govan, Richard Thomas, *OBE, pce, psc*	CDR(FTC)	X	PWO(U)	30.06.92	SULTAN
Gower, John Howard James, *OBE, BSc, MNI, pce, pce(sm)*	CAPT(FTC)	X	SM	31.12.99	MOD (LONDON)
Grace, Nicholas John	LT RM(FTC)	BS		01.01.98	RM SCHOOL MUSIC
Grace, Trevor Paul, *LRSM*	LT CDR(FTC)	E	WE	01.10.98	SOUTHAMPTON
Gracey, Peter Pequignot, *BEng, AMIEE*	LT CDR(FTC)	E	WESM	01.07.96	SUPERB
Grafton, Martin Nicholas, *BSc, CEng, MIMechE, MINucE*	CDR(FTC)	E	MESM	31.12.96	NEPTUNE FD
Graham, Alastair Neil Spencer, *BSc*	LT(FTC)	E	WESM	01.08.93	MOD (LONDON)
Graham, David Edward, *pce*	LT CDR(FTC)	X	PWO(A)	01.10.91	FOSF
Graham, David Winston Stuart, *BEng, CEng, MIMechE*	LT CDR(FTC)	E	MESM	01.08.97	VICTORIOUS(PORT)
Graham, Gordon Russell, *BSc, psc(m)*	CDR(FTC)	E	WE	30.06.97	*BDS* WASHINGTON
Graham, Ian Edmund, *n*	LT CDR(FTC)	X	PWO(A)	01.08.98	GRAFTON
Graham, James, *MA, MSc, CEng, MIEE*	LT CDR(FTC)	E	WE	01.12.97	MOD (LONDON)
Graham, James Edward	CDR(FTC)	S	SM	30.06.00	EXCHANGE SPAIN
Graham, Mark Alexander, *pcea*	LT(CC)	X	O	01.10.90	702 SQN HERON
Graham, Penelope Jane, *BA*	LT CDR(FTC)	W	S	01.10.99	FONA
Graham, Robert	LT CDR(FTC)	E	ME	01.10.97	ARK ROYAL
Graham, Stephen William, *OBE, BSc, CEng, MIMarE, jsdc (COMMODORE)*	CAPT(FTC)	E	ME	31.12.91	NBC PORTSMOUTH
Grainge, Christopher Leonard	SURG LT	-		04.08.99	INM ALVERSTOKE
Grainger, Adam Lennox, *MA*	CAPT RM(FTC)	RM		01.09.97	CTCRM
Grandison, John Alexander Steele	LT CDR(FTC)	X	PWO(A)	01.03.86	DRYAD
Granger, Christopher Ronald	LT CDR(FTC)	E	MESM	01.10.97	DRAKE CFM
Grant, Alan Kenneth, *OBE, MA, pcea, pce*	CDR(FTC)	X	O	30.06.93	MOD (BATH)
Grant, Brian Gerald	LT(TC)	E	MESM	10.06.94	CLYDE MIXMAN2
Grant, David James	LT(FTC)	E	MESM	14.06.96	NEPTUNE NT
Grant, Ian William, *psc(m), psc(j)*	LT COL(FTC)	RM	LC	30.06.91	HQRM
Grant, Roland Stephen, *MBE, psc*	LT COL(FTC)	RM		30.06.90	CTCRM
Grant, Wayne Graham, *BEng*	SLT(FTC)	E	AE	01.01.98	SOMERSET

Name	Rank	Branch	Spec	Seniority	Where Serving
Grantham, Stephen Mark , *BSc, MSc, CEng, MIMechE, MCGI*	LT CDR(FTC)	E	MESM	01.07.93	CSST SEA
Gratton, Stephen William	LT CDR(FTC)	E	WE	01.10.96	CDRE MFP(SEA)
Graves, Michael Edward Linsan , *BSc*	CAPT(FTC)	E	WESM	30.06.98	MOD (BATH)
Gray, Anthony James , *MA, psc(j)*	CDR(FTC)	E	AE(P)	31.12.98	ES AIR BRISTOL
Gray, Anthony John , *BSc, MSc, CEng, MIMechE*	LT CDR(FTC)	E	MESM	01.07.93	VANGUARD(PORT)
Gray, Dennis	LT CDR(FTC)	E	ME	01.10.93	FOST SEA
Gray, David Kingston , *BEng, AMIEE*	LT CDR(FTC)	E	WE	01.04.95	FOSF
Gray, Emma Jane , *BA*	SLT(IC)	S		01.09.98	DARTMOUTH BRNC
Gray, John Allan , *BEng*	LT(FTC)	X	PWO(A)	01.06.92	DRYAD
Gray, John Arthur , *BSc*	LT(IC)	X	SM	01.03.98	VICTORIOUS(PORT)
Gray, James Alan	CAPT RM(FTC)	RM		29.04.97	CTCRM
Gray, James	LT(CC)	X	O	01.04.95	815 FLT 234
Gray, Karl Daniel	2LT(GRAD)(FTC)	RM		29.04.98	40 CDO RM
Gray, Michael John Henry *(Act Lt)*	SLT(FTC)	X	AV	09.01.98	SULTAN
Gray, Mark Nicholas , *MA, osc(us)*	MAJ(FTC)	RM		01.09.97	PJHQ
Gray, Nathan John , *BEng*	LT(CC)	X	P U/T	01.12.99	DHFS
Gray, Paul Reginald	LT(CC)	X	P	01.08.91	820 SQN
Gray, Richard	LT CDR(FTC)	X	SM	01.03.99	VICTORIOUS(STBD)
Gray, Robert Stanley , *BSc (BARRISTER)*	CDR(FTC)	S	BAR	31.12.99	2SL/CNH
Gray, Yvonne Michelle , *BEd*	LT(FTC)	X	MW	01.02.95	CROMER
Grears, Jonathan , *BSc*	LT CDR(FTC)	E	IS	01.09.99	INVINCIBLE
Greatwood, Ian Mark , *BEng*	LT CDR(FTC)	E	WESM	01.01.99	LN DERA PRTSDWN
Greaves, Michael Jonathan , *BA, pce, pcea*	LT CDR(FTC)	X	P	01.04.94	815 SQN HQ
Greedus, David Arthur	MAJ(FTC)	RM	SO(LE)	01.10.96	JSCSC
Green, Andrew John , *BA*	LT CDR(FTC)	E	TMSM	01.05.98	PJHQ
Green, Andrew Michael	LT(FTC)	E	ME	01.07.93	MOD (BATH)
Green, Adrian Richard , *BSc, MSc, MIMechE, MCGI, CEng*	CDR(FTC)	E	MESM	31.12.98	NP BRISTOL
Green, Catherine Margaret , *BEng*	LT(FTC)	E	WE	01.06.91	SSA/CWTA PORTS
Green, David Paul	LT CDR(FTC)	X	SM	13.08.93	FOSM GOSPORT
Green, David Patrick Savage , *BEng, MSc*	LT CDR(FTC)	E	WESM	01.05.95	MOD (LONDON)
Green, Gary Edward	CAPT RM(FTC)	RM	SO(LE)	01.01.96	HQ 3 CDO BDE RM
Green, Gareth Mark , *BA*	MAJ(FTC)	RM		01.09.98	NELSON (PAY)
Green, Ian Andrew	LT(CC)	X	ATC	01.04.97	EXCHANGE RAF UK
Green, Jonathan	LT CDR(FTC)	X		01.06.98	COMSTRIKFORSTH
Green, John	CHAPLAIN	CE		04.06.91	2SL/CNH
Green, Jonathan	SLT(IC)	X	P U/T	01.01.00	RAF CRANWELL EFS
Green, John Anthony , *BSc, CEng, MIEE, MInstP, AMInstP, CDipAF, jsdc*	CAPT(FTC)	E	WESM	31.12.97	NEPTUNE NT
Green, James Erskines	MID(UCE)(IC)	E		01.09.99	SHEFFIELD
Green, Jayne Hannah , *BSc*	LT(CC)	X		01.09.99	DRYAD
Green, Janette Lesley	LT(FTC)	W	AV	11.12.92	JS PHOT SCHOOL
Green, Michael Gerald Hamilton , *MA, psc(j)*	MAJ(FTC)	RM	LC	01.09.95	CINCFLEET
Green, Michael Ronald	MAJ(FTC)	RM	SO(LE)	01.10.99	CTCRM
Green, Peter Andrew	SLT(IC)	X		01.04.99	CUMBERLAND
Green, Philip Daniel , *BSc*	LT(CC)	X	P	16.10.97	819 SQN
Green, Peter James , *pce(sm)*	LT CDR(FTC)	X	SM	01.07.96	MOD (LONDON)
Green, Roger Richard , *BA*	SLT(IC)	X		01.09.98	DARTMOUTH BRNC
Green, Selina Katherine , *BA*	LT(IC)	X		01.02.94	NELSON
Green, Stephen Noel , *BSc, CEng, MIEE, psc*	CDR(FTC)	E	WE	31.12.98	JSCSC
Green, Timothy Cooper , *BA*	LT(FTC)	X	SM	01.04.94	VENGEANCE(PORT)
Green, Timothy John , *pce(sm), psc(a)*	CDR(FTC)	X	SM	31.12.98	VIGILANT(STBD)
Greenaway, Nicholas Mark , *pce*	LT CDR(FTC)	X	PWO(A)	01.08.95	LIVERPOOL
Greenberg, Neil , *BM, BSc, MRCPsych*	SURG LTCDR	-		01.08.99	INVINCIBLE
Greene, Michael John , *BEd, MSc, psc*	CDR(FTC)	E	TM	31.12.99	DRYAD
Greener, Carl , *MEng, CEng, MIEE*	LT CDR(FTC)	E	WE	01.09.99	COLLINGWOOD
Greenfield, David Peter	LT CDR(FTC)	X		21.09.92	2SL/CNH FOTR
Greenfield, Kenneth	LT CDR(FTC)	E	ME	01.10.93	FOST SEA
Greenish, Philip Duncan , *ADC, BSc, CEng, MIEE, rcds, jsdc (COMMODORE)*	CAPT(FTC)	E	WE	31.12.91	MOD (LONDON)
Greenland, Michael Richard , *pce, pcea*	LT CDR(FTC)	X	P	16.04.95	FONA SEAGOING
Greenlees, Iain Wallace , *BSc, pce*	CDR(FTC)	X	PWO(A)	30.06.93	SSA/CWTA PORTS
Greenop, Jeremy Peter Spencer , *OBE, jsdc, pce, psc*	CDR(FTC)	X	P	31.12.89	SACLANT USA
Greenshields, Frazer Newhams , *BA(OU)*	SLT(FTC)	E	MESM	02.05.97	SCEPTRE
Greenway, Stephen Anthony , *BEng, CEng*	LT CDR(FTC)	E	ME	01.02.00	NEPTUNE NT
Greenwood, Antony Wyn , *BSc*	LT(CC)	X		01.09.99	DRYAD

Name	Rank	Branch	Spec	Seniority	Where Serving
Greenwood, Benjamin Charles John , *BEng*	SLT(IC)	X	O U/T	01.09.98	DARTMOUTH BRNC
Greenwood, Michael John , *BA*	LT CDR(FTC)	X	METOC	01.09.91	RNAS YEOVILTON
Greenwood, Peter , *pce*	LT CDR(FTC)	X	MCD	29.04.93	GRAFTON
Greenwood, Peter Adam	LT(CC)	X	P	16.10.99	820 SQN
Greenwood, Stephen , *BSc, CEng, MRAeS, MDA*	CDR(FTC)	E	AE(P)	31.12.97	ES AIR YEO
Greer, James Patrick , *MB, BCh*	SURG CDR	-	GMPP	31.12.94	RN GIBRALTAR
Greetham, Clare Elizabeth , *LLB*	LT(IC)	X		01.08.96	CAPTAIN RNP TEAM
Gregan, David Carl , *psc*	CDR(FTC)	X	H CH	30.06.92	MOD (LONDON)
Gregory, Alexander Michael , *OBE, jsdc, pce(sm)*	RADM	-	SM	30.09.97	FOSNNI/NBC CLYDE
Gregory, Alastair Stuart , *BEng, MSc, CEng, MIMarE, AMIMechE*	LT CDR(FTC)	E	ME	01.06.00	ASTUTE IPT
Gregory, Ian Stuart , *pce, pcea, psc*	CDR(FTC)	X	P	30.06.89	HQ DCSA
Gregory, James , *MB, ChB (Act Surg Lt)*	SURG SLT	-		05.08.96	DARTMOUTH BRNC
Gregory, Mark , *BEng, AMIEE*	LT CDR(FTC)	E	WE	01.01.00	OCLC BIRM
Gregory, Timothy Maurice , *BA, rcds, psc(m)*	COL(FTC)	RM	C	30.06.96	BDS WASHINGTON
Greig, Judith Anne , *BEng*	LT(FTC)	E	ME	01.05.99	GLOUCESTER
Grenfell-Shaw, Mark Christopher , *MA*	LT CDR(FTC)	E	WESM	01.06.95	TORBAY
Grennan, Eamonn Fergal , *BEng, MSc*	LT(IC)	E	AE	01.05.98	810 SQN SEAHAWK
Grey, Christopher Sidney , *BSc*	SLT(IC)	X		01.01.99	DARTMOUTH BRNC
Grey, Edward John William , *BA*	SLT(IC)	X	O U/T	01.05.98	DARTMOUTH BRNC
Grieve, Steven Harry , *BSc, CEng, MRAeS, psc*	LT CDR(FTC)	E	AE	01.11.92	RNAS YEOVILTON
Griffen, David John , *BSc*	SLT(IC)	X		01.01.98	BERKELEY
Griffin, Niall Robert	LT(CC)	X	P	01.03.93	846 SQN
Griffin, Peter	SLT(FTC)	X	ATC	19.09.97	RNAS CULDROSE
Griffin, Stephen	SLT(IC)	X	AV	19.09.98	RFANSU (ARGUS)
Griffin, William Forrester Griffith , *MA, pce, psc(m) (Act Capt)*	CDR(FTC)	X	AWO(C)	30.06.81	DRAKE CBP(CNH)
Griffiths, Anthony	LT CDR(FTC)	X	MW	01.10.97	EXCHANGE AUSTLIA
Griffiths, Andrew John , *BSc, MSc, psc(j)*	LT CDR(FTC)	E	TM	26.07.94	2SL/CNH
Griffiths, Alan Richard	LT(FTC)	E	WE	09.06.89	CFM PORTSMOUTH
Griffiths, Christopher John James	SLT(IC)	E	ME	29.04.98	SULTAN
Griffiths, Colin Stuart Henry , *BSc*	SLT(CC)	X	P U/T	01.05.97	RNAS YEOVILTON
Griffiths, David Anthony	LT CDR(FTC)	MS	SM	01.10.99	DRAKE CBS
Griffiths, David Brett	SLT(CC)	X	ATCU/T	01.04.98	RAF SHAWBURY
Griffiths, David Michael , *BSc, CEng, FIMarE, MIMarE*	LT CDR(FTC)	E	ME	01.06.91	MOD (BATH)
Griffiths, David Price , *BEng*	LT(CC)	E	WE	01.09.97	YORK
Griffiths, David Thomas , *BSc, pce*	LT CDR(FTC)	X	MCD	01.04.90	ENDURANCE
Griffiths, Gareth Heaton , *BSc*	LT(IC)	X		01.10.98	QUORN
Griffiths, Lloyd , *MEng*	LT(FTC)	E	MESM	01.09.98	TURBULENT
Griffiths, Neil , *BA*	LT(IC)	X		01.09.98	ALDERNEY
Griffiths, Nicholas Alan	LT RM(CC)	RM		01.05.00	CTCRM
Griffiths, Richard Hywel	LT(FTC)	X	SM	01.06.96	SCEPTRE
Griffiths, Timothy George	SLT(FTC)	X	FC	01.09.97	801 SQN
Grigg, Shelton Kent	SLT(IC)	S	(W)	19.09.98	RNAS CULDROSE
Grimley, Daemon Marcus John , *pce, pce(sm)*	LT CDR(FTC)	X	SM	01.11.89	MOD (LONDON)
Grindel, David John , *BEd, MA(Ed), MSc*	LT CDR(FTC)	E	TM	01.09.94	JSCSC
Grindon, Matthew Guy , *BEng*	LT(CC)	X	P	16.01.91	845 SQN
Grixoni, Martin Reynold Roberto	MAJ(FTC)	RM		01.09.90	HQRM
Grocott, Peter Clark	LT(FTC)	S	(W)	08.04.94	RALEIGH
Groom, Ian Stuart , *BEng, CEng, MIMarE*	LT CDR(FTC)	E	ME	01.03.99	NOTTINGHAM
Groom, Mark Richard , *MB, BCh, ChB, DipAvMed, MRAeS, MRCGP, AFOM,* aws	SURG CDR	-	GMPP	30.06.00	NELSON (PAY)
Grosse, Sarah Elizabeth Kingsbury , *BSc, BDS*	SG LT(D)	-		25.06.99	DRYAD
Groves, Christopher Keith	LT CDR(FTC)	X	SM	01.04.99	CSST SHORE DEVPT
Gubbins, Victor Robert , *BSc, CEng, MIMarE, fsc*	CDR(FTC)	E	ME	31.12.93	MOD (BATH)
Guild, Nigel Charles Forbes , *BA, PhD, MIEE, AFIMEE, jsdc*	RADM	-	WE	06.01.00	DGSS BRISTOL *AFIMA*
Guilfoyle, Victoria Marion	SLT(IC)	X		01.04.98	KENT
Guiver, Paul , *BEM*	LT(FTC)	X	MCD	03.04.97	BANGOR
Gullett, Humphrey Richard , *MA*	LT(IC)	S		01.02.97	TIRELESS
Gulley, Trevor James , *BSc, MSc, CEng, MCGI*	CDR(FTC)	E	ME	30.06.98	MOD (BATH)
Gulliford, Kerry Anne , *BA, BSc*	LT(IC)	S		01.08.99	RALEIGH
Gunn, William John Simpson , *BSc, PGDip*	LT CDR(FTC)	X	METOC	01.11.94	CINCFLEET
Gunther, Paul Thomas	LT CDR(FTC)	E	WESM	01.10.99	SSA/CWTA PORTS
Gurmin, Stephen John Albert	LT CDR(FTC)	X	PWO(C)	18.05.95	PJHQ
Gurr, Andrew William George	LT(FTC)	X	PWO(A)	01.05.92	WESTMINSTER
Gutteridge, Jeffrey David James	LT(FTC)	E	WE	20.12.90	MCM3 SEA

Name	Rank	Branch	Spec	Seniority	Where Serving
Guy, Charles Richard, *BA*	LT(IC)	X		01.03.98	EDINBURGH
Guy, Mark Andrew, *BEng*	LT CDR(FTC)	E	WE	13.11.98	SSA BRISTOL
Guy, Philip Stuart, *BA*	CAPT RM(FTC)	RM		01.09.97	CTCRM
Guy, Richard John, *MB, BCh*	SURG LTCDR	-	(GS)UT	15.08.93	NELSON (PAY)
Guy, Terry John, *MIExpE, psc*	CDR(FTC)	E	WESM	30.06.93	MOD (BATH)
Guy, Thomas Justin, *n*	LT(FTC)	X	PWO(U)	01.05.92	MONTROSE
Guyatt, Anthony Edward, *BA*	CDR(FTC)	S		30.06.86	NMA PORTSMOUTH
Guyer, Simon Thomas Glode, *psc(m)*	LT COL(FTC)	RM	LC	30.06.95	HQRM
Guyver, Paul, *MB, BS (Act Surg Lt)*	SURG SLT	-		15.11.97	DARTMOUTH BRNC
Gwatkin, Nicholas John	SLT(IC)	X	C	29.04.98	DRYAD
Gwillim, Vivian George	MAJ(FTC)	RM	ML2	01.09.93	JACIG

H

Name	Rank	Branch	Spec	Seniority	Where Serving
Habershon, David Broadhurst, *pce, psc*	CDR(FTC)	X	PWO(U)	30.06.90	AGRIPPA NAVSOUTH
Hackland, Andrew Stuart	SLT(IC)	X	P U/T	01.05.98	DARTMOUTH BRNC
Haddacks, *Sir* Paul (Kenneth), *rcds, pce, psc, hcsc*	VADM	-	PWO(N)†	24.02.97	UKMILREP BRUSS
Haddon, Richard, *MB, BS, DipAvMed, LRCP, MRCS, MRECGP, AFOM, MRAeS, MRCA*	SURG LTCDR	-	GMPP	19.10.87	NELSON (PAY)
Haddow, Fraser, *psc*	COL(FTC)	RM	MLDR	30.06.00	CINCFLEET
Haddow, Timothy Rowat, *BEng*	LT(FTC)	E	WE	01.03.97	ARGYLL
Hadfield, David, *MSc, CEng, MIMarE*	CDR(FTC)	E	MESM	30.06.99	MOD (LONDON)
Hadland, Giles	SLT(CC)	X		01.04.98	NEWCASTLE
Hadlow, David Keith	CAPT RM(FTC)	RM	SO(LE)	01.01.99	RM Poole
Haggard, Amanda, *BA*	LT(FTC)	S		01.03.98	INVINCIBLE
Haggart, Peter Dewar	LT(FTC)	X	C	01.12.91	COLLINGWOOD
Haggerty, Shaun Michael, *BEng*	LT(CC)	E	AE	01.10.97	899 SQN HERON
Haggo, Jamie Robert, *BSc*	LT(IC)	X	P	16.07.98	FONA VALLEY
Haigh, Alastair James, *BSc*	LT(CC)	X	P	01.12.92	DHFS
Haigh, Julian Joseph, *BA*	LT(IC)	S		01.02.98	VIGILANT(STBD)
Haill, Simon John Jackson, *pce, psc, MInsD*	CDR(FTC)	X	PWO(U)	31.12.93	NMA GOSPORT
Hailstone, Jonathan Henry Steven, *BA, pce, pcea, psc(m)*	LT CDR(FTC)	X	O	16.05.94	MOD (LONDON)
Haines, Paul Roger	LT CDR(FTC)	E	WE	09.12.94	CINCFLEET
Haines, Russell James	LT(IC)	S		01.02.99	FOSNNI/NBC CLYDE
Haines, Steven William, *MA, PhD, FNI, FRGS, FRSA, MRIN, MIMgt, psc*	CDR(FTC)	E	TM	30.06.93	JDCC
Hains, Justin, *BSc*	LT(FTC)	X	MCD	01.04.96	SANDOWN
Hainsworth, Pauline Mary	LT	Q	OPHTH	30.03.94	RH HASLAR
Hale, John Nathan, *BSc*	CAPT RM(FTC)	RM	LC	27.04.96	539 ASLT SQN RM
Haley, Colin William, *pce, psc(a)*	CDR(FTC)	X	PWO(A)	30.06.99	JSCSC
Haley, Timothy John, *MSc, CEng, FIMarE*	CDR(FTC)	E	ME	30.06.96	CAPT F6 (SEA)
Hall, Andrew Jeremy, *BSc*	LT CDR(FTC)	E	AE	01.08.98	MERLIN IPT
Hall, Alexander Peter, *BSc, pce, pcea*	LT CDR(FTC)	X	O	01.03.93	CINCFLEET
Hall, Barry James, *MSc, BEng*	LT CDR(FTC)	E	MESM	01.11.98	MOD (BATH)
Hall, Christopher John	SLT(IC)	X		01.01.98	EXETER
Hall, Christopher Mark Ian *(Act Capt Rm)*	LT RM(IC)	RM		01.04.98	COMACCHIO GP RM
Hall, Darren	LT(CC)	X	P	16.08.96	846 SQN
Hall, David Allen, *MSc, CEng, FIMgt, MIMarE (COMMODORE)*	CAPT(FTC)	E	MESM	31.12.91	SSA DEVONPORT
Hall, Derek Alexander	LT(FTC)	S	(W)	02.04.93	EXCELLENT
Hall, David James, *BDS, MSc, MGDS RCSEd*	SGCDR(D)	-		31.12.99	DDA HALTON
Hall, David William, *BSc, gdas*	LT CDR(FTC)	X	O	01.10.90	RNAS CULDROSE
Hall, Elizabeth Clair, *BSc, PGCE*	LT CDR(FTC)	S		01.05.96	NMA PORTSMOUTH
Hall, Eleanor Louise, *BA*	LT(FTC)	S		01.05.95	DGSS BRISTOL
Hall, John	LT(CS)	-		19.09.97	2SL/CNH FOTR
Hall, Jeremy William Morris, *BSc, MSc, FIMarE, jsdc*	CDR(FTC)	E	MESM	31.12.92	FOSM NWOOD HQ
Hall, Kilian John Darwin, *BSc*	SLT(IC)	X	O U/T	01.05.98	FEARLESS
Hall, Neil Jeremy, *pce*	LT CDR(FTC)	X	PWO(A)	01.03.93	OCEAN
Hall, Robert Langford, *BSc, pce (Act Cdr)*	LT CDR(FTC)	X	PWO(C)	01.05.93	MOD (LONDON)
Hall, Richard Mark, *MA, psc*	MAJ(FTC)	RM		01.09.90	CDO LOG REGT RM
Hall, Stephen, *BEng*	LT CDR(FTC)	E	AE	01.12.98	824 NAS
Hall, Steven Brian, *BSc*	CAPT RM(IC)	RM		28.04.95	CTCRM
Hall, Simon Jeremy, *BSc, MSc, psc*	LT COL(FTC)	RM	MLDR	31.12.99	HQRM
Hall, Thane Trent, *BEng*	LT(FTC)	E	WESM	01.04.95	SPARTAN
Hallett, Simon John, *BSc*	LT(FTC)	S		01.03.93	RALEIGH

Name	Rank	Branch	Spec	Seniority	Where Serving
Halliday, David Alistair , *BA, jsdc, pce*	CAPT(FTC)	X	PWO(A)	30.06.00	2SL/CNH
Halliwell, David Colin , *BEng, MSc*	LT CDR(FTC)	E	MESM	01.03.00	VIGILANT(PORT)
Halls, Bernard Charles , *IEng, MIEEIE*	LT(FTC)	E	WE	18.10.85	RMCS SHRIVENHAM
Hally, Philip John , *BSc*	LT(FTC)	S		01.11.92	FOSM NWOOD HQ
Halsey, Karen Elizabeth , *BSc*	LT(IC)	X	P U/T	01.09.99	DHFS
Halsted, Benjamin Erik , *BA*	2LT(GRAD)(IC)	RM		01.09.99	RE ENTRY(ARMY)
Halton, Paul Vincent , *pce*	LT CDR(FTC)	X	SM	01.12.97	SPLENDID
Hambly, Brian John , *BEng*	LT(CC)	E	WESM	01.09.95	TRENCHANT
Hamilton, Angus John Burnside , *BEng*	LT CDR(FTC)	E	AE(P)	01.04.98	RNAS CULDROSE
Hamilton, Alexander	2LT(GRAD)(IC)	RM		28.04.99	CTCRM LYMPSTONE
Hamilton, Graham Douglas	SLT(IC)	E	AE	29.04.98	SULTAN
Hamilton, Gregory Robert	LT CDR(FTC)	X		01.10.94	PJHQ
Hamilton, Ivan James	LT(CC)	X	P	16.11.91	849 SQN HQ
Hamilton, Mark Ian , *BEng*	LT(CC)	E	ME	01.11.99	SULTAN
Hamilton, Richard Alexander , *BSc, MSc, CEng,*	LT CDR(FTC)	E	IS	01.10.93	IMS BRUSSELS MBCS
Hamilton, Susanna Mary , *BEng*	LT(CC)	E	ME	01.07.94	OCLC ROSYTH
Hamilton-Bruce, Emma Catherine , *BEng, MSc*	LT(CC)	E	AE	01.06.99	SULTAN
Hammersley, James Michael , *BSc, MSc*	LT CDR(FTC)	E	IS	01.10.94	NELSON RNSETT
Hammett, Barry Keith , *QHC, MA*	CHAPLAIN	CE		11.07.77	CINCFLEET
Hammock, Simon George , *BEng*	LT(CC)	X	P	16.12.98	845 SQN
Hammon, Mark Alexander , *BSc*	SLT(IC)	X		01.05.97	DRYAD
Hammond, David Evan , *BSc*	CAPT RM(FTC)	RM	P	01.09.96	DRYAD
Hammond, Mark Christopher *(Act Maj)*	CAPT RM(FTC)	RM	P	26.04.94	JHCHQ
Hammond, Meirion Mark , *BSc*	SLT(IC)	X	P U/T	01.09.97	RAF CRANWELL EFS
Hammond, Nicholas John , *MBE, BTech, PGCE, psc*	LT CDR(FTC)	X	METOC	01.09.85	SACLANT USA
Hammond, Paul Adrian , *BEng, MSc, MIEE, gw*	CDR(FTC)	E	AE	31.12.99	MOD (LONDON)
Hammond, Paul John , *n*	LT(FTC)	X		01.05.96	DARTMOUTH BRNC
Hamp, Colin John , *BSc, pce, pcea, psc*	CDR(FTC)	X	O	31.12.96	MOD (LONDON)
Hampshire, Tony	SLT(CC)	X		01.04.98	DRYAD
Hancock, Andrew Philip , *pce*	LT CDR(FTC)	X	PWO(U)	01.01.99	COMATG SEA
Hancock, James Henry , *BA*	SLT(IC)	X		01.01.98	HERALD
Hancock, Robert Thomas Alexander , *BEng, AMIEE*	LT(FTC)	E	WE	22.12.93	COLLINGWOOD
Hancox, Michael John , *BEng, CEng, MIMarE*	LT CDR(FTC)	E	MESM	01.02.99	SPLENDID
Hand, Christopher John , *MB, BS, FRCS*	SURG LTCDR	-		04.01.95	NELSON (PAY)
Handley, Jonathan Mark , *jsdc, pce, psc(j)*	CDR(FTC)	X	PWO(U)	31.12.96	DRYAD
Hands, Anthony James , *BDS*	SG LT(D)	-		26.06.97	RNAS YEOVILTON
Hands, Adrian Peter , *pcea*	LT CDR(FTC)	X	P	01.10.94	FONA SULTAN
Hanks, Paul Eric , *BSc*	LT(CC)	X	P U/T	01.04.99	FONA VALLEY
Hannaford, William Craig , *MBE*	LT CDR(FTC)	E	WE	01.10.90	COLLINGWOOD
Hannah, William Fergusson	CAPT RM(FTC)	RM	SO(LE)	01.01.96	CTCRM
Hannam, Darrell Brett , *BSc*	LT(IC)	X	O U/T	01.12.99	849 SQN HQ
Hanneman, Martin Nicholas , *BSc*	LT(CC)	X	P	01.10.95	FONA VALLEY
Hannigan, Paul Francis , *pcea*	LT(CC)	X	P	16.01.91	848 SQN HERON
Hanrahan, Martin , *pcea*	LT(FTC)	X	P	08.01.90	848 SQN HERON
Hanslip, Michael Richard	LT CDR(FTC)	E	WE	01.10.91	NELSON
Hanson, Mark Nicholas , *BA*	LT(FTC)	S		01.03.96	MOD (LONDON)
Hanson, Nicholas Anthony , *BEng, CEng, MIMarE, AMIEE*	LT CDR(FTC)	E	WE	01.06.98	MOD (BATH)
Hanson, Sven	2LT(GRAD)(IC)	RM		28.04.99	CTCRM LYMPSTONE
Harborth, Julia Ann	LT(IC)	X	P U/T	01.11.99	DHFS
Harbour, John Robert MacKay , *jsdc, psc*	CDR(FTC)	S		31.12.93	NEPTUNE CFS
Harbroe-Bush, Robert Douglas , *BSc, CEng, MIEE,*	CDR(FTC)	E	WESM	31.12.88	2SL/CNH *psc*
Harcombe, Andrew , *BSc*	SLT(IC)	X	P U/T	01.05.97	RAF CRANWELL EFS
Harcourt, Robert James , *BSc, PGCE, PGDip*	LT CDR(FTC)	X	METOC	01.01.00	DRYAD
Hardacre, Paul Vincent , *BSc*	LT CDR(FTC)	X	SM	01.06.94	MOD (LONDON)
Hardern, Simon Paul , *MNI, pce, psc(j)*	LT CDR(FTC)	X	PWO(U)	01.11.96	SACLANT USA
Hardie, Mark John , *BA*	2LT(GRAD)(IC)	RM		29.04.98	COMACCHIO GP RM
Hardiman, Nicholas Anthony , *BEng*	LT(FTC)	E	MESM	01.05.95	MOD (BATH)
Harding, Carl Sinclair , *BEng, MBA*	LT(CC)	E	TM	01.09.92	DEF SCH OF LANG
Harding, David John	LT(FTC)	S	SM	01.06.96	NEPTUNE SM1
Harding, David Malcolm , *BSc, CEng*	LT CDR(FTC)	E	AE	01.05.95	899 SQN HERON
Harding, Gary Alan , *BEng, AMIEE, psc*	LT CDR(FTC)	E	WE	01.12.94	MOD (LONDON)
Harding, Hadrian Robert , *BEng*	LT(CC)	E	ME	01.04.97	ARK ROYAL
Harding, Russell George , *BSc, pce, pcea*	CDR(FTC)	X	O	31.12.95	MOD (LONDON)

Name	Rank	Branch	Spec	Seniority	Where Serving
Hardman, Mathew James, *BSc*	SLT(FTC)	X		01.09.97	DRYAD
Hardwick, Mark	LT(CC)	S	SM	01.09.98	VICTORIOUS(PORT)
Hardy, Duncan Mark	CAPT RM(FTC)	RM	C	24.04.96	RM Poole
Hardy, Leslie Brian	LT(FTC)	X	PWO(U)	16.12.94	MANCHESTER
Hardy, Lee Charles, *pce*	LT CDR(FTC)	X	PWO(A)	01.12.92	DRYAD
Hardy, Robert John	SLT(IC)	E	ME	29.04.98	SULTAN
Hare, John Herbert, *BA, PGDip*	LT CDR(CC)	X	METOC	01.09.97	RNAS YEOVILTON
Hare, Nigel James, *pce*	LT CDR(FTC)	X	PWO(N)	01.01.94	CROMER
Hare, Timothy William, *BSc, CEng, MIEE, jsdc (COMMODORE)*	CAPT(FTC)	E	WESM	30.06.93	MOD (LONDON)
Harford Cross, Peter James, *MA*	SLT(IC)	X		01.09.97	DRYAD
Hargraves, John, QHDS, *BDS, MSc, MFGDP(UK), LDS RCS(Eng), psc (COMMODORE)*	SGCAPT(D)	-		31.12.91	DDA HALTON
Hargreaves, Neale	LT CDR(FTC)	X	O	01.10.97	LOAN DERA BSC DN
Harland, Nicholas Jonathan Godfrey, *BSc, jsdc, pce*	CAPT(FTC)	X	O	30.06.99	SACLANT BELGIUM
Harlow, Simon Richard	LT(CC)	X	P	01.05.93	702 SQN HERON
Harman, Michael John	CHAPLAIN	CE		20.09.79	ILLUSTRIOUS
Harmer, Jason Neil Jonathon	LT CDR(FTC)	X	P	01.10.97	FONA
Harms, James Graeme	LT(CC)	X	P	01.03.95	801 SQN
Harold, Richard St John, *BSc*	LT(IC)	X		01.04.99	VICTORIOUS(STBD)
Harper, Andrew Charles, *BEng*	LT CDR(FTC)	E	WESM	01.07.97	MOD CSSE USA
Harper, Christopher Hodges, *BSc*	LT CDR(FTC)	X	H CH	01.09.95	ENDURANCE
Harper, Ian Lorimer	LT(FTC)	X	AV	23.07.93	ILLUSTRIOUS
Harper, James Andrew	LT CDR(FTC)	X	O	01.10.97	815 SQN HQ
Harper, Philip Robert, *BA*	LT(FTC)	X	SM	01.02.97	RALEIGH
Harradine, Paul Anthony, *psc(j)*	MAJ(FTC)	RM	SO(LE)	01.10.94	HQ 3 CDO BDE RM
Harrall, Phillip Anthony Robertson, *AFC, MPhil, MRAeS, MRIN, MIMgt, psc (Act Cdr)*	LT CDR(FTC)	X	O	03.03.85	FONA
Harrap, Nicholas Richard Edmund, *OBE, jsdc, pce, pce(sm)*	CDR(FTC)	X	SM	31.12.95	FOSM NWOOD HQ
Harries, Jon Michael Henry, *BSc, CEng, FIEE,*	CAPT(FTC)	E	WE	31.12.91	DRAKE CFM *jsdc*
Harriman, Peter	LT(FTC)	X	C	26.04.99	CNOCS GROUP
Harriman, Suzanne Jane	LT	Q	IC	20.02.96	RH HASLAR
Harrington, Jonathan Barratt, *BEng*	LT(FTC)	E	WE	01.08.95	SSA BRISTOL
Harrington, Lee, *BEng*	LT(FTC)	E	ME	01.10.98	SULTAN
Harris, Andrew Gordon, *BEng, MAPM, AMIEE*	LT CDR(FTC)	E	WE	12.04.97	DGSS BRISTOL
Harris, Andrew Ian, *pce, pcea*	CDR(FTC)	X	O	31.12.99	JSCSC
Harris, Carl Christian, *BA*	CAPT RM(FTC)	RM		01.09.95	FOST SEA
Harris, Keri John, *BEng*	LT CDR(FTC)	X	O	01.04.99	MONTROSE
Harris, Melvin, *MITE*	CDR(FTC)	E	WE	30.06.89	FOSF
Harris, Maxwell	LT(CC)	X	P	01.08.95	819 SQN
Harris, Michael Trevor	LT CDR(FTC)	S	CA	01.10.99	RNAS YEOVILTON
Harris, Nicholas Henry Linton, *MBE, pce, pce(sm), ocds(US) (COMMODORE)*	CAPT(FTC)	X	SM	30.06.95	BDS WASHINGTON
Harris, Philip Norman, *OBE, MPhil, MNI, pce, psc*	CDR(FTC)	X	O	31.12.85	LOAN KUWAIT
Harris, Richard Paul, *BA*	LT(CC)	S		01.09.96	SOMERSET
Harris, Tristan	CAPT RM(FTC)	RM	MLDR	01.09.96	HQ 3 CDO BDE RM
Harris, Timothy Ronald, *pce*	CAPT(FTC)	X	PWO(U)	31.12.98	CAMPBELTOWN
Harrison, Adrian, *BEng*	LT(FTC)	E	MESM	01.02.93	NP BRISTOL
Harrison, Andrew David	SLT(IC)	E	AE	29.04.98	SULTAN
Harrison, Clive Anthony, *AIL, pce*	LT CDR(FTC)	X	PWO(A)	01.03.94	FOST SEA
Harrison, David	LT CDR(FTC)	E	WESM	05.01.97	MOD (BATH)
Harrison, James, *MB, BS (Act Surg Lt)*	SURG SLT	-		01.10.96	DARTMOUTH BRNC
Harrison, Mark Andrew, *BEng, AMIEE*	LT(CC)	E	WESM	01.07.98	DOLPHIN *SM* SCHL
Harrison, Matthew Sean, *BEng, MSc, CEng, MIEE, gw*	CDR(FTC)	E	WE	31.12.99	JSCSC
Harrison, Paul Dominic, *gdas*	LT(CC)	X	O	01.10.90	LOAN DERA BSC DN
Harrison, Paul Geoffrey, *BTech*	LT CDR(FTC)	E	AE(L)	12.09.96	RNAS YEOVILTON
Harrison, Richard Anthony, *MSc, CDipAF, psc, gw*	CDR(FTC)	E	WESM	31.12.89	TORPEDO IPT
Harrison, Richard Frederick	LT CDR(FTC)	X	PWO(A)	22.03.87	COMATG SEA
Harrison, Roger Geoffrey, *psc*	CDR(FTC)	X	P	31.12.87	FONA
Harrison, Richard Simon, *BA*	LT(CC)	X	P	15.09.95	845 SQN
Harrison, Thomas Iain, *BEng, MPhil*	LT(IC)	E	TM	01.01.96	COLLINGWOOD
Harrop, Ian, *BEng, MIMarE*	LT CDR(FTC)	E	MESM	01.05.96	VICTORIOUS(STBD)
Harry, Andrew David, *BEng*	LT CDR(FTC)	X		01.04.96	RNAS CULDROSE
Harry, Peter Norman, *MILog, AMIAM*	CDR(FTC)	S	(S)	01.10.98	RHQ AFNORTH
Hart, Acland	2LT(GRAD)(IC)	RM		28.04.99	CTCRM LYMPSTONE

Name	Rank	Branch	Spec	Seniority	Where Serving
Hart, Camilla Louise	LT(FTC)	S		11.06.93	EXCELLENT
Hart, Derek John, *BSc, CEng, MIEE*	CDR(FTC)	E	WE	30.06.94	COLLINGWOOD
Hart, Jonathan, *MSc, CEng, MIEE, psc*	CAPT(FTC)	E	WESM	31.12.99	ASTUTE IPT
Hart, Mark Alan, *BSc, pce*	LT CDR(FTC)	X	PWO(A)	01.12.94	JSCSC
Hart, Neil Lawrence Whynden	LT(CC)	S	SM	01.05.94	AFPAA(CENTURION)
Hart, Paul Andrew, *BSc*	LT CDR(CC)	E	TM	01.10.98	LOAN BRUNEI
Hart, Robert	LT CDR(FTC)	E	WE	01.10.94	COLLINGWOOD
Hart, Steven David	SLT(FTC)	X		01.04.00	DARTMOUTH BRNC
Hart, Stephen John Eric, *BA*	CAPT RM(FTC)	RM		01.09.99	40 CDO RM
Hart, Tobin Giles De Burgh	LT(FTC)	X	P	01.07.91	CHFHQ
Hart, Willem Cornelis, *IEng, MIMgt, AMIMarE*	CDR(FTC)	E	ME	01.10.98	CAPT D3 SEA
Hartley, Andrew Paul, *BEng*	LT CDR(FTC)	E	ME	02.03.00	UNOMIG
Hartley, Barrie Howard	LT(FTC)	X	AV	03.05.85	FONA
Hartley, Benjamin Paul Iles, *BSc*	LT(IC)	X	P	01.04.99	RNAS CULDROSE
Hartley, John Laurence, *BSc*	LT CDR(FTC)	X	P	01.10.99	EXCHANGE DENMARK
Hartley, Stephen William, *BSc, PGCE*	LT CDR(CC)	E	TM	01.10.96	EXCHANGE ARMY UK
Hartnell, Stephen Thomas, *OBE, MA, psc*	COL(FTC)	RM		30.06.98	CTCRM
Harvey, Barrie, *BEng*	LT(FTC)	E	ME	01.06.97	ILLUSTRIOUS
Harvey, Colin Ashton, *BSc*	CDR(FTC)	E	MESM	30.06.00	CSST SEA
Harvey, Gary	LT(FTC)	E	ME	01.07.92	KENT
Harvey, Keith, *pce*	CDR(FTC)	X	MCD	30.06.93	MOD (LONDON)
Harvey, Paul Anthony, *BSc*	LT CDR(FTC)	X	ATC	01.10.91	RNAS YEOVILTON
Harvey, Paul John	SLT(IC)	S	CA	19.09.98	AFPAA(CENTURION)
Harvey, Robert Matthew Malvern Jolyon, *pce*	LT CDR(FTC)	X	PWO(A)	01.03.97	FOST SEA
Harwood, Christopher George, *BTech*	LT(FTC)	E	WE	24.02.95	KENT
Harwood, Lee Brian	LT(IC)	X		01.02.00	BANGOR
Haseldine, Stephen George	LT CDR(FTC)	X	ATC	01.02.98	MOD (LONDON)
Haskell, Eric Thomas	LT CDR(FTC)	E	WE	01.10.94	SSA/CWTA PORTS
Haslam, Philip James, *pce*	LT CDR(FTC)	X	PWO(A)	01.10.98	ILLUSTRIOUS
Hassall, Harry, *BSc, MEng, MSc*	LT CDR(CC)	E	TM	01.10.95	NELSON RNSETT
Hassall, Ian, *BEng*	LT(CC)	E	ME	01.01.98	LIVERPOOL
Hasted, Daniel	CAPT RM(IC)	RM		01.05.99	CDO LOG REGT RM
Hastilow, Nicholas, *BA*	LT(CC)	X	P	01.12.94	815 FLT 221
Hatch, Giles William Hellesdon, *pce*	CDR(FTC)	X	PWO(A)	31.12.98	MOD (LONDON)
Hatchard, Peter John, *BSc, jsdc, pce*	CDR(FTC)	X	PWO(C)	30.06.94	COLLINGWOOD
Hatcher, Rhett Slade	LT CDR(FTC)	X	P	01.03.98	815 SQN HQ
Hatcher, Timothy Robert	LT(FTC)	E	WESM	19.02.93	2SL/CNH FOTR
Hattersley, Jonathan Peter George, *LLB, CDipAF (BARRISTER)*	LT CDR(FTC)	S	BAR	01.02.87	2SL/CNH
Hattle, Prideaux	SLT(IC)	X	MW	29.04.98	DRYAD
Haughey, John	SLT(FTC)	MS		01.04.98	NEPTUNE CFS
Havron, Paul Richard	SLT(FTC)	E	WE	01.04.98	COLLINGWOOD
Haw, Christopher Edward, *BSc*	CAPT RM(IC)	RM		01.05.98	40 CDO RM
Hawes, Grace Elaine, *psc*	LT CDR(FTC)	W	C	01.01.91	RHQ AFNORTH
Hawkes, Jonathan Derrick	LT(FTC)	X	PT	23.07.93	NEPTUNE CFS
Hawkins, Catherine Elizabeth, *BA*	LT(IC)	X		01.05.98	CAPT F2(SEA)
Hawkins, Ian	CDR(FTC)	E	AE	31.12.98	DHP BRISTOL
Hawkins, John David, *BSc*	SLT(IC)	X		01.05.98	OCEAN
Hawkins, James Seymour, *pcea*	LT CDR(FTC)	X	O	16.08.98	FONA
Hawkins, Martin Adam Jeremy, *pce, pcea*	LT CDR(FTC)	X	O	01.05.95	CAMPBELTOWN
Hawkins, Richard Culworth, *BA, jsdc, pcea*	CDR(FTC)	X	P	30.06.92	HQ3GP HQSTC
Hawkins, Robert Henry	LT CDR(FTC)	X	MCD	01.10.91	LOAN INDUSTRY
Hawkins, Stuart	SLT(IC)	E	WE	27.01.99	COLLINGWOOD
Hawkins, Shane Robert, *BEng*	LT(CC)	E	WE	01.12.97	CUMBERLAND
Hawley, Stephen Christopher, *BEng*	LT(FTC)	E	ME	01.03.94	LN DERA HASLAR
Haworth, John, *IEng, MIMechIE*	CDR(FTC)	E	ME	30.06.99	CDRE MFP(SEA)
Haworth, Jonathan Hywel Tristan, *BEng*	LT(FTC)	E	WE	01.10.96	SSA ROSYTH
Haworth, Stephen	LT(FTC)	E	WE	18.02.94	CFM PORTSMOUTH
Hawthorn, Emma Maudie, *BA*	LT(IC)	S		01.12.98	700M MERLIN IFTU
Hawthorne, Michael John, *pce, pce(sm), psc(j)*	CDR(FTC)	X	SM	31.12.97	TIRELESS
Hay, James Donald, *BSc*	CDR(FTC)	E	WE	30.06.97	MOD (LONDON)
Hay, Michael, *BEng*	LT(FTC)	E	WE	01.03.98	SHEFFIELD
Hayashi, Luke Ronald, *BSc*	LT(CC)	X		01.04.00	DRYAD
Haycock, John Edward, *psc(m)*	LT COL(FTC)	RM	C	30.06.83	NMA PORTSMOUTH

Name	Rank	Branch	Spec	Seniority	Where Serving
Haycock, Timothy Paul , *pce, pcea, psc*	LT CDR(FTC)	X	O	01.06.94	NEWCASTLE
Hayde, Phillip John , *BSc, MRAeS*	LT CDR(FTC)	X	P	01.10.99	LOAN DERA BSC DN
Hayden, Timothy William , *BSc*	LT(CC)	X	P	01.05.97	814 SQN
Hayes, Brian John	LT(FTC)	X	PT	03.04.98	FONA
Hayes, Claire Louise , *BSc*	LT(FTC)	S		01.09.97	NMA GOSPORT
Hayes, David John	LT CDR(FTC)	MS	(AD)	01.10.90	MOD (LONDON)
Hayes, James Victor Buchanan , *BSc, psc(j)*	CDR(FTC)	E	WESM	31.12.98	DSWS BRISTOL
Hayes, Mark Andrew	SLT(IC)	X		01.01.00	DARTMOUTH BRNC
Hayes, Sean , *BSc*	SLT(IC)	X	O U/T	01.09.97	750 SQN OBS SCH
Hayes, Stuart John , *pce*	CDR(FTC)	X	MCD	30.06.00	LOAN OMAN
Hayle, Elizabeth Anne , *BA*	LT CDR(FTC)	W	X	01.10.98	CINCFLEET
Hayle, James Kenneth	LT CDR(FTC)	S	SM	01.04.96	NEPTUNE CFS
Hayles, Nicholas Clive	LT CDR(FTC)	S	CMA	01.09.87	MOD (LONDON)
Hayman, Paul Stephen	SLT(FTC)	E	WE	09.01.98	NORTHUMBERLAND
Haynes, John William	LT CDR(FTC)	X	PT	01.10.98	TEMERAIRE
Hayton, James , *MB, BA, ChB (Act Surg Lt)*	SURG SLT	-		08.08.96	DARTMOUTH BRNC
Hayton, Stephen	LT(CC)	X	O	05.09.95	824 NAS
Hayward, Andrew Leonard	LT(IC)	X	FC	01.07.97	YORK
Hayward, Clive Edward William , *BA*	LT CDR(FTC)	X	SM	01.06.96	DEF SCH OF LANG
Hayward, Geoffrey	LT(CC)	X	O	16.07.91	EXCHANGE USA
Hayward, Peter James	LT CDR(FTC)	S		01.04.86	RH HASLAR
Haywood, Guy , *pce, pcea*	LT CDR(FTC)	X	P	01.10.95	DRYAD
Haywood, Peter James , *BEng*	LT(CC)	X	P	01.01.94	824 NAS
Haywood, Simon Anthony	LT CDR(FTC)	E	WESM	01.10.94	CSST SEA
Hazelwood, Christopher David	CAPT RM(FTC)	RM	SO(LE)	01.01.00	NMA WHALE ISLAND
Head, Rupert Richmond D Esterre	CDR(FTC)	S		30.06.89	MOD (LONDON)
Head, Steven Andrew , *BEng*	LT(FTC)	E	WE	01.03.93	RMC OF SCIENCE
Head, Stephen Geoffrey , *BEng*	LT(IC)	E	WE	01.03.98	COLLINGWOOD
Headley, Mark James , *BSc*	SLT(IC)	X		01.01.98	CHIDDINGFOLD
Heal, Jeremy Phillip Carlton , *psc*	COL(FTC)	RM		31.12.99	RMB STONEHOUSE
Heal, Tristan Stephen , *MEng*	SLT(IC)	E	WE	01.09.98	ILLUSTRIOUS
Healey, Mark Jon	LT(CC)	E	AE	01.10.99	DARTMOUTH BRNC
Healy, Anthony John	CDR(FTC)	X	EW	31.12.99	RNEAWC
Heames, Richard Mark , *BM*	SURG LTCDR	-		01.08.99	NELSON (PAY)
Heaney, Martin Joseph , *BSc*	LT(CC)	X	O	16.04.97	814 SQN
Heap, Justin Timothy , *BEng*	LT(FTC)	X	SM	01.05.98	SPLENDID
Hearn, Samuel Peter , *BA*	SLT(IC)	X		01.01.98	YORK
Hearnden, Graham Eric , *pce*	LT CDR(FTC)	X	AWO(C)	01.04.79	DRYAD
Heath, Craig William , *MB, ChB, DObstRCOG*	SURG LTCDR	-		01.08.99	JSU NORTHWOOD
Heather, Christopher Vernon Stewart , *TEng*	LT(FTC)	E	WE	29.10.82	COLLINGWOOD
Heatly, Robert Johnston , *MBE, osc(us)*	LT COL(FTC)	RM		31.12.95	LN BMATT SAFRICA
Heaver, David Gerard Verney , *MA, psc(m)*	COL(FTC)	RM		30.06.96	RM POOLE
Hedgecox, David Colin , *BEng*	LT(FTC)	E	WE	01.06.96	RALEIGH
Hedger, Neil Alexander , *MB, BSc, BCh, MRCP, AFOM*	SURG CDR	-	(CM)	30.06.97	RH HASLAR
Hedges, Justin William , *BSc*	CAPT RM(FTC)	RM		01.09.95	RM Poole
Hedworth, Anthony Joseph , *BComm*	LT(IC)	X	P	01.06.94	810 SQN SEAHAWK
Hefford, Christopher John , *BSc*	LT(CC)	S		01.03.97	CAPT IST STAFF
Heighway, Martin Richard , *BSc, MEng, MSc*	LT(IC)	E	TM	01.01.96	NELSON RNSETT
Heirs, Gavin George , *MA*	LT(CC)	X	P	16.12.98	RNAS CULDROSE
Helby, Philip Faulder Hasler , *MBE, BSc, MBA, AMIEE, CDipAF*	LT CDR(FTC)	E	MESM	16.07.82	2SL/CNH
Heley, David Nicolas , *pce*	CDR(FTC)	X	PWO(U)	30.06.00	DRYAD
Heley, Jonathan Mark , *MSc, BEng, CEng, MIMarE*	LT CDR(FTC)	E	MESM	01.11.94	NP BRISTOL
Helliwell, Michael Andrew , *BEng*	LT CDR(FTC)	E	AE	01.05.98	FONA
Helliwell, Martyn Gregory	LT CDR(FTC)	X	AV	01.10.99	SULTAN
Hellyn, David Robert	LT CDR(FTC)	E	WE	01.10.97	PORTLAND
Helps, Adrian Richard , *BEng*	LT(FTC)	E	MESM	01.06.92	NP BRISTOL
Hember, Marcus James Christopher	SLT(IC)	X		01.01.98	ALDERNEY
Hembrow, Terence	MAJ(FTC)	RM	SO(LE)	01.10.97	RMB STONEHOUSE
Hemingway, Ross	SURG SLT	-		20.11.98	DARTMOUTH BRNC
Hempsell, Adrian Michael , *n*	LT(FTC)	X		01.06.94	DRYAD
Hemsworth, Kenneth John , *BEng, CEng*	LT CDR(FTC)	E	ME	01.01.98	MANCHESTER
Hemsworth, Michael Kim , *BSc*	CAPT(FTC)	S		30.06.97	2SL/CNH
Henderson, Andrew David , *LRAM*	CAPT RM(FTC)	BS		01.01.93	HQ BAND SERVICE

Name	Rank	Branch	Spec	Seniority	Where Serving
Henderson, Elizabeth Mary , *BEng*	LT(FTC)	E	AE	01.07.92	ARK ROYAL
Henderson, Iain Robert , *CBE, pce, pcea, psc*	RADM	-	P	06.10.98	JSU NORTHWOOD
Henderson, Peter Philip	LT(FTC)	E	WE	24.02.95	COLLINGWOOD
Henderson, Robert John	LT(FTC)	E	AE(M)	04.09.98	RNAS YEOVILTON
Henderson, Sam Charles , *BA*	SLT(IC)	S		01.01.98	SHEFFIELD
Henderson, Stuart Philip , *BEng, MSc*	LT CDR(FTC)	E	ME	01.03.99	MOD (BATH)
Henderson, Thomas Maxwell Philip , *BSc, pce*	LT CDR(FTC)	X	PWO(U)	01.04.91	DRYAD
Hendrickx, Christopher John , *BEng*	LT(FTC)	E	WE	01.01.96	SSA/CWTA PORTS
Hendy, Laurence Samuel , *BEng*	LT(FTC)	E	WE	28.09.92	COLLINGWOOD
Hendy, Richard	LT(FTC)	S		23.09.97	MOD (LONDON)
Heneghan, John Francis , *BEng, adp*	LT CDR(CC)	E	IS	01.10.97	PJHQ
Henley, Simon Michael , *MBE, BSc, jsdc*	CAPT(FTC)	E	AE	30.06.97	MOD PE USA
Hennell, Nigel Jeffrey , *AFC, pcea*	LT CDR(FTC)	X	P	01.03.80	810 SQN SEAHAWK
Hennessey, Timothy Patrick David , *BSc, pce, psc*	CDR(FTC)	X	O	30.06.93	ELANT/NAVNORTH
Henry, Gavin Paul , *BA*	SLT(IC)	X		01.01.99	DARTMOUTH BRNC
Henry, Mark Frederick , *MB, BCh*	SURG LT	-		06.08.97	RALEIGH
Henry, Timothy Michael	LT(FTC)	X	PWO(A)	01.09.93	WESTMINSTER
Henty, Iain , *BSc, pcea*	LT(CC)	X	O	01.08.86	EXCHANGE RAF UK
Hepburn, John , *BA, LLB, MInstAM, MIMgt*	LT CDR(FTC)	S		01.02.83	CINCFLEET
Hepplewhite, Mark Barrie	LT(CC)	E	AE	01.09.99	DARTMOUTH BRNC
Hepworth, Andrew W D , *BEng*	LT CDR(FTC)	E	IS	01.05.98	HQRM
Herington, Paul Wilfred , *rcds, jsdc, pce, hcsc*	CAPT(FTC)	X	AWO(A)	30.06.92	FOSF (*COMMODORE*)
Heritage, Lee James , *BSc, CEng, MIMarE, psc*	CDR(FTC)	E	ME	30.06.96	KENT
Herman, Thomas Rolf , *OBE, BSc, pce(sm)*	CDR(FTC)	X	SM	30.06.92	FOSM NWOOD OPS
Hermer, Jeremy Peter	CAPT RM(FTC)	RM		01.09.95	NP 1066
Herridge, Peter Gary , *BSc, MA, MRAeS, psc*	CDR(FTC)	E	AE	31.12.95	MOD DHSA
Herriman, John Andrew	LT(CC)	X	MCD	01.04.91	DEF DIVING SCHL
Herring, Jonathan James Auriol , *BSc, MA, psc*	LT COL(FTC)	RM		30.06.98	CTCRM
Heselton, Branden Lawrence , *MA, CEng, MIEE, psc*	CAPT(FTC)	E	WE	30.06.96	MOD (BATH)
Hesling, Gary , *n*	LT(FTC)	X	H2	28.02.94	NP 1008 OFS SVY
Hester, James Francis William , *BA*	2LT(GRAD)(IC)	RM		01.09.99	CTCRM LYMPSTONE
Hett, David Anthony , *BSc, DA, LRCP, FFARCS,*	SURG CDR	-	(CA)	31.12.93	RH HASLAR *MRCS*
Heward, Alan Frank *(Act Maj)*	CAPT RM(FTC)	RM	SO(LE)	01.01.95	RMDIV LECONFIELD
Hewit, Stephanie	*MID*(NE)(IC)	X		01.09.99	DARTMOUTH BRNC
Hewitson, Jonathan George Austin , *BSc*	SLT(IC)	X		01.01.98	BRECON
Hewitt, Antony , *BEng*	LT CDR(FTC)	E	MESM	01.06.95	SPLENDID
Hewitt, David Leslie	LT CDR(FTC)	X	PWO(A)	26.02.96	MWC PORTSDOWN
Hewitt, Ian Rhoderick , *OBE, nadc, jsdc, pce, pce(sm), odc(US)*	CAPT(FTC)	X	SM	31.12.93	SACLANT USA
Hewitt, Lloyd Russell	LT(FTC)	S		01.07.93	RALEIGH
Hewitt, Mark John	SLT(IC)	E	ME	29.04.98	SULTAN
Heyworth, James Edward , *BSc*	SLT(IC)	X		01.09.97	PEMBROKE
Hibberd, Karen Michelle , *BA*	LT(FTC)	X		01.05.97	GLOUCESTER
Hibberd, Nicholas James , *pce(sm)*	LT CDR(FTC)	X	SM	01.11.97	FOSM NWOOD OPS
Hibbert, Martin Christopher	LT CDR(FTC)	X		01.10.96	RM CHIVENOR
Hibbert, Nicola Jane	LT CDR(FTC)	S		29.07.96	RALEIGH
Hibbert, Peter Nigel , *MNI, MInsD, jsdc, pce, pce(sm)*	CDR(FTC)	X	SM	31.12.90	NMA PORTSMOUTH
Hibbert, Richard John Norman , *CBE, CEng, FIMechE, MIMarE, psc (COMMODORE)*	CAPT(FTC)	E	ME	31.12.89	NMA PORTSMOUTH
Hicking, Neil , *BSc*	LT CDR(FTC)	X	METOC	01.10.94	PRESTWICK
Hickman, Simon Michael , *BEd*	CAPT RM(FTC)	RM		01.09.94	CTCRM
Hicks, Anna	SURG SLT	-		22.09.97	DARTMOUTH BRNC
Hicks, Nicholas John Ivatts , *BSc*	LT(IC)	X	SM	01.06.98	TALENT
Hickson, Craig Julian	LT(CC)	X	P	01.04.89	FONA
Hickson, Michael Stuart Harris , *BEng, MRAeS*	LT(FTC)	E	(AE)	01.08.95	EXCHANGE CANADA
Higgins, Andrew John	LT(CC)	X	FC	01.08.95	EXCHANGE RAF UK
Higgins, Godfrey Nigel , *BEng*	LT CDR(FTC)	E	AE	01.11.96	800 SQN
Higginson, Nicholas John , *BEng*	SLT(IC)	X		01.01.98	MARLBOROUGH
Higgs, Robert James *(Act Lt Cdr)*	LT(FTC)	X	C	27.07.90	RHQ SOUTHLANT
Higgs, Thomas Arthur , *BSc*	LT(FTC)	S		01.02.94	RALEIGH
Higham, Anthony , *pce, psc*	CDR(FTC)	X	PWO	30.06.89	SHAPE BELGIUM
Higham, James Godfrey , *BEng, AMIEE*	LT(FTC)	E	WE	01.01.93	T45 IPT
Higham, Stephen William James , *BA*	LT(FTC)	X		01.05.98	CARDIFF
Higson, Beverly Lynn , *BSc, PGDip, MIMA, CMath*	LT(CC)	E	TM	01.01.93	ILLUSTRIOUS

Name	Rank	Branch	Spec	Seniority	Where Serving
Hill, Adrain Jason , *BSc*	LT(CC)	X	O	01.10.96	849 SQN A FLT
Hill, David , *BEng*	LT CDR(FTC)	E	AE	01.03.99	NELSON
Hill, Elizabeth Carol Anne	LT(IC)	S		12.12.91	DRAKE DPL
Hill, Graham Alan , *MB, ChB, FRCS, FRCS(ORTH)*	SURG LTCDR	-	O/S UT	01.08.91	NELSON (PAY)
Hill, George Alexander	LT CDR(FTC)	E	WESM	01.10.98	NMA GOSPORT
Hill, Giulian Francis , *BEng, MSc, MCGI, MIMarE*	LT CDR(FTC)	E	ME	01.01.98	MONTROSE
Hill, John	CHAPLAIN	CE		17.01.94	INVINCIBLE
Hill, Jonathan Paul , *BSc*	CAPT RM(FTC)	RM		01.05.99	42 CDO RM
Hill, Mark Robert , *pcea*	LT CDR(FTC)	X	P	22.06.96	INVINCIBLE
Hill, Nigel George	LT CDR(FTC)	X	MCD	01.10.97	DRYAD
Hill, Philip John , *BEng*	LT CDR(FTC)	E	WESM	01.06.96	DPA BRISTOL
Hill, Richard Andrew	LT CDR(FTC)	X	MW	01.09.95	DRYAD
Hill, Roy Keith John	LT CDR(FTC)	S	CMA	16.02.97	JSCSC
Hill, Simon Patrick , *OBE, MPhil, psc(m) (BRIGADIER)*	COL(OF6)(FTC)	RM		31.12.94	HQRM
Hilliard, Robert Godfrey , *DipTh*	CHAPLAIN	CE		01.08.80	CDRE MFP(SEA)
Hillier, John , *MMus, LRAM, ARCM, pdm*	CAPT RM(FTC)	BS		01.01.90	HQRM
Hillier, Nicholas John , *BSc, CDipAF, nadc, jsdc*	CDR(FTC)	E	WE	30.06.84	LOAN BMATT(EC)
Hills, Anthony Alexander , *pce*	LT CDR(FTC)	X	P	01.12.94	FONA NORTHWOOD
Hills, Ian Edward	LT(IC)	X	P	01.09.97	819 SQN
Hills, Michael John	CHAPLAIN	CE		21.04.98	CDRE MFP(SEA)
Hills, Richard Brian , *BA*	MAJ(FTC)	RM		01.05.99	HQ 3 CDO BDE RM
Hilson, Steven Millar	LT(CC)	X	O	01.10.91	815 FLT 212
Hilton, David , *MNI, psc*	CDR(FTC)	X	MCD	01.10.95	SUPT OF DIVING
Hilton, Simon Thomas , *BEng*	LT(IC)	X	O	01.09.99	849 SQN B FLT
Hinch, David Graham William	LT(FTC)	X	P	01.07.91	899 SQN HERON
Hinch, Neil Eric	LT CDR(FTC)	X	PT	01.10.93	SHAPE BELGIUM
Hinchcliffe, Alan , *BSc*	LT(IC)	X	P	01.03.94	814 SQN
Hinchliffe, Peter Brenton , *OBE, BSc, MNI, pce(sm), psc*	CDR(FTC)	X	SM	30.06.94	VIGILANT(PORT)
Hindmarch, Stephen Andrew , *BA*	LT(CC)	X	P	01.09.96	820 SQN
Hindson, Craig Lee , *BEng*	LT(CC)	E	ME	01.04.94	RALEIGH
Hine, Nicholas William , *pce, pce(sm)*	CDR(FTC)	X	SM	30.06.00	JSCSC
Hinks, Karl James , *BEng, CEng, MIMarE*	LT CDR(FTC)	E	ME	25.08.98	EXETER
Hinton, Lee , *BSc*	LT(IC)	X	ATCU/T	01.09.99	RNAS YEOVILTON
Hinxman, Matthew Alex , *LLB*	SLT(IC)	S		01.09.97	DRYAD
Hipkin, Simon Richard Charles , *BSc*	SLT(IC)	X		01.05.98	MARLBOROUGH
Hipsey, Stephen Jon , *BSc*	LT CDR(CC)	X	METOC	01.10.89	HQ NORTH
Hird, Richard Peter , *BSc*	LT(FTC)	X	MW	01.01.95	BICESTER
Hirons, Francis Durham , *BSc*	LT(CC)	X		01.02.99	DULVERTON
Hirst, Robert Thomas	LT CDR(FTC)	X	SM	01.09.88	DISC
Hirstwood, John	SLT(IC)	X		19.09.98	DRYAD
Hiscock, Fabian Henry , *OBE, BSc, pce, pce(sm)* (*COMMODORE*)	CAPT(FTC)	X	SM	31.12.91	CINCFLEET
Hiscock, Stephen Richard Blackler , *BEng*	LT(FTC)	E	WE	01.05.96	COLLINGWOOD
Hitchings, Deborah Louise , *BA*	LT(IC)	X	FC	01.01.94	DARTMOUTH BRNC
Hoare, Dion Wyn	SLT(FTC)	E	WE	09.01.98	CARDIFF
Hoare, Peter	LT(CC)	X	O	01.05.94	815 FLT 209
Hoath, Moira Elizabeth Jane , *MA, MSc, CEng, CMath, MBCS, MIMA*	CDR(FTC)	W	E	01.10.96	AFPAA(CENTURION)
Hoather, Martin Stephen	LT(FTC)	E	WE	01.10.98	SUTHERLAND
Hobbs, Alan Ronald	LT CDR(FTC)	X	PWO(A)	01.04.93	DPA BRISTOL
Hobbs, Richard , *IEng, MIEEIE*	CDR(FTC)	E	WE	01.10.98	MOD (BATH)
Hobbs, Thomas Peter	MID(UCE)(IC)	E	WE	01.09.99	MARLBOROUGH
Hobson, Charles William Peter , *psc*	COL(FTC)	RM		31.12.98	CDO LOG REGT RM
Hobson, Ian Stuart , *BTech*	LT(FTC)	E	WESM	18.02.94	NEPTUNE SM1
Hobson, Peter , *psc, BA, MSc, FIMgt*	CDR(FTC)	X	HCH	31.12.90	LOAN HYDROG
Hocking, Christopher Bernard , *BA*	LT(FTC)	X		01.03.94	DNR PRES TEAMS
Hocking, Mark John Eldred	SLT(FTC)	E	WE	01.04.98	IRON DUKE
Hockley, Christopher John , *MSc, CEng, MIMarE, psc*	CAPT(FTC)	E	ME	30.06.99	CV(F) IPT
Hockley, Graham Peter , *BSc, CEng, MIMarE, psc*	CDR(FTC)	E	ME	30.06.92	MOD (LONDON)
Hockley, Samantha Leigh	SLT(IC)	X		01.01.98	SOUTHAMPTON
Hodge, Christopher Michael , *MSc*	LT(FTC)	E	MESM	01.09.94	SULTAN
Hodgkins, Jonathan Mark , *pce, pcea, psc(j)*	LT CDR(FTC)	X	O	01.12.92	MOD (LONDON)
Hodgson, Jonathan Richard	SLT(FTC)	E	ME	02.05.97	INVINCIBLE
Hodgson, Richard Stephen , *BSc*	SLT(IC)	X		01.05.97	DRYAD
Hodgson, Timothy Charles , *MBE, BSc, MA, CEng, MIMarE, MIMechE*	CDR(FTC)	E	MESM	31.12.99	JSCSC

Name	Rank	Branch	Spec	Seniority	Where Serving
Hodkinson, Christopher Brian , *BA, pce*	LT CDR(FTC)	X	PWO(A)	01.10.96	CAPT F6 (SEA)
Hodsdon, Robin Euan , *BSc*	CDR(FTC)	E	TM	31.12.90	LOAN OMAN
Hofman, Alison Jayne , *BSc*	LT	Q	IC	26.10.94	MODHU DERRIFORD
Hogan, David , *BSc, CEng, MIEE*	LT CDR(FTC)	E	WE	19.10.90	EXCELLENT
Hogan, Terence *(Act Lt Cdr)*	LT(FTC)	X	AV	15.12.89	MOD (BATH)
Hogben, Andrew Lade	LT CDR(FTC)	X	PWO(A)	01.03.99	GLOUCESTER
Hogg, Andrew	LT(CC)	X	ATC	16.03.96	RNAS CULDROSE
Hogg, Anthony John Marsden , *AFC, pce (COMMODORE)*	CAPT(FTC)	X	P	30.06.91	RNAS CULDROSE
Hogg, Christopher William , *BSc*	LT CDR(FTC)	X	PWO(A)	01.03.97	CAMBRIDGE
Holberry, Anthony Paul , *psc, psc(j)*	CDR(FTC)	E	WE	31.12.94	FOST SEA
Holden, John Lloyd , *BA*	LT(IC)	X		01.11.99	DRYAD
Holden, John Thomas , *TEng, IEng, MIMgt, AMRINA*	LT CDR(FTC)	E	HULL	01.10.94	CNSA BRISTOL
Holden, Neil	LT(CC)	X	MCD	01.04.89	CDRE MFP
Holden, Paul Andrew	LT(FTC)	E	AE(L)	07.09.95	INVINCIBLE
Holden, Robert John	LT CDR(FTC)	X	O	01.10.99	EXCHANGE USA
Holden, Simon David , *BEng*	LT CDR(FTC)	E	AE	24.08.97	815 SQN HQ
Holder, John Michael , *BSc*	LT(IC)	X	P	01.12.97	814 SQN
Holder, Richard John	CDR(FTC)	S	(W)	01.10.94	MOD (BATH)
Holder, Shaun Richard , *MSc*	LT CDR(FTC)	MS	SM	01.10.97	FOSM NWOOD HQ
Holdsworth, Howard William	CDR(FTC)	E	AE	30.06.97	FONA
Holford, Stephen James , *BEng*	SLT(IC)	E	ME	01.05.98	MARLBOROUGH
Holgate, Christopher James	CDR(FTC)	E	ME	31.12.91	2SL/CNH FOTR
Holgate, James Alan	SLT(CC)	X		01.04.00	DARTMOUTH BRNC
Holihead, Philip Wedgwood , *pce, psc(a)*	CDR(FTC)	X	PWO(A)	30.06.93	RNAS YEOVILTON
Holland, John Vallis , *BDS, LDS, FDS, FDS RCS(Eng)*	SGCAPT(D)	-	(COSM)	30.06.93	RH HASLAR
Holland, Nicholas Roy	LT CDR(FTC)	S	(S)	01.10.99	MOD (BATH)
Holland, Simon Martin Walkington , *BSc*	LT(CC)	E	TM	01.05.89	NELSON RNSETT
Holley, Andrew John , *pcea*	LT CDR(CC)	X	P	01.10.95	DHFS
Hollidge, John Howard , *BSc, psc, CEng, FIMarE,*	CAPT(FTC)	E	ME	30.06.98	SUP SHIPS PTSMTH MBIM
Holliehead, Craig Lewis , *BSc*	SLT(IC)	X		01.01.99	DARTMOUTH BRNC
Hollingdale, Ross Alan	SLT(IC)	X	O U/T	01.05.99	DARTMOUTH BRNC
Hollins, Rupert Patrick , *MA*	LT CDR(FTC)	S	BAR	01.12.96	NELSON
Hollis, Christopher , *BEng, AMIEE*	LT CDR(FTC)	E	WE	01.04.97	MARLBOROUGH
Holloway, Jonathan Toby , *BSc, MSc, CEng, MIMechE, jsdc*	CDR(FTC)	E	MESM	31.12.95	MOD (LONDON)
Holloway, Nicholas , *BEM*	CAPT RM(FTC)	RM	SO(LE)	01.01.98	45 CDO RM
Holloway, Steven Andrew	LT(CC)	X		01.10.97	DRYAD
Holmes, Annabel Mary , *BMus*	SLT(CC)	X	ATCU/T	01.09.97	RNAS YEOVILTON
Holmes, Ashley Neil , *BA*	SLT(IC)	X	P U/T	01.01.98	RNAS YEOVILTON
Holmes, Christopher John	MAJ(FTC)	RM	C	01.05.98	HQRM
Holmes, Graham , *pce(sm)*	LT CDR(FTC)	X	SM	01.12.87	MWC PORTSDOWN
Holmes, Jonathan David	LT(FTC)	X	H2	01.07.93	GLEANER
Holmes, Mark Daniel	MID(IC)	X	P U/T	01.04.98	DARTMOUTH BRNC
Holmes, Michael John , *BSc, CEng, MIEE, MIMgt, jsdc (COMMODORE)*	CAPT(FTC)	E	WESM	30.06.94	DSWS BRISTOL
Holmes, Matthew John , *BA*	MAJ(FTC)	RM		01.09.96	JSCSC
Holmes, Paul Stewart , *BDS*	SG LT(D)	-		20.07.98	RALEIGH
Holmes, Robert , *pce, psc(a)*	CDR(FTC)	X	PWO(A)	31.12.95	MWC SOUTHWICK
Holmes, Robert Andrew Gordon , *BEng*	LT(FTC)	E	AE	01.03.95	FONA
Holmes, Rupert Womack , *BEng*	LT CDR(FTC)	E	AE	01.04.95	MOD (BATH)
Holmwood, Mark Alan , *BEng*	LT(CC)	E	ME	01.01.00	SULTAN
Holroyd, Jonathon Edward James , *BSc*	LT(CC)	X	O	16.02.98	820 SQN
Holt, Andrew Frederick , *BSc*	LT CDR(FTC)	X	H CH	01.10.88	MOD (LONDON)
Holt, Justin Sefton , *MA, psc(j)*	MAJ(FTC)	RM	LC	27.08.99	EXCHANGE ARMY UK
Holt, Steven , *pce*	LT CDR(FTC)	X	PWO(N)	01.04.97	CATTISTOCK
Holvey, Paul Jonathan	SLT(FTC)	E	MESM	01.04.98	TALENT
Holyer, Raymond John , *MSc*	CDR(FTC)	MS	(P)	01.10.98	NMA PORTSMOUTH
Honey, John Philip , *BSc, CEng, MIMarE, MIMechE*	LT CDR(FTC)	E	MESM	01.03.88	DRAKE CBS
Honnoraty, Mark Robert , *SM(n)*	LT CDR(FTC)	X	SM	11.01.97	VANGUARD(PORT)
Hood, Cherry Kathleen	LT(IC)	W	S	23.10.92	2SL/CNH FOTR
Hood, Kevin Christopher	LT CDR(FTC)	S		16.01.98	COMUKTG/CASWSF
Hood, Kevin Michael , *BEng*	LT CDR(FTC)	E	MESM	01.04.98	SULTAN
Hood, Matthew John	MAJ(FTC)	RM		25.04.96	45 CDO RM
Hook, David Arnold , *psc(m)*	LT COL(FTC)	RM	C	31.12.97	MOD (LONDON)
Hookway, Brian Charles , *BSc, MEng, PGCE, MA(Ed) (Act Cdr)*	LT CDR(FTC)	E	TM	12.09.79	JSCSC

Name	Rank	Branch	Spec	Seniority	Where Serving
Hoole, Robert John	LT CDR(FTC)	X	MCD	01.03.84	MWC PORTSDOWN
Hooley, Roland George , *BSc*(Eng), *MSc*, *CEng*,	CDR(FTC)	E	ME	31.12.98	ILLUSTRIOUS *MCGI*
Hooper, Gary Peter	LT(FTC)	E	WE	18.02.94	OCEAN
Hooper, Johanna	LT(FTC)	S		01.01.00	CAMBRIDGE
Hooton, Daniel Alexander Spangler Homer	LT(IC)	X		01.07.96	FONA SUPPORT
Hooton, David Richard , *BA*	LT(CC)	X	P	01.12.97	819 SQN
Hope, Karl , *BSc*	LT CDR(CC)	E	IS	01.09.96	FOSM NWOOD HQ
Hope, Mark Roger	LT(FTC)	E	AE(L)	01.07.96	849 SQN HQ
Hoper, Paul Roger , *pcea*	LT CDR(FTC)	X	O	01.10.96	RNAS YEOVILTON
Hopkins, Anthony Edward Tobin , *BSc*	SLT(IC)	X		01.01.99	DARTMOUTH BRNC
Hopkins, Catherine	SLT(IC)	X	ATCU/T	01.05.98	RAF SHAWBURY
Hopkins, Laurence Charles , *pce*, *psc*, *psc(m)* (*COMMODORE*)	CAPT(FTC)	X	P	30.06.91	NELSON
Hopkins, Rhys , *BA*, *BSc*	2LT(GRAD)(IC)	RM		01.09.99	CTCRM LYMPSTONE
Hopkins, Richard Michael Edward	CAPT RM(IC)	RM		01.09.99	RMR TYNE
Hopkins, Steven David	LT(CC)	X	P	16.07.94	848 SQN HERON
Hopley, David Alan , *OBE*, *jsdc*, *psc*	COL(FTC)	RM		31.12.96	RHQ AFNORTH
Hopper, Ian Michael	LT(FTC)	X	MW	09.04.94	RAMSEY
Hopper, Simon Mallam , *BA*, *n*	LT(FTC)	X	PWO(A)	01.02.93	SOMERSET
Hopper, Stephen Owen , *pce*, *psc(j)*	CDR(FTC)	X	PWO(N)	31.12.99	CINCFLEET
Hore, Robert Charles , *psc*	CDR(FTC)	E	ME	31.12.93	MOD (LONDON)
Horn, Peter Barrick , *MBE*, *pce*	CDR(FTC)	X	PWO(A)	30.06.99	PJHQ OSISOSEAS
Horne, Archibald	LT CDR(FTC)	X	C	01.10.99	EXCHANGE CANADA
Horne, Coralie Ann	LT(IC)	S		01.12.99	BEAGLE
Horne, Jason Richard , *SM(n)*	LT(FTC)	X		01.10.95	EXCHANGE AUSTLIA
Horne, Timothy George , *MA*, *MSc*, *pce*, *psc*	CDR(FTC)	X	PWO(A)	30.06.97	JSCSC
Horne, Trevor Kingsley , *MA*, *MRIN*, *ARICS*, *pce*, *psc*	CDR(FTC)	X	H CH	31.12.94	SCOTT
Horner, Patrick Andrew , *pce*	LT CDR(FTC)	X	PWO(A)	01.08.94	CHATHAM
Horrell, Michael Ian , *OBE*, *BSc*, *psc*	CAPT(FTC)	E	ME	30.06.97	MOD (BATH)
Horrocks, Christopher Carl (*Act Lt Cdr*)	LT(FTC)	X	EW	23.07.93	SCU LEYDENE ACNS
Horsley, Alan Malcolm Ronald , *pce*	LT CDR(FTC)	X	PWO(N)	01.07.94	FOST SEA
Horsted, Peter James , *MAPM*, *MSc*, *CEng*, *FIMarE*, *MIMechE*, *MINucE*, *psc*, *Eur Ing*	CAPT(FTC)	E	ME	31.12.96	RCDS
Horswill, Mark Nicholas	LT CDR(FTC)	S		01.08.97	DARTMOUTH BRNC
Horton, James Robert , *BEng*	SLT(IC)	X	P U/T	01.09.98	DARTMOUTH BRNC
Horton, Peter Adam , *BSc*, *MBA*, *CEng*, *MIEE*	LT CDR(FTC)	E	WE	01.01.94	MOD (BATH)
Horton, Simon , *BA*	SLT(IC)	X		01.09.98	DARTMOUTH BRNC
Horwell, Brian Bernard	LT(FTC)	E	WE	13.06.91	MCM1 SEA
Horwood, Neil Anthony	SLT(IC)	S		01.01.99	DARTMOUTH BRNC
Hosker, Timothy James , *MA*, *psc*	CDR(FTC)	S		30.06.92	MOD (LONDON)
Hosking, David Blaise , *MBE*, *MA*, *pce*, *psc*	CDR(FTC)	X	PWO(U)	31.12.94	MOD (LONDON)
Hoskins, Alan Bruce , *BSc*, *CEng*, *MIEE*, *psc*	CDR(FTC)	E	WESM	31.12.88	MOD (BATH)
Hough, Clive Charles	CAPT RM(IC)	RM		29.04.94	CTCRM
Houghton, Philip John , *MA*, *pce*	LT CDR(FTC)	X	PWO(U)	01.07.94	PJHQ
Houlberg, Kristian Anthony Niels , *BM*	SURG LTCDR	-		01.08.99	MODHU DERRIFORD
Houlberg, Kenneth Mark Torben , *pce*, *n*	LT CDR(FTC)	X	PWO(A)	01.11.97	DARTMOUTH BRNC
Hounsom, Timothy Rogers	LT(FTC)	X		01.04.97	WESTMINSTER
Hourigan, Mark Peter	LT(CC)	X	P	16.06.96	846 SQN
House, Nigel Patrick Joseph , *psc*, *jssc*	LT COL(FTC)	RM		31.12.91	2SL/CNH
Houston, Darren John McCaw , *n*	LT(FTC)	X		01.10.93	EXCHANGE NORWAY
Houvenaghel, Ian Michael	CAPT RM(CC)	RM		01.09.98	DRYAD
Howard, Benjamin Peter , *BA*	LT(IC)	X		01.04.98	LEDBURY
Howard, Charles William Wykeham	CHAPLAIN	CE		28.09.82	FEARLESS
Howard, Daniel Gordon , *MIL*	LT CDR(FTC)	X	ATC	01.10.99	RNAS YEOVILTON
Howard, Keith Anthony , *BSc*, *MSc*, *CEng*, *MIMarE*	LT CDR(FTC)	E	ME	01.07.90	FOSF ENG DEVPT
Howard, Neil , *BEng*	LT CDR(FTC)	E	AE	31.10.94	NELSON
Howard, Naomi Avice , *BSc*	LT(IC)	X		01.01.99	BEAGLE
Howard, Nicholas Henry , *BSc* (*Act Lt Cdr*)	LT(FTC)	E	AE	01.06.92	ES AIR BRISTOL
Howard, Oliver Melbourne , *MB*, *BS*, *FRCP*, *OStJ*	SURG CAPT	-	(CM)	31.12.94	NELSON (PAY)
Howard, Peter MacArthy	LT CDR(FTC)	X	P	16.08.96	CAPT D5 SEA
Howard, Richard David	2LT(GRAD)(IC)	RM		29.04.98	42 CDO RM
Howard, Roderick Graeme , *TEng*, *AMIMarE*	LT CDR(FTC)	E	ME	01.10.91	MOD (LONDON)
Howarth, Dillon Wharton , *MSc*, *pce*, *pcea*	LT CDR(FTC)	X	O	01.06.90	RNAS YEOVILTON
Howarth, John	CAPT RM(FTC)	RM	SO(LE)	01.01.00	42 CDO RM

Name	Rank	Branch	Spec	Seniority	Where Serving
Howarth, Stephen Joseph	CAPT RM(FTC)	RM		01.09.99	847 SQN
Howden, Allan James, *pcea*	LT CDR(FTC)	X	P	01.10.89	MERLIN IPT
Howe, Craig Michael, *BSc*	LT(IC)	X	P	01.01.99	RNAS CULDROSE
Howe, Douglas Lawrence	LT CDR(FTC)	E	WE	23.11.81	2SL/CNH
Howe, Julian Peter, *BA*	LT(FTC)	X	FC	01.05.94	BITER
Howe, Paul Alfred, *BSc, MA, psc(j)*	MAJ(FTC)	RM	MLDR	01.05.94	JHQ NORTHEAST
Howe, Scott *(Act Capt Rm)*	LT RM(IC)	RM		01.04.98	CDO LOG REGT RM
Howe, Sarah Elizabeth, *BDS*	SGCDR(D)	-		31.12.98	RNAS YEOVILTON
Howe, Thomas, *BSc*	LT(FTC)	X	SM	01.11.97	VICTORIOUS(STBD)
Howe, Tokunbo Akinlabi Irorunola Olusegun, *BA*	LT(IC)	X		01.12.98	MARLBOROUGH
Howell, Gwynne Evan Daniel, *MB, BS, FRCS, FRCS(ORTH)*	SURG CDR	-	(CO/S)	30.06.98	RH HASLAR
Howell, Henry Roderick Gwynn, *BSc, MSc, PGDip*	LT(CC)	X	METOC	25.09.91	EXCHANGE USA
Howell, Michael	LT CDR(FTC)	S	(W)	01.10.93	CAMBRIDGE
Howell, Michael Alfred, *MB, BS, MA, FRCS*	SURG CDR	-	(CA/E)	30.06.99	RH HASLAR
Howell, Simon Brooke, *pce*	LT CDR(FTC)	X	PWO(A)	01.11.93	ARGYLL
Howells, Gary Russell, *BSc, CEng, MIMarE, adp*	LT CDR(CC)	E	IS	01.10.90	AFPAA(CENTURION)
Howells, John, *BSc*	LT CDR(FTC)	E	TM	01.01.93	EXCHANGE AUSTLIA
Howells, Martin John	LT(FTC)	MS	SM	29.07.94	JSCSC
Howells, Sian Louise, *BEng*	LT(IC)	E	TM	01.05.96	DRAKE CBP(DLO)
Howells, Simon Murray	SLT(FTC)	X	EW	19.09.97	CHIDDINGFOLD
Howes, Francis Hedley Roberton, *BSc, MA, psc*	LT COL(FTC)	RM	MLDR	30.06.96	MOD (LONDON)
Howes, Nicholas James	LT CDR	Q	ACC/EM	01.10.99	MOD (LONDON)
Howick, Stephen William, *MSc, CEng, MIEE (Act Capt)*	CDR(FTC)	E	WE	30.06.87	LN DERA PRTSDWN
Howorth, Georgina Mary Rumney	MID(CC)	X		01.04.98	PENZANCE
Howorth, Keith, *BSc, pce, pcea*	LT CDR(FTC)	X	O	01.12.92	SOMERSET
Hoyle, John Jefferson	LT CDR(FTC)	E	AE(M)	01.10.99	NMA GOSPORT
Hubbarde, Simon David *(Act Lt)*	SLT(FTC)	S	(W)	09.01.98	HQRM
Hubschmid, Spencer Raymond, *BSc*	LT(IC)	E		01.11.99	COLLINGWOOD
Hudson, Andrew Ian	SLT(IC)	X	SM	01.04.98	TRIUMPH
Hudson, Jeremy David, *MA, psc(j)*	MAJ(FTC)	RM	MLDR	01.09.93	HQ 3 CDO BDE RM
Hudson, Jonathan David Piers, *MB, ChB, Dip FFP, (Act Surg Lt Cdr) MRCGP*	SURG LT	-		02.08.95	NELSON
Hudson, Nicholas Graeme, *jsdc, pce*	CDR(FTC)	X	PWO(U)	30.06.91	NMA PORTSMOUTH
Hudson, Peter Derek, *pce*	CDR(FTC)	X	PWO(N)	31.12.95	MOD (LONDON)
Hudson, Peter John, *BA*	LT(IC)	X		01.10.99	DRYAD
Hudson, Philip Trevor	LT CDR(FTC)	X	AV	01.10.96	FONA
Huggett, Clare Louise	MID(UCE)(IC)	E	WE	01.09.99	ILLUSTRIOUS
Huggins, Geoffrey Edward, *BSc, CEng, MIEE*	LT CDR(FTC)	E	WE	15.09.82	MOD (LONDON)
Hughes, Andrew Simon, *MB, BCh, MRCGP*	SURG CDR	-	GMPP	31.12.95	JSU NORTHWOOD
Hughes, Christopher Bryan, *BSc*	LT(IC)	X	O U/T	01.12.99	849 SQN HQ
Hughes, Daniel Colin, *BA*	CAPT RM(IC)	RM		01.09.97	CDO LOG REGT RM
Hughes, David James, *MB, ChB*	SURG LTCDR	-	SM	01.08.99	MODHU DERRIFORD
Hughes, Gareth David, *BEng*	SLT(IC)	E	ME	01.01.99	DARTMOUTH BRNC
Hughes, Gary George Henry	LT CDR(FTC)	X	C	01.10.98	HQ DCSA
Hughes, Gareth Llewelyn, *psc*	LT CDR(FTC)	S		01.05.92	NMA PORTSMOUTH
Hughes, John James, *BEng*	LT(IC)	X	P U/T	01.08.99	DHFS
Hughes, Jon-Paul Hudson	MAJ(FTC)	RM	C	01.09.97	HQRM
Hughes, Mark Jonathan	CAPT RM(FTC)	RM		01.09.95	LN BMATT (CEE)
Hughes, Nicholas David	LT(FTC)	E	ME	01.12.95	SUPT OF DIVING
Hughes, Nicholas Justin, *pce, pce(sm)*	CDR(FTC)	X	SM	31.12.96	SOVEREIGN
Hughes, Paul Antony, *MB, BS, DObstRCOG, Dip FFP, MRCGP*	SURG CDR	-	GMPP	30.06.98	RN GIBRALTAR
Hughes, Peter John, *LVO, pce, psc*	CDR(FTC)	X	PWO(N)†	31.12.87	2SL/CNH FOTR
Hughes, Robert Ian, *BSc, jsdc*	CDR(FTC)	E	WESM	31.12.92	FASM IPT
Hughes, Stephen John, *psc(m)*	LT COL(FTC)	RM		30.06.94	CDO LOG REGT RM
Hughes, Scott Maurice, *BSc*	LT(CC)	X	P	01.12.97	814 SQN
Hughes, Timothy	SLT(FTC)	E	MESM	01.04.98	SPLENDID
Hughesdon, Mark Douglas, *BEng, MSc, AMIEE*	LT CDR(FTC)	E	WE	01.02.98	MONMOUTH
Hugo, Ian David, *pce, pce(sm)*	CDR(FTC)	X	SM	31.12.96	AGRIPPA AFSOUTH
Hulme, Christian Anthony	SLT(IC)	X		01.05.99	DARTMOUTH BRNC
Hulme, Timothy Mark, *BA, pce, pcea*	LT CDR(FTC)	X	O	01.03.97	FOST SEA
Hulse, Anthony William	LT RM(CC)	RM		01.04.98	COMACCHIO GP RM
Hulston, Lauren Marie, *BSc*	SLT(IC)	X	O U/T	01.09.98	DARTMOUTH BRNC
Hume, Charles Bertram, *BSc, CEng, MIMechE*	CDR(FTC)	E	MESM	31.12.91	NEPTUNE SM1
Hume, Kenneth John, *BEng*	LT(IC)	X		01.01.00	RNSOMO

Name	Rank	Branch	Spec	Seniority	Where Serving
Humphery, Duncan , *BEng*	LT(IC)	E	ME	01.06.98	NORTHUMBERLAND
Humphrey, David Roger *(BARRISTER) (COMMODORE)*	CAPT(FTC)	S	BAR	30.06.92	2SL/CNH
Humphrey, Ivor James	LT(FTC)	E	WE	01.03.94	SSA PORTSMOUTH
Humphrey, Ian Robert	SLT(IC)	X		01.04.99	CHIDDINGFOLD
Humphreys, John Illingworth , *MNI, pce(sm)*	CDR(FTC)	X	SM	30.06.94	CSST SEA
Humphreys, Robert James , *pce*	LT CDR(FTC)	X	PWO(A)	01.01.94	PJHQ
Humphries, Graham David	SLT(IC)	X	P U/T	01.05.98	DARTMOUTH BRNC
Humphries, Jason Eric , *n*	LT(CC)	X		01.04.95	CAPT IST STAFF
Humphries, Mark , *MSc*	SLT(IC)	X	P U/T	01.09.97	RAF CRANWELL EFS
Humphrys, James Alan , *BSc, MA, pce, psc*	CDR(FTC)	X	PWO(U)	31.12.93	MOD (LONDON)
Hunkin, David John	LT CDR(FTC)	X	PWO(A)	01.12.99	INVINCIBLE
Hunt, Charles James , *BEng*	LT CDR(CC)	X	METOC	01.10.97	EXCHANGE USA
Hunt, Darren , *MM*	LT RM(IC)	RM		24.01.00	847 SQN
Hunt, Fraser Brain George	LT(CC)	X	P	01.03.96	824 NAS
Hunt, Gerald Clive , *pce (Act Capt)*	CDR(FTC)	X	O	30.06.85	JSU NORTHWOOD
Hunt, Jeremy Simon Paul , *BSc, PGDip*	LT CDR(FTC)	X	METOC	05.02.95	FOSM NWOOD HQ
Hunt, Patrick Edward Robin David	LT(FTC)	E	WE	05.06.92	SSA BRISTOL
Hunt, Patrick Simon , *BEng*	LT(FTC)	E	WE	01.09.99	NORFOLK
Hunt, Stephen Christopher	LT(FTC)	X	O	01.07.94	EXCHANGE RAF UK
Hunt, Stella Sachiko , *BSc*	LT(FTC)	X		01.02.97	RICHMOND
Hunter, Bruce John , *BSc, CEng, MIMarE*	LT CDR(FTC)	E	MESM	01.07.90	CAPTAIN SM2
Hunter, Jeremy Grant , *BA*	CAPT RM(FTC)	RM		01.09.96	CTCRM
Hunter, Kevin Patrick , *BSc, CEng, MIMarE, MIMechE*	LT CDR(FTC)	E	ME	01.08.87	HQRM
Hunter, Nicholas John , *BEng*	LT(IC)	E	TM	01.09.95	SULTAN
Hunter, *N H* (Neil Mitchell) , *QCBA, BSc, pce, pcea*	LT CDR(FTC)	X	P	01.01.94	DARTMOUTH BRNC
Hunter, Toby Charles Graeme , *psc(m)*	LT COL(FTC)	RM		30.06.90	SHAPE BELGIUM
Huntingford, Damian Jon , *BA*	2LT(GRAD)(IC)	RM		02.09.98	42 CDO RM
Huntington, Simon Peter , *BSc, n*	LT CDR(FTC)	X	PWO(U)	01.10.98	CUMBERLAND
Huntley, Ian Philip , *BA, psc(m)*	LT COL(FTC)	RM		30.06.97	JSCSC
Hunwicks, Sarah Elizabeth , *BEng*	LT(CC)	E	AE	01.01.97	ES AIR BRISTOL
Hurford, Peter Giles , *BSc, FIMechE*	CAPT(FTC)	E	MESM	31.12.94	CNNRP BRISTOL
Hurley, Christopher , *BSc*	LT(FTC)	X	MW	01.06.94	JSCSC
Hurley, Karl Antony	LT	Q	ACC/EM	26.05.99	MODHU DERRIFORD
Hurrell, Piers Richard	LT CDR(FTC)	X	PWO(A)	01.07.98	NEWCASTLE
Hurry, Andrew Patridge	LT CDR(FTC)	X	P	01.11.94	FOST SEA
Hurst, Charles Nicholas Somerville	SLT(IC)	X		01.09.98	ATHERSTONE
Hussain, Amjad Mazhar , *MSc, CEng, MIEE, jsdc*	CAPT(FTC)	E	WE	31.12.97	MOD (LONDON)
Hussain, Shayne , *BSc, PhD, PGDip*	LT CDR(FTC)	X	METOC	01.03.99	JSCSC
Hussey, Stephen John , *pce(sm)*	LT CDR(FTC)	X	SM(G)	15.07.93	PJHQ
Hussey, Steven John , *BSc*	MAJ(FTC)	RM	P	01.09.99	AACC MID WALLOP
Hutchings, Justin Robert , *MA*	LT(IC)	X		01.04.99	TALENT
Hutchings, James Stewart	LT(FTC)	E	AE(M)	16.10.92	FONA
Hutchings, Richard Peter Hugh , *BA*	LT(FTC)	X	SM	01.12.97	VICTORIOUS(PORT)
Hutchings, Sam David , *BM, DipIMC RCSED*	SURG LT	-		06.08.97	VICTORIOUS(STBD)
Hutchins, Iain David MacKenzie	LT(FTC)	X		01.09.98	EXETER
Hutchins, Richard Frank , *BEng*	LT(FTC)	E	MESM	01.06.93	SULTAN
Hutchins, Timothy Paul , *BSc*	LT CDR(FTC)	E	AE(P)	01.06.96	NARO GOSPORT
Hutchins, Timothy Simon , *BSc*	LT(CC)	X	O	16.06.96	814 SQN
Hutchinson, Christopher John , *BSc, PGDip*	LT(CC)	X	METOC	01.09.88	ILLUSTRIOUS
Hutchinson, Nicholas James , *BA*	SLT(IC)	X		01.01.99	DARTMOUTH BRNC
Hutchinson, Oliver James Procter	LT CDR(FTC)	X	PWO(A)	01.09.97	INVINCIBLE
Hutchinson, Peter , *IEng, AMIMarE*	LT(FTC)	E	ME	14.06.96	ILLUSTRIOUS
Hutchinson, Philip Ian	CAPT RM(IC)	RM	P	01.09.98	847 SQN
Hutchinson, Timothy James , *BSc, CEng, MIMarE, MINucE*	CDR(FTC)	E	MESM	30.06.91	ASTUTE IPT
Hutchinson, Thomas Stanley	LT CDR(FTC)	S	SM	01.07.83	GANNET
Hutchison, George Bruce , *pcea*	LT CDR(FTC)	X	O	01.02.95	849 SQN B FLT
Hutchison, Paul Gordon , *MSc, CEng, MIMarE*	LT CDR(FTC)	E	MESM	01.05.98	SULTAN
Hutton, Graham , *pcea*	LT(CC)	X	O	01.11.91	849 SQN HQ
Hutton, James Kyle , *psc(m)*	LT COL(FTC)	RM		30.06.97	OCEAN
Hutton, Katharine Denise , *BEd*	LT(CC)	E	TM	01.09.90	EXCELLENT
Hutton, Simon John , *pce*	LT CDR(FTC)	X	SM	01.11.95	RMC OF SCIENCE
Huxford, Stephen , *BSc*	SLT(IC)	X		01.05.98	INVINCIBLE
Huxtable, Barrie James , *BChD*	SG LT(D)	-		22.07.97	42 CDO RM

Name	Rank	Branch	Spec	Seniority	Where Serving
Huynh, Cuong Chuong , *BA*	SLT(IC)	S		01.01.99	DARTMOUTH BRNC
Hyde, Debra Marie , *BSc(Hons)*	SLT	Q	ONC	22.06.96	MODHU DERRIFORD
Hyde, Trevor	LT CDR(FTC)	E	WESM	01.10.94	BDS WASHINGTON
Hygate, Alison Margaret , *BEng*	LT(FTC)	X		01.05.94	PJHQ
Hyland, Roger Alan , *BSc*	LT(FTC)	E	WE	22.02.96	MOD (BATH)
Hyldon, Christopher John , *BSc, jsdc*	CAPT(FTC)	E	AE	30.06.99	HARRIER IPT
Hynde, Claire Louise , *BSc*	SLT(IC)	S		01.09.97	INVINCIBLE
Hynett, William Anthony	LT(CC)	X	P	16.05.95	899 SQN HERON

I

Name	Rank	Branch	Spec	Seniority	Where Serving
Ibbotson, Richard Jeffery , *DSC, MSc, CGIA, pce*	CAPT(FTC)	X	PWO(U)	30.06.97	MOD (LONDON)
Iliffe, David Ian , *BD, MLITT*	LT(IC)	X	O	16.11.98	849 SQN B FLT
Imrie, Peter Blain , DSM	LT(FTC)	X	AV	14.12.90	ILLUSTRIOUS
Ince, David Peter	LT CDR(FTC)	X	MCD	01.12.97	FOST SEA
Inge, Daniel	LT(CC)	X	ATC	01.05.95	RNAS CULDROSE
Ingham, Andrew Richard , *BEng*	LT(FTC)	X		01.09.99	DRYAD
Ingham, Ivan Michael	LT CDR(FTC)	X	PWO(A)	01.05.99	DRYAD
Ingham, Lee-Anne Elizabeth , *LLB*	SLT(IC)	X		01.09.98	INVINCIBLE
Ingham, Nicholas Hampshire	MID(NE)(IC)	X		01.09.99	DARTMOUTH BRNC
Ingham, Phillip Clayton , *pce, psc*	CDR(FTC)	X	PWO(N)	30.06.92	IMS BRUSSELS
Inglis, David John , *BSc*	SLT(IC)	X		01.01.99	DARTMOUTH BRNC
Ingram, Gareth John , *BSc*	LT(FTC)	X	O U/T	01.12.95	702 SQN HERON
Ingram, Richard Gordon , *pce, psc(a)*	CDR(FTC)	X	PWO(A)	30.06.98	CINCFLEET
Instone, Malcolm John , *BA*	LT(IC)	X		01.11.98	SANDOWN
Ireland, Alasdair Robbie , *pce, psc(j)*	CDR(FTC)	X	PWO(A)	30.06.99	GLASGOW
Ireland, John Mitchell	LT(FTC)	E	MESM	15.10.93	MOD (BATH)
Ireland, Philip Charles , *pce*	LT CDR(FTC)	X	PWO(U)	01.03.97	FOSNNI OPS CFS
Ireland, Roger Charles , *MBE, MILT, ACIS*	CDR(FTC)	S	SM	31.12.95	DRYAD
Irons, Paul Andrew	LT CDR(FTC)	X		01.07.97	PJHQ
Irons, Rupert Charles St John , *BSc*	LT(FTC)	X		01.10.95	DRYAD
Irving, David	LT(FTC)	X	C	10.01.00	JSCSC
Irwin, Mark Andrew , *BEng*	LT CDR(FTC)	E	ME	09.01.97	FOSF
Irwin, Stuart Gordon	SLT(IC)	X		01.04.98	SHEFFIELD
Isaac, Philip , *ACIS*	CDR(FTC)	S		31.12.99	COLLINGWOOD
Isbister, Elspeth	SURG SLT			01.08.99	DARTMOUTH BRNC
Issitt, Barry David	SLT(IC)	X		01.01.99	DARTMOUTH BRNC
Issitt, David James , *BA, BSc, jsdc*	CDR(FTC)	E	AE(P)	30.06.90	CINCFLEET
Ives, David Jonathan , *BSc*	SLT(CC)	X		01.01.98	BANGOR

J

Name	Rank	Branch	Spec	Seniority	Where Serving
Jack, Peter John , *adp*	LT CDR(FTC)	S		01.10.97	MOD (LONDON)
Jackman, Andrew Warren , *pce*	CDR(FTC)	X	PWO(C)	30.06.98	MWC SOUTHWICK
Jackman, Richard William , *BSc, psc*	CAPT(FTC)	E	WE	31.12.98	HQ DCSA
Jackson, Andrew Stephen , *BSc, MSc*	LT CDR(FTC)	E	MESM	01.01.97	TRAFALGAR
Jackson, David John , *BEng, MSc*	LT CDR(FTC)	E	AE	01.03.00	ILLUSTRIOUS
Jackson, Gary Kevin , *psc(j), MA*	LT CDR(FTC)	X	REG	01.10.96	EXCELLENT
Jackson, Howard , *BEng*	SLT(IC)	X	P U/T	01.05.98	DARTMOUTH BRNC
Jackson, Ian	LT(CC)	X	SM	01.03.97	SPLENDID
Jackson, Ian Anthony , *BSc*	LT CDR(FTC)	E	ME	01.04.96	2SL/CNH FOTR
Jackson, Michael Anthony , *BEd, FRMS, psc*	LT CDR(FTC)	X	METOC	25.07.84	LN DERA FARN
Jackson, Mark Harding	CHAPLAIN	CE		19.04.83	RNAS YEOVILTON
Jackson, Matthew John Andrew , *MA*	CAPT RM(FTC)	RM		01.09.96	JSCSC
Jackson, Peter , *FBIM, MRIN, pce, pcea, ocds(Pak), psc*	CAPT(FTC)	X	O	31.12.93	*DA* BRIDGETOWN
Jackson, Pamela	SLT(CC)	X		01.09.97	DRYAD
Jackson, Paul Anthony , *MISM*	LT(FTC)	S	(W)	13.12.95	CARDIFF
Jackson, Peter Neil , *BEng, MIEE*	LT CDR(FTC)	E	AE	01.02.99	SULTAN
Jackson, Stuart Harry , *BSc, MBA, MRAeS (Act Cdr)*	LT CDR(FTC)	E	AE	01.07.89	2SL/CNH
Jackson, Stevan Kenneth , *FRGS*	LT CDR(FTC)	MS		01.10.93	CINCFLEET
Jackson, Stephen Michael	LT CDR(FTC)	E	ME	09.02.89	LOAN BMATT(EC)
Jackson, Stephen Norman , *BSc*	LT(IC)	E	TM	01.01.00	COLLINGWOOD
Jackson-Smith, Stuart Paul	SLT(IC)	X	ATC	19.09.98	RNAS CULDROSE

Name	Rank	Branch	Spec	Seniority	Where Serving
Jacob, Andrew William, *BA*	SLT(CC)	X		01.01.98	HURWORTH
Jacobs, Joseph Mark, *MSc*	LT(IC)	X	PU/T	01.12.99	DHFS
Jacobs, Matthew Philip, *BEng*	LT(IC)	E	ME	01.02.98	SOUTHAMPTON
Jacques, Marcus James	LT(FTC)	X	FC	01.07.94	DRYAD
Jacques, Nicholas Adrian	LT(CC)	X	O	01.06.93	815 FLT 216
Jagger, Charles Edward, *BSc, pcea, psc*	LT CDR(FTC)	X	P	16.04.83	FAAIT MAN ORG VL
Jagger, Paul Richard Albert, *MSc, AMIEE*	CDR(FTC)	E	WESM	30.06.95	MOD CSSE USA
Jaggers, Gary George	LT(FTC)	X	O	16.12.94	810 SQN SEAHAWK
Jaini, Andrew	LT(IC)	X		01.10.96	MOD (LONDON)
James, Adam Jon	LT CDR(FTC)	X	HCH	01.10.97	FOST MPV(SEA)
James, Alexander Williams, *BSc*	LT(FTC)	X		01.01.00	RNAS YEOVILTON
James, Christopher, *BSc, CEng, MIMarE, MIMechE*	LT CDR(FTC)	E	MESM	01.06.91	CSST SEA
James, Christopher William, *pce*	LT CDR(FTC)	X	PWO(A)	27.10.93	COMUKTG/CASWSF
James, David Russell, *pce, pcea, psc*	CDR(FTC)	X	O	31.12.94	BDS WASHINGTON
James, Ian, *BChD*	SGLTCDR(D)			09.01.99	RNAS YEOVILTON
James, Katherine Jeanette	LT	Q	CC	26.11.96	RN GIBRALTAR
James, Mark	SLT(FTC)	E	WE	01.04.98	COLLINGWOOD
James, Michael Ashton, *pce, psc (Act Capt)*	CDR(FTC)	X	AWO(C)†	31.12.84	CINCFLEET CIS
James, Paul Edward	LT CDR(FTC)	E	AE(M)	01.10.98	RNAS YEOVILTON
James, Paul Melvyn	CAPT RM(FTC)	RM		01.09.95	40 CDO RM
James, Stuart Alain	MAJ(FTC)	RM		01.09.96	HQBF CYPRUS
James, Timothy Edward, *BEng*	LT(IC)	E	ME	01.04.94	SULTAN
Jameson, Andrew Charles, *LLB, psc(j)*	CDR(FTC)	S	BAR	31.12.98	2SL/CNH
Jameson, Andrew John, *BA*	LT(IC)	E		01.09.98	GLOUCESTER
Jameson, Roger Mark, *BSc*	LT(CC)	X	P	16.07.92	815 FLT 212
Jamieson, Roger Euan, *BSc*	LT(FTC)	X		01.12.95	SHETLAND
Janaway, Paul, *BSc, CEng, MIEE*	LT CDR(FTC)	E	WE	01.10.93	SSA/CWTA PORTS
Janzen, Alexander Nicholas, *BA*	CAPT RM(FTC)	RM		01.09.97	42 CDO RM
Jappy, Gavin William George, *BA*	LT(IC)	X		01.08.97	OCLC ROSYTH
Jaques, David Anthony	LT(CC)	X	O	16.08.92	CMSA UK
Jardine, Darren Scott, *n*	LT(FTC)	X		01.11.95	DRYAD
Jardine, Graham Andrew, *pce, pcea, psc(j)*	CDR(FTC)	X	O	30.06.98	PJHQ
Jarman, Paul	SLT(IC)	E	WESM	27.01.99	COLLINGWOOD
Jarrett, Michael Thomas John, *n*	LT(FTC)	X		01.06.95	DRYAD
Jarvis, David John, *BSc, CEng, MIEE, psc*	CAPT(FTC)	E	WESM	31.12.99	MOD (LONDON)
Jarvis, Ian Lawrence, *BSc, psc*	CAPT(FTC)	E	WE	30.06.97	LN DERA PORTN DN
Jarvis, Lionel John, *MB, BS, LRCP, FRCR, MRCS*	SURG CAPT	-	CPDATE	31.12.99	MODHU PORTSMOUTH
Jarvis, Laurence Richard, *BSc*	LT CDR(FTC)	E	ME	01.05.96	EXETER
Jay, Kenneth George, *MA*	CDR(FTC)	E	AE(P)	31.12.86	LN DERA FARN
Jayes, Neil John	SLT(FTC)	X	REG	01.04.98	2SL/CNH
Jaynes, Peter Robert William, *BSc, CEng, FIMechE, psc*	CAPT(FTC)	E	ME	30.06.99	NBC PORTSMOUTH
Jeffcoat, Stewart Murray, *BA, GradIMA, MIMgt, MDA*	CDR(FTC)	E	ME	31.12.93	FOST SEA
Jefferson, Peter Mark	LT CDR(FTC)	X	O	01.10.96	849 SQN HQ
Jefferson, Toby Simon, *BEng*	LT(FTC)	E	AE	01.02.97	SULTAN
Jeffrey, Ian, *BA, BSc, CEng, MIEE, MIL, nadc, psc*	CDR(FTC)	E	WE	30.06.85	UKMILREP BRUSS
Jellyman, Paul Anthony, *BSc, psc*	CDR(FTC)	X	METOC	30.06.89	2SL/CNH
Jenkin, Alastair Michael Hugh, *BSc, MA, CEng, MIEE, psc(m)*	CDR(FTC)	E	WE	31.12.96	CAPT F6 (SEA)
Jenkin, James Richard Saint Lawrence, *MSc*	LT CDR(FTC)	X	SM	01.05.92	MOD (LONDON)
Jenking-Rees, Damian, *LLB*	LT(IC)	S		01.10.97	RNAS CULDROSE
Jenkins, Alastair Rodney, *BSc*	LT(IC)	X	P	01.12.98	845 SQN
Jenkins, David Gareth, *BSc*	SLT(IC)	X		01.09.98	DARTMOUTH BRNC
Jenkins, Edward James	CAPT RM(FTC)	RM	C	28.04.99	JSCSC
Jenkins, Gwyn	CAPT RM(FTC)	RM		01.09.95	RM Poole
Jenkins, Gari Wyn, *BEng, MSc, gw*	LT CDR(FTC)	E	WE	01.09.95	MOD (BATH)
Jenkins, Ian Francis, *BSc, CEng, MIEE, psc*	CAPT(FTC)	E	WE	31.12.96	MOD (LONDON)
Jenkins, Ian Lawrence, *CVO, MB, BCh, FRCS, OStJ*	SURG RADM	-	CPDATE	13.04.99	2SL/CNH
Jenkins, Robert Christopher, *BSc*	LT(IC)	X	PU/T	01.12.99	DHFS
Jenks, Anthony William Jervis	LT CDR(FTC)	X	HCH	16.04.87	RN HYDROG SCHL
Jenner, Andrew Christopher, *BEng*	LT(IC)	E	TM	16.09.97	SULTAN
Jennings, Matthew Paul, *BTech, MA, MRAeS, pcea, psc*	LT CDR(FTC)	X	P	01.10.89	MOD (LONDON)
Jennings, William, *BEng*	LT(FTC)	E	ME	01.03.95	MOD (BATH)
Jenrick, Martin Frederick	LT CDR(FTC)	X	MCD	01.10.95	SUPT OF DIVING
Jepson, Nicholas Henry Martin	CAPT RM(FTC)	RM	C	01.09.97	HQRM

Name	Rank	Branch	Spec	Seniority	Where Serving
Jermy, Stephen Charles, *BSc, MPhil, pce*	CAPT(FTC)	X	O	31.12.97	MOD (LONDON)
Jermyn, Nicholas Charles, *BA*	CAPT RM(FTC)	RM	LC	01.09.94	COMATG SEA
Jervis, Neil David, *pce(sm)*	CDR(FTC)	X	SM	30.06.99	SHAPE BELGIUM
Jess, Aran Ernest Kingston, *BSc, MPhil*	CAPT RM(IC)	RM		01.09.98	40 CDO RM
Jess, Ian Michael, *MA, MA, MSc, CEng, MIMarE, psc*	CDR(FTC)	E	ME	31.12.94	MOD (LONDON)
Jessiman, Sarah Irene, *BDS*	SG LT(D)	-		20.06.97	DRAKE CBP(CNH)
Jessop, Paul Edward, *BEng, MSc, CEng, MIMechE*	LT CDR(FTC)	E	MESM	01.03.95	TIRELESS
Jewitt, Charles James Bagot	LT CDR(FTC)	S		01.07.96	DRAKE DPL
John, Gareth David, *BSc, CEng, MIEE*	LT CDR(FTC)	E	WE	01.09.92	COLLINGWOOD
John, Michael Leyshon	CDR(FTC)	E	WESM	30.06.91	JSCSC
Johns, Adrian James, *BSc, pce, pcea, psc* *(COMMODORE)*	CAPT(FTC)	X	P	31.12.94	MOD (LONDON)
Johns, Andrew William, *SM(n)*	LT(FTC)	X	SM	01.03.98	RALEIGH
Johns, Leslie Ernest	LT(FTC)	X	REG	23.07.98	NEPTUNE 2SL/CNH
Johns, Michael Glynn, *BSc, pcea*	LT CDR(FTC)	X	O	01.10.99	700M MERLIN IFTU
Johns, Tony, *BSc, MSc, psc*	CDR(FTC)	E	MESM	31.12.95	MOD (BATH)
Johnson, Amanda Constance *(Act Lt)*	SLT(IC)	S		01.05.98	MWC PORTSDOWN
Johnson, Alan David, *BSc*	LT(IC)	X		01.08.97	NOTTINGHAM
Johnson, Alex David, *BSc*	LT(CC)	X	P U/T	01.08.99	RNAS YEOVILTON
Johnson, Alan David	MAJ(IC)	RM		29.05.97	JACIG
Johnson, Anthony Robert	LT(CC)	X	O	16.02.95	815 FLT 217
Johnson, Andrew Stephen, *pce*	CDR(FTC)	X	PWO(A)	31.12.99	CINCFLEET
Johnson, Bryan, *BSc, pce*	LT CDR(FTC)	X	PWO(U)	01.05.88	CNOCS GROUP
Johnson, Chad Colin Burnett, *BEng*	LT(FTC)	E	AE(P)	01.04.94	JSCSC
Johnson, Graham Andrew Halsted, *MB, BSc, BS, DObstRCOG, MRCGP*	SURG LTCDR	-	GMPP	01.08.96	UKSU AFSOUTH
Johnson, Grenville Philip, *MBE, jsdc, pce*	CDR(FTC)	X	MCD	31.12.91	LOAN ABU DHABI
Johnson, Graham Robert, *BPharm (Act Capt)*	CDR(FTC)	X	AWO(C)	30.06.87	HQ DCSA
Johnson, James Charles, *MBE, BEng, CEng, MIEE*	CDR(FTC)	E	WESM	31.12.99	CSST SEA
Johnson, Jeremy David, *BSc*	LT(IC)	E	TM	01.01.98	SULTAN
Johnson, Kevin, *MBE*	SLT(FTC)	S	(S)	09.01.98	RNAS CULDROSE
Johnson, Lee Samuel, *n*	LT CDR(FTC)	X		01.03.00	DRYAD
Johnson, Mark	CAPT RM(IC)	RM		01.09.99	NP 1002 DIEGOGA
Johnson, Michael Anthony, *pce*	CAPT(FTC)	X	G	31.12.91	MOD (LONDON)
Johnson, Michael David, *AIMgt*	LT(FTC)	S	(W)	17.12.93	MOD (LONDON)
Johnson, Michael John	LT(FTC)	E	WE	19.02.93	FOST SEA
Johnson, Mark Ralph Edward, *BSc*	LT(FTC)	X		01.07.98	GRAFTON
Johnson, Peter Richard, *FFA, MIMgt, MIPD*	LT CDR(FTC)	S		01.11.83	RM BICKLEIGH
Johnson, Paul Raymond, *BEng*	LT(CC)	E	AE	01.02.99	820 SQN
Johnson, Scott	LT(IC)	X	SM	01.09.99	TRIUMPH
Johnson, Symon Roger David	LT(CC)	X	P	01.07.96	848 SQN HERON
Johnson, Voirrey	LT	Q		25.01.96	RH HASLAR
Johnston, Alan George, *BEng*	SLT(IC)	E	WE	01.09.99	GLASGOW
Johnston, Charles Gardner, *MB, BCh, BAO, FFARCS, FFARCSI* *(Act Surg Capt)*	SURG CDR	-	(CA)	31.12.87	MODHU DERRIFORD
Johnston, Gavin Stewart, *MA*	LT(IC)	X	P	01.04.99	MOD (LONDON)
Johnston, James Angus, *BEng*	LT(FTC)	X	SM	01.01.96	RALEIGH
Johnston, Richard Patrick, *MB, BS, DipAvMed, MRCP, AFOM*	SURG CDR	-	(CO/M)	30.06.97	RNAS CULDROSE
Johnston, Timothy Alan, *pce, pcea*	LT CDR(FTC)	X	P	01.06.95	HURWORTH
Johnstone, Clive Charles Carruthers, *BA, BSc, pce*	CDR(FTC)	X	PWO(A)	31.12.97	MOD (LONDON)
Johnstone, Ian Stuart, *BSc, CEng, MRAeS, adp*	LT CDR(FTC)	E	AE	01.04.89	IMS BRUSSELS
Johnstone-Burt, Charles Anthony, *OBE, MA, pce,*	CAPT(FTC)	X	P	31.12.97	DRYAD *pcea*
Joll, Simon Mark, *BA*	LT(FTC)	S	SM	01.10.93	RALEIGH
Jolliffe, Graham Edward, *BSc*	LT CDR(FTC)	E	AE	01.08.90	JHCHQ
Jolly, John Edward Ian *(Act Cdr)*	LT CDR(FTC)	X	HCH	16.12.84	LOAN OMAN
Jones, Anthony, *psc*	CDR(FTC)	S		31.12.91	ELANT/NAVNORTH
Jones, Alun David, *BA, pcea*	LT CDR(FTC)	X	P	01.11.97	815 FLT 203
Jones, Adam Edward, *BEng*	LT(FTC)	X	P	01.12.94	845 SQN
Jones, Alan Frank, *MSc*	LT(CC)	E	TM	01.09.91	2SL/CNH FOTR
Jones, Anthony William, *BSc*	LT CDR(FTC)	E	WE	01.07.77	2SL/CNH FOTR
Jones, Barry Andrew, *BSc, pcea*	LT CDR(FTC)	X	P	01.10.91	FONA SEAHAWK
Jones, Bryn Sherwood, *BSc*	LT CDR(FTC)	X	PWO(U)	16.11.81	DRYAD
Jones, Craig Anthony, *n*	LT CDR(FTC)	X	PWO(C)	01.11.99	FEARLESS

Name	Rank	Branch	Spec	Seniority	Where Serving
Jones, Christopher	SLT(IC)	E	WE	27.01.99	COLLINGWOOD
Jones, Carolyn Jane	LT(IC)	S		28.04.95	FONA
Jones, Collin Raymond	LT(CS)	-		08.01.99	DNR MANW
Jones, David Allen	LT CDR(FTC)	E	MESM	01.10.99	SULTAN
Jones, David Bryan, *MSc, AMIMechE*	LT CDR(FTC)	E	MESM	01.07.99	SUPERB
Jones, David Clement, *BSc*	LT CDR(FTC)	E	MESM	01.06.91	FOSM NWOOD HQ
Jones, Derrick John	SLT(IC)	X	SM	01.04.98	TRAFALGAR
Jones, David Lloyd, *BTech*	LT(FTC)	E	WE	24.02.95	FOSF
Jones, David Leonard, *BEM*	CAPTCS)RM	-		16.10.88	DNR RCHQ SOUTH
Jones, David Michael, *BEng, AMIEE*	LT(FTC)	E	WE	01.07.96	SOUTHAMPTON
Jones, Ernest John	LT CDR(FTC)	X	AV	01.10.98	FOST FTG SEA
Jones, Gareth David, *BSc*	LT(CC)	E	TM	01.09.91	NELSON
Jones, Gary James	CAPT RM(FTC)	RM	SO(LE)	01.01.97	HQ 3 CDO BDE RM
Jones, Glyn Robert, *MA, pce*	LT CDR(FTC)	X	METOC	01.09.95	MOD (LONDON)
Jones, Huw Ashton, *BSc, MSc*	LT CDR(FTC)	E	MESM	01.03.94	CNNRP BRISTOL
Jones, Ian Michael, *BEng*	LT(CC)	E	AE	01.11.99	SULTAN
Jones, Jenny, *BA*	LT(IC)	X		01.05.97	DRYAD
Jones, Lyndsey Helan, *BEng*	LT()	E	WE	14.02.99	NELSON RNSETT
Jones, Michael	LT CDR(FTC)	X	PWO(A)	01.03.95	DRYAD
Jones, Mark Andrew	LT(FTC)	S	(W)	10.12.98	EXCELLENT
Jones, Martin Clifford, *BSc, n*	LT CDR(FTC)	X	H CH	01.10.93	MOD (LONDON)
Jones, Martin David, *BA*	LT(FTC)	X	FC	01.01.95	LEEDS CASTLE
Jones, Mark Douglas, *BEng*	LT(CC)	X	O	16.01.95	815 FLT 239
Jones, Mark Roger	SLT(CC)	E	WE	01.04.98	DARTMOUTH BRNC
Jones, Matthew Russell, *BA*	MAJ(FTC)	RM		01.09.98	CTCRM
Jones, Matthew Robert, *BSc*	SLT(IC)	X		01.01.99	DARTMOUTH BRNC
Jones, Nigel Patrick	LT CDR(FTC)	X	SM	01.02.99	TRIUMPH
Jones, Nikki Sarah	SLT(IC)	S		01.04.98	WESTMINSTER
Jones, Paul, *pce*	LT CDR(FTC)	X	PWO(A)	01.07.92	CDRE MFP
Jones, Philip Andrew, *MA, jsdc, pce*	CAPT(FTC)	X	PWO(C)	31.12.99	COVENTRY
Jones, Paul Andrew	SLT(FTC)	E	WE	09.01.98	YORK
Jones, Paul David	LT(CC)	X	SM	01.11.95	VICTORIOUS(PORT)
Jones, Peter Haydn, *OBE, jsdc (Act Capt)*	CDR(FTC)	X	H CH	30.06.89	DA BRUNEI
Jones, Paul Ivan	LT(CC)	X	P	01.09.94	702 SQN HERON
Jones, Richard James, *BSc*	SLT(IC)	X		01.09.97	DRYAD
Jones, Richard John, *BA*	SLT(IC)	X		01.05.98	GLASGOW
Jones, Russell Keenan, *IEng, MIEE*	LT(FTC)	E	MESM	19.06.98	SPARTAN
Jones, Richard Oliver	SLT(IC)	X		01.04.99	COTTESMORE
Jones, Robert Peter Martyn, *BSc*	2LT(UCE)(FTC)	RM		02.09.98	CTCRM LYMPSTONE
Jones, Roderick Vernon	LT(FTC)	E	ME	14.06.96	FOST MPV(SEA)
Jones, Richard William, *BSc, MSc, CEng, MIMarE*	LT CDR(FTC)	E	ME	01.03.93	FOSF
Jones, Samantha Ann, *BA*	LT(CC)	X		01.11.97	NORFOLK
Jones, Simon Sean	SLT(FTC)	X	AV	01.04.98	RNAS YEOVILTON
Jones, Timothy	SLT(FTC)	MS		18.09.98	DRAKE CBS
Jones-Thompson, Michael John	SLT(FTC)	X		01.04.98	SHETLAND
Jordan, Andrew Aidan, *BA, n*	LT(FTC)	X	PWO(U)	01.09.93	CORNWALL
Jordan, Anna Frances, *LLB*	LT(FTC)	X		01.01.99	ORWELL
Jordan, Adrian Mark, *BDS, LDS RCS(Eng)*	SGCDR(D)	-		31.12.98	NELSON (PAY)
Jordan, Craig, *BEng, MSc*	LT(IC)	E	TM	01.01.95	DISC
Jordan, Louis *(Act Lt Cdr)*	LT(FTC)	E	ME	18.06.93	LIVERPOOL
Jordan, Mark David, *BSc*	SLT(IC)	E	WE	01.05.98	DARTMOUTH BRNC
Jordan, Nicholas Stuart	LT CDR(FTC)	E	WE	01.10.98	MOD (BATH)
Jordan, Peter David, *BEng*	LT CDR(FTC)	E	MESM	01.12.95	MOD (LONDON)
Jose, Steven, *BA*	LT(FTC)	E	P U/T	01.03.94	815 FLT 217
Joyce, David Andrew, *BEng, MSc, CEng, MIEE*	LT(FTC)	E	WE	01.12.92	COLLINGWOOD
Joyce, Philip, *BSc, psc(j)*	MAJ(FTC)	RM		25.04.98	MOD (LONDON)
Joyce, Thomas Jeremy	LT CDR(FTC)	X	P	01.11.99	815 FLT 244
Joyner, Adam, *pce, pcea*	LT CDR(FTC)	X	P	01.05.89	RNAS YEOVILTON
Juckes, Martin Anthony	LT(FTC)	E	AE(L)	01.07.92	ES AIR BRISTOL
Judd, Simon Alexander	LT CDR(FTC)	X	P	01.10.96	848 SQN HERON
Julian, Timothy Mark	LT(CC)	X	P	16.11.92	820 SQN

Name	Rank	Branch	Spec	Seniority	Where Serving

K

Name	Rank	Branch	Spec	Seniority	Where Serving
Kadinopoulos, Benjamin Alexander	MID(UCE)(FTC)	E	WE	01.09.98	DARTMOUTH BRNC
Karsten, Thomas Michael, *BA, jsdc, pce*	CDR(FTC)	X	PWO(U)	31.12.94	FOSF SEA PTSMTH
Kassapian, David Lee, *BA*	MAJ(FTC)	RM		01.09.97	EXCHANGE NLANDS
Kay, Paul Stuart	SLT(FTC)	X	SM	01.04.98	SOVEREIGN
Kearney, Paul Leonard, *BDS*	CAPT RM(FTC)	RM		27.04.96	HQ 3 CDO BDE RM
Kearney, Thomas Mark, *BSc*	SLT(IC)	X		01.01.99	DARTMOUTH BRNC
Keay, Howard, *BA(OU), MA, FBIM, FIMgt, pce, pce(sm), psc*	CAPT(FTC)	X	SM	30.06.94	ACDS(POL) USA
Keble, Kenneth Wayne Latimer, *jsdc, pce, pcea*	CDR(FTC)	X	O	31.12.95	FOST DPORT SHORE
Keefe, Patrick Charles, *BSc*	CDR(FTC)	S		31.12.95	MOD (LONDON)
Keefe, Sally-Anne, *BA*	LT CDR(FTC)	W	S	30.04.92	DEF SCH OF LANG
Keegan, William John, *BSc, CEng, MIEE, psc*	CAPT(FTC)	E	WE	31.12.98	DLO LONDON
Keeley, Stephen Peter	LT(FTC)	E	MESM	15.06.95	TORBAY
Keen, Neil, *BEng, AMIEE*	LT(FTC)	E	WE	01.06.93	SSA BRISTOL
Keeping, Daniel James, *BEng*	SLT(IC)	X	P U/T	01.09.97	RAF CRANWELL EFS
Kehoe, Anthony Desmond	SURG LT	-		01.12.95	45 CDO RM
Keillor, Stuart James	MID(NE)(IC)	X		01.09.99	DARTMOUTH BRNC
Keith, Benjamin Charles, *BSc*	SLT(CC)	X	P U/T	01.09.97	RNAS YEOVILTON
Keith, Donald, *BD, MA*	CHAPLAIN	SF		15.05.84	COMACCHIO GP RM
Kelbie, Ewan, *BA, pce, pcea*	LT CDR(FTC)	X	P	01.11.93	JSCSC
Kellett, Andrew, *BEng*	LT(FTC)	E	ME	01.02.95	DARTMOUTH BRNC
Kellow, Stephen John	LT CDR(FTC)	E	WESM	01.10.98	RALEIGH
Kelly, Anthony Paul *(Act Maj)*	CAPT RM(FTC)	RM	SO(LE)	01.01.96	40 CDO RM
Kelly, Grant Jason, *BA, MSc*	LT(IC)	E	TM	01.09.96	COLLINGWOOD
Kelly, Howard Clifton	LT(FTC)	E	MESM	01.04.94	NEPTUNE SM1
Kelly, John Anson, *BEng*	LT CDR(FTC)	E	ME	01.02.00	EXCHANGE CANADA
Kelly, Joseph	CHAPLAIN	RC		07.09.97	CAPT F6 (SEA)
Kelly, Martin Dominic Richard	LT CDR(FTC)	S		01.04.85	EXCELLENT
Kelly, Nigel	CHAPLAIN	CE		26.05.92	FOST SEA
Kelly, Philip Michael, *BEng, MSc*	CAPT RM(FTC)	RM	P	01.09.96	RNAS YEOVILTON
Kelly, Richard, *pce(sm)*	LT CDR(FTC)	X	SM	03.04.91	CNSA BRISTOL
Kelly, Simon Peter, *BA*	SLT(FTC)	X		01.05.97	NEWCASTLE
Kelly, Thomas	LT(FTC)	X	MCD	16.12.94	NELSON
Kelly, Thomas James, *BA*	2LT(GRAD)(IC)	RM		02.09.98	45 CDO RM
Kelynack, Mark Trevellyan	LT(CC)	X	O	16.04.95	810 SQN SEAHAWK
Kemp, Alexander Charles	LT RM(IC)	RM		01.04.99	EXCHANGE ARMY UK
Kemp, Michael Stanley	LT CDR(FTC)	E	AE(M)	01.10.95	819 SQN
Kemp, Peter John	MAJ(FTC)	RM	MLDR	01.09.98	EXCHANGE NLANDS
Kempsell, Ian, *BSc, CEng, MIMarE*	LT CDR(FTC)	E	ME	26.06.96	GLOUCESTER
Kendrick, Alexander Michael, *BEng*	LT(FTC)	E	WE	01.02.97	MANCHESTER
Kenealy, Timothy Michael	LT CDR(FTC)	X	PT	01.10.92	PRESIDENT
Kennaugh, Alastair John, *BSc, PGCE, psc*	CDR(FTC)	E	TM	31.12.88	SULTAN AIB
Kenneally, Sean Joseph	CAPT RM(FTC)	RM	SO(LE)	01.01.00	RM Poole
Kennedy, Angelina, *LLB*	LT(IC)	S		08.01.98	CAMPBELTOWN
Kennedy, Ian, *BEng*	LT(FTC)	E	WESM	01.07.97	SPLENDID
Kennedy, Inga	LT CDR	Q		31.03.97	RE ENTRY(RN)
Kennedy, Ian James Andrew, *BEng*	LT CDR(FTC)	E	ME	01.08.95	MOD (BATH)
Kennedy, Nigel Henry, *BSc, MIMarE, psc*	LT CDR(FTC)	E	ME	01.05.92	MOD (BATH)
Kennedy, Roger John, *BEng*	LT(CC)	X	O	01.07.99	849 SQN A FLT
Kenney, Ronald Paul	LT CDR(FTC)	MS		01.10.97	RN GIBRALTAR
Kennington, Lee Alexander, *BSc*	LT(CC)	X	O	01.05.94	819 SQN
Kenny, Stephen James, *pce*	CDR(FTC)	X	PWO(A)	31.12.97	EXCHANGE USA
Kent, Alan James, *BA*	LT(CC)	X	O	16.06.94	815 FLT 204
Kent, Isabel Maria, *BEd*	LT CDR(FTC)	W	X	01.10.96	NELSON
Kent, Martin David, *pce*	LT CDR(FTC)	X	PWO(N)	01.05.89	EXCHANGE AUSTLIA
Kent, Matthew John	SLT(IC)	E	ME	01.05.98	DARTMOUTH BRNC
Kenward, Peter David, *BSc, MA, CEng, MRAeS, psc*	CDR(FTC)	E	AE(P)	30.06.95	INVINCIBLE
Kenworthy, Richard Alan	MAJ(FTC)	RM		30.04.98	CDO LOG REGT RM
Kenyon, Carolyn Marie, *LLB*	SLT(IC)	S		01.05.98	RICHMOND
Keogh, Joanna Mary Elizabeth, *MB, BS*	SURG LT	-		04.08.99	CFLT MED(SEA)
Kerchey, Stephen John Victor, *BSc, MIEE, (Act Cdr)*	LT CDR(FTC)	E	WE	20.01.91	MOD (BATH)
Kern, Alastair Seymour	CAPT RM(FTC)	RM		01.09.94	42 CDO RM

Name	Rank	Branch	Spec	Seniority	Where Serving
Kerr, Adrian Nicholas , *BEng, AMIEE*	LT(FTC)	E	WESM	01.01.93	ASTUTE IPT
Kerr, Alan Thomas Frederick	LT(FTC)	X	MW	06.04.95	FOST MPV(SEA)
Kerr, Jack (*Act Lt Cdr*)	LT(FTC)	X	PR	17.12.93	INVINCIBLE
Kerr, Mark William Graham , ADC, *BA, pce, psc (COMMODORE)*	CAPT(FTC)	X	PWO	31.12.93	DARTMOUTH BRNC
Kerr, William Malcolm McTaggart	LT CDR(FTC)	X	MCD	09.03.90	EXCHANGE CANADA
Kershaw, Christopher Robert , *MB, BCh, ChB, MA, DCH, LRCP, FRCP, MRCS*	SURG CDR	-	(CC)	30.06.85	RH HASLAR
Kershaw, Damian James Edward , *MB, BS*	SURG LT			06.08.97	VANGUARD(PORT)
Kershaw, Richard	SURG SLT			29.06.98	DARTMOUTH BRNC
Kershaw, Steven	LT CDR(FTC)	E	WESM	01.11.96	TIRELESS
Kerslake, Richard William	LT CDR(FTC)	X	P	01.02.99	LIVERPOOL
Kerwood, Richard John	LT(FTC)	S	CA	25.07.91	MOD (BATH)
Kessler, Mark Lance	LT CDR(CC)	X	MCD	01.10.97	EXCHANGE CANADA
Ketteringham, Michael John , *BA, n*	LT(FTC)	X		01.03.94	DRYAD
Kettle, Richard Andrew , *BA*	MAJ(FTC)	RM		24.04.99	EXCHANGE FRANCE
Kewley, Ian David , *BA*	LT(CC)	X		01.08.98	LEEDS CASTLE
Key, Benjamin John , *BSc, pce*	CDR(FTC)	X	O	31.12.99	DRYAD
Key, David Frank , *pce, pcea (Act Cdr)*	LT CDR(FTC)	X	P	01.11.91	OCEAN
Khan, Liaqat Ali , *BSc*	LT(IC)	X		01.09.99	SANDOWN
Khan, Mansoor	SURG SLT	-		07.01.98	DARTMOUTH BRNC
Kidd, Clive John Charles , *Eur Ing, BSc, CEng, MIEE*	LT CDR(FTC)	E	WE	01.12.82	SCU LEYDENE ACNS
Kidd, James Christian , *MSc, CDipAF, psc, gw*	CAPT(FTC)	E	WE	30.06.99	T45 IPT
Kidner, Peter Jonathan , *BSc, CEng, FRAeS, psc, psc(m) (COMMODORE)*	CAPT(FTC)	E	AE	31.12.93	SULTAN
Kierstan, Simon Janusz James , *BEng*	SLT(IC)	X	O U/T	01.09.97	750 SQN OBS SCH
Kies, Lawrence Norman , *BSc, PGCE*	LT(CC)	E	TM	01.01.94	CDO LOG REGT RM
Kilby, Stewart Edward , *pce, pcea, psc(j)*	LT CDR(FTC)	X	O	01.04.96	PENZANCE
Kilgour, Niall Stuart Roderick , *pce, pce(sm), psc (COMMODORE)*	CAPT(FTC)	X	SM	30.06.92	COMATG SEA
Kilmartin, Andrew , *BSc*	LT(IC)	E	ME	01.09.99	SULTAN
Kimberley, Robert , *BSc, n*	LT CDR(FTC)	X	PWO(U)	01.07.98	ARGYLL
Kimmons, Michael , *BA*	CAPT(FTC)	S		30.06.97	MOD (LONDON)
King, Anthony Michael , *BSc, MDA, CEng, MRAeS*	CDR(FTC)	E	AE(P)	31.12.91	FONA
King, Antony Richard , *gdas*	LT(CC)	X	O	01.03.92	LN DERA MALVERN
King, Charles Edward William , *BA, MILT, jsdc*	CDR(FTC)	S		30.06.96	NMA PORTSMOUTH
King, David Christopher Michael , *BSc, psc(j)*	MAJ(FTC)	RM		01.09.96	45 CDO RM
King, Dean Stewart	LT(FTC)	E	WE	22.02.96	DCSA RADIO FAS
King, Edward Michael , *BSc, MSc, CEng, MIEE, gw*	CDR(FTC)	E	WE	31.12.96	MOD (LONDON)
King, Gordon Charles	LT(FTC)	E	MESM	14.06.96	SCEPTRE
King, John Nicholas Gaunt , *BSc, pce*	CDR(FTC)	X	PWO(U)	30.06.97	CAPTAIN RNP TEAM
King, Nigel Alan , *pcea, psc(m)*	LT CDR(FTC)	X	P	01.12.84	RAF HANDLING SQN
King, Nicholas William , *BEng, MSc*	LT CDR(FTC)	E	MESM	01.05.97	SCEPTRE
King, Paul Christopher , *BSc, MSc*	LT CDR(FTC)	E	ME	01.09.92	SULTAN
King, Richard James , *BSc, pcea*	LT CDR(FTC)	X	P	01.10.99	771 SK5 SAR
King, Richard John , *BSc (Act Maj)*	CAPT RM(FTC)	RM		28.04.95	45 CDO RM
King, Richard William , *BSc, pce, pcea*	LT CDR(FTC)	X	P	16.09.92	846 SQN
King, Steven John	LT(CC)	X	P	16.06.92	810 SQN SEAHAWK
King, William Robert Charles , *BSc*	SLT(IC)	X		01.09.98	WESTMINSTER
King, William Thomas Poole , *BEng*	SLT(IC)	X		01.09.99	DARTMOUTH BRNC
Kingdom, Mark Andrew , *BEng*	LT(CC)	E	AE	01.02.97	HARRIER IPT
Kingdon, Simon	SLT(IC)	S		27.01.99	DARTMOUTH BRNC
Kings, Simon John Nicholson , *MBE, pce, pcea*	CDR(FTC)	X	PWO(A)	30.06.98	EDINBURGH
Kingsbury, James Arthur Timothy , *BSc (BARRISTER)*	LT CDR(FTC)	S	BAR	01.02.91	2SL/CNH
Kingsbury, Simon Hugh , *BEng, MSc, AMIEE*	LT CDR(FTC)	E	WE	01.04.96	DRAKE CFM
Kingwell, John Matthew Leonard , *BA, pce*	CDR(FTC)	X	PWO(U)	30.06.99	JSCSC
Kirby, Stephen Redvers , *BSc, MA, pce, pcea, psc, ocds(USN)*	CAPT(FTC)	X	O	30.06.98	MOD (LONDON)
Kirk, Adrian Christopher , *BEng*	LT(FTC)	E	AE	01.05.97	845 SQN
Kirk, Trevor Leslie , *BSc, psc*	LT CDR(FTC)	E	WE	01.06.87	OSG BRISTOL
Kirkbright, Keith Leslie Mellor	LT(CS)	-		17.02.91	DNR WROUGHTON
Kirkham, Simon Philip	LT(IC)	X	P	16.08.94	INVINCIBLE
Kirkpatrick, John , *OBE, BSc, AMIEE, jsdc*	CAPT(FTC)	E	WESM	31.12.95	TORPEDO IPT
Kirkup, John Paul , *BSc, psc(j)*	LT CDR(FTC)	E	TM	01.03.94	SULTAN
Kirkwood, James Alistair Delange , *LLB, pce*	LT CDR(FTC)	X	PWO(A)	01.04.90	LOAN BMATT(EC)
Kirkwood, Tristram Andrew Harry , *BSc*	LT(FTC)	X	P	01.11.94	RNAS CULDROSE
Kirwan, John	SLT(IC)	S		27.01.99	DARTMOUTH BRNC
Kissane, Robert Edward Thomas , *BEng, MSc*	LT CDR(FTC)	E	WE	01.04.97	MANCHESTER

Name	Rank	Branch	Spec	Seniority	Where Serving
Kitchen, Bethan , *BEng*	SLT(IC)	E	AE	01.09.97	CORNWALL
Kitchen, Stephen Anthony , *BEng*	LT CDR(FTC)	E	AE(P)	01.01.98	NARO GOSPORT
Kitt, Robert George	LT(FTC)	E	WE	01.09.99	CORNWALL
Kitteridge, Daniel James , *BA*	LT(IC)	X	P U/T	01.01.00	DHFS
Klidjian, Michael Jeffrey , *BSc*	SLT(IC)	X		01.05.98	MONMOUTH
Knibbs, Mark , *BA, pce, psc(j)*	CDR(FTC)	X	PWO(U)	30.06.99	JSCSC
Knight, Alastair Cameron Fergus , *BSc*	LT(IC)	X	P	01.03.94	810 SQN SEAHAWK
Knight, Andrew Robert	LT(FTC)	X	P	01.10.90	810 SQN B FLIGHT
Knight, Anthony William , *BSc, pce*	LT CDR(FTC)	X	PWO(C)	01.02.90	T45 IPT
Knight, Damon Ashley , *pce*	LT CDR(FTC)	X	PWO(A)	01.04.92	CNOCS GROUP
Knight, David John , *psc, rcds*	CDR(FTC)	S		31.12.89	RCDS
Knight, Diane Joy	LT	Q	IC	18.01.94	UKSU IBERLANT
Knight, Daniel Simon , *BSc*	SLT(FTC)	X		01.09.97	DRYAD
Knight, David William , *BSc*	LT(FTC)	X	PWO(A)	01.06.93	LANCASTER
Knight, Emma , *MB, ChB*	SURG LT	-		05.08.98	CFLT MED(SEA)
Knight, Jeremy Denis	LT(FTC)	X	EW	13.12.95	ILLUSTRIOUS
Knight, Keith John , *BTech*	LT(FTC)	E	WESM	24.02.95	MOD (BATH)
Knight, Matthew Richard , *BA*	LT(IC)	X	P	01.01.99	FONA SULTAN
Knight, Paul James , *BSc, psc(j)*	LT CDR(FTC)	E	AE	01.05.97	846 SQN
Knight, Paul Richard , *BSc, psc*	LT CDR(FTC)	E	MESM	01.09.93	SULTAN
Knight, Robert Harry	LT(FTC)	E	MESM	15.06.95	NEPTUNE DSQ
Knight, Stephen David , *MEng*	LT(CC)	X	P U/T	01.09.99	FONA VALLEY
Knights, Robin	LT CDR(FTC)	X	PWO(U)	01.10.99	CNOCS GROUP
Knill, Robin Lloyd	LT CDR(FTC)	S	(S)	01.10.97	NOTTINGHAM
Knock, Gareth Paul	LT(FTC)	S	SM	01.10.93	HQBF CYPRUS
Knott, Michael Bruce , *AMNI*	LT(FTC)	X	PWO(A)	01.02.93	SOUTHAMPTON
Knowles, Christopher James , *BSc*	SLT(IC)	X	P U/T	01.09.98	DARTMOUTH BRNC
Knowles, John Michael , *pce, pcea, psc*	CAPT(FTC)	X	P	30.06.99	DHFS
Knowles, Michael Mark	LT(FTC)	S	(W)	24.07.92	RN GIBRALTAR
Knowling, Philip John , *MSc, CEng, MIEE, jsdc*	CDR(FTC)	E	AE	31.12.91	MOD (BATH)
Knox, Graeme Peter , *LLB*	SLT(CC)	S		01.09.97	RALEIGH
Knox, Margaret Mary	LT(FS)	FS		17.04.89	HQRM
Knox, Nicolas Oliver Gunning , *BSc, CEng, MIMarE, pce, psc*	CDR(FTC)	E	MESM	30.06.86	FOSM FASLANE
Kohler, Andrew Philip	LT(FTC)	X	FC	01.04.94	RNAS YEOVILTON
Kohn, Patricia Anne	SLT(FTC)	X		01.04.98	BRIDPORT
Kongialis, James Allyn , *BSc*	CAPT(FTC)	E	WESM	30.06.97	OSG BRISTOL
Kroon, Zoe	SLT(IC)	X		01.05.98	GUERNSEY
Krosnar-Clarke, Steven Matthew , *BSc, MSc*	LT CDR(FTC)	E	TM	01.10.98	RALEIGH
Kyd, Jeremy Paul , *pce, n*	LT CDR(FTC)	X	PWO(N)	01.08.97	CAPT D3 SEA
Kyte, Andrew Jeffery , *BA*	LT CDR(FTC)	S		16.12.96	JSCSC

L

Name	Rank	Branch	Spec	Seniority	Where Serving
Lacey, Ian Nigel , *BSc, MSc, PhD*	LT CDR(FTC)	E	IS	16.06.91	EXCHANGE USA
Lacey, Stephen Patrick , *pcea*	LT CDR(FTC)	X	O	16.05.93	750 SQN OBS SCH
Lacy, Lynne Helen , *BEng*	LT(IC)	X		01.12.96	GRAFTON
Lade, Christopher John , *BSc, pce*	CDR(FTC)	X	MCD	30.06.98	BDS WASHINGTON
Ladislaus, Cecil James , *BEng*	SLT(IC)	X		01.01.99	DARTMOUTH BRNC
Laggan, Peter John	LT CDR(FTC)	S	(W)	01.10.98	SULTAN
Laing, Iain , *BEng, AMIEE*	LT(FTC)	E	WE	01.09.93	COLLINGWOOD
Laird, Colin Rory , *pce, pcea, psc*	CDR(FTC)	X	O	31.12.85	DNR RCHQ NORTH
Lake, Peter Howard	LT(FTC)	E	ME	15.02.91	SCOTT
Lake, Richard Victor , *MA, MSc (Act Capt)*	CDR(FTC)	X	O	31.12.86	2SL/CNH
Lamb, Andrew Gordon , *n*	LT(FTC)	X		01.12.94	CDRE MFP
Lamb, Caroline Jayne , *BEng*	LT(FTC)	X		01.09.99	NORFOLK
Lamb, Robert , *jsdc, pce, pcea, psc*	CDR(FTC)	X	P	31.12.90	SHAPE BELGIUM
Lambert, Allison	LT(CC)	X	ATC	09.08.92	FOST DPORT SHORE
Lambert, Anthony Wayne , *MB, BS, FRCS, FRCS, MS*	SURG CDR	-	(GS)UT	30.06.99	NELSON (PAY)
Lambert, Brian , *pce*	CDR(FTC)	X	PWO(A)	31.12.96	MWC PORTSDOWN
Lambert, Kevin John , *pcea, psc*	LT CDR(FTC)	X	P	16.11.88	MOD (LONDON)
Lambert, Nicholas Richard , *BSc, pce*	CAPT(FTC)	X	PWO(A)	30.06.00	RHQ AFNORTH
Lambert, Paul , *BSc, MPhil, pce, pce(sm)*	CAPT(FTC)	X	SM	30.06.96	RCDS
Lambert-Humble, Stephen , *BDS, MSc, DGDP(UK)*	SGCAPT(D)	-		31.12.95	DDA HALTON

Name	Rank	Branch	Spec	Seniority	Where Serving
Lambie, Timothy James	LT(CC)	X	MCD	01.09.91	NORTH DIVING GRP
Lambourn, Peter Neil, *pce, pcea, psc*	CDR(FTC)	X	O	31.12.96	MOD (LONDON)
Lambourne, David John, *BSc*	LT CDR(FTC)	X	P	01.10.97	FONA SEAHAWK
Lamont, Samuel *(Act Surg Lt)*	SURG SLT	-		17.09.97	DARTMOUTH BRNC
Lancashire, Antony Craig, *MA*	CAPT RM(IC)	RM		01.09.97	539 ASLT SQN RM
Lancaster, Barrie-John, *BSc*	SLT(IC)	X		01.09.97	DRYAD
Lancaster, Craig, *BSc*	CAPT RM(FTC)	RM		01.09.96	EXCELLENT
Lancaster, Neil, *n*	LT(FTC)	X		01.04.97	DRYAD
Lander, Daniel Timothy James, *BEng*	SLT(IC)	X	P U/T	01.01.98	RNAS YEOVILTON
Lander, Martin Christopher, *MA, pce, pcea, psc,*	CDR(FTC)	X	O	30.06.95	JSCSC *psc(j)*
Landrock, Graham John, *pce*	LT CDR(FTC)	X	MCD	01.09.93	CDRE MFP NWOOD
Lane, David Fredrick	CDR(FTC)	S		30.06.92	FONA
Lane, Michael George, *BSc, FIMgt, rcds, psc*	CAPT(FTC)	S		31.12.95	AFPAA(CENTURION)
Lane, Nicholas, *BSc*	SLT(IC)	S		01.09.97	RALEIGH
Lane, Roger Guy Tyson, *OBE, FIMgt, jsdc, psc(m), fsc*	BRIG(FTC)	RM	WTO	30.06.99	RCDS
Lane, Robert Michael	LT(FTC)	E	ME	18.02.88	NBC PORTSMOUTH
Lane, Richard Norton	LT CDR(FTC)	X	PWO(U)	01.04.97	EXCHANGE CANADA
Lang, Andrew James Nicholas, *BEng*	LT(CC)	E	AE	01.04.89	HARRIER IPT
Lang, Justine Suzanne	LT	Q		30.09.94	DRAKE CBP(DLO)
Langbridge, David Charles, *BSc, MSc, MCGI, jsdc*	CDR(FTC)	E	MESM	30.06.93	NMA PORTSMOUTH
Langhorn, Nigel, *pce*	CDR(FTC)	X	PWO(A)	30.06.96	MWC SOUTHWICK
Langley, Eric Steven, *pce*	LT CDR(FTC)	X	PWO(A)	01.02.93	DRYAD
Langrill, Mark Philip, *BEng, MSc*	LT(FTC)	E	AE	01.06.93	801 SQN
Langrill, Tracey Jane, *MA*	LT(IC)	X		01.02.95	OCEAN
Langrish, Gary James	LT(CC)	X	P	01.10.92	800 SQN
Langrishe, James Hoadly, *pce*	LT CDR(FTC)	X	PWO(U)	16.04.81	CNOCS GROUP
Lanigan, Ben Ryan	SLT(IC)	S		01.04.00	OCEAN
Lankester, Peter, *BTech, pce, pcea, psc*	CDR(FTC)	X	P	30.06.92	RALEIGH
Lankester, Timothy John, *BSc, CEng, MIMechE, psc*	CDR(FTC)	E	ME	30.06.92	SSA BRISTOL
Lanni, Martin Nicholas	LT(CC)	X	P	01.09.95	771 SK5 SAR
Lanning, Roderick MacGregor, *BSc*	SLT(CC)	X		01.09.97	LEDBURY
Large, John Lawrence	LT CDR(FTC)	S	SM	17.01.90	2SL/CNH FOTR
Large, Stephen Andrew, *BEng*	LT(FTC)	E	ME	01.03.95	MOD (BATH)
Larmour, David Rutherford, *pce*	CAPT(FTC)	X	O	30.06.98	MOD (LONDON)
Latham, Lynne Barbara *(Act Lt)*	SLT(FTC)	S	(S)	01.05.98	NEPTUNE NT
Latham, Neil Degge, *BSc, MSc, CEng, MIMechE, jsdc*	CAPT(FTC)	E	ME	30.06.96	MOD (BATH)
Latus, Simon Harry, *BSc*	SLT(IC)	X		01.01.99	DARTMOUTH BRNC
Lauchlan, Robert Alexander, *BSc*	LT(FTC)	E	WESM	01.08.92	SSA BRISTOL
Laughton, Peter	LT(FTC)	X	MCD	01.04.96	CROMER
Launchbury, Stephen Joseph, *psc(j)*	MAJ(FTC)	RM	SO(LE)	01.10.95	2SL/CNH
Laurence, Simon Timothy	SLT(IC)	X	O	01.09.98	820 SQN
Laurence, Timothy James Hamilton, *MVO, BSc, pce (COMMODORE)*	CAPT(FTC)	X	PWO(U)	30.06.95	JSCSC
Lauste, William Emile, *BA*	LT CDR(CC)	E	TM	01.03.99	RNAS YEOVILTON
Laverty, Robert Edwin, *BA, SM(n)*	LT(FTC)	X	SM	01.02.95	SOVEREIGN
Lavery, John Patrick, *MVO*	CDR(FTC)	S		30.06.99	FOST DPORT SHORE
Lavin, Gerard Joseph, *BEng, CEng, MIMechE*	LT(IC)	E	ME	01.03.93	HQ 3 CDO BDE RM
Law, John	LT CDR(FTC)	X	MCD	27.03.95	CDRE MFP
Law, Richard, *BEng*	SLT(FTC)	E	WE	01.09.97	COLLINGWOOD
Lawler, Jon Andrew	LT CDR(CC)	X	P	01.10.95	MOD (LONDON)
Lawrance, Gregory Michael	LT(CC)	X	P	16.05.92	815 FLT 228
Lawrence, Linda Jane, *BA*	LT(IC)	X		01.09.99	ORWELL
Lawrence, Marc Andrew, *BSc*	SLT(IC)	X	O U/T	01.05.98	750 SQN OBS SCH
Lawrence, Stephen Paul, *n*	LT CDR(FTC)	X	H CH	01.10.93	RN HYDROG SCHL
Lawrence, Stuart Peter	LT(FTC)	S		01.03.94	LIVERPOOL
Lawrence, Steven Raymond	LT CDR(FTC)	E	ME	01.10.97	SSA DEVONPORT
Laws, Anthony	SLT(IC)	X		27.01.99	750 SQN OBS SCH
Laws, Philip Eric Arthur, *LLB, FCMA, ACMA (Act Cdr)*	LT CDR(FTC)	S	CMA	16.02.93	2SL/CNH FOTR
Lawson, Geoffrey John	LT(FTC)	X	tas	13.12.95	DUMBARTON CASTLE
Lawson, Robin Ian, *n*	LT CDR(FTC)	X	H CH	02.08.93	BULLDOG
Lawson, Richard Keith	LT(CC)	X	O	16.03.96	819 SQN
Lawson, Stephen Jonathan, *pce, pce(sm)*	LT CDR(FTC)	X	SM	01.09.91	DRYAD
Lawton, Andrew Charles Richard, *BSc*	LT CDR(FTC)	E	ME	01.11.85	FOSF
Lawton, Michael Joseph, *DEH, MIOSH*	LT(FTC)	MS		26.04.99	MOD (BATH)

Name	Rank	Branch	Spec	Seniority	Where Serving
Lawton, Peter , *MBE*	CAPT RM(FTC)	RM	SO(LE)	01.01.99	RM Poole
Laycock, Antony , *BSc*	LT(IC)	X	O	16.07.94	815 FLT 244
Layland, Stephen , *pce*	LT CDR(FTC)	X	PWO(N)	01.03.92	LANCASTER
Layton, Christopher , *BEng*	SLT(IC)	E	ME	01.05.98	MANCHESTER
Le Gassick, Peter James , *BEng*	LT(CC)	E	TM	01.09.95	COMACCHIO GP RM
Lea, John , *pcea*	LT CDR(FTC)	X	O	01.01.98	849 SQN B FLT
Lea, Jeffrey Henry Arthur , *BSc, CEng, MIMarE, psc*	CDR(FTC)	E	ME	31.12.94	DRAKE CFM
Lea, Sebastian Augustine Pollard , *n*	LT(FTC)	X		01.11.91	DRYAD
Leach, John Foster Jeffery , *BSc*	CAPT RM(IC)	RM		01.05.98	40 CDO RM
Leach, Sarah Jane	LT(FTC)	E	ME	01.07.96	DARTMOUTH BRNC
Leadbetter, Andrew John , *BA*	LT(IC)	X		01.11.97	ANGLESEY
Leaman, Adrian Richard , *BSc*	SLT(IC)	X		01.09.98	CORNWALL
Leaman, Richard Derek , *OBE, pce*	CAPT(FTC)	X	PWO(A)	31.12.96	MOD (LONDON)
Leaney, Michael John , *BSc*	LT CDR(FTC)	X	MCD	01.03.90	SDG PLYMOUTH
Leaning, David John	LT(FTC)	E	MESM	15.10.93	DRAKE CFM
Leaning, Mark Vincent , *MA, MIMgt, pcea, psc*	LT CDR(FTC)	X	P	01.09.91	FONA SEAGOING
Lear, Stuart Francis , *BA*	SLT(IC)	S		01.09.97	FOSF
Leason, Nicholas Charles	SLT(IC)	X		01.12.97	ANGLESEY
Leatherby, James Hawton	CDR(FTC)	S	SM	31.12.90	CALEDONIA CFS
Leaver, Andrew Michael	LT(FTC)	E	AE(M)	02.09.99	824 NAS
Leaver, Charmian Elizabeth Lucy , *MA, MSc, PGDip*	LT(FTC)	X	METOC	01.07.91	FOSM NWOOD OPS
Ledingham, Herbert John , *pcea, psc(m)*	CDR(FTC)	X	P	30.06.90	JHCHQ
Ledward, Karen Louise	SLT(IC)	S		01.04.98	DARTMOUTH BRNC
Lee, Daniel John , *pce, psc*	CDR(FTC)	X	PWO(A)	31.12.96	RMC OF SCIENCE
Lee, Jonathan Coling	LT CDR(FTC)	X	MW	01.10.94	DRYAD
Lee, Matthew Martin , *MRAeS*	LT CDR(FTC)	X	ATC	01.10.91	DISC SEA
Lee, Nigel David	LT(FTC)	X	FC	16.06.95	CAMPBELTOWN
Lee, Nicholas Foden , *BEng, MIMechE, pcea*	LT CDR(FTC)	X	P	01.03.99	FONA DARTMOUTH
Lee, Oliver Andrew , *BA*	CAPT RM(FTC)	RM		01.05.98	CTCRM
Lee, Peter Alan , *BEng, AMIMechE*	LT CDR(FTC)	E	ME	01.08.99	SULTAN
Lee, Philip Marsden , *BSc*	LT(IC)	X	P	01.10.94	EXCHANGE RAF UK
Lee, Steven Edward , *MEng, MSc*	LT(CC)	E	WE	01.12.99	COLLINGWOOD
Lee, Steven Patrick , *MA*	CAPT RM(FTC)	RM		27.04.96	NMA WHALE ISLAND
Lee, Steven Yiu Lam , *BEng*	LT(FTC)	E	WE	01.12.95	COLLINGWOOD
Lee, Warren , *BEng*	LT(FTC)	E	WE	01.06.97	GRAFTON
Leeder, Roger John	LT(CS)	-		17.02.91	DNR SOUTH EAST
Leeder, Timothy Rupert	MID(IC)	X		01.05.98	DARTMOUTH BRNC
Leeming, Robert John , *BSc, CEng*	CAPT(FTC)	E	ME	30.06.00	MOD (BATH)
Leeper, James Stephen , *BSc*	SLT(IC)	X		01.01.99	DARTMOUTH BRNC
Lees, Edward Charles , *n*	LT CDR(FTC)	X	PWO(C)	01.02.99	INVINCIBLE
Lees, Rodney Burnett *(BARRISTER)* , n	RADM	-	BAR	21.02.95	MOD (LONDON)
Lees, Simon Neville , *BEd*	LT(CC)	E	TM	02.09.93	2SL/CNH FOTR
Leeson, Antony Richard	SLT(IC)	X		01.04.00	INVINCIBLE
Legg, Malcolm Robert , *pcea, psc(a), ocds(Can)*	CDR(FTC)	X	O	30.06.90	AST(E)
Leggett, Christopher Charles , *MBE, TEng, AMINucE*	CDR(FTC)	E	MESM	01.10.96	NEPTUNE NT
Leggett, Stephen Edward , *MBE*	LT CDR(FTC)	E	AE	13.01.88	DHP BRISTOL
Leigh, John , *osc(us)*	LT COL(FTC)	RM	MLDR	31.12.96	SACLANT USA
Leigh, Siobhan	LT(CC)	W		25.07.91	OCLC BRISTOL
Leightley, Simon Mark	MID(IC)	X		01.01.00	IRON DUKE
Leighton, Matthew Richard , *BA*	LT(IC)	X	P	01.12.97	846 SQN
Leitch, Iain Robertson , *BSc*	LT CDR(FTC)	X	PWO(A)	01.10.96	DRYAD
Leivers, Andrew James	LT(CC)	E	ME	01.09.99	DARTMOUTH BRNC
Lemkes, Paul Douglas , *pce*	CDR(FTC)	X	PWO(A)	31.12.97	FOSF
Lemon, Robert Gordon Arthur , *BSc*	LT CDR(FTC)	E	WESM	01.09.84	MOD (LONDON)
Lemon, Robin William George	CAPT RM(FTC)	RM		01.09.94	UNOMIG
Leonard, Mark , *BEng*	LT CDR(FTC)	E	WE	01.10.97	CAMBRIDGE
Lester, Rodney Leslie	LT(FTC)	X	g	10.01.00	DRYAD
Lett, Jonathan David , *n*	LT(FTC)	X		01.07.93	JSCSC
Letts, Andrew John , *BEng, AMIEE*	LT(FTC)	E	WE	01.08.95	DRAKE CFM
Levine, Andrew John	CAPT RM(FTC)	RM		29.04.97	CTCRM
Lew-Gor, Simione Tomasi Warren , *MB, ChB*	SURG LT	-		05.09.95	RH HASLAR
Lewins, Grant	LT(FTC)	S	(W)	08.04.94	RALEIGH
Lewis, Andrew James , *BA, BEng*	LT(FTC)	E	MESM	01.03.96	SOVEREIGN

Name	Rank	Branch	Spec	Seniority	Where Serving
Lewis, Benjamin Charles, *BSc*	LT(IC)	X	P	01.12.97	846 SQN
Lewis, Daniel, *BEng*	LT(CC)	E	TM	19.07.98	SULTAN
Lewis, David Arthur, *MNI, rcds, pce, psc, hcsc (COMMODORE)*	CAPT(FTC)	X	AWO(A)	30.06.93	PJHQ
Lewis, David James	LT CDR(CC)	X	O	01.10.98	815 SQN HQ
Lewis, David John, *BEng, AMIEE*	LT(FTC)	E	WE	01.09.93	SSA BRISTOL
Lewis, David Malcolm John, *MBE, FIMgt*	CDR(FTC)	E	ME	31.12.96	ILLUSTRIOUS
Lewis, Gary David *(Act Cdr)*	LT CDR(FTC)	S		01.09.89	MOD (BATH)
Lewis, Guy David, *BEng*	LT CDR(FTC)	E	ME	03.02.00	FOSF
Lewis, John Keene, *BSc, BEng, MDA*	CDR(FTC)	E	WESM	30.06.99	EXCHANGE AUSTLIA
Lewis, Jennifer Lucy Mary, *BA*	LT(CC)	X	O U/T	01.04.00	702 SQN HERON
Lewis, Keith Alan	LT(FTC)	X	PWO(C)	03.04.97	OCEAN
Lewis, Neil Melwyn, *BSc, CDipAF*	LT CDR(FTC)	E	TM	27.10.91	FOST DPORT SHORE
Lewis, Paul *(Act Lt)*	SLT(IC)	X	tas	19.09.98	RNU ST MAWGAN
Lewis, Peter Reginald, *MBE, pce, (A Cdr)*	LT CDR(FTC)	X	PWO(U)	21.11.86	EXC BRISTOL
Lewis, Stephen Bernard, *pce, psc*	LT CDR(FTC)	X	PWO(U)	01.01.87	JSCSC
Lewis, Simon John, *BSc, MSc*	LT(CC)	E	TM	01.01.93	COLLINGWOOD
Lewis, Timothy John	LT CDR(FTC)	X	PWO(U)	05.02.95	GRIMSBY
Lewis, Timothy John	CHAPLAIN	CE		28.11.89	DARTMOUTH BRNC
Ley, Alastair Blevins	LT(FTC)	X	SM	01.11.95	TRAFALGAR
Ley, Jonathan Ashley, *n*	LT(FTC)	X	PWO(A)	01.08.92	NORTHUMBERLAND
Leyden, Tristan Neil	CAPT RM(FTC)	RM		01.09.99	RM Poole
Leyland, Emma Margaret, *BEng*	SLT(IC)	E	WE	01.09.98	NEWCASTLE
Leyshon, Brian Stuart, *pce, pcea*	LT CDR(FTC)	X	P	16.03.83	PJHQ
Leyshon, Robert John, *BDS*	SGLTCDR(D)	-		09.01.99	CTCRM
Lias, Carl David, *BEng*	LT CDR(FTC)	E	MESM	01.10.96	VIGILANT(STBD)
Lidbetter, Scott, *pce, hcsc*	CAPT(FTC)	X	P	31.12.92	OCEAN
Liddell, Matthew Lewis	SLT(FTC)	E	ME	02.05.97	CHATHAM
Liddle, Richard David, *BEng*	SLT(CC)	X	P U/T	01.09.97	RAF CRANWELL EFS
Liddle, Stephen Johnstone, *BA*	CAPT RM(FTC)	RM		01.09.95	DRYAD
Liggins, Michael Philip, *BSc*	LT(CC)	X	P	01.03.90	848 SQN HERON
Liggins, Steven John, *BDS, MB, BCh, FDS RCSEdin, FRCS, BSc*	SGCDR(D)	-	(COSM)	31.12.97	MODHU DERRIFORD
Lightfoot, Charles David, *BSc, pce, pce(sm), psc(j)*	LT CDR(FTC)	X	SM	01.07.90	UPHLDER TRG TEAM
Lightfoot, Christopher Morrison, *pce, psc, psc(j)*	CDR(FTC)	X	PWO(N)†	30.06.89	JSCSC
Lightfoot, Richard	SLT(IC)	X	O U/T	29.04.98	750 SQN OBS SCH
Lilburn, Lawrence Kevin, *BSc*	LT(IC)	X	P	01.12.92	EXCHANGE USA
Lilley, David John, *BSc, pce, pcea, psc(m)*	CDR(FTC)	X	O	31.12.96	MOD (LONDON)
Lilly, David Mark, *BSc*	LT(IC)	X	P U/T	01.08.99	DHFS
Lincoln, Keith James, *BEng*	LT(FTC)	E	WE	01.07.95	DRYAD
Lincoln, Peter Wesley	MID(NE)(IC)	X		01.01.00	DARTMOUTH BRNC
Linderman, Ian Ronald, *BSc, MBA*	LT CDR(CC)	E	TM	01.10.99	HQRM
Lindley, Nicholas Paul, *BSc, psc(m)*	LT COL(FTC)	RM		31.12.99	CTCRM
Lindley, Richard Anthony, *MIEE, MIMgt, psc*	CDR(FTC)	E	WE	30.06.88	2SL/CNH FOTR
Lindsay, David Joseph, *BEng*	LT(CC)	X	P	01.08.91	EXCHANGE RAF UK
Lindsay, Gordon	LT CDR(FTC)	E	WESM	01.10.97	FOSM FASLANE
Lindsay, Ian Barry	LT(CC)	X	ATC	01.06.96	RNAS YEOVILTON
Lindsay, Irvine Graham, *MA, pce(sm), psc(j)*	LT CDR(FTC)	X	SM	01.04.96	RN GIBRALTAR
Lindsay, Jonathan	2LT(GRAD)(IC)	RM		28.04.99	CTCRM LYMPSTONE
Lindsey, Richard	LT CDR(FTC)	X	SM	30.04.00	TRIUMPH
Lineker, Robert John, *BSc, Eur Ing, CEng, MIEE*	CDR(FTC)	E	WESM	30.06.93	MOD (LONDON)
Lines, James Micheal	LT CDR(FTC)	S		16.11.95	NMA PORTSMOUTH
Ling, Christopher, *BSc*	LT(FTC)	E	AE	01.03.96	NELSON (PAY)
Ling, John William Legrys, *BEng*	LT(CC)	X	O	16.09.94	849 SQN HQ
Lintern, Robert David, *PGDip, n*	LT(FTC)	X	H2	01.10.94	RN HYDROG SCHL
Lippiett, Richard John, *MBE, rcds, jsdc, pce, psc*	RADM	-	PWO	07.07.97	AGRIPPA NAVSOUTH
Lippitt, Simon Thomas, *BEng*	LT(CC)	X	ATCU/T	01.04.98	RNAS YEOVILTON
Lipscomb, Paul, *BSc, CEng, MIMarE*	LT CDR(FTC)	E	MESM	01.11.95	VIGILANT(STBD)
Lison, Andrew Christopher, *BEng, MSc, AMIEE*	LT CDR(FTC)	E	AE	01.05.99	HARRIER IPT
Lister, Andrew Robert, *BSc*	LT(CC)	X	P	16.06.93	815 SQN HQ
Lister, John Andrew, *pce*	CDR(FTC)	X	O	31.12.88	2SL/CNH FOTR
Lister, Mark, *pce(sm)*	LT CDR(FTC)	X	SM	01.01.97	CSST SEA
Lister, Simon	LT(FTC)	X	SM	08.04.94	SCEPTRE
Lister, Simon Robert, *MSc, AMIMechE*	CAPT(FTC)	E	MESM	31.12.99	MOD (LONDON)
Lister, Stephen Richard	LT CDR(FTC)	S	SM	01.04.93	CSST SEA

Name	Rank	Branch	Spec	Seniority	Where Serving
Litchfield, Julian Felix	CDR(FTC)	S		30.06.98	NMA PORTSMOUTH
Litster, Alan , *MBE, BSc*	MAJ(FTC)	RM	LC	01.09.98	HQ 3 CDO BDE RM
Little, Charles Stewart Anderson , *BSc, pce, pce(sm)*	LT CDR(FTC)	X	SM	01.02.90	CSST SHORE DEVPT
Little, Graeme Terence , *BEng, MSc*	CDR(FTC)	E	ME	30.06.00	JSCSC
Little, Matthew Iain Graham , *BSc*	SLT(IC)	X		01.05.98	LANCASTER
Little, Nicholas Richmond , *BSc, pce*	LT CDR(FTC)	X	PWO(U)	01.06.88	NMA PORTSMOUTH
Little, Rhoderick McKeand , *BSc, CDipAF, CEng, MIEE, psc*	CAPT(FTC)	E	WESM	31.12.98	SSIP IPT
Littleboy, Martin Nelson , *MPhil, pce, psc*	CAPT(FTC)	X	AWO(A)	31.12.94	DA KIEV
Liva, Anthony John , *BSc*	2LT(GRAD)(IC)	RM		01.09.99	CTCRM LYMPSTONE
Livesey, John Edward	LT(CC)	X	SM	01.07.97	RALEIGH
Livingstone, Alan James , *MBE*	MAJ(FTC)	RM		01.09.97	HQ NORTH
Livsey, Andrew Everard John , *BA*	LT(FTC)	X		01.09.99	ANGLESEY
Llewellyn, Jonathan Gwyn *(Act Lt)*	SLT(FTC)	X	AV	20.09.96	RNAS CULDROSE
Llewelyn, Barry	LT CDR(FTC)	S	CA	01.10.95	EDINBURGH
Llewelyn, Kevin	LT CDR(FTC)	X	ATC	01.10.97	RNAS YEOVILTON
Lloyd, Bruce Jeremy , *BSc*	LT(CC)	X	P U/T	01.04.00	RNAS YEOVILTON
Lloyd, Christopher John	LT CDR(FTC)	MS		01.10.96	NMA GOSPORT
Lloyd, David Philip John	LT CDR(FTC)	S		01.09.91	MONTROSE
Lloyd, Paul Robert , *pce, psc(j)*	CDR(FTC)	X	PWO(N)	31.12.97	PJHQ
Lloyd, Stephen John , *MSc, CEng, MIMarE, psc*	CAPT(FTC)	E	MESM	30.06.00	SSA DEVONPORT
Lloyd, Susan Jane , *BSc*	LT(IC)	E	TM	01.09.90	NELSON RNSETT
Loane, Michael MacAire	LT(CC)	X	MCD	01.06.93	FDU2
Lochrane, Alexandre Edmond Ross , *pce*	LT CDR(FTC)	X	PWO(U)	01.07.95	SOMERSET
Lock, Andrew Glen David	CAPT RM(FTC)	RM		28.04.98	DARTMOUTH BRNC
Lock, Willam Robert , *BDS, MSc, DGDP RCS(UK), LDS RCS(Eng)*	SGCAPT(D)	-		30.06.97	DDA PORTSMOUTH
Lockett, David John	LT(FTC)	X		01.04.96	DRYAD
Lockwood, Roger Graham , *BA, rcds, jsdc (COMMODORE)*	CAPT(FTC)	S		31.12.91	RALEIGH
Lodge, Christopher Norman , *BEng*	LT(IC)	E	TM	01.02.93	CTCRM
Lofthouse, Ian , *MA*	CDR(FTC)	E	MESM	31.12.96	MOD (BATH)
Logan, Joseph Majella	LT(FTC)	X	FC	01.10.91	INVINCIBLE
Lokai, Dario Steffan	SLT	Q		14.09.96	RH HASLAR
Lombard, Didier , *pce, pce(sm), odc(Fr)*	CDR(FTC)	X	SM	31.12.91	MOD (LONDON)
London, Martin Richard , *MBE*	LT CDR(FTC)	X	P	01.03.99	801 SQN
Long, Anthony Donald , *pce, pcea*	LT CDR(FTC)	X	O	16.05.98	JMOTS NORTHWOOD
Long, Adrian Montague , *BEng, MIEE*	LT CDR(FTC)	E	WE	01.04.00	RMC OF SCIENCE
Long, Derek Ray	LT CDR(FTC)	X	PWO(A)	17.02.83	NMA GOSPORT
Long, Michael Selden	LT(FTC)	X	MW	01.04.96	GRIMSBY
Long, Nicholas Andrew , *BSc, MSc, CEng, MIEE (Act Cdr)*	LT CDR(FTC)	E	WE	01.05.91	SHAPE BELGIUM
Long, Philip John , *MBE, jsdc, pce*	CDR(FTC)	X	PWO(U)	30.06.94	MOD (LONDON)
Long, Stuart Gemmell , *BSc*	LT(CC)	X	HM	01.11.94	GLEANER
Long, William Gerald Hanslip	LT(CC)	X	P	01.12.93	810 SQN SEAHAWK
Longbottom, Christopher John , *MSc, CEng, MIMarE, MIMechE, psc (Act Capt)*	CDR(FTC)	E	MESM	30.06.95	NEPTUNE FD
Longstaff, Richard , *MSRP*	LT(FTC)	E	WE	13.06.86	COLLINGWOOD
Longstaff, Thomas William	SLT(FTC)	S	CA	19.09.97	TRAFALGAR
Lonsdale, Robert James , *MA*	CAPT RM(IC)	RM		01.09.98	OCLC MANCH
Lord, Andrew Stephen , *BA, MA(Ed), PGCE*	LT CDR(FTC)	E	TM	01.09.87	EXCELLENT
Lord, Martin	LT CDR(FTC)	E	WE	01.10.98	GLASGOW
Lord, Richard John , *MSc, jsdc (COMMODORE)*	CAPT(FTC)	E	WE	30.06.92	FOSNNI/NBC CLYDE
Lord, Richard James	LT(CC)	X	P	01.10.94	815 FLT 209
Loring, Andrew , *BSc, CEng, MIMechE*	LT CDR(FTC)	E	ME	01.03.93	NORTHUMBERLAND
Louden, Carl Alexander	LT(FTC)	X	C	23.07.98	FEARLESS
Loughrey, Neil Charles	SLT(IC)	E	AE	29.04.98	SULTAN
Louis, David Richard Anthony	MID(UCE)(FTC)	X		01.09.98	DARTMOUTH BRNC
Louw, Len	SLT(IC)	E	WE	01.01.99	DARTMOUTH BRNC
Lovatt, Graham John	LT(FTC)	X	FC	01.04.95	DRYAD
Love, Julie Dawn	SLT(FTC)	S	(W)	19.09.97	GLOUCESTER
Love, Richard J , *BEng*	LT(CC)	E	AE	01.08.98	814 SQN
Love, Robert Thomas , *BSc, CEng, FIMarE, psc*	CAPT(FTC)	E	ME	30.06.98	MOD (BATH)
Love, Tristram Simon Nicholas , *BEng*	LT(FTC)	E	WESM	01.07.93	FOSM NWOOD HQ
Lovegrove, Raymond Anthony , *MSc, CEng, MIEE, gw*	LT CDR(FTC)	E	WE	01.10.96	WESTMINSTER
Lovelock, Richard Benjamin , *psc(m)*	LT COL(FTC)	RM		30.06.94	JDCC
Loveridge, Paul James , *MA*	SLT(IC)	X		01.01.99	DARTMOUTH BRNC

Name	Rank	Branch	Spec	Seniority	Where Serving
Lovering, Tristan Timothy Alan , *BSc*	LT(IC)	E	TM	01.01.95	SULTAN
Lovett, Andrew Robert	SLT(CC)	E	AE	01.04.98	DARTMOUTH BRNC
Lovett, Michael John , *BSc*	CDR(FTC)	E	WE	30.06.96	CAPT F2(SEA)
Lovett, Stephen Andrew	LT(FTC)	X	SM	26.04.99	RALEIGH
Low, Christopher David Tullis , *MB, BCh, ChB, FRCSEd*	SURG CDR	-	(CO)	31.12.99	RH HASLAR
Low, Mark Edward	LT(FTC)	E	WESM	13.06.91	MOD (BATH)
Lowe, Christopher	SLT(FTC)	E	MESM	02.05.97	VICTORIOUS(PORT)
Lowe, Julian Charles , *BEng, BTech, MSc*	LT CDR(FTC)	E	ME	01.08.99	EXCHANGE CANADA
Lowe, Stanley Alan , *MBE*	LT CDR(FTC)	S	CA	01.10.94	FOSF
Lowe, Stuart Michael , *BEng, MSc, AMIEE*	LT(FTC)	E	WE	01.12.92	LOAN DERA ADAC
Lowe, Timothy Miles , *jsdc, pce*	CDR(FTC)	X	PWO(N)	31.12.95	SHEFFIELD
Lower, Iain Stuart , *BSc, n*	LT CDR(FTC)	X	PWO(A)	01.10.99	DRYAD
Lowes, Christopher	LT CDR(FTC)	E	WE	01.10.99	MOD (LONDON)
Lown, David	LT CDR(RETL	E	WE	06.07.89	MOD (LONDON)
Lowson, Roderick Mark , *pce*	LT CDR(FTC)	X	PWO(A)	01.04.97	CINCFLEET
Lowther, James Marcus , *BA, n*	LT CDR(FTC)	X	PWO(U)	01.07.98	RICHMOND
Loxdale, Patrick Henry , *MB, BS, FRCS*	SURG CDR	-	(CO/S)	30.06.97	MODHU DERRIFORD
Luard, James Richard , *BSc, CEng, MRAeS, psc*	CAPT(FTC)	E	AE	30.06.90	NELSON
Lucas, Simon Ulrick	LT RM(FTC)	RM	SO(LE)	01.01.98	RMB STONEHOUSE
Lucey, Richard Noel , *pce*	CDR(FTC)	X	PWO(C)	30.06.89	LOAN DERA ADAC
Luckraft, Christopher John , *BD, AKC*	CHAPLAIN	CE		05.08.87	ILLUSTRIOUS
Lucocq, Nicholas James , *BSc*	LT(CC)	X		01.08.95	RICHMOND
Ludlow, Julian Andrew	SLT(IC)	X		01.04.99	DARTMOUTH BRNC
Lugg, John Charles	CAPT RM(FTC)	RM	SO(LE)	01.01.98	RMB STONEHOUSE
Luker, Geoffrey Peter , *MBE*	LT CDR(FTC)	X	PWO(A)	01.03.83	LANG TRNG(UK)
Lumsden, Peter Imrie , *BEng*	LT(FTC)	X	P U/T	01.04.97	RAF CRANWELL EFS
Lunn, Adam Christopher , *pce, pcea*	LT CDR(FTC)	X	P	01.06.94	DRYAD
Lunn, David Vaughan , *MB, BCh, ChB, DA, FFARCS*	SURG CDR	-	(CA)	30.06.91	MODHU DERRIFORD
Lunn, James Francis Clive , *BSc, CEng, MIMarE, MIMechE, psc*	CDR(FTC)	E	MESM	31.12.93	2SL/CNH
Lunn, Mark Henry Bernard , *BSc, MSc, CEng, MIMarE*	LT(FTC)	E	MESM	01.07.92	MOD (BATH)
Lunn, Thomas Ramsay	LT(FTC)	X		01.01.95	INVINCIBLE
Luscombe, Michael David , *pcea*	LT CDR(FTC)	X	P	01.10.99	810 SQN SEAHAWK
Lusted, Roy Peter (*Act Lt Cdr*)	LT(FTC)	E	AE(L)	13.10.89	RNAS YEOVILTON
Lustman, Arnold Marc	LT CDR(FTC)	S	SM	25.09.97	FOSF
Lutman, Charles Robert , *BEng*	SLT(IC)	E		01.01.98	DARTMOUTH BRNC
Lyall, Alistair Jonathan , *MBE, jsdc, pce(sm)* (*COMMODORE*)	CAPT(FTC)	X	SM	30.06.92	BDLS AUSTRALIA
Lydiate, Gary , *pce*	LT CDR(FTC)	X	PWO(A)	01.01.95	NORFOLK
Lye, David James , *OBE, psc*	CDR(FTC)	X	H CH	31.12.92	RN HYDROG SCHL
Lygo, Martin Howard , *MB, BS, MA, MSc, MFOM*	SURG CDR	-	(CO/M)	30.06.98	NEPTUNE CFS
Lynas, Jonathan Francis Alistair	SLT(CC)	X	P	01.01.98	845 SQN
Lynch, Michael , *MA, psc*	LT CDR(FTC)	S	SM	24.03.91	RNAS CULDROSE
Lynch, Paul Patrick , *BA*	CAPT RM(CC)	RM		01.05.98	40 CDO RM
Lynch, Rory Denis Fenton , *BA*	LT(CC)	X		16.04.90	CHFHQ
Lynch, Stephen , *pcea*	LT(CC)	X	O	01.08.91	ILLUSTRIOUS
Lynn, Henry William	SLT(FTC)	X	tas	19.09.97	CATTISTOCK
Lynn, Ian Herbert	LT(FTC)	X		30.06.95	JSCSC
Lynn, Steven Robert , *BEng*	LT CDR(FTC)	E	WE	01.04.98	LIVERPOOL
Lynskey, Matthew Lee , *BEng*	SLT(IC)	E	WE	01.09.98	ILLUSTRIOUS
Lyons, Alan Gordon , *BEng*	LT(CC)	E	MESM	01.10.98	SULTAN
Lyons, Michael John , *BEng*	LT(FTC)	E	MESM	01.01.97	VENGEANCE(PORT)

M

Name	Rank	Branch	Spec	Seniority	Where Serving
Mabbott, Keith , *BSc*	SLT(CC)	X		01.09.97	DRYAD
Mac Donald, Stuart Brewey	SLT(IC)	S		01.04.98	SHEFFIELD
MacAskill, Colin Hugh	LT(FTC)	S	CA	11.12.92	NEPTUNE CFS
Macaulay, Neil	LT CDR(FTC)	E	WE	01.10.95	CFM PORTSMOUTH
MacBean, Christopher Ciaran	LT CDR(FTC)	X	P	01.10.93	RNAS CULDROSE
MacColl, Andrew	LT(CC)	X	ATC	01.05.96	EXCHANGE GERMANY
MacCormick, Alexander Wright , *psc*	COL(FTC)	RM	C	31.12.95	HQRM
MacCorquodale, Mairi Ann , *MA, MPhil*	LT(IC)	E		01.09.98	INVINCIBLE
MacDonald, Alasdair Iain , *BSc, CEng, MIEE, MIMgt,*	CDR(FTC)	E	WE	30.06.98	COLLINGWOOD *MDA*
MacDonald, Alastair James , *BEng*	LT(FTC)	E	WE	01.09.94	MOD (BATH)

Name	Rank	Branch	Spec	Seniority	Where Serving
MacDonald, Douglas Hugh Lawson, *BSc, MA, MNI, pce, ocds(US)*	CDR(FTC)	X	MCD	30.06.91	MWC SOUTHWICK
MacDonald, Glen Dey, *BA*	LT CDR(FTC)	X		01.05.91	ARK ROYAL
MacDonald, George Ewen, *LLB*	CAPT(FTC)	S		30.06.00	DPA BRISTOL
MacDonald, Ian Robert, *MBE*	MAJ(FTC)	RM		08.02.93	HQ NORTH
MacDonald, John Robert, *BSc, MSc, gw*	LT CDR(FTC)	E	WESM	01.07.97	JSCSC
MacDonald Watson, Alastair Ian, *BSc, CEng, MIEE, MIExpE, psc*	CDR(FTC)	E	WE	31.12.83	STG BRISTOL
MacDonald-Robinson, Nicholas Ulric Spencer	LT CDR(FTC)	X	PWO(A)	01.04.98	EXETER
MacDougall, Gavin Ross	LT CDR(FTC)	S		01.10.98	DRAKE DPL
MacDougall, Stewart John	LT(FTC)	E	WESM	19.02.93	RALEIGH
Mace, Stephen Barry, *BEng*	LT CDR(FTC)	E	WE	01.02.96	FOSF
MacFarlane, Iain Stuart David, *BSc*	LT(CC)	X	P	01.11.93	820 SQN
MacGillivray, Ian, *BEng*	LT CDR(FTC)	E	WE	01.04.98	ST ALBANS
MacIntyre, Ian	SLT(IC)	E	WESM	27.01.99	COLLINGWOOD
MacIver, George, *BSc, pce, pce(sm)*	LT CDR(FTC)	X	SM	01.02.98	NEPTUNE SM1
MacKay, Andrew Colin, *BA*	LT(FTC)	S		01.02.96	CORNWALL
MacKay, Colin Ross, *BSc*	LT CDR(FTC)	E	TM	01.09.91	2SL/CNH FOTR
MacKay, David Hugh	LT CDR(FTC)	X	P	01.10.93	899 SQN HERON
MacKay, Graeme Angus, *pce, pcea, ocds(Can)*	CDR(FTC)	X	O	31.12.97	FOSF NORTHWOOD
MacKay, Peter, *BEng*	LT CDR(FTC)	E	WE	01.12.98	EDINBURGH
MacKenzie, Hannah Louise, *LLB*	SLT(IC)	S		01.01.99	DARTMOUTH BRNC
MacKenzie, Jessica-Rose, *BA*	LT(IC)	S		01.07.99	NBC PORTSMOUTH
MacKenzie, Kenneth Donald, *psc*	CDR(FTC)	X	O	30.06.83	NELSON
MacKenzie, Michael David, *BSc, pce(sm)*	LT CDR(FTC)	X	SM	01.11.95	MWC PORTSDOWN
MacKett, Duncan Geoffrey, *pce*	LT CDR(FTC)	X	PWO(A)	01.05.88	RHQ AFNORTH
Mackey, Martin Christopher	LT CDR(FTC)	X	MCD	01.06.99	DRYAD
Mackie, David Francis Sarsfield, *BEng, MSc*	LT CDR(FTC)	E	WE	01.03.99	MOD (LONDON)
Mackie, Simon, *MB, BS*	SURG LT	-		12.08.96	NELSON (PAY)
MacKinnon, Anne, *BSc*	LT(CC)	E	TM	01.09.97	RALEIGH
MacKinnon, Donald James, *BEng*	LT(FTC)	X		01.01.93	SMITER
MacLaughlin, Richard Adrian, *BA*	LT(IC)	X	P	16.12.98	RNAS CULDROSE
MacLean, David James, *BTech, MSc, MRINA, jsdc (COMMODORE)*	CAPT(FTC)	E	ME	30.06.94	LPD(R) IPT
MacLean, Malcolm Thomas	LT(FTC)	E	ME	02.09.99	SULTAN
MacLean, Shamus MacFarlane	MID(NE)(IC)	X		01.09.99	DARTMOUTH BRNC
MacLennan, Iain Ross, *MB, BCh, DTM&H, MRCGP*	SURG LTCDR	-	GMPP	01.07.89	CINCFLEET
Macleod, James Norman, *BEng, AMIEE*	LT CDR(FTC)	E	WE	01.03.00	RMC OF SCIENCE
Macleod, Mark Stuart, *BEng*	LT(FTC)	E	AE(P)	01.02.94	814 SQN
Macleod, Roderick, *BA, BD, MBA*	CHAPLAIN	SF		20.02.98	CTCRM
MacNaughton, Francis George, *MBE, BA, pce*	LT CDR(FTC)	X	PWO(A)	01.05.87	FOST DPORT SHORE
MacNeil, Stephen William	LT(CC)	X	P	01.03.93	824 NAS
MacOwan, Andrew Stewart, *MA*	2LT(GRAD)(IC)	RM		02.09.98	COMACCHIO GP RM
MacRae, Kirsteen Louise, *BSc*	LT(CC)	X		01.10.99	DRYAD
Madders, Brian Richard, *MBE*	CHAPLAIN	RC		09.09.85	NELSON
Maddick, Mark Jeremy, *psc(j)*	MAJ(FTC)	RM	LC	26.05.95	HQ 3 CDO BDE RM
Maddison, John David	CAPT RM(FTC)	RM	SO(LE)	01.01.98	CTCRM
Madge, Anthony Willian John	LT CDR(FTC)	X	PR	01.10.94	DCSA PLYMOUTH
Madge, Richard, *BSc, jsdc*	CAPT(FTC)	E	WE	30.06.98	MOD (LONDON)
Madgwick, Edward Charles Cowtan, *BDS*	SG LT(D)	-		23.07.96	40 CDO RM
Madigan, Lee, *BA*	SLT(IC)	X		01.01.98	ROEBUCK
Maese, Philip Andrew	MAJ(FTC)	RM	SO(LE)	01.10.97	RM Poole
Magan, Michael James Christopher, *BEng, MSc, AMIEE, psc(j), gw*	LT CDR(FTC)	E	WE	01.03.95	CINCFLEET
Magill, Thomas Eugene	LT(FTC)	X	AV	24.07.97	ILLUSTRIOUS
Magill, William John, *BSc, CEng, MIEE*	CDR(FTC)	E	WE	30.06.89	SSA BRISTOL
Magowan, Robert Andrew, *BSc*	MAJ(FTC)	RM		01.09.97	BDS WASHINGTON
Magrath, Alan Richard	LT(TC)	S	(S)	01.05.98	FOREST MOOR
Maguire, Anton Paul Duncan, *MIPD*	LT CDR(FTC)	S		01.11.81	DRAKE CBP(DLO)
Maher, Anthony Michael	MAJ(FTC)	RM	SO(LE)	01.10.96	JSU NORTHWOOD
Maher, Michael Patrick, *pce*	LT CDR(FTC)	X	PWO(A)	16.05.96	EXCHANGE USA
Mahony, David Grehan, *pce, pcea*	LT CDR(FTC)	X	O	16.04.96	NMA PORTSMOUTH
Maidment, Keith Charles, *BSc, MSc, CEng, MIMarE*	LT CDR(FTC)	E	ME	01.03.87	SSA DEVONPORT
Maidment, Phillip Charles	LT CDR(FTC)	E	WE	01.10.95	HQ DCSA
Mailes, Ian Robert Arthur	LT(CC)	X	O	16.04.94	824 NAS
Main, Edward Stafford, *BSc, CEng, MIMarE*	CDR(FTC)	E	ME	30.06.98	FOSF
Mair, Brian, *pce*	LT CDR(FTC)	X	MCD	05.03.93	PEMBROKE

Name	Rank	Branch	Spec	Seniority	Where Serving
Makepeace, Philip Andrew , *BEng, AMIEE*	LT CDR(FTC)	E	WE	24.12.98	MOD (LONDON)
Malbon, Fabian Michael , *rcds, pce, psc*	VADM	-	PWO(N)†	06.01.99	CINCFLEET
Malcolm, Stephen Robert , *MA, pce, psc(j)*	LT CDR(FTC)	X	H CH	01.06.91	NMA PORTSMOUTH
Maley, Catherine Elizabeth , *LLB*	LT(CC)	X	O	16.01.98	815 FLT 210
Malin, Michael John	LT CDR(FTC)	X	H CH	01.04.88	MOD (LONDON)
Malins, Damian Joseph Holland , *BSc*	LT(FTC)	S		01.03.95	NMA PORTSMOUTH
Malkin, Sharon Louise , *BA*	LT(FTC)	E	AE	01.05.95	HARRIER IPT
Mallabone, James John Kenneth , *BSc*	LT(IC)	E	TM	01.08.97	COLLINGWOOD
Mallalieu, Adam John , *MA, psc*	LT COL(FTC)	RM		31.12.98	CTCRM
Mallard, Elizabeth	LT	Q		07.11.99	RH HASLAR
Mallen, David John	LT(CC)	E	AE(P)	01.12.95	814 SQN
Malley, Mark Paul , *BEng*	LT(FTC)	E	WESM	01.01.93	DARTMOUTH BRNC
Mallinson, Robert , *BEng, psc(j)*	LT CDR(FTC)	E	AE(O)	01.03.97	700M MERLIN IFTU
Malone, Mick	SLT(IC)	X	g	29.04.98	DRYAD
Maltby, Michael Robert James , *BSc*	CDR(FTC)	E	ME	31.12.99	CINCFLEET
Maltby, Richard James	CAPT RM(FTC)	RM		29.04.97	RM Poole
Manchanda, Keith Sajir , *OBE, pce, pcea (Act Cdr)*	LT CDR(FTC)	X	O	01.03.84	MOD (LONDON)
Mandley, Philip John , *BSc, MSc*	LT(CC)	E	TM	01.05.90	DITMTC SHRIVNHAM
Manfield, Michael David , *pce(sm)*	LT CDR(FTC)	X	SM	01.01.99	VICTORIOUS(PORT)
Manger, Garth Stuart Cunningham , *osc(us)*	MAJ(FTC)	RM	C	25.04.96	EXCHANGE ARMY UK
Mann, Andrew	SLT(IC)	E	WE	27.01.99	COLLINGWOOD
Mann, Colin Andrew	SLT(UCE)(CC)	E	AE	01.09.99	DARTMOUTH BRNC
Mann, David Michael , *BEng*	LT(IC)	X		01.06.99	LANCASTER
Mann, Gary Digby , *BA, FCMA*	LT CDR(CC)	E	TMSM	01.10.97	CSST SHORE DEVPT
Manning, Duncan , *MA*	CAPT RM(FTC)	RM		01.09.97	RM Poole
Manning, Gary Paul	SLT(IC)	S		01.09.98	DARTMOUTH BRNC
Manning, Martin Graham Bickley , *AFC, pce, pcea, psc, psc(j)*	CAPT(FTC)	X	O	31.12.95	NMA PORTSMOUTH
Mannion, Robert Victor , *pce*	LT CDR(FTC)	X	SM	01.06.95	MWC PORTSDOWN
Mannion, Timothy Shaun	LT CDR(FTC)	X	P	01.09.86	HQ3GP HQSTC
Manoy, Stephen , *BSc*	LT(IC)	X		01.01.00	CHIDDINGFOLD
Mansell, Paul Robert , *MA, MPhil, psc(m)*	LT COL(FTC)	RM		31.12.97	MOD (LONDON)
Manser, Darren	LT(IC)	X	P	01.04.94	771 SK5 SAR
Mansergh, Andrew Christopher , *BA*	2LT(GRAD)(IC)	RM		01.09.99	CTCRM LYMPSTONE
Mansergh, Michael Peter , *BA, pce*	CDR(FTC)	X	PWO(C)	30.06.94	NMA PORTSMOUTH
Mansergh, Robert James , *LLB, pce, pce(sm)*	CAPT(FTC)	X	SM	30.06.00	CINCFLEET
Mansfield, Ian , *BSc*	LT(IC)	E		01.01.00	DARTMOUTH BRNC
Mansfield, James Alexander , *BA*	LT(CC)	X		01.10.97	IRON DUKE
Manson, Colin Robert , *BSc, PGDip*	LT CDR(FTC)	X	METOC	01.10.98	CINCFLEET
Manson, Paul David	LT(IC)	X		01.05.94	JARIC
Manson, Peter Duncan , *BA*	MAJ(FTC)	RM	P	01.09.99	847 SQN
Manson, Thomas Edward , *BSc, psc(j)*	LT CDR(FTC)	E	AE(P)	07.09.98	RNAS YEOVILTON
Mant, James Nicholas , *BSc, CEng*	LT CDR(FTC)	E	WE	01.10.89	COLLINGWOOD
Mantella, Dante Nevil , *BSc*	CAPT RM(IC)	RM		01.09.98	42 CDO RM
Mantle, Mark , *MB, BS*	SURG LT	-		07.08.96	MODHU DERRIFORD
Mantri, Anand Harishankar , *BEng*	LT(IC)	X	P U/T	01.01.00	DHFS
Manwaring, Roy Geoffrey	LT(FTC)	MS		26.04.99	NEPTUNE CFS
Maples, Andrew	SURG SLT	-		25.06.99	DARTMOUTH BRNC
Marchant, Timothy Alan Cardew , *pce*	LT CDR(FTC)	X	PWO(U)	01.02.91	FOST SEA
Mardlin, Stephen Andrew	LT CDR(FTC)	S		01.04.99	RICHMOND
Mardon, Karl Fraser	LT CDR(FTC)	X	PWO(U)	02.09.92	DRYAD
Marini, Tristan Antonio , *BSc*	LT(CC)	X		01.09.99	MOD (LONDON)
Marino, David Jones , *MBE, MA, psc*	LT COL(FTC)	RM	SO(LE)	01.10.98	HQRM
Marjoram, Gareth Keri , *BEng*	LT(CC)	E	WESM	01.05.96	TIRELESS
Marjoram, Joseph William , *BSc*	SLT(CC)	X		01.09.97	DRYAD
Mark, Robert Alan , *BSc, MNI, MRIN*	CAPT(FTC)	X	H CH	31.12.96	MOD (LONDON)
Markey, Adrian Philip , *BEng*	LT(FTC)	X	O	01.08.93	815 FLT 207
Marks, Nicholas , *BSc, MDA, CEng, MRAeS*	CAPT(FTC)	E	AE	31.12.97	MOD DHSA
Marland, Eunice Elizabeth , *BSc*	SLT(IC)	X		01.01.99	DARTMOUTH BRNC
Marley, Peter Shaun , *BSc, MA, PGCE, FIMgt, MIPD, jsdc, psc(m)*	CDR(FTC)	E	TM	31.12.87	EXCELLENT
Marmont, Kerry Lewis , *BSc*	LT CDR(FTC)	E	WESM	01.05.92	CSST SEA
Marok, Jani , *BSc, MA, psc(j)*	MAJ(FTC)	RM		30.04.95	JSCSC
Marquis, Adrian Colin , *BEng*	LT(CC)	X	P	01.12.93	810 SQN SEAHAWK
Marr, James , *BEng*	LT(FTC)	E	MESM	01.05.97	VICTORIOUS(STBD)

Name	Rank	Branch	Spec	Seniority	Where Serving
Marratt, Richard James, *BSc*	LT(CC)	E	TM	01.09.90	RM POOLE
Marriott, Matthew James	SLT(UCE)(FTC)	X		01.09.99	DARTMOUTH BRNC
Marriott, Mark Nicholas, *BEng, MSc*	LT CDR(FTC)	E	AE	01.04.99	ES AIR BRISTOL
Marriott, Neil Kenneth	LT(CC)	X	MCD	01.12.95	HURWORTH
Marsh, Brian Henry, *MBE, BSc, pcea*	LT CDR(FTC)	X	O	01.10.99	DRYAD
Marsh, David Julian, *BSc, MIMgt*	CDR(FTC)	S		31.12.93	FOSF
Marsh, Michael Peter Alan	LT(FTC)	X	PR	13.12.95	FOSNNI OPS CFS
Marshall, Alistair John, *BA*	LT(IC)	X		01.12.99	RALEIGH
Marshall, Colin George	MID(UCE)(FTC)	E	WE	01.09.98	DARTMOUTH BRNC
Marshall, Fleur Tiffany, *MB, ChB*	SURG LT	-		07.08.96	MODHU DERRIFORD
Marshall, Gavin Peter, *MEng*	SLT(IC)	E	ME	01.01.99	DARTMOUTH BRNC
Marshall, Jonathan Paul, *psc*	LT CDR(FTC)	S		01.01.83	MOD (LONDON)
Marshall, Matthew, *BEng*	LT(IC)	X	P	01.09.98	845 SQN
Marshall, Paul, *BEng, MSc*	LT(FTC)	E	ME	01.03.93	MOD (LONDON)
Marshall, Richard Anthony, *pce, psc(m)*	CDR(FTC)	X	MCD	31.12.92	DARTMOUTH BRNC
Marshall, Richard George Carter	LT CDR(FTC)	X	PWO(C)	01.05.95	COLLINGWOOD
Marson, Gary Michael	LT(FTC)	E	WE	01.03.94	SSA BRISTOL
Marston, Peter Alan, *BA*	LT CDR(FTC)	S		16.04.96	PORTLAND
Marston, Sarah Alice Bedford, *BSc, MSc*	LT CDR(FTC)	E	IS	01.10.96	CINCFLEET
Marten, Andrew	LT(CC)	X	ATC	01.04.95	RNAS YEOVILTON
Martin, Antony John	LT(FTC)	X	C	10.12.98	MARLBOROUGH
Martin, Bruce Anthony, *BSc, CEng*	LT CDR(FTC)	E	MESM	01.05.97	VANGUARD(PORT)
Martin, Christopher Charles Roger	*MID*(IC)	X		01.09.98	DARTMOUTH BRNC
Martin, Colin John, *pce, pcea, ocds(Can)*	CDR(FTC)	X	O	30.06.00	BFFI
Martin, David	SLT(IC)	X	NO-S/S	19.09.98	DRYAD
Martin, Elizabeth Janet, *BSc*	LT CDR(FTC)	E	TM	01.04.91	NP 1061
Martin, John Henry	LT(TC)	S	(S)	18.06.93	MWC SOUTHWICK
Martin, Michael Peter	LT CDR(FTC)	E	AE(L)	01.10.93	ES AIR YEO
Martin, Michael Terence, *BEng, psc*	LT CDR(FTC)	E	ME	12.05.92	FOST SEA
Martin, Neil, *MB, BSc, ChB*	SURG LT	-		04.08.99	INM ALVERSTOKE
Martin, Nigel	LT(FTC)	X	C	20.09.99	HQ DCSA
Martin, Nathan Alan	CAPT RM(IC)	RM		01.09.99	CTCRM
Martin, Neil Douglas, *BSc, pcea, psc, gdas*	LT CDR(FTC)	X	O	01.06.87	LOAN DERA BSC DN
Martin, Nicholas Peter	SURG LT	-		26.08.99	INM ALVERSTOKE
Martin, Paul John, *BSc, psc(m)*	LT COL(FTC)	RM	C	31.12.93	MOD (LONDON)
Martin, Ronald Charles John Richard	CHAPLAIN	SF		03.09.96	DARTMOUTH BRNC
Martin, Roger Graham	LT CDR(FTC)	X	PWO(A)	01.09.95	EXCHANGE CANADA
Martin, Robert James, *BEng*	LT(CC)	E	AE	01.01.00	SULTAN
Martin, Simon Charles, *LVO, pce, pce(sm), psc*	CAPT(FTC)	X	SM	30.06.98	MOD (LONDON)
Martin, Simon James, *BEng*	LT CDR(FTC)	E	WESM	01.02.00	MWC PORTSDOWN
Martin, Stuart William, *BSc, MSc*	LT(IC)	E	AE	01.06.99	SULTAN
Martin, Timothy Frederick Wilkins, *LLB (BARRISTER)*	CAPT(FTC)	S	BAR	31.12.98	MOD (LONDON)
Martyn, Alan Wallace, *MSc, CEng, MRAeS*	LT CDR(FTC)	E	AE	01.07.93	MOD (LONDON)
Martyn, Daniel, *BA, MSc*	SLT(IC)	X		01.05.98	EXETER
Maskell, John Malcolm, *adp (Act Lt Cdr)*	LT(FTC)	E	MESM	16.02.84	2SL/CNH FOTR
Mason, Andrew Clive, *BSc*	LT(IC)	X		01.07.98	COTTESMORE
Mason, Andrew Harold, *BSc, MSc*	CDR(FTC)	E	AE	31.12.99	ES AIR YEO
Mason, Alexander Malcolm, *OBE, ocds(No), fsc*	COL(OF6)(FTC)	RM	RL	30.06.94	MOD (LONDON)
Mason, Colin Edward, *ACMA*	LT CDR(FTC)	S	CMA	16.11.83	2SL/CNH
Mason, Darren Jon, *BEng*	LT(FTC)	X	SM	01.03.97	RALEIGH
Mason, Jeffrey Sinclair, *psc*	LT COL(FTC)	RM	LC	31.12.95	HQ 3 CDO BDE RM
Mason, Martin	LT CDR(FTC)	E	AE(M)	01.10.99	FONA
Mason, Maxwell James, *BA*	LT(IC)	X	H2	01.05.98	ENDURANCE
Mason, Mark John, *BSc*	LT(IC)	X		01.01.00	DUMBARTON CASTLE
Mason, Michael Miles David, *BSc, pce, pcea*	CDR(FTC)	X	O	30.06.93	NELSON (PAY)
Mason, Nicholas Hugh, *BSc, MinstP, C PHYS*	CDR(FTC)	E	TM	31.12.98	JSCSC
Mason, Richard William, *BSc, MA, CEng, MIEE, psc*	CDR(FTC)	E	WE	30.06.93	FOSF
Mason-Matthews, Angela	MID(NE)(IC)	X		01.09.99	DARTMOUTH BRNC
Massey, Alan Michael, *BA, rcds, pce, psc (COMMODORE)*	CAPT(FTC)	X	PWO(A)	30.06.96	SACLANT USA
Massey, Paul	LT(FTC)	X	AV	23.07.93	DISC SEA
Massie-Taylor, Christopher Gerald, *OBE, pce, psc*	CAPT(FTC)	X	MCD/MW	31.12.93	SAUDI AFPS SAUDI
Masson, Neil Graham, *BSc*	SLT(IC)	X		01.01.99	DARTMOUTH BRNC
Masters, James Christopher	LT CDR(FTC)	X	PWO(A)	01.05.96	DRYAD

Name	Rank	Branch	Spec	Seniority	Where Serving
Masters, Nicholas Norman John , *MA, MRCVS*	CAPT RM(IC)	RM		01.09.98	40 CDO RM
Masters, Richard Hilary , *BTech, MIPD, MA*	LT CDR(FTC)	E	TM	01.01.92	2SL/CNH FOTR
Mather, Graeme Philip	LT CDR(FTC)	E	ME	01.07.97	GRAFTON
Mather, Richard Hedley , *BM, BS, BMS*	SURG LT	-		07.08.96	RH HASLAR
Mathews, Andrew David Hugh , *MSc, CEng, MIMechE,*	CAPT(FTC)	E	MESM	30.06.97	RCDS *psc*
Mathias, Philip Bentley , *MBE, pce, pce(sm), psc*	CAPT(FTC)	X	SM	31.12.99	MOD (LONDON)
Mathias-Jones, Peter David , *pce*	LT CDR(FTC)	X	PWO(U)	01.09.90	DRYAD
Mathieson, Kevin Richard , *pcea*	LT CDR(FTC)	X	P	01.10.95	824 NAS
Mathieson, Neil Braid , *BEng*	LT(CC)	E	AE	01.02.00	SULTAN
Matters, Andrew Charles , *BSc, CEng, FIMechE*	CDR(FTC)	E	ME	30.06.92	MOD (BATH)
Matthew, Mark Jonathan *(Act Lt)*	SLT(CC)	S		01.05.97	TRIUMPH
Matthews, Duncan Neil , *MBE, BSc, pce, pcea*	CDR(FTC)	X	P	31.12.99	JSCSC
Matthews, David William , *BEng, MSc*	LT CDR(FTC)	E	WESM	01.01.98	RALEIGH
Matthews, George , *psc*	MAJ(FTC)	RM	SO(LE)	01.10.95	MOD (LONDON)
Matthews, Gary Anthony , *MB, BCh, MRCP*	SURG LTCDR	-		01.08.98	NELSON (PAY)
Matthews, Graham Gavin , *BA*	LT(CC)	X	P	01.03.86	RAF SHAWBURY
Matthews, Justin	LT(CC)	X	O	16.05.94	849 SQN HQ
Matthews, Jonathan James , *MB, ChB*	SURG LT	-		01.08.96	MODHU DERRIFORD
Matthews, Peter , *BSc, pce, jsdc*	CDR(FTC)	X	AWO(A)	30.06.89	LN DERA CDA HLS
Matthews, Paul Brian , *BEng*	LT CDR(FTC)	E	TM	01.10.99	NELSON RNSETT
Matthews, Paul Kinley	LT(FTC)	S		01.10.95	DRAKE DPL
Matthews, Peter Ronald	SLT(FTC)	E	AE(M)	01.04.98	815 SQN HQ
Matthews, Quentin Stacey , *n*	LT(FTC)	X		01.08.93	CINCFLEET
Matthews, Stuart Grendon , *pce*	LT CDR(FTC)	X	PWO(N)	01.06.95	ENDURANCE
Matthews, William	CHAPLAIN	SF		12.08.91	NELSON
Mattin, Paul Roger	CAPT RM(FTC)	RM	MLDR	26.04.94	EXCHANGE ARMY UK
Mattock, Damian Brian	LT(FTC)	X	SM	01.04.98	FOSM NWOOD OPS
Maude, Christopher Philip , *pcea*	LT CDR(FTC)	X	P	01.10.92	700M MERLIN IFTU
Maude, David Howard	LT CDR(FTC)	E	AE(L)	01.10.99	FONA
Maughan, Jonathan Mortimer Collingwood , *LVO, OBE, MRIN, MNI, pce*	CDR(FTC)	X	PWO(N)†	31.12.92	SACLANT USA
Maw, Martyn John , *BSc, CEng, MIEE*	LT CDR(FTC)	E	WESM	01.12.90	RALEIGH
Mawdsley, Gareth Richard	SLT(UCE)(FTC)	X		01.09.99	DARTMOUTH BRNC
Mawson, John Robert , *BA*	CAPT RM(IC)	RM		01.05.99	CTCRM
Maxwell, Alan Brian Crawford , *BDS, MSc, MGDS, RCSEd*	SGCDR(D)	-		31.12.97	RALEIGH
Maxwell, Alexander Matthew	CAPT(CS)RM	-		10.01.97	DNR N SCOTLAND
Maxwell, Rachel , *BA, n*	LT(FTC)	X		01.05.94	DRYAD
Maxwell-Cox, Michael James , *IEng, AMIMarE*	LT CDR(FTC)	E	ME	01.10.98	NEWCASTLE
May, Colin	LT(FTC)	X		01.07.96	DRYAD
May, Damien John	LT RM(IC)	RM		01.04.99	42 CDO RM
May, Dominic Peter	CAPT RM(FTC)	RM		26.04.94	HQRM
May, John William	LT(CC)	X	P	01.07.95	815 SQN HQ
May, Nigel Peter , *pcea*	LT CDR(FTC)	X	P	01.09.98	LIVERPOOL
May, Phillip	CAPT RM(IC)	RM		01.09.97	CTCRM
May, Steven Charles , *BEng*	LT(FTC)	E	ME	01.07.95	SULTAN
May-Clingo, Martin Stephen	LT(FTC)	X	AV	04.04.91	FOSF PHOT UNIT
Maybery, James Edward	MAJ(FTC)	RM		01.05.97	RM Poole
Mayhew, Nicholas Morvaren , *pce, pcea, psc*	LT CDR(FTC)	X	P	16.08.90	MERLIN IPT
Maynard, Andrew Thomas Westenborg , *osc(us)*	MAJ(FTC)	RM		01.09.97	MOD (LONDON)
Maynard, Charles Ian , *BA, n*	LT(FTC)	X		01.02.95	EDINBURGH
Maynard, Paul Andrew , *BSc*	2LT(GRAD)(IC)	RM		01.09.99	CTCRM LYMPSTONE
Mayne, Charles William Erskine , *BEng*	CAPT RM(IC)	RM		01.09.96	CTCRM
Maze, Andrew Terence , *BSc*	CHAPLAIN	SF		11.09.79	2SL/CNH
Mc Allister, Steven Edward	SLT(IC)	X		01.01.99	DARTMOUTH BRNC
Mc Currach, Robert Henry	SLT(IC)	X		01.05.98	DRYAD
Mc Laren, James Patrick	MAJ(FTC)	RM		30.04.98	PJHQ
McAlpine, Paul Anthony , *pce, psc(j)*	CDR(FTC)	X	MCD	31.12.98	SOMERSET
McAnally, John Henry Stuart , *CB, LVO, MNI, MRIN, rcds, pce, psc, hcsc*	RADM	-	N†	12.08.98	RCDS
McArdell, Steven James Ronald , *pcea*	LT(CC)	X	P	01.04.90	RAF CRANWELL EFS
McArthur, Calum James Gibb , *BM, BCh, BAO, DObstRCOG, Dip FFP, LRCP, MRCGP*	SURG CDR	-	GMPP	30.06.92	HQ 3 CDO BDE RM
McAulay, Paul John , *BSc*	SLT(IC)	X		01.09.97	DRYAD
McAuslin, Thomas McDonald , *MSc*	LT CDR(FTC)	MS	SM	01.10.98	DEF MED TRG CTR
McBain, Mandy Sheila	LT(CC)	W	S	11.12.92	NMA PORTSMOUTH

Name	Rank	Branch	Spec	Seniority	Where Serving
McBarnet, Thomas Francis, *BSc, pce*	CDR(FTC)	X	PWO(U)	31.12.97	IRON DUKE
McBratney, James Alexander Grant	LT(FTC)	X	SM	01.11.96	VIGILANT(STBD)
McCabe, Daniel Stewart	LT(FTC)	E	WE	19.02.93	MCM2 SEA
McCabe, Garry Patrick, *BA*	CAPT RM(IC)	RM		01.09.97	40 CDO RM
McCabe, Joseph, *BA, psc*	LT COL(FTC)	RM		31.12.92	NMA PORTSMOUTH
McCabe, Shane Edward Thomas, *MB, BSc, BS*	SURG LT	-		01.08.95	MODHU DERRIFORD
McCaffery, George Frederick	LT CDR(FTC)	E	AE(M)	01.10.98	FONA
McCall, Gary, *BA*	LT(CC)	X	P	01.05.99	702 SQN HERON
McCall, Iain Robert, *pce*	LT CDR(FTC)	X	PWO(N)	01.07.96	CAPT F4 (SEA)
McCallum, Neil Ritchie, *BEng*	LT(FTC)	E	ME	01.06.97	RICHMOND
McCamphill, Paul Joseph, *BEng*	SLT(IC)	E	WE	01.01.99	DARTMOUTH BRNC
McCann, Toby, *BEng*	LT(FTC)	E	AE	01.12.98	RNAS CULDROSE
McCardle, John Alexander, *BSc, jsdc*	MAJ(FTC)	RM	P	01.08.92	JHCHQ
McCartain, Michael Brendon William, *BSc, pce, pcea, psc*	CDR(FTC)	X	O	31.12.98	FONA
McCarthy, Patrick John, *MILog*	CDR(FTC)	S		31.12.91	2SL/CNH
McCarthy, Steven James, *BEng*	LT(FTC)	E	ME	01.01.95	MOD (BATH)
McCaughey, Vincent Joseph, *BComm, PGCE*	LT(CC)	E	TM	01.03.93	AFPAA(CENTURION)
McCauley, Linda Jane, *BA*	SLT(IC)	X		01.05.98	CHATHAM
McClay, William Jason, *BEng*	CAPT RM(IC)	RM		01.09.97	RMR SCOTLAND
McCleary, Simon Paul, *BEng*	LT(CC)	E	WESM	01.03.98	VENGEANCE(PORT)
McClement, Duncan, *BEng*	LT(FTC)	E	MESM	01.09.99	SULTAN
McClement, Timothy Pentreath, *OBE, jsdc, pce, pce(sm), hcsc*	CAPT(FTC)	X	SM	30.06.92	CORNWALL
McCloskey, Ian Michael	LT(CC)	E	ME	01.06.96	JSCSC
McCombe, John	LT(FTC)	E	ME	01.09.96	DRAKE CFM
McConochie, Andrew David, *BSc*	LT CDR(FTC)	S		16.04.96	CORNWALL
McCorkindale, Peter Robin, *BDS*	SGLTCDR(D)	-		13.06.96	NELSON
McCormack, Conor Patrick	MAJ(FTC)	RM	LC	30.04.98	COMACCHIO GP RM
McCormack, Gary	MID(UCE)(FTC)	E	ME	01.09.98	DARTMOUTH BRNC
McCormick, John Patrick, *BEng*	LT CDR(FTC)	E	AE	20.09.93	MOD DHSA
McCormick, Peter Edward, *BSc*	LT(CC)	X	P	01.08.98	RNAS CULDROSE
McCowan, David James	LT(CC)	X	P	16.06.95	846 SQN
McCowen, Polly Anne Charlotte, *BA*	SLT(IC)	S		01.05.98	DARTMOUTH BRNC
McCoy, Mark	LT(CC)	E	AE	01.11.98	SULTAN
McCready, Geoffrey Alan Roy, *MBE, FBIM, AIL, pce, pce(sm) (Act Capt)*	CDR(FTC)	X	SM	31.12.90	SA MOSCOW
McCue, Duncan, *MA, MSc, CEng, MIMarE*	LT CDR(FTC)	E	ME	01.10.98	ILLUSTRIOUS
McCulley, Steven Cameron *(Act Capt Rm)*	LT RM(IC)	RM		01.04.98	45 CDO RM
McCulloch, Isla Dunbar, *BSc*	LT(IC)	X		01.09.96	BRIDPORT
McCutcheon, Graeme	LT(CC)	X	P	01.02.95	815 SQN HQ
McDermott, Mark, *pcea*	LT(CC)	X	P	01.01.90	819 SQN
McDermott, Owen David, *BEng*	LT CDR(FTC)	E	WE	01.10.99	NORFOLK
McDermott, Paul Andrew	LT(FTC)	X	MW	24.07.97	CHIDDINGFOLD
McDermott, William Martin, OBE, pcs	COL RM(FTC)	RM	RM MOR	31.12.99	CTCRM
McDicken, Ian Neil, *BDS*	SG LT(D)	-		25.06.98	DRAKE CBP(CNH)
McDonald, Andrew, *BEng*	LT(CC)	E	AE	01.03.00	SULTAN
McDonald, Duncan James, *BEng*	LT(IC)	E		01.09.98	NOTTINGHAM
McDonald, Damien Niall, *BA*	LT(CC)	X		01.10.98	COTTESMORE
McDonald, Ian Gordon	LT(CC)	X	O	01.05.91	771 SK5 SAR
McDonald, James	LT(CS)	-		06.02.94	DNR S SCOTLAND
McDonald, John James Bruce	LT CDR(FTC)	X	P	01.05.84	RNAS YEOVILTON
McDonald, Norman	LT(CC)	X	P	01.09.94	819 SQN
McDonnell, David Shaw, *PGDip*	LT CDR(FTC)	X	METOC	01.03.99	LOAN DERA ADAC
McDonnell, Peter William, *pce, pce(sm)*	CDR(FTC)	X	SM	30.06.98	VICTORIOUS(STBD)
McDonough, Ambrose Gerrard, *BSc*	LT CDR(FTC)	X	PWO(U)	01.07.96	JMOTS NORTHWOOD
McDougall, David William, *BSc, SM(n)*	LT(CC)	X	SM	01.03.96	SOVEREIGN
McElwaine, Richard Ian, *BSc*	CDR(FTC)	E	AE(P)	31.12.94	MOD (LONDON)
McEvoy, Lee Patrick	LT(FTC)	X	EW	24.07.97	PJHQ
McEwan, Andrea Morrison, *BA*	LT(IC)	X		01.10.96	SOMERSET
McFadden, Andrew	CHAPLAIN	RC		01.09.98	CAPT F4 (SEA)
McFadyen, Howard, *OBE, BSc, MSc, CEng, MIMechE*	CAPT(FTC)	E	MESM	31.12.96	MOD (BATH)
McFadzean, Iain	CHAPLAIN	SF		01.07.99	NEPTUNE 2SL/CNH
McFarlane, Andrew Lennox, *OBE, BSc, CEng, MIMechE*	CAPT(FTC)	E	MESM	30.06.00	NEPTUNE DSQ
McFarlane, Robert William Archibald	SLT	Q		02.07.97	RH HASLAR
McGannity, Colin Stephen, *BEng*	SLT(CC)	X	O U/T	01.09.97	849 SQN HQ

Name	Rank	Branch	Spec	Seniority	Where Serving
McGarel, David Francis	LT CDR(FTC)	S	CA	01.10.96	FOSF
McGhee, Craig, *BEng*	CAPT RM(FTC)	RM	P	01.09.96	847 SQN
McGhie, Ian Andrew, *pce, pce(sm)*	CDR(FTC)	X	SM	31.12.99	DRYAD
McGill, Emma Jane, *BDS*	SG LT(D)	-		17.06.98	RALEIGH
McGinley, Christopher Thomas, *BSc, PGCE*	LT(IC)	E	TM	01.05.97	COLLINGWOOD
McGlory, Stephen Joseph, *BA*	LT(FTC)	X	FC	01.06.94	ILLUSTRIOUS
McGowan, Angela Bridget, *BA*	SLT(IC)	X	O U/T	01.09.98	DARTMOUTH BRNC
McGrane, Richard	LT(FTC)	X	C	03.04.97	MOD (LONDON)
McGrath, Wayne James	SLT(IC)	S	(S)	19.09.98	RALEIGH
McGrenary, Andrew	LT CDR(FTC)	X		01.01.94	DISC
McGuire, James, *SM(n)*	LT(CC)	X	SM	01.10.96	VIGILANT(STBD)
McGuire, Michael Joseph, *pce, n*	LT CDR(FTC)	X	PWO(A)	31.08.98	EXCHANGE GERMANY
McGunigall, Roy	LT(FTC)	MS	(AD)	03.04.97	NEPTUNE NT
McHale, Gareth John, *BSc, pce, pcea*	LT CDR(FTC)	X	O	01.12.91	COMUKTG/CASWSF
McHale, Kevan	LT CDR(FTC)	E	AE(M)	01.10.97	848 SQN HERON
McHugh, Richard Henry, *BEng*	LT(FTC)	E	ME	01.03.97	CAMPBELTOWN
McHugh, Terence Patrick, *BSc*	LT(CC)	X		01.08.89	2SL/CNH FOTR
McInerney, Andrew Jonathon, *BSc*	MAJ(FTC)	RM		01.09.99	HQRM
McInnes, James Gerald Kenneth, *BSc*	LT CDR(FTC)	E	WESM	01.06.95	CSST SEA
McIntosh, James Declan, *MB, BS, BA(Hons)*	SURG LT	-		26.08.97	DRAKE CBP(DLO)
McIntyre, Alastair William *(Act Lt Cdr)*	LT(FTC)	X	tas	25.07.91	PJHQ
McIntyre, Louise, *MA*	SLT(CC)	X		01.09.97	DRYAD
McJarrow, Duncan James, *BDS, MDGS, RCS, LDS RCS(Eng)*	SGCDR(D)	-		30.06.00	LOAN BRUNEI
McKay, Paul Anthony, *pcea*	LT CDR(FTC)	X	O	16.08.85	MOD (LONDON)
McKay, Thomas Westley, *LLB*	SLT(IC)	X		01.01.99	DARTMOUTH BRNC
McKeating, John Brendan, *BM, BSc, BCh, MSc*, Dip *FP, DipIMC RCSED, MRCGP, JCPTGP*	SURG CDR	-	GMPP	30.06.00	JSU NORTHWOOD
McKee, Hamish McLeod, *BA, BComm*	LT(IC)	X	O	01.07.97	820 SQN
McKellar, Robert Archibald, *pcea, psc*	LT CDR(FTC)	X	O	01.06.81	RNAS YEOVILTON
McKendrick, Andrew Michael, *pce, pce(sm)*	CDR(FTC)	X	SM	31.12.98	MWC PORTSDOWN
McKenna, Danelle Rosanne	*MID*(IC)	X	O U/T	01.01.99	MONTROSE
McKenzie, David, *BSc, CEng, MIMarE*	CDR(FTC)	E	ME	30.06.00	CINCFLEET
McKenzie, Ian Scott, *MBE, jsdc, pce*	CDR(FTC)	X	P	31.12.87	MOD (LONDON)
McKenzie, Malcolm	LT CDR(FTC)	X	PWO(A)	03.03.98	FONA
McKeown, Justin Reaney	MAJ(FTC)	RM		01.09.97	CTCRM
McKernan, James	LT(FTC)	X	C	27.07.95	COLLINGWOOD
McKie, Andrew, *MBE, MA, pcea, psc*	LT CDR(FTC)	X	P	01.10.89	FONA
McKillop, Helenora Elisabeth Lang	LT	Q	OTSPEC	14.02.86	RH HASLAR
McKinlay, Stuart, *BEM, MSc*	LT CDR(FTC)	MS	(LT)	01.10.93	MOD (LONDON)
McKinney, Mark Douglas	MAJ(FTC)	RM	MLDR	01.05.97	NP 1066
McKnight, Derekjames Stewart	LT(FTC)	X	MCD	01.07.91	DRYAD
McKnight, Nicholas William	LT CDR(FTC)	S		01.10.93	AFPAA WTHY DOWN
McLachlan, Jennifer Kim, *MB, ChB*	SURG LT	-		17.08.95	MODHU DERRIFORD
McLachlan, Michael Paul, *AMIMarE*	LT(FTC)	E	ME	18.06.93	OCEAN
McLarnon, Christopher Patrick Charles, *BSc*	LT CDR(FTC)	E	TM	01.09.99	HQRM
McLaughlan, Charles John, *MBA (Act Lt Cdr)*	LT(FTC)	MS	(PD)	08.04.94	2SL/CNH
McLaughlan, Claire Louise, *MA(Ed)*	LT CDR	Q	IC	01.10.98	RDMC BLOCKHOUSE
McLean, David	CHAPLAIN	RC		18.09.96	NEPTUNE 2SL/CNH
McLean, Rory Alistair Ian, *OBE, pce, hcsc*	CAPT(FTC)	X	P	30.06.92	INVINCIBLE
McLellan, James Douglas, *BEng, AMIEE*	LT(CC)	E	WE	01.11.97	EXETER
McLennan, Andrew	LT(CC)	X	O	01.04.95	824 NAS
McLennan, Richard Glenn, *BSc, fsc*	CDR(FTC)	E	AE	30.06.98	AIS SW
McLintock, Mark William, *MA*	LT(IC)	X		01.05.94	FOSNNI OPS CFS
McLocklan, Lee Michael	LT(IC)	S		01.04.00	NELSON WF
McMenamin, Diarmaid	SURG SLT	-		01.10.99	DARTMOUTH BRNC
McMichael, James Stewart, *BSc*	LT(CC)	X	O	01.01.98	815 FLT 241
McMichael-Phillips, Scott James, *BSc, ARICS*	CDR(FTC)	X	H CH	31.12.99	DRYAD
McMillan, George Harrison Grant, *QHP, MD, MSc, BCh, FRCP, FRCPGlas, FFOM, MRCP, AFOM, jsdc, GB*, O *(COMMODORE)*	SURG CAPT	-	(CO/M)	31.12.92	2SL/CNH
McMillan, Nelson	MID(NE)(IC)	X		01.09.99	DARTMOUTH BRNC
McMulkin, John Patrick, *BA*	CAPT RM(IC)	RM		01.09.98	RM Poole
McMullan, Neil Leslie, *BA, MSc*	LT(FTC)	E	TM	01.01.93	SULTAN
McNair, Euan Alan, *AFC, pce, pcea, psc*	CDR(FTC)	X	P	30.06.95	GANNET

Name	Rank	Branch	Spec	Seniority	Where Serving
McNair, James *(Act Lt)*	SLT(FTC)	E	AE	02.05.97	702 SQN HERON
McNally, Neville James	LT CDR(FTC)	S		01.11.98	HERALD
McNamara, Ian Martin, *BEng*	LT(FTC)	E	WESM	01.08.96	VIGILANT(PORT)
McNaughton, John Alistair	LT CDR(FTC)	X	SM	01.07.93	CNOCS GROUP
McNeice, Anna Louise	MID(NE)(IC)	X		01.01.00	DARTMOUTH BRNC
McNeile, Rory Hugh, *BA, pce*	CDR(FTC)	X	P	30.06.00	820 SQN
McNeill, Ian, *BA, psc(m) (BRIGADIER)*	COL(OF6)(FTC)	RM		31.12.96	HQ NORTH
McNeill Love, *The Hon* Robin (Michael Cox), *MB, BS, DA, DObstRCOG, BS, DA, DObstRCOG, DipAvMed, Dip FFP, MRCGP*	SURG CDR	-	GMPP	30.06.96	NBC PORTSMOUTH
McQuaker, Stuart Ross, *pce, psc(j)*	CDR(FTC)	X	PWO(N)	31.12.98	NORTHUMBERLAND
McQueen, Jason Bedwell, *BSc, n*	LT(IC)	E	TM	01.07.93	COLLINGWOOD
McRae, Philip Compton, *BEng, CEng, MIEE*	LT CDR(FTC)	E	WESM	01.12.99	MOD (LONDON)
McTaggart, Douglas Alexander	LT(FTC)	E	WE	07.02.97	SSA BRISTOL
McTear, Karen, *BSc*	LT CDR(FTC)	E	TM	16.05.93	SULTAN
McTear, Nigel James	LT(FTC)	X	AV	11.12.92	RFANSU
McTeer, Ian James, *BA*	LT(IC)	X	P	01.01.99	RNAS YEOVILTON
McWilliams, Adrian	LT(CC)	X	O	01.05.98	815 FLT 201
McWilliams, Jacqueline Elizabeth, *BA, MSc*	LT(FTC)	X	MW	01.09.95	WALNEY
Meachin, Michael Charles	CHAPLAIN	SF		07.07.97	RALEIGH
Meadows, Brian	LT CDR(FTC)	X	PT	01.10.98	FORWARD
Meaken, John, *BSc, CEng, MIEE, psc*	CDR(FTC)	E	MESM	31.12.89	DRAKE CBS
Meakin, Brian Richard, *BSc, MBA, pcea*	LT CDR(FTC)	X	O	01.10.96	FONA NORTHWOOD
Mealing, David William, *BEng*	LT(FTC)	E	AE	01.04.97	815 SQN HQ
Mealing, Steven, *BEng*	LT(CC)	E	ME	01.09.98	SULTAN
Meardon, Sarah Beth, *MA*	LT(IC)	S		01.11.99	RALEIGH
Mearns, Craig McDonald, *MA*	LT CDR(FTC)	S		01.05.97	MOD (LONDON)
Mears, Kristian, *BA, BMS*	SURG SLT	-		29.06.99	DARTMOUTH BRNC
Mears, Richard John, *BSc*	2LT(GRAD)(IC)	RM		29.04.98	COMACCHIO GP RM
Meatyard, Christopher George Brandon, *psc*	CDR(FTC)	X	MCD	31.12.88	2SL/CNH
Meeds, Kevin, *pcea*	LT CDR(FTC)	X	O	16.12.95	DRYAD
Meek, Camilla Simpson, *BEng*	LT(FTC)	E	ME	01.03.94	EXCELLENT
Meeking, Christopher George	LT CDR(FTC)	X	PWO(A)	09.01.00	CAMPBELTOWN
Mehta, Raj Philip, *BEng*	LT(IC)	E	WE	01.12.93	MOD (BATH)
Meikle, Kevin Edward James	SLT(FTC)	X	C	01.04.98	KENT
Meikle, Robert	SLT(IC)	X		01.04.98	SANDOWN
Meikle, Stuart Andrew	SLT(FTC)	E	AE(L)	01.04.98	814 SQN
Mellor, Adrian John, *MB, BCh, FRCA*	SURG LTCDR	-	SM	06.09.96	NELSON (PAY)
Mellor, Barry John, *MA, MIMgt, psc(j)*	LT CDR(FTC)	S		16.05.93	ELANT/NAVNORTH
Melly, Richard Graham, *MSc, CEng, MIMarE, psc*	CAPT(FTC)	E	ME	31.12.95	RCDS
Melrose, John, *BSc, adp*	LT CDR(FTC)	E	IS	27.10.83	2SL/CNH
Melton, Colin, *BEng, MSc, AMIEE*	LT CDR(FTC)	E	WE	01.05.99	DGSS BRISTOL
Melville-Brown, Martin Giles	LT(FTC)	S	CA	08.04.94	MOD (BATH)
Menlove-Platt, Christopher John, *BSc, CEng, FIMarE*	CDR(FTC)	E	ME	31.12.93	AMC
Menzies, Angus	CAPT(FTC)	S	SM	31.12.98	CINCFLEET
Menzies, Anthony John, *BSc*	LT CDR(FTC)	E	AE(P)	01.05.90	RNAS CULDROSE
Menzies, Bruce, *BSc*	SLT(IC)	X	P U/T	01.09.97	RAF CRANWELL EFS
Mercer, Andrew	SURG SLT	-		27.01.99	DARTMOUTH BRNC
Mercer, David Crispian	LT(CC)	X	P	16.01.93	815 FLT 215
Mercer, Paul John	LT(IC)	X	O	01.04.96	819 SQN
Mercer, Stuart James, *BM, BCh*	SURG LT	-		03.08.95	MODHU DERRIFORD
Mercer, Simon, *MB, ChB (Act Surg Lt)*	SURG SLT	-		06.04.98	DARTMOUTH BRNC
Merchant, Ian Charles	LT CDR(FTC)	S		05.01.94	FOST SEA
Merchant, Jeremy Mark	CAPT RM(FTC)	RM	SO(LE)	01.01.98	CHFHQ
Meredith, Nicholas, *BSc, pce(sm)*	LT CDR(FTC)	X	SM	01.04.94	DALRIADA
Merewether, Henry Alworth Hamilton, *pce, pcea*	LT CDR(FTC)	X	O	01.05.98	CAPT F4 (SEA)
Merrett, Gordon James, *LLB, pce, psc, psc(m)*	CDR(FTC)	X	AWO(A)	30.06.88	JSSU OAKLEY
Merriman, Malcolm Roy, *BA*	LT CDR(FTC)	E	MESM	01.10.99	DRAKE CBS
Merriman, Peter Orrill, *BSc, MIMechE*	CDR(FTC)	E	MESM	30.06.99	NEPTUNE DSQ
Merritt, Jonathan James, *BEng, MSc, CEng, MCGI, FIMarE ocds(Can)*	LT CDR(FTC)	E	ME	01.05.96	CINCFLEET
Mervik, Christopher Fields, *OBE, pce, pcea,*	CAPT(FTC)	X	P	31.12.99	FONA
Messenger, Gordon Kenneth, *BSc, psc*	LT COL(FTC)	RM	MLDR	30.06.97	HQ 3 CDO BDE RM
Metcalf, Robin	LT(FTC)	E	ME	10.06.94	OCEAN
Metcalf, Stephen William, *IEng*	SLT(FTC)	E	MESM	01.04.98	VIGILANT(STBD)

Name	Rank	Branch	Spec	Seniority	Where Serving
Metcalfe, Anthony Paul Warren , *BA, pce*	LT CDR(FTC)	X	PWO(U)	01.12.91	CINCFLEET
Metcalfe, Michael Peter , *BEM*	LT(FTC)	X	EW	25.07.96	HQ 3 CDO BDE RM
Metcalfe, Philip Geoffrey , *BEng, MSc, MIEE*	LT CDR(FTC)	E	WESM	01.02.96	VANGUARD(PORT)
Metcalfe, Philip Ian , *BEng*	LT(FTC)	E	WE	01.07.93	2SL/CNH FOTR
Metcalfe, Richard John	LT(FTC)	E	WE	04.09.98	ARK ROYAL
Methven, Paul , *BEng, MIMarE*	LT CDR(FTC)	E	MESM	01.11.99	MOD (BATH)
Meyer, Alexander James , *BA*	LT(CC)	X		01.12.98	YORK
Meyer, Stephen Richard , *pce, psc, hcsc*	RADM	-	PWO(N)	01.07.99	COMUKTG/CASWSF
Michie, Anthony Richard , *BSc*	CDR(FTC)	E	WE	30.06.99	SSA BRISTOL
Mickleburgh, Allan	LT CDR(FTC)	X	REG	01.10.97	2SL/CNH
Middlebrook, Mark Simon , *pce*	LT CDR(FTC)	X	PWO(U)	30.03.95	RALEIGH
Middlemas, Simon Robert , *BSc, CEng, MIMechE*	CDR(FTC)	E	MESM	30.06.96	NP DNREAY
Middleton, Christopher Sydney , *BEd*	CAPT RM(CC)	RM		01.09.98	RM POOLE
Middleton, Judith , *BSc(Hons)*	SLT	Q		26.04.97	RH HASLAR
Middleton, Simon	SURG SLT	-		30.04.99	DARTMOUTH BRNC
Middleton, Toby Patrick Windsor , *BSc, psc(m)*	MAJ(FTC)	RM	LC	01.05.94	EXCHANGE ARMY UK
Middleton, Wayne Trevor	SLT(IC)	S		01.04.98	RALEIGH
Midmore, Martin Jonathan	LT(FTC)	E	AE(M)	14.10.94	RNAS CULDROSE
Midwinter, Mark John , *MB, BSc, BS, FRCS*	SURG CDR	-	(GS)	31.12.98	RH HASLAR
Mifflin, Michelle Jane	MID(NE)(IC)	S		01.01.00	DARTMOUTH BRNC
Miklinski, Anthony Stanley , *BSc, DipEd, psc*	CAPT(FTC)	E	TM	31.12.98	MOD (LONDON)
Milburn, Philip Kenneth , *pce*	LT CDR(FTC)	X	PWO(A)	01.01.95	LEEDS CASTLE
Milburn, Victoria *(Act Lt)*	SLT(FTC)	MS	(AD)	18.09.98	DRAKE CBP(DLO)
Miles, Graham John , *BSc, BEng (Act Lt Cdr)*	LT(FTC)	E	AE	07.08.92	ES AIR BRISTOL
Miles, Philip John , *BA*	LT(IC)	S		01.08.98	COLLINGWOOD
Miles, Richard , *MB, BS, MRCP*	SURG LTCDR	-	(X) UT	01.08.96	NELSON (PAY)
Miles, Rebecca Lewis , *BSc*	LT(FTC)	X		01.01.97	BULLDOG
Millar, Gordon Craig , *BEng*	LT CDR(FTC)	E	AE	15.05.98	2SL/CNH FOTR
Millar, Kevin Ian , *MIEEIE*	LT(FTC)	E	MESM	02.09.99	VENGEANCE(PORT)
Millar, Sean Jason	LT(FTC)	X	MCD	01.09.94	JSCSC
Millar, Stuart William Sinclair , *MB, BS, Dip FFP, MRCGP*	SURG LTCDR	-	GMPP	01.08.96	OCEAN
Millard, Andrew Robert	LT CDR(FTC)	X		01.01.99	CINCFLEET
Millard, Jeremy Robert , *BEng, AMIEE*	LT(IC)	E	ME	01.02.98	GLASGOW
Millen, Ian Stuart	LT CDR(FTC)	X	EW	01.10.99	COMUKTG/CASWSF
Millen, Stuart Charles William	LT(CC)	X	P	01.04.93	DHFS
Miller, Andrew David , *MB, BS*	SURG LT	-		04.08.99	CTCRM
Miller, Andrew James Gildard , *pce*	CAPT(FTC)	X	PWO(A)	31.12.94	FOST SEA
Miller, Colin Robert , *pcea*	LT CDR(FTC)	X	O	01.10.99	MWC PORTSDOWN
Miller, David Edward	LT(FTC)	MS	(AD)	25.07.96	DRAKE CBS
Miller, Gary	LT(FTC)	X	AV	17.12.93	ES AIR YEO
Miller, Ian , *MEng*	SLT(FTC)	E	MESM	01.09.97	SULTAN
Miller, John Charles , *IEng, MIMarE*	LT(FTC)	E	MESM	17.10.86	SULTAN
Miller, Kevin Roy	SLT(IC)	E	WE	01.05.98	DARTMOUTH BRNC
Miller, Mandy Catherine , *BEng*	LT(FTC)	E	WE	01.02.97	SHEFFIELD
Miller, Nicholas William Henry , *BSc, SM(n)*	LT(FTC)	X	SM	01.08.96	TURBULENT
Miller, Paul David	LT(FTC)	X	FC	01.02.93	DRYAD
Miller, Richard Hugh , *BEng*	LT CDR(FTC)	E	WESM	01.03.98	MOD (LONDON)
Milles, Olivia Kate , *BA*	SLT(IC)	X	P U/T	01.01.98	RNAS YEOVILTON
Milligan, Robert James Charles , *pcea*	LT(CC)	X	O	16.04.92	815 FLT 229
Milliner, Christopher Liam , *BSc*	CAPT RM(IC)	RM		01.09.95	CTCRM
Millington, Isobel	LT(FS)	FS		08.01.99	NELSON
Millman, Dominic John , *BSc, PGDip*	LT(CC)	X	METOC	01.01.92	INVINCIBLE
Mills, Andrew , *BEng*	LT CDR(FTC)	E	WESM	01.05.95	NEPTUNE SM1
Mills, Barrie , *BMus, BA(Hons), LRAM, ARCM*	MAJ(FTC)	BS		01.10.99	RM BAND PLYMOUTH
Mills, Gary Anthony	SLT(FTC)	X	PT	19.09.97	DRYAD
Mills, Gordon William	LT CDR(FTC)	E	WE	01.10.98	CORNWALL
Mills, Ian , *BEng*	LT(FTC)	E	WE	01.08.92	HQ DCSA
Mills, Sydney David Gareth	LT(CC)	X	P	01.01.95	FONA VALLEY
Mills, Thomas Clark , *BSc, psc(j)*	LT CDR(FTC)	E	TM	01.10.93	MOD (LONDON)
Millward, Jeremy , *MBE*	CDR(FTC)	X	P	31.12.99	MOD (LONDON)
Milne, Andrew Richard , *BA (Act Lt Col)*	MAJ(FTC)	RM	MLDR	01.09.88	SEA CADET CORPS
Milne, David Murray Ferguson , *BSc, AMIEE*	LT CDR(FTC)	E	WE	16.08.79	MOD (BATH)
Milne, James William	LT CDR(FTC)	E	WE	01.10.92	SSA BRISTOL

Name	Rank	Branch	Spec	Seniority	Where Serving
Milne, Peter Barkes , *BEng*	LT(CC)	X	P	16.09.91	FONA VALLEY
Milne, Simon Stephen , *MBE, BSc, psc*	LT COL(FTC)	RM	C	31.12.93	MOD (LONDON)
Milne, William John Connington , *BEng*	SLT(FTC)	E	ME	01.09.97	OCEAN
Milner, Hugh Christopher , *ocds(No)*	MAJ(FTC)	RM		01.09.89	ELANT/NAVNORTH
Milner, Robert , *MB, BS*	SURG LT	-		07.08.96	MODHU DERRIFORD
Milnes, John Lee , *nadc, pce, pce(sm)*	CAPT(FTC)	X	SM	31.12.93	SA ATHENS
Milsom, Jonathan , *BEng*	LT CDR(FTC)	E	AE	01.10.99	ES AIR MASU
Milton, Anthony Arthur , *OBE, MPhil, rcds, jsdc, psc(m)*	MAJ GEN	RM	C	01.04.99	JDCC
Milton, Graham Boyd McCullough , *pcea*	LT CDR(FTC)	X	P	01.10.89	RNAS CULDROSE
Milton, George James Gordon , *BSc, CEng, MIEE, psc*	CDR(FTC)	E	WESM	31.12.90	SSA ROSYTH
Milton, Gary Peter	LT(CC)	X	O	01.05.93	814 SQN
Mimpriss, Graham Donald , *n*	LT CDR(FTC)	X	H1	01.04.99	ROEBUCK
Mincher, David Joseph Francis	LT(FTC)	E	MESM	01.07.94	NEPTUNE SM1 SEA
Minns, Peter Frank , *MA, pce, psc(j)*	CDR(FTC)	X	PWO(U)	31.12.97	MOD (LONDON)
Mitchell, Bernard Anthony , *BSc, MIEE*	LT CDR(FTC)	E	WESM	01.11.79	MOD (BATH)
Mitchell, Christopher David	LT(FTC)	X		01.12.96	PENZANCE
Mitchell, Henry George Murray , *pcea*	LT CDR(FTC)	X	P	16.10.93	801 SQN
Mitchell, Jamie Dundas	SLT(IC)	X		01.09.98	DARTMOUTH BRNC
Mitchell, Jamie Murray , *BSc*	SLT(IC)	X		01.01.99	DARTMOUTH BRNC
Mitchell, James Robert , *BA*	LT(IC)	X	P	01.07.95	810 SQN SEAHAWK
Mitchell, Michael	LT(FTC)	X	AV	11.12.92	801 SQN
Mitchell, Patrick , *IEng, MIEEIE*	LT(FTC)	E	WESM	05.06.92	NEPTUNE SWS
Mitchell, Richard Hannay , *pce*	CDR(FTC)	X	FC	31.12.88	CINCFLEET
Mitchell, Stephen Derek , *IEng, AMIMarE*	LT(FTC)	E	MESM	15.06.95	NBC PORTSMOUTH
Mitchell, William John , *BA*	SLT(IC)	X		01.09.98	DARTMOUTH BRNC
Mitchinson, Leslie	LT CDR(FTC)	X	C	01.10.96	MOD (LONDON)
Moberly, Nigel George Hamilton , *BSc, MIEE, psc*	CDR(FTC)	E	WE	30.06.91	NMA PORTSMOUTH
Mockford, James Arthur	LT CDR(FTC)	E	AE(M)	01.10.96	849 SQN HQ
Moffat, John William , *BEng*	CAPT RM(IC)	RM	NO-S/S	23.04.99	COMACCHIO GP RM
Moffatt, Neil Robert , *BSc, CEng, MIMarE*	LT CDR(FTC)	E	MESM	01.11.93	TALENT
Moffatt, Roger , *pcea, tp*	LT CDR(FTC)	X	P	01.10.95	MERLIN IPT
Moir, Simon , *BSc, CEng, MIEE, jsdc*	CDR(FTC)	E	WESM	30.06.87	SSA DEVONPORT
Moll, Andrew Gerald , *jsdc, pce*	CAPT(FTC)	X	PWO(A)	30.06.00	MOD (LONDON)
Mollard, Michael Joseph , *BSc*	LT(IC)	X	P	01.07.94	815 FLT 227
Molloy, Lynne , *BSc*	SLT(IC)	X	ATCU/T	01.09.99	DARTMOUTH BRNC
Molnar, Richard Mark	SLT(FTC)	X	EW	01.04.98	CARDIFF
Molyneaux, Dean George , *BSc, CEng, MIEE, psc*	CDR(FTC)	E	WE	30.06.94	T45 IPT
Molyneux, Ian Thomas	LT(CC)	E	WESM	01.08.99	DARTMOUTH BRNC
Monachello, Paolo Gino , *BSc*	LT(IC)	X		01.05.99	SCEPTRE
Moncrieff, Ian , *BA, pce*	CAPT(FTC)	X	PWO(C)	30.06.99	HQRM
Monday, Julia Elizabeth , *BA*	SLT(IC)	S		01.09.98	DARTMOUTH BRNC
Money, Christopher John , *BA*	SLT(IC)	X		01.01.98	HERALD
Monger, Paul David , *BSc*	LT CDR(FTC)	X	METOC	01.10.94	RNSOMO
Monk, Christopher David , *BSc*	LT CDR(FTC)	E	TM	01.10.97	RNSR BOVINGTON
Monk, Colin Roy , *BSc*	LT(FTC)	X	P U/T	01.06.96	702 SQN HERON
Monnox, Jill	SLT(IC)	X		19.09.98	DRYAD
Montague, Richard James , *BSc*	SLT(IC)	X		01.09.98	DARTMOUTH BRNC
Montgomery, Charles Percival Ross , *BEng, pce, psc*	CAPT(FTC)	X	PWO(U)	31.12.97	2SL/CNH FOTR
Montgomery, Michael Henry	LT CDR(FTC)	X	SM	01.12.97	SCEPTRE
Moodie, Graeme Russell , *jsdc, pce, pcea*	CAPT(FTC)	X	O	31.12.96	LOAN OMAN
Moody, Alistair Charles , *BEng, MSc*	LT(FTC)	E	MESM	01.01.00	SULTAN
Moody, David Christopher , *BEng, AMIEE*	LT(FTC)	E	WE	01.07.92	MOD (LONDON)
Moon, Ian Langland	SLT(IC)	E	ME	01.05.98	DARTMOUTH BRNC
Moore, Christian Benedict	MAJ(FTC)	RM		01.09.96	RM Poole
Moore, Christopher Ian , *pce*	CDR(FTC)	X	PWO(A)	30.06.99	PJHQ
Moore, Christopher , *BA*	LT CDR(CC)	X		05.12.99	FEARLESS
Moore, David Duncan Vincent	LT CDR(FTC)	S	(W)	01.10.99	RMB STONEHOUSE
Moore, Martin , *BA*	LT(FTC)	X		01.06.92	DRYAD
Moore, Matthew James	SLT(IC)	X		01.04.98	IRON DUKE
Moore, Martin Nicholas , *MBE*	LT CDR(FTC)	E	WESM	01.10.95	SSA/CWTA PORTS
Moore, Michael Ronald	LT(FTC)	E	WE	29.10.82	MOD (BATH)
Moore, Nicholas James , *BSc*	SLT(IC)	X	P U/T	01.05.97	RNAS YEOVILTON
Moore, Paul Grenville , *BDS*	SGLTCDR(D)	-		31.12.98	LOAN BRUNEI

Name	Rank	Branch	Spec	Seniority	Where Serving
Moore, Piers Henry George	LT CDR(FTC)	X	SM	01.06.96	RN GIBRALTAR
Moore, Simon , *CB, pce, psc*	RADM	-	PWO	04.11.97	MOD (LONDON)
Moore, Sean Barry , *BA, LLB*	LT(FTC)	S		01.04.95	SCOTT
Moore, Suzanne Kathryn , *BEd, n*	LT(FTC)	X		01.11.93	DRYAD
Moore, Simon Paul , *BA*	LT(IC)	X		01.10.95	FOST DPORT SHORE
Moores, Colin Peter , *BEng, CEng, MIMarE*	LT(CC)	E	ME	01.09.91	SULTAN
Moores, John	LT(FTC)	S	(S)	03.04.97	INVINCIBLE
Moores, John Keith , *BSc, pce, pce(sm)*	CDR(FTC)	X	SM	30.06.97	COMUKTG/CASWSF
Moorey, Christopher George , *pce*	LT CDR(FTC)	X	PWO(A)	01.03.94	PORTLAND
Moorhouse, Dominic , *BSc*	CAPT RM(IC)	RM		01.09.94	CTCRM
Moorhouse, Edward James	CAPT RM(FTC)	RM		24.04.96	COMACCHIO GP RM
Moorhouse, Stephen Mark Richard , *BSc*	LT(FTC)	X	O	01.02.96	849 SQN B FLT
Moran, Benjamin Michael	SLT(IC)	X		01.01.99	DARTMOUTH BRNC
Moran, Craig Andrew	LT(FTC)	X	REG	10.01.00	2SL/CNH
Moran, Julian Toby	CAPT RM(CC)	RM		28.04.99	OCLC BRISTOL
Moran, Russell James	LT(IC)	X		01.06.99	BICESTER
Moreby, Martin Francis	LT(FTC)	X	AV	02.04.93	RNAS YEOVILTON
Moreland, Michael John , *BSc, CEng, MIMarE, psc(m)*	CDR(FTC)	E	MESM	30.06.00	FOSM FASLANE
Morey, Kevin Norton	SLT(UCE)(FTC)	X		01.09.98	DARTMOUTH BRNC
Morgan, Andrew Kevin Glyn , *MSc, Cert Ed*	LT CDR(FTC)	E	IS	06.02.92	2SL/CNH
Morgan, Benjamin Penoyre , *BSc*	SLT(IC)	X		01.01.99	DARTMOUTH BRNC
Morgan, Charles Edward William , *MA*	CAPT RM(IC)	RM		01.09.98	HQ 3 CDO BDE RM
Morgan, David , *BSc, MBA, CEng, MRAeS, jsdc*	CDR(FTC)	E	AE	30.06.90	2SL/CNH FOTR
Morgan, David Henry , *BSc*	LT(FTC)	X		01.10.94	EXPRESS
Morgan, Frances Antonia , *BA*	LT(FTC)	X		01.08.98	SOMERSET
Morgan, Forbes Scott , *BEng*	LT CDR(FTC)	E	ME	01.11.97	NORFOLK
Morgan, Gareth Lee	MID(NE)(IC)	X	P U/T	01.09.99	DARTMOUTH BRNC
Morgan, Huw Lloyd , *BSc*	2LT(GRAD)(IC)	RM		01.09.99	CTCRM LYMPSTONE
Morgan, John Hutchinson , *jsdc, pce (COMMODORE)*	CAPT(FTC)	X	AWO(A)	30.06.93	MOD (BATH)
Morgan, Nicholas Vaughan , *MB, BS, FRCSEd, jsdc*	SURG CAPT	-	GMPP	30.06.00	MOD (LONDON)
Morgan, Peter , *MIMarE*	LT(FTC)	E	ME	19.06.98	RM POOLE
Morgan, Peter Thomas , *DSC, pce, psc*	CDR(FTC)	X	PWO(A)	30.06.97	MOD (LONDON)
Morgan, Rachel Sara	LT	Q	REGM	06.09.99	RN GIBRALTAR
Morgan, Stephen Alexander	LT CDR(FTC)	E	WE	01.10.97	GLOUCESTER
Morgan-Hosey, John Noel , *BEng, CEng, MIMarE*	LT(FTC)	E	MESM	01.01.92	FOSM NWOOD HQ
Morisetti, Neil , *BSc, jsdc, pce*	CAPT(FTC)	X	PWO(A)	31.12.97	CARDIFF
Morland, Robert Michael	LT CDR(FTC)	X	C	01.10.95	MOD (LONDON)
Morley, Adrian , *BA*	CAPT RM(FTC)	RM	P U/T	29.04.97	DHFS
Morley, Anthony Derek , *BSc*	CDR(FTC)	E	IS	31.12.99	SACLANT USA
Morley, Dominic Stuart , *LLB*	LT(IC)	X	SM	01.05.97	RALEIGH
Morley, James David	LT CDR(FTC)	X	FC	01.08.99	DRYAD
Morley, James Ian , *BSc*	LT(FTC)	E	ME	01.11.97	COVENTRY
Morley, Samantha , *PGDip*	LT(CC)	X	H2	01.03.97	CAPT F4 (SEA)
Morley-Smith, Nigel Humphrey , *MA*	LT CDR(FTC)	E	WE	01.02.78	HQ DCSA
Morphet, Kathryn , *BSc, MA*	SLT(IC)	E		01.01.98	DARTMOUTH BRNC
Morrell, Andrew John	LT(FTC)	X	SM	25.07.91	COLLINGWOOD
Morris, Andrew Julian , *BSc, MDA*	CDR(FTC)	E	WESM	31.12.99	CINCFLEET
Morris, Anthony Martin	LT(CC)	X	P	01.07.93	815 FLT 239
Morris, Daniel Rowland	SLT(IC)	X		01.04.00	DARTMOUTH BRNC
Morris, David Simon , *pce, pce(sm)*	CDR(FTC)	X	SM	30.06.91	CINCFLEET
Morris, Daniel William , *BEng*	SLT(IC)	E	ME	01.01.99	DARTMOUTH BRNC
Morris, Frank	CDR(FTC)	X	EW	01.10.90	RNEAWC
Morris, James Andrew John , *BSc*	MAJ(FTC)	RM		01.09.98	40 CDO RM
Morris, John	CHAPLAIN	CE		06.10.92	DRAKE CBP(CNH)
Morris, Kevin Ian	LT(FTC)	S	CA	24.07.97	FOST SEA
Morris, Nigel Jonathan , *BSc, CEng, MIEE*	CDR(FTC)	E	WE	30.06.00	RMCS SHRIVENHAM
Morris, Paul , *BSc, Cert Ed*	LT CDR(CC)	E	TM	01.10.99	NELSON RNSETT
Morris, Paul Edward Mannering	MAJ(FTC)	RM	P	01.05.97	847 SQN
Morris, Peter John , *BEng, AMIEE*	LT CDR(FTC)	E	WESM	10.06.92	MOD (BATH)
Morris, Philip John	LT CDR(FTC)	X	C	01.10.97	COLLINGWOOD
Morris, Paul John , *BA*	SLT(IC)	X		01.09.98	DARTMOUTH BRNC
Morris, Paul Nigel , *BSc, MSc*	CDR(FTC)	E	TM	31.12.90	BRNC RNSU SOTON
Morris, Richard John	LT CDR(FTC)	X	PWO(A)	01.04.97	PJHQ

Name	Rank	Branch	Spec	Seniority	Where Serving
Morris, Simon Timothy , *BEng, CEng, MIEE*	LT CDR(FTC)	E	WESM	01.10.97	MOD (BATH)
Morrison, Bruce	LT(CC)	X	P	01.12.90	RAF CRANWELL EFS
Morrison, Christopher John Neill , *nadc, pce,*	CAPT(FTC)	X	PWO(N)†	31.12.91	SULTAN AIB,*psc*
Morrison, Calum Petter , *BSc*	CAPT RM(IC)	RM		29.04.94	RM POOLE
Morrison, Graham Lindsay , *BDS, MBA, DRD, FDS RCSEdin, jsdc*	SGCAPT(D)	-		31.12.96	DDA HALTON
Morrison, George Ross	LT CDR(FTC)	E	AE(M)	01.10.95	ES AIR MASU
Morrison, Gordon William	LT(IC)	X	P	01.10.91	JATEBRIZENORTON
Morrison, Kenneth William , *IEng, AMIMarE*	CDR(FTC)	E	ME	31.12.99	MOD (BATH)
Morrison, Paul	LT(FTC)	X	O	13.12.95	700M MERLIN IFTU
Morrison, Robert William	LT CDR(FTC)	E	ME	01.10.97	FOST SEA
Morritt, Dain Cameron , *BEng, MA, MSc, psc*	CDR(FTC)	E	WE	31.12.98	MOD (LONDON)
Morrow, Daniel George , *BA*	SLT(IC)	X		01.01.99	DARTMOUTH BRNC
Morse, Andrew Charles , *pcea*	LT CDR(FTC)	X	O	01.01.92	RNAS YEOVILTON
Morse, Jeremy , *BSc*	SLT(IC)	X	P U/T	01.05.97	RNAS YEOVILTON
Morse, James Anthony , *BSc, pce*	CDR(FTC)	X	PWO(N)	30.06.97	PJHQ
Mortimer, Richard Peter , *BEd*	LT(FTC)	X	HM	01.08.94	SCOTT
Mortlock, Philip Alun , *BEng*	LT(CC)	E	WESM	01.01.00	RALEIGH
Morton, Nigel Peter Bradshaw , *BSc, psc*	CDR(FTC)	S		30.06.99	FOSNNI/NBC CLYDE
Morton, Thomas , *nadc, pce (COMMODORE)*	CAPT(FTC)	X	AWO(C)	31.12.91	RHQ SOUTHLANT
Moss, Alexander David	LT CDR(FTC)	E	ME	06.10.91	MOD (BATH)
Moss, Peter , *psc(m)*	LT CDR(FTC)	X	O	18.02.92	OCLC BIRM
Moss, Patrick John	LT(FTC)	E	WESM	13.06.91	DSWS BRISTOL
Moss, Richard Ashley , *BSc*	LT CDR(FTC)	X	PWO(U)	01.03.99	YORK
Moss, Timothy Edward , *IEng, AMIMarE*	LT CDR(FTC)	E	ME	01.10.97	MOD (BATH)
Moughton, John Robert , *IEng, MIEEIE*	LT(FTC)	E	WE	03.11.83	MOD (BATH)
Mould, Philip	LT(CC)	X	P	01.05.93	899 SQN HERON
Mould, Timothy Paul	LT(FTC)	E	WE	01.03.94	SSA BRISTOL
Moules, Matthew Alexander John , *BSc, SM(n)*	LT(FTC)	X	SM	01.08.96	TURBULENT
Moult, Richard Michael , *BSc, psc*	LT CDR(FTC)	X	METOC	09.01.80	RNAS CULDROSE
Moulton, Simon John , *BSc*	LT(CC)	X	O	01.01.92	810 SQN SEAHAWK
Mount, James Bruce	SLT(CC)	X	P	01.01.98	820 SQN
Mountford, Penny Claire , *BEng*	LT(FTC)	E	ME	01.04.98	MANCHESTER
Mountjoy, Brian John , *MIOSH*	LT(FTC)	E	WESM	05.06.92	CMSA UK
Mountney, Gemma Ann , *BSc*	SLT(IC)	X		01.01.99	DARTMOUTH BRNC
Mowatt, Patrick	LT(FTC)	X	HM	01.05.96	BULLDOG
Mowlam, David John Mark , *nadc, pce, psc (COMMODORE)*	CAPT(FTC)	X	AWO(C)	31.12.93	AGRIPPA AFSOUTH
Moxey, David Erskine , MCIT	LT CDR(FTC)	S	SM	01.04.91	ES AIR BRISTOL
Moy, David Keith	SLT(FTC)	E	ME	02.05.97	FEARLESS
Moyo, Themba Kabelo , *BSc*	LT(IC)	X	P U/T	01.01.00	DHFS
Moys, Andrew John	LT CDR(FTC)	X	METOC	01.10.97	OCEAN
Moyse, Robert Edward , *BSc*	MAJ(FTC)	RM		01.09.86	RM POOLE
Muddiman, Andrew Robert , *BA*	CAPT RM(FTC)	RM		01.09.97	42 CDO RM
Mudford, Hugh Christopher , *psc*	LT COL(FTC)	RM		30.06.99	HQRM
Mudge, Adrian Michael , *BSc*	LT(CC)	X	O	01.07.93	750 SQN OBS SCH
Mugridge, Anthony Robert , *MB, ChB, FRCSEd*	SURG CAPT	-	(CGS)	30.06.98	RH HASLAR
Mugridge, David Robert , *BA, MNI, pce*	LT CDR(FTC)	X	PWO(C)	01.02.98	OCEAN
Muir, Keith , *pce, pcea, psc(j)*	CDR(FTC)	X	O	31.12.98	SACLANT USA
Muirhead, Barry George , *BEng*	LT(CC)	X	P	16.12.98	RNAS CULDROSE
Mules, Anthony John , *n*	LT CDR(FTC)	X	H2	01.03.98	SCOTT
Mullen, Andrew John , *psc, psc(j)*	CDR(FTC)	S	SM	30.06.95	MOD (BATH)
Mullen, Jason John , *BA*	LT(FTC)	X	MCD	01.10.94	BERKELEY
Mullen, Matthew Lee , *BA*	SLT(IC)	X		01.09.97	DRYAD
Mullins, Andrew Dominic	LT(FTC)	E	MESM	01.12.96	VIGILANT(PORT)
Mullowney, Paul , *BEng*	LT(CC)	X	O	01.08.99	849 SQN A FLT
Mulvaney, Paul Andrew , *BSc*	LT(FTC)	E	AE	01.06.92	815 SQN HQ
Muncer, Richard A , *BSc*	2LT(GRAD)(IC)	RM		02.09.98	42 CDO RM
Munday, Ian Vernon , *MBE, pce, pcea, psc*	LT CDR(FTC)	X	O	01.04.85	824 NAS
Munden, Cathryn Sarah	LT	Q	OTSPEC	07.07.95	MODHU DERRIFORD
Mundin, Adrian John , *BSc, CEng, MIMechE*	LT CDR(FTC)	E	ME	01.04.92	MOD (BATH)
Munns, Adrian , *OBE, rcds (COMMODORE)*	CAPT(FTC)	S		31.12.92	EXCELLENT
Munns, Andrew Robert , *BEng*	LT CDR(FTC)	E	ME	01.01.96	SULTAN
Munns, Christopher Ronald , *jsdc, pce, pce(sm), hcsc*	CA-PT(FTC)	X	SM	31.12.96	ELANT/NAVNORTH
Munro, Kenneth , *BEng, CEng, MIMarE*	LT CDR(FTC)	E	ME	01.04.95	FOSF

Name	Rank	Branch	Spec	Seniority	Where Serving
Munro, Niall Frank Hamilton , *LLB*	LT(IC)	X		01.01.99	CATTISTOCK
Munro-Lott, Peter Robert John , *BA, pcea*	LT CDR(FTC)	X	O	01.10.96	824 NAS
Murch, Julian David , *MSc, CEng, MIEE, psc*	CDR(FTC)	E	WE	30.06.90	MOD (LONDON)
Murchie, Alistair Duncan , *BEng*	LT(FTC)	E	ME	01.05.97	INVINCIBLE
Murchison, Ewen Alexander , *BSc*	CAPT RM(FTC)	RM		01.09.94	NP 1061
Murdoch, Andrew Peter , *BSc*	LT(FTC)	S		01.11.94	2SL/CNH
Murdoch, Andrew William , *BSc, MSc, AMIEE*	LT CDR(FTC)	E	WESM	01.06.93	MOD (LONDON)
Murdoch, Gillian Agnes , *BDS*	SG LT(D)	-		20.07.98	DRAKE CBP(CNH)
Murdoch, Stephen John	CDR(FTC)	S		31.12.99	MOD (LONDON)
Murgatroyd, Andrew Clive , *MBE, BSc, jsdc, pce*	CDR(FTC)	X	PWO(A)	31.12.94	MOD (LONDON)
Murgatroyd, Kevin John , *BEng*	LT(IC)	X	O U/T	01.04.00	RNAS CULDROSE
Murison, Lisa Campbell , *MA*	LT(FTC)	X		01.05.95	CUMBERLAND
Murnane, Paul Martin , *MBE, pce*	CDR(FTC)	X	PWO(A)	01.10.98	ELANT/NAVNORTH
Murns, Nicolas Peter , *BSc*	CAPT RM(IC)	RM	LC	28.04.95	42 CDO RM
Murphie, John Dermot Douglas , *pce, psc(m)*	CDR(FTC)	X	MCD	31.12.95	MCM1 SEA
Murphy, Anthony , *MBA*	LT CDR(FTC)	MS		01.10.96	DMTO HQ
Murphy, Andrew	SLT(FTC)	E	WE	09.01.98	MANCHESTER
Murphy, Diccon Andrew , *BSc*	LT(CC)	X	P	01.04.92	815 FLT 211
Murphy, James , *BSc*	LT CDR(FTC)	S	SM	01.06.92	RALEIGH
Murphy, Kian Stuart , *BA*	CAPT RM(CC)	RM		01.05.98	RM Poole
Murphy, Nicholas , *MNI, pce*	LT CDR(FTC)	X	PWO(U)	01.09.90	FOSF
Murphy, Paul Anthony , *BA*	LT CDR(FTC)	S	SM	01.03.00	FOSM NWOOD HQ
Murphy, Peter John , *BA, PGCE*	LT CDR(CC)	E	TM	01.10.91	HQRM
Murphy, Peter William , *MSc, BEng*	LT CDR(FTC)	E	MESM	01.09.95	VENGEANCE(PORT)
Murphy, Richard James , *BA*	LT(IC)	X		01.01.00	RNAS YEOVILTON
Murphy, Stephen Mark , *BEng*	LT(FTC)	E	ME	01.08.96	DUMBARTON CASTLE
Murphy, Steven Robert Anthony , *BA*	LT CDR(FTC)	X	SM	01.09.98	CSST SHORE DEVPT
Murray, Alister	SLT(IC)	MS		19.09.98	DEF MED TRG CTR
Murray, Alexander Bruce	CAPT RM(FTC)	RM		26.04.94	EXCHANGE USA
Murray, Andrew Sidney	LT CDR(CC)	X	P	01.10.99	810 SQN SEAHAWK
Murray, David	LT(FTC)	X	PT	07.01.88	EXCELLENT
Murray, Grant McNiven	LT CDR(FTC)	E	WESM	01.06.98	ASTUTE IPT
Murray, Robert Henry , *MBE, BSc, MIMechE*	LT CDR(FTC)	E	MESM	01.01.82	DRAKE NBSD
Murray, Stephen	LT(FTC)	E	MESM	15.10.93	ASTUTE IPT
Murray, Simon Christopher , *BSc*	LT(IC)	E	TM	01.01.98	NEPTUNE 2SL/CNH
Murray, Stephen John , *pcea, gdas*	LT CDR(FTC)	X	O	01.10.89	700M MERLIN IFTU
Murray, William Richard Charles , *BA*	CAPT RM(FTC)	RM		01.09.95	LOAN BALBAT
Murrison, Andrew William , *MB, BCh, ChB, MD, DPH, MFOM, GB*	SURG CDR	-	(CO/M)	31.12.97	CINCFLEET
Murrison, Richard Anthony	LT CDR(FTC)	S		01.03.97	FOSF
Murton, William Maurice , *BSc*	LT CDR(FTC)	X	P	01.10.92	848 SQN HERON
Muscroft, Paul James Victor	LT CDR(FTC)	E	WE	01.10.93	2SL/CNH FOTR
Musters, John Basil Auchmuty , *osc (COMMODORE)*	CAPT(FTC)	S		30.06.93	NMA GOSPORT
Musto, Edward Charles , *BA, psc(m)*	LT COL(FTC)	RM		31.12.96	HQRM
Mutch, Jonathan Rocliffe , *BSc*	LT(CC)	X	P	01.09.94	815 FLT 229
Muxworthy, Angela Mary Blythe , *psc*	CDR(FTC)	W	IS	31.12.95	MOD (BATH)
Myers, Geoffrey William , *OBE, BChD, MSc, DGDP RCS(UK), LDS RCS(Eng), jsdc*	SGCAPT(D)	-		31.12.94	MOD (LONDON)
Myerscough, Andrew Paul	LT CDR(FTC)	E	AE(P)	01.10.96	RNAS CULDROSE
Myres, Peter John Lukis	LT CDR(FTC)	X	O	01.07.98	CARDIFF

N

Name	Rank	Branch	Spec	Seniority	Where Serving
Naden, Andrew Charles Keith , *BSc, CEng, MIMarE*	LT CDR(FTC)	E	ME	01.09.92	PJHQ
Naden, James Ralph , *BA, Cert Ed*	LT CDR(FTC)	E	IS	01.10.94	AFPAA(CENTURION)
Nail, Vaughan Anthony , *MA, psc*	CDR(FTC)	X	H CH	31.12.97	DGSS BRISTOL
Nailor, Andrew	LT CDR(FTC)	E	ME	01.10.95	CFM PORTSMOUTH
Nairn, Alan Barclay , *BSc*	LT CDR(FTC)	S		01.02.99	SOMERSET
Nairn, Robert , *psc*	CDR(FTC)	S		31.12.96	HQ3GP HQSTC
Naismith, David Hamilton , *BSc, pcea*	LT CDR(FTC)	X	O	01.05.91	MERLIN IPT
Naldrett, Geoffrey	SLT(IC)	X		19.09.98	HQ DCSA
Nance, Adrian Ralph , *OBE, BSc, pce*	CAPT(FTC)	X	PWO(A)	30.06.97	MWC SOUTHWICK
Napier, Graham Andrew	LT(FTC)	E	AE(M)	01.07.93	ES AIR BRISTOL
Nash, Philip David , *BSc*	LT(CC)	X	O	01.08.95	815 FLT 218

Name	Rank	Branch	Spec	Seniority	Where Serving
Nash, Robin David Cory , *BSc*	SLT(IC)	X		01.01.99	DARTMOUTH BRNC
Nash, Rubin Piero , *BSc*	SLT(IC)	X		01.01.99	DARTMOUTH BRNC
Nason, Sarah Marie	*MID*(IC)	X		01.01.99	DARTMOUTH BRNC
Nathanson, Helen , *BA*	LT(IC)	S		01.02.97	RALEIGH
Naylor, Andrew James	LT(IC)	X	P	16.06.94	819 SQN
Naylor, Ian Frederick , *BA, AKC*	CHAPLAIN	CE		16.09.86	EXCELLENT
Neal, Alistair John Duncan , *MB, ChB, DipAvMed*	SURG CDR	-	GMPP	30.06.96	MOD (LONDON)
Neal, Simon Matthew , *pcea*	LT(CC)	X	O	16.01.92	EXCHANGE USA
Neave, Andrew Michael	LT CDR(FTC)	X	ATC	01.10.98	RNAS YEOVILTON
Neave, Christopher Bryan , *BSc, pcea*	CDR(FTC)	E	AE(P)	31.12.94	RNAS YEOVILTON
Necker, Carl Dominic	LT CDR(FTC)	X	PWO(A)	01.11.99	CUMBERLAND
Needham, Phillip David , *DSC, MCGI, gdas*	LT CDR(FTC)	X	O	01.10.92	815 SQN OEU
Neil, Simon John , *MA, pce, psc(j)*	CDR(FTC)	X	MCD	31.12.97	CDRE MFP
Neild, Timothy	LT(FTC)	X		01.11.95	COVENTRY
Nelson, Andrew	LT CDR(FTC)	E	WESM	01.10.95	COLLINGWOOD
Nelson, Christopher Stuart , *BSc, n*	LT(FTC)	X		01.03.93	CAPT IST STAFF
Nelson, Dominic Edward , *BSc*	LT CDR(FTC)	X	PWO(A)	01.04.88	DRAKE CFM
Nelson, David Lawrence	LT CDR(FTC)	X	P	01.10.92	FONA
Nelson, Digby Theodore , *BSc, psc*	CDR(FTC)	S		30.06.94	EXCHANGE AUSTLIA
Nelson, Lisa Marie , *BEng*	LT(FTC)	E	ME	01.01.95	MOD (LONDON)
Nelson, Matthew	LT(CC)	X	P	01.03.99	810 SQN B FLIGHT
Nelson, Paul Moffat , *BA, Cert Ed*	LT(CC)	E	TM	01.01.97	DEF DIVING SCHL
Nelson, Timothy Brian , *pce*	LT CDR(FTC)	X	PWO(A)	16.06.83	CV(F) IPT
Nelson, Victoria , *BA*	LT(CC)	S		01.03.96	RNAS YEOVILTON
Nelstrop, Andrew Marcus	SURG LT	-		10.02.99	HQ 3 CDO BDE RM
Neofytou, Andrew George Klropas , *BEng*	LT(IC)	X	P U/T	01.08.99	FONA LINTON/OUSE
Nethercott, Eoin Robert , *BEng*	LT(IC)	X		01.01.00	BRECON
Nethercott, Lyndon Raymond	LT CDR(FTC)	E	AE(L)	01.10.94	LOAN DERA BSC DN
Netherwood, Lyndsey Dawn , *BA*	LT(FTC)	X		15.09.99	LIVERPOOL
Neve, Piers Charles , *pce(sm)*	LT CDR(FTC)	X	SM	11.02.94	EXCHANGE AUSTLIA
New, Christopher Maxwell , *BEng*	LT CDR(FTC)	E	ME	01.04.97	EXCELLENT
New, Richard Ashley	SLT(IC)	S		01.04.98	DARTMOUTH BRNC
Newall, Jeremy Andrew	LT CDR(CC)	X	ATC	01.03.94	NAIC NORTHOLT
Newby Stubbs, Rebecca Louise	LT	Q	IC	15.08.99	MODHU DERRIFORD
Newell, Gary David	SLT(IC)	E	ME	29.04.98	SULTAN
Newell, Jonathan Michael , *BSc, MSc, CEng, FIMarE, MIL, fsc*	CDR(FTC)	E	ME	31.12.97	MOD (BATH)
Newell, Phillip Russell , *BEng*	LT(FTC)	X	H1	01.06.93	EXCHANGE AUSTLIA
Newing, Stephen Geoffrey , *psc*	LT COL(FTC)	RM	MOR	30.06.98	NMA WHALE ISLAND
Newland, Mark Ian , *BSc*	LT CDR(FTC)	X	PWO(U)	01.10.96	ILLUSTRIOUS
Newlands, George Alexander , *pce, pcea, psc*	LT CDR(FTC)	X	O	01.02.89	824 NAS
Newman, David	LT(CC)	E	AE	01.01.99	DARTMOUTH BRNC
Newman, Paul Henry , *BSc*	LT CDR(FTC)	X	METOC	01.05.89	RHQ SOUTHLANT
Newman, Sally	LT	Q	OTSPEC	18.08.97	MODHU DERRIFORD
Newport, Janet Daveen McDiarmid	LT(CS)	-		09.01.98	DNR STH CENTRAL
Newth, Christopher , *BSc*	SLT(IC)	E	TM	01.05.97	COLLINGWOOD
Newton, Bryan James , *BSc, CEng, MIMechE*	LT CDR(FTC)	E	TM	01.05.91	EXCELLENT
Newton, David John , *pce, psc*	CDR(FTC)	X	P	31.12.98	MOD (LONDON)
Newton, Garry Arnold , *pce(sm)*	CDR(FTC)	X	SM	30.06.00	DRYAD
Newton, James	LT(CC)	X	P	16.09.95	848 SQN HERON
Newton, Michael Ronald , *FIEIE*	LT CDR(FTC)	E	WE	22.09.87	DRAKE CFM
Newton, Nicholas	SURG SLT	-		11.01.00	DARTMOUTH BRNC
Nicholas, Bryan John , *BSc, pcea*	LT(FTC)	X	P	16.05.90	849 SQN B FLT
Nicholas, Stephen Paul	LT(CC)	E	MESM	01.04.94	OCLC MANCH
Nicholl, Stuart , *MB, BS*	SURG LT	-		21.03.96	RNAS YEOVILTON
Nicholls, Barry Austin	CAPT RM(FTC)	RM	SO(LE)	01.01.95	42 CDO RM
Nicholls, David Vernon , *psc(m), hcsc (BRIGADIER)*	COL(OF6)(FTC)	RM	MLDR	30.06.95	EXCELLENT
Nicholls, Guy Anthony	LT CDR(FTC)	E	WE	01.10.99	MOD (BATH)
Nichols, Elizabeth Anne , *MB, BS, DObstRCOG, MRCGP*	SURG LTCDR	-	GMPP	01.08.96	DRAKE CBP(DLO)
Nicholson, Brian Harold	SLT(IC)	E	AE	29.04.98	SULTAN
Nicholson, Bridget Rachel , *BA*	LT(CC)	S		14.07.92	SULTAN AIB
Nicholson, David Andrew Gore , *BEng*	SLT(IC)	X		01.01.99	DARTMOUTH BRNC
Nicholson, David Jeremy	LT(FTC)	X	P	16.06.89	FONA SEAHAWK
Nicholson, David Peter , *BSc*	CAPT RM(FTC)	RM		01.09.99	NEPTUNE

Name	Rank	Branch	Spec	Seniority	Where Serving
Nicholson, Graeme, *MB, BCh, MRCGP, AFOM*	SURG LTCDR	-	GMPP	01.08.92	INM ALVERSTOKE
Nicholson, Heather, *BSc*	LT CDR(FTC)	S		06.04.97	OCLC ROSYTH
Nicholson, Jonathan Craig	LT(FTC)	E	WE	02.09.99	SSA BRISTOL
Nicholson, Kristin James, *BA*	LT(FTC)	S		01.08.94	SCOTT
Nicholson, Paul James	LT(FTC)	E	WE	10.06.88	DCSA RADIO PLY
Nicholson, Simon Charles Lawrence, *pce*	CDR(FTC)	X	MCD	30.06.96	CDRE MFP
Nicholson, Shaun Raymond	LT(FTC)	X		22.11.94	DRYAD
Nickisson, David John	CAPT(CS)RM	-		02.05.97	DNR NWENI
Nicklas, Colin James, *BEng, MSc, CEng, MIEE*	LT(FTC)	E	WE	01.06.92	LN DERA FRT HAL
Nicklin, Gareth James Edward, *BEng*	LT(CC)	E	MESM	01.01.00	SULTAN
Nickolls, Kevin Paul, *BEng*	LT CDR(FTC)	E	AE	01.01.00	SULTAN
Nicol, Peter James Stewart, *MB, BS, LRCP, MRCS*	SURG CDR	-	GMPP	30.06.94	SULTAN
Nicoll, Andrew John, *BEng*	LT(FTC)	E	WESM	01.04.97	VENGEANCE(PORT)
Nicoll, Anthony John Keay, *pce, pce(sm)*	CDR(FTC)	X	SM	30.06.87	NELSON
Nicoll, Steve Kenneth	CAPT RM(FTC)	RM	SO(LE)	01.01.96	RMR LONDON
Nimmo-Scott, Sarah Jane, *BEng*	SLT(FTC)	X		01.09.97	DRYAD
Nimmons, Paul, *BEng*	LT(CC)	E	MESM	01.06.96	TRIUMPH
Nisbet, James Henry Thomas, *pce*	LT CDR(FTC)	X	PWO(U)	01.07.95	DRYAD
Nitsch, Karl David	LT(IC)	X		01.10.99	CORNWALL
Niven, Graham David *(Act Cdr)*	LT CDR(FTC)	X	AWO(A)	01.03.81	SEA CADET CORPS
Nixon, Michael Charles, *OBE, jsdc, pcea, pce*	CAPT(FTC)	X	P	31.12.99	MOD (LONDON)
Nixon, Paul William, *BSc, CEng, MIMechE*	CDR(FTC)	E	MESM	30.06.96	MOD (BATH)
Noakes, Kevin Massie, *BEng, CEng, MIEE, AMIEE*	LT(FTC)	E	WE	01.05.94	RMC OF SCIENCE
Noble, Mark Jonathan Dean, *psc*	COL(FTC)	RM	P	31.12.99	COMACCHIO GP RM
Noblett, Peter Gordon Arthur, *pce*	LT(FTC)	X	SM	01.11.91	SUPERB
Nolan, Anthony Laurence	LT CDR(FTC)	X	C	01.10.95	MOD (LONDON)
Nolton, James Raymond, *MBE, BSc*	LT CDR(FTC)	E	ME	01.02.86	SCOTIA
Noon, David	LT(FTC)	S	CA	23.07.98	NELSON
Noonan, Charles Daniel, *BA*	SLT(IC)	X		01.05.98	SUTHERLAND
Norford, Michael	LT(FTC)	X	PT	03.04.97	EXCELLENT
Norgan, David James, *BA, n*	LT(FTC)	X		01.07.93	DRYAD
Norgate, Andrew Thomas, *BSc*	LT(FTC)	X		01.11.98	VENGEANCE(PORT)
Norgate, Perry Raymond Edward	LT(FTC)	E	ME	19.06.98	DRAKE CFM
Norman, Alison Esther Phyllis	CHAPLAIN	SF		01.10.92	FEARLESS
Norman, Phillip Douglas	LT CDR(FTC)	E	WE	01.10.99	INVINCIBLE
Norman, Peter Gilford, *MA, FRGS, psc*	MAJ(FTC)	RM	LC	01.09.92	MOD (LONDON)
Norman, Shaun Lindsay, *BEng*	LT CDR(FTC)	E	AE	01.10.98	MOD DHSA
Norman-Walker, Belinda Sophie, *BA*	LT(IC)	S		01.05.95	JSU NORTHWOOD
Norris, Guy Patrick	LT(CC)	X	O	16.07.93	810 SQN SEAHAWK
Norris, James Garnet, *BA*	LT(FTC)	E	AE	01.11.92	HARRIER IPT
Norris, Richard Edward, *BDS, MGDS RCS, LDS RCS(Eng)*	SGCDR(D)	-		30.06.96	DRAKE CBP(CNH)
Norris, Robert John, *pce*	CDR(FTC)	X	PWO(A)	30.06.95	DNR RCHQ SOUTH
Norris, William Desmond, *MB, BSc, ChB, PhD*	SURG LT	-		20.05.97	VIGILANT(STBD)
Northcote, Kevin Hendon	LT(FTC)	X	PT	04.01.85	DRAKE CBP(DLO)
Northcote, Mark Richard	SLT(IC)	X		01.05.98	DRYAD
Northcott, Michael Kevin, *BEng*	LT(CC)	E	WE	01.03.99	CUMBERLAND
Northeast, Paul *(Act Lt)*	SLT(FTC)	S	CA	18.09.98	SUPERB
Northover, Adam Frederick, *BSc, n*	LT(FTC)	X		01.08.97	DUMBARTON CASTLE
Northwood, Gerard Rodney, *pce*	CDR(FTC)	X	PWO(A)	30.06.99	PJHQ
Norton, Andrew Jonathan, *BSc, CEng, MIEE, psc*	CDR(FTC)	E	WE	30.06.87	AGRIPPA AFSOUTH
Norton, Thomas Charles Horatio	2LT(UCE)(FTC)	RM		01.09.97	CTCRM
Notley, Louis Paul	LT CDR(FTC)	S	SM	01.03.96	RMC OF SCIENCE
Nottley, Simon Matthew	SLT(FTC)	E	WESM	01.04.98	RALEIGH
Nowosielski, Frank	LT CDR(FTC)	X	AV	01.10.93	VICTORY
Noyce, Nigel Roderick	LT CDR(FTC)	X		15.01.97	COLLINGWOOD
Noyce, Roger Grenville, *MRINA*	LT(CC)	X		01.06.95	PJHQ
Noyce, Vincent Robert Amos	LT(FTC)	X	FC	01.11.93	NOTTINGHAM
Noye, Charles Lovell, *MBE, AMINucE*	LT CDR(FTC)	E	MESM	21.02.84	CAPTAIN SM2
Noyes, David James	LT CDR(FTC)	S		01.12.96	MOD (LONDON)
Nugent, Colin James *(Act Lt Cdr)*	LT(FTC)	X	EW	29.07.94	ELANT/NAVNORTH
Nunn, Christopher John, *OBE, nadc, psc(a)*	LT COL(FTC)	RM	P	30.06.88	SHAPE BELGIUM
Nunn, Gerald Eric, *BSc, PGCE*	LT CDR(CC)	E	TM	01.10.95	SULTAN
Nunnen, Catherine Rebecca, *MA*	SLT(IC)	X	O U/T	01.05.98	750 SQN OBS SCH

Name	Rank	Branch	Spec	Seniority	Where Serving
Nurse, Michael Talbot, *BSc*	LT CDR(FTC)	E	AE	01.06.88	HQ3GP HQSTC
Nursey, Adrian Paul, *MIEEIE*	LT(FTC)	E	MESM	02.09.99	TURBULENT
Nurton, Katherine Emma, *BDS*	SG LT(D)	-		08.08.95	EXCELLENT

O

Name	Rank	Branch	Spec	Seniority	Where Serving
O'Brien, Kieran John, *BEng*	LT CDR(FTC)	E	AE	01.02.00	ES AIR YEO
O'Brien, Peter Charles, *BSc, PGCE, adp*	LT CDR(FTC)	E	IS	23.04.88	EXCHANGE USA
O'Brien, Patrick Michael Christopher, *BEng, MSc, MIEE*	LT CDR(FTC)	E	IS	01.10.96	MOD (LONDON)
O'Byrne, Patrick Barry Mary	LT(FTC)	X	SM	01.11.92	CSST SHORE DEVPT
O'Callaghan, Sean Tiernan *(Act Lt Cdr)*	LT(FTC)	MS		03.04.92	CDO LOG REGT RM
O'Donnell, Ian Mark, *MA, psc*	MAJ(FTC)	RM	P	01.10.97	847 SQN
O'Donnell, James Kirk Patrick, *BA*	LT(IC)	X		01.10.97	CARDIFF
O'Flaherty, Christopher Patrick John	LT CDR(FTC)	X	PWO(U)	01.03.99	NORTHUMBERLAND
O'Grady, Matthew James, *fsc*	LT CDR(FTC)	S	SM	16.11.92	RALEIGH
O'Hara, Gerard Connor	CAPT RM(FTC)	RM		01.09.97	JSCSC
O'Kane, Robert James, *BSc*	SLT(IC)	X	O U/T	01.09.97	750 SQN OBS SCH
O'Neill, Conor Mark	MID(UCE)(IC)	X		01.09.99	INVINCIBLE
O'Neill, James, *BA*	LT(IC)	X		22.11.99	BULLDOG
O'Neill, Patrick John, *MA, MSc*	CDR(FTC)	E	WESM	30.06.97	FOSM NWOOD HQ
O'Neill, Paul Joseph, *BEng*	LT(FTC)	E	MESM	01.10.95	TRAFALGAR
O'Neill, Richard Kim, *pce, psc*	CDR(FTC)	X	O	31.12.89	SHAPE BELGIUM
O'Nyons, Yorick Ian, *BA*	LT(FTC)	X	SM	01.07.94	TALENT
O'Reilly, Sean Anthony, *pce, psc*	CDR(FTC)	X	MCD	31.12.95	SAUDI AFPS SAUDI
O'Reilly, Terence Michael, *MRAeS*	CDR(FTC)	E	AE	31.12.98	JSCSC
O'Shaughnessy, David John, *BEng*	LT(FTC)	E	ME	01.05.97	FEARLESS
O'Shaughnessy, Paul Charles, *BEng*	LT(CC)	E	WE	01.01.99	SOMERSET
O'Shaughnessy, Patrick Joseph	LT CDR(FTC)	E	WE	01.10.99	CV(F) IPT
O'Shea, Eamon Patrick, *BEng*	LT CDR(FTC)	E	AE	01.07.98	AIS(SW)
O'Shea, Matthew, *BSc*	SURG SLT	-		17.05.99	DARTMOUTH BRNC
O'Sullivan, Aidan Marian	LT CDR(FTC)	X	O	01.10.92	849 SQN HQ
O'Sullivan, Barrie Oliver *(Act Lt Cdr)*	LT(FTC)	X	P	16.11.90	MWC PORTSDOWN
O'Sullivan, Michael Louis James, *BSc*	LT(FTC)	X	H2	01.08.93	RN HYDROG SCHL
O'Sullivan, Matthew Richard John	2LT(IC)	RM		01.09.99	CTCRM LYMPSTONE
O'Toole, Mathew Charles, *BEng*	LT(FTC)	E	MESM	01.11.97	SULTAN
Oakes, Ian James	LT(CC)	X	P	16.06.94	815 FLT 234
Oakes, Raymond Leslie	LT CDR(FTC)	X	C	01.10.94	FONA
Oakley, Claire Marie	SLT(IC)	X		01.05.98	NORTHUMBERLAND
Oakley, Nicholas George, *BSc, MSc, MIEE*	CDR(FTC)	E	WESM	31.12.97	ASTUTE IPT
Oakley, Sarah Ellen, *BA*	LT(FTC)	X		01.05.97	KENT
Oatley, Timothy	LT(CC)	X	O	16.07.94	820 SQN
Obrien, Ian Patrick, *BTech, IEng, MIEIE*	LT(FTC)	E	WE	24.02.95	CFM PORTSMOUTH
Obrien, Paul Terence, *BSc*	LT(CC)	X	SM	01.05.97	DRYAD
Oddy, David Mark	LT(FTC)	X	P	16.08.90	EXCHANGE USA
Oden, Mark, *BA*	CAPT RM(IC)	RM		01.09.99	JSU NORTHWOOD
Officer, Robert Lennie	LT(CC)	X	MW	01.02.96	NELSON
Offord, Matthew Ronald	LT(FTC)	X	MCD	01.04.94	HURWORTH
Oflaherty, John Stephen, *BEng*	LT CDR(FTC)	E	ME	03.10.97	MOD (BATH)
Ogden, Braddan	LT(CC)	X	O	01.04.95	702 SQN HERON
Oherlihy, Simon Ian, *MA*	CAPT RM(FTC)	RM		01.09.96	45 CDO RM
Okukenu, Dele	LT(IC)	X	P	01.01.96	846 SQN
Oldfield, Paul Henry, *BSc, MSc, MBCS*	LT CDR(CC)	E	IS	01.10.95	CINCFLEET CIS
Oliphant, William	LT CDR(FTC)	S		01.10.98	GRAFTON
Olive, Peter Nicholas, *pce, n*	LT CDR(FTC)	X	PWO(A)	01.11.98	FOSF SEA PTSMTH
Oliver, Graham, *PGDip*	LT(CC)	X	METOC	01.05.91	PRESTWICK
Oliver, Graeme John, *BSc*	LT(IC)	S		01.01.00	RALEIGH
Oliver, Kevin Brian, *BA, mdtc*	MAJ(FTC)	RM	MLDR	01.09.97	JSCSC
Ollerton, Justin Clive	LT(CC)	X	P	16.11.96	820 SQN
Ollis, Victoria	SLT(IC)	S		01.05.98	DARTMOUTH BRNC
Olliver, Adrian John	LT CDR(FTC)	S	SM	01.10.96	RALEIGH
Oneill, Timothy James	SLT(IC)	X		01.01.99	DARTMOUTH BRNC
Onions, Judith Mary, *ARRC*	LT CDR	Q	IC	11.02.91	MODHU DERRIFORD
Onyike, Chinyere Eme, *BEng, MSc, MIEE*	LT(FTC)	E	WE	01.01.94	JSCSC

Name	Rank	Branch	Spec	Seniority	Where Serving
Orchard, Adrian Paul	LT CDR(FTC)	X	P	16.01.99	EXCHANGE USA
Ordway, Christopher Norman Maurice Patrick	CAPT RM(FTC)	RM		01.09.99	CDO LOG REGT RM
Oriordan, Michael Patrick , *BSc, pce, pcea*	LT CDR(FTC)	X	P	01.04.89	SA MALAYSIA
Ormshaw, Richard John , *pcea, tp*	LT CDR(FTC)	X	P	01.10.90	MERLIN IPT
Orr, Keith John , *BEng*	LT(IC)	E	MESM	01.12.99	SULTAN
Orton, David Michael , *BSc, DPhil*	LT(CC)	E	TM	01.05.91	VIGILANT(PORT)
Osbaldestin, Richard Alan	LT(FTC)	X	MCD	01.10.98	INVERNESS
Osborn, Colvin Graeme , *BSc*	LT(FTC)	X	SM	01.06.94	JARIC
Osborn, Richard Marcus	LT CDR(FTC)	X	PWO(A)	01.02.99	LN DERA CDA HLS
Osbourn, Simon Edwin John , *pce*	LT CDR(FTC)	X	PWO(U)	01.04.93	DRYAD
Osman, Mark Ronald , *pcea, psc*	LT CDR(FTC)	X	P	01.09.86	824 NAS
Osmond, Justin Bruce , *BEng*	LT CDR(FTC)	E	AE	01.02.99	JF HARROLE OFF
Ottewell, Paul Steven , *BSc*	LT(FTC)	X	SM	01.01.97	TORBAY
Oulds, Keith Antony , *BEng*	LT(FTC)	X	MCD	01.09.92	FDU3
Oura, Adrian Nicholas , *BA*	2LT(GRAD)(FTC)	RM		02.09.98	40 CDO RM
Ouvry, Janet Elisabeth Delahaize	LT	Q		25.03.93	JSU NORTHWOOD
Ovenden, Neil Stephen Paul , *pce*	LT CDR(FTC)	X	PWO(U)	01.02.95	CAPT F2(SEA)
Ovens, Jeremy John , *QCVS, BSc, pce, pcea, psc*	CDR(FTC)	X	O	31.12.99	JSCSC
Ovens, Michael James	LT CDR(FTC)	X	PWO(U)	20.08.97	FOST SEA
Overington, Nigel , *BSc, pce*	CDR(FTC)	X	PWO(U)	31.12.90	FOSF
Owen, Glyn	LT(CC)	X	O	16.02.97	815 FLT 212
Owen, Nigel Richard , *jsdc, pce, psc(j) (COMMODORE)*	CAPT(FTC)	X	AWO(U)	30.06.93	NATO DEF COL
Owen, Peter Clive , *pcea*	LT CDR(FTC)	X	P	01.10.91	MERLIN IPT
Owen, Samuel Thomas Louis	SLT(IC)	X		01.04.98	DRYAD
Owens, Daniel Tudor , *BEng, CEng, MIMechE*	LT CDR(FTC)	E	ME	01.08.99	CNSA BRISTOL
Oxlade, Andrew Thomas , *BSc*	SLT(IC)	X		01.09.98	DARTMOUTH BRNC

P

Name	Rank	Branch	Spec	Seniority	Where Serving
Pacey, Peter John , *MA, MSc, CEng, FIEE, nadc*	CAPT(FTC)	E	WE	31.12.91	SA MADRID
Packham, Craig Nicholas Ronald	LT(CC)	X	P	01.03.96	819 SQN
Page, Durward Charles Miller , *BSc*	CAPT RM(FTC)	RM		01.09.95	RM Poole
Page, David Michael , *BSc, CEng, MIEE*	CDR(FTC)	E	WE	30.06.97	CINCFLEET
Page, Lewis , *BA*	LT(CC)	X	MCD	01.04.94	BRIDPORT
Page, Michael Christian , *MA, psc*	LT COL(FTC)	RM	LC	30.06.99	MWC SOUTHWICK
Page, Mark Robert	SLT(CC)	X	O	01.05.97	849 SQN B FLT
Page, Simon Peter , *BEd, MSc*	LT CDR(FTC)	E	TM	01.03.97	MOD (LONDON)
Page, Trevor Andrew	LT(FTC)	E	ME	10.06.94	ENDURANCE
Paget, Simon James	SLT(FTC)	X	PT	02.05.97	DRAKE CBP(DLO)
Painter, Christopher John , *BSc*, MInstPS, *MIMgt, MILog*	LT CDR(FTC)	S		23.02.87	RHQ AFNORTH
Pakes, Danyel Tobias , *BEng*	LT(FTC)	E	WESM	01.01.96	VICTORIOUS(PORT)
Palethorpe, Nicholas , *BSc*	LT(CC)	X		01.09.97	IRON DUKE
Palframan, Ian Martin , *MEng*	SLT(IC)	X	O U/T	01.09.98	DARTMOUTH BRNC
Palin, Giles Roland , *LLB*	LT(FTC)	X		01.12.97	GLOUCESTER
Pallot, Marcus Louis Alexander , *LLB*	LT CDR(FTC)	S	BAR	01.03.00	FOSM NWOOD HQ
Palmer, Alan Charles , *MB, ChB*	SURG LTCDR	-		01.03.97	CTCRM
Palmer, Christopher Laurence , *BSc, MIMgt, pce, pcea, psc (Act Capt)*	CDR(FTC)	X	O	30.06.91	MOD (LONDON)
Palmer, Christopher	SLT(IC)	E	MESM	19.09.98	SULTAN
Palmer, Geoffrey David	LT CDR(FTC)	X	PR	01.10.88	NMA GOSPORT
Palmer, John , *MA, CEng, MIEE*	LT(CC)	E	WE	01.07.95	IRON DUKE
Palmer, James Ernest , *BSc, MSc, MPhil, CEng, FRINA, MIEE*	CDR(FTC)	E	WE	31.12.96	MOD (LONDON)
Palmer, Michael Edward , *BEng*	LT(FTC)	E	WE	01.11.93	COLLINGWOOD
Palmer, Phillip Alan , *BA*	LT CDR(FTC)	X	SM	01.07.89	MOD (LONDON)
Palmer, Rhoderick Adrian Nigel , *BSc, ACGI, psc*	CAPT(FTC)	E	AE	31.12.96	ES AIR YEO
Pamphilon, Michael John , *pcea, psc*	LT CDR(FTC)	X	P	01.03.88	824 NAS
Pancott, Brian Michael , *BSc, mdtc, MCGI, psc*	CDR(FTC)	E	WE	31.12.91	2SL/CNH
Panic, Alexander , *BSc*	LT(IC)	E	TM	15.04.95	CSST SHORE FSLN
Pannett, Leonard William , *BSc, BEng, AIL, AMIEE*	LT(CC)	E	WESM	01.06.97	SCEPTRE
Panther, Andrew Mark , *BEng*	LT(FTC)	E	WE	01.07.92	LN DERA FARN
Pardoe, Elton , *BSc*	SURG SLT	-		12.09.99	DARTMOUTH BRNC
Paris, William , *BEng*	LT CDR(FTC)	E	WE	15.04.98	SSA BRISTOL
Park, Brian Campbell , *BA*	LT(CC)	S		01.06.94	HQ 3 CDO BDE RM
Park, Ian David , *MA*	LT(IC)	S		01.08.98	JMOTS NORTHWOOD

Name	Rank	Branch	Spec	Seniority	Where Serving
Parker, George Patrick , *BEd, MBA, PGCE, jsdc*	CDR(FTC)	E	TM	31.12.90	MOD (LONDON)
Parker, Henry Hardyman , *MA, PhD, CEng, MIEE, psc*	CDR(FTC)	E	WESM	30.06.97	MOD (LONDON)
Parker, Ian Robert , *BSc, MIMechE*	CDR(FTC)	E	MESM	31.12.93	NMA PORTSMOUTH
Parker, Jeremy William , *pce, ocds(USN), (Commodore)*	CAPT(FTC)	X	AWO(A)	31.12.94	NELSON
Parker, Jeremy Vaugn Vernham , *BSc, psc(m)*	LT COL(FTC)	RM		30.06.92	COMSTRIKFORSTH
Parker, Mark Neal , *BEng, MSc, CEng, FIMarE, MCGI*	LT CDR(FTC)	E	ME	01.03.91	RMCS SHRIVENHAM
Parker, Matthew Sheldon	SLT(IC)	X	O U/T	01.05.98	DARTMOUTH BRNC
Parker, Sarah Anne Marie , *BA*	SLT(IC)	X		01.01.98	GUERNSEY
Parker, Stephen John , *MB, BSc, BS, FRCS, FRCSEd, FRCPglas, ms*	SURG LTCDR	-	(GS)UT	01.08.94	NELSON (PAY)
Parker, Timothy Stephen , *BSc, CMath*	LT(CC)	E	TM	01.11.95	JSCSC
Parkin, James Miles Benjamin , *BA*	LT(FTC)	X		01.09.98	BERKELEY
Parkin, Malcolm Ian , *BEng*	LT CDR(FTC)	E	ME	01.07.99	MOD (BATH)
Parkinson, Andrew	LT(FTC)	X	AV	23.07.98	RNAS YEOVILTON
Parkinson, Henry Michael Larissa	MID(UCE)(FTC)	E	AE	01.09.98	DARTMOUTH BRNC
Parkinson, James Hugh George	SLT(UCE)(FTC)	X		01.09.98	DARTMOUTH BRNC
Parkinson, Richard Ian , *BA*	LT CDR(FTC)	E	AE	01.01.00	FONA
Parks, Edward Patrick , *jsdc*	MAJ(FTC)	RM		01.09.90	PJHQ
Parmenter, Alan John	SLT(FTC)	E	AE(M)	01.04.98	848 SQN HERON
Parnell, Adam David , *BEng (Act Lt Cdr)*	LT(FTC)	E	WE	01.04.93	CORNWALL
Parr, Matthew John , *BSc, pce, pce(sm)*	CDR(FTC)	X	SM	31.12.96	PJHQ
Parr, Michael John Edward	LT(FTC)	X	HM	01.10.96	RNSOMO
Parr, Nicola Karen	LT(IC)	X		01.05.97	OCLC BIRM
Parrett, John William	LT(FTC)	E	MESM	16.10.92	SPARTAN
Parris, Kevin John , *BSc, jsdc, pce*	CDR(FTC)	X	PWO(U)	31.12.88	CNSA BRISTOL
Parrock, Neil Graham	LT(CC)	X	P	01.07.95	RNAS YEOVILTON
Parrott, James Philip	LT(FTC)	X	FC	01.07.96	800 SQN
Parry, Alexander Keith Illiam , *BSc*	LT CDR(FTC)	S		01.02.98	PJHQ
Parry, Christopher Adrian , *MB, BSc, BS, PhD*	SURG LTCDR	-		12.08.99	RH HASLAR
Parry, Christopher John , *MA, rcds, pce, pcea, psc*	CAPT(FTC)	X	O	30.06.97	FEARLESS
Parry, David Reginald *(Act Lt Cdr)*	LT(FTC)	X	EW	03.04.92	JSSU OAKLEY
Parry, Jonathan Allan , *BSc*	CAPT RM(IC)	RM	P	27.04.96	847 SQN
Parry, Jonathan David Frank	LT(FTC)	X	P	01.05.92	815 FLT 214
Parry, Mark Roderick Raymond , *BEng*	LT(FTC)	E	AE	01.09.96	RMC OF SCIENCE
Parry, Nicholas Thomas , *BSc, AMIEE, CGIA, psc, mdtc*	CDR(FTC)	E	WESM	31.12.94	NEPTUNE NT
Parry, Roger John	LT(FTC)	E	AE(M)	16.10.92	819 SQN
Parry, Robin Wyn , *BSc, CEng, MIMechE, psc*	CDR(FTC)	E	ME	31.12.93	EXCHANGE USA
Parry, Sophie Joanna , *BSc*	SLT(IC)	X		01.05.97	SHETLAND
Parsonage, Robert James	LT CDR(FTC)	E	MESM	07.10.89	NP DNREAY
Parsons, Andrew David , *BSc, n*	LT CDR(FTC)	X	PWO(C)	01.01.00	CAMPBELTOWN
Parsons, Brian Robert , *BSc*	LT CDR(FTC)	E	AE	01.02.93	ES AIR YEO
Parsons, Christopher Graham , *BSc, MDA, CEng, MIEE*	LT CDR(FTC)	E	WE	01.03.92	MOD (LONDON)
Parsons, Geoffrey , *MSc, CEng, MIEE, MIMgt, gw*	CDR(FTC)	E	WE	30.06.93	DEF SCH OF LANG
Parsons, Gareth James , *BA*	SLT(IC)	X		01.05.97	DRYAD
Parsons, Patrick Hugh , *osc(us)*	LT COL(FTC)	RM	MLDR	31.12.92	HQ NORTH
Parsons, Philip Kelvin Charles , *MSc, BSc, adp*	LT CDR(FTC)	E	IS	29.07.85	EXCHANGE USA
Parsons, Robert John , *BSc*	SLT(IC)	X		01.01.98	LINDISFARNE
Parsons, Robert Martin James	SLT(IC)	X		01.01.99	DARTMOUTH BRNC
Parton, Alan	SLT(FTC)	X	MCD	19.09.97	INVINCIBLE
Parton, Stephen Lewis	LT CDR(FTC)	S		11.11.94	MOD (LONDON)
Partridge, Simon Christopher , *BSc*	SLT(IC)	X		01.01.98	SHEFFIELD
Parvin, Philip Stanley , *BEng, MSc, CEng, MIMarE, MIMechE*	LT CDR(FTC)	E	MESM	01.02.97	TORBAY
Parvin, Richard Alan	CAPT RM(FTC)	RM		01.05.97	EXCHANGE ARMY UK
Passingham, Rodney Edris , *MSc, CEng, MIEE*	CDR(FTC)	E	WE	31.12.89	SSA/CWTA PORTS
Pate, Christopher Michael	MID(IC)	X		01.01.99	DARTMOUTH BRNC
Paterson, Fergus James Blair	LT CDR(FTC)	X	PWO(C)	01.08.99	COLLINGWOOD
Paterson, Michael Paul , *n*	LT(FTC)	X	PWO(U)	01.06.93	SHEFFIELD
Paton, Alan John Malcolm	LT(FTC)	E	ME	19.06.98	CFM PORTSMOUTH
Paton, Christopher Mark , *BSc*	CAPT RM(FTC)	RM		01.09.96	HQ 3 CDO BDE RM
Paton, David William	SLT(CC)	E	WE	01.05.98	DARTMOUTH BRNC
Patrick, James , *BSc, MSc, psc*	CAPT(FTC)	E	TM	31.12.97	NMA PORTSMOUTH
Patterson, Andrew James , *BSc*	LT(IC)	X	P	16.11.92	819 SQN
Patterson, David , *BEng*	LT(FTC)	E	WE	01.12.94	SSA BRISTOL
Patterson, John David , *BSc*	LT(FTC)	X		01.08.96	EXCHANGE ITALY

Name	Rank	Branch	Spec	Seniority	Where Serving
Patterson, Scott Douglas, *BEng*	LT(FTC)	E	WE	01.07.97	GLASGOW
Pattinson, Ian Howard, *BSc, MSc*	CDR(FTC)	S		30.06.98	MOD (BATH)
Pattison, Kelvin, *BA(OU)*	LT CDR(FTC)	E	TM	01.10.89	NELSON RNSETT
Paul, Russell William Fordyce, *MA, psc*	MAJ(FTC)	RM	LC	01.09.90	COMUKTG/CASWSF
Paulet, Michael Raoul	SLT(IC)	X	P U/T	01.04.98	RNAS YEOVILTON
Paulson, Richard Brian, *AMIEE*	LT(FTC)	E	WE	01.08.95	RMC OF SCIENCE
Pavey, Emma Lesley, *LLB*	LT(IC)	X	H2	01.05.97	CAPT F2(SEA)
Payne, Daniel	LT CDR(FTC)	E	ME	01.10.99	FEARLESS
Payne, John Durley, *BSc, pce, n*	LT CDR(FTC)	X	PWO(U)	01.06.98	DARTMOUTH BRNC
Payne, Matthew John	LT(FTC)	X	PWO(C)	01.05.93	INVINCIBLE
Payne, Philip John, *BA*	LT(FTC)	X	H2	01.07.94	RN HYDROG SCHL
Payne, Richard Charles, *pce, pcea*	LT CDR(FTC)	X	P	16.04.93	YORK
Payne-Hanlon, Peter Norman, *FIEIE, MIMgt*	CDR(FTC)	E	WESM	31.12.90	2SL/CNH FOTR
Peace, Richard William	LT(FTC)	E	MESM	01.07.92	DRAKE CBS
Peach, Christopher Charles, *pce*	CAPT(FTC)	X	O	30.06.97	*DA* MANILA
Peach, Graham Leslie, *BSc, psc*	CAPT(FTC)	E	WE	30.06.00	SSA/CWTA PORTS
Peachey, Richard, *BSc*	LT(IC)	X	P	01.03.95	819 SQN
Peacock, Michael Robert	LT CDR(FTC)	E	MESM	01.10.96	DRAKE CBS
Peacock, Stephen, *BSc, MIEE*	LT CDR(FTC)	E	WESM	01.06.92	MOD (BATH)
Peacock, Timothy James, *MA, pcea*	LT CDR(FTC)	X	P	01.01.98	SHEFFIELD
Peak, Martyn	LT(FTC)	X	g	03.04.98	CAMBRIDGE
Pear, Ian Keith, *BSc, CEng, MIMarE*	LT CDR(FTC)	E	MESM	01.04.96	TALENT
Pearce, Jonathan Kenneth Charles	CAPT(FTC)	S		31.12.97	MOD (BATH)
Pearce, Lucy	SURG LT	-		05.08.98	FOSM GOSPORT
Pearce, Rebecca Anne	LT(IC)	S		01.11.97	MOD (BATH)
Pearce, Robert James, *BA*	SLT(IC)	X		01.01.99	DARTMOUTH BRNC
Pearch, Sean	LT(FTC)	X	ATC	26.04.99	RAF SHAWBURY
Pearey, Michael Scott, *DSC, BSc, jsdc, pce,*	CDR(FTC)	X	O	31.12.96	PJHQ *pcea*
Pearmain, Stephanie Rosina, *BSc*	SLT(IC)	X		01.01.99	DARTMOUTH BRNC
Pears, Ian James, *BSc*	LT(FTC)	E	IS	01.01.91	CAPT IST STAFF
Pearson, Charles Peter Bellamy, *BEng*	LT(FTC)	E	ME	01.08.93	MOD (BATH)
Pearson, Christopher Robert, *MB, BCh, BChir, MA, DLO, FRCS* (*Act* Surg *Cdr*)	SURG LTCDR	-	(CE)	15.05.89	RH HASLAR
Pearson, Gareth, *BEng*	CAPT RM(IC)	RM		01.09.98	CTCRM
Pearson, James Carden	SLT(CC)	X		01.04.98	GUERNSEY
Pearson, Jon Richard	LT CDR(FTC)	E	WE	01.10.98	DGSS BARROW
Pearson, Michael Forbes	LT(FTC)	X	O	01.03.93	URNU SUSSEX
Pearson, Neil, *BEng, CEng, MIMarE*	LT CDR(FTC)	E	ME	01.08.97	SHEFFIELD
Pearson, Rebekah	LT(IC)	W		01.05.96	NELSON
Pearson, Stephen John, *MA, pce, psc(j)*	CDR(FTC)	X	O	30.06.00	NEWCASTLE
Peck, Ian John, *BSc, CEng, MRAeS, MDA*	CDR(FTC)	E	AE	31.12.97	MOD (LONDON)
Peckham, David Reginald, *BSc, Eur Ing, CEng, MIEE, psc*	CDR(FTC)	E	WE	31.12.94	PAAMS PARIS
Pedler, Mark David, *BEng*	LT(IC)	X	P	01.12.97	846 SQN
Pedre, Robert George, *BSc*	LT(FTC)	X		01.10.97	SOUTHAMPTON
Peel, Giles Robert, *BSc, FCIS*	CDR(FTC)	S		31.12.96	NELSON
Peerman, Stephen John	LT CDR(FTC)	E	WE	01.10.95	HQ DCSA
Pegden, Clive, *BSc, MSc*	LT CDR(FTC)	E	AE	16.02.81	SULTAN
Pegg, Russell Montfort, *pce, fsc*	CDR(FTC)	X	PWO(U)	31.12.95	MOD (LONDON)
Pegg, Stephen Michael, *pce, psc*	CDR(FTC)	X	AWO(A)	30.06.88	SA ANKARA
Pegrum, Terrence Allen	LT CDR(FTC)	X	P	01.10.99	845 SQN
Peilow, Benjamin Francis, *BA, MILT, psc*	CDR(FTC)	S		31.12.92	AGRIPPA AFSOUTH
Pelly, Gilbert Ralph	MAJ(FTC)	RM		25.04.96	NEPTUNE CFS
Pelly, Richard Cecil, *MA, MSc, CEng, FIMarE, MIMechE, MInsD* (*COMMODORE*)	CAPT(FTC)	E	ME	31.12.93	LN DERA FARN
Penalver, Warren Craig	MID(UCE)(FTC)	E	AE	01.09.98	DARTMOUTH BRNC
Pendle, Martin Erle John, *BSc, CEng, MIMarE, jsdc*	CDR(FTC)	E	ME	30.06.95	CAPT F2(SEA)
Penfold, Michael Jamie	LT(FTC)	E	WE	18.02.94	CFM PORTSMOUTH
Pengelly, Steven	SURG SLT	-		16.05.99	DARTMOUTH BRNC
Penketh, Mark Geoffrey	LT(FTC)	E	ME	02.09.99	SULTAN
Penkman, William Alfred Vincent, *BSc*	CAPT RM(FTC)	RM	P U/T	01.09.98	FONA SULTAN
Penn-Barwell, Jowan	SURG SLT	-		11.01.00	DARTMOUTH BRNC
Pennefather, William Jonathan Richard, *jsdc*	CAPT(FTC)	S		31.12.96	CINCFLEET
Pennington, Charles Edmond, *BSc*	2LT(GRAD)(IC)	RM		01.09.99	CTCRM LYMPSTONE

Name	Rank	Branch	Spec	Seniority	Where Serving
Penniston, John Raymond , *BSc*	CDR(FTC)	E	MESM	31.12.97	FOSNNI/NBC CLYDE
Penny, Anthony David , *BSc, MSc, CEng, MIEE, AMIEE*	CDR(FTC)	E	WE	31.12.95	CNSA BRISTOL
Penprase, Jason Michael	LT(CC)	X		01.10.94	RALEIGH
Penrice, Ian William	LT(CC)	X	P	01.08.94	EXCHANGE RAF UK
Penson, Jonathan George	SLT(IC)	X	O U/T	01.09.98	DARTMOUTH BRNC
Pentreath, Jonathan Patrick , *BSc, psc(j)*	LT CDR(FTC)	X	P	01.12.95	JHCHQ
Peppe, Alasdair George	LT(FTC)	X		01.06.95	ALDERNEY
Pepper, Martin Richard , *BSc, pce, pcea, psc*	CDR(FTC)	X	O	31.12.92	JDCC
Pepper, Philip Michael	SLT(IC)	X	P U/T	01.09.98	DARTMOUTH BRNC
Percey, Steven John , *BA*	CAPT RM(IC)	RM		01.09.94	CTCRM
Percharde, Michael Robert , *BSc, pce, psc(j)*	CDR(FTC)	X	PWO(A)	31.12.98	MOD (LONDON)
Percival, Andrew William , *BA*	LT(FTC)	X		01.03.95	COTTESMORE
Percival, Fiona	LT(FTC)	S		01.09.96	MOD (LONDON)
Percival, Michael Christopher	LT CDR(FTC)	S		01.07.99	WESTMINSTER
Percy, Nicolas Andrew , *BSc*	LT(CC)	X		01.04.99	GLOUCESTER
Perkins, Ben , *BEng*	SLT(IC)	E	AE	01.09.98	INVINCIBLE
Perkins, John Robert , *MMus, ARAM, ARCM, LGSM, LRAM, pdm*	MAJ(FTC)	BS		01.10.93	RM BAND PTSMTH
Perkins, Michael Jonathan , *BA, pce, MDA*	CDR(FTC)	X	PWO(A)	30.06.96	MOD (BATH)
Perkins, Ross John	LT(FTC)	E	ME	01.01.96	CFM PORTSMOUTH
Perks, James Le Seelleur , *SM(n) (Act Lt Cdr)*	LT(FTC)	X	SM	01.03.93	TALENT
Perowne, Benjamin Brian , *CDipAF, rcds, pce, psc*	RADM	-	AWO(C)	06.11.96	MOD (BATH)
Perowne, *Sir* James (Francis) , *KBE, rcds, pce(sm)*	ADM	-	SM	09.05.00	SACLANT USA
Perrin, Mark	2LT(GRAD)(IC)	RM		28.04.99	CTCRM LYMPSTONE
Perry, Andrew James	LT CDR(FTC)	S	SM	16.07.99	MONMOUTH
Perry, Emma Marie , *BSc*	LT(IC)	X		01.08.98	GRIMSBY
Perry, Jonathan Neil , *MB, ChB, FRCR*	SURG CDR	-	(CX)	31.12.96	MODHU DERRIFORD
Perry, Richard , *BSc, psc*	LT CDR(FTC)	E	MESM	01.11.90	MOD (BATH)
Perry, Russell John	LT(CC)	X	MW	01.11.93	INVINCIBLE
Perry, Robert William *(Act Maj)*	CAPT RM(FTC)	RM	SO(LE)	01.01.94	NMA WHALE ISLAND
Perry-Evans, Sean Patrick Alfred , *BSc, CEng, MIMarE, psc*	LT CDR(FTC)	E	ME	01.06.90	NMA PORTSMOUTH
Perryment, Claire Patricia	SLT(CC)	X		01.04.99	DRYAD
Peters, Adam John Urlin , *BSc*	LT CDR(FTC)	X	SM	01.08.87	DRYAD
Peters, William Richard , *BA*	LT(FTC)	X		01.03.96	DRYAD
Petheram, Anthony John , *pce*	LT CDR(FTC)	X	PWO(C)	01.09.97	PJHQ
Petheram, Michael John , *pce, psc(j), MA*	LT CDR(FTC)	X	PWO(U)	29.06.92	PJHQ
Petherick, Jason Stewart	LT CDR(FTC)	X	PWO(A)	01.04.98	INVINCIBLE
Pethybridge, Richard Alan , *pce, n*	LT CDR(FTC)	X	PWO(N)	01.05.97	FOST SEA
Petitt, Simon Richard , *BEng, MBA, CEng, MIEE*	LT CDR(FTC)	E	WE	01.02.98	CHATHAM
Pett, Jeremy Graham , *BSc, MInstP, C PHYS*	CDR(FTC)	E	TM	30.06.99	FOSM NWOOD HQ
Pettigrew, Thomas Robert , *BEng*	LT(IC)	E	TM	01.09.97	SULTAN
Pettitt, Gary William , *pce*	CDR(FTC)	X	PWO(U)	31.12.97	BDS WASHINGTON
Petzer, Garth Stephen , *MBE*	CHAPLAIN	CE		09.01.96	SULTAN
Peyman, Tracy Anne	SLT(IC)	S		01.04.98	DARTMOUTH BRNC
Pheasant, John Christian Stephen , *BSc*	LT(FTC)	S		01.10.93	2SL/CNH
Phenna, Andrew , *BEng*	LT CDR(FTC)	E	WE	01.03.96	FOSF
Phesse, John Paul Lloyd , *IEng, AMRAeS*	LT(FTC)	E	AE(M)	15.10.93	JF HARROLE OFF
Philip, Alistair David , *BSc*	LT(CC)	X		01.03.97	ROEBUCK
Phillips, Andrew Ralph , *IEng, MIMechIE*	LT(FTC)	E	AE(M)	07.09.95	ES AIR MASU
Phillips, Christopher John , *BA*	SLT(IC)	X		01.09.97	CUMBERLAND
Phillips, David Alan , *rcds, pce, psc, hcsc COMMODORE)*	CAPT(FTC)	X	AWO(U)	30.06.93	ELANT/NAVNORTH
Phillips, David George , *pce, pce(sm)*	CDR(FTC)	X	SM	30.06.95	MWC SOUTHWICK
Phillips, Ian Michael	LT(FTC)	MS		29.07.94	MODHU DERRIFORD
Phillips, James	SURG SLT	-		12.12.99	DARTMOUTH BRNC
Phillips, James Nicholas , *BEng, AMIEE, AIMgt*	LT(FTC)	E	WE	01.03.95	MOD (LONDON)
Phillips, Jason Peter , *pcea*	LT(FTC)	X	O	01.03.91	EXCHANGE AUSTLIA
Phillips, Laura Claire	MID(NE)(IC)	X		01.09.99	DARTMOUTH BRNC
Phillips, Matthew Benjamin , *BSc*	LT(IC)	X	P	01.04.96	800 SQN
Phillips, Mark Christopher	CAPT RM(FTC)	RM	SO(LE)	01.01.99	RM Poole
Phillips, Richard Edward	MID(IC)	X	P U/T	01.09.98	DARTMOUTH BRNC
Phillips, Richard Mark , *BSc, MSc*	SLT(CC)	X		01.09.97	DRYAD
Phillips, Stephen John , *MA, psc*	MAJ(FTC)	RM		01.09.90	MOD (LONDON)
Phillis, Ian Richard , *MRAeS*	LT(CC)	X	P	16.09.90	824 NAS
Philo, Julian Quentin , *BEng*	LT CDR(FTC)	E	ME	01.06.98	IRON DUKE

Name	Rank	Branch	Spec	Seniority	Where Serving
Philpot, David John, *BEng*	LT(FTC)	E	WESM	18.07.92	TRAFALGAR
Philpott, Ashley Michael	LT(FTC)	X	SM	01.03.96	RALEIGH
Philpott, Geoffrey Richard, *BA*	CDR(FTC)	S		30.06.90	AFPAA(CENTURION)
Philpott, Nigel Edward	LT CDR(FTC)	S		01.11.96	JSCSC
Phipps, Tracey Anne, *BA*	LT(CC)	X	H2	01.02.94	RN HYDROG SCHL
Piaggesi, Gareth Fiorenzo	MID(UCE)(IC)	E	AE	01.09.99	EXETER
Pickard, David Malcolm	CAPT RM(FTC)	RM	SO(LE)	01.01.99	RM Poole
Pickard, Donna Marie, *BA*	LT(IC)	S		01.03.99	RNAS CULDROSE
Pickard, Stephen Richard	SLT(CC)	E	AE	01.05.98	DARTMOUTH BRNC
Pickbourne, Martin, *IEng, AMIMarE*	LT CDR(FTC)	E	ME	01.10.95	MOD (BATH)
Picken, Jeffrey David	LT CDR(FTC)	E	MESM	01.10.90	DRAKE CFM
Pickering, David Hal, *MA*	LT(IC)	X	SM	01.03.98	SUPERB
Pickering, Ian Jeffery	LT(CC)	X	SM	01.07.96	VANGUARD(PORT)
Pickering, Martin John, *BA*	CDR(FTC)	X	METOC	01.10.92	SEA CADET CORPS
Pickering-Wheeler, Christopher William, *BSc*	LT(FTC)	X	SM	01.01.98	TURBULENT
Pickles, David Richard	SLT(CC)	X	ATCU/T	01.05.98	RNAS YEOVILTON
Pickles, Ian Seaton, *pce, pce(sm)*	CDR(FTC)	X	SM	30.06.97	MOD (LONDON)
Pickles, Martin Richard, *BSc*	SLT(IC)	X	P U/T	01.05.98	DARTMOUTH BRNC
Picksley, Michael Raymond	LT(FTC)	E	WE	15.06.90	SSA BRISTOL
Pickthall, David Nicholas, *BSc, CEng, MIEE*	CDR(FTC)	E	WE	31.12.97	DGSS BRISTOL
Pickup, Richard Allan, *BSc, MA, psc(m)*	LT COL(FTC)	RM		31.12.97	HQ NORTH
Picton, Annette Mary, *psc*	CAPT(FTC)	W	SEC	30.06.96	MOD (LONDON)
Pierce, Adrian Kevern Maxwell, *n*	LT CDR(FTC)	X	PWO(U)	01.02.00	CAMPBELTOWN
Pierson, Matthew Fraser	MAJ(FTC)	RM		01.09.99	NELSON (PAY)
Piggott, Graham David, *MNI, pce, psc (Act Capt)*	CDR(FTC)	X	AWO(C)	30.06.86	HQ DCSA
Pike, Martin Stephen, *BSc*	LT CDR(FTC)	S		01.03.91	JHQ NORTHEAST
Pile, Kenneth James, *IEng, MIEEIE*	LT CDR(FTC)	E	WE	01.10.91	MOD (BATH)
Pillar, Andrew Robert, *OBE, ADC, psc(a) (BRIGADIER)*	COL(OF6)(FTC)	RM		30.06.98	CTCRM
Pillar, Christopher David, *pce*	LT CDR(FTC)	X	PWO(U)	01.03.95	CHATHAM
Pilley, Michael Anthony, *pce*	LT CDR(FTC)	X	PWO(U)	16.09.84	DRYAD
Pilsworth, Dermod Scott, *BSc, CGIA*	LT CDR(FTC)	E	WE	01.06.85	MOD (BATH)
Pimpalnerkar, Ashvin	SURG LTCDR	-		04.01.98	NELSON (PAY)
Pinckney, Matthew	2LT(UCE)(IC)	RM		01.09.99	CTCRM LYMPSTONE
Pinder, Christopher David, *BEng*	LT(IC)	E	TM	01.02.96	RALEIGH
Pine, Paul Martin, *BSc*	LT(IC)	E	TM	06.12.98	NELSON RNSETT
Pinhey, Andrew	SLT(IC)	MS		27.01.99	MOD (BATH)
Pink, Simon Edward, *n*	LT(FTC)	X	PWO(A)	01.01.94	GLOUCESTER
Piper, Neale Derek, *ARRC*	LT	Q	IC	23.11.95	RDMC BLOCKHOUSE
Pipkin, Christopher, *MB, BS*, MRCPath	SURG CDR	-	CPDATE	30.06.94	RH HASLAR
Pipkin, Peter John, *BEng*	LT(FTC)	E	WE	01.04.00	COLLINGWOOD
Pipkin, Simon Christian	LT CDR(FTC)	X	P	01.10.95	DHFS
Pirie, Scott Keith	CAPT RM(IC)	RM		01.05.99	CDO LOG REGT RM
Pirrie, James Alexander	SLT(FTC)	X	C	19.09.97	COLLINGWOOD
Pitcher, James	LT CDR(FTC)	E	AE(L)	01.10.93	FONA
Pitcher, Paul, *BA*	LT(FTC)	X		01.11.94	EXCHANGE GERMANY
Pitchford, Ian Charles, *BEng*	LT(FTC)	E	AE	01.07.95	845 SQN
Pitt, Johnathan Mark	LT CDR(FTC)	X	SM	17.02.99	TRAFALGAR
Pittard, David Campbell, *BSc*	LT(IC)	X		01.06.99	EDINBURGH
Pittard, Peter Michael, *TEng, IEng, MITE*	LT CDR(FTC)	E	WE	01.10.91	SULTAN
Plackett, Andrew John, *MA*	LT(CC)	E	TM	01.05.92	RALEIGH
Plaice, Graham Conyers	LT(FTC)	S	SM	12.12.91	ES AIR YEO
Plant, Ian Robert, *BSc*	LT CDR(FTC)	E	AE	01.07.90	OCEAN
Plant, Jeremy Neil Melrose, *BSc*	CDR(FTC)	E	AE	31.12.99	RMCS SHRIVENHAM
Plant, Martin Gary	LT CDR(FTC)	E	WE	13.06.91	MOD (BATH)
Platt, Jonathan Howard, *BSc*	LT(CC)	X	P	16.06.96	820 SQN
Platt, Nicola	LT(FTC)	S	(W)	03.04.98	NELSON
Platt, Timothy Samuel, *BSc*	LT CDR(FTC)	X	MCD	01.04.00	DRYAD
Pledger, David	LT(FTC)	X	AV	16.12.94	RNU ST MAWGAN
Plewes, Andrew Burns, *BSc*	CAPT RM(FTC)	RM		27.04.96	HQRM
Plumb, Michael Christopher Mark, *BSc*	LT(FTC)	X		01.05.98	DRYAD
Pnematicatos, Nicholas	CHAPLAIN	CE		01.09.98	CAPT D3 SEA
Pocock, David *(Act Lt Cdr)*	LT(CC)	S		16.10.88	NEPTUNE CFS
Podger, Kevin Gordon Ray, *BSc, psc*	CDR(FTC)	E	MESM	30.06.95	MOD (BATH)

Name	Rank	Branch	Spec	Seniority	Where Serving
Podmore, Anthony, *BSc*	LT CDR(FTC)	E	TM	01.09.94	DEF DIVING SCHL
Polding, Martin, *BA*	LT(IC)	X	P	01.11.93	846 SQN
Poll, Martin	CHAPLAIN	CE		14.06.90	NEPTUNE 2SL/CNH
Pollard, Alexandra Eleanor, *BA*	LT(IC)	X		01.05.99	NORFOLK
Pollard, Andrew John	SLT(FTC)	E	ME	01.04.98	EXETER
Pollard, Jonathan Richard	LT(CC)	E	WE	01.03.00	DARTMOUTH BRNC
Pollitt, David Nigel Anthony, *pce(sm), psc*	LT CDR(FTC)	X	SM	01.04.89	JMOTS NORTHWOOD
Pollock, Christopher Jon	SLT(IC)	X		01.09.97	DRYAD
Pollock, David John, *BSc, pce, pce(sm)*	CDR(FTC)	X	SM	30.06.99	SUPERB
Pollock, Malcolm Philip, *pce, pcea*	LT CDR(FTC)	X	O	01.07.95	CAPT F4 (SEA)
Pomeroy, Mark Anthony	LT CDR(FTC)	E	ME	01.10.98	SUTHERLAND
Pomeroy, Philippa Mary, *BEd*	LT CDR(FTC)	S		01.02.00	CAMPBELTOWN
Pond, David William, *BEd, MIMgt*	CAPT(FTC)	X	METOC	30.06.98	RCDS
Ponsford, Philip Kevin	LT CDR(FTC)	X	SM	01.01.99	CSST SHORE DEVPT
Poole, Jason Lee, *pce*	LT CDR(FTC)	X	MCD	01.04.94	KENT
Poole, Timothy, *BSc, pcea*	LT(CC)	X	O	16.01.92	RNAS YEOVILTON
Pooley, Steven William, *BSc*	LT CDR(FTC)	E	WESM	01.07.96	SOVEREIGN
Pope, Catherine Manuela, *BSc, MSc, psc*	CDR(FTC)	X	METOC	31.12.97	CINCFLEET
Porrett, Johnathan Anthony	LT CDR(FTC)	S	SM	14.11.95	2SL/CNH
Port, Leslie Alan, *MBE*	LT CDR(FTC)	X	P	15.04.83	CHFHQ
Porter, Andrew James, *BEM*	LT CDR(FTC)	E	WE	01.10.99	SHEFFIELD
Porter, Christopher William	LT CDR(FTC)	X	O	01.10.94	ES AIR YEO
Porter, Derek Lowry, *BA*	LT(IC)	S	SM	01.06.97	VANGUARD(PORT)
Porter, Matthew Edward, *MBE, BSc*	MAJ(FTC)	RM		01.05.98	RM Poole
Porter, Suzanne, *MB, BSc, ChB*	SURG LT	-		01.08.96	MODHU DERRIFORD
Porter, Simon Paul, *pce, psc(j)*	CDR(FTC)	X	PWO(A)	31.12.99	YORK
Porter, Timothy Benedict, *BA*	LT(FTC)	S		01.05.94	RALEIGH
Pothecary, Richard Edward, *MNI, pce*	CDR(FTC)	X	PWO(A)	31.12.93	RNAS CULDROSE
Potiphar, Darren Wayne, *MB, ChB*	SURG LTCDR	-		01.08.99	NELSON (PAY)
Potter, David John	LT(FTC)	X	O	24.07.97	810 SQN SEAHAWK
Potter, Michael John, *MA, MSc, CEng, MIMarE, MINucE, MinstP, C PHYS, psc*	CAPT(FTC)	E	TM	30.06.97	2SL/CNH FOTR
Potter, Stephen	MAJ(FTC)	RM	SO(LE)	01.10.98	RM Poole
Potts, Duncan Laurence, *BSc, pce*	CAPT(FTC)	X	PWO(U)	30.06.00	FOST SEA
Potts, Gary, *BEng*	LT(FTC)	E	WESM	01.06.96	TALENT
Potts, Kevin Maxwell	LT CDR(FTC)	X	P	01.02.92	RAF CRANWELL EFS
Poulter, Anthony Mervyn, *OBE, pce, pce(sm)*	CAPT(FTC)	X	SM	30.06.92	SHAPE BELGIUM
Pounder, Adam, *pce*	CDR(FC)	X		01.10.93	FOSNNI/NBC CLYDE
Pounder, George William James, *BA*	2LT(GRAD)(IC)	RM		01.09.99	CTCRM LYMPSTONE
Pounder, Michael	LT CDR(FTC)	X	H1	01.10.98	SCOTT
Pounds, Nicholas Ernest, *psc(m)*	BRIG(FTC)	RM	A/TK	31.12.99	HQRM
Powell, David Charles, *MSc*	CDR(FTC)	E	ME	31.12.95	MOD (LONDON)
Powell, Mark Andrew, *BSc*	LT CDR(FTC)	E	WESM	01.03.98	RALEIGH
Powell, Rebecca Jane	SLT(IC)	X		01.04.98	DARTMOUTH BRNC
Powell, Richard Laurence, *pce, pcea*	LT CDR(FTC)	X	P	01.11.92	JSCSC
Powell, Roger Norman, *BA, BSc, CEng, psc*	CDR(FTC)	E	AE	31.12.94	RNAS YEOVILTON
Powell, Steven, *MA, pce, pcea, psc(a)*	LT CDR(FTC)	X	O	16.04.92	FONA
Powell, Steven Richard	LT CDR(FTC)	X	MW	01.07.98	DRYAD
Powell, William Glyn	LT CDR(FTC)	X	O	16.12.98	702 SQN HERON
Powis, Jonathan, *pce, pce(sm)*	CDR(FTC)	X	SM	31.12.92	MOD (LONDON)
Powles, Derek Anthony, *MEng*	LT(FTC)	E	ME	01.02.96	FOSF
Pratt, Ian Heggie, *BSc, CEng, MIEE*	LT CDR(FTC)	E	WE	01.03.93	SSA/CWTA PORTS
Preece, David Graeme, *BA*	LT(FTC)	S	SM	01.08.93	NEPTUNE CFS
Preece, David Wyndham, *BEng, CEng, AMRAeS*	LT(FTC)	E	AE(L)	15.10.93	MOD DHSA
Prendergast, Matthew Patrick, *BM, BS, BMS*	SURG LT	-		04.08.99	CTCRM
Prendergast, Sally Ann, *BSc, PGDip*	LT(CC)	E	TM	26.02.90	SULTAN
Prentice, David Charles, *QCVS*	LT CDR(FTC)	X	PWO(C)	22.12.97	CARDIFF
Prescott, Shaun, *BEng, CEng, MIEE*	LT CDR(FTC)	E	WE	01.11.96	JSCSC
Pressdee, Simon John	LT(IC)	X	SM	01.07.98	TRIUMPH
Pressly, James Winchester, *BSc*	MAJ(FTC)	RM		25.04.98	HQRM
Prest, Neal Andrew	LT(FTC)	S	(W)	10.12.98	JMOTS NORTHWOOD
Prest, Stephen Frederick, *MEng*	SLT(IC)	E	WE	01.06.98	IRON DUKE
Preston, Mark Richard, *BEng, CEng, MIMechE*	LT CDR(FTC)	E	ME	01.10.99	SOMERSET
Preston, Ross Walker, *BSc*	CAPT RM(FTC)	RM		01.09.96	CTCRM

Name	Rank	Branch	Spec	Seniority	Where Serving
Preston-Jones, Noel Clisby *(COMMODORE)*	CAPT(FTC)	S		31.12.94	MOD (LONDON)
Price, Andrew Michael	MAJ(FTC)	RM	C	01.05.97	CTCRM
Price, David Glyn *(Act Capt Rm)*	LT RM(FTC)	RM	SO(LE)	01.01.98	845 SQN
Price, David John , *pce*	LT CDR(FTC)	X	PWO(A)	01.04.93	SA MALAYSIA
Price, David William	LT CDR(FTC)	X	REG	01.10.98	NELSON
Price, Frederick Earle Francis , *MBE, MA, MSc, PhD, CEng, psc*	CDR(FTC)	E	TM	30.06.95	MOD (LONDON)
Price, Graham	LT CDR(FTC)	S	(S)	01.10.94	FONA
Price, Joseph Charles , *BSc*	LT(IC)	X		01.01.98	PEMBROKE
Price, John Philip , *MA, psc*	CDR(FTC)	E	ME	30.06.96	SULTAN
Price, Julian Stanton	LT(IC)	X	O	16.11.94	RNAS CULDROSE
Price, Martin John , *MA, psc*	LT COL(FTC)	RM	MLDR	31.12.98	JACIG
Price, Timothy Andrew , *n*	LT CDR(FTC)	X	PWO(A)	01.07.98	EDINBURGH
Price, Tracie Evelyn , *BSc*	LT(IC)	E	TM	01.12.93	COLLINGWOOD
Price, Tania Lucille , *BSc, MA(Ed), MEng, Cert Ed, MIPD*	LT CDR(FTC)	W	TM	01.10.92	DEF SCH OF LANG
Price, Terence Peter	LT CDR(FTC)	E	WE	01.10.97	SOMERSET
Price, Trevor William , *BSc*	LT CDR(FTC)	X	METOC	01.01.92	DRYAD
Price, Victoria Juliette , *MB, BSc, ChB*	SURG LT	-		04.08.99	CFLT MED(SEA)
Prideaux, David Martin	LT CDR(FTC)	E	WE	01.10.87	DGCIS BRISTOL
Priest, James Edward , *BEng*	LT(CC)	X	P U/T	01.09.98	846 SQN
Prime, John Roger Martin , *pce, psc, psc(a)*	CDR(FTC)	X	PWO(N)†	30.06.88	SEA CADET CORPS
Prince, Andrew Charles Vaughan , *pce, pcea*	LT CDR(FTC)	X	O	16.02.88	DARTMOUTH BRNC
Prince, Mark Edward , *BEng*	LT(FTC)	E	MESM	01.07.93	NP DNREAY
Pring, Stuart James , *BA*	LT(IC)	S		14.08.97	CTCRM
Pringle, Anthony , *pce, pcea*	LT CDR(FTC)	X	P	01.07.90	CINCFLEET
Prinsep, Timothy John , *BEng, CEng, MIEE*	LT(FTC)	E	WE	01.06.92	LPD(R) IPT
Prior, Grant Michael	LT CDR(FTC)	E	WE	02.06.96	COLLINGWOOD
Prior, Iain Alexander	SLT(FTC)	E	ME	01.04.98	ARGYLL
Prior, Kate Rebecca Edna Jane , *MB, BS*	SURG LT	-		06.08.97	CFLT MED(SEA)
Pritchard, Alison Margaret , *BA*	SLT(IC)	X		01.01.98	DUMBARTON CASTLE
Pritchard, Gavin Scrimgeour , *pce*	LT CDR(FTC)	X	PWO(U)	01.01.95	CINCFLEET
Pritchard, Irene Joanne , *BSc*	SLT(IC)	S		01.05.97	RALEIGH
Pritchard, Rayson Cann	MAJ(FTC)	RM		01.08.85	42 CDO RM
Pritchard, Simon Andrew , *MA, psc*	MAJ(FTC)	RM		18.04.94	HQRM
Procter, Jamie Edward , *BEng, MSc*	LT(CC)	E	TM	01.09.92	RALEIGH
Procter, Kathryn Joanne	SLT	Q	CC	15.01.97	MODHU DERRIFORD
Proctor, William John Gibbon , *BEng, AMIEE*	LT(FTC)	E	WE	01.03.94	NEPTUNE NT
Proffitt Burnham, Julia Marie , *BSc*	LT(IC)	E	TM	01.09.95	DEF SCH OF LANG
Prole, Nicholas Mark	LT(CC)	X	P	16.09.98	845 SQN
Prosser, Matthew James	SLT(CC)	X		01.04.98	BRIDPORT
Proud, Andrew Douglas , *BEng*	LT CDR(FTC)	E	AE	11.06.99	SANS IPT
Prowse, David George	SLT(FTC)	E	ME	01.04.98	MONTROSE
Pruden, Ian , *BSc*	CAPT RM(IC)	RM		01.05.98	RM Poole
Pryde, Colin Swinton , *BEng, CEng, Eur Ing*	LT CDR(FTC)	E	AE	01.07.94	700M MERLIN IFTU
Pugh, Jonathan	LT CDR(FTC)	E	WE	08.03.00	COLLINGWOOD
Pugh, Martin Reginald	LT(FTC)	X	C	08.04.94	SHAPE BELGIUM
Pulvertaft, Rupert James , *odc(Fr)*	MAJ(FTC)	RM		01.05.97	40 CDO RM
Punch, Gerard Kevin , *BEng, AMIMechE*	LT(IC)	E	MESM	01.03.96	SPLENDID
Punch, John Matthew , *BSc*	SLT(IC)	X	P U/T	01.09.98	DARTMOUTH BRNC
Punton, Ian Matthew , *BEng*	LT CDR(FTC)	E	AE	01.09.99	HARRIER IPT
Purdy, Richard John	MID(UCE)(IC)	E	AE	01.09.99	CUMBERLAND
Purvis, David Mark	LT(FTC)	E	P	01.12.96	RNAS YEOVILTON
Puxley, Michael Edward , *BEng*	LT(FTC)	E	WESM	01.09.96	VANGUARD(PORT)
Pye, Philip Martin	LT CDR(FTC)	S	CA	01.10.98	MOD (LONDON)
Pyne, Robert	CHAPLAIN	CE		23.01.90	EXCELLENT

Q

Name	Rank	Branch	Spec	Seniority	Where Serving
Quade, Nicholas Alexander Clive , *BEng*	LT(FTC)	E	MESM	01.12.97	VIGILANT(PORT)
Quantrill, Steven William , *BSc*	LT(IC)	S		01.03.97	ILLUSTRIOUS
Quaye, Duncan Thomas George , *BSc, MSc*	CDR(FTC)	E	ME	30.06.98	SULTAN
Quekett, Ian Peter Scott , *BEng, MSc, AMIEE*	LT CDR(FTC)	E	WE	01.08.99	FOSF
Quick, Neville Hellins , *BSc, CEng, MIEE*	LT CDR(FTC)	E	WE	01.05.91	NMA PORTSMOUTH
Quick, Stephen James , *BA*	SLT(IC)	X		01.05.98	FEARLESS

Name	Rank	Branch	Spec	Seniority	Where Serving
Quine, Nicholas John , *MA, psc*	LT CDR(FTC)	E	WE	01.12.88	MOD (LONDON)
Quinn, Martin Edward	LT(CC)	S	SM	01.02.92	OCLC ROSYTH
Quinn, Michael Gerard , *BA*	SLT(IC)	X		01.01.99	DARTMOUTH BRNC
Quinn, Paul Anthony , *BA, MHCIMA, MIMgt, jsdc*	CAPT(FTC)	S	SM	30.06.00	FONA
Quinn, Shaun Andrew	LT(CC)	X	O	16.05.92	824 NAS
Quirk, Anthony Thomas	LT(FTC)	E	WE	02.09.99	FEARLESS

R

Name	Rank	Branch	Spec	Seniority	Where Serving
Raby, Nigel John Francis , *BSc, MSc, jsdc* (*COMMODORE*)	CAPT(FTC)	E	WE	30.06.95	DPA BRISTOL
Race, Nigel James , *MA, pce, psc(j)*	CDR(FTC)	X	PWO(C)	31.12.99	MOD (LONDON)
Rackham, Anthony David Henry , *BSc*	LT(FTC)	X	FC	01.11.95	BRECON
Rackham, Katharine , *BSc*	LT(FTC)	X		01.03.97	GLASGOW
Radakin, Antony David , *pce*	LT CDR(FTC)	X	PWO(U)	01.11.96	JSCSC
Radbourne, Neville Ian	LT(FTC)	E	WE	05.06.92	HQ DCSA
Radcliffe, Nicholas , *LLB, LMIPD*	LT CDR(FTC)	S		16.02.91	CINCFLEET
Radford, Andrew , *BEng*	LT(CC)	X	P	01.06.92	849 SQN B FLT
Radmore, Keith Vernon	LT CDR(FTC)	X	SM	23.09.91	RM BICKLEIGH
Rae, Anthony James William , *BSc*	LT CDR(FTC)	X	P	01.10.99	EXCHANGE RAF UK
Rae, Alistair Lewis , *BEng, AMIEE,*	LT(FTC)	E	WE	01.04.97	ILLUSTRIOUS
Rae, Derek Gordon , *BSc*	LT(FTC)	X	HM	01.03.96	EXCHANGE N ZLAND
Rae, Fraser , *BEng*	SLT(IC)	X		01.01.98	PENZANCE
Rae, Stephen Gordon , *AGSM*	LT CDR(FTC)	S		01.02.00	RALEIGH
Rae, Scott MacKenzie , *MBE, BD*	CHAPLAIN	SF		02.02.81	AFCC
Raeburn, Craig , *BSc, SM(n)*	LT(FTC)	X	SM	01.09.96	TIRELESS
Raeburn, Mark , *n*	LT(FTC)	X		01.07.94	EXAMPLE
Raeburn, Timothy Jon , *BSc*	CAPT RM(FTC)	RM		01.05.97	DRYAD
Raffaelli, Philip Iain , *MB, BA, BSc, BCH, BCh, MSc, FFOM, MFOM, MRCGP, AFOM, jsdc*	SURG CAPT	-	CPDATE	31.12.98	2SL/CNH
Raffle, Anthony John	LT CDR(FTC)	E	WE	01.10.92	MOD (LONDON)
Raggett, Andrew , *MVO, pcea*	LT CDR(FTC)	X	P	01.09.87	702 SQN HERON
Rahman, Junia , *MB, BS*	SURG LT	-		06.08.97	FONA SULTAN
Railton, Andrew Stuart , *BSc*	SLT(IC)	X		01.01.99	DARTMOUTH BRNC
Rainbow, John , *MRIN, MIM*	LT CDR(FTC)	X		14.09.81	AST(N)
Raisbeck, Adrian Bruce , *BSc*	CAPT RM(IC)	RM		01.09.98	OCEAN
Raisbeck, Paul Temple , *MA, pce, psc(j)*	LT CDR(FTC)	X	MCD	01.11.93	BANGOR
Raitt, James Edwin , *BSc*	CAPT RM(FTC)	RM		01.09.97	42 CDO RM
Ralph, Andrew Philip	LT(FTC)	X	FC	01.04.96	ILLUSTRIOUS
Ralphson, Mark David , *BEng*	LT(FTC)	E	WE	01.06.93	RMC OF SCIENCE
Ramm, Steven Charles , *pce, pce(sm), psc*	CAPT(FTC)	X	SM	31.12.98	MOD (LONDON)
Ramsay, Graham Patrick , *pce*	CDR(FTC)	X	PWO(N)	30.06.92	EXCHANGE ITALY
Ramsey, Jeremy Stephen , *BSc*	LT CDR(FTC)	S		16.04.89	RDMC BLOCKHOUSE
Ramsey, Ryan Trevor , *SM(n)*	LT(FTC)	X	SM	01.11.92	RALEIGH
Ramshaw, George William Lilwall , *BSc, CEng, FIMgt, MIEE*	CDR(FTC)	E	WE	30.06.99	CAPT D3 SEA
Rance, Maxwell George William , *MA, psc(j)*	CDR(FTC)	S		31.12.99	FOSM NWOOD HQ
Rand, Mark	SLT(IC)	E	WESM	27.01.99	COLLINGWOOD
Rand, Marc James , *BEng*	LT(FTC)	E	ME	01.05.93	SULTAN
Randall, David Frederick , *BA, MSc (Act Cdr)*	LT CDR(FTC)	S		16.01.94	AFPAA WTHY DOWN
Randall, Nicholas John , *BSc, pce*	LT CDR(FTC)	X	PWO(N)	01.10.97	INVINCIBLE
Randall, Richard David , *BSc*	LT CDR(FTC)	E	MESM	01.08.92	MOD (BATH)
Randles, Steven , *BA*	SLT(IC)	X		01.01.98	COTTESMORE
Ranger, John Leonard *(Act Lt Cdr)*	LT(FTC)	E	WE	18.10.85	SSA BRISTOL
Rankin, Graham	SLT(IC)	X		19.09.98	DRYAD
Rankin, Ian Gordon , *MSc, CEng, MIEE, CGIA, mdtc*	CAPT(FTC)	E	WESM	31.12.96	MOD (BATH)
Rankin, Suzanne Jayne	LT	Q	ONC		RH HASLAR
Rankine, Ivor Matthew	LT(FTC)	E	MESM	19.06.98	JSCSC
Ransom, Benjamin Robert James	SLT(IC)	X		01.04.98	INVINCIBLE
Ranson, Christopher David , *MSc, CEng, MIEE*	CDR(FTC)	E	WE	30.06.99	CINCFLEET
Rant, Oliver James , *BA*	SLT(IC)	X		01.05.97	DRYAD
Rapp, James Campsie , ADC, *pce, pcea, psc (COMMODORE)*	CAPT(FTC)	X	O	31.12.92	CINCFLEET
Rasor, Andrew Martin	LT(CC)	X	P	01.07.92	DRYAD
Ratcliffe, John Paul , *BSc*	CDR(FTC)	E	TM	30.06.92	NELSON RNSETT

Name	Rank	Branch	Spec	Seniority	Where Serving
Rawal, Krishna , *MB, BS*	SURG LTCDR	-		01.11.96	CDO LOG REGT RM
Rawles, Julian	LT(CC)	X	ATC	01.12.98	RNAS CULDROSE
Rawlings, Damian Paul , *BEng, CEng, MIMarE*	LT CDR(FTC)	E	ME	01.08.95	SULTAN
Rawlings, Gary Andrew	SLT(FTC)	E	ME	01.04.98	SUTHERLAND
Rawlings, Gary Charles , *HND, MIPD*	LT CDR(CC)	E	TM	01.10.89	2SL/CNH
Rawlins, Simon Terence	SLT(IC)	X	P U/T	01.04.99	RNAS YEOVILTON
Rawlinson, David	LT(IC)	X	P	16.03.95	846 SQN
Rawlinson, Stephen James , *BEng, MIMarE*	LT CDR(FTC)	E	MESM	01.03.99	SOVEREIGN
Rawson, Clive , *AFC*	LT CDR(FTC)	X	O	01.10.94	824 NAS
Rawson, Scott Michael	LT(FTC)	E	MESM	01.04.95	SSA BATH
Ray, Martin William , *LLB*	LT(IC)	S		01.10.97	ROEBUCK
Raybould, Adrian Glyn , *BSc, CEng, MIEE, psc(j)*	LT CDR(FTC)	E	WESM	01.01.93	MOD (LONDON)
Rayner, Brett Nicholas , *psc*	CAPT(FTC)	S		30.06.99	IMS BRUSSELS
Raynes, Christopher , *BSc*	LT(IC)	X	P	01.01.99	RNAS YEOVILTON
Raynor, Sean David	LT(FTC)	E	WE	04.09.98	COLLINGWOOD
Rea, Stephen Dennis	SLT(IC)	X		01.04.98	ARGYLL
Read, Alistair , *BSc, MSc*	LT CDR(CC)	X	METOC	01.10.94	CINCFLEET
Read, Alun John	LT(CC)	X	P	01.09.84	RNAS YEOVILTON
Read, Clinton Derek *(Act Capt Rm)*	LT RM(FTC)	RM		01.05.97	HQRM
Read, Crispin , *BA*	LT(IC)	X	P	16.05.92	849 SQN HQ
Read, Jonathon Asher Jason Marcus	SURG LT	-	O U/T	04.08.99	INM ALVERSTOKE
Read, Jonathan , *BSc, MSc, CEng*	LT CDR(FTC)	E	WESM	23.05.97	MOD (LONDON)
Read, Matthew Richard	LT(FTC)	E	ME	01.02.96	DUMBARTON CASTLE
Read, Paul Steven , *BEng, AMIEE*	LT(CC)	E	WE	01.03.97	CAMPBELTOWN
Read, Richard Harold , *BSc, ARICS, psc*	LT CDR(FTC)	X	H CH	01.09.81	RN HYDROG SCHL
Read, Richard John , *BA*	CAPT RM(FTC)	RM	LC	01.09.96	539 ASLT SQN RM
Readwin, Roger Roy , *BA*	LT(FTC)	X	MCD	01.04.96	MIDDLETON
Reah, Stephen , *BEng (Act Lt Cdr)*	LT(FTC)	E	ME	01.06.92	MOD (LONDON)
Rearden, Richard Joseph *(Act Maj)*	CAPT RM(FTC)	RM	SO(LE)	01.01.96	FEARLESS
Reason, Ian Malcolm , *MSc, BEng*	CDR(FTC)	E	AE	30.06.00	HARRIER IPT
Redford, Duncan Edward MacDonald	LT(FTC)	X	SM	01.06.96	TIRELESS
Redgrove, Mark Anthony	LT(FTC)	E	WE	01.09.99	LIVERPOOL
Redman, Christopher Douglas Jeremy , *BDS, LDS RCS(Eng), MGDS, MFDS, RCS*	SGLTCDR(D)	-		19.07.93	NELSON (PAY)
Redman, Charles Jeremy Rufus , *n*	LT CDR(FTC)	X		23.11.98	FOSNNI OPS CFS
Redmayne, Mark Edward , *BA*	LT(IC)	X		01.06.99	QUORN
Redstone, Colin	CDR(FTC)	S	SM	31.12.98	2SL/CNH FOTR
Reece, Nigel David , *BEng, CEng, MIMechE*	LT CDR(FTC)	E	MESM	01.03.00	MOD (BATH)
Reed, Andrew William , *BSc, pce*	LT CDR(FTC)	X	PWO(A)	01.10.94	MONTROSE
Reed, Darren Keith , *BA*	LT(FTC)	S		01.12.96	2SL/CNH
Reed, Frank , *BA, MSc, psc*	CAPT(FTC)	MS	(P)	31.12.99	DEF MED TRG CTR
Reed, Jonathan Charles	LT(FTC)	E	AE(M)	07.09.95	EXCHANGE GERMANY
Reed, James Hamilton , *pce, pcea*	LT CDR(FTC)	X	P	01.04.95	815 SQN HQ
Reed, James William	MAJ(FTC)	RM	SO(LE)	01.10.99	CTCRM
Reed, Mark , *BSc, PGDip*	LT CDR(CC)	X	METOC	01.10.98	CINCFLEET
Reed, Matthew Trevor , *n*	LT(FTC)	X		01.10.93	NORFOLK
Reed, Nicholas	LT(FTC)	S	(W)	26.04.99	RALEIGH
Reed, Peter Kirby	MID(UCE)(IC)	E	ME	01.09.99	CUMBERLAND
Reeder, Robert , *OBE, BSc, MIMechE*	CDR(FTC)	E	AE	31.12.91	HARRIER IPT
Reen, Stephen Charles	LT(CC)	X	P	01.11.92	848 SQN HERON
Rees, Adam Martin , *BA, MSc*	LT(IC)	E	TM	01.09.98	MANCHESTER
Rees, John Blain Minto , *BSc, jsdc*	CAPT(FTC)	E	TM	31.12.99	2SL/CNH FOTR
Rees, Justin Harrington , *BSc, MILog, AMIAM*	CDR(FTC)	S	SM	30.06.99	COMUKTG/CASWSF
Rees, John Patrick	LT CDR(FTC)	S		29.06.99	IRON DUKE
Rees, Paul Stuart Chadwick , *MB, BS*	SURG LT	-		06.08.97	VIGILANT(PORT)
Rees, Richard Thomas , *BEng*	LT(FTC)	X		01.12.95	BFFI
Reese, David Michael , *BSc*	LT(FTC)	X	O	01.09.94	815 FLT 235
Reeve, Jonathon , *MA, CEng, MIEE, rcds, psc*	RADM	-	MESM	13.03.00	CINCFLEET
Reeves, Andrew Philip	MID(IC)	X	(X)	01.09.98	ALDERNEY
Reeves, Kurt , *BEng (Act Lt Cdr)*	LT(FTC)	E	ME	04.12.92	MOD (BATH)
Reeves, Paul Kieth	SLT(CC)	E	ME	01.05.98	DARTMOUTH BRNC
Regan, Vanessa Lorraine , *BSc*	LT(CC)	X		01.07.97	LIVERPOOL
Reid, Charles Ian , *BSc, pce, pce(sm)*	CDR(FTC)	X	SM	31.12.99	JSCSC
Reid, Christopher Joseph , *MB, BS*	SURG LTCDR	-		01.08.98	RM POOLE

Name	Rank	Branch	Spec	Seniority	Where Serving
Reid, Duncan , *MBE, BA, BA(OU)*	CDR(FTC)	E	AE(L)	01.10.96	HARRIER IPT
Reid, Jason Charles James , *BEng*	LT(FTC)	E	WESM	01.04.93	FOSM FASLANE
Reid, James Lyle , *BSc*	SLT(IC)	X		01.01.98	SOUTHAMPTON
Reid, Martyn , *pce, pcea, psc*	CDR(FTC)	X	O	30.06.94	INVINCIBLE
Reid, Martyn Richard	LT(CC)	X		01.04.95	OCLC MANCH
Reid, Paul Frederick *(Act Lt Cdr)*	LT(FTC)	X	SM	24.07.92	FOSM NWOOD OPS
Reid, William Andrew , *BA*	LT(FTC)	X	SM	01.06.96	VENGEANCE(PORT)
Reidy, Paul Alan , *pce(sm)*	LT CDR(FTC)	X	SM	01.11.98	DARTMOUTH BRNC
Reilly, Thomas Gerald *(Act Lt Cdr)*	LT(FTC)	X	C	03.06.92	HQ DCSA
Reindorp, David Peter , *PGDIPAN, pce*	LT CDR(FTC)	X	PWO(N)	01.07.96	DRYAD
Relf, Kerry Marie , *BA*	LT(IC)	S		01.01.00	CINCFLEET
Renaud, Gavin Andrew Richard	SLT(IC)	X	O	01.04.99	810 SQN SEAHAWK
Rendell, Derrick John , *BSc*	LT(FTC)	E	MESM	14.06.96	SULTAN
Rennie, James Gibson	CAPT(CS)RM	-		18.09.98	MOD (LONDON)
Rennison, William Ross , *OBE, BSc, MSc*	CDR(FTC)	E	TM	31.12.86	NMA PORTSMOUTH
Renwick, John	LT CDR(FTC)	S	SM	23.08.95	2SL/CNH
Resheph, Amelia	SLT(FTC)	E	WE	01.09.97	DARTMOUTH BRNC
Reston, Samuel Craig , *MB, ChB*	SURG LT	-		07.08.96	RH HASLAR
Retter, Rachael Louise , *BA*	LT(IC)	X		01.02.00	DRYAD
Revens, Carl Andrew	CAPT RM(FTC)	RM		01.05.97	EXCHANGE ARMY UK
Rex, Colin	LT(IC)	X	P U/T	01.10.99	845 SQN
Reynolds, Andrew Graham , *BEng, MSc, CEng, MIMechE, MCGI*	LT CDR(FTC)	E	ME	01.08.97	MONMOUTH
Reynolds, Christopher Herbert , *BSc, MIMgt, pce(sm) (Act Cdr)*	LT CDR(FTC)	X	SM	01.04.87	FOSM NWOOD HQ
Reynolds, Mark Edward	MID(UCE)(FTC)	E	ME	01.09.98	DARTMOUTH BRNC
Reynolds, Matthew Jowan	SLT(IC)	X		01.04.98	DARTMOUTH BRNC
Reynolds, Peter Anthony , *BSc, psc*	COL(FTC)	RM		30.06.97	SA CARACAS
Reynolds, Richard	SURG SLT	-		30.11.98	DARTMOUTH BRNC
Reynolds, Timothy Edward , *MA*	CDR(FTC)	X	METOC	30.06.98	SACLANT USA
Reynolds, Timothy Paul , *BSc*	LT CDR(FTC)	E	IS	30.04.95	DRAKE CBP(DLO)
Rhodes, Andrew Gregory , *BEng*	LT CDR(FTC)	E	WE	01.07.95	COLLINGWOOD
Rhodes, Andrew William	SLT(FTC)	E	WE	01.04.98	COLLINGWOOD
Rhodes, Martin	LT(CC)	X	O	01.09.95	RNAS CULDROSE
Rich, Alvin Arnold , *pce, pcea*	CDR(FTC)	X	O	30.06.90	TEMERAIRE
Rich, David Charles , *pce*	LT CDR(FTC)	X	SM	20.05.97	TIRELESS
Rich, Jonathan George , *MIPD, pcea, psc(j)*	LT CDR(FTC)	X	P	01.10.89	MOD (LONDON)
Richards, Alan David , *jsdc, pce, pcea*	CAPT(FTC)	X	P	31.12.98	MOD (LONDON)
Richards, Anthony Jeremy	SLT(IC)	S		01.04.98	RALEIGH
Richards, Adam Vivian , *BA*	LT(IC)	X		01.03.99	MONMOUTH
Richards, Bryan Robert , *DEH, MIOSH (Act Lt Cdr)*	LT(FTC)	MS	(AD)	23.07.93	2SL/CNH
Richards, Christopher Martin , *pce, psc*	CDR(FTC)	X	PWO(A)	30.06.95	EXETER
Richards, Fraser	LT(FTC)	X	SM	25.07.96	MOD DIS SEA
Richards, Gregory Bernard , *BA, n*	LT(FTC)	X		01.05.93	MONMOUTH
Richards, James Ian Hanson , *BEng*	LT(FTC)	E	WESM	01.07.97	VANGUARD(PORT)
Richards, Paul	SLT(IC)	E	ME	29.04.98	SULTAN
Richards, Steven	SLT(IC)	E	WE	27.01.99	COLLINGWOOD
Richards, Stephen William	MAJ(FTC)	RM	SO(LE)	01.10.99	CHFHQ
Richardson, Adrian Paul	SLT(CC)	E	WE	01.05.98	DARTMOUTH BRNC
Richardson, Daniel , *BEng, AMIEE*	LT(FTC)	E	WE	01.01.94	LN DERA PRTSDWN
Richardson, Douglas , *BEng*	LT(FTC)	E	MESM	01.10.94	SULTAN
Richardson, Gavin Andrew , *pcea*	LT(CC)	X	O	01.04.92	824 NAS
Richardson, Geoffrey , *BSc*	LT(CC)	X	P	01.08.91	846 SQN
Richardson, George Nicholas , *BA*	LT(FTC)	S		01.07.93	HQRM
Richardson, Ian Hayden	LT(IC)	X		01.03.00	CHIDDINGFOLD
Richardson, Ian James Ward , *BSc, CEng, MIEE, psc*	CAPT(FTC)	E	WE	31.12.95	MOD (LONDON)
Richardson, Mark Anthony , *BSc*	LT CDR(CC)	E	IS	01.09.97	PJHQ
Richardson, Michael Colin	CAPT RM(FTC)	RM	SO(LE)	01.01.95	EXCH ARMY SC(G)
Richardson, Michael Peter , *FHCIMA*	CDR(FTC)	S		30.06.97	MOD (BATH)
Richardson, Peter	LT(CC)	X	P	16.01.92	848 SQN HERON
Richardson, Philip Charles , *BSc*	LT(FTC)	X		01.09.98	INVERNESS
Richardson, Peter Stephen Mark , *BEng, AMIEE*	LT CDR(FTC)	E	WE	01.08.99	NEWCASTLE
Richardson, Sophie Charlotte	MID(UCE)(FTC)	S		01.09.98	DARTMOUTH BRNC
Richardson, Stephen Frank *(Act Lt Cdr)*	LT(FTC)	E	WE	18.06.87	MOD (BATH)
Riches, Ian Charles , *pce(sm)*	LT CDR(FTC)	X	SM	01.10.90	FOSM FASLANE

Name	Rank	Branch	Spec	Seniority	Where Serving
Richford, Terence Fitzpatrick	LT CDR(FTC)	X	C	01.10.92	FOSNNI OPS CFS
Richings, Peter Charles, *pcea*	LT CDR(FTC)	X	P	01.03.87	771 SK5 SAR
Richman, Paul George, *BA*	LT(IC)	X	P	16.02.98	RNAS YEOVILTON
Richman, Philip Jonathan	LT(FTC)	E	WESM	13.06.91	RALEIGH
Richmond, Iain James Martin, *BA, pce, pcea*	CDR(FTC)	X	P	31.12.96	SACLANT USA
Richter, Alwyn Stafford Byron, *BEng, AMIEE*	LT(FTC)	E	WE	01.09.92	SSA/CWTA PORTS
Rickard, Hugh Wilson, *CBE, BSc, psc, rcds*	RADM	-	METOC	20.04.98	RCDS
Rickard, Rory Frederick, *MB, BCh, BAO, FRCSEd*	SURG LTCDR	-		03.08.98	NELSON (PAY)
Riden, Donald Keith, *BM, BDS, LDS, FRCS, FDS RCS(Eng) (Act Sgcdr(D))*	SGLTCDR(D)	-	(COSM)	01.08.90	NP 1067 KOSOVO
Rider, John Charles Raymon, *BSc*	SLT(IC)	X		01.01.99	DARTMOUTH BRNC
Rider, Mary Catherine Elizabeth, *BA*	LT(FTC)	X		01.04.99	GRAFTON
Ridge, Mervyn Henry	LT(FTC)	E	WESM	07.02.97	DRAKE CFM
Ridland, Keith	CAPT(FTC)	S		30.06.94	BDLS INDIA
Ridley, Steven Andrew, *BEng*	SLT(CC)	X	O U/T	01.01.98	DARTMOUTH BRNC
Ridley, William Kenneth, *BSc, CEng, FIMarE, psc*	CDR(FTC)	E	ME	30.06.87	2SL/CNH FOTR
Rigby, Jeremy Conrad, *BA, MILDM*	LT CDR(FTC)	S		16.01.94	JSCSC
Riggall, Andrew Derek	LT(CC)	X	P	01.05.96	848 SQN HERON
Riley, Graeme Alexander	LT(FTC)	E	MESM	14.06.96	DRAKE CBS
Riley, Jansen	SLT(FTC)	X	AV	09.01.98	RFANSU
Riley, Michael Jaeger, *BSc, jsdc, pce*	CDR(FTC)	X	PWO(A)	31.12.93	BDS WASHINGTON
Rimington, Anthony Kingsmill, *BA*	LT(FTC)	X	P	01.02.96	815 FLT 210
Rimington, John Anthony, *jsdc, pce*	CAPT(FTC)	X	AWO(U)	31.12.92	2SL/CNH FOTR
Rimmer, Heather Elizabeth, *BA*	LT CDR(FTC)	E	TM	22.07.96	COLLINGWOOD
Rimmer, Michael, *pce*	CDR(FTC)	X	PWO(C)	31.12.97	BDS WASHINGTON
Rimmer, Owen Francis, *BA*	SLT(IC)	X		01.01.99	DARTMOUTH BRNC
Rimmer, Robin	LT CDR(FTC)	E	WE	01.10.98	FOSF
Ripley, Benjamin Edward, *n*	LT(FTC)	X	H1	01.11.94	DRYAD
Rippingale, Stuart Nicholas, *BSc, MSc*	LT CDR(FTC)	E	IS	01.10.95	2SL/CNH
Risdall, Jane Elizabeth, *MB, BS, MA, DA, FFARCSI*	SURG CDR	-	(CA)	31.12.98	NELSON (PAY)
Risley, Jonathan, *BSc, MA, CEng, MBCS, CDipAF, (Act Cdr)*	LT CDR(FTC)	E	IS	01.10.92	CINCFLEET CIS
Risley, James Grant, *BEng*	LT(CC)	E	MESM	01.03.00	SULTAN
Ritchie, Douglas	SLT(IC)	E	MESM	19.09.98	SULTAN
Ritchie, David Michael	LT(FTC)	X	P	16.03.90	899 SQN HERON
Ritchie, Iain David, *BSc*	SLT(IC)	X		01.01.99	DARTMOUTH BRNC
Ritchie, John Noble	LT(FTC)	X	SM	01.04.90	CSST SHORE DEVPT
Ritchie, William James	MAJ(FTC)	RM	SO(LE)	01.10.97	HQ 3 CDO BDE RM
Ritsperis, Athos, *BSc, MSc,* DIC, *PGCE, MIL, ACGI, ARCS*	LT(IC)	E	TM	01.01.92	NEPTUNE 2SL/CNH
Rix, Anthony John, *pce, psc*	CAPT(FTC)	X	PWO(U)	30.06.97	MARLBOROUGH
Robb, Matthew Cruickshanks, *OBE, BA, CGIA, psc, mdtc (Act Capt)*	CDR(FTC)	E	WE	30.06.92	T45 IPT
Robb, Michael Edward, *BA*	LT(CC)	S		01.08.97	AGRIPPA NAVSOUTH
Robbins, Harry Vincent	LT RM(IC)	RM		24.01.00	847 SQN
Robbins, Julian Garth, *BSc, MSc*	LT CDR(FTC)	E	AE	01.03.84	LOAN DERA BSC DN
Robbins, Jeremy Matthew Francis, *MBE, BSc, psc(m)*	COL(FTC)	RM	C	30.06.99	COMSTRIKFORSTH
Robbins, Margaret Joy, *psc*	CDR(FTC)	W	X	31.12.92	MOD (LONDON)
Robert, Iain Andrew	SLT(IC)	E	AE	29.04.98	SULTAN
Roberts, Annabel Mary, *BSc*	LT(IC)	E	TM	01.01.95	COLLINGWOOD
Roberts, Antony Paul, *MB, BS, DObstRCOG*	SURG CDR	-	GMPP	31.12.97	NELSON (PAY)
Roberts, Dean	LT CDR(FTC)	E	WE	04.04.99	SSA BRISTOL
Roberts, David Alan, *pce*	LT CDR(FTC)	X	PWO(A)	01.05.92	EXCHANGE NLANDS
Roberts, David Howard Wyn, *BA, pce*	LT CDR(FTC)	X	PWO(A)	01.04.91	JMOTS NORTHWOOD
Roberts, Ellis William	LT CDR(FTC)	E	AE(M)	01.10.95	MOD (BATH)
Roberts, Grant Michael Frank	LT(IC)	X		01.09.98	DRYAD
Roberts, Iain Gordon, *BSc, BEng*	LT(CC)	E	WESM	01.10.91	DCS *SM* BRISTOL
Roberts, Ian Thomas, *pce(sm)*	LT CDR(FTC)	X	SM	18.01.93	FOSM NWOOD HQ
Roberts, Kenneth Eric, *BEng, MSc, CEng, MIEE*	LT CDR(FTC)	E	WE	01.01.99	MOD (LONDON)
Roberts, Martyn, *BEng*	LT(CC)	X	O	01.10.88	EXCHANGE RAF UK
Roberts, Martin Alan	LT(CC)	X	O	01.11.94	820 SQN
Roberts, Nigel David	LT(IC)	X	O	10.02.98	815 FLT 229
Roberts, Nicholas Steven, *BEng, MSc*	CDR(FTC)	E	WE	30.06.99	JSCSC
Roberts, Peter Stafford	LT(FTC)	X	PWO(A)	01.10.95	MONMOUTH
Roberts, Stephen *(Act Lt Cdr)*	LT(FTC)	X	AV	12.12.91	CHFHQ
Roberts, Suzi, *BA*	SLT(IC)	X		01.05.98	ILLUSTRIOUS
Roberts, Selvin Clive, *BEng*	LT CDR(FTC)	E	MESM	01.10.99	SULTAN

Name	Rank	Branch	Spec	Seniority	Where Serving
Roberts, Stephen David, *BEng, MSc, CEng, MIEE*	LT CDR(FTC)	E	WE	01.04.98	SUTHERLAND
Roberts, Suzanne Marie, *BA*	LT(FTC)	S		01.06.94	ILLUSTRIOUS
Roberts, Timothy John, *BEng, MSc*	LT CDR(FTC)	E	MESM	01.07.95	TRAFALGAR
Robertshaw, Ian Weston, *BEng*	LT(FTC)	E	WESM	01.04.96	TRIUMPH
Robertson, David Colin, *BSc*	LT CDR(FTC)	E	AE	01.10.90	DGSS BRISTOL
Robertson, David Cameron, *n*	LT CDR(FTC)	X	H1	01.06.97	LEDBURY
Robertson, Douglas Malcolm, *BSc*	LT CDR(FTC)	X	ATC	01.10.93	RNAS YEOVILTON
Robertson, Frederick William, *pcea*	LT CDR(FTC)	X	P	01.03.86	847 SQN
Robertson, Kevin Francis, *pce*	CDR(FTC)	X	PWO(C)	30.06.98	MOD (LONDON)
Robertson, Michael George, *BSc, pce*	LT CDR(FTC)	X	O	01.04.94	FOSF
Robertson, Malcolm Nairn	LT CDR(FTC)	E	MESM	01.10.99	SULTAN
Robertson, Neil Bannerman *(Act Maj)*	CAPT RM(FTC)	RM		26.04.94	40 CDO RM
Robertson, Paul Noel, *pcea*	LT(FTC)	X	O	01.11.90	FONA SEAHAWK
Robertson, Stuart Thomas, *BA*	LT(IC)	S		01.03.99	SULTAN
Robertson Gopffarth, Alexander Alistair John, *BSc, SM(n)*	LT(FTC)	X	SM	01.02.97	EXCHANGE NLANDS
Robey, James Christopher	SLT(IC)	X		01.04.98	YORK
Robin, Christopher Charles Edward, *pce, pcea, psc(j)*	LT CDR(FTC)	X	P	01.09.94	MANCHESTER
Robin, Julie *(Act Surg Lt)*	SURG SLT	-		30.04.99	DARTMOUTH BRNC
Robins, Mark Duncan, *MBE (Act Lt)*	SLT(IC)	X	C	29.04.98	BOWMAN IPT
Robinson, Andrew, *BSc, jsdc*	CDR(FTC)	X	METOC	30.06.97	ELANT/NAVNORTH
Robinson, Andrew *(Act Lt)*	SLT(FTC)	MS		01.05.98	CDO LOG REGT RM
Robinson, Bruce Douglas, *BSc, MIMgt*	LT CDR(CC)	X	METOC	01.10.93	RALEIGH
Robinson, Charles Edward Thayne, *pce*	CDR(FTC)	X	PWO(U)	30.06.99	JSCSC
Robinson, Christopher Paul, *MBE, pce, pcea, psc (Act Capt)*	CDR(FTC)	X	O	31.12.87	SA SEOUL
Robinson, David Ian, *MSc, MIEE, psc, gw*	LT CDR(FTC)	E	WE	01.02.84	T45 IPT
Robinson, David Paul	SLT(FTC)	E	WESM	01.04.98	RALEIGH
Robinson, Guy Antony, *pce*	LT CDR(FTC)	X	PWO(A)	01.05.97	GUERNSEY
Robinson, James Stuart, *pce*	CDR(FTC)	X	PWO(U)	31.12.97	CINCFLEET
Robinson, Michael Peter, *BSc, MSc, CEng, MIMarE*	LT CDR(FTC)	E	MESM	01.11.96	TRENCHANT
Robinson, Michael Steven, *BSc*	LT(CC)	X	ATC	01.05.94	RNAS YEOVILTON
Robinson, Melanie Suzanne, *BSc*	LT(FTC)	X		01.06.94	DRYAD
Robinson, Pollyanna, *BEng*	LT(CC)	E	AE	01.01.00	SULTAN
Robinson, Paul Henry, *pce, pce(sm)*	CAPT(FTC)	X	SM	30.06.00	JDCC
Robinson, Philip James Owen, *BSc*	2LT(GRAD)(IC)	RM		01.09.99	CTCRM LYMPSTONE
Robinson, Richard John	SLT(FTC)	X	ATC	01.04.98	RNAS CULDROSE
Robinson, Steven Leslie, *BEng*	SLT(IC)	E	WE	01.09.98	MANCHESTER
Robison, Garry Stuart, *MPhil, psc(m), psc(j)*	COL(FTC)	RM		31.12.98	45 CDO RM
Robley, William Forster	LT(CC)	X	P	01.06.96	771 SK5 SAR
Robson, Christine Jane	LT	Q	IC/CC	01.03.91	RH HASLAR
Roddy, Michael Patrick, *BSc*	CAPT RM(FTC)	RM		27.04.96	45 CDO RM
Rodgers, Darren	LT(CC)	X	P	01.07.93	EXCHANGE RAF UK
Rodgers, Steven	LT CDR(FTC)	E	WE	01.10.96	FOST SEA
Rodley, John Frederick, *pce, psc (COMMODORE)*	CAPT(FTC)	X	AWO(U)	31.12.92	DRYAD
Rodrigues, Martin Tadeu	LT(FTC)	S	(W)	07.01.83	AFPAA WTHY DOWN
Rodwell, Toby Richard James, *BSc*	LT(FTC)	E	WESM	01.02.94	CSST SHORE FSLN
Rogers, Alan	LT(FTC)	X	AV	03.04.92	OCEAN
Rogers, Anthony George, *AFC*	CDR(FTC)	X	O	31.12.85	MOD (LONDON)
Rogers, Andrew Gavin, *BEng, CEng, MIEE*	LT CDR(FTC)	E	WE	01.02.98	CARDIFF
Rogers, Christopher Mark, *BEng*	LT(FTC)	E	WE	01.06.92	SSA BRISTOL
Rogers, Ian Arthur, *BSc, MSc, CEng, MIMechE*	LT CDR(FTC)	E	MESM	01.01.96	VENGEANCE(PORT)
Rogers, Julian Charles Everard	LT(CC)	X	SM	01.03.91	VENGEANCE(PORT)
Rogers, Malcolm Stuart, *BSc*	CDR(FTC)	E	TM	30.06.90	AGRIPPA AFSOUTH
Rogers, Philip Scott, *BSc*	LT(IC)	E	TM	01.01.95	CTCRM
Rogers, Roland Jeremy, *BSc, MSc*	LT CDR(FTC)	X	METOC	01.10.91	LN DERA WNFRITH
Rogers, Simon James Peter, *BA*	LT(CC)	X		01.07.98	CROMER
Rogers, Timothy Hugh Goddard	LT CDR(FTC)	X		04.12.98	NEPTUNE
Rollason, Caroline Anne	SLT(IC)	S		01.04.98	RALEIGH
Rolph, Andrew Peter Mark, *pce*	LT CDR(FTC)	X	PWO(C)	16.11.97	BROCKLESBY
Rom, Stephen Paul	LT(FTC)	E	WE	02.09.99	COVENTRY
Romney, Paul David, *pce*	LT CDR(FTC)	X	PWO(N)	01.01.98	OCEAN
Ronaldson, Gordon Ian, *BEng, AMIMechE*	LT(FTC)	E	ME	01.12.94	FOSF ROSYTH
Rook, David John	LT CDR(FTC)	E	WE	01.10.96	COLLINGWOOD
Rook, Graeme Inglis, *BSc*	LT CDR(FTC)	E	WE	01.04.98	SOUTHAMPTON

Name	Rank	Branch	Spec	Seniority	Where Serving
Rooney, Michael	SLT(CC)	E	WE	01.05.98	DARTMOUTH BRNC
Root, William Richard	CDR(FTC)	X	C	01.10.92	ELANT/NAVNORTH
Roots, Sally, *BEng*	LT CDR(FTC)	E	AE	01.08.98	DNAS CRAWLEY
Roper, Martin, *pcea*	LT CDR(FTC)	X	O	01.11.90	AGRIPPA NAVSOUTH
Roscoe, Robert David, *BEng*	LT CDR(FTC)	E	WE	01.04.99	MOD (LONDON)
Rose, Alan	2LT(GRAD)(IC)	RM		28.04.99	CTCRM LYMPSTONE
Rose, Andrew Donald, *BA*	LT(IC)	X	O	01.04.98	849 SQN A FLT
Rose, Caroline Mary, *BEng, MSc, AMIMarE*	LT(FTC)	E	ME	01.03.94	FOSF
Rose, Emily Kate	MID(IC)	X		01.05.98	DARTMOUTH BRNC
Rose, John Gordon, *MBE, psc(m)*	BRIG(FTC)	RM		30.06.00	MOD (LONDON)
Rose, Michael Frederick, *BEng, MSc, CEng, MIMarE*	LT(FTC)	E	ME	01.09.92	SULTAN
Roskilly, Martyn	2LT(GRAD)(IC)	RM		28.04.99	CTCRM LYMPSTONE
Ross, Angus Allan, *BA, MSc (Act Capt)*	CDR(FTC)	S		30.06.91	AFPAA WTHY DOWN
Ross, Andrew Charles Paterson, *BSc, ocds(No), ptsc, psc*	MAJ(FTC)	RM		25.04.96	42 CDO RM
Ross, Andrew Duncan	SLT(FTC)	X	EW	01.04.98	TIRELESS
Ross, Bruce James	LT CDR(FTC)	X	PWO(U)	16.11.89	FOSF
Ross, Gawain	CAPT RM(FTC)	RM	SO(LE)	01.01.99	RM Poole
Ross, Ian, *BEng, CEng, MIMarE*	LT(FTC)	E	ME	01.08.92	DRAKE CFM
Ross, Jonathan Hubert, *BSc, MA, ACGI, psc(j)*	MAJ(FTC)	RM		01.09.95	40 CDO RM
Ross, Robert Alasdair, *MB, BS, Dip FFP, FRCS*	SURG CDR	-	GMPP	31.12.99	CTCRM
Ross, Sarah Joanne, *MB, BCH, BCh, MRCGP, psc(j)*	SURG CDR	-	GMPP	14.10.99	RALEIGH
Rossiter, Mark Anthony, *BEng*	LT CDR(FTC)	E	ME	01.10.99	LOAN DERA PYSTCK
Roster, Shaun	LT(CC)	X	O	16.11.94	702 SQN HERON
Rostron, David William, *BEng*	LT(CC)	E	MESM	01.01.92	DRAKE CBS
Rothwell, John Francis	LT CDR(FTC)	X	PWO(A)	01.09.82	SSA/CWTA PORTS
Rothwell, Mark Kinsey, *BSc, MNI, pce*	CDR(FTC)	X	PWO(N)	30.06.94	DRYAD
Routledge, William David	LT(FTC)	X	PT	10.12.98	LINDISFARNE
Rowan, Mark Edward	LT(FTC)	X	C	24.07.97	DCSA COMMCEN PLY
Rowan, Nicholas Anthony, *BEng*	LT(FTC)	E	MESM	01.12.93	NEPTUNE NT
Rowberry, Adrian Graham, *BSc*	SLT(IC)	X		01.01.99	DARTMOUTH BRNC
Rowe, Andrew James	LT(FTC)	E	WE	19.02.93	FOSM NWOOD OPS
Rowe, Hannah, *BA*	LT(IC)	S		01.04.95	RALEIGH
Rowe, Kevin Christopher	LT(CC)	X	O	01.01.93	849 SQN B FLT
Rowe, Paula Elizabeth, *MBA*	LT CDR(CC)	E	TM	01.10.97	DARTMOUTH BRNC
Rowe, Vivian Noel, *psc(m)*	LT COL(FTC)	RM	MLDR	31.12.88	RM POOLE
Rowell, Graham Edward, *BSc, MSc*	CDR(FTC)	E	AE	30.06.94	RNAS CULDROSE
Rowland, Paul Nicholas, *BEng, CEng, MIMarE*	LT CDR(FTC)	E	MESM	01.01.00	NP 1066
Rowlands, Andrew Richard, *BEng*	LT(FTC)	E	WE	01.06.96	BRNC RNSU SOTON
Rowlands, Geoffrey Alan, *BA, BSc, FRMS*	LT CDR(FTC)	X	METOC	01.09.85	CINCFLEET
Rowlands, Kevin, *BSc*	LT(FTC)	X	FC	01.03.92	ILLUSTRIOUS
Rowley, Sean	LT(IC)	X	O	16.11.94	815 SQN HQ
Rowse, Mark Lawrence, *BEng, CEng*	LT CDR(FTC)	E	WE	01.07.97	FOST SEA
Rowson, Marcus Jonathan, *BSc*	SLT(IC)	X	P U/T	01.05.97	RNAS YEOVILTON
Roy, Alexander Campbell, *osc(us)*	LT COL(FTC)	RM		31.12.90	RM Poole
Roy, Christopher	MID(IC)	X	P U/T	01.01.99	RNAS YEOVILTON
Roylance, Jaimie Fraser, *MA*	CAPT RM(FTC)	RM	P	01.09.95	DRYAD
Royston, Stuart James, *pce*	LT CDR(FTC)	X	PWO(C)	01.05.98	COMUKTG/CASWSF
Rudd, Vanessa Jane, *BA*	LT(CC)	X		01.01.00	WESTMINSTER
Ruddock, Gordon William David, *n*	LT(FTC)	X		01.07.95	PUNCHER
Rudman, Christopher John, *BSc*	LT CDR(FTC)	E	TM	15.05.90	NMA PORTSMOUTH
Rule, Stuart James, *LLB*	CAPT RM(FTC)	RM		01.05.99	FEARLESS
Runchman, Phillip Charles, *BM, BCh, FRCS*	SURG CDR	-	(CGS)	30.06.85	NELSON (PAY)
Rundle, Anthony Littlejohns, *BEng*	LT(FTC)	E	WE	19.02.93	SSA DEVONPORT
Rundle, Robert Mark, *BSc, psc(m)*	LT COL(FTC)	RM		30.06.87	NS OBERAMMERGAU
Rusbridger, Robert Charles, *MSc, psc*	CDR(FTC)	E	ME	30.06.95	CINCFLEET
Rushworth, Benjamin John, *BSc*	LT(FTC)	X		01.05.98	YORK
Russell, Bruce, *BEng, CEng, MIEE*	LT(FTC)	E	WESM	01.05.92	DCS SM BRISTOL
Russell, Colin	SLT(FTC)	E	AE	01.05.97	DARTMOUTH BRNC
Russell, David John, *rcds, pce, pce(sm), hcsc (COMMODORE)*	CAPT(FTC)	X	SM	31.12.93	FOSM NWOOD HQ
Russell, Gillian Spence, *BEng(Hons)*	LT(FTC)	S		01.08.95	2SL/CNH
Russell, Martin Simon, *BA*	SLT(IC)	X		01.01.99	DARTMOUTH BRNC
Russell, Nigel Anthony David	LT(FTC)	X	FC	01.12.94	DRYAD
Russell, Paul	LT(FTC)	X	PWO(A)	01.05.93	IRON DUKE

Name	Rank	Branch	Spec	Seniority	Where Serving
Russell, Philip Robert, *BTech, MSc, CEng, MIMarE*	LT CDR(FTC)	E	ME	01.02.98	CAMPBELTOWN
Russell, Simon Jonathon, *AMRAeS, psc*	CDR(FTC)	E	AE	30.06.98	ES AIR BRISTOL
Russell, Thomas, *pce*	LT CDR(FTC)	X	MCD	01.07.93	NMA PORTSMOUTH
Russell, Timothy James, *BSc*	LT(CC)	X	MW	01.07.90	DRYAD
Ruston, Mark Robert, *BEng, MSc*	LT(CC)	E	WE	01.01.99	NEWCASTLE
Rutherford, Kevin John, *BSc*	LT(CC)	X	P	01.10.93	771 SK5 SAR
Rutherford, Timothy James, *BEng*	LT(FTC)	E	AE	30.12.92	700M MERLIN IFTU
Ruthven, Stuart	SURG SLT	-		22.05.98	DARTMOUTH BRNC
Ryan, Dennis Graham, *BSc*	LT CDR(FTC)	E	AE(P)	01.03.93	MOD DHSA
Ryan, John Benedict	LT(CC)	S		01.06.90	NEPTUNE CFS
Ryan, Jennifer Helen, *BSc*	LT(IC)	X		01.03.98	ORWELL
Ryan, John Peter	SLT(FTC)	E	MESM	02.05.97	TIRELESS
Ryan, Nicholas, *BEng*	LT(FTC)	E	ME	01.07.95	SULTAN
Ryan, Patrick Douglas Blackwood	SLT(UCE)(FTC)	X		01.09.99	DARTMOUTH BRNC
Ryan, Richard Michael, *BSc, pcea*	LT CDR(FTC)	X	O	01.04.97	FOST SEA
Ryan, Sean Joseph, *BA, SM(n)*	LT(FTC)	X	SM	01.04.93	SOVEREIGN
Rycroft, Alan Edward, *pce, pcea*	CDR(FTC)	X	O	30.06.96	BDS WASHINGTON
Ryder, Steven John, *MB, BCh, FRCS, FRCSEd, AFOM, MFOM*	SURG CDR	-	(CO/M)	30.06.90	NBC PORTSMOUTH
Ryder, Stephen Maurice, *TEng, IEng, AMIMarE*	LT CDR(FTC)	E	ME	01.10.94	CUMBERLAND
Ryder, Timothy John	LT(FTC)	MS	(AD)	23.07.93	NELSON (PAY)
Rydiard, David Martin, *BSc, AMNI, pce, psc*	LT CDR(FTC)	X	PWO(N)†	01.12.81	DRYAD
Rye, John Walter, *MA, psc*	MAJ(FTC)	RM	C	01.09.84	CTCRM
Rymer, Alan Robert, *BSc, CEng, MIMarE, psc*	CAPT(FTC)	E	ME	30.06.99	MOD (LONDON)

S

Name	Rank	Branch	Spec	Seniority	Where Serving
Saddleton, Andrew David	MAJ(FTC)	RM	LC	01.09.96	NELSON
Sadler, Christopher John, *pce, pcea*	LT CDR(FTC)	X	O	01.02.90	RNAS CULDROSE
Sage, David Ian, *n*	LT CDR(FTC)	X	H1	04.11.97	BULLDOG
Salim, Muttahir, *BSc*	LT(IC)	E	TM	01.09.98	SULTAN
Salisbury, David Peter, *pce*	LT CDR(FTC)	X	P	01.02.96	EDINBURGH
Salmon, Andrew, *MA, psc*	COL(FTC)	RM		30.06.00	42 CDO RM
Salmon, Michael Alan, *pcea*	LT CDR(FTC)	X	O	01.10.96	HQ3GP HQSTC
Salmon, Robert David	LT(FTC)	X	EW	23.07.98	JSSU OAKLEY
Salt, Hedley Stephen	LT(CC)	X	P	01.09.93	RAF CRANWELL EFS
Salter, Jeffrey Alan, *BEng*	LT CDR(FTC)	E	WE	10.02.94	FOST SEA
Salter, Mark David, *pcea*	CDR(FTC)	X	P	01.10.95	CHFHQ
Saltonstall, Philip James Rous, *BA*	LT(CC)	X	P U/T	01.12.99	DHFS
Salzano, Gerard Mark, *psc*	LT COL(FTC)	RM		30.06.00	CTCRM
Samborne, Michael David Palmer, *pce, pce(sm)*	CDR(FTC)	X	SM	30.06.87	MOD (LONDON)
Sambrooks, Richard John, *BEng*	LT(CC)	X	P U/T	01.08.99	FONA LINTON/OUSE
Sampson, Philip Henry, *psc(m)*	LT COL(FTC)	RM	-	30.06.97	MOD (LONDON)
Samuel, Christopher	2LT(GRAD)(IC)	RM		28.04.99	CTCRM LYMPSTONE
Samuel, Katja Lilian Hamilton, *BA*	LT(FTC)	S	BAR	01.08.93	2SL/CNH
Samways, Michael James	MID(IC)	X		01.09.98	DARTMOUTH BRNC
Sanders, Andrew William Tyrrell, *BSc*	LT CDR(FTC)	E	WE	01.08.80	2SL/CNH FOTR
Sanderson, Christopher Peter, *MA*	SLT(FTC)	X		01.05.97	DRYAD
Sanderson, Lee David, *BEng*	LT(FTC)	E	WE	01.10.96	DRAKE CFM
Sanderson, Peter Charles, *MSc, CEng, MIEE (COMMODORE)*	CAPT(FTC)	E	MESM	31.12.92	CINCFLEET
Sanderson, Robert Christopher, *BDS, FDS RCPSGlas*	SGCAPT(D)	-	(COSM)	30.06.00	RH HASLAR
Sandle, Neil David, *BEng, AMIMechE*	LT(FTC)	E	ME	01.08.95	INVINCIBLE
Sandover, Richard John, *BSc, pce, pcea, psc, gdas*	LT CDR(FTC)	X	O	20.04.87	MERLIN IPT
Sangha, Randeep Singh, *BEng*	LT(CC)	E	AE	01.12.98	RNAS CULDROSE
Sanguinetti, Hector Robert, *pce, psc(j)*	CDR(FTC)	X	PWO(C)	30.06.98	GRAFTON
Sansford, Adrian James, *BEng, MSc*	LT CDR(FTC)	E	MESM	27.05.99	TRIUMPH
Santrian, Karl	LT(FTC)	X	AV	01.01.97	EXCHANGE RAF UK
Santry, Paul Matthew	SLT(FTC)	X	C	01.04.98	ATHERSTONE
Sargent, David Reginald	SLT(IC)	X		01.01.99	DARTMOUTH BRNC
Sargent, David, *BSc*	SURG SLT	-		29.07.99	DARTMOUTH BRNC
Sargent, Kevin Stephen, *MBE*	LT(FTC)	E	AE(M)	29.04.97	DARA
Sargent, Nicholas Matthew, *BEng*	LT(CC)	E	AE	01.09.98	SULTAN
Sargent, Philippa Mary, *MA, n*	LT(IC)	X		01.12.92	DRYAD
Satterly, Robert James, *BEng*	SLT(IC)	E		01.09.98	ARGYLL

Name	Rank	Branch	Spec	Seniority	Where Serving
Satterthwaite, Benjamin John , *BA*	LT(CC)	X	MW	01.02.95	CHIDDINGFOLD
Saunders, Alice Caroline , *BSc, PGDip*	LT(IC)	X	METOC	25.04.89	RNAS YEOVILTON
Saunders, Christopher Edmund Maurice , *BSc*	LT(FTC)	X		01.06.97	CUMBERLAND
Saunders, Jason Mervin , *BEng*	LT(IC)	E	TM	01.09.94	NELSON
Saunders, John Nicholas	LT CDR(FTC)	X	N	01.10.90	CDRE MFP
Saunders, Peter William , *BEng, CEng*	LT(FTC)	E	AE	01.06.92	EXCHANGE AUSTLIA
Saunders, Timothy Mark , *BSc*	LT CDR(FTC)	E	TMSM	01.09.94	JSCSC
Sauze, Martin James , *BEd, MSc*	LT CDR(FTC)	X	METOC	01.10.88	AGRIPPA NAVSOUTH
Savage, Alan Paul , *BSc*	LT(IC)	E	IS	01.07.91	2SL/CNH
Savage, Daniel McLaughlan , *BSc*	LT(IC)	X	P	01.09.98	815 FLT 234
Savage, Mark Roger	LT CDR(FTC)	X	PWO(U)	01.09.98	MCM3 SEA
Savage, Nigel David	CAPT(FTC)	S		30.06.95	SACLANT USA
Savage, Shane , *BSc*	LT CDR(FTC)	X	ATC	01.10.94	FOST DPORT SHORE
Saward, Justin Robert Ernest , *BEng*	LT(IC)	E	AE	01.07.97	848 SQN HERON
Sawford, Gavin	SLT(IC)	E	WE	27.01.99	COLLINGWOOD
Sawyer, Trevor James	MAJ(FTC)	RM	SO(LE)	01.10.94	COMACCHIO GP RM
Saxby, Christopher James , *BEng, MSc, MIMarE, MCGI*	LT CDR(FTC)	E	ME	01.11.94	CAPT(H) DEVPT
Saxby, David George	LT(CS)	-		25.04.93	RNSR BOVINGTON
Saxby, Keith Alan	LT CDR(FTC)	X	PWO(A)	24.02.94	LN DERA PRTSDWN
Sayer, David Julian , *pce, psc*	CDR(FTC)	X	AWO(A)	31.12.88	DRAKE DPM
Sayer, Jamie Michael , *BA, BEng*	LT(CC)	E	AE	01.06.97	JF HARROLE OFF
Sayles, Stephen	CDR(FTC)	E	ME	31.12.91	2SL/CNH
Saynor, Roger Michael	LT CDR(FTC)	X	PT	01.10.96	TEMERAIRE
Saywell-Hall, Stephen Eric	LT(FTC)	E	AE(L)	02.09.99	FONA SEAGOING
Scandling, Rachel Jane	LT(FTC)	S		01.05.96	INVINCIBLE
Scanlon, Michael Jon	2LT(GRAD)(IC)	RM		28.04.99	CTCRM LYMPSTONE
Scarth, William , *BSc, jsdc, pce*	CDR(FTC)	X	MCD	30.06.97	JSCSC
Schillemore, Paul Colin *(Act Lt Cdr)*	LT(FTC)	E	WE	18.10.85	PJHQ
Schmidt, James Frederick Kurt , *BSc*	LT CDR(FTC)	E	MESM	01.03.91	FOSNNI/NBC CLYDE
Schnadhorst, James Charles , *pce*	LT CDR(FTC)	X	PWO(U)	01.05.95	EXCHANGE AUSTLIA
Schofield, Julie Claire	MID(NE)(IC)	X		01.09.99	DARTMOUTH BRNC
Scholes, Neil Andrew	LT(FTC)	E	MESM	02.09.99	DRAKE CFM
Schreier, Paul Jakob Robert , *MA, MEng, DPhil*	LT(FTC)	X	FC	01.01.96	RAIDER
Schunmann, Ceri Peter Ingo , *BSc*	LT(IC)	X	MCD	01.12.93	INVERNESS
Schwab, Robert Anthony	LT CDR(FTC)	X	P	01.10.97	FONA
Schwarz, Paul Michael Gunter	LT CDR(FTC)	X	ATC	01.10.88	MOD (LONDON)
Scivier, John Stapleton , *MIMgt*	LT(FTC)	X	ATC	01.02.91	EXCHANGE RAF GER
Scoles, Jonathon Charles , *OBE, FIMgt, pce, psc*	CDR(FTC)	X	PWO(U)	31.12.89	2SL/CNH
Scopes, David , *BEng*	LT(FTC)	E	AE	01.12.94	LN DERA BEDFORD
Scorer, Samuel James , *jsdc, pce*	CAPT(FTC)	X	PWO(U)	30.06.00	NATO DEF COL
Scott, Christopher Ralph , *OBE, psc*	LT COL(FTC)	RM		30.06.98	PJHQ
Scott, Jason Andrew , *BA, pce*	LT CDR(FTC)	X	PWO(U)	01.04.97	QUORN
Scott, Juliet Anna , *BA*	LT(IC)	X	O U/T	01.04.00	750 SQN OBS SCH
Scott, James Baxter , *BEng, MIMechE*	LT CDR(FTC)	E	MESM	01.05.96	TORBAY
Scott, Michael , *BEng, CEng, MIEE*	LT CDR(FTC)	E	WESM	01.05.99	COLLINGWOOD
Scott, Michael , *BA, BEng*	LT(IC)	X	P	16.08.97	820 SQN
Scott, Melvyn Anthony George	LT(FTC)	E	ME	27.02.87	LN DERA PRTSDWN
Scott, Mark Robert	LT(CC)	X	P	16.12.93	815 FLT 207
Scott, Neil	SLT(IC)	X	NO-S/S	01.09.98	DARTMOUTH BRNC
Scott, Nigel Leonard James , *BEng, CEng, MIMarE, ACGI, psc(j)*	LT CDR(FTC)	E	WESM	01.04.96	TRIUMPH
Scott, Peter James Douglas Sefton	CHAPLAIN	CE		03.09.91	CTCRM
Scott, Richard Antony , *BEng*	LT(CC)	E	WE	01.08.94	EXCHANGE RAF UK
Scott, Roderick Cameron , *MB, BSc, ChB, FFARCS, FRCA*	SURG CDR	-	(CA)	31.12.96	RH HASLAR
Scott, Robert John , *pcea*	LT CDR(FTC)	X	O	02.03.98	COMATG SEA
Scott, Robert Munro , *psc*	LT CDR(FTC)	S		01.05.84	2SL/CNH FOTR
Scott, Stephen Charles	CAPT RM(FTC)	RM	SO(LE)	01.01.98	CDO LOG REGT RM
Scott, Simon John	MAJ(FTC)	RM	LC	01.09.96	RMCS SHRIVENHAM
Scott, Timothy Edward , *MB, BS*	SURG LT	-		04.08.99	MCM2 SEA
Scott-Dickins, Charles Angus , *BSc*	LT CDR(FTC)	X	METOC	01.10.94	MWC PORTSDOWN
Screaton, Richard Michael , *BEng*	LT(FTC)	E	ME	01.03.96	SULTAN
Screech, Michael Courtney , FInstAM	LT CDR(FTC)	S	SM	01.08.81	PJHQ
Scruton, Neil , *BSc, psc*	LT CDR(FTC)	X	H CH	16.03.84	MOD (LONDON)
Seabrook, Ian	LT(FTC)	X	P	16.03.91	EXCHANGE USA

Name	Rank	Branch	Spec	Seniority	Where Serving
Seabrooke-Spencer, David John, *BA, pce*	LT CDR(FTC)	X	PWO(A)	01.07.94	MOD (LONDON)
Seager, Andrew Keith	SLT(IC)	X	ATCU/T	19.09.98	RNAS YEOVILTON
Seagrave, Suzanna Jane, *BA, BEng*	SLT(IC)	E		01.09.98	CORNWALL
Sealey, Nicholas Peter, *BSc, CEng, MIMarE, psc*	CDR(FTC)	E	ME	30.06.94	FOSF
Seaman, Philip John	LT(FTC)	E	WE	19.02.93	RHQ SOUTHLANT
Sear, Jonathan Jasper	MAJ(FTC)	RM		01.09.98	45 CDO RM
Searight, Mark Frederick Chamney	MAJ(FTC)	RM		01.05.97	JSCSC
Searle, Edward Francis, *BSc, CEng, MIEE, MIMarE, psc*	CAPT(FTC)	E	ME	31.12.95	NELSON
Searle, Michael Philip, *BSc*	SLT(IC)	X	O U/T	01.09.97	750 SQN OBS SCH
Searle, Russell John, *BSc, pce*	CDR(FTC)	X	PWO(C)	30.06.91	SCU LEYDENE ACNS
Seatherton, Elliot Frazer Kingston, *MBE, pce, ocds(US)*	CDR(FTC)	X	PWO(N)	31.12.95	INVINCIBLE
Secretan, Simon James, *BEd, pce, n*	LT CDR(FTC)	X	PWO(U)	01.08.96	EXCHANGE USA
Seddon, John Stephen Maurice	LT CDR(FTC)	S	SM	16.10.88	DRAKE DPL
Seed, Gareth James, *BA, BEng*	SLT(IC)	E		01.01.99	DARTMOUTH BRNC
Seekings, Andrew Laurence, *BSc*	LT(CC)	X	METOC	01.06.89	EXCHANGE NLANDS
Segebarth, Robert Andrew	LT(CC)	X	P	16.02.96	899 SQN HERON
Sellar, Trevor Jefferson	CAPT RM(FTC)	RM	SO(LE)	01.01.97	RM POOLE
Sellars, Scott John, *BA*	LT(CC)	S	FC	01.07.94	SCEPTRE
Sellers, Graham Donald, *BEng, CEng, MIEE*	LT(FTC)	E	WE	01.02.93	RMC OF SCIENCE
Selman, Toby Roger, *BSc*	CAPT RM(FTC)	RM		01.09.99	45 CDO RM
Selway, Mark Anthony, *BEng*	LT(FTC)	E	AE	01.07.97	ES AIR MASU
Selwyn, Peter David, *BSc*	LT CDR(FTC)	E	WESM	01.07.90	ASTUTE IPT
Semple, Brian	SLT(IC)	X		01.01.00	DARTMOUTH BRNC
Sennitt, John William, *BSc*	LT CDR(FTC)	E	WE	01.08.92	CINCFLEET CIS
Sephton, John Richard, *BSc, psc*	CDR(FTC)	X	METOC	30.06.00	RNSOMO
Sergeant, Nicholas Robin	LT CDR(FTC)	E	WE	01.10.99	MOD (BATH)
Seward, Stafford Allan	LT(FTC)	X	g	06.04.95	RNAS YEOVILTON
Sewed, Michael Antony, *BSc*	LT CDR(FTC)	X	O	01.10.94	EXCHANGE N ZLAND
Sewell, Iain Timothy Tait, *OBE, BSc, psc*	CDR(FTC)	X	H CH	31.12.90	MOD (LONDON)
Sewell, Mark Anthony Philip	LT(IC)	X	P	16.10.96	819 SQN
Sewry, Michael Ronald, *BSc, CEng, MIEE, psc(a)*	CDR(FTC)	E	AE	31.12.95	MOD (LONDON)
Sexton, Michael John	CDR(FTC)	E	WE	30.06.98	AGRIPPA AFSOUTH
Seymour, Kevin William, *pcea*	LT CDR(FTC)	X	P	01.10.96	EXCHANGE USA
Shackleton, (Scott James Sinclair)	CHAPLAIN	SF		20.04.93	RMB STONEHOUSE
Shadbolt, Simon Edward, *MBE, BSc, psc(m)*	COL(FTC)	RM	C	31.12.98	PJHQ
Shallcroft, John Edward, *pcea*	LT CDR(FTC)	X	P	01.10.98	824 NAS
Shand, Christopher Michael, *BSc*	LT CDR(FTC)	E	WESM	01.11.82	DRAKE CBP(DLO)
Shanks, Graeme John, *BA*	LT(IC)	X	FC	01.04.98	GLASGOW
Shanks, Steven Andrew, *BSc*	SLT(IC)	X		01.09.97	DRYAD
Sharkey, Elton Richard, *BEng*	LT(FTC)	E	MESM	01.06.95	VIGILANT(PORT)
Sharkey, Michael	CHAPLAIN	RC		01.10.90	CTCRM
Sharland, Simon Patrick, *BA*	MAJ(FTC)	RM	LC	01.09.90	NMA PORTSMOUTH
Sharman, David John Thomas, *BSc, MSc, CEng, AMIEE*	LT CDR(FTC)	E	WE	01.03.94	EXCHANGE CANADA
Sharp, Colin Carlisle Gwinnett, *rcds, nadc, psc*	CDR(FTC)	S		31.12.88	JHCHQ
Sharp, John Vivian	MID(CC)	X	P U/T	01.01.99	RNAS YEOVILTON
Sharp, Lee Dominic, *MA*	LT(IC)	X		01.09.99	DRYAD
Sharpe, Gary Anthony	CAPT RM(FTC)	RM	SO(LE)	01.01.93	FEARLESS
Sharpe, Grantley James, *pce*	LT CDR(FTC)	X	PWO(U)	01.02.88	RNU ST MAWGAN
Sharpe, Thomas Grenville	LT(FTC)	X	FC	01.10.94	LINDISFARNE
Sharpley, John Guy, *MB, BCh, MA, MRCPsych*	SURG LTCDR			08.02.96	NELSON (PAY)
Sharrocks, Ian James	LT(CC)	X	P	16.05.98	RNAS YEOVILTON
Shaughnessy, Toby Edward	LT(FTC)	X	FC	01.10.97	RNAS YEOVILTON
Shaw, Graeme Roberts, *BEng, AMIEE*	LT CDR(FTC)	E	WE	01.05.00	DARTMOUTH BRNC
Shaw, Ian Brian, *BEng*	LT CDR(FTC)	E	WESM	15.09.91	NEPTUNE SWS
Shaw, Kevin Norman Graham, *MA, PhD, CEng, MIEE, MRIN, psc(j)*	LT CDR(FTC)	E	WE	01.02.94	HQ DCSA
Shaw, Michael Leslie, *BEng*	LT(FTC)	E	AE	01.05.93	824 NAS
Shaw, Neil Andrew	SLT(FTC)	E	WE	01.04.98	COLLINGWOOD
Shaw, Philip Anthony, *MVO, pce, pcea*	CDR(FTC)	X	P	01.10.89	FONA
Shaw, Philip Andrew George, *MBE, BSc, MA, pce, pcea, psc*	CDR(FTC)	X	P	31.12.99	824 NAS
Shaw, Paul James	LT CDR(FTC)	S		17.03.95	PJHQ
Shaw, Stuart Lawson, *MB, BSc, BS*	SURG LT	-		06.08.97	ENDURANCE
Shaw, Steven Matthew, *MA, psc(j)*	LT CDR(FTC)	S		01.03.95	MOD (BATH)
Shawcross, Paul Kenneth, *BSc, pcea*	LT CDR(FTC)	X	P	01.10.91	JHCHQ

Name	Rank	Branch	Spec	Seniority	Where Serving
Shearn, Matthew Arthur, *BA*	SLT(IC)	X		01.01.98	LEDBURY
Sheedy, Kim Louise, *BEng*	LT(IC)	E	TM	01.09.95	SULTAN
Sheehan, Mark Andrew, *pce, pcea, psc*	LT CDR(FTC)	X	O	01.07.92	702 SQN HERON
Sheikh, Nabil, *BSc*	LT(FTC)	S		01.11.97	LANCASTER
Sheils, Damian Edmund Tyrie	LT(CC)	X	P	16.07.94	849 SQN A FLT
Sheldon, Mark Laurence	LT(FTC)	E	WE	07.02.97	COLLINGWOOD
Sheldrake, James Peter, *BEng*	LT(IC)	X	SM	01.08.96	VICTORIOUS(STBD)
Sheldrake, Terence William, *BSc, pce, pcea, gdas*	LT CDR(FTC)	X	O	29.04.83	RNAS CULDROSE
Shellard, Graeme Iain, *BEng*	LT(IC)	E	WE	01.03.94	SSA BRISTOL
Shepherd, Alan	LT CDR(FTC)	E	WE	01.10.92	MOD (LONDON)
Shepherd, Charles Scott, *BSc, pce(sm)*	LT CDR(FTC)	X	SM	01.01.97	EXCHANGE USA
Shepherd, Fiona Rosemary, *BSc*	LT(IC)	S		01.10.99	RALEIGH
Shepherd, Iain, *BSc, pce*	CDR(FTC)	X	PWO(A)	30.06.92	NELSON
Shepherd, Martin Paul	LT(FTC)	X	P	01.04.96	815 FLT 208
Shepherd, Paul Rodney, *pcea*	LT CDR(FTC)	X	O	01.10.92	RNAS CULDROSE
Shepherd, Roger Guy, *BEng, AMIEE*	LT CDR(FTC)	E	WESM	01.05.96	TURBULENT
Shepherd, Sarah Louise	MID(NE)(IC)	S		01.01.00	DARTMOUTH BRNC
Sheppard, David George, *adp*	LT CDR(FTC)	E	WE	01.10.99	NMA PORTSMOUTH
Sheppard, Suzy Helen, *BA*	LT(FTC)	S		01.03.99	FOST DPORT SHORE
Shergold, Paul James	CAPT RM(FTC)	RM	SO(LE)	01.01.97	CTCRM
Sherlock, Francis Christopher Edwin, *MSc, CEng, MIMarE, psc*	CDR(FTC)	E	ME	31.12.92	FOST SEA
Sherriff, David Anthony, *pce, pcea*	LT CDR(FTC)	X	P	01.01.96	814 SQN
Sherwood, Gideon Andrew Francis	SLT(IC)	X		01.05.98	DARTMOUTH BRNC
Shield, Simon James, *pce(sm), psc*	CDR(FTC)	X	SM	31.12.98	TALENT
Shields, Carole Tracey	LT CDR(FTC)	S		01.10.99	NEPTUNE CFS
Shipperley, Ian, *BSc, CEng, MIMechE*	CDR(FTC)	E	ME	30.06.98	CINCFLEET
Shirley, Andrew John, *BEng*	LT(FTC)	E	MESM	01.08.89	FOSM NWOOD HQ
Shirley, Wayne Peter, *MA, psc(j)*	LT CDR(FTC)	E	WE	12.10.93	2SL/CNH FOTR
Shore, Elizabeth Anne, *MA*	SLT(IC)	X		01.01.99	DARTMOUTH BRNC
Shorland-Ball, Timothy John, *BA*	LT(FTC)	X		01.04.98	DRYAD
Short, Gavin Conrad, *BEng, AMIEE*	CDR(FTC)	E	WESM	30.06.00	JSCSC
Short, John Jeffrey, *BEng*	LT CDR(FTC)	E	ME	01.06.96	LANCASTER
Shrimpton, Helen Diane, *MB, BA, BCh*	SURG LTCDR	-		04.02.98	NELSON (PAY)
Shrimpton, Matthew William	LT(CC)	X	P	01.04.92	815 FLT 212
Shrives, Michael Peter, *pce, pcea, psc, psc(j)*	CDR(FTC)	X	P	30.06.95	2SL/CNH FOTR
Shrubsole, Steven John, *BEng*	LT CDR(FTC)	E	WE	01.12.99	T45 IPT
Shuttleworth, Stephen	LT(FTC)	E	ME	13.06.97	FOSF
Shutts, David, *BEng, AMIMechE, psc(j)*	LT CDR(FTC)	E	ME	01.06.98	WESTMINSTER
Sibbit, Neil Thomas, *pce, pcea, psc*	CDR(FTC)	X	O	30.06.96	BDS WASHINGTON
Sibley, Andrew Keith	LT(FTC)	E	ME	02.09.99	CFM PORTSMOUTH
Sibley, Graeme Paul, *BA*	CAPT RM(FTC)	RM		27.04.96	RM Poole
Sidebotham, Michael John, *PGDip, MHCIMA*	LT(FTC)	S	CA	28.07.89	VICTORY
Sidoli, Giovanni Eugenio, *BDS, MSc, MGDS RCS*	SGCDR(D)	-		31.12.95	NEPTUNE CFS
Sienkiewicz, Maryla Krystyna, *LLB*	SLT(IC)	X		01.05.98	CORNWALL
Silcock, Christopher Anthony James, *BA, rcds, pce, psc(m)*	CAPT(FTC)	X	PWO(A)	31.12.95	FOSF
Sillars, Malcolm Crawford, *MVO, MA, MNI, pce, psc*	CDR(FTC)	X	PWO(A)	31.12.95	CINCFLEET
Sillers, Barry, *BSc, SM(n)*	LT(FTC)	X	SM	01.12.94	SPLENDID
Silver, Christina Kay	LT CDR(FTC)	W	C	01.10.93	MOD (LONDON)
Sim, Donald Leslie Whyte, *MA, FIMgt, MNI, pce, pcea, ocds(USN)*	CDR(FTC)	X	O	30.06.90	SA PRETORIA
Simbeye, Martin, *BEng*	SLT(IC)	E	ME	01.01.99	DARTMOUTH BRNC
Simcock, Julia Louise	LT(FTC)	X		01.07.97	DRYAD
Simcox, Paul Alan, *MBE, MCGI, mdtc*	MAJ(FTC)	RM		19.06.99	JSCSC
Simm, Craig, *BEng*	LT(CC)	E	AE	01.07.98	899 SQN HERON
Simmonds, Daniel Douglas Harold	MID(IC)	X		01.05.98	DARTMOUTH BRNC
Simmonds, Gary Fredrick	LT CDR(FTC)	E	AE(L)	01.10.98	RNAS CULDROSE
Simmonds, Peter Bruce, *psc(a)*	MAJ(FTC)	RM		01.08.83	RM POOLE
Simmonds, Richard Michael, *OBE, jsdc, pce, psc(a)*	CDR(FTC)	X	MCD	31.12.90	SHAPE BELGIUM
Simmonite, Gavin Ian	SLT(CC)	X	P	01.01.98	846 SQN
Simmons, Nigel Douglas, *BSc, MSc, CEng, MIEE*	CDR(FTC)	E	WESM	30.06.99	DGCIS BRISTOL
Simms, David	LT(CC)	X	O	16.03.96	EXCHANGE RAF UK
Simpson, Alister Clive, *LLB*	CAPT RM(IC)	RM		01.05.98	CHFHQ
Simpson, Antonia Mary, *LLB*	LT(CC)	S		01.12.95	RALEIGH
Simpson, Colin Chisholm	LT(CC)	X	P	01.03.93	702 SQN HERON

Name	Rank	Branch	Spec	Seniority	Where Serving
Simpson, David Keith	LT(CC)	X	O	16.11.93	824 NAS
Simpson, Emma Jane , *BA*	LT(FTC)	W	X	04.04.90	MOD (LONDON)
Simpson, Erin Leona	MID(UCE)(IC)	E		01.09.99	CHATHAM
Simpson, Ian Heaton , *psc(j)*	LT CDR(FTC)	S		01.06.93	MOD (LONDON)
Simpson, Martin Joseph , *pce*	LT CDR(FTC)	X	PWO(N)	01.07.96	EXCHANGE USA
Simpson, Peter	LT(FTC)	MS	(CDO)	04.04.91	INM ALVERSTOKE
Simpson, Paul Emmanuel	SLT	Q		27.10.96	MODHU DERRIFORD
Simpson, Scott Forsyth	SLT(CC)	X	O U/T	01.04.98	750 SQN OBS SCH
Simpson, William James Stuart , *BEng*	SLT(IC)	X		01.01.99	DARTMOUTH BRNC
Sims, Alexander Richard	SLT(IC)	X	O U/T	01.01.98	RNAS CULDROSE
Sinclair, Andrew Bruce , *odc(Aus)*	LT CDR(FTC)	X	P	01.02.84	ILLUSTRIOUS
Sinclair, Angus Hugh , *BA, jsdc*	CAPT(FTC)	S	SM	30.06.96	SA ROME
Singleton, Mark Donald	LT(FTC)	X	AV	10.12.98	SULTAN
Sitton, John Barry , *BEng*	LT(CC)	E	MESM	01.11.95	TURBULENT
Skeer, Martyn Robert , *MBE, pce, pcea*	LT CDR(FTC)	X	P	04.04.94	814 SQN
Skelley, Alasdair Neil Murdoch , *MA, n*	LT(FTC)	X		01.03.95	DARTMOUTH BRNC
Skelton, John Steven , *BEng*	LT(CC)	E	ME	01.07.94	CFM PORTSMOUTH
Skidmore, Christopher Mark , *BA*	CDR(FTC)	S	SM	31.12.98	DARTMOUTH BRNC
Skidmore, Paul James , *BSc*	LT(FTC)	X		01.01.98	LANCASTER
Skidmore, Rodney Peter	LT(CC)	X	P	01.09.92	702 SQN HERON
Skinner, John Richard , *pce, psc, psc(a)*	CDR(FTC)	X	P	30.06.89	FONA
Skinner, Neil Peter Francis	LT CDR(FTC)	E	WE	01.10.92	SSA BRISTOL
Skipper, James Alexander	MID(FTC)	X		01.09.98	DARTMOUTH BRNC
Skipworth, Fiona Marianne , *BSc*	LT(FTC)	S		01.12.97	2SL/CNH
Skittrall, Steven , *BEng*	LT(FTC)	E	O U/T	01.12.97	750 SQN OBS SCH
Skuse, Matthew , *BSc*	MAJ(FTC)	RM	MLDR	01.09.99	COMACCHIO GP RM
Slack, Jeremy Mark	MAJ(FTC)	RM	LC	01.05.97	RM POOLE
Slade, Christopher , *pcea*	LT CDR(FTC)	X	P	01.10.90	824 NAS
Slade, Neil Richard , *BEng*	SLT(IC)	X		01.01.98	HERALD
Slater, Dougal Gordon , *BEng*	SLT(IC)	E		01.09.98	CARDIFF
Slater, Peter	LT CDR(FTC)	E	WE	01.10.92	RNEAWC
Slattery, Damian John , *BSc*	LT(IC)	X		01.12.99	DEF DIVING SCHL
Slavin, David Eric , *MB, BS, MSc, DObstRCOG, LRCP, MRCS, AFOM, MFOM*	SURG CDR	-	(CO/M)	31.12.96	EXCHANGE USA
Slawson, James Mark , *BSc, psc*	CDR(FTC)	E	ME	31.12.97	OCEAN
Slimmon, Kevan William	LT(FTC)	E	WESM	02.09.99	VIGILANT(STBD)
Sloan, Daniel Jan , *BEng*	LT(IC)	E	TM	01.09.91	EXCHANGE RAF UK
Sloan, Graham Daniel	SLT(IC)	X		01.04.00	DARTMOUTH BRNC
Sloan, Ian Alexander , *BEng*	LT(CC)	X	P U/T	01.12.99	FONA LINTON/OUSE
Sloan, Mark Usherwood , *BSc, pce, psc*	CAPT(FTC)	X	PWO(U)	31.12.99	FOSF
Slocombe, Christopher Alwyn	LT CDR(FTC)	X	P	01.10.96	COMATG SEA
Slocombe, Jane Scriven	LT(CC)	X	ATC	01.07.96	RNAS YEOVILTON
Slocombe, Nicholas Richard	LT(FTC)	X	ATC	01.11.91	INVINCIBLE
Slowther, Stuart John , *BA, BEng*	SLT(IC)	E		01.09.98	INVINCIBLE
Small, Richard James , *BSc*	LT(FTC)	X	SM	01.03.97	RALEIGH
Smallman, Laurence Delaney , *BSc, pce*	CDR(FTC)	X	PWO(U)	31.12.96	NORFOLK
Smallwood, Justin Patrick , *MA*	MAJ(FTC)	RM		05.09.95	539 ASLT SQN RM
Smallwood, Richard Iain	LT(FTC)	X	SM	12.10.93	RALEIGH
Smart, Mark James *(Act Lt)*	SLT(FTC)	E	AE	02.05.97	847 SQN
Smart, Steven Joe	LT(FTC)	E	ME	23.02.90	SULTAN
Smee, Norman Lee , *pce, psc*	CDR(FTC)	X	AWO(A)	30.06.92	EXCELLENT
Smerdon, Christopher David Edward , *BA*	LT CDR(FTC)	S	SM	01.07.94	MARLBOROUGH
Smith, Andrew , *BSc, psc*	CDR(FTC)	E	WE	30.06.88	CV(F) IPT
Smith, Andrew , *BA*	LT(IC)	X		01.04.99	NEWCASTLE
Smith, Austin Bernard Dudley	LT(CC)	X	P	01.05.96	847 SQN
Smith, Adrian Charles , *BSc*	LT CDR(FTC)	E	AE	16.03.84	ES AIR BRISTOL
Smith, Adrian Gerard , *BA*	LT CDR(FTC)	E	WE	01.02.99	DRYAD
Smith, Andrew Paul	LT CDR(FTC)	X	PWO(A)	01.04.98	MWC PORTSDOWN
Smith, Barbara Carol	LT CDR	Q	SCM	01.10.92	RH HASLAR
Smith, Brian Joseph , *AMNI, n*	LT CDR(FTC)	X		01.12.99	DRYAD
Smith, Brian Stephen , *BDS, MGDS RCSEd (Act Sgcdr(D))*	SGLTCDR(D)	-		13.09.93	RN GIBRALTAR
Smith, Christopher Julian	LT CDR(FTC)	S		16.03.96	DARTMOUTH BRNC
Smith, Christopher John Hilton , *BEng, AMIEE*	LT(CC)	E	WE	01.09.97	INVINCIBLE
Smith, Clive Peter	LT CDR(FTC)	X	PWO(U)	26.04.95	MCM1 SEA

Name	Rank	Branch	Spec	Seniority	Where Serving
Smith, Clive Sherrif, *OBE, MSc, CEng, MIMarE*	CDR(FTC)	E	MESM	30.06.92	MOD (BATH)
Smith, David Andrew Harry McGregor, *ADC, FHCIMA, rcds (COMMODORE)*	CAPT(FTC)	S		31.12.92	2SL/CNH
Smith, Daniel James, *BA*	LT(CC)	X	P	01.11.93	771 SK5 SAR
Smith, David Leslie	LT(CC)	X	FC	01.03.96	RNAS YEOVILTON
Smith, David Munro	CAPT RM(FTC)	RM	SO(LE)	01.01.99	RMR SCOTLAND
Smith, David Thomas	LT(CC)	X	O	16.06.91	RNAS CULDROSE
Smith, Gregory Charles Stanley, *pcea*	LT CDR(FTC)	X	O	01.01.98	849 SQN A FLT
Smith, Graeme Douglas James, *BSc*	LT(FTC)	X		01.01.93	DRYAD
Smith, Gregory Kenneth, *BSc, CEng, MBCS, MIProdE, adp*	LT CDR(FTC)	E	IS	01.10.93	SHAPE BELGIUM
Smith, Graham Kenneth, *BComm*	MAJ(FTC)	RM		24.04.99	COMACCHIO GP RM
Smith, Gordon Kenneth	2LT(GRAD)(IC)	RM		29.04.98	COMACCHIO GP RM
Smith, Helen Louise, *BA*	LT(IC)	S		01.01.00	CINCFLEET
Smith, John Charles, *BSc, pcea, gdas*	LT CDR(FTC)	X	O	06.01.87	LOAN DERA BSC DN
Smith, Jason Edward, *MB, BS, MRCP*	SURG LTCDR	-		01.08.98	MODHU FRIMLEY
Smith, Jason James, *MB, BS*	SURG LT	-		07.08.96	RH HASLAR
Smith, Kevin Alexander, *BSc*	LT CDR(FTC)	E	MESM	01.04.95	NMA PORTSMOUTH
Smith, Kevin Bernard Albert	LT CDR(FTC)	X	PWO(A)	01.04.96	MWC PORTSDOWN
Smith, Kevin Donlan, *BEng, MA, MEng*	LT(IC)	E	TM	01.02.97	SULTAN
Smith, Keven John, *pcea*	LT CDR(FTC)	X	P	01.10.95	OCEAN
Smith, Kenneth Marshall	LT CDR(FTC)	X	TAS	16.11.88	AGRIPPA NAVSOUTH
Smith, Kirsten Mary Louise	LT(FTC)	X		01.12.96	MOD (LONDON)
Smith, Lynnette	SLT(IC)	S		27.01.99	DARTMOUTH BRNC
Smith, Malcolm	CDR(FTC)	S	SM	30.06.96	DRAKE DPL
Smith, Melvin Andrew, *MSc, mdtc*	CDR(FTC)	E	WE	31.12.95	HQ DCSA
Smith, Michael Daren	LT(FTC)	X	O	01.02.96	702 SQN HERON
Smith, Michael James	LT(FTC)	E	WE	13.06.91	COLLINGWOOD
Smith, Michael John, *BSc*	LT(FTC)	E	WESM	01.05.96	VIGILANT(STBD)
Smith, Martin Linn, *MBE, BSc, psc*	LT COL(FTC)	RM		31.12.99	MOD (LONDON)
Smith, Mark MacFarlane, *BEng*	LT CDR(FTC)	E	AE	01.11.98	AIS(SW)
Smith, Mark Peter	LT(FTC)	MS		26.04.99	DEF MED TRG CTR
Smith, Mark Richard, *BEng*	LT CDR(FTC)	E	ME	14.07.95	CORNWALL
Smith, Martin Russell Kingsley, *BA, PGDip*	LT CDR(FTC)	X	METOC	01.09.93	RMC OF SCIENCE
Smith, Nicholas Derek, *psc*	MAJ(FTC)	RM		01.03.80	DISC
Smith, Neville Edward Philip, *BA*	LT(IC)	X		01.08.98	SCOTT
Smith, Nigel John	LT(FTC)	X	PWO(U)	25.07.96	DRYAD
Smith, Nicholas James Dominic	LT(CC)	X	O	01.04.98	815 SQN HQ
Smith, Nigel Paul, *BA, pce, psc*	CDR(FTC)	X	PWO(U)	31.12.89	SACLANT BELGIUM
Smith, Nigel Peter, *BA, pce*	LT CDR(FTC)	X	PWO(U)	01.07.91	CINCFLEET
Smith, Nicholas Peter, *BSc*	LT(IC)	E	TM	01.05.92	COLLINGWOOD
Smith, Owen John	SLT(CC)	X	ATCU/T	01.04.98	SULTAN
Smith, Paul	SLT(FTC)	X	WE	01.04.98	INVERNESS
Smith, Peter Geoffrey, *BSc*	LT CDR(CC)	X	O	01.10.98	LOAN DERA BSC DN
Smith, Rudi Adam	SLT(IC)	X		01.09.98	DARTMOUTH BRNC
Smith, Robert Charles Vernon	LT(FTC)	X	O	16.04.91	815 FLT 208
Smith, Richard David	LT(FTC)	X	H2	22.07.95	CAPT F6 (SEA)
Smith, Robert Edward	LT(FTC)	X	O	10.12.98	814 SQN
Smith, Richard William Robertson	LT CDR(FTC)	X	PWO(U)	01.05.93	EXCHANGE NLANDS
Smith, Stephen Bower, *BEng, CEng, MIMarE, AMIMechE*	LT CDR(CC)	E	TMSM	01.10.99	NELSON RNSETT
Smith, Stuart Frederick	LT CDR(FTC)	X	ATC	01.09.82	RNAS YEOVILTON
Smith, Stephen Frank	CAPT RM(FTC)	RM	SO(LE)	01.01.95	CDO LOG REGT RM
Smith, Steven Luigi, *pce*	LT CDR(FTC)	X	PWO(A)	01.02.92	MWC SOUTHWICK
Smith, Steven, *MB, BCh, ChB*	SURG LTCDR	-		01.08.95	NELSON (PAY)
Smith, Vincent Ivan Peregrine	MID(UCE)(IC)	X		01.09.99	SOUTHAMPTON
Smith-Jaynes, Ernest Royston	CDR(FTC)	E	WESM	01.10.94	CNSA BRISTOL
Smithson, Peter Edward, *BSc, MSc, CEng, MRAeS*	CDR(FTC)	E	AE	30.06.97	BDS WASHINGTON
Smye, Malcolm Alexander, *BEng*	SLT(IC)	E	AE	01.01.99	DARTMOUTH BRNC
Smyth, Michael James	LT CDR(FTC)	E	WE	01.10.94	CINCFLEET CIS
Sneddon, Russell Neil	LT(FTC)	X	P	16.06.92	DHFS
Snell, David Micheal	SLT(IC)	E	WE	27.01.99	COLLINGWOOD
Snelling, Paul Douglas, *BEng*	LT(FTC)	E	MESM	01.10.94	NP BRISTOL
Snelson, David George, *FIMgt, MNI, pce, psc (COMMODORE)*	CAPT(FTC)	X	AWO(A)	30.06.94	MOD(LONDON)
Sneyd, Eric Patrick Bartholomew, *MBE, BEng, MSc*	LT CDR(FTC)	E	TM	20.06.93	ELANT/NAVNORTH

Name	Rank	Branch	Spec	Seniority	Where Serving
Snook, Raymond Edward , *pce, pcea, psc(j)*	CDR(FTC)	X	O	30.06.98	MOD (LONDON)
Snow, Christopher Allen , *BA, pce*	CAPT(FTC)	X	PWO(U)	30.06.98	MOD (LONDON)
Snow, Maxwell Charles Peter , *BSc, pce, pcea, psc*	CDR(FTC)	X	P	30.06.93	EXCHANGE USA
Snow, Paul Frederick , *BSc*	LT CDR(FTC)	E	ME	01.10.94	MOD (BATH)
Snowball, Simon John , *MA, psc*	CDR(FTC)	X	PWO(N)	30.06.00	EXCHANGE CANADA
Snowden, Michael Brian Samuel , *MB, ChB, DObstRCOG, Dip FFP*	SURG LTCDR	-		01.08.99	NELSON (PAY)
Soar, Gary	LT(CC)	X	O	16.04.93	700M MERLIN IFTU
Soar, Trevor Alan , *OBE, pce, pce(sm)*	CAPT(FTC)	X	SM	31.12.96	MOD (LONDON)
Solly, Matthew MacDonald , *BSc*	LT(CC)	E	TMSM	22.05.92	CSST SHORE FSLN
Somerville, Angus James Dunmore , *LLB, rcds, pce (COMMODORE)*	CAPT(FTC)	X	PWO(A)	30.06.94	MOD (LONDON)
Somerville, Nigel John Powell , *MA*	CAPT RM(FTC)	RM		01.05.98	RM Poole
Somerville, Stuart James *(Act Lt)*	SLT(FTC)	S	CA	18.09.98	SOVEREIGN
Sopinski, Gregory Francis	LT(CC)	X	P	16.09.90	815 FLT 202
Soul, Nicholas John , *BEng*	LT(CC)	X	P	01.12.94	DRYAD
South, David John	LT(FTC)	X	PWO(A)	01.03.94	GLASGOW
Southern, Peter John	LT CDR(FTC)	E	MESM	01.10.90	UPHLDER TRG TEAM
Southern, Paul Jonathan , *BSc, IEng, AMIMarE*	LT CDR(FTC)	E	ME	27.02.99	SAUDI AFPS SAUDI
Southorn, M	LT CDR(FTC)	X	PWO(U)	21.07.99	EXCHANGE FRANCE
Southwell, Neil Peter	LT(FTC)	X	C	24.07.97	CINCFLEET CIS
Soutter, Laurence Donald Lister , *BSc*	CDR(FTC)	E	WESM	30.06.87	CAPTAIN SM2
Sowden, Lesley Margaret , *MB, ChB, Dip FFP*	SURG LT	-		02.08.95	RH HASLAR
Spalding, Richard Edmund Howden , *BSc, CEng, MIEE, MRIN, jsdc*	CDR(FTC)	E	WE	30.06.97	SSA BRISTOL
Spalding, Timothy John Wallis , *MB, BS, FRCS*	SURG CDR	-	(CO/S)	30.06.94	RH HASLAR
Spalton, Gary Marcus Sean , *BSc, pce*	CDR(FTC)	X	PWO(U)	31.12.92	MOD (LONDON)
Spanner, Paul	CAPT RM(FTC)	RM		01.05.95	JARIC
Sparke, Philip Richard William , *BA*	LT CDR(FTC)	S		01.03.00	RALEIGH
Sparkes, Peter James , *BSc, pce, n*	LT CDR(FTC)	X	PWO(C)	01.06.99	FEARLESS
Sparkes, Simon Nicholas , *pcea*	LT(FTC)	X	P	01.04.92	700M MERLIN IFTU
Sparrow, Mark , *BSc*	LT(IC)	X	P	16.04.99	FONA VALLEY
Spayne, Nicholas John	LT CDR(FTC)	X	PWO(U)	01.10.98	FOST DPORT SHORE
Speake, Jonathan , *BEng*	LT(CC)	X	O	01.12.90	EXCHANGE CANADA
Spears, Andrew Graeme	SLT(CC)	X		01.04.99	DRYAD
Speller, Nicholas Simon Ford , *pce(sm)*	LT CDR(FTC)	X	SM	01.05.88	FOSF
Spence, Andrei Barry , *BSc*	CDR(FTC)	S	BAR	30.06.00	FOSF
Spence, Nicholas Anthony , *pce*	CDR(FTC)	X	PWO(U)	30.06.97	JDCC
Spence, Robert Graeme , *BA*	LT(CC)	X	P	16.12.93	EXCHANGE ARMY UK
Spencer, Ashley Carver , *BA*	SLT(IC)	X		01.05.98	CAMPBELTOWN
Spencer, Elizabeth Anne , *BSc, BEd, MA, psc(j)*	CDR(FTC)	X	METOC	30.06.99	RHQ SOUTHLANT
Spencer, Jeremy Charles	LT(FTC)	E	ME	02.09.99	SULTAN
Spencer, Peter , *ADC, MA, MSc, jsdc*	VADM	-	WE	19.01.00	2SL/CNH
Spencer, Richard Anthony Winchcombe , *BA*	LT COL(FTC)	RM	C	31.12.99	CTCRM
Spencer, Steven John	LT	Q	CC	12.10.91	2SL/CNH FOTR
Spens-Black, Gerard Peter , *pce, pcea*	LT CDR(FTC)	X	P	16.01.86	FAAIT MAN ORG VL
Spicer, Clive Graham , *BSc, CEng, MIMarE*	CDR(FTC)	E	ME	31.12.95	MOD (BATH)
Spicer, Mark Nicholas , *BSc, psc*	COL(FTC)	RM		31.12.97	HQRM
Spillane, Paul	LT(CC)	X	O	01.07.96	849 SQN HQ
Spiller, Michael Francis , *BSc, psc*	CDR(FTC)	S		31.12.98	MOD (LONDON)
Spiller, Stephen Nicholas , *BEng*	LT(FTC)	E	WE	01.08.97	NEWCASTLE
Spiller, Vanessa Jane	LT CDR(FTC)	X	PWO(U)	28.07.97	CAPT F6 (SEA)
Spinks, David William	LT(FTC)	X	FC	01.08.97	DRYAD
Spinks, Robert John , *BSc*	SLT(IC)	X	P U/T	01.05.98	DARTMOUTH BRNC
Spires, Trevor Allan , *BSc, CDipAF, nadc (COMMODORE)*	CAPT(FTC)	E	TM	31.12.94	AFPAA HQ
Spofforth-Jones, Martyn Aubrey , *IEng, MIPlantE*	LT(FTC)	E	ME	13.06.97	SULTAN
Spooner, Peter David	LT CDR(FTC)	E	AE(M)	01.10.98	RNAS CULDROSE
Spooner, Ross Sydney	LT(FTC)	E	P	01.04.96	820 SQN
Spooner, Sophie Louise , *BEng*	LT(CC)	E	ME	01.05.95	SULTAN
Spoors, Brendan Mark , *BEng*	LT(CC)	X	P U/T	01.08.98	RNAS CULDROSE
Spring, Andrew Ralph James , *pce, n*	LT CDR(FTC)	X	PWO(U)	01.03.98	CAPT F2(SEA)
Spring, Jeremy Mark , *BEng*	LT CDR(FTC)	E	AE	03.08.97	814 SQN
Springett, Julia Katherine	LT CDR(CC)	W	C	01.10.99	RN GIBRALTAR
Springett, Simon	CHAPLAIN	CE		10.09.91	RALEIGH
Spurdle, Andrew Peter	LT(FTC)	X	C	20.09.99	HQ DCSA
Squibb, Clifford John , *BSc, pcea, psc*	LT CDR(FTC)	X	P	16.01.84	RNAS CULDROSE

Name	Rank	Branch	Spec	Seniority	Where Serving
Squire, Paul Anthony, *BSc, MIEE, MBCS, CDipAF, adp*	LT CDR(FTC)	E	WE	01.10.90	DRYAD
St Aubyn, John David Erskine, *BSc*	LT CDR(FTC)	E	WESM	01.12.95	VIGILANT(PORT)
Stace, Ivan Spencer, *BEng, MSc*	LT CDR(FTC)	E	WESM	01.07.96	TURBULENT
Stacey, Andrew Michael, *BSc*	LT(FTC)	X	PWO(A)	01.06.94	KENT
Stacey, Hugo Alister	LT CDR(FTC)	X	P	01.10.93	LOAN DERA BSC DN
Stafford, Benjamin Robert, *MEng*	SLT(FTC)	E	MESM	01.09.96	SULTAN
Stafford, Derek Bryan	CAPT RM(IC)	RM	P	27.04.96	846 SQN
Stafford, Wayne	SLT(FTC)	E	WESM	09.01.98	TORBAY
Stagg, Antony Robert, *BEng*	LT(FTC)	E	AE	01.03.95	MOD DHSA
Stait, Benjamin Geoffrey	LT(CC)	X		01.04.99	DRYAD
Stait, Carolyn Jane, *OBE, psc*	CAPT(FTC)	W	S	31.12.98	2SL/CNH
Staley, Simon Peter Lee	LT CDR(FTC)	X	O	01.02.99	SUTHERLAND
Stallion, Ian Michael, *BA, pce, pce(sm)*	CDR(FTC)	X	SM	31.12.94	FOSM NWOOD HQ
Stamp, Derek William	LT(TC)	E	ME	10.06.94	CLYDE MIXMAN2
Stamp, Gordon, *MA, pce, psc*	CDR(FTC)	X	MCD	30.06.95	SACLANT USA
Stamper, Jonathan Charles Henry, *BSc*	LT CDR(FTC)	E	TM	01.01.00	AFPAA(CENTURION)
Standen, Colin Anthony	LT RM(FTC)	RM	SO(LE)	01.01.98	CDO LOG REGT RM
Stanesby, David Laurence, *BSc, BA(OU), PGCE, psc*	CDR(FTC)	X	METOC	30.06.88	SA OSLO
Stanford, Christopher David, *MA, MNI, rcds, pce, psc*	RADM	-	AWO(C)	04.01.99	MOD (LONDON)
Stanford, Jeremy Hugh, *BA, jsdc, pce*	CDR(FTC)	X	P	31.12.94	NMA PORTSMOUTH
Stangroom, Alastair, *pce*	LT CDR(FTC)	X	MCD	24.03.95	CORNWALL
Stanham, Christopher Mark	LT(FTC)	E	AE(M)	06.09.96	CINCFLEET
Stanhope, Mark, *OBE, ADC, MA, MNI, rcds, pce, pce(sm), psc, hcsc*	RADM	-	SM	01.06.00	RHQ AFNORTH
Stanley, Christopher Edward, *pce, psc*	CDR(FTC)	X	PWO(A)	30.06.94	MOD (LONDON)
Stanley, Nicholas James	LT(CC)	X	O	16.09.93	702 SQN HERON
Stanley, Nicholas Paul, *pce, psc*	CDR(FTC)	X	PWO(U)	30.06.95	MOD (LONDON)
Stanley, Paul, *BEd, jsdc, ODC(SWISS)*	CDR(FTC)	E	TM	30.06.92	MOD (LONDON)
Stanley-Whyte, Berkeley John, *BSc, MA, CEng, MIEE, psc(j)*	CDR(FTC)	E	WESM	31.12.98	IMS BRUSSELS
Stannard, Adam, *MB, BSc, ChB (Act Surg Lt)*	SURG SLT	-		15.03.97	DARTMOUTH BRNC
Stannard, Mark Philip	LT CDR(FTC)	X		01.08.97	EXCHANGE FRANCE
Stanton, David Vernon, *pcea*	LT CDR(FTC)	X	O	01.10.91	810 SQN SEAHAWK
Stanton, Paul Charles Maund, *BSc, ACMA*	LT CDR(FTC)	S	CMA	16.02.97	2SL/CNH
Stanton-Brown, Peter James, *BSc*	LT(FTC)	X	SM	01.02.93	TIRELESS
Stanway, Charles Adrian, *BSc*	SLT(IC)	X		01.09.98	KENT
Stapley, Sarah Ann, *MB, ChB, FRCS*	SURG LTCDR	-		01.08.95	NELSON (PAY)
Stark, Trevor Alan, *psc*	MAJ(FTC)	RM		01.12.82	AST(E)
Starks, Michael Robert, *BSc, MA, CEng, MRAeS, psc*	CDR(FTC)	E	AE	30.06.97	JSCSC
Startup, Helen Jane, *BSc*	SLT(IC)	X		01.01.99	DARTMOUTH BRNC
Staveley, John Richard	LT CDR(FTC)	X	MCD	01.01.87	SACLANT ITALY
Stead, John Arthur, *BSc*	LT(TC)	E	WESM	02.09.99	CLYDE MIXMAN1
Stead, Richard Alexander	LT(FTC)	MS	(AD)	06.04.95	2SL/CNH
Stead, Steven Neil	SLT(IC)	X		01.09.98	DARTMOUTH BRNC
Steadman, Robert Paul, *BA*	LT(FTC)	X	FC	01.05.96	EXETER
Stear, Timothy James Fletcher	CAPT RM(IC)	RM		01.09.97	42 CDO RM
Stearns, Rupert Paul, *MA, psc*	LT COL(FTC)	RM	LC	30.06.96	JSCSC
Steeds, Sean Michael, *pce, pcea, psc(j)*	CDR(FTC)	X	P	30.06.98	RHQ AFNORTH
Steel, Christopher Michael Howard, *BSc, CEng, MIEE, MIMgt, jsdc*	CDR(FTC)	E	WESM	31.12.92	MOD (LONDON)
Steel, David George, *BA, jsdc (BARRISTER)*	CDR(FTC)	S	BAR	31.12.94	NMA PORTSMOUTH
Steel, David Goodwin	LT CDR(FTC)	MS	(CDO)	01.10.98	HQRM
Steel, Peter St Clair, *BSc, jsdc, pce (Act Capt)*	CDR(FTC)	X	P	30.06.91	MOD (LONDON)
Steel, Robert Ali, *BEng, CEng, MIMarE*	LT(FTC)	E	ME	01.09.93	MOD (BATH)
Steel, Rodney James, *BSc, CEng, MIMechE, jsdc*	CDR(FTC)	E	AE(P)	31.12.90	MERLIN IPT
Steele, Karen Sheila	LT(IC)	S		01.07.92	CDRE MFP
Steele, Richard Martin, *BSc*	LT(IC)	X		01.06.99	DOLPHIN SM SCHL
Steele, Trevor Graeme	LT(FTC)	X	O	11.12.92	819 SQN
Steen, Kieron Malcolm, *BSc*	LT(CC)	X	P	16.06.98	FONA VALLEY
Steer, Andrew David	LT(FTC)	X		01.02.98	FOSM NWOOD OPS
Steil, Cameron Wellesley Rutherford	LT(FTC)	X		01.02.93	DRYAD
Stein, Graham Kenneth, *BSc*	LT(CC)	X	P	01.04.99	RNAS YEOVILTON
Stellingworth, Jill Pamela, *rcds, psc*	CDR(FTC)	W	SEC	01.04.89	DCTA
Stembridge, Daniel Patrick Trelawney	LT(CC)	X	P	16.04.94	801 SQN
Stemp, Justin Edward, *BA*	CAPT RM(FTC)	RM		01.09.98	HQ 3 CDO BDE RM
Stenhouse, Nicholas John, *BSc, MA, CEng, MIEE, psc*	CDR(FTC)	E	WE	31.12.93	FOSF ROSYTH

Name	Rank	Branch	Spec	Seniority	Where Serving
Stenhouse, Ronald Cowan, *MA, pce*	LT CDR(FTC)	X	PWO(A)	01.05.91	BFFI
Stephen, Barry Mark, *BA, n*	LT(FTC)	X		01.03.94	TRACKER
Stephens, Andrew William	SLT(FTC)	E	WE	09.01.98	NOTTINGHAM
Stephens, Richard John, *BSc, PGDip*	LT(CC)	X	METOC	01.09.90	CINCFLEET
Stephens, Richard James, *MBE, MA, psc(j)*	MAJ(FTC)	RM		01.05.97	HQRM
Stephens, Richard Philip	LT CDR(FTC)	X	EW	01.10.99	DRYAD
Stephenson, Christopher John, *BSc*	SLT(IC)	X		01.05.98	NORFOLK
Stephenson, David, *BEng, MSc*	LT CDR(FTC)	E	ME	22.11.95	MOD (BATH)
Stephenson, Edward Kenneth	LT(FTC)	S	(W)	17.09.82	AFPAA(CENTURION)
Stephenson, Frederick, *BSc, CEng, MIMechE*	LT CDR(FTC)	E	AE	16.05.80	ES AIR WYTON
Stephenson, Geoffrey Thomas	LT CDR(FTC)	X	P	01.03.87	DHFS
Stephenson, Keith James MacFarlane, *BA*	LT(CC)	E	TM	01.05.94	2SL/CNH FOTR
Stephenson, Philip George	LT(FTC)	S	(S)	23.07.98	RALEIGH
Sterry, Jasen	SLT(IC)	X		19.09.98	EXCELLENT
Stevens, Anthony, BA	LT(IC)	E		04.12.97	RALEIGH
Stevens, Andrew Mark Robert	LT(CC)	X	MCD	01.10.97	INVINCIBLE
Stevens, Robert Patrick, *CB, pce, pce(sm)*	RADM	-	SM(N)	04.08.98	FOSM NWOOD HQ
Stevenson, Aubrey, *AMIMarE*	LT(FTC)	E	ME	23.02.90	FOSF
Stevenson, Charles Bernard Hilton, *BSc, psc*	CAPT(FTC)	X	METOC	31.12.95	MOD (LONDON)
Stevenson, Julian Patrick	LT(CC)	E	MESM	01.11.93	JSCSC
Stevenson, Robert MacKinnon, *BDS, MSc, MGDS RCS*	SGCDR(D)	-		31.12.90	DDA PORTSMOUTH
Stevenson, Simon Richard	SLT(IC)	X		01.01.99	DARTMOUTH BRNC
Stewart, Annabel Barbara, *BSc*	LT(FTC)	X		01.02.95	NELSON
Stewart, Andrew Carnegie, *pce*	CDR(FTC)	X	PWO(C)	30.06.00	MOD (LONDON)
Stewart, Alastair Malcolm, *MSc, BEng, MIMechE*	LT CDR(FTC)	E	MESM	01.11.98	VIGILANT(STBD)
Stewart, Charles Edward, *QHC, BSc, BD, PhD*	DGNCS SF	SF		29.02.76	2SL/CNH
Stewart, Charles Hardie	SLT(IC)	X		19.09.98	RNAS CULDROSE
Stewart, David James, *OBE, MC, BSc, MA, psc*	LT COL(FTC)	RM	C	30.06.95	MOD (LONDON)
Stewart, James, *psc*	LT COL(FTC)	RM	SO(LE)	01.10.97	RMR SCOTLAND
Stewart, James Neil, *BSc, psc(j)*	LT CDR(FTC)	E	TMSM	01.09.93	DARTMOUTH BRNC
Stewart, Kenneth Currie, *BSc*	LT CDR(FTC)	E	TM	01.09.98	CSST SHORE FSLN
Stewart, Michael David, *MB, ChB, MRCP*	SURG LTCDR	-	(M) UT	03.08.93	NELSON (PAY)
Stewart, Peter Charles, *BEng, MSc, CEng, MIMechE*	LT CDR(FTC)	E	MESM	01.02.97	SPLENDID
Stewart, Robert Gordon, *BSc, psc*	CDR(FTC)	X	H CH	30.06.97	MOD (LONDON)
Stewart, Robert Murray, *BSc ARRC*	MAJ(FTC)	RM		01.03.89	HQ
Stewart, Rory William, *BSc*	LT CDR(FTC)	E	MESM	01.07.91	MOD (BATH)
Stickland, Charles Richard, *BSc*	MAJ(FTC)	RM	LC	30.04.98	RMCS SHRIVENHAM
Stidston, Ian James, *BSc*	LT CDR(FTC)	E	TM	01.09.91	COLLINGWOOD
Stiles, Faye Elizabeth, *BEng*	LT(IC)	E		01.05.98	SULTAN
Stillwell, Andrew James, *BEd, adp*	LT CDR(FTC)	E	IS	01.09.87	SHAPE BELGIUM
Stillwell-Cox, Andrew David Robert, *MHCIMA, MCFA*	LT(FTC)	S	CA	17.12.93	ILLUSTRIOUS
Stilwell, James Michael, *BA, LLB*	LT(IC)	X	SM	01.01.98	RALEIGH
Stinton, Carol Ann	LT CDR	Q	OTSPEC	01.10.99	RH HASLAR
Stirzaker, Mark, *BSc*	LT CDR(FTC)	E	MESM	01.11.96	SOVEREIGN
Stiven, Timothy David, *BSc*	LT(FTC)	E	ME	01.03.96	SULTAN
Stobie, Ian Charles Angus, *MBE*	LT CDR(FTC)	S		28.07.88	SAUDI AFPS SAUDI
Stobie, Paul Lionel	LT(FTC)	E	AE(L)	16.10.92	JSCSC
Stock, Christopher Mark	LT(CC)	X	O	01.05.93	700M MERLIN IFTU
Stockbridge, Antony Julian, *MA*	LT(CC)	S		01.03.97	VICTORIOUS(STBD)
Stocker, Nicholas John, *BSc*	CAPT RM(IC)	RM		01.09.94	HQ 3 CDO BDE RM
Stockings, Timothy Mark, *BSc, pce, pcea*	CDR(FTC)	X	P	30.06.00	MONMOUTH
Stockman, Colin David, *BA, pce, pce(sm), psc*	CDR(FTC)	X	SM	31.12.90	CAPTAIN SM2
Stockton, James Philip, *psc*	CDR(FTC)	X	SM	01.10.98	MOD (LONDON)
Stockton, Kevin Geoffrey	LT(FTC)	X	MCD	19.11.92	DRYAD
Stoffell, David Peter	LT CDR(FTC)	S	SM	27.11.98	CUMBERLAND
Stokes, Alan William	LT CDR(FTC)	E	WESM	01.10.98	DRAKE CFM
Stokes, Richard, *BSc, CEng, MDA, MIEE*	CDR(FTC)	E	WESM	31.12.98	NEPTUNE SM1
Stone, Colin Robert Macleod, *pce*	LT CDR(FTC)	X	PWO(U)	01.05.85	ELANT/NAVNORTH
Stone, Nicholas Joseph John, *BA*	SLT(IC)	S		01.01.98	ILLUSTRIOUS
Stone, Paul Christopher Julian, *BSc, tp*	LT CDR(FTC)	X	P	01.10.98	LOAN DERA BSC DN
Stone, Richard James	LT(FTC)	E	ME	19.06.98	SULTAN
Stoneman, Timothy John, *BSc, MA, pce, psc*	CDR(FTC)	X	PWO(A)	31.12.91	MWC SOUTHWICK
Stonier, Paul Leslie	LT RM(FTC)	RM	SO(LE)	01.01.98	40 CDO RM

Name	Rank	Branch	Spec	Seniority	Where Serving
Stonor, Philip Francis Andrew, *pce, pcea, odc(Fr)*	CDR(FTC)	X	P	31.12.95	IMS BRUSSELS
Storey, Ceri Leigh, *BEng*	LT(FTC)	E	MESM	01.08.95	VICTORIOUS(STBD)
Storrs-Fox, Roderick Noble, *BSc*	CDR(FTC)	S		31.12.95	RNAS YEOVILTON
Stott, John Antony	LT CDR(FTC)	E	WESM	26.05.91	ASTUTE IPT
Stovin-Bradford, Matthew	MAJ(FTC)	RM	C	01.09.99	HQ 3 CDO BDE RM
Stowe, Elisabeth Jane, *BA*	LT(FTC)	S		01.08.97	ILLUSTRIOUS
Stowell, Perry Ivan Mottram, *n*	LT CDR(FTC)	X	PWO(U)	01.04.98	DRYAD
Stowell, Robin Barnaby Mottram, *BEng*	LT(FTC)	E	ME	01.09.95	ILLUSTRIOUS
Strain, Justin Damian Russell, *BA*	LT(FTC)	X		01.05.98	NEWCASTLE
Strange, Steven Paul, *BEng*	LT(CC)	E	WESM	01.09.97	VICTORIOUS(STBD)
Stratford, Peter John	LT(CC)	X	ATCU/T	01.04.95	RNAS CULDROSE
Strathern, Roderick James	LT CDR(FTC)	X	PWO(U)	01.10.98	EDINBURGH
Strathie, Gavin Scott	LT(CC)	X	ATC	01.06.96	RNAS YEOVILTON
Stratton, John Denniss, *BSc, psc*	CDR(FTC)	E	AE(P)	30.06.93	MOD DHSA
Stratton, Matthew Paul	LT(CC)	E	WE	01.06.99	DARTMOUTH BRNC
Stratton, Nicholas Charles	SLT(CC)	X	SM	01.10.97	TIRELESS
Stratton, Stuart John	SLT(IC)	E	MESM	01.05.98	DARTMOUTH BRNC
Straughan, Christopher John, *MBE, pce*	LT CDR(FTC)	X	PWO(U)	01.12.90	FOST SEA
Straughan, Harry, *BSc, psc*	CDR(FTC)	E	TM	31.12.97	DITMTC SHRIVNHAM
Straughan, Kerry Elizabeth	LT CDR(CC)	W	C		2SL/CNH
Straughan, Scott, *BEng*	LT(CC)	X	P	01.05.97	RNAS CULDROSE
Straw, Andrew Nicholas	LT CDR(FTC)	S		16.03.96	2SL/CNH
Street, James John, *BA*	CAPT RM(IC)	RM		01.09.99	42 CDO RM
Streeten, Christopher Mark, *BSc*	LT CDR(FTC)	E	WESM	01.06.95	FOSM NWOOD HQ
Streets, Christopher George, *MB, BSc, BCh*	SURG LTCDR	-		01.08.98	NELSON (PAY)
Stretton, Darrell George	LT(FTC)	X	AV	03.04.97	DARTMOUTH BRNC
Strick, Charles Gordon, *BSc, MDA*	LT CDR(FTC)	E	WESM	01.02.93	MOD (LONDON)
Stride, James Alan, *BSc*	LT(FTC)	X	H2	01.02.96	CAPT F4 (SEA)
Stride, Jamieson Colin	LT(FTC)	X	O	01.04.95	815 FLT 214
Stringer, Graeme Ellis	SLT(FTC)	X	ATC	19.09.97	RNAS YEOVILTON
Stringer, Karl David Paul	LT(IC)	X	P	16.03.97	845 SQN
Stringer, Michael Charles, *MILDM*	CDR(FTC)	S		31.12.89	2SL/CNH FOTR
Stringer, Roger Andrew, *pcea*	LT CDR(FTC)	X	P	01.10.97	819 SQN
Stroude, Paul Addison, *BEng*	LT(FTC)	X		01.08.96	SUTHERLAND
Strudwick, Russell	LT(FTC)	S	(W)	24.07.97	FEARLESS
Strutt, Jason Fearnley, *BEng, MSc*	LT(FTC)	E	WE	01.05.92	COLLINGWOOD
Stuart, Charles William McDonald	LT CDR(FTC)	S		01.03.83	CFLT COMMAND SEC
Stuart, Euan Edward Andrew, *BA, MEng*	LT(FTC)	X	FC	01.10.96	INVINCIBLE
Stubbings, Paul Richard	CDR(FTC)	E	MESM	31.12.99	SULTAN
Stubbs, Gary Andrew	LT(CC)	X	P	16.09.94	848 SQN HERON
Stubbs, Ian	LT(CC)	X	O	16.05.95	819 SQN
Stubbs, Martin Andrew	LT(FTC)	E	WESM	22.02.96	SCU LEYDENE ACNS
Stuchbury, Robert John, *BEng*	LT(IC)	X	SM	01.10.97	VIGILANT(PORT)
Studley, Steven Alan	LT(CC)	X	MCD	01.10.97	EXCHANGE FRANCE
Sturdy, Clive Charles Markus	LT(FTC)	X	MCD	14.06.96	PENZANCE
Sturman, Matthew, *OBE, MPhil, CDipAF, psc(m), osc*	COL(FTC)	RM		31.12.94	NMA PORTSMOUTH
Sturman, Richard William, *BSc*	SLT(CC)	X	P U/T	01.01.98	RNAS YEOVILTON
Stuttard, Mark Christopher, *pce*	LT CDR(FTC)	X	PWO(A)	01.07.94	CUMBERLAND
Stuttard, Stephen Eric	LT CDR(FTC)	X	AV	01.10.97	MOD (LONDON)
Style, Charles Rodney, *MA, rcds, pce, hcsc*	CAPT(FTC)	X	PWO(U)	30.06.93	ILLUSTRIOUS
Suckling, Paul Morris, *BSc, CEng, MIMarE*	LT CDR(FTC)	E	MESM	01.10.94	VIGILANT(PORT)
Suckling, Robin Leslie, *pcea*	LT(FTC)	X	O	16.08.90	RNAS CULDROSE
Suddes, Lesley Ann, *BA*	LT CDR(FTC)	X	METOC	01.10.92	MOD (LONDON)
Suddes, Thomas	LT CDR(FTC)	X	AV	01.10.94	CAMBRIA
Sudding, Catherine Duncan, *BA*	LT(IC)	X		01.08.99	DRYAD
Sugden, Michael Rodney, *BSc, MBA*	LT CDR(FTC)	E	ME	01.10.94	MOD (BATH)
Sugden, Stephen Robert, *HNC*	LT CDR(FTC)	E	WE	01.10.99	SSA/CWTA PORTS
Suggett, Peter Roger	LT(FTC)	X	SM	20.09.99	PJHQ
Sullivan, Anne Gillian, *BSc*	CDR(FTC)	X	METOC	31.12.99	JSCSC
Sullivan, Colin, *BA, psc*	CDR(FTC)	X	METOC	31.12.96	CINCFLEET
Sullivan, Mark, *BEng*	LT(FTC)	E	WE	01.07.93	SOUTHAMPTON
Sullivan, Mark Nigel, *BEng*	LT(CC)	E	ME	01.12.97	MONMOUTH
Sullivan, Timothy, *BA(OU), DEH, MIOSH*	SLT(IC)	MS		29.04.98	CINCFLEET

Name	Rank	Branch	Spec	Seniority	Where Serving
Summerfield, David Edward , *osc(us)*	LT COL(FTC)	RM		30.06.00	RM Poole
Summers, Alastair John	SLT(CC)	X	P U/T	01.04.98	RAF CRANWELL EFS
Summers, James Alexander Edward , *BEd*	LT(CC)	E	TM	24.05.90	CTCRM
Summerton, Duncan John , *MB, BSc, ChB, FRCS, FRCSEd*	SURG LTCDR	-	(U) UT	01.08.93	NELSON (PAY)
Sumner, Denise June	SLT(FTC)	S	(S)	01.04.98	FONA
Sumner, Michael Dennis	LT CDR(FTC)	E	WESM	01.10.94	NEPTUNE SM1
Sunderland, John Dominic , *MSc, CEng, MIEE*	CDR(FTC)	E	WESM	31.12.97	MOD (LONDON)
Sutcliffe, Edward Diccon , *BA*	LT(IC)	S		01.05.98	RALEIGH
Sutcliffe, John , *pce, pcea*	LT CDR(FTC)	X	O	21.12.94	DRYAD
Sutcliffe, Mark Richard , *n*	LT(FTC)	X		01.03.97	DRYAD
Sutcliffe, Roy William	LT(FTC)	E	WESM	15.06.90	VENGEANCE(PORT)
Suter, Francis Thomas	SLT(IC)	X		01.01.99	DARTMOUTH BRNC
Sutherland, Gayl	SLT	Q		25.10.96	MODHU DERRIFORD
Sutherland, Neil	CAPT RM(FTC)	RM	C	24.04.96	EXCHANGE ARMY UK
Sutherland, William Murray , *MA, PGCE*	CDR(FTC)	E	TM	30.06.93	MOD (LONDON)
Sutton, David	LT RM(IC)	RM	P U/T	01.04.98	DHFS
Sutton, Gary Brian , *pce*	CDR(FTC)	X	PWO(N)	30.06.98	MCM2 SEA
Sutton, Gareth David , *BSc, CEng, MIMarE*	LT CDR(FTC)	E	ME	01.06.93	MOD (BATH)
Sutton, Richard Michael John	LT(CC)	X	P	01.06.93	846 SQN
Sutton, Robert William	LT CDR(FTC)	X	AV	01.10.95	FONA COLLINGWOOD
Sutton, Stephen John	CAPT RM(IC)	RM	P	29.04.97	846 SQN
Sutton-Scott-Tucker, Jonathan James , *BSc*	LT CDR(FTC)	S		01.03.96	NBC PORTSMOUTH
Swain, Andrew Vincent	LT CDR(FTC)	X	H1	05.03.97	CDRE MFP
Swain, David Michael , *BSc, MNI, pce, pcea*	CDR(FTC)	X	O	31.12.91	PJHQ
Swain, Timothy Guy , *BA, BEng*	LT CDR(FTC)	E	AE(O)	01.02.00	RNAS CULDROSE
Swainson, David John , *CEng, FIMechE*	CDR(FTC)	E	MESM	31.12.91	MOD (BATH)
Swan, Peter William Hewett , *pce (COMMODORE)*	CAPT(FTC)	X	AWO(C)	30.06.93	MOD (LONDON)
Swan, Wendy	LT(CC)	W		09.07.95	DRYAD
Swann, John Ivan	LT(FTC)	X	EW	28.07.89	EXCHANGE USA
Swannick, Derek John , *BSc*	LT CDR(FTC)	X	METOC	01.09.96	COMUKTG/CASWSF
Swarbrick, Richard James , *BA, pcea, psc(j)*	LT CDR(FTC)	X	P	01.12.94	DRYAD
Sweeney, Craig , *BSc*	LT(IC)	X	P U/T	01.08.99	DHFS
Sweeney, Keith Patrick Michael , *BEng*	LT(FTC)	E	ME	01.08.95	DNR PRES TEAMS
Sweeny, Brian Donald , *IEng, AMIMarE*	LT CDR(FTC)	E	HULL	01.10.93	SULTAN
Sweet, Paul , *BSc*	LT(FTC)	X		01.12.94	FOSM NWOOD OPS
Swift, Robin David , *pce*	LT CDR(FTC)	X	PWO(U)	28.08.94	EXCHANGE AUSTLIA
Swigciski, David Phillip , *n*	LT(FTC)	X		01.02.95	DULVERTON
Swigciski, Lucinda Anderson , *BDS*	SG LT(D)	-		21.06.96	NEPTUNE CFS
Swindells, Mark , *BEng*	LT(CC)	X	P U/T	01.12.99	702 SQN HERON
Sykes, Jeremy James William , *MB, ChB, MSc, FRCP, FFOM, MFOM*	SURG CAPT	-	(CO/M)	31.12.98	MOD (LONDON)
Sykes, Malcolm , *BEng, MSc, psc*	LT CDR(FTC)	E	MESM	16.11.92	MOD (BATH)
Sykes, Matthew John	MID(UCE)(FTC)	X		01.09.98	DARTMOUTH BRNC
Sykes, Robert Alan	LT CDR(CC)	X	O	01.10.96	815 SQN HQ
Symington, Zena Marie Alexandrea	LT(IC)	X		01.11.97	CORNWALL
Syrett, Matthew Edward , *BSc, n*	LT(FTC)	X	H2	01.08.95	HERALD
Syvret, Mark Edward Vibert , *BSc*	MAJ(FTC)	RM		01.09.93	COMACCHIO GP RM

T

Name	Rank	Branch	Spec	Seniority	Where Serving
Tabberer, Ian Craig , *BSc*	LT(FTC)	X	SM	01.04.96	FOSM NWOOD HQ
Tabeart, George William	LT CDR(FTC)	X	SM	01.11.97	RN HYDROG SCHL
Tacey, Richard Haydn	LT(CC)	X		01.12.95	ANGLESEY
Tait, Martyn David , *BEng*	LT(CC)	E	MESM	01.01.00	SULTAN
Tait, Stacey Jane , *BSc*	SLT(IC)	X		01.01.99	DARTMOUTH BRNC
Talbot, Christopher Martin	LT CDR(FTC)	X	C	01.10.99	ELANT/NAVNORTH
Talbot, George Keith , *BSc, PGCE, MA(Ed)*, MITD	LT CDR(FTC)	E	TM	01.09.86	COLLINGWOOD
Talbot, Nigel Adrian , *BSc, MEng, PGCE, MA(Ed)*	LT CDR(CC)	E	TM	01.10.93	2SL/CNH FOTR
Talbot, Richard Paul , *pce*	CDR(FTC)	X	PWO(A)	30.06.00	JSCSC
Talbott, Aidan Hugh	LT CDR(FTC)	S		01.12.99	LANCASTER
Tall, David Michael , *OBE, jsdc, pce, pce(sm)*	CAPT(FTC)	X	SM	31.12.94	DRAKE CBP(DLO)
Tamayo, Brando Christian Craig , *MB, ChB, DipIMC RCSEd*	SURG LTCDR	-		01.08.99	RH HASLAR
Tamlyn, Stephen	2LT(GRAD)(IC)	RM		28.04.99	CTCRM LYMPSTONE
Tanner, Michael John *(Act Maj)*	CAPT RM(FTC)	RM		01.09.96	BDS WASHINGTON

Name	Rank	Branch	Spec	Seniority	Where Serving
Tanner, Richard Carlisle	LT(FTC)	X	SM	01.03.95	SPLENDID
Tanser, Susan Jane, *MB, BS*	SURG LTCDR	-		01.08.96	MODHU DERRIFORD
Tapp, Steven John *(Act Capt Rm)*	LT RM(FTC)	RM	SO(LE)	01.01.98	CHFHQ
Tappin, Simon John, *BEng*	SLT(IC)	X		01.01.99	DARTMOUTH BRNC
Tapping, Kenneth, *MSc*	LT CDR(FTC)	E	AE(M)	01.10.97	ES AIR BRISTOL
Tarr, Barry Stuart, *BEng, CEng, MIMarE*	LT CDR(FTC)	E	MESM	01.07.92	MOD (BATH)
Tarr, Michael Douglas, *BSc, pce, psc(a)*	CDR(FTC)	X	PWO(A)	30.06.93	COMATG SEA
Tarr, Richard Nicholas Vaughan, *BSc*	LT CDR(FTC)	E	MESM	01.08.93	VICTORIOUS(PORT)
Tarrant, David Charles, *pce*	LT CDR(FTC)	X	PWO(C)	01.08.93	COLLINGWOOD
Tarrant, Robert Kenneth, *pce, pce(sm)*	CDR(FTC)	X	SM	30.06.97	FOSM NWOOD HQ
Tasker, Greg, *psc(m)*	LT COL(FTC)	RM		31.12.95	DISC
Tate, Andrew John, *BSc, AMIEE, psc*	CDR(FTC)	E	WESM	31.12.92	MOD (LONDON)
Tate, Graeme	LT(CC)	X	P	01.02.95	849 SQN A FLT
Tate, Simon John, *BSc*	CDR(FTC)	E	AE	31.12.99	ES AIR YEO
Tatham, Peter Hugh, *BSc, CEng, FCIS, MBCS, MILog*	CAPT(FTC)	S		31.12.96	FOSF
Tatham, Stephen Alan, *BSc*	LT CDR(FTC)	E	TM	01.09.99	ILLUSTRIOUS
Tatlow, Joanne Mary, *BA*	LT(IC)	E	TM	20.09.95	DRYAD
Tattersall, Philip David	LT CDR(FTC)	X	SM	01.07.96	FOSM NWOOD OPS
Tattersall, Richard Brian	LT(FTC)	X	P	01.07.91	899 SQN HERON
Tatton-Brown, Hugh Trelawny	MID(UCE)(IC)	E		01.09.98	YORK
Tawse, Alistair Robert James, *BSc*	SLT(IC)	X	P U/T	01.09.98	DARTMOUTH BRNC
Tayler, James Ralph Newton, *pcea*	LT(FTC)	X	P	01.05.90	700M MERLIN IFTU
Taylor, Anna, *PGDip, HND*	LT(CC)	E	IS	01.09.89	MOD (LONDON)
Taylor, Anthony Frederick Murray, *FBIM, MNI, pce(sm)*	CDR(FTC)	X	SM	31.12.86	RH HASLAR
Taylor, Andrew Ian, *BSc*	SLT(IC)	X		01.09.97	DRYAD
Taylor, Andrew Lyndon, *BA, MSc*	LT(CC)	E	TM	01.05.91	2SL/CNH FOTR
Taylor, Anthony Richard, *SM(n)*	LT CDR(FTC)	X	SM	01.11.98	DRYAD
Taylor, Brian David	LT CDR(FTC)	X		01.07.96	CFPS SEA
Taylor, Christopher David, *BSc, pcea*	LT CDR(FTC)	X	P	01.04.89	LOAN DERA BSC DN
Taylor, Christopher Nigel John	2LT(UCE)(FTC)	RM		04.09.96	CTCRM LYMPSTONE
Taylor, Christopher Paul, *BSc*	LT(IC)	X	O	16.05.98	819 SQN
Taylor, Carl Richard	LT(FTC)	S		25.08.94	DRYAD
Taylor, Christopher Simon, *MA*	LT(IC)	E	TM	01.01.97	SULTAN
Taylor, Gordon David, *BA*	SLT(IC)	X		01.01.99	DARTMOUTH BRNC
Taylor, Hazel Jane	LT(CC)	E	WE	01.03.96	SCU LEYDENE ACNS
Taylor, Ian John, *BEng*	LT(IC)	E	TM	05.05.96	RALEIGH
Taylor, Ian Kennedy	LT(FTC)	S	(S)	16.12.94	HARRIER IPT
Taylor, John Basil, *BA*	LT(IC)	S		01.02.99	801 SQN
Taylor, John Jeremy, *BSc, MSc, CEng, MIMarE*	CDR(FTC)	E	MESM	30.06.96	CSST SEA
Taylor, Jonathan Paul	LT(FTC)	X	SM	24.07.97	VICTORIOUS(STBD)
Taylor, John William, *MIPM*	LT CDR(FTC)	X	ATC	01.09.87	FONA
Taylor, Keith, *BEng*	LT CDR(FTC)	E	WESM	01.10.97	SPLENDID
Taylor, Kenneth Alistair, *BSc, pce, pcea, psc*	CDR(FTC)	X	O	31.12.97	MOD (LONDON)
Taylor, Kenneth John	LT CDR(FTC)	E	WESM	01.10.99	DGSS BRISTOL
Taylor, Keith Milbrun, *BEng*	LT(CC)	E	WE	01.08.98	RICHMOND
Taylor, Leslie, *MBE*	LT CDR(FTC)	X	P	01.10.94	824 NAS
Taylor, Lester Geoffrey	LT CDR(FTC)	X	SM	15.11.92	FOSM NWOOD OPS
Taylor, Lisa	LT	Q		05.07.99	RH HASLAR
Taylor, Mark Andrew	LT CDR(FTC)	X	PWO(C)	01.02.99	COVENTRY
Taylor, Marcus Anthony Beckett	CAPT RM(FTC)	RM	LC	01.09.95	RM WARMINSTER
Taylor, Martin Kenneth, *osc*	LT COL(FTC)	RM	C	30.06.94	MOD (LONDON)
Taylor, Mark Richard	LT(FTC)	X	C	29.07.94	STRS IPT
Taylor, Nigel, *MIOSH*	LT(IC)	MS		06.03.96	HQ 3 CDO BDE RM
Taylor, Nicholas Frederick, *MA, pce*	LT CDR(FTC)	X	PWO(C)	16.02.87	HQ DCSA
Taylor, Neville Graham, *BSc, pce, pce(sm)*	LT CDR(FTC)	X	SM	01.04.89	CALLIOPE
Taylor, Neil Robert, *BEng*	LT(CC)	E	ME	01.06.91	FEARLESS
Taylor, Peter George David, *BSc, mdtc*	MAJ(FTC)	RM		25.04.96	JSCSC
Taylor, Paul James, *BSc, PGCE, adp*	LT CDR(FTC)	E	IS	01.10.92	SACLANT USA
Taylor, Robert, *BEng, MSc, AMIEE*	LT CDR(FTC)	E	WE	01.09.99	IRON DUKE
Taylor, Rodney Hemingfield, *MB, BSc, BS, MBA, MD, LRCP, FRCP, MRCS, MRCP, DPhil, DHMSA*	SURG CAPT	-	CPDATE	30.06.99	RH HASLAR
Taylor, Robert James	LT(CC)	X	O	16.02.94	RNAS YEOVILTON
Taylor, Spencer Alan, *BSc, MSc, CEng, MIEE, AMIEE*	CDR(FTC)	E	IS	09.06.98	MOD (LONDON)

Name	Rank	Branch	Spec	Seniority	Where Serving
Taylor, Stephen Bryan, *CQSW*	LT(FS)	FS		01.05.96	DRAKE CBP(CNH)
Taylor, Stuart David, *BSc*	CAPT RM(CC)	RM		01.09.97	CDO LOG REGT RM
Taylor, Stephen John, *BEng, CEng, MIEE*	LT(CC)	E	WE	02.10.90	SSA/CWTA PORTS
Taylor, Stephen John, *BA (BARRISTER)*	LT CDR(FTC)	S	BAR	16.04.96	NEPTUNE 2SL/CNH
Taylor, Stephen Mark	LT CDR(FTC)	S		01.11.93	RNAS CULDROSE
Taylor, Timothy Jon, *BSc*	LT(FTC)	X	P	14.03.89	899 SQN HERON
Taylor, Terence Peter	SLT(CC)	X	ATCU/T	01.04.98	RNAS CULDROSE
Taylor, William John, *osc*	LT COL(FTC)	RM		31.12.96	42 CDO RM
Tazewell, Matthew Robert, *BEng*	LT(IC)	X	O	01.05.99	815 FLT 217
Teasdale, Derrick, *MBE*	LT CDR(FTC)	E	WESM	01.10.97	SPARTAN
Teasdale, Robert Mark, *BA*	LT CDR(FTC)	S		16.01.93	RNAS CULDROSE
Tebbet, Paul Nicholas	LT CDR(FTC)	X	PWO(U)	01.09.97	FOST SEA
Teer, David Raymond Dennis, *OBE, MIMgt, pce*	CDR(FTC)	X	PWO(A)	30.06.88	2SL/CNH FOTR
Teideman, Ian Charles, *BEng*	LT CDR(FTC)	E	WE	01.03.00	MOD (BATH)
Temple, David Christopher	SLT(FTC)	E	WE	01.04.98	COLLINGWOOD
Templeton, Thomas Appleyard Molison, *IEng, MIEEIE*	LT CDR(FTC)	E	WE	01.10.98	ILLUSTRIOUS
Tennant, Michael Ian, *MB, BS*	SURG LT	-		14.09.95	MODHU DERRIFORD
Tennuci, Robert George	LT CDR(FTC)	X	PWO(A)	01.12.99	NEWCASTLE
Terrill, Keith William, *BA, gdas (Act Cdr)*	LT CDR(FTC)	X	O	01.03.85	LOAN DERA BSC DN
Terry, Judith Helen, *BSc*	LT(IC)	S		01.09.99	NEPTUNE CFS
Terry, John Michael, *BSc, MSc, CEng, MIMarE*	CDR(FTC)	E	ME	31.12.96	MOD (BATH)
Terry, Nigel Patrick	LT(CC)	X	P	01.09.96	DARTMOUTH BRNC
Tetley, Mark	LT(CC)	X	O	01.07.91	820 SQN
Tetlow, Hamish Stuart Guy, *BA, pce(sm)*	LT CDR(FTC)	X	SM	01.07.96	FOSM NWOOD HQ
Tew, John Philip, *MA*	LT CDR(FTC)	S	BAR	16.04.97	FONA
Thain, Julie	LT CDR	Q		31.03.99	RE ENTRY(RN)
Thatcher, Louise Frances Victoria, *BA*	SLT(FTC)	X		01.09.97	DRYAD
Thatcher, Robert Peter, *BSc, CEng, MIEE, psc*	CDR(FTC)	E	WE	30.06.89	NBC PORTSMOUTH
Theakston, Sally	CHAPLAIN	CE		03.06.96	JSU NORTHWOOD
Thicknesse, Philip John, *MA, pce, pcea, psc*	CDR(FTC)	X	P	31.12.96	WESTMINSTER
Thirkettle, Julian Andrew, *BEng*	LT(FTC)	E	AE	01.02.94	LN DERA BEDFORD
Thistlethwaite, Mark Halford, *BSc, psc*	CDR(FTC)	E	AE(O)	31.12.96	DARTMOUTH BRNC
Thoburn, Ross, *OBE, pce*	CDR(FTC)	X	O	30.06.92	JMOTS NORTHWOOD
Thom, Mathew Frank, *BA*	SLT(IC)	X		01.01.99	DARTMOUTH BRNC
Thomas, Andrew Giles, *BSc*	SLT(IC)	X		01.09.98	CORNWALL
Thomas, Ann Louise, *BEng*	LT(CC)	E	TM	01.01.91	INVINCIBLE
Thomas, Daniel Huw	LT(CC)	X	P	01.07.99	702 SQN HERON
Thomas, David Jonathan	LT(FTC)	S	(S)	10.12.98	SHEFFIELD
Thomas, David Lynford, *BDS, MSc, LDS RCS(Eng), MGDS RCS, MGDS RCSEd*	SGCDR(D)	-		30.06.87	SULTAN
Thomas, David William, *BEng*	LT(CC)	X	P	16.12.98	RNAS CULDROSE
Thomas, David William Wallace, *BA*	CHAPLAIN	CE		18.10.88	RM POOLE
Thomas, Francis Stephen	CDR(FTC)	S	(SM)	30.06.99	MOD (BATH)
Thomas, Geoffrey Charles, *OBE, BSc, pce, pce(sm)*	CDR(FTC)	X	SM	30.06.95	RALEIGH
Thomas, Jeffrey Evans	LT CDR(FTC)	X	EW	01.10.98	MOD (LONDON)
Thomas, Jeremy Huw	LT CDR(FTC)	E	WESM	01.02.98	PJHQ
Thomas, Jeremy Hywel, *psc(m), hcsc*	COL(FTC)	RM	WTO	30.06.97	PJHQ
Thomas, Kevin Ian, *BSc*	LT CDR(FTC)	X	METOC	01.10.92	RNSOMO
Thomas, Leslie	LT CDR(FTC)	X	C	01.10.99	STRS IPT
Thomas, Lynn Marie, *MB, BSc, BS*	SURG LTCDR	-		01.08.98	RH HASLAR
Thomas, Mark, *BSc*	LT(IC)	X		01.05.99	PENZANCE
Thomas, Martyn George, *IEng, AMIMarE*	LT(FTC)	E	ME	17.02.89	CFM PORTSMOUTH
Thomas, Matthew Norman, *BSc, BA(OU), MSc*	LT CDR(FTC)	X		01.01.89	2SL/CNH
Thomas, Neal Raymond *(Act Lt Cdr)*	LT(FTC)	X	EW	23.07.93	JSSU DIGBY
Thomas, Neill Wynell, *DSC, nadc, jsdc, pce (COMMODORE)*	CAPT(FTC)	X	P	31.12.92	SHAPE BELGIUM
Thomas, Owen Hopkin, *BSc*	LT(IC)	X		01.01.00	DULVERTON
Thomas, Paul Geraint, *pce*	LT CDR(FTC)	X	PWO(U)	01.11.94	JSCSC
Thomas, Patrick William	MAJ(FTC)	RM	SO(LE)	01.10.96	HQRM
Thomas, Richard Anthony Aubrey, *pce*	LT CDR(FTC)	X	PWO(U)	01.03.98	INVINCIBLE
Thomas, Richard Charles, *MB, BS, FRCA*	SURG LTCDR	-		05.08.97	NELSON (PAY)
Thomas, Richard Kevin, *BSc, pce, ocds(USN)*	LT CDR(FTC)	X	PWO(U)	01.06.96	MIDDLETON
Thomas, Robert Paul, *pce, pcea, psc*	CDR(FTC)	X	O	30.06.95	ELANT/NAVNORTH
Thomas, Simon Alan, *MA, pce, pcea, psc(a)*	CDR(FTC)	X	P	31.12.93	MWC PORTSDOWN
Thomas, Stephen Mark, *BEng*	LT(FTC)	E	ME	01.01.93	FEARLESS

Name	Rank	Branch	Spec	Seniority	Where Serving
Thomas, Stephen Michael	LT(CC)	X	P	16.02.96	819 SQN
Thomas, William Gwynne, *BSc, pce, pcea*	LT CDR(FTC)	X	O	16.06.92	819 SQN
Thompson, Andrew, *BSc*	LT CDR(FTC)	E	AE(M)	06.08.95	JF HARROLE OFF
Thompson, Andrew Joseph, *BSc, BEng*	LT(FTC)	E	AE	01.01.95	824 NAS
Thompson, Andrew Robert	LT(CC)	X	O	01.02.92	815 FLT 200
Thompson, Bernard Dominic, *BA, pce*	LT CDR(FTC)	X	MCD	01.09.94	RICHMOND
Thompson, David Anthony, *BSc*	LT(IC)	X	P U/T	16.08.99	RNAS YEOVILTON
Thompson, David Huw	CAPT RM(FTC)	RM		01.09.99	RM Poole
Thompson, David William, *BEng*	LT(CC)	E	MESM	01.06.97	SOVEREIGN
Thompson, Gary	CDR(FTC)	X	C	30.06.00	DGCIS BRISTOL
Thompson, Graham Michael, *BEM*	CAPT RM(FTC)	RM	SO(LE)	01.01.97	CHFHQ
Thompson, Geoffrey Norman	LT CDR(FTC)	E	WE	25.01.88	OCLC MANCH
Thompson, John Andrew	SLT(TC)	X	ATC	09.01.98	RNAS CULDROSE
Thompson, James Peter Bibby	2LT(GRAD)(IC)	RM		29.04.98	COMACCHIO GP RM
Thompson, Mark George, *SM(n)*	LT(FTC)	X	SM	01.03.95	DRYAD
Thompson, Michael James, *BEng*	LT(FTC)	E	ME	01.01.96	FOST SEA
Thompson, Neil James, *pcea*	LT CDR(FTC)	X	P	01.10.94	845 SQN
Thompson, Paul, *BSc*	2LT(GRAD)(IC)	RM		01.09.99	CTCRM LYMPSTONE
Thompson, Robert Anthony	LT CDR(FTC)	X	O	01.10.98	810 SQN SEAHAWK
Thompson, Richard Charles, *BEng, psc(j)*	LT CDR(FTC)	E	AE	01.02.97	820 SQN
Thompson, Robert Joseph, *BSc, jsdc*	CDR(FTC)	E	ME	30.06.95	INVINCIBLE
Thompson, Stephen John, *BSc, MSc, MCGI*	CDR(FTC)	E	ME	31.12.99	JSCSC
Thompson, William Alistair, *BEng*	SLT(IC)	X	P U/T	01.09.97	RAF CRANWELL EFS
Thomsen, Lavinia Lisa, *BSc*	LT(IC)	X		01.02.97	SOUTHAMPTON
Thomsett, Harry Fergus James, *BA*	CAPT RM(FTC)	RM		01.09.95	CHFHQ
Thomson, Allan Brown, *fsc, osc (Act Col)*	LT COL(FTC)	RM	MLDR	31.12.92	HQRM
Thomson, Colin Douglas, *BSc*	LT(FTC)	X	H2	01.02.93	BEAGLE
Thomson, Duncan, *pce*	LT CDR(FTC)	X	PWO(U)	23.05.95	NMA PORTSMOUTH
Thomson, David Forbes	SLT(FTC)	E	AE(M)	01.04.98	800 SQN
Thomson, Iain Rodger, *BSc*	LT CDR(FTC)	E	WESM	22.05.97	NEPTUNE NT
Thomson, Ian Wallace	SLT(FTC)	E	WESM	01.04.98	RALEIGH
Thomson, James Christopher, *BSc*	LT(CC)	X		01.01.99	BRECON
Thomson, Michael Lee, *BEng*	LT(CC)	E	ME	01.05.99	MARLBOROUGH
Thomson, Paul Damian, *BSc*	LT(IC)	E	TM	24.02.97	SULTAN
Thorburn, Andrew	LT CDR(FTC)	X	AV	01.10.96	RFANSU (ARGUS)
Thornback, John Gordon *(Act Lt Cdr)*	LT(FTC)	E	WE	02.11.84	SAUDI AFPS UK
Thorne, Dain Jason, *BEng*	LT(FTC)	E	AE	01.03.97	ES AIR BRISTOL
Thornewill, Simon Clive, *DSC, MRAeS, tp (COMMODORE)*	CAPT(FTC)	X	P	30.06.91	COMNA
Thornhill, Andrew Philip	CAPT RM(FTC)	BS		01.01.00	BRNC BAND
Thornton, Brian Patrick	LT(FTC)	S	CA	03.04.97	OCEAN
Thornton, Charles Exley, *BA, pcea, gdas*	LT CDR(FTC)	X	O	01.02.84	LOAN DERA BSC DN
Thornton, Michael Crawford, *pce, pcea, psc*	LT CDR(FTC)	X	P	08.02.84	RNAS YEOVILTON
Thornton, Philip John, *pcea*	LT CDR(FTC)	X	P	01.10.93	702 SQN HERON
Thorp, Benjamin Thomas	LT(FTC)	E	ME	01.07.96	SULTAN
Thorp, David Brian, *BEng, AMIEE*	LT(FTC)	E	WE	01.03.98	CHATHAM
Thorpe, Conrad Dermot Biltcliffe, *psc(j)*	MAJ(FTC)	RM		01.09.98	NMA WHALE ISLAND
Thorpe, Christopher Robert, *BSc, psc*	CDR(FTC)	E	WE	31.12.92	DRAKE CBP(DLO)
Thorpe, Ian, *pce, pcea, psc*	CAPT(FTC)	X	P	31.12.94	2SL/CNH
Thrippleton, Mark Graham, *BEng*	LT(FTC)	E	AE	15.08.92	MOD DHSA
Thurstan, Richard William Farnall	MAJ(FTC)	RM	LC	01.05.97	HQ 3 CDO BDE RM
Thwaites, Gerard James, *BSc, CEng, MIMechE, psc*	CAPT(FTC)	E	MESM	31.12.97	FOSM NWOOD HQ
Tibbitt, Ian Peter Gordon, *MA, CEng, MIEE, jsdc*	CAPT(FTC)	E	AE	31.12.97	FONA
Tidball, Ian, *BEng*	LT(CC)	X	P	01.02.92	800 SQN
Tidbury, Neil, *pce(sm) (Act Cdr)*	LT CDR(FTC)	X	SM	05.07.85	FOSM NWOOD HQ
Tighe, Gary, *BA, pcea*	LT CDR(FTC)	X	P	01.02.91	750 SQN (HERON)
Tighe, John Geoffrey Hugh, *OBE, nadc, jsdc, pce*	CAPT(FTC)	X	AWO(A)	31.12.95	MOD (LONDON)
Tighe, Simon	LT(IC)	X	SM	30.03.99	FOSNNI OPS CFS
Tigwell, Nigel Keith, *BSc, CEng, MDA*	CDR(FTC)	E	MESM	31.12.98	CNNRP BRISTOL
Tilden, Philip James Edward	LT(FTC)	X		01.03.97	DRYAD
Tilley, Duncan Scott Jamieson, *pce*	CDR(FTC)	X	HCH	30.06.00	HERALD
Tillion, Andrew Malcolm	LT CDR(CC)	X	P	01.10.98	848 SQN HERON
Tilney, Duncan Edward, *BA*	LT(FTC)	X		01.01.97	BERKELEY
Timbrell, Ian Philip James, *BEng*	SLT(FTC)	E	MESM	01.09.97	SULTAN

Name	Rank	Branch	Spec	Seniority	Where Serving
Timms, Deborah Ann, *BA*	LT(IC)	X		01.05.99	GLASGOW
Timms, Stephen John, *OBE, MBA, MSc, CEng, MIMarE, MIMechE, jsdc*	CAPT(FTC)	E	MESM	31.12.98	RN GIBRALTAR
Tindal, Nicolas Henry Charles, *pce, pcea*	LT CDR(FTC)	X	P	01.02.96	NMA PORTSMOUTH
Tindall-Jones, Lee Douglas, *BSc, MA, CEng, MIEE, psc*	CDR(FTC)	E	WESM	31.12.99	NW IPT
Tindell, Richard William, *BA*	SLT(IC)	X		01.01.99	DARTMOUTH BRNC
Tinsley, Glenn Nigel	CDR(FTC)	S		31.12.96	SULTAN
Titcomb, Andrew Charles, *BEng, MSc*	LT CDR(FTC)	E	WESM	01.06.97	RALEIGH
Titcomb, Mark Richard, *BSc, pce, pce(sm)*	LT CDR(FTC)	X	SM	01.02.98	TRAFALGAR
Titcombe, Adam James, *BA*	LT(IC)	S		01.01.00	TRENCHANT
Tite, Anthony	LT(CC)	X	O	01.02.94	EXCHANGE USA
Titmus, Garry David, *pce, psc*	CDR(FTC)	X	PWO(N)†	30.06.82	LOAN OMAN
Titmuss, Julian Francis, *BA*	LT(FTC)	S		01.12.94	JSU NORTHWOOD
Titterton, Phillip James, *pce, pce(sm)*	CDR(FTC)	X	SM	30.06.99	SCEPTRE
Todd, Clare Francesca Jane, *BSc, PGCE*	LT(IC)	E	TM	01.09.88	RALEIGH
Todd, Donald, *pce*	LT CDR(FTC)	X	AWO(A)	01.01.82	2SL/CNH FOTR
Todd, James William, *BSc*	2LT(GRAD)(IC)	RM		29.04.98	45 CDO RM
Todd, Michael Anthony	CAPT RM(FTC)	RM	SO(LE)	01.01.97	RMR BRISTOL
Todd, Oliver James, *LLB*	2LT(GRAD)(IC)	RM		02.09.98	COMACCHIO GP RM
Toft, Michael David, *BEng*	LT CDR(FTC)	E	WE	01.03.96	DGCIS BRISTOL
Tofts, Christopher, *BEng*	SLT(FTC)	E	AE	01.09.97	SULTAN
Tok, Chantelle Fen Lynne, *BSc*	SLT(IC)	X	ATCU/T	01.05.97	RAF SHAWBURY
Tolley, Dominic Mark	SLT	Q		25.07.96	RH HASLAR
Tolley, Peter Frederick Richmond, *MB, BCh*	SURG CAPT	-	GMPP	31.12.95	NMA PORTSMOUTH
Tomes, Adrian Carl	LT(CC)	X		01.04.00	DEF SCH OF LANG
Tomkins, Alan Brian	LT(FTC)	E	WE	19.02.93	SSA BRISTOL
Tomlin, Peter Dawson, *MBE*	LT CDR(FTC)	X	PT	01.10.98	NELSON
Tomlinson, David Charles	LT(FTC)	X	AV	03.04.97	RFANSU
Tomlinson, James Henry	LT(FTC)	X	PR	27.07.95	RALEIGH
Toms, Robert James, *BSc*	LT CDR(FTC)	X	PWO(U)	16.01.83	CINCFLEET
Toms, Trevor Martyn	LT CDR(FTC)	X	P	01.10.90	810 SQN SEAHAWK
Tong, David Keith, *BA, rcds, psc(m)*	LT COL(FTC)	RM		31.12.90	MOD (LONDON)
Toomey, Nicholas John, *BSc*	LT CDR(FTC)	S	SM	01.11.96	KENT
Toon, John Richard	LT CDR(FTC)	E	AE(M)	01.10.92	ES AIR YEO
Toon, Paul Graham	LT(FTC)	X	AV	26.04.99	RNAS CULDROSE
Toone, Stephen Anthony	SLT(FTC)	E	WE	01.04.98	COLLINGWOOD
Toor, Jeevan Jyoti Singh, *BSc, PGDip*	LT CDR(FTC)	X	METOC	01.09.98	CAPT F6 (SEA)
Toothill, John Samuel, *SM(n)*	LT CDR(FTC)	X	SM	01.04.97	DRYAD
Tooze, Lee	LT(IC)	X	P	01.04.94	771 SK5 SAR
Topping, James Russell	LT(FTC)	E	AE(L)	02.09.99	ES AIR BRISTOL
Torney, Colin James	LT(FTC)	E	MESM	02.09.99	VANGUARD(PORT)
Torvell, Matthew David Bingham, *BSc, psc*	LT CDR(FTC)	E	WE	01.08.89	MOD (BATH)
Tothill, Nicholas Michael	CDR(FTC)	S		30.06.00	RMC OF SCIENCE
Totten, Philip Mark	2LT(GRAD)(IC)	RM		29.04.98	40 CDO RM
Tougher, Raymond	LT CDR(FTC)	E	AE(L)	01.10.93	ES AIR MASU
Towell, Peter James	LT(FTC)	E	ME	01.07.93	SULTAN
Towler, Alison, *BSc*	LT CDR(FTC)	S	BAR	14.12.97	NELSON
Towler, Perrin James Bryher, *BSc, pce*	LT CDR(FTC)	X	PWO(A)	01.06.94	NOTTINGHAM
Towns, Andrew Richard, *BSc*	LT(IC)	X		01.01.99	GLOUCESTER
Townsend, David John, *BEng*	LT(CC)	E	WE	01.03.96	COLLINGWOOD
Townsend, Graham Peter	LT(CC)	X	O	01.05.94	810 SQN SEAHAWK
Townsend, Jonathan James	SLT(IC)	X	P U/T	01.04.98	RNAS YEOVILTON
Townsend, John Robert	CDR(FTC)	E	WE	31.12.88	LOAN HYDROG
Townshend, Jeremy John, *BSc, MBA*	LT CDR(FTC)	E	TMSM	03.04.92	COLLINGWOOD
Toy, Malcolm John, *BEng, MRAeS*	CDR(FTC)	E	AE	30.06.98	ES AIR BRISTOL
Tozer, Colin Vinson	LT CDR(FTC)	X	PWO(A)	01.10.88	FOSF
Tracey, Alan David, *BEng*	LT(CC)	E	AE	01.05.97	SULTAN
Tracey, Wayne Sean, *BSc*	SLT(IC)	X		01.01.99	DARTMOUTH BRNC
Trasler, Mark Farnham *(Act Lt Cdr)*	LT(FTC)	MS	(LT)	03.04.92	MOD (LONDON)
Trathen, Neil Charles, *BSc, pce*	LT CDR(FTC)	X	PWO(N)	01.02.92	FOSF SEA PTSMTH
Treanor, Martin Andrew, *BSc, psc*	CDR(FTC)	E	AE	31.12.99	RMCS SHRIVENHAM
Tredray, Thomas Patrick, *BA*	LT(FTC)	X		01.02.93	DRYAD
Treffry-Kingdom, Michael, *BA*	2LT(GRAD)(IC)	RM		01.09.99	CTCRM LYMPSTONE
Tregaskis, Nicola Suzanne, *BA*	LT(FTC)	X		01.11.95	DRYAD

Name	Rank	Branch	Spec	Seniority	Where Serving
Tregunna, Gary Andrew	LT(FTC)	X	SM	08.08.95	RNU ST MAWGAN
Treharne, Mark Adrian, *BEng*	SLT(CC)	E	ME	01.09.97	539 ASLT SQN RM
Tremelling, Paul Nicholas, *BEng*	LT(CC)	X	P	01.07.98	FONA VALLEY
Trevithick, Andrew Richard, *BSc, MA*	CDR(FTC)	X	METOC	31.12.93	CINCFLEET
Trevor, Mark Gerard, *pce, psc(j)*	CDR(FTC)	X	PWO(C)	31.12.98	SOUTHAMPTON
Trewhella, Graham Gilbey, *BSc, psc*	LT CDR(FTC)	E	TM	01.05.91	2SL/CNH FOTR
Tribe, Jeremy David, *BSc*	LT(FTC)	X	P	16.10.87	815 FLT 204
Trinder, Stephen John	LT(FTC)	S	CA	30.01.96	DRAKE DPL
Tritschler, Edwin Lionel, *BEng, BTech, psc(j)*	LT CDR(FTC)	E	AE	01.10.98	801 SQN
Trott, Craig Michael James, *BEng*	LT(CC)	X	P	01.02.93	EXCH ARMY SC(G)
Trott, Edward Alan, *BEng*	LT(FTC)	E	AE	01.12.94	CV(F) IPT
Trott, Peter Alan, *BSc, MSc, AMIEE*	LT CDR(FTC)	E	WE	19.05.83	MOD (BATH)
Trotter, Steven, *BSc, MSc, CEng, MIMarE*	LT CDR(FTC)	E	ME	01.12.87	DRAKE CFM
Trueman, Brian David	SLT(CC)	E	AE	01.04.98	DARTMOUTH BRNC
Trump, Nigel William	LT CDR(FTC)	S		16.01.98	MOD (LONDON)
Trundle, David Jonathan William	LT CDR(FTC)	S	SM	01.01.95	FOSNNI/NBC CLYDE
Trundle, Nicholas Reginald Edward, *pce, pcea, psc(j)*	CDR(FTC)	X	O	31.12.98	RMCS SHRIVENHAM
Tucker, Kevin Michael	LT(CC)	S		01.08.91	MWC SOUTHWICK
Tucker, Robin Simon	LT(FTC)	S	CA	17.12.93	NELSON
Tudor-Thomas, Richard James, *BSc*	LT(CC)	X		01.03.98	BROCKLESBY
Tuffley, Christopher Robin, *LVO, pce, osc*	CAPT(FTC)	X	P	30.06.91	TEMERAIRE
Tulley, James Robert, *BSc*	CDR(FTC)	S		31.12.99	2SL/CNH
Tulloch, Frederik Martin, *BSc*	LT CDR(FTC)	E	WE	01.04.93	SSA BRISTOL
Tulloch, Stuart William	CAPT RM(FTC)	RM	SO(LE)	01.01.97	CTCRM
Tumelty, Gerwyn Charles, *BEng, MSc*	LT(CC)	E	ME	01.11.97	CORNWALL
Tunnicliffe, Peter Alan, *BEng, PhD*	LT CDR(FTC)	X	METOC	01.03.87	RNAS CULDROSE
Tupman, Keith Campbell	MAJ(FTC)	RM	SO(LE)	01.10.99	HQ 3 CDO BDE RM
Tuppen, Russell Mark, *pce, pcea, psc*	CDR(FTC)	X	O	31.12.99	BICESTER
Tupper, Robert William	LT CDR(FTC)	S	SM	01.10.98	CSSG (SEA)
Turle, Paul James, *IEng, AMIMechE*	LT(FTC)	E	ME	13.06.97	DEF DIVING SCHL
Turnbull, Graham David	LT CDR(FTC)	X	HCH	01.04.94	ROEBUCK
Turnbull, Nicholas Robin, *BSc, BDS, FDS RCSEdin*	SGLTCDR(D)	-		02.01.97	DDA TE
Turnbull, Paul Sands, *MB, BS, AFOM*	SURG LTCDR	-	GMPP	01.08.92	NEPTUNE CFS
Turnbull, Simon Jonathan Lawson, *MNI, pce, psc(j)*	LT CDR(FTC)	X	PWO(U)	01.01.94	CARDIFF
Turner, Allan James	SLT(FTC)	E	ME	01.04.98	FEARLESS
Turner, Antony Richard, *BA*	2LT(GRAD)(FTC)	RM		02.09.98	42 CDO RM
Turner, David, *pce*	LT CDR(FTC)	X	MCD	03.06.91	NORTH DIVING GRP
Turner, Derek Bayard, *BSc, ARICS, pce*	LT CDR(FTC)	X	HCH	01.04.95	BEAGLE
Turner, David James, *LLB*	SLT(FTC)	S		01.01.98	GLOUCESTER
Turner, David Neil	LT(CC)	X	P	01.06.95	RNAS YEOVILTON
Turner, Geoffrey Keith	LT CDR(RETL	E	WE	17.11.89	CNSA BRISTOL
Turner, Henry Charles James, *BSc*	2LT(GRAD)(IC)	RM		02.09.98	COMACCHIO GP RM
Turner, Ian, *BSc, psc*	CDR(FTC)	X	HCH	31.12.91	MOD (LONDON)
Turner, Jonathan Anthony Edward, *BEng*	LT CDR(FTC)	E	WE	01.08.96	YORK
Turner, Jonathan Stephen, *BA*	SLT(CC)	X	O U/T	01.01.98	DARTMOUTH BRNC
Turner, Joseph Seymour Hume, *MA*	LT CDR(FTC)	S	BAR	01.04.99	NORFOLK
Turner, Kerry Ann, *BEng, PGDip*	LT(CC)	X	METOC	01.09.90	RNSOMO
Turner, Roger Bentley, *BSc, CEng, FIMarE*	CAPT(FTC)	E	MESM	30.06.95	SA BRAZIL
Turner, Robert Francis, *BSc*	LT(FTC)	S	(W)	11.12.92	DRAKE DPL
Turner, Simon Alexander, *BSc*	CAPT RM(FTC)	RM		01.09.96	42 CDO RM
Turner, Stephen Edward, *pce*	CDR(FTC)	X	PWO(U)	31.12.93	FCS IPT
Turner, Shaun Mark, *jsdc, pce, pce(sm)*	CDR(FTC)	X	SM	30.06.90	DRAKE DPL
Turton, Trevor Martyn Howard, *MBE, MA, psc(m)*	LT CDR(FTC)	S		16.11.79	MOD (LONDON)
Tutchings, Andrew	SLT(FTC)	X	PT	01.04.98	RNAS YEOVILTON
Tweed, Christopher James, *BSc*	LT CDR(FTC)	E	WE	01.02.89	2SL/CNH
Twigg, Katherine Louise, *MSc*	LT(IC)	X		01.04.99	BULLDOG
Twigg, Neil Robert, *BEng*	SLT(IC)	X	P U/T	01.09.98	DARTMOUTH BRNC
Twine, John Harold, *BA*	LT CDR(FTC)	E	TM	01.01.99	NELSON RNSETT
Twist, David Charles	LT CDR(FTC)	S	(W)	01.10.99	CINCFLEET
Twist, Martin Thomas, *BSc*	CAPT RM(FTC)	RM		01.09.95	JSCSC
Twitchen, Richard Christopher, *pce, psc, psc(m)*	CAPT(FTC)	X	PWO(A)	30.06.99	LIVERPOOL
Tyack, Terence James	LT CDR(FTC)	X	P	01.10.98	EXCHANGE AUSTLIA
Tyce, David John	CAPT RM(FTC)	RM	SO(LE)	01.01.96	CTCRM

Name	Rank	Branch	Spec	Seniority	Where Serving
Tyler, Jeremy Charles	LT(FTC)	X	FC	01.07.96	EXCHANGE FRANCE
Tyler, Peter Leslie	LT CDR(FTC)	S		10.07.93	SCU LEYDENE ACNS
Tyrrell, Patrick John , *OBE, LLB, GradInstPS, MIMgt, rcds, jsdc (COMMODORE)*	CAPT(FTC)	E	IS	31.12.92	HQ DCSA
Tyrrell, Richard Kim	MAJ(FTC)	RM	LC	01.09.86	DRAKE CBP(DLO)

U

Name	Rank	Branch	Spec	Seniority	Where Serving
Ubhi, Wayne Gurdial	LT(FTC)	E	ME	01.06.96	SULTAN
Udensi, Ernest Andrew Anene Anderson , *BEng, MSc, CEng, MIEE*	LT CDR(FTC)	E	WE	01.09.93	EXCHANGE USA
Underwood, Andrew Gavin Howard , *BSc, FNI, MNI, MIMgt, pce, pcea*	CDR(FTC)	X	O	31.12.91	AGRIPPA AFSOUTH
Underwood, Nicholas John , *BSc, psc(a)*	MAJ(FTC)	RM		01.09.88	CTCRM
Underwood, Paul John	CAPT RM(FTC)	RM	SO(LE)	01.01.95	RM Poole
Upright, Stephen William , *BSc, pce, pce(sm)*	CDR(FTC)	X	SM	30.06.93	VENGEANCE(PORT)
Upton, Iain David , *BSc, CEng, MIEE*	LT CDR(FTC)	E	WE	01.02.93	2SL/CNH FOTR
Urry, Simon Richard , *BSc*	CAPT RM(IC)	RM		01.09.98	COMACCHIO GP RM
Urwin, Stuart James , *BA*	SLT(IC)	X		01.01.98	CROMER
Usborne, Andre Christopher , *BSc, FIMgt, psc*	CDR(FTC)	E	WE	31.12.92	NMA PORTSMOUTH
Usborne, Christopher Martin , *BSc, CEng, MIEE*	CDR(FTC)	E	WE	30.06.94	SSA BRISTOL
Utley, Michael Keith , *n*	LT(FTC)	X	PWO(A)	01.05.93	NORFOLK

V

Name	Rank	Branch	Spec	Seniority	Where Serving
Vale, Andrew	SURG SLT	-		30.04.99	DARTMOUTH BRNC
Vallance, Michael Stefan , *BSc*	LT(IC)	X	P	16.08.98	845 SQN
Vamplew, David	LT CDR(FTC)	E	AE(L)	01.10.91	SULTAN
Van Beek, Dirk , *BSc, CEng, MIEE, psc*	CDR(FTC)	E	WE	30.06.96	MOD (LONDON)
Van Beek, Luke , *BSc, MBA, psc, psc(m)*	CAPT(FTC)	E	WE	31.12.98	FAAIT MAN ORG VL
van der Horst, Richard Evert , *BSc, psc(j)*	MAJ(FTC)	RM		01.09.95	MOD (LONDON)
Van Duin, Martin Ivar Alexander , *BSc*	SLT(IC)	X		01.01.99	DARTMOUTH BRNC
Van-Den-Bergh, William Lionel	LT CDR(FTC)	X	FC	01.10.96	RNAS YEOVILTON
Van-Nijkerk, Eleanor Beth , *BA, BSc*	LT(CC)	X		01.01.00	FEARLESS
Vanderpump, David John , *BEng, psc(j)*	CDR(FTC)	E	ME	30.06.00	T45 IPT
Vandome, Andrew Michael , *BSc, AMIEE, psc(j)*	CDR(FTC)	E	WE	30.06.99	LN DERA MALVERN
Varley, Ian Guy , *BEng, pcea*	LT(FTC)	X	P	01.01.93	849 SQN A FLT
Varley, Peter George Sidney , *BSc*	SLT(IC)	X		01.01.98	INVERNESS
Vartan, Mark Richard , *BSc*	LT(CC)	X	HM	01.10.94	DRYAD
Varty, Jason Alan , *BSc*	LT(CC)	X		01.10.98	HURWORTH
Vaughan, David Michael , *BA, MSc, MNI, pce, pce(sm)*	CDR(FTC)	X	SM	31.12.90	CAPT PORT CLYDE
Veal, Alan Edward , *BEng*	LT(FTC)	E	WE	01.08.95	MONTROSE
Veal, Dominic Joseph	SLT(IC)	X		01.01.99	DARTMOUTH BRNC
Venables, Adrian Nicholas	LT CDR(FTC)	X	PWO(C)	01.12.97	DRYAD
Ventura, Don Clark	LT CDR(FTC)	X	H CH	01.01.94	LOAN HYDROG
Verney, Kirsty Hilary , *BSc, BDS*	SG LT(D)	-		09.07.97	NELSON
Verney, Peter Scott	LT CDR(FTC)	X	PWO(A)	01.08.99	CHATHAM
Vickers, Carl Geoffrey	LT(FTC)	E	WESM	02.09.99	VICTORIOUS(PORT)
Vickers, John , *BEng, MSc*	LT CDR(FTC)	E	AE	01.11.98	EXCHANGE USA
Vickery, Ben Robert , *BA*	SLT(IC)	X		01.05.98	CORNWALL
Vickery, Kay Elisabeth	SLT(IC)	X		01.05.97	COVENTRY
Vickery, Robert James	LT(FTC)	E	AE(M)	02.09.99	HQ3GP HQSTC
Vickery, Timothy Kenneth , *BSc*	LT CDR(FTC)	X	PWO(U)	01.11.95	LN DERA CDA HLS
Vincent, Adrian , *BEng, MPhil, CEng, MIMechE,*	LT(CC)	E	TM	01.09.90	SULTAN *MRAeS*
Vincent, Daniel , *BSc, PhD*	LT(IC)	E	TM	01.09.95	SULTAN
Vincent, Peter Hedley	MID(UCE)(FTC)	X		01.09.98	DARTMOUTH BRNC
Viner, Timothy Robin , *BSc*	CAPT RM(IC)	RM		01.05.97	CTCRM
Viney, Peter	SLT(IC)	S	(W)	29.04.98	FOSM NWOOD HQ
Vink, James Dingeman	LT(FTC)	X		20.03.93	FOSF
Vitali, Robert Charles , *pce*	LT CDR(FTC)	X	PWO(A)	01.08.97	CARDIFF
Vogel, Lanning David	LT(FTC)	S	SM	01.06.97	VENGEANCE(PORT)
Vollentine, Lucy	LT(FTC)	S		01.04.98	CAPTAIN SM2
Von Hoven, Anthony Christopher , *BA, pcea*	LT(CC)	X	P	01.08.85	DHFS
Vorley, Simon William , *BSc*	LT(CC)	X	P	15.06.96	702 SQN HERON
Vosper, Iain Attrill , *BA, psc(m), MPhil*	CDR(FTC)	S		30.06.85	SA RIYADH
Vowles, Mitchell John	LT(FTC)	X	PR	24.07.97	OCEAN

Name	Rank	Branch	Spec	Seniority	Where Serving
Vowles, Timothy John	LT(CC)	S		01.09.92	MAS BRUSSELS
Voyce, John Edington, *BEng*	LT(FTC)	E	ME	01.09.94	MOD (BATH)

W

Name	Rank	Branch	Spec	Seniority	Where Serving
Waddington, Andrew Kennneth	LT CDR(FTC)	X	H1	01.12.95	WALNEY
Waddington, John, *BSc*	LT CDR(FTC)	E	WESM	01.05.94	DSWS BRISTOL
Wade, Andrew	SLT(IC)	MS		19.09.98	CDO LOG REGT RM
Wade, Claire Victoria	SG SLT(D)	-		01.04.98	DARTMOUTH BRNC
Wade, Jonathan Mark Robertson, *BA*	LT(IC)	X	P	01.05.99	BFFI
Wade, Nicholas Charles, *BSc*	LT CDR(FTC)	X	PWO(C)	01.01.90	2SL/CNH FOTR
Wadge, Guy, *BSc*	SLT(IC)	E		01.01.97	DARTMOUTH BRNC
Wadham, John, *psc*	CDR(FTC)	E	ME	30.06.92	SULTAN
Wadsworth, Richard York, *BEng*	LT(CC)	E	ME	01.04.99	SULTAN
Wagstaff, Neil	LT(FTC)	MS	(LT)	10.04.95	CINCFLEET
Wain, Robin Nicholas, *jsdc, pcea, psc, ocds(Can), psc(j) psc(j)*	CDR(FTC)	X	O	31.12.95	NMA PORTSMOUTH
Wainhouse, Michael James, *pce*	LT CDR(FTC)	X	PWO(A)	01.07.97	NMA PORTSMOUTH
Wainwright, Barnaby George, *BA, MNI, pce, pcea*	LT CDR(FTC)	X	P	01.09.89	815 SQN OEU
Wainwright, Paul Albert	LT CDR(FTC)	X	PWO(A)	16.03.85	DRYAD
Waite, Christopher William, *pce, psc, psc(m) (COMMODORE)*	CAPT(FTC)	X	P	30.06.95	RNAS CULDROSE
Waite, Jeremy Nicholas *(Com 2lt)*	SLT(IC)	X		01.05.97	NEPTUNE
Waite, Tobias George, *BSc*	SLT(IC)	X		01.05.98	NEWCASTLE
Wakefield, Gary Malcolm, *pcea, psc(j)*	LT CDR(FTC)	X	P	01.03.93	HQ DCSA
Wakeford, Ian Frederick, *MEng*	LT(FTC)	X	FC	01.02.98	LIVERPOOL
Wakeling, Jonathan Lee, *MA*	CDR(FTC)	E	TM	31.12.94	NMA PORTSMOUTH
Wakely, Stephen Argent, *MC*	MAJ(FTC)	RM	SO(LE)	01.10.94	RM Poole
Wales, Benjamin David, *BSc*	LT(FTC)	S		01.03.95	NELSON
Walker, Alasdair James, *MB, ChB, FRCSEd*	SURG CDR	-	(CGS)	30.06.91	MODHU DERRIFORD
Walker, Andrew John, *BA*	CAPT RM(FTC)	RM		28.04.95	CTCRM
Walker, Clive Leslie *(Act Cdr)*	LT CDR(FTC)	S		16.10.93	HQRM
Walker, Carl Stephen, *psc*	CDR(FTC)	S		30.06.95	RALEIGH
Walker, Donald William Alexander, *BA*	LT(FTC)	S		01.05.94	MOD (LONDON)
Walker, Ellis George	LT(FTC)	X	REG	17.12.93	JSCSC
Walker, George	LT(FTC)	E	WE	02.09.99	COLLINGWOOD
Walker, Gavin Stewart Logan	MAJ(FTC)	RM		01.09.90	MOD (LONDON)
Walker, James John	*MID*(UCE)(CC)	X		01.09.98	DARTMOUTH BRNC
Walker, Louise Linda, *MB, BS*	SURG LTCDR	-		01.08.99	NELSON (PAY)
Walker, Martin, *BEng, MSc*	CDR(FTC)	E	WE	30.06.00	JSCSC
Walker, Mark Christopher, *pcea*	LT CDR(FTC)	X	P	01.10.94	846 SQN
Walker, Mark Justin, *BEng*	LT(CC)	E	TM	01.01.91	RM POOLE
Walker, Michael John	LT(FTC)	X	g	04.04.96	SHETLAND
Walker, Nigel Albert	LT(FTC)	S	CA	27.07.90	RALEIGH
Walker, Nicholas John, *BSc, MSc*	CDR(FTC)	E	MESM	30.06.00	JSCSC
Walker, Nicholas Lee, *pce*	LT CDR(FTC)	X	PWO(U)	01.02.93	LOAN DERA ADAC
Walker, Nicholas MacLaren, *BSc*	LT CDR(FTC)	X	P	01.01.00	801 SQN
Walker, Nicholas Michael Cleveland	SLT(CC)	X	P U/T	01.04.00	RAF CRANWELL EFS
Walker, Patrick John, *FIMgt, MNI, pce, pce(sm)*	CAPT(FTC)	X	SM	31.12.93	NEPTUNE SM1
Walker, Peter Richard, *BSc, MBA*	LT CDR(FTC)	E	TM	01.05.96	CTCRM
Walker, Robbie Andrew, *BEng, MSc, CEng, MIEE*	LT(IC)	E	TM	01.09.90	SULTAN
Walker, Robert Dixon	LT CDR(FTC)	E	WESM	01.10.97	TRAFALGAR
Walker, Richard Eden, *MA, psc*	LT COL(FTC)	RM	C	31.12.97	40 CDO RM
Walker, Robin Stuart	SLT(FTC)	X		19.09.97	MONTROSE
Walker, Stephen Paul	LT(FTC)	X	SM	09.03.94	TIRELESS
Wall, Steven Nicholas, *BSc*	LT(CC)	X		01.02.99	RAMSEY
Wallace, Allan, *BSc, pce*	LT CDR(FTC)	X	PWO(N)	01.12.95	DRYAD
Wallace, Anthony Robert, *BEng*	SLT(IC)	X		01.01.99	DARTMOUTH BRNC
Wallace, David James, *BSc*	LT CDR(CC)	E	TM	01.10.98	40 CDO RM
Wallace, George William Alexander, *AFC, BSc, pce, pcea, ocds(Can), osc*	CDR(FTC)	X	P	30.06.94	ILLUSTRIOUS
Wallace, Kirsty Gayle, *MA*	SLT(IC)	S		01.09.98	DARTMOUTH BRNC
Wallace, Kenneth Neil, *BDS*	SGLTCDR(D)	-		31.01.98	NEPTUNE CFS
Wallace, Michael Rupert Barry, *BA, jsdc, pce*	CDR(FTC)	X	PWO(U)	30.06.95	SUTHERLAND
Wallace, Richard Stuart	2LT(IC)	RM		29.04.98	45 CDO RM
Wallace, Stewart Andrew, *BSc*	LT(FTC)	X	ATC	01.12.97	RNAS CULDROSE

Name	Rank	Branch	Spec	Seniority	Where Serving
Wallace, Simon Jonathan	LT(FTC)	X	FC	01.03.94	JSCSC
Wallace, Scott Peter, *BSc*	2LT(GRAD)(IC)	RM		01.09.99	CTCRM LYMPSTONE
Waller, Steven Adrian	LT CDR(FTC)	X	SM	01.03.99	SCEPTRE
Walliker, Michael John Delane, *pce, pce(sm)*	CDR(FTC)	X	SM	31.12.99	DRYAD
Wallis, Adrian John, *pce, pcea*	LT CDR(FTC)	X	O	16.04.96	JDCC
Wallis, Jonathan Spencer	LT(CC)	X	P	01.08.92	846 SQN
Wallis, Lee Allan, *MB, ChB, DipIMC RCSED, FRCS(Ed)*	SURG LTCDR	-		01.08.99	MODHU DERRIFORD
Walls, Kevin Finlay	CAPT RM(FTC)	RM	MLDR	26.04.94	CTCRM
Walmsley, Elizabeth Ann	LT CDR(FTC)	S		08.02.96	2SL/CNH
Walpole, Peter Kenneth, *BSc, pce*	CAPT(FTC)	X	PWO(C)	31.12.98	MOD (LONDON)
Walsh, Andrew Harwood, *BEng*	LT(IC)	E		01.12.98	SULTAN
Walsh, Andrew James, *BSc*	LT(IC)	X		01.05.98	MIDDLETON
Walsh, Andrew Stephen James	LT CDR(FTC)	X	P	01.10.96	899 SQN HERON
Walsh, Dennis Gerard	LT(FTC)	E	AE(L)	07.09.95	LOAN DERA BSC DN
Walsh, Damian Martin, *BSc*	LT(IC)	E	TM	12.01.97	SULTAN
Walsh, Jane Sabina	LT(CC)	W		11.12.92	RALEIGH
Walsh, Kevin Michael, *BSc*	LT(FTC)	X		01.11.96	WESTMINSTER
Walsh, Mark Anthony	LT(FTC)	S	CA	01.07.92	NORTHUMBERLAND
Walsh, Sean Christopher	LT(CC)	X	ATC	01.11.91	ILLUSTRIOUS
Walters, Jonathan, *BSc, gdas*	LT CDR(CC)	X	O	01.10.96	LOAN DERA BSC DN
Walters, Richard John, *BEng, n*	LT(FTC)	X	PWO(U)	01.02.93	EXETER
Walton, Anthony Frederick, *BSc, psc*	CDR(FTC)	E	ME	30.06.91	EXCELLENT
Walton, Andrew Paul	LT(FTC)	MS	(AD)	04.04.96	INM ALVERSTOKE
Walton, Colin Peter, *BEng*	LT(FTC)	E	WE	01.09.92	COLLINGWOOD
Walton, Christopher Paul, *BEng, CEng, MIMarE*	LT(FTC)	E	MESM	01.04.93	DRAKE CBS
Walton, David	LT CDR(FTC)	X	PWO(U)	01.09.84	DRYAD
Walton, Jonathan Charles, *BSc, MSc, mdtc*	LT CDR(FTC)	E	WE	01.12.90	LN DERA PRTSDWN
Walton, Stephen David	LT(FTC)	X		01.04.97	LANCASTER
Walton, Stephen Paul	LT(FTC)	E	AE(L)	14.10.94	ES AIR BRISTOL
Walton, Simon Phillip	LT(FTC)	X	MW	01.10.97	BROCKLESBY
Wappner, Gary Dean, *BA*	LT(IC)	X	P	01.01.99	RNAS CULDROSE
Ward, Andrew James	LT(FTC)	X	MCD	01.06.95	DARTMOUTH BRNC
Ward, Andrew James, *BSc*	2LT(GRAD)(IC)	RM		02.09.98	COMACCHIO GP RM
Ward, Colin David	CAPT RM(FTC)	RM	SO(LE)	01.01.98	HQ 3 CDO BDE RM
Ward, Douglas John, *BSc*	LT(FTC)	S		01.11.98	ROSYTH SOSM(R)
Ward, David Steven	LT CDR(FTC)	X	PT	01.10.97	DRAKE CBP(DLO)
Ward, Emma Jane	SLT(IC)	X	O U/T	01.04.98	750 SQN OBS SCH
Ward, Francis Stanley *(Act Cdr)*	LT CDR(FTC)	X	PWO(U)	01.03.85	SAUDI AFPS UK
Ward, John Emlyn, *pce, pcea*	CDR(FTC)	X	O	31.12.94	RNAS CULDROSE
Ward, Joanne Erien, *BSc*	LT(IC)	X		01.08.98	MANCHESTER
Ward, Jason George	MAJ(FTC)	RM		01.05.99	HQRM
Ward, Kristian	LT(IC)	X	P	13.02.98	FONA
Ward, Michelle Therese, *MA*	LT(IC)	X		01.04.99	CAMPBELTOWN
Ward, Nigel Anthony, *IEng, MIEEIE*	LT(FTC)	E	WE	02.09.99	GLOUCESTER
Ward, Nicholas John	CDR(FTC)	X	PWO(A)	01.10.94	CINCFLEET
Ward, Rees Graham John, *MA, MSc, CEng, FIEE, rcds, jsdc, gw, hcsc*	RADM	-	WE	27.04.99	MOD (LONDON)
Ward, Simon	LT(FTC)	X	P	01.09.97	847 SQN
Ward, Stephen David, *BEng*	LT CDR(FTC)	E	ME	01.01.98	NORTHUMBERLAND
Ward, Simon Ira, *pce*	LT CDR(FTC)	X	PWO(A)	01.10.98	CARDIFF
Ward, Timothy John, *BEng, MIMarE*	LT CDR(FTC)	E	MESM	11.01.99	DARTMOUTH BRNC
Warde, Nicholas Andrew	SLT(CC)	X	O U/T	01.04.98	RNAS CULDROSE
Warden, John Mitchell, *BA, BSc, MSc, CEng, MinstP, C PHYS*	LT CDR(FTC)	E	TMSM	01.09.92	RALEIGH
Wardle, Mark	LT(FTC)	X	C	17.12.93	HQ DCSA
Ware, Samuel Arthur	LT(CC)	X	P	01.01.95	NEPTUNE CFS
Wareham, Michael Paul, *BEng, MSc*	CDR(FTC)	E	MESM	31.12.99	MOD (BATH)
Waring, John Robert, *BSc, PhD*	LT CDR(FTC)	E	TM	01.04.99	CFPS SHORE
Warlow, Mark Richard Norman	LT CDR(FTC)	X	MCD	01.05.93	DEF DIVING SCHL
Warn, Christopher John	LT CDR(FTC)	X	SM	01.07.98	RALEIGH
Warne, Emma Jane, *BSc*	LT(FTC)	E	ME	01.07.97	NEPTUNE NT
Warneken, Andrew Ellery, *BEng*	LT(FTC)	E	MESM	01.10.94	VICTORIOUS(PORT)
Warneken, Alison Jane, *BDS*	SGLTCDR(D)	-		09.01.99	NEPTUNE CFS
Warnett, Derek Louis, *BSc, MSc, CEng, MIEE, MIMarE, jsdc (COMMODORE)*	CAPT(FTC)	E	MESM	30.06.94	NP BRISTOL
Warnock, Gavin, *BSc*	LT CDR(CC)	X	P	01.10.95	824 NAS

Name	Rank			Date	Unit
Warr, Richard Frank	LT(FTC)	E	WESM	19.02.93	SSA BRISTOL
Warren, Brian Howard, *BSc, pce*	CDR(FTC)	X	PWO(U)	30.06.96	FOST MPV(SEA)
Warren, Martin Kenneth, *MSc, MIMarE, adp, HND*	LT CDR(CC)	E	IS	01.01.96	DITMTC SHRIVNHAM
Warren, Thomas Stephen Evrall, *DEH*	MAJ(FTC)	RM	SO(LE)	01.10.95	HQRM
Warrender, William Jonathan	LT CDR(FTC)	X	FC	01.11.99	DRYAD
Warrington, Paul Thomas, *BEng*	LT CDR(FTC)	E	MESM	01.01.99	VANGUARD(PORT)
Warwick, Philip David, *pce*	LT CDR(FTC)	X	PWO(U)	01.04.96	COMUKTG/CASWSF
Washer, Nicholas Barry John, *BSc*	LT CDR(FTC)	X	PWO(C)	01.01.00	ILLUSTRIOUS
Wass, Martin James, *BSc*	LT CDR(FTC)	X	PWO(A)	01.08.90	SSA/CWTA PORTS
Waterer, Richard Alan, *OBE, MMus, LRAM, pdm*	LT COL(FTC)	BS		29.07.94	HQ BAND SERVICE
Waterfield, Simon Jon	LT(FTC)	X		01.06.94	DULVERTON
Waterhouse, Phillip	LT(FTC)	S		01.04.93	COMATG SEA
Waterman, David Leslie	LT(FTC)	E	ME	10.06.94	SULTAN
Waterman, John Henry, *BSc, MA, CEng, MIMarE, psc*	CDR(FTC)	E	ME	31.12.97	NMA PORTSMOUTH
Waters, Christopher David, *BSc, CEng, MIEE, MIMgt, nadc*	CDR(FTC)	E	WESM	31.12.87	MOD (LONDON)
Waters, Nigel Roger, *BSc*	LT CDR(FTC)	S	SM	16.04.96	MOD (BATH)
Waterworth, Stephen Norman, *BEng*	LT(IC)	E	WE	01.04.93	MOD (LONDON)
Waterworth, Terence Jack	LT(CS)	-		05.09.93	DNR YORKSHIRE
Watkins, Andrew Patrick Leonard, *BSc*	CAPT RM(FTC)	RM		01.05.97	NP 1061
Watkins, Colin Francis Frederick, *pce, psc*	CDR(FTC)	X	O	31.12.89	SEA CADET CORPS
Watkins, Kevin John, *BEng*	LT(CC)	E	ME	01.02.98	FEARLESS
Watkins, Timothy Crispin, *BSc*	LT(CC)	X	P	16.09.89	COMATG SEA
Watson, Andrew Herbert, *BEng*	LT(CC)	X	O	01.06.95	814 SQN
Watson, Anthony Peter	LT(FTC)	E	MESM	02.09.99	SULTAN
Watson, Bradley Lawrence, *BSc*	SLT(IC)	X	O U/T	01.05.98	RNAS CULDROSE
Watson, Brian Robert	LT RM(IC)	RM		24.01.00	847 SQN
Watson, Christopher Charles, *BA, pce*	LT CDR(FTC)	X	PWO(A)	16.05.86	*BDS* WASHINGTON
Watson, Clive Raymond, *BTech*	LT(FTC)	E	WE	24.02.95	SSA ROSYTH
Watson, Charles Robert	LT(FTC)	E	WE	22.02.96	FOREST MOOR
Watson, David Robert, *BSc, MSc, CEng, MIEE*	LT CDR(FTC)	E	WESM	01.12.89	MOD (LONDON)
Watson, Ian, *n*	LT(FTC)	X		01.03.95	MANCHESTER
Watson, Malcolm	LT CDR(FTC)	E	AE(M)	01.10.91	FONA
Watson, Philip Frank, BA(Hons), BSc, LRAM, ARCM	CAPT RM(FTC)	BS		01.01.95	JSCSC
Watson, Peter Gerald Charles, *BEng, CEng, MIMarE*	LT CDR(FTC)	E	MESM	25.10.96	SULTAN
Watson, Patrick Halfdan, *pce, psc*	CAPT(FTC)	X	PWO	30.06.96	AGRIPPA NAVSOUTH
Watson, Richard Ian	CAPT RM(FTC)	RM	SO(LE)	01.01.98	RM Poole
Watson, Richard John, *MSc*	LT CDR(FTC)	X	SM	01.08.89	MOD DIS SEA
Watson, Stuart Benedict Cooper	LT(FTC)	S	SM	23.07.98	VIGILANT(STBD)
Watt, Anthony James Landon	LT CDR(FTC)	X	PWO(U)	01.11.99	SUTHERLAND
Watt, Stuart, *pce (Act Cdr)*	LT CDR(FTC)	X	PWO(A)	29.09.88	NP 1002 DIEGOGA
Watts, Alun David	LT CDR(FTC)	S	SM	01.01.94	DRYAD
Watts, Alexandra Jane, *BA*	LT(IC)	S		01.11.94	2SL/CNH
Watts, Andrew Peter, *pcea*	LT CDR(FTC)	X	O	01.10.93	ILLUSTRIOUS
Watts, David John	LT CDR(FTC)	S	SM	01.10.97	DDA HALTON
Watts, Graham Michael, *BSc, CEng, FIMarE, psc*	CDR(FTC)	E	ME	31.12.95	NMA GOSPORT
Watts, Jason Neil, *BSc*	LT(CC)	X	P	01.02.96	820 SQN
Watts, Matthew Alan, *BSc, MSc*	SLT(IC)	X		01.09.97	DRYAD
Watts, Margaret Dora	LT CDR	Q	CC	01.10.99	RH HASLAR
Watts, Robert	LT(FTC)	X	SM	01.07.93	VIGILANT(PORT)
Watts, Richard Dennis, *psc(m)*	LT COL(FTC)	RM		31.12.99	MOD (LONDON)
Watts, Raymond Frederick, *BSc, psc (Act Capt)*	CDR(FTC)	E	WE	31.12.92	SSA BRISTOL
Watts, Sandra Fay	LT(CC)	W	S	01.12.95	NELSON
Watts, Zoe Abigail, *BSc*	LT(CC)	X		01.01.99	CAMPBELTOWN
Waugh, Peter John, *MB, BCh, MA, DipAvMed, LRCP, LRCS, AFOM, MFOM*	SURG CDR	-	(CO/M)	30.06.90	FONA SULTAN
Weale, John Stuart, *pce(sm)*	CDR(FTC)	X	SM	30.06.99	TRAFALGAR
Weall, Elizabeth Mary, *ARRC*	CDR	Q	OTSPEC	31.12.99	RH HASLAR
Weare, Jonathan Bran, *BA, MSc*	SLT(FTC)	S		01.05.97	RALEIGH
Wearmouth, Paul William Anthony, *IEng*	CDR(FTC)	E	WE	01.10.95	DCSA RADIO HQ
Weaver, Neil	LT(FTC)	E	MESM	13.06.97	FOSM NWOOD HQ
Weaver, Simon	LT(CC)	X	H2	01.10.99	BEAGLE
Webb, Andrew James, *BSc, pce*	LT CDR(FTC)	X	PWO(C)	01.05.95	DRYAD
Webb, Christopher McDonald, *pcea*	LT CDR(FTC)	X	O	01.10.96	814 SQN
Webb, Daniel, *BEng*	SLT(IC)	E	ME	01.01.99	DARTMOUTH BRNC

Name	Rank	Branch	Spec	Seniority	Where Serving
Webb, Matthew David	LT(FTC)	X		01.06.97	MARLBOROUGH
Webb, Martin Robert, *BSc*	SLT(IC)	X		01.09.98	DARTMOUTH BRNC
Webber, Christopher John, *BEng, FRMS*	LT CDR(FTC)	X	METOC	26.08.97	FOSF
Webber, Joanne Patricia, *BA*	LT(CC)	X	O	01.09.94	819 SQN
Webber, Kerry Jane	LT(CC)	X		01.11.96	JSCSC
Webber, Richard James, *MB, BS*	SURG LT	-		01.02.96	NELSON (PAY)
Webber, Shaun Anthony	MAJ(FTC)	RM	PT	01.09.96	JSCSC
Webber, Steven John Anthony Maltravers, *MA, FCIS, FCMA (Act Cdr)*	LT CDR(FTC)	S	CMA	01.02.94	MOD (LONDON)
Webster, Andrew Philip, *BA*	LT(CC)	X		01.11.94	ENDURANCE
Webster, Graham, *pce(sm)*	CDR(FTC)	X	SM	31.12.89	JHQ NORTHEAST
Webster, Richard John, *BA*	LT(FTC)	S		01.12.97	JMOTS NORTHWOOD
Webster, Richard James, *BSc*	LT(IC)	X		01.12.98	EXETER
Webster, Timothy John Cook, *psc(m)*	LT COL(FTC)	RM	C	30.06.00	HQRM
Weedon, Grant Antony	MID(UCE)(FTC)	E	ME	01.09.98	DARTMOUTH BRNC
Weedon, Kevin Donald	LT CDR(FTC)	E	ME	19.06.94	FOSF
Weeks, Deborah Clare, *BEd*	LT(IC)	S		01.03.99	CSST SHORE FSLN
Weightman, Nicholas Ellison	LT(FTC)	X	P	16.02.94	800 SQN
Weil, Daniel Gerard	MID(UCE)(IC)	E		01.09.99	LANCASTER
Weir, Scott Duncan	LT CDR(FTC)	E	WESM	01.10.99	CSST RNSSS
Welborn, Colin George, *pce, psc(m)*	CDR(FTC)	X	PWO(A)	31.12.92	HQRM
Welburn, Ross Coates	LT(FTC)	X	EW	04.04.96	JSSU OAKLEY
Welburn, Roy Stuart, *BSc*	LT CDR(FTC)	E	AE	01.03.91	ES AIR BRISTOL
Welch, Andrew, *MBE*	LT CDR(FTC)	X	O	13.10.95	815 FLT 226
Welch, Alan *(Act Lt)*	SLT(FTC)	MS	(AD)	20.09.96	DEF MED TRG CTR
Welch, Andrew Timothy, *FNI, pce (Act Capt)*	CDR(FTC)	X	AWO(A)	31.12.88	SA ISLAMABAD
Welch, David Alexander	LT(FTC)	X	MCD	05.07.94	LEDBURY
Welch, Jonathan, *BSc, jsdc, pce*	CAPT(FTC)	X	PWO(U)	31.12.95	JMOTS NORTHWOOD
Welch, James, *MB, BMS, ChB*	SURG LT	-		05.08.98	CFLT MED(SEA)
Welch, Katherine Alice	LT(CC)	S		01.07.97	SULTAN AIB
Welford, Robert Clive, *BEng*	LT CDR(FTC)	X	PWO(C)	01.02.99	STANAVFORLANT
Wellesley, Richard Charles Robert, *pce, pcea*	CDR(FTC)	X	O	31.12.94	ARGYLL
Wellington, Stuart, *BEng, HNC*	LT CDR(FTC)	E	WE	01.02.98	LANCASTER
Wells, Barry Charles	LT(FTC)	E	WESM	18.02.94	FOSM NWOOD HQ
Wells, Barrie Ivor	LT(FTC)	X	C	03.06.98	COLLINGWOOD
Wells, David Andrew Hester, *pcea*	LT CDR(FTC)	X	O	29.11.86	AGRIPPA NAVSOUTH
Wells, David George	LT CDR(FTC)	X		01.10.98	CAMBRIDGE
Wells, Jamie Duncan, *BSc*	SLT(IC)	X		01.09.98	SHEFFIELD
Wells, Justin Harrington	SLT(IC)	X	P U/T	01.04.98	RAF CRANWELL EFS
Wells, Michael Peter, *BSc, PGCE*	LT(FTC)	S		01.03.97	EDINBURGH
Wells, Simon Peter	SLT(FTC)	S	(W)	01.04.98	CFPS SHORE
Welsh, Richard Michael Karl	SLT(CC)	E	AE	01.05.98	DARTMOUTH BRNC
Welton, William Brodie Dexter	LT CDR(FTC)	X	PWO(C)	01.09.94	LPD(R) IPT
Wenger, Nicholas Andrew, *BDS*	SG LT(D)	-		23.07.96	RH HASLAR
West, Anthony Bernard	LT(FTC)	X	REG	29.07.94	COLLINGWOOD
West, Andrew William	LT(FTC)	S	(W)	11.12.92	NMA GOSPORT
West, *Sir* Alan (William John), *KCB, DSC, rcds, pce, psc, hcsc*	VADM	-	AWO(A)	23.10.97	MOD (LONDON)
West, Darren Colin, *BSc*	LT(CC)	X	MCD	01.12.95	CATTISTOCK
West, Graham George, *BEng, CEng, MIMarE*	LT CDR(FTC)	E	ME	06.06.99	DRAKE CFM
West, Michael Wallace, *pce*	LT CDR(FTC)	X	PWO(A)	05.08.92	FOSF SEA PTSMTH
West, Nicholas Kingsley, *BA*	SLT(IC)	S		01.01.98	RALEIGH
West, Philip James, *BA*	LT(CC)	X	O	16.05.93	750 SQN OBS SCH
West, Ronald James, *BA(OU), MInsD*	LT CDR(FTC)	X	C	01.10.87	LN DERA CDA HLS
West, Rory Julian, *BSc*	LT(FTC)	X	O	01.06.94	814 SQN
Westbrook, Jonathan Simon, *MBE, pce(sm), pce*	CDR(FTC)	X	SM	30.06.95	MOD (LONDON)
Westermann, Richard	SURG SLT	-		22.06.99	DARTMOUTH BRNC
Western, William John Harry, *BTech, CEng, MIMechE, psc*	CDR(FTC)	E	AE(O)	30.06.89	AIS(SW)
Westlake, Simon Richard	CAPT RM(FTC)	RM	SO(LE)	01.01.00	42 CDO RM
Westley, David Richard	LT(CC)	X	P	16.08.91	847 SQN
Westoby, Richard Malcolm	MAJ(FTC)	RM	LC	01.09.90	EXCHANGE AUSTLIA
Weston, Karl Nicholas Neville, *BEng*	LT(IC)	X	O U/T	01.12.99	702 SQN HERON
Weston, Mark William, *BDS, MSc, DGDP RCS(UK) (Act Sgcapt(D))*	SGCDR(D)	-		31.12.88	DDA PLYMOUTH
Weston, Paul Andrew, *pdm*	CAPT RM(FTC)	BS		01.01.99	CTCRM BAND
Westwood, Mark Robin Timothy, *BEng, MSc, CEng, MIMarE, MIMechE,*	LT CDR(FTC)	E	MESM	01.07.94	VANGUARD(PORT)

Name	Rank	Branch	Spec	Seniority	Where Serving
MCGI, psc(j), Eur Ing					
Westwood, Martin William *,pce,pcea,psc*	CDR(FTC)	X	P	30.06.95	JSCSC
Westwood, Stephen Philip Charles *,BSc, CEng, MIMarE, MCGI*	CAPT(FTC)	E	ME	31.12.96	DRAKE CBP(CNH)
Whale, Victoria Alice	SLT(IC)	S		01.04.99	RALEIGH
Whalley, Kathryn Jane *,BSc, PGDip*	LT(CC)	X	METOC	21.10.92	CINCFLEET
Whalley, Richard James	LT(FTC)	S		01.04.93	FONA
Whalley, Simon David *,psc*	CDR(FTC)	S	SM	31.12.94	PJHQ
Wharrie, Craig George *,BEng*	SLT(CC)	E	ME	01.01.98	CORNWALL
Wharrie, Ewan Killen Balnave *,BSc*	LT(CC)	E	TMSM	01.09.92	OCLC ROSYTH
Whatling, Kevin Micheal	SLT(FTC)	X	REG	09.01.98	WALNEY
Whatmough, David Edward *,CEng, MIMechE, jsdc*	CAPT(FTC)	E	ME	30.06.96	2SL/CNH
Wheadon, Philip Charles *,BEng, HNC*	LT(IC)	E	TM	01.03.96	SULTAN
Wheal, Adrian Justin *,BEng*	LT(FTC)	E	MESM	01.09.92	RM Poole
Wheatley, Ian	CHAPLAIN	CE		08.04.97	OCEAN
Wheatley, Wendy Joy *,BA, PGDip*	LT CDR(FTC)	X	METOC	04.10.97	RNSOMO
Wheaton, Bowden James Stewart	LT CDR(CC)	X	O	01.10.98	750 SQN OBS SCH
Wheeldon, Thomas Bertram	LT(FTC)	E	ME(L)	15.02.91	DGSS BARROW
Wheeler, Nicholas Jules *,SM(n)*	LT(FTC)	X	SM	01.10.95	VICTORIOUS(PORT)
Whetter, Richard Scott *,BSc*	SLT(IC)	X		01.09.98	DARTMOUTH BRNC
Whetton, Julia Barbara Dawn	LT CDR(FTC)	W	S	01.10.96	JSCSC
Whild, Aaron Alexander	LT(FTC)	E	WESM	01.02.90	FOSM GOSPORT
Whild, Douglas James	LT(FTC)	X	PR	24.07.97	CINCFLEET
Whitaker, Hugh Rudkin *,jsdc*	CAPT(FTC)	S		31.12.95	NMA PORTSMOUTH
Whitaker, Michael John *,BSc, CEng, MIMechE, MDA*	CDR(FTC)	E	AE	30.06.97	ILLUSTRIOUS
White, Andrew Raymond *,BSc, CEng, MIEE*	CDR(FTC)	E	WESM	31.12.94	MOD (LONDON)
White, David John *,BSc*	LT(IC)	X	P	01.03.98	819 SQN
White, David Simon Haydon *,OBE, FRIN, MNI, jsdc, pce(sm)*	CAPT(FTC)	X	SMTAS	31.12.97	RCDS
White, Graham John *,BEng*	LT(IC)	E	TM	01.08.96	42 CDO RM
White, Haydn John	MAJ(FTC)	RM	LC	01.05.97	BDS WASHINGTON
White, Ian Frank	LT(FTC)	X	SM	01.03.94	SPLENDID
White, Jonathan Andrew Paul *,pce(sm)*	LT CDR(FTC)	X	SM	01.11.97	LINDISFARNE
White, Jonathan Eric *,BSc*	LT(FTC)	S		01.11.94	GANNET
White, Jason Paul	SLT(CC)	X		01.05.98	WESTMINSTER
White, Kevin Frederick *,BEng*	LT(CC)	E	ME	01.07.97	CARDIFF
White, Melvyn Andrew *,MBE, BEM*	CDR(FTC)	MS	(RGN)	31.12.99	DEF MED TRG CTR
White, Martin Eugene	CDR(FTC)	X	ATC	01.10.98	FONA
White, Mark William *,BSc, MA, pce, psc*	CDR(FTC)	X	PWO(U)	31.12.98	COMSTRIKFORSTH
White, Peter *(Act Cdr)*	LT CDR(FTC)	X	PWO(A)	01.02.87	SEA CADET CORPS
White, Philip Alan *,MSc, CEng, FIMarE*	LT CDR(FTC)	E	MESM	16.02.92	NEPTUNE DSQ
White, Robert Fredrick	LT CDR(FTC)	E	WE	01.10.97	FOSF
White, Robert Leonard	LT(FTC)	E	AE(L)	14.10.94	815 SQN OEU
White, Simon Henry Wilmot *,BA*	LT(CC)	X	P	16.06.93	849 SQN HQ
White, Stephen James	SLT(FTC)	X	C	09.01.98	ARGYLL
White, Sarah Michelle *,n*	LT(IC)	X		01.02.98	CORNWALL
White, Stephen Noel *,BA*	CDR(FTC)	S		31.12.97	OCEAN
White, Stephen Paul *,IEng, MIEEIE (Act Lt Cdr)*	LT(FTC)	E	WESM	10.06.88	JSSU OAKLEY
Whitehall, Sally *,BSc*	SLT(IC)	X		01.09.97	DRYAD
Whitehead, Darryl *,pcea*	LT CDR(FTC)	X	P	01.10.92	771 SK5 SAR
Whitehead, Peter James	LT(CC)	X	O	01.12.98	849 SQN A FLT
Whitehead, Steven John *,BEng*	LT CDR(FTC)	E	AE	01.03.00	LN DERA BEDFORD
Whitehorn, Iain James *,BSc, CEng, MIMarE*	CDR(FTC)	E	MESM	30.06.94	NMA PORTSMOUTH
Whitehouse, Dominic Patrick	SURG LTCDR	-	(CM)	01.05.92	INM ALVERSTOKE
Whitehouse, David Spencer	LT(IC)	X	SM	01.04.00	VIGILANT(PORT)
Whitehouse, Mark Justin *,BSc, MEng*	LT CDR(FTC)	E	WE	01.03.94	JSCSC
Whitehouse, Niall Robert	LT(FTC)	E	P	01.01.97	RNAS YEOVILTON
Whitehouse, Simon Robert	SLT(FTC)	E	WE	01.04.98	COLLINGWOOD
Whitelaw, David Andrew	MID(NE)(IC)	X		01.09.99	DARTMOUTH BRNC
Whitelaw, Victoria Leigh *,BSc*	SLT(IC)	E		01.09.97	RICHMOND
Whitfield, Joe Alexander	LT(FTC)	X	P	16.06.91	COMATG SEA
Whitfield, Kenneth David *,BEng*	LT CDR(FTC)	E	AE	01.03.00	SULTAN
Whitfield, Philip Mark *,BSc*	CAPT RM(FTC)	RM	PU/T	01.09.97	DHFS
Whitfield, Robert Matthew Patrick *,BSc*	LT(FTC)	X	P	01.05.95	899 SQN HERON
Whiting, Elizabeth Ann *,BSc, MSc*	LT(IC)	E	TM	05.05.96	NMA PORTSMOUTH

Name	Rank	Branch	Spec	Seniority	Where Serving
Whitlam, John (*Act Lt Cdr*)	LT(FTC)	X	PWO(A)	16.12.94	DRYAD
Whitley, Ian Derek Brake , *n*	LT CDR(FTC)	X	PWO(C)	01.06.99	STANAVFORMED
Whitlum, Andrew Colin , *BEng*	LT(CC)	X	P	16.08.96	814 SQN
Whitlum, Sarah , *BSc*	LT(IC)	X		01.11.96	SHEFFIELD
Whitmee, Michael James	LT(CC)	X		01.08.95	EXCHANGE NLANDS
Whitson-Fay, Craig David	SLT(FTC)	X	O U/T	01.04.98	849 SQN HQ
Whittaker, Mark Adrian , *BM*	SURG LTCDR	-		01.08.97	NELSON (PAY)
Whittaker, Neill James , *BEng, CEng, MIEE, MIERE, jsdc*	CDR(FTC)	E	WESM	31.12.96	MOD (LONDON)
Whittingham, Debra Jayne	LT CDR(FTC)	W	X	01.10.98	EXCHANGE ARMY UK
Whitwell, Nicholas Shaun	LT(IC)	X		01.07.99	DRYAD
Whitworth, Robert Maitland	LT CDR(FTC)	X	PWO(U)	01.10.99	KENT
Whybourn, Lesley Ann , *MB, ChB*	SURG LT	-		28.11.97	COLLINGWOOD
Whyntie, Adrian , *BSc, CEng, MIEE, jsdc (Act Capt)*	CDR(FTC)	E	WE	30.06.94	LARONE IPT
Whyte, Iain Paul , *BA*	LT(FTC)	E	TM	01.04.93	RM Poole
Wick, Harry Mark Stephen	SLT(CC)	X		01.04.98	CAMPBELTOWN
Wickham, Robert James , *BEng*	SLT(IC)	X		01.05.98	GRAFTON
Wicking, Geoffrey Steven , *BEng*	LT(FTC)	E	AE	01.05.94	EXCHANGE ARMY UK
Wielopolski, Mark Leszek Christopher Carpenter	SLT(IC)	X	P U/T	01.05.98	DARTMOUTH BRNC
Wiffin, Anthony Francis	LT CDR(FTC)	E	AE(M)	01.10.97	RFANSU
Wigham, Timothy Walter	CAPT RM(IC)	RM		01.09.97	42 CDO RM
Wightwick, Katherine Helen Torr , *BA, BD*	SLT(IC)	X		01.01.98	FEARLESS
Wilcocks, Philip Lawrence , *DSC, BSc, AMRINA, pce, psc(a) (COMMODORE)*	CAPT(FTC)	X	PWO(A)	30.06.95	MOD (LONDON)
Wilcockson, Roy ,	CAPT(CS)RM	-		08.05.00	NEW ENTRY
Wild, Gareth , *BMS*	SURG SLT	-		16.09.97	DARTMOUTH BRNC
Wild, Richard James , *LLB*	SLT(IC)	S		01.01.99	DARTMOUTH BRNC
Wildin, Andrew , *BEng*	LT(FTC)	E	WE	01.04.97	EDINBURGH
Wiles, Stephen John , *BSc, MSc, CEng, MRAeS*	CDR(FTC)	E	AE	30.06.98	DARA
Wilkie, Andrew Robert (*Act Maj*)	CAPT RM(FTC)	RM	SO(LE)	01.01.94	HQRM
Wilkie, Neil , *BDS*	SGLTCDR(D)	-		11.06.93	RDMC BLOCKHOUSE
Wilkie, Suzanne Ellen	LT CDR(CC)	W	TM	01.10.99	2SL/CNH
Wilkins, David Paul	SLT(IC)	X		01.04.98	DARTMOUTH BRNC
Wilkins, Richard Ronald , *BEng*	LT(CC)	E	MESM	01.06.92	SULTAN
Wilkinson, Antonio	LT CDR(FTC)	E	AE(M)	01.10.91	FONA
Wilkinson, Andrew Charles	SLT(FTC)	E	WESM	09.01.98	VIGILANT(STBD)
Wilkinson, Andrew John , *BSc*	LT CDR(FTC)	X		16.12.86	CFPS SHORE
Wilkinson, David Henry	LT(FTC)	X	PWO(U)	01.06.92	MARLBOROUGH
Wilkinson, Georgina	LT	Q	OTSPEC	06.10.97	RH HASLAR
Wilkinson, Jane	LT(FTC)	X	REG	04.04.96	NP 1061
Wilkinson, Michael French	LT(CC)	X	P U/T	16.09.96	EXCHANGE RAF UK
Wilkinson, Peter John , *BA, pce, pce(sm)*	CAPT(FTC)	X	SM	31.12.95	CAPTAIN SM2
Wilkinson, Peter McConnell	LT CDR(FTC)	X	P	01.10.96	EXCHANGE USA
Wilkinson, Richard Murray , *BSc, PGCE, MDA, jsdc*	CAPT(FTC)	E	TM	30.06.00	NELSON
Wilkinson, Robin Nicholas	LT CDR(FTC)	X	P	01.10.98	RAF SHAWBURY
Wilkinson, Timothy Lindow , *BA*	CHAPLAIN	SF		04.03.97	RNAS CULDROSE
Will, Andrew Watt , *MBE, BSc*	LT CDR(FTC)	E	WE	01.06.84	GANNET
Willett, Roger John , *BA*	LT CDR(FTC)	X	METOC	04.01.81	FOSM NWOOD OPS
Williams, Andrew Bruce , *BSc, MIMechE*	LT CDR(CC)	E	TMSM	01.10.93	CSST SEA
Williams, Andrew David Justin , *BSc, psc(a)*	LT COL(FTC)	RM	P	30.06.96	NMA PORTSMOUTH
Williams, Andrew John , *BEng*	LT CDR(FTC)	E	MESM	01.02.98	VICTORIOUS(STBD)
Williams, Anthony Peter , *DSC, pce*	LT CDR(FTC)	X	MCD	01.11.93	JSCSC
Williams, Anthony Stephen	LT(FTC)	X	FC	01.09.98	GLOUCESTER
Williams, Bruce Nicholas Bromley , *BSc, pce, psc*	CDR(FTC)	X	PWO(U)	30.06.93	MOD (LONDON)
Williams, Caroline Mary Alexandra , *BA(Hons)*	LT CDR	Q	IC	01.10.98	RDMC BLOCKHOUSE
Williams, Colin Nicholas Owen , *BSc*	LT(FTC)	X		01.06.93	DRYAD
Williams, David	LT CDR(FTC)	S	SM	01.10.99	JHCHQ
Williams, Deborah , *BEd*	LT CDR(CC)	E	TM	16.12.99	DRAKE CBP(CNH)
Williams, Darrell Anthony	LT(FTC)	E	WE	13.06.86	COLLINGWOOD
Williams, David Clifford , *BSc, MEng, PGCE*	LT(CC)	E	TM	01.09.91	2SL/CNH
Williams, David Ian , *pce*	LT CDR(FTC)	X	PWO(A)	29.05.92	PJHQ
Williams, Daniel Leslie , *BA*	LT(CC)	X	P U/T	01.01.00	FONA LINTON/OUSE
Williams, David Spencer , *BEng, pce*	LT CDR(FTC)	X	PWO(U)	01.09.95	JSCSC
Williams, Geraint Michael Glyn	LT(CC)	X	SM	01.10.99	VANGUARD(PORT)
Williams, Ivan , *BSc, n*	LT(FTC)	X		01.06.95	GRAFTON

Name	Rank	Branch	Spec	Seniority	Where Serving
Williams, Ian Richard , *psc*	CDR(FTC)	X	H CH	30.06.94	MOD (LONDON)
Williams, Julian Llewelyn , *BA, rcds, jsdc*	CAPT(FTC)	S		30.06.94	MOD (BATH)
Williams, James Phillip	LT(FTC)	X	FC	01.06.92	DRYAD
Williams, James Robert , *BSc*	SLT(IC)	X	O U/T	01.01.98	750 SQN OBS SCH
Williams, Leo Douglas	MAJ(FTC)	RM	MLDR	01.08.78	RM CHIVENOR
Williams, Lucinda Emma , *BSc*	LT(FTC)	X		01.02.97	EXETER
Williams, Linda Jean , *BA*	LT(IC)	X		01.05.98	CAMPBELTOWN
Williams, Mark , *BEng*	LT(FTC)	E	MESM	01.06.93	NEPTUNE NT
Williams, Mark Adrian	LT(FTC)	X	O	01.06.90	815 SQN HQ
Williams, Mark Henry , *MSc, pce, pce(sm), psc(j)*	CDR(FTC)	X	SM	31.12.98	FOSM NWOOD HQ
Williams, Martyn Jon , *MA, MIEE*	CDR(FTC)	E	WESM	30.06.00	TRENCHANT
Williams, Mervyn John , *BSc*	LT(FTC)	X	MCD	01.12.93	INVERNESS
Williams, Malcolm Stephen , *BA, pce (COMMODORE)*	CAPT(FTC)	X	PWO(N)	30.06.94	CINCFLEET
Williams, Mark Stuart , *BSc*	LT CDR(FTC)	S		29.03.97	RALEIGH
Williams, Nigel David Blackstone , *BSc, jsdc, pce*	CDR(FTC)	X	PWO(U)	31.12.91	MOD (LONDON)
Williams, Nigel Lamplough , *BSc, CEng, MIMarE*	CAPT(FTC)	E	ME	30.06.00	2SL/CNH
Williams, Paul Allan , *BEng*	SLT(IC)	E	ME	01.01.99	DARTMOUTH BRNC
Williams, Paul Glynn , *BA*	SLT(IC)	X		01.05.98	SOMERSET
Williams, Peter Mark , *BEng*	LT(CC)	E	TM	01.01.91	SULTAN
Williams, Roderick Charles , *BSc*	LT CDR(FTC)	E	ME	01.10.89	EXCHANGE AUSTLIA
Williams, Robert Evan , *LLB (BARRISTER)*	CDR(FTC)	S	BAR	30.06.93	2SL/CNH
Williams, Richard Ivor	LT(CC)	X	P	16.05.92	848 SQN HERON
Williams, Robert John Stirling , *n*	LT(CC)	X		01.09.96	KENT
Williams, Stephen John , *BSc*	LT CDR(FTC)	E	AE(P)	18.10.85	SULTAN
Williams, Stephen Martin , *BSc, CEng, FIMechE, rcds, jsdc (COMMODORE)*	CAPT(FTC)	E	ME	30.06.92	NMA PORTSMOUTH
Williams, Simon Paul , *BSc, pce*	CDR(FTC)	X	PWO(C)	31.12.97	MOD (LONDON)
Williams, Simon Thomas , *BSc, pce, pce(sm)*	CDR(FTC)	X	SM	30.06.93	MOD (LONDON)
Williams, Sian	SURG SLT	-		16.05.99	DARTMOUTH BRNC
Williams, Stephen Wayne Leonard	LT(CC)	S		01.04.89	CTCRM
Williams, Thomas Alun	CDR(FTC)	X	PWO(C)	31.12.90	SACLANT USA
Williams, Timothy Nicholas Edward , *BSc, pce, pcea, psc*	CDR(FTC)	X	P	31.12.89	BDS WASHINGTON
Williamson, Alexander Karl , *BSc, MSc*	CAPT RM(FTC)	RM		01.05.98	40 CDO RM
Williamson, Peter James	SLT(IC)	X		01.04.00	GLASGOW
Williamson, Stephen John , *BSc*	LT(CC)	X	P	01.03.89	815 FLT 241
Williamson, Stephen Michael	LT(FTC)	X	MCD	01.11.94	FDU1
Williamson, Tobias Justin Lubbock , *MVO, BEng, pce, pcea*	LT CDR(FTC)	X	O	01.10.94	SHETLAND
Willing, Nigel Phillip , *BSc*	LT(CC)	X	P	16.08.93	702 SQN HERON
Willis, Alistair James , *MA, MILT, psc(j)*	LT CDR(FTC)	S		01.12.95	JSCSC
Willis, Andrew Stephen	LT(CC)	X		01.01.98	GRIMSBY
Willis, Martyn Stephen	LT CDR(FTC)	S	CA	02.05.95	RALEIGH
Willmett, Andrew Malcolm , *BSc, pce, psc (COMMODORE)*	CAPT(FTC)	X	AWO(A)	31.12.93	RN GIBRALTAR
Wills, John Robert , *BSc, CEng, MIMarE*	CAPT(FTC)	E	ME	31.12.97	NBC PORTSMOUTH
Wills, Michael Vincent	MAJ(FTC)	RM		05.09.88	RMB STONEHOUSE
Wills, Philip , *BSc*	LT(FTC)	X	O	01.01.93	815 FLT 246
Willson, Neil Julian	MAJ(FTC)	RM		01.09.96	CTCRM
Wilman, David Mark , *BA*	LT(FTC)	S		01.02.94	2SL/CNH
Wilmott, Sarah	SURG SLT	-		14.05.98	DARTMOUTH BRNC
Wilson, Alexander Charles , *MA, psc*	LT COL(FTC)	RM	LC	31.12.95	539 ASLT SQN RM
Wilson, Adrian Clive	CAPT RM(FTC)	RM	SO(LE)	01.01.97	HQ 3 CDO BDE RM
Wilson, Allan John , *n*	LT(FTC)	X		01.08.97	MONTROSE
Wilson, Andrew Stott	LT(CC)	X	P	16.09.96	819 SQN
Wilson, Charles Dominick , *BSc, jsdc, pce*	CDR(FTC)	X	MCD	30.06.95	PJHQ
Wilson, Christopher Gordon Talbot , *pce, pcea*	LT CDR(FTC)	X	P	01.08.85	ES AIR BRISTOL
Wilson, Christopher John , *BEng, CEng, MIMarE*	LT CDR(FTC)	E	MESM	01.12.96	FOSNNI/NBC CLYDE
Wilson, Christopher , *MB, ChB*	SURG LT	-		25.02.98	RNAS YEOVILTON
Wilson, Christopher Ward , *BEng*	LT(FTC)	E	WESM	01.08.94	SOVEREIGN
Wilson, David , *OBE, MID, psc(m), hcsc*	MAJ GEN	RM		22.11.99	HQ NORTH
Wilson, David Robert , *n*	LT(FTC)	X	PWO(A)	01.05.92	YORK
Wilson, David Timothy	LT CDR(FTC)	E	WE	01.10.98	MOD (BATH)
Wilson, David William Howard , *psc(j)*	MAJ(FTC)	RM		25.04.96	45 CDO RM
Wilson, Graham John	LT(FTC)	X	MCD	27.07.95	SDG PORTSMOUTH
Wilson, Geoffrey	SLT(FTC)	X	REG	19.09.97	LINDISFARNE
Wilson, Gary Leonard , *pce, pce(sm)*	LT CDR(FTC)	X	SM	01.04.92	LOAN DERA ADAC

Name	Rank	Branch	Spec	Seniority	Where Serving
Wilson, Ian Peter , *BA*	SLT(IC)	X		01.01.99	DARTMOUTH BRNC
Wilson, John , *BEng*	LT(CC)	X	P	01.12.97	846 SQN
Wilson, James Andrew	LT(FTC)	E	ME	15.06.95	FOSTSEA NBCDPSMH
Wilson, Julian , *BSc*	CAPT RM(FTC)	RM		01.09.98	45 CDO RM
Wilson, James Robert , *psc*	LT COL(FTC)	RM	MLDR	30.06.87	RMR BRISTOL
Wilson, Kevin Paul , *BSc, MDA, CEng, MIEE*	CDR(FTC)	E	WESM	31.12.96	HQ DCSA
Wilson, Marcus Alaric , *gdas*	LT(CC)	X	O	16.07.87	LOAN DERA BSC DN
Wilson, Philip Anthony , *psc*	LT COL(FTC)	RM		30.06.88	LN BMATT (CEE)
Wilson, Robert , *ARICS*	LT CDR(FTC)	X	H CH	01.07.83	LOAN HYDROG
Wilson, Robert	LT(FTC)	X	PWO(A)	01.09.92	MONTROSE
Wilson, Robert Paul , *pcea*	LT CDR(FTC)	X	O	01.10.95	DARTMOUTH BRNC
Wilson, Stephen Gordon , *MNI, pce, psc*	CDR(FTC)	X	PWO(A)	31.12.91	DRYAD
Wilson, Stephen Richard , *psc*	LT COL(FTC)	RM		30.06.94	JDCC
Wilson-Chalon, Louis Michael , *BSc, pcea*	LT CDR(FTC)	X	P	01.04.97	CAPT F2(SEA)
Wiltcher, Ross Alexander , *BA*	LT CDR(FTC)	S		01.08.93	MOD (LONDON)
Wiltshire, Graham John , *MA, MSc, CEng, MIEE, nadc, psc*	CAPT(FTC)	E	WESM	31.12.93	NELSON
Winand, Francis Michael John , *BA*	SLT(IC)	X		01.01.98	ROEBUCK
Winbolt, Neil	LT(IC)	X	P U/T	01.04.00	RAF CRANWELL EFS
Winch, Emma Jane , *BDS*	SGLTCDR(D)	-		24.01.99	CAPTAIN SM2
Winchurch, Michael Roy Glen , *ARICS, psc, n*	LT CDR(FTC)	X	H CH	16.11.83	DRAKE DPL
Windebank, Stephen John , *pcea*	LT(FTC)	X	P	01.10.91	700M MERLIN IFTU
Window, Stephen Harvey	LT CDR(FTC)	X	MCD	01.09.95	2SL/CNH
Windsar, Paul Andrew	LT CDR(FTC)	E	WESM	27.11.98	MOD (LONDON)
Windsor, Mark , *BSc, MA, MIMechE, psc*	CDR(FTC)	X	METOC	30.06.96	MOD (LONDON)
Wines, David Anthony , *MCFA, psc*	CAPT(FTC)	S		31.12.93	BDLS NEW ZEALAND
Wingfield, Melissa Helen , *BDS*	SG LT(D)	-		01.07.96	FEARLESS
Wingfield, Michael James , *BEng*	LT(CC)	X	O	16.07.94	EXCHANGE RAF UK
Winkle, Sean James , *BA*	LT CDR(FTC)	E	TM	01.05.96	HQRM
Winn, John Paul	SLT(IC)	X		01.04.98	CUMBERLAND
Winsor, James , *BSc*	SLT(IC)	X		01.05.97	DRYAD
Winstanley, Keith , *MBE, pce*	CAPT(FTC)	X	PWO(N)	31.12.99	JSCSC
Winston, Lionel Angelo , *MBE*	LT CDR(FTC)	E	ME	01.10.99	MOD (BATH)
Winter, Richard Jason , *BEng*	LT(FTC)	E	WE	01.08.93	RMCS SHRIVENHAM
Winter, Timothy McMahon , *BEng, CEng, MIMarE*	LT CDR(FTC)	E	ME	01.05.98	CHATHAM
Winterbon, Andrew Richard	SLT(IC)	X		01.05.98	DARTMOUTH BRNC
Wintle, Geoffrey Lawrence	LT CDR(FTC)	S	SM	01.02.97	COMATG SEA
Wise, Graham John , *BEng, MSc, CEng, MIEE*	LT CDR(FTC)	E	WE	01.04.96	LN DERA PRTSDWN
Wise, Simon David , *BSc, MAPM, CDipAF*	CDR(FTC)	E	WE	31.12.96	CAPT D5 SEA
Wiseman, George Richard	CAPT RM(FTC)	RM	SO(LE)	01.01.00	40 CDO RM
Wiseman, Ian Carl , *n*	LT(FTC)	X		01.02.95	ARCHER
Wiseman, Neil Christopher	LT(CC)	X	O	16.06.96	702 SQN HERON
Wiseman, Wayne Theodore , *BSc, CEng, MIEE, jsdc*	CDR(FTC)	E	WE	30.06.84	T45 IPT
Withers, James Warren , *BEng, MIEE*	LT CDR(FTC)	E	WE	01.04.96	MOD (BATH)
Witt, Alister Kevin	SLT(IC)	E		01.09.98	DARTMOUTH BRNC
Witte, Richard Hugh , *LLB*	LT(FTC)	X		01.12.97	NORTHUMBERLAND
Wittich, Thomas Steven , *OBE, MBA, MSc, gw (COMMODORE)*	CAPT(FTC)	E	WE	30.06.91	T45 IPT
Witton, James William , *pce*	LT CDR(FTC)	X	PWO(U)	01.06.93	FOSF SEA PTSMTH
Wolfe, David Edward , *pce, pcea, fsc*	CDR(FTC)	X	O	30.06.96	MOD (LONDON)
Wolsey, Mark Andrew Ronald , *BA, psc(m) (Act Lt Col)*	MAJ(FTC)	RM		30.06.99	HQRM
Wombwell, John Frederick , *MA, MSc, CGIA*	LT CDR(FTC)	E	WE	19.02.88	MOD (LONDON)
Wood, Allan Cawsey MacDonald , *BSc, MDA, CDipAF*	CDR(FTC)	E	TM	31.12.86	COLLINGWOOD
Wood, Andrew Graeme , *BEng*	LT(IC)	E	AE	01.08.97	801 SQN
Wood, Alexander , *BMS*	SURG SLT	-		21.08.98	DARTMOUTH BRNC
Wood, Craig , *n*	LT(FTC)	X		01.08.93	TRUMPETER
Wood, Christopher	MID(NE)(IC)	X		01.01.00	DARTMOUTH BRNC
Wood, Charles Andrew	LT CDR(FTC)	X	PWO(U)	09.01.88	MOD (LONDON)
Wood, Christopher Henry , *BSc*	SLT(IC)	X		01.01.97	DRYAD
Wood, Christopher Richard	LT(FTC)	X	P U/T	01.01.97	DHFS
Wood, Frank Douglas	LT CDR(FTC)	X	AV	01.10.99	FONA
Wood, Gregory , *MB, BS*	SURG LTCDR	-	GMPP	01.08.94	NELSON (PAY)
Wood, Graham Richard , *BA*	LT(IC)	S		01.02.98	RALEIGH
Wood, Ian Derrick , *IEng, AMIMarE*	LT CDR(FTC)	E	ME	01.10.96	FOSF
Wood, Iain Leslie	LT(IC)	X		01.01.99	SUTHERLAND

Name	Rank	Branch	Spec	Seniority	Where Serving
Wood, Joseph Albert	LT(FTC)	X	PT	03.04.98	COTTESMORE
Wood, John Lindsay , *BSc, MSc, MCGI*	LT CDR(FTC)	E	ME	01.03.94	JSCSC
Wood, Justin Noel Alexander , *BSc, MRAeS, MNI, MIMgt, pce, pcea, psc*	CDR(FTC)	X	P	30.06.96	INVINCIBLE
Wood, Jonathan Richard	MID(UCE)(IC)	E		01.09.99	INVINCIBLE
Wood, Joanne Tamar , *BSc*	SLT(IC)	X		01.01.99	DARTMOUTH BRNC
Wood, Michael George , *CBE, BSc, CEng, FIMechE, rcds, jsdc*	RADM	-	ME	09.03.99	MOD (BATH)
Wood, Michael Leslie , *BSc, MPhil*	LT(FTC)	X		01.12.96	CAMPBELTOWN
Wood, Nicholas Robert	SLT(FTC)	X	tas	01.04.98	RICHMOND
Wood, Robert	LT CDR(FTC)	S	BAR	01.03.98	MANCHESTER
Wood, Simon Andrew Hall , *BEng*	SLT(IC)	X	P U/T	01.09.97	RAF CRANWELL EFS
Wood, Stephen Graham	LT(FTC)	X	O	11.12.92	EXCHANGE RAF UK
Wood, Stephanie Jane	SLT(IC)	X		01.04.99	FEARLESS
Wood, Uvedale George Singleton	LT CDR(FTC)	X	P	01.04.99	MWC PORTSDOWN
Woodard, Jolyon Robert Alban , *BSc*	LT(IC)	X	P	01.11.92	845 SQN
Woodard, Neil Antony , *BSc*	LT(CC)	S		01.04.96	MANCHESTER
Woodbridge, Graham Francis , *MBE, psc*	LT CDR(FTC)	X	PWO(U)	01.11.82	DRYAD
Woodbridge, Richard George , *BEng*	LT(CC)	E	ME	01.08.92	NEPTUNE FD
Woodcock, Nicholas	CHAPLAIN	CE		31.03.92	NELSON
Woodcock, Simon Jonathan , *BSc, CEng, MIMechE, psc(j)*	CDR(FTC)	E	ME	31.12.99	MOD (BATH)
Woodford, Geoffrey Ian , *MBE, BEng*	LT CDR(FTC)	E	WESM	01.09.96	VENGEANCE(PORT)
Woodham, Robert Henry , *BSc, MSc, PGDip*	LT CDR(FTC)	X	METOC	01.03.99	HERALD
Wooding, Graham Allen	LT(FTC)	E	WE	19.02.93	MOD (LONDON)
Woodrow, Kevin	LT(FTC)	X	SM	13.12.95	ELANT/NAVNORTH
Woodruff, Anthony Desmond	LT CDR(FTC)	X	PWO(U)	01.10.99	DRYAD
Woodruff, Dean Aaron , *BEng, MSc*	LT CDR(FTC)	E	ME	01.12.99	LN DERA HASLAR
Woods, Jeremy Billing , *pce*	LT CDR(FTC)	X	PWO(A)	01.07.97	NMA PORTSMOUTH
Woods, Michael James Peter , *BEng*	SLT(IC)	E		01.09.98	SOMERSET
Woods, Roland Philip , *AMIAM, pce*	CDR(FTC)	X	PWO(A)	31.12.98	CINCFLEET
Woods, Roland Steven , *BDS*	SG LT(D)	-		20.07.98	NELSON
Woods, Timothy Christopher , *BA (Act Lt Cdr)*	LT(FTC)	E	TMSM	01.02.93	CSST SHORE FSLN
Woodward, Darroch John , *BA, BSc*	LT CDR(FTC)	X	MCD	01.07.95	FDU2
Wookey, Mark	LT(CC)	X	O	01.02.96	815 FLT 206
Woolhead, Andrew Lyndon , *BA, n*	LT(CC)	X		01.10.94	YORK
Woolhead, Craig Morton , *BA*	SLT(IC)	X		01.09.97	ILLUSTRIOUS
Woollcombe-Gosson, David James , *pce*	LT CDR(FTC)	X	PWO(A)	01.06.97	COMUKTG/CASWSF
Wooller, Mark Adrian Hudson , *BA*	LT(FTC)	S	SM	01.10.92	VICTORIOUS(STBD)
Woolley, Martin James	LT CDR(FTC)	X	MCD	01.01.93	ELANT/NAVNORTH
Woolliams, Michael Frank , *MNI, psc*	LT CDR(FTC)	X		01.12.84	RALEIGH
Woollven, Andrew Howard	LT CDR(FTC)	X	PWO(U)	01.08.97	ILLUSTRIOUS
Woollven, Christopher David , *BSc*	LT(IC)	X	O U/T	01.12.99	810 SQN SEAHAWK
Woolsey, Kevin Edward Keith	LT(CC)	X	ATC	16.05.95	INVINCIBLE
Wormald, Robert Edward , *MSc, CEng, FIMarE, psc*	CDR(FTC)	E	MESM	31.12.92	NP BRISTOL
Worman, Robin , *BSc*	LT CDR(CC)	X	P	01.10.98	848 SQN HERON
Wort, Roland	CHAPLAIN	SF		27.07.93	CAPT D5 SEA
Worthington, Jonathan Michael Francis , *MA*	LT CDR(FTC)	E	TM	01.05.96	JSCSC
Wotherspoon, Steven Robert , *psc*	LT COL(FTC)	RM		30.06.94	HQRM
Wotton, John Charles Lawson , *BSc, jsdc, pce*	CAPT(FTC)	X	FC	30.06.98	2SL/CNH FOTR
Woznicki, Stanley James	LT CDR(FTC)	X	PWO(A)	16.06.88	SACLANT USA
Wragg, Gareth Terence	SLT(CC)	X		01.04.98	DARTMOUTH BRNC
Wraith, Neil	CAPT RM(FTC)	RM	LC	01.09.94	RM Poole
Wray, Arthur Douglas	LT(FTC)	E	WESM	05.06.92	RALEIGH
Wrenn, Michael Reader William , *FIEEIE, MIOSH*	LT(FTC)	E	WE	18.02.94	SSA/CWTA PORTS
Wrennall, Eric Paul	SLT(IC)	E	ME	29.04.98	SULTAN
Wright, Antony John	LT CDR(FTC)	X	O	01.10.97	JSCSC
Wright, Anna Louise	LT(IC)	S		02.05.92	DRYAD
Wright, Bradley Lee , *BEng, MAPM, AMIEE*	LT CDR(FTC)	E	WE	01.06.99	RMCS SHRIVENHAM
Wright, David Anthony	LT(FTC)	X	MCD	29.07.94	EXCHANGE USA
Wright, David Ian , *BEng*	LT(FTC)	E	WE	01.09.96	SSA BRISTOL
Wright, Daniel James , *LLB*	LT(CC)	X		01.12.98	SPLENDID
Wright, Geoffrey Neil , *MBE, BSc*	CDR(FTC)	E	MESM	30.06.93	MOD (BATH)
Wright, John , *BSc*	LT CDR(CC)	E	TM	01.10.90	NELSON
Wright, John Vincent , *CEng, MIMechE*	CAPT(FTC)	E	ME	30.06.93	SULTAN AIB
Wright, John William Talbot , *BA, pce, pcea (Act Capt)*	CDR(FTC)	X	O	30.06.87	IMS BRUSSELS

Name	Rank	Branch	Spec	Seniority	Where Serving
Wright, Michael John , *MBE*	LT CDR(FTC)	X		01.09.85	LOAN SAUDI ARAB
Wright, Nicholas Peter , *LVO, jsdc*	CAPT(FTC)	S		31.12.97	SACLANT USA
Wright, Nigel Seymour , *BEng, MSc, CEng, MIMarE*	LT CDR(FTC)	E	ME	01.02.99	COVENTRY
Wright, Stuart Hugh	LT CDR(FTC)	S	BAR	16.07.97	GLASGOW
Wright, Toby John , *BSc*	SLT(IC)	X	P U/T	01.01.98	DARTMOUTH BRNC
Wright, Timothy Mark , *BA*	LT(IC)	S		01.04.98	NEPTUNE CFS
Wrighton, Christopher Russell , *pce, psc*	LT CDR(FTC)	X	P	16.09.80	RNAS YEOVILTON
Wrightson, Hugh Mawson , *BSc, MA, CEng, MIEE, psc(j)*	CDR(FTC)	E	ME	31.12.97	CAPT F4 (SEA)
Wrigley, Bradley Stephen *(Act Lt)*	SLT(IC)	S		01.05.98	FOSM NWOOD HQ
Wrigley, Peter James	LT CDR(FTC)	X		16.10.88	RHQ AFNORTH
Wroblewski, Jefferey Andre	LT(FTC)	E	MESM	16.10.92	TRENCHANT
Wunderle, Charles Albert	CDR(FTC)	S	(W)	30.06.00	2SL/CNH
Wyatt, Christopher	LT(FTC)	S	(S)	17.12.93	NEPTUNE
Wyatt, David James , *pce*	LT CDR(FTC)	X	H CH	01.11.93	ANGLESEY
Wyatt, Julian Michael , *BSc, CEng, FIMarE, MIMechE*	LT CDR(FTC)	E	MESM	01.10.90	2SL/CNH FOTR
Wyatt, Steven Patrick , *BSc*	CDR(FTC)	E	WESM	31.12.95	DPA BRISTOL
Wykeham-Martin, Peter Charles *(COMMODORE)*	CAPT(FTC)	S	(S)	30.06.91	NELSON
Wyld, Anthony Wallace	LT(FTC)	E	WE	18.02.94	CAPT(H) DEVPT
Wylie, David	CHAPLAIN	CE		01.12.98	CHFHQ
Wylie, Ian Charles Henfrey , *BEng, AMIEE*	LT(FTC)	E	WESM	01.11.92	JSCSC
Wyness, Roger Simon	LT(CC)	X	P	01.07.96	815 SQN OEU
Wynn, Simon Christopher	LT(CC)	X		01.11.97	LEDBURY
Wynn, Simon Raymond , *BSc, MEng, PGDip*	LT CDR(FTC)	X	METOC	01.09.97	CINCFLEET
Wyper, James Robert , *BSc*	LT(FTC)	X	SM	01.09.92	VANGUARD(PORT)

Y

Name	Rank	Branch	Spec	Seniority	Where Serving
Yardley, Andrew Philip	LT CDR(FTC)	X	METOC	01.10.99	RFANSU
Yarker, Daniel Lawrence , *pce*	LT CDR(FTC)	X	PWO(A)	01.10.97	FOST SEA
Yarnall, Nicholas John , *MB, BCh, DObstRCOG*	SURG LTCDR	-	GMPP	01.08.97	NEPTUNE CFS
Yates, David	CHAPLAIN	RC		01.09.98	DRAKE CBP(CNH)
Yates, Elizabeth	SURG SLT	-		18.12.97	DARTMOUTH BRNC
Yates, Michael Leslie , *MHCIMA*	LT(TC)	S	CA	18.06.90	NELSON
Yates, Neal Peter , *pce, pcea, psc*	LT CDR(FTC)	X	O	01.06.89	RNAS YEOVILTON
Yates, Stuart Edward , *BSc*	LT(CC)	X		01.05.98	LIVERPOOL
Yelland, Christopher Brian	LT(CC)	X	O	16.05.87	848 SQN HERON
Yeomans, Paul Andrew	LT(CC)	X		01.09.93	PJHQ
York, Gideon Rufus James , *BEng*	LT(FTC)	E	MESM	01.05.96	TRAFALGAR
York, H R H, The Duke Of , *pce, pcea, psc(m)*	CDR(FTC)	X	P	27.04.99	MOD (LONDON)
Youldon, Louisa Jane , *BSc*	SLT(IC)	X		01.05.98	DARTMOUTH BRNC
Young, Andrew , *BSc, CEng, MIMechE*	CDR(FTC)	E	ME	31.12.90	SSA BRISTOL
Young, Angus , *n*	LT CDR(FTC)	X	PWO(U)	01.06.99	NEWCASTLE
Young, Andrew Park , *BSc*	LT CDR(FTC)	S		16.06.95	NEPTUNE CFS
Young, Christopher John , *BEd, HND*	LT(CC)	E	TM	18.06.92	2SL/CNH FOTR
Young, Gavin Lee , *pce*	LT CDR(FTC)	X	PWO(A)	01.01.98	FOST SEA
Young, Ian James , *BSc, MIL, AMIEE (Act Cdr)*	LT CDR(FTC)	E	WE	16.12.80	T45 IPT
Young, John Nicholas	LT(FTC)	X	AV	24.07.97	EXCELLENT
Young, Keith Hunter	LT(FTC)	E	ME	23.02.90	SULTAN
Young, Mark James	LT(CC)	X	O	16.09.91	EXCHANGE BRAZIL
Young, Michael Stephen , *BSc, MA, psc(j)*	LT CDR(FTC)	E	TM	01.09.96	CICHM
Young, Nigel Alan , *BSc*	LT(IC)	E	TM	01.01.96	SULTAN
Young, Peter	SLT(FTC)	E	ME	02.05.97	YORK
Young, Philip Charles , *MB, BS, FRCA*	SURG CDR	-	(CA)	31.12.99	ILLUSTRIOUS
Young, Robin	LT(FTC)	E	ME	13.02.92	SULTAN
Young, Rachel , *BA*	LT(IC)	X		01.12.94	DRYAD
Young, Richard Arthur Sinclair , *BSc, CDipAF, CEng, MAPM, MIEE*	CDR(FTC)	E	WESM	30.06.89	MOD (LONDON)
Young, Stephen Andrew , *BEng*	LT CDR(FTC)	E	WESM	01.02.00	TORPEDO IPT
Young, Stuart Sheldon , *BSc, MEng, MSc, CEng, MIMechE, jsdc*	CDR(FTC)	E	ME	30.06.95	DGSS BRISTOL
Young, Stephen William	LT(FTC)	S	SM	16.12.94	NELSON
Youp, Allan Thomas , *BSc, PGCE*	LT(IC)	E	TM	01.06.95	45 CDO RM
Yuill, Ian Alexander , *BSc, adp*	CDR(FTC)	E	IS	01.10.96	2SL/CNH

RFA OFFICERS

COMMODORE

P. J. LANNIN

COMMODORE (ENGINEERS)

N. K. BALL

Captains

J.R.J. Carew, OBE
C.J. Fell
S.F. Hodgson psc
C.R. Knapp
C.A. Mitchell psc
D.M. Pitt
G.D. Pursall
A.T. Roach
P.J.G. Roberts, DSO
P.A. Taylor, OBE
J.P. Thompson, OBE
B.J. Waters, OBE
L.M Coupland
N. A. Jones
J. Stones
D. Worthington
M. T. Jarvis
W.M. Walworth OBE
R. L. Williams
F. Brady
I.. N. Pilling
R. A. Bliss
S. H. Cant
R. G. Ferris
J. P. Huxley
M. T . Jarvis
I.E. Johnson
J. Murchie
R. Robinson-Brown
R.C. Thornton
P. M. Farmer
D. I. Gough
R. H. Allan

Captain (Engineers)

T. Adam
G.R. Axworthy
D.E. Bass
P.J. Beer, MBE
D.W. Birkett
R.J. Brewer
P.C.M. Daniels
R.W. Donkin
A. Edworthy
M. Ellam
I. W. Finlayson
I.E. Hall
K. Holder
H.R. Hurley
R. Kirk
R.W. Langton
J.W. Leach
S.J. Mathews
M. Mission
K. Nicholls
W. Pearce
D. W. G. Phasey
R. Settle
K. Smeaton
C.S. Smith
D.C. Smith
R.J. Smith
N.C. Springer
A.D. Wills
M. D. Norfolk
E. M. Quigley
G. T. Turner
K. R. C. Moore
A.C. Bowditch
J. E. Collins
I.M. Doolan-Phillip
A.J. Grant
B.S. Layson
J.J. Oakey
D.S. Simpson
D. Preston
I. Dunbar
P.I Henney
A.G. Sinclair

SENIORITY LIST

ADMIRALS OF THE FLEET

(This rank is now held in abeyance in peacetime (1996))

Edinburgh, *His Royal Highness The Prince* Philip, *Duke Of, KG, KT, OM, GBE, AC, QSO* .... 15 Jan 53

Hill-Norton, The Lord, *GCB* .... 12 Mar 71

Pollock, Sir Michael, (Patrick), *GCB, LVO, DSC, psc* .... 1 Mar 74

Ashmore, Sir Edward (Beckwith), *GCB, DSC, IRs, jssc, psc* .... 9 Feb 77

Leach, Sir Henry (Conyers), *GCB, DL, jssc, psc* .... 1 Dec 82

Oswald, Sir (John) Julian (Robertson), *GCB, rcds, psc* .... 2 Mar 92

Bathurst, Sir (David) Benjamin, *GCB, rcds* .... 10 Jul 95

FORMER FIRST SEA LORD

Slater, Sir Jock (John Cunningham Kirkwood), GCB, LVO, rcds, pce .... 20 Jan 91
(remains on the Active List)

ADMIRALS

Boyce, *Sir* Michael (Cecil) , *GCB, OBE, ADC, rcds, psc* .... 25 May 95
(CHIEF OF NAVAL STAFF AND FIRST SEA LORD OCT 98)

Abbott, *Sir* Peter (Charles) , *GBE, KCB, MA, rcds, pce* .... 03 Oct 95
(VICE CHIEF OF THE DEFENCE STAFF OCT 97)

Essenhigh, *Sir* Nigel (Richard) , *KCB, rcds, pce, psc, hcsc* .... 11 Sep 98
(COMMANDER-IN-CHIEF FLEET, CINC EAST ATLANTIC, COMMANDER NAVAL FORCES NORTH EUROPE SEP 98)

Perowne, *Sir* James (Francis) , *KBE, rcds, pce, psc* .... 9 May 00
(DEPUTY SACLANT NOV 98)

VICE ADMIRALS

Garnett, *Sir* Ian (David Graham) , *KCB, psc* .... 24 Aug 95
(CHIEF OF JOINT OPERATIONS FEB 99)

Haddacks, *Sir* Paul (Kenneth) , *KCB, rcds, pce, psc, hcsc* .... 24 Feb 97
(UK MILITARY REPRESENTATIVE BRUSSELS FEB 97)

Blackham, *Sir* Jeremy (Joe) , *KCB, BA, rcds, pce, psc* .... 24 Jun 97
(DEP CHIEF OF DEFENCE STAFF (EQUIPMENT CAPABILITY) SEP 99)

West, *Sir* Alan (William John) , *KCB, DSC, rcds, pce, psc, hcsc* .... 23 Oct 97
(CHIEF OF DEFENCE INTELLIGENCE OCT 97)

Malbon, Fabian Michael , *rcds*, *pce*, *psc* .... 06 Jan 99
(DEPUTY COMMANDER FLEET JAN 99)

Band, Jonathon , *BA*, *jsdc*, *pce*, *hcsc* .... 11 Jan 00
(TEAM LEADER DEFENCE TRAINING REVIEW JAN 00)

Spencer, Peter , *ADC, MA, MSc*, *jsdc* .... 19 Jan 00
(SECOND SEA LORD AND CINCNAVHOME JAN 00)

REAR ADMIRALS

Clarke, John Patrick , *CB*, *LVO*, *MBE*, *pce* .... 14 Mar 94
(HYDROGRAPHER APR 96)

Lees, Rodney Burnett (Barrister) , *n* .... 21 Feb 95
(DEFENCE SERVICES SECRETARY MAR 98)

Perowne, Benjamin Brian , *CDipAF*, *rcds*, *pce*, *psc* .... 06 Nov 96
(CHIEF EXECUTIVE NAVAL BASES AND SUPPLY AGENCY MAR 99, CHIEF OF FLEET SUPPORT APR 00)

Forbes, Ian Andrew , *CBE*, *rcds*, *pce*, *psc*(a) .... 04 Dec 96
(FLAG OFFICER SURFACE FLOTILLA APR 00)

Lippiett, Richard John , *MBE*, *rcds*, *jsdc*, *pce*, *psc* .... 07 Jul 97
(CHIEF OF STAFF TO COMMANDER ALLIED NAVAL FORCES SOUTHERN.EUROPE OCT 99)

Gregory, Alexander Michael , *OBE*, *jsdc*, *pce(sm)* .... 30 Sep 97
(FOSNNI SEP 97)

Moore, Simon , *CB*, *pce*, *psc* .... 04 Nov 97
(ASSISTANT CHIEF OF DEF STAFF (OPS) NOV 97)

Dunt, Peter Arthur , *rcds* .... 05 Jan 98
(DIRECTOR GENERAL NAVAL PERSONNEL STRATEGY AND PLANS, COS 2SL/CNH JAN 98)

Rickard, Hugh Wilson , *CBE*, *BSc*, *psc*, *rcds* .... 20 Apr 98
(SENIOR DIRECTING STAFF (NAVY) - RCDS APR 98)

Chadwick, John , *CEng*, *FIEE*, *MIEE*, *jsdc* .... 23 Jul 98
(FLAG OFFICER TRAINING & RECRUITING, CHIEF EXECUTIVE NAVAL RECRUITING AND TRAINING AGENCY DEC 99)

Stevens, Robert Patrick , *CB*, *pce*, *pce(sm)* .... 04 Aug 98
(FLAG OFFICER SUBMARINES & COMMANDER SUBMARINES EAST ATLANTIC, COMMANDER SUBMARINE FORCES NORTH AUG 98)

McAnally, John Henry Stuart , *CB*, *LVO*, *MNI*, *MRIN*, *rcds*, *pce*, *psc*, *hcsc* .... 12 Aug 98
(COMMANDANT RCDS as Acting Vice Admiral AUG 98)

Henderson, Iain Robert , *CBE*, *pce*, pcea, *psc* .... 06 Oct 98
(AOC 3GP/FOMA APR 00)

de Halpert, Jeremy Michael , *MRIN, jsdc, pce* .... 09 Dec 98
(NAVAL SECRETARY, CHIEF EXECUTIVE NAVAL MANNING AGENCY DEC 98)

Stanford, Christopher David , *MA, MNI, rcds, pce, psc* .... 04 Jan 99
(CHIEF OF STAFF TO THE SURGEON GENERAL JAN 99)

Wood, Michael George , *CBE, BSc, CEng, FIMechE, rcds, jsdc* .... 09 Mar 99
(DIRECTOR GENERAL DEFENCE LOGISTICS (OPERATIONS AND BUSINESS DEVELOPMENT) MAY 00)

Ward, Rees Graham John , *MA, MSc, CEng, FIEE, rcds, jsdc*, gw, *hcsc* .... 27 Apr 99
(CAPABILITY MANAGER (STRATEGIC DEPLOYMENT) APR 99)

Meyer, Stephen Richard , *pce, psc, hcsc* .... 01 Jul 99
(COMMANDER UK TASK GROUP FEB 00)

Clare, Roy Alexander George , *rcds, pce, psc* .... 23 Aug 99
(DIRECTOR OPERATIONAL MANAGEMENT HQ AFCENT MAR 00)

Backus, Alexander Kirkwood , *OBE, jsdc, pce* .... 07 Sep 99
(FLAG OFFICER SEA TRAINING SEP 99)

Burnell-Nugent, James Michael , *CBE, MA, jsdc, pce, pce(sm)* .... 06 Dec 99
(ASSISTANT CHIEF OF THE NAVAL STAFF DEC 99)

Guild, Nigel Charles Forbes , *BA*, PhD, *MIEE, AFIMA, jsdc* .... 06 Jan 00
(DPA EXECUTIVE DIRECTOR 4, CONTROLLER OF THE NAVY JAN 00)

Dymock, Anthony Knox , *BA, pce, psc* .... 19 Jan 00
(DEPUTY COMSTRIKFORSTH MAR 00)

Reeve, Jonathon , *MA, CEng, MIEE, rcds, psc* .... 13 Mar 00
(CHIEF OF STAFF (CORPORATE DEVELOPMENT) MAR 00)

Stanhope, Mark , *OBE, ADC, MA, MNI, rcds, pce, pce(sm), psc, hcsc* .... 01 Jun 00
(DIRECTOR OPERATIONAL MANAGEMENT HQ AFCENT JUN 00)

CAPTAINS

1983

X Burns, B. .... 30 Jun

1989

E Hibbert, R.J.N. .... 31 Dec
X Bradshaw, R.J. .... 31 Dec

1990

E Luard, J.R. .... 30 Jun
X Conley, D. .... 31 Dec

1991

E Wittich, T.S. .... 30 Jun
X Tuffley, C.R. .... 30 Jun
E Day, K J C .... 30 Jun
X Thornewill, S.C. .... 30 Jun
S Wykeham-Martin, P.C. .... 30 Jun
X Hopkins, L.C. .... 30 Jun
X Anthony, D.J. .... 30 Jun
X Hogg, A.J.M. .... 30 Jun
E Clayden, J.W.A. .... 31 Dec
E Hall, D.A. .... 31 Dec
X Bishop, R.ST.J.S. .... 31 Dec
X Edwardes, G.H. .... 31 Dec
E Graham, S.W. .... 31 Dec
X Morrison, C.J.N. .... 31 Dec
X Chilton, A.L. .... 31 Dec
X Johnson, M.A. .... 31 Dec
E Pacey, P.J. .... 31 Dec
S Lockwood, R.G. .... 31 Dec
X Morton, T. .... 31 Dec
E Harries, J.M.H. .... 31 Dec
X Hiscock, F.H. .... 31 Dec
E Greenish, P.D. .... 31 Dec

1992

S Humphrey, D.R. .... 30 Jun
X Lyall, A.J. .... 30 Jun
X Ellison, C.V. .... 30 Jun
X Goldman, B.A.L. .... 30 Jun
X Poulter, A.M. .... 30 Jun
X Herington, P.W. .... 30 Jun
X Ellis, P.J. .... 30 Jun
E Lord, R.J. .... 30 Jun
E Williams, S.M. .... 30 Jun
X Kilgour, N.S.R. .... 30 Jun

X McLean, R.A.I. 30 Jun
E Challands, G.D. 30 Jun
X McClement, T.P. 30 Jun
X Thomas, N.W. 31 Dec
E Brougham, M.J.D. 31 Dec
X Du Port, A.N. 31 Dec
X Rimington, J.A. 31 Dec
S Smith, D.A.H.M. 31 Dec
E Broadhurst, M.J. 31 Dec
X Rodley, J.F. 31 Dec
X Bryant, B.W. 31 Dec
E Sanderson, P.C. 31 Dec
S Munns, A. 31 Dec
X Rapp, J.C. 31 Dec
E Brooks, B.P.S. 31 Dec
E Tyrrell, P.J. 31 Dec
X Lidbetter, S. 31 Dec

1993

X Benbow, W.K. 30 Jun
S Musters, J.B.A. 30 Jun
X Morgan, J.H. 30 Jun
E Wright, J.V. 30 Jun
X Owen, N.R. 30 Jun
E Davies, P.R. 30 Jun
E Hare, T.W. 30 Jun
X Swan, P.W.H. 30 Jun
X Phillips, D.A. 30 Jun
E Cheadle, R.F. 30 Jun
X Lewis, D.A. 30 Jun
X Style, C.R. 30 Jun
X Mowlam, D.J.M. 31 Dec
X Jackson, P. 31 Dec
S Wines, D.A. 31 Dec
X Milnes, J.L. 31 Dec
E Pelly, R.C. 31 Dec
X Walker, P.J. 31 Dec
X Massie-Taylor, C.G. 31 Dec
E Goodall, S.R.J. 31 Dec
X Hewitt, I.R. 31 Dec
E Kidner, P.J. 31 Dec
X Edleston, H.A.H.G. 31 Dec
X Willmett, A.M. 31 Dec
X Kerr, M.W.G. 31 Dec
E Wiltshire, G.J. 31 Dec
X Russell, D.J. 31 Dec

1994

X Cosby, R.A.DE.S. 30 Jun
S Ridland, K. 30 Jun
X Cust, D.R. 30 Jun
E Holmes, M.J. 30 Jun
X Keay, H. 30 Jun
X Barton, T.J. 30 Jun
X Williams, M.S. 30 Jun
X Snelson, D.G. 30 Jun
E Brokenshire, L.P. 30 Jun
E Warnett, D.L. 30 Jun
S Williams, J.L. 30 Jun
E MacLean, D.J. 30 Jun
X Somerville, A.J.D. 30 Jun
X Boissier, R.P. 30 Jun
X Thorpe, I. 31 Dec
E Hurford, P.G. 31 Dec
X Tall, D.M. 31 Dec
X Ainsley, R.S. 31 Dec
E Spires, T.A. 31 Dec
X Parker, J W 31 Dec
E Chittenden, T.C. 31 Dec
X Littleboy, M.N. 31 Dec
S Preston-Jones, N.C. 31 Dec
E Clark, A.I.H. 31 Dec
X Johns, A.J. 31 Dec
E Finlayson, R.D. 31 Dec
X Miller, A.J.G. 31 Dec

1995

X Booth, M.D. 30 Jun
X Bray, N.G.H. 30 Jun
E Fitzgerald, M.P. 30 Jun
X Waite, C.W. 30 Jun
X Harris, N.H.L. 30 Jun
E Raby, N.J.F. 30 Jun
S Savage, N.D. 30 Jun
X Clapp, R.J. 30 Jun
X Auty, S.J. 30 Jun
E Fairbairn, W.D.M. 30 Jun
X Laurence, T.J.H. 30 Jun
X Wilcocks, P.L. 30 Jun
E Turner, R.B. 30 Jun
E Searle, E.F. 31 Dec
X Manning, M.G.B. 31 Dec
X Tighe, J.G.H. 31 Dec
S Whitaker, H.R. 31 Dec
E Kirkpatrick, J. 31 Dec
X Batho, W.N.P. 31 Dec
X Stevenson, C.B.H. 31 Dec
E Dawson, E.W. 31 Dec
E Richardson, I.J.W. 31 Dec
X Welch, J. 31 Dec
X Clayton, C.H.T. 31 Dec
S Lane, M.G. 31 Dec
X Cooke, D.J. 31 Dec
E Melly, R.G. 31 Dec
X Silcock, C.A.J. 31 Dec
E Borley, K.J. 31 Dec
X Wilkinson, P.J. 31 Dec

1996

E Whatmough, D.E. 30 Jun
X Fifield, D.J. 30 Jun
E Eastley, B.R. 30 Jun
X Watson, P.H. 30 Jun
X Fanshawe, J.R. 30 Jun
X Barritt, M.K. 30 Jun
E Heselton, B.L. 30 Jun
X Boyd, J.A. 30 Jun
X Dickson, A.P. 30 Jun
S Sinclair, A.H. 30 Jun
X Massey, A.M. 30 Jun
X Lambert, P. 30 Jun
W Picton, A.M. 30 Jun
E Latham, N.D. 30 Jun
E Westwood, S.P.C. 31 Dec
S Pennefather, W.J.R. 31 Dec
X Daglish, H.B. 31 Dec
E McFadyen, H. 31 Dec
X Moodie, G.R. 31 Dec
X Baxter, G.F. 31 Dec
S Tatham, P.H. 31 Dec
X Covington, W.M. 31 Dec
E Jenkins, I.F. 31 Dec
E Horsted, P.J. 31 Dec
X Munns, C.R. 31 Dec
E Palmer, R.A.N. 31 Dec
X Mark, R.A. 31 Dec
X Leaman, R.D. 31 Dec
E Rankin, I.G. 31 Dec
X Soar, T.A. 31 Dec

1997

X Eberle, P.J.F. 30 Jun
X Peach, C.C. 30 Jun
E Jarvis, I.L. 30 Jun
X Fergusson, D.C.M. 30 Jun
E Kongialis, J.A. 30 Jun
S Hemsworth, M.K. 30 Jun
X Parry, C.J. 30 Jun
E Potter, M.J. 30 Jun
X Nance, A.R. 30 Jun
X Gass, C.J. 30 Jun
E Horrell, M.I. 30 Jun
X Ibbotson, R.J. 30 Jun
S Kimmons, M. 30 Jun
E Bowker, M.A. 30 Jun
E Henley, S.M. 30 Jun
X Rix, A.J. 30 Jun
E Mathews, A.D.H. 30 Jun
X Goddard, I.K. 31 Dec
E Wills, J.R. 31 Dec
E Patrick, J. 31 Dec

E Green, J.A. 31 Dec
S Wright, N.P. 31 Dec
X White, D.S.H. 31 Dec
E Marks, N. 31 Dec
X Avery, M.B. 31 Dec
E Tibbitt, I.P.G. 31 Dec
X Jermy, S.C. 31 Dec
X Montgomery, C.P.R. 31 Dec
X Butler, N.A.M. 31 Dec
E Thwaites, G.J. 31 Dec
S Pearce, J.K.C. 31 Dec
X Johnstone-Burt, C.A. 31 Dec
X Morisetti, N. 31 Dec
E Hussain, A.M. 31 Dec

1998

E Madge, R. 30 Jun
X Adair, A.A.S. 30 Jun
X Martin, S.C. 30 Jun
E Hollidge, J.H. 30 Jun
X Kirby, S.R. 30 Jun
X Larmour, D.R. 30 Jun
X Cameron, A.J.B. 30 Jun
X Bennett, A.R.C. 30 Jun
E Love, R.T. 30 Jun
X Wotton, J.C.L. 30 Jun
X Pond, D.W. 30 Jun
E Graves, M.E.L. 30 Jun
S Blackett, J. 30 Jun
X Cooling, R.G. 30 Jun
E Alabaster, M.B. 30 Jun
E Branch-Evans, S.J. 30 Jun
X Snow, C.A. 30 Jun
X Goodall, D.C. 31 Dec

E Miklinski, A.S. 31 Dec
X Docherty, P.T. 31 Dec
E Little, R.M. 31 Dec
S Menzies, A. 31 Dec
X Harris, T.R. 31 Dec
E Timms, S.J. 31 Dec
X Ramm, S.C. 31 Dec
E Van Beek, L. 31 Dec
X Walpole, P.K. 31 Dec
X Davies, P.N.M. 31 Dec
E Jackman, R.W. 31 Dec
S Martin, T.F.W. 31 Dec
W Stait, C.J. 31 Dec
X Brooks, A.S. 31 Dec
X Richards, A.D. 31 Dec
E Keegan, W.J. 31 Dec

1999

E Kidd, J.C. 30 Jun
X Knowles, J.M. 30 Jun
X Freeman, D.A.K. 30 Jun
S Rayner, B.N. 30 Jun
E Jaynes, P.R.W. 30 Jun
X Twitchen, R.C. 30 Jun
E Hyldon, C.J. 30 Jun
X Harland, N.J.G. 30 Jun
X Croke, A. 30 Jun
X Moncrieff, I. 30 Jun
E Rymer, A.R. 30 Jun
E Hockley, C.J. 30 Jun
X Corder, I.F. 30 Jun
X Zambellas, G.M. 30 Jun
X Nixon, M.C. 31 Dec
E Rees, J.B.M. 31 Dec

E Jarvis, D.J. 31 Dec
E Ellins, S.J. 31 Dec
X Mervik, C.F. 31 Dec
E Hart, J. 31 Dec
X Sloan, M.U. 31 Dec
S Fraser, R.W. 31 Dec
X Anderson, M. 31 Dec
X Mathias, P.B. 31 Dec
MS Reed, F. 31 Dec
E Lister, S.R. 31 Dec
X Jones, P.A. 31 Dec
E Baldwin, S.F. 31 Dec
X Gower, J.H.J. 31 Dec
X Winstanley, K. 31 Dec

2000

X Scorer, S.J. 30 Jun
E Williams, N.L. 30 Jun
S Quinn, P.A. 30 Jun
E Leeming, R.J. 30 Jun
X Mansergh, R.J. 30 Jun
E Wilkinson, R.M. 30 Jun
X Robinson, P.H. 30 Jun
S MacDonald, G.E. 30 Jun
E McFarlane, A.L. 30 Jun
X Cleary, S.P. 30 Jun
E Lloyd, S.J. 30 Jun
X Moll, A.G. 30 Jun
X Charlier, S.B. 30 Jun
E Peach, G.L. 30 Jun
X Lambert, N.R. 30 Jun
X Halliday, D.A. 30 Jun
X Potts, D.L. 30 Jun

COMMANDERS

1981

X Griffin, W.F.G. 30 Jun

1982

X Titmus, G.D. 30 Jun

1983

E Fulford, N.J.D. 30 Jun
X MacKenzie, K.D. 30 Jun
E Fenwick, J. 30 Jun
E MacDonald Watson, A.I. 31 Dec
E Darch, B.N. 31 Dec

1984

E Blake, R.M. 30 Jun
S Abbott, C.P.G. 30 Jun
E Hillier, N.J. 30 Jun
E Wiseman, W.T. 30 Jun
E Curran, M.G.S. 31 Dec

X James, M.A. 31 Dec

1985

X Hunt, G.C. 30 Jun
S Vosper, I.A. 30 Jun
E Jeffrey, I. 30 Jun
X Gordon Lennox, A.C. 30 Jun
X Laird, C.R. 31 Dec
X Rogers, A.G. 31 Dec
S Evans, M.J. 31 Dec
X Harris, P.N. 31 Dec

1986

E Knox, N.O.G. 30 Jun
S Guyatt, A.E. 30 Jun
X Piggott, G.D. 30 Jun
E Wood, A.C.M. 31 Dec
E Barltrop, J.A. 31 Dec

E Rennison, W.R. 31 Dec
X Taylor, A.F.M. 31 Dec
X Lake, R.V. 31 Dec
E Jay, K.G. 31 Dec
S Endersby, R.J.S. 31 Dec
X Bateman, G. 31 Dec
X Bennett, S.H.G. 31 Dec
X Fyfe, P.M. 31 Dec
X Galloway, P. 31 Dec

1987

S Farquhar, J.W. 30 Jun
X Nicoll, A.J.K. 30 Jun
E Dennis-Jones, M. 30 Jun
E Moir, S. 30 Jun
E Soutter, L.D.L. 30 Jun
X Baudains, D.P. 30 Jun
E Howick, S.W. 30 Jun

E Binns, J.B. .... 30 Jun
E Norton, A.J. .... 30 Jun
X Samborne, M.D.P. .... 30 Jun
E Edwards, I. .... 30 Jun
X Wright, J.W.T. .... 30 Jun
S Barge, M.A. .... 30 Jun
X Johnson, G.R. .... 30 Jun
E Ridley, W.K. .... 30 Jun
X Edmonds, G.J.L. .... 31 Dec
E Marley, P.S. .... 31 Dec
E Garland, J.M.R. .... 31 Dec
E Waters, C.D. .... 31 Dec
S Cordner, K. .... 31 Dec
X Harrison, R.G. .... 31 Dec
X Forsyth, A.W. .... 31 Dec
X Robinson, C.P. .... 31 Dec
X Hughes, P.J. .... 31 Dec
X McKenzie, I.S. .... 31 Dec
E Bailie, D.J. .... 31 Dec

1988

X Merrett, G.J. .... 30 Jun
X Prime, J.R.M. .... 30 Jun
E Cirin, W.R.J. .... 30 Jun
E Barnacle, C.A. .... 30 Jun
E Smith, A. .... 30 Jun
X Pegg, S.M. .... 30 Jun
X Stanesby, D.L. .... 30 Jun
E Lindley, R.A. .... 30 Jun
X Gale, H.N. .... 30 Jun
X Banting, Q.C.L. .... 30 Jun
E English, C.R. .... 30 Jun
X Teer, D.R. .... 30 Jun
S Sharp, C.C.G. .... 31 Dec
E Harbroe-Bush, R.D. .... 31 Dec
E Butler, R.J. .... 31 Dec
S Cole, C.M. .... 31 Dec
E Egerton, P.M. .... 31 Dec
E Kennaugh, A.J. .... 31 Dec
X Mitchell, R.H. .... 31 Dec
X Sayer, D.J. .... 31 Dec
X Welch, A.T. .... 31 Dec
S Gill, M. .... 31 Dec
E Townsend, J.R. .... 31 Dec
X Lister, J.A. .... 31 Dec
X Forster, T.J.A. .... 31 Dec
X Meatyard, C.G.B. .... 31 Dec
E Hoskins, A.B. .... 31 Dec
E Binns, J.B.H. .... 31 Dec
X Parris, K.J. .... 31 Dec

1989

W Stellingworth, J.P. .... 01 Apr
E Harris, M. .... 30 Jun
X Gregory, I.S. .... 30 Jun
X Higham, A. .... 30 Jun
X Ewins, G.P. .... 30 Jun
E Young, R.A.S. .... 30 Jun
X Skinner, J.R. .... 30 Jun
X Lightfoot, C.M. .... 30 Jun
X Jellyman, P.A. .... 30 Jun
X Chapman-Andrews, P.C. .. 30 Jun
E Doxsey, R.A. .... 30 Jun
E Magill, W.J. .... 30 Jun
S Ainslie, A.A. .... 30 Jun
S Head, R.R.D'E. .... 30 Jun
X Bailey, J. .... 30 Jun
X Matthews, P. .... 30 Jun
X Jones, P.H. .... 30 Jun
E Western, W.J.H. .... 30 Jun
E Thatcher, R.P. .... 30 Jun
X Lucey, R.N. .... 30 Jun
X Shaw, P.A. .... 01 Oct
X Watkins, C.F.F. .... 31 Dec
S Carter, S.F. .... 31 Dec
X Webster, G. .... 31 Dec
E Meaken, J. .... 31 Dec
S Stringer, M.C. .... 31 Dec
X Cowley, N.J. .... 31 Dec
X O'Neill, R.K. .... 31 Dec
E Douglas, F.R. .... 31 Dec
E Passingham, R.E. .... 31 Dec
E Antcliffe, G.A. .... 31 Dec
E Bell, A.D. .... 31 Dec
X Greenop, J.P.S. .... 31 Dec
X Smith, N.P. .... 31 Dec
S Knight, D.J. .... 31 Dec
X Scoles, J.C. .... 31 Dec
X Williams, T.N.E. .... 31 Dec
E Harrison, R.A. .... 31 Dec

1990

S Philpott, G.R. .... 30 Jun
X Rich, A.A. .... 30 Jun
E Banks, R.G. .... 30 Jun
E Broad, R.O. .... 30 Jun
X Craig, R.W.W. .... 30 Jun
E Rogers, M.S. .... 30 Jun
E Arthur, J.C.W. .... 30 Jun
X Habershon, D.B. .... 30 Jun
E Murch, J.D. .... 30 Jun
E Coles, G.W.G. .... 30 Jun
X Eltringham, T.J. .... 30 Jun
X Legg, M.R. .... 30 Jun
E Morgan, D. .... 30 Jun
X Sim, D.L.W. .... 30 Jun
X Turner, S.M. .... 30 Jun
X Ledingham, H.J. .... 30 Jun
E Issitt, D.J. .... 30 Jun
E Geddes, W.B. .... 30 Jun
X Morris, F. .... 01 Oct
X Hobson, P. .... 31 Dec
E Payne-Hanlon, P.N. .... 31 Dec
X Lamb, R. .... 31 Dec
X Stockman, C.D. .... 31 Dec
E Craig, D.M. .... 31 Dec
X McCready, G.A.R. .... 31 Dec
X Dodds, M. .... 31 Dec
X Williams, T.A. .... 31 Dec
S Backhouse, A.W. .... 31 Dec
E Steel, R.J. .... 31 Dec
E Milton, G.J.G. .... 31 Dec
X Overington, N. .... 31 Dec
E Young, A. .... 31 Dec
E Morris, P.N. .... 31 Dec
E Hodsdon, R.E. .... 31 Dec
X Sewell, I.T.T. .... 31 Dec
X Dedman, N.J.K. .... 31 Dec
X Hibbert, P.N. .... 31 Dec
X Bearne, J.P. .... 31 Dec
S Leatherby, J.H. .... 31 Dec
E Parker, G.P. .... 31 Dec
S Davis, B.J. .... 31 Dec
X Simmonds, R.M. .... 31 Dec
X Crabtree, I.M. .... 31 Dec
E Firth, S.K. .... 31 Dec
X Vaughan, D.M. .... 31 Dec

1991

E Walton, A.F. .... 30 Jun
X Clark, T.H.V. .... 30 Jun
E Hutchinson, T.J. .... 30 Jun
X Ewing, A.D. .... 30 Jun
X Chambers, N.M.C. .... 30 Jun
X Foster, G.R.N. .... 30 Jun
X Morris, D.S. .... 30 Jun
X Boxall-Hunt, B.P. .... 30 Jun
X Searle, R.J. .... 30 Jun
E Dodd, J.S.C. .... 30 Jun
E John, M.L. .... 30 Jun
E Moberly, N.G.H. .... 30 Jun
X Butcher, M.W. .... 30 Jun
X Steel, P.S.T.C. .... 30 Jun
X Ferguson, J.N. .... 30 Jun
X Palmer, C.L. .... 30 Jun
X MacDonald, D.H.L. .... 30 Jun
X Hudson, N.G. .... 30 Jun
S Ross, A.A. .... 30 Jun
E Swainson, D.J. .... 31 Dec
E Holgate, C.J. .... 31 Dec
X Underwood, A.G.H. .... 31 Dec

X Wilson, S.G. 31 Dec
X Bishop, R.J. 31 Dec
E Sayles, S. 31 Dec
E Bowker, E.A. 31 Dec
E Reeder, R. 31 Dec
E Hume, C.B. 31 Dec
S Day, N.R. 31 Dec
X Williams, N.D.B. 31 Dec
E Pancott, B.M. 31 Dec
X De Sa, P.J. 31 Dec
X Stoneman, T.J. 31 Dec
X Swain, D.M. 31 Dec
E Knowling, P.J. 31 Dec
X Bramley, S. 31 Dec
X Fortescue, P.W. 31 Dec
X Armstrong, C.A. 31 Dec
S Jones, A. 31 Dec
X Johnson, G.P. 31 Dec
X Turner, I. 31 Dec
E Bailey, J.W. 31 Dec
S McCarthy, P.J. 31 Dec
E Gibb, R.W. 31 Dec
E King, A.M. 31 Dec
X Lombard, D. 31 Dec

1992

X Burston, R. 30 Jun
X Govan, R.T. 30 Jun
S Lane, D.F. 30 Jun
X Shepherd, I. 30 Jun
X Ingham, P.C. 30 Jun
E Ratcliffe, J.P. 30 Jun
E Stanley, P. 30 Jun
X Ramsay, G.P. 30 Jun
E Matters, A.C. 30 Jun
X Gregan, D.C. 30 Jun
E Adams, R.A.S. 30 Jun
E Robb, M.C. 30 Jun
X Smee, N.L. 30 Jun
E Lankester, T.J. 30 Jun
E Dyer, S.J. 30 Jun
X Durston, D.H. 30 Jun
X Lankester, P. 30 Jun
X Donaldson, J. 30 Jun
E Smith, C.S. 30 Jun
S Hosker, T.J. 30 Jun
E Wadham, J. 30 Jun
X Hawkins, R.C. 30 Jun
E Hockley, G.P. 30 Jun
X Herman, T.R. 30 Jun
S Cornberg, M.A. 30 Jun
X Thoburn, R. 30 Jun
X Pickering, M.J. 01 Oct
X Arnall-Culliford, N.D. 01 Oct
X Root, W.R. 01 Oct
X Pepper, M.R. 31 Dec
X Maughan, J.M.C. 31 Dec
E Usborne, A.C. 31 Dec
X Arrow, J.W. 31 Dec
E Ayers, R.P.B. 31 Dec
X Aitken, F.J. 31 Dec
X Marshall, R.A. 31 Dec
E Cooper, J.A. 31 Dec
S Peilow, B.F. 31 Dec
E Thorpe, C.R. 31 Dec
X Lye, D.J. 31 Dec
W Robbins, M.J. 31 Dec
X Spalton, G.M.S. 31 Dec
E Arnold, B.W.H. 31 Dec
E Sherlock, F.C.E. 31 Dec
X Brocklebank, G.P. 31 Dec
X Bartholomew, I.M. 31 Dec
X Welborn, C.G. 31 Dec
X Gibson, I.A. 31 Dec
E Wormald, R.E. 31 Dec
E Watts, R.F. 31 Dec
X Powis, J. 31 Dec
E Tate, A.J. 31 Dec
E Hall, J.W.M. 31 Dec
X Dickens, D.J.R. 31 Dec
E Steel, C.M.H. 31 Dec
X Collins, P.N. 31 Dec
E Hughes, R.I. 31 Dec

1993

E Parsons, G. 30 Jun
E Febbrarro, N.R. 30 Jun
E Lineker, R.J. 30 Jun
S Williams, R.E. 30 Jun
X Dale, M.J. 30 Jun
X Andrew, W.G. 30 Jun
E Bateman, R.D. 30 Jun
X Grant, A.K. 30 Jun
E Guy, T.J. 30 Jun
X Bell-Davies, R.W. 30 Jun
X Mason, M.M.D. 30 Jun
X Chambers, W.J. 30 Jun
E Stratton, J.D. 30 Jun
X Upright, S.W. 30 Jun
E Sutherland, W.M. 30 Jun
E Bishop, P.R. 30 Jun
X Snow, M.C.P. 30 Jun
X Holihead, P.W. 30 Jun
E Wright, G.N. 30 Jun
E Haines, S.W. 30 Jun
S Cowdrey, M.C. 30 Jun
X Hennessey, T.P.D. 30 Jun
X Tarr, M.D. 30 Jun
X Williams, S.T. 30 Jun
X Harvey, K. 30 Jun
E Mason, R.W. 30 Jun
E Cox, P.W.S. 30 Jun
E Dannatt, T.M. 30 Jun
X Greenlees, I.W. 30 Jun
E Langbridge, D.C. 30 Jun
X Williams, B.N.B. 30 Jun
S Albon, R. 30 Jun
X Bateman, S.J.F. 30 Jun
X Pounder, A.G.P. 01 Oct
E Alexander, S.J. 01 Oct
X Connell, J.A. 01 Oct
X Haill, S.J.J. 31 Dec
E Gubbins, V.R. 31 Dec
X Turner, S.E. 31 Dec
E Coombes, D. 31 Dec
X Goodwin, D.R. 31 Dec
X Thomas, S.A. 31 Dec
E Jeffcoat, S.M. 31 Dec
X Bevan, S. 31 Dec
E George, S.A. 31 Dec
X Pothecary, R.E. 31 Dec
E Stenhouse, N.J. 31 Dec
E Menlove-Platt, C.J. 31 Dec
S Harbour, J.R.M. 31 Dec
E Lunn, J.F.C. 31 Dec
X Curd, T.A. 31 Dec
E Allwood, C. 31 Dec
X Trevithick, A.R. 31 Dec
X Bosshardt, R.G. 31 Dec
E Coulthard, J.K. 31 Dec
X Churchill, T.C. 31 Dec
E Parker, I.R. 31 Dec
X Humphrys, J.A. 31 Dec
X Edgell, J.N. 31 Dec
E Parry, R.W. 31 Dec
E Hore, R.C. 31 Dec
S Marsh, D.J. 31 Dec
E Coverdale, A. 31 Dec
E Costello, G.T. 31 Dec
X Riley, M.J. 31 Dec
S Crabtree, P.D. 31 Dec

1994

X Long, P.J. 30 Jun
S Cooper, S.N. 30 Jun
X Hatchard, P.J. 30 Jun
E Fisher, M.A.L. 30 Jun
X Stanley, C.E. 30 Jun
E Fox, K.A. 30 Jun
E Brockwell, P.E.N. 30 Jun
X Evans, D.M. 30 Jun
E Usborne, C.M. 30 Jun

S Forsyth, A.R. .... 30 Jun
E Whitehorn, I.J. .... 30 Jun
X Hinchliffe, P.B. .... 30 Jun
E Hart, D.J. .... 30 Jun
X Wallace, G.W.A. .... 30 Jun
S Nelson, D.T. .... 30 Jun
X Cutt, J.J.D. .... 30 Jun
E Molyneaux, D.G. .... 30 Jun
X Reid, M. .... 30 Jun
E Sealey, N.P. .... 30 Jun
E Whyntie, A. .... 30 Jun
X Humphreys, J.I. .... 30 Jun
E Christie, C.S. .... 30 Jun
X Rothwell, M.K. .... 30 Jun
E Rowell, G.E. .... 30 Jun
S Chelton, S.R.L. .... 30 Jun
X Arthur, I.D. .... 30 Jun
X Finney, M.E. .... 30 Jun
X Mansergh, M.P. .... 30 Jun
X Williams, I.R. .... 30 Jun
X Archibald, B.R. .... 30 Jun
E Gosden, S.R. .... 30 Jun
X Brown, M.K. .... 20 Sep
X Ward, N.J. .... 01 Oct
E Smith-Jaynes, E.R. .... 01 Oct
S Holder, R.J. .... 01 Oct
E Lea, J.H.A. .... 31 Dec
X James, D.R. .... 31 Dec
X Brown, R.A.M. .... 31 Dec
E Wakeling, J.L. .... 31 Dec
S Whalley, S.D. .... 31 Dec
X Hosking, D.B. .... 31 Dec
E Parry, N.T. .... 31 Dec
X Murgatroyd, A.C. .... 31 Dec
E Faulconbridge, D. .... 31 Dec
X Fletcher, N.E. .... 31 Dec
X Davies, A.R. .... 31 Dec
E McElwaine, R.I. .... 31 Dec
X Horne, T.K. .... 31 Dec
X Fraser, E. .... 31 Dec
X Evans, M.C. .... 31 Dec
E Powell, R.N. .... 31 Dec
X Stallion, I.M. .... 31 Dec
E Peckham, D.R. .... 31 Dec
X Ward, J.E. .... 31 Dec
X Clark, K.I.M. .... 31 Dec
X Wellesley, R.C.R. .... 31 Dec
E Holberry, A.P. .... 31 Dec
E Neave, C.B. .... 31 Dec
X Stanford, J.H. .... 31 Dec
X Burrows, M.J. .... 31 Dec
E White, A.R. .... 31 Dec
S Airey, S.E. .... 31 Dec
E Couch, P.J. .... 31 Dec
X Karsten, T.M. .... 31 Dec
E Jess, I.M. .... 31 Dec
S Steel, D.G. .... 31 Dec
X Gillanders, F.G.R. .... 31 Dec

1995

X Carter, K. .... 30 Jun
E Podger, K.G.R. .... 30 Jun
S Mullen, A.J. .... 30 Jun
X Stamp, G. .... 30 Jun
X Phillips, D.G. .... 30 Jun
X McNair, E.A. .... 30 Jun
E Longbottom, C.J. .... 30 Jun
X Wilson, C.D. .... 30 Jun
X Shrives, M.P. .... 30 Jun
X Norris, R.J. .... 30 Jun
E Evans, D.J. .... 30 Jun
X Thomas, R.P. .... 30 Jun
X Westwood, M.W. .... 30 Jun
X Gasson, N.S.C. .... 30 Jun
X Thomas, G.C. .... 30 Jun
E Kenward, P.D. .... 30 Jun
E Pendle, M.E.J. .... 30 Jun
X Cunningham, T.A. .... 30 Jun
S Walker, C.S. .... 30 Jun
E Burrell, P.M. .... 30 Jun
X Stanley, N.P. .... 30 Jun
E Price, F.E.F. .... 30 Jun
E Young, S.S. .... 30 Jun
X Lander, M.C. .... 30 Jun
X Richards, C.M. .... 30 Jun
E Rusbridger, R.C. .... 30 Jun
X Clarke, C.M.L. .... 30 Jun
E Jagger, P.R.A. .... 30 Jun
X Wallace, M.R.B. .... 30 Jun
E Thompson, R.J. .... 30 Jun
X Westbrook, J.S. .... 30 Jun
X Salter, M.D. .... 01 Oct
X Bull, A.J. .... 01 Oct
E Wearmouth, P.W.A. .... 01 Oct
X Hilton, D. .... 01 Oct
MS Bootland, E.G. .... 01 Oct
W Muxworthy, A.M.B. .... 31 Dec
X Wain, R.N. .... 31 Dec
X Holmes, R. .... 31 Dec
E Cummin, M.A. .... 31 Dec
E Smith, M.A. .... 31 Dec
E Spicer, C.G. .... 31 Dec
X Doyne-Ditmas, P.S. .... 31 Dec
S Ireland, R.C. .... 31 Dec
E Sewry, M.R. .... 31 Dec
X Stonor, P.F.A. .... 31 Dec
X Seatherton, E.F.K. .... 31 Dec
E Penny, A.D. .... 31 Dec
E Burton, D.S. .... 31 Dec
X Beaumont, I.H. .... 31 Dec
X Harrap, N.R.E. .... 31 Dec
S Storrs-Fox, R.N. .... 31 Dec
X Davis-Marks, M.L. .... 31 Dec
E Herridge, P.G. .... 31 Dec
X Sillars, M.C. .... 31 Dec
E Powell, D.C. .... 31 Dec
X Best, R.R. .... 31 Dec
S Keefe, P.C. .... 31 Dec
E Anderson, R.G. .... 31 Dec
E Forsey, C.R. .... 31 Dec
X O'Reilly, S.A. .... 31 Dec
X Harding, R.G. .... 31 Dec
E Holloway, J.T. .... 31 Dec
X Murphie, J.D.D. .... 31 Dec
E Brunton, S.B. .... 31 Dec
E Wyatt, S.P. .... 31 Dec
E Fulford, J.P.H. .... 31 Dec
X Pegg, R.M. .... 31 Dec
X Keble, K.W.L. .... 31 Dec
S Bullock, M.P. .... 31 Dec
E Watts, G.M. .... 31 Dec
X Hudson, P.D. .... 31 Dec
E Johns, T. .... 31 Dec
X Lowe, T.M. .... 31 Dec

1996

X Nicholson, S.C.L. .... 30 Jun
E Nixon, P.W. .... 30 Jun
E Farrington, S.P. .... 30 Jun
E Heritage, L.J. .... 30 Jun
X Betteridge, J.T. .... 30 Jun
E Middlemas, S.R. .... 30 Jun
X Langhorn, N. .... 30 Jun
X Windsor, M. .... 30 Jun
X Ayres, C.P. .... 30 Jun
E Van Beek, D. .... 30 Jun
E Lovett, M.J. .... 30 Jun
X Funnell, N.C. .... 30 Jun
E Price, J.P. .... 30 Jun
E Bridger, D.W. .... 30 Jun
X Sibbit, N.T. .... 30 Jun
E Drake, E.D. .... 30 Jun
X Furness, S.B. .... 30 Jun
X Wood, J.N.A. .... 30 Jun
E Haley, T.J. .... 30 Jun
S Smith, M. .... 30 Jun
X Rycroft, A.E. .... 30 Jun
X Warren, B.H. .... 30 Jun
E Gourlay, J.S. .... 30 Jun

X Perkins, M.J. .... 30 Jun
X Corrigan, N.R. .... 30 Jun
E Da Gama, J.A.J. .... 30 Jun
S Finlayson, A.G. .... 30 Jun
E Taylor, J.J. .... 30 Jun
X Wolfe, D.E. .... 30 Jun
X Chick, S.J. .... 30 Jun
X Farrington, R. .... 30 Jun
E Erskine, P.A. .... 30 Jun
X Blunden, J.J.F. .... 30 Jun
S King, C.E.W. .... 30 Jun
E Beverstock, M.A. .... 30 Jun
X Doggett, R.A. .... 01 Oct
E Yuill, I.A. .... 01 Oct
E Burgess, W.C. .... 01 Oct
W Hoath, M.E.J. .... 01 Oct
MS Chandler, M. .... 01 Oct
S Anderson, M.J. .... 01 Oct
E Leggett, C.C. .... 01 Oct
X Easton, R.W. .... 01 Oct
E Reid, D. .... 01 Oct
X Bowen, G.P. .... 01 Oct
X Lee, D.J. .... 31 Dec
E Palmer, J.E. .... 31 Dec
E Grafton, M.N. .... 31 Dec
X Sullivan, C. .... 31 Dec
E Terry, J.M. .... 31 Dec
S Nairn, R. .... 31 Dec
X Lambert, B. .... 31 Dec
E Lofthouse, I. .... 31 Dec
X Hamp, C.J. .... 31 Dec
X Handley, J.M. .... 31 Dec
X Lambourn, P.N. .... 31 Dec
S Church, A.D. .... 31 Dec
E Wilson, K.P. .... 31 Dec
X Cochrane, M.C.N. .... 31 Dec
X Edney, A.R. .... 31 Dec
E Lewis, D.M.J. .... 31 Dec
X Pearey, M.S. .... 31 Dec
X Thicknesse, P.J. .... 31 Dec
X Hughes, N.J. .... 31 Dec
E Dearden, S.R. .... 31 Dec
S Tinsley, G.N. .... 31 Dec
E Thistlethwaite, M.H. .... 31 Dec
X Buckley, P.J.A. .... 31 Dec
X Richmond, I.J.M. .... 31 Dec
X Lilley, D.J. .... 31 Dec
X Hugo, I.D. .... 31 Dec
E Jenkin, A.M.H. .... 31 Dec
X Abraham, P. .... 31 Dec
E Wise, S.D. .... 31 Dec
X Parr, M.J. .... 31 Dec
E Farrage, M.E. .... 31 Dec
X Fraser, T.P. .... 31 Dec
E King, E.M. .... 31 Dec
E Whittaker, N.J. .... 31 Dec
S Peel, G.R. .... 31 Dec
X Smallman, L.D. .... 31 Dec

1997

X Horne, T.G. .... 30 Jun
X Robinson, A. .... 30 Jun
X Balston, D.C.W. .... 30 Jun
E Spalding, R.E.H. .... 30 Jun
E Whitaker, M.J. .... 30 Jun
E Derrick, G.G.J. .... 30 Jun
X Moores, J.K. .... 30 Jun
E Foster, M.A. .... 30 Jun
X Stewart, R.G. .... 30 Jun
E Graham, G.R. .... 30 Jun
E Page, D.M. .... 30 Jun
X Morgan, P.T. .... 30 Jun
X Spence, N.A. .... 30 Jun
E Starks, M.R. .... 30 Jun
E Holdsworth, H.W. .... 30 Jun
X Scarth, W. .... 30 Jun
X Baum, S.R. .... 30 Jun
X Pickles, I.S. .... 30 Jun
S Richardson, M.P. .... 30 Jun
X Barker, R.D.J. .... 30 Jun
X Brand, S.M. .... 30 Jun
X Tarrant, R.K. .... 30 Jun
E Dolton, A. .... 30 Jun
S Crook, A.S. .... 30 Jun
E O'Neill, P.J. .... 30 Jun
X Bell, A.S. .... 30 Jun
E Braham, S.W. .... 30 Jun
X Garratt, M.D. .... 30 Jun
X Morse, J.A. .... 30 Jun
E Hay, J.D. .... 30 Jun
E Smithson, P.E. .... 30 Jun
X King, J.N.G. .... 30 Jun
E Parker, H.H. .... 30 Jun
X Beardall, J. .... 01 Oct
MS Baker, K. .... 01 Oct
E Foster, S. .... 01 Oct
E Brazier, F.W.T. .... 01 Oct
E Waterman, J.H. .... 31 Dec
X Nail, V.A. .... 31 Dec
S Charlton, C.R.A.M. .... 31 Dec
E Greenwood, S. .... 31 Dec
E Wrightson, H.M. .... 31 Dec
E Penniston, J.R. .... 31 Dec
E Straughan, H. .... 31 Dec
E Peck, I.J. .... 31 Dec
X Rimmer, M. .... 31 Dec
X Brooksbank, R.J. .... 31 Dec
X Robinson, J.S. .... 31 Dec
E Slawson, J.M. .... 31 Dec
X Taylor, K.A. .... 31 Dec
X Neil, S.J. .... 31 Dec
X MacKay, G.A. .... 31 Dec
E Newell, J.M. .... 31 Dec
S White, S.N. .... 31 Dec
E Sunderland, J.D. .... 31 Dec
X McBarnet, T.F. .... 31 Dec
X Minns, P.F. .... 31 Dec
S Cunningham, P. .... 31 Dec
X Garrett, S.W. .... 31 Dec
X Williams, S.P. .... 31 Dec
E Pickthall, D.N. .... 31 Dec
X Lloyd, P.R. .... 31 Dec
X Blazeby, N.J. .... 31 Dec
X Ameye, C.R. .... 31 Dec
X Pope, C.M. .... 31 Dec
X Hawthorne, M.J. .... 31 Dec
X Lemkes, P.D. .... 31 Dec
E Carter, A.F.R. .... 31 Dec
E Oakley, N.G. .... 31 Dec
S Atherton, M.J. .... 31 Dec
X Kenny, S.J. .... 31 Dec
X Pettitt, G.W. .... 31 Dec
E Beckett, K.A. .... 31 Dec
X Johnstone, C.C.C. .... 31 Dec

1998

E Taylor, S.A. .... 09 Jun
X Snook, R.E. .... 30 Jun
E Enticknap, K. .... 30 Jun
E Clark, D.K. .... 30 Jun
X Jardine, G.A. .... 30 Jun
X Lade, C.J. .... 30 Jun
E McLennan, R.G. .... 30 Jun
X Steeds, S.M. .... 30 Jun
X Jackman, A.W. .... 30 Jun
X Gaunt, N.R. .... 30 Jun
E Russell, S.J. .... 30 Jun
E Main, E.S. .... 30 Jun
X Ewence, M.W. .... 30 Jun
E MacDonald, A.I. .... 30 Jun
X Cassar, A.P.F. .... 30 Jun
S Pattinson, I.H. .... 30 Jun
E Quaye, D.T.G. .... 30 Jun
X Robertson, K.F. .... 30 Jun
X McDonnell, P.W. .... 30 Jun
E Wiles, S.J. .... 30 Jun
X Reynolds, T.E. .... 30 Jun
E Shipperley, I. .... 30 Jun
X Ingram, R.G. .... 30 Jun

X	Cree, M.C.	30 Jun
S	Flanagan, J.	30 Jun
X	Alcock, C.	30 Jun
X	Kings, S.J.N.	30 Jun
X	Ancona, S.J.	30 Jun
E	Elford, D.G.	30 Jun
S	Litchfield, J.F.	30 Jun
E	Gulley, T.J.	30 Jun
X	Sutton, G.B.	30 Jun
E	Danbury, I.G.	30 Jun
X	Bennett, P.M.	30 Jun
X	Darlington, M.R.	30 Jun
E	Sexton, M.J.	30 Jun
E	Toy, M.J.	30 Jun
X	Sanguinetti, H.R.	30 Jun
X	Murnane, P.M.	01 Oct
X	White, M.E.	01 Oct
S	Harry, P.N.	01 Oct
X	Stockton, J.P.	01 Oct
E	Collins, R.J.	01 Oct
E	Hart, W.C.	01 Oct
MS	Holyer, R.J.	01 Oct
E	Hobbs, R.	01 Oct
X	Trundle, N.R.E.	31 Dec
E	Hawkins, I.	31 Dec
E	Dodgson, S.J.	31 Dec
E	Davies, T.G.	31 Dec
S	Spiller, M.F.	31 Dec
X	Newton, D.J.	31 Dec
X	White, M.W.	31 Dec
X	Percharde, M.R.	31 Dec
E	Mason, N.H.	31 Dec
E	Curnow, M.D.	31 Dec
E	Gray, A.J.	31 Dec
X	Woods, R.P.	31 Dec
X	Clark, A.W.C.	31 Dec
E	Stanley-Whyte, B.J.	31 Dec
S	Beard, G.T.C.	31 Dec
E	Fry, J.M.S.	31 Dec
X	Williams, M.H.	31 Dec
S	Redstone, C.	31 Dec
X	Hatch, G.W.H.	31 Dec
E	Tigwell, N.K.	31 Dec
X	Evans, K.N.M.	31 Dec
E	Green, A.R.	31 Dec
X	McKendrick, A.M.	31 Dec
E	Chidley, T.J.	31 Dec
X	Muir, K.	31 Dec
E	Green, S.N.	31 Dec
X	McCartain, M.B.W.	31 Dec
X	Shield, S.J.	31 Dec
X	Cook, P.R.	31 Dec
E	Hooley, R.G.	31 Dec
S	Skidmore, C.M.	31 Dec
E	Stokes, R.	31 Dec
X	Adams, A.J.	31 Dec
X	Green, T.J.	31 Dec
E	O'Reilly, T.M.	31 Dec
X	McAlpine, P.A.	31 Dec
X	McQuaker, S.R.	31 Dec
E	Morritt, D.C.	31 Dec
S	Jameson, A.C.	31 Dec
E	Hayes, J.V.B.	31 Dec
X	Trevor, M.G.	31 Dec
S	Brown, N.L.	31 Dec
	1999	
X	The Duke Of York, H.R.H.	27 Apr
E	Merriman, P.O.	30 Jun
E	Hadfield, D.	30 Jun
S	Rees, J.H.	30 Jun
X	Drewett, R.E.	30 Jun
X	Haley, C.W.	30 Jun
E	Ellis, R.W.	30 Jun
E	Fear, R.K.	30 Jun
X	Alexander, R.S.	30 Jun
E	Ranson, C.D.	30 Jun
E	Darwent, A.	30 Jun
E	Pett, J.G.	30 Jun
X	Clarke, N.J.	30 Jun
E	Haworth, J.	30 Jun
E	Bisson, I.J.P.	30 Jun
E	Vandome, A.M.	30 Jun
X	Spencer, E.A.	30 Jun
X	Knibbs, M.	30 Jun
X	Jervis, N.D.	30 Jun
E	Michie, A.R.	30 Jun
S	Thomas, F.S.	30 Jun
X	Carden, P.D.	30 Jun
X	Northwood, G.R.	30 Jun
E	Ramshaw, G.W.L.	30 Jun
E	Simmons, N.D.	30 Jun
X	Ireland, A.R.	30 Jun
X	Horn, P.B.	30 Jun
S	Morton, N.P.B.	30 Jun
X	Robinson, C.E.T.	30 Jun
X	Moore, C.I.	30 Jun
E	Lewis, J.K.	30 Jun
E	Barton, P.G.	30 Jun
X	Titterton, P.J.	30 Jun
E	Daws, R.P.A.	30 Jun
X	Allen, R.M.	30 Jun
X	Clink, J.R.H.	30 Jun
X	Pollock, D.J.	30 Jun
X	Weale, J.S.	30 Jun
E	Roberts, N.S.	30 Jun
S	Lavery, J.P.	30 Jun
X	Kingwell, J.M.L.	30 Jun
X	Millward, J.P.	31 Dec
E	Morley, A.D.	31 Dec
E	Tindall-Jones, L.D.	31 Dec
X	Buckland, R.J.F.	31 Dec
X	Ovens, J.J.	31 Dec
E	Treanor, M.A.	31 Dec
E	Maltby, M.R.J.	31 Dec
S	Isaac, P.	31 Dec
E	Crossley, C.C.	31 Dec
S	Tulley, J.R.	31 Dec
E	Greene, M.J.	31 Dec
X	Chalmers, D.P.	31 Dec
X	Matthews, D.N.	31 Dec
E	Mason, A.H.	31 Dec
X	Tuppen, R.M.	31 Dec
X	Johnson, A.S.	31 Dec
E	Plant, J.N.M.	31 Dec
X	Shaw, P.A.G.	31 Dec
X	Doyle, G.L.	31 Dec
E	Thompson, S.J.	31 Dec
E	Morrison, K.W.	31 Dec
E	Woodcock, S.J.	31 Dec
X	Harris, A.I.	31 Dec
S	Gray, R.S.	31 Dec
X	Reid, C.I.	31 Dec
S	Murdoch, S.J.	31 Dec
X	Race, N.J.	31 Dec
E	Hodgson, T.C.	31 Dec
X	Brown, H.S.	31 Dec
X	Hopper, S.O.	31 Dec
E	Morris, A.J.	31 Dec
X	McMichael-Phillips, S.J.	31 Dec
E	Stubbings, P.R.	31 Dec
S	Gardner, C.R.S.	31 Dec
E	Harrison, M.S.	31 Dec
E	Johnson, J.C.	31 Dec
X	Sullivan, A.G.	31 Dec
E	French, S.A.	31 Dec
E	Wareham, M.P.	31 Dec
E	Hammond, P.A.	31 Dec
X	Porter, S.P.	31 Dec
MS	White, M.A.	31 Dec
X	Healy, A.J.	31 Dec
X	Walliker, M.J.D.	31 Dec
S	Rance, M.G.W.	31 Dec
X	Bone, D.N.	31 Dec
E	Tate, S.J.	31 Dec
X	Key, B.J.	31 Dec
X	McGhie, I.A.	31 Dec

2000

X Daniels, S.A. 30 Jun
E Blake, G.E. 30 Jun
E McKenzie, D. 30 Jun
E Moreland, M.J. 30 Jun
X Snowball, S.J. 30 Jun
X Stewart, A.C. 30 Jun
S Graham, J.E. 30 Jun
X Tilley, D.S.J. 30 Jun
X Newton, G.A. 30 Jun
X Sephton, J.R. 30 Jun
X Cunningham, R.A. 30 Jun
E Basson, A.P. 30 Jun
X Broadley, K.J. 30 Jun
E Atkinson, S.R. 30 Jun
E Argent-Hall, D. 30 Jun
E Baker, P.G. 30 Jun
E Short, G.C. 30 Jun
X Martin, C.J. 30 Jun
E Morris, N.J. 30 Jun
S Tothill, N.M. 30 Jun
S Fergusson, H.J. 30 Jun
E Harvey, C.A. 30 Jun
X McNeile, R.H. 30 Jun
X Hayes, S.J. 30 Jun
E Vanderpump, D.J. 30 Jun
S Wunderle, C.A. 30 Jun
X Entwistle, S.C. 30 Jun
S Spence, A.B. 30 Jun
E Gilbert, S.A. 30 Jun
X Carter, I.P. 30 Jun
X Stockings, T.M. 30 Jun
X Chivers, P.A. 30 Jun
E Walker, N.J. 30 Jun
E Walker, M. 30 Jun
X Heley, D.N. 30 Jun
X Pearson, S.J. 30 Jun
X Allibon, M.C. 30 Jun
X Thompson, G. 30 Jun
S Bath, M.A.W. 30 Jun
E Williams, M.J. 30 Jun
E Little, G.T. 30 Jun
X Talbot, R.P. 30 Jun
E Dyer, M.D.J. 30 Jun
X Hine, N.W. 30 Jun
E Reason, I.M. 30 Jun

LIEUTENANT COMMANDERS

1976

E Eitzen, R.P. 01 Nov

1977

E Jones, A.W. 01 Jul

1978

E Morley-Smith, N.H. 01 Feb

1979

X Hearnden, G.E. 01 Apr
E Milne, D.M.F. 16 Aug
X Cullen-Jones, H. 01 Sep
E Hookway, B.C. 12 Sep
E Mitchell, B.A. 01 Nov
S Turton, T.M.H. 16 Nov

1980

X Moult, R.M. 09 Jan
X Hennell, N.J. 01 Mar
E Stephenson, F. 16 May
E Sanders, A.W.T. 01 Aug
X Wrighton, C.R. 16 Sep
X Brimley, K.S. 01 Dec
E Young, I.J. 16 Dec
X Budd, P.R. 16 Dec

1981

X Willett, R.J. 04 Jan
X Brady, M.R. 16 Jan
X Engeham, P.R. 16 Jan
E Pegden, C. 16 Feb
X Niven, G.D. 01 Mar
X Cuming, B.H.D. 16 Mar
X Langrishe, J.H. 16 Apr
X McKellar, R.A. 01 Jun
S Screech, M.C. 01 Aug
X Read, R.H. 01 Sep
X Rainbow, J. 14 Sep
X Flynn, P.J. 31 Oct
E Budge, R.G. 01 Nov
S Maguire, A.P.D. 01 Nov
X Jones, B.S. 16 Nov
E Howe, D.L. 23 Nov
E Broadbent, A. 29 Nov
X Rydiard, D.M. 01 Dec

1982

E Murray, R.H. 01 Jan
X Todd, D. 01 Jan
E Chadwick, G.E. 01 Apr
X Dickinson, P.N. 01 May
E Helby, P.F.H. 16 Jul
E Ager, R.G. 01 Aug
X Farmer, J.R. 16 Aug
X Smith, S.F. 01 Sep
X Rothwell, J.F. 01 Sep
E Huggins, G.E. 15 Sep
E Debenham, L.A. 20 Oct
X Woodbridge, G.F. 01 Nov
X Bent, G.R. 01 Nov
E Shand, C.M. 01 Nov
E Kidd, C.J.C. 01 Dec
E Fernihough, M.R. 08 Dec
S Austin, S.J. 16 Dec

1983

S Marshall, J.P. 01 Jan
E Flockhart, D.N. 01 Jan
X Toms, R.J. 16 Jan
S Hepburn, J. 01 Feb
X Long, D.R. 17 Feb
X Luker, G.P. 01 Mar
S Stuart, C.W.M. 01 Mar
X Leyshon, B.S. 16 Mar
X Port, L.A. 15 Apr
X Jagger, C.E. 16 Apr
X Sheldrake, T.W. 29 Apr
X Felgate, H. 01 May
X Gooder, S.P. 01 May
E Trott, P.A. 19 May
X Nelson, T.B. 16 Jun
S Hutchinson, T.S. 01 Jul
X Wilson, R. 01 Jul
X Cook, H.C. 10 Aug
X Davies, I.H. 16 Oct
E Melrose, J. 27 Oct
S Johnson, P.R. 01 Nov
S Mason, C.E. 16 Nov
X Winchurch, M.R.G. 16 Nov

1984

X Squibb, C.J. 16 Jan
X Sinclair, A.B. 01 Feb
X Thornton, C.E. 01 Feb
E Robinson, D.I. 01 Feb
X Thornton, M.C. 08 Feb
E Noyc, C.L. 21 Feb
X Manchanda, K.S. 01 Mar
X Eagles, A.J. 01 Mar
X Hoole, R.J. 01 Mar
E Robbins, J.G. 01 Mar
X Scruton, N. 16 Mar
E Smith, A.C. 16 Mar
E Aubrey-Rees, A.W. 16 Apr
X Coley, A.R. 16 Apr
S Scott, R.M. 01 May
X Buckley, P. 01 May
X McDonald, J.J.B. 01 May

E Will, A.W. .... 01 Jun
E Dixon, R.F. .... 08 Jun
X Fraser, D.K. .... 01 Jul
X Jackson, M.A. .... 25 Jul
X Fewtrell, M. .... 01 Sep
X Walton, D. .... 01 Sep
E Lemon, R.G.A. .... 01 Sep
X Pilley, M.A. .... 16 Sep
X Easton, R.N. .... 16 Nov
X Woolliams, M.F. .... 01 Dec
X King, N.A. .... 01 Dec
X Jolly, J.E.I. .... 16 Dec

1985

X Terrill, K.W. .... 01 Mar
X Ward, F.S. .... 01 Mar
X Harrall, P.A.R. .... 03 Mar
X Archdale, P.M. .... 16 Mar
X Brown, P.R. .... 16 Mar
X Wainwright, P.A. .... 16 Mar
X Munday, I.V. .... 01 Apr
X Brown, D.J. .... 01 Apr
S Kelly, M.D.R. .... 01 Apr
E Fergusson, R.R. .... 01 May
X Bebbington, S.P. .... 01 May
X Stone, C.R.M. .... 01 May
X Bourn, K.E. .... 09 May
X Buckley, M.J. .... 16 May
E Pilsworth, D.S. .... 01 Jun
S Edwards, C.C. .... 01 Jul
S Gopsill, B.R. .... 01 Jul
X Tidbury, N. .... 05 Jul
E Parsons, P.K.C. .... 29 Jul
X Wilson, C.G.T. .... 01 Aug
X Edmonds, G. .... 02 Aug
X McKay, P.A. .... 16 Aug
X Wright, M.J. .... 01 Sep
X Hammond, N.J. .... 01 Sep
X Rowlands, G.A. .... 01 Sep
S Craven, J.A.G. .... 01 Sep
E Williams, S.J. .... 18 Oct
E Lawton, A.C.R. .... 01 Nov
X Butcher, M.C. .... 16 Nov
E Franks, J.P. .... 01 Dec
E Coulson, J.R. .... 08 Dec

1986

X Spens-Black, G.P. .... 16 Jan
E Nolton, J.R. .... 01 Feb
X Alexander, G.E. .... 15 Feb
X Evans, M.J.G. .... 01 Mar
X Grandison, J.A.S. .... 01 Mar
X Robertson, F.W. .... 01 Mar
E Carr, G. .... 06 Mar
S Edwards, J.M. .... 01 Apr
S Hayward, P.J. .... 01 Apr
S Fishlock, G.N. .... 16 Apr
E Baker, A.P. .... 26 Apr
X Blair, S.R. .... 01 May
X Evans, J.W. .... 06 May
X Watson, C.C. .... 16 May
E Talbot, G.K. .... 01 Sep
X Mannion, T.S. .... 01 Sep
X Osman, M.R. .... 01 Sep
X Field, S.N.C. .... 01 Sep
X Daykin, P.M. .... 09 Sep
X Browning, M.L.C. .... 21 Sep
E Churchill, W.J. .... 01 Oct
X Lewis, P.R. .... 21 Nov
X Wells, D.A.H. .... 29 Nov
X Forrester, T.R. .... 01 Dec
S Erskine, R.N. .... 16 Dec
X Wilkinson, A.J. .... 16 Dec

1987

X Staveley, J.R. .... 01 Jan
X Chandler, S.A. .... 01 Jan
X Lewis, S.B. .... 01 Jan
X Dobson, M.F. .... 01 Jan
X Smith, J.C. .... 06 Jan
E Fiander, P.J. .... 01 Feb
X Dickens, M.G.C. .... 01 Feb
S Hattersley, J.P.G. .... 01 Feb
X White, P. .... 01 Feb
X Taylor, N.F. .... 16 Feb
S Painter, C.J. .... 23 Feb
X Tunnicliffe, P.A. .... 01 Mar
X Richings, P.C. .... 01 Mar
X Stephenson, G.T. .... 01 Mar
E Maidment, K.C. .... 01 Mar
X Gibson, T.A. .... 16 Mar
E Brook, J.G. .... 21 Mar
X Harrison, R.F. .... 22 Mar
X Creates, K.I. .... 01 Apr
X Reynolds, C.H. .... 01 Apr
X Jenks, A.W.J. .... 16 Apr
X Field, J.D. .... 16 Apr
X Sandover, R.J. .... 20 Apr
X MacNaughton, F.G. .... 01 May
X Martin, N.D. .... 01 Jun
E Kirk, T.L. .... 01 Jun
E Hunter, K.P. .... 01 Aug
X Peters, A.J.U. .... 01 Aug
E Lord, A.S. .... 01 Sep
X Crudgington, P. .... 01 Sep
X Taylor, J.W. .... 01 Sep
X Brown, C.D. .... 01 Sep
S Hayles, N.C. .... 01 Sep
X Raggett, A. .... 01 Sep
E Stillwell, A.J. .... 01 Sep
E Newton, M.R. .... 22 Sep
X West, R.J. .... 01 Oct
X Goddard, D.J.S. .... 01 Oct
E Prideaux, D.M. .... 01 Oct
X Gaskin, S.E. .... 01 Nov
X Holmes, G. .... 01 Dec
X Allen, M.J. .... 01 Dec
X Franks, K.B. .... 01 Dec
E Trotter, S. .... 01 Dec

1988

X Wood, C.A. .... 09 Jan
E Leggett, S.E. .... 13 Jan
E Baker, G.R. .... 15 Jan
E Thompson, G.N. .... 25 Jan
S Billington, N.S. .... 01 Feb
E Edwards, A.D.P. .... 01 Feb
X Sharpe, G.J. .... 01 Feb
X Prince, A.C.V. .... 16 Feb
E Wombwell, J.F. .... 19 Feb
X Pamphilon, M.J. .... 01 Mar
E Honey, J.P. .... 01 Mar
E Cross, M.G. .... 01 Apr
X Nelson, D.E. .... 01 Apr
X Malin, M.J. .... 01 Apr
E O'Brien, P.C. .... 23 Apr
X MacKett, D.G. .... 01 May
X Johnson, B. .... 01 May
X Speller, N.S.F. .... 01 May
X Little, N.R. .... 01 Jun
E Nurse, M.T. .... 01 Jun
X Appleyard, T.P. .... 05 Jun
X Woznicki, S.J. .... 16 Jun
S Clark, R.W. .... 01 Jul
X Davis, M.P. .... 01 Jul
S Stobie, I.C.A. .... 28 Jul
X Adams, R.J. .... 01 Aug
E Boyes, N. .... 11 Aug
X Ewers, A.M. .... 20 Aug
X Hirst, R.T. .... 01 Sep
X Watt, S. .... 29 Sep
X Bristow, G.D. .... 01 Oct
X Sauze, M.J. .... 01 Oct
X Schwarz, P.M.G. .... 01 Oct
X Clark, M.A.S. .... 01 Oct
X Tozer, C.V. .... 01 Oct
X Cooper, J.A. .... 01 Oct
E Cooke, R.G. .... 01 Oct
X Abbey, M.P. .... 01 Oct

E Dinham, A.C. .... 01 Oct
X Chambers, T.G. .... 01 Oct
X Holt, A.F. .... 01 Oct
X Palmer, G.D. .... 01 Oct
X Wrigley, P.J. .... 16 Oct
S Seddon, J.S.M. .... 16 Oct
X Lambert, K.J. .... 16 Nov
X Smith, K.M. .... 16 Nov
E Quine, N.J. .... 01 Dec
E Gabriel, C.J. .... 01 Dec
E Gillam, R.L. .... 01 Dec

1989

X Thomas, M.N. .... 01 Jan
S Dwane, C.M.R. .... 01 Jan
X Newlands, G.A. .... 01 Feb
E Tweed, C.J. .... 01 Feb
X Gibbs, P.N.C. .... 01 Feb
E Denison, A.R.V.T. .... 01 Feb
E Jackson, S.M. .... 09 Feb
S Cass, P.S. .... 11 Feb
X Oriordan, M.P. .... 01 Apr
X Pollitt, D.N.A. .... 01 Apr
X Baudains, T.J. .... 01 Apr
E Johnstone, I.S. .... 01 Apr
X Taylor, C.D. .... 01 Apr
X Taylor, N.G. .... 01 Apr
X Foale, S.J. .... 01 Apr
S Ramsey, J.S. .... 16 Apr
E Cooper, P.F. .... 21 Apr
X Newman, P.H. .... 01 May
E Carver, A.G. .... 01 May
X Joyner, A. .... 01 May
X Kent, M.D. .... 01 May
E Davey, P.J. .... 01 Jun
X Yates, N.P. .... 01 Jun
S Burton, N.J. .... 16 Jun
S Almond, D.E.M. .... 01 Jul
E Jackson, S.H. .... 01 Jul
X Palmer, P.A. .... 01 Jul
E Lown, D.P. .... 06 Jul
E Faulkner, R.I. .... 01 Aug
E Torvell, M.D.B. .... 01 Aug
X Watson, R.J. .... 01 Aug
S Lewis, G.D. .... 01 Sep
X Wainwright, B.G. .... 01 Sep
X Boast, M.T. .... 01 Sep
X Milton, G.B.M. .... 01 Oct
E Clement, C.J. .... 01 Oct
X Jennings, M.P. .... 01 Oct
X Howden, A.J. .... 01 Oct
E Rawlings, G.C. .... 01 Oct
E Eastaugh, A.C. .... 01 Oct
X Murray, S.J. .... 01 Oct
X Rich, J.G. .... 01 Oct
X Hipsey, S.J. .... 01 Oct
E Pattison, K. .... 01 Oct
X Booker, G.R. .... 01 Oct
X McKie, A. .... 01 Oct
X Gill, C.M. .... 01 Oct
X Carr, D.L. .... 01 Oct
X Dawson, P.J. .... 01 Oct
E Williams, R.C. .... 01 Oct
E Mant, J.N. .... 01 Oct
X Carroll, P.W.M. .... 01 Oct
X Carlton, I.P. .... 01 Oct
E Parsonage, R.J. .... 07 Oct
X Grimley, D.M.J. .... 01 Nov
X Ross, B.J. .... 16 Nov
E Turner, G.K. .... 17 Nov
X Baileff, R.I. .... 01 Dec
E Watson, D.R. .... 01 Dec

1990

X Wade, N.C. .... 01 Jan
S Large, J.L. .... 17 Jan
X Croome-Carroll, M.P.J. .... 27 Jan
X Knight, A.W. .... 01 Feb
X Sadler, C.J. .... 01 Feb
X Little, C.S.A. .... 01 Feb
X Beats, K.A. .... 16 Feb
X Leaney, M.J. .... 01 Mar
X Kerr, W.M.M. .... 09 Mar
X Currie, D.W. .... 01 Apr
X Britton, N.J. .... 01 Apr
E Fowler, P.J.S. .... 01 Apr
X Kirkwood, J.A.D. .... 01 Apr
E Dickinson, R.J. .... 01 Apr
X Griffiths, D.T. .... 01 Apr
E Boraston, P.J. .... 01 Apr
S Gorsuch, P.G. .... 16 Apr
X Chapple, C.P. .... 01 May
E Menzies, A.J. .... 01 May
X Barker, N.J. .... 01 May
X Chapman, N.J. .... 01 May
E Rudman, C.J. .... 15 May
S Cropper, M.A.K. .... 16 May
X Howarth, D.W. .... 01 Jun
X Clegg, M.L. .... 01 Jun
E Perry-Evans, S.P.A. .... 01 Jun
E Howard, K.A. .... 01 Jul
E Hunter, B.J. .... 01 Jul
X Chatwin, N.J. .... 01 Jul
E Plant, I.R. .... 01 Jul
X Pringle, A. .... 01 Jul
E Selwyn, P.D. .... 01 Jul
X Lightfoot, C.D. .... 01 Jul
X Finnemore, R.A. .... 09 Jul
E Jolliffe, G.E. .... 01 Aug
X Wass, M.J. .... 01 Aug
X Mayhew, N.M. .... 16 Aug
X Davies, C.S. .... 01 Sep
X Mathias-Jones, P.D. .... 01 Sep
E Carpenter, C.J. .... 01 Sep
X Murphy, N. .... 01 Sep
S Bostock, C.E. .... 09 Sep
E Dawson, S.L. .... 12 Sep
X Hall, D.W. .... 01 Oct
E Wright, J. .... 01 Oct
E Hannaford, W.C. .... 01 Oct
X Burgess, S. .... 01 Oct
E Howells, G.R. .... 01 Oct
X Ormshaw, R.J. .... 01 Oct
X Riches, I.C. .... 01 Oct
X Saunders, J.N. .... 01 Oct
X Buckett, E.J. .... 01 Oct
X Toms, T.M. .... 01 Oct
X Slade, C. .... 01 Oct
E Picken, J.D. .... 01 Oct
E Southern, P.J. .... 01 Oct
MS Hayes, D.J. .... 01 Oct
E Squire, P.A. .... 01 Oct
E Robertson, D.C. .... 01 Oct
X Bell, R.P.W. .... 01 Oct
X Chichester, M.A.R. .... 01 Oct
E Wyatt, J.M. .... 01 Oct
E Coles, G.J.V. .... 01 Oct
E Godwin, J.C. .... 01 Oct
E Elliott, T.F. .... 01 Oct
E Hogan, D. .... 19 Oct
E Perry, R. .... 01 Nov
X Roper, M. .... 01 Nov
E Drake, R.W. .... 16 Nov
X Straughan, C.J. .... 01 Dec
X Corner, G.C. .... 01 Dec
X Evans, G.R. .... 01 Dec
E Maw, M.J. .... 01 Dec
E Walton, J.C. .... 01 Dec
X Ferguson, R.G. .... 12 Dec

1991

W Hawes, G.E. .... 01 Jan
E Kerchey, S.J.V. .... 20 Jan
S Kingsbury, J.A.T. .... 01 Feb
X Tighe, G. .... 01 Feb
X Marchant, T.A.C. .... 01 Feb
S Radcliffe, N. .... 16 Feb
E Welburn, R.S. .... 01 Mar
S Faulks, D.J. .... 01 Mar

S Pike, M.S. .... 01 Mar
E Schmidt, J.F.K. .... 01 Mar
X Backhouse, J.R. .... 01 Mar
X Eedle, R.J. .... 01 Mar
E Parker, M.N. .... 01 Mar
S Lynch, M. .... 24 Mar
X Crowther, K.W. .... 29 Mar
E Martin, E.J. .... 01 Apr
X Henderson, T.M.P. .... 01 Apr
X Dobson, R.A. .... 01 Apr
X Dunlop, P.F. .... 01 Apr
E Gascoyne, D.J. .... 01 Apr
S Moxey, D.E. .... 01 Apr
X Roberts, D.H.W. .... 01 Apr
X Kelly, R. .... 03 Apr
S Barnwell, K.L. .... 23 Apr
X Edwards, P.J. .... 01 May
X Naismith, D.H. .... 01 May
E Newton, B.J. .... 01 May
E Trewhella, G.G. .... 01 May
X Stenhouse, R.C. .... 01 May
E Barclay, J.H.B. .... 01 May
E Long, N.A. .... 01 May
X MacDonald, G.D. .... 01 May
E Quick, N.H. .... 01 May
E Stott, J.A. .... 26 May
E Griffiths, D.M. .... 01 Jun
E Gibson, D.T. .... 01 Jun
X Gomm, K. .... 01 Jun
E James, C. .... 01 Jun
E Jones, D.C. .... 01 Jun
X Malcolm, S.R. .... 01 Jun
X Turner, D. .... 03 Jun
E Gibson, A. .... 08 Jun
E Plant, M.G. .... 13 Jun
E Lacey, I.N. .... 16 Jun
E Stewart, R.W. .... 01 Jul
X Smith, N.P. .... 01 Jul
X Faulkner, J.J. .... 05 Jul
E Cochrane, M.D. .... 09 Aug
X Greenwood, M.J. .... 01 Sep
E MacKay, C.R. .... 01 Sep
E Stidston, I.J. .... 01 Sep
E Canty, N.R. .... 01 Sep
X Lawson, S.J. .... 01 Sep
E Ball, M.P. .... 01 Sep
S Lloyd, D.P.J. .... 01 Sep
X Donaldson, S.B. .... 01 Sep
X Leaning, M.V. .... 01 Sep
E Clark, A.N. .... 01 Sep
E Dumbell, P. .... 01 Sep
E Shaw, I.B. .... 15 Sep
X Radmore, K.V. .... 23 Sep

X Jones, B.A. .... 01 Oct
X Rogers, R.J. .... 01 Oct
X Lee, M.M. .... 01 Oct
E Pile, K.J. .... 01 Oct
E Pittard, P.M. .... 01 Oct
X Owen, P.C. .... 01 Oct
X Corbett, W.R. .... 01 Oct
X Harvey, P.A. .... 01 Oct
E Hanslip, M.R. .... 01 Oct
E Wilkinson, A. .... 01 Oct
X Hawkins, R.H. .... 01 Oct
X Stanton, D.V. .... 01 Oct
X Bunn, M.E. .... 01 Oct
X Carrington-Wood, C.G. ...... 01 Oct
E Cowton, E.N. .... 01 Oct
E Howard, R.G. .... 01 Oct
E Murphy, P.J. .... 01 Oct
X Shawcross, P.K. .... 01 Oct
X Graham, D.E. .... 01 Oct
E Ballantyne, M.C. .... 01 Oct
E Vamplew, D. .... 01 Oct
E Brown, M.E. .... 01 Oct
E Watson, M. .... 01 Oct
E Moss, A.D. .... 06 Oct
E Birchall, S.J. .... 21 Oct
E Lewis, N.M. .... 27 Oct
X Burden, J.C. .... 01 Nov
X Key, D.F. .... 01 Nov
X Bernau, J.C. .... 01 Nov
E Body, H.J. .... 01 Dec
X Metcalfe, A.P.W. .... 01 Dec
X McHale, G.J. .... 01 Dec

1992

E Masters, R.H. .... 01 Jan
X Morse, A.C. .... 01 Jan
X Price, T.W. .... 01 Jan
E Gordon, D. .... 09 Jan
X Drylie, A.J. .... 01 Feb
X Potts, K.M. .... 01 Feb
X Smith, S.L. .... 01 Feb
X Flanagan, M.E.A. .... 01 Feb
X Trathen, N.C. .... 01 Feb
S Emerton, M.S. .... 01 Feb
E Morgan, A.K.G. .... 06 Feb
E White, P.A. .... 16 Feb
X Moss, P. .... 18 Feb
X Layland, S. .... 01 Mar
X Blakey, A.L. .... 01 Mar
X Connolly, C.J. .... 01 Mar
E Dullage, B. .... 01 Mar
E Parsons, C.G. .... 01 Mar
X Wilson, G.L. .... 01 Apr

X Knight, D.A. .... 01 Apr
E Mundin, A.J. .... 01 Apr
S Blain, R.G. .... 01 Apr
E Townshend, J.J. .... 03 Apr
X Powell, S. .... 16 Apr
W Keefe, S-A. .... 30 Apr
E Marmont, K.L. .... 01 May
X Jenkin, J.R.S.L. .... 01 May
E Deaney, M.N. .... 01 May
X Deighton, D.S. .... 01 May
S Hughes, G.L. .... 01 May
E Kennedy, N.H. .... 01 May
X Roberts, D.A. .... 01 May
X Giles, K.D.L. .... 01 May
E Bone, C.J. .... 01 May
E Martin, M.T. .... 12 May
E Abbey, M.K. .... 16 May
X Bromige, T.R.J. .... 19 May
E Clarke, R.D. .... 27 May
X Williams, D.I. .... 29 May
X Abbott, S.S.C. .... 01 Jun
E Burdett, R.W. .... 01 Jun
E Peacock, S. .... 01 Jun
X Bridger, R.J. .... 01 Jun
X Emmerson, G.J. .... 01 Jun
S Murphy, J. .... 01 Jun
E Morris, P.J. .... 10 Jun
X Thomas, W.G. .... 16 Jun
E Cheesman, C.J. .... 28 Jun
X Petheram, M.J. .... 29 Jun
X Jones, P. .... 01 Jul
E Tarr, B.S. .... 01 Jul
X Sheehan, M.A. .... 01 Jul
X Barnes-Yallowley, J.J.H. ..... 16 Jul
S Giles, A.R. .... 21 Jul
E Randall, R.D. .... 01 Aug
E Sennitt, J.W. .... 01 Aug
X West, M.W. .... 05 Aug
E Warden, J.M. .... 01 Sep
E John, G.D. .... 01 Sep
E Naden, A.C.K. .... 01 Sep
X Blowers, M.D. .... 01 Sep
E King, P.C. .... 01 Sep
X Mardon, K.F. .... 02 Sep
X King, R.W. .... 16 Sep
X Greenfield, D.P. .... 21 Sep
X Thomas, K.I. .... 01 Oct
E Slater, P. .... 01 Oct
E Taylor, P.J. .... 01 Oct
X Richford, T.F. .... 01 Oct
X Murton, W.M. .... 01 Oct
X Shepherd, P.R. .... 01 Oct
X Austin, J.D. .... 01 Oct

W Price, T.L. 01 Oct
E Brunink, J.W. 01 Oct
X Edwards, E.G. 01 Oct
X Fox, R.G. 01 Oct
X Nelson, D.L. 01 Oct
X Dunn, N.G. 01 Oct
E Risley, J. 01 Oct
E Skinner, N.P.F. 01 Oct
E Toon, J.R. 01 Oct
X Maude, C.P. 01 Oct
S Chapman, N.P. 01 Oct
X Kenealy, T.M. 01 Oct
X Needham, P.D. 01 Oct
X Suddes, L.A. 01 Oct
X Whitehead, D. 01 Oct
E Bright, D.A. 01 Oct
S Davies, J.P. 01 Oct
E Milne, J.W. 01 Oct
E Shepherd, A. 01 Oct
W Crumplin, C.A. 01 Oct
E Coppin, P.D. 01 Oct
E Raffle, A.J. 01 Oct
X O'Sullivan, A.M. 01 Oct
E Dalton, D.J. 01 Oct
E Grieve, S.H. 01 Nov
X Powell, R.L. 01 Nov
X Taylor, L.G. 15 Nov
E Sykes, M. 16 Nov
S O'Grady, M.J. 16 Nov
X Hardy, L.C. 01 Dec
X Hodgkins, J.M. 01 Dec
X Howorth, K. 01 Dec

1993

E Howells, J. 01 Jan
X Bilson, J.M.F. 01 Jan
E Raybould, A.G. 01 Jan
X Woolley, M.J. 01 Jan
S Teasdale, R.M. 16 Jan
X Roberts, I.T. 18 Jan
X Baines, M.D. 01 Feb
X Walker, N.L. 01 Feb
E Cargen, M.R. 01 Feb
X Chesterman, G.J. 01 Feb
X Langley, E.S. 01 Feb
E Parsons, B.R. 01 Feb
E Strick, C.G. 01 Feb
E Upton, I.D. 01 Feb
S Laws, P.E.A. 16 Feb
E Claxton, M.G. 18 Feb
E Dustan, A.J. 19 Feb
X Fortescue, R.C. 01 Mar
E Ryan, D.G. 01 Mar
X Hall, N.J. 01 Mar
S Chilman, P.W.H. 01 Mar
X Hall, A.P. 01 Mar
E Loring, A. 01 Mar
E Pratt, I.H. 01 Mar
X Wakefield, G.M. 01 Mar
E Jones, R.W. 01 Mar
X Mair, B. 05 Mar
S Cooter, M.P. 16 Mar
E Crago, P.T. 01 Apr
X Hobbs, A.R. 01 Apr
S Lister, S.R. 01 Apr
X Osbourn, S.E.J. 01 Apr
X Price, D.J. 01 Apr
E Tulloch, F.M. 01 Apr
E Fogg, D.S. 01 Apr
S Drabble, R.C. 16 Apr
X Payne, R.C. 16 Apr
X Greenwood, P. 29 Apr
X Fitter, I.S.T. 01 May
S Bond, N.D. 01 May
X Dodds, R.S. 01 May
X Smith, R.W.R. 01 May
X Warlow, M.R.N. 01 May
X Hall, R.L. 01 May
E McTear, K. 16 May
X Lacey, S.P. 16 May
S Mellor, B.J. 16 May
X Durkin, M.T.G. 01 Jun
E Sutton, G.D. 01 Jun
X Collier, A.S. 01 Jun
S Simpson, I.H. 01 Jun
E Murdoch, A.W. 01 Jun
X Witton, J.W. 01 Jun
E Sneyd, E.P.B. 20 Jun
E Grantham, S.M. 01 Jul
E Martyn, A.W. 01 Jul
X Bennett, G.L.N. 01 Jul
X Aiken, S.R. 01 Jul
E Giles, D.W. 01 Jul
X McNaughton, J.A. 01 Jul
X Russell, T. 01 Jul
E Gray, A.J. 01 Jul
X French, K.L. 09 Jul
S Tyler, P.L. 10 Jul
X Hussey, S.J. 15 Jul
E Burnip, J.M. 01 Aug
E Tarr, R.N.V. 01 Aug
X Tarrant, D.C. 01 Aug
S Wiltcher, R.A. 01 Aug
X Ashcroft, C. 01 Aug
X Lawson, R.I. 02 Aug
X Green, D.P. 13 Aug
X Davies, J.H. 01 Sep
X Godfrey, K.R. 01 Sep
X Smith, M.R.K. 01 Sep
E Stewart, J.N. 01 Sep
E Knight, P.R. 01 Sep
X Landrock, G.J. 01 Sep
E Udensi, E.A.A.A. 01 Sep
E McCormick, J.P. 20 Sep
X Anderson, F.B. 01 Oct
X MacBean, C.C. 01 Oct
X Burgess, J.D.A. 01 Oct
X Thornton, P.J. 01 Oct
X Bate, C. 01 Oct
X Doherty, K. 01 Oct
E Mills, T.C. 01 Oct
E Talbot, N.A. 01 Oct
X Lawrence, S.P. 01 Oct
X MacKay, D.H. 01 Oct
X Bradburn, S.J. 01 Oct
E Smith, G.K. 01 Oct
X Drury, M.H. 01 Oct
E Ford, N.P. 01 Oct
E Williams, A.B. 01 Oct
E Franks, P.D. 01 Oct
X Stacey, H.A. 01 Oct
E Hamilton, R.A. 01 Oct
E Tougher, R. 01 Oct
X Robertson, D.M. 01 Oct
X Bowker, G.N. 01 Oct
E Burrows, J.A. 01 Oct
E Pitcher, J. 01 Oct
X Robinson, B.D. 01 Oct
X Bird, D.E. 01 Oct
E Sweeny, B.D. 01 Oct
X Eastaugh, T.C. 01 Oct
X Clark, P.M.C. 01 Oct
W Silver, C.K. 01 Oct
E Janaway, P. 01 Oct
S McKnight, N.W. 01 Oct
X Croft, M. 01 Oct
X Jones, M.C. 01 Oct
X Watts, A.P. 01 Oct
X Davies, C.J. 01 Oct
X Acland, D.D. 01 Oct
E Goodrich, D.L. 01 Oct
E Muscroft, P.J.V. 01 Oct
MS Jackson, S.K. 01 Oct
X Hinch, N.E. 01 Oct
E Gray, D. 01 Oct
E Greenfield, K. 01 Oct
MS McKinlay, S. 01 Oct
S Burt, P.R. 01 Oct
S Howell, M. 01 Oct

E Martin, M.P. .... 01 Oct
X Nowosielski, F. .... 01 Oct
E Shirley, W.P. .... 12 Oct
X Mitchell, H.G.M. .... 16 Oct
S Walker, C.L. .... 16 Oct
X James, C.W. .... 27 Oct
S Batty, M.J. .... 01 Nov
X Cobb, D.R. .... 01 Nov
X Conway, J.J. .... 01 Nov
E Moffatt, N.R. .... 01 Nov
X Raisbeck, P.T. .... 01 Nov
S Taylor, S.M. .... 01 Nov
X Wyatt, D.J. .... 01 Nov
X Williams, A.P. .... 01 Nov
S Flynn, M.T. .... 01 Nov
X Kelbie, E. .... 01 Nov
X Howell, S.B. .... 01 Nov
X Elvin, A.J. .... 06 Nov
X Gladwell, T.J. .... 01 Dec
X Cooper, S.J. .... 01 Dec
X Cunningham, J.G. .... 01 Dec
S Forer, T.J. .... 01 Dec

1994

E Adams, P. .... 01 Jan
X Brown, W.C. .... 01 Jan
S Watts, A.D. .... 01 Jan
E Glennie, A.M.G. .... 01 Jan
X McGrenary, A. .... 01 Jan
X Ventura, D.C. .... 01 Jan
E Blackman, N.T. .... 01 Jan
E Denovan, P.A. .... 01 Jan
E Horton, P.A. .... 01 Jan
X Humphreys, R.J. .... 01 Jan
X Hunter, N.M. .... 01 Jan
X Turnbull, S.J.L. .... 01 Jan
X Hare, N.J. .... 01 Jan
S Buchan-Steele, M.A. .... 05 Jan
S Merchant, I.C. .... 05 Jan
E Brads, W. .... 14 Jan
S Rigby, J.C. .... 16 Jan
S Randall, D.F. .... 16 Jan
E Corry, S.M. .... 01 Feb
X Gordon, S.R. .... 01 Feb
X Barrand, S.M. .... 01 Feb
E Charlesworth, G.K. .... 01 Feb
X Cluett-Green, S.M. .... 01 Feb
E Shaw, K.N.G. .... 01 Feb
S Webber, S.J.A.M. .... 01 Feb
X Doolan, M. .... 01 Feb
E Salter, J.A. .... 10 Feb
X Neve, P.C. .... 11 Feb
X Saxby, K.A. .... 24 Feb

X Newall, J.A. .... 01 Mar
E Kirkup, J.P. .... 01 Mar
E Wood, J.L. .... 01 Mar
X Moorey, C.G. .... 01 Mar
X Harrison, C.A. .... 01 Mar
E Cattroll, I.M. .... 01 Mar
X Deller, M.G. .... 01 Mar
E Jones, H.A. .... 01 Mar
E Sharman, D.J.T. .... 01 Mar
E Whitehouse, M.J. .... 01 Mar
X Gething, J.B. .... 06 Mar
X Falk, B.H.G. .... 01 Apr
X Turnbull, G.D. .... 01 Apr
S Crozier, S.R.M. .... 01 Apr
E Depledge, I.G. .... 01 Apr
X Meredith, N. .... 01 Apr
X Poole, J.L. .... 01 Apr
X Robertson, M.G. .... 01 Apr
E Blount, D.R. .... 01 Apr
X Crispin, T.A.B. .... 01 Apr
X Greaves, M.J. .... 01 Apr
E Archer, G.W. .... 01 Apr
X Skeer, M.R. .... 04 Apr
E Waddington, J. .... 01 May
E Float, R.A. .... 01 May
X Hailstone, J.H.S. .... 16 May
X Eaton, P.G. .... 01 Jun
E Bolam, A.G. .... 01 Jun
X Andrews, P.N. .... 01 Jun
E Duncan, I.S. .... 01 Jun
X Fields, D.G. .... 01 Jun
X Lunn, A.C. .... 01 Jun
X Hardacre, P.V. .... 01 Jun
X Haycock, T.P. .... 01 Jun
X Towler, P.J.B. .... 01 Jun
E Weedon, K.D. .... 19 Jun
E Pryde, C.S. .... 01 Jul
X Horsley, A.M.R. .... 01 Jul
X Houghton, P.J. .... 01 Jul
E Borland, S.A. .... 01 Jul
E Dabell, G.L. .... 01 Jul
X Seabrooke-Spencer, D.J. .... 01 Jul
S Smerdon, C.D.E. .... 01 Jul
X Stuttard, M.C. .... 01 Jul
E Westwood, M.R.T. .... 01 Jul
X Abernethy, L.J.F. .... 11 Jul
E Griffiths, A.J. .... 26 Jul
X Horner, P.A. .... 01 Aug
E Dowell, P.H.N. .... 01 Aug
X Denholm, I.G. .... 13 Aug
X Swift, R.D. .... 28 Aug
E Cropley, A. .... 01 Sep
E Grindel, D.J. .... 01 Sep

E Podmore, A. .... 01 Sep
E Saunders, T.M. .... 01 Sep
X Glass, J.E. .... 01 Sep
X Robin, C.C.E. .... 01 Sep
X Thompson, B.D. .... 01 Sep
X Welton, W.B.D. .... 01 Sep
X Fleming, S.A. .... 30 Sep
X Davis, A.R. .... 01 Oct
X Rawson, C. .... 01 Oct
E Day, T.M. .... 01 Oct
E Bryce, C.G. .... 01 Oct
X Hands, A.P. .... 01 Oct
E Alison, L.A. .... 01 Oct
E Haskell, E.T. .... 01 Oct
X Monger, P.D. .... 01 Oct
X Scott-Dickins, C.A. .... 01 Oct
S Lowe, S.A. .... 01 Oct
E Holden, J.T. .... 01 Oct
E Ryder, S.M. .... 01 Oct
X Davison, A.P. .... 01 Oct
X Taylor, L. .... 01 Oct
X Hicking, N. .... 01 Oct
X Sewed, M.A. .... 01 Oct
X Porter, C.W. .... 01 Oct
X Walker, M.C. .... 01 Oct
X Oakes, R.L. .... 01 Oct
X Dowdell, R.E.J. .... 01 Oct
E Suckling, P.M. .... 01 Oct
E Smyth, M.J. .... 01 Oct
S Franks, D.I. .... 01 Oct
X Davis, P.B. .... 01 Oct
E Hammersley, J.M. .... 01 Oct
E Naden, J.R. .... 01 Oct
X Read, A. .... 01 Oct
X Burrows, M.J. .... 01 Oct
X Fraser, P.T. .... 01 Oct
X Thompson, N.J. .... 01 Oct
X Madge, A.W.J. .... 01 Oct
E Hart, R. .... 01 Oct
E Sugden, M.R. .... 01 Oct
X Savage, S. .... 01 Oct
X Suddes, T. .... 01 Oct
X Lee, J.C. .... 01 Oct
X Elliman, S.M. .... 01 Oct
E Barnden, M.J. .... 01 Oct
E Hyde, T. .... 01 Oct
X Dane, R.M.H. .... 01 Oct
E Snow, P.F. .... 01 Oct
S De La Mare, R.M. .... 01 Oct
X Hamilton, G.R. .... 01 Oct
X Disney, P.W. .... 01 Oct
X Reed, A.W. .... 01 Oct
E Gilbert, L.G. .... 01 Oct

	Name	Date
X	Williamson, T.J.L.	01 Oct
X	Denham, N.J.	01 Oct
E	Nethercott, L.R.	01 Oct
X	Blake, K.B.	01 Oct
E	Sumner, M.D.	01 Oct
X	Bryant, D.J.	01 Oct
S	Price, G.	01 Oct
E	De Jonghe, P.T.	01 Oct
E	Haywood, S.A.	01 Oct
X	Francis, J.	01 Oct
S	David, S.E.J.	16 Oct
X	Evans, W.Q.F.	20 Oct
E	Howard, N.	31 Oct
X	Gunn, W.J.S.	01 Nov
E	Clark, K.C.	01 Nov
E	Heley, J.M.	01 Nov
X	Thomas, P.G.	01 Nov
X	Hurry, A.P.	01 Nov
E	Bull, G.C.	01 Nov
E	Saxby, C.J.	01 Nov
E	Clark, I.D.	01 Nov
S	Parton, S.L.	11 Nov
E	Harding, G.A.	01 Dec
X	Hills, A.A.	01 Dec
X	Ashcroft, A.C.	01 Dec
X	Swarbrick, R.J.	01 Dec
X	Hart, M.A.	01 Dec
E	Haines, P.R.	09 Dec
E	Gardiner, D.A.	13 Dec
X	Sutcliffe, J.	21 Dec

1995

	Name	Date
X	Lydiate, G.	01 Jan
X	Pritchard, G.S.	01 Jan
S	Trundle, D.J.W.	01 Jan
X	Milburn, P.K.	01 Jan
X	George, A.P.	16 Jan
X	Hutchison, G.B.	01 Feb
E	Campbell, R.D.H.	01 Feb
X	Ovenden, N.S.P.	01 Feb
X	Hunt, J.S.P.	05 Feb
X	Lewis, T.J.	05 Feb
X	Baldwin, C.M.	01 Mar
S	Shaw, S.M.	01 Mar
E	Boyd, N.	01 Mar
E	Dathan, T.J.	01 Mar
X	Fulton, C.R.	01 Mar
E	Jessop, P.E.	01 Mar
E	Magan, M.J.C.	01 Mar
X	Pillar, C.D.	01 Mar
X	Firth, N.R.	01 Mar
X	Jones, M.	01 Mar
S	Shaw, P.J.	17 Mar
X	Stangroom, A.	24 Mar
X	Law, J.	27 Mar
S	Andrews, S.G.	28 Mar
X	Middlebrook, M.S.	30 Mar
E	Gray, D.K.	01 Apr
E	Munro, K.	01 Apr
X	Egeland-Jensen, F.A.	01 Apr
E	Gill, M.R.	01 Apr
E	Gillan, G.M.	01 Apr
E	Holmes, R.W.	01 Apr
X	Reed, J.H.	01 Apr
E	Smith, K.A.	01 Apr
X	Turner, D.B.	01 Apr
X	Greenland, M.R.	16 Apr
X	Smith, C.P.	26 Apr
E	French, J.T.	29 Apr
E	Reynolds, T.P.	30 Apr
X	Birley, J.H.	01 May
X	Amphlett, N.G.	01 May
E	Mills, A.	01 May
E	Harding, D.M.	01 May
X	Hawkins, M.A.J.	01 May
X	Marshall, R.G.C.	01 May
X	Goldsmith, S.V.W.	01 May
X	Webb, A.J.	01 May
E	Green, D.P.S.	01 May
X	Schnadhorst, J.C.	01 May
S	Willis, M.S.	02 May
X	Gurmin, S.J.A.	18 May
X	Thomson, D.	23 May
E	Hewitt, A.	01 Jun
E	Brown, P.S.J.	01 Jun
E	Grenfell-Shaw, M.C.	01 Jun
X	Johnston, T.A.	01 Jun
X	Matthews, S.G.	01 Jun
E	McInnes, J.G.K.	01 Jun
X	Mannion, R.V.	01 Jun
E	Streeten, C.M.	01 Jun
S	Young, A.P.	16 Jun
X	Woodward, D.J.	01 Jul
X	Cornish, M.C.	01 Jul
X	Foster, D.G.S.	01 Jul
E	Gibbs, N.D.	01 Jul
E	Rhodes, A.G.	01 Jul
X	Foreman, J.L.R.	01 Jul
X	Lochrane, A.E.R.	01 Jul
X	Pollock, M.P.	01 Jul
X	Nisbet, J.H.T.	01 Jul
E	Roberts, T.J.	01 Jul
E	Smith, M.R.	14 Jul
X	Coomber, M.A.	18 Jul
E	Rawlings, D.P.	01 Aug
X	Greenaway, N.M.	01 Aug
E	Kennedy, I.J.A.	01 Aug
E	Thompson, A.	06 Aug
S	Renwick, J.	23 Aug
E	Collins, P.R.	01 Sep
X	Harper, C.H.	01 Sep
X	Jones, G.R.	01 Sep
X	Beardall, M.J.D.	01 Sep
X	Burke, M.C.	01 Sep
X	Hill, R.A.	01 Sep
E	Jenkins, G.W.	01 Sep
X	Williams, D.S.	01 Sep
X	Window, S.H.	01 Sep
X	Fitzsimmons, M.B.	01 Sep
X	Martin, R.G.	01 Sep
E	Murphy, P.W.	01 Sep
X	Evans, M.J.	01 Sep
X	Burton, A.J.	01 Sep
X	Evans, A.W.	01 Oct
X	Gobey, C.G.	01 Oct
X	Moffatt, R.	01 Oct
E	Oldfield, P.H.	01 Oct
E	Macaulay, N.	01 Oct
E	Morrison, G.R.	01 Oct
X	Dean, W.M.H.	01 Oct
X	Daniels, I.J.R.	01 Oct
E	Nunn, G.E.	01 Oct
E	Goble, I.J.	01 Oct
X	Holley, A.J.	01 Oct
E	Chapman, G.J.D.	01 Oct
X	Fulford, M.K.	01 Oct
X	Wilson, R.P.	01 Oct
X	Carter, R.I.	01 Oct
E	Day, T.S.	01 Oct
E	Edwards, R.A.	01 Oct
X	Smith, K.J.	01 Oct
W	Buchanan, A.J.	01 Oct
X	Callister, D.R.	01 Oct
E	Cunningham, C.	01 Oct
E	Hassall, H.	01 Oct
X	Pipkin, S.C.	01 Oct
X	Lawler, J.A.	01 Oct
X	Mathieson, K.R.	01 Oct
X	Warnock, G.	01 Oct
X	Brundle, P.R.	01 Oct
X	Carretta, M.V.	01 Oct
X	Collins, D.A.	01 Oct
E	Nelson, A.	01 Oct
W	Davis, S.B.	01 Oct
X	Daniell, C.J.	01 Oct
E	Rippingale, S.N.	01 Oct
X	Cox, J.P.	01 Oct
E	Clifford, T.J.	01 Oct
X	Fincher, K.J.	01 Oct

X Bate, D.I.G. .... 01 Oct
X Haywood, G. .... 01 Oct
E Andrews, I. .... 01 Oct
E Roberts, E.W. .... 01 Oct
X Sutton, R.W. .... 01 Oct
E Pickbourne, M. .... 01 Oct
E Peerman, S.J. .... 01 Oct
E Brazendale, C. .... 01 Oct
E Kemp, M.S. .... 01 Oct
S Dobson, B.J. .... 01 Oct
E Dorricott, A.J. .... 01 Oct
E Nailor, A. .... 01 Oct
E Maidment, P.C. .... 01 Oct
X Daniel, A.G. .... 01 Oct
X Jenrick, M.F. .... 01 Oct
S Llewelyn, B. .... 01 Oct
X Nolan, A.L. .... 01 Oct
E Baxter, K.C. .... 01 Oct
E Moore, M.N. .... 01 Oct
X Morland, R.M. .... 01 Oct
X Welch, A. .... 13 Oct
X MacKenzie, M.D. .... 01 Nov
S Garland, N. .... 01 Nov
E Lipscomb, P. .... 01 Nov
X Vickery, T.K. .... 01 Nov
E Burlingham, B.L. .... 01 Nov
X Hutton, S.J. .... 01 Nov
E Allen, D.R. .... 01 Nov
S Porrett, J.A. .... 14 Nov
S Lines, J.M. .... 16 Nov
E Stephenson, D. .... 22 Nov
E St Aubyn, J.D.E. .... 01 Dec
S Willis, A.J. .... 01 Dec
E Jordan, P.D. .... 01 Dec
X Aspden, A.M. .... 01 Dec
X Waddington, A.K. .... 01 Dec
X Wallace, A. .... 01 Dec
X Pentreath, J.P. .... 01 Dec
X Cunningham, D.A. .... 15 Dec
X Boddington, J.D.L. .... 16 Dec
X Meeds, K. .... 16 Dec
X Bath, E.G. .... 27 Dec

1996

E Warren, M.K. .... 01 Jan
E Frankham, P.J. .... 01 Jan
X Cramp, A.M. .... 01 Jan
E Rogers, I.A. .... 01 Jan
X Sherriff, D.A. .... 01 Jan
E Munns, A.R. .... 01 Jan
X Craig, P.D. .... 01 Feb
X Dyke, C.L. .... 01 Feb
X Atkinson, M. .... 01 Feb
S Carter, S.N. .... 01 Feb
E Casson, P.R. .... 01 Feb
E Metcalfe, P.G. .... 01 Feb
X Tindal, N.H.C. .... 01 Feb
X Salisbury, D.P. .... 01 Feb
E Mace, S.B. .... 01 Feb
X Entwisle, W.N. .... 01 Feb
S Walmsley, E.A. .... 08 Feb
X Bankier, S. .... 19 Feb
X Draper, S.P. .... 26 Feb
X Barker, D.C.K. .... 28 Feb
S Sutton-Scott-Tucker, J.J. ... 01 Mar
X Burke, P.D. .... 01 Mar
E Fieldsend, M.A. .... 01 Mar
X Furlong, K. .... 01 Mar
E Phenna, A. .... 01 Mar
E Toft, M.D. .... 01 Mar
S Notley, L.P. .... 01 Mar
E Gilbert, P.D. .... 01 Mar
S Smith, C.J. .... 16 Mar
S Straw, A.N. .... 16 Mar
X Cooper, M.A. .... 01 Apr
X Harry, A.D. .... 01 Apr
S Hayle, J.K. .... 01 Apr
E Jackson, I.A. .... 01 Apr
X Lindsay, I.G. .... 01 Apr
X Smith, K.B.A. .... 01 Apr
X Warwick, P.D. .... 01 Apr
E Wise, G.J. .... 01 Apr
E Withers, J.W. .... 01 Apr
X Chrishop, T.I. .... 01 Apr
X Kilby, S.E. .... 01 Apr
E Kingsbury, S.H. .... 01 Apr
E Pear, I.K. .... 01 Apr
E Scott, N.L.J. .... 01 Apr
X Collins, G.J.S. .... 07 Apr
S Waters, N.R. .... 16 Apr
X Wallis, A.J. .... 16 Apr
S Marston, P.A. .... 16 Apr
S McConochie, A.D. .... 16 Apr
S Taylor, S.J. .... 16 Apr
X Mahony, D.G. .... 16 Apr
E Clough, C.R. .... 28 Apr
E Walker, P.R. .... 01 May
E Worthington, J.M.F. .... 01 May
E Winkle, S.J. .... 01 May
E Jarvis, L.R. .... 01 May
E Fitzjohn, D. .... 01 May
E Merritt, J.J. .... 01 May
E Harrop, I. .... 01 May
X Masters, J.C. .... 01 May
E Scott, J.B. .... 01 May
E Shepherd, R.G. .... 01 May
E Childs, D.G. .... 01 May
S Hall, E.C. .... 01 May
X Maher, M.P. .... 16 May
E Carter, J.M. .... 01 Jun
X Thomas, R.K. .... 01 Jun
X Moore, P.H.G. .... 01 Jun
X Gazzard, J.H. .... 01 Jun
E Hill, P.J. .... 01 Jun
X Corbett, A.S. .... 01 Jun
X Freeman, D.R. .... 01 Jun
X Hayward, C.E.W. .... 01 Jun
E Hutchins, T.P. .... 01 Jun
E Short, J.J. .... 01 Jun
E Prior, G.M. .... 02 Jun
S Goldthorpe, M. .... 06 Jun
X Hill, M.R. .... 22 Jun
E Kempsell, I.D. .... 26 Jun
X Clayton, S. .... 01 Jul
X Taylor, B.D. .... 01 Jul
X Bellfield, R.J.A. .... 01 Jul
E Buckle, I.L. .... 01 Jul
X Bucknell, D.I. .... 01 Jul
E Chubb, J.J. .... 01 Jul
E Gracey, P.P. .... 01 Jul
X McDonough, A.G. .... 01 Jul
X Reindorp, D.P. .... 01 Jul
X Simpson, M.J. .... 01 Jul
X Tetlow, H.S.G. .... 01 Jul
X Green, P.J. .... 01 Jul
S Jewitt, C.J.B. .... 01 Jul
X McCall, I.R. .... 01 Jul
E Pooley, S.W. .... 01 Jul
X Tattersall, P.D. .... 01 Jul
E Stace, I.S. .... 01 Jul
E Rimmer, H.E. .... 22 Jul
S Hibbert, N.J. .... 29 Jul
E Geary, T.W. .... 01 Aug
X Fancy, R. .... 01 Aug
E Turner, J.A.E. .... 01 Aug
E Adams, A.M. .... 01 Aug
E Berryman, C.B. .... 01 Aug
X Coles, A.L. .... 01 Aug
X Secretan, S.J. .... 01 Aug
X Abernethy, J.R.G. .... 01 Aug
X Howard, P.M. .... 16 Aug
E Hope, K. .... 01 Sep
X Benton, A.M. .... 01 Sep
X Swannick, D.J. .... 01 Sep
E Young, M.S. .... 01 Sep
E Geddis, R.D. .... 01 Sep
X Brady, S.E. .... 01 Sep
X Bark, J.S. .... 01 Sep
E Woodford, G.I. .... 01 Sep

E	Coles, C.J.	01 Sep
E	Harrison, P.G.	12 Sep
E	Goodings, G.J.	01 Oct
X	Corbett, G.J.	01 Oct
X	Conway, T.A.	01 Oct
X	Meakin, B.R.	01 Oct
X	Hibbert, M.C.	01 Oct
X	Creech, R.D.	01 Oct
X	Jefferson, P.M.	01 Oct
E	Gratton, S.W.	01 Oct
E	Hartley, S.W.	01 Oct
X	Bickerton, R.E.	01 Oct
E	Anderson, J.J.	01 Oct
E	Marston, S.A.B.	01 Oct
X	Sykes, R.A.	01 Oct
X	Dickson, J.P.E.	01 Oct
X	Munro-Lott, P.R.J.	01 Oct
X	Walters, J.	01 Oct
X	Hoper, P.R.	01 Oct
X	Biggs, D.M.	01 Oct
X	Webb, C.M.	01 Oct
E	O'Brien, P.M.C.	01 Oct
S	Bridgeman, J.W.T.	01 Oct
X	Wilkinson, P.M.	01 Oct
X	Attrill, A.A.	01 Oct
E	Ashton Jones, G.	01 Oct
X	Walsh, A.S.J.	01 Oct
X	Armstrong, N.P.B.	01 Oct
X	Judd, S.A.	01 Oct
W	Whetton, J.B.D.	01 Oct
E	Clarke, R.	01 Oct
W	Kent, I.M.	01 Oct
E	Chamberlain, T.I.	01 Oct
X	Slocombe, C.A.	01 Oct
E	Lias, C.D.	01 Oct
X	Salmon, M.A.	01 Oct
E	Ashton, R.D.	01 Oct
E	Bracher, H.	01 Oct
E	Rook, D.J.	01 Oct
MS	Murphy, A.	01 Oct
X	Hudson, P.T.	01 Oct
MS	Lloyd, C.J.	01 Oct
S	Olliver, A.J.	01 Oct
X	Hodkinson, C.B.	01 Oct
E	Lovegrove, R.A.	01 Oct
X	Newland, M.I.	01 Oct
E	Foster, G.J.	01 Oct
X	Seymour, K.W.	01 Oct
X	Leitch, I.R.	01 Oct
E	Myerscough, A.P.	01 Oct
E	Peacock, M.R.	01 Oct
E	Dobbin, V.W.	01 Oct
MS	Coulton, I.C.	01 Oct
X	Evans, D.J.	01 Oct
X	Jackson, G.K.	01 Oct
X	Saynor, R.M.	01 Oct
E	Wood, I.D.	01 Oct
E	Galvin, D.	01 Oct
E	Rodgers, S.	01 Oct
S	Aitken, K.M.	01 Oct
X	Mitchinson, L.	01 Oct
X	Thorburn, A.	01 Oct
X	Van-Den-Bergh, W.L.	01 Oct
E	Mockford, J.A.	01 Oct
S	Ewen, R.J.	01 Oct
E	Cooper, K.P.	01 Oct
E	Fraser, W.C.	01 Oct
S	McGarel, D.F.	01 Oct
X	Edgley, A.D.	15 Oct
E	Watson, P.G.C.	25 Oct
E	Burwin, H.L.	01 Nov
S	Toomey, N.J.	01 Nov
X	Gale, S.P.	01 Nov
E	Prescott, S.	01 Nov
E	Stirzaker, M.	01 Nov
X	Bowen, N.T.	01 Nov
X	Briers, M.P.	01 Nov
X	Hardern, S.P.	01 Nov
E	Robinson, M.P.	01 Nov
S	Philpott, N.E.	01 Nov
E	Kershaw, S.	01 Nov
X	Radakin, A.D.	01 Nov
E	Higgins, G.N.	01 Nov
X	Dible, J.H.	16 Nov
E	Wilson, C.J.	01 Dec
S	Blackwell, R.E.	01 Dec
E	Cran, B.C.	01 Dec
S	Hollins, R.P.	01 Dec
S	Noyes, D.J.	01 Dec
X	Barnbrook, J.C.	16 Dec
S	Kyte, A.J.	16 Dec
	1997	
X	Shepherd, C.S.	01 Jan
X	Lister, M.	01 Jan
X	Adam, I.K.	01 Jan
X	Carson, N.D.E.	01 Jan
E	Jackson, A.S.	01 Jan
E	Harrison, D.	05 Jan
E	Irwin, M.A.	09 Jan
X	Noyce, N.R.	15 Jan
X	Davies, M.B.	24 Jan
E	Thompson, R.C.	01 Feb
S	Wintle, G.L.	01 Feb
X	Blount, K.E.	01 Feb
X	Drysdale, S.R.	01 Feb
E	Gillies, R.R.	01 Feb
E	Parvin, P.S.	01 Feb
E	Stewart, P.C.	01 Feb
E	Course, A.J.	01 Feb
S	Hill, R.K.J.	16 Feb
S	Stanton, P.C.M.	16 Feb
X	Hulme, T.M.	01 Mar
X	Ireland, P.C.	01 Mar
X	Bell, R.D.	01 Mar
E	Bartlett, D.S.G.	01 Mar
X	Chandler, N.J.	01 Mar
S	Chapell, A.	01 Mar
X	Cummings, A.T.	01 Mar
X	Hogg, C.W.	01 Mar
E	Mallinson, R.	01 Mar
S	Murrison, R.A.	01 Mar
E	Page, S.P.	01 Mar
E	Bull, C.M.S.	01 Mar
X	Harvey, R.M.M.J.	01 Mar
X	Swain, A.V.	05 Mar
S	Williams, M.S.	29 Mar
X	Cowley, R.M.	01 Apr
E	New, C.M.	01 Apr
X	Scott, J.A.	01 Apr
X	Morris, R.J.	01 Apr
E	Hollis, C.	01 Apr
X	Toothill, J.S.	01 Apr
X	Barker, P.T.	01 Apr
X	Bowbrick, R.C.	01 Apr
X	Bower, N.S.	01 Apr
X	Holt, S.	01 Apr
E	Kissane, R.E.T.	01 Apr
X	Lane, R.N.	01 Apr
X	Lowson, R.M.	01 Apr
E	Dailey, P.G.J.	01 Apr
X	Ryan, R.M.	01 Apr
X	Wilson-Chalon, L.M.	01 Apr
X	Davison, J.E.	06 Apr
S	Nicholson, H.	06 Apr
E	Harris, A.G.	12 Apr
S	Tew, J.P.	16 Apr
E	Fairbrass, J.F.	28 Apr
E	Evans, M.	01 May
E	Finch, R.L.	01 May
E	Feeney, M.L.	01 May
E	Clark, S.R.	01 May
E	Annett, I.G.	01 May
E	Knight, P.J.	01 May
X	Pethybridge, R.A.	01 May
E	Carrick, R.J.	01 May
E	King, N.W.	01 May
E	Martin, B.A.	01 May
S	Mearns, C.M.	01 May

X Robinson, G.A. .... 01 May
X Rich, D.C. .... 20 May
E Thomson, I.R. .... 22 May
E Read, J.M. .... 23 May
X Robertson, D.C. .... 01 Jun
E Titcomb, A.C. .... 01 Jun
X Dutton, D. .... 01 Jun
X Woollcombe-Gosson,D.J. .. 01 Jun
S Edge, J.H. .... 01 Jun
X Breckenridge, I.G. .... 01 Jul
E Harper, A.C. .... 01 Jul
X Irons, P.A. .... 01 Jul
E Rowse, M.L. .... 01 Jul
X Wainhouse, M.J. .... 01 Jul
X Woods, J.B. .... 01 Jul
E Corderoy, J.R. .... 01 Jul
E MacDonald, J.R. .... 01 Jul
X Bewick, D.J. .... 01 Jul
E Mather, G.P. .... 01 Jul
S Wright, S.H. .... 16 Jul
X Ellis, N.M. .... 18 Jul
X Forester-Bennett, R.M.W. .... 24 Jul
X Spiller, V.J. .... 28 Jul
E Pearson, N. .... 01 Aug
X Woollven, A.H. .... 01 Aug
X Stannard, M.P. .... 01 Aug
E Graham, D.W.S. .... 01 Aug
S Horswill, M.N. .... 01 Aug
X Vitali, R.C. .... 01 Aug
X Kyd, J.P. .... 01 Aug
E Reynolds, A.G. .... 01 Aug
E Spring, J.M. .... 03 Aug
S Evans, E.M. .... 16 Aug
X Bourne, C.M. .... 16 Aug
E Folwell, M.W. .... 20 Aug
X Ovens, M.J. .... 20 Aug
E Holden, S.D. .... 24 Aug
X Webber, C.J. .... 26 Aug
X Hare, J.H. .... 01 Sep
E Richardson, M.A. .... 01 Sep
E Cree, A.M. .... 01 Sep
X Wynn, S.R. .... 01 Sep
X Petheram, A.J. .... 01 Sep
X Tebbet, P.N. .... 01 Sep
E Gaitley, I. .... 01 Sep
X Hutchinson, O.J.P. .... 01 Sep
X Bazley, J.C. .... 01 Sep
S Lustman, A.M. .... 25 Sep
X Llewelyn, K. .... 01 Oct
W Gent, S.J. .... 01 Oct
E Evans, S.J. .... 01 Oct
E Mann, G.D. .... 01 Oct
E Granger, C.R. .... 01 Oct
X Kessler, M.L. .... 01 Oct
X Broster, P.T. .... 01 Oct
X Edwards, J.P.T. .... 01 Oct
X Stringer, R.A. .... 01 Oct
E Heneghan, J.F. .... 01 Oct
X Schwab, R.A. .... 01 Oct
X Daw, S.J. .... 01 Oct
W Cobb, J.E. .... 01 Oct
X Mickleburgh, A. .... 01 Oct
X Lambourne, D.J. .... 01 Oct
E Cooper, N.P. .... 01 Oct
X Clucas, M.R. .... 01 Oct
E Morris, S.T. .... 01 Oct
X James, A.J. .... 01 Oct
E Morgan, S.A. .... 01 Oct
X Moys, A.J. .... 01 Oct
X Fleming, K.P. .... 01 Oct
X Brooks, M.L. .... 01 Oct
X Ford, G.H. .... 01 Oct
E Monk, C.D. .... 01 Oct
X Wright, A.J. .... 01 Oct
E Lawrence, S.R. .... 01 Oct
X Dawkins, M.W. .... 01 Oct
X Cook, D.J. .... 01 Oct
E Lindsay, G. .... 01 Oct
E Price, T.P. .... 01 Oct
X Barling, N.R. .... 01 Oct
X Cornick, R.M. .... 01 Oct
X Harmer, J.N.J. .... 01 Oct
X Hill, N.G. .... 01 Oct
X Hunt, C.J. .... 01 Oct
X Hargreaves, N. .... 01 Oct
E Leonard, M. .... 01 Oct
E Rowe, P.E. .... 01 Oct
W Campbell, K.L. .... 01 Oct
S Jack, P.J. .... 01 Oct
E Davies, T.M. .... 01 Oct
S Watts, D.J. .... 01 Oct
E Wiffin, A.F. .... 01 Oct
E Taylor, K. .... 01 Oct
X Randall, N.J. .... 01 Oct
E Cole, S.P. .... 01 Oct
E Downie, A.J. .... 01 Oct
E Teasdale, D. .... 01 Oct
S Brier, C.A.C. .... 01 Oct
X Harper, J.A. .... 01 Oct
MS Holder, S.R. .... 01 Oct
MS Kenney, R.P. .... 01 Oct
X Yarker, D.L. .... 01 Oct
X Stuttard, S.E. .... 01 Oct
E Barrs, H.A. .... 01 Oct
E Tapping, K. .... 01 Oct
S Bennett, A.J. .... 01 Oct
S Finch, T.S.A. .... 01 Oct
X Morris, P.J. .... 01 Oct
E Graham, R. .... 01 Oct
E Moss, T.E. .... 01 Oct
E Hellyn, D.R. .... 01 Oct
E McHale, K. .... 01 Oct
X Ward, D.S. .... 01 Oct
E Morrison, R.W. .... 01 Oct
X Griffiths, A. .... 01 Oct
E Walker, R.D. .... 01 Oct
E White, R.F. .... 01 Oct
S Knill, R.L. .... 01 Oct
E Oflaherty, J.S. .... 03 Oct
X Wheatley, W.J. .... 04 Oct
X Tabeart, G.W. .... 01 Nov
X Hibberd, N.J. .... 01 Nov
X Jones, A.D. .... 01 Nov
E Morgan, F.S. .... 01 Nov
X Blackmore, M.S. .... 01 Nov
X White, J.A.P. .... 01 Nov
X Houlberg, K.M.T. .... 01 Nov
X Sage, D.I. .... 04 Nov
S Gibson, A.D. .... 16 Nov
S Asbridge, J.I. .... 16 Nov
X Rolph, A.P.M. .... 16 Nov
E Faulkner, D.W. .... 29 Nov
X Barber, A.S. .... 01 Dec
X Allen, S.M. .... 01 Dec
E Baker, G.C. .... 01 Dec
X Dale-Smith, G. .... 01 Dec
E Graham, J. .... 01 Dec
X Ince, D.P. .... 01 Dec
X Montgomery, M.H. .... 01 Dec
X Venables, A.N. .... 01 Dec
X Halton, P.V. .... 01 Dec
X Gilmour, C.J.M. .... 01 Dec
E Coulson, P. .... 01 Dec
S Towler, A. .... 14 Dec
S Anderson, H.A. .... 16 Dec
X Prentice, D.C. .... 22 Dec

1998

X Carroll, P.J. .... 01 Jan
X Peacock, T.J. .... 01 Jan
E Bartlett, I.D. .... 01 Jan
S Burningham, M.R. .... 01 Jan
E Kitchen, S.A. .... 01 Jan
X Lea, J. .... 01 Jan
E Matthews, D.W. .... 01 Jan
X Romney, P.D. .... 01 Jan
X Smith, G.C.S. .... 01 Jan
E Ward, S.D. .... 01 Jan
X Young, G.L. .... 01 Jan

E Hemsworth, K.J. .... 01 Jan
E Hill, G.F. .... 01 Jan
X Dunn, R.P. .... 02 Jan
S Trump, N.W. .... 16 Jan
S Hood, K.C. .... 16 Jan
X Haseldine, S.G. .... 01 Feb
X Allen, A.D. .... 01 Feb
E Williams, A.J. .... 01 Feb
X Beadsmoore, J.E. .... 01 Feb
X Bence, D.E. .... 01 Feb
X Carroll, B.J. .... 01 Feb
E Hughesdon, M.D. .... 01 Feb
X MacIver, G. .... 01 Feb
X Mugridge, D.R. .... 01 Feb
S Parry, A.K.I. .... 01 Feb
E Petitt, S.R. .... 01 Feb
E Rogers, A.G. .... 01 Feb
E Russell, P.R. .... 01 Feb
E Thomas, J.H. .... 01 Feb
X Titcomb, M.R. .... 01 Feb
E Wellington, S. .... 01 Feb
E Franks, C.S. .... 01 Feb
E Blackburn, S.A. .... 01 Mar
X Hatcher, R.S. .... 01 Mar
X Goodman, A.T. .... 01 Mar
X Mules, A.J. .... 01 Mar
E Powell, M.A. .... 01 Mar
X Spring, A.R.J. .... 01 Mar
E Miller, R.H. .... 01 Mar
X Thomas, R.A.A. .... 01 Mar
S Wood, R. .... 01 Mar
X Dainton, S. .... 01 Mar
X Scott, R.J. .... 02 Mar
X McKenzie, M. .... 03 Mar
X Stowell, P.I.M. .... 01 Apr
E Hamilton, A.J.B. .... 01 Apr
E Lynn, S.R. .... 01 Apr
X MacDonald-Robinson, N.U.S. .... 01 Apr
X Petherick, J.S. .... 01 Apr
E Roberts, S.D. .... 01 Apr
E Rook, G.I. .... 01 Apr
X Smith, A.P. .... 01 Apr
X Chapman, S.J. .... 01 Apr
E Hood, K.M. .... 01 Apr
E MacGillivray, I. .... 01 Apr
E Biggs, W.P.L. .... 01 Apr
E Ferris, D.P.S. .... 01 Apr
E Paris, W. .... 15 Apr
E Bone, R.C. .... 01 May
E Green, A.J. .... 01 May
E Fawcett, F.P. .... 01 May
E Hepworth, A.W.D. .... 01 May
X Merewether, H.A.H. .... 01 May
X Goodacre, I.R. .... 01 May
E Helliwell, M.A. .... 01 May
E Hutchison, P.G. .... 01 May
E Short, A.S.J. .... 01 May
E Winter, T.M. .... 01 May
X Burns, D.I. .... 01 May
E Dunn, G.R. .... 01 May
X Royston, S.J. .... 01 May
X Anstey, R.J. .... 01 May
E Christian, D. .... 01 May
E Millar, G.C. .... 15 May
S Evans, M.D. .... 16 May
X Long, A.D. .... 16 May
E Philo, J.Q. .... 01 Jun
E Murray, G.M. .... 01 Jun
E Baker, M.J. .... 01 Jun
E Bosustow, A.M. .... 01 Jun
X Davidson, A.M. .... 01 Jun
E Evans, G. .... 01 Jun
X Green, J. .... 01 Jun
X Payne, J.D. .... 01 Jun
E Shutts, D. .... 01 Jun
X Deacon, S. .... 01 Jun
E Hanson, N.A. .... 01 Jun
X Kimberley, R. .... 01 Jul
X Lowther, J.M. .... 01 Jul
X Powell, S.R. .... 01 Jul
X Beech, C.M. .... 01 Jul
X Price, T.A. .... 01 Jul
X Warn, C.J. .... 01 Jul
X Axon, D.B. .... 01 Jul
X Bird, R.A.J. .... 01 Jul
E O'Shea, E.P. .... 01 Jul
X Myres, P.J.L. .... 01 Jul
X Hurrell, P.R. .... 01 Jul
X Badrock, B. .... 05 Jul
E Roots, S. .... 01 Aug
E Hall, A.J. .... 01 Aug
X Cryar, T.M.C. .... 01 Aug
X Graham, I.E. .... 01 Aug
X Ford, M.J. .... 05 Aug
X Albon, M. .... 12 Aug
X Hawkins, J.S. .... 16 Aug
E Hinks, K.J. .... 25 Aug
X McGuire, M.J. .... 31 Aug
E Band, J.W. .... 01 Sep
E Stewart, K.C. .... 01 Sep
X Toor, J.J.S. .... 01 Sep
X Cartwright, D. .... 01 Sep
X Murphy, S.R.A. .... 01 Sep
X Savage, M.R. .... 01 Sep
X May, N.P. .... 01 Sep
E Manson, T.E. .... 07 Sep
W Straughan, K.E. .... 08 Sep
E Bowden, M.N. .... 01 Oct
E Forer, D.A. .... 01 Oct
E Wallace, D.J. .... 01 Oct
E Hart, P.A. .... 01 Oct
X Cooper, C.J. .... 01 Oct
E Spooner, P.D. .... 01 Oct
W Hayle, E.A. .... 01 Oct
X Manson, C.R. .... 01 Oct
X Reed, M. .... 01 Oct
X Jones, E.J. .... 01 Oct
X Worman, R. .... 01 Oct
E Carr, M.P. .... 01 Oct
E Wilson, D.T. .... 01 Oct
E Biggs, C.R. .... 01 Oct
X Haynes, J.W. .... 01 Oct
E Davies, L.J. .... 01 Oct
X Stone, P.C.J. .... 01 Oct
E Krosnar-Clarke, S.M. .... 01 Oct
E Norman, S.L. .... 01 Oct
X Tyack, T.J. .... 01 Oct
E Darling, J.I. .... 01 Oct
E Mills, G.W. .... 01 Oct
E Templeton, T.A.M. .... 01 Oct
MS Steel, D.G. .... 01 Oct
W Whittingham, D.J. .... 01 Oct
X Neave, A.M. .... 01 Oct
X Thompson, R.A. .... 01 Oct
E Bourne, D.S. .... 01 Oct
E James, P.E. .... 01 Oct
X Wilkinson, R.N. .... 01 Oct
X Shallcroft, J.E. .... 01 Oct
X Spayne, N.J. .... 01 Oct
X Tomlin, P.D. .... 01 Oct
E Dawson, S.N. .... 01 Oct
X Smith, P.G. .... 01 Oct
X Ffrench, D.J. .... 01 Oct
S Cunane, J.R. .... 01 Oct
X Chapman, D.A. .... 01 Oct
X Franklin, B.J. .... 01 Oct
X Tillion, A.M. .... 01 Oct
X Wheaton, B.J.S. .... 01 Oct
E Hill, G.A. .... 01 Oct
E Kellow, S.J. .... 01 Oct
E Lord, M. .... 01 Oct
X Lewis, D.J. .... 01 Oct
X Barrick, P.V. .... 01 Oct
X Dann, A.S. .... 01 Oct
W Eastlake, A.C. .... 01 Oct
S Gilbert, S.K. .... 01 Oct
E Foster, J.S. .... 01 Oct
X Wells, D.G. .... 01 Oct

E Tritschler, E.L. .... 01 Oct
X Haslam, P.J. .... 01 Oct
S MacDougall, G.R. .... 01 Oct
X Strathern, R.J. .... 01 Oct
X Ward, S.I. .... 01 Oct
E McCue, D. .... 01 Oct
S Oliphant, W. .... 01 Oct
E Simmonds, G.F. .... 01 Oct
X Price, D.W. .... 01 Oct
S Tupper, R.W. .... 01 Oct
E Bennett, M.J. .... 01 Oct
E Maxwell-Cox, M.J. .... 01 Oct
MS McAuslin, T.M. .... 01 Oct
MS Derby, P.J. .... 01 Oct
E Clarke, J. .... 01 Oct
E Grace, T.P. .... 01 Oct
E Jordan, N.S. .... 01 Oct
X Cottingham, N.P.S. .... 01 Oct
X Thomas, J.E. .... 01 Oct
X Huntington, S.P. .... 01 Oct
X Meadows, B. .... 01 Oct
E Birbeck, K. .... 01 Oct
E Pearson, J.R. .... 01 Oct
E Rimmer, R. .... 01 Oct
E Stokes, A.W. .... 01 Oct
E Arnell, S.J. .... 01 Oct
E Ferguson, G.H. .... 01 Oct
E McCaffery, G.F. .... 01 Oct
S Case, P. .... 01 Oct
X Forsyth, D.C. .... 01 Oct
S Laggan, P.J. .... 01 Oct
S Pye, P.M. .... 01 Oct
X Hughes, G.G.H. .... 01 Oct
E Pomeroy, M.A. .... 01 Oct
X Pounder, M. .... 01 Oct
S Fisher, C.R.A. .... 06 Oct
X Dawson, W. .... 01 Nov
X Davison, J.C. .... 01 Nov
S McNally, N.J. .... 01 Nov
X Reidy, P.A. .... 01 Nov
S Clark, M.T. .... 01 Nov
E Hall, B.J. .... 01 Nov
X Olive, P.N. .... 01 Nov
E Smith, M.M. .... 01 Nov
E Stewart, A.M. .... 01 Nov
X Taylor, A.R. .... 01 Nov
E Vickers, J. .... 01 Nov
E Davey, G.S. .... 01 Nov
S Aplin, A.T. .... 01 Nov
X Bark, A.M. .... 01 Nov
E Guy, M.A. .... 13 Nov
E Boulton, N.A. .... 20 Nov
E Donnelly, J.S. .... 22 Nov
X Redman, C.J.R. .... 23 Nov
S Stoffell, D.P. .... 27 Nov
E Windsar, P.A. .... 27 Nov
X Davies, I.E. .... 01 Dec
E MacKay, P. .... 01 Dec
S Clark, S.M. .... 01 Dec
E Hall, S. .... 01 Dec
X Rogers, T.H.G. .... 04 Dec
E Foster, B.M.T. .... 07 Dec
X Powell, W.G. .... 16 Dec
E Makepeace, P.A. .... 24 Dec

1999

S Dudley, S.M.T. .... 01 Jan
X Millard, A.R. .... 01 Jan
E Twine, J.H. .... 01 Jan
X Hancock, A.P. .... 01 Jan
X Manfield, M.D. .... 01 Jan
E Greatwood, I.M. .... 01 Jan
E Warrington, P.T. .... 01 Jan
X Ponsford, P.K. .... 01 Jan
E Roberts, K.E. .... 01 Jan
E Ward, T.J. .... 11 Jan
X Orchard, A.P. .... 16 Jan
X Lees, E.C. .... 01 Feb
X Osborn, R.M. .... 01 Feb
X Staley, S.P.L. .... 01 Feb
E Copeland, S.N. .... 01 Feb
X Godwin, C.A. .... 01 Feb
X Goodsell, C.D. .... 01 Feb
E Hancox, M.J. .... 01 Feb
E Jackson, P.N. .... 01 Feb
X Jones, N.P. .... 01 Feb
X Kerslake, R.W. .... 01 Feb
S Nairn, A.B. .... 01 Feb
E Osmond, J.B. .... 01 Feb
E Smith, A.G. .... 01 Feb
X Taylor, M.A. .... 01 Feb
X Welford, R.C. .... 01 Feb
E Wright, N.S. .... 01 Feb
X Betton, A. .... 01 Feb
E Fergusson, N.A. .... 01 Feb
E Crofts, D.J. .... 01 Feb
X Pitt, J.M. .... 17 Feb
E Southern, P.J. .... 27 Feb
X London, M.R. .... 01 Mar
X Lee, N.F. .... 01 Mar
E Lauste, W.E. .... 01 Mar
E Casson, N.P. .... 01 Mar
X Hussain, S. .... 01 Mar
X Woodham, R.H. .... 01 Mar
X Burns, R.D.J. .... 01 Mar
X McDonnell, D.S. .... 01 Mar
X Bingham, D.S. .... 01 Mar
E Hill, D. .... 01 Mar
X Waller, S.A. .... 01 Mar
E Currass, T.D. .... 01 Mar
E Douglass, M.C.M. .... 01 Mar
X Gray, R. .... 01 Mar
E Groom, I.S. .... 01 Mar
E Henderson, S.P. .... 01 Mar
E Mackie, D.F.S. .... 01 Mar
E Rawlinson, S.J. .... 01 Mar
X Moss, R.A. .... 01 Mar
X O'Flaherty, C.P.J. .... 01 Mar
E Bywater, R.L. .... 01 Mar
X Hogben, A.L. .... 01 Mar
S Turner, J.S.H. .... 01 Apr
X Brooks, G.L. .... 01 Apr
X Beck, S.K. .... 01 Apr
X Collighan, G.T. .... 01 Apr
X Dodd, K.M. .... 01 Apr
E Goldman, P.H.L. .... 01 Apr
S Mardlin, S.A. .... 01 Apr
E Marriott, M.N. .... 01 Apr
X Mimpriss, G.D. .... 01 Apr
E Roscoe, R.D. .... 01 Apr
S Dodd, N.C. .... 01 Apr
E Foster, S.J.H. .... 01 Apr
X Harris, K.J. .... 01 Apr
X Wood, U.G.S. .... 01 Apr
E Waring, J.R. .... 01 Apr
X Groves, C.K. .... 01 Apr
S Athayde Banazol, C.V.N. .... 04 Apr
E Roberts, D. .... 04 Apr
X Foster, D.H. .... 01 May
X Ingham, I.M. .... 01 May
E Bowhay, S. .... 01 May
X Burstow, R.S. .... 01 May
E Scott, M. .... 01 May
X Bravery, M.A.E. .... 01 May
E Cooper, S.S. .... 01 May
X Duffy, H. .... 01 May
X Garratt, J.K. .... 01 May
E Melton, C. .... 01 May
E Lison, A.C. .... 01 May
E Sansford, A.J. .... 27 May
X Golden, D.S.C. .... 01 Jun
X Bush, A.J.T. .... 01 Jun
X Allen, P.L. .... 01 Jun
S Ferns, T.D. .... 01 Jun
X Mackey, M.C. .... 01 Jun
X Sparkes, P.J. .... 01 Jun
X Whitley, I.D.B. .... 01 Jun
E Wright, B.L. .... 01 Jun
X Young, A. .... 01 Jun

E West, G.G. 06 Jun
E Proud, A.D. 11 Jun
S Rees, J.P. 29 Jun
X Hewitt, D.L. 01 Jul
E Jones, D.B. 01 Jul
E Parkin, M.I. 01 Jul
S Percival, M.C. 01 Jul
X Honnoraty, M.R. 01 Jul
X Bushell, G.R. 09 Jul
S Perry, A.J. 16 Jul
X Allen, R. 20 Jul
X Southorn, M.D. 21 Jul
E Richardson, P.S.M. 01 Aug
E Lee, P.A. 01 Aug
X Churcher, J.E. 01 Aug
E Collis, M.J. 01 Aug
E Currie, S.M. 01 Aug
X Dreelan, M.J. 01 Aug
E Owens, D.T. 01 Aug
E Quekett, I.P.S. 01 Aug
X Verney, P.S. 01 Aug
X Brown, P.A.E. 01 Aug
E Lowe, J.C. 01 Aug
X Paterson, F.J.B. 01 Aug
X Barnes, J.R. 01 Aug
X Morley, J.D. 01 Aug
E Dyer, J.D.T. 01 Sep
E Grears, J. 01 Sep
E McLarnon, C.P.C. 01 Sep
E Tatham, S.A. 01 Sep
E Bolton, J.P. 01 Sep
X Cameron, I. 01 Sep
X Goode, A.N. 01 Sep
X Beard, H.D. 01 Sep
E Greener, C. 01 Sep
E Taylor, R. 01 Sep
E Punton, I.M. 01 Sep
W Springett, J.K. 01 Oct
X Whitworth, R.M. 01 Oct
X Luscombe, M.D. 01 Oct
E Merriman, M.R. 01 Oct
X Johns, M.G. 01 Oct
X King, R.J. 01 Oct
X Marsh, B.H. 01 Oct
X Fraser, J.A. 01 Oct
X Hartley, J.L. 01 Oct
X Callaghan, P.F. 01 Oct
X Hayde, P.J. 01 Oct
E Morris, P. 01 Oct
X Howard, D.G. 01 Oct
E Sergeant, N.R. 01 Oct
E Barrett, S.J. 01 Oct
X Rae, A.J.W. 01 Oct
X Goldsmith, D. 01 Oct
X Anderson, S.C. 01 Oct
W Edge, P.A. 01 Oct
X Cooke, G.J. 01 Oct
X Wood, F.D. 01 Oct
E Preston, M.R. 01 Oct
X Holden, R.J. 01 Oct
E Weir, S.D. 01 Oct
E Winston, L.A. 01 Oct
E Ford, A. 01 Oct
X Yardley, A.P. 01 Oct
X Deeney, S.J. 01 Oct
E Smith, S.B. 01 Oct
E Dolby, M.J. 01 Oct
E O'Shaughnessy, P.J. 01 Oct
E Sheppard, D.G. 01 Oct
X Barker, J.W. 01 Oct
E Mason, M. 01 Oct
E Robertson, M.N. 01 Oct
X Pegrum, T.A. 01 Oct
X Cowie, K.M. 01 Oct
E Linderman, I.R. 01 Oct
E Matthews, P.B. 01 Oct
E Rossiter, M.A. 01 Oct
X Avison, M.J. 01 Oct
E Burnett, G.A. 01 Oct
E Roberts, S.C. 01 Oct
X Murray, A.S. 01 Oct
W Graham, P.J. 01 Oct
W Wilkie, S.E. 01 Oct
X Miller, C.R. 01 Oct
E Gunther, P.T. 01 Oct
E Nicholls, G.A. 01 Oct
X Ash, T.C.V. 01 Oct
S Moore, D.D.V. 01 Oct
S Shields, C.T. 01 Oct
E Milsom, J. 01 Oct
E Appelquist, P. 01 Oct
X Blythe, P.C. 01 Oct
E Bougourd, M.A. 01 Oct
X Chalmers, P. 01 Oct
X Lower, I.S. 01 Oct
E McDermott, O.D. 01 Oct
E Gazard, P.N. 01 Oct
E Hoyle, J.J. 01 Oct
S Bryant, G.D. 01 Oct
X Talbot, C.M. 01 Oct
E Payne, D. 01 Oct
E Atherton, G. 01 Oct
E Dutton, P.J. 01 Oct
E Glennie, B.W. 01 Oct
E Lowes, C. 01 Oct
E Porter, A.J. 01 Oct
S Freegard, I.P. 01 Oct
MS Griffiths, D.A. 01 Oct
S Williams, D. 01 Oct
E Maude, D.H. 01 Oct
X Edwards, R. 01 Oct
S Twist, D.C. 01 Oct
X Woodruff, A.D. 01 Oct
E Bassett, N.E. 01 Oct
MS Durning, W.M. 01 Oct
X Thomas, L. 01 Oct
E Jones, D.A. 01 Oct
X Helliwell, M.G. 01 Oct
X Knights, R. 01 Oct
X Stephens, R.P. 01 Oct
X Horne, A. 01 Oct
E Norman, P.D. 01 Oct
E Sugden, S.R. 01 Oct
E Taylor, K.J. 01 Oct
S Harris, M.T. 01 Oct
S Holland, N.R. 01 Oct
X Millen, I.S. 01 Oct
X Jones, C.A. 01 Nov
X Necker, C.D. 01 Nov
X Baker, A.P. 01 Nov
X Joyce, T.J. 01 Nov
E Edmonds, R.M. 01 Nov
X Watt, A.J.L. 01 Nov
S Ackland, H.K. 01 Nov
E Methven, P. 01 Nov
X Warrender, W.J. 01 Nov
E Chapman, C.L. 29 Nov
X Balchin, D.J. 30 Nov
X Smith, B.J. 01 Dec
E Easterbrook, K.I.E. 01 Dec
E McRae, P.C. 01 Dec
E Shrubsole, S.J. 01 Dec
X Tennuci, R.G. 01 Dec
E Woodruff, D.A. 01 Dec
X Boynton, S.J. 01 Dec
X Hunkin, D.J. 01 Dec
E Gayfer, M.E. 01 Dec
S Talbott, A.H. 01 Dec
X Moore, C.R. 05 Dec
E Williams, D. 16 Dec

2000

E Campbell, M.A. 01 Jan
X Harcourt, R.J. 01 Jan
E Stamper, J.C.H. 01 Jan
E Gregory, M. 01 Jan
E Nickolls, K.P. 01 Jan
E Baxter, I.M. 01 Jan
X Bryan, R.J.L. 01 Jan

E	Parkinson, R.I.	01 Jan
X	Parsons, A.D.	01 Jan
E	Rowland, P.N.	01 Jan
X	Walker, N.M.	01 Jan
X	Washer, N.B.J.	01 Jan
X	Connell, M.J.	01 Jan
S	Dunthorne, J.A.	04 Jan
X	Meeking, C.G.	09 Jan
X	Aylott, P.R.F.D.	29 Jan
E	Swain, T.G.	01 Feb
E	Young, S.A.	01 Feb
X	Crosbie, D.E.F.	01 Feb
X	Pierce, A.K.M.	01 Feb
E	Burgess, G.T.M.	01 Feb
E	Gale, M.A.	01 Feb
E	Greenway, S.A.	01 Feb
E	Kelly, J.A.	01 Feb
E	Martin, S.J.	01 Feb
E	O'Brien, K.J.	01 Feb
S	Rae, S.G.	01 Feb
S	Cole, A.C.	01 Feb
E	Dinsdale, A.M.	01 Feb
S	Pomeroy, P.M.	01 Feb
E	Lewis, G.D.	03 Feb
E	Bolton, M.T.W.	06 Feb
S	Ashman, R.G.	28 Feb
S	Sparke, P.R.W.	01 Mar
E	Cotterill, B.M.	01 Mar
E	Balhetchet, A.S.	01 Mar
X	Dominy, D.J.D.	01 Mar
E	Halliwell, D.C.	01 Mar
S	Murphy, P.A.	01 Mar
S	Pallot, M.L.A.	01 Mar
E	Reece, N.D.	01 Mar
E	Teideman, I.C.	01 Mar
E	Whitehead, S.J.	01 Mar
E	Jackson, D.J.	01 Mar
X	Johnson, L.S.	01 Mar
E	Whitfield, K.D.	01 Mar
E	Macleod, J.N.	01 Mar
E	Hartley, A.P.	02 Mar
E	Pugh, J.	08 Mar
S	Fletcher, R.J.	16 Mar
E	Cameron, M.J.	01 Apr
E	Bedding, S.W.E.	01 Apr
E	Bignell, S.	01 Apr
X	Bruford, R.M.C.	01 Apr
X	Buck, J.E.	01 Apr
E	Curlewis, A.J.	01 Apr
E	Long, A.M.	01 Apr
X	Platt, T.S.	01 Apr
X	Burns, A.P.	01 Apr
X	Firth, R.J.G.	08 Apr
X	Lindsey, R.J.	30 Apr
E	Shaw, G.R.	01 May
E	Gregory, A.S.	01 Jun

LIEUTENANTS

1982

S	Stephenson, E.K.	17 Sep
E	Heather, C.V.S.	29 Oct
E	Moore, M.R.	29 Oct

1983

S	Rodrigues, M.T.	07 Jan
E	Arnold, M.E.	03 Nov
E	Dorset, W.	03 Nov
E	Moughton, J.R.	03 Nov

1984

E	Maskell, J.M.	16 Feb
X	Ellett, K.G.	01 Jun
X	Read, A.J.	01 Sep
E	Gamble, J.	02 Nov
E	Thornback, J.G.	02 Nov

1985

X	Northcote, K.H.	04 Jan
E	Bryant, P.	15 Feb
X	Hartley, B.H.	03 May
X	Von Hoven, A.C.	01 Aug
X	Bentley, D.A.	06 Sep
X	Gorrod, P.C.A.	06 Sep
E	Curtis, P.A.	18 Oct
E	Dyche, T.	18 Oct
E	Halls, B.C.	18 Oct
E	Ranger, J.L.	18 Oct
E	Schillemore, P.C.	18 Oct

1986

X	Matthews, G.G.	01 Mar
E	Davison, T.J.	13 Jun
E	Longstaff, R.	13 Jun
E	Williams, D.A.	13 Jun
X	Henty, I.	01 Aug
E	Miller, J.C.	17 Oct

1987

E	Scott, M.A.G.	27 Feb
X	Goram, M.	01 May
X	Carne, R.J.P.	16 May
X	Yelland, C.B.	16 May
E	Foubister, R.	18 Jun
E	Richardson, S.F.	18 Jun
X	Wilson, M.A.	16 Jul
X	Tribe, J.D.	16 Oct

1988

X	Murray, D.	07 Jan
E	Lane, R.M.	18 Feb
E	Fisher, R.	10 Jun
E	Gamble, R.	10 Jun
E	Nicholson, P.J.	10 Jun
E	White, S.P.	10 Jun
E	Collins, S.J.	27 Jun
X	Dearling, P.C.	29 Jul
X	Hutchinson, C.J.	01 Sep
E	Todd, C.F.J.	01 Sep
X	Roberts, M.	01 Oct
S	Pocock, D.	16 Oct
X	Fedorowicz, R.	16 Oct
E	Evans, C.H.	01 Nov

1989

E	Cogdell, P.C.	01 Jan
X	Bance, N.D.	16 Feb
E	Thomas, M.G.	17 Feb
X	Williamson, S.J.	01 Mar
X	Coupland, M.B.	01 Mar
X	Boyes, R.A.	01 Mar
X	Taylor, T.J.	14 Mar
X	Hickson, C.J.	01 Apr
E	Lang, A.J.N.	01 Apr
S	Williams, S.W.L.	01 Apr
X	Holden, N.	01 Apr
X	Saunders, A.C.	25 Apr
E	Holland, S.M.W.	01 May
X	Seekings, A.L.	01 Jun
E	Griffiths, A.R.	09 Jun
X	Nicholson, D.J.	16 Jun
X	Swann, J.I.	28 Jul
S	Sidebotham, M.J.	28 Jul
X	McHugh, T.P.	01 Aug
E	Shirley, A.J.	01 Aug
X	Eatwell, R.A.	01 Aug
E	Campbell, J.C.	01 Sep
E	Taylor, A.	01 Sep
X	Watkins, T.C.	16 Sep
X	Cook, G.E.	16 Sep
E	Lusted, R.P.	13 Oct
E	Bulcock, L.C.	01 Nov
E	George, J.M.	01 Nov
X	Bithell, I.S.	01 Nov
X	Castle, A.S.	01 Dec
X	Hogan, T.	15 Dec
X	Currie, D.G.	16 Dec

1990

E	Browning, R.S.	01 Jan
X	McDermott, M.	01 Jan

X Hanrahan, M.W. 08 Jan
E Whild, A.A. 01 Feb
E Smart, S.J. 23 Feb
E Stevenson, A. 23 Feb
E Young, K.H. 23 Feb
E Prendergast, S.A. 26 Feb
X Liggins, M.P. 01 Mar
E Arthur, A.W. 15 Mar
X Ritchie, D.M. 16 Mar
X McArdell, S.J.R. 01 Apr
X Ritchie, J.N. 01 Apr
W Simpson, E.J. 04 Apr
X Lynch, R.D.F. 16 Apr
X Brotherton, J.D. 16 Apr
E Flint, H.A. 01 May
E Mandley, P.J. 01 May
X Tayler, J.R.N. 01 May
X Nicholas, B.J. 16 May
X Clarke, A.P. 16 May
X Cobbett, J.F. 16 May
E Summers, J.A.E. 24 May
S Ryan, J.B. 01 Jun
X Williams, M.A. 01 Jun
E Allen, D.P. 15 Jun
E Picksley, M.R. 15 Jun
E Sutcliffe, R.W. 15 Jun
X Bhattacharya, D. 16 Jun
X Booker, S.R. 16 Jun
S Yates, M.L. 18 Jun
E Cook, M.C. 01 Jul
X Ford, J.A. 01 Jul
X Russell, T.J. 01 Jul
X Higgs, R.J. 27 Jul
S Walker, N.A. 27 Jul
X Davies, A.J.A. 01 Aug
E Fraser, I.D. 01 Aug
X Suckling, R.L. 16 Aug
X Oddy, D.M. 16 Aug
X D'Arcy, P.A. 16 Aug
E Critchley, M.S. 01 Sep
X Crockatt, S.R.J. 01 Sep
E Hutton, K.D. 01 Sep
E Lloyd, S.J. 01 Sep
E Marratt, R.J. 01 Sep
X Stephens, R.J. 01 Sep
X Turner, K.A. 01 Sep
E Vincent, A. 01 Sep
E Walker, R.A. 01 Sep
E Choules, B. 01 Sep
X Gardiner, P.F.D. 01 Sep
S Church, C.R. 01 Sep
X Sopinski, G.F. 16 Sep
X Phillis, I.R. 16 Sep
X Deverson, R.T.M. 01 Oct
X Harrison, P.D. 01 Oct
X Graham, M.A. 01 Oct
X Knight, A.R. 01 Oct
E Taylor, S.J. 02 Oct
E Forward, D.J. 19 Oct
X Adams, I. 01 Nov
X Robertson, P.N. 01 Nov
X O'Sullivan, B.O. 16 Nov
S Cottis, M.C. 16 Nov
X Speake, J. 01 Dec
X Morrison, B. 01 Dec
X Imrie, P.B. 14 Dec
E Gutteridge, J.D.J. 20 Dec

1991

E Diver, P.H. 01 Jan
E Frost, M.A. 01 Jan
E Pears, I.J. 01 Jan
E Thomas, A.L. 01 Jan
E Walker, M.J. 01 Jan
E Williams, P.M. 01 Jan
X Grindon, M.G. 16 Jan
X Hannigan, P.F. 16 Jan
X Scivier, J.S. 01 Feb
E Bosustow, B.F. 01 Feb
E Lake, P.H. 15 Feb
E Wheeldon, T.B. 15 Feb
X Bowers, J.P. 01 Mar
X Crimmen, D.J. 01 Mar
X Phillips, J.P. 01 Mar
X Rogers, J.C.E. 01 Mar
X Seabrook, I. 16 Mar
X Davison, G.J. 01 Apr
X Eldridge, T.J. 01 Apr
X Herriman, J.A. 01 Apr
S Atkinson, I.N. 01 Apr
X Duncan, J. 01 Apr
X Davidson, N.R. 01 Apr
X Clucas, P.R. 04 Apr
W Ambler, K.K. 04 Apr
X May-Clingo, M.S. 04 Apr
MS Simpson, P. 04 Apr
X Carr, R.A. 13 Apr
X Forster, R.A. 16 Apr
X Smith, R.C.V. 16 Apr
E Cook, C.B. 01 May
X Oliver, G. 01 May
E Orton, D.M. 01 May
E Taylor, A.L. 01 May
X McDonald, I.G. 01 May
X Allen, P.M. 01 May
E Coulthard, A.J. 11 May
X Adams, B.M. 16 May
X Bucklow, S.P. 01 Jun
E Taylor, N.R. 01 Jun
X Beirne, S. 01 Jun
X Abson, I.T. 01 Jun
X Brunskill, J.E.T. 01 Jun
E Green, C.M. 01 Jun
E Gilliland, S.S. 13 Jun
E Horwell, B.B. 13 Jun
E Low, M.E. 13 Jun
E Moss, P.J. 13 Jun
E Smith, M.J. 13 Jun
E Richman, P.J. 13 Jun
X Whitfield, J.A. 16 Jun
X Smith, D.T. 16 Jun
X Duffy, J.B. 01 Jul
X Gladston, S.A. 01 Jul
X Leaver, C.E.L. 01 Jul
E Savage, A.P. 01 Jul
X Tetley, M. 01 Jul
X McKnight, D.J.S. 01 Jul
X Hinch, D.G.W. 01 Jul
X Tattersall, R.B. 01 Jul
X Hart, T.G.DEB. 01 Jul
X Hayward, G. 16 Jul
X Bennett, W.D. 25 Jul
X Garlick, E.C. 25 Jul
S Kerwood, R.J. 25 Jul
W Leigh, S. 25 Jul
X McIntyre, A.W. 25 Jul
X Morrell, A.J. 25 Jul
S Tucker, K.M. 01 Aug
X Gray, P.R. 01 Aug
X Lynch, S. 01 Aug
X Lindsay, D.J. 01 Aug
X Richardson, G.L. 01 Aug
X Christmas, S.P. 16 Aug
X Bullen, M.P. 16 Aug
X Westley, D.R. 16 Aug
E Jones, G.D. 01 Sep
E Sloan, D.J. 01 Sep
E Williams, D.C. 01 Sep
X Lambie, T.J. 01 Sep
E Jones, A.F. 01 Sep
X Carnell, G.J. 01 Sep
E Moores, C.P. 01 Sep
X Young, M.J. 16 Sep
X Milne, P.B. 16 Sep
X Howell, H.R.G. 25 Sep
X Morrison, G.W. 01 Oct
X Logan, J.M. 01 Oct
X Hilson, S.M. 01 Oct
E Roberts, I.G. 01 Oct

X Windebank, S.J. .... 01 Oct
E Bissett, I.M. .... 17 Oct
E Bissett, P.K. .... 17 Oct
E Bissett, R.W. .... 17 Oct
X Walsh, S.C. .... 01 Nov
X Lea, S.A.P. .... 01 Nov
X Noblett, P.G.A. .... 01 Nov
E Donovan, P. .... 01 Nov
X Slocombe, N.R. .... 01 Nov
X Hutton, G. .... 01 Nov
X Finch, C.R. .... 16 Nov
X Hamilton, I.J. .... 16 Nov
X Haggart, P.D. .... 01 Dec
X Dunn, P.E. .... 12 Dec
S Gill, S.C. .... 12 Dec
S Hill, E.C.A. .... 12 Dec
S Plaice, G.C. .... 12 Dec
X Roberts, S. .... 12 Dec

1992

E Baines, D.M.L. .... 01 Jan
E Beadnell, R.M. .... 01 Jan
X Millman, D.J. .... 01 Jan
E Ritsperis, A. .... 01 Jan
E Morgan-Hosey, J.N. .... 01 Jan
E Rostron, D.W. .... 01 Jan
X Moulton, S.J. .... 01 Jan
X Richardson, P. .... 16 Jan
X Chan-A-Sue, S.S. .... 16 Jan
X Neal, S.M. .... 16 Jan
X Poole, T.J. .... 16 Jan
S Quinn, M.E. .... 01 Feb
X Thompson, A.R. .... 01 Feb
X Brown, A.P. .... 01 Feb
X Atkinson, G.C. .... 01 Feb
X Tidball, I.C. .... 01 Feb
E Ball, S.J. .... 13 Feb
E Young, R. .... 13 Feb
X Dale, A. .... 23 Feb
X King, A.R. .... 01 Mar
X Rowlands, K. .... 01 Mar
X Canning, C.P. .... 01 Mar
X Sparkes, S.N. .... 01 Apr
X Murphy, D.A. .... 01 Apr
X Shrimpton, M.W. .... 01 Apr
X Richardson, G.A. .... 01 Apr
X Gough, S.R. .... 03 Apr
MS O'Callaghan, S.T. .... 03 Apr
X Parry, D.R. .... 03 Apr
X Rogers, A. .... 03 Apr
MS Trasler, M.F. .... 03 Apr
X Milligan, R.J.C. .... 16 Apr
X Birse, G.J. .... 01 May

E Plackett, A.J. .... 01 May
E Smith, N.P. .... 01 May
X Gurr, A.W.G. .... 01 May
X Bird, J.M. .... 01 May
X Guy, T.J. .... 01 May
X Parry, J.D.F. .... 01 May
E Russell, B. .... 01 May
E Strutt, J.F. .... 01 May
X Wilson, D.R. .... 01 May
E Bye, M.D. .... 01 May
E Chambers, I.R. .... 01 May
X Foreman, S.L. .... 01 May
S Wright, A.L. .... 02 May
X Quinn, S.A. .... 16 May
X Brunsden-Brown, SE .... 16 May
X Lawrance, G.M. .... 16 May
X Read, C.T. .... 16 May
X Williams, R.I. .... 16 May
E Solly, M.M. .... 22 May
E Prinsep, T.J. .... 01 Jun
X Gray, J.A. .... 01 Jun
E Bradley, P.M. .... 01 Jun
E Helps, A.R. .... 01 Jun
E Howard, N.H. .... 01 Jun
E Reah, S. .... 01 Jun
E Rogers, C.M. .... 01 Jun
E Wilkins, R.R. .... 01 Jun
X Radford, A.J. .... 01 Jun
S Barton, A.J. .... 01 Jun
S Burns, R.C. .... 01 Jun
E Fleisher, S.M. .... 01 Jun
X Moore, M. .... 01 Jun
E Mulvaney, P.A. .... 01 Jun
E Nicklas, C.J. .... 01 Jun
E Saunders, P.W. .... 01 Jun
X Wilkinson, D.H. .... 01 Jun
X Williams, J.P. .... 01 Jun
X Reilly, T.G. .... 03 Jun
E Craib, A.G. .... 05 Jun
E Davies, S.P. .... 05 Jun
E Dyer, G.R. .... 05 Jun
E Hunt, P.E.R.D. .... 05 Jun
E Mitchell, P. .... 05 Jun
E Mountjoy, B.J. .... 05 Jun
E Radbourne, N.I. .... 05 Jun
E Wray, A.D. .... 05 Jun
E Bond, A.J. .... 09 Jun
X Sneddon, R.N. .... 16 Jun
X King, S.J. .... 16 Jun
E Young, C.J. .... 18 Jun
X Campbell, L.M. .... 01 Jul
E Elliott, S. .... 01 Jul
X Rasor, A.M. .... 01 Jul

X Gardner, J.E. .... 01 Jul
S Steele, K.S. .... 01 Jul
E Barton, M.A. .... 01 Jul
E Crundell, R.J. .... 01 Jul
X Diggle, W.N.N. .... 01 Jul
X Finn, G.J. .... 01 Jul
E Henderson, E.M. .... 01 Jul
E Lunn, M.H.B. .... 01 Jul
E Moody, D.C. .... 01 Jul
E Panther, A.M. .... 01 Jul
S Walsh, M.A. .... 01 Jul
E Gillham, P.R. .... 01 Jul
S Brenchley, N.G. .... 01 Jul
E Harvey, G. .... 01 Jul
E Juckes, M.A. .... 01 Jul
E Peace, R.W. .... 01 Jul
E Etchells, S.B. .... 03 Jul
W Coulton, J.A. .... 14 Jul
S Nicholson, B.R. .... 14 Jul
X Jameson, R.M. .... 16 Jul
E Philpot, D.J. .... 18 Jul
S Knowles, M.M. .... 24 Jul
X Reid, P.F. .... 24 Jul
E Bulcock, M. .... 28 Jul
E Lauchlan, R.A. .... 01 Aug
E Donovan, M.C. .... 01 Aug
E Mills, I. .... 01 Aug
X Wallis, J.S. .... 01 Aug
X Brian, N. .... 01 Aug
X Dando, J.N. .... 01 Aug
X Ley, J.A. .... 01 Aug
E Ross, I. .... 01 Aug
E Woodbridge, R.G. .... 01 Aug
X Gillespie, C.D. .... 01 Aug
E Miles, G.J. .... 07 Aug
X Lambert, A. .... 09 Aug
E Thrippleton, M.G. .... 15 Aug
X Jaques, D.A. .... 16 Aug
E Bee, M.T. .... 01 Sep
E Harding, C.S. .... 01 Sep
E Procter, J.E. .... 01 Sep
E Richter, A.S.B. .... 01 Sep
X Skidmore, R.P. .... 01 Sep
S Vowles, T.J. .... 01 Sep
X Duff, A.P. .... 01 Sep
E Wharrie, E.K.B. .... 01 Sep
X Flynn, L.P. .... 01 Sep
X Oulds, K.A. .... 01 Sep
E Walton, C.P. .... 01 Sep
E Wheal, A.J. .... 01 Sep
X Wyper, J.R. .... 01 Sep
E Rose, M.F. .... 01 Sep
X Wilson, R. .... 01 Sep

E Hendy, L.S. 28 Sep
E Carr, R.G. 01 Oct
S Bell, M. 01 Oct
X Langrish, G.J. 01 Oct
S Wooller, M.A.H. 01 Oct
X Allen, L.B. 01 Oct
E Dyke, K.A. 01 Oct
X Gibbons, N.P. 01 Oct
S Adlam, G.M. 01 Oct
W Clark, A.C. 06 Oct
E Cheseldine, D. 16 Oct
E Cooke, M.J. 16 Oct
E Dunn, A.J.P. 16 Oct
E Hutchings, J.S. 16 Oct
E Parrett, J.W. 16 Oct
E Parry, R.J. 16 Oct
E Stobie, P.L. 16 Oct
E Wroblewski, J.A. 16 Oct
X Curtis, R.J. 19 Oct
X Whalley, K.J. 21 Oct
W Hood, C.K. 23 Oct
E Dickens, D.S. 01 Nov
E Gordon, N.L. 01 Nov
E Norris, J.G. 01 Nov
X Ramsey, R.T. 01 Nov
S Cogan, R.E.C. 01 Nov
S Fogell, A.D. 01 Nov
X O'Byrne, P.B.M. 01 Nov
X Reen, S.C. 01 Nov
E Wylie, I.C.H. 01 Nov
S Hally, P.J. 01 Nov
X Woodard, J.R.A. 01 Nov
X Julian, T.M. 16 Nov
X Patterson, A.J. 16 Nov
X Stockton, K.G. 19 Nov
X Fitzgerald, N.J. 01 Dec
E Ballard, M.L. 01 Dec
E Daly, A. 01 Dec
E Lowe, S.M. 01 Dec
X Broadhurst, M.R. 01 Dec
X Haigh, A.J. 01 Dec
E Joyce, D.A. 01 Dec
X Lilburn, L.K. 01 Dec
X Sargent, P.M. 01 Dec
X Douglas, P.G. 03 Dec
E Reeves, K. 04 Dec
W Elborn, T.K. 11 Dec
W Green, J.L. 11 Dec
S MacAskill, C.H. 11 Dec
W McBain, M.S. 11 Dec
X McTear, N.J. 11 Dec
X Mitchell, M. 11 Dec
X Steele, T.G. 11 Dec
S Turner, R.F. 11 Dec
W Walsh, J.S. 11 Dec
S West, A.W. 11 Dec
X Wood, S.G. 11 Dec
S Beresford-Green, P.M. 16 Dec
S Gale, C.V. 24 Dec
E Rutherford, T.J. 30 Dec

1993

E Boston, J. 01 Jan
E Lewis, S.J. 01 Jan
E McMullan, N.L. 01 Jan
X Rowe, K.C. 01 Jan
E Higson, B.L. 01 Jan
E Kerr, A.N. 01 Jan
E Malley, M.P. 01 Jan
X Smith, G.D.J. 01 Jan
E Thomas, S.M. 01 Jan
E Atkins, I. 01 Jan
S Donovan, R.J. 01 Jan
E Ewen, A.P. 01 Jan
E Higham, J.G. 01 Jan
X MacKinnon, D.J. 01 Jan
X Varley, I.G. 01 Jan
X Wills, P.J. 01 Jan
E Clarke, A.R. 03 Jan
W Daly, J.M. 04 Jan
X Brown, S.H. 15 Jan
X Mercer, D.C. 16 Jan
E Lodge, C.N. 01 Feb
E Sellers, G.D. 01 Feb
X Binstead, K.N. 01 Feb
E Cleminson, M.D. 01 Feb
X Stanton-Brown, P.J. 01 Feb
X Steil, C.W.R. 01 Feb
X Black, J.J.M. 01 Feb
E Harrison, A. 01 Feb
X Hopper, S.M. 01 Feb
X Knott, M.B. 01 Feb
X Miller, P.D. 01 Feb
X Thomson, C.D. 01 Feb
X Tredray, T.P. 01 Feb
X Trott, C.M.J. 01 Feb
X Walters, R.J. 01 Feb
E Woods, T.C. 01 Feb
E Bowker, I.C. 13 Feb
E Bannister, A.N. 19 Feb
E Batten, A.J. 19 Feb
E Bedelle, S.J. 19 Feb
E Burge, R.G. 19 Feb
E Gisborne, W.C. 19 Feb
E Hatcher, T.R. 19 Feb
E Johnson, M.J. 19 Feb
E MacDougall, S.J. 19 Feb
E McCabe, D.S. 19 Feb
E Rowe, A.J. 19 Feb
E Rundle, A.L. 19 Feb
E Seaman, P.J. 19 Feb
E Tomkins, A.B. 19 Feb
E Warr, R.F. 19 Feb
E Wooding, G.A. 19 Feb
E Lavin, G.J. 01 Mar
E McCaughey, V.J. 01 Mar
X Perks, J.LE'S. 01 Mar
X MacNeil, S.W. 01 Mar
X Simpson, C.C. 01 Mar
X Chaston, S.P. 01 Mar
X Cox, R.J. 01 Mar
X Darwent, S.A. 01 Mar
X Griffin, N.R. 01 Mar
S Hallett, S.J. 01 Mar
E Head, S.A. 01 Mar
E Marshall, P. 01 Mar
X Nelson, C.S. 01 Mar
X Pearson, M.F. 01 Mar
X Bristowe, P.A. 01 Mar
X Giles, R.K. 01 Mar
X George, D.M. 13 Mar
X Gates, N.S. 16 Mar
X Vink, J.D. 20 Mar
S Waterhouse, P. 01 Apr
E Whyte, I.P. 01 Apr
E Adams, G.H. 01 Apr
X Bramwell, J.G. 01 Apr
S Butterworth, N.G. 01 Apr
X Millen, S.C.W. 01 Apr
E Parnell, A.D. 01 Apr
X Ryan, S.J. 01 Apr
E Walton, C.P. 01 Apr
E Waterworth, S.N. 01 Apr
E Drywood, T. 01 Apr
E Reid, J.C.J. 01 Apr
S Whalley, R.J. 01 Apr
X Barron, P.J. 02 Apr
X Billington, T.J. 02 Apr
MS Chilcott, P.L.H. 02 Apr
X Clements, S.J. 02 Apr
S Hall, D.A. 02 Apr
X Moreby, M.F. 02 Apr
X Soar, G. 16 Apr
W Gale, S.L. 25 Apr
X Milton, G.P. 01 May
X Harlow, S.R. 01 May
X Mould, P. 01 May
X Payne, M.J. 01 May
E Rand, M.J. 01 May

X Richards, G.B. .... 01 May
X Russell, P. .... 01 May
X Stock, C.M. .... 01 May
X Utley, M.K. .... 01 May
E Shaw, M.L. .... 01 May
E Davies, J.W. .... 11 May
X Crossley, G.A. .... 16 May
X West, P.J. .... 16 May
E Langrill, M.P. .... 01 Jun
E Aniyi, C.B.J. .... 01 Jun
X Bessell, D.A. .... 01 Jun
X Douglas, P.J. .... 01 Jun
X Durham, P.C.L. .... 01 Jun
X Paterson, M.P. .... 01 Jun
X Williams, C.N.O. .... 01 Jun
E Baller, C.R. .... 01 Jun
E Bonnar, J.A. .... 01 Jun
E Hutchins, R.F. .... 01 Jun
E Keen, N. .... 01 Jun
X Knight, D.W. .... 01 Jun
X Loane, M.M. .... 01 Jun
X Newell, P.R. .... 01 Jun
E Ralphson, M.D. .... 01 Jun
E Williams, M. .... 01 Jun
X Jacques, N.A. .... 01 Jun
X Sutton, R.M.J. .... 01 Jun
S Hart, C.L. .... 11 Jun
X White, S.H.W. .... 16 Jun
X Lister, A.R. .... 16 Jun
X Austin, I. .... 18 Jun
E Byrne, A.C. .... 18 Jun
E Jordan, L. .... 18 Jun
S Martin, J.H. .... 18 Jun
E McLachlan, M.P. .... 18 Jun
E Cropper, F.B.N. .... 24 Jun
E Elliott, S. .... 01 Jul
E Love, T.S.N. .... 01 Jul
X Morris, A.M. .... 01 Jul
X Norgan, D.J. .... 01 Jul
X Watts, R. .... 01 Jul
X Dunn, P.E. .... 01 Jul
X Lett, J.D. .... 01 Jul
E Metcalfe, P.I. .... 01 Jul
X Mudge, A.M. .... 01 Jul
E Prince, M.E. .... 01 Jul
S Richardson, G.N. .... 01 Jul
X Geary, M.D. .... 01 Jul
X Rodgers, D. .... 01 Jul
E McQueen, J.B. .... 01 Jul
E Green, A.M. .... 01 Jul
X Holmes, J.D. .... 01 Jul
E Napier, G.A. .... 01 Jul
E Sullivan, M. .... 01 Jul
S Hewitt, L.R. .... 01 Jul
E Towell, P.J. .... 01 Jul
X Brosnan, M.A. .... 16 Jul
X Norris, G.P. .... 16 Jul
X Crascall, S.J. .... 23 Jul
MS Dell, I.M. .... 23 Jul
X Harper, I.L. .... 23 Jul
X Hawkes, J.D. .... 23 Jul
X Horrocks, C.C. .... 23 Jul
X Massey, P. .... 23 Jul
MS Richards, B.R. .... 23 Jul
MS Ryder, T.J. .... 23 Jul
X Thomas, N.R. .... 23 Jul
E Pearson, C.P.B. .... 01 Aug
X Bower, A.J. .... 01 Aug
S Finch, B.A. .... 01 Aug
X O'Sullivan, M.L.J. .... 01 Aug
E Broadbent, A.C. .... 01 Aug
X Coyle, G.J. .... 01 Aug
E Graham, A.N.S. .... 01 Aug
X Matthews, Q.S. .... 01 Aug
S Preece, D.G. .... 01 Aug
E Winter, R.J. .... 01 Aug
X Wood, C. .... 01 Aug
X Markey, A.P. .... 01 Aug
S Samuel, K.L.H. .... 01 Aug
E Downer, M.J. .... 01 Aug
X Cox, S.A.J. .... 16 Aug
X Choat, J.H. .... 16 Aug
X Willing, N.P. .... 16 Aug
E Ellis, J.P. .... 01 Sep
E Lewis, D.J. .... 01 Sep
E Laing, I. .... 01 Sep
X Salt, H.S. .... 01 Sep
E Steel, R.A. .... 01 Sep
X Yeomans, P.A. .... 01 Sep
X Corney, A.D. .... 01 Sep
X Dowsett, P.G. .... 01 Sep
X Henry, T.M. .... 01 Sep
X Jordan, A.A. .... 01 Sep
X Duncan, C.J. .... 01 Sep
E Chapman, P. .... 01 Sep
X Downes, C.H. .... 01 Sep
E Lees, S.N. .... 02 Sep
X Elwell-Deighton, D.C. .... 16 Sep
X Stanley, N.J. .... 16 Sep
X Beattie, P.S. .... 01 Oct
X Dennis, M.J. .... 01 Oct
S Knock, G.P. .... 01 Oct
X Reed, M.T. .... 01 Oct
X Houston, D.J.M. .... 01 Oct
S Joll, S.M. .... 01 Oct
X Rutherford, K.J. .... 01 Oct
X Cooke, G.S. .... 01 Oct
S Pheasant, J.C.S. .... 01 Oct
X Smallwood, R.I. .... 12 Oct
E Barrett, D.L. .... 15 Oct
E Bell, D.P. .... 15 Oct
E Bowness, P. .... 15 Oct
E Burrows, J.C. .... 15 Oct
E Butler, L.P. .... 15 Oct
E Ireland, J.M. .... 15 Oct
E Leaning, D.J. .... 15 Oct
E Murray, S. .... 15 Oct
E Phesse, J.P.L. .... 15 Oct
E Preece, D.W. .... 15 Oct
X Bolton, S.J. .... 16 Oct
X Perry, R.J. .... 01 Nov
X Gamble, N. .... 01 Nov
E Stevenson, J.P. .... 01 Nov
X MacFarlane, I.S.D. .... 01 Nov
X Moore, S.K. .... 01 Nov
X Noyce, V.R.A. .... 01 Nov
E Palmer, M.E. .... 01 Nov
X Polding, M. .... 01 Nov
X Smith, D.J. .... 01 Nov
X Curry, R.E. .... 01 Nov
E Chamberlain, N.R.L. .... 01 Nov
X Simpson, D.K. .... 16 Nov
X Long, W.G.H. .... 01 Dec
X Blackburn, P.R. .... 01 Dec
X Buckingham, G. .... 01 Dec
E Mehta, R.P. .... 01 Dec
E Price, T.E. .... 01 Dec
E Ford, J.D. .... 01 Dec
E Rowan, N.A. .... 01 Dec
X Edey, M.J. .... 01 Dec
E Howse, R.J. .... 01 Dec
X Marquis, A.C. .... 01 Dec
X Schunmann, C.P.I. .... 01 Dec
X Williams, M.J. .... 01 Dec
E Crawford, L. .... 05 Dec
X Scott, M.R. .... 16 Dec
X Bing, N.A. .... 16 Dec
X Spence, R.G. .... 16 Dec
S Arnold, A.S. .... 17 Dec
X Coyne, J.D. .... 17 Dec
X Doyle, N.P. .... 17 Dec
S Johnson, M.D. .... 17 Dec
X Kerr, J. .... 17 Dec
X Miller, G. .... 17 Dec
S Stillwell-Cox, A.D.R. .... 17 Dec
S Tucker, R.S. .... 17 Dec
X Walker, E.G. .... 17 Dec
X Wardle, M. .... 17 Dec
S Wyatt, C. .... 17 Dec

	Name	Date
E	Hancock, R.T.A.	22 Dec
	1994	
E	Baggaley, J.A.L.	01 Jan
X	Campbell, P.R.	01 Jan
E	Davies, L.	01 Jan
E	Onyike, C.E.	01 Jan
X	Pink, S.E.	01 Jan
E	Kies, L.N.	01 Jan
E	Farrington, J.L.	01 Jan
E	Goldsmith, D.T.	01 Jan
X	Haywood, P.J.	01 Jan
X	Hitchings, D.L.	01 Jan
E	Richardson, D.	01 Jan
X	Allen, D.J.K.	16 Jan
X	Gotke, C.T.	16 Jan
E	Evans, A.J.	01 Feb
X	Buckley, D.D.G.	01 Feb
X	Tite, A.D.	01 Feb
X	Phipps, T.A.	01 Feb
E	Thirkettle, J.A.	01 Feb
E	Barnett, A.C.	01 Feb
X	Carpenter, P.J.	01 Feb
E	Cheshire, T.E.	01 Feb
X	Fryer, A.C.	01 Feb
E	Game, P.G.	01 Feb
E	Goddard, A.S.N.	01 Feb
X	Green, S.K.	01 Feb
S	Higgs, T.A.	01 Feb
E	Macleod, M.S.	01 Feb
E	Rodwell, T.R.J.	01 Feb
S	Wilman, D.M.	01 Feb
X	Weightman, N.E.	16 Feb
X	Taylor, R.J.	16 Feb
E	Bradshaw, K.T.	18 Feb
E	Brothers, A.H.G.	18 Feb
E	Chambers, P.	18 Feb
E	Dewsnap, M.D.	18 Feb
E	Dymond, N.R.J.	18 Feb
E	Haworth, S.	18 Feb
E	Hobson, I.S.	18 Feb
E	Hooper, G.P.	18 Feb
E	Penfold, M.J.	18 Feb
E	Wells, B.C.	18 Feb
E	Wrenn, M.R.W.	18 Feb
E	Wyld, A.W.	18 Feb
X	Hesling, G.	28 Feb
X	Chadfield, L.J.	01 Mar
X	Bryson, S.A.	01 Mar
E	Carroll, P.C.	01 Mar
E	Clarke, R.W.	01 Mar
E	Finn, I.R.	01 Mar
X	Hinchcliffe, A.	01 Mar
E	Jose, S.	01 Mar
X	Ketteringham, M.J.	01 Mar
X	Knight, A.C.F.	01 Mar
E	Meek, C.S.	01 Mar
E	Proctor, W.J.G.	01 Mar
E	Rose, C.M.	01 Mar
E	Shellard, G.I.	01 Mar
X	Stephen, B.M.	01 Mar
X	Wallace, S.J.	01 Mar
E	Cunnane, K.J.	01 Mar
E	Hawley, S.C.	01 Mar
X	Hocking, C.B.	01 Mar
E	Humphrey, I.J.	01 Mar
X	White, I.F.	01 Mar
S	Brock, R.F.	01 Mar
E	Bugg, K.J.	01 Mar
E	Marson, G.M.	01 Mar
E	Mould, T.P.	01 Mar
X	South, D.J.	01 Mar
S	Lawrence, S.P.	01 Mar
E	Broadbent, P.S.	01 Mar
E	Corps, S.D.	01 Mar
S	Burns, A.C.	04 Mar
X	Walker, S.P.	09 Mar
X	Clarke, D.	16 Mar
E	Derby, B.D.	01 Apr
X	Corbett, T.J.	01 Apr
X	Barnes, P.A.L.	01 Apr
X	Kohler, A.P.	01 Apr
E	James, T.E.	01 Apr
E	Cubbage, J.	01 Apr
S	Goudge, S.D.P.	01 Apr
E	Hindson, C.L.	01 Apr
E	Johnson, C.C.B.	01 Apr
E	Kelly, H.C.	01 Apr
E	Nicholas, S.P.	01 Apr
X	Offord, M.R.	01 Apr
X	Tooze, L.V.	01 Apr
X	Manser, D.N.	01 Apr
X	Childs, J.R.	01 Apr
X	Dineen, J.M.G.	01 Apr
X	Green, T.C.	01 Apr
X	Page, L.	01 Apr
S	Austen, R.M.	08 Apr
MS	Gerrell, F.J.	08 Apr
S	Grocott, P.C.	08 Apr
S	Lewins, G.	08 Apr
X	Lister, S.	08 Apr
MS	McLaughlan, C.J.	08 Apr
S	Melville-Brown, M.G.	08 Apr
X	Pugh, M.R.	08 Apr
X	Hopper, I.M.	09 Apr
X	Mailes, I.R.A.	16 Apr
X	Stembridge, D.P.T.	16 Apr
E	Blacow, C.	24 Apr
X	Manson, P.D.	01 May
X	Cull, I.	01 May
X	Townsend, G.P.	01 May
E	Wicking, G.S.	01 May
X	Foreman, T.P.	01 May
S	Hart, N.L.W.	01 May
X	Hoare, P.J.E.	01 May
X	Blackburn, S.J.	01 May
X	Hygate, A.M.	01 May
X	Maxwell, R.	01 May
X	Robinson, M.S.	01 May
X	Bradley, M.T.	01 May
X	Craig, J.A.	01 May
E	Stephenson, K.J.M.	01 May
X	Howe, J.P.	01 May
X	Kennington, L.A.	01 May
X	McLintock, M.W.	01 May
E	Noakes, K.M.	01 May
S	Porter, T.B.	01 May
S	Walker, D.W.A.	01 May
X	Matthews, J.	16 May
X	Billcliff, N.	16 May
X	West, R.J.	01 Jun
X	Osborn, C.G.	01 Jun
X	Clark, J.L.	01 Jun
X	Fuller, J.P.	01 Jun
X	Hedworth, A.J.	01 Jun
E	Cox, D.J.	01 Jun
X	Hempsell, A.M.	01 Jun
X	Hurley, C.	01 Jun
X	McGlory, S.J.	01 Jun
S	Park, B.C.	01 Jun
S	Roberts, S.M.	01 Jun
X	Robinson, M.S.	01 Jun
X	Stacey, A.M.	01 Jun
X	Waterfield, S.J.	01 Jun
E	Cowper, I.R.	10 Jun
E	Dunningham, S.	10 Jun
E	Grant, B.G.	10 Jun
E	Metcalf, R.	10 Jun
E	Page, T.A.	10 Jun
E	Stamp, D.W.	10 Jun
E	Waterman, D.L.	10 Jun
X	Collicutt, J.M.	16 Jun
X	Naylor, A.J.	16 Jun
X	Clink, A.D.	16 Jun
X	Kent, A.J.	16 Jun
X	Oakes, I.J.	16 Jun
X	Hunt, S.C.	01 Jul
E	Campbell-Balcombe AA	01 Jul

E	Doran, S.E.	01 Jul
X	O'Nyons, Y.I.	01 Jul
X	Raeburn, M.	01 Jul
X	Balmain, S.S.	01 Jul
X	Jacques, M.J.	01 Jul
E	Block, A.W.G.	01 Jul
X	Chaloner, A.C.	01 Jul
E	Garland, D.S.	01 Jul
X	Gill, M.H.	01 Jul
E	Hamilton, S.M.	01 Jul
E	Mincher, D.J.F.	01 Jul
X	Mollard, M.J.	01 Jul
X	Payne, P.J.	01 Jul
S	Sellars, S.J.	01 Jul
E	Skelton, J.S.	01 Jul
X	Welch, D.A.	05 Jul
X	Hopkins, S.D.	16 Jul
X	Sheils, D.E.T.	16 Jul
X	Oatley, T.P.	16 Jul
X	Wingfield, M.J.	16 Jul
X	Laycock, A.	16 Jul
X	Carter, K.S.	29 Jul
X	Ellwood, P.G.	29 Jul
MS	Howells, M.J.	29 Jul
X	Nugent, C.J.	29 Jul
MS	Phillips, I.M.	29 Jul
X	Taylor, M.R.	29 Jul
X	West, A.B.	29 Jul
X	Wright, D.A.	29 Jul
X	Penrice, I.W.	01 Aug
X	Bunney, G.J.	01 Aug
X	Garner, S.M.	01 Aug
E	Wilson, C.W.	01 Aug
E	Bonner, N.	01 Aug
E	Combe, G.R.	01 Aug
X	Goldstone, R.S.	01 Aug
X	Mortimer, R.P.	01 Aug
S	Nicholson, K.J.	01 Aug
E	Scott, R.A.	01 Aug
S	Dickson, J.I.	01 Aug
X	Dufosee, S.W.	06 Aug
X	Kirkham, S.P.	16 Aug
S	Taylor, C.R.	25 Aug
E	Dawson, N.J.F.	01 Sep
E	Saunders, J.M.	01 Sep
X	Cottee, B.R.J.	01 Sep
E	Hodge, C.M.	01 Sep
X	Jones, P.I.	01 Sep
X	McDonald, N.	01 Sep
X	Aitken, A.J.	01 Sep
E	Beautyman, A.J.	01 Sep
E	Entwistle, C.	01 Sep
E	MacDonald, A.J.	01 Sep
X	Mutch, J.R.	01 Sep
X	Ahlgren, E.G.	01 Sep
E	Ajala, A.A.	01 Sep
E	Balcombe, J.S.	01 Sep
X	Millar, S.J.	01 Sep
E	Voyce, J.E.	01 Sep
X	Edmonds, L.A.	01 Sep
S	Goldsworthy, P.J.	01 Sep
X	Reese, D.M.	01 Sep
X	Webber, J.P.	01 Sep
X	Downing, I.M.	16 Sep
X	Birmingham, T.C.	16 Sep
X	Stubbs, G.A.	16 Sep
X	Ling, J.W.L.	16 Sep
E	Warneken, A.E.	01 Oct
X	Drodge, A.P.F.	01 Oct
X	Lee, P.M.	01 Oct
X	Lintern, R.D.	01 Oct
X	Mullen, J.J.	01 Oct
X	Penprase, J.M.	01 Oct
E	Richardson, D.	01 Oct
E	Snelling, P.D.	01 Oct
E	Boyle, J.B.	01 Oct
S	Bryant, D.J.G.	01 Oct
E	Earl, N.J.C.	01 Oct
S	Goodman, P.R.	01 Oct
X	Lord, R.J.	01 Oct
X	Morgan, D.H.	01 Oct
X	Sharpe, T.G.	01 Oct
X	Vartan, M.R.	01 Oct
X	Woolhead, A.L.	01 Oct
X	Barry, J.P.	11 Oct
E	Bryce, N.A.	14 Oct
E	Ford, G.R.	14 Oct
E	Midmore, M.J.	14 Oct
E	Walton, S.P.	14 Oct
E	White, R.L.	14 Oct
X	Brayson, M.	16 Oct
X	Ellerton, P.	16 Oct
X	Pitcher, P.P.	01 Nov
X	Williamson, S.M.	01 Nov
X	Roberts, M.A.	01 Nov
X	Brown, S.D.	01 Nov
E	Cummings, D.J.	01 Nov
E	Davidson, M.	01 Nov
X	Long, S.G.	01 Nov
X	Webster, A.P.	01 Nov
E	Bird, M.G.J.	01 Nov
X	Ripley, B.E.	01 Nov
S	White, J.E.	01 Nov
E	Doull, D.J.M.	01 Nov
X	Kirkwood, T.A.H.	01 Nov
S	Murdoch, A.P.	01 Nov
S	Watts, A.J.	01 Nov
X	Allison, G.	16 Nov
X	Rowley, S.A.C.	16 Nov
X	Roster, S.P.	16 Nov
X	Price, J.S.	16 Nov
X	Bratby, S.P.	16 Nov
X	Nicholson, S.R.	22 Nov
X	Russell, N.A.D.	01 Dec
S	Birse, B.L.	01 Dec
X	Jones, A.E.	01 Dec
X	Lamb, A.G.	01 Dec
X	Sillers, B.	01 Dec
X	Brodie, R.W.J.	01 Dec
X	Young, R.	01 Dec
E	Patterson, D.	01 Dec
E	Craggs, S.	01 Dec
E	Burbridge, D.J.	01 Dec
X	Hastilow, N.H.	01 Dec
E	Ronaldson, G.I.	01 Dec
E	Scopes, D.	01 Dec
X	Soul, N.J.	01 Dec
X	Sweet, P.	01 Dec
S	Titmuss, J.F.	01 Dec
E	Trott, E.A.	01 Dec
X	Beaumont, S.J.	16 Dec
X	Elston, A.J.	16 Dec
X	Hardy, L.B.	16 Dec
X	Jaggers, G.G.	16 Dec
X	Kelly, T.	16 Dec
X	Pledger, D.	16 Dec
S	Taylor, I.K.	16 Dec
X	Whitlam, J.	16 Dec
S	Young, S.W.	16 Dec
X	Dembrey, M.N.S.	16 Dec

1995

E	Carpenter, B.H.	01 Jan
E	Deakin, J.	01 Jan
E	Jordan, C.	01 Jan
E	Lovering, T.T.A.	01 Jan
E	Roberts, A.M.	01 Jan
E	Rogers, P.S.	01 Jan
E	Thompson, A.J.	01 Jan
X	Braithwaite, J.S.	01 Jan
X	Lunn, T.R.	01 Jan
X	Mills, S.D.G.	01 Jan
X	Ware, S.A.	01 Jan
E	Cooper, A.	01 Jan
X	Allfree, J.	01 Jan
X	Bishop, D.J.	01 Jan
E	Cragg, R.D.	01 Jan
X	Drake-Wilkes, N.J.	01 Jan
X	Hird, R.P.	01 Jan

X Jones, M.D. .... 01 Jan
E McCarthy, S.J. .... 01 Jan
E Nelson, L.M. .... 01 Jan
E Benn, S.W. .... 01 Jan
X Duncan, G.S. .... 16 Jan
X Jones, M.D. .... 16 Jan
X Laverty, R.E. .... 01 Feb
X Tate, G.A. .... 01 Feb
E Kellett, A. .... 01 Feb
X Satterthwaite, B.J. .... 01 Feb
X Gray, Y.M. .... 01 Feb
X Stewart, A.B. .... 01 Feb
E Bowden, M.T.E. .... 01 Feb
E Boyes, M.R. .... 01 Feb
S Dutton, A.C. .... 01 Feb
E Eccleston, J.M. .... 01 Feb
X Franklin, G.D. .... 01 Feb
E Gair, S.D.H. .... 01 Feb
X Langrill, T.J. .... 01 Feb
X Maynard, C.I. .... 01 Feb
X McCutcheon, G. .... 01 Feb
X Swigciski, D.P. .... 01 Feb
X Wiseman, I.C. .... 01 Feb
X Barber, C.J.H. .... 01 Feb
X Borbone, N. .... 06 Feb
X Johnson, A.R. .... 16 Feb
X Cooke, J.E. .... 18 Feb
E Abbott, D.A. .... 24 Feb
E Dawson, A.J. .... 24 Feb
E Eddie, A.G.W. .... 24 Feb
E Evans, S. .... 24 Feb
E Fallowfield, J.P. .... 24 Feb
E Harwood, C.G. .... 24 Feb
E Henderson, P.P. .... 24 Feb
E Jones, D.L. .... 24 Feb
E Knight, K.J. .... 24 Feb
E Obrien, I.P. .... 24 Feb
E Watson, C.R. .... 24 Feb
E Adams, R.J. .... 01 Mar
X Bellis, B.M. .... 01 Mar
E Carlisle, C.R. .... 01 Mar
X Foulis, N.D.A. .... 01 Mar
S Gennard, A. .... 01 Mar
S Malins, D.J.H. .... 01 Mar
X Peachey, R.M. .... 01 Mar
X Tanner, R.C. .... 01 Mar
X Bainbridge, S.D. .... 01 Mar
E Burvill, J.P. .... 01 Mar
E Coope, P.J. .... 01 Mar
E Fisher, P.C. .... 01 Mar
X Goulding, J.P. .... 01 Mar
X Harms, J.G. .... 01 Mar
E Holmes, R.A.G. .... 01 Mar
E Jennings, W. .... 01 Mar
E Large, S.A. .... 01 Mar
E Phillips, J.N. .... 01 Mar
E Stagg, A.R. .... 01 Mar
X Thompson, M.G. .... 01 Mar
S Wales, B.D. .... 01 Mar
X Watson, I. .... 01 Mar
X Percival, A.W. .... 01 Mar
X Skelley, A.N.M. .... 01 Mar
X Rawlinson, D. .... 16 Mar
X Gray, J.N.S. .... 01 Apr
X Marten, A.D. .... 01 Apr
E Rawson, S.M. .... 01 Apr
X Ogden, B.P. .... 01 Apr
X Humphries, J.E. .... 01 Apr
X Foster, T.G. .... 01 Apr
X Stratford, P.J. .... 01 Apr
E Hall, T.T. .... 01 Apr
X Lovatt, G.J. .... 01 Apr
S Moore, S.B. .... 01 Apr
X Reid, M.R. .... 01 Apr
S Rowe, H. .... 01 Apr
X Stride, J.C. .... 01 Apr
X McLennan, A. .... 01 Apr
X Atkinson, C.P. .... 01 Apr
X Ayers, T.P. .... 01 Apr
E Bowman, R.J. .... 01 Apr
S Bunt, K.J. .... 06 Apr
X Gold, J.W. .... 06 Apr
X Kerr, A.T.F. .... 06 Apr
X Seward, S.A. .... 06 Apr
MS Stead, R.A. .... 06 Apr
MS Wagstaff, N. .... 10 Apr
E Panic, A. .... 15 Apr
X Kelynack, M.T. .... 16 Apr
S Jones, C.J. .... 28 Apr
E Hardiman, N.A. .... 01 May
X Cooke-Priest, N.C.R. .... 01 May
S Hall, E.L. .... 01 May
S Norman-Walker, B.S. .... 01 May
X Whitfield, R.M.P. .... 01 May
X Ingc, D.J. .... 01 May
X Byron, J.D. .... 01 May
E Malkin, S.L. .... 01 May
X Murison, L.C. .... 01 May
E Spooner, S.L. .... 01 May
X Hynett, W.A. .... 16 May
X Stubbs, I. .... 16 May
X Woolsey, K.E.K. .... 16 May
E Youp, A.T. .... 01 Jun
X Noyce, R.G. .... 01 Jun
X Peppe, A.G. .... 01 Jun
X Asquith, S.P. .... 01 Jun
E Eastwood, L. .... 01 Jun
X Euden, C.P. .... 01 Jun
X Jarrett, M.T.J. .... 01 Jun
E Barrows, D.M. .... 01 Jun
E Sharkey, E.R. .... 01 Jun
X Turner, D.N. .... 01 Jun
X Ward, A.J. .... 01 Jun
X Watson, A.H. .... 01 Jun
X Williams, I.J. .... 01 Jun
E Berry, P. .... 15 Jun
E Dunsby, N.B. .... 15 Jun
E Keeley, S.P. .... 15 Jun
E Knight, R.H. .... 15 Jun
E Mitchell, S.D. .... 15 Jun
E Wilson, J.A. .... 15 Jun
X Day, M.K. .... 15 Jun
X Coulton, J.R.S. .... 16 Jun
X McCowan, D.J. .... 16 Jun
X Lee, N.D. .... 16 Jun
X Lynn, I.H. .... 30 Jun
S Cowan, C.J. .... 01 Jul
X May, J.W. .... 01 Jul
E Pitchford, I.C. .... 01 Jul
E May, S.C. .... 01 Jul
X Parrock, N.G. .... 01 Jul
X Beacham, P.R. .... 01 Jul
X Clarke, I.B. .... 01 Jul
E Dalton, F.J. .... 01 Jul
X Deavin, M.J. .... 01 Jul
X Doran, I.A.G. .... 01 Jul
E Edward, G.J. .... 01 Jul
E Lincoln, K.J. .... 01 Jul
X Mitchell, J.R. .... 01 Jul
X Ruddock, G.W.D. .... 01 Jul
E Ryan, N. .... 01 Jul
E Palmer, J. .... 01 Jul
W Swan, W. .... 09 Jul
X Smith, R.D. .... 22 Jul
X Bishop, G.C. .... 27 Jul
X Cunningham, N.J.W. .... 27 Jul
X Elsom, G.K. .... 27 Jul
X McKernan, J. .... 27 Jul
X Tomlinson, J.H. .... 27 Jul
X Wilson, G.J. .... 27 Jul
E Bagwell, P. .... 01 Aug
X Harris, M.J. .... 01 Aug
S Goldsworthy, E.T. .... 01 Aug
X Higgins, A.J. .... 01 Aug
E Paulson, R.B. .... 01 Aug
E Harrington, J.B. .... 01 Aug
E Sandle, N.D. .... 01 Aug
X Syrett, M.E. .... 01 Aug
X Whitmee, M.J.C. .... 01 Aug

X Cahill, K.A. .... 01 Aug
E Hickson, M.S.H. .... 01 Aug
E Letts, A.J. .... 01 Aug
X Lucocq, N.J. .... 01 Aug
S Russell, G.S. .... 01 Aug
E Storey, C.L. .... 01 Aug
E Sweeney, K.P.M. .... 01 Aug
E Veal, A.E. .... 01 Aug
X Nash, P.D. .... 01 Aug
X Tregunna, G.A. .... 08 Aug
X Brooman, M.J. .... 16 Aug
X Armstrong, S.T. .... 16 Aug
E Blow, P.T. .... 01 Sep
E Hunter, N.J. .... 01 Sep
E Le Gassick, P.J. .... 01 Sep
E Proffitt Burnham, J.M. .... 01 Sep
E Sheedy, K.L. .... 01 Sep
E Vincent, D. .... 01 Sep
X Brennan, A.J. .... 01 Sep
E Edwards, A.G. .... 01 Sep
E Foster, P.J. .... 01 Sep
E Hambly, B.J. .... 01 Sep
X Rhodes, M.J. .... 01 Sep
X Cullen, N.L. .... 01 Sep
X Lanni, M.N. .... 01 Sep
X McWilliams, J.E. .... 01 Sep
E Stowell, R.B.M. .... 01 Sep
S Curry, A.H. .... 01 Sep
X Hayton, S.R.C. .... 05 Sep
E Brown, P.A. .... 07 Sep
E Holden, P.A. .... 07 Sep
E Phillips, A.R. .... 07 Sep
E Reed, J.C. .... 07 Sep
E Walsh, D.G. .... 07 Sep
X Harrison, R.S. .... 15 Sep
X Newton, J.L. .... 16 Sep
E Tatlow, J.M. .... 20 Sep
X Baxter, J.C. .... 27 Sep
X Brown, S.J. .... 01 Oct
X Aspden, M.C. .... 01 Oct
X Moore, S.P. .... 01 Oct
E O'Neill, P.J. .... 01 Oct
X Horne, J.R. .... 01 Oct
S Dean, J.R. .... 01 Oct
X Roberts, P.S. .... 01 Oct
X Hanneman, M.N. .... 01 Oct
X Irons, R.C.S. .... 01 Oct
S Matthews, P.K. .... 01 Oct
X Wheeler, N.J. .... 01 Oct
E Sitton, J.B. .... 01 Nov
X Jardine, D.S. .... 01 Nov
X Jones, P.D. .... 01 Nov
X Ley, A.B. .... 01 Nov

E Parker, T.S. .... 01 Nov
X Bassett, D.A. .... 01 Nov
X Neild, T. .... 01 Nov
X Tregaskis, N.S. .... 01 Nov
X Rackham, A.D.H. .... 01 Nov
X Chick, N.S. .... 16 Nov
E Lee, S.Y.L. .... 01 Dec
W Watts, S.F. .... 01 Dec
E Mallen, D.J. .... 01 Dec
E Deeks, P.J. .... 01 Dec
X Jamieson, R.E. .... 01 Dec
X Marriott, N.K. .... 01 Dec
X Tacey, R.H. .... 01 Dec
X West, D.C. .... 01 Dec
S Simpson, A.M. .... 01 Dec
X Brown, C.L. .... 01 Dec
E Hughes, N.D. .... 01 Dec
X Ingram, G.J. .... 01 Dec
X Rees, R.T. .... 01 Dec
X Byrne, T.M. .... 13 Dec
S Fearnley, A.T. .... 13 Dec
S Jackson, P.A. .... 13 Dec
X Knight, J.D. .... 13 Dec
X Lawson, G.J. .... 13 Dec
X Marsh, M.P.A. .... 13 Dec
X Morrison, P. .... 13 Dec
X Woodrow, K.J. .... 13 Dec
X Evans, D.A. .... 20 Dec

1996

E Collins, T.L. .... 01 Jan
E Harrison, T.I. .... 01 Jan
E Heighway, M.R. .... 01 Jan
E Young, N.A. .... 01 Jan
S Bollen, J.M. .... 01 Jan
X Okukenu, D. .... 01 Jan
E Pakes, D.T. .... 01 Jan
E Hendrickx, C.J. .... 01 Jan
X Bratt, A.R. .... 01 Jan
E Field, C.R.H. .... 01 Jan
X Gibson, J.B. .... 01 Jan
X Johnston, J.A. .... 01 Jan
E Perkins, R.J. .... 01 Jan
E Thompson, M.J. .... 01 Jan
E Bailey, J.J. .... 01 Jan
X Schreier, P.J.R. .... 01 Jan
S Trinder, S.J. .... 30 Jan
E Pinder, C.D. .... 01 Feb
X Officer, R.L. .... 01 Feb
E Powles, D.A. .... 01 Feb
X Wookey, M. .... 01 Feb
S MacKay, A.C. .... 01 Feb
X Moorhouse, S.M.R. .... 01 Feb

E Read, M.R. .... 01 Feb
X Rimington, A.K. .... 01 Feb
X Stride, J.A. .... 01 Feb
X Watts, J.N. .... 01 Feb
X Smith, M.D. .... 01 Feb
X Segebarth, R.A. .... 16 Feb
X Thomas, S.M. .... 16 Feb
E Edson, M.A. .... 22 Feb
E Hyland, R.A. .... 22 Feb
E King, D.S. .... 22 Feb
E Stubbs, M.A. .... 22 Feb
E Watson, C.R. .... 22 Feb
E Wheadon, P.C. .... 01 Mar
X Smith, D.L. .... 01 Mar
X Hunt, F.B.G. .... 01 Mar
X Peters, W.R. .... 01 Mar
X Packham, C.N.R. .... 01 Mar
X Clark, M.H. .... 01 Mar
X Clay, J.C. .... 01 Mar
E Gardner, M.E.F. .... 01 Mar
S Hanson, M.N. .... 01 Mar
E Ling, C. .... 01 Mar
S Nelson, V. .... 01 Mar
X Philpott, A.M. .... 01 Mar
E Punch, G.K. .... 01 Mar
X Rae, D.G. .... 01 Mar
E Screaton, R.M. .... 01 Mar
E Stiven, T.D. .... 01 Mar
E Taylor, H.J. .... 01 Mar
E Townsend, D.J. .... 01 Mar
X Backus, R.I.K. .... 01 Mar
X McDougall, D.W. .... 01 Mar
E Lewis, A.J. .... 01 Mar
MS Taylor, N.A. .... 06 Mar
X Hogg, A. .... 16 Mar
X Lawson, R.K. .... 16 Mar
X Simms, D.M. .... 16 Mar
X Flintham, J.E. .... 16 Mar
X Long, M.S. .... 01 Apr
X Mercer, P.J. .... 01 Apr
X Lockett, D.J. .... 01 Apr
X Phillips, M.B. .... 01 Apr
S Barber, R.W. .... 01 Apr
X Capes, S.G. .... 01 Apr
X Donnan, H.M. .... 01 Apr
X Ralph, A.P. .... 01 Apr
X Readwin, R.R. .... 01 Apr
X Shepherd, M.P. .... 01 Apr
S Woodard, N.A. .... 01 Apr
X Battrick, R.R. .... 01 Apr
X Crabb, A.J. .... 01 Apr
E Fitzsimmons, S.M. .... 01 Apr
X Hains, J. .... 01 Apr

X Laughton, P. 01 Apr
E Robertshaw, I.W. 01 Apr
E Spooner, R.S. 01 Apr
X Tabberer, I.C. 01 Apr
MS Blocke, A.D. 04 Apr
MS Bradford, T.H.C. 04 Apr
X Brailey, I.S.F. 04 Apr
S Carter, S.P. 04 Apr
X Easton, D.W. 04 Apr
X Ford, A.J. 04 Apr
X Walker, M.J. 04 Apr
MS Walton, A.P. 04 Apr
X Welburn, R.C. 04 Apr
X Wilkinson, J. 04 Apr
X Campbell, I.A. 16 Apr
X Fraser, I.E. 16 Apr
E Evans, P.C. 01 May
X MacColl, A.A.J. 01 May
E Marjoram, G.K. 01 May
W Pearson, R. 01 May
E Hiscock, S.R.B. 01 May
X Smith, A.B.D. 01 May
E Fraser, P. 01 May
X Hammond, P.J. 01 May
X Riggall, A.D. 01 May
S Scandling, R.J. 01 May
E Bell, J.M. 01 May
E Blair, G.J.L. 01 May
E Howells, S.L. 01 May
E Smith, M.J. 01 May
E York, G.R.J. 01 May
E Flynn, A. 01 May
X Mowatt, P. 01 May
X Steadman, R.P. 01 May
E Taylor, I.J. 05 May
E Whiting, E.A. 05 May
X Robley, W.F. 01 Jun
E Nimmons, P. 01 Jun
X Strathie, G.S. 01 Jun
X Griffiths, R.H. 01 Jun
E Potts, G. 01 Jun
S Evans, C.A. 01 Jun
X Redford, D.E.M. 01 Jun
X Reid, W.A. 01 Jun
E Ubhi, W.G. 01 Jun
X Criddle, G.D.J. 01 Jun
X Fisher, R.J. 01 Jun
X Gilmore, M.P. 01 Jun
S Harding, D.J. 01 Jun
E Hedgecox, D.C. 01 Jun
E McCloskey, I.M. 01 Jun
X Monk, C.R. 01 Jun
E Rowlands, A.R. 01 Jun
X Lindsay, I.B. 01 Jun
E Clare, K. 01 Jun
X Sturdy, C.C.M. 14 Jun
E Grant, D.J. 14 Jun
E Hutchinson, P. 14 Jun
E Jones, R.V. 14 Jun
E King, G.C. 14 Jun
E Rendell, D.J. 14 Jun
E Riley, G.A. 14 Jun
X Vorley, S.W. 15 Jun
X Hourigan, M.P. 16 Jun
X Wiseman, N.C. 16 Jun
X Hutchins, T.S. 16 Jun
X Platt, J.H. 16 Jun
X Slocombe, J.S. 01 Jul
X Adams, P.N.E. 01 Jul
X Fox, T.M. 01 Jul
X Johnson, S.R.D. 01 Jul
X Spillane, P.W. 01 Jul
X Wyness, R.S. 01 Jul
X Atkinson, R.J. 01 Jul
E Fraser, H.L. 01 Jul
X Hooton, D.A.S.H. 01 Jul
E Hope, M.R. 01 Jul
E Jones, D.M. 01 Jul
E Leach, S.J. 01 Jul
X Parrott, J.P. 01 Jul
X Pickering, I.J. 01 Jul
X Davies, H.G.A. 01 Jul
X Armstrong, N.S. 01 Jul
X Burke, D.E. 01 Jul
X May, C. 01 Jul
E Thorp, B.T. 01 Jul
X Tyler, J.C. 01 Jul
S Bagworth, J.F. 01 Jul
X Dennis, P.E. 01 Jul
X Church, S.C. 16 Jul
X Forbes, P.T. 16 Jul
X Brember, P.B. 25 Jul
X Dale, N.R. 25 Jul
X Metcalfe, M.P. 25 Jul
MS Miller, D.E. 25 Jul
X Richards, F.C. 25 Jul
X Smith, N.J. 25 Jul
E McNamara, I.M. 01 Aug
X Miller, N.W.H. 01 Aug
X Stroude, P.A. 01 Aug
E Murphy, S.M. 01 Aug
X Patterson, J.D. 01 Aug
X Greetham, C.E. 01 Aug
X Moules, M.A.J. 01 Aug
X Sheldrake, J.P. 01 Aug
E White, G.J. 01 Aug
X Abel, N.P. 16 Aug
X Clarke, R.J. 16 Aug
X Hall, D. 16 Aug
X Whitlum, A.C. 16 Aug
X Everitt, T.W. 19 Aug
E Ahern, H. 01 Sep
E Edwards, J. 01 Sep
E Kelly, G.J. 01 Sep
W Dobie, F.E. 01 Sep
X Terry, N.P. 01 Sep
X Boorman, J.C. 01 Sep
E McCombe, J. 01 Sep
E Parry, M.R.R. 01 Sep
X Enever, S.A. 01 Sep
X McCulloch, I.D. 01 Sep
X Williams, R.J.S. 01 Sep
E Wright, D.I. 01 Sep
S Harris, R.P. 01 Sep
X Hindmarch, S.A. 01 Sep
S Percival, F. 01 Sep
E Puxley, M.E. 01 Sep
X Raeburn, C. 01 Sep
E Bottomley, S. 06 Sep
E Stanham, C.M. 06 Sep
X Wilson, A.S. 16 Sep
X Wilkinson, M.F. 16 Sep
E Donnelly, S. 17 Sep
X Clifford, C.T. 25 Sep
X McGuire, J. 01 Oct
E Sanderson, L.D. 01 Oct
X Byrne, T.F. 01 Oct
X Edge, K.L. 01 Oct
X Jaini, A. 01 Oct
X McEwan, A.M. 01 Oct
X Parr, M.J.E. 01 Oct
X Donegan, C.L. 01 Oct
E Haworth, J.H.T. 01 Oct
X Hill, A.J. 01 Oct
E Day, S.N. 01 Oct
X Stuart, E.E.A. 01 Oct
X Sewell, M.A.P. 16 Oct
X Bonnar, S.M. 01 Nov
E Davis, S.R. 01 Nov
E Gothard, A.M. 01 Nov
X Balletta, R.J. 01 Nov
X McBratney, J.A.G. 01 Nov
X Walsh, K.M. 01 Nov
X Webber, K.J. 01 Nov
X Bradley, R.L. 01 Nov
X Black, S.A. 01 Nov
X Dickins, B.R. 01 Nov
X Essenhigh, A.N.P. 01 Nov
X Whitlum, S. 01 Nov

X Ollerton, J.C. .... 16 Nov
E Mullins, A.D. .... 01 Dec
E Purvis, D.M. .... 01 Dec
X Wood, M.L. .... 01 Dec
X Donworth, D.M.J. .... 01 Dec
X Mitchell, C.D. .... 01 Dec
E Ankah, G.K.E. .... 01 Dec
S Coaker, S.A. .... 01 Dec
X Smith, K.M.L. .... 01 Dec
E Ashworth, H.J. .... 01 Dec
E Brown, A.M. .... 01 Dec
X Lacy, L.H. .... 01 Dec
S Reed, D.K. .... 01 Dec

1997

E Collins, D.R. .... 01 Jan
E Dennis, M.J. .... 01 Jan
E Dick, C.M. .... 01 Jan
E Nelson, P.M. .... 01 Jan
E Taylor, C.S. .... 01 Jan
E Lyons, M.J. .... 01 Jan
X Santrian, K. .... 01 Jan
S Coley, J.M. .... 01 Jan
S Dow, C.S. .... 01 Jan
E Hunwicks, S.E. .... 01 Jan
X Miles, R.L. .... 01 Jan
X Ottewell, P.S. .... 01 Jan
X Tilney, D.E. .... 01 Jan
E Whitehouse, N.R. .... 01 Jan
X Wood, C.R. .... 01 Jan
E Walsh, D.M. .... 12 Jan
E Smith, K.D. .... 01 Feb
X Caldicott-Barr, V.A. .... 01 Feb
X Harper, P.R. .... 01 Feb
X Hunt, S.S. .... 01 Feb
X Codd, JS. .... 01 Feb
X Field, J.S. .... 01 Feb
E Jefferson, T.S. .... 01 Feb
X Cutler, A.R. .... 01 Feb
X Foster, N.P. .... 01 Feb
S Gullett, H.R. .... 01 Feb
E Kendrick, A.M. .... 01 Feb
E Kingdom, M.A. .... 01 Feb
E Miller, M.C. .... 01 Feb
S Nathanson, H. .... 01 Feb
X Robertson Gopffarth, A.A.J. .... 01 Feb
X Thomsen, L.L. .... 01 Feb
X Williams, L.E. .... 01 Feb
E Cain, C.W. .... 07 Feb
E Collins, S.A. .... 07 Feb
E Eardley, J.M. .... 07 Feb
E Fulford, R.N. .... 07 Feb
E McTaggart, D.A. .... 07 Feb
E Ridge, M.H. .... 07 Feb
E Sheldon, M.L. .... 07 Feb
X Owen, G. .... 16 Feb
E Thomson, P.D. .... 24 Feb
X Barlow, M.J. .... 01 Mar
E Haddow, T.R. .... 01 Mar
E Read, P.S. .... 01 Mar
X Sutcliffe, M.R. .... 01 Mar
X Morley, S. .... 01 Mar
X Bone, J. .... 01 Mar
X Butterworth, P.G. .... 01 Mar
X Clague, J.J. .... 01 Mar
S Hefford, C.J. .... 01 Mar
X Jackson, I. .... 01 Mar
X Mason, D.J. .... 01 Mar
E McHugh, R.H. .... 01 Mar
X Philip, A.D. .... 01 Mar
S Quantrill, S.W. .... 01 Mar
S Stockbridge, A.J. .... 01 Mar
E Thorne, D.J. .... 01 Mar
X Tilden, P.J.E. .... 01 Mar
S Wells, M.P. .... 01 Mar
X Rackham, K.L.M. .... 01 Mar
X Small, R.J. .... 01 Mar
X Stringer, K.D.P. .... 16 Mar
E Rae, A.L. .... 01 Apr
E Cumming, R.A. .... 01 Apr
E Foreman, S.M. .... 01 Apr
E Wildin, A. .... 01 Apr
X Campbell, M.A.M. .... 01 Apr
X Lancaster, N. .... 01 Apr
X Walton, S.D. .... 01 Apr
X Bernard, R.A. .... 01 Apr
E Boxall, P. .... 01 Apr
X Brooks, G.C.G. .... 01 Apr
X Green, I.A. .... 01 Apr
E Harding, H.R. .... 01 Apr
X Hounsom, T.R. .... 01 Apr
X Lumsden, P.I. .... 01 Apr
E Mealing, D.W. .... 01 Apr
E Nicoll, A.J. .... 01 Apr
X Cole, D.J. .... 01 Apr
S Barratt, S.M. .... 03 Apr
X Bennetts, N. .... 03 Apr
X Clark, A.S. .... 03 Apr
X Conway, M.J. .... 03 Apr
S Darlow, P.R. .... 03 Apr
X Dunne, M.G. .... 03 Apr
MS Finn, D.W. .... 03 Apr
X Guiver, P. .... 03 Apr
X Lewis, K.A. .... 03 Apr
X McGrane, R.J. .... 03 Apr
MS McGunigall, R.J. .... 03 Apr
S Moores, J. .... 03 Apr
X Norford, M.A. .... 03 Apr
X Stretton, D.G. .... 03 Apr
S Thornton, B.P. .... 03 Apr
X Tomlinson, D.C. .... 03 Apr
X Heaney, M.J. .... 16 Apr
E Sargent, K.S. .... 29 Apr
E Bennett, D.P. .... 01 May
E McGinley, C.T. .... 01 May
E Adams, G. .... 01 May
X Straughan, S.R. .... 01 May
X Hayden, T.W. .... 01 May
E Marr, J. .... 01 May
E Tracey, A.D. .... 01 May
X Birkett, C.L. .... 01 May
X Hibberd, K.M. .... 01 May
X Oakley, S.E. .... 01 May
X Parr, N.K. .... 01 May
X Jones, J. .... 01 May
E Kirk, A.C. .... 01 May
X Morley, D.S. .... 01 May
E Murchie, A.D. .... 01 May
E O'Shaughnessy, D.J. .... 01 May
X Obrien, P.T. .... 01 May
X Pavey, E.L. .... 01 May
S Berisford, A.W. .... 01 Jun
E Briggs, M.D. .... 01 Jun
E Thompson, D.W. .... 01 Jun
E Pannett, L.W. .... 01 Jun
X Clark, J.M. .... 01 Jun
S Dobbins, S.J. .... 01 Jun
S Exworthy, D.A.G. .... 01 Jun
E Lee, W. .... 01 Jun
E McCallum, N.R. .... 01 Jun
E Sayer, J.M. .... 01 Jun
X Webb, M.D. .... 01 Jun
E Duesbury, C.L. .... 01 Jun
E Edwards, J.E. .... 01 Jun
X Ellison, T.G. .... 01 Jun
E Harvey, B. .... 01 Jun
S Porter, D.L. .... 01 Jun
X Saunders, C.E.M. .... 01 Jun
S Vogel, L.D. .... 01 Jun
E Cattroll, D. .... 13 Jun
E Finnie, H.M. .... 13 Jun
E Shuttleworth, S. .... 13 Jun
E Spofforth-Jones, M.A. .... 13 Jun
E Turle, P.J. .... 13 Jun
E Weaver, N. .... 13 Jun
E Warne, E.J. .... 01 Jul
X Donovan, S.J. .... 01 Jul
E Boyes, G.A. .... 01 Jul

X Hayward, A.L. 01 Jul
S Welch, K.A. 01 Jul
E White, K.F. 01 Jul
X Arden, V.G. 01 Jul
X Fitzpatrick, J.A.J. 01 Jul
X Livesey, J.E. 01 Jul
E Brutton, J.H. 01 Jul
X Crookes, W.A. 01 Jul
E Kennedy, I. 01 Jul
X McKee, H.M. 01 Jul
E Patterson, S.D. 01 Jul
E Richards, J.I.H. 01 Jul
E Saward, J.R.E. 01 Jul
E Selway, M.A. 01 Jul
X Simcock, J.L. 01 Jul
X Birrell, G.C. 01 Jul
X Canale, A.J. 01 Jul
X Regan, V.L. 01 Jul
S Cox, M.B. 03 Jul
E Driscoll, R. 22 Jul
X Barraclough, C.D. 24 Jul
S Bower, J.W. 24 Jul
X Collins, M.C. 24 Jul
X Corkett, K.S. 24 Jul
X Magill, T.E. 24 Jul
X McDermott, P.A. 24 Jul
X McEvoy, L.P. 24 Jul
S Morris, K.I. 24 Jul
X Potter, D.J. 24 Jul
X Rowan, M.E. 24 Jul
X Southwell, N.P. 24 Jul
S Strudwick, R. 24 Jul
X Taylor, J.P. 24 Jul
X Vowles, M.J. 24 Jul
X Whild, D.J. 24 Jul
X Young, J.N. 24 Jul
E Mallabone, J.J.K. 01 Aug
E Edwards, J. 01 Aug
X Chawira, D.N. 01 Aug
X Spinks, D.W. 01 Aug
X Jappy, G.W.G. 01 Aug
X Northover, A.F. 01 Aug
E Spiller, S.N. 01 Aug
E Burley, M.R. 01 Aug
S Burnham, J.A.I. 01 Aug
X Clemson, A.J. 01 Aug
S Stowe, E.J. 01 Aug
E Wood, A.G. 01 Aug
X Johnson, A.D. 01 Aug
S Robb, M.E. 01 Aug
X Wilson, A.J. 01 Aug
S Pring, S.J. 14 Aug
X Fuller, C.E. 16 Aug
X Scott, M. 16 Aug
E Clark, S.R. 01 Sep
E Pettigrew, T.R. 01 Sep
E Smith, C.J.H. 01 Sep
E Ashby, K.J. 01 Sep
E Griffiths, D.P. 01 Sep
E Strange, S.P. 01 Sep
E Elsey, D.J. 01 Sep
E MacKinnon, A. 01 Sep
X Coles, S.C. 01 Sep
X Doyle, G.B. 01 Sep
X Ward, S. 01 Sep
S Hayes, C.L. 01 Sep
X Hills, I.E. 01 Sep
X Palethorpe, N. 01 Sep
E Butler, I.A. 12 Sep
E Fitzgerald, C. 12 Sep
E Jenner, A.C. 16 Sep
S Hendy, R. 23 Sep
X Collins, P.W. 24 Sep
E Haggerty, S.M. 01 Oct
X Stevens, A.M.R. 01 Oct
E Evans, M.E. 01 Oct
X Holloway, S.A. 01 Oct
X Daveney, D.A. 01 Oct
X Gatenby, C.D. 01 Oct
X Shaughnessy, T.E. 01 Oct
X Studley, S.A. 01 Oct
X Walton, S.P. 01 Oct
X Duff, E.T. 01 Oct
S Jenking-Rees, D. 01 Oct
X Mansfield, J.A. 01 Oct
X O'Donnell, J.K.P. 01 Oct
S Ray, M.W. 01 Oct
X Stuchbury, R.J. 01 Oct
X Bramall, K.S. 01 Oct
X Davey, T.J. 01 Oct
X Pedre, R.G. 01 Oct
X Green, P.D. 16 Oct
X Alexander, O.D.D. 01 Nov
S Pearce, R.A. 01 Nov
E O'Toole, M.C. 01 Nov
X Symington, Z.M.A. 01 Nov
X Brockington, G.C. 01 Nov
E Tumelty, G.C. 01 Nov
X Wynn, S.C. 01 Nov
S Bull, C.V.R. 01 Nov
X Goulder, J.D. 01 Nov
X Howe, T. 01 Nov
X Jones, S.A. 01 Nov
X Leadbetter, A.J. 01 Nov
E McLellan, J.D. 01 Nov
E Morley, J.I. 01 Nov
S Sheikh, N. 01 Nov
S Ashby, M.K. 01 Dec
E Hawkins, S.R. 01 Dec
E Quade, N.A.C. 01 Dec
E Sullivan, M.N. 01 Dec
E Banham, A.W.D. 01 Dec
X Davies, G.W.T. 01 Dec
X Frean, J.P. 01 Dec
X Gamble, S.B. 01 Dec
X Holder, J.M. 01 Dec
X Hooton, D.R. 01 Dec
X Hughes, S.M. 01 Dec
X Leighton, M.R. 01 Dec
X Lewis, B.C. 01 Dec
X Pedler, M.D. 01 Dec
E Skittrall, S.D. 01 Dec
X Wilson, J. 01 Dec
X Witte, R.H. 01 Dec
S Allsford, K.M. 01 Dec
X Carrick, J.P. 01 Dec
E Collen, S.J. 01 Dec
X Wallace, S.A. 01 Dec
X Anderson, M.E.J. 01 Dec
X Doig, B.J. 01 Dec
X Hutchings, R.P.H. 01 Dec
X Palin, G.R. 01 Dec
S Webster, R.J. 01 Dec
S Skipworth, F.M. 01 Dec

1998

E Hassall, I. 01 Jan
X Baines, A.R. 01 Jan
E Darkins, C.R. 01 Jan
E Johnson, J.D. 01 Jan
X Skidmore, P.J. 01 Jan
X Pickering-Wheeler, C.W. 01 Jan
X Price, J.C. 01 Jan
X Stilwell, J.M. 01 Jan
E Ablett, S.D. 01 Jan
S Carrigan, J.A. 01 Jan
E Chestnutt, J.M. 01 Jan
S Gillies, E.M. 01 Jan
X McMichael, J.S. 01 Jan
X Willis, A.S. 01 Jan
E Murray, S.C. 01 Jan
S Kennedy, A. 08 Jan
X Blackwell, J.M. 16 Jan
X Maley, C.E. 16 Jan
X Boughton, T.F. 24 Jan
E Auld, D.M. 01 Feb
X Wakeford, I.F. 01 Feb
E Watkins, K.J. 01 Feb
S Haigh, J.J. 01 Feb

	Name	Date
X	Steer, A.D.	01 Feb
X	Curry, J.H.	01 Feb
E	D'Silva, D.M.	01 Feb
S	Drake, C.L.	01 Feb
E	Jacobs, M.P.	01 Feb
E	Millard, J.R.	01 Feb
X	White, S.M.	01 Feb
S	Wood, G.R.	01 Feb
X	Roberts, N.D.	10 Feb
X	Ward, K.N.	13 Feb
X	Richman, P.G.	16 Feb
X	Holroyd, J.E.J.	16 Feb
E	McCleary, S.P.	01 Mar
E	Head, S.G.	01 Mar
X	Allison, G.J.	01 Mar
X	Guy, C.R.	01 Mar
S	Haggard, A.	01 Mar
E	Hay, M.	01 Mar
X	Johns, A.W.	01 Mar
X	Pickering, D.H.	01 Mar
X	Ryan, J.H.	01 Mar
E	Thorp, D.B.	01 Mar
X	Tudor-Thomas, R.J.	01 Mar
X	White, D.J.	01 Mar
X	Gray, J.A.	01 Mar
X	Adamson, D.D.	01 Apr
X	Alcindor, D.J.	01 Apr
X	Lippitt, S.T.	01 Apr
X	Rose, A.D.	01 Apr
X	Brotton, P.J.	01 Apr
X	Howard, B.P.	01 Apr
X	Mattock, D.B.	01 Apr
E	Mountford, P.C.	01 Apr
X	Shorland-Ball, T.J.	01 Apr
S	Vollentine, L.	01 Apr
X	Smith, N.J.D.	01 Apr
S	Cox, G.F.	01 Apr
X	Shanks, G.J.	01 Apr
S	Wright, T.M.	01 Apr
S	Goodwin, L.B.	03 Apr
X	Hayes, B.J.	03 Apr
X	Peak, M.	03 Apr
S	Platt, N.	03 Apr
X	Wood, J.A.	03 Apr
E	Connor, M.	09 Apr
E	Buck, S.R.	01 May
E	Stiles, F.E.	01 May
X	Rushworth, B.J.	01 May
X	McWilliams, A.R.	01 May
E	Clarke, M.D.	01 May
X	Clay, T.C.D.C.	01 May
X	Denton, A.M.	01 May
X	Fitzgerald, G.D.	01 May
S	Magrath, A.R.	01 May
X	Plumb, M.C.M.	01 May
X	Strain, J.D.R.	01 May
X	Williams, L.J.	01 May
E	Bartlett, M.J.	01 May
E	Beaver, R.M.S.	01 May
E	Grennan, E.F.	01 May
X	Hawkins, C.E.	01 May
X	Mason, M.J.	01 May
X	Heap, J.T.	01 May
X	Higham, S.W.J.	01 May
S	Sutcliffe, E.D.	01 May
X	Walsh, A.J.	01 May
X	Yates, S.E.	01 May
X	Sharrocks, I.J.	16 May
X	Taylor, C.P.	16 May
X	Full, R.J.	01 Jun
E	Humphery, D.	01 Jun
X	Denham, D.J.	01 Jun
S	Gilbert, R.G.	01 Jun
X	Hicks, N.J.I.	01 Jun
X	Wells, B.I.	03 Jun
X	Steen, K.M.	16 Jun
E	Austin, C.J.	19 Jun
E	Jones, R.K.	19 Jun
E	Morgan, P.	19 Jun
E	Norgate, P.R.E.	19 Jun
E	Paton, A.J.M.	19 Jun
E	Rankine, I.M.	19 Jun
E	Stone, R.J.	19 Jun
E	Simm, C.W.	01 Jul
X	Blackmore, J.	01 Jul
X	Johnson, M.R.E.	01 Jul
X	Tremelling, P.N.	01 Jul
X	Mason, A.C.	01 Jul
X	Pressdee, S.J.	01 Jul
E	Harrison, M.A.	01 Jul
X	Rogers, S.J.P.	01 Jul
X	Haggo, J.R.	16 Jul
E	Lewis, D.	19 Jul
X	Beale, M.D.	23 Jul
X	Clelland, G.	23 Jul
X	Deam, P.A.V.	23 Jul
MS	Follington, D.C.	23 Jul
X	Johns, L.E.	23 Jul
X	Louden, C.A.	23 Jul
S	Noon, D.	23 Jul
X	Parkinson, A.P.	23 Jul
X	Salmon, R.D.	23 Jul
S	Stephenson, P.G.	23 Jul
S	Watson, S.B.C.	23 Jul
X	Kewley, I.D.	01 Aug
E	Love, R.J.	01 Aug
E	Taylor, K.M.	01 Aug
X	Ward, J.E.	01 Aug
E	Burns, E.P.	01 Aug
X	Carolan, K.S.	01 Aug
X	Gibbs, D.J.E.	01 Aug
X	McCormick, P.E.	01 Aug
X	Morgan, F.A.	01 Aug
X	Spoors, B.M.	01 Aug
S	Cooper, A.	01 Aug
X	Dale, W.D.J.	01 Aug
X	Ellis, N.J.	01 Aug
X	Perry, E.M.	01 Aug
X	Smith, N.E.P.	01 Aug
S	Miles, P.J.	01 Aug
S	Park, I.D.	01 Aug
X	Bates, A.J.	16 Aug
X	Beech, D.J.	16 Aug
X	Vallance, M.S.	16 Aug
E	Bird, T.S.V.	01 Sep
E	Jameson, A.J.	01 Sep
E	MacCorquodale, M.A.	01 Sep
E	Rees, A.M.	01 Sep
E	Salim, M.	01 Sep
E	Griffiths, L.	01 Sep
S	Hardwick, M.J.	01 Sep
X	Allan, C.R.	01 Sep
X	Amey, J.M.	01 Sep
X	Bagshaw, J.R.W.	01 Sep
E	Bamforth, C.J.M.	01 Sep
E	Benstead, N.W.J.	01 Sep
X	Birchall, J.C.	01 Sep
X	Calhaem, R.T.	01 Sep
X	Davies, N.M.S.	01 Sep
X	Eastwood, R.N.	01 Sep
X	Marshall, M.	01 Sep
X	Priest, J.E.	01 Sep
X	Richardson, P.C.	01 Sep
X	Savage, D.M.	01 Sep
X	Roberts, G.M.F.	01 Sep
X	Berry, T.J.	01 Sep
X	Griffiths, N.	01 Sep
X	Hutchins, I.D.M.	01 Sep
E	McDonald, D.J.	01 Sep
X	Williams, A.S.	01 Sep
X	Burbidge, K.	01 Sep
E	Chambers, P.D.	01 Sep
E	Chilton, J.	01 Sep
X	Colin-Thome, N.J.	01 Sep
E	Goodship, M.T.	01 Sep
E	Mealing, S.P.	01 Sep
E	Sargent, N.M.	01 Sep
X	Parkin, J.M.B.	01 Sep
E	Brodier, M.I.	04 Sep

E Curtis, D. .... 04 Sep
E Henderson, R.J. .... 04 Sep
E Metcalfe, R.J. .... 04 Sep
E Raynor, S.D. .... 04 Sep
X Prole, N.M. .... 16 Sep
X Osbaldestin, R.A. .... 01 Oct
E Lyons, A.G. .... 01 Oct
X Anderson, G.S. .... 01 Oct
X Fletcher, I.J. .... 01 Oct
X Gould, J.D. .... 01 Oct
X Griffiths, G.H. .... 01 Oct
X Varty, J.A. .... 01 Oct
X Densham, M.P.J. .... 01 Oct
E Harrington, L.B. .... 01 Oct
X McDonald, D.N. .... 01 Oct
X Doubleday, S. .... 16 Oct
X Gillett, D.A. .... 01 Nov
X Downing, S.J. .... 01 Nov
X Instone, M.J. .... 01 Nov
X Bembridge, S.R. .... 01 Nov
X Chacksfield, E.N. .... 01 Nov
E McCoy, M.J. .... 01 Nov
X Norgate, A.T. .... 01 Nov
S Ward, D.J. .... 01 Nov
X Iliffe, D.I. .... 16 Nov
X Whitehead, P.J. .... 01 Dec
X Howe, T.A.I.O. .... 01 Dec
X Jenkins, A.R. .... 01 Dec
E Sangha, R.S. .... 01 Dec
E Walsh, A.H. .... 01 Dec
X Astle, D.S. .... 01 Dec
E Blackburn, A.R.J. .... 01 Dec
X Crabbe, R.J. .... 01 Dec
S Hawthorn, E.M. .... 01 Dec
E McCann, T. .... 01 Dec
X Meyer, A.J. .... 01 Dec
X Webster, R.J. .... 01 Dec
X Wright, D.J. .... 01 Dec
E Pine, P.M. .... 06 Dec
X Beard, R.G. .... 10 Dec
X Egerton, S.B. .... 10 Dec
S Jones, M.A. .... 10 Dec
X Martin, A.J. .... 10 Dec
X Routledge, W.D. .... 10 Dec
X Singleton, M.D. .... 10 Dec
X Smith, R.E. .... 10 Dec
S Thomas, D.J. .... 10 Dec
S Prest, N.A. .... 10 Dec
X Crane, O.R. .... 16 Dec
X Craven, M.W. .... 16 Dec
X Gaskell, H.D. .... 16 Dec
X Hammock, S.G. .... 16 Dec
X Heirs, G.G. .... 16 Dec
X MacLaughlin, R.A. .... 16 Dec
X Muirhead, B.G. .... 16 Dec
X Thomas, D.W. .... 16 Dec

1999

E Gibson, S.J. .... 01 Jan
X Ball, A.D. .... 01 Jan
E Burns, J.E. .... 01 Jan
E Cartwright, J.A. .... 01 Jan
E Cross, A.L. .... 01 Jan
X Davis, R. .... 01 Jan
X Burdett, R.W. .... 01 Jan
E Carroll, S.L. .... 01 Jan
X Clarke, D. .... 01 Jan
X Conlin, J.A. .... 01 Jan
E Goodall, M.A. .... 01 Jan
X Howard, N.A. .... 01 Jan
X Howe, C.M. .... 01 Jan
X Knight, M.R. .... 01 Jan
X McTeer, I.J. .... 01 Jan
X Raynes, C. .... 01 Jan
X Wappner, G.D. .... 01 Jan
X Wood, I.L. .... 01 Jan
E Newman, D.J. .... 01 Jan
E Ruston, M.R. .... 01 Jan
X Towns, A.R. .... 01 Jan
X Ansell, C.N. .... 01 Jan
S Arend, F.M. .... 01 Jan
X Bradburn, J.A. .... 01 Jan
X Carrington, V.L. .... 01 Jan
X Coackley, J. .... 01 Jan
X Munro, N.F.H. .... 01 Jan
E O'Shaughnessy, P.C. .... 01 Jan
X Thomson, J.C. .... 01 Jan
X Watts, Z.A. .... 01 Jan
E Dry, I. .... 31 Jan
X Dempsey, S.P. .... 01 Feb
X Downing, P.L. .... 01 Feb
S Haines, R.J. .... 01 Feb
X Alsop, S.H. .... 01 Feb
E Barr, C.J.G. .... 01 Feb
X Bell, C.M. .... 01 Feb
X Benson, R.A. .... 01 Feb
X Hirons, F.D. .... 01 Feb
E Johnson, P.R. .... 01 Feb
S Taylor, J.B. .... 01 Feb
X Wall, S.N. .... 01 Feb
E Jones, L.H. .... 14 Feb
E Northcott, M.K. .... 01 Mar
X Barton, J.E. .... 01 Mar
S Collacott, J.S. .... 01 Mar
X Nelson, M.R. .... 01 Mar
X Boswell, D.J. .... 01 Mar
X Corden, M. .... 01 Mar
S Pickard, D.M. .... 01 Mar
X Richards, A.V. .... 01 Mar
S Robertson, S.T. .... 01 Mar
S Sheppard, S.H. .... 01 Mar
S Weeks, D.C. .... 01 Mar
E Barton, K.J.A. .... 01 Mar
X Tighe, S. .... 30 Mar
X Dodds, M.L. .... 01 Apr
X Harold, R.S.J. .... 01 Apr
X Dann, A. .... 01 Apr
X Rawles, J.R. .... 01 Apr
X Twigg, K.L. .... 01 Apr
X Ward, M.T. .... 01 Apr
X Arkle, N.J. .... 01 Apr
X Ashlin, J.M. .... 01 Apr
X Benzie, N.J.E. .... 01 Apr
X Brazier, L.F. .... 01 Apr
X Cowin, T.J. .... 01 Apr
X Drodge, K.N. .... 01 Apr
X Hanks, P.E. .... 01 Apr
X Hartley, B.P.I. .... 01 Apr
X Johnston, G.S. .... 01 Apr
X Smith, A. .... 01 Apr
X Stait, B.G. .... 01 Apr
X Stein, G.K. .... 01 Apr
X Beavis, J.A. .... 01 Apr
S Finn, E.J. .... 01 Apr
X Rider, M.C.E. .... 01 Apr
E Wadsworth, R.Y. .... 01 Apr
X Hutchings, J.R. .... 01 Apr
X Percy, N.A. .... 01 Apr
X Gibbs, A.M. .... 16 Apr
X Sparrow, M.J. .... 16 Apr
X Blacklock, J.F. .... 26 Apr
X Calter, M. .... 26 Apr
S Case, A. .... 26 Apr
X Dunkley, S.C. .... 26 Apr
X Harriman, P. .... 26 Apr
MS Lawton, M.J. .... 26 Apr
X Lovett, S.A. .... 26 Apr
MS Manwaring, R.G. .... 26 Apr
X Pearch, S.M. .... 26 Apr
S Reed, N. .... 26 Apr
MS Smith, M.P. .... 26 Apr
X Toon, P.G. .... 26 Apr
X Ellis, A.C. .... 01 May
X Tazewell, M.R. .... 01 May
X Thomas, M. .... 01 May
X Baldie, S.A.H. .... 01 May
S Clements, E.J. .... 01 May
S Coyle, P.J. .... 01 May
X Felters, A.W. .... 01 May

	Name	Date
E	Greig, J.A.	01 May
X	McCall, G.	01 May
X	Monachello, P.G.	01 May
X	Pollard, A.E.	01 May
E	Thomson, M.L.	01 May
X	Timms, D.A.	01 May
X	Wade, J.M.R.	01 May
X	Daly, P.	01 May
X	Mann, D.M.	01 Jun
X	Pittard, D.C.	01 Jun
E	Deal, C.	01 Jun
E	Hamilton-Bruce, E.C.	01 Jun
E	Martin, S.W.	01 Jun
X	Moran, R.J.	01 Jun
X	Redmayne, M.E.	01 Jun
X	Steele, R.M.	01 Jun
E	Stratton, M.P.	01 Jun
X	Kennedy, R.J.	01 Jul
S	MacKenzie, J.R.E.	01 Jul
E	Ford, J.S.	01 Jul
X	Gillard, V.A.	01 Jul
X	Thomas, D.H.	01 Jul
S	Caple, J.N.	01 Jul
X	Whitwell, N.S.	01 Jul
X	Cox, M.J.	01 Aug
E	Bailey, S.	01 Aug
X	Bewley, N.J.	01 Aug
X	Edwards, A.W.	01 Aug
X	Flatman, T.D.	01 Aug
X	Hughes, J.J.	01 Aug
X	Johnson, A.D.	01 Aug
X	Lilly, D.M.	01 Aug
X	Mullowney, P.	01 Aug
X	Neofytou, A.G.K.	01 Aug
X	Sambrooks, R.J.	01 Aug
X	Sweeney, C.	01 Aug
X	Clark, R.A.	01 Aug
X	Crowe, D.M.	01 Aug
S	Gulliford, K.A.	01 Aug
X	Frazer, H.F.	01 Aug
E	Molyneux, I.T.	01 Aug
X	Sudding, C.D.	01 Aug
X	Thompson, D.A.	16 Aug
X	Bussey, E.L.	01 Sep
E	Hoather, M.S.	01 Sep
X	Jordan, A.F.	01 Sep
X	Knight, S.D.	01 Sep
S	Curwood, J.E.	01 Sep
X	Greenwood, A.W.	01 Sep
X	Khan, L.A.	01 Sep
E	Alexander, A.L.	01 Sep
X	Barr, S.P.	01 Sep
X	Birleson, P.D.	01 Sep

	Name	Date
X	Brewin, D.J.	01 Sep
X	Carnie, M.J.	01 Sep
X	Croft, D.F.	01 Sep
X	Deighton, A.W.G.	01 Sep
X	Denney, J.R.	01 Sep
E	Derrick, M.J.G.	01 Sep
X	Fisher, S.J.	01 Sep
X	Halsey, K.E.	01 Sep
X	Hilton, S.T.	01 Sep
X	Hinton, L.	01 Sep
E	Hunt, P.S.	01 Sep
X	Ingham, A.R.	01 Sep
E	Kilmartin, A.	01 Sep
X	Lamb, C.J.	01 Sep
X	Lawrence, L.J.	01 Sep
X	Livsey, A.E.J.	01 Sep
X	Marini, T.A.	01 Sep
E	McClement, D.L.	01 Sep
S	Terry, J.H.	01 Sep
E	Kitt, R.G.	01 Sep
E	Redgrove, M.A.	01 Sep
X	Buchan, J.A.	01 Sep
X	Green, J.H.	01 Sep
E	Hepplewhite, M.B.	01 Sep
X	Johnson, S.	01 Sep
E	Leivers, A.J.	01 Sep
X	Sharp, L.D.	01 Sep
E	Benn, J.	02 Sep
E	Booth, W.N.	02 Sep
E	Brennan, P.A.	02 Sep
E	Brunell, P.J.	02 Sep
E	Flatt, L.D.	02 Sep
E	Forshaw, D.R.	02 Sep
E	Leaver, A.M.	02 Sep
E	MacLean, M.T.	02 Sep
E	Millar, K.I.	02 Sep
E	Nicholson, J.C.	02 Sep
E	Nursey, A.P.	02 Sep
E	Penketh, M.G.	02 Sep
E	Quirk, A.T.	02 Sep
E	Rom, S.P.	02 Sep
E	Saywell-Hall, S.E.	02 Sep
E	Scholes, N.A.	02 Sep
E	Sibley, A.K.	02 Sep
E	Slimmon, K.W.	02 Sep
E	Spencer, J.C.	02 Sep
E	Stead, J.A.	02 Sep
E	Topping, J.R.	02 Sep
E	Torney, C.J.	02 Sep
E	Vickers, C.G.	02 Sep
E	Vickery, R.J.	02 Sep
E	Walker, G.	02 Sep
E	Ward, N.A.	02 Sep

	Name	Date
E	Watson, A.P.	02 Sep
X	Bull, M.A.J.	11 Sep
X	Netherwood, L.D.	15 Sep
X	Spurdle, A.P.	20 Sep
X	Suggett, P.R.	20 Sep
X	Martin, N.	20 Sep
E	Buckenham, P.J.	01 Oct
E	Healey, M.J.	01 Oct
X	Hudson, P.J.	01 Oct
X	MacRae, K.L.	01 Oct
X	Nitsch, K.D.	01 Oct
X	Rex, C.A.	01 Oct
X	Weaver, S.	01 Oct
X	Williams, G.M.G.	01 Oct
S	Shepherd, F.R.	01 Oct
X	Greenwood, P.A.	16 Oct
X	Barker, T.J.	16 Oct
X	Ackerley, R.S.J.	01 Nov
E	Clear, N.J.	01 Nov
X	Finch, I.R.	01 Nov
X	Harborth, J.A.	01 Nov
X	Cable, P.M.	01 Nov
S	Cutler, T.P.	01 Nov
X	Holden, J.L.	01 Nov
E	Hubschmid, S.R.	01 Nov
S	Meardon, S.B.	01 Nov
E	Hamilton, M.I.	01 Nov
E	Jones, I.M.	01 Nov
X	Currie, M.J.	16 Nov
X	O'Neill, J.	22 Nov
X	Gates, D.A.	01 Dec
X	Alderwick, J.R.C.	01 Dec
E	Cessford, R.I.	01 Dec
X	Marshall, A.J.	01 Dec
X	Birchfield, G.M.	01 Dec
X	Chambers, C.P.	01 Dec
X	Doyle, A.B.	01 Dec
X	Dransfield, J.A.J.	01 Dec
X	Dunn, R.A.P.	01 Dec
X	Gray, N.J.	01 Dec
X	Hannam, D.B.	01 Dec
X	Hughes, C.B.	01 Dec
X	Jacobs, J.M.	01 Dec
X	Jenkins, R.C.	01 Dec
X	Saltonstall, P.J.R.	01 Dec
X	Sloan, I.A.	01 Dec
X	Swindells, M.	01 Dec
X	Weston, K.N.N.	01 Dec
X	Woollven, C.D.	01 Dec
S	Ames, K.M.M.	01 Dec
E	Ball, M.P.	01 Dec
X	Bowen, C.N.	01 Dec
S	Horne, C.A.	01 Dec

E Orr, K.J. .... 01 Dec
X Slattery, D.J. .... 01 Dec
E Lee, S.E. .... 01 Dec

2000

E Mansfield, I.L. .... 01 Jan
E Aston, J.A. .... 01 Jan
S Burchell, H.E. .... 01 Jan
X Fisher, G.E.M. .... 01 Jan
X Hume, K.J. .... 01 Jan
X James, A.W. .... 01 Jan
X Kitteridge, D.J. .... 01 Jan
X Mantri, A.H. .... 01 Jan
X Mason, M.J. .... 01 Jan
X Moyo, T.K. .... 01 Jan
S Titcombe, A.J. .... 01 Jan
X Brewer, C.E. .... 01 Jan
X Butler, R. .... 01 Jan
X Crew, J.M. .... 01 Jan
X Deakin, D.J. .... 01 Jan
S Downing-Waite, J.A. .... 01 Jan
E Holmwood, M.A.G. .... 01 Jan
S Hooper, J. .... 01 Jan
E Jackson, S.N. .... 01 Jan
X Manoy, S. .... 01 Jan
E Moody, A.C. .... 01 Jan
X Murphy, R.J. .... 01 Jan
X Nethercott, E.R. .... 01 Jan
S Oliver, G.J. .... 01 Jan
S Relf, K.M. .... 01 Jan
X Rudd, V.J. .... 01 Jan
S Smith, H.L. .... 01 Jan
E Tait, M.D. .... 01 Jan
X Thomas, O.H. .... 01 Jan
X Van-Nijkerk, E.B. .... 01 Jan
X Williams, D.L. .... 01 Jan
X Bloska, R.M. .... 01 Jan
E Andrew, P. .... 01 Jan
S Carcone, P.N. .... 01 Jan
E Mortlock, P.A. .... 01 Jan
E Martin, R.J. .... 01 Jan
E Nicklin, G.J.E. .... 01 Jan
E Robinson, P. .... 01 Jan
X Francis, D.E. .... 10 Jan
X Irving, D. .... 10 Jan
X Lester, R.L. .... 10 Jan
X Moran, C.A. .... 10 Jan
X Harwood, L.B. .... 01 Feb
E Mathieson, N.B. .... 01 Feb
X Retter, R.L. .... 01 Feb
X Bevan, J.R. .... 16 Feb
X Cobban, M.J. .... 01 Mar
E George, S.D. .... 01 Mar
E Pollard, J.R. .... 01 Mar
E McDonald, A.W. .... 01 Mar
X Richardson, I.H. .... 01 Mar
E Risley, J.G. .... 01 Mar
X Brown, A.R.A. .... 01 Mar
X Barritt, O.D. .... 01 Apr
S Brimacombe, L.M. .... 01 Apr
E Pipkin, P.J. .... 01 Apr
X Winbolt, N.I. .... 01 Apr
X Adams, E.S. .... 01 Apr
X Beveridge, G. .... 01 Apr
X Cornford, M. .... 01 Apr
X Hayashi, L.R. .... 01 Apr
X Lloyd, B.J. .... 01 Apr
X Murgatroyd, K.J. .... 01 Apr
X Scott, J.A. .... 01 Apr
E Gilmore, S.J. .... 01 Apr
X Lewis, J.L.M. .... 01 Apr
X Tomes, A.C. .... 01 Apr
X Whitehouse, D.S. .... 01 Apr
S McLocklan, L.M. .... 01 Apr

SUB LIEUTENANTS

1996

E Corderoy, R.I. .... 01 Sep
E Stafford, B.R. .... 01 Sep
MS Goodrum, S.E. .... 19 Sep
S Baker, N.J. .... 20 Sep
S Burns, R.J. .... 20 Sep
X Llewellyn, J.G. .... 20 Sep
MS Welch, A. .... 20 Sep

1997

X Bagshaw, E.F. .... 01 Jan
X Fennell, C.B. .... 01 Jan
E Wadge, G.D.E. .... 01 Jan
X Wood, C.H. .... 01 Jan
E Andrews, C. .... 01 May
X Andrews, C.J. .... 01 May
E Baillie, R.W. .... 01 May
X Cannell, G.M. .... 01 May
S Carter, G.R. .... 01 May
X Coverdale, P. .... 01 May
X Davies, T.C. .... 01 May
X Firth, J.S. .... 01 May
X Forge, S.M. .... 01 May
X Gardner, M.P. .... 01 May
X Griffiths, C.S.H. .... 01 May
X Hammon, M.A. .... 01 May
X Harcombe, A. .... 01 May
X Hodgson, R.S. .... 01 May
X Kelly, S.P. .... 01 May
S Matthew, M.J. .... 01 May
X Moore, N.J. .... 01 May
X Morse, J. .... 01 May
E Newth, C.S. .... 01 May
X Page, M.R. .... 01 May
X Parry, S.J. .... 01 May
X Parsons, G.J. .... 01 May
S Pritchard, I.J. .... 01 May
X Rant, O.J. .... 01 May
X Rowson, M.J. .... 01 May
E Russell, C.M.L. .... 01 May
X Sanderson, C.P. .... 01 May
X Tok, C.F.L. .... 01 May
X Vickery, K.E. .... 01 May
S Weare, J.B. .... 01 May
X Winsor, J. .... 01 May
E Austin, S.T. .... 02 May
S Benfell, N.A. .... 02 May
E Bowser, N.J. .... 02 May
E Burton, P.R. .... 02 May
E Collins, D.A. .... 02 May
E Edwins, M.R. .... 02 May
X Evans, B.D. .... 02 May
X Fairnie, D.W. .... 02 May
E Greenshields, F.N. .... 02 May
E Hodgson, J.R. .... 02 May
E Liddell, M.L. .... 02 May
E Lowe, C. .... 02 May
E McNair, J. .... 02 May
E Moy, D.K. .... 02 May
X Paget, S.J. .... 02 May
E Ryan, J.P. .... 02 May
E Smart, M.J. .... 02 May
E Young, P. .... 02 May
X Brown, S.G. .... 04 Aug
X Aldous, B.W. .... 01 Sep
X Armstrong, S.M. .... 01 Sep
E Barker, P.D. .... 01 Sep
X Bates, N.S. .... 01 Sep
X Beanland, P.L. .... 01 Sep
X Bedding, D. .... 01 Sep
X Bennett, C.D. .... 01 Sep
E Bennett, W.E. .... 01 Sep
E Blackburn, L.R. .... 01 Sep
X Campbell, T.R. .... 01 Sep
X Chambers, R. .... 01 Sep
X Chester, A.D.M. .... 01 Sep
S Clarke, A.G. .... 01 Sep
E Coles, C.P. .... 01 Sep

X Considine, K.J. .... 01 Sep
S Curtis, S.E.H. .... 01 Sep
X Dawson, G.A.E. .... 01 Sep
E Dickinson, P.H. .... 01 Sep
X Duncan, K.C.L. .... 01 Sep
X Edgington, S.P. .... 01 Sep
E Ellis, C.R. .... 01 Sep
X Feeney, M.B. .... 01 Sep
X Finlay, M.S. .... 01 Sep
X Gadsden, A.C. .... 01 Sep
X Gare, C.J. .... 01 Sep
X Gill, C.D. .... 01 Sep
X Griffiths, T.G. .... 01 Sep
X Hammond, M.M.V. .... 01 Sep
X Hardman, M.J. .... 01 Sep
X Harford Cross, P.J. .... 01 Sep
X Hayes, S. .... 01 Sep
X Heyworth, J.E. .... 01 Sep
S Hinxman, M.A. .... 01 Sep
X Holmes, A.M. .... 01 Sep
X Humphries, M. .... 01 Sep
S Hynde, C.L. .... 01 Sep
X Jackson, P. .... 01 Sep
X Jones, R.J. .... 01 Sep
X Keeping, D.J. .... 01 Sep
X Keith, B.C. .... 01 Sep
X Kierstan, S.J.J. .... 01 Sep
E Kitchen, B. .... 01 Sep
X Knight, D.S. .... 01 Sep
S Knox, G.P. .... 01 Sep
X Lancaster, B.J. .... 01 Sep
S Lane, N. .... 01 Sep
X Lanning, R.M. .... 01 Sep
E Law, R. .... 01 Sep
S Lear, S.F. .... 01 Sep
X Liddle, R.D. .... 01 Sep
X Mabbott, K.I. .... 01 Sep
X Marjoram, J.W. .... 01 Sep
X McAulay, P.J. .... 01 Sep
X McGannity, C.S. .... 01 Sep
X McIntyre, L. .... 01 Sep
X Menzies, B. .... 01 Sep
E Miller, I. .... 01 Sep
E Milne, W.J.C. .... 01 Sep
X Mullen, M.L. .... 01 Sep
X Nimmo-Scott, S.J. .... 01 Sep
X O'Kane, R.J. .... 01 Sep
X Phillips, C.J. .... 01 Sep
X Phillips, R.M. .... 01 Sep
X Pollock, C.J. .... 01 Sep
E Resheph, A.A. .... 01 Sep
X Searle, M.P. .... 01 Sep
X Shanks, S.A. .... 01 Sep
X Taylor, A.I. .... 01 Sep
X Thatcher, L.F.V. .... 01 Sep
X Thompson, W.A. .... 01 Sep
E Timbrell, I.P.J. .... 01 Sep
E Tofts, C. .... 01 Sep
E Treharne, M.A. .... 01 Sep
X Watts, M.A. .... 01 Sep
X Whitehall, S. .... 01 Sep
E Whitelaw, V.L. .... 01 Sep
X Wood, S.A.H. .... 01 Sep
X Woolhead, C.M. .... 01 Sep
X Boon, G.J. .... 19 Sep
X Castle, C.D. .... 19 Sep
X Cowan, A.R. .... 19 Sep
X Griffin, P.J. .... 19 Sep
X Howells, S.M. .... 19 Sep
S Longstaff, T.W. .... 19 Sep
S Love, J.D. .... 19 Sep
X Lynn, H.W. .... 19 Sep
X Mills, G.A. .... 19 Sep
X Parton, A. .... 19 Sep
X Pirrie, J.A. .... 19 Sep
X Stringer, G.E. .... 19 Sep
X Walker, R.S. .... 19 Sep
X Wilson, G.J. .... 19 Sep
X Stratton, N.C. .... 01 Oct
X Leason, N.C. .... 01 Dec

1998

X Aitken, S.R. .... 01 Jan
E Alexander, P.M.D. .... 01 Jan
X Bailes, K.P. .... 01 Jan
X Bane, N.S.J. .... 01 Jan
X Banks, M.C. .... 01 Jan
X Bodman, S.A. .... 01 Jan
X Boeckx, T.J.F. .... 01 Jan
S Bommert, J.K. .... 01 Jan
X Bradbury, J.E.D. .... 01 Jan
X Brearley, R.L. .... 01 Jan
X Brooks, A.M. .... 01 Jan
X Brown, J.A. .... 01 Jan
X Bull, L.P. .... 01 Jan
X Bullock, R.A. .... 01 Jan
X Butler, P.M. .... 01 Jan
X Conyers, W.L. .... 01 Jan
X Cromie, J.M. .... 01 Jan
X Daulby, D.J. .... 01 Jan
X Davies, M.C. .... 01 Jan
X England, P.M. .... 01 Jan
X Evans, D.J. .... 01 Jan
X Finn, J.S. .... 01 Jan
S Fleming, R.E. .... 01 Jan
X Gauld, M.G.R. .... 01 Jan
X Gladwin, M.D. .... 01 Jan
E Grant, W.G. .... 01 Jan
X Griffen, D.J. .... 01 Jan
X Hall, C.J. .... 01 Jan
X Hancock, J.H. .... 01 Jan
X Headley, M.J. .... 01 Jan
X Hearn, S.P. .... 01 Jan
X Hember, M.J.C. .... 01 Jan
S Henderson, S.C. .... 01 Jan
X Hewitson, J.G.A. .... 01 Jan
X Higginson, N.J. .... 01 Jan
X Hockley, S.L. .... 01 Jan
X Holmes, A.N. .... 01 Jan
X Ives, D.J. .... 01 Jan
X Jacob, A.W. .... 01 Jan
X Lander, D.T.J. .... 01 Jan
E Lutman, C.R. .... 01 Jan
X Lynas, J.F.A. .... 01 Jan
X Madigan, L. .... 01 Jan
X Milles, O.K. .... 01 Jan
X Money, C.J. .... 01 Jan
E Morphet, K. .... 01 Jan
X Mount, J.B. .... 01 Jan
X Parker, S.A.M. .... 01 Jan
X Parsons, R.J. .... 01 Jan
X Partridge, S.C. .... 01 Jan
X Pritchard, A.M. .... 01 Jan
X Rae, F. .... 01 Jan
X Randles, S. .... 01 Jan
X Reid, J.L. .... 01 Jan
X Ridley, S.A. .... 01 Jan
X Shearn, M.A. .... 01 Jan
X Simmonite, G.I. .... 01 Jan
X Sims, A.R. .... 01 Jan
X Slade, N.R. .... 01 Jan
S Stone, N.J.J. .... 01 Jan
X Sturman, R.W. .... 01 Jan
S Turner, D.J. .... 01 Jan
X Turner, J.S. .... 01 Jan
X Urwin, S.J. .... 01 Jan
X Varley, P.G.S. .... 01 Jan
S West, N.K. .... 01 Jan
E Wharrie, C.G. .... 01 Jan
X Wightwick, K.H.T. .... 01 Jan
X Williams, J.R. .... 01 Jan
X Winand, F.M.J. .... 01 Jan
X Wright, T.J. .... 01 Jan
E Austin, P.N. .... 09 Jan
E Collins, D. .... 09 Jan
E Collins, M.A. .... 09 Jan
E Conneely, S.A. .... 09 Jan
E Cope, M.A. .... 09 Jan
E Donaldson, A.M. .... 09 Jan

E	Emms, S.M.	09 Jan
X	Flynn, S.J.	09 Jan
X	Goodman, D.F.	09 Jan
X	Gray, M.J.H.	09 Jan
E	Hayman, P.S.	09 Jan
E	Hoare, D.W.	09 Jan
S	Hubbarde, S.D.	09 Jan
S	Johnson, K.	09 Jan
E	Jones, P.A.	09 Jan
E	Murphy, A.	09 Jan
X	Riley, J.	09 Jan
E	Stafford, W.	09 Jan
E	Stephens, A.W.	09 Jan
X	Thompson, J.A.	09 Jan
X	Whatling, K.M.	09 Jan
X	White, S.J.	09 Jan
E	Wilkinson, A.C.	09 Jan
X	Bartram, R.J.	01 Apr
X	Bouyac, D.R.L.	01 Apr
S	Challis, S.E.	01 Apr
S	Clark, C.L.	01 Apr
S	Cotton, E.L.	01 Apr
X	Fagan, J.S.	01 Apr
X	Fyfe, K.S.	01 Apr
X	Gamble, M.J.	01 Apr
X	Guilfoyle, V.M.	01 Apr
X	Hadland, G.V.	01 Apr
X	Hampshire, T.	01 Apr
X	Irwin, S.G.	01 Apr
E	Jones, M.R.	01 Apr
X	Kohn, P.A.	01 Apr
S	Mac Donald, S.B.	01 Apr
X	Meikle, K.E.J.	01 Apr
X	Meikle, R.B.	01 Apr
X	Owen, S.T.L.	01 Apr
X	Paulet, M.R.	01 Apr
X	Prosser, M.J.	01 Apr
S	Rollason, C.A.	01 Apr
X	Summers, A.J.	01 Apr
X	Taylor, T.P.	01 Apr
E	Trueman, B.D.	01 Apr
X	Ward, F.J.	01 Apr
X	Warde, N.A.	01 Apr
X	Wells, J.H.	01 Apr
X	Wilkins, D.P.	01 Apr
S	Brint, I.	29 Apr
X	Carter, N.R.	29 Apr
S	Christie, A.B.	29 Apr
E	Cooke, R.N.	29 Apr
X	Dainty, R.C.	29 Apr
E	Finch, S.	29 Apr
E	Griffiths, C.J.J.	29 Apr
X	Gwatkin, N.J.	29 Apr
E	Hamilton, G.D.	29 Apr
E	Hardy, R.J.	29 Apr
E	Harrison, A.D.	29 Apr
X	Hattle, P.M.	29 Apr
E	Hewitt, M.J.	29 Apr
X	Lightfoot, R.A.	29 Apr
E	Loughrey, N.C.	29 Apr
X	Malone, J.M.	29 Apr
E	Newell, G.D.	29 Apr
E	Nicholson, B.H.	29 Apr
E	Richards, P.	29 Apr
E	Robert, I.A.	29 Apr
X	Robins, M.D.	29 Apr
MS	Sullivan, T.E.	29 Apr
S	Viney, P.M.	29 Apr
E	Wrennall, E.P.	29 Apr
X	Aldridge, D.	01 May
X	Anderson, S.R.	01 May
X	Barnes, P.I.	01 May
X	Barron, J.M.	01 May
E	Baxter, F.J.	01 May
X	Binns, J.F.	01 May
X	Broster, M.	01 May
E	Buchanan, R.M.	01 May
X	Burghall, R.C.	01 May
S	Bussell, S.L.	01 May
S	Carthew, R.J.	01 May
E	Casson, R.F.	01 May
X	Cave, J.H.J.	01 May
X	Chandler, G.E.	01 May
X	Corbett, M.T.	01 May
E	Crawley, D.A.	01 May
X	Crosby, M.P.	01 May
X	Crouch, M.	01 May
E	Dawson, P.	01 May
X	Day, C.P.	01 May
X	Dean, L.J.	01 May
X	Dodd, S.E.	01 May
X	Duce, M.	01 May
X	Dunn, A.	01 May
X	Edge, J.M.	01 May
E	Elliott, J.A.	01 May
S	Epps, M.P.	01 May
X	Evans, L.S.	01 May
X	Fabik, A.N.	01 May
X	Fillmore, R.J.	01 May
E	Foote, A.S.	01 May
E	Freeman, M.J.	01 May
X	Gallimore, R.M.C.	01 May
X	Garreta, C.E.	01 May
X	George, J.E.	01 May
E	Gibson, M.J.S.	01 May
X	Gordon, D.I.	01 May
S	Gosling, D.J.	01 May
X	Grey, E.J.W.	01 May
X	Hackland, A.S.	01 May
X	Hall, K.J.D.	01 May
X	Hawkins, J.D.	01 May
X	Hipkin, S.R.C.	01 May
E	Holford, S.J.	01 May
E	Holvey, P.J.	01 May
X	Hopkins, C.	01 May
E	Hughes, T.	01 May
X	Humphries, G.D.	01 May
X	Huxford, S.	01 May
X	Jackson, H.C.	01 May
S	Johnson, A.C.	01 May
X	Jones, R.J.	01 May
X	Jones-Thompson, M.J.	01 May
E	Jordan, M.D.	01 May
E	Kent, M.J.	01 May
S	Kenyon, C.M.	01 May
X	Klidjian, M.J.	01 May
X	Kroon, Z.	01 May
S	Latham, L.B.	01 May
X	Lawrence, M.A.	01 May
E	Layton, C.	01 May
X	Little, M.I.G.	01 May
E	Lovett, A.R.	01 May
X	Martyn, D.	01 May
E	Matthews, P.R.	01 May
X	Mc Currach, R.H.	01 May
X	McCauley, L.J.	01 May
S	McCowen, P.A.C.	01 May
E	Meikle, S.A.	01 May
E	Metcalf, S.W.	01 May
E	Miller, K.R.	01 May
E	Moon, I.L.	01 May
S	New, R.A.	01 May
X	Noonan, C.D.	01 May
X	Northcote, M.R.	01 May
X	Nunnen, C.R.	01 May
X	Oakley, C.M.	01 May
S	Ollis, V.	01 May
X	Parker, M.S.	01 May
E	Parmenter, A.J.	01 May
E	Paton, D.W.	01 May
E	Pickard, S.R.	01 May
X	Pickles, D.R.	01 May
X	Pickles, M.R.	01 May
E	Pollard, A.J.	01 May
E	Prior, I.A.	01 May
E	Prowse, D.G.	01 May
X	Quick, S.J.	01 May
E	Rawlings, G.A.	01 May
E	Reeves, P.K.	01 May

X Reynolds, M.J. .... 01 May
S Richards, A.J. .... 01 May
E Richardson, A.P. .... 01 May
X Roberts, S. .... 01 May
MS Robinson, A. .... 01 May
E Rooney, M. .... 01 May
X Santry, P.M. .... 01 May
X Sherwood, G.A.F. .... 01 May
X Sienkiewicz, M.K. .... 01 May
X Spencer, A.C. .... 01 May
X Spinks, R.J. .... 01 May
X Stephenson, C.J. .... 01 May
E Stratton, S.J. .... 01 May
S Sumner, D.J. .... 01 May
E Thomson, D.F. .... 01 May
E Turner, A.J. .... 01 May
X Vickery, B.R. .... 01 May
X Waite, T.G. .... 01 May
X Watson, B.L. .... 01 May
E Welsh, R.M.K. .... 01 May
X White, J.P. .... 01 May
X Wickham, R.J. .... 01 May
X Wielopolski, M.L.C.C. .... 01 May
X Williams, P.G. .... 01 May
X Winterbon, A.R. .... 01 May
X Wragg, G.T. .... 01 May
S Wrigley, B.S. .... 01 May
X Youldon, L.J. .... 01 May
E Prest, S.F. .... 01 Jun
X Barnes, A.W.G. .... 01 Aug
X Abbott, R.J. .... 01 Sep
X Agnew, R.L.P. .... 01 Sep
X Andrews, I.S. .... 01 Sep
X Andrews, J.P. .... 01 Sep
X Armstrong, C.D. .... 01 Sep
X Atkinson, A.N.C. .... 01 Sep
X Barlow, B.M. .... 01 Sep
E Billington, S. .... 01 Sep
E Bland, C.D. .... 01 Sep
X Boullin, J.P. .... 01 Sep
E Breen, J.E. .... 01 Sep
E Brooks, N.R. .... 01 Sep
X Brown, A.S. .... 01 Sep
E Bulter, D.B. .... 01 Sep
X Burton, A. .... 01 Sep
E Buxton, D.A. .... 01 Sep
E Cantellow, S.J. .... 01 Sep
S Chapman, M.S. .... 01 Sep
S Chesters, D.M.B. .... 01 Sep
E Cheyne, R.D. .... 01 Sep
X Christie, D.W. .... 01 Sep
X Clapham, G.T. .... 01 Sep
S Cole, B.B. .... 01 Sep

X Collins, A.C. .... 01 Sep
X Collins, S.J.P. .... 01 Sep
X Crawford, K. .... 01 Sep
X Crompton, P.J. .... 01 Sep
S De La Rue, A.N. .... 01 Sep
X Dermody, R.T. .... 01 Sep
E Dixon, A.K. .... 01 Sep
X Dixon, R.A. .... 01 Sep
E Dodd, L. .... 01 Sep
X Doran, K.E. .... 01 Sep
X Dowling, A.J. .... 01 Sep
X Filtness, D.M. .... 01 Sep
E Finley, P.M. .... 01 Sep
X Finn, S.A. .... 01 Sep
X Fisher, A.I. .... 01 Sep
E Flegg, M.J. .... 01 Sep
X Fraser, M.J.S. .... 01 Sep
X Goddard, I.A. .... 01 Sep
S Gray, E.J. .... 01 Sep
X Green, R.R. .... 01 Sep
X Greenwood, B.C.J. .... 01 Sep
X Griffiths, D.B. .... 01 Sep
E Heal, T.S. .... 01 Sep
X Horton, J.R. .... 01 Sep
X Horton, S. .... 01 Sep
X Hulston, L.M. .... 01 Sep
X Hurst, C.N.S. .... 01 Sep
X Ingham, L.E. .... 01 Sep
X Jenkins, D.G. .... 01 Sep
X Jones, D.J. .... 01 Sep
X Kay, P.S. .... 01 Sep
X King, W.R.C. .... 01 Sep
X Knowles, C.J. .... 01 Sep
X Laurence, S.T. .... 01 Sep
X Leaman, A.R. .... 01 Sep
S Ledward, K.L. .... 01 Sep
E Leyland, E.M. .... 01 Sep
E Lynskey, M.L. .... 01 Sep
S Manning, G.P. .... 01 Sep
X McGowan, A.B. .... 01 Sep
X Mitchell, J.D. .... 01 Sep
X Mitchell, W.J. .... 01 Sep
S Monday, J.E. .... 01 Sep
X Montague, R.J. .... 01 Sep
X Moore, M.J. .... 01 Sep
X Morris, P.J. .... 01 Sep
X Oxlade, A.T. .... 01 Sep
X Palframan, I.M. .... 01 Sep
X Pearson, J.C. .... 01 Sep
X Penson, J.G. .... 01 Sep
X Pepper, P.M. .... 01 Sep
E Perkins, B. .... 01 Sep
S Peyman, T.A. .... 01 Sep

X Punch, J.M. .... 01 Sep
E Robinson, S.L. .... 01 Sep
E Satterly, R.J. .... 01 Sep
X Scott, N. .... 01 Sep
E Seagrave, S.J. .... 01 Sep
E Slater, D.G. .... 01 Sep
E Slowther, S.J. .... 01 Sep
X Smith, R.A. .... 01 Sep
X Stanway, C.A. .... 01 Sep
X Stead, S.N. .... 01 Sep
X Tawse, A.R.J. .... 01 Sep
X Thomas, A.G. .... 01 Sep
X Townsend, J.J. .... 01 Sep
X Twigg, N.R. .... 01 Sep
S Wallace, K.G. .... 01 Sep
X Webb, M.R. .... 01 Sep
X Wells, J.D. .... 01 Sep
X Whetter, R.S. .... 01 Sep
X Winn, J.P. .... 01 Sep
E Witt, A.K. .... 01 Sep
E Woods, M.J.P. .... 01 Sep
S Bell, S.W. .... 18 Sep
S Brady, T.W. .... 18 Sep
X Clarke, M. .... 18 Sep
X Daniels, S.P. .... 18 Sep
X Gallimore, J.M. .... 18 Sep
X Godfrey, S.D.W. .... 18 Sep
X Jayes, N.J. .... 18 Sep
X Jones, S.S. .... 18 Sep
MS Jones, T.M. .... 18 Sep
MS Milburn, V. .... 18 Sep
S Northeast, P. .... 18 Sep
X Ross, A.D. .... 18 Sep
S Somerville, S.J. .... 18 Sep
X Tutchings, A. .... 18 Sep
S Wells, S.P. .... 18 Sep
X Wood, N.R. .... 18 Sep
E Beadling, D.J. .... 19 Sep
X Colley, R. .... 19 Sep
E Cunningham, D.B. .... 19 Sep
MS Davies, J.L. .... 19 Sep
X Griffin, S. .... 19 Sep
S Grigg, S.K. .... 19 Sep
S Harvey, P.J. .... 19 Sep
X Hirstwood, J.L. .... 19 Sep
X Jackson-Smith, S.P. .... 19 Sep
X Lewis, P.L. .... 19 Sep
X Martin, D.C.S. .... 19 Sep
S McGrath, W.J. .... 19 Sep
X Monnox, J. .... 19 Sep
MS Murray, A. .... 19 Sep
X Naldrett, G.C. .... 19 Sep
E Palmer, C.R. .... 19 Sep

X Rankin, G.J. 19 Sep
E Ritchie, D.B. 19 Sep
X Seager, A.K. 19 Sep
X Sterry, J.E.B. 19 Sep
X Stewart, C.H. 19 Sep
MS Wade, A. 19 Sep
X Cust, S.A. 01 Nov

1999

X Ainsley, A.M.J. 01 Jan
S Ashley, P.D. 01 Jan
X Barnard, T.J. 01 Jan
X Barr, D.D. 01 Jan
X Barrow, C.M. 01 Jan
X Beswick, S.D. 01 Jan
S Boardman, S.J. 01 Jan
X Boulind, M.A. 01 Jan
E Bradley, T.A. 01 Jan
X Briggs, H.C. 01 Jan
X Brock, M.J. 01 Jan
E Brodie, D.J. 01 Jan
E Bukhory, H. 01 Jan
X Burgon, R. 01 Jan
E Calver, B.J. 01 Jan
S Chadwick, K. 01 Jan
X Chandler, P.J. 01 Jan
X Chapman, J.L.J. 01 Jan
X Chapman, S.J. 01 Jan
X Clarke, M. 01 Jan
X Cooke, S.N. 01 Jan
X Cowie, A.D. 01 Jan
X Crawford, V.E. 01 Jan
X Dadwal, R.K. 01 Jan
X Dallamore, R.A. 01 Jan
X Dawson, P.M.D. 01 Jan
X Day, B.T. 01 Jan
X Dowie, M.E. 01 Jan
X Eaton, D.C. 01 Jan
X Edmondson, J.A. 01 Jan
X Farr, I.R. 01 Jan
X Filshie, S.J. 01 Jan
X French, J.H. 01 Jan
S Garbutt, H.J. 01 Jan
S Gilbert, S.L. 01 Jan
X Grey, C.S. 01 Jan
X Henry, G.P. 01 Jan
X Holliehead, C.L. 01 Jan
X Hopkins, A.E.T. 01 Jan
S Horwood, N.A. 01 Jan
X Hudson, A.I. 01 Jan
E Hughes, G.D. 01 Jan
X Hutchinson, N.J. 01 Jan
S Huynh, C.C. 01 Jan
X Inglis, D.J. 01 Jan
X Issitt, B.D. 01 Jan
X Jones, M.R. 01 Jan
S Jones, N.S. 01 Jan
X Kearney, T.M. 01 Jan
X Ladislaus, C.J. 01 Jan
X Latus, S.H. 01 Jan
X Leeper, J.S. 01 Jan
E Louw, L. 01 Jan
X Loveridge, P.J. 01 Jan
S MacKenzie, H.L. 01 Jan
X Marland, E.E. 01 Jan
E Marshall, G.P. 01 Jan
X Masson, N.G. 01 Jan
X Mc Allister, S.E. 01 Jan
E McCamphill, P.J. 01 Jan
X McKay, T.W. 01 Jan
S Middleton, W.T. 01 Jan
X Mitchell, J.M. 01 Jan
X Moran, B.M. 01 Jan
X Morgan, B.P. 01 Jan
E Morris, D.W. 01 Jan
X Morrow, D.G. 01 Jan
X Mountney, G.A. 01 Jan
X Nash, R.D.C. 01 Jan
X Nash, R.P. 01 Jan
X Nicholson, D.A.G. 01 Jan
X Oneill, T.J. 01 Jan
X Parsons, R.M.J. 01 Jan
X Pearce, R.J. 01 Jan
X Pearmain, S.R. 01 Jan
X Powell, R.J. 01 Jan
X Quinn, M.G. 01 Jan
X Railton, A.S. 01 Jan
X Ransom, B.R.J. 01 Jan
X Rea, S.D. 01 Jan
X Rider, J.C.R. 01 Jan
X Rimmer, O.F. 01 Jan
X Ritchie, I.D. 01 Jan
X Robey, J.C. 01 Jan
X Rowberry, A.G. 01 Jan
X Russell, M.S. 01 Jan
X Sargent, D.R. 01 Jan
E Seed, G.J. 01 Jan
X Shore, E.A. 01 Jan
E Simbeye, M. 01 Jan
X Simpson, S.F. 01 Jan
X Simpson, W.J.S. 01 Jan
X Smith, O.J. 01 Jan
E Smye, M.A. 01 Jan
X Startup, H.J. 01 Jan
X Stevenson, S.R. 01 Jan
X Suter, F.T. 01 Jan
X Tait, S.J. 01 Jan
X Tappin, S.J. 01 Jan
X Taylor, G.D.L. 01 Jan
X Thom, M.F. 01 Jan
X Tindell, R.W. 01 Jan
X Tracey, W.S. 01 Jan
X Van Duin, M.I.A. 01 Jan
X Veal, D.J. 01 Jan
X Wallace, A.R. 01 Jan
E Webb, D. 01 Jan
X Wick, H.M.S. 01 Jan
S Wild, R.J. 01 Jan
E Williams, P.A. 01 Jan
X Wilson, I.P. 01 Jan
X Wood, J.T. 01 Jan
E Alberts, P.W. 08 Jan
E Blois, S.D. 08 Jan
E Carter, P. 08 Jan
X Dingley, P.A. 08 Jan
E Dumbleton, D.W. 08 Jan
MS Haughey, J.P. 08 Jan
E Havron, P.R. 08 Jan
E Hocking, M.J.E. 08 Jan
E James, M. 08 Jan
X Molnar, R.M. 08 Jan
E Nottley, S.M. 08 Jan
E Rhodes, A.W. 08 Jan
E Robinson, D.P. 08 Jan
X Robinson, R.J. 08 Jan
E Shaw, N.A. 08 Jan
X Smith, P.A. 08 Jan
E Temple, D.C. 08 Jan
E Thomson, I.W. 08 Jan
E Toone, S.A. 08 Jan
E Whitehouse, S.R. 08 Jan
X Whitson-Fay, C.D. 08 Jan
X Beegan, C.F. 27 Jan
E Berry, S.M. 27 Jan
E Binns, J.R. 27 Jan
E Carbery, S.J. 27 Jan
S Cleary, C.M. 27 Jan
E Creek, S.B. 27 Jan
X Davis, G.R. 27 Jan
MS Edwards, D. 27 Jan
X Evans, I.C. 27 Jan
E Fitzgerald, G.S. 27 Jan
E Fry, T.G. 27 Jan
E Gibson, T.A. 27 Jan
E Godley, D. 27 Jan
E Hawkins, S. 27 Jan
E Jarman, P.R. 27 Jan
E Jones, C.D. 27 Jan
S Kingdon, S.C. 27 Jan

S Kirwan, J.A. .... 27 Jan
X Laws, A.P. .... 27 Jan
E MacIntyre, I.D. .... 27 Jan
E Mann, A.W. .... 27 Jan
MS Pinhey, A.D. .... 27 Jan
E Rand, M.A. .... 27 Jan
E Richards, S.C. .... 27 Jan
E Sawford, G.N. .... 27 Jan
S Smith, L. .... 27 Jan
E Snell, D.M. .... 27 Jan
X Blythe, J. .... 01 Apr
X Fuller, J.E. .... 01 Apr
X Green, P.A. .... 01 Apr
X Humphrey, I.R. .... 01 Apr
X Jones, R.O. .... 01 Apr
X Ludlow, J.A. .... 01 Apr
X Perryment, C.P. .... 01 Apr
X Rawlins, S.T. .... 01 Apr
X Renaud, G.A.R. .... 01 Apr
X Spears, A.G. .... 01 Apr
S Whale, V.A. .... 01 Apr
X Wood, S.J. .... 01 Apr
X Fergusson, I.B. .... 01 May
X Fraser, A.G. .... 01 May
X Hollingdale, R.A. .... 01 May
X Hulme, C.A. .... 01 May
X Bush, N. .... 01 Sep
X Evans, L. .... 01 Sep
X Farrell, J.A. .... 01 Sep
X Garner, M.E. .... 01 Sep
E Johnston, A.G. .... 01 Sep
X King, W.T.P. .... 01 Sep
X Molloy, L. .... 01 Sep

2000

X Bullock, J.R. .... 01 Jan
E Gaytano, R.T.M. .... 01 Jan
X Green, J. .... 01 Jan
X Hayes, M.A. .... 01 Jan
X Semple, B. .... 01 Jan
X Bannister, J. .... 01 Apr
X Braithwaite, G.C. .... 01 Apr
S Dobson, A.C. .... 01 Apr
X Ewer, J.E. .... 01 Apr
X Farmer, P.A. .... 01 Apr
X Hart, S.D. .... 01 Apr
X Holgate, J.A. .... 01 Apr
S Lanigan, B.R. .... 01 Apr
X Leeson, A.R. .... 01 Apr
X Morris, D.R. .... 01 Apr
X Sloan, G.D. .... 01 Apr
X Walker, N.M.C. .... 01 Apr
X Williamson, P.J. .... 01 Apr

SUB LIEUTENANTS (UCE)

1998

X Morey, K.N. .... 01 Sep
X Parkinson, J.H.G. .... 01 Sep

1999

X Carpenter, G.E. .... 01 Sep
E Dyter, R.C. .... 01 Sep
X Feasey, I.D. .... 01 Sep
E Mann, C.A. .... 01 Sep
X Marriott, M.J. .... 01 Sep
X Mawdsley, G.R. .... 01 Sep
X Ryan, P.D.B. .... 01 Sep

MIDSHIPMEN

1998

X Holmes, M.D. .... 01 Apr
X Howorth, G.M.R. .... 01 Apr
X Leeder, T.R. .... 01 May
X Rose, E.K. .... 01 May
X Simmonds, D.D.H. .... 01 May
E Anderson, L.C. .... 01 Sep
E Bailey, I.J. .... 01 Sep
X Benarr, C.M. .... 01 Sep
S Farrant, J.D. .... 01 Sep
E Faulkner, S.G. .... 01 Sep
X Gilmore, J.E. .... 01 Sep
E Gordon, A.J. .... 01 Sep
E Gosden, D.R. .... 01 Sep
E Kadinopoulos, B.A. .... 01 Sep
X Louis, D.R.A. .... 01 Sep
E Marshall, C.G. .... 01 Sep
X Martin, C.C.R. .... 01 Sep
E McCormack, G. .... 01 Sep
E Parkinson, H.M.L. .... 01 Sep
E Penalver, W.C. .... 01 Sep
X Phillips, R.E. .... 01 Sep
X Reeves, A.P. .... 01 Sep
E Reynolds, M.E. .... 01 Sep
S Richardson, S.C. .... 01 Sep
X Samways, M.J. .... 01 Sep
X Skipper, J.A. .... 01 Sep
X Sykes, M.J. .... 01 Sep
E Tatton-Brown, H.T. .... 01 Sep
X Vincent, P.H. .... 01 Sep
X Walker, J.J. .... 01 Sep
E Weedon, G.A. .... 01 Sep

1999

X Barron, P.R. .... 01 Jan
X Blair, L.D. .... 01 Jan
X Leightley, S.M. .... 01 Jan
X McKenna, D.R. .... 01 Jan
X Nason, S.M. .... 01 Jan
X Pate, C.M. .... 01 Jan
X Roy, C.A. .... 01 Jan
X Sharp, J.V. .... 01 Jan
E Amorosi, R.G.F.L. .... 01 Sep
X Ballard, A.P.V. .... 01 Sep
E Bell, F.J. .... 01 Sep
X Bond, R.D.A. .... 01 Sep
E Bowen, R.J. .... 01 Sep
E Colley, I.P. .... 01 Sep
X Dacombe, C.A. .... 01 Sep
X Dale, N.A. .... 01 Sep
E Dalglish, K.M. .... 01 Sep
E Dart, D.J. .... 01 Sep
S Deacon, P.R. .... 01 Sep
X Elliott, T.D. .... 01 Sep
E Fisher, N.D. .... 01 Sep
E Golden, C.A. .... 01 Sep
E Green, J.E. .... 01 Sep
X Hewit, S. .... 01 Sep
E Hobbs, T.P. .... 01 Sep
E Huggett, C.L. .... 01 Sep
X Ingham, N.H. .... 01 Sep
X Keillor, S.J. .... 01 Sep
X MacLean, S.M. .... 01 Sep
X Mason-Matthews, A. .... 01 Sep
X McMillan, N. .... 01 Sep
X Morgan, G.L. .... 01 Sep
X O'Neill, C.M. .... 01 Sep
X Phillips, L.C. .... 01 Sep
E Piaggesi, G.F. .... 01 Sep
E Purdy, R.J. .... 01 Sep
E Reed, P.K. .... 01 Sep
X Schofield, J.C. .... 01 Sep
E Simpson, E.L. .... 01 Sep
X Smith, V.I.P. .... 01 Sep

E Weil, D.G. .... 01 Sep
X Whitelaw, D.A. .... 01 Sep
E Wood, J.R. .... 01 Sep

2000

X Barnes, J.C. .... 01 Jan
S Brooksbank, R. .... 01 Jan
E Chaudhary, R. .... 01 Jan
X Lincoln, P.W. .... 01 Jan
X McNeice, A.L. .... 01 Jan
S Mifflin, M.J. .... 01 Jan
S Shepherd, S.L. .... 01 Jan
X Wood, C. .... 01 Jan

MEDICAL OFFICERS

SURGEON REAR ADMIRALS

Jenkins, Ian Lawrence , *CVO, MB, BCh, FRCS, OStJ* .... 13 Apr 99
(MEDICAL DIRECTOR GENERAL(NAVAL) APR 99)

SURGEON CAPTAINS
(Full Career Commission)

1989
- Evans, C.W. .... 30 Jun

1992
- Curr, R.D. .... 30 Jun
- Baldock, N.E. .... 31 Dec
- McMillan, G.H.G. .... 31 Dec

1993
- Farquharson-Roberts, M.A. .... 30 Jun
- Carne, J.R.C. .... 30 Jun

1994
- Cunningham, D.A. .... 30 Jun
- Howard, O.M. .... 31 Dec

1995
- Tolley, P.F.R. .... 31 Dec

1996
- Edmondstone, W.M. .... 30 Jun
- Douglas-Riley, T.R. .... 31 Dec

1997
- Churcher-Brown, C.J. .... 31 Dec

1998
- Mugridge, A.R. .... 30 Jun
- Sykes, J.J.W. .... 31 Dec
- Raffaelli, P.I. .... 31 Dec

1999
- Taylor, R.H. .... 30 Jun
- Bevan, N.S. .... 31 Dec
- Jarvis, L.J. .... 31 Dec

2000
- Morgan, N.V. .... 30 Jun

SURGEON COMMANDERS
(Full Career Commission)

1985
- Kershaw, C.R. .... 30 Jun
- Runchman, P.C. .... 30 Jun
- Ashton, R.E. .... 31 Dec

1987
- Gabb, J.H. .... 31 Dec
- Johnston, C.G. .... 31 Dec

1989
- Barker, C.P.G. .... 31 Dec

1990
- Ryder, S.J. .... 30 Jun
- Waugh, P.J. .... 30 Jun

1991
- Lunn, D.V. .... 30 Jun
- Allison, A.S.C. .... 30 Jun
- Walker, A.J. .... 30 Jun
- Brown, D.C. .... 31 Dec
- Dale, R.F. .... 31 Dec

1992
- Campbell, J.K. .... 30 Jun
- McArthur, C.J.G. .... 30 Jun
- Butterfield, N.P. .... 31 Dec

1993
- Dean, M.R. .... 30 Jun
- Balmer, A.V. .... 31 Dec
- Benton, P.J. .... 31 Dec
- Hett, D.A. .... 31 Dec

1994
- Nicol, P.J.S. .... 30 Jun
- Baker, A.B. .... 30 Jun
- Pipkin, C. .... 30 Jun
- Spalding, T.J.W. .... 30 Jun
- Greer, J.P. .... 31 Dec
- Cripps, N.P.J. .... 31 Dec

1995
- Hughes, A.S. .... 31 Dec
- Buxton, P.J. .... 31 Dec

1996
- Burgess, A.J. .... 30 Jun
- Neal, A.J.D. .... 30 Jun
- McNeill Love, R.M.C. .... 30 Jun
- Slavin, D.E. .... 31 Dec
- Scott, R.C. .... 31 Dec
- Perry, J.N. .... 31 Dec

1997
- Hedger, N.A. .... 30 Jun
- Johnston, R.P. .... 30 Jun
- Loxdale, P.H. .... 30 Jun
- Roberts, A.P. .... 31 Dec
- Edwards, C.J.A. .... 31 Dec
- Murrison, A.W. .... 31 Dec

1998
- Howell, G.E.D. .... 30 Jun
- Hughes, P.A. .... 30 Jun
- Lygo, M.H. .... 30 Jun
- Crawford, P.I. .... 31 Dec
- Midwinter, M.J. .... 31 Dec
- Risdall, J.E. .... 31 Dec

1999
- Lambert, A.W. .... 30 Jun
- Howell, M.A. .... 30 Jun

- Ross, S.J. 14 Oct
- Low, C.D.T. 31 Dec
- Ross, R.A. 31 Dec
- Young, P.C. 31 Dec
- Gent, R.P.ST.J. 31 Dec

2000

- Groom, M.R. 30 Jun
- Bree, S.E.P. 30 Jun
- McKeating, J.B. 30 Jun
- Dashfield, A.K. 30 Jun

SURGEON LIEUTENANT COMMANDERS
(Full Career & Medium Career Commission)

1987

- Haddon, R.W.J. 19 Oct

1989

- Pearson, C.R. 15 May
- MacLennan, I.R. 01 Jul

1990

- Campbell, D.J. 01 May

1991

- Hill, G.A. 01 Aug

1992

- Nicholson, G. 01 Aug
- Turnbull, P.S. 01 Aug

1993

- Glover, M.A. 01 Aug
- Summerton, D.J. 01 Aug
- Stewart, M.D. 03 Aug
- Guy, R.J. 15 Aug
- Foster, C.R.M. 19 Sep

1994

- Parker, S.J. 01 Aug
- Wood, G. 01 Aug
- Clarke, J.M. 01 Aug
- Birt, D.J. 25 Aug

1995

- Hand, C.J. 04 Jan
- Smith, S.R.C. 01 Aug
- Stapley, S.A. 01 Aug
- Edwards, P.D. 21 Dec

1996

- Sharpley, J.G. 08 Feb
- Miles, R. 01 Aug
- Tanser, S.J. 01 Aug
- Millar, S.W.S. 01 Aug
- Nichols, E.A. 01 Aug
- Mellor, A.J. 06 Sep

1997

- Palmer, A.C. 01 Mar
- Whittaker, M.A. 01 Aug
- Blair, D.G.S. 01 Aug
- Yarnall, N.J. 01 Aug
- Cannon, L.B. 01 Aug
- Fisher, N.G. 01 Aug
- Connor, D.J. 01 Aug

1998

- Dowdeswell, K.A. 01 Aug
- Craner, M.J. 01 Aug
- Matthews, G.A. 01 Aug
- Thomas, L.M. 01 Aug
- Streets, C.G. 01 Aug
- Smith, J.E. 01 Aug
- Rickard, R.F. 03 Aug
- Freshwater, D.A. 09 Aug

1999

- Bowie, A.N. 11 Mar
- Walker, L.L. 01 Aug
- Dekker, B.J. 01 Aug
- Heames, R.M. 01 Aug
- Counter, P.R. 01 Aug
- Snowden, M.B.S. 01 Aug
- Brinsden, M.D. 01 Aug
- Tamayo, B.C.C. 01 Aug
- Houlberg, K.A.N. 01 Aug
- Wallis, L.A. 01 Aug
- Gibson, A.R. 01 Aug
- Hughes, D.J. 01 Aug
- Parry, C.A. 12 Aug

SURGEON LIEUTENANT COMMANDERS
(Short Career Commission)

1992

- Whitehouse, D.P. 01 May

1996

- Johnson, G.A.H. 01 Aug
- Rawal, K.M. 01 Nov
- Evershed, M.C. 02 Nov

1997

- Thomas, R.C. 05 Aug

1998

- Pimpalnerkar, A.L. 04 Jan
- Every, M. 03 Feb
- Shrimpton, H.D. 04 Feb
- Reid, C.J. 01 Aug

1999

- Greenberg, N. 01 Aug
- Heath, C.W. 01 Aug
- Potiphar, D.W. 01 Aug
- Clarke, M.D. 04 Aug

SURGEON LIEUTENANTS
(Medium Career Commission)

1995

- Coltman, T.P. 01 Aug
- McCabe, S.E.T. 01 Aug
- Sowden, L.M. 02 Aug
- Dickson, S.J. 02 Aug
- Mercer, S.J. 03 Aug
- Ayers, D.E.B. 03 Aug
- McLachlan, J.K. 17 Aug
- Tennant, M.I. 14 Sep

1996

- Matthews, J.J. 01 Aug
- Porter, S. 01 Aug
- Reston, S.C. 07 Aug
- Davies, S.R. 08 Aug

1997

- Rees, P.S.C. 06 Aug

SURGEON LIEUTENANTS

(Short Career Commission)

1995

- Ahling-Smith, H.E.M. ...... 01 Aug
- Bateman, R.M. .... 02 Aug
- Lew-Gor, S.T.W. .... 05 Sep
- Kehoe, A.D. .... 01 Dec

1996

- Webber, R.J. .... 01 Feb
- Nicholl, S. .... 21 Mar
- Atkinson, P.A. .... 01 Aug
- Clarkson, S.J. .... 01 Aug
- Mantle, M. .... 07 Aug
- Marshall, F.T. .... 07 Aug
- Denholm, J.L. .... 07 Aug
- Smith, J.J. .... 07 Aug
- Bland, S.A. .... 07 Aug
- Milner, R.A. .... 07 Aug
- Mather, R.H. .... 07 Aug
- Mackie, S.J. .... 12 Aug

1997

- Armstrong, E.M. .... 05 Feb
- Norris, W.D. .... 20 May
- Prior, K.R.E.J. .... 06 Aug
- Hutchings, S.D. .... 06 Aug
- Beadsmoore, E.J. .... 06 Aug
- Henry, M.F. .... 06 Aug
- Dow, W.A.M. .... 06 Aug
- Shaw, S.L. .... 06 Aug
- Rahman, J. .... 06 Aug
- Kershaw, D.J.E. .... 06 Aug
- McIntosh, J.D. .... 26 Aug
- Whybourn, L.A. .... 28 Nov

1998

- Wilson, C.J.F. .... 25 Feb
- Brown, A. .... 05 Aug
- Carty, J. .... 05 Aug
- Fitzsimons, D.E. .... 05 Aug
- Pearce, L.A. .... 05 Aug
- Welch, J.F. .... 05 Aug
- Brims, F.J.H. .... 05 Aug
- Knight, E.M. .... 05 Aug
- Allsop, A.R.L. .... 05 Aug
- Evans, G.C. .... 05 Aug
- Cormack, A.J.R. .... 05 Aug
- Collett, S.M. .... 05 Aug

1999

- Nelstrop, A.M. .... 10 Feb
- Gay, D.A.T. .... 01 Aug
- Prendergast, M.P. .... 04 Aug
- Price, V.J. .... 04 Aug
- Miller, A.D. .... 04 Aug
- Barton, S.J. .... 04 Aug
- Martin, N. .... 04 Aug
- Scott, T.E. .... 04 Aug
- Grainge, C.L. .... 04 Aug
- Brodribb, T.J. .... 04 Aug
- Keogh, J.M.E. .... 04 Aug
- Read, J.A.J.M. .... 04 Aug
- Coates, P.J.B. .... 04 Aug
- Martin, N.P. .... 26 Aug

2000

- Hudson, J.D.P. .... 12 Jan

ACTING SURGEON LIEUTENANTS

1999

- Gregory, J.R.C. .... 25 Jun
- Dew, A.M. .... 06 Jul
- Lamont, S.N.J. .... 08 Jul
- Guyver, P.M. .... 15 Jul
- Harrison, J.C. .... 15 Jul
- Mercer, S.J. .... 15 Jul
- Robin, J.I. .... 16 Jul
- Stannard, A. .... 16 Jul
- Baden, J.M. .... 19 Jul
- Cooke, J.M. .... 19 Jul
- Gardner, C.B. .... 19 Jul
- Hayton, J.C. .... 19 Jul
- Bains, B.S. .... 22 Dec

MEDICAL CADETS SURGEON SUB LIEUTENANTS RN

1997

- Bennett, S.A.F.J. .... 01 Sep
- Wild, G. .... 16 Sep
- Hicks, A.R. .... 22 Sep
- Bonner, T.J. .... 09 Oct
- Yates, E.H. .... 18 Dec

1998

- Khan, M.A. .... 07 Jan
- Bray, K.E. .... 12 Feb
- Wilmott, S.C. .... 14 May
- Ruthven, S.C. .... 22 May
- Kershaw, R.J. .... 29 Jun
- Allcock, E.C. .... 24 Jul
- Wood, A.M. .... 21 Aug
- Evans, T.E. .... 01 Oct
- Edward, A.M. .... 03 Oct
- Beard, D.J. .... 11 Oct
- Hemingway, R. .... 20 Nov
- Reynolds, R.H. .... 30 Nov
- Barker, V.S. .... 24 Dec

1999

- Mercer, A.J. .... 27 Jan
- Middleton, S.W.F. .... 30 Apr
- Vale, A.J. .... 30 Apr
- Pengelly, S.P. .... 16 May
- Williams, S.W. .... 16 May
- O'Shea, M.K. .... 17 May
- Cordner, M.A. .... 20 May
- Westermann, R.W. .... 22 Jun
- Gardiner, D.R.C. .... 24 Jun
- Maples, A.T. .... 25 Jun
- Mears, K.P. .... 29 Jun
- Sargent, D.S. .... 29 Jul
- Isbister, E.J. .... 01 Aug
- Pardoe, E.R. .... 12 Sep
- McMenamin, D.M. .... 01 Oct
- Gilmartin, K.P. .... 04 Oct
- Phillips, J.C. .... 12 Dec

2000

- Newton, N.J.P. .... 11 Jan
- Penn-Barwell, J.G. .... 11 Jan
- Ambrose, R.E.F. .... 20 Feb

DENTAL OFFICERS

SURGEON CAPTAINS(D)
(Full Career Commission)

1991
- Hargraves, J. .... 31 Dec

1993
- Holland, J.V. .... 30 Jun

1994
- Myers, G.W. .... 31 Dec

1995
- Lambert-Humble, S. ...... 31 Dec

1996
- Morrison, G.L. .... 31 Dec

1997
- Lock, W.R. .... 30 Jun

2000
- Sanderson, R.C. .... 30 Jun

SURGEON COMMANDERS(D)
(Full Career & Medium Career Commission)

1987
- Thomas, D.L. .... 30 Jun

1988
- Weston, M.W. .... 31 Dec

1990
- Stevenson, R.M. .... 31 Dec

1995
- Gall, M.R.C. .... 30 Jun
- Sidoli, G.E. .... 31 Dec

1996
- Norris, R.E. .... 30 Jun
- Culwick, P.F. .... 31 Dec

1997
- Aston, M.W. .... 30 Jun
- Maxwell, A.B.C. .... 31 Dec
- Liggins, S.J. .... 31 Dec

1998
- Howe, S.E. .... 31 Dec
- Jordan, A.M. .... 31 Dec

1999
- Hall, D.J. .... 31 Dec

2000
- McJarrow, D.J. .... 30 Jun

SURGEON LIEUTENANT COMMANDERS(D)
(Full Career & Medium Career Commission)

1990
- Riden, D.K. .... 01 Aug

1993
- Redman, C.D.J. .... 19 Jul
- Smith, B.S. .... 13 Sep

1994
- Elmer, T.B. .... 15 Dec

1995
- Fenwick, J.C. .... 03 Sep

1997
- Turnbull, N.R. .... 02 Jan
- Davenport, N.J. .... 16 Jan
- Everitt, C.J. .... 11 Mar

1998
- Denny, A.M. .... 05 Jan
- Wallace, K.N. .... 31 Jan
- Moore, P.G. .... 31 Dec

1999
- James, I. .... 09 Jan

SURGEON LIEUTENANT COMMANDERS(D)
(Short Career Commission)

1993
- Wilkie, N. .... 11 Jun

1996
- McCorkindale, P.R. .... 13 Jun

1999
- Francis, J.M. .... 09 Jan
- Leyshon, R.J. .... 09 Jan
- Warneken, A.J. .... 09 Jan

SURGEON LIEUTENANTS(D)
(Medium Career Commission)

1996
- Wenger, N.A. .... 23 Jul
- Madgwick, E.C.C. .... 23 Jul

SURGEON LIEUTENANTS(D)

(Short Career Commission)

1995

- Nurton, K.E. .... 08 Aug

1996

- Swigciski, L.A. .... 21 Jun
- Wingfield, M.H. .... 01 Jul

1997

- Jessiman, S.I. .... 20 Jun
- Hands, A.J. .... 26 Jun
- Verney, K.H. .... 09 Jul
- Chittick, W.B.O. .... 10 Jul
- Dean, T.C. .... 22 Jul
- Huxtable, B.J. .... 22 Jul

1998

- McGill, E.J. .... 17 Jun
- McDicken, I.N. .... 25 Jun
- Drummond, K.B. .... 13 Jul
- Holmes, P.S. .... 20 Jul
- Murdoch, G.A. .... 20 Jul
- Woods, R.S. .... 20 Jul

1999

- Foulger, T.E. .... 11 Jun
- Grosse, S.E.K. .... 25 Jun
- Burton, T.J. .... 05 Jul
- Anderton, S.W. .... 06 Sep

SURGEON SUB LIEUTENANTS(D)

(Short Career Commission)

1998

- Wade, C.V. .... 01 Apr

1999

- Bryce, G.E. .... 01 Jan

CHAPLAINS

DIRECTOR GENERAL NAVAL CHAPLAINCY SERVICE AND THE CHAPLAIN OF THE FLEET

Golding, Simon Jefferies , *QHC* .... 03 May 77
(DIRECTOR GENERAL NAVAL CHAPLAINCY SERVICE.MAY 00)

PRINCIPAL ANGLICAN CHAPLAIN

Golding, Simon Jefferies , *QHC* .... 03 May 77
(DIRECTOR GENERAL NAVAL CHAPLAINCY SERVICE. MAY 00)

CHAPLAINS

1975
CE Ames, J.P .... 19 Jun

1977
CE Hammett, B.K. .... 11 Jul

1978
CE Barlow, D. .... 04 Apr

1979
CE Harman, M.J. .... 20 Sep

1980
CE Hilliard, R.G. .... 01 Aug

1981
CE Clarke, B.R. .... 30 Jun

1982
CE Howard, C.W.W. .... 28 Sep

1983
CE Jackson, M.H. .... 19 Apr
CE Baxendale, R.D. .... 14 Jul

1984
CE Brotherton, M. .... 04 Sep

1986
CE Naylor, I.F. .... 16 Sep
CE Elmore, G.M. .... 30 Sep

1987
CE Eglin, I. .... 27 Jan
CE Luckraft, C.J. .... 05 Aug

1988
CE Thomas, D.W.W. .... 18 Oct

1989
CE Franklin, W.H. .... 10 Jan
CE Lewis, T.J. .... 28 Nov

1990
CE Pyne, R.L. .... 23 Jan
CE Callon, A.M. .... 05 Jun
CE Poll, M.G. .... 14 Jun

1991
CE Green, J. .... 04 Jun
CE Fairbank, B.D.S. .... 03 Sep
CE Scott, P.J.D.S. .... 03 Sep
CE Springett, S.P .... 10 Sep

1992
CE Woodcock, N.E. .... 31 Mar
CE Kelly, N.J. .... 26 May
CE Bromage, K.C. .... 02 Aug
CE Morris, J.O. .... 06 Oct

1993
CE Beveridge, S.A.R. .... 28 Apr

1994
CE Hill, J. .... 17 Jan

1996
CE Petzer, G.S. .... 09 Jan
CE Theakston, S.M. .... 03 Jun

1997
CE Wheatley, I.J. .... 08 Apr

1998
CE Hills, M.J. .... 21 Apr
CE Catherall, M.L. .... 01 Sep
CE Evans, M.L. .... 01 Sep
CE Gough, M.J. .... 01 Sep
CE Pnematicatos, N.P.A. .... 01 Sep
CE Wylie, D.V. .... 01 Dec

2000
CE Phillips, A G .... 14 Feb 00

PRINCIPAL CHURCH OF SCOTLAND AND FREE CHURCHES CHAPLAIN

Maze, Andrew Terence, *QHC*, *BSc* .... 11 Sep 79
(DIRECTOR GENERAL NAVAL CHAPLAINCY SERVICE. MAY 00)

CHAPLAINS

1984
SF Keith, D. .... 15 May

1990
SF Eglin, C.A. .... 10 Sep

1981
SF Rae, S.M. .... 02 Feb

1991
SF Matthews, W.J.J. .... 12 Aug

1992
SF Britchfield, A E P .... 01 Oct

1993
SF Brown, S.J. .... 20 Apr
SF Shackleton, S.J.S. .... 20 Apr
SF Wort, R.S. .... 27 Jul

1995

SF Beadle, J.T. .... 30 Mar

1996

SF Martin, R.C.J.R. .... 03 Sep

1997

SF Wilkinson, T.L. .... 04 Mar
SF Meachin, M.C. .... 07 Jul

1998

SF Macleod, R.A.R. .... 20 Feb

1999

SF McFadzean, I. .... 01 Jul

2000

SF Ellingham, R E .... 17 Apr 00
SF Grimshaw, E .... 02 May 00

PRINCIPAL ROMAN CATHOLIC CHAPLAIN

Burns, Thomas Matthew, *SM, QHC,VG,* BA, MBIM .... 04 Jan 94
(DIRECTOR NAVAL CHAPLAINCY SERVICE (MANNING) MAY 00)

CHAPLAINS

1985

RC Donovan, P.A. .... 22 Apr
RC Madders, B.R. .... 09 Sep

1990

RC Sharkey, M. .... 01 Oct

1992

RC Couch, P.H.R.B. .... 05 May

1994

RC Forster, S. .... 08 Aug

1996

RC Bradbury, S. .... 18 Sep
RC McLean, D. .... 18 Sep

1997

RC Kelly, J.T. .... 07 Sep

1998

RC McFadden, A. .... 01 Sep
RC Yates, D.M. .... 01 Sep

NAVAL CAREERS SERVICE OFFICERS (RN)

LIEUTENANTS

1988
- Armstrong, P.W. ....13 Dec

1989
- Bennetts, M. .... 16 Apr

1990
- Breslin, M.J. ....07 Jan

1991
- Kirkbright, K.L.M. .... 17 Feb
- Leeder, R.J. .... 17 Feb

1993
- Saxby, D.G. .... 25 Apr
- Waterworth, T.J. ....05 Sep

1994
- McDonald, J. .... 06 Feb

1997
- Connolly, M.H. ....19 Sep
- Hall, J. ....19 Sep

1998
- Newport, J.D.M. .... 09 Jan
- Concarr, D.T. ....19 Sep
- Drewett, C.E. ....19 Sep

1999
- Jones, C.R. ....08 Jan

NAVAL CAREERS SERVICE OFFICERS (RM)

LIEUTENANTS (C.S)

1988
- Jones, D.L. .... 16 Oct

1997
- Maxwell, A.M. ....10 Jan
- Nickisson, D.J. ....02 May

1998
- Barker, J.E. ....01 May
- Rennie, J.G. ....18 Sep

FAMILY SERVICE

LIEUTENANT F.S.

1989

FS Knox, M.M. .... 17 Apr

1996

FS Taylor, S.B. ....01 May

1997

FS Buckley, N.C. ....19 Sep

1999

FS Millington, I.R. ....08 Jan

FS Butterworth, L. ....27 Jan

ROYAL MARINES

CREST.- The Globe surrounded by a Laurel wreath and surmounted by the Crowned Lion and Crown with 'Gibraltar' on a scroll. The Fouled Anchor imposed on the wreath below the Globe. Motto - 'Per Mare Per Terram'.

THE QUEEN'S COLOUR. - The Union. In the centre the Fouled Anchor with the Royal Cypher interlaced ensigned with the St Edward's Crown and 'Gibraltar' above; in base the Globe surrounded by a Laurel wreath. Motto - 'Per Mare Per Terram'. In the case of Royal Marines Commando units the distinguishing colour of the units is interwoven in the gold cords and tassles.

THE REGIMENTAL COLOUR. - Blue. In the centre the Fouled Anchor interlaced with the Royal Cypher 'G.R.IV' ensigned with the St Edward's Crown and 'Gibraltar' above, in base the Globe surrounded by a Laurel wreath. Motto - 'Per Mare Per Terram'. In the dexter canton the Union in the remaining three corners the Royal Cypher. In the case of Royal Marines Commando units the numerical designation of the unit is shown immediately below the insignia. The distinguishing colour of the unit is interwoven in the gold cords and tassles.

ROYAL MARINES SECRETARY. - Whale Island, Portsmouth Hants PO2 8ER.

CORPS JOURNAL.- 'The Globe and Laurel,' Whale Island Portsmouth, Hants PO2 8ER

ROYAL MARINES ASSOCIATION. - General Secretary, Southsea, Hants, PO4 9PX.

ROYAL MARINES MUSEUM. - Southsea, Hants, PO4 9PX.

THE ROYAL MARINES

CAPTAIN GENERAL

His Royal Highness The Prince Philip Duke of Edinburgh, KG, KT, OM, GBE, AC, QSO

HONORARY COLONEL

His Majesty King Harald V of Norway, GCVO

COLONELS COMMANDANT

Major General A M Keeling, CB, CBE .... 6 Nov 98
(REPRESENTATIVE COLONEL COMMANDANT ROYAL MARINES)

Major General P T Stevenson , *OBE* .... 8 Aug 89
(COLONEL COMMANDANT ROYAL MARINES)

MAJOR GENERALS

Fulton, Robert Henry Gervase , *BA, rcds, psc(m), hcsc* .... 23 Oct 98
(COMMANDANT GENERAL OCT 98)

Milton, Anthony Arthur , *OBE, MPhil, rcds, jsdc, psc(m)* .... 01 Apr 99
(DIRECTOR GENERAL JOINT DOCTRINE CONCEPTS MAR 00)

Wilson, David , *OBE, MID, psc(m), hcsc* .... 22 Nov 99
(CHIEF OF STAFF JOINT HEADQUARTERS HQ NORTH DEC 99)

BRIGADIERS

1996

- Nicholls, D V .... 20 May
- Hill, S P .... 23 Sep

1997

- McNeill, I .... 30 Jun
- Fry, R A .... 21 Oct

1998

- Gardiner, I R .... 12 Jan
- Dutton, J B .... 3 Nov
- Pillar, A R .... 18 Dec

1999

- Lane, R G T .... 17 Dec
- Pounds, N.E. .... 31 Dec

2000

- Rose, J.G. .... 30 Jun

COLONELS

1994

- Mason, A.M (as OF6) .. 30 Jun

1993

- Downton, J M G .... 31 Dec

1994

- Sturman, M. .... 31 Dec

1995

- McDermott, W M .... 31 Dec
- MacCormick, A.W. .... 31 Dec
- Gregory, T.M. .... 30 Jun
- Heaver, D.G.V. .... 30 Jun
- Bowkett, R.M. .... 31 Dec
- Hopley, D.A. .... 31 Dec

1997

- Reynolds, P.A. .... 30 Jun
- Thomas, J.H. .... 30 Jun
- Spicer, M.N. .... 31 Dec

1998

- Hartnell, S.T. .... 30 Jun

Robison, G.S. .... 31 Dec
- Hobson, C.W.P. .... 31 Dec
- Shadbolt, S.E. .... 31 Dec

1999

- Cox, S.J. .... 30 Jun
- Robbins, J.M.F. .... 30 Jun
- Capewell, D.A. .... 31 Dec
- Heal, J.P.C. .... 31 Dec
- Noble, M.J.D. .... 31 Dec

2000
- Haddow, F. 30 Jun
- Salmon, A. 30 Jun

LIEUTENANT COLONELS

1983
- Haycock, J.E. 30 Jun

1986
- Babbington, P.M. 30 Jun
- de Val, K.L. 31 Dec
- Bush, S.J.D. 31 Dec

1987
- Wilson, J.R. 30 Jun
- Rundle, R.M. 30 Jun

1988
- Wilson, P.A. 30 Jun
- Nunn, C.J. 30 Jun

1989
- George, P.D. 30 Jun

1990
- Grant, R.S. 30 Jun
- Hunter, T.C.G. 30 Jun
- Tong, D.K. 31 Dec
- Roy, A.C. 31 Dec

1991
- Cooke, M.Y. 30 Jun
- Crawford, R.L. 30 Jun
- Grant, I.W. 30 Jun
- House, N.P.J. 31 Dec
- de Jager, H. 31 Dec

1992
- Baxter, J.S. 30 Jun
- Bibbey, M.W. 30 Jun
- Parker, J.V.V. 30 Jun
- Balm, S.V. 30 Jun
- Parsons, P.H. 31 Dec
- McCabe, J. 31 Dec
- Armstrong, R.I. 31 Dec
- Thomson, A.B. 31 Dec

1993
- Crosby, J.P. 30 Jun
- Canning, W.A. 30 Jun
- Gelder, G.A. 31 Dec
- Martin, P.J. 31 Dec

1994
- Beadon, C.J.A. 30 Jun
- Hughes, S.J. 30 Jun
- Lovelock, R.B. 30 Jun
- Wilson, S.R. 30 Jun
- Wotherspoon, S.R. 30 Jun
- Taylor, M.K. 30 Jun

BS Waterer, R.A. 29 Jul

1995
- Guyer, S.T.G. 30 Jun
- Getgood, J.A. 30 Jun
- Stewart, D.J. 30 Jun
- Wilson, A.C. 31 Dec
- Tasker, G. 31 Dec
- Chicken, S.T. 31 Dec
- Mason, J.S. 31 Dec
- Heatly, R.J. 31 Dec

1996
- Bruce, S.L. 30 Jun
- Stearns, R.P. 30 Jun
- Williams, A.D.J. 30 Jun
- Howes, F.H.R. 30 Jun
- Leigh, J. 31 Dec
- Dunham, M.W. 31 Dec
- Musto, E.C. 31 Dec
- Taylor, W.J. 31 Dec
- Denning, P.R. 31 Dec

1997
- Conway, S.A. 30 Jun
- Sampson, P.H. 30 Jun
- Huntley, I.P. 30 Jun
- Hutton, J.K. 30 Jun
- Messenger, G.K. 30 Jun
- Stewart, J. 01 Oct
- Foster, G.R. 31 Dec
- Pickup, R.A. 31 Dec
- Mansell, P.R. 31 Dec
- Walker, R.E. 31 Dec
- Hook, D.A. 31 Dec

1998
- Herring, J.J.A. 30 Jun
- Arding, N.M.B. 30 Jun
- Brown, N.P. 30 Jun
- Newing, S.G. 30 Jun
- Scott, C.R. 30 Jun
- Marino, D.J. 01 Oct
- Ellis, M.P. 31 Dec
- Davies, J.R. 31 Dec
- Price, M.J. 31 Dec
- Davis, E.G.M. 31 Dec
- Mallalieu, A.J. 31 Dec
- Bevis, T.J. 31 Dec

1999
- Cusack, N.J. 30 Jun
- Mudford, H.C. 30 Jun
- Page, M.C. 30 Jun
- Dechow, W.E. 30 Jun
- Wolsey, M.A.R. 30 Jun
- Smith, M.L. 31 Dec
- Hall, S.J. 31 Dec
- Watts, R.D. 31 Dec
- Lindley, N.P. 31 Dec
- Spencer, R.A.W. 31 Dec
- Clark, D.M.J. 31 Dec

2000
- Summerfield, D.E. 30 Jun
- Webster, T.J.C. 30 Jun
- Cawthorne, M.W.S. 30 Jun
- Salzano, G.M. 30 Jun

MAJORS

1978
- Fletcher, R.J. 01 Mar
- Williams, L.D. 01 Aug
- Gillson, D.M. 01 Nov

1979
- Craven-Phillips, T.C.D. 01 Feb

1980
- Smith, N.D. 01 Mar

1981
- Cailes, M.J. 10 Feb
- Gordon, J.P.M. 13 Dec

1982

- Bailey, A.M.S. 01 Aug
- Stark, T.A. 01 Dec

1983

- Simmonds, P.B. 01 Aug
- Corner, I.L.F. 01 Nov

1984

- Rye, J.W. 01 Sep

1985

- Clapson, K. 01 Jul
- Pritchard, R.C. 01 Aug
- Ellis, M.A.H. 01 Sep

1986

- Dunn, I.L. 01 Sep
- Moyse, R.E. 01 Sep
- Tyrrell, R.K. 01 Sep

1987

- Ebbens, A.J. 01 Sep

1988

- Underwood, N.J. 01 Sep
- Gidney, N. 01 Sep
- Milne, A.R. 01 Sep
- Wills, M.V. 05 Sep
- Curtis, B.J. 01 Oct

1989

- Stewart, R.M. 01 Mar
- Milner, H.C. 01 Sep

1990

- Walker, G.S.L. 01 Sep
- Gittoes, M.A.W. 01 Sep
- Hall, R.M. 01 Sep
- Parks, E.P. 01 Sep
- Paul, R.W.F. 01 Sep
- Phillips, S.J. 01 Sep
- Westoby, R.M. 01 Sep
- Grixoni, M.R.R. 01 Sep
- Sharland, S.P. 01 Sep

1991

- Burnell, J.R.J. 01 Sep

1992

- Cook, P.W.J. 01 May
- Barnes, R.W. 01 May
- McCardle, J.A. 01 Aug
- Corrin, C.ST.J. 01 Sep
- Bruce-Jones, N.W. 01 Sep
- Bentham-Green, N.R.H. 01 Sep
- Norman, P.G. 01 Sep
- Glaze, J.W. 01 Oct
- Brown, R.J. 01 Oct

1993

- MacDonald, I.R. 08 Feb
- Daniels, T.N. 01 Sep
- Evans, M.A. 01 Sep
- Syvret, M.E.V. 01 Sep
- Hudson, J.D. 01 Sep
- Gwillim, V.G. 01 Sep
- Allen, R.J. 01 Sep
- Evans, D.M.M. 01 Sep

BS Perkins, J.R. 01 Oct

1994

- Pritchard, S.A. 18 Apr
- Middleton, T.P.W. 01 May
- Howe, P.A. 01 May
- Anthony, N.M.K. 01 Sep
- Copinger-Symes,R.S. 01 Sep
- Forster, R.M. 01 Sep
- Wakely, S.A. 01 Oct
- Harradine, P.A. 01 Oct
- Sawyer, T.J. 01 Oct

1995

- Marok, J. 30 Apr
- Maddick, M.J. 26 May
- van der Horst, R.E. 01 Sep
- Cameron, P.S. 01 Sep
- Green, M.G.H. 01 Sep
- Ross, J.H. 01 Sep
- Smallwood, J.P. 05 Sep
- Atkinson, J.C. 01 Oct
- Warren, T.S.E. 01 Oct
- Launchbury, S.J. 01 Oct
- Matthews, G. 01 Oct

1996

- Allison, K.R. 25 Apr
- Hood, M.J. 25 Apr
- Pelly, G.R. 25 Apr
- Taylor, P.G.D. 25 Apr
- Manger, G.S.C. 25 Apr
- Wilson, D.W.H. 25 Apr
- Cullis, C.J. 25 Apr
- Curry, B.R. 25 Apr
- Francis, S.J. 25 Apr
- Ross, A.C.P. 25 Apr
- Scott, S.J. 01 Sep
- Freeman, M.E. 01 Sep
- Cundy, R.G. 01 Sep
- Webber, S.A. 01 Sep
- Saddleton, A.D. 01 Sep
- Willson, N.J. 01 Sep
- Moore, C.B. 01 Sep
- James, S.A. 01 Sep
- Bennett, N.M. 01 Sep
- Birrell, S.M. 01 Sep
- Holmes, M.J. 01 Sep
- King, D.C.M. 01 Sep
- Cooper, R.T. 01 Oct
- Anderson, S.T. 01 Oct
- Collins, P.R. 01 Oct
- Greedus, D.A. 01 Oct
- Maher, A.M. 01 Oct
- Thomas, P.W. 01 Oct

1997

- Bell, D.W.A. 26 Apr
- Pulvertaft, R.J. 01 May
- Coldrick, S.A. 01 May
- Gadie, P.A. 01 May
- Maybery, J.E. 01 May
- Thurstan, R.W.F. 01 May
- McKinney, M.D. 01 May
- Morris, P.E.M. 01 May
- Price, A.M. 01 May
- Searight, M.F.C. 01 May
- Slack, J.M. 01 May
- Stephens, R.J. 01 May
- White, H.J. 01 May
- Johnson, A.D. 29 May
- Gray, M.N. 01 Sep
- Livingstone, A.J. 01 Sep
- Maynard, A.T.W. 01 Sep
- Hughes, J-P.H. 01 Sep
- Magowan, R.A. 01 Sep
- Cook, T.A. 01 Sep
- Kassapian, D.L. 01 Sep
- Oliver, K.B. 01 Sep
- McKeown, J.R. 01 Sep
- Disbury, B.N. 01 Oct
- Hembrow, T. 01 Oct
- Maese, P.A. 01 Oct
- Ritchie, W.J. 01 Oct
- Corbidge, S.J. 01 Oct
- O'Donnell, I.M. 01 Oct

1998

- Pressly, J.W. 25 Apr
- Joyce, P. 25 Apr
- McCormack, C.P. 30 Apr

	Name	Date
-	Stickland, C.R.	30 Apr
-	Kenworthy, R.A.	30 Apr
-	Mc Laren, J.P.	30 Apr
-	Porter, M.E.	01 May
-	Chandler, M.F.H.	01 May
-	Holmes, C.J.	01 May
-	Litster, A.	01 Sep
-	Morris, J.A.J.	01 Sep
-	Kemp, P.J.	01 Sep
-	Sear, J.J.	01 Sep
-	Amos, J.H.J.	01 Sep
-	Thorpe, C.D.B.	01 Sep
-	Gilding, D.R.	01 Sep
-	Green, G.M.	01 Sep
-	Chapman, S.	01 Sep
-	Jones, M.R.	01 Sep
-	Fitzgerald, B.	01 Oct
-	Cunningham, J.S.	01 Oct
-	Potter, S.	01 Oct
-	Crouden, S.F.	01 Oct
-	Everritt, R.	01 Oct
BS	Davis, C.J.	01 Oct
-	Ford, D.	01 Oct
	1999	
-	Dewar, D.A.	01 Mar
-	Case, A.C.	24 Apr
-	Kettle, R.A.	24 Apr
-	Smith, G.K.	24 Apr
-	Fergusson, A.C.	01 May
-	Cunningham, J.T.	01 May
-	Hills, R.B.	01 May
-	Armour, G.A.	01 May
-	Ward, J.G.	01 May
-	Simcox, P.A.	19 Jun
-	Holt, J.S.	27 Aug
-	Ashby, P.J.C.	01 Sep
-	Corn, R.A.F.	01 Sep
-	Manson, P.D.	01 Sep
-	Beach, J.M.	01 Sep
-	Pierson, M.F.	01 Sep
-	Evans, P.J.	01 Sep
-	McInerney, A.J.	01 Sep
-	Baxendale, R.F.	01 Sep
-	Hussey, S.J.	01 Sep
-	Skuse, M.	01 Sep
-	Stovin-Bradford, M.	01 Sep
-	Green, M.R.	01 Oct
BS	Mills, B.	01 Oct
-	Tupman, K.C.	01 Oct
-	Richards, S.W.	01 Oct
-	Beazley, P.	01 Oct
-	Reed, J.W.	01 Oct
	2000	
-	Robertson, N.B.	1 May
-	Mattin, P.R.	1 May
-	Bucknall, R.J.W.	1 May
-	Cooper-Simpson, R.J.	1 May
-	Hammond, M.C.	1 May
-	Murray, A.B.	1 May
-	Walls, K.F.	1 May
-	May, D.P.	1 May
-	Chattin, A.P.	1 May
-	Congreve, S.C.	1 May
-	Cook, M.F.	1 May

CAPTAINS

	Name	Date
	1990	
BS	Hillier, J.	01 Jan
	1993	
-	Devlin, H.F.G.	01 Jan
-	Bain, D.I.	01 Jan
-	Sharpe, G.A.	01 Jan
-	Goodridge, T.J.	01 Jan
BS	Henderson, A.D.	01 Jan
	1994	
-	Bulmer, R.J.	01 Jan
-	Perry, R.W.	01 Jan
-	Hough, C.C.	29 Apr
-	Morrison, C.P.	29 Apr
-	Murchison, E.A.	01 Sep
-	Blythe, T.S.	01 Sep
-	Wraith, N.	01 Sep
-	Kern, A.S.	01 Sep
-	Lemon, R.W.G.	01 Sep
-	Bakewell, T.D.	01 Sep
-	Jermyn, N.C.	01 Sep
-	Hickman, S.M.	01 Sep
-	Stocker, N.J.	01 Sep
-	Bailey, J.J.	01 Sep
-	Davies, H.C.A.	01 Sep
-	Moorhouse, D.	01 Sep
-	Percey, S.J.	01 Sep
	1995	
-	Ginn, R.N.	01 Jan
-	Heward, A.F.	01 Jan
-	Nicholls, B.A.	01 Jan
-	Richardson, M.C.	01 Jan
-	Smith, S.F.	01 Jan
-	Underwood, P.J.	01 Jan
BS	Watson, P.F.	01 Jan
-	Geldard, M.A.	25 Apr
-	Bestwick, M.C.	25 Apr
-	Bennett, R.W.	25 Apr
-	Bray, M.R.	25 Apr
-	Walker, A.J.	28 Apr
-	Craig, K.M.	28 Apr
-	Ethell, D.R.	28 Apr
-	Hall, S.B.	28 Apr
-	King, R.J.	28 Apr
-	Murns, N.P.	28 Apr
-	Spanner, P.	01 May
-	Page, D.C.M.	01 Sep
-	Daukes, N.M.	01 Sep
-	Dowd, J.W.	01 Sep
-	Hedges, J.W.	01 Sep
-	Liddle, S.J.	01 Sep
-	Murray, W.R.C.	01 Sep
-	Hermer, J.P.	01 Sep
-	Hughes, M.J.	01 Sep
-	Jenkins, G.	01 Sep
-	Taylor, M.A.B.	01 Sep
-	Fuller, S.R.	01 Sep
-	James, P.M.	01 Sep
-	Coomber, J.M.	01 Sep
-	De Reya, A.L.	01 Sep
-	Fraser, G.W.	01 Sep
-	Franks, J.A.	01 Sep
-	Ginnever, M.S.M.	01 Sep
-	Harris, C.C.	01 Sep
-	Milliner, C.L.	01 Sep
-	Roylance, J.F.	01 Sep
-	Thomsett, H.F.J.	01 Sep
-	Twist, M.T.	01 Sep
	1996	
-	Nicoll, S.K.	01 Jan
-	Bourne, P.J.	01 Jan
-	Green, G.E.	01 Jan
-	Hannah, W.F.	01 Jan
-	Kelly, A.P.	01 Jan
-	Rearden, R.J.	01 Jan
-	Tyce, D.J.	01 Jan
-	Brighouse, N.G.	24 Apr
-	Dresner, R.J.	24 Apr
-	Everett, E.J.	24 Apr
-	Moorhouse, E.J.	24 Apr
-	Balmer, G.A.	24 Apr
-	Sutherland, N.	24 Apr

-	Hardy, D.M.	24 Apr
-	Kearney, P.L.	27 Apr
-	Hale, J.N.	27 Apr
-	Plewes, A.B.	27 Apr
-	Sibley, G.P.	27 Apr
-	Lee, S.P.	27 Apr
-	Roddy, M.P.	27 Apr
-	Stafford, D.B.	27 Apr
-	Parry, J.A.	27 Apr
-	Tanner, M.J.	01 Sep
-	Ashton, C.N.	01 Sep
-	Blanchford, D.	01 Sep
-	Read, R.J.	01 Sep
-	Turner, S.A.	01 Sep
-	Bailey, D.S.	01 Sep
-	Harris, T.	01 Sep
-	Hammond, D.E.	01 Sep
-	Ballard, S.A.	01 Sep
-	Beeley, W.T.	01 Sep
-	Campbell, L.G.	01 Sep
-	Cunningham, A.N.	01 Sep
-	Hunter, J.G.	01 Sep
-	Jackson, M.J.A.	01 Sep
-	Kelly, P.M.	01 Sep
-	Mayne, C.W.E.	01 Sep
-	McGhee, C.	01 Sep
-	Paton, C.M.	01 Sep
-	Preston, R.W.	01 Sep
-	Oherlihy, S.I.	01 Sep
-	Lancaster, C.	01 Sep

1997

-	Wilson, A.C.	01 Jan
-	Shergold, P.J.	01 Jan
-	Thompson, G.M.	01 Jan
-	Todd, M.A.	01 Jan
-	Sellar, T.J.	01 Jan
-	Jones, G.J.	01 Jan
-	Tulloch, S.W.	01 Jan
-	Clark, P.A.	01 Jan
-	Gray, J.A.	29 Apr
-	Levine, A.J.	29 Apr
-	Maltby, R.J.	29 Apr
-	Morley, A.	29 Apr
-	Sutton, S.J.	29 Apr
-	Parvin, R.A.	01 May
-	Revens, C.A.	01 May
-	Cole, S.R.	01 May
-	Douglas, A.M.	01 May
-	Fenwick, R.J.	01 May
-	Raeburn, T.J.	01 May
-	Viner, T.R.	01 May
-	Watkins, A.P.L.	01 May
-	Brown, L.A.	01 Sep
-	O'Hara, G.C.	01 Sep
-	Jepson, N.H.M.	01 Sep
-	Stear, T.J.F.	01 Sep
-	Wigham, T.W.	01 Sep
-	May, P.	01 Sep
-	Muddiman, A.R.	01 Sep
-	Raitt, J.E.	01 Sep
-	Whitfield, P.M.	01 Sep
-	Manning, D.	01 Sep
-	Atherton, B.W.	01 Sep
-	Bowra, M.A.	01 Sep
-	Brady, S.P.	01 Sep
-	Chilvers, M.I.	01 Sep
-	Clayton, M.J.	01 Sep
-	Combe, S.A.N.	01 Sep
-	Devereux, M.E.	01 Sep
-	Gordon, M.W.	01 Sep
-	Grainger, A.L.	01 Sep
-	Guy, P.S.	01 Sep
-	Hughes, D.C.	01 Sep
-	Janzen, A.N.	01 Sep
-	Lancashire, A.C.	01 Sep
-	McCabe, G.P.	01 Sep
-	McClay, W.J.	01 Sep
-	Taylor, S.D.	01 Sep

1998

BS	Best, P.	01 Jan
-	Cockton, P.G.	01 Jan
-	Daniel, I.R.	01 Jan
-	Holloway, N.	01 Jan
-	Lugg, J.C.	01 Jan
-	Maddison, J.D.	01 Jan
-	Merchant, J.M.	01 Jan
-	Scott, S.C.	01 Jan
-	Ward, C.D.	01 Jan
-	Watson, R.I.	01 Jan
-	Burrell, A.M.G.	28 Apr
-	Friendship, P.G.	28 Apr
-	Collin, M.	28 Apr
-	Lock, A.G.D.	28 Apr
-	Lee, O.A.	01 May
-	Alderson, R.J.	01 May
-	Churchward, M.J.	01 May
-	Crawford, A.T.S.	01 May
-	Duncan, G.S.	01 May
-	Haw, C.E.	01 May
-	Leach, J.F.J.	01 May
-	Lynch, P.P.	01 May
-	Pruden, I.	01 May
-	Simpson, A.C.	01 May
-	Somerville, N.J.F.	01 May
-	Murphy, K.S.	01 May
-	Williamson, A.K.	01 May
-	Atherton, J.R.	01 Sep
-	Houvenaghel, I.M.	01 Sep
-	Hutchinson, P.I.	01 Sep
-	Cheesman, D.J.E.	01 Sep
-	Wilson, J.G.	01 Sep
-	Baker, M.B.	01 Sep
-	Cantrill, R.J.	01 Sep
-	Coats, D.S.	01 Sep
-	Darling, R.J.C.	01 Sep
-	Fisher, A.G.	01 Sep
-	Jess, A.E.K.	01 Sep
-	Lonsdale, R.J.	01 Sep
-	Mantella, D.N.	01 Sep
-	Masters, N.N.J.	01 Sep
-	McMulkin, J.P.	01 Sep
-	Middleton, C.S.	01 Sep
-	Morgan, C.E.W.	01 Sep
-	Pearson, G.D.	01 Sep
-	Penkman, W.A.V.	01 Sep
-	Raisbeck, A.B.	01 Sep
-	Stemp, J.E.	01 Sep
-	Urry, S.R.	01 Sep

1999

-	Lawton, P.	01 Jan
-	Hadlow, D.K.	01 Jan
-	Clare, J.F.	01 Jan
-	Smith, D.M.	01 Jan
-	Pickard, D.M.	01 Jan
-	Ross, G.	01 Jan
-	Phillips, M.C.	01 Jan
-	Gosney, C.J.	01 Jan
BS	Weston, P.A.	01 Jan
-	Cowan, K.G.	23 Apr
-	Moffat, J.W.	23 Apr
-	Cleaver, J.P.	24 Apr
-	Moran, J.T.	28 Apr
-	Blyth, M.	28 Apr
-	Jenkins, E.J.	28 Apr
-	Davies, C.R.	01 May
-	Alexander, G.D.	01 May
-	Bubb, J.D.	01 May
-	Edmondson, S.P.	01 May
-	Garnham, S.W.	01 May
-	Gibson, A.J.	01 May
-	Hasted, D.	01 May
-	Hill, J.P.	01 May
-	Mawson, J.R.	01 May
-	Pirie, S.K.	01 May
-	Rule, S.J.	01 May
-	Nicholson, D.P.	01 Sep

- Bird, G.M. .... 01 Sep
- Boschi, P.H. .... 01 Sep
- Dennis, J.A. .... 01 Sep
- Fuller, J.B. .... 01 Sep
- Hart, S.J.E. .... 01 Sep
- Johnson, M. .... 01 Sep
- Oden, M. .... 01 Sep
- Selman, T.R. .... 01 Sep
- Street, J.J. .... 01 Sep
- Cambridge, G.A. .... 01 Sep
- Hopkins, R.M.E. .... 01 Sep
- Leyden, T.N. .... 01 Sep
- Martin, N.A. .... 01 Sep
- Ordway, C.N.M.P. .... 01 Sep
- Thompson, D.H. .... 01 Sep
- Howarth, S.J. .... 01 Sep

2000

- Hazelwood, C.D. .... 01 Jan
- Wiseman, G.R. .... 01 Jan
- Garland, A.N. .... 01 Jan
- Howarth, J. .... 01 Jan
- Cooper, N. .... 01 Jan
- Kenneally, S.J. .... 01 Jan
- Westlake, S.R. .... 01 Jan

BS Thornhill, A.P. .... 01 Jan

LIEUTENANTS

1997

- Fomes, C.J.H. .... 23 Apr
- Read, C.D. .... 01 May

1998

- Stonier, P.L. .... 01 Jan
- Baines, G.A. .... 01 Jan
- Adcock, G.E. .... 01 Jan
- Collins, J. .... 01 Jan
- Fitzpatrick, P.S. .... 01 Jan
- Standen, C.A. .... 01 Jan
- Lucas, S.U. .... 01 Jan
- Giles, G.J. .... 01 Jan

BS Grace, N.J. .... 01 Jan

- Price, D.G. .... 01 Jan
- Tapp, S.J. .... 01 Jan
- Sutton, D. .... 01 Apr
- Hulse, A.W. .... 01 Apr
- Hall, C.M.I. .... 01 Apr
- McCulley, S.C. .... 01 Apr
- Howe, S. .... 01 Apr

1999

- Kemp, A.C. .... 01 Apr
- May, D.J. .... 01 Apr

2000

- Clarke, P.M. .... 24 Jan
- Cross, E.J. .... 24 Jan
- Frost, M.J. .... 24 Jan
- Hunt, D. .... 24 Jan
- Robbins, H.V. .... 24 Jan
- Watson, B.R. .... 24 Jan
- Bowyer, R.J. .... 01 May
- Griffiths, N.A. .... 01 May

SECOND LIEUTENANTS(GRAD)

- Atkinson, N.C. .... 29 Apr
- Edye, R.F. .... 29 Apr
- Foster, N.P. .... 29 Apr
- Gray, K.D. .... 29 Apr
- Hardie, M.J. .... 29 Apr
- Howard, R.D. .... 29 Apr
- Mears, R.J. .... 29 Apr
- Smith, G.K. .... 29 Apr
- Thompson, J.P.B. .... 29 Apr
- Todd, J.W. .... 29 Apr
- Totten, P.M. .... 29 Apr
- Waite, J.N. .... 01 May
- Foster, B. .... 08 May
- Oura, A.N. .... 02 Sep
- Turner, A.R. .... 02 Sep
- Brain, W.J. .... 02 Sep
- Durup, J.M.S. .... 02 Sep
- Huntingford, D.J. .... 02 Sep
- Kelly, T.J. .... 02 Sep
- MacOwan, A.S. .... 02 Sep

1998

- Muncer, R.A. .... 02 Sep
- Todd, O.J. .... 02 Sep
- Turner, H.C.J. .... 02 Sep
- Ward, A.J. .... 02 Sep

1999

- Black, E.J. .... 28 Apr
- Cavill, N.R.D. .... 28 Apr
- Hamilton, A.O.F. .... 28 Apr
- Hanson, S.C. .... 28 Apr
- Hart, A.P.W. .... 28 Apr
- Lindsay, J.M. .... 28 Apr
- Perrin, M.S. .... 28 Apr
- Rose, A. .... 28 Apr
- Roskilly, M. .... 28 Apr
- Samuel, C.D.R. .... 28 Apr
- Scanlon, M.J. .... 28 Apr
- Tamlyn, S.J. .... 28 Apr
- Bonney, J.E. .... 01 Sep
- Brown, J.R. .... 01 Sep
- Darley, M.E. .... 01 Sep
- Dean, M.C. .... 01 Sep
- Forbes, D.G. .... 01 Sep
- Francis, T.D.H. .... 01 Sep
- Halsted, B.E. .... 01 Sep
- Hester, J.F.W. .... 01 Sep
- Hopkins, R. .... 01 Sep
- Thompson, P.L. .... 01 Sep
- Mansergh, A.C. .... 01 Sep
- Maynard, P.A. .... 01 Sep
- Morgan, H.L. .... 01 Sep
- Pennington, C.E. .... 01 Sep
- Pounder, G.W.J. .... 01 Sep
- Robinson, P.J.O. .... 01 Sep
- Treffry-Kingdom, M.J.D. .... 01 Sep
- Wallace, S.P. .... 01 Sep
- Liva, A.J. .... 01 Sep

SECOND LIEUTENANTS

1996

- Taylor, C.N.J. .... 04 Sep

1997

- Norton, T.C.H. .... 01 Sep

1998

- Wallace, R.S. .... 29 Apr
- Brading, R.D. .... 02 Sep
- Jones, R.P.M. .... 02 Sep

1999

- O'Sullivan, M.R.J. ..... 01 Sep
- Pinckney, M.R.N. .... 01 Sep

QUEEN ALEXANDRA'S ROYAL NAVAL NURSING SERVICE

CAPTAIN

1996
Hambling, P.M. .... 20 Dec

1999
Brown, J.C. .... 31 Dec

COMMANDER

1998
Bowen, M. .... 31 Dec

1999
Weall, E.M. .... 31 Dec

LIEUTENANT COMMANDER

1988
Butcher, L.J. .... 08 Jan
Gibbon, L. .... 05 Oct

1991
Onions, J.M. .... 11 Feb

1992
Smith, B.C. .... 01 Oct

1996
Duke, R.M. .... 31 Dec

1997
Allkins, H.L. .... 31 Dec

1999
Broom, N.J. .... 01 Oct

LIEUTENANT COMMANDER
(Medium Career Commission)

1998
McLaughlan, C.L. .... 01 Oct
Williams, C.M.A. .... 01 Oct

1999
Watts, M.D. .... 01 Oct
Howes, N.J. .... 01 Oct
Stinton, C.A. .... 01 Oct

LIEUTENANT COMMANDER
(Short Career Commission)

1997
Kennedy, I.J. .... 31 Mar

1999
Thain, J.C. .... 31 Mar

LIEUTENANT
(Medium Career Commission)

McKillop, H.E.L. .... 14 Feb

1991
England, L. .... 11 Jan
Robson, C.J. .... 01 Mar
Aldwinckle, T.W. .... 23 Jun

1986
Spencer, S.J. .... 12 Oct

1994
Knight, D.J. .... 18 Jan
Hainsworth, P.M. .... 30 Mar

1995
Ferguson, V.S. .... 21 Jan
Piper, N.D. .... 23 Nov

LIEUTENANT
(Short Career Commission)

1986
Rankin, S.J. .... 17 Jul

1992
Dilloway, P.J. .... 07 Dec

1993
Ouvry, J.E.D. .... 25 Mar

Coleman, A.A. .... 18 Jun

1994

Float, S.M. .... 18 Jan
Lang, J.S. .... 30 Sep
Hofman, A.J. .... 26 Oct

1995

Munden, C.S. .... 07 Jul

1996

Johnson, V. .... 25 Jan
Harriman, S.J. .... 20 Feb
Bagnall, S.A.E. .... 28 May
James, K.J. .... 26 Nov

1997

Armstrong, M.A. .... 28 Apr
Newman, S.A. .... 18 Aug
Wilkinson, G. .... 06 Oct
Beare, A.L. .... 10 Oct

1998

Downey, K. .... 03 Feb
Gardner, S.L. .... 05 Nov
Carnell, R.P. .... 06 Nov
Blakeley, A.L. .... 17 Nov

1999

Hurley, K.A. .... 26 May
Taylor, L.M. .... 05 Jul
Newby Stubbs, R.L. .... 15 Aug
France, S.C. .... 25 Aug
Morgan, R.S. .... 06 Sep
Mallard, E. .... 07 Nov
Chilvers, L.D. .... 14 Nov

SUB LIEUTENANT

1996

Brown, B.C. .... 11 Jun
Hyde, D.M. .... 22 Jun
Tolley, D.M. .... 25 Jul
Lokai, D.S. .... 14 Sep
Sutherland, G. .... 25 Oct
Simpson, P.E. .... 27 Oct

1997

Procter, K.J. .... 15 Jan
Middleton, J.E. .... 26 Apr
McFarlane, R.W.A. .... 02 Jul
Bryce, F.L.S. .... 16 Jul

KEY ROYAL NAVAL PERSONNEL, ATTACHES AND ADVISERS

(See Sec. 1 for Admiralty Board Members and Defence Council Members)

COMMANDERS-IN-CHIEF, FLAG OFFICERS AND OTHER SENIOR OFFICERS

Command or Station	*Officers*	*Address*
NAVAL HOME COMMAND	Second Sea Lord and Commander in Chief Naval Home Command Vice Admiral P Spencer ADC	Victory Building HM Naval Base PORTSMOUTH PO1 3LS
	Chief of Staff to Second Sea Lord and Commander in Chief Naval Home Command Rear Admiral P A Dunt	
FLEET	Commander-in-Chief Fleet, Commander-in-Chief East Atlantic and Commander Allied Naval Forces North Europe Admiral Sir Nigel Essenhigh KCB	Northwood HQ Sandy Lane NORTHWOOD Middlesex HA6 3HP
	Deputy Commander Fleet/Chief of Staff Vice Admiral F M Malbon	
	Chief of staff (Coperate Development) Rear Admiral J Reave	
	Commander United Kingdom Task Group and Commander Anti Submarine Warfare Striking Force Rear Admiral S R Meyer	BFPO 200
	Commander Amphibious Task Group and Commander UK/NL Amphibious Striking Force Commodore N S R Kilgour	RM Barracks Stonehouse PLYMOUTH PL1 3QS
SURFACE FLOTILLA	Flag Officer Surface Flotilla Rear Admiral I A Forbes CBE Deputy Flag Officer Surface Flotilla Commodore P W Herington	Jago Road HM Naval Base PORTSMOUTH PO1 3NB
	Commodore Mine Warfare & Patrol Vessels, Diving & Fishery Protection Commodore R A I Goldman	HM Naval Base PORTSMOUTH PO1 3NH
MARITIME AVIATION	Air Officer Commanding 3 Group/Flag Officer Maritime Aviation Rear Admiral I R Henderson CBE	hqstc RAF High Wycombe Buckinghamshire HP14 4UE
	Commodore Naval Aviation Commodore C H T Clayton	Yeovilton ILCHESTER Somerset BA22 8HL

Command or Station	*Officers*	*Address*
SUBMARINES	Flag Officer Submarines, Chief of Staff Operations, Commander Submarines East Atlantic and Commander Submarine Forces North Rear Admiral R P Stevens CB	Northwood HQ Sandy Lane NORTHWOOD Middlesex HA6 3HP
	Deputy Flag Officer Submarines Commodore D J Russell	
SEA TRAINING	Flag Officer Sea Training Rear Admiral A K Backus OBE	Grenville Block HMS DRAKE Devonport PLYMOUTH PL2 2BG
ROYAL MARINES	Commandant General Major General R H G Fulton	HQRM West Battery Whale Island PORTSMOUTH PO2 8DX
PORTSMOUTH	Naval Base Commander Commodore S W Graham OBE	HM Naval Base PORTSMOUTH Hants PO1 3LT
PLYMOUTH	Naval Base Commander Commodore R F Cheadle	HM Naval Base DEVONPORT Devon PL2 2BG
SCOTLAND NORTHERN ENGLAND AND NORTHERN IRELAND	Flag Officer Scotland Northern England and Northern Ireland Naval Base Commander Clyde Rear Admiral A M Gregory, OBE	HM Naval Base Clyde Faslane HELENSBURGH Dunbartonshire G84 8HL
CLYDE	Director Naval Base Commodore R J Lord	HM Naval Base Clyde Faslane HELENSBURGH Dunbartonshire G84 8HL
GIBRALTAR	Commander British Forces Gibraltar, and COMGIBMED Commodore A M Willmett	BFPO 52

NATO

Deputy SACLANT	Admiral Sir James Perowne KBE
UK Military Representative Brussels	Vice Admiral Sir Paul Haddacks KCB
UK National Liaison Representative to SACLANT	Commodore D J Anthony MBE
Assistant Chief of Staff (Policy & Requirements) to the Supreme Allied Commander, Europe	Rear Admiral A.B. Gough CB
Chief of Staff to Commander Allied Naval Forces Southern Europe	Rear Admiral R J Lippiett MBE
COMGIBMED	Commodore A M Willmett
CINCEASTLANT and COMNAVNORTH	Admiral Sir Nigel Essenhigh KCB
COMUKTG/COMASWSF	Rear Admiral S R Meyer
COMUKNLPHIBGRU	Commodore R S Ainsley
Dep COMSTRIKFORSOUTH	Rear Admiral A K Dymock
DOM HQ AFCENT	Rear Admiral M Stanhope
COS JHQ NORTH	Major General D Wilson OBE

MINISTRY OF DEFENCE (NAVY DEPARTMENT)

Chief of the Naval Staff and First Sea Lord	Admiral Sir Michael Boyce GCB, OBE, ADC
Assistant Chief of Naval Staff	Rear Admiral J M Burnell-Nugent CBE
Second Sea Lord and Commander in Chief Naval Home Command	Vice Admiral P Spencer ADC
Chief of Staff to 2SL/CNH	Rear Admiral P A Dunt
Naval Secretary/Director General Naval Manning/ CE NMA	Rear Admiral J M de Halpert
Flag Officer Training and Recruiting/ CE NRTA	Rear Admiral J Chadwick
CE NBSA/Chief of Fleet Support	Rear Admiral B B Perowne
Director General Defence Logistics (Operations and Business Development)	Rear Admiral M G Wood CBE
Controller of the Navy	Rear Admiral N C F Guild
Hydrographer of the Navy	Rear Admiral J P Clarke CB, LVO, MBE

HEADS OF SERVICE (ROYAL NAVY)

Medical Director General (N)	Surgeon Rear Admiral I L Jenkins CVO, QHS
Director Naval Dental Services	Surgeon Commodore J. Hargraves QHDS, Royal Navy
Director Naval Nursing Services & Matron-in-Chief	Captain J C Brown ARRC, QHNS, QARNNS
Director General Naval Chaplaincy Services and Chaplain of the Fleet	The Venerable S J Golding QHC
Chief Naval Warfare Officer	Vice Admiral F M Malbon
Chief Naval Engineer Officer	Rear Admiral J Chadwick
Chief Naval Supply Officer	Rear Admiral R B Lees

FLAG OFFICERS CURRENTLY SERVING IN THE MINISTRY OF DEFENCE CENTRAL AND OPERATIONAL STAFFS

Vice Chief of Defence Staff	Admiral Sir Peter Abbott GBE, KCB
Chief of Defence Intelligence	Vice Admiral Sir Alan West KCB, DSC
Deputy Chief of Defence Staff (Equipment Capability)	Vice Admiral Sir Jeremy Blackham KCB
Chief of Joint Operations	Vice Admiral Sir Ian Garnet KCB
Capability Manager (Strategic Deployment)	Rear Admiral R G J Ward
Chief of Staff/ Surgeon General	Rear Admiral C D Stanford
Director General Joint Doctrine and Concepts	Major General A A Milton OBE
Assistant Chief of the Defence Staff, (Operations)	Rear Admiral S Moore CB

FLAG OFFICERS CURRENTLY SERVING IN OTHER APPOINTMENTS

Commandant RCDS	Acting Vice Admiral J H S McAnally LVO CB
Senior Directing Staff (Navy) RCDS	Rear Admiral H W Rickard CBE

ATTACHES AND ADVISERS

NAVAL ATTACHES IN FOREIGN COUNTRIES

Service Mail
All official service mail is to be forwarded in accordance with current instructions.

OFFICERS PROVIDING A NAVAL SERVICE IN FOREIGN COUNTRIES

Argentina
Naval & Air Attaché
Buenos Aires

Austria
Defence Attaché
Vienna

Bahrain
Defence Attaché
Manama

Belgium
Defence Attaché
Brussels

Brazil
Naval Attaché
Brasilia

Bulgaria
Defence Attaché
Sofia

Chile
Defence Attaché
Santiago

China
Naval Attaché
Peking

Colombia
Defence Attaché
Bogota

Croatia
Defence Attaché
Zagreb

Czech Republic
Defence Attaché
Prague

Denmark
Defence Attaché
Copenhagen

Egypt
Naval & Air Attaché
Cairo

Finland
Defence Attaché
Helsinki

France
Naval Attaché
Paris

Georgia
Defence Attaché
Tbilisi

Germany
Naval Attaché
Bonn

Greece
Naval & Air Attaché
Athens

Guatemala
Defence Attaché
Guatemala City

Hungary
Defence Attaché
Budapest

Indonesia
Defence Attaché
Jakarta

Irish Republic
Defence Attaché
Dublin

Israel
Naval & Air Attaché
Tel Aviv

Italy
Naval Attaché
Rome

Japan
Defence & Naval Attaché
Tokyo

Jordan
Defence, Naval & Military Attaché
Amman

Korea
Naval & Air Attaché
Seoul

Kuwait
Defence Attaché
Kuwait City

Latvia
Defence Attaché
Riga

Lebanon
Defence Attaché
Beirut

Macedonia
Defence Attaché
Skopje

Mexico
Defence Attaché
Mexico City

Morocco
Defence Attaché
Rabat

Nepal
Defence Attaché
Kathmandu

Netherlands
Defence & Naval Attaché
The Hague

Norway
Defence & Naval Attaché
Oslo

Oman
Naval & Air Attaché
Muscat

Philippines
Defence Attaché
Manila

Poland
Naval & Military Attaché
Warsaw

Portugal
Defence Attaché
Lisbon

Qatar
Defence Attaché
Doha

Romania
Defence Attaché
Bucharest

Russia
Naval Attaché
Assistant Naval Attaché
Moscow

Saudi Arabia
Naval Attaché
Riyadh

Slovakia
Defence Attaché
Bratislava

Spain
Defence & Naval Attaché
Madrid

Sweden
Naval & Military Attaché
Stockholm

Switzerland
Defence Attaché
Berne

Syria
Defence Attaché
Damascus

Thailand
Defence Attaché
Bangkok

Turkey
Naval & Air Attaché
Ankara

Ukraine
Defence Attaché
Kiev

United Arab Emirates
Defence Attaché
Abu Dhabi

United States of America
Naval Attaché
Assistant Naval Attaché
Washington DC

Venezuela
Defence Attaché
Caracas

Yugoslavia (Federal Republic)
Defence Attaché
Belgrade
(Embassy remains closed for the forseeable future)
[Info dated April 2000]

OFFICERS PROVIDING A NAVAL SERVICE IN COMMONWEALTH COUNTRIES

Australia
Defence & Naval Adviser
Canberra

Barbados
Defence Adviser
Bridgetown

Brunei
Defence Adviser
Bandar Seri Begawan

Canada
Naval & Air Adviser
Ottawa

Cyprus
Defence Adviser
Nicosia

Ghana
Defence Adviser
Accra

India
Naval and Air Adviser
New Delhi

Jamaica
Defence Adviser
Kingston

Kenya
Defence Adviser
Nairobi

Malaysia
Defence Adviser
Kuala Lumpur

New Zealand
Defence Adviser
Wellington

Nigeria
Defence Adviser
Abuja

Pakistan
Naval & Air Adviser
Islamabad

Singapore
Assistant Defence Adviser & Royal Navy Liaison Officer
Singapore

South Africa
Naval & Air Adviser
Pretoria

Sri Lanka
Defence Adviser
Colombo

Uganda
Defence Adviser
Kampala

Zimbabwe
Defence Adviser
Harare

NON-RESIDENTIAL ACCREDITATIONS

Attaches accredited to the following countries are non-residential

Albania
(Is resident Macedonia)

Algeria
(Is resident London (DOMA))

Angola
(Is resident London (DOMA))

Anguilla
(Is resident Barbados)

Antigua & Barbuda
(Is resident Barbados)

Armenia
(Is resident Georgia)

Azerbaijan
(Is resident Georgia)

Bahamas
(Is resident Jamaica)

Bangladesh
(Is resident India)

Belarus
(Is resident Russia)

Belize
(Is resident Mexico)

Bermuda
(Is resident USA)

Botswana
(Is resident Zimbabwe)

British Virgin Islands
(Is resident Barbados)

Burundi
(Is resident Uganda)

Cayman Islands
(Is resident Jamaica)

Cuba
(Is resident Mexico)

Curacao
(Is resident Barbados)

Dominica
(Is resident Barbados)

Ecuador
(Is resident Venezuela)

El Salvador
(Is resident Guatemala)

Eritrea
(Is resident Kenya)

Estonia
(Is resident Finland)

Ethiopia
(Is resident Kenya)

Fiji
(Is resident New Zealand)

Granada
(Is resident Barbados)

Guadeloupe
(Is resident Barbados)

Guyana
(Is resident Barbados)

Honduras
(Is resident Guatemala)

Ivory Coast
(Is resident Ghana)

Kazakhstan
(Is resident Russia)

Kyrgyzstan
(Is resident Russia)

Lesotho
(Is resident South Africa)

Lithuania
(Is resident Latvia)

Luxembourg
(Is resident Belgium)

Madagascar
(Is resident London (DOMA))

Malawi
(Is resident Zimbabwe)

Mauritania
(Is resident Morocco)

Mauritius
(Is resident Kenya)

Moldova
(Is resident Romania)

Mongolia
(Is resident China)

Montserrat
(Is resident Barbados)

Mozambique
(Is resident Zimbabwe)

Namibia
(Is resident South Africa)

Nicaragua
(Is resident Guatemala)

Panama
(Is resident Venezuela)

Papua New Guinea
(Is resident Australia)

Paraguay
(Is resident Argentina)

Peru
(Is resident Colombia)

Rwanda
(Is resident Uganda)

St Kitts & Nevis
(Is resident Barbados)

St Lucia
(Is resident Barbabos)

St Vincent
(Is resident Barbados)

Senegal
(Is resident Morocco)

Seychelles
(Is resident Kenya)

Sierra Leone
(Is resident Ghana)

Slovenia
(Is resident Austria)

Suriname
(Is resident Barbados)

Swaziland
(Is resident South Africa)

Tajikistan
(Is resident Russia)

Tanzania
(Kenya)

Togo
(Is resident Ghana)

Trinidad & Tobago
(Is resident Barbados)

Tunisia
(Is resident London (DOMA))

Turkmenistan
(Is resident Russia)

Turks & Caicos Islands
(Is resident Jamaica)

Uruguay
(Is resident Argentina)

Uzbekistan
(Is resident Russia)

Vietnam
(Is resident Malaysia)

Yemen
(Is resident Saudi Arabia)

Zambia
(Is resident London (DOMA))

INTERPRETERS

Name	Rank	Date Of Qualifying or Re-qualifying
ARABIC		
Pearce, J.K.C.	CAPT	Mar 90
Vosper, I.A.	CDR	Feb 73
CHINESE		
Gopsill, B.R.	LT CDR	Sep 84
Rayner, B.N.	CAPT	Dec 83
White, S.N.	CDR	Sep 90
DUTCH		
Davies, A.R.	CDR	Mar 84
Ewence, M.W.	CDR	Mar 88
Shipperley, I.	CDR	Oct 93
FRENCH		
Airey, S.E.	CDR	Mar 80
Craven, J.A.G.	LT CDR	Mar 90
Cree, M.C.	CDR	Feb 95
Dermody, R.T.	SLT	Mar 98
Ewence, M.W.	CDR	Mar 98
Fieldsend, M.A.	LT CDR	May 95
Gubbins, V.R.	CDR	Jul 96
Hollins, R.P.	LT CDR	Apr 99
Jeffrey, I.	CDR	Sep 72
Keefe, S-A.	LT CDR	Mar 89
Kettle, R.A.	MAJ	Jun 98
Mansergh, M.P.	CDR	Mar 91
Newell, J.M.	CDR	Mar 89
Stonor, P.F.A.	CDR	Mar 88
Stride, J.A.	LT	Apr 99
Turner, J.S.H.	LT CDR	Mar 94
Young, I.J.	A/CDR	Mar 93
Bussey, E.L	LT	Apr 99
GERMAN		
Airey, S.E.	CDR	Apr 81
Dashfield, A.K.	SURG CDR	Mar 90
Davis, P.B.	LT CDR	Mar 92
Durston, D.H.	CDR	Mar 83
Eberle, P.J.F.	CDRE	Mar 77
Finch, B.A.	LT	Mar 96
Hill, D.	LT CDR	Mar 98
Hollins, R.P.	LT CDR	Mar 98
Knight, P.J.	LT CDR	Apr 97
Massey, A.M.	CDRE	Mar 80
Nurse, M.T.	LT CDR	Mar 86

Name	Rank	Date Of Qualifying or Re-qualifying
Robertson Gopffarth, A.A.J.	LT	Mar 95
Robin, C.C.E.	LT CDR	Mar 98
Sparke, P.R.W.	LT CDR	Mar 92
Williams, N.L.	CAPT	Mar 85
Wiseman, W.T.	CDR	May 87
Pitcher, P.P	LT	Nov 97
ITALIAN		
Jeffrey, I.	CDR	Oct 97
JAPANESE		
Chelton, S.R.L.	CDR	Oct 88
NORWEGIAN		
Stallion, I.M.	CDR	Mar 79
Taylor, W.J.	LT COL	Mar 91
PORTUGUESE		
Harrison, R.A.	CDR	Mar 83
Pannett, L.W.	LT	Jul 96
RUSSIAN		
Airey, S.E.	CDR	Mar 94
Connolly, C.J.	LT CDR	Mar 89
Davies, A.R.	CDR	Mar 89
Drewett, R.E., *MBE*	CDR	Mar 91
Fairbrass, J.E.	LT CDR	Mar 94
Fields, D.G.	LT CDR	Mar 90
Foreman, J.L.R.	LT CDR	Mar 92
Green, T.J.	CDR	Mar 89
Gwillim, V.G.	MAJ	Mar 94
Hodgson, T.C., *MBE*	CDR	Mar 94
Lister, S.R.	CAPT	Mar 90
McTear, K.	LT CDR	Mar 91
Newton, C.A.	CDR	Mar 94
Ross, A.D.	SLT	Nov 99
Simpson, E.J.	LT	Mar 91
Watson, C.C.	LT CDR	Mar 88
Peters, W.R	LT	Mar 00
SPANISH		
Adam, I.K.	LT CDR	Mar 91
Bussey, E.L.	LT	Mar 98
Curry, B.R.	MAJ	Mar 98
Dedman, N.J.K.	CDR	Mar 86
Eedle, R.J.	LT CDR	Sep 98

Name	Rank	Date Of Qualifying or Re-qualifying
Graham, J.E.	CDR	Jun 99
Harrison, C.A.	LT CDR	Mar 89
Humphrys, J.A.	CDR	Mar 98
Lynch, R.D.F.	LT	Mar 91
McGlory, S.J.	LT	Mar 94
McLennan, R.G.	CDR	Mar 94
Pacey, P.J.	CAPT	Jun 99
Sanguinetti, H.R.	CDR	Mar 90
Turner, J.S.H.	LT CDR	Nov 94
Wolfe, D.E.	CDR	Mar 95

SWEDISH

Name	Rank	Date Of Qualifying or Re-qualifying
Rigby, J.C.	LT CDR	Mar 86

HM SHORE ESTABLISHMENTS

CAMBRIDGE
HMS CAMBRIDGE
Wembury
nr *PLYMOUTH*
Devon
PL9 0AZ

CALEDONIA
HMS CALEDONIA
ROSYTH
FIFE
SCOTLAND
KY11 2XH

CENTURION
CENTURION BUILDING
GOSPORT
Hants
PO13 9XA

COLLINGWOOD
HMS COLLINGWOOD
Newgate Lane
FAREHAM
Hants
PO14 1AS

DARTMOUTH BRNC
Britannia Royal Naval College
DARTMOUTH
Devon
TQ6 0HJ

DRAKE
HMS DRAKE
PLYMOUTH
Devon
PL2 2BG

DRYAD
HMS DRYAD
Southwick
Fareham
Hants
PO17 6EJ

EXCELLENT
HMS EXCELLENT
Whale Island
PORTSMOUTH
Hants
PO2 8ER

FOREST MOOR
HMS FOREST MOOR
Menwith Hill Road
Darley
HARROGATE
HG3 2RE

GANNET
HMS GANNET
RNAS Prestwick
Greensite
MONKTON
Ayrshire
KA9 2RZ

HERON
RNAS YEOVILTON
Ilchester
Nr YEOVIL
Somerset
BA22 8HT

NELSON
HMS NELSON
PORTSMOUTH
Hants
PO1 3HH

NEPTUNE CFS
HMS NEPTUNE
HM Naval Base Clyde
FASLANE
Argyll and Bute
Scotland
G84 8HL

RALEIGH
HMS RALEIGH
TORPOINT
Cornwall
PL11 2PD

SEAHAWK
RNAS CULDROSE
HELSTON
Cornwall
TR12 7RH

SULTAN
HMS SULTAN
GOSPORT
Hants
PO12 3BY

SULTAN AIB
Admiralty Interview Board
HMS SULTAN
GOSPORT
Hants
PO12 3BY

TEMERAIRE
HMS TEMERAIRE
Burnaby Road
PORTSMOUTH
Hants
PO1 2HB

VICTORY
HMS VICTORY
HM Naval Base
PORTSMOUTH
Hants
PO1 3PZ

JSU NORTHWOOD
JOINT SUPPORT UNIT
NORTHWOOD
Middlesex
HA6 3HP

HM SHIPS

ALDERNEY (Island)
BFPO 203
LT CDR .... X A S Barber

ANGLESEY (Island)
BFPO 207
LT CDR .... X D J Wyatt

ARCHER (P2000)
BFPO 208
LT .... X I C Wiseman

ARGYLL (Type 23)
BFPO 210
CDR .... X R C R Wellesley

ARK ROYAL (Invincible)
BFPO 212
CDR .... X T M Dannatt

ATHERSTONE (Hunt)
BFPO 215
LT CDR .... X M T G Durkin

BANGOR (Sandown)
BFPO 222
LT CDR .... X P T Raisbeck

BEAGLE (Bulldog)
BFPO 224
LT CDR .... X D B Turner

BERKELEY (Hunt)
BFPO 226
LT CDR .... X R C Bowbrick

BICESTER (Hunt)
BFPO 227
CDR .... X R M Tuppen

BITER (P2000)
BFPO 229
LT .... X J P Howe

BLAZER (P2000)
BFPO 231
LT .... X P N E Adams

BRECON (Hunt)
BFPO 235
LT .... X A D H Rackham

BRIDPORT (Sandown)
BFPO 236
LT CDR .... X D J Bewick

BROCKLESBY (Hunt)
BFPO 241
LT CDR .... X A P M Rolph

BULLDOG (Bulldog)
BFPO 242
LT CDR .... X D I Sage

CAMPBELTOWN (Type 22)
BFPO 248
CAPT .... X T R Harris

CARDIFF (Type 42)
BFPO 249
CAPT .... X N Morisetti

CATTISTOCK (Hunt)
BFPO 251
LT CDR .... X S Holt

CHARGER (P2000)
BFPO 252
LT .... X R K Giles

CHATHAM (Type 22)
BFPO 253
CAPT .... X G M Zambellas

CHIDDINGFOLD (Hunt)
BFPO 254
LT CDR .... X C R Fulton

CORNWALL (Type 22)
BFPO 256
CAPT .... X T P McClement OBE

COTTESMORE (Hunt)
BFPO 257
LT .... X A W Percival

COVENTRY (Type 22)
BFPO 259
CAPT .... X P A Jones

CROMER (Sandown)
BFPO 260
LT CDR .... X N J Hare

CUMBERLAND (Type 22)
BFPO 261
CAPT .... X D J Cooke MBE

DASHER (P2000)
BFPO 271
LT .... X D A Bassett

DULVERTON (Hunt)
BFPO 273
LT .... X D P Swigciski

DUMBARTON CASTLE (Castle)
BFPO 274
LT CDR .... X J L R Foreman

EDINBURGH (Type 42)
BFPO 277
CDR .... X S J N Kings MBE

ENDURANCE (Ice patrol)
BFPO 279
CAPT .... X A P Dickson

EXAMPLE (P2000)
BFPO 281
LT .... X M Raeburn

EXETER (Type 42)
BFPO 278
CDR .... X C M Richards

EXPLOIT (P2000)
BFPO 285
LT .... X P J Douglas

EXPLORER (P2000)
BFPO 280
LT .... X E G Ahlgren

EXPRESS (P2000)
BFPO 282
LT .... X D H Morgan

FEARLESS (Fearless)
BFPO 283
CAPT .... X C J Parry

GLASGOW (Type 42)
BFPO 287
CDR .... X A R Ireland

GLEANER (Gleaner)
BFPO 288
LT .... X J D Holmes

GLOUCESTER (Type 42)
BFPO 289
CDR .... X P R Cook

GRAFTON (Type 23)
BFPO 291
CDR .... X H R Sanguinetti

GRIMSBY (Sandown)
BFPO 292
LT CDR .... X T J Lewis

GUERNSEY (Island)
BFPO 290
LT CDR .... X G A Robinson

HERALD (Hecla)
BFPO 296
CDR .... X D S J Tilley

HURWORTH (Hunt)
BFPO 300
LT CDR .... X T A Johnston

ILLUSTRIOUS (Invincible)
BFPO 305
CAPT .... X C R Style

INVERNESS (Sandown)
BFPO 307
LT CDR .... X A J Burton

INVINCIBLE (Invincible)
BFPO 308
CAPT .... X R A I McLean OBE

IRON DUKE (Type 23)
BFPO 309
CDR .... X T F McBarnet

KENT (Type 23)
BFPO 318
CDR .... X J R H Clink

LANCASTER (Type 23)
BFPO 323
CDR .... X R J F Buckland

LEDBURY (Hunt)
BFPO 324
LT CDR .... X D C Robertson

LEEDS CASTLE (Castle)
BFPO 325
LT CDR .... X P K Milburn

LINDISFARNE (Island)
BFPO 326
LT CDR .... X J A P White

LIVERPOOL (Type 42)
BFPO 327
CAPT .... X R C Twitchen

MANCHESTER (Type 42)
BFPO 331
CDR .... X R A M Brown OBE

MARLBOROUGH (Type 23)
BFPO 333
CAPT .... X A J Rix

MIDDLETON (Hunt)
BFPO 335
LT CDR .... X R K Thomas

MONMOUTH (Type 23)
BFPO 338
CDR .... X T M Stockings

MONTROSE (Type 23)
BFPO 339
CAPT .... X R G Cooling

NEWCASTLE (Type 42)
BFPO 343
CDR .... X S J Pearson

NORFOLK (Type 23)
BFPO 344
CDR .... X L D Smallman

NORTHUMBERLAND (Type 23)
BFPO 345
CDR .... X S R McQuaker

NOTTINGHAM (Type 42)
BFPO 346
LT CDR .... X G T Collighan

OCEAN (Ocean)
BFPO 350
CAPT .... X S Lidbitter

ORWELL (River)
BFPO 355
LT .... X I B Clarke

PEMBROKE (Sandown)
BFPO 357
LT CDR .... X B Mair

PENZANCE (Sandown)
BFPO 358
LT CDR .... X S E Kilby

PUNCHER (P2000)
BFPO 362
LT .... X G W D Ruddock

PURSUER (P2000)
BFPO 363
LT .... X M F Pearson

QUORN (Hunt)
BFPO 366
LT CDR .... X J A Scott

RAIDER (P2000)
BFPO 377
LT .... X P J R Schreier

RANGER (P2000)
BFPO 369
LT CDR .... X J E Davison

RICHMOND (Type 23)
BFPO 375
CDR .... X A J Adams

ROEBUCK (Roebuck)
BFPO 376
LT CDR .... X G D Turnbull

SANDOWN (Sandown)
BFPO 379
LT CDR .... X J R G Abernethy

SCEPTRE (Swiftsure)
BFPO 380
CDR .... X P J Titterton

SCOTT (Scott)
BFPO 381
CDR .... X T K Horne

SHEFFIELD (Type 22)
BFPO 383
CDR .... X T M Lowe

SHETLAND (Island)
BFPO 385
LT CDR .... X T J L Williamson MVO

SMITER (P2000)
BFPO 387
LT .... X D J MacKinnon

SOMERSET (Type 23)
BFPO 395
CDR .... X P A McAlpine

SOUTHAMPTON (Type 42)
BFPO 389
CDR .... X M G Trevor

SOVEREIGN (Swiftsure)
BFPO 390
CDR .... X N J Hughes

SPARTAN (Swiftsure)
BFPO 391
LT CDR .... E G A Brough

SPLENDID (Swiftsure)
BFPO 393
CDR .... X R D J Barker OBE

SUPERB (Swiftsure)
BFPO 396
CDR .... X D J Pollock

SUTHERLAND (Type 23)
BFPO 398
CDR .... X M R B Wallace

TALENT (Trafalgar)
BFPO 401
CDR .... X S J Shield

TIRELESS (Trafalgar)
BFPO 402
CDR .... X M J Hawthorne

TORBAY (Trafalgar)
BFPO 403
LT CDR .... E S R Aiken

TRACKER (P2000)
BFPO 409
LT .... X B M Stephen

TRAFALGAR (Trafalgar)
BFPO 404
CDR .... X J S Weale

TRENCHANT (Trafalgar)
BFPO 405
CDR .... E M J Williams

TRIUMPH (Trafalgar)
BFPO 406
CDR .... X P J A Buckley

TRUMPETER (P2000)
BFPO 407
LT .... X C Wood

TURBULENT (Trafalgar)
BFPO 408
CDR .... X S W Garrett

VANGUARD(PORT) (Trident)
BFPO 418
CDR .... X K N M Evans

VENGEANCE(PORT) (Trident)
BFPO 421
CDR .... X S W Upright

VICTORIOUS(PORT) (Trident)
BFPO 419
CDR .... X R M Allen

VICTORIOUS(STBD) (Trident)
BFPO 419
CDR .... X P W McDonnell

VIGILANT(PORT) (Trident)
BFPO 420
CDR .... X J J Cutt

VIGILANT(STBD) (Trident)
BFPO 420
CDR .... X T J Green

WALNEY (Sandown)
BFPO 423
LT CDR .... X A K Waddington

WESTMINSTER (Type 23)
BFPO 426
CDR .... X P J Thicknesse

YORK (Type 42)
BFPO 430
CDR .... X S P Porter

RN FISHERY PROTECTION & MINE COUNTERMEASURES SQUADRONS

FIRST MCM SQN
CDR .... X J D D Murphie

SECOND MCM SQN
CDR .... X D N Bone

THIRD MCM SQN
CDR .... X C M L Clarke

FISHERY PROTECTION SQN
CDR .... X M W Butcher MBE

FIRST PATROL BOAT SQUADRON
CDR .... X N J Blaxeby

ROYAL NAVAL AIR SQUADRONS

CHFHQ
CDR .... X M D Salter

700M SQN CULDROSE
LT CDR .... X P Cruddgington AFC

702 SQN HERON
LT CDR .... X M Sheehan

705 SQN RAF SHAWBURY
LT CDR .... X S Burgess

750 SQN CULDROSE (Jetsteam)
LT CDR .... X S P Powell

771 SQN CULDROSE (Sea King)
LT CDR .... X D Whitehead

800 SQN HERON (Sea Harrier)
BFPO 200
LT CDR .... X T C Eastaugh

801 SQN HERON (Sea Harrier)
BFPO 200
LT CDR .... X H G M Mitchell

810 SQN CULDROSE (Sea King Mk6)
LT CDR .... X D V Stanton

814 SQN CULDROSE (Sea King Mk6)
BFPO 200
LT CDR .... X M R Skeer MBE

815 SQN HERON (Lynx)
LT CDR .... X J H Reed

819 SQN HERON (Sea King Mk5)
CDR .... X R A Cunningham MBE

820 SQN CULDROSE (Sea King Mk6)
BFPO 200
LT CDR .... X R J Bridger

824 SQN CULDROSE (Merlin)
CDR .... X P A G Shaw MBE

845 SQN HERON(Sea King Mk4)
LT CDR .... X S R Gordon

846 SQN CULDROSE (Sea King Mk4)
LT CDR .... X R W King

847 SQN HERON (Lynx AN7 and Gazelle)
LT CDR .... X F W Robertson

848 SQN HERON (Sea King Mk 4)
LT CDR .... X M D Baines

849 SQN HQ CULDROSE
LT CDR .... X A M O'Sullivan

849 SQN A FLT (Sea King AEW)
BFPO 200
LT CDR .... X M E A Flanagan

849 SQN B FLT (Sea King AEW)
BFPO 200
LT CDR .... X G B Hutchison

899 SQN HERON (Sea Harrier)
LT CDR .... X D H MacKay

ROYAL NAVAL RESERVE UNITS

HMS CALLIOPE
South Shore Road
GATESHEAD
Tyne & Wear
NE8 2BE

HMS CAMBRIA
Hayes Point
Sully
SOUTH GLAMORGAN
CF6 2XU

HMS CAROLINE
BFPO 806

HMS DALRIADA
Navy Buildings
Eldon Street
GREENOCK
PA16 7SL

HMS EAGLET
RNHQ Merseyside
East Brunswick Dock
LIVERPOOL
L3 4DZ

HMS FERRET
DISC
Chicksands
SHEFFORD
Beds
SG17 5PR

HMS FLYING FOX
Winterstoke Road
BRISTOL
BS3 2NS

HMS FORWARD
42 Tilton Road
BIRMINGHAM
B9 4PP

HMS KING ALFRED
Fraser Building
Whale Island
PORTSMOUTH
PO2 8ER

HMS WILDFIRE
Brackenhill House
The Woods
NORTHWOOD
HA6 3EX

HMS PRESIDENT
72 St Katherine's Way
LONDON
E1 9UQ

HMS SCOTIA
RNSE Caledonia
Hilton Road
ROSYTH
KY11 2X

HMS SHERWOOD
Chalfont Drive
NOTTINGHAM
NG8 3LT

HMS WILDFIRE
Brakenhill House
The Woods
NORTHWOOD
HA6 3EX

HMS VIVID
Mount Wise Court
DEVONPORT
PL1 4JJ

ROYAL MARINES UNITS AND ESTABLISHMENTS

HQRM
Headquarters Royal Marines
West Battery
Whale Island
PORTSMOUTH
Hants
PO2 8DX

40 CDO RM
40 Commando Royal Marines
Norton Monor Camp
TAUNTON
Somerset
TA2 6PF

42 CDO RM
42 Commando Royal Marines
Bickleigh Barracks
Shaugh Prior
nr PLYMOUTH
Devon
PL6 7AJ

45 CDO RM
45 Commando Royal Marines
RM CONDOR
ARBROATH
Angus
Scotland
DD11 3SJ

CDO LOG REGT RM
Commando Logistics Regiment
Royal Marines
RMB Chivenor
BARNSTAPLE
Devon
EX31 1AZ

HQ 3 CDO BDE RM
Headquarters 3 Commando Brigade
Royal Marines
RM Barracks
Stonehouse
PLYMOUTH
Devon
PL1 3QS

539 ASSLT SQN RM
539 Assault Squadron Royal Marines
RM Turnchapel
Barton Road
Turnchapel
PLYMOUTH
PL9 9XD

RM STONEHOUSE
Royal Marines Stonehouse
RM Barracks
Stonehouse
PLYMOUTH
Devon
PL1 3QS

COMACCHIO GP RM
COMACCHIO Group Royal Marines
Royal Marines Condor
ARBROATH
Angus
Scotland
DD11 3SJ

RM POOLE
Royal Marines Poole
Hamworthy
POOLE
Dorset
BH15 4NQ

CTCRM
Commando Training Centre Royal Marines
Lympstone
EXMOUTH
Devon
EX8 5AR

ATTURM
Instow
BIDEFORD
Devon
EX39 4JH

HQ BAND SERVICE RM
Headquarters Band Service Royal Marines
Eastney Block
HMS NELSON
Queen Street
PORTSMOUTH
Hants
PO1 3HH

RM BAND PORTSMOUTH
Royal Marines Band Portsmouth
Eastney Block
HMS NELSON
Queen Street
PORTSMOUTH
Hants
PO1 3HH

RM BAND SCOTLAND
Royal Marines Band Scotland
HMS CALEDONIA
ROSYTH
Fife
Scotland
KY11 2XH

RM BAND BRNC
Royal Marines Band BRNC
BRNC
DARTMOUTH
Devon
TQ6 0HJ

RMSM
Royal Marines School of Music
Gibraltar Block
HMS NELSON
Queen Street
PORTSMOUTH
Hants
PO1 3HH

RM BAND PLYMOUTH
Royal Marines Band Plymouth
HMS RALEIGH
TORPOINT
East Cornwall
PL11 2PD

RM BAND CTCRM
Royal Marines Band CTCRM
CTCRM
Lympstone
EXMOUTH
Devon
EX8 5AR

ROYAL MARINES RESERVE UNITS

RMR BRISTOL
Royal Marines Reserve Bristol
Dorset House
Litfield Place
BRISTOL
BS8 3NA

RMR LONDON
Royal Marines Reserve
City of London
2 Old Jamaica Road
Bermondsey
LONDON
SE16 4AN

RMR MERSEYSIDE
Royal Marines Reserve Merseyside
RNHQ Merseyside
East Brunswick Dock
LIVERPOOL
Merseyside
L3 4DZ

RMR SCOTLAND
Royal Marines Reserve Scotland
37-51 Birkmyre Road
Govan
GLASGOW
G51 3JH

RMR TYNE
Royal Marines Reserve Tyne
Anzio House
Quayside
NEWCASTLE-UPON-TYNE
NE6 1BU

ROYAL FLEET AUXILIARY SERVICE

ARGUS, *Aviation Training Ship (AG)*

BAYLEAF, *Support Tanker, (AO)*

BLACK ROVER, *Small Fleet Tanker, (AORL)*

BRAMBLELEAF, *Support Tanker, (AO)*

DILIGENCE, *Forward Repair Ship, (AR)*

FORT AUSTIN, *Solid Support Ship (AFS)*

FORT ROSALIE, *Solid Support Ship, (AFS)*

FORT VICTORIA, *Auxiliary Oiler Replenishment, (AOR)*

FORT GEORGE, *Auxiliary Oiler Replenishment, (AOR)*

GOLD ROVER, *Small Fleet Tanker, (AORL)*

GREY ROVER, *Small Fleet Tanker, (AORL)*

OAKLEAF, *Support Tanker, ((AO)*

OLNA, *Fleet Tanker, (AO)*

OLWEN, *Fleet Tanker, (AO)*

ORANGELEAF, *Support Tanker, (AO)*

SIR BEDIVERE, *Landing Ship Logistics, (LSL)*

SIR GALAHAD, *Landing Ship Logistics, (LSL)*

SIR GERAINT, *Landing Ship Logistics, (LSL)*

SIR PERCIVALE, *Landing Ship Logistics, (LSL)*

SIR TRISTRAM, *Landing Ship Logistics, (LSL)*

SEA CRUSADER, *RO RO*

SEA CENTURION, *RO RO*

KEY ADDRESSES

ARMED FORCES PERSONNEL ADMINISTRATION AGENCY HEADQUARTERS (AFPAA HQ)

AFPAA (Central Office)
Building 182
RAF Innsworth
GLOUCESTER
Gloucestershire
GL3 1EZ

AFPAA (CENTURION)
Centurion Building
Grange Road
GOSPORT
Hants
PO13 9XA

COMBINED CADET FORCE

Director of Naval Reserves
Victory Building
HM Naval Base
PORTSMOUTH
Hants
PO1 3LS

COMMITTEES

UNITED KINGDOM COMMANDERS IN CHIEF COMMITTEES (UKCICC)

Erskine Barracks
Wilton
SALISBURY
Wiltshire
SP2 0AG
(01722-433208)

COMMONWEALTH LIAISON OFFICES

AUSTRALIA
Australia House
Strand
London
WC2B 4LA

BANGLADESH
28 Queens Gate
LONDON
SW7 5JA

CANADA
Macdonald House
Grosvenor Square
LONDON
W1X 0AB

GHANA
13 Belgrave Square
LONDON
SW1X 8PN

INDIA
India House
Aldwych
LONDON
WC2B 4NA

MALAYSIA
45 Belgrave Square
LONDON
SW1X 8QT

NEW ZEALAND
New Zealand House
Haymarket
LONDON
SW1Y 4TQ

NIGERIA
Nigeria House
9 Northumberland Avenue
LONDON
WC2N 5BX

EDUCATIONAL ESTABLISHMENTS

THE ROYAL COLLEGE OF DEFENCE STUDIES
Seaford House
37 Belgrave Square
LONDON
SW1 X8NS
(020 7915 4804)

THE JOINT SERVICES COMMAND AND STAFF TRAINING COLLEGE
BRACKNELL
Berkshire
RG12 9DD
(01344 457271)

BRITANNIA ROYAL NAVAL COLLEGE
Dartmouth
Devon
TQ6 0HJ
(01803-832141)

MEDICAL SERVICES

The Medical Director General (Naval)
Victory Building
HM Naval Base
PORTSMOUTH
PO1 3LS

Royal Hospital
Haslar
GOSPORT
Hants
PO12 2AA

Royal Naval Defence Hospital Unit
Derriford Hospital
PLYMOUTH
Devon
PL6 8DH

Institute of Naval Medicine
ALVERSTOKE
Hants
PO12 2DL

MINISTRY OF DEFENCE POLICE HEADQUARTERS

Ministry of Defence Police Headquarters
MDP Wethersfield
BRAINTREE
Essex
CM7 4AZ
(01371 854000)

NAVAL BASES AND SUPPLY AGENCY

CHIEF EXECUTIVE, NAVAL BASES & SUPPLY AGENCY
Management Suite
Block C
ENSLEIGH
Bath
BA1 5AB

NAVAL BASE COMMANDER CLYDE
HM Naval Base
Clyde
Dunbartonshire
G84 8HL

BEITH(RN Armament Depot)
Ayrshire
KA15 1JT

CAMBELTOWN(NATO POL Depot)
Argyll
PA28 6RD

COULPORT (RN Armament Depot)
PO Box 1
Cove
Helensburgh
Dunbartonshire
G84 0PD

CROMBIE (RN Armament Depot)
Dunfermline
Fife
KY12 8LA

FASLANE (RN Store Depot)
HM Naval Base
Faslane
G84 8HL

GLEN DOUGLAS (NATO Ammunition Depot)
PO Box 1
Arrochar
Dunbartonshire
G83 7BA

LOCH EWE (NATO POL Depot)
Aulbea
Achnasheen
Ross Shire
IV22 2HU

LOCH STRIVEN (NATO POL Depot)
Toward
Argyll
PA23 7UL

ROSYTH (RN Store Depot)
Fife
KY11 2XP

NAVAL BASE COMMANDER DEVONPORT
HM Naval Base
Devonport
Plymouth
PL1 4SL

Devonport (RN Store Depot)
HM Naval Base
DEVON PORT
Plymouth
PL1 4SL

Ernesettle (RN Armament Depot)
Ernesettle Lane
PLYMOUTH
PL5 2TX

Exeter (Support Engineering Facility)
Topsham
EXETER
Devon

NAVAL BASE COMMANDER PORTSMOUTH
HM Naval Base
PROTSMOUTH
Hants
PO1 3LT

DIRECTOR SUPPLY (SOUTH)
South Office Block
HM Naval Base
PORTSMOUTH
PO1 3LU

Colerne (RN Store Depot)
Nr CHPPENHAM
Wiltshire
SN14 8QR

Dean Hill (RN Armament Depot)
West Dean
SALISBURY
Wiltshire
SP5 1EY

GOSPORT (RN Armament Depot)
Hants
PO13 0AH

PORTSMOUTH(RN Armament Depot)
Hants
PO1 3LU

MARINE SERVICES SUPPORT

Deputy Director Marine Services Support
Room 92A
Block E
ENSLEIGH
Bath
BA1 5AB

General Manager
HM Mooring Depot
Pembroke Dock
Pembrokeshire
SA72 6TB

Singapore (OFD Senko)
RNSTO Singapore
NP1022
BFPO 489
LONDON

NAVY, ARMY AND AIR FORCE INSTITUTES

NAAFI HQ
LONDON Road
Amesbury
SALISBURY
Wiltshire
SP4 7EN
(01980-627000)

NATO HEADQUARTERS-MILITARY COMMITTEE (UKMILREP)

UKMILREP
NATO Headquarters
BFPO 49

SUPREME ALLIED COMMANDER ATLANTIC(SACLANT)

HEADQUARTERS, SUPREME ALLIED COMMANDER ATLANTIC (SACLANT)
Naval Party 1964
(Saclant)
BFPO Ships

REGIONAL HEADQUARTERS
SOUTH ATLANTIC
(RHQ SOUTHLANT)
BFPO 6

CENTRAL SUB-AREA (CENTLANT)
Mountwise
PLYMOUTH
Devon

NORTHERN SUB-AREA (NORLANT)
Clyde Naval Base
HELENSBURGH
Dunbartonshire
Scotland
G84 8HL

SUBMARINE FORCES EASTERN ATLANTIC
(SUBEASTLANT)
Eastbury Park
NORTHWOOD
Middlesex
HA6 3HP

ANTI-SUBMARINE WARFARE STRIKING FORCE
Office of COMUKTG
7-8 The Parade
HM Naval Base
PORTSMOUTH
Hants
PO17 6AR

SACLANT UNDERSEA RESEARCH CENTRE
Viale San Bartolomeo 400
I-19026 San Bartolomeo
Italy

SUPREME ALLIED COMMANDER EUROPE (SACEUR)

SUPREME HEADQUARTERS ALLIED POWERS EUROPE (SHAPE)
BFPO 26

NATO SCHOOL (SHAPE)
Oberammergau
Box 2003
BFPO 105

REGIONAL HEADQUARTERS
AFSOUTH
BFPO 8

COMSTRIKFORSOUTH
COMSUBMED
U.K. NATIONAL SUPPORT UNIT RHQ
AFSOUTH
BFPO 8

HQ ALLIED NAVAL FORCES SOUTHERN EUROPE
(HQ NAVSOUTH)
BFPO 8

Office of COMNAVSOUTHREP
JOINT HQ SOUTHEAST
Sirinyer
Izmir
Turkey

FRENCH COMMANDER-IN-CHIEF MEDITERRANEAN
(CECMED)
Prefecture Maritime
83800 Toulon Naval
France

REGIONAL HEADQUARTERS AFNORTH
BPFO 28

JHQ NORTHEAST
c/o UK Support Element
HQ BALTAP
Naval Party 1004
BFPO 486

ALLIED COMMANDER-IN-CHIEF EASTERN ATLANTIC AREA (CINCEASTLANT)

REGIONAL HEADQUARTERS EASTLANT
Eastbury Park
NORTHWOOD
Middlesex
HA6 3HP

NORTH ATLANTIC AREA (NORLANT)
MHQ
Clyde Naval Base
HELENSBURGH
Dunbartonshire
Scotland

CENTRAL ATLANTIC AREA (CENTLANT)
MHQ
PLYMOUTH
Devon

NAVAL PERSONAL AND FAMILY SERVICE (NFPS)

Area Office (NPFS) Eastern
Swiftsure Block
HMS Nelson
PORTSMOUTH
Hants
PO1 3HH

Area Office (NPFS) Western
Fenner Block
HMS DRAKE
PLYMOUTH
Devon
PL2 2BJ

Area Office (NPFS) Northern
Triton House
1-5 Churchill Square
HELENSBURGH
Argyll and Bute
G84 9HL

NAVAL REGIONAL OFFICES

SCOTLAND & NORTHERN IRELAND REGIONS
HMS CALEDONIA
ROSYTH
Fife
KY11 2XH
(01383 425532)

NORTHERN ENGLAND REGION
Royal Naval Headquarters Merseyside
Brunswick Dock
LIVERPOOL
L3 4DZ
(0151-707-3400)

Naval Regional Sub-Office
HMS CALLIOPE
South Shore Road
GATESHEAD
Tyne & Wear
NE8 2BE
(0191-477-2536)

WALES & WESTERN REGIONS
HMS FLYING FOX
Winterstoke Road
BRISTOL
BS3 2NS
(0117 953 0996)

EASTERN ENGLAND REGION
HMS PRESIDENT
72 St Katherines Way
LONDON
E1 9UQ
(020 7481 7219)

REGULAR FORCES EMPLOYMENT ASSOCIATION

(NATIONAL ASSOCIATION FOR EMPLOYMENT OF REGULAR SAILORS SOLDIERS AND AIRMEN)
49 Pall Mall
LONDON
SW1Y 5JG
(020 7321 2011)

ABERDEEN
46A Union Street
ABERDEEN
AB10 1BD

BEDFORD
TA Centre
28 Bedford Road
KEMPSTON
Beds
MK42 8AJ

BELFAST
Northern Ireland War Memorial Building
Waring Street
BELFAST
BT1 2EU

BIRMINGHAM
2nd Floor, City Gate
25 Moat Lane
BIRMINGHAM
B5 6BH

BRISTOL
Unit 24 Apex Court
Woodlands Lane
Almondsbury
BRISTOL
BS32 4JT

BURY ST. EDMUNDS
Room 4
90 Guildhall Street
BURY ST EDMUNDS
IP33 1PR

CARDIFF
Maindy Barracks
CARDIFF
CF4 3YE

CARLISLE
The Castle
CARLISLE
Cumbia
CA3 8UR

CHATHAM
9 New Road
ROCHESTER
Kent
ME1 1BG

CHELMSFORD
The Gate House
AMT Centre
Upper Chase
Writtle Road
CHELMSFORD
CM2 0BN

CHELTENHAM
Potter House
St Annes Road
CHELTENHAM
Glos
GL52 2SS

CHESTER
156 Percival Road
The Dale
CHESTER
Cheshire
CH2 4AN

DARLINGTON
4th Floor
Northgate House
St Augustine's Way
DARLINGTON
DL1 1XA

DERBY
Room 18
The College Business Centre
Uttoxeter New Road
DERBY
DE22 3WZ

EDINBURGH
New Haig House
Logie Green Road
EDINBURGH
EH7 4HQ

EXETER
Wyvern Barracks
EXETER
Devon
EX2 6AF

GLASGOW
Haig House
1 Fitzroy Place
GLASGOW
G3 7RJ

HULL
34-38 Beverley Road
HULL
East Yorkshire
HU3 1YE

LEEDS
Harewood Barracks
Regent Street
LEEDS
LS7 1AT

LINCOLN
Cobb Hall Centre
St. Pauls Lane
Bailgate
LINCOLN

LIVERPOOL
Suite 43 Oriel Chambers
14 Water Street
LIVERPOOL
L2 8TD

LONDON
49 Pall Mall
LONDON
SW1Y 5JG

MANCHESTER
TA Centre
Belle Vue Street
MANCHESTER
M12 5PW

NEWCASTLE-ON-TYNE
Stanegate House
2 Groat Market
NEWCASTLE-UPON-TYNE
NE1 1UQ

NORTHAMPTON
TA Centre
Clare Street
NORTHAMPTON
NN1 3JQ

NORWICH
TA Centre
Britannia House
325 Aylsham Road
NORWICH
NR3 2AB

NOTTINGHAM
19 Malvern Road
NOTTINGHAM
NG3 5HA

PERTH
Room 5
Lower Ground Floor
4 Atholl Place
PERTH
PH1 5ND

PLYMOUTH
Raglan Cottage
MOD Mt Wise Business Park
Devonport
PLYMOUTH
PL1 4JH

PORTSMOUTH
2B Tipner Road
Stamshaw
PORTSMOUTH
PO2 8QS

PRESTON
Fulwood Barracks
Fulwood
PRESTON
Lancs
PR2 8AA

READING
Watlington House
Watlington Street
READING
RG1 4RJ

SALISBURY
27 Castle Street
SALISBURY
Wilts
SP1 1TT

SHEFFIELD
2nd Floor
9 Paradise Square
SHEFFIELD
S1 2DE

SHREWSBURY
Building 4
Copthorne Barracks
Copthorne Road
SHREWSBURY
SY3 7LT

STOKE-ON-TRENT
Martin Leake House
TA Centre
Waterloo Road
Cobridge
STOKE-ON-TRENT
ST6 3HJ

SWANSEA
TA Centre
The Grange
West Cross
SWANSEA
SA3 5LB

DERA (DEFENCE EVALUATION AND RESEARCH AGENCY) MAJOR ESTABLISMENTS

HEAD OFFICE

DERA Farnborough
Ively Road
FARNBOROUGH
Hampshire
GU14 0LX

DERA Portsdown West
Portsdown Hill Road
FAREHAM
Hampshire
PO17 6AD

DERA Winfrith
Winfrith Technology Centre
Newburgh
DORCHESTER
Dorset
DT2 8XJ

DERA Porton Down
SALISBURY
Wiltshire
SP4 0JQ

DERA Malvern
St Andrews Road
MALVERN
Worcs
WR14 3PS

DERA Fort Halstead
SEVENOAKS
Kent
TN14 7BP

DERA Boscombe Down
SALISBURY
Wilts
SP4 0JF

NAVAL AIRCRAFT REPAIR ORGANISATION

Fleetlands Division
Gosport
Hants
PO13 0AA

Almondbank Division
Perth
PH1 3NQ

DIRECTORATE OF NAVAL RECRUITING REGIONAL CAREERS HEADQUARTERS (RCHQS) AND ARMED FORCE CAREERS OFFICES (AFCOs)

RCHQ NORTH
RN Support Establishment
HMS Caledonia
ROSYTH
KY11 2XH
(0138-425510)

AFCOs NORTH REGION
63 Belmont Street
ABERDEEN
AB10 1JS
(01224-639999)

Palace Barracks
Holywood
BELFAST
BT18 9RA
(02890-427040/1)

94-96 English Street
CARLISLE
CA3 8ND
(01228-523958)

29/31 Bank Street
PO BOX 81
DUNDEE
DD1 1RW
(01382-227198)

67-83 Shandwick Place
EDINBURGH
EH2 4SN
(0131-221-1111)

Charlotte House
78 Queen Street
GLASGOW
G1 3DN
(0141-221-6110/9)

Britannia Suite
Norwich House
Savile Street
KINGSTON-UPON-HULL
HU1 3ES
(01482 325902)

3 Bridge Street
INVERNESS
IV1 1HG
(01463 233668)

Graeme House
Derby Square
LIVERPOOL
L2 7SD
(0151 2271764)

Petersfield House
29 Peters Street
MANCHESTER
M2 5QL
(0161 8352923)

67 Borough Road
MIDDLESBROUGH
Cleveland
TS1 3AE
(01642 211749/230677)

New England House
20 Ridley Place
NEWCASTLE UPON TYNE
NE1 8JW
(0191-2327048)

63 College Street
St Helens
MERSEYSIDE
WA1D 1TN
(01744 753560)

Halkyn House
21 Rhosddu Road
WREXHAM
LL11 1NF
(01978 263334)

RCHQ SOUTH
Ladywood House
45/46 Stephenson Street
BIRMINGHAM
B2 4DY
(0121-6065102)

AFCOs SOUTH REGION
Unit 46
The Pallasades
BIRMINGHAM
B2 4XD
(0121-6334995)

244 Holdenhurst Road
BOURNEMOUTH
BH8 8AZ
(01202 311224)

120 Queen's Road
BRIGHTON
BN1 3XE
(01273 325386)

4 Colston Avenue
BRISTOL
BS1 4TY
(0117 9260233)

82-88 Hills Road
CAMBRIDGE
CB2 1LQ
(01223 315118)

South Gate House
Wood Street
CARDIFF
CF1 1GR
(02920 726805)

1 Dock Road
CHATHAM
ME4 4JR
(01634 826206)

1 - 3 Dorset House
CHELMSFORD
Essex
CM1 1HQ
(01245 355134)

60 Hertford Street
COVENTRY
CV1 1LB
(02476 226513)

35 - 36 Castlefield
Main Centre
DERBY
DE1 2PE
(01332 348120)

Fountain House
Western Way
EXETER
EX1 2DQ
(01392 2274040)

Britannia Buildings
The Docks
GLOUCESTER
GL1 2EH
(01452 521676)

37 Silent Street
IPSWICH
IP1 1TF
(01473 254450)

Rutland Centre
Yeoman Street
LEICESTER
LE1 1UT
(01162 620284)

Sibthorpe House
350/352 High Street
LINCOLN
LN5 7BN
(01522 525661)

Iverna Gardens
Kensington
LONDON
W8 6TN
(020 7937 3493/0749)

453/454 Strand
LONDON
WC2R 0RG
(020 7839 4643)

Dunstable House
Dunstable Road
LUTON
LU1 1EA
(01582 721501)

22 Unthank Road
NORWICH
NR2 2RA
(01603 620033)

70 Milton Road
Victoria Centre
NOTTINGHAM
NG1 3QX
(01159 419503)

35 St Giles
OXFORD
OX1 3LJ
(01865 515098)

21 - 23 Hereward Centre
PETERBOROUGH
PE1 1TB
(01733 568833)

Mount Wise
Devonport
PLYMOUTH
PL1 4JH
(01752 501750)

Cambridge Road
PORTSMOUTH
PO1 2EN
(023 9282 6536)

Oak House
Chapel Street
REDRUTH
TR15 2BY
(01209 314143)

2nd Floor
Princess House
The Square
SHREWSBURY
Shropshire
SY1 1JZ
(01743 232541)

36 - 38 Old Hall Street
Hanley
STOKE-ON-TRENT
ST1 3ZY
(01782 214688)

Llanfair Buildings
19 Castle Street
SWANSEA
SA1 1JF
(01792 654208/642516)

35 East Street
TAUNTON
Somerset
TA1 3LS
(01823 354430)

OFFICER CAREERS LIAISON CENTRES (OCLCs)

OCLCs NORTH REGION

RN Support Establishment
HMS CALEDONIA
ROSYTH
KY11 2XH
(01383 425522)

Petersfield House
29 St Peter's Street
MANCHESTER
M2 5QL
(0161 8352916

OCLCs SOUTH REGION

Ladywood House
45/46 Stephenson Street
BIRMINGHAM
B2 4DY
(0121 6065099)

Iverna Gardens
Kensington
LONDON
W8 6TN
(020 7938 4646)

HMS FLYING FOX
Wintersoke Road
BRISTOL
BS3 2NS
(0117 9664246)

ROYAL NAVAL FILM CORPORATION

Registered Office
HM Naval Base (PP23)
PORTSMOUTH
PO1 3NH
(023 9272 3108)

SEA CADET CORPS

HEADQUARTERS
202 Lambeth Road
LONDON
SE1 7JF
(020 7928 8978)

NORTHERN AREA
HMS CALEDONIA
ROSYTH
Fife
KY11 2XH
(01383 416300)

NORTH WEST AREA
Royal Naval Headquarters Merseyside
East Bruswick Dock
LIVERPOOL
L3 4DZ
(0151-707-3440)

SOUTH WEST AREA
HMS FLYING FOX
Winterstoke Road
BRISTOL
Avon
BS3 2NS
(0117 953 1991)

EASTERN AREA
The Drill Hall
Ropery Road
GAINSBOROUGH
Lincolnshire
DN21 2NS
(01427-614441)

LONDON AREA
HMS PRESIDENT
72 St. Katherine's Way
LONDON
E1W 1UQ
(020 7481 7371)

SOUTHERN AREA
HMS NELSON
PORTSMOUTH
Hants
PO1 3HH
(023 9272 4263)

SHIPPING POLICY DIVISION (SEA TRANSPORT)

Department of the Environment, Transport and Regions
Zone 2/24
Great Minster House
76 Marsham Street
LONDON
SW1P 4DR
(020 7944 5121)

SHIPYARD OVERSEEING SERVICE

CLYDE
c/o BAE Systems Marine (YSL) Ltd
South Street
Scotstoun
GLASGOW
G14 0XN
(0141-4355200)

SOUTHAMPTON
c/o Vosper Thornycroft (UK) Ltd
Victoria Road
Woolston
SOUTHAMPTON
SO9 5GR
(023 8044 4853)

BARROW
c/o BAE Systems Marine Ltd
BARROW-IN-FURNESS
Cumbria
LA14 1AF
(01229-823366)

HONORARY OFFICERS OF THE ROYAL NAVAL RESERVE

Honorary Commodore HRH The Prince Michael of Kent, KCVO .... 01 Apr 94

Honorary Captain The Lord Sterling of Plaistow, Kt CBE .... 15 Jan 91

Honorary Captain (Supernumerary) The Duke of Buccleugh and Queensferry Kt .... 02 Feb 88

Honorary Captain (Supernumerary) Sir Donald Gosling Kt .... 27 Jun 93

Honorary Commander E J Billington

Honorary Commander F A Mason MBE

Honorary Commander P R Moore RD*

Honorary Commander (Supernumerary) R D P Gilbert

Honorary Chaplain (Supernumerary) The Right Reverend D G Hawker, MA, (CofE)

Honorary Chaplain (Supernumerary) The Right Reverend M A P Woods, DSc, MA, (CofE)

HONORARY OFFICERS OF THE ROYAL MARINE RESERVE

Honorary Colonel E P R Cautley .... 1 Jul 99

Honorary Colonel G M Simmers, CBE, CA .... 01 Apr 00

Honorary Colonel J N Tidmarsh, MBE, JP .... 01 Jan 98

Honorary Colonel Sir David Trippier RD JP DL .... 01 Jan 96

Honorary Colonel Sir Neville Trotter, FCA, JP, DL .... 1 Sep 98

OFFICERS OF THE ACTIVE LIST OF THE ROYAL NAVAL RESERVE, ROYAL MARINES RESERVE, THE QUEEN ALEXANDRA'S ROYAL NAVAL NURSING RESERVE, SEA CADET CORPS AND COMBINED CADET FORCE

ROYAL NAVAL RESERVE

Name	Rank	Branch	Unit	Seniority
A				
Abbotts, Michael	Mid	URNU	Brnc Rnr Soton	08.09.97
Ackerman, Richard	Lt	OPS(SM)	Cambria	09.05.99
Ackland, Simon Robert	Slt	NCS	Cambria	10.12.88
Adams, A C, *RD*	Capt	AW	President	30.09.99
Adams, David	Lt	NCS	Wildfire	23.02.81
Ahmed, Iftikhar	Lt	LOGS	Forward	19.03.93
Ainsworth, Jeffery	Lt	AIR	Rnr Air Br VI	16.11.85
Aitchison, Ian James	Lt	PA	President	02.06.94
Aitken, Lee	Mid	URNU	Urnu Glasg	10.10.97
Aitken, Rebecca	Mid	URNU	Urnu Soton	08.10.98
Alcock, Charles Edward	Lt Cdr	SEA	President	31.03.00
Alcock, David John, *RD*	Lt Cdr	MW	King Alfred	18.02.87
Alcock, Marisa Luisa	Lt	INTR	Ferret	14.01.94
Alder, Mark Christian	ASl	NE	Wildfire	09.12.98
Aldous, Georgina	Mid	URNU	Urnu Londn	13.10.97
Aldous, Robert	Mid	URNU	Urnu Soton	07.10.99
Alexander, William	Mid	URNU	U/A	08.10.98
Ali, Imran	Mid	URNU	Urnu anch	07.10.99
Ali, Muhammed	Mid	URNU	Urnu Londn	12.10.99
Allan, Nicholas	Mid	URNU	U/A	08.10.98
Allan, Richard Michael	Lt	INTR	Ferret (Rnr)	20.05.94
Allan, Sophie	Mid	URNU	U/A	08.10.98
Allan, William, *RD*	Lt Cdr	HQ	Scotia	02.09.88
Allaway, Edward	Mid	URNU	U/A	21.10.99
Allen, Caroline	Mid	URNU	U/A	20.10.99
Allen, Elinor Jane	Lt Cdr	HQ	Vivid	30.09.91
Allen, *I J* (James Ian)	Lt Cdr	MW	Caroline	31.03.97
Allinson, Matthew	Mid	URNU	U/A	16.10.97
Almond, Nicholas	Mid	URNU	Urnu Manch	07.10.99
Altoft, Kerry	Mid	URNU	U/A	21.10.99

Name	Rank	Branch	Unit	Seniority
Amure, Mark	Mid	URNU	U/A	14.10.99
Anderson, Adrian	Lt	AIR	Rnr Air Br VI	15.05.89
Anderson, Clare	Mid	URNU	Urnu Livp	14.10.99
Anderson, John Christopher	Lt	MW	Dalriada	06.03.99
Anderson, Kerry McGowan, *BSC*	Lt Cdr	HQ	Caroline	31.03.99
Anderson, Roderick Gavin Adam	ASl	NE	President	16.06.98
Andersson, James	Mid	URNU	Urnu Livp	14.10.99
Andrews, Mark David	Slt	SEA	Flying Fox	29.02.92
Arbeid, Mark	ASl	NE	Forward	19.11.98
Arthurs, Cedric James, *RD, JP*	Cdr	NCS	Eaglet	30.09.95
Ashpole, Richard David	Sg Ltcdr	MED	Sherwood	01.08.90
Ashton, James	Mid	URNU	Brnc Rnr Soton	08.09.97
Ashton, Samantha	ASl	URNU	Urnu (Rnr) Manch	16.06.99
Ashworth, Andrew John	Sg Ltcdr	MED	Scotia	23.04.93
Ashworth, Lorna Elizabeth, *BSC, RD*	Lt Cdr	HQ	Scotia	31.03.99
Aslam, Zabeada	Mid	URNU	U/A	22.10.98
Aspinell, Charles Jonathan, *RD**	Cdr	NCS	King Alfred	30.09.97
Aspinell, Pamela Ann	Lt Cdr	Q	King Alfred	31.03.96
Aston, Christopher	Mid	URNU	Urnu (Rnr) Ssx	20.10.98
Aston, Dora Ann	ALt	CEW	Flying Fox	05.06.99
Atherton, Mark	Mid	URNU	Urnu (Rnr) Glasg	14.10.95
Atkinson, Susan Mary	Lt Cdr	PA	President	31.03.94
Attwood, Keith	Mid	URNU	Urnu (Rnr) Livp	14.10.99
Auld, Alasdair	Mid	URNU	Urnu (Rnr) Glasg	08.10.98
Austin, Kevin	Lt Cdr	AW	Sherwood	31.03.98
Avery, Philip	Lt Cdr	AIR	Rnr Air Br VI	31.03.97
Avis, Robert Graeme, *RD**	Cdr	AW	President	30.09.97
Awenat, William	Lt Cdr	AIR	Rnr Air Br VI	31.03.95

B

Name	Rank	Branch	Unit	Seniority
Bacon, James	Mid	URNU	Brnc Rnr Soton	06.09.98
Bagley, Catherine	Mid	URNU	U/A	22.10.97
Bailey, Stuart	Mid	URNU	Urnu (Rnr) Ssx	12.10.99
Baillie, Andren	Lt	AIR	Rnr Air Br VI	01.01.91
Baird, Andrew	Lt	HQ	Caroline	07.09.90
Baird, Elaine Harper	Lt Cdr	Q	King Alfred	31.03.96
Baker, James	Mid	URNU	U/A	16.10.97
Baker, Johanna	Mid	URNU	Urnu (Rnr) Londn	13.10.97
Baker, Peter Alan	Lt Cdr	NCS	President	31.03.94
Baker, Vikki	Mid	URNU	U/A	06.10.97
Bamford, Joanne	Mid	URNU	Urnu (Rnr) Manch	01.10.98
Bancroft, David Gideon	Lt	AW	Calliope	20.12.94
Bankhead, Maurice	Lt Cdr	NCS	Caroline	31.03.95
Banks, Iain	Lt	AIR	Rnr Air Br VI	01.06.91
Barbour, Abigail	ASl	NE	Caroline	02.12.98
Barclay, Neil Howard	Lt	AW	Vivid	18.09.93
Barden, Edward	Mid	URNU	Urnu (Rnr) Londn	01.11.97
Barfield, Kevin Lloyd, *RD*	Lt Cdr	OPS(CEW)	Forward	31.01.96
Barfoot, Peter	Mid	URNU	U/A	08.10.98
Barker, Amy	Mid	URNU	Urnu (Rnr) Brstl	26.10.99
Barker, Alison	Mid	URNU	U/A	22.10.98
Barker, Caroline	Mid	URNU	U/A	19.10.98
Barker, Elizabeth Charlotte	ASl	NE	President	13.10.98
Barker, Tamsin	Mid	URNU	U/A	15.10.98
Barnes, David	Mid	URNU	Urnu (Rnr) Soton	07.10.99
Barnes, Judith Margaret	ASl	NE	Eaglet	05.10.99
Barnwell, Andrew	Lt Cdr	AIR	Rnr Air Br VI	11.11.90
Barr, Andrew	Mid	URNU	Urnu (Rnr) Glasg	08.10.98
Barr, Calum	Mid	URNU	Brnc Rnr Soton	06.09.98
Barrand, William	Mid	URNU	Urnu (Rnr) Londn	07.10.98
Barrett, Lee	Mid	URNU	U/A	21.10.99
Barrett, Mark	Lt	AIR	Rnr Air Br VI	01.06.91

Name	Rank	Branch	Unit	Seniority
Barton, Christopher James, *RD*	Lt Cdr	HQ	Cambria	30.09.87
Barton, Matthew	Mid	URNU	U/A	15.10.98
Bass, Claire	Mid	URNU	Urnu (Rnr) Ssx	20.10.98
Bassett, Nigel Peter	Lt Cdr	AW	Flying Fox	31.03.97
Bassford, Stephanie	Mid	URNU	U/A	23.10.97
Bates, Jodie	Mid	URNU	Urnu (Rnr) Manch	07.10.99
Batki, Cavus	Mid	URNU	Urnu (Rnr) Brstl	26.10.99
Baughan, Philip John, *RD*	Lt Cdr	HQ	Sherwood	02.07.89
Baxter, Ross John, *RD*	Lt	NCS	Forward	01.09.91
Baylis, Clive	Lt Cdr	AIR	Rnr Air Br VI	01.10.90
Bean, Maurice	Lt Cdr	SEA	Flying Fox	15.02.93
Beaton, Iain William	ASl	NE	Dalriada	24.03.99
Beattie, Jane Elizabeth, RD	Lt Cdr	Q	Wildfire	31.03.93
Beauchamp, Martyn	Mid	URNU	Urnu (Rnr) Manch	01.10.98
Beaumont, Andrew John	Lt	MW	Eaglet	31.07.95
Bedford, Jonathan	Sg Ltcdr		Scotia	26.03.92
Beech, Eric Edward, *RD*	Lt Cdr	DIS	Ferret (Rnr)	31.03.98
Beedall, Richard Anthony	Lt	HQ	Sherwood	24.03.95
Beeharry, Neil	Mid	URNU	Urnu (Rnr) Ssx	21.10.97
Bellamy, Philippa	Mid	URNU	U/A	16.10.97
Bellamy, Simon	Lt	URNU	Urnu (Rnr) Londn	01.10.97
Benn, Peter Quentin	Lt	PA	Wildfire	28.02.98
Bentall, Estelle	Mid	URNU	U/A	07.10.98
Bereznyckyj, Susan Dorothy	Lt Cdr	Q	Sherwood	31.03.94
Bernard, David Maurice, *RD*	Cdr	AWNIS	Flying Fox	30.09.84
Bernays, Annie	Mid	URNU	U/A	08.10.98
Berry, Ian, *RD*	Lt Cdr	MW	Calliope	31.03.96
Bevan, Gillian Lesley	Slt	LOGS	Vivid	05.11.96
Bevan, Philip Alexander	ASl	NE	Vivid	16.04.97
Bewley, Geoffrey	Lt Cdr	MW	King Alfred	31.03.99
Bickerton, Lisa	Mid	URNU	U/A	14.10.99
Bicknell, Richard Anthony	Lt	MW	King Alfred	14.07.90
Biddlecombe, Amy	Mid	URNU	U/A	14.10.99
Biggerstaff, Adam Graham, *RD*	Lt Cdr	HQ	Dalriada	03.04.85
Biggerstaff, Fiona Joyce	ASl	NE	Scotia	10.03.98
Biggs, Nigel	Lt	SEA	President	31.07.95
Birch, Anthony	Lt Cdr	AIR	Rnr Air Br VI	31.03.99
Bird, Amy	Mid	URNU	Urnu (Rnr) Soton	07.10.99
Bird, Graham	Mid	URNU	Urnu (Rnr) Aberd	30.09.99
Bird, Stephen Peter Glover	Sg Ltcdr	MED	Scotia	01.08.90
Bishop, Jonathan	Mid	URNU	U/A	21.10.99
Bishop, Jonathan	Lt Cdr	AIR	Rnr Air Br VI	31.03.96
Black, Simon Mitchell, *RD*	Lt Cdr	HQ	Scotia	30.06.83
Blackhurst, Kelly	Mid	URNU	U/A	20.10.99
Blackler, Steven	Mid	URNU	Urnu (Rnr) Aberd	09.10.97
Blake, Jonathan	Mid	URNU	Urnu (Rnr) Manch	07.10.99
Bloom, Michael	ASl	URNU	U/A	04.03.97
Bloy, Michael William	Lt	OPS(CEW)	Wildfire	20.07.88
Blyth, Anne Scotland	Sg Ltcdr	MED	President	14.08.83
Blythe, Wendy Elizabeth	Lt	LOGS	Vivid	29.01.96
Boag, Kyle Ian	Lt	SEA	Dalriada	12.01.96
Boal, Michael Alexander	Lt	MW	Caroline	23.02.98
Boardman, Sarah	Mid	URNU	U/A	16.10.97
Boath, Gerard	Mid	URNU	U/A	21.10.99
Bomby, David	Lt Cdr	AIR	Rnr Air Br VI	26.03.90
Bond, Joanne	Mid	URNU	U/A	20.10.98
Bonham-Smith, Rupert	Mid	URNU	U/A	05.11.98
Booth, Mark	Mid	URNU	U/A	16.09.97
Boothroyd, Susan Elizabeth	ASl	NE	Calliope	02.06.99
Bosanquet, Elinor	Mid	URNU	Urnu (Rnr) Aberd	09.10.97
Boughton, Jonathan	Mid	URNU	Brnc Rnr Soton	06.09.98
Boughton, John, *QGM*	Lt Cdr	AIR	Rnr Air Br VI	07.04.92
Boulton, Jeremy Charles	Lt	SM	President	14.12.90

Name	Rank	Branch	Unit	Seniority
Bowen, Michael Leslie	ASgltcdr	MED	Wildfire	30.09.98
Bowles, William	Lt Cdr	MW	Scotia	31.03.98
Bown, Anthony Mark	Lt Cdr	HQ	Cambria	08.03.91
Boyd, Edward Russell	Lt	AWNIS	King Alfred	13.03.96
Boyden, Simon	Mid	URNU	U/A	16.10.97
Boyes, James	Mid	URNU	Urnu (Rnr) Londn	13.10.98
Brabner, Susan, RD	Lt Cdr	DIS	Ferret (Rnr)	31.03.99
Brace, Anna	Mid	URNU	U/A	14.10.99
Bradbury, Miles	ASl	URNU	Urnu (Rnr) Brstl	29.09.98
Bradford, Christine Mary Patricia	Lt Cdr	NCS	Eaglet	31.03.93
Bradford, Michelle	Mid	URNU	U/A	21.10.99
Bradford, Nigel Stuart	Lt	SM	Eaglet	18.12.87
Bradley, Bradley	Mid	URNU	Urnu (Rnr) Aberd	11.11.99
Bradshaw, Francis John C, *LVO*	Cdr	MA	Eaglet	01.02.82
Brady, Matthew`	Mid	URNU	U/A	14.10.99
Braine, David	Lt Cdr	AIR	Rnr Air Br VI	31.03.98
Brampton, Susan	Lt	Q	President	08.01.97
Branyan, Lawrence	Lt	HQ	Eaglet	06.09.89
Brayfield, Rosalind Marion	Lt Cdr	PA	Wildfire	26.12.84
Breyley, Nigel	Lt Cdr	AIR	Rnr Air Br VI	31.03.98
Bridge, Benedict Lenthall	Lt	INTR	Ferret (Rnr)	01.10.96
Bridgen, Andrew Urquhart	Lt	INTR	Ferret (Rnr)	23.07.92
Bridgen, Kevin	Lt Cdr	AIR	Rnr Air Br VI	16.04.92
Briggs, Charmody	Mid	URNU	Urnu (Rnr) Brstl	12.11.97
Broadhurst, Audrey	Lt	CEW	Wildfire	17.02.97
Brockie, Brian	ACdr	MS	Scotia	31.03.96
Brodie, Hazel	Mid	URNU	Urnu (Rnr) Soton	08.10.98
Brogan, Gary Edward	ASl	NE	Eaglet	29.09.98
Bromwell, Mark	Mid	URNU	U/A	14.10.99
Brook, Roger	Lt	AIR	Rnr Air Br VI	22.02.97
Brooking, Stephen	Lt Cdr	AIR	Rnr Air Br VI	11.05.87
Brooks, Alexandra	ASl	NE	Flying Fox	03.02.99
Brooks, Richard	Mid	URNU	U/A	14.10.99
Broughton, Robert Bruce Knight, *RD*	Sg Cdr		Cambria	30.09.82
Browett, Jon	Mid	URNU	U/A	08.10.98
Brown, Alastair	Mid	URNU	U/A	30.09.99
Brown, Andrew	Mid	URNU	Urnu (Rnr) Glasg	08.10.98
Brown, Andrew	Lt Cdr	AIR	Rnr Air Br VI	01.10.90
Brown, Colin	Lt Cdr	AIR	Rnr Air Br VI	30.04.97
Brown, Charles David	Lt	X	U/A	01.10.81
Brown, Hilary	Mid	URNU	Urnu (Rnr) Soton	08.10.98
Brown, John Erskine	Lt Cdr	AWNIS	Wildfire	31.03.96
Brown, Katharine	Lt Cdr	PA	Wildfire	12.03.86
Brown, Karl	Lt Cdr	AIR	Rnr Air Br VI	31.03.98
Brown, Malcolm Stuart, *RD*	Lt Cdr	AW	Scotia	02.07.84
Brown, Nicholas	Mid	URNU	U/A	25.11.99
Brown, Sabrina	Mid	URNU	Urnu (Rnr) Livp	15.10.98
Brown, Timothy	Lt Cdr	AIR	Rnr Air Br VI	19.03.93
Browne, Emma	Mid	URNU	U/A	16.10.97
Browne, Thomas	Mid	URNU	U/A	14.10.99
Brunswick, Robert	Lt	AIR	Rnr Air Br VI	16.10.90
Bryning, Christopher	Lt Cdr	AIR	Rnr Air Br VI	01.03.85
Buchanan, Helen	Mid	URNU	U/A	19.10.98
Buckingham, Ann	Slt	NCS	King Alfred	02.04.97
Buckley, Jonathan Mark	Lt	MW	Cambria	08.11.97
Bugler, Martin	Lt Cdr	AIR	Rnr Air Br VI	31.03.97
Bullen, Louise	Mid	URNU	Urnu (Rnr) Ssx	12.10.99
Bunn, Toby	Mid	URNU	U/A	14.10.99
Burchinshaw, Philip	Mid	URNU	Urnu (Rnr) Soton	07.10.99
Burden, Fraser	Lt	AIR	Rnr Air Br VI	01.04.88
Burden, Simon	Mid	URNU	U/A	14.10.99
Burgess, David	Mid	URNU	U/A	12.03.99
Burgess, Philip	Mid	URNU	Brnc Rnr Soton	06.09.99

Name	Rank	Branch	Unit	Seniority
Burne, Penelope Jane, *RD*	Lt Cdr	INTR	Ferret (Rnr)	30.09.91
Burnet, Alexander	Mid	URNU	Urnu (Rnr) Aberd	30.09.99
Burton, Grahame Anthony, *RD**	Cdr	AW	Flying Fox	30.09.90
Butterworth, James	Mid	URNU	Urnu (Rnr) Soton	08.10.98
Button, Edward	Mid	URNU	U/A	21.10.99

C

Name	Rank	Branch	Unit	Seniority
Cadden, Edward	SLt	URNU	Urnu (Rnr) Glasg	11.08.94
Caddock, Matthew	Mid	URNU	Urnu (Rnr) Soton	09.10.97
Cain, Neal	Lt	AIR	Rnr Air Br Vl	17.10.91
Caine, Samantha	Mid	URNU	Urnu (Rnr) Brstl	21.10.98
Callahan, David Robert	ASl	NE	Scotia	09.12.97
Cambridge, Aaron Russell	Lt Cdr	PA	King Alfred	20.02.89
Cameron, Anne Louise, *RD*	Lt	NCS	King Alfred	28.10.91
Cameron, Christopher	ASl	URNU	Urnu (Rnr) Brstl	08.12.95
Cameron, Fiona	ASl	NE	Caroline	09.06.98
Campbell, Mairi	Mid	URNU	Urnu (Rnr) Glasg	08.10.98
Campbell, William	Lt Cdr	AIR	Rnr Air Br Vl	01.04.92
Campbell-Burt, Robin	Mid	URNU	U/A	20.10.98
Camwell, Barry	Mid	URNU	U/A	07.10.98
Caney, Jonathan	Mid	URNU	Urnu (Rnr) Soton	07.10.99
Canham, Wendy Jacqueline	Lt Cdr	CEW	Sherwood	31.03.98
Canty, Thomas	Mid	URNU	Brnc Rnr Soton	08.09.97
Carman, Felix	Mid	URNU	U/A	08.10.98
Carpenter, David, *RD*	Lt Cdr	PA	Scotia	05.06.85
Carre, Jane	ASl	SEA	Urnu (Rnr) Ssx	21.01.97
Carrott, Deborah	Mid	URNU	Urnu (Rnr) Livp	14.10.99
Carss, George Alexander	Sg Ltcdr		King Alfred	09.12.81
Carter, David	ASl	AW	Eaglet	13.10.98
Carter, Richard	Lt	AIR	Rnr Air Br Vl	06.01.87
Carvasso-White, Anna-Louise	Mid	URNU	U/A	14.10.99
Carvasso-White, Helen	Mid	URNU	U/A	21.10.99
Carver, Andrew	Lt Cdr	AIR	Rnr Air Br Vl	31.03.98
Casey, Graham Peter	Lt Cdr	DIS	Ferret (Rnr)	31.03.00
Casey, Neil	Lt	AIR	Rnr Air Br Vl	23.12.90
Caskie, Iain Neil	Lt Cdr	SM	Scotia	16.05.92
Casson, Hilary Patricia	Lt Cdr	NCS	Vivid	31.03.96
Caulfield, Lee	Mid	URNU	Urnu (Rnr) Aberd	30.09.99
Cendrowicz, Agata	Mid	URNU	Urnu (Rnr) Soton	11.11.99
Chadwick, Jillian	Lt	LOGS	Eaglet	20.05.91
Chaffin-Laird, Madeleine	Mid	URNU	U/A	20.10.98
Chalmers, Amalia Lourdes, *RD*	Lt Cdr	INTR	Ferret (Rnr)	31.03.95
Chamberlain, Moira	ASl	Q	King Alfred	02.06.99
Chambers, Catherine Louise	ASl	NE	Flying Fox	17.11.99
Chan, Aaron	Mid	URNU	Urnu (Rnr) Londn	12.10.99
Chan, Chung	Mid	URNU	U/A	20.10.98
Chapman, Anthony	Lt	MW	President	31.07.95
Chapman, David Ralph	Lt	AW	Calliope	05.12.87
Chapman, Graham Philip	Lt	AW	President	14.11.92
Chapman, Kate	Mid	URNU	Urnu (Rnr) Londn	12.10.99
Chapman, David Quentin	Lt Cdr	X	Rnr Air Br Vl	01.10.90
Chatterton, Robert Martin	Lt Cdr	AW	President	31.03.95
Chauvelin, David Coulson Wyllie	Lt	MW	Scotia	26.11.98
Cheang, Tia	Mid	URNU	Urnu (Rnr) Brstl	26.10.99
Cheyne, Steven	Lt Cdr	AIR	Rnr Air Br Vl	01.04.93
Chishick, Harry Benjamin James	Sg Ltcdr	MED	President	17.09.90
Chua, Jimmy	Mid	URNU	Urnu (Rnr) Brstl	26.10.99
Church, Elizabeth Ann, *RD*	Lt	SM	President	16.11.88
Churchley, Richard	Lt Cdr	AIR	Rnr Air Br Vl	26.04.98
Clark, Suzanne	Lt Cdr	AIR	Rnr Air Br Vl	31.03.97
Clarke, Amanda Lesley	Lt	PA	President	07.10.90
Clarke, Peter	Lt Cdr	AIR	Rnr Air Br Vl	01.10.90

Name	Rank	Branch	Unit	Seniority
Clarke, Roger Derek, *RD*	Lt Cdr	NCS	Vivid	31.03.96
Clarke, Steven David	Lt	AW	Calliope	09.06.90
Clarke, William Stephen	Lt Cdr	MW	Caroline	31.03.00
Classey, Mark	Lt	AIR	Rnr Air Br VI	01.12.91
Claxton, David	Mid	URNU	U/A	21.10.99
Cleary, Deidre Ann	Lt Cdr	PA	President	31.03.99
Clegg, David	Mid	URNU	Urnu (Rnr) Manch	01.10.98
Clegg, Tina Sandra	ASl	NE	Cambria	30.08.93
Cliffe, Daniela Maria	ALt	Q	Vivid	14.07.99
Clissold-Jones, Catherine	Mid	URNU	Urnu (Rnr) Brstl	21.10.98
Cloney, Justin	Mid	URNU	Urnu (Rnr) Livp	15.10.98
Coad, Ivan Harry, *RD*	Lt Cdr	AW	Flying Fox	13.03.88
Coates, Lorna	Mid	URNU	U/A	04.01.99
Cobb, Gary	Mid	URNU	U/A	14.10.99
Cobbold, Andrew Reginald, *MA*	Lt	INTR	Ferret (Rnr)	12.11.95
Cochrane, Christopher	Mid	URNU	Urnu (Rnr) Brstl	26.10.99
Cockburn, Frank	Lt Cdr	PA	Calliope	01.10.99
Cockcroft, John Paul	Lt	SM	Wildfire	14.09.89
Coe, Morgan	ASl	NE	President	02.06.99
Coffey, Ralph	Mid	URNU	U/A	15.10.98
Cohen, James Seymour Lionel, *BSC, RD*	Lt Cdr	NCS	President	31.03.97
Cohen, Rachel	Mid	URNU	U/A	22.10.97
Coke, Jim	Mid	URNU	U/A	18.11.99
Colborne, Raymond	Lt Cdr	AIR	U/A	01.01.89
Coldham, David	Mid	URNU	U/A	21.10.99
Cole, James	Lt Cdr	AIR	Rnr Air Br VI	01.09.84
Coleman, Timothy	Mid	URNU	Brnc Rnr Soton	06.09.98
Coles, Victoria	Mid	URNU	U/A	21.10.99
Colley, Derek Peter	Lt Cdr	AW	Forward	31.03.94
Colley, Mark	Mid	URNU	U/A	04.01.99
Collie, James	Mid	URNU	Urnu (Rnr) Soton	07.10.99
Collings, Benjamin	Mid	URNU	Urnu (Rnr) Brstl	21.10.98
Collins, Charles	Mid	URNU	U/A	14.10.99
Collins, David	Mid	URNU	Urnu (Rnr) Ssx	12.10.99
Collins, Steven Mark	Lt Cdr	AW	Forward	31.03.94
Collinson, James	ASl	NE	King Alfred	02.12.99
Colquhoun, Alastair	Mid	URNU	Brnc Rnr Soton	06.09.98
Colquhoun, Rodger	Lt	AIR	Rnr Air Br VI	01.06.89
Colquhoun-Flannery, William	Sg Ltcdr		King Alfred	31.03.98
Colton, Ian	Lt Cdr	AIR	Rnr Air Br VI	22.11.92
Condy, Sallie Louise	Lt	INT	Ferret (Rnr)	30.09.89
Connell, John	Lt Cdr	AIR	Rnr Air Br VI	01.10.91
Constant, David	Lt	AIR	Rnr Air Br VI	27.03.97
Conway, Carl	Lt	AIR	Rnr Air Br VI	01.06.91
Conway, Keith Alexander, RD	Lt Cdr	MW	Scotia	31.03.99
Cook, David, *RD*	Lt Cdr	AW	Flying Fox	31.03.93
Cook, Simon	Mid	URNU	Urnu (Rnr) Livp	15.10.98
Cook, Simon Hugh Home	Lt	MW	President	31.03.98
Cook, William John	Lt Cdr	AW	Scotia	01.03.85
Coombes, Helen	Mid	URNU	Urnu (Rnr) Manch	07.10.99
Coombes, Kirsty	Mid	URNU	Urnu (Rnr) Soton	26.10.98
Coombes, Stewart	Lt Cdr	AIR	Rnr Air Br VI	31.03.95
Cooper, Adam	Mid	URNU	Brnc Rnr Soton	06.09.98
Cooper, David John	Lt Cdr	HQ	President	31.03.99
Cooper, Susan, *BSC*	Lt	HQ	President	21.07.91
Copeland-Davis, Terence	Lt	AIR	Rnr Air Br VI	01.05.88
Corcoran, Robert	Mid	URNU	U/A	21.10.99
Corminboeuf-Clarke, Philip	Lt	URNU	U/A	01.08.94
Cornell, Patricia Jane	Lt	Q	King Alfred	02.04.91
Cornes, John	Lt	URNU	U/A	01.01.92
Corson, Robert John	PSgltcdr	MED	Calliope	13.10.98
Costin, Matthew	Mid	URNU	Urnu (Rnr) Ssx	12.10.99
Cottam, Simon Roscoe, RD	Lt Cdr	AWNIS	Flying Fox	31.03.97

Name	Rank	Branch	Unit	Seniority
Cotterill, Thomas	Mid	URNU	Brnc Rnr Soton	06.09.98
Cotton, Michael	Mid	URNU	U/A	14.10.99
Coulson, James Robert Bradley	Lt	LOGS	Sherwood	02.05.92
Coultate, Anthony	Mid	URNU	U/A	16.09.97
Council, Robert	Mid	URNU	Urnu (Rnr) Livp	18.11.99
Couper, Donald	Sg Ltcdr		Eaglet	01.02.99
Cowan, Andrew Stuart, *RD*	Lt Cdr	MW	Dalriada	31.03.97
Cox, Darren	Mid	URNU	U/A	21.10.99
Cox, Rhoderick	Lt Cdr	AIR	Rnr Air Br VI	01.12.88
Coyle, Mark Francis	Slt	SEA	Calliope	15.02.94
Craig, Graeme	ALt	URNU	U/A	29.04.98
Craig, John Terence, *RA, RD*	Cdr	NA	Wildfire	30.09.95
Craig, Wendy	ALt	URNU	U/A	01.10.98
Craik, Lorna	Mid	URNU	Urnu (Rnr) Glasg	10.10.97
Crawford, Andrew John	Lt Cdr	AW	Vivid	01.06.91
Crawford, Judith	Mid	URNU	Urnu (Rnr) Aberd	01.10.98
Cribley, Michael	Lt Cdr	AIR	Rnr Air Br VI	01.10.91
Critchley, Julian Arthur John Hall	Sg Ltcdr		Scotia	07.08.83
Crockett, Victor Andrew, *RD*	Lt Cdr	DIS	Ferret (Rnr)	31.03.95
Crombie, Nicholas	Lt	AIR	Rnr Air Br VI	01.02.93
Crone, David James Edward, *RD*	ACdr	MW	Caroline	26.02/90
Crossley, Samuel Neil Thomas	ASl	NE	President	07.01.99
Crossman, Kate	Mid	URNU	U/A	16.10.97
Crowdy, Karen Ann	ASl	NE	Flying Fox	24.07.98
Crump, Peter Charles, *RD**	Cdr	AW	King Alfred	30.09.97
Culver, Peter Charles Leonard	Lt	SEA	President	08.08.89
Cunningham, Rachael	Mid	URNU	Brnc Rnr Soton	06.09.98
Curley, Ronald Robertson	Lt	MW	Scotia	17.10.90
Currie, Katherine	Mid	URNU	Urnu (Rnr) Brstl	15.10.97

D

Name	Rank	Branch	Unit	Seniority
Dace, Katherine Elizabeth, *RD*	Lt Cdr	INTR	Ferret (Rnr)	31.03.95
Dady, Simon James	ASl	NE	President	29.09.98
Dale, Marcus	Mid	URNU	Urnu (Rnr) Ssx	12.10.99
Dale, Rebecca	Mid	URNU	Urnu (Rnr) Londn	13.10.98
Dalton, Neil Jarvis	Lt	PA	President	02.06.92
Daly, Paul	Lt Cdr	AIR	Rnr Air Br VI	31.03.95
Dalziel, Simon Anthony Cannon	Lt Cdr	PA	King Alfred	16.02.89
Danby, Sarah	Mid	URNU	Urnu (Rnr) Manch	22.01.98
Daros, Aloysia	Mid	URNU	Urnu (Rnr) Ssx	12.10.99
Dasgupta, Tanya	Mid	URNU	Urnu (Rnr) Londn	13.10.97
Davies, Andrew	Mid	URNU	U/A	19.10.98
Davies, Dennis James	Lt Cdr	AWNIS	President	31.03.98
Davies, George	Lt	AIR	Rnr Air Br VI	01.07.91
Davies, John Lawrence	Lt	AWNIS	Flying Fox	30.10.95
Davies, Richard	Mid	URNU	Brnc Rnr Soton	06.09.98
Davies,Robert Michael	Lt Cdr	SEA	Sherwood	31.03.00
Davies, Richard Myall	ASl	NE	President	23.04.97
Davies, Sarah Elizabeth	Lt	AWNIS	King Alfred	19.02.99
Davies, Simon Lovat	Lt	MW	King Alfred	15.09.95
Davies, Taavi	Mid	URNU	U/A	14.10.99
Davies, William	Slt	URNU	U/A	31.07.95
Davis, Peter	Mid	URNU	Urnu (Rnr) Londn	12.10.99
Dawes, Gawaine	Mid	URNU	U/A	14.10.99
Day, James	Mid	URNU	U/A	22.10.98
Day, James	Mid	URNU	U/A	19.06.98
Daye, Angela	Mid	URNU	Urnu (Rnr) Glasg	22.10.98
Deacon, Christopher	Lt	URNU	Urnu (Rnr) Londn	09.03.91
Dear, Joanna	Mid	URNU	Urnu (Rnr) Manch	07.10.99
Delderfield, Mark	Mid	URNU	Urnu (Rnr) Manch	01.10.98
Delf, Jeannie	Mid	URNU	Urnu (Rnr) Glasg	14.10.99
Denison-Davies, Edward	Mid	URNU	Urnu (Rnr) Londn	12.10.99

Name	Rank	Branch	Unit	Seniority
Denman, Rachel	Mid	URNU	U/A	14.10.99
Dennard, Kieron	Mid	URNU	U/A	14.10.99
Denslow, Paul	Mid	URNU	Urnu (Rnr) Brstl	15.10.97
Derrick, Malcom	Lt Cdr	AIR	Rnr Air Br VI	10.12.91
Devereaux, James	Lt Cdr	AIR	Rnr Air Br VI	31.03.98
Dewar, Michael	Mid	URNU	Urnu (Rnr) Livp	14.10.99
Dickinson, Faye	Mid	URNU	Urnu (Rnr) Livp	15.10.98
Dilks, Paul David Peter, *RD*	Lt Cdr	AW	King Alfred	05.04.87
Dillon, Ben	Mid	URNU	Brnc Rnr Soton	26.09.98
Dingwall, Donald	Mid	URNU	Urnu (Rnr) Glasg	08.10.98
Dismore, Oliver	Lt Cdr	AIR	Rnr Air Br VI	01.01.88
Divers, Barry	Mid	URNU	Urnu (Rnr) Aberd	30.09.99
Dixon, Mark	Mid	URNU	Brnc Rnr Soton	08.09.97
Dodds, Nicholas	Mid	URNU	Urnu (Rnr) Brstl	26.10.99
Doe, James	Mid	URNU	Urnu (Rnr) Brstl	26.10.99
Donaldson, John Richard	Lt Cdr	SM	Flying Fox	12.08.94
Doran, Claire-Marie	Mid	URNU	Urnu (Rnr) Ssx	20.10.98
Dorman, Nicholas Roger Vause, *RD*	Lt Cdr	MW	Scotia	31.03.97
Dorrian, Georgina	Mid	URNU	U/A	22.10.98
Douglas, Norman	Lt	SEA	Calliope	19.01.96
Downer, Samuel	Mid	URNU	Urnu (Rnr) Londn	17.12.97
Downie, Anne Louise, *RD*	Lt	SEA	Scotia	01.12.95
Downing, Carl	Lt Cdr	AIR	Rnr Air Br VI	16.11.92
Downing, Neil Edmond	Lt Cdr	MW	Caroline	31.03.00
Downs, Stuart	ASl	NE	Forward Rnr	05.10.99
Doyle, Lucie	Mid	URNU	U/A	14.10.99
Drake, Jonathan	Mid	URNU	U/A	14.10.99
Drake, Roderick Allan	Lt Cdr	NCS	Flying Fox	31.03.98
Drever, Lisa	Mid	URNU	U/A	14.10.99
Drewett, Brian	Mid	URNU	U/A	12.03.99
Driscoll, Mark	Mid	URNU	U/A	01.12.99
Dudill, William	ASl	NE	Sherwood	20.04.99
Duffield, Gary	Lt Cdr	AIR	Rnr Air Br VI	01.02.90
Duggan, Paul	Mid	URNU	U/A	22.10.98
Duggua, Rodney, *RD*	Lt Cdr	CEW	King Alfred	31.03.93
Dukes,	Lt Cdr	AIR	Rnr Air Br VI	01.10.93
Duncan, Barbara Mary	Lt	AWNIS	Eaglet	14.03.91
Duncan, Keith Julian, *RD*	Lt Cdr	AW	Eaglet	31.03.94
Dunford, Victoria	Mid	URNU	U/A	14.10.99
Dunkley, Ian Max, *RD*	ACdr	AW	President	01.10.88
Dunn, Jonathan	Mid	URNU	U/A	14.10.99
Dunn, Josephine	Slt	URNU	Urnu (Rnr) Londn	11.11.98
Dunn, Matthew John	PSg Ltcdr	MED	Forward	24.11.99
Dunne, James	Mid	URNU	Urnu (Rnr) Soton	07.10.99
Dunne, Lawrence John	Lt	SEA	Forward	01.12.95
Duthie, David	Lt Cdr	AIR	Rnr Air Br VI	01.10.89
Duthie, David James Ralph	Sg Ltcdr	MED	Sherwood	31.03.95
Duthie, Ruth Mary Mitchell	Lt	AWNIS	Flying Fox	16.04.94
Dutt, Trevor Peter, *RD*	Sg Cdr	MED	President	30.09.89

E

Name	Rank	Branch	Unit	Seniority
Eagles, Susan Jane	Cdr	PA	Flying Fox	30.09.95
Ealey, Nicholas	Mid	URNU	Urnu (Rnr) Londn	12.10.99
Earle-Payne, Gareth	Mid	URNU	U/A	19.10.98
Eastham, Allan Michael, *BSC, RD*	Lt Cdr	NCS	Forward	31.03.94
Easton-Corke, Gillian	Mid	URNU	U/A	19.10.98
Eaton, Kadi	Mid	URNU	Urnu (Rnr) Soton	11.02.98
Eccles, Alan	Mid	URNU	Urnu (Rnr) Glasg	10.10.97
Edge, Helen	Mid	URNU	Urnu (Rnr) Londn	13.10.97
Eduam-Baiden, Abena	Mid	URNU	Urnu (Rnr) Livp	09.10.97
Edwards, Michael Steven De La Warr	ASgltcdr	MED	Sherwood	07.09.98
Ehlers, Richard	Mid	URNU	U/A	15.10.98
Eling, Richard	Mid	URNU	Urnu (Rnr) Livp	14.10.99

Name	Rank	Branch	Unit	Seniority
Elliott, Robin	Lt Cdr	AIR	Rnr Air Br Vl	01.04.97
Ellis, John Anthony, *RD*	Capt	MW	Flying Fox	30.09.99
Ellis, Richard Alliyn, RD	Lt	HQ	President	18.08.90
Ellis, Verrill	ASl	URNU	U/A	01.04.98
Emsley, Richard John Paul	Lt	MW	Sherwood	31.03.96
England, Robert Frederick Charles	Lt	QMQ	King Alfred	30.08.96
Esam, Laura	Mid	URNU	U/A	16.10.97
Esfahani, Shahrokh	Lt	HQ	Wildfire	27.01.95
Evans, Ann, *RD*	Lt Cdr	DIS	Forward	31.03.94
Evans, Alex	Lt Cdr	AIR	Rnr Air Br Vl	31.03.99
Evans, Carol	Lt	PA	Flying Fox	12.01.92
Evans, Charlotte	Mid	URNU	U/A	08.10.98
Evans, Ewan	Mid	URNU	Urnu (Rnr) Manch	01.10.98
Evans, Nichael	Lt Cdr	AIR	Rnr Air Br Vl	17.05.88
Ewing, Simon	Lt Cdr	AIR	Rnr Air Br Vl	31.03.93

F

Name	Rank	Branch	Unit	Seniority
Farmer, Gary Gordon	Lt	HQ	Dalriada	28.06.92
Farquhar, Rosie	Mid	URNU	U/A	23.10.97
Farrand, Rachel, *RD**	ACdr	NA	Sherwood	30.09.89
Faulkner, Keith Michael	Lt Cdr	LOGS	Wildfire	26.05.90
Faulks, Robert	Lt Cdr	AIR	Rnr Air Br Vl	17.06.84
Fearnley, David George, *B.ED, RD**	Lt Cdr	MW	Eaglet	31.03.89
Fearon, David	Mid	URNU	Urnu (Rnr) Livp	15.10.98
Fearon, John	ASl	NE	Eaglet	12.07.99
Fenix, Aisling	Mid	URNU	Urnu (Rnr) Livp	15.10.98
Fenn, Deborah	Mid	URNU	U/A	20.10.99
Ferebee, Joanne	Mid	URNU	U/A	20.10.99
Ferguson, Emily	Mid	URNU	Urnu (Rnr) Aberd	09.10.97
Ferguson, Neil	Lt	HQ	Caroline	20.08.89
Ferguson, Nicholas Alistair Malcolm	Lt Cdr	HQ	Vivid	31.03.99
Fernandez, Adam	Mid	URNU	U/A	20.10.98
Fickling, James	Mid	URNU	Brnc Rnr Soton	06.09.99
Fiddock, Matthew	Mid	URNU	Urnu (Rnr) Livp	15.10.98
Filtness, Rosemary Jane, *RD*	Lt Cdr	DIS	Ferret (Rnr)	31.03.93
Findlay, Alan	Lt	AIR	Rnr Air Br Vl	28.10.90
Finley, Sarah	Mid	URNU	Urnu (Rnr) Londn	12.10.99
Finnie, Scott	Mid	URNU	Urnu (Rnr) Aberd	01.10.98
Fitchsampson, Steven R	Slt	SEA	Flying Fox	16.11.94
Flaxman, Edward William	Lt	SEA	Calliope	26.09.92
Flegg, William	Mid	URNU	U/A	08.10.98
Fleming, Samuel Andrew	Lt	HQ	Sherwood	20.01.92
Fletcher, Richard Paul	ASl	CEW	Eaglet	04.03.99
Flower, Clare	Mid	URNU	Urnu (Rnr) Ssx	12.10.99
Floyd, Robert	Mid	URNU	Urnu (Rnr) Brstl	26.10.99
Flynn, Joanna	Mid	URNU	Urnu (Rnr) Londn	12.10.99
Forster, Catherine	Mid	URNU	Urnu (Rnr) Londn	13.10.97
Fortey, Louise	Mid	URNU	Urnu (Rnr) Ssx	20.10.98
Forward, Kirsty	Mid	URNU	Urnu (Rnr) Brstl	26.10.99
Foster, David	Mid	URNU	Urnu (Rnr) Glasg	08.10.98
Foster, Stephen Edward, RD	ACdr	NCS	Forward	31.03.95
Fouracre, Andrew Mark George	ASl	NE	Cambria	22.09.99
Fowler, Alan	Lt Cdr	AIR	Rnr Air Br Vl	01.06.78
Fowler, Darren Joseth	Psg Lt	MED	President	04.09.96
Fox, Vickie	Mid	URNU	Urnu (Rnr) Aberd	01.10.98
Foxwell, David	Mid	URNU	U/A	25.11.99
Franks, Edward	Mid	URNU	Urnu (Rnr) Brstl	26.10.99
Franks, James	Mid	URNU	U/A	22.10.98
Fraser, James	Mid	URNU	Urnu (Rnr) Ssx	20.10.98
Freeman, Claire	Mid	URNU	Urnu (Rnr) Glasg	10.10.97
Freeman, Helen	Mid	URNU	Urnu (Rnr) Manch	07.10.99

Name	Rank	Branch	Unit	Seniority
Fry, Christopher Wesley	Lt	HQ	Forward	28.07.95
Fry, Stephen Michael	Lt	NCS	Cambria	15.06.95
Futcher, Paul	Mid	URNU	Urnu (Rnr) Brstl	02.12.98

G

Name	Rank	Branch	Unit	Seniority
Galloway, Richard	Mid	URNU	U/A	03.12.99
Galway, Ian, *QCVSA*	Lt Cdr	AIR	Rnr Air Br VI	11.10.89
Gamble, Alexandra	Mid	URNU	Urnu (Rnr) Soton	09.10.97
Gamble, Deborah	Lt	AIR	Rnr Air Br VI	14.03.90
Gandy, Paul	Mid	URNU	U/A	16.10.97
Gardiner, George	Sg Ltcdr	MED	Caroline	31.03.97
Gardner, Louis	Mid	URNU	U/A	08.10.98
Garner, Philip	Lt Cdr	AIR	Rnr Air Br VI	31.03.97
Garrod, Michael	Mid	URNU	Brnc Rnr Soton	06.09.98
Gater, James	Mid	URNU	Urnu (Rnr) Londn	13.10.98
Gausden, Christine	Lt Cdr	SM	President	31.03.00
Gavey, Stephen John	Lt Cdr	HQ	Vivid	01.08.88
Georgeson, Ian	Lt Cdr	AIR	Rnr Air Br VI	01.06.91
Geraghty, Felicity Roseleen	ASl	Q	Scotia	29.04.98
Ghaibi, Adam	Mid	URNU	Urnu (Rnr) Livp	14.10.99
Ghouini, Mira	Mid	URNU	Urnu (Rnr) Londn	11.10.99
Gibb, Peter	Lt Cdr	AIR	Rnr Air Br VI	24.01.98
Gibbs, Mark	Mid	URNU	Brnc Rnr Soton	08.09.97
Gibson, Michael	Mid	URNU	Urnu (Rnr) Manch	09.10.97
Gibson, Stephen	Lt Cdr	AIR	Rnr Air Br VI	31.03.94
Gillett, Andrew	Mid	URNU	Urnu (Rnr) Brstl	21.10.98
Gleave, James	Lt	OEW	Dalriada	15.09.95
Glover, David	Mid	URNU	U/A	06.11.97
Glover, Martyn Richard Timothy, *MA*	Lt	NCS	President	04.10.90
Goatman, Emma	Mid	URNU	Urnu (Rnr) Brstl	15.10.97
Gobey, Richard	Mid	URNU	U/A	08.10.98
Godfrey, Thomas	Mid	URNU	U/A	21.10.99
Goldby, Philip David	ASl	NE	President	09.12.98
Goldthorpe, Sally Louise	Lt Cdr	PA	Eaglet	31.03.95
Goodenough, Robert	Mid	URNU	Brnc Rnr Soton	08.09.97
Goodes, Simon Newbury, *RD*	Lt Cdr	NCS	Wildfire	31.03.97
Goodman, Chantal	Mid	URNU	Urnu (Rnr) Manch	07.10.99
Goodwin, Jonathan Paul Kerr	Lt Cdr	SM	President	31.03.97
Gough, Nicholas William	Lt	MW	President	11.05.90
Gould, Andrew Edward	Cdr	LOGS	Scotia	30.09.97
Gow, Neil Henry Keefe	Lt	SM	Calliope	21.03.94
Goward, Jennifer	Mid	URNU	U/A	14.12.99
Goward, Rachel Jane	ASl	NE	Eaglet	09.06.99
Grace, Jonathan	Lt	AIR	Rnr Air Br VI	01.05.89
Graham, Adrian William	Lt Cdr	DIS	Ferret (Rnr)	31.03.98
Graham, Jennifer	Mid	URNU	Urnu (Rnr) Brstl	26.10.99
Graham, Nadia	Mid	URNU	U/A	30.09.99
Graham, Stephen	Lt Cdr	AIR	Rnr Air Br VI	31.03.94
Grainger, Serena	Mid	URNU	Urnu (Rnr) Ssx	21.10.97
Grant, Shoni	Mid	URNU	Urnu (Rnr) Soton	08.10.98
Grattan-Cooper, David	Mid	URNU	U/A	07.10.98
Graves, Malcolm Harold, *RD**	Lt Cdr	AW	Cambria	19.07.82
Graveson, Allan	Lt Cdr	AW	King Alfred	09.07.92
Gray, Andrew Crispian	Lt Cdr	AW	President	31.03.99
Gray, James	Mid	URNU	Urnu (Rnr) Brstl	21.10.98
Gray, Susan Kathryn	Lt Cdr	PA	Scotia	01.10.93
Greaves, Christopher	Lt Cdr	AIR	Rnr Air Br VI	01.10.95
Greaves, Jeremy Justin	Lt	PA	Flying Fox	13.06.95
Green, Toby	Mid	URNU	Urnu (Rnr) Ssx	30.10.98
Greenacre, Richard Paul, *RD*	Lt Cdr	AWNIS	Vivid	31.03.97
Greenhall, Christopher	Mid	URNU	U/A	07.10.98
Greenwood, Elizabeth	Lt Cdr	PA	President	31.03.99

Name	Rank	Branch	Unit	Seniority
Greenwood, Jeanette	Slt	LOGS	Forward	16.01.96
Greenwood, Stephen	Mid	URNU	Urnu (Rnr) Livp	14.10.99
Gregory, Jonathan	Mid	URNU	U/A	14.10.99
Gregory, Simon	Lt	AIR	Rnr Air Br VI	01.02.90
Gresty, David	Mid	URNU	Urnu (Rnr) Livp	14.10.99
Grice, Matthew	Mid	URNU	Urnu (Rnr) Livp	15.10.98
Grierson, Andrew	ASl	URNU	U/A	30.09.99
Griffin, Alexandra	Mid	URNU	U/A	21.10.99
Griffin, Danielle	Mid	URNU	U/A	08.10.98
Griffiths, Andrew Derek	Lt	AW	Flying Fox	26.02.94
Griffiths, Michael Edward, *BSC, RD*	Lt	SM	Cambria	03.05.89
Griffiths, Sara Louise	Lt	Q	King Alfred	11.11.91
Grimes, Matthew	Mid	URNU	Urnu (Rnr) Ssx	21.10.97
Grist, David Francis Neil	Slt	MS(M)	King Alfred	08.11.96
Gross, Hamilton	Mid	URNU	Urnu (Rnr) Brstl	26.10.99
Grove, Sarah	Mid	URNU	U/A	07.10.97
Groves, Clare Julia	Sg Lt	MED	Eaglet	31.03.92
Gubby, Adrian	Mid	URNU	Brnc Rnr Soton	08.09.97
Guild, Malcolm Donald	Sg Ltcdr	MED	Scotia	12.07.87
Gunn, Debra Ann, *RD*	Lt Cdr	HQ	Scotia	31.03.94
Gunning, Hollie	Mid	URNU	U/A	14.10.99
Gupta, Anshul	Mid	URNU	Urnu (Rnr) Ssx	12.10.99

H

Name	Rank	Branch	Unit	Seniority
Haffenden, Simon, *BSC, MIEE, C.ENG*	Lt	SM	Flying Fox	26.04.96
Hagan, Annelise	Mid	URNU	Urnu (Rnr) Soton	09.10.97
Haigh, Julie Ann	Lt	AWNIS	Cambria	13.10.90
Haikin, Peter Harry, *BSC*	Lt	HQ	Vivid	02.02.96
Hain, Douglas	Mid	URNU	Urnu (Rnr) Manch	07.10.99
Halblander, Craig James Michael, *BA, LLB, LLM*	Lt	MW	Eaglet	06.05.94
Hale, Amanda	Mid	URNU	U/A	23.10.97
Hall, Euan James Armstrong, *RD*	Lt Cdr	LOGS	Eaglet	16.11.92
Hall, Naomi	Mid	URNU	Urnu (Rnr) Manch	01.10.98
Hall, Tracey	Slt	URNU	U/A	15.09.94
Hall, Victoria	ASl	URNU	Urnu (Rnr) Ssx	21.03.96
Haller, Pauline Mary, *RD*	Lt Cdr	NCS	Wildfire	31.03.93
Hallett, Daniel	Mid	URNU	Urnu (Rnr) Brstl	21.10.98
Halliday, Ian	Lt Cdr	AIR	Rnr Air Br VI	01.09.90
Halls, Tamasin Amaelia	ASl	NE	Vivid	23.02.99
Halpin, Andrew	Mid	URNU	Urnu (Rnr) Aberd	11.10.99
Hamilton, Andrew Robert	Sg Ltcdr	MED	Scotia	01.08.86
Hamilton, Lee	Mid	URNU	Urnu (Rnr) Manch	22.01.98
Hamilton, Neil	Mid	URNU	U/A	19.10.98
Hamilton, Ronald	Lt	LOGS	Dalriada	14.10.95
Hancock, Angela	Lt Cdr	PA	Vivid	31.03.00
Handley, Dane	Lt Cdr	AIR	Rnr Air Br VI	31.03.96
Hands, Carolyn, *RD*	Lt Cdr	NCS	Flying Fox	30.09.85
Hankey, Mark Harold	Lt	SEA	President	31.07.95
Hankin, Robert	Mid	URNU	U/A	30.09.99
Hannah, Marcus	Mid	URNU	Urnu (Rnr) Ssx	21.10.97
Hansom, Edward John	Lt	PA	President	25.11.91
Harding, Janet Elizabeth, *RD**	Lt Cdr	HQ	Wildfire	31.03.93
Hardinge, Christopher Harry	Lt Cdr	SM	King Alfred	31.03.98
Hardy, Simon	Lt	SEA	Vivid	12.06.91
Hardy, Stephen	Mid	URNU	U/A	21.10.99
Hargrave, Anthony James	Lt Cdr	SM	Flying Fox	31.03.93
Hargreaves, Simon	Lt Cdr	AIR	Rnr Air Br VI	01.10.89
Hargreaves, Tony	Mid	URNU	Urnu (Rnr) Ssx	20.10.98
Harman, Stephen	Mid	URNU	Urnu (Rnr) Brstl	15.10.97
Harper, Robert Simon	Lt	HQ	Caroline	27.01.95
Harper, Stephen	Mid	URNU	U/A	16.10.97
Harrington, Anthony Christopher Robert	Lt Cdr	INTR	Ferret (Rnr)	31.03.97

Name	Rank	Branch	Unit	Seniority
Harris, Adrian James	Lt	SM	President	30.07.95
Harris, Richard	Mid	URNU	Brnc Rnr Soton	06.09.99
Harris, Raymond Leo, *RD*	Lt Cdr	ME	U/A	23.10.80
Harrison, Eileen	Mid	URNU	Urnu (Rnr) Glasg	08.10.98
Harrison, Peter	Lt Cdr	SEA	King Alfred	30.05.90
Harrison, Richard William	Sg Ltcdr		Sherwood	30.09.96
Harrower, William	Lt Cdr	AIR	Rnr Air Br VI	15.01.88
Hart, Daniel	Mid	URNU	Urnu (Rnr) Soton	07.10.99
Hart, Keith, *RD*	Lt Cdr	AWNIS	Wildfire	31.03.93
Hart, Shelia Maria	ASl	NE	Sherwood	26.11.98
Hartley, Ann Theresa, *RD*	Lt Cdr	DIS	Wildfire	06.12.96
Hartley, David	Lt Cdr	SM	Dalriada	01.06.91
Hartley, Philip Terence	Lt Cdr	SM	Ferret (Rnr)	16.12.88
Hartley, Sheila Ann, *RD*	Lt	HQ	Vivid	20.01.89
Hartley, Sarah Boyt	Lt	NCS	President	06.12.96
Harvey, Paul	Mid	URNU	Urnu (Rnr) Aberd	01.10.98
Harwood, Steven	Lt Cdr	PA	President	31.03.96
Haslam, David	Mid	URNU	Urnu (Rnr) Manch	01.10.98
Hatchard, John	Lt	AIR	Rnr Air Br VI	12.03.91
Hathway, Steven	Lt Cdr	AIR	Rnr Air Br VI	31.03.98
Hawes, Alison Linda	Lt Cdr	PA	King Alfred	31.03.98
Hawkins, Duncan	ASl	URNU	U/A	26.11.98
Hawkins, James	Mid	URNU	U/A	14.10.99
Hayman, Matthew Robert	ASg Lt		Wildfire	09.09.97
Haynes, Zoe	Mid	URNU	U/A	08.10.98
Hayton, Carrie Jane	Lt Cdr	PA	Wildfire	30.09.91
Hayward, James Douglas, *MA, B.ENG*	Lt Cdr	LOGS	Forward	31.03.00
Healy, Joanne	Mid	URNU	U/A	16.10.97
Healy, Pamela Joyce, *BSC*	Lt Cdr	PA	King Alfred	30.09.90
Heath, Stephen	Mid	URNU	Urnu (Rnr) Brstl	12.11.97
Heathcote, Paul	Lt Cdr	AIR	Rnr Air Br VI	31.03.96
Heffron, Kirsty	Mid	URNU	Urnu (Rnr) Glasg	14.11.95
Helsby, Edward	Lt Cdr	AIR	Rnr Air Br VI	31.03.96
Henderson, Andrew	Mid	URNU	U/A	21.10.99
Henwood, A, *RD*	Cdr	AW	President	30.09.98
Hesketh, John	Mid	URNU	Urnu (Rnr) Soton	09.10.97
Hess, Daniel	Mid	URNU	U/A	14.10.99
Hetherington, Simon	Mid	URNU	Urnu (Rnr) Brstl	15.10.97
Hewins, Clive William, RD	Lt Cdr	AW	Sherwood	20.05.91
Hewitt, Shirley Angela	Lt Cdr	PA	Wildfire	21.07.94
Hewitt, Stephen	Mid	URNU	Urnu (Rnr) Brstl	02.12.98
Hick, David	Lt	AIR	Rnr Air Br VI	20.11.91
Hickey, Gurney	Lt Cdr	AIR	Rnr Air Br VI	31.03.99
Hicks, John David	Lt	HQ	Eaglet	31.03.90
Hicks, Mark	Mid	URNU	U/A	21.10.99
Higgins, Peter	Mid	URNU	Urnu (Rnr) Soton	09.10.97
Higgs-Goodwin, Marilyn Lee, *BA, MA*	Lt Cdr	NCS	Wildfire	31.03.95
Highett, David Francis Trevor	Lt Cdr	LOGS	King Alfred	02.08.83
Hill, Matthew Charles	Lt	SEA	President	25.01.91
Hill, Paul Terence, RD	Lt Cdr	SM	President	31.03.00
Hill-Tout, Laurence	Mid	URNU	Urnu (Rnr) Livp	15.10.98
Hills, Stephen John	ALt	AW	Vivid	08.04.99
Hilton, Caroline	Mid	URNU	Urnu (Rnr) Aberd	27.01.00
Hindle, Sean	Lt	SM	Eaglet	18.09.91
Hines, Richard	Mid	URNU	U/A	22.11.99
Hines, Stephen Frederick, *RD*	Lt Cdr	AW	King Alfred	01.08.86
Hitchings, Joseph	Mid	URNU	Urnu (Rnr) Manch	07.10.99
Hodgkinson, Rosemary	Mid	URNU	Urnu (Rnr) Brstl	21.10.98
Hodgson, Jane Lee	Lt	PA	Flying Fox	04.04.90
Hogan, Francis John, *RD*	Lt	MW	Eaglet	16.07.88
Hogg, Michael	Mid	URNU	U/A	21.10.99
Holborn, Carl	Lt	AIR	Rnr Air Br VI	16.09.90
Holbrook, Bryony	Mid	URNU	Urnu (Rnr) Soton	21.01.00

Name	Rank	Branch	Unit	Seniority
Hollard, Jeremy	Mid	URNU	Urnu (Rnr) Soton	18.02.99
Hollis, Robert Leslie Graham	Lt	AWNIS	Eaglet	11.07.89
Holloway, Stephen Leslie	Lt	AW	Eaglet	17.09.88
Holloway, Sophia Rebecca Frances	ASl	NE	President	29.09.98
Holman, Matthew	Mid	URNU	Brnc Rnr Soton	06.09.99
Holmes, David Grindall, *RD*	Lt Cdr	NCS	Flying Fox	30.12.89
Holmes, Sandra	Mid	URNU	Urnu (Rnr) Aberd	01.10.98
Hooper, Nicholas Robert Joseph, *RD*	Sg Capt		Flying Fox	30.09.98
Hope, Nigel Charles Dawson, *RD**	Cdr	AW	Scotia	30.09.96
Hopkins, Paul	Mid	URNU	Urnu (Rnr) Soton	07.10.99
Hopps, Francis	Lt Cdr	AIR	Rnr Air Br VI	31.03.98
Horne, Martin	Lt	FTRS	President	01.04.98
Horner, Benjamin Brian Harold	ASl	NE	President	10.02.99
Horner, Ian David	Lt Cdr	DIS	Ferret (Rnr)	01.11.83
Horrell, Stephen Peter	Lt Cdr	CEW	Vivid	31.03.00
Horseman, Kevin	Mid	URNU	Brnc Rnr Soton	06.09.98
Horsey, Justin	Mid	URNU	Urnu (Rnr) Soton	09.10.97
Horton, Bruce Andrew, *BSC*	Lt	AWNIS	President	15.04.91
Houghton, Nicholas	Lt Cdr	AIR	Rnr Air Br VI	31.03.96
Houghton, Philip Arthur, *BSC, LBIOL, FCA, RD**	Cdr	LOGS	Eaglet	30.09.86
Houston, Nicola	Mid	URNU	Urnu (Rnr) Glasg	14.10.99
How, Wilfrid	Mid	URNU	U/A	21.10.99
Howard, Ben	Mid	URNU	Urnu (Rnr) Ssx	20.10.98
Howard, Claire	Mid	URNU	U/A	22.10.97
Howard, The Hon Alexander	Lt Cdr	AIR	Rnr Air Br VI	31.03.94
Howard, William Jonathon, *RD**	Cdr	AW	King Alfred	30.09.92
Howarth, Alison	Mid	URNU	Urnu (Rnr) Livp	15.10.98
Howell, Colin, *RD*	Lt Cdr	HQ	King Alfred	31.03.99
Howes, Georgina	Mid	URNU	Urnu (Rnr) Livp	15.10.98
Howes, Simon Tee, RD	Lt Cdr	DIS	Ferret (Rnr)	28.03.84
Hoyle, Stephen	Lt	SM	Eaglet	20.11.95
Hubbard, Paul	Lt Cdr	LOGS	Scotia Rnr	22.05.98
Hubber, Keith Michael	Lt Cdr	AW	Flying Fox	31.03.96
Hubbert, Sherard	Mid	URNU	Urnu (Rnr) Aberd	30.09.99
Hudson, Graham Francis Grenville	Lt	INTR	Ferret (Rnr)	07.08.86
Hughes, Angharad	Mid	URNU	U/A	15.10.98
Hughes, Clare Yvonne, *RD**	Lt Cdr	CEW	President	30.09.90
Hughes, Josephine	Mid	URNU	Urnu (Rnr) Londn	12.10.99
Hughes, Jill Elizabeth	Lt Cdr	NCS	Caroline	31.03.95
Hughes, John Fraser	Lt Cdr	PA	King Alfred	14.05.92
Hughes, Kai	Lt Cdr	INT	Ferret (Rnr)	31.05.92
Hughes, Paul James, *RD*	Sg Cdr		King Alfred	30.09.95
Hulett, Peter, *AFC*	Lt Cdr	AIR	Rnr Air Br VI	26.06.87
Hulse, Rebecca	Mid	URNU	U/A	21.10.99
Hulse, Royston	Mid	URNU	U/A	16.10.97
Humphreys, John Martyn, *PHD, BSc*	Lt	MW	Wildfire	25.06.90
Hunt, Phillippa	Mid	URNU	Urnu (Rnr) Brstl	26.10.99
Hunt, Rachel	Mid	URNU	Urnu (Rnr) Glasg	14.10.95
Hunter, Clare	Mid	URNU	Urnu (Rnr) Londn	12.10.99
Hunter, Karl	Mid	URNU	Urnu (Rnr) Londn	13.10.97
Huntly, Victoria	Mid	URNU	U/A	14.10.99
Hurndall, Dominic	Lt	PA	Calliope	31.08.94
Hutchings, Carol	Mid	URNU	Urnu (Rnr) Soton	07.10.99
Hutchinson, Janice Elizabeth	Lt Cdr	NCS	Eaglet	31.03.93
Hutton, Miles	Lt	AIR	Rnr Air Br VI	09.07.90
Hyre, Stephanie	Mid	URNU	Urnu (Rnr) Ssx	12.10.99

I

Name	Rank	Branch	Unit	Seniority
Idiens, Estelle	Mid	URNU	Urnu (Rnr) Soton	09.10.97
Ilott, Simon	Mid	URNU	Urnu (Rnr) Manch	01.10.98
Imrie, Samantha	Mid	URNU	U/A	08.10.98
Induruwana, Chinthaka	Mid	URNU	Urnu (Rnr) Manch	07.10.99

Name	Rank	Branch	Unit	Seniority
Inkpin, Julie Anne	Slt	Q	King Alfred	22.01.92
Inness, Matthew	Mid	URNU	U/A	22.10.98
Insley, Andrew	Mid	URNU	U/A	20.10.99
Inwood, John	Sg Cdr		Scotia	30.09.98
Irons, Oliver	Mid	URNU	U/A	14.10.99
Irvine, Morag Mary	ASl	NE	Dalriada	02.12.98
Irving-Robertson, Georgina	Mid	URNU	U/A	20.10.98
Ivory, Daniel	Mid	URNU	U/A	31.10.99

J

Name	Rank	Branch	Unit	Seniority
Jachnik, Clive	Lt Cdr	INTR	Ferret (Rnr)	31.03.99
Jack, Andrew	ASl	URNU	Urnu (Rnr) Glasg	24.03.99
Jackson, Graham	Lt Cdr	AIR	Rnr Air Br Vl	01.10.88
Jackson, Iain	Mid	URNU	Urnu (Rnr) Livp	15.10.98
Jackson, Trevor	Lt Cdr	AIR	Rnr Air Br Vl	01.10.94
Jacques, Kathryn	Mid	URNU	Urnu (Rnr) Livp	15.10.98
Jaffier, Robert Gary	ASl	NE	Forward	13.10.98
James, Andrew George	ASl	NE	Scotia	09.07.97
James, Christopher Henry, *RD*	Lt Cdr	AW	Flying Fox	01.07.82
James, Edwin	Mid	URNU	U/A	07.10.98
James, John	Mid	URNU	U/A	22.10.97
James, Roy Arthur, *BSC*	ACdr	SM	Forward	01.03.83
James, Victoria	Mid	URNU	U/A	05.11.97
Jameson, Susan Catherine	Lt Cdr	HQ	Flying Fox	31.03.00
Jardine, Corriene Marie	Lt	AWNIS	Wildfire	12.10.93
Jarrett, Catherine	Mid	URNU	U/A	26.01.00
Jasper, Mark Jonathan	Lt	MW	Sherwood	01.01.96
Jeffries, Megan	Mid	URNU	U/A	16.10.97
Jenkins, Adele Elizabeth	Lt	HQ	Cambria	14.10.89
Jenner, Alexander	Mid	URNU	Urnu (Rnr) Ssx	20.10.98
Jermy, Richard Alexander	Lt	INTR	Ferret (Rnr)	13.12.91
Jewell, Chris	Mid	URNU	Urnu (Rnr) Livp	15.10.98
John, Peter Martin	Lt Cdr	AW	Cambria	11.06.92
Johns, Gavin Haydn	Lt	SEA	Cambria	01.01.93
Johnson, Catherine	Mid	URNU	Urnu (Rnr) Glasg	14.10.99
Johnson, Craig Rothwell	Lt	LOGS	Sherwood	19.04.89
Johnson, Edward	Mid	URNU	U/A	20.10.99
Johnson, Jill Ena	Lt	Q	Cambria	09.10.88
Johnston, Michael	Mid	URNU	Urnu (Rnr) Glasg	14.10.99
Johnstone, James Oliver	Slt	SEA	President	27.02.93
Johnstone, Peter Hughes, *RD*	Lt Cdr	LOGS	President	31.03.97
Jones, Andrew	Mid	URNU	U/A	22.01.98
Jones, Christopher, *RD*	Lt Cdr	AW	President	01.05.88
Jones, Charles David, *RD*	Lt Cdr	SM	Dalriada	31.03.00
Jones, Gordon	Mid	URNU	U/A	19.10.98
Jones, Geoffrey Mark	ALt	AW	Eaglet	20.01.92
Jones, Kathryn	Mid	URNU	U/A	16.10.97
Jones, Keith William	ASl	NE	Forward	22.04.99
Jones, Pauline	Lt Cdr	LOGS	Calliope	31.03.98
Joshi, Tejas	Mid	URNU	Urnu (Rnr) Londn	26.01.00
Journeaux, Simon Francis	ASgltcdr		Eaglet	28.09.99
Joyce, David	Mid	URNU	Brnc Rnr Soton	06.09.99
Jubb, Caroline	Mid	URNU	Urnu (Rnr) Livp	14.10.99
Jutley, Jasdeep	Mid	URNU	Urnu (Rnr) Aberd	30.09.99

K

Name	Rank	Branch	Unit	Seniority
Kadera, Stephen John	Lt	PA	Wildfire	02.04.86
Kassell, Marie	Mid	URNU	U/A	21.10.99
Kay, David	Lt Cdr	LOGS	Flying Fox	31.03.97
Kay, Ivan Charles Michael	Lt	SEA	King Alfred	12.11.88
Kay, Timothy	Mid	URNU	Urnu (Rnr) Livp	14.10.99
Kay, Victoria	Mid	URNU	U/A	14.10.99

Name	Rank	Branch	Unit	Seniority
Kearney, Melian Jane	Lt Cdr	HQ	Vivid	31.03.97
Keith, Rory	Mid	URNU	Urnu (Rnr) Soton	07.10.99
Kelly, Timothy	Lt Cdr	X	Rnr Air Br VI	01.04.98
Kelly, William	Mid	URNU	Urnu (Rnr) Brstl	15.10.97
Kembery, Simon John	Lt	AW	Cambria	11.06.93
Kemp, Richard	Mid	URNU	Urnu (Rnr) Soton	07.10.99
Kemp, Simon Michael	Lt Cdr	DIS	Ferret (Rnr)	31.03.99
Kenney, Dawn Elizabeth, RD	Cdr	Q	Vivid	30.09.99
Kenny, Luke	Mid	URNU	U/A	03.02.00
Kent, Thomas William Henry, *RD*	Cdr	AW	Sherwood	30.09.99
Kenyon, Christopher	Lt Cdr	HQ	President	03.04.82
Kerr, Gordon	Mid	URNU	Urnu (Rnr) Brstl	21.10.98
Khan, Basit	Mid	URNU	Urnu (Rnr) Londn	12.10.99
King, Andrew Stephen	Lt Cdr	MW	King Alfred	31.03.99
King, Charles Guy Hall	Lt	SEA	King Alfred	16.08.92
King, David	Mid	URNU	U/A	14.10.99
King, Ian	Lt	HQ	Eaglet	05.12.97
Kinsella, Kevin, *QVRM, RD**	Lt Cdr	MW	King Alfred	30.09.96
Kirby, Kier	Mid	URNU	Urnu (Rnr) Ssx	12.10.99
Kirk, William Walter	Lt	NCS	Sherwood	31.03.96
Kirkham, Anna	Mid	URNU	Urnu (Rnr) Manch	07.10.99
Kirkpatrick, Alasdair	ASl	NE	Wildfire Rnr	18.11.99
Kirkpatrick, David	Mid	URNU	Urnu (Rnr) Aberd	01.10.98
Kirkpatrick, Robin	Mid	URNU	Urnu (Rnr) Soton	08.10.98
Kistruck, David	Lt	AIR	Rnr Air Br VI	01.06.89
Kitchen, Catherine Anne	Lt	HQ	Wildfire	12.12.92
Knight, David	Lt Cdr	AIR	Rnr Air Br VI	01.10.88
Knott, Clive	Lt Cdr	AIR	Rnr Air Br VI	31.03.98
Knotts, George William	Lt	CEW	Calliope	27.09.93
Knowles, Donna Maureen	Lt	SEA	Caroline	28.10.91
Knowles, Thomas	Mid	URNU	U/A	14.10.99

L

Name	Rank	Branch	Unit	Seniority
Ladislaus, Paul	Mid	URNU	U/A	16.10.97
Lai Hung, Jeremy	Mid	URNU	Urnu (Rnr) Londn	13.10.98
Laird, William	Mid	URNU	Urnu (Rnr) Brstl	26.10.99
Lancaster, Leonie	Lt	SEA	Scotia	23.05.97
Langdon, Simon	Mid	URNU	Urnu (Rnr) Ssx	12.10.99
Langmead, Clive Francis, *RD*	Lt Cdr	AW	Forward	01.07.90
Lapage-Norris, Thomas	Slt	LOGS	Flying Fox	31.10.97
Lasham, Caroline	Mid	URNU	Urnu (Rnr) Ssx	12.10.99
Last,	Lt Cdr	AIR	Rnr Air Br VI	01.10.91
Lathrope, Jennifer	Mid	URNU	Urnu (Rnr) Aberd	30.09.99
Lauretani, Andrew Stephen David	Lt	PA	Vivid	05.10.90
Laverick, Helen Tanya	ASl	NE	President	02.06.99
Lawson, Alexandra	Mid	URNU	Urnu (Rnr) Londn	13.10.98
Lea, Carey	Mid	URNU	U/A	16.12.97
Leather, Roger James, *RD*	Lt Cdr	AW	Eaglet	01.06.87
Leaver, Claire	Mid	URNU	U/A	07.10.98
Ledwidge, Francis Andrew	Lt	INTR	Ferret (Rnr)	15.01.95
Lee, David Anthony	Lt Cdr	SM	Dalriada	31.03.98
Lee, Daren	Mid	URNU	Urnu (Rnr) Manch	07.10.99
Lee, John	ACdr	NCS	Calliope	31.03.94
Lee, Robert	Lt	AIR	Rnr Air Br VI	01.10.91
Lee, Thomas William Robert	Lt	INTR	Ferret (Rnr)	03.09.95
Lees, Sarah	Mid	URNU	U/A	04.02.99
Legge, Fiona	Mid	URNU	U/A	14.10.99
Leigh-Smith, Simon John	Sg Ltcdr		Scotia	21.01.97
Lemon, John	ALt	X	Urnu (Rnr) Aberd	09.02.88
Leonard, John Francis	Sg Ltcdr		King Alfred	14.07.85
Leonard, Maria	Mid	URNU	U/A	20.10.99
Leslie, Sarah	Mid	URNU	Urnu (Rnr) Aberd	30.09.99

Name	Rank	Branch	Unit	Seniority
Lewis, Ann	Mid	URNU	Brnc Rnr Soton	08.09.97
Lewis, John Charles	Lt	SEA	President	20.01.94
Lewis, Justine	Mid	URNU	Urnu (Rnr) Brstl	26.10.99
Lewis, Kathryn Elizabeth	Lt	MW	President	31.07.95
Lewis, Mark	Mid	URNU	U/A	14.10.99
Lewis, Richard	Lt	AIR	Rnr Air Br VI	01.05.86
Lewis, Simon, RD	Lt	LOGS	King Alfred	01.02.95
Lewtas, Andrew	Mid	URNU	U/A	29.10.98
Leyshon, Sally Louise	Lt Cdr	AWNIS	Flying Fox	31.03.93
Lindsley, Michael James	Lt Cdr	AW	Calliope	31.03.99
Lines, Jessica	Mid	URNU	Urnu (Rnr) Manch	07.10.99
Lippell, Sabrina Rose, *BSC*	Lt Cdr	PA	Wildfire	30.09.89
Livey, Kate	Mid	URNU	Urnu (Rnr) Ssx	21.10.97
Livingstone, Michael Jeremy	Lt	MW	Eaglet	26.12.89
Llewellyn, Sarah	Mid	URNU	Urnu (Rnr) Ssx	20.10.98
Lloyd, Conrad Michael Rawlings, *RD***	Cdr	AW	King Alfred	31.12.79
Lloyd, David Vernon	Lt Cdr	AW	King Alfred	31.03.99
Lloyd, Gareth, RD	Lt Cdr	HQ	Eaglet	31.03.98
Lloyd, Peter John	Lt	AW	King Alfred	27.11.86
Loates, Mark	Slt	URNU	Urnu (Rnr) Manch	22.01.98
Logan, John	ASl	Q	Calliope	21.01.92
Lomas, Hugh, DSC	Lt Cdr	AIR	Rnr Air Br VI	01.04.80
Longmore, David	Mid	URNU	Urnu (Rnr) Soton	08.10.98
Lord, Richard	Mid	URNU	Urnu (Rnr) Aberd	30.09.99
Lort, Timothy	Lt Cdr	AIR	Rnr Air Br VI	01.10.95
Lorton, Jonathan, *RD*	Lt Cdr	HQ	Flying Fox	31.03.94
Loughran, Cedric Grenville, *RD*	Cdr	AW	Eaglet	30.09.98
Lovell, James	Mid	URNU	U/A	22.10.97
Lovelock, Adam	Mid	URNU	U/A	17.02.00
Lovett, Clare	Mid	URNU	Urnu (Rnr) Soton	26.10.98
Lowry, Claire	Mid	URNU	Urnu (Rnr) Livp	15.10.98
Luke, Warren Munro, *RD*	Sg Cdr		Scotia	30.09.99
Lund, Christian	Mid	URNU	U/A	25.01.99
Lunt, Dean	Lt Cdr	AIR	Rnr Air Br VI	03.12.86
Lupini, James	Mid	URNU	U/A	08.10.98
Lusher, Catherine	Mid	URNU	U/A	22.10.97
Lyall, Kenneth Alexander, RD	Lt Cdr	HQ	Scotia	31.03.97
Lydon, Michael	Lt	LOGS	Calliope	30.09.96
Lynch, Suzanne Marie	ASl	NE	Cambria	31.10.95
Lynn, Sarah	Mid	URNU	Urnu (Rnr) Londn	13.10.97
Lyons, Eleanore	Mid	URNU	U/A	20.10.98

M

Name	Rank	Branch	Unit	Seniority
Mccallum, Andrew	Mid	URNU	Urnu (Rnr) Glasg	10.10.97
MacDonald, Angus	Lt Cdr	AIR	Rnr Air Br VI	31.03.98
MacDonald, Alastair	Mid	URNU	Urnu (Rnr) Manch	07.10.99
MacDonald, Colin	ASl	NE	Scotia	07.01.98
MacDonald, Clare	Mid	URNU	U/A	23.10.97
MacDonald, Fiona	Mid	URNU	Urnu (Rnr) Glasg	14.10.99
Machin, Peter Charles Clive, *RD**	Lt Cdr	HQ	Cambria	21.12.87
MacKay, Evan George	Palt	AW	Dalriada	06.12.96
MacKay, Graham	Mid	URNU	Urnu (Rnr) Aberd	01.10.98
MacKenzie, Cailean	Mid	URNU	Urnu (Rnr) Aberd	30.09.99
MacKenzie, Luke	Mid	URNU	Urnu (Rnr) Manch	09.10.97
MacKenzie-Philps, Linda	Lt Cdr	PA	King Alfred	31.03.99
Mackie, Robert Charles Gordon	ASl	NE	Forward	19.05.99
MacKintosh, Zemma	Mid	URNU	Urnu (Rnr) Livp	15.10.98
MacLean, Nicholas Peter	Lt Cdr	SM	President	31.03.97
Macleod, Alistair David	Sg Ltcdr		Scotia	17.10.78
MacMillan, Alasdair Iain Macaulay	Sg Ltcdr		Scotia	04.03.99
MacRae, Kirk	Mid	URNU	Urnu (Rnr) Glasg	14.10.99
MacTaggart, Alasdair Donald, *RD*	Lt Cdr	COMM	Dalriada	31.03.94

Name	Rank	Branch	Unit	Seniority
Maddison, Hugh	Mid	URNU	Brnc Rnr Soton	08.09.97
Maddocks, Sian	Mid	URNU	U/A	16.10.97
Magnay, Claire Georgina	Slt	SM	Forward	16.07.94
Mahony, Christopher	Lt Cdr	AIR	Rnr Air Br VI	26.09.96
Maitland, John, *RD**	Sg Capt		Dalriada	30.09.95
Major, Christopher	Mid	URNU	Urnu (Rnr) Livp	14.10.99
Malkin, Emma Mary, *BA*	Lt	SEA	President	14.09.95
Malkin, Roy Vyvian	Palt	AW	President	02.06.99
Mallinson, Ian	Mid	URNU	U/A	21.10.99
Mallinson, Stuart Jeffry, *MSC*	Lt	MW	President	31.03.96
Malone, Keith	PSgltcdr		Eaglet	07.01.00
Malpas, Peter	Lt	NCS	King Alfred	22.03.92
Manley, John Preston	ALt	NE	Vivid	29.02.00
Mann, Barbara	Lt	PA	Vivid	24.12.93
Manning, Jacquline Vera, RD	Lt	SM	President	11.02.89
Manson, Adrian	Mid	URNU	Urnu (Rnr) Glasg	14.10.99
Manson, Peter	Mid	URNU	Urnu (Rnr) Brstl	26.10.99
Manzoor, Asim	Mid	URNU	Urnu (Rnr) Londn	12.10.99
Marandola, Stefan	Lt	AIR	Rnr Air Br VI	17.01.96
March, Marisa	Mid	URNU	Urnu (Rnr) Londn	13.10.98
Markham, Paul Anthony	Lt	SM	President	28.07.92
Marland, Helen	Mid	URNU	U/A	14.12.99
Marlow, Stephen, *QGM*	Lt Cdr	AIR	Rnr Air Br VI	31.03.97
Marr, David	Lt Cdr	AIR	Rnr Air Br VI	01.10.94
Marsh, Timothy	Lt	AIR	Rnr Air Br VI	06.07.87
Marshall, Peter John	Lt Cdr	MW	Flying Fox	31.03.96
Marshall, Stephen Michael	Lt	MCDO	U/A	17.04.88
Martin, Darren Hinna	Lt	SEA	President	16.12.90
Martin, Gareth	Mid	URNU	Urnu (Rnr) Livp	05.11.99
Martin, Lisa	Mid	URNU	Urnu (Rnr) Londn	13.10.98
Martin, Nicholas John, *RD*	Lt Cdr	MW	Calliope	31.03.95
Maryon, Karen Anne	Lt	Q	Sherwood	24.12.87
Maryon, Michael Ian	Lt Cdr	PA	Sherwood	31.03.98
Mason, Ann Margaret, RD	Lt Cdr	LOGS	Eaglet	31.03.99
Mason, Andrew Robert	ASl	NE	President	11.06.99
Mason, Grace	Mid	URNU	Urnu (Rnr) Manch	01.10.98
Mason, Richard	Mid	URNU	Urnu (Rnr) Livp	17.02.00
Mason, Thomas	Lt Cdr	AIR	Rnr Air Br VI	01.10.88
Massey, Steven	Lt	AIR	Rnr Air Br VI	01.02.91
Mathias, Menna	Mid	URNU	U/A	14.10.99
Maude, Colin	Mid	URNU	Brnc Rnr Soton	06.09.98
Maurin, Claudine	Mid	URNU	Urnu (Rnr) Soton	08.10.98
Mawer, Kieren	Mid	URNU	Brnc Rnr Soton	06.09.99
Maxwell, Andrew Alistair, *RD*	Lt Cdr	INTR	Ferret (Rnr)	05.08.88
May, Jennifer	Mid	URNU	U/A	22.10.98
May, Sarah	Mid	URNU	Brnc Rnr Soton	06.09.99
May, Victoria	Mid	URNU	Urnu (Rnr) Livp	26.10.95
Maynard, Alison	Mid	URNU	Urnu (Rnr) Glasg	08.10.98
McAllister, Donald*D, MCALISTER, MBA, BSC*	Lt Cdr	HQ	Dalriada	21.02.90
McBride, Maurice, *BSC*	Lt Cdr	AIR	Rnr Air Br VI	02.08.86
McCabe, Jeremy Charles	Lt	AW	Vivid	31.07.94
McCarthy, Daniel	Mid	URNU	U/A	19.10.98
McCartney, William Robert	ASl	NE	President	10.06.97
McCloghrie, Paul	Mid	URNU	U/A	20.10.99
McClurg, Robert James	Slt	SEA	Vivid	12.07.98
McConn, Dervla	ASl	NE	Caroline	23.07.98
McCormack, Patrick, *RD*	Lt Cdr	NCS	Dalriada	15.07.92
McCormick, Damion Kevin	ASl	NE	Sherwood	20.04.99
McCreery, Robert George	Lt	SEA	Caroline	20.06.89
McDermott Evans, Rachel	Mid	URNU	U/A	29.10.98
McDonald, Roger	Lt Cdr	AIR	Rnr Air Br VI	01.09.87
McGhee, Stephen James	Slt	HQ	Dalriada	16.03.91
McGrath, Gerard Francis	Slt	SEA	President	23.10.95

Name	Rank	Branch	Unit	Seniority
McHugh De Clare, Abigail	Mid	URNU	U/A	20.10.99
McKenzie, Alexander	Mid	URNU	Urnu (Rnr) Glasg	14.10.99
McKetty, Paul	Mid	URNU	Urnu (Rnr) Aberd	30.09.99
McKinnell, Soraya Jane	ASl	NE	Calliope	08.06.99
McKinnon, Laura	Mid	URNU	Urnu (Rnr) Glasg	08.10.98
McKnight, Edward	ASl	X	Urnu (Rnr) Glasg	17.10.90
McLaren, Alastair, *QCVSA*	Lt Cdr	AIR	Rnr Air Br VI	09.03.92
McLaughlin, Vincent	Mid	URNU	Brnc Rnr Soton	06.09.99
McLaverty, Karen Anne	Lt	NCS	Caroline	17.03.99
McManus, Peter	Lt Cdr	AIR	Rnr Air Br VI	01.10.89
McMinn, Sandra	ASl	URNU	Urnu (Rnr) Aberd	01.10.98
McMurran, Robert Campbell	Lt Cdr	HQ	Caroline	31.03.97
McNaught, Edward William Gordon	Lt Cdr	MW	Calliope	31.03.97
McNeish, A S	Lt	SM	President	05.09.94
McPhail, Alastair John, *RD**	Lt Cdr	NCS	President	14.03.85
McQueen, Patrick	Mid	URNU	Urnu (Rnr) Aberd	01.10.98
Meacher, Paul	Mid	URNU	Urnu (Rnr) Londn	13.10.98
Meekins, Timothy	Lt Cdr	AIR	Rnr Air Br VI	06.12.89
Meerza, Andrew	Lt	AWNIS	Vivid	16.04.93
Meharg, Neil	Lt	MW	Caroline	11.08.96
Meldram, Sheryl Christine Anne	Lt	Q	President	30.10.93
Melson, Janet	Lt	LOGS	King Alfred	25.02.96
Mercer, Ian S	Slt	SEA	Ferret (Rnr)	21.02.97
Mercer, Lara	Mid	URNU	Urnu (Rnr) Manch	07.10.99
Merrington, Matthew	Mid	URNU	Urnu (Rnr) Londn	12.10.99
Mettam, Samuel Richard	ASl	NE	Scotia	31.07.98
Meyer, Amme Marie	Mid	URNU	Urnu (Rnr) Londn	05.11.98
Meyers, Philip	Mid	URNU	Urnu (Rnr) Livp	15.10.98
Miall, Merlin	Mid	URNU	Urnu (Rnr) Ssx	21.10.97
Millar, Peter	Mid	URNU	U/A	15.10.99
Miller, Charles	Mid	URNU	U/A	22.10.98
Miller, Carol Diane, *BA, RD*	Lt	HQ	King Alfred	30.01.96
Miller, David	Lt Cdr	AIR	Rnr Air Br VI	01.04.95
Miller, Gary	Mid	URNU	Urnu (Rnr) Manch	01.10.98
Milligan, Kevin	Mid	URNU	U/A	14.10.99
Mills, Mary Kathleen, RD	Lt Cdr	CEW	Flying Fox	31.03.93
Millward, Jonathan	Lt Cdr	SM	King Alfred	01.09.91
Milne-Home, Elizabeth Mary	Lt	SEA	King Alfred	23.05.97
Milner, Lisa	Mid	URNU	U/A	07.10.97
Minehane, Claire	Mid	URNU	Urnu (Rnr) Ssx	12.10.99
Minter, Louise Inglis Hood	Lt Cdr	Q	Dalriada	01.08.83
Miskin, Peter	Lt Cdr	AIR	Rnr Air Br VI	31.03.94
Misra, Suneet	Mid	URNU	Urnu (Rnr) Livp	14.10.99
Mitchell, Colin	Lt	NCS	Ferret (Rnr)	05.08.94
Mitchell, Robert	Lt Cdr	AIR	Rnr Air Br VI	31.03.93
Mitchell, Shouna	Mid	URNU	Urnu (Rnr) Soton	07.10.99
Mochar, Melanie	Mid	URNU	Urnu (Rnr) Aberd	30.09.99
Moffat, Linda Winifred, RD	Lt Cdr	INTR	Ferret (Rnr)	30.09.88
Moghraby, Chetal	Mid	URNU	Urnu (Rnr) Ssx	20.10.98
Montgomery, William George	Lt Cdr	SEA	Flying Fox	31.03.00
Moorthy, Roham Michael	SLt	SM	President	09.02.95
Moran, Simon	Lt	AIR	Rnr Air Br VI	18.02.94
Morden, Hayley	Mid	URNU	Urnu (Rnr) Aberd	30.09.99
Morgan, Eugene Peter	Lt	MW	President	31.07.95
Morgan, Gareth William	Lt	LOGS	Cambria	29.06.90
Morgan, Linda Frances	Lt	Q	Wildfire	26.09.96
Morgan, Sian	Mid	URNU	Urnu (Rnr) Ssx	21.10.97
Morgans, Daniel James	Lt	MW	President	09.05.99
Moriarty, Helen Jean	ASl	Q	President	03.09.98
Morison, Julian Ronald	ASl	NE	King Alfred	17.11.99
Morland, Andrew	Mid	URNU	Urnu (Rnr) Soton	08.10.98
Morley, Dietmar Allen	Lt	NCS	Sherwood	20.10.98
Morley, Graham David, *RD**	Cdr	MW	King Alfred30.09.93	

Name	Rank	Branch	Unit	Seniority
Morley, Jane Mary, RD	Cdr	Q	President	30.09.97
Morris, David John	Lt Cdr	SM	Wildfire	02.08.82
Morris, Jessica	Mid	URNU	U/A	14.10.99
Morris, Louise	Mid	URNU	Urnu (Rnr) Londn	12.10.99
Morris, Paul	Mid	URNU	Brnc Rnr Soton	06.09.98
Morris, Richard	Mid	URNU	Urnu (Rnr) Soton	08.10.98
Morris, William Alexander	Lt	MW	Scotia	19.07.89
Morrison, Susan	ASl	NE	Dalriada	24.11.99
Mortlock, Alison Jane	Lt	SEA	President	17.05.98
Moseley, Allison	ASl	NE	Calliope	10.03.98
Moss, Eleanor	Mid	URNU	Urnu (Rnr) Ssx	21.10.97
Mowbray, Roger, *QCVSA*	Lt Cdr	AIR	Rnr Air Br Vl	01.10.88
Moyes, Peter	ASl	URNU	Urnu (Rnr) Glasg	24.03.99
Mulheirn, Ian	Mid	URNU	U/A	25.10.99
Mullins, Natalie	Mid	URNU	Brnc Rnr Soton	06.09.99
Munday, Stephen	Mid	URNU	Urnu (Rnr) Soton	07.10.99
Munson, Eileen Patricia	Lt	Q	Cambria	23.09.95
Munt, Marcus	Mid	URNU	Urnu (Rnr) Brstl	08.10.98
Murray, Abigail	Mid	URNU	U/A	08.10.98
Murray, Christine	Mid	URNU	Urnu (Rnr) Glasg	15.11.99
Murray, Edward Charles, *RD*	Lt Cdr	INTR	Ferret (Rnr)	31.03.99
Murrison, M P	Lt Cdr	AW	President	31.03.99
Myers, Margaret Cynthia, *RD**	Lt Cdr	CEW	Vivid	31.03.93
Myers, Paul	Lt	AIR	Rnr Air Br Vl	01.08.84
Myers, Verity	Mid	URNU	U/A	08.10.98
Myles, Ian	Mid	URNU	Urnu (Rnr) Glasg	14.10.99

N

Name	Rank	Branch	Unit	Seniority
Nadin, Robert	Lt Cdr	AIR	Rnr Air Br Vl	01.09.95
Nanji, Karim	Mid	URNU	Urnu (Rnr) Londn	13.10.98
Neal, Ellen	Mid	URNU	U/A	14.10.99
Neale, Kirsty A	Lt	NCS	Scotia	30.11.94
Neate, James	Mid	URNU	Urnu (Rnr) Ssx	20.10.98
Nelson, Victoria	Mid	URNU	Urnu (Rnr) Glasg	08.10.98
Nettleton, Philip James	Lt	PA	Wildfire	23.08.88
Newby-Grant, William Robert, *RD**	Lt Cdr	INTR	Ferret (Rnr)	26.03.80
Newland, Anthony D	Sg Ltcdr		Eaglet	23.11.97
Newton, David Jason	Lt	SEA	President	28.03.96
Newton, Ingrid Catherine	Lt Cdr	LOGS	Eaglet	31.03.99
Newton, Mark	Lt	AIR	Rnr Air Br Vl	01.08.91
Nichol, R C F	Lt Cdr	PA	President	18.09.75
Nicholson, Emma	ASl	NE	Dalriada	22.01.98
Nicholson, Jeremy David, *RD**	Lt Cdr	AW	Flying Fox	01.10.84
Nicholson, Peter Adrian, *RD**	Lt Cdr	INTR	Ferret (Rnr)	19.02.87
Noakes, David Anthony	Slt	LOGS	Eaglet	18.01.93
Noble, Robert Howard, *BSC*	Lt Cdr	NCS	Forward	31.03.97
Northcott, John	Lt Cdr	LOGS	Calliope	31.03.98
Northcott, Phillip	Mid	URNU	Brnc Rnr Soton	09.09.96
Norton, Rachel	Lt	Q	Wildfire	30.10.94
Norwood, Jeffrey Michael	Sg Cdr		Forward	30.09.97
Nunn, James	Lt Cdr	AIR	Rnr Air Br Vl	31.03.99
Nurse, Alan Vincent Pigott	ASl	NE	President	13.05.97

O

Name	Rank	Branch	Unit	Seniority
O'Callaghan, Penelope Jane	Lt Cdr	Q	King Alfred	31.03.96
O'Driscoll, Edward Hugh	ASl	NE	President	10.03.99
O'Hagan, Helen	Mid	URNU	Urnu (Rnr) Ssx	21.10.97
O'Neill, George Paul	Lt	INTR	Ferret (Rnr)	08.08.93
O'Sullivan, Kathryn Winifred, *RD*	Lt	SEA	Vivid	26.07.96
O'Sullivan, Paul	Mid	URNU	Brnc Rnr Soton	06.09.98
Oag, Denis Cairns	Lt Cdr	MW	Scotia	31.03.00
Oakley, Richard	ALt	AW	President	29.09.98

Name	Rank	Branch	Unit	Seniority
Oakley, Ruth	Mid	URNU	Urnu (Rnr) Manch	07.10.99
Oaten, Timothy	Lt	CEW	Sherwood	03.06.87
Oates, Edward	Lt Cdr	AIR	Rnr Air Br VI	16.02.93
Odujinrin, Dolapo	Mid	URNU	U/A	16.10.97
Okubanjo, Adewale	Mid	URNU	Urnu (Rnr) Manch	01.10.98
Oleary, Catherine	Mid	URNU	Urnu (Rnr) Ssx	12.10.99
Olivant, David Francis	Lt Cdr	CEW	Sherwood	31.03.99
Ormshaw, Andrew	Lt Cdr	AIR	Rnr Air Br VI	23.06.87
Osborn, Anthony	Mid	URNU	U/A	20.10.99
Osborne, Laura	Mid	URNU	Urnu (Rnr) Glasg	10.10.97
Otto, Antoni	Mid	URNU	Urnu (Rnr) Livp	14.10.99
Owen, Paul	Mid	URNU	U/A	07.10.98
Owen, Sarah Elizabeth	ASl	NE	Presedent	29.09.98

P

Name	Rank	Branch	Unit	Seniority
Paddock, Lee David	Lt	SM	Forward	01.03.94
Padget, Joanna Louise	Slt	NCS	King Alfred	10.02.95
Padgham, Philip	ALt	URNU	Urnu (Rnr) Ssx	30.06.97
Pain, Sarah Louise	ASl	NE	King Alfred	14.10.98
Palmer, Alon, *RD*	Lt Cdr	AW	Scotia	09.05.91
Palmer, Helen	ASl	URNU	Urnu (Rnr) Manch	01.10.90
Palmer, James	Mid	URNU	U/A	14.10.99
Papaioannou, Theodore	Mid	URNU	Urnu (Rnr) Soton	07.10.99
Pardoe, Christopher Richard	Lt Cdr	PA	Vivid	13.09.86
Parirenyatwa, Tawanda	Mid	URNU	U/A	07.10.97
Park, Alyson Marie	ASl	NE	Eaglet	21.01.98
Park, Kenneth	ASl	SM	Eaglet	10.06.97
Parker, David	Mid	URNU	U/A	21.10.99
Parker, Jonathan	Mid	URNU	Brnc Rnr Soton	06.09.98
Parker, Philip	Mid	URNU	U/A	23.10.97
Parkins, Jennifer	Mid	URNU	U/A	20.10.98
Parkinson, Gemma	Mid	URNU	Urnu (Rnr) Ssx	20.10.98
Parnell, Nicola	Mid	URNU	Urnu (Rnr) Soton	09.10.97
Parris, John Stewart, *RD*	Lt Cdr	PA	Flying Fox	31.03.93
Parsonage, Neil David, *LLM*	Lt Cdr	NCS	Eaglet	31.03.00
Parsons, Laura	Mid	URNU	U/A	19.10.98
Passmore, Susan Margaret, *RD*	Cdr	HQ	Flying Fox	30.09.97
Paterson, Gordon Laird	Lt Cdr	AWNIS	King Alfred	02.11.84
Paterson, Matthew	Mid	URNU	U/A	22.10.98
Patten, Nicholas William	Lt Cdr	NCS	Forward	131.03.00
Patterson, Jarrod Lee	Lt	PA	President	07.07.91
Paxton, Alan	Mid	URNU	Urnu (Rnr) Glasg	14.10.99
Payne, Gareth	Mid	URNU	Urnu (Rnr) Glasg	14.10.99
Payton, Philip John	ACdr	PA	Vivid	24.07.86
Peace, Alexander	Mid	URNU	U/A	06.10.97
Pearson, Ian	Mid	URNU	U/A	01.04.99
Pearson, Paul Austin Kevin	Lt Cdr	SM	Presedent	31.03.00
Pendlebury, Ruth	Mid	URNU	Urnu (Rnr) Livp	14.10.99
Percival, Victoria	Mid	URNU	Urnu (Rnr) Brstl	26.10.99
Perkins, Lucy	Mid	URNU	U/A	14.10.99
Perks, Edward	Mid	URNU	U/A	14.10.99
Perks, Simon	Mid	URNU	Urnu (Rnr) Brstl	15.10.97
Peskett, Daniel	Mid	URNU	Brnc Rnr Soton	06.09.98
Petch, Alan	Mid	URNU	U/A	07.10.97
Peters, Charlotte	Mid	URNU	U/A	19.10.98
Pethick, Ian	Lt	LOGS	Vivid	25.09.96
Petrie, Melville	Lt Cdr	LOGS	Flying Fox	09.01.87
Philcox, Zoe	Mid	URNU	U/A	20.10.99
Phillips, Lucy	Mid	URNU	U/A	10.10.97
Phillips, Matthew	Mid	URNU	U/A	14.10.99
Phillips, Victoria	Mid	URNU	U/A	05.01.00
Philpott, Sally Anne	ASl	NE	King Alfred	04.01.95

Name	Rank	Branch	Unit	Seniority
Pickup, David Julian	Lt Cdr	PA	Wildfire	17.09.75
Pike, Christine Margaret	Lt Cdr	DIS	Ferret (Rnr)	31.03.95
Pike, Daniella	Mid	URNU	Urnu (Rnr) Ssx	20.10.98
Pimm, Anthony	Mid	URNU	U/A	14.10.99
Pirie, Katherine	Lt	AIR	Rnr Air Br Vl	15.12.89
Pitman, Lisa	Mid	URNU	U/A	15.10.98
Pittaway, Ernest	Mid	URNU	Urnu (Rnr) Ssx	21.10.97
Player, Rodney	Lt	AIR	Rnr Air Br Vl	09.06.88
Plumtree, Matthew James Thomas	ASl	NE	President	26.11.98
Pockett, Gemma	Mid	URNU	Urnu (Rnr) Brstl	15.10.97
Pollock, Susan	Mid	URNU	Urnu (Rnr) Manch	01.10.98
Posnett, Dickon	Lt	AIR	Rnr Air Br Vl	01.08.88
Poulton-Watt, Andrew Ritchie	ALt	CEW	Scotia	10.09.95
Powell, Emma	Mid	URNU	Urnu (Rnr) Soton	07.10.99
Powell, Jonathan Charles Boyd	Lt Cdr	MW	Wildfire	31.03.97
Powell, Stephen	Lt Cdr	AIR	Rnr Air Br Vl	01.10.93
Powell, William	Lt Cdr	AIR	Rnr Air Br Vl	31.03.99
Powley, Simon Owen Maxwell	Lt Cdr	INTR	Ferret (Rnr)	31.03.98
Poynton, Claire	Mid	URNU	Urnu (Rnr) Aberd	30.09.99
Preece, Adam	Mid	URNU	U/A	01.02.00
Pressagh, John Patterson, *RD*	Lt Cdr	INTR	Ferret (Rnr)	02.04.78
Preston, Thomas	Mid	URNU	Urnu (Rnr) Glasg	10.10.97
Price, Edward	Mid	URNU	Urnu (Rnr) Manch	09.10.97
Price, Naomi	Mid	URNU	Urnu (Rnr) Aberd	30.09.99
Price, Susan, RD	Lt Cdr	NCS	Flying Fox	31.03.97
Proctor, Caroline	Mid	URNU	Urnu (Rnr) Aberd	01.10.98
Pryce, Simon	Lt	AIR	Rnr Air Br Vl	05.10.88
Pugh, Hywel Jones	ALt	AW	President	10.06.90
Pugh, Neil	Lt	LOGS	Cambria	15.05.91
Pugsley, Andrew	Mid	URNU	Urnu (Rnr) Londn	12.10.99
Purdy, Helen	Mid	URNU	U/A	25.11.99
Pye, Steven	ALt	URNU	U/A	21.10.97
Pyman, John	Mid	URNU	U/A	14.10.99

R

Name	Rank	Branch	Unit	Seniority
Rahman, Farhana	Mid	URNU	Urnu (Rnr) Ssx	12.10.99
Rainey, Peter	Lt Cdr	AIR	Rnr Air Br Vl	01.03.90
Ramsay, Brian P., *MA*	Lt	SM	President	17.08.90
Ramsdale, Timothy	Lt	AIR	Rnr Air Br Vl	16.04.89
Rankin, Ben	Mid	URNU	Urnu (Rnr) Brstl	21.10.98
Rankin, John Graham, *RD*	Cdr	AW	Vivid	30.09.95
Rayment, Lucy	Mid	URNU	U/A	07.10.97
Rayne, Jeremy	Mid	URNU	Urnu (Rnr) Londn	02.11.99
Read, David Arthur, *RD, BSC*	Lt Cdr	HQ	President	31.03.97
Read, Emily	Mid	URNU	U/A	14.10.99
Redmond, Robert	Lt Cdr	CEW	President	31.03.00
Reece, Christopher	Lt	AIR	Rnr Air Br Vl	01.11.90
Rees, Nicola	ASl	NE	King Alfred	07.01.00
Reid, Iain	Lt	AIR	Rnr Air Br Vl	01.06.88
Reid, Joseph	Mid	URNU	Urnu (Rnr) Brstl	21.10.98
Reid, Jonothan	Lt	AIR	Rnr Air Br Vl	16.04.90
Reid, Robert Downie	Cdr	HQ	Cambria	30.09.98
Reilly, Donna	Mid	URNU	Urnu (Rnr) Glasg	08.10.98
Rennell, Ian Joseph	Lt	SEA	Eaglet	26.06.88
Reubens, Edwin George Oliver	Cdr	NCS	Vivid	30.09.82
Reynolds, Huw	Mid	URNU	Brnc Rnr Soton	08.09.97
Reynolds, James	ASl	NE	Vivid	23.06.99
Reynolds, Louisa	Mid	URNU	Urnu (Rnr) Livp	09.10.97
Reynolds, Nelson James Elliott, *RD*	Capt	MW	Caroline	30.09.99
Reynoldson, Howard	Lt Cdr	AIR	Rnr Air Br Vl	30.11.90
Ribeiro, Naa Lamley	Mid	URNU	Urnu (Rnr) Aberd	01.10.98
Richard-Dit-Leschery, Stanley Ernest, *RD*	Lt Cdr	AW	Vivid	22.11.92

Name	Rank	Branch	Unit	Seniority
Richardosn, Mark	Mid	URNU	Urnu (Rnr) Manch	07.10.99
Richards, Aneurin	Mid	URNU	Urnu (Rnr) Ssx	12.10.99
Richards, Guy	Lt	SEA	Cambria	26.08.94
Richardson, Ian John	Lt Cdr	INTR	Ferret (Rnr)	15.01.91
Richardson, John	Mid	URNU	U/A	14.10.99
Richardson, Margaret Lynda Maither, *RD*	Lt Cdr	Q	Dalriada	31.03.98
Richardson, Nicholas	Lt Cdr	AIR	Rnr Air Br VI	01.10.96
Richmond, Joel	Mid	URNU	U/A	16.09.97
Rickard, Ian	Mid	URNU	Urnu (Rnr) Glasg	14.10.99
Rickard, Margaret Mary	Lt	MS(F)	King Alfred	15.05.94
Riddett, Adam	Mid	URNU	U/A	21.10.99
Riley, Peter John	Lt Cdr	AW	Calliope	18.02.00
Rimay-Muranyi, Gary	Lt	INTR	Ferret	24.04.95
Roberts, David	ASl	URNU	Urnu (Rnr) Londn	22.11.94
Roberts, Vicky	Mid	URNU	Urnu (Rnr) Aberd	01.10.98
Robertson, Lorne, *RD*	Lt Cdr	MW	Dalriada	17.11.97
Robertson, Wendy Mary Anne	Lt	Q	Dalriada	08.12.95
Robinson, Anthony Michael, *RD*	Lt Cdr	AW	Cambria	16.06.92
Robinson, Ian Michael, *RD*	Cdr	NCS	Sherwood	30.09.89
Robinson, James Brian	Lt	AW	Calliope	24.02.90
Robinson, Jonathon Charles King	Lt Cdr	AIR	Rnr Air Br VI	01.11.91
Robinson, Michael	Lt Cdr	AIR	Rnr Air Br VI	31.03.96
Robinson, Nigel	Lt Cdr	AIR	Rnr Air Br VI	31.03.94
Roche, Philip Brynley	Lt Cdr	HQ	President	31.03.93
Rodgers, Beth	Mid	URNU	Urnu (Rnr) Glasg	14.10.99
Rogers, Stella	Mid	URNU	U/A	29.01.98
Rollings, David Jonathon, *RD**	Lt Cdr	HQ	Cambria	30.10.87
Rooke, Adam	Mid	URNU	Brnc Rnr Soton	06.09.99
Rooke, Zoe	Mid	URNU	U/A	17.01.99
Rose, Norman, *RD*			Urnu (Rnr) Aberd	23.02.90
Rosindale, Philip Michael, *RD*	Lt	SEA	Vivid	19.05.97
Ross, Jonathan Anthony Duncan	Lt Cdr	MW	Dalriada	31.03.98
Ross, Rosanna	Mid	URNU	Urnu (Rnr) Aberd	09.10.97
Rowe, Susan Margaret	Lt	NCS	Vivid	23.11.91
Rowell, Nina	Mid	URNU	U/A	20.10.99
Rowles, Joanne	Lt	CEW	Cambria	21.07.96
Royston, James	Mid	URNU	Urnu (Rnr) Glasg	10.10.97
Rudkin, Adam	Mid	URNU	Urnu (Rnr) Brstl	26.10.99
Ruglys, Matthew	Lt	AIR	Rnr Air Br VI	16.11.86
Rule, John Stewart	Lt	MW	Eaglet	23.04.90
Rushworth, Andrew	Mid	URNU	Urnu (Rnr) Glasg	14.10.99
Russ, Philip, John, RD	Lt Cdr	MW	Eaglet	31.03.96
Russell, David Robert	Lt Cdr	PA	King Alfred	19.03.89
Rutherford, Lesley Ann	ASl	NE	Sherwood	06.11.96
Rutledge, Janice	Mid	URNU	Urnu (Rnr) Ssx	12.10.99
Ryan, Paul	Mid	URNU	U/A	14.10.99
Ryan, Simon John D Arcy	Lt Cdr	HQ	Eaglet	31.03.99

S

Name	Rank	Branch	Unit	Seniority
Saffell, Thomas	Mid	URNU	U/A	15.10.98
Salji, Sean	Mid	URNU	U/A	15.10.98
Salmon, Lindsay	Mid	URNU	U/A	23.10.97
Sambrook, Mitchell	Lt Cdr	AIR	Rnr Air Br VI	31.03.93
Samuel, Laurence	Mid	URNU	Urnu (Rnr) Aberd	09.10.97
Samuels, Nicholas John	Lt	SM	Vivid	02.10.92
Samwell, Michael	Mid	URNU	U/A	21.10.99
San, Howald Kin Hong	Lt	SM	President	15.12.90
Sandeman, Lillian	Mid	URNU	Urnu (Rnr) Aberd	30.09.99
Sanderson, Jennifer Patricia	Lt	HQ	King Alfred	08.07.96
Sargent, Sara	Mid	URNU	U/A	14.10.99
Satchell, Peter James	Lt Cdr	MW	Dalreriada	31.03.00
Saunders, David James, *RD*	Lt Cdr	MW	President	31.03.95

Name	Rank	Branch	Unit	Seniority
Saunders, Duncan	ASl	URNU	Urnu (Rnr) Soton	10.10.96
Scanlon, Michael Stephen	ASl	NE	President	13.01.99
Scarth, Martin Richard	Slt	SM	President	09.09.95
Scott, Edward Martin, RD**, FNI	Capt			
Scott, J G	Lt Cdr	AW	President	31.03.99
Scott, Samantha	Mid	URNU	Urnu (Rnr) Soton	08.10.98
Scribbins, Christopher John, *RD*	Lt Cdr	HQ	Calliope	11.10.91
Scriven, Josella	Mid	URNU	Urnu (Rnr) Ssx	21.10.97
Scutt, Martin	Mid	URNU	Urnu (Rnr) Soton	08.10.98
Seakins, Patrick Edward	Lt Cdr	INTR	Ferret (Rnr)	31.03.00
Searle, Geoffrey Derek	Lt Cdr	MW	King Alfred	31.03.90
Seaton, Christopher Shaun Tudor	Lt Cdr	AW	Flying Fox	01.11.91
Seaton, Judith	ASg Lt		Vivid	20.06.95
Seewooruttun, Gavin	Mid	URNU	Brnc Rnr Soton	04.01.99
Seldon, John	Mid	URNU	U/A	22.10.97
Sellar, Susan	Mid	URNU	Urnu (Rnr) Glasg	14.10.99
Sendall, Sharron	Mid	URNU	U/A	05.11.98
Service, Brian	Lt Cdr	AIR	Rnr Air Br Vl	31.03.99
Shah, Punit	Mid	URNU	Urnu (Rnr) Manch	09.10.97
Shah, Shameer	Mid	URNU	Urnu (Rnr) Manch	01.10.98
Shakespeare, Martin, *RD*	Lt Cdr	DIS	Ferret (Rnr)	31.03.97
Shanahan, Patrick	Mid	URNU	Urnu (Rnr) Manch	01.10.98
Shannon, Tom, *RD*			Urnu (Rnr) Glasg	01.11.95
Sharples, Derek	Lt Cdr	AIR	Rnr Air Br Vl	01.06.91
Shaw, James Elliot, *RD**	Cdr	AW	President	30.09.97
Shaw, Mark	Mid	URNU	Urnu (Rnr) Livp	14.10.99
Shawcross, Jayne	Lt Cdr	AIR	Rnr Air Br Vl	03.01.95
Shearman, Elizabeth	Mid	URNU	Urnu (Rnr) Londn	12.10.99
Shears, Gary	Mid	URNU	Urnu (Rnr) Londn	13.10.97
Shears, Stephen	Lt	AIR	Rnr Air Br Vl	05.09.86
Sheffield, Raphael	Mid	URNU	U/A	17.03.99
Sherman, Christopher James	Lt Cdr	MCDO	King Alfred	24.11.91
Sherwin, Anthony	Mid	URNU	U/A	14.10.99
Shinner, Patrick Anthony, RD	Lt Cdr	SM	President	31.03.99
Shinner, Stephanie Katherine Fleur	Lt Cdr	NCS	Wildfire	31.03.00
Sibcy, James	Mid	URNU	Urnu (Rnr) Soton	26.05.98
Sides, Susan C.	Lt Cdr	HQ	Forward	30.09.91
Sigley, Arthur David Martin	ASl	NE	Scotia	04.08.98
Sim, Daniel	Mid	URNU	Urnu (Rnr) Soton	08.10.98
Simmonds, Richard Charles Kenneth	Lt	AWNIS	Wildfire	15.11.94
Simmonds, Timothy Paul	Lt	MW	Eaglet	23.05.97
Simpkins, Daniel	Mid	URNU	Brnc Rnr Soton	06.09.99
Simpson-Hayes, Gizella	Mid	URNU	Urnu (Rnr) Livp	12.11.99
Sims, Richmal Jane	Lt	SM	King Alfred	16.08.98
Sinclair, James	Mid	URNU	Urnu (Rnr) Aberd	30.09.99
Skade, James	Mid	URNU	U/A	20.01.99
Skimming, Joseph Thomas	Lt	NCS	Calliope	18.10.91
Skinner, Nigel Guy, *BSC, M.ENG*	Lt	NCS	Sherwood	15.11.99
Skuriat, Olenka	Mid	URNU	U/A	23.10.97
Sleeman, Robin	Lt Cdr	AIR	Rnr Air Br Vl	01.09.87
Sloan, Wesley	Mid	URNU	U/A	16.10.97
Small, Peter Kenneth	Sg Cdr		Calliope	30.09.97
Small, Stuart	Mid	URNU	Urnu (Rnr) Londn	13.10.98
Small, Tracy Sharon	Slt	LOGS	Wildfire	17.12.92
Smith, David	Lt	AIR	Rnr Air Br Vl	01.11.85
Smith, Dominic	Mid	URNU	U/A	14.10.99
Smith, Gordon	Lt	AIR	Rnr Air Br Vl	04.05.84
Smith, Hannah	Mid	URNU	Urnu (Rnr) Manch	01.10.98
Smith, Jillian	Mid	URNU	Urnu (Rnr) Ssx	12.10.99
Smith, James	Mid	URNU	U/A	08.10.98
Smith, Lesley Gay Isabel, *RD**	Cdr	LOGS	Vivid	30.09.96
Smith, Neil L, *RD**	Lt Cdr	AWNIS	Dalriada	31.03.81
Smith, William Charles	ASl	NE	Scotia	02.12.99

Name	Rank	Branch	Unit	Seniority
Smith, Wilfred Donald Fitzroy, *RD*	Sg Cdr		Eaglet	30.09.99
Smyth, Kiaran	ASl	URNU	Urnu (Rnr) Ssx	06.10.98
Smyth, Michael Paul	Lt	MW	President	05.06.89
Sneddon, Laura	Mid	URNU	Urnu (Rnr) Glasg	06.01.98
Snell, Douglas	Mid	URNU	U/A	12.02.98
Snoddon, Robert	Lt	CEW	Calliope	06.05.93
Souter, Michael David, *RD*	Lt Cdr	PA	Wildfire	01.01.84
Southern, Carl	Mid	URNU	U/A	07.10.98
Southworth, Mika	Mid	URNU	U/A	23.10.97
Spaine, Victor	Mid	URNU	Urnu (Rnr) Glasg	14.10.99
Speake, John Graham	Sg Ltcdr		Vivid	03.07.83
Spence, Jeremy	Lt Cdr	AIR	Rnr Air Br VI	01.10.92
Spencer, Dominic	Mid	URNU	Urnu (Rnr) Brstl	26.10.99
Spencer, Gary	Lt Cdr	AIR	Rnr Air Br VI	21.10.94
Spray, Alison	Lt Cdr	NCS	Vivid	31.03.93
Spring, Avril Ann	Slt	LOGS	Vivid	04.12.96
Sprowles, K J, *RD*	Lt Cdr	NCS	President	04.11.90
Squire, Elizabeth Jane	Lt	INTR	Ferret (Rnr)	17.06.96
Stack, Eleanor Frances	ASl	NE	Scotia	07.10.98
Stacpoole, Sybil	Mid	URNU	U/A	15.10.98
Stafford-Smith, Karen Julie, *RD*	Lt Cdr	SM	King Alfred	31.03.98
Stammers, George J	ASl	NE	Sherwood	03.03.98
Stanley, Dermot Alan	Lt	SEA	Calliope	12.01.96
Staples, David	ASl	URNU	U/A	20.10.98
Starkey, Peter Gordon, *RD*	Cdr	AW	President	30.09.85
Steer, Colin Nigel	Lt	HQ	Wildfire	25.07.90
Stephenson, Michael Edward	ASl	NE	Calliope	19.11.98
Stephenson, Richard	Lt Cdr	AIR	Rnr Air Br VI	01.03.80
Stevens, Andrew	ASl	QMQ	Vivid Rnr	05.01.00
Stevens, Anthony	Lt	URNU	U/A	26.12.90
Stevens, Richard	Mid	URNU	U/A	22.10.97
Stevenson, Adam	Mid	URNU	U/A	20.10.99
Stevenson, Paul	Mid	URNU	Brnc Rnr Soton	08.09.99
Stewart, Allan	Lt	SM	Eaglet	17.03.89
Stewart, Iain Alexander, *RD*	Lt Cdr	LOGS	Scotia	21.03.87
Stewart, Rachel	Mid	URNU	U/A	15.10.98
Stewart, William Roderick, *BSC, RD*	Lt Cdr	NA	Scotia	06.12.86
Stickland, Anthony Charles Robert	Lt Cdr	AW	King Alfred	31.03.98
Stidston, David	Lt Cdr	AIR	Rnr Air Br VI	01.10.94
Stock, Patrick	Mid	URNU	U/A	06.10.97
Stocker, Jeremy Richard	Lt Cdr	HQ	Calliope	01.06.89
Stones, Nicholas	Lt	SEA	Forward	09.10.95
Stopps, Claire	Mid	URNU	Urnu (Rnr) Livp	14.10.99
Strachan, Robin Kinnear	Sg Cdr		President	30.09.95
Strangways, Jane Caroline	ALt	INTR	Ferret (Rnr)	05.01.99
Strawbridge, Chantal	Mid	URNU	Urnu (Rnr) Soton	07.10.99
Street, Adam Matthew	ASl	NE	President	08.01.97
Streeter, Pamela	Mid	URNU	U/A	04.02.99
Strudwick, Peggy Barbara	Lt	LOGS	Vivid	17.12.96
Sturgeon, Mark	Mid	URNU	Urnu (Rnr) Glasg	08.10.98
Subramaniam, Suresh	Mid	URNU	Urnu (Rnr) Aberd	30.09.99
Suffolk, Lily	Mid	URNU	Urnu (Rnr) Ssx	20.10.98
Surgey, Ian Christopher	Lt Cdr	SM	Vivid	21.03.97
Surrey, Andrew	Mid	URNU	U/A	08.10.98
Sutton, Kevin	Lt Cdr	AIR	Rnr Air Br VI	16.08.92
Swabey, Matthew	Mid	URNU	Brnc Rnr Soton	06.09.98
Swann, Adam	Mid	URNU	U/A	21.10.99
Swann, Judith Helen, *RD*, JP*	Cdr	NCS	Sherwood	03.09.90
Sweenie, John Fraser	Sg Ltcdr		Dalriada	13.02.90
Swiatek, Simon	ASl	URNU	U/A	01.11.97
Swift, James	Mid	URNU	Urnu (Rnr) Londn	12.10.99
Sykes, Robin	Mid	URNU	U/A	14.10.99
Syme, Allan, *RD*	Lt Cdr	HQ	Dalriada	11.02.83

Name	Rank	Branch	Unit	Seniority
Symington, Anna	Mid	URNU	U/A	08.10.98

T

Name	Rank	Branch	Unit	Seniority
Tabner, Reuben	Mid	URNU	Urnu (Rnr)	30.09.99
Taborda, Matthew	Mid	URNU	U/A	14.10.99
Talbot-Weiss, Melanie	Mid	URNU	Urnu (Rnr) Soton	07.10.99
Tall, Louisa	Mid	URNU	Urnu (Rnr) Ssx	20.10.98
Tall, Richard Edward	Lt	SM	Flying Fox	14.12.97
Tantam, Robert	Mid	URNU	Urnu (Rnr) Londn	13.10.97
Tapley, Richard	Lt Cdr	AIR	Rnr Air Br VI	31.03.97
Tarmey, Sarah	Mid	URNU	Urnu (Rnr) Glasg	08.10.98
Taub, Aidan	Mid	URNU	U/A	07.10.98
Taylor, Christopher, RD	Mid	URNU	Urnu (Rnr) Soton	07.10.99
Taylor, Dale	Mid	URNU	U/A	21.10.99
Taylor, David Paul, *RD*	Lt Cdr	MS(M)	Flying Fox	11.08.89
Taylor, Gareth	Mid	URNU	Urnu (Rnr) Manch	07.10.99
Taylor, James	Mid	URNU	Urnu (Rnr) Soton	09.10.97
Taylor, Karolina	Mid	URNU	U/A	08.10.98
Taylor, Louise Elizabeth	Lt Cdr	NCS	Eaglet	31.03.00
Taylor, Nicholas Robert	Psg Lt		Flying Fox	14.04.99
Taylor, Nicholas	Mid	URNU	Urnu (Rnr) Ssx	20.10.98
Taylor, Rupert James, RD	Lt Cdr	AW	King Alfred	31.03.99
Taylor, Robert	Mid	URNU	U/A	07.10.98
Teasdale, David Andrew	Lt	SM	Calliope	01.12.93
Telfer, Alison Averil, *RD*	Lt Cdr	NCS	Eaglet	30.09.91
Temple, Miles	Lt	SEA	President	01.11.94
Templeton, Susan Marie, RD	Lt Cdr	LOGS	Flying Fox	31.03.96
Thomas, Adam	Mid	URNU	Brnc Rnr Soton	06.09.98
Thomas, David Graham	Slt	COMM	King Alfred	21.07.96
Thomas, Emma Margaret	Lt	PA	Wildfire	26.07.86
Thomas, Neil	Mid	URNU	U/A	25.11.99
Thomas, Peter Glyn	Lt Cdr	MW	Eaglet	31.03.99
Thomas, Stephen Paul	Lt	MW	Cambria	26.01.97
Thomas, Tenny	Mid	URNU	U/A	20.10.99
Thomason, Michael	Lt	LOGS	Eaglet	18.09.96
Thompson, Alastair	Mid	URNU	Urnu (Rnr) Soton	18.02.99
Thompson, Andrew, *RD*	Lt Cdr	NCS	Vivid	31.03.94
Thompson, Edwina	Mid	URNU	Urnu (Rnr) Londn	13.10.98
Thompson, Elizabeth	Mid	URNU	Brnc Rnr Soton	06.09.98
Thompson, Glenn	Lt Cdr	AIR	Rnr Air Br VI	31.03.99
Thompson, Stuart	ASl	NE	Flying Fox	19.01.99
Thompson, Trisha	Mid	URNU	Urnu (Rnr) Manch	07.10.99
Thomson, Paul	Mid	URNU	Urnu (Rnr) Manch	07.10.99
Thomson, Susie	Lt Cdr	PA	Flying Fox	31.03.00
Thomson, Sheena, *BA*	Lt Cdr	PA	Dalriada	31.03.00
Thorne, Brian John, *RD**	Cdr	CEW	Cambria	30.09.97
Thorne, Lee	Lt	MW	Sherwood	01.11.96
Thorne, Stephen Paul, *RD*	Cdr	COMM	King Alfred	30.09.98
Thorogood, Daniel	Mid	URNU	Urnu (Rnr) Londn	13.10.98
Thorp, Thomas	Mid	URNU	U/A	23.10.97
Tidbury, Fiona	Mid	URNU	Urnu (Rnr) Ssx	12.10.99
Tighe, Christopher	Mid	URNU	U/A	21.10.99
Tindall-Jones, Julia, *BA*	Lt Cdr	LOGS	Vivid	31.03.94
Todd, Andrew Harry Campbell, RD	Lt Cdr	NCS	Scotia	31.03.98
Todd, Craig,	Mid	URNU	Urnu (Rnr) Glasg	14.10.99
Todd, Emily	Mid	URNU	Urnu (Rnr) Livp	09.10.97
Todd, Matthew	ASl	URNU	Urnu (Rnr) Londn	21.06.96
Todd, Susan	ASl	URNU	Urnu (Rnr) Livp	05.03.96
Tomlin, Ian	Mid	URNU	Brnc Rnr Soton	06.09.98
Tomlinson, Christopher	Mid	URNU	U/A	22.10.98
Tonkin, Neil	Lt Cdr	AIR	Rnr Air Br VI	01.10.90
Tonks, Jennifer	Mid	URNU	Urnu (Rnr) Soton	07.10.99

Name	Rank	Branch	Unit	Seniority
Topping, Mark, RD	Lt Cdr	HQ	Cambria	31.03.97
Tornambe, Richard	Mid	URNU	Urnu (Rnr) Manch	07.10.99
Townsend, John Stafford	Sg Ltcdr		Sherwood	11.02.85
Toy, John Michael, *RD*	Lt Cdr	NA	Caroline	03.07.80
Trangmar, Paul	Lt	NCS	Wildfire Rnr	22.11.93
Traynor, Holly	Mid	URNU	Urnu (Rnr) Brstl	26.10.99
Trelawny, Christopher Charles	Lt	SEA	President	14.12.89
Trelinska, Victoria Jane, *RD*	Lt Cdr	NCS	Sherwood	30.09.91
Treloar, Philip Michael	Lt Cdr	PA	Wildfire	16.09.88
Trevail, Jill	Mid	URNU	Urnu (Rnr) Aberd	09.10.97
Trewinnard, Robin	Mid	URNU	Urnu (Rnr) Brstl	15.10.97
Tribe, David	Lt Cdr	AIR	Rnr Air Br VI	31.03.99
Trimmer, Patrick David Mark	Lt Cdr	HQ	Calliope	31.03.96
Trosh, Nicholas	Mid	URNU	U/A	30.09.99
Truscott, Rena Julie	Lt	HQ	Vivid	12.09.96
Tulloch, Alan	Slt	X	Urnu (Rnr) Aberd	08.04.87
Tuppen, Heather Jill	Lt	PA	Wildfire	24.10.94
Turner, Jonathan Andrew McMahon, *RD*	Sg Cdr		King Alfred	30.09.99
Turner, Philip	Mid	URNU	Urnu (Rnr) Soton	07.10.99
Turner, Simon John	Lt Cdr	AWNIS	Vivid	31.03.99
Turtill, Lisa Helen	ASl	NE	Flying Fox	07.10.99
Tutton, Amanda	Mid	URNU	U/A	14.10.99
Tweed, Susan Linda, *JP*, *RD**	Cdr	NCS	Vivid	30.09.99
Twigg, Kathryn	Mid	URNU	Urnu (Rnr) Livp	15.10.98
Tyrrell, Carol Marguerite	Lt Cdr	INT	Ferret (Rnr)	11.04.90

U

Name	Rank	Branch	Unit	Seniority
Unejeyah, Irene	Mid	URNU	Urnu (Rnr) Ssx	20.10.98
Upchurch, Victoria	Mid	URNU	Urnu (Rnr) Livp	15.10.98
Ure, Fiona, *RD*	Lt	Q	Scotia	04.03.99
Utting, Penelope Anne	Lt	PA	King Alfred	09.12.90

V

Name	Rank	Branch	Unit	Seniority
Valentine, Robert Innes	Lt Cdr	SEA	Scotia	31.03.99
Van Asch, Alexandra	Mid	URNU	Urnu (Rnr) Ssx	12.10.99
Van Den Bergh, *M*(Mark), RD	Lt	HQ	Wildfire	16.12.92
Van Onselen, Ian	Lt Cdr	AIR	Rnr Air Br VI	31.03.98
Varley, Peter	Lt Cdr	AIR	Rnr Air Br VI	07.09.81
Vaughan, James	Mid	URNU	Brnc Rnr Soton	06.09.98
Venton, Paul Adrian	ASl	NE	Flying Fox	13.10.98
Vernon, Michael A, *RD*	Lt Cdr	CEW	Vivid	27.08.90
Versallion, Mark	ASl	NE	Wildfire	09.12.99
Vincent, Claire Elaine	Lt	AWNIS	King Alfred	23.04.92
Visram, Adrian	Mid	URNU	U/A	22.10.98

W

Name	Rank	Branch	Unit	Seniority
Waddell, Verity Noeline, *RD*	Lt Cdr	NCS	Calliope	31.03.93
Waddington, Christopher	Mid	URNU	U/A	14.10.99
Wain, Alexis	Mid	URNU	U/A	05.07.99
Waite, Stephen	Slt	QMQ	Vivid	16.06.99
Wake, Thomas Baldwin	Lt Cdr	CEW	Sherwood	14.05.89
Wakeford, Mark Warren	Lt	PA	King Alfred	10.03.92
Walden, Geoffery George	Lt	SM	Sherwood	10.12.90
Walder, Karen	Mid	URNU	Urnu (Rnr) Livp	15.10.98
Wale, Martin Charles Johnson	Lt Cdr	DIS	Ferret (Rnr)	01.08.86
Wales, Frederick Anthony, RD	Lt Cdr	AW	King Alfred	31.03.98
Walker, David, RD	Lt Cdr	LOGS	President	31.03.97
Walker, Gail	Mid	URNU	Urnu (Rnr) Glasg	14.10.99
Walker, Jamie	Mid	URNU	U/A	01.02.00
Walker, Paul MacKenzie	ASl	NE	President	17.03.98
Walker, Stephen	Mid	URNU	Brnc Rnr Soton	08.09.97

Name	Rank	Branch	Unit	Seniority
Walker-Spicer, Ian Edward, RD*	Lt Cdr	AW	President	12.11.84
Wallace, Richard	Mid	URNU	U/A	16.10.97
Wallace, Stuart Iain	Lt	AW	President	23.07.99
Waller, James	Mid	URNU	U/A	07.10.98
Waller, Vincent Francis, *RD*	Lt Cdr	AW	Calliope	01.09.88
Wallom, Anne	Lt	PA	Scotia	13.09.97
Walmsley, Stephen Graham	Lt	HQ	Caroline	01.10.97
Walthall, Fiona Elizabeth	Lt	NCS	Scotia	17.11.88
Walton, Katherine	Mid	URNU	U/A	24.10.96
Walworth, William Michael	Cdr	AW	President	30.09.95
Ward, Eleanore	Mid	URNU	U/A	08.10.98
Ward, Joanna	Mid	URNU	Urnu (Rnr) Manch	01.10.98
Ward, Suzanne	Mid	URNU	Urnu (Rnr) Aberd	30.09.97
Ware, James Robert	Lt	MW	Caroline	20.08.89
Warren, Matthew	Mid	URNU	Urnu (Rnr) Manch	09.10.97
Warrick, Mark	Mid	URNU	Brnc Rnr Soton	06.09.99
Waters, Michael	Mid	URNU	U/A	14.10.99
Waterworth, Kathryn	Mid	URNU	Urnu (Rnr) Aberd	11.11.99
Watson, Catherine Jennifer, *RD*	Lt Cdr	HQ	Eaglet	31.03.98
Watson, Ian	Lt Cdr	AIR	Rnr Air Br VI	01.10.92
Watson, Karen Marie	Lt Cdr	INTR	Ferret (Rnr)	31.03.99
Watson, Lloyd	Lt Cdr	AIR	Rnr Air Br VI	01.10.94
Waugh, Richard	Mid	URNU	Urnu (Rnr) Brstl	21.10.98
Way, Katherine	Mid	URNU	Urnu (Rnr) Manch	07.10.99
Weate, Sally	Mid	URNU	U/A	27.01.00
Webb, Avril	Mid	URNU	Urnu (Rnr) Soton	09.10.97
Webber, Michael	Cdr	AIR	Rnr Air Br VI	30.09.98
Webster, Patrick	Lt	AIR	Rnr Air Br VI	20.01.87
Weeden, Alexandra Louise	ASl	NE	President	09.12.97
Weldon, Helen Wright, RD	Lt	HQ	Dalriada	16.03.89
Weller, Thomas	Mid	URNU	Urnu (Rnr) Londn	12.10.99
Wells, Christopher Michael	Lt Cdr	AW	President	31.03.94
Wells, Jonathan	Lt Cdr	AIR	Rnr Air Br VI	01.12.91
Wells, Rebecca	Mid	URNU	U/A	22.10.98
Welsh, John	Lt	CEW	Wildfire	12.10.95
Welsh, Nicholas	Mid	URNU	Urnu (Rnr) Londn	09.11.99
Wesley, John, RD	Lt Cdr	HQ	President	12.11.89
West, Nicholas	Lt Cdr	AIR	Rnr Air Br VI	31.03.99
West, Susan Elizabeth	Sg Ltcdr		President	27.09.84
Weston, Andrew	Mid	URNU	U/A	16.10.97
Westwood, Andrew	Mid	URNU	Urnu (Rnr) Soton	28.01.99
Westwood, Steve	Lt Cdr	AIR	Rnr Air Br VI	01.10.92
Whawell, Peter Gerald Maber	Lt	MW	President	09.02.94
Wheeldon, Matthew	Mid	URNU	Urnu (Rnr) Brstl	26.10.99
Wheeler, Louise	Mid	URNU	U/A	12.02.98
Wheeler, Robert Alec	Sg Cdr		King Alfred	30.09.98
Whitaker, Gary	Lt Cdr	AIR	Rnr Air Br VI	31.03.97
Whitby, David John, *RD**	Cdr	AW	President	30.09.84
Whitby, Philip	Lt Cdr	SM	Wildfire	26.12.90
Whitby, Stephen	Lt Cdr	HQ	Scotia	01.0192
White, Antony	Mid	URNU	U/A	23.10.97
White, Ian Roy	Lt Cdr	HQ	Calliope	31.03.96
White, Paul Donald	ASl	NE	Flying Fox	07.10.99
White, Stephen	Mid	URNU	U/A	26.11.98
Whitehead, Keith Stuart, *BSC*, RD	Lt Cdr	HQ	King Alfred	31.03.00
Whitehouse, Andrew	Mid	URNU	U/A	25.11.99
Whitehouse, Marie	Mid	URNU	U/A	21.10.99
Whiteley, Philip	Mid	URNU	Urnu (Rnr) Brstl	21.10.98
Whitlock, Michael Anthony	Lt	SEA	King Alfred	27.01.92
Whittall, Andrew	Lt	AIR	Rnr Air Br VI	15.10.90
Wickens, Ian	Lt	AIR	Rnr Air Br VI	24.12.91
Wigley, Ellen	Mid	URNU	U/A	08.10.98
Wigley, Laura	Mid	URNU	U/A	07.10.97

Name	Rank	Branch	Unit	Seniority
Wilkins, Georgina	Mid	URNU	U/A	22.10.98
Wilkinson, Lynn	Lt	Q	Eaglet	11.01.92
Williams, Anthony	Mid	URNU	U/A	14.10.99
Williams, Brett	Mid	URNU	U/A	14.10.99
Williams, Cassandra	Mid	URNU	Brnc Rnr Soton	08.09.97
Williams, Mark Jeremy	Lt	NCS	Eaglet	27.10.92
Williams, Michele Louise	ASl	NE	Wildfire	23.12.98
Williams, Owain	Mid	URNU	Urnu (Rnr) Glasg	08.10.98
Williams, Paul David	Lt Cdr	AW	Calliope	05.08.86
Williams, Peter Lunt, *RD*	Lt Cdr	CRW	Eaglet	11.05.90
Williams, Simon	Mid	URNU	U/A	26.01.00
Williams, Simon	Mid	URNU	Urnu (Rnr) Brstl	21.10.98
Williams, Thomas	Mid	URNU	Urnu (Rnr) Ssx	20.10.98
Williams, Timothy Paul	Lt	MW	Wildfire	14.09.95
Wills, Robert	Mid	URNU	Brnc Rnr Soton	06.09.98
Wilson, Gary			U/A	10.10.95
Wilson, Gerard	Mid	URNU	Brnc Rnr Soton	08.09.97
Wilson, Jennifer Maureen	Lt Cdr	Q	Flying Fox	31.03.95
Wilson, Karyn Stewart	Lt	NCS	Flying Fox	19.07.90
Wilson, Stephen John	Sg Ltcdr		Wildfire	30.09.98
Winfield, Adrian	Lt Cdr	AIR	Rnr Air Br VI	31.03.99
Winstanley, Nichola Ann	Lt Cdr	PA	Vivid	31.03.95
Wiseman, Jane	Lt	AIR	Rnr Air Br VI	01.09.89
Wolstenholme, David	Lt Cdr	AIR	Rnr Air Br VI	01.10.93
Wood, Allison	Mid	URNU	Urnu (Rnr) Livp	14.10.99
Wood, Daniel James	ASl	NE	Eaglet	23.10.96
Wood, Gerald Norman, ADC *RD**	Cdre	NA	Flying Fox	30.09.93
Wood, John	ALt Cdr	CEW	Calliope	05.03.98
Wood, James	Mid	URNU	Urnu (Rnr) Aberd	01.10.98
Wood, Louisa	Mid	URNU	U/A	16.10.97
Wood, Richard	Mid	URNU	U/A	20.10.99
Wood, Suzanne	Lt	HQ	President	05.04.93
Woodham, Jeremy	Lt Cdr	AIR	Rnr Air Br VI	02.07.92
Woodman, Clive Andrew	Lt Cdr	PA	Vivid	01.09.87
Woodman, Daniel	Mid	URNU	Brnc Rnr Soton	06.09.98
Woodruffe, Jonathan	Mid	URNU	Urnu (Rnr) Manch	07.10.99
Woods, Amber	Mid	URNU	U/A	15.10.98
Woods, Fergus	Lt Cdr	AIR	Rnr Air Br VI	01.10.88
Woods, Martin	Mid	URNU	Urnu (Rnr) Londn	14.10.98
Wordie, Andrew George Lyon, *RD*	Lt Cdr	CEW	Sherwood	31.03.95
Worsley, Alistair Louis	Lt Cdr	PA	Wildfire	31.03.96
Wray, Ronald Maurice	Lt Cdr	NCS	Caroline	31.03.99
Wreford, Katrine	Lt Cdr	PA	Scotia	31.03.93
Wrigglesworth, Peter John	Sg Ltcdr		Sherwood	02.08.88
Wright, Alan Howard	Lt Cdr	AW	Eaglet	01.11.91
Wright, Douglas John	ALt	DIS	Ferret (Rnr)	11.12.95
Wright, Gordon, *MSC, RD*	Lt Cdr	AIR	Rnr Air Br VI	17.04.86
Wright, Georgina	Mid	URNU	Urnu (Rnr) Manch	01.10.98
Wright, Iain Alistair MacKay	Lt Cdr	DIS	Ferret (Rnr)	18.08.97
Wright, Nicola Anne	ASl	NE	Vivid	05.08.99
Wright, Peter	Mid	URNU	Urnu (Rnr) Soton	09.10.97
Wright, Stephen	Lt Cdr	CEW	King Alfred	31.03.00
Wright, Stephen, *GM*	Lt	AIR	Rnr Air Br VI	17.12.93
Wring, Matthew Anthony	Lt	MW	Flying Fox	25.01.95
Wuidart Gray, Spencer	Lt	SEA	King Alfred	07.12.93
Wyatt, Mark Edward, *RD*	Cdr	MW	King Alfred	30.09.99
Wyglendacz, Jan Andrew	Lt	LOGS	Cambria	28.01.90
Wyness, Sharon	Lt	AIR	Rnr Air Br VI	01.09.96

Y

Name	Rank	Branch	Unit	Seniority
Yardley, Ian	Mid	URNU	U/A	21.10.99
Yates, Steven, RD	Lt Cdr	MW	Flying Fox	31.03.00

Name	Rank	Branch	Unit	Seniority
Yavuz, Aslan	Mid	URNU	Urnu (Rnr) Ssx	20.10.98
Yetman, Philip John, *RD*	Cdr	NCS	King Alfred	30.09.98
Yibowei, Amaebi	Mid	URNU	Urnu (Rnr) Londn	13.10.98
Yong, Andrew	Mid	URNU	U/A	19.10.98
Young, Carl	Lt Cdr	AIR	Rnr Air Br Vl	31.03.98
Young, Duncan Alexander, *RD*	Lt Cdr	MW	Calliope	31.03.98
Young, Deborah Joy	ALt	NCS	Calliope	12.07.99
Young, Gregory Christian	ASl	NE	President	29.10.97
Young, William David	Lt	LOGS	King Alfred	11.05.93

ROYAL MARINES RESERVE

Name	Rank	Branch	Unit	Seniority
A				
Adcock, Brian	Maj	M1	LONDON	01/07/99
Ardron, Andrew	Lt	M2	LONDON	01.09.98
B				
Baker, Alastair	Lt	M1	LONDON	08.03.00
Barnwell, Barry	Lt Col	M1	SCOTLAND	01.12.90
Bates, Nigel	2lt	M1	LONDON	01.07.99
Billington, Edward	Capt	M1	MERSEYSIDE	07.06.92
Blyth, Alexander	Lt Col	M2	TYNE	30.06.98
Board, Michael	Capt	M1	LONDON	01.04.97
Bristow, Paul	2lt	M1	TYNE	13.01/00
Brocklehurst, Kelly	2lt	M1	BRISTOL	
Brooker-Gillespie, Robin	Capt	M1	LONDON	04.01.95
Brown, Roger	Capt	M1	MERSEYSIDE	15.07.90
Brownhill, Terence	Maj	M1	MERSEYSIDE	17.10.88
Bruce, Rory	Lt Col	M1	BRISTOL	30.06.98
Brunskill, Michael	2lt	M1	MERSEYSIDE	01.07.99
C				
Campbell, Michael	Act Maj	M1	TYNE	01.04.95
Carpenter, Nicholas	Maj	M1	MERSEYSIDE	30.06.98
Chamberlain, Henry	Capt	M1	SBS POOLE	28.04.94
Churchill, Colin	2lt	M1	SCOTLAND	19.04.97
Coard, John	Maj	M1	SCOTLAND	30.06.98
D				
Day, Jason	Lt	M1	LONDON	01.07.99
Dixon, Iain	Maj	M1	BRISTOL	30.06.98
Dugard, Peter , RD	Maj	M1	MERSEYSIDE	08.08.87
Doubleday, Iain	Capt	M1	LONDON	01.04.97
F				
Fielder, David	Maj	M1	BRISTOL	01.04.99
Figgins, Phillip	Maj	M2	LONDON	01.04.91
G				
Galley, Christopher	Capt	M1	SCOTLAND	25.05.93
Gardiner, Andrew	Capt	M1	SBS POOLE	03.08.98
Guest, Simon	Capt	M1	LONDON	29.04.93
H				
Hall, David	Lt	M1	TYNE	01.10.99
Halls, Montagu	Act Maj	M1	LONDON	09.11.99
Hawkins, Russell	Lt	M1	MERSEYSIDE	
Hebron, Bryan	Capt	M1	TYNE	22.05.90
Holt, Andrew	Lt Col	M1	MERSEYSIDE	31.12.93
Hough, Brian, *RD*	Col	M1	MERSEYSIDE	01.08.99
Hudson, Thomas	Lt	M1	TYNE	01.08.98
Hunter, Benjamin	Lt	M2	LONDON	15.01.98
I				
Ing, John	Maj	M1	SBS POOLE	01.09.94

Name	Rank	Branch	Unit	Seniority
J				
Jackson, Fraser	Capt	M1	SCOTLAND	01.10.92
Jobbins, Paul	Col	M2	BRISTOL	28.01.94
Johnson, Ian	Lt	M1	MERSEYSIDE	08.12.96
K				
Kinninmonth, Craig	2lt	M1	SCOTLAND	14.09.99
Knox, David	Maj	M1	TYNE	01.05.99
L				
Lacy, Robert	Capt	M1	MERSEYSIDE	01.04.91
Lang, Tom	Col	M1	BRISTOL	28.02.95
Langford, Haj	2lt	M1	LONDON	25.11.99
Lewis, Robbie	Capt	M1	BRISTOL	01.07.98
Lindfield, Barry	Maj	M1	MERSEYSIDE	25.10.91
Loynes, Philip	Lt Col	M1	MERSEYSIDE	31.12.94
M				
Mannion, Stephen	Maj	M2	LONDON	26.03.96
March, Jefreey	Lt Col	M1	MERSEYSIDE	01.07.99
Mason, Andrew	Capt	M1	BRISTOL	16.12.96
Mather, Nicholas	Maj	M1	LONDON	19.05.97
Mawhood, Christopher	Maj	M1	MERSEYSIDE	01.09.87
McGovern, James	2lt	M1	SCOTLAND	14.05.99
McLaughlin, Stephen	Capt	M1	SCOTLAND	18.09.91
McNeil, David	Capt	M2	LONDON	01.06.94
Mirtle, Frank, *RD*	Col	M1	LONDON	01.06.99
Moulton, Frederick	Maj	M1	BRISTOL	27.04.92
Murray, Ian	Maj	M1	MERSEYSIDE	14.02.89
P				
Phillips, Andrew	Maj	M1	BRISTOL	01.09.95
Pike, Andrew	Lt	M1	TYNE	30.07.95
Pilkington, Alex	Capt	M1	MERSEYSIDE	01.07.96
Player, Hugh	Col	M2	LONDON	01.08.96
Pollock, Andrew	Capt	M1	LONDON	01.04.96
R				
Radford, Barry	Col	M1	BRISTOL	30.06.94
Reynolds, Stephen	Maj	N2A	RNR AIR BR VL	01.05.98
Richards, Gavin, *RD*	Maj	M1	LONDON	16.09.93
Roberts, John	Capt	M1	SCOTLAND	22.08.92
Robinson, David	Maj	M1	TYNE	14.11.95
Rochester, Richard	Capt	M1	BRISTOL	07.07.99
Rogers, Alastair	Lt Col	M1	BRISTOL	30.06.91
Rowland, Johnny	Maj	M1	BRISTOL	25.06.96
Rowlstone, David	Maj	M1	MERSEYSIDE	01.04.97
S				
Scott, John	Maj	M1	BRISTOL	01.03.96
Sharp, Gordon	Maj	M1	LONDON	30.06.98
Smith, Anthony	Loc Col	M1	BRISTOL	18.07.96
Smith, Frazer	Capt	M1	LONDON	03.08.96
Storrie, Richard	Capt	M1	BRISTOL	24.04.91
T				
Tarnowski, Thomas	Lt	M1	LONDON	12.01.95
Tayler, Harry	Capt	M1	LONDON	01.07.94

Name	Rank	Branch	Unit	Seniority
Terry, Stuart	Maj	M1	FERRET (RNR)	01.02.93
Thompson, Joseph	Lt	M1	TYNE	07.12.98
Tompkins, Richard	Maj	M2	LONDON	30.06.98
Tonner, Raymond	Maj	M1	BRISTOL	03.05.95
Travis, Adrian	Maj	M1	LONDON	01.05.96

W

Name	Rank	Branch	Unit	Seniority
Waddell, Ian	Capt	M1	SCOTLAND	01.08.91
Watkinson, Neil	Maj	M1	LONDON	02.09.99
Watt, David	Capt	M1	BRISTOL	22.01.95
Wilson, Alan	Lt	M1	SBS POOLE	01.05.97

X

Name	Rank	Branch	Unit	Seniority
Xiberras, Maurice	2Lt	M1	MERSEYSIDE	23.05.00

SEA CADET CORPS

Name	Rank	Seniority
A		
Adams, Michael	Lt	5. 2.83
Adams, Thomas	Lt	7. 9.83
Agar, Andrew	Lt	22. 3.91
Agnew, Anthony	Lt RMR	5. 6.98
Allam, John	Lt	31. 8.87
Allen, Karen	Lt(SCC)	8.10.88
Allen, Leslie	Alt Cdr	1. 1.99
Allo, David	Lt Cdr	6. 5.72
Alston-Pottinger, Brian	Lt	5. 3.99
Andersen, Kim	Lt RMR	1. 7.99
Anderson, Alex	S/Lt	29. 1.97
Anderson, Robert	Lt	1. 4.99
Andrews, Colin	Lt Cdr	18. 2.87
Appleby, Keith	Lt	21. 2.98
Archbold, Dennis	Alt Cdr	11. 8.99
Archbold, Theresa	Lt	20.11.97
Archer, Barry	Lt	8. 3.94
Archer, Lynn	Lt	14.11.96
Atherton, John	S/Lt	2. 6.96
Atkins, Doreen	Lt	8. 4.92
Attwood, Anthony	Lt	22. 2.89
Attwood, Robert	A/Lt Cdr	8.11.87
Avill, Susan	Lt	1.11.89
Ayers, William	S/Lt	4. 1.00
B		
Baddley, Stephen	Lt	28.11.95
Bagley, Bruce	Lt Cdr	1. 7.81
Bailey, Robert	Lt	12. 3.91
Bailey, Terence	Lt	1.12.95
Baillie, Janet	Lt	21. 3.96
Bainbridge, Patricia	Lt	3.11.98
Baker, Michael	Lt RMR	1.7.99
Baker, Roy	A/Maj RMR	18. 5.82
Bancroft, David	S/Lt	6. 5.94
Banks, Michael	Lt Cdr	6. 9.88
Banks, Paul	Lt	6. 6.96
Banner, Peter	S/Lt	30. 3.92
Barber, Anthony	Lt	12. 3.91
Barker, David	Lt	21. 6.99
Barker, Sandra	Lt	7.10.98
Barons, Simon	Lt	28. 4.99
Barr, William	S/Lt	15. 2.98
Barras, Hugh	Lt	1. 1.94
Barritt, Richard	Alt Cdr	5. 3.89
Barron, Edward	Capt RMR	15.10.91
Barron, Valery	A/Lt Cdr	1.11.92
Barrow, Joan	Lt	5.11.97
Bartlett, Jonathan	Lt	21. 9.96
Bartlett, Peter	Lt Cdr	5. 1.78
Bartlweman, Alexander	Lt	25.11.72
Barton, William	Lt Cdr	1.3.83
Bassett, Gary	Lt	28.10.96
Bayley, George	Lt	24. 3.99
Bayliss, John	Lt Cdr	18. 2.87
Bayliss, Peter	Lt Cdr	1. 8.91
Bayly, Peter	S/Lt	23. 3.91
Bayton, Trevor	Lt	25.2.00
Beach, Andrew	Lt	18. 7.87
Beal, Peter	Lt	26. 3.85
Beaumont, Marilyn	Lt	28. 2.95
Bedford, Michael	Lt	1. 4.86
Bell, Brian	Lt	25.2.00
Bell, Joseph	S/Lt	13. 9.99
Bell, Veronica	Lt	29. 1.98
Bennett, Paul	S/Lt	25.10.99
Benton, Anthony	Capt RMR	1. 8.99
Benton, Ruth	Lt	8.10.91
Bereznyckyj, Nicholas	Capt RMR	3.11.94
Bickle, Margaret	S/Lt	5. 5.96
Billinghay, Sandra	Lt(W)	1. 7.85

Name	Rank	Seniority
Bilverstone, Brian	Lt	24. 3.91
Bingham, Keith	Lt	1. 3.95
Bingham, Maurice	Lt	1. 1.85
Birch, Paul	Lt Cdr	5. 7.88
Bishop, Peter	Lt	1.11.95
Black, Magdalene	A/Lt Cdr	1. 1.96
Blackburn, Alan	S/Lt	3. 3.91
Blackwood, Alan	Lt	9. 1.92
Blaker, Carol	A/Lt Cdr	1.10.81
Blaker, Malcolm	Lt Cdr	3. 1.79
Bloor, John	Capt RMR	15. 1.97
Board, Brian	Lt	15.11.91
Boardman, Richard	Lt Cdr	27. 4.86
Bodycote, Stephen	Lt	24. 9.91
Bolton, David	S/Lt	5. 2.99
Bond, Paul	Lt	1. 4.85
Bonfield, Christopher	Lt	6.11.96
Bonjour, Andre	Lt	27. 5.92
Boorman, Nicholas	Lt	12.11.88
Booth, Christina	Lt	3.12.91
Bowen, Terrence	Lt	3. 3.83
Bowman, Thomas	A/Lt Cdr	21.11.98
Bowskill, Michael	Lt	10.11.87
Boxall, Alan	Lt	2. 8.89
Boyes, Stephen	Lt	25. 2.99
Boyle, Alexander	Lt	30. 9.91
Boyne, John	S/Lt	16. 3.94
Bradbury, David	Lt	1. 1.85
Bradbury, Jason	Lt	5. 5.98
Bradbury, Scott	S/Lt	5.12.99
Bradford, David	Lt	8.10.85
Bradford, William	Lt	21.10.99
Bradley, John	Lt	10. 9.91
Bratley, Charles	Lt	9.10.90
Bratley, Norma	Lt	11. 6.97
Bray, John	Lt	7.12.99
Brayford, John	Lt Cdr	2. 2.84
Brazier, Colin	Lt	29. 9.84
Brentnall, Charles	S/Lt	24. 9.94
Bridle, Stephen	Lt	12.11.93
Briggs, Donald	Lt Cdr	1. 9.77
Brimelow, Michael	Lt	1. 2.99
Briscoe, Robert	Lt	14.11.96
Broadbent, Graham	Lt Cdr	1. 1.84
Broadfoot, Robert	Lt Cdr	1. 7.85
Brockwell, Graham	Lt	21. 9.90
Brooks, Henry	Lt Cdr	2. 5.87
Brotherton, Stephen	Lt	3. 7.97
Broughton, Carol	S/Lt	28. 3.99
Brown, Alexander	Lt	22. 9.88
Brown, Anthony	Lt	4. 2.89
Brown, David	Lt Cdr	30. 3.80
Brown, David	Lt Cdr	2. 6.86
Brown, Jeffrey	Lt	25. 2.92
Brown, Jeremy	S/Lt	4. 2.00
Brown, John	Lt Cdr	4. 7.78
Brown, Keith	Lt	26.10.84
Brown, Norman	Lt	1. 6.91
Brown, Sylvia	Lt	9.11.88
Brown, William	Lt	14. 4.92
Browning, Martin	S/Lt	1. 9.98
Browning, Tony	Lt	19.12.93
Broxham, Roy	Lt	21. 9.90
Bryant, Charles	Lt	19. 12.87
Budd, Anthony	A/Lt Cdr	1. 1.91
Bullock, Geoffrey	Lt Cdr	1. 7.87
Bullock, Lynn	Lt (W)	1.12.84
Burbridge, Lee	S/Lt	8.11.98
Burden, John	Lt Cdr	19. 4.78
Burdeyron-Dyster, Ian	Lt Cdr	18. 1.86
Burnett, Peter	Lt	12. 2.99
Burns, Clifford	Lt	1.11.93
Burns, Desmond	Lt	18. 2.78
Burns, Philip	Lt	20. 7.82
Burr, Peter	Lt	3.11.93
Burrage, Richard	Lt	25. 6.90
Burt, Christopher	Lt	20. 8.99
Burton, Craig	S/Lt	29. 1.00
Busby, Roger	Lt	19. 2.99
Bushen, Martyn	Lt	28.11.95
Butler, Colin	S/Lt	5.12.99
Butler, John	Lt	20.11.97
Butterworth, John	Lt	23. 3.87

C

Name	Rank	Seniority
Cade, John	Lt	26.11.87
Cadman, Julie	Lt	7.10.89
Cadman, John	Lt Cdr	26.11.86
Cadman, Leslie	Lt Cdr	30. 6.99
Calvert, Martin	Lt	19. 8.92
Campbell, Diane	S/Lt	5. 6.92
Campbell, William	Lt	20.8.87
Carney, Robert	Lt	8. 8.97
Carpenter, Michael	Lt Cdr	1.12.83
Carr, Leonard	Lt Cdr	19. 2.76
Carroll, Paul	Capt RMR	28.10.97
Carter, David	Lt	4. 3.92
Caslaw, Paul	Lt	1. 8.94
Catterall, Susan	Lt	20. 1.87
Cauley, John	Lt Cdr	1. 1.95
Cea, Franklin	Lt	18. 7.92
Chadwick, Heather	2/O	26. 2.93
Challacombe, Jonathan	Lt Cdr	27. 6.90
Chalmers, Janette	Lt	1. 1.90
Chambers, John	Lt Cdr	12. 12.95
Chantler, Michael	S/Lt	1. 1.00
Chaplin, Edwin	Lt	16. 7.97
Charlton, Adrian	Lt	8. 9.86
Chesworth, Howard	Lt	3.12.91
Childs, Paul	S/Lt	28. 9.98
Chinn, John	Lt Cdr	1. 1.83
Chittock, Michael	Lt	25. 3.94
Chitty, Rosemary	Lt	14. 4.98
Critchlow, Julian	Lt	8. 9.95
Cioma, Antoni	Lt Cdr	1. 7.90
Clark, Anne	Lt	5.11.97
Clark, Ian	Lt Cdr	1. 3.92
Clarke, Judith	Lt	6. 7.87
Clarke, Leonard	S/Lt	9. 6.94
Clarke, Mark	Lt	3.11.98
Clarke, Reuben	Lt	30.12.89
Clay, John	Lt Cdr	1. 4.99
Clissold, Mark	Lt	1. 4.93
Coast, Philip	Lt Cdr	9. 7.90

Name	Rank	Seniority
Cockell, Richard	Lt Cdr	4.12.96
Coffin, Roney	S/Lt	25. 6.97
Cole, Ian	S/Lt	8. 6.95
Coleman, Keith	Lt	26.11.98
Coles, Thomas	Lt Cdr	19.12.87
Collier, David	Alt	1. 9.88
Collins, Ann	Lt	25. 1.91
Collins, David, *CENG, MRINA*	Lt Cdr	1. 2.82
Collins, Raymond	S/Lt	31. 8.94
Compton, Paul	Lt Cdr	14.11.81
Constable, David	Lt	1. 3.81
Cooling, Philip	Lt	4.11.91
Coombes, Paul	Lt	25. 1.94
Cope, Derek	Lt Cdr	16. 2.82
Copelin, Maureen	Lt	5.10.88
Corbett, Sandra	Lt	23. 4.99
Cormack, Raymond	Lt	20.11.97
Cornish, Michael	Lt	15. 9.89
Cotton, Colin	Lt	21. 1.79
Cowell, Christopher	Lt RMR	1.7.99
Cowell, Ian	Lt Cdr	1. 1.92
Cowell, John	Lt	1. 4.91
Craig, Neil	Lt	1. 4.86
Craighead, Roderick	Lt	8. 3.93
Crawley, Stephen	Capt RMR	4. 6.95
Creighton, Edward William	Lt	26.11.92
Crick, Kenneth	Lt	20.10.92
Critchlow, Jonathan	Lt	19. 2.89
Cross, Stuart	Lt	5.12.97
Crowley, Derek	Lt	4.1.74
Cruse, Gillian	Lt	16.10.98
Cruse, Malcolm	Lt Cdr	17.10.89
Cummins, Sheila	Lt	1.11.86
Cumper, Alan	Lt	1.12.98
Curran, Paul	Lt	1. 2.88
Curtis, Owen	Lt	25. 6.85

D

Name	Rank	Seniority
Dale, Philip	S/Lt	1. 3.99
Daly, Martin	Lt	19.11.91
Daniels, Roger	Lt Cdr	14. 1.91
Dann, John	Lt	9. 7.95
Davies, Bruno	Lt Cdr	15. 4.86
Davies, Frederick	S/Lt	24. 4.94
Davies, Richard	Lt Cdr	7.12.81
Davies, William	Lt	18.1.84
Davis, Brian	Lt Cdr	21. 2.89
Davison, Henry	Lt	30.1.00
Daw, Clifford	Lt Cdr	8.8.84
Dawson, James, *BED(HONS), M1PM, TENG*	Lt Cdr	24.10.87
Day, Jean Stevenson	Lt	5. 2.91
Deacon, Maureen	S/Lt	7. 9.98
Delin, Roual	Lt RMR	1.11.93
Demellweek, Gilbert	Lt	1. 1.92
Derbyshire, David	Lt	3. 6.92
Devenish, Ian	S/Lt	5.11.95
Devereux, Edwin	Lt Cdr	1.5.87
Dibben, Michael	Lt	3.11.88
Dibben, Nigel	Lt Cdr	19.10.98
Dibnah, Robert	Lt	29.10.95
Dickinson, Keith	Lt	10.11.87
Dickson, James	Lt	1. 9.92
Dixie, Colin	S/Lt	14.10.98
Doggart, James	S/Lt	21. 1.99
Doggart, Norman	Lt	1. 7.88
Donovan, Terence	Lt	6.11.96
Dorricott, Peter	Lt	2.11.85
Dougal, Alexander	Lt	2.10.81
Dowdeswell, Robin	Lt	12. 7.86
Dowding-Vesey, Julie	S/Lt	25. 6.98
Doyle, Ellen	Lt Cdr	31. 3.80
Draper, Philip	Lt	20.12.99
Dryden, Stephen	Lt	1.3.81
Duncan, Niall	S/Lt	1. 3.89
Dunkeld, Brian	Lt	4. 6.97
Dunn, Simon	Lt	20. 3.96
Dunne, Lawrence	Lt	24. 2.97
Dyer, Geoffrey	Act Maj RMR	1. 5.99
Dyer, Gillian	Lt	21. 6.94
Dyer, Roger	Lt	7. 6.97
Dyer, Trevor	Lt	3.11.93

E

Name	Rank	Seniority
Eagles, Alan	Lt	5. 2.94
Eaton, Trevor	Lt	1. 9.96
Edmondson, Denis	S/Lt	28. 3.99
Edwards, Stuart	S/Lt	4. 6.95
Egan, Terence	Lt	1. 1.86
Eland, Robert	Lt	22.5.86
Elbrow, Kevin	Lt	14. 4.99
Ellicker, Robert	Lt	7. 5.83
Ellis, Henry	Lt	27.11.94
Ellis, Kenneth	S/Lt	24. 3.97
Ellis, Wininfred	Lt	21. 4.93
Ellison, Michael	Lt Cdr	1. 5.76
Ellsmore-Creed, Derek	Lt Cdr	1. 1.85
English, Michael	Lt Cdr	30.3.88
Erskine, Richard	Lt	1.4.97
Evans, Ivor	S/Lt	17. 7.97
Evans, Janet	Lt Cdr	1. 7.94
Evans, John	S/Lt	28. 9.98
Evans, Mark	Capt RMR	10. 4.99
Evans, Richard	Lt Cdr	16. 9.96
Evans, Wendy	Lt Cdr	1. 4.90
Everard, Gordon	Lt	11. 8.89
Every, Paul David	Lt	17. 4.92

F

Name	Rank	Seniority
Farrant, Paul	Lt	1. 6.96
Farrell, Martin	Lt	16. 9.85
Feist, Ivor	Lt Cdr	12. 7.80
Fenn, Paul	S/Lt	29.11.99
Fifield, Mark	Lt	14. 6.97
Finister, Anthony	Capt RMR	15. 8.95
Finlay, David	Lt	21. 2.98
Finley, Martin	Capt RMR	27. 4.96
Fisher, Hazel	Lt	26. 1.92
Fitch, Michael	S/Lt	16. 1.00
Fitzgerald, Terence	Capt RMR	1. 8.99

Name	Rank	Seniority
Flack, Brian	Lt	4. 9.96
Fleet, Gordon	Capt RMR	21. 3.97
Fleming, Alan	Lt	10. 7.93
Fletcher, Carol	Lt Cdr	1. 3.80
Fletcher, David	Lt	1. 3.99
Fletcher, John	Lt Cdr	6.3.87
Fletcher, Malcolm	Lt	20. 2.84
Flett, William	Capt RMR	17.11.96
Flynn, John, *MBE*	Lt Cdr	9.11.75
Forbes, John	Lt	18. 9.89
Ford, Stuart	Lt	2. 9.96
Fordy, Cyril	Lt Cdr	1. 6.79
Foreman, Waleria	Lt	20.10.95
Forrester, Michael	Lt	1. 8.81
Forster, Thomas	Lt	13.5.79
Fortune, Colin	Lt	1.10.99
Foster, Andrew	Lt	19.11.91
Foster, David	Lt	5.11.97
Foster, Ian	Lt	5. 8.85
Fowler, Alison	Lt	16. 1.97
Fox, Jane	S/Lt	27. 3.92
Fraser, Garry	Lt	1. 5.93
Freeman, Brian	Lt	16. 6.95
Freestone, Andrew	Lt	7.11.95
Fry, Brian	Lt	25. 9.80
Fulcher, Diane	Lt	6. 9.94
Fulcher, Graham	S/Lt	24. 4.94
Fuller, Keith Duncan	Lt	4. 5.92
Fussell, Christopher	Lt	1.990

G

Name	Rank	Seniority
Gale, Ronnie	Lt	1.11.90
Gallagher, Eamon	Lt	23. 6.92
Gambell, Mark	Lt	14.12.96
Gardinerr, John	Lt	4. 8.97
Gardner, Keith	Lt	1. 5.94
Gardner, Robert	Lt	6. 2.82
Garner, James	Lt	4. 8.97
Garnsworthy, Derek	S/Lt	25. 2.90
Garrett, John	Lt	7. 5.89
Garrett, Robert	S/Lt	6.11.94
Gathergood, John	Lt	17. 4.98
Gearing, Robert	Lt Cdr	1. 9.77
Gell, Dorothy	Lt	16.10.87
George, Brian	Lt	1. 9.85
Gerald, Anthony	Lt	1. 9.98
Gerrard, David	Lt Cdr	1.12.88
Gerrard, Mary	Lt Cdr	1. 9.98
Gibson, Peter	Lt	22. 5.93
Gilbert, John	Lt Cdr	31.12.75
Gilbert, Robin	Maj RMR	1. 6.99
Giles, Roger	Lt Cdr	30. 6.94
Gill, Jacqueline	Lt	28. 2.95
Gillard, Terence	Lt Cdr	1. 1.95
Gillert, Valerie	Lt	19.11.91
Gilliam, Kevin	Lt	1. 7.93
Gillies, Malcolm	S/Lt	30.11.97
Gillott, Peter	S/Lt	23. 5.99
Gittens, Adrian	S/Lt	5. 2.99
Glanfield, Mark	Lt	6. 2.82
Glanville, Barry	Lt	9. 2.91
Glanville, Debra	S/Lt	23. 5.99
Glendinning, Michael	Lt	7. 7.99
Goode, Eric	Lt	13.12.97
Goode, Victoria	S/Lt	4.11.98
Gooding, Peter	Lt Cdr	1. 1.81
Goodwin, Michael	S/Lt	29.11.99
Gordon, Andrew	Lt	19. 2.89
Govier, Adrian Terry	Alt Cdr	27. 9.99
Grace, Roger	Lt Cdr	13. 7.84
Graham, Robert	Lt Cdr	1. 2.87
Grainge, Andrew	S/Lt	2. 9.98
Grant, Malcolm	Lt	28. 2.95
Gratwick, Geffrey	Lt	29. 3.95
Gravestock, Denise	Lt Cdr	31. 3.80
Gray, Brian	Lt	12.12.87
Green, Cecilia	S/Lt	2.12.87
Green, Malcom	Lt	16. 8.97
Green, Paul	Lt	1. 9.86
Greenfield, Stephen	S/Lt	23. 5.99
Greenhalgh, Peter, *ENGTECH, MINSKSCE, AM*	Lt	30. 4.86
Greer, John	Lt Cdr	7.7.76
Gresty, Stephen	Lt	7.10.98
Grice, Robert	Lt Cdr	8.3.89
Griffin, Paul	Lt	24.10.86
Griffiths, Meirion	Lt Cdr	4.11.88
Grocott, Alan	Lt	22. 5.97
Grogan, Kenneth	Lt	16. 9.78
Groves, Richard	Lt Cdr	9. 9.99
Guiver, Carl	Maj RMR	1. 1.96
Guppy, Graham	Maj RMR	20. 6.84

H

Name	Rank	Seniority
Hackett, Clive	Lt Cdr	12.10.90
Hadfield, Philip	Capt	9. 4.91
Hagan, George	S/Lt	29.11.92
Hailwood, Paul	Lt Cdr	1.12.92
Haines, Linda	Lt	1.11.89
Hale, Carol	Lt	21. 1.99
Hale, Ronald	Lt Cdr	11.2.85
Hall, Allan	Lt	1. 2.76
Hall, Derek	Lt Cdr	19. 2.98
Hamilton, Kerry	Lt	1. 5.92
Hammond, Stephen	Lt	30. 5.97
Hanky, Carolyne	Lt	29. 9.99
Hanley, David	Lt	18.11.93
Hanna, June	S/Lt	20. 6.96
Hanson, David	Lt Cdr	26. 7.88
Hardick, Roger	Lt	13.10.93
Hargreaves, Andrew	Lt Cdr	1. 11.85
Harman, Robert	Lt	4. 8.90
Harmer, Robert	Lt	28.10.99
Harries, Mark	S/Lt	5. 6.94
Harris, Brian Stanley	Lt	4. 7.92
Harris, Peter	Lt	27.10.94
Harris, Stephen	Lt	1.10.91
Harris, Trevor	S/Lt	5.12.99
Hartley, Jacqueline	Lt Cdr	1.4.87
Harvey, Brian	S/Lt	1.11.94
Harvey, Lawrence	Lt	27. 8.87
Hatrick, James	Lt	29. 7.93

Name	Rank	Seniority
Hawes, Sandra	Lt	6.11.95
Hawkins, Leslie	S/Lt	8.11.99
Hayes, Stephen	S/Lt	1.11.92
Hayton, Alan	Lt	20.7.89
Hayward, Kenneth	S/Lt	1.12.98
Hazeldon, Donald	S/Lt	28.4.93
Hazzard, Keith	Lt	2.6.98
Headen, Geoffrey	S/Lt	28.9.98
Hearl, James	Lt	21.12.89
Heathcote, Victoria	Lt	1.5.98
Hebbes, Margaret	Lt	5.6.96
Hebbes, Peter	S/Lt	1.9.91
Helkin, Margaret	Lt	7.12.85
Henwood, Martin	Lt Cdr	21.10.80
Herbert, Michael	Alt Cdr	1.1.00
Hercock, Norman	Lt	3.11.93
Heward, Paul	Lt	1.5.86
Hewitt, Graham	Lt Cdr	7.4.92
Higman, Roger	Lt	26.7.83
Hill, Anthony	S/Lt	26.6.85
Hill, Ian	Lt	15.3.89
Hill, Monica	Lt	18.11.93
Hill, Reginald	Lt Cdr	1.3.88
Hinds, Michael	Lt	10.11.95
Hiscock, Andrew	Lt	17.2.83
Hithersay, John	Lt	28.10.78
Hodgson, Ian	Lt	4.1.92
Hoey, David	Lt	10.11.94
Holland, Donald	Lt	15.9.84
Holliday, Anthony	Lt	21.4.93
Hollywell, Gary	Alt Cdr	1.5.99
Holman, John	Maj RMR	1.1.94
Holmes, Kevin	Lt	9.11.90
Holt, Martin	Lt	10.9.83
Holt, Wendy	Lt	29.11.97
Hopper, Colin	Lt	20.9.97
Horne, Allan	Lt	16.9.89
Horner, John	Lt Cdr	16.9.92
Horner, Lynda	S/Lt	7.8.88
Houghton, Steven	A Maj RMR	1.194
Houlden, Paul	Lt	1.9.91
Houlden, Wendy	S/Lt	1.3.98
Howe, Margaret	Lt Cdr	1.10.85
Howie, Thomas	Lt Cdr	1.11.88
Hoyle, Keith	S/Lt	1.10.86
Hudson, Christopher	S/Lt	29.11.95
Hughes, Thomas	Lt Cdr	1.8.83
Hulonce, Michael, *AMS*	Lt Cdr	1.3.82
Hunt, Claire	Lt	14.6.97
Hunter, Lesley	Lt	5.5.98
Hurst, Paul	S/Lt	29.9.93
Hurst, Thomas	Lt Cdr	1.6.85
Hurst, Walter	Lt	30.9.91
Hutchings, Andrew	S/Lt	16.11.98
Huttley, Kenneth	Lt	13.11.87
Huyton, Gillian	Lt	7.10.98

I

Name	Rank	Seniority
Iggo, David	Lt	26.1.96
Ingham, Anthony	S/Lt	24.2.99
Ingham, David	Lt Cdr	28.4.98
Izzard, Michael	Lt	25.6.98

J

Name	Rank	Seniority
Jackson, Graeme	Lt	18.9.94
Jaconelli, Nicholas	S/Lt	10.12.97
James, George	Lt	22.8.78
James, Kevin	Lt	6.9.94
James, Robert	Lt Cdr	1.1.95
Jardine, Roderick	Lt	5.10.95
Jeffcoate, John	Lt	30.11.73
Jeffrey, Andrew	S/Lt	30.8.94
Jehan, Paula	S/Lt	19.5.91
Jenkins, Ian	Capt RMR	1.9.91
Jennings, William	Lt	19.10.84
Jepson, David	Lt	26.9.91
Jezzard, Kevin	S/Lt	12.4.99
Johns, Bevan	Lt Cdr	21.5.91
Johns, Deirdre	Lt	1.11.88
Johns, Nicholas	Lt	8.4.92
Johnson, Andrew	Lt	17.2.96
Johnson, Laurence	Lt Cdr	2.8.87
Johnson-Paul, David	Lt	18.4.92
Johnston, Peter	Lt	2.11.84
Johnstone, James	Lt Cdr	1.1.97
Jones, Antony	S/Lt	23.7.81
Jones, Christopher	Alt Cdr	11.8.99
Jones, Dorothy Edwina	Lt	22.10.94
Jones, Kelvin	Lt	6.5.92
Jones, Lily	Lt	9.4.91
Jones, Margaret	Lt	5.11.97
Jones, Mark	Lt	6.11.96
Jones, Neil	Lt	24.3.94
Jones, Neil	Lt	3.1.96
Jones, Peter	Lt	17.6.89
Jones, Trevor	S/Lt	7.4.97
Jordan, Robert	Alt Cdr	1.1.95
Jordan, Roger	Lt	22.6.87
Jordan, Sheila	Lt	26.7.90
Jupe, Paul	Lt	2.3.88
Justice, David, *GIFE, JP*	Lt	7.2.84

K

Name	Rank	Seniority
Kaye, Malcolm	Lt	1.11.89
Kayne, Robert	S/Lt	22.11.92
Kean, Robert	Lt	26.11.79
Keegan, William	Lt Cdr	16.7.84
Keenan, Robert	Alt Cdr	1.4.91
Keery, Neil	S/Lt	21.3.99
Keery, William	Lt Cdr	1.1.83
Kelsall, Alan	Lt Cdr	30.4.75
Kemp, David	Lt	23.9.94
Kempton, Edward	Lt Cdr	1.5.97
Kenna, Bryan	Lt Cdr	18.11.87
Kennedy, Ivan	Lt	1.11.89
Kenrick, Peter	Lt	23.11.94
Kerwin, James	Lt	9.5.97
Ketch, Roy	Lt	2.11.89
Killick, Peter	Lt	8.10.87
King, David	S/Lt	1.8.98
King, Leslie	Lt Cdr	15.3.98
Kinghorn, Jason	Lt	14.4.98
Kirkham, Stephen	Lt	12.12.87

Name	Rank	Seniority
Kissock, Robert Frederick	S/Lt	4.11.90
Knight, Nicholas	Lt	1.11.91
Knight, Robert	Lt	15. 2.00
Knill, Colin	Lt	1. 5.89
Korth, David	S/Lt	23.11.92
Kyle, Raymond	S/Lt	1.11.90

L

Name	Rank	Seniority
Lamb, David	Lt	1. 4.71
Lamb, Maureen	A/Lt Cdr	15. 3.95
Lamkin, John	Lt	15. 2.96
Lampert, Brian	Lt Cdr	17.10.79
Lampert, Susan	Lt	1.11.89
Lamport, John	S/Lt	1. 7.98
Lane, John	Lt	31. 5.91
Larsen, Colin	Lt	9. 5.97
Lawes, Sonia	Lt	8. 3.94
Lawrence, Barrie	Lt	4.10.92
Lawrence, Kevin	S/Lt	12. 4.99
Lawrence, Marion	S/Lt	20. 3.94
Lazenby, George	Lt Cdr	1. 5.97
Lazenby, Pauline	Lt	5.12.89
Lea, Garry	S/Lt	5. 5.99
Leatherbarrow, Ronald	Lt	29. 3.95
Ledgeton, Anthony	Capt RMR	24. 1.91
Lee, Arthur	Lt	1. 3.87
Lee, Terry	Lt	14. 7.98
Lees, Martin	S/Lt	19. 9.92
Lentle, Robert	Lt	1.11.90
Leslie, Harry	S/Lt	3. 3.91
Lewis, Alan	Lt	5. 5.85
Lewis, Clifford Bruce	Lt	4.11.92
Lewis, David	Lt	14. 4.98
Lewis, Eleanor	Lt	23.11.94
Lewis, John	Capt RMR	17.11.98
Lewis, Peter	Lt	31.10.90
Lewis, Robert	Lt	16. 6.90
Lewis, Walter	Lt	6. 5.79
Lincoln, David	Lt	1. 1.96
Lincoln, John	Lt	13. 9.96
Lock, Keith	S/Lt	1.12.92
Locke, David	Lt	10. 9.88
Login, Brenda	Lt	10.11.89
Login, Derek	Lt Cdr	12.12.88
Long, Adam	Lt	1. 4.97
Lonsdale, Bryan	Lt Cdr	1. 9.90
Lorimer, Deirdre	Lt	24. 6.98
Louden, Elizabeth Jane	S/Lt	1. 7.90
Loveland, John	Lt	21. 4.93
Loveridge, Anthony	Lt Cdr	1.12.89
Low, William	S/Lt	5. 4.94
Lowe, David	Lt	23. 7.77
Lucas, Peter	Lt	24. 3.99
Luckman, Bruce Innes	Lt	1.10.92
Ludford, Samuel	Lt	3.11.87
Lumley, Margaret	Lt	14. 6.97
Luxton, Phillip	S/Lt	5.11.98
Luxton, Peter	Lt Cdr	15.4.80

M

Name	Rank	Seniority
Mac Iver, Lynn	Lt	19. 4.96
MacAusland, Iain	Alt Cdr	1. 9.98
MacCallum, James	Lt	18. 1.98
MacDonald, Peter	Lt	7.11.91
MacDonald, William	Lt	9.10.76
Macey, Mark	Lt	13.11.93
Machin, Ian	Act Maj RMR	1. 8.96
MacKay, Charles	S/Lt	1.12.97
MacKay, David	Lt	1. 7.84
MacKay, Norman	Lt Cdr	1.7.80
MacKay, Norman	Lt	20.10.93
MacKinlay, Colin	Lt	8. 4.92
MacKinlay, Sherie	Lt	1. 9.93
MacKrell, Roger	Lt Cdr	1.8.87
MacLean, Colin, *M, INST, T, T*	Lt Cdr	14.6.83
MacLean, Donald	Lt	28. 3.90
Madden, Brian	Lt Cdr	1.11.88
Magnall, Edward	Lt Cdr	2. 4.80
Mahoney, Jane	Lt	4.11.93
Main, Paul	Lt	12. 3.91
Mair, Brian	Lt	24. 9.87
Malik, Camron	S/Lt	31. 1.96
Mannough, John	Lt	14. 5.90
Mansell, Nicholas	Lt	7.10.92
Mars, Victoria	Lt	7.11.92
Martin, John	Lt Cdr	1. 1.87
Martin, Kevin	Lt	14. 3.94
Mathers, David	Lt	15. 2.96
Matson, Christopher	Lt	16.11.97
Mattey, Barry John	Lt Cdr	4. 2.91
Matthews, Christopher	Lt	26. 1.95
Matthews, John	Lt	19. 6.95
Matthews, Philip Kenneth	Lt Cdr	1. 2.89
Matthews, Ronald	Lt	14. 1.97
Mayhew, Anthony	Lt	6.11.95
Maynard, Robert	Lt Cdr	31.3.84
Mc Williams, Zoe	Lt	27. 7.93
McAvady, Andrew	Lt	12. 6.98
McAvennie, John	Lt	3. 2.90
McAvoy, William	Lt	16.3.84
McCune, Barry	Lt	4. 6.88
McDonald, Alexander	S/Lt	1. 9.87
McDonald, Duncan	Lt	17.8.79
McDonald, Peter	Lt	29. 6.92
McGarry, George	Lt	3. 9.82
McGlashan, Robert	S/Lt	5. 5.96
McGuire, Gerald	S/Lt	12.11.97
McIntyre, Rosamund	Lt Cdr	1. 1.90
McKaig, Alexander	Lt	8. 1.87
McKee, David	Lt Cdr	27.9.87
McKenna, Paul	Lt	14. 3.96
McKeown, Glenda	Lt	24. 4.96
McLaren, George	S/Lt	2.12.95
McMahon, Thomas	Lt RMR	1.7.99
McMaster, George	Lt	6.10.88
McNee, Julia	Lt	4. 8.88
McRobb, Brian	Lt	6. 4.85
McVinnie, Elizabeth	S/Lt	6.11.98
Meadows, Paul	Lt	29. 1.99
Meldon, Michael	Lt Cdr	1. 3.88
Menhams, Angela	Lt	1.12.90

Name	Rank	Seniority
Meyer, Jonathan	Lt	16.11.90
Milby, Stuart	Lt Cdr	27. 7.93
Miles, Gail	Lt	1.10.83
Mills, William	Lt	23. 6.93
Milner, Anna	Lt Cdr	28.3.86
Mitchell, David	Lt	15. 5.98
Mitchell, Jane	S/Lt	4. 1.89
Mitchell, Ray	Lt	20. 7.86
Moffitt, Andrew	Lt Cdr	1. 4.99
Moffitt, Joan	Lt	3. 7.90
Mohammed, Barbara	Lt	7.12.83
Mohammed, John	Lt Cdr	9. 9.87
Moir, Brian	Lt	18. 9.95
Money, Alan	Lt	25. 3.94
Monkcom, Susan	Lt	1. 1.98
Mons-White, John Michael	Lt Cdr	15. 8.83
Mons-White, Margaret	Lt	1. 9.92
Moody, Roger	Lt Cdr	1. 4.74
Moore, Antony	Lt	7.12.85
Moore, Robert	Lt	3. 7.90
Morgan, John	Lt	10. 2.90
Morgan, Norman	Lt	1. 1.95
Morgan, Stephen	Lt	13. 4.96
Morley, Andrew	Lt	7.10.98
Morley, Michael	Lt	16. 3.88
Morrin, Kevin	Lt	5. 4.97
Morris, William	S/Lt	1. 7.98
Morton, Rita	Lt	13. 5.98
Mould, Peter	Lt Cdr	1. 8.78
Moulton, Nicholas	Alt Cdr	21.11.98
Mountier, Peter	Lt	19.11.90
Moyse, Janet	Lt	5. 6.95
Muggeridge, Edwin	Lt	6. 5.84
Mugridge, Toni	S/Lt	21. 7.99
Mulholland, Ross	Lt Cdr	1 6 .5.87
Mullin, Margaret	Lt	5.7.86
Mullin, William	Lt	10.11.86
Munro, Gordon	S/Lt	20. 3.91
Murchison, Donald	Lt Cdr	12.12.67
Murdock, Gordon	Lt Cdr	11. 2.76
Murphy, William	S/Lt	24. 5.99
Murray, Donald	Lt	1. 5.93

N

Name	Rank	Seniority
Newman, Raymond	Lt	27.10.82
Nice, David	Lt	1.5.84
Nichols, David	S/Lt	15. 7.99
Nixon, Joseph	Lt	30. 6.84
Norman, David	Lt	1. 4.86
Norman, John	Lt Cdr	1. 8.87
Norris, Norman Terence	Lt	1. 4.92

O

Name	Rank	Seniority
O Brien, Gary	Lt	30. 1.96
O Neill, Dawn	Lt	2.12.94
O'Connor, Brian	Lt	30. 7.87
O'Connor, Roy	Lt RMR	19.10.96
O'Donnell, Adrian	Lt	6.11.90
O'Donnell, Dominic	Lt	11.3.83
O'Hagan, William	Lt	1.12.85
O'Keefe, Richard	Lt	29. 4.89
O'Neill, Terence	Lt	26. 4.97
O'Shaughnessy, Helen	S/Lt	22. 5.95
Orton, Adrian	Capt RMR	1. 7.99
Osborne, Brian	Lt	1.1.87
Osborne, Dawn	Lt	1.2.86
Osborne, James	Lt Cdr	1.12.78
Owen, John	Lt	1. 1.84
Owen, William	Lt	5. 6.96
Owens, Christopher	Lt	30. 5.97
Owens, Michael	Capt RMR	6. 4.79

P

Name	Rank	Seniority
Packwood, Shelagh	Lt Cdr	1.12.86
Page, Helen	Lt	1.10.90
Painter, Lorretta	Lt	10. 6.92
Painting, Peter	Lt	10.3.79
Paling, John	Alt Cdr	1.10.96
Palmer, Alan	Lt RMR	20.11.99
Palmer, Robert	Lt	18.11.93
Palmer, Richard	Lt	23. 9.97
Parker, David	S/Lt	9.11.94
Parker, Derek	Alt Cdr	1. 6.90
Parker, Ian	Lt	20. 9.97
Parker, Simon	Lt	1. 3.90
Parkin, William	Lt	9.12.98
Parks, Edwin	Lt	2.12.95
Parks, Martyn	Lt	1. 5.99
Parr, Geoffrey Lawrenc	Lt	28.11.92
Parr, John	Capt RMR	1. 7.99
Parris, Stephen	Capt RMR	30. 1.99
Parry, Michael	Lt	1.5.87
Pascoe, William	Lt	26. 7.84
Paterson, Gordon	Alt Cdr	1.12.99
Patterson, Alexander	Lt Cdr	1.10.83
Patterson, Phillip	Lt	21. 1.99
Patterson, Paul	S/Lt	26.10.97
Paul, Patrick	S/Lt	12. 8.99
Payne, David	Lt	26.11.98
Payne, Derek	Lt	16.10.86
Payne, David	Lt	18. 3.00
Payne, Joseph	Lt	1. 7.90
Pearce, Peter	Lt	1. 6.98
Pearson, James	Lt	9. 3.93
Peck, John	Lt	23. 4.96
Penny, Carl	Capt RMR	1. 7.99
Perkins, Jonathon	S/Lt	14. 8.86
Perkins, Kevin	Lt	5.11.97
Perrins, John	Lt Cdr	15.2.81
Perry, Paul	Lt Cdr	4. 2.94
Peters, Kenneth	S/Lt	25. 9.98
Pether, Phillip	Lt	2.12.72
Pettit, Nicholas	Lt	9. 3.99
Phelps, Joanne	Lt	2. 4.99
Phillips, Pamela	S/Lt	5.11.95
Pickering, Jean	Lt	3. 7.90
Picton, Janet	Lt Cdr	18. 9.87
Piercy, Peter	Lt Cdr	25.10.86
Pike, John	Lt	31. 5.96
Plummer, Thomas	Lt	24.5.91
Pocock, Stewart	Lt Cdr	1. 7.88

Name	Rank	Seniority
Pogson, Godfrey	Lt Cdr	11.12.85
Poke, David	Capt RMR	1. 7.99
Pollard, Colin William	A/Lt	24. 7.90
Pool, Adam	S/Lt	8. 6.94
Pope, Darren	Lt	22. 4.93
Porter, John	Lt	3. 2.84
Postill, John	Lt RMR	1.799
Poth, Anthony	Lt Cdr	17. 3.86
Pow, David John	Lt	6.10.92
Powell, Denise	Lt Cdr	19. 1.94
Powell, Robert	Lt RMR	1.7.99
Power, Fiona	Lt	5. 3.99
Preston, Frank	S/Lt	1. 6.94
Priestley, Gary	S/Lt	18. 9.94
Prince, Ramon	S/Lt	13. 4.97
Pritchard, Carol	Lt	6. 9.94
Pritchard, David	A/Lt Cdr	1. 1.95
Pugh, Heather	Lt Cdr	28. 4.98
Pugh, John	Lt RMR	1.7.99
Pusill, David	Lt	7. 2.92

R

Name	Rank	Seniority
Radcliffe, Brian	Lt Cdr	15. 1.89
Rattenbury, John	Lt	10.11.94
Rawcliffe, Michael	Lt	17. 4.98
Rawlinson, Martin	Lt	1. 3.98
Rayner, Miranda	S/Lt	14. 4.97
Rayson, Trevor	Lt	20.10.81
Reddecliffe, Phillip	Lt	13. 4.91
Redhead, Gavin	S/Lt	28. 9.98
Redhead, Julie	S/Lt	28. 3.99
Redmond, Lee	Lt	1.12.96
Rees, Andrew	Lt	14. 7.86
Rees, Celia	Lt Cdr	1. 1.94
Rees, Susan	Lt	5. 4.97
Reeve, John	Lt	19.11.91
Reeve, Sydney	Lt Cdr	1.10.88
Reeves, Angela	Lt	12. 9.90
Reeves, Mark	S/Lt	3. 3.99
Regan, Paul	Maj RMR	1.10.96
Reid, Jeffery	S/Lt	4.11.98
Reid, Morag	S/Lt	21. 3.99
Richards, Philip	S/Lt	12. 4.99
Richings, David	Lt	15. 4.99
Richmond, Peter	Lt	1. 1.00
Ridley, Christoher	Lt	14. 6.87
Ridsdale, Lorna	Lt	10.11.95
Rimmer, David	Lt	1. 2.80
Rimmer, Kevin	Lt	30. 3.94
Roaf, Alistair	S/Lt	7. 6.96
Robbins, Allan	Lt	17. 6.88
Roberts, Evphemia	Lt	3.11.98
Roberts, Ronald	Lt Cdr	6. 1.86
Robins, William	Lt	1. 9.76
Robinson, Eric	Lt	18. 3.99
Robinson, Paul	Lt	1. 2.99
Rock, William	S/Lt	12.11.98
Rockey, David	S/Lt	11. 3.98
Roden, John	Lt RMR	1. 7.99
Roe, Graham	Capt RMR	1. 7.99
Rogers, Neil	S/Lt	30. 9.98
Rogers, Sallyanne	Lt	22.11.97
Rolfe, Victor	Lt	2. 8.91
Rollins, Linda	Lt	3.11.98
Rooney, Frederick	S/Lt	14.11.96
Roots, Joseph	S/Lt	16.11.98
Ross, David	Lt	13.10.90
Ross, Malcoln	Lt	9. 5.95
Rotherham, Thomas	Lt	10. 1.98
Rothwell, Jacquelyn	Lt	12. 3.91
Rowe, Raymond	Lt	2. 4.99
Rowland, Victor	Lt	21.3.87
Rowles, David	Lt Cdr	3.5.74
Rummins, Ann	Lt	13.12.85
Rushton, Steven	Lt	15. 3.95
Rusiecki, Lawrence Joseph	Capt RMR	10.12.93
Russell, Audrey	Lt	1. 3.99
Russell, John	Lt	1.11.89
Russett, Terence	Lt	9.10.90
Rutter, Thomas	Lt	30.10.87
Rycroft, Paul	Lt Cdr	8. 9.89
Ryder, Ruth	Lt	3.11.93

S

Name	Rank	Seniority
Salisbury, Linda	Lt	2. 4.99
Salveson, Anthony	Lt Cdr	1. 3.79
Saunders, Donald	Lt	28. 8.94
Saupe, Peter	Lt	1. 7.87
Sawford, Michael	Lt	3.12.85
Sayer, Janet	Lt	30. 1.87
Scanlan, John	Lt	1.4.89
Scarisbrick-Wright, Alan	S/Lt	15. 2.98
Scarratt, Leslie	Lt RMR	1.7.99
Schembri, Winifred	Lt Cdr	7. 2.97
Schofield, George	S/Lt	1. 4.91
Scholes, David	Capt RMR	1.7.99
Scholes, Stephen	Lt RMR	1.7.99
Scott, Francis	Lt Cdr	1. 4.92
Scott, Gordon	Lt Cdr	1.12.98
Scourfield, Royston	Lt	1. 6.91
Scrivens, Stuart	Lt	3.12.91
Seabury, Paul	Lt	16. 8.97
Searles, Andrew	Lt	9.11.96
Sedgwick, Mark	S/Lt	3. 6.98
Servis, Thomas	Lt	20. 8.85
Shakespeare, William	Lt Cdr	1. 4.99
Sharp, Christine	Lt Cdr	1.4.83
Sharp, Terence	Lt Cdr	8. 9.80
Shaw, David	Lt	14.5.84
Shaw, Geoff	Lt	12. 6.98
Shaw, James	Lt	21. 4.93
Shelton, Clive	Lt Cdr	24. 4.98
Sherwin, *P W*(Peter), *MBE*	Lt Cdr	30.10.80
Shiels, Robert	Lt Cdr	8. 9.86
Shone, Michael	Lt	15. 6.98
Short, Keith	Lt Cdr	6. 4.86
Sickelmore, Barry	Alt Cdr	5. 4.99
Sidney, Gerald	Maj RMR	1. 1.96
Sigley, Dermid	Lt	1. 5.89
Silverthorne, Robert	Lt	31.10.91
Simister, Alan	Lt	10.11.95

Name	Rank	Seniority
Simmons, Melvyn	Lt	10. 4.93
Simpson, Alfred	Lt Cdr	8.2.84
Simpson, Leonard	S/Lt	1. 5.93
Simpson, Timothy	Lt	1. 2.95
Skingle, Stephen	S/Lt	14. 7.96
Skinner, Angela	S/Lt	8.11.98
Skinner, John	Lt	14. 7.98
Smales, Geoffrey	Lt Cdr	1. 1.97
Smart, Claude	Lt Cdr	26. 4.79
Smith, Adrian	Lt	21. 8.92
Smith, Alan	S/Lt	1. 1.88
Smith, Deborah	Lt	29. 3.95
Smith, Graham	Lt	5. 4.97
Smith, John	S/Lt	12.11.98
Smith, James	Lt	5.10.98
Smith, James	Lt	9. 5.94
Smith, Kathleen	Lt	27. 9.99
Smith, Robin	Lt	6. 7.89
Smith, Victoria	Lt Cdr	31.3.80
Smith-Gosling, Malcolm	Lt	15. 6.95
Soards, Sonia	Lt Cdr	15. 4.93
Soilleux, Peter	S/Lt	12. 4.99
Southcott, Michael	Lt	13.10.95
Sparks, Alison	S/Lt	17. 3.97
Speariett, Gail	Lt Cdr	16.11.91
Spencer, Allan	Lt	15.10.93
Spencer, Edward	Lt	9. 9.76
Spicer, Janice	Lt	1.7.87
Spindler, William	Maj RMR	1. 5.85
Spink, James	Lt	2.3.88
Spong, Victor	Lt Cdr	20. 7.76
Sprogis, Alfred	Lt	22. 4.94
Squires, John	Lt	6.12.88
Stacey, Stephen	Lt	16. 2.87
Stafford, Rita	Lt	21.10.94
Standen, Roy	Lt Cdr	31.12.67
Steggall, Mark	Lt	19.11.91
Steggall, Stephen	Lt	19. 11.91
Stevens, Alan	S/Lt	1. 7.98
Stevenson, Ian	Lt	31. 3.87
Steward, Karen	Lt	14. 2.98
Stewart, David	Lt Cdr	10. 2.96
Stewart, James	Lt	22. 5.79
Stewart, Patrick	Lt Cdr	27. 7.83
Stewart, Rosaleen	S/Lt	1.10.90
Stone, Terrence	Lt	26. 2.91
Stott, Barry	Lt	19. 1.96
Straderick, Barbara	Lt	10.11.95
Street, Brenda	Lt	18.7.84
Street, Steven	Lt	14. 4.99
Streete, Brenda	Lt	17. 5.84
Stringman, Michael	Lt	1. 8.98
Strutt, Dupre	Lt Cdr	28. 1.98
Stubbs, Edward	Lt	18.11.93
Sturt, Lisa	Lt	20.3.96
Sumner, Robert	Lt	6.12.99
Sutherland, Shane	Lt	1. 7.94
Svendsen, Peter	Lt	23.11.90
Swan, Gordon	Lt	11. 3.96
Swarbrick, David	Lt	16. 6.83

T

Name	Rank	Seniority
Tait, Graham	Lt	12. 5.97
Tanner, Roland	Lt Cdr	21. 7.87
Tannock, Andrew	Capt RMR	30. 1.99
Tapp, Maria	Lt	23.10.95
Taylor, Brian	Capt RMR	1. 7.91
Taylor, Duncan	Lt	22.11.97
Taylor, John	S/Lt	1. 3.96
Taylor, Pauline	Lt Cdr	1. 3.89
Taylor, William	Lt	1. 4.91
Tearle, Kevin	Lt Cdr	5. 1.92
Tebby, Alan	S/Lt	23. 5.99
Tebby, Christine	Lt	5. 9.89
Temple, Edward	Lt Cdr	14.10.91
Thackery, Richard	Lt	2. 3.96
Theobald, Robert	Lt	10.11.87
Theobald, Wendy Margaret	A/Lt Cdr	1. 1.96
Thomas, Alan	Lt	14. 4.98
Thomas, Adrian	Capt RMR	9. 7.85
Thomas, Derek	Lt	10.10.94
Thomas, Jacqueline	Lt	31. 5.93
Thomas, Michael	Lt	19. 7.80
Thomas, Roderick Leslie	Lt	26.11.92
Thomas, Valerie	Lt	22.11.97
Thomas, William	Lt	1. 1.84
Thompson, Robert	S/Lt	5. 5.98
Thompson, Andrew	S/Lt	15.10.99
Thompson, Joan	Lt	10.02.82
Thompson, Michael	Lt Cdr	31.12.83
Thompson, Peter	Lt Cdr	1.12.74
Thomson, Andrew	Lt	7. 4.95
Thomson, Rose	S/Lt	26.10.97
Thomson, Robert	Lt	17. 3.71
Thorne, Christopher	Lt	13. 7.90
Thwaites, David	Lt Cdr	1. 1.95
Tilley, Lorna	Lt	9. 6.93
Timothy, Emile	Maj RMR	20. 4.92
Titley, John	Lt	4. 7.93
Tomlinson, Alan	S/Lt	29. 9.97
Totty, Paul	Capt RMR	10.9.89
Townley, Frederick	Lt Cdr	4. 9.89
Townsend, Graham	Lt	1. 5.98
Townshend, Shella	Lt	3.11.98
Trahair, Estelle	Lt	24. 4.96
Tranter, Gary	Lt Cdr	1. 3.87
Treverton, Mary	Lt	21. 3.96
Trojan, Margaret	Alt	30.11.99
Trott, Peter	Lt Cdr	15.3.83
Truelove, Gary	Lt	26.11.89
Truscott, Gary	Lt Cdr	1. 1.96
Tubbs, Sean	S/Lt	16.10.96
Tubman, Vernon	S/Lt	18.10.91
Tucker, Neil	Lt	3.11.95
Turnbull, Peter	Lt	16. 2.78
Turnell, Terence	Lt	19. 4.97
Turner, Ian	Lt	4.11.97
Tuson, Barry	S/Lt	24. 3.97
Tuson, Denise	Lt	30. 3.94
Tweed, Alan Campbell	Lt	6. 1.93
Tyrrell, Richard	Lt Cdr	19. 6.91
Tyson, Michael	Lt	22. 3.83

U

Name	Rank	Seniority
Ulrich, Geoffrey	Lt Cdr	27.11.82
Unwin, Mark	S/Lt	24. 2.99
Urquhart, John	Lt	5. 5.97
Utting, Joseph	S/Lt	22. 1.98

V

Name	Rank	Seniority
Vallois, Neil	Lt RMR	1.7.99
Vanns, Jonathan	Lt	4. 5.92
Vaughan, Jeffery	Lt	10.11.95
Villa, Nina	S/Lt	8.11.99
Vincett, Shirley	Lt	12. 1.99

W

Name	Rank	Seniority
Waddleton, Michael	Lt	17.3.79
Wade, John	Lt	1.7.78
Wagstaff, Melvin	S/Lt	21. 6.92
Wain, Alan	Lt Cdr	1.10.87
Wakeham, David	S/Lt	16.11.99
Walker, Keith	Lt	5. 2.88
Walker, Pamela	S/Lt	5.12.99
Wall, Margaret	Lt	26.10.84
Wallace, Iain	Alt Cdr	1. 4.95
Wallis, Alexander	Lt	7. 6.95
Walsh, Barry	S/Lt	1. 3.95
Walsh, Edward	Lt Cdr	1. 6.82
Walsh, Maxwell	Lt Cdr	1. 3.91
Ward, John	Lt	2. 3.88
Waring, Peter	Lt	14.11.96
Waring, Paula	S/Lt	22. 5.95
Warner, Peter	Capt RMR	10. 3.96
Warwick, Stephen	Lt	12. 3.98
Waters, Alan	Lt Cdr	1. 1.81
Waters, Scott	Lt	21. 4.94
Watson, Ian	Lt	20. 7.91
Watson, Sheila	Lt	4. 2.00
Watts, Reginald	Lt Cdr	27.10.91
Waugh, John	Lt	6. 9.80
Way, Christopher	S/Lt	23.11.99
Waylett, Graham	S/Lt	15. 2.00
Webb, Colin	Lt	17.11.95
Webb, John	Lt Cdr	9.11.85
Webb, John	Alt Cdr	21. 4.99
Webb, Martin	Lt	7. 6.96
Webster, Jonathan	S/Lt	23. 5.99
Webster, John	Lt Cdr	14.12.90
Weightman, Eric	Lt	22. 5.85
Welsh, John	Lt	7.11.93
Welsh, Michelle	Lt	7.11.95
Weobley, Malcolm	Maj RMR	28. 8.86
Weston, Mark	Lt	7.11.95
Westover, Robert	Lt	9.6.78
Wheatley, Noel	Lt Cdr	1. 1.95
Wheeler, Deanna	S/Lt	12. 4.99
Wheeler, Michael	Lt	22. 3.75
White, David	S/Lt	2.12.95
White, Robert	Lt	29.10.99
Whitehead, William	Lt RMR	5.12.99
Whiteman, Mark	Lt	5.8.85
Whiteman, Paul	Lt Cdr	27. 3.90
Whitley, Glenda	Lt	8. 5.87
Whitley, Roger	Lt	14. 4.99
Whitworth, Duncan	Alt Cdr	1. 9.94
Whorwood, Julia	Lt	7. 5.97
Whyte, Lawrence	Lt Cdr	1. 3.98
Wickenden, Frances	Lt	1. 9.98
Wigley, Grahame	S/Lt	12. 4.99
Wilcock, David	Lt	20. 1.93
Wilde, James	S/Lt	1. 3.93
Wilkinson, Christopher	Lt	4.11.97
Wilks, Stephen	S/Lt	3. 3.99
Willett, Marion	Lt	21.12.86
Williams, Alan	Lt Cdr	1. 5.84
Williams, Derek	Lt	13.12.88
Williams, David	Lt	15. 3.98
Williams, Deborah Karen	Lt	4.11.92
Williams, Peter John	Lt	16.11.92
Williams, Suzanne	Lt	18. 3.81
Williamson, William	Lt Cdr	26.5.87
Wilson, Brian	Lt	21. 9.96
Wilson, Edward	S/Lt	8. 5.89
Wilson, Ethel	Lt	1.11.98
Wilson, George	Lt	5. 6.96
Wilson, George	Lt	1.11.95
Wilson, Ian	Lt	21. 2.82
Wilson, Ian	Capt RMR	24. 5.90
Wilson, Michael	Lt	14. 4.99
Wilson, Paul	Lt	8.10.91
Wilson, William	Lt	1.7.87
Wilton, Christopher	Lt	2.10.92
Windle, John	Lt	13. 7.90
Winn, Julie	S/Lt	28. 9.98
Wood, Christopher	Lt	27.10.92
Wood, Mclhael	Lt	1. 6.84
Wood, Norman	Lt Cdr	1. 3.90
Woods, Edward Arthur	Lt	4.11.92
Wooldridge, Donald	Lt	3. 2.94
Woolgar, Victor	Lt Cdr	1. 4.88
Worrall, Ian	Capt RMR	1. 7.99
Wrin, Jane Frances	Lt	26.11.92
Wylie, William	Lt Cdr	5.12.83
Wynne, David	Lt	21. 4.93
Wythe, Kay	Lt	20.11.92

Y

Name	Rank	Seniority
Yeomans, Roy	Lt	10. 4.97
Yorke, Barrie	Lt	1. 7.87
Young, Jean	Lt	1.12.95
Young, Steven	Lt	5. 5.95

COMBINED CADET FORCE

Name	Rank	Seniority	School/College
A			
Abrahams, Ian	S/Lt	7. 3.99	Framlingham
Adams, Mark	S/Lt	1. 6.99	Churchers
Adams, Neil	Asl	5. 9.99	Haileybury
Adams, Thomas	Lt	1. 9.81	Cheltenham
Agutter, Neil	S/Lt	8. 8.94	St Bartholomews
Aldridge, Mark	Lt	1. 4.95	St Dunstans
Allen, Brian	S/Lt	28. 2.84	Elizabeth
Allen, Philip	Lt	26. 7.99	Perse
Allison, Peter	Lt RMR	1. 7.99	Charterhouse
Andrews, Jacqueline	Lt	29.11.96	Dundee High Sch
Arkieson, David	Lt	1. 9.98	Ellesmore
Armitage, David	S/Lt	1.10.98	Wellington
Armstrong, Ivan	Lt Cdr	31. 5.95	Cambell
Ashfield, Noel	S/Lt	28.11.99	Cambell
Aston, Paul	Lt Cdr	25. 7.97	Loretto Sch
B			
Baker, Michael	Lt	25. 9.97	Plymouth
Baker, Piers	S/Lt	14. 7.86	Victoria
Barker, Janet	S/Lt	5. 3.91	Recall
Barker, Simon	Lt	20. 3.92	RGS High Sch
Batchelder, Mark	S/Lt	4. 3.99	Berkhamsted
Belcher, John	Lt	1. 9.88	Solihull
Benson, Derek	Cdr	10. 3.79	Recall
Benson, Roger	Lt	1. 9.95	Nottingham High
Bird, Elizabeth	S/Lt	1. 7.98	Recall
Bird, Jason	S/Lt	31. 7.99	Trinity
Bird, Stephen	S/Lt	1. 1.98	Recall
Bond, Esther	S/Lt	1. 5.99	Batley
Bone, Robert	S/Lt	27. 2.00	Mill Hill
Borking, Graham	Lt	9. 1.90	Queen Victoria
Boughton, Charles	S/Lt	8. 8.95	RHS
Boulton, Martin	A/Lt RMR	1. 7.99	Sherbourne
Bowles, Michael	Lt	21. 9.86	Brentwood
Brazier, Colin	Lt	19. 6.97	HQCCF
Bridgeman, Keith	Lt Cdr	1. 7.95	MTS Northwood
Brittain, Norman	Lt	1. 8.75	Oundle
Brooks, John	Lt Cdr	19. 2.80	St Peters Cof E
Brown, Anthony	Cdr	26. 4.98	Recall
Brown, Simon	S/Lt	1.10.99	Shiplake Col
Brown, Stephen	Lt	26. 7.99	Milton Abbey
Browne, Nialle	S/Lt	12.10.98	Kelly
Browne, Victoria	S/Lt	12. 7.98	Dollar
Buchanan, Katy	S/Lt	28.11.99	RGS High Sch
Burden, Richard	A/Lt RMR	1. 7.99	Harrow
Burns, Dereck	Lt Cdr		Recall
Burrowes, Christopher	Lt	12. 8.91	Winchester
C			
Callow, Martin	:Lt RMR	1. 7.99	Royal Hospital
Cardwell, Alexander	Lt	30.10.94	Bangor
Carless, Barry	Lt	16. 6.83	Recall
Carley, Jonathan	Lt	1. 7.94	Recall
Carpenter, Richard	S/Lt	1.11.98	Nottingham High
Carter, Ian	S/Lt	1. 2.88	Cheltenham
Carter, Michael	Lt Cdr	21. 6.95	Kelly
Carter, Nicholas	Lt Cdr	20. 7.98	Newcastle High
Carter, Steven	Lt Cdr	1. 9.93	Recall
Cartmell, Keith	S/Lt	16.11.98	Arnold
Caves, Richard	S/Lt	7.12.98	Strathallan
Chalcraft, Christopher	S/Lt	12.10.98	Solihull
Chapman, Kenneth	S/Lt	19. 6.84	Stamford
Chetwood, James	Lt	1. 9.97	Portsmouth
Clark, Timothy	S/Lt	11. 8.97	Brighton
Clarke, Rueben	Lt	1. 5.96	Recall
Clayton, Fiona	S/Lt	1. 8.99	sutton Valence
Clough, Howard	Lt	1. 9.99	Scarborough
Collier, Anthony	S/Lt	8. 8.94	Christs Hospital
Collins, Micheal	S/Lt	28. 2.83	Magdalen
Collins, Wendy	S/Lt	27. 9.93	RGS Newcastle
Collins, Wendy	S/Lt		Recall
Connor, Simon	A/Lt RMR	1. 7.99	Uppingham

Name	Rank	Seniority	School/College
Copleston, Michael	S/Lt	28. 3.99	Taunton
Copp, Anthony	Lt RMR	1. 7.99	Canford
Copplestone, Neil	S/Lt	1. 1.91	Brentwood
Corbould, Leigh	S/Lt	10.10.99	Canford
Costin, Robert	S/Lt	11. 8.98	Worksop
Couch, Patrick	S/Lt	8. 8.95	St Lawrence
Cox, James	Lt	17. 9.97	Birkenhead
Crabtree, John	Lt Cdr	1.11.89	Kings Col Taunton
Creasey, Peter	S/Lt	10. 8.92	Royal Hospital
Crees, David	Cdr	1.11.92	Recall
Crook, Patricia	S/Lt	28. 3.99	Haileybury
Crook, Stephen	S/Lt	11. 2.00	City of London
Curtis, Berwick	Lt	1. 9.81	Epsom
Cuthbertson, James	S/Lt	1. 2.97	Kelvinside
D			
Daniel, Martine	S/Lt	8. 8.95	Ryde
Davies, Jonathon	Lt	7.10.99	Seaford
Day, Anita	S/Lt	1.12.99	Alleynes
Delpech, Daniel	Lt	30. 1.92	Haberdashers Askes
Dewey, Peter	Lt RMR	1. 7.99	Rugby
Dolman, Clare	S/Lt	1.10.97	Recall
Dore, Karen	Lt	1. 9.96	Stowe Sch
Dubbins, Keith	Lt	17. 7.93	Ryde
Dunn, Alexander	Cdr	16. 3.95	HQCCF(Sailing)
Durrans, Howard	Lt	13. 1.98	Bridlington
Durrant, Robert	Cdr	1. 3.92	Ruthin
Dyster, Sabine	A/3/O	15. 2.99	Christ's Hospital
E			
Eames, Andrew	Lt Col RMR	1. 7.99	Hereford Cathedral
Ecclestone, Kay	S/Lt	28. 2.00	Eastbourne
Elbourne, Nicholas	Cdr	1.11.97	Wellingborough
Elkington, Herbert	Cdr	12. 1.87	Wellington Sch
Ellis, Timothy	Lt	1. 9.94	Hereford Cathedral
Emms, Peter	S/Lt	11. 8.98	Magdalan
Ettinger, Damian	Lt	1. 9.92	Downside
Evans, Richard	Lt Cdr	16. 9.96	Raleigh
Everest, Derek	Lt	1. 4.74	Kings Edwards
Eyles, Mark	S/Lt	18.10.99	Colstons
Eyles, Ruth	S/Lt	8. 8.95	Recall
F			
Finn, Mark	Lt Cdr	9.11.93	HQCCF(ATO)
Fischer, Andrew	Asl	18.10.99	St Lawrence
Fletcher, Richard	Lt	17. 7.93	Recall
Foster, Stella	S/Lt	8. 8.95	Recall
Foulger, Tim	Lt	1. 9.97	Recall
Fox, Stephen	Lt RMR	1. 7.99	Shrewsbury
Francis-Jones, Anthony	S/Lt	10. 8.93	Kings Taunton Col
Freedman, Stephen	Lt Cdr	5. 9.99	MTS Crosby
Friend, David	Lt	1.10.96	Kings Bruton Sch
Frost, Rex	Cdr	1. 8.92	Exeter
Fullarton, Ian	Asl	7. 3.99	Bedford Modern
Fuller, David	S/Lt	26. 6.99	Oundle
Fulton-Peebles, Peter	Lt	30. 3.81	King Williams
Funston, Bryan	Lt	12. 8.91	Campbell
G			
Georgiakakis, Nikos	Lt	20. 8.90	Charterhouse
Glasby, Martyn	S/Lt	5. 9.91	Ryde

Name	Rank	Seniority	School/College
Glasspoole, Paul	Lt Cdr	4. 5.89	Hele's
Glimm, Klaus	Act Maj RMR	1. 7.99	Recall
Glover, William	S/Lt	8. 8.95	Recall
Goodwin, Michael	S/Lt	28. 8.92	Reading Blue Coat
Gosnell, Nicholas	Lt	21.10.95	Recall
Gray, David	Lt Cdr	20. 9.98	Bradfield
Green, George	Cdr	1. 1.94	Brighton
Greenhough, Clive	S/Lt	1. 9.99	Mill Hill
Griffin, Paul	S/Lt	5. 1.99	Downside
Guise, Nicola	3/O	1. 9.95	Recall
H			
Hall, Austin	Lt	15. 7.88	Recall
Hamilton, Lesley	S/Lt	1. 9.98	Liverpool
Hamon, Christopher	Lt	1. 9.96	Sherbourne
Harding, Clare	Lt Cdr	7. 7.95	Kelly
Hardman, Thomas	Lt	7. 7.99	Haberdashers
Harris, Steven	Lt	1. 8.98	Exeter
Harrison, Anthony	Lt	8. 2.94	Sandbach
Harrod, Samantha	S/Lt	11. 8.98	Pangbourne
Hartley, George	S/Lt	1. 1.92	Ruthin
Harvey, Peter	Lt Cdr	1. 8.97	Kings Rochester Sch
Harvey, Stephen	Lt	17. 8.97	Bedford Modern
Hawkins, Keith	Lt Cdr	1. 4.93	Recall
Hellier, Jeremy	Lt Cdr	1. 3.90	Wellington
Henderson, Joan	Lt	1.10.98	RGS High Wycombe
Hendry, Alastair	S/Lt	8. 8.94	Reigate Sch
Hewett, Michael	Lt	23. 5.79	Recall
Hewitt, Richard	Lt	31. 7.83	Durham
Hey, Richard	Lt	1. 4.98	Oratory
Hill, Charles	Lt	1. 3.77	Winchester
Hill, Peter	Lt	12. 3.98	Sevenoaks
Hobbs, Andrew	Lt RMR	1. 7.99	Canford
Hocking, Barry	Asl	20. 3.99	Royal Hospital
Hocking, John	S/Lt	8. 8.94	Plymouth
Holland, Clare	S?Lt	12.10.98	Calday Grange
Holmes, Matthew	S/Lt	17.11.98	Langley
Horley, Philip	Asl	28. 6.99	Sutton Valence
Houghton, Philip	Asl	7. 3.99	Fettes
Hudson, John	Lt Cdr	1. 9.95	Kings Taunton Col
Hutchings, Jonathan	S/Lt	1. 5.97	Recall
Hutchinson, Jeremy	Cdr	12. 8.96	Recall
I			
Ibbertson-Price, William	Lt Cdr	14.11.91	Oratory
Iles, Terence	Lt Cdr	9. 7.99	Recall
Ing, John	Capt RMR	1. 7.99	Harrow
Iredale, Judy	Lt	1. 7.98	Taunton
J			
Jacklin, John	Lt Cdr	8.10.99	HQCCF
Jackson, Andrew	S/Lt	1. 1.98	WoodBridge
Jackson, Howard	Lt	15. 7.88	Worksop Col
Jackson, David	Lt	1. 6.81	Bedford
Jago, Peter	S/Lt	21. 1.97	RGS Lancaster
Jeans-Jakobsson, Michael	Lt	1. 5.92	Recall
Jenkins, David	Lt Cdr	1. 9.92	Recall
Jethwa, Ashok	S/Lt	26. 1.98	Arnold
Johnson, Marcus	S/Lt	8. 8.95	Exeter
Johnston, Hilary	S/Lt	1. 5.99	Haberdashers Askes

Name	Rank	Seniority	School/College
Johnston, Kirsten	S/Lt	1. 9.97	MTS Northwood
Jolliff, Timothy	S/Lt	18.10.95	Loughborough
Jones, Philip	Lt RMR	1. 7.99	Bedford Modern

K

Name	Rank	Seniority	School/College
Kay, Anne	S/Lt	7. 4.96	HQCCF
Kennedy, Karen	S/Lt	28. 3.99	PLymouth
Kent, Iain	S/Lt	11. 8.98	St Batholomews
Kermode, Erica	S/Lt	8. 8.94	Recall
Kidwell, Montserrat	S/Lt	20.11.99	St Johns
Kilbey, Susan	S/Lt	10.11.98	Cheltenham
Killgren, Carl	Lt Cdr	1.11.98	Stamford
Kingsland, Jennifer	Lt	1. 1.91	Bradfield Col
Kirton, Stephanie	S/Lt	3. 7.98	Birkhamsted
Kirwin, Christopher	Cdr	1. 2.91	Kelly

L

Name	Rank	Seniority	School/College
Lankester, Robert	Lt RMR	1. 7.99	Uppingham
Larby, John	Lt Cdr	1. 9.95	Kelly
Law, Brendan	Lt	1.12.97	Bedford
Lawson, Edward	Lt Cdr	28. 1.97	Arnold
Lawson, Grant	S/Lt	6. 9.98	Shiplake
Lawson, Matthew	S/Lt	1. 9.99	St Johns
Lea, Ruth	S/Lt	1. 1.98	Dean Close
Lee, John	Lt	1. 9.90	Ruthin
Leigh, Richard	S/Lt	27. 6.99	King Williams
Lemieux, Simon	Lt	1. 9.93	Portsmouth
Lewis, Andrew Robert	S/Lt	10. 8.93	Christs Hospital
Lingard, David	Cdr	8. 3.99	Recall
Little, John	Lt Cdr	1. 9.91	Eastbourne
Lloyd, Theo	Lt	22.11.99	Churchers
Lofthouse, John	S/Lt	25. 2.97	Alleyn's
Loudon, Iain	S/Lt	18.10.95	Russell
Lovell, Keith	S/Lt	21. 7.89	Recall
Lovell, Stephen	Lt	8. 1.92	RHS
Low, Frances	S/Lt	27. 2.00	Edinborough Academy
Lowles, Ian	Lt	1. 4.97	Cliffton Col
Lucas, Ian	Lt	26. 4.88	Recall
Lucas, Stuart	S/Lt	27. 2.00	Loretto
Lucius-Clarke, David	Lt	1. 9.97	RGS Newcastle

M

Name	Rank	Seniority	School/College
MacDonald, Fraser	Lt	1. 9.71	Trinity
MacIntosh, Colin	A/Lt	15. 7.99	Shrewsbury
Mackie, Alan	Lt Cdr	19. 6.96	Bangor
Magor, Brian	Cdr	14.10.85	Calday Grange
Manners, David	Lt	1. 9.93	Woodroffe
Marchant, Nicholas	Lt RMR	1. 7.99	Harrow
Marsh, Lesley	Lt Cdr	19. 1.93	Recall
Marshall, Michelle	S/Lt	27. 2.00	Heles
Martin, Steven	Lt	1. 1.87	Kelly
Matson, Christopher	Lt	26.11.99	Recall
May, Edward	S/Lt	1. 7.98	Recall
Maynard, Rachel	S/Lt	1.10.99	Wellingborough
McConnell, Susan	Lt	31. 8.92	Kings Canterbury Sch
McConnell, William	Lt	6. 5.92	Kings Sch Canterbury
McCormick, Ian	Lt	5.10.67	Liverpool
McDermott, Robert	Lt RMR	1. 7.99	Kelly
McDonald, Colin	S/Lt	1. 9.88	Bangor
McDonald, Richard	Lt RMR	1. 9.86	Whitgift
McGuff, Neil	S/Lt	4. 9.91	Wellinton Sch
McKee, Mark	S/Lt	10. 8.93	Cambell
McLaughlin, Steven	S/Lt	4.10.99	Perse
Meierdirk, Charlotte	S/Lt	1. 9.99	Lancing
Melville, Graham	S/Lt	10. 8.93	Birkenhead
Mercer, Jane	S/Lt	18. 7.99	Russell
Mercer, Louise	Lt	10. 9.97	Prior Park
Merrett, Nicholas	S/Lt	29.11.90	Uppingham
Millard, Michelle	S/Lt	8. 8.95	Victoria Jersey
Mills, Anita	S/Lt	1. 1.00	Monkton Combe
Mills, Stephen	S/Lt	8. 8.95	Sandbach
Milne, Stewart	S/Lt	25. 6.97	Recall
Minto, Neil	S/Lt	8. 1.91	Recall
Mitchell, Ian	Lt	1. 9.99	Wellington Col
Mitchell, Robert	Lt Cdr	1. 9.88	Kings Col Sc Wimbledon
Montgomery, Paul	S/Lt	25. 7.97	Dean Close
Moody, Susan	Lt Cdr	15.12.95	Recall
Moore, David John	Lt	21. 4.85	Recall
Moore, Terry	S/Lt	11. 7.83	Recall
Morgan, Bryn	Lt	1. 1.91	Brentwood
Morgan, James	S/Lt	1. 4.96	Sedburgh
Moss-Gibbons, David	Cdr	6. 1.00	Bradfield Col
Mundill, Robin	Lt	1. 7.90	Recall

N

Name	Rank	Seniority	School/College
Newton, John	Lt	1. 1.84	Recall
Newton, Robert	Lt Cdr	1. 1.96	Recall
Nicholson, Robert	Lt Cdr	1. 3.95	Milton Abbey
Nurser, Graham	S/Lt	28.11.99	Wellington Col
Nye, Jenny	S/Lt	2. 5.98	Colstons'

O

Name	Rank	Seniority	School/College
O Hagan, Gerard	S/Lt	18. 7.99	Victoria
Ogilvie, Fergus	Lt RMR	1. 7.99	Giggleswick
Oldbury, David	Cdr	1. 1.93	Kings Sch Rochester
Osmond, Stephen	Lt	11.10.99	RGS Worcestor
Othick, Anthony	S/Lt	25. 5.99	Scarborough
Owen, Elizabeth	S/Lt	19. 1.98	HQCCF(ADVT TRG)
Owen, John	Lt Cdr	1.12.84	HQCCF(ADVT TRG)

P

Name	Rank	Seniority	School/College
Packer, Thomas	Lt Cdr	13. 1.95	Recall
Paris, David	S/Lt	11. 8.98	RGS Newcastle
Parker, Ann	S/Lt	2. 9.92	St Bartholomews
Parkinson, Micheal	S/Lt	1. 6.99	Kings Rochester
Parkinson, Kenneth	Lt	1. 9.90	Recall
Paton, Gordon	Lt Cdr	1. 1.81	Recall
Payne, Anthony	Lt	1.12.73	Loughborough
Pearson, Andrew	Lt	1.10.97	St Dunstons
Pegg, Joanna	S/Lt	1. 1.00	Exeter
Phillips, Adrian	S/Lt	20. 9.90	Stathallen
Pidowx, John	S/Lt	1. 1.86	Maidstone
Pilbeam, Jeremy	Lt	16. 7.94	Recall
Pollard, Eric	Acdr	1. 1.89	HQCCF (NCFBO)
Poulet-Bowden, Geraldine	S/Lt	18. 7.99	Exeter
Povey, Philip	S/Lt	12. 3.98	Batley
Powell, Andrew	Lt	14.11.94	Reigate Sch
Powell, John	S/Lt	8. 8.95	Pangbom
Price, Thelma	S/Lt	28. 6.99	Dulwich
Prior, Anthony	Lt	1. 8.82	Milton Abbey
Prior, Stephen	S/Lt	10. 8.93	Westbuckland
Prosser, Nicholas, *MBE*	Lt Cdr	1. 9.77	Tonbridge

Name	Rank	Seniority	School/College
R			
Raines, David	Lt	5. 8.79	Elizabeth Col
Reed, Louise	S/Lt	1. 7.99	St Batholomews
Reid, David	Lt RMR	1. 9.98	Wellington
Rennison, Christopher	Lt RMR	1. 7.99	Royal Hospital
Reynolds, Christopher	Lt	1.10.73	Bournemouth
Rhodes, Terry	S/Lt	20. 9.94	Kimbolton
Richard, Peter	Lt	1. 1.93	Recall
Richards, Philip	Lt	16. 2.94	Fettes
Ridley Thomas, Michael	Lt	1. 9.92	Calday Grange
Ripley, Myles	Lt	1. 9.83	Sedbergh
Roberts, Derek	Lt	11. 7.94	Brighton
Roberts, Martin	Lt Cdr	1. 4.96	Recall
Roby, Ronald	Acdr	1. 9.86	Recall
Rooms, Lindsay	Cdr	1.12.97	Oundle
Rothwell, George	Lt Cdr	6. 4.95	HQCCF (Sailing)
Rule, Peter	Cdr	1. 6.98	Trinity
Russell, James	/j RMR	1. 7.99	Malvern
S			
Sanders, Bryant	Cdr	15.11.86	Bournemouth
Sanders, Robert	S/Lt	16. 9.99	Oratory
Savage, Anthony	Cdr	1. 1.97	Portsmouth
Scorgie, Helen	S/Lt	30. 4.91	Recall
Scorgie, Stuart	Lt	13.11.91	Cliffton Col
Sell, Roger	Lt	1. 9.97	Hereford
Shannon, Lorna	S/Lt	1.10.97	Recall
Shannon, Tom	Lt	2. 9.86	Queen Victoria
Sharman, Deborah	Lt Cdr	1. 9.90	West Buckland
Shone, Michael	S/Lt	1. 3.99	Raleigh
Shorrocks, Jonathan	Lt Cdr	1. 9.96	RGS Worcester
Sibley, Peter	Lt Cdr	25. 2.87	Recall
Simpson, Philip	Lt	1. 1.98	Ellesmere
Sissons, Stewart	S/Lt	9. 4.98	HQCCF
Skidmore, Mark	A/Lt RMR	1. 7.99	RHS
Smith, Alison	S/Lt	11. 8.98	Kelinside
Smith, Nicolas	S/Lt	28.11.99	Woodbridge
Smith, Ronald	Lt	1.11.95	Kelvinside
Solly, Raymond	Lt Cdr	16. 5.90	St Lawrence
Somerville, Nicholas	S/Lt	9. 8.99	Harrow
Sparks, Alison	S/Lt	17. 3.98	Recall
Spence, Donna	S/Lt	29. 7.96	Bangor
Spence, Richard	S/Lt	1.12.98	Bangor
Spike, Nigel	Lt	4.11.89	Glasgow Academy
Stacey, Margaret	S/Lt	1. 9.96	Gordons Sch
Stacey, William	S/Lt	1. 9.96	Gordons Sch
Stansbury, William	S/Lt	1. 9.96	MTS Northwood
Stevens, Laurence	Lt	1. 9.85	St Bartholomews
Stevens, Peter	Cdr	1. 9.93	Plymouth
Stilwell, Valerie	S/Lt	8. 8.94	Recall
Stocker, Paul	S/Lt	10. 9.91	Uppingham
Stocks, David	Lt RMR	6. 1.00	Bradfield
Stratton-Brown, Colin	Lt Cdr	1. 9.90	Maidstone
Stringer, Christopher	Lt RMR	1. 7.99	Malvern
Strong, Gillian	S/Lt	8. 8.95	Wellingborough
Sunderland, Susan	S/Lt	12.10.98	Kings Rochester
Sutherland, Peter	S/Lt	9. 8.99	Whitgift
T			
Taylor, Liam	Lt RMR	1. 7.99	Winchester Col
Taylor, Penelope	S/Lt	27. 2.00	Canford

Name	Rank	Seniority	School/College
Tear, Richard	Lt	1. 9.99	Portsmouth
Tennant, David	Lt	30. 9.92	Tonbridge
Tetley, Neil	S/Lt	18.10.99	Kings Wimbledon
Thorn, Simon	S/Lt	17.10.98	Radley
Tinker, Christopher	Cdr	30. 5.96	Whitgift
Tiplady, Rodney	S/Lt	1. 9.96	Edinburgh Academy
Todd, Milke	Lt Cdr	1. 1.93	HQCCF (Diving Offcier)
Tolhurst, Aidan	Lt Cdr	1. 9.81	City of London
Trelawny, Giles	S/Lt	8. 8.94	Exeter
Trigg, Duncan	S/Lt	12. 7.98	Ruthin
Trundle, Simon	Lt	1. 9.94	RGS Worcester
Tucker, Vivian	S/Lt	12.10.98	Hereford
Tudor, Catherine	S/Lt	10. 8.93	King Edwards
Turner, Clive	S/Lt	30. 8.99	Lancing
Turner, Mark	S/Lt	29. 6.98	Recall
Tutton, Sarah	S/Lt	1. 3.99	Camell
Tyas, Kristian	Lt	25.11.96	Arnold
V			
Van Der Werff, Tanya	Lt	1. 9.95	Reading Blue Coat
Van Zwanenberg, Louise	Lt	25. 1.99	Woodbridge
Vaughan, Piers	Lt Cdr	5. 1.98	Sevonoaks
Vickery, David	Lt Cdr	2. 9.97	Monkton Combe
Vigers, Rosemary	Lt	20. 7.94	Kings Bruton
Vine, Roger	Lt	21. 7.95	Dulwich
W			
Walker, Colin	Capt(PD CDR)	1. 1.88	Strathallan
Walsh, George	S/Lt	30. 9.99	Liverpool
Walters, Dominic	S/Lt	6.10.91	Uppingham
Ward, David	Lt	17. 7.93	Kimbolton
Warren, Clive	S/Lt	18. 5.98	Colston's
Waugh, Patric	Lt	1.12.97	Wellingborough
Whale, Andrew	Lt	1. 4.89	Pangbourne
Whitfield, John	Lt	2. 8.84	West Buckland
Whitlock, Scott	S/Lt	18. 7.99	Epson
Whittaker, Douglas	Acdr	30. 6.85	Haberdashers Askes
Wightman, Martin	Lt RMR	1. 9.99	Strathallan
Wigley, Graham	Lt	31. 8.95	Framlingham
Wilkes, Justin	Lt Cdr	29. 6.98	Dollar
Wilkins, Peter	Lt	31. 1.85	St Peters C of E
Williams, Adam	A/Lt RMR	1. 7.99	Bradfield
Williams, Robert	Lt	1. 9.84	Glasgow Academy
Windsor, Michael	S/Lt	12.10.98	Kings Wimbledon
Woodley, Stephen	S/Lt	26. 6.99	St Edwards
Worrall, Stuart	Lt RMR	1. 9.99	Kings Taunton
Wylie, John	Lt	31. 7.93	Radley
Y			
Yates, Christopher	Lt RMR	1. 7.99	Winchester
Yorath, James	A/Lt RMR	1. 7.99	Pangbourne

OBITUARY

ROYAL NAVAL SERVICE

Captain
Cotton, R A 09.08.99

Captain
Prior, M F 04.09.99

Commander
Weberstadt, R R 12.06.99

Lieutenant Commander
Acton, J S 19.08.99

Lieutenant
Murphy, B

Lieutenant
Thomson, R H L 14.12.99

Lieutenant
Kirby, C J 19.09.99

Sub Lieutenant
James, R 23.11.99

ABBREVIATIONS OF RANKS AND LISTS

A ..... Acting
A/ ..... Acting
ACT ..... Acting
ADM ..... Admiral
ADM OF FLEET ..... Admiral of the Fleet
ASL ..... Acting Sub-Lieutenant
AT ..... Acting Temporary
BRIG ..... Brigadier
CAND ..... Candidate
CAPT ..... Captain
CDT ..... Cadet
CHAPLAIN-FLT ..... Chaplain of the Fleet
CDR ..... Commander
CDRE ..... Commodore
CNO ..... Chief Nursing Officer
COL ..... Colonel
COMDT ..... Commandant
(CS) ..... Careers Service
(D) ..... Dental
E ..... Engineering
(FS) ..... Family Service
GEN ..... General
(GRAD) ..... Graduate
HON ..... Honorary
I ..... Instructor
LOC ..... Local
LT ..... Lieutenant
LCDR ..... Lieutenant-Commander
LT CDR ..... Lieutenant-Commander
LT COL ..... Lieutenant-Colonel
LT GEN ..... Lieutenant-General
MAJ ..... Major
MAJ GEN ..... Major-General
MID ..... Midshipman
(NE) ..... New Entry
NO ..... Nursing Officer
OFF ..... Officer
OFFR ..... Officer
P/ ..... Probationary
PNO ..... Principal Nursing Officer
PR ..... Principal
RADM ..... Rear-Admiral
REV ..... Reverend
RM ..... Royal Marines
S ..... Supply & Secretariat

(SD) .... Special Duties List
(SDT) .... Special Duties List Temporary
SG .... Surgeon
SURG .... Surgeon
(SL) .... Supplementary List
SLT .... Sub-Lieutenant
SNO .... Senior Nursing Officer
SUPT NO .... Superintendent Nursing Officer
T .... Temporary
T/ .... Temporary
TLT .... Temporary Lieutenant
TSLT .... Temporary Sub-Lieutenant
(UCE) .... University Cadet Entrant
VADM .... Vice-Admiral
X .... Seaman
2LT .... Second Lieutenant, Royal Marines

ABBREVIATIONS OF SPECIALISATIONS & QUALIFICATIONS

(Eur Ing) .... European Engineer
A/TK .... Heavy Weapons Anti-Tank
AC .... Aircraft Controller
ACC/EM .... Accident and Emergency
ACGI .... Associate, City and Guilds London Institute
ACIS .... Associate of The Institute of Chartered Secretaries and Administrators
ACMA .... Associate, Institute of Cost & Management Accountants
(AD) .... Medical and Dental Administration
ADIPM .... Associate, Institute of Data Processing Management
adp .... Passed Advanced Adp Course Dadptc
AE .... Air Engineering
AE(L) .... Air Engineering (Electrical)
AE(M) .... Air Engineering (Mechanical)
AE(O) .... Air Engineering (Observer)
AE(P) .... Air Engineering (Pilot)
(AE) .... Assault Engineer
AFIMA .... Associate Fellow, Institute Mathematics & Its Applications
AFOM .... Associate, Faculty of Occupational Medicine
AGSM .... Associate of The Guildhall School of Music and Drama
AIL .... Associate, Institute of Linguists
AIM .... Associate, Institute of Metallurgists
AIMgt .... Associate of The Institute of Management
AInstP .... Associate, Institute of Physics
AKC .... Associate, King's College London
ALCD .... Associate, London College of Divinity
AMASEE .... Associate Member, Association of Electrical Engineers
AMBCS .... Associate Member, British Computing Society

AMBIM .... Associate Member, British Institute of Management
AMHCIMA .... Associate Member, Hotel Catering & Institutional Management Association
AMIAM .... Associate Member, Institute of Administrative Management
AMICE .... Associate Member, Institute of Civil Engineers
AMIEE .... Associate Member, Institute of Electrical Engineers
AMIERE .... Associate Member, Institution of Electronic and Radio Engineers
AMIIE .... Associate Member, Institute of Industrial Engineers
AMIMarE .... Associate Member, Institute of Marine Engineers
AMIMechE .... Associate Member, Institution of Mechanical Engineers
AMInstP .... Associate Member, Institute of Physics
AMINucE .... Associate Member, Institution of Nuclear Engineers
AMIPIE .... Associate Member, Institution of Plant Engineers
AMNI .... Associate Member, Nautical Institute
AMRAeS .... Associate Member, Royal Aeronautical Society
AMRINA .... Associate Member. Royal Institution of Naval Architects
ARAM .... Associate, Royal Academy of Music
ARCM .... Associate, Royal College of Music
ARCS .... Associate, Royal College of Science
ARCST .... Associate, Royal College of Science and Technology (Glasgow)
ARIC .... Associate, Royal Institute of Chemistry
ARICS .... Professional Asssociate, Royal Institution of Chartered Surveyors
ATC .... Air Traffic Control Officer
ATCU/T .... Air Traffic Control Officer Under Training
AV .... Aviation
AWO(A) .... Advanced Warfare Officer(Above Water)
AWO(C) .... Advanced Warfare Officer(Communications)
AWO(U) .... Advanced Warfare Officer(Underwater)
aws .... Qualified Air Warfare College
BA .... Bachelor of Arts
BA(OU) .... Bachelor of Arts, Open University
BAO .... Bachelor of Art of Obstetrics
BAR .... Barrister
BCH .... Bachelor of Surgery (Bch)
BCh .... Bachelor of Surgery
BChD .... Bachelor of Dentistry
BChir .... Bachelor of Surgery
BComm .... Bachelor of Commerce
BD .... Bachelor of Divinity
BDS .... Bachelor of Dental Surgery
BEd .... Bachelor of Education
BEng .... Bachelor of Engineering
BM .... Bachelor of Medicine
BMedSc .... Bachelor of Medical Science
BMS .... Bachelor of Medical Science
BMus .... Bachelor of Music
BPh .... Bachelor of Philosophy
BPharm .... Bachelor of Pharmacy

BS ... Bachelor of Surgery
BSc ... Bachelor of Science
BSc(Eng) ... Bachelor of Science (Engineering)
BTech ... Bachelor of Technology
C ... Communications
C PHYS ... Chartered Physicist
C/T ... Clinical Teacher
CA ... Caterer
(CA) ... Consultant in Anaesthetics
(CA/E) ... Consultant in Accident/Emergency
CC ... Coronary Care
(CC) ... Consultant in Paediatrics
CDipAF ... The Certified Diploma in Accounting and Finance
(CDO) ... Commando Trained
(CE) ... Consultant in Otorhinolaryngology
CEng ... Chartered Engineer
Cert Ed ... Certificate of Education
CertTh ... Certificate in Theology
CGIA ... Insignia Award of The City & Guilds of London Insitute
(CGS) ... Consultant in General Surgery
CHB ... Bachelor of Surgery (Chb)
ChB ... Bachelor of Surgery
ChM ... Chartered Mathematician
(CK) ... Consultant in Dermatology
(CL) ... Consultant in Pathology
(CM) ... Consultant in General Medicine
CMA ... Management Accountant
CMath ... Chartered Mathematician
(CN/P) ... Consultant in Neuro-Psychiatry
(CO) ... Consultant in Opthalmology
(CO/M) ... Consultant in Occupational Medicine
(CO/S) ... Consultant in Orthopaedic Surgery
(COSM) ... Consultant in Oral Surgery/Oral Medicine
CPDATE ... This Is A 'pay' Only Sq. It Will Not Be Awarded To Personnel.
CPN ... Community Psychiatric Nurse
CQSW ... Certificate of Qualification in Social Work
(CU) ... Consultant in Urology
(CX) ... Consultant in Radiology
D ... Direction Officer
DA ... Diploma in Anaesthesia
DAppDy ... Diploma in Applied Dynamics
DCH ... Diploma in Child Health
DCL ... Doctor of Civil Law
DCP ... Diploma in Clinical Pathology
DD ... Doctor of Divinity
DDPH ... Diploma in Public Dental Health
DEH ... Diploma in Environmental Health

df .... Qualified Defence Fellowship
DGDP RCS(UK) .... Diploma in General Dental Practice Rcs (Uk)
DGDP(UK) .... Diploma in General Dental Practice (Uk)
DGDPRCS(Eng) .... Diploma General Dental Practice Rcs(Eng)
DHMSA .... Diploma in The History of Medicine (Society of Apothecaries)
DIC .... Diploma of The Imperial College
DIH .... Diploma in Industrial Health
Dip FFP .... Diploma of The Facalty of Family Planning
DipAvMed .... Diploma in Aviation Medicine
DipEd .... Diploma in Education
DipIMC RCSED .... Diploma in Immmediate Medical Care of Royal College Surgeons (Edinburgh)
DipTh .... Diploma in Theology
DLitt .... Doctor of Letters
DLO .... Diploma in Laryngology and Otology
DM .... Doctor of Medicine
DMRD .... Diploma in Medical Radiological Diagnosis
DO .... Diploma in Ophthalmology
DObstRCOG .... Diploma Royal College of Obstetricians and Gynaecologists
DOrth .... Diploma in Orthodontics
DPH .... Diploma in Public Health
DPhil .... Doctor of Philosophy
DPhysMed .... Diploma in Physical Medicine
DPM .... Diploma in Psychological Medicine
DRD .... Diploma in Restorative Dentistry
DSc .... Doctor of Science
DTM&H .... Diploma in Tropical Medicine and Hygiene
E .... Engineer
Eur Ing .... European Engineer
EW .... Electronic Warfare
F .... Pilot and Observer
FA .... Fleet Analyst
FBCS .... Fellow, British Computer Society
FBIM .... Fellow, British Institute of Management
FC .... Fighter Controller
FCIS .... Fellow, Institute Chartered Secretaries & Administrators
FCMA .... Fellow, Chartered Institute of Management Accountants
FDS .... Fellow in Dental Surgery
FDS RCPSGlas .... Fellow in Dental Surgery Royal College of Physicians & Surgeons (Glasgow)
FDS RCS(Eng) .... Fellow in Dental Surgery, Royal College of Surgeons of England
FDS RCS(Irl) .... Fellow in Dental Surgery Royal College of Surgeons in Ireland
FDS RCSEdin .... Fellow in Dental Surgery Royal College of Surgeons of Edinburgh
FDS(RCS) .... Fellow in Dental Surgery, Royal College of Surgeons of England
FFA .... Fellow, Institute of Financial Accountants
FFARCS .... Fellow, Faculty of Anaesthetists, Royal College of Surgeons of England
FFARCSI .... Fellow, Faculty of Anaesthetists, Royal College of Surgeons in Ireland
FFOM .... Fellow, Faculty of Occupational Medicine
FHCIMA .... Fellow of The Hotel and Catering Management Association

FIAA ..... Fellow, Institute of Actuaries of Australia
FIEE ..... Fellow, Institute of Electrical Engineers
FIEEIE ..... Fellow of The Institute of Electrical and Electronic Incorparated Engineer
FIEIE ..... Fellow, Institute of Electrical and Electronic Incorporated Engineers
FIERE ..... Fellow, Institution of Electronic and Radio Engineers
FIL ..... Fellow, Institute of Linguists
FIM ..... Fellow of The Institute of Metals
FIMA ..... Fellow, Institute of Mathematics and Its Applications
FIMarE ..... Fellow, Institute of Marine Engineers
FIMechE ..... Fellow, Institution of Mechanical Engineers
FIMgt ..... Fellow of The Institute of Management
FIMS ..... Fellow, Institute of Management Specialists Or Mathematical Statistics
FInstAM ..... Fellow Institute of Administrative Management
FINucE ..... Fellow, Institute of Nuclear Engineers
FIPM ..... Fellow of The Institute of Personnel Management
FISM ..... Fellow of The Institute of Supervision and Management
FITE ..... Fellow, Institution Electrical & Electronics Technician Engineers
FNI ..... Fellow, Nautical Institute
FRAeS ..... Fellow, Royal Aeronautical Society
FRAM ..... Fellow, Royal Academy of Music
FRC.Psych ..... Fellow of The Royal College of Psychiatrists
FRCA ..... Fellow of The Royal College of Anaesthetists
FRCGP ..... Fellow Royal College General Practioners
FRCOG ..... Fellow, Royal College of Obstetricians and Gynaecologists
FRCP ..... Fellow, Royal College of Physicians, London
FRCPath ..... Fellow, Royal College of Pathologists
FRCPEd ..... Fellow, Royal College of Physicians, Edinburgh
FRCPGlas ..... Fellow, Royal College of Physicians and Surgeons of Glasgow
FRCR ..... Fellow, Royal College of Radioligists
FRCS ..... Fellow, Royal College of Surgeons of England
FRCS(ORTH) ..... Fellow Royal College Surgeons (Orthopaedics)
FRCSEd ..... Fellow, Royal College of Surgeons of Edinburgh
FRCSGlas ..... Fellow, Royal College of Physicians and Surgeons of Glasgow
FRCSTr&Orth ..... Fellowship of The Royal College of Surgeons (Trauma & Orthopaedics)
FRGS ..... Fellow, Royal Geographical Society
FRHistS ..... Fellow Royal Historical Society
FRICS ..... Fellow Royal Institute Chartered Surveyors
FRIN ..... Fellow of The Royal Institute of Navigation
FRINA ..... Fellow, Royal Institute of Naval Architects
FRMS ..... Fellow, Royal Meteorological Society
FRSA ..... Fellow, Royal Society of Arts
fsc ..... Qualified Foreign Staff College
G ..... Gunnery
..... Gunnery (Mortar Course)
GB ..... The Gilbert Blane Medal
GCIS ..... Graduate of The Institute of Chartered Secretaries and Administrators
gdas ..... General Duties Areo Systems

GISVA .... Graduate Institute of Surveyors, Valuers and Auctioneers
GMPP .... General Medical Practitioner
GradIMA .... Graduate Member, Institute of Mathematics and Its Applications
GradIMS .... Graduate Institute of Management Specialists
GradInstPS .... Graduate Institute of Purchasing and Supply
(GS) .... Specialist in General Surgery
(GS)UT .... Senior Registrar in General Surgery - Under Training
GU .... Genito Urinary
gw .... Guided Weapons Systems Course Rmcs Shrivenham
H CH .... Hydrographer (Charge)
hcsc .... Higher Command & Staff College
Hf .... Hudson Fellowship
HM .... Hydrographer Metoc
HNC .... Higher National Certificate
HND .... Higher National Diploma
HULL .... Hull Engineering
HW .... Heavy Weapons
H1 .... Hydrographer (First Class)
H2 .... Hydrographer (Second Class)
I(1)Ab .... Interpreter 1st Class Arabic
I(1)Ch .... Interpreter 1st Class Chinese
I(1)Da .... Interpreter 1st Class Danish
I(1)Du .... Interpreter 1st Class Dutch
I(1)Fi .... Interpreter 1st Class Finnish
I(1)Fr .... Interpreter 1st Class French
I(1)Ge .... Interpreter 1st Class German
I(1)Id .... Interpreter 1st Class Indonesian
I(1)It .... Interpreter 1st Class Italian
I(1)Ja .... Interpreter 1st Class Japanese
I(1)Ma .... Interpreter 1st Class Malayan
I(1)No .... Interpreter 1st Class Norwegian
I(1)Pl .... Interpreter 1st Class Polish
I(1)Po .... Interpreter 1st Class Portugese
I(1)Ru .... Interpreter 1st Class Russian
I(1)Sh .... Interpreter 1st Class Swahili
I(1)Sp .... Interpreter 1st Class Spanish
I(1)Sw .... Interpreter 1st Class Swedish
I(1)Tu .... Interpreter 1st Class Turkish
I(1)Ur .... Interpreter 1st Class Urdu
I(2)Ab .... Interpreter 2nd Class Arabic
I(2)Ch .... Interpreter 2nd Class Chinese
I(2)Da .... Interpreter 2nd Class Danish
I(2)Du .... Interpreter 2nd Class Dutch
I(2)Fi .... Interpreter 2nd Class Finnish
I(2)Fr .... Interpreter 2nd Class French
I(2)Ge .... Interpreter 2nd Class German
I(2)Id .... Interpreter 2nd Class Indonesian

I(2)It .... Interpreter 2nd Class Italian
I(2)Ja .... Interpreter 2nd Class Japanese
I(2)Ma .... Interpreter 2nd Class Malayan
I(2)No .... Interpreter 2nd Class Norwegian
I(2)Pl .... Interpreter 2nd Class Polish
I(2)Po .... Interpreter 2nd Class Portugese
I(2)Ru .... Interpreter 2nd Class Russian
I(2)Sh .... Interpreter 2nd Class Swahili
I(2)Sp .... Interpreter 2nd Class Spanish
I(2)Sw .... Interpreter 2nd Class Swedish
I(2)Tu .... Interpreter 2nd Class Turkish
I(2)Ur .... Interpreter 2nd Class Urdu
IC .... Intensive Care
IC/CC .... Intensive Care and Coronary Care
idc .... Qualified Imperial Defence College
IEng .... Incorporated Engineer
ifp .... Qualified, International Fellows Programme
IS .... Information Systems
JCPTGP .... Certificate of Prescribed Experience in General Practice
jsdc .... Joint Service Defence College
jssc .... Joint Services Staff College
LC .... Landing Craft
LDS .... Licentiate in Dental Surgery
LDS RCPSGlas .... Licenciate in Dental Surgery Royal College of Physicians & Surgeons (Glasgow)
LDS RCS(Eng) .... Licentiate in Dental Surgery, Royal College of Surgeons of England
LDS RCS(Irl) .... Licenciate in Dental Surgery Royal College of Surgeons in Ireland
LDS RCSEdin .... Licenciate in Dental Surgery Royal College of Surgeons of Edinburgh
LGSM .... Licentiate, Guildhall School of Music and Drama
LHCIMA .... Licentiate Hotel, Catering and Institutional Management Assn
LICG .... Licentiate of City and Guilds Institute
LIEE .... Licentiate, Institute Electrical Engineers
LIMA .... Licentiate Institute Mathematics & Its Applications
LLB .... Bachelor of Law
LLD .... Doctor of Laws
LMCC .... Licentiate, Medical Council of Canada
LMHCIMA .... Licentiate Member of Hotel,Catering and Institutional Management Assn
LMIPD .... Licentiate Member To The Institute of Personnel and Development
LMSSA .... Licentiate in Medicine & Surgery, Society of Apothecaries
LRAM .... Licentiate, Royal Academy of Music
LRCP .... Licentiate, Royal College of Physicians, London
LRCPSGlas .... Licentiate, Royal College of Physicians and Surgeons of Glasgow
LRCS .... Licentiate, Royal College of Surgeons of England
LRPS .... Licentiate, Royal Photographic Society
(LT) .... Laboratory Technician
LTh .... Licentiate in Theology
M.Univ .... Master of The University (Ou)
(M) .... Specialist in General Medicine

(M) UT .... Senior Registrar in General Medicine - Under Training
MA .... Master of Arts
MA(Ed) .... Master of Arts in Education
MAPM .... Member of The Association of Project Managers
MB .... Bachelor of Medicine
MBA .... Master of Business Administration
MBCS .... Member, British Computer Society
MBIM .... Member, British Institute of Management
MCD .... Mine Warfare Clearance Diver
MCD/MW .... Mine Clearance Diving & Mine Warfare
MCFA .... Member of The Catering and Food Association
MCGI .... Member of City and Guilds Institiute
MCh .... Master in Surgery
MChOrth .... Master of Orthopaedic Surgery
MCIT .... Member, Institute of Training Officers
MD .... Doctor of Medicine
MDA .... Master of Defence Administration
MDSc .... Master of Dental Science
mdtc .... Maritime Defence Technology Course
ME .... Marine Engineering
ME(L) .... Marine Engineering (Electrical)
MEng .... Master of Engineering
MESM .... Marine Engineering (Submarine)
METOC .... Meteorology & Oceanography
MFCM .... Member, Faculty of Community Medicine
MFOM .... Member, Faculty of Occupational Medicine
MFPM .... Member of Faculty of Pharmaceutical Medicine
MGDS RCS .... Member in General Dental Surgery, Royal College of Surgeons of England
MGDS RCSEd .... Member in General Dental Surgery, Royal College of Surgeons of Edinburgh
MHCIMA .... Member, Hotel Catering & Institutional Management Association
MHSM .... Member of The Institute of Health Services Mamagement
MICE .... Member, Institution Civil Engineers
MIDPM .... Member Institute of Data Processing Management
MIEE .... Member, Insitution of Electrical Engineers
MIEEE .... Member of The Institution of Electrical and Electronic Engineers
MIEEIE .... Member of The Institute of Electrical and Electronic Incorporated Engineers
MIERE .... Member, Institution of Electrical & Radio Engineers
MIExpE .... Member, Institute of Explosives Engineers
MIL .... Member, Institute of Linguists
MILDM .... Member of The Institute of Logistics and Distribution Management
MILog .... Member of The Institue of Logistics
MILT .... Member of The Institute of Logistics and Transport
MIM .... Member, Institute of Metals
MIMA .... Member of The Institute of Mathematics and Applications
MIMarA .... Member, Institute of Marine Architects
MIMarE .... Member, Institute of Marine Engineers
MIMechE .... Member, Institution of Mechanical Engineers

MIMechIE .... Member of The Institute of Mechanical Incorporayed Engineers
MIMgt .... Member of The Institute of Management
MIMS .... Member, Institute of Management Specialists
MInsD .... Member of The Institute of Directors
MinstAM .... Member, Institute of Administrative Management
MInstFM .... Member, Institute of Facilities/Resources Management
MinstP .... Member, Institute of Physics
MInstPS .... Member, Institute of Purchasing and Supply
MINucE .... Member, Institute of Nuclear Engineers
MIOSH .... Member, Institute of Occupational Safety and Health
MIPD .... Member of The Institute of Personnel and Development
MIPlantE .... Member, Plant Engineers
MIPM .... Member, Institute of Personnel Management
MIProdE .... Member, Institute of Production Engineers
MISecM .... Member of The Institute of Security Management
MISM .... Member of The Institute of Supervisory Management
MITD .... Member Institute of Training and Development
MITE .... Member, Institute of Technical Engineers
MLDR .... Mountain Leader
MLITT .... Master of Letters
ML2@ .... Mountain Leader 2 (Rm)
MNI .... Member, Nautical Institute
MNZIS .... Member of The New Zealand Institute of Surveyors
MOR .... Heavy Weapons Mortar Course
MOrth .... Master of Orthodontics
MPH .... Master of Public Health
MPhil .... Master of Philosophy
MPS .... Member, Pharmaceutical Society
MRAeS .... Member, Royal Aeronautical Society
MRCGP .... Member, Royal College of General Practitioners
MRCOG .... Member, Royal College Obstetricians & Gynaecologists
MRCP .... Member, Royal College of Physicians, London
MRCP(UK) .... Member, Royal College of Physicians
MRCPath .... Member, Royal College of Pathologists
MRCPE .... Member, Royal College of Physicians, Edinburgh
MRCPGlas .... Member, Royal College of Physicians and Surgeons of Glasgow
MRCPI .... Member, Royal College of Physicians of Ireland
MRCPsych .... Member, Royal College of Phsyciatrists
MRCS .... Member, Royal College of Surgeons of England
MRCVS .... Member of The Royal College of Veterinary Surgeons
MRIC .... Member, Royal Institute of Chemistry
MRIN .... Member, Royal Institute of Navigation
MRINA .... Member, Royal Institute of Naval Architects
MS .... Master of Surgery
MSc .... Master of Science
MScD .... Master of Dental Science
MSE .... Member, Society of Engineers

MSRP .... Member of The Society For Radiological Protection
MTh .... Master of Theology
MTO .... Motor Transport Officer
MW .... Mine Warfare
n .... Frigate Navigating Officer's Course
N .... Navigation
nadc .... Nato Defence College Course
NCS(A) .... Naval Control Shipping
NCS(B) .... Nsc (B)
NCS(C) .... Ncs (C)
ndc .... National Defence College
NInstC .... Nuclear Instrument Calibration Course
NO-S/S .... No Specialisation
nrf .... Qualified, Nato Research Fellowship
O .... Observer
O U/T .... Observer Under Training
O/S UT .... Senior Registrar in Orthopaedic Surgery - Under Training
ocds(Can) .... Qualified Canadian National Defence College
ocds(Ind) .... Qualified Indian National Defence College
OCDS(JAP) .... Overseas National Defence College Japanese
ocds(No) .... Qualified, Norwegian Defence College
ocds(Pak) .... Qualified Pakistan National Defence College
ocds(US) .... Qualified The United States National War College
ocds(USN) .... Qualified, United States Naval War College
odc(Aus) .... Qualified Australia Joint Services Staff College
odc(Fr) .... Qualified French Cours Superieur Interarmees
ODC(SWISS) .... International Training in Security and Arms Control
odc(US) .... Qualified United States Armed Forces Staff College
ONC .... Orthopaedic Nursing
OPHTH .... Opthalmic
osc .... Qualified Overseas Staff College
osc(Nig) .... Qualified Nigerian Command & Staff College
osc(us) .... Qualified, Usmc Command & Staff College
OSM UT .... Senior Registrar in Oral Surgery/Oral Medicine - Under Training
OStJ .... Order of St. John
OTSPEC .... Operating Theatre Specialist
P .... Pilot
P U/T .... Pilot Under Training
(P) .... Physiotherapist
pce .... Passed Command Examinations
pce(sm) .... Passed Command Examinations (Sm)
pcea .... Passed Command Examinations (Air)
(PD) .... Pharmacy Dispenser
pdm .... Principal Director of Music
PFOM .... President Faculty of Occupational Medicine
PGCE .... Post Graduate Certificate of Education
PGDip .... Post Graduate

PGDIP ..... Post Graduate Diploma
PGDIPAN ..... Post Graduate Diploma in Applied Navigation
PH ..... Helicopter Pilot
PhD ..... Doctor of Philosophy
PI ..... Photographic Interpreter
PR ..... Plotting & Radar
psc ..... Passed Staff Course
psc(a) ..... Passed Staff Course (Raf)
psc(j) ..... Passed Staff Course (Joint)
psc(m) ..... Passed Staff Course (Army)
PT ..... Physical Training
ptsc ..... Completed Technical Staff Course at The Rmsc Shrivenham
PWO ..... Principal Warfare Officer
PWO(A) ..... Principal Warfare Officer Above Water
PWO(C) ..... Principal Warfare Officer Communications
PWO(N) ..... Principal Warfare Officer Navigation
PWO(U) ..... Principal Warfare Officer Underwater
rcds ..... Royal College of Defence Studies
RCPS(Glas) ..... Royal College of Phsicians and Surgeons of Glasgow
RCS ..... Royal College of Surgeons of England
RCSEd ..... Royal College of Surgeons of Edinburgh
REG ..... Regulating
REGM ..... Registered Midwife
(RGN) ..... Registered General Nurse
RL ..... Reconnaissance Leader
RMN ..... Registered Mental Nurse
RMP1 ..... Pilot 1
RMP2 ..... Pilot 2
RNT ..... Registered Nurse Tutor
S ..... S
(S) ..... Stores
(SA) ..... Senior Specialist in Anaesthetics
SALT ..... Salt - Nmmis Only
SBS ..... Special Boat Squadron
SCM ..... State Certified Midwife
SEC ..... Secretarial
(SGS) ..... Senior Specialist in General Surgery
SM ..... Submariner
SM ..... Sm Qualified
SM(G) ..... Submarine (Gunnery)
SM(n) ..... Submarine Navigating Officer
SM(N) ..... Submarine (Navigation)
(SM) ..... Senior Specialist in General Medicine
SMTAS ..... Submarine Torpedo Anti-Submarine
SO(LE) ..... Staff Officer Personnel and Logistics
(SO/M) ..... Senior Specialist in Occupational Medicine
(SO/S) ..... Senior Specialist in Orthopaedic Surgery

sowc .... Senior Officer's War Course
sq .... Rm Major Staff Qualified After Holding Two Specified Staff Appointments
tacsc .... Territorial Army Command and Staff Course
TAS .... Torpedo Anti-Submarine
AS# .... Torpedo Anti-Submarine Basic
TEng .... Certificate of Technical Engineering
TM .... Training Management
TMSM .... Training Management (Sm)
tp .... Qualified Test Pilots Course
(U) UT .... Senior Registrar in Urology - Under Training
(W) .... Writer
(X) .... Specialist in Radiology
(X) UT .... Senior Registrar in Radiology - Under Training
WE .... Weapons Engineering
WESM .... Weapon Engineering (Submarine)
WTO .... Weapon Training Officer
X X

ABBREVIATIONS OF PLACE WHERE OFFICER IS SERVING WHEN NOT SERVING AT SEA

AACC MID WALLOP .... HQ School of Army Aviation Middle Wallop
ACDS OR (SEA) .... Assistant Chief of Defence Staff Operational Requirement (Sea Systems)
ACDS OR(AIR) .... Assistant Chief of the Defence Staff Operational Requirements (Air)
ACDS OR(LAND) .... Assistant Chief of the Defence Staff Operational Requirements (Land Sytems)
ACDS(OPS) .... Assistant Chief of Defence Staff (Operations)
ACDS(POL) USA .... Assistant Chief of Defence Staff (Policy and Nuclear) USA
ACDS(POL) .... Assistant Chief of Defence Staff (Policy)
ACDS(RP) .... Assistant Chief of Defence Staff (Resources & Plans)
ACE SRGN GIBLTAR .... Allied Forces Southern Europe (Gibraltar)
ACE SRGN TURKEY .... Allied Forces Southern Europe (Turkey)
AFCC .... ARMED FORCES CHAPLAINCY CENTRE
AFPAA HQ .... ARMED FORCES PERSONNEL ADMINISTRATION AGENCY HEADQUARTERS
AFPAA WTHY DOWN .... AFPAA (Worthy Down)
AFPAA(CENTURION) .... Directorate of AFPAA (CENTURION)
AGRIPPA AFSOUTH .... HMS Agrippa (Allied Forces S. Europe (Italy))
AGRIPPA NAVSOUTH .... HMS Agrippa (Allied Naval Forces S. Europe (Italy))
AMC .... Aquisition Management Cell
ASC CAMBERLEY .... Joint Service Command and Staff College Camberley
AST(E) ....
AST(N) ....
AST(W) .... Area Security Team (West)
ASTUTE IPT .... Director Submarines
ATTURM .... Amphibious Training & Trials Unit Royal Marines
BDLS AUSTRALIA .... British Defence Liaison Staff Australia
BDLS CANADA .... British Defence Liaison Staff Canada

BDLS INDIA .... British Defence Liaison Staff India
BDLS NEW ZEALAND .... British Defence Liaison Staff New Zealand
BDMT .... Arms CIS Group/Bowman Military Team
BDS WASHINGTON .... British Defence Staff Washington
BOWMAN IPT .... BOWMAN Integrated Project Team
BRNC BAND .... Band of HM Royal Marines Britannia Royal Naval College
BRNC RNSU SOTON .... Royal Naval Support Unit - University of Southampton
CABINET OFFICE .... Cabinet Office
CALEDONIA CFS .... HMS Caledonia
CALLIOPE .... Royal Naval Reserve Tyne (RN Staff)
CAMBRIA .... Royal Naval Reserve South Wales (RN Staff)
CAPT(H) DEVPT .... Captain (Hydrographic) Devonport
CAPTAIN RNP TEAM .... Captain Royal Naval Presentation Team
CAPTAIN SM2 .... Captain Second Submarine Squadron
CAPTPORT CLYDE .... Captain of the Port (Clyde)
CDL .... Chief of Defence Logistics
CDO LOG REGT RM .... Commando Logistics Regiment Royal Marines
CDP OFFICE .... Chief of Defence Procurement's Office
CDRE MFP NWOOD .... Commodore Mine Warefare and Patrol Vessels (NORTHWOOD)
CDRE MFP .... Commodore Minewarfare & Patrol Vessels, Diving & Fishery Protection
CDS/VCDS/COSSEC .... Chief of Defence Staff and Vice Chief of Defence Staff
CESO(N) .... Directorate of Naval Environment and Safety
CFC .... MOD Corporate Finance Controller
CFLT COMMAND SEC .... Commander-in-Chief Fleet Command Secretary's Division
CFM PORTSMOUTH .... Captain Fleet Maintenance (Portsmouth)
CFPS SHORE .... Commander Fishery Protection Squadron (Shore)
CFS BATH .... Chief of Fleet Support (Bath)
CHF AED .... CDO Helo Force Air Eng Dept
CINCFLEET CIS .... Northwood Communications Information Systems
CINCFLEET FIMU .... FLEET INFORMATION MANAGEMENT UNIT
CINCFLEET .... Commander-in-Chief Fleet
CJPS .... Allied Forces Europe Reaction Forces Planning Staff
CLYDE MIXMAN2 .... Clyde Mixed Manning 2
CMSA UK .... Cruise Missile Support Activity (UK)
CNNRP BRISTOL .... Chairman Naval Nuclear Regulatory Panel
CNOCS GROUP .... Captain Naval Operational Combat Systems Group
CNS/ACNS .... Chief of Naval Staff and Assistant Chief of Naval Staff
CNSA BRISTOL .... Commodore Naval Ship Acceptance
COMACCHIO GP RM .... Comacchio Group Royal Marines
COMSTRIKFORSTH .... Commander Strike Force South
CSSE USA .... Chief Strategic Systems Executive (USA)
CSST RNSSS .... CSST Royal Navy Strategic Systems School
CSST SHORE DEVPT .... Captain Sea & Shore Submarine Training (Devonport)
CSST SHORE FSLN .... Captain Sea & Shore Submarine Training (Faslane)
CTCRM BAND .... Band of HM Royal Marines Commando Training Centre Royal Marines
CTCRM .... Commando Training Centre Royal Marines
CV(F) IPT .... CVF Integrated Project Team

D DEF SYSTEMS .... Directorate of Defence Systems
DA BAHRAIN .... Defence Attache Bahrain
DA BRIDGETOWN .... Defence Attache Bridgetown
DA BRUNEI .... Defence Attache Brunel
DA KIEV .... Defence Attache Kiev
DA MANILA .... Defence Attache Manila
DA PEKING .... Defence Attache Peking
DA SINGAPORE .... Defence Attache Singapore
DAP .... Directorate of Air Space Policy
DARTMOUTH BRNC .... Britannia Royal Naval College Dartmouth
DCDS(C) .... Deputy Chief of Defence Staff (Commitments)
DCDS(P&P) .... Deputy Chief of Defence Staff (Programmes and Personnel)
DCDS(S) .... Deputy Chief of Defence Staff (Systems)
DCEE .... Directorate Central & Eastern Europe
DCIS(FS) .... Directorate of Communications & Information Systems (Fleet Support)
DCIS(N) .... Directorate of Communication & Information Systems (Navy)
DCS SM BRISTOL .... Director Combat Systems/Submarines
DCSA COMMCEN FAS .... DCSA COMMCEN FASLANE
DCSA COMMCEN FSK .... DCSA COMMCEN FORT SOUTHWICK
DCSA COMMCEN PLY .... DCSA COMMCEN PLYMOUTH
DCSA COMMCEN WHI .... DCSA COMMCEN WHITEHALL
DCSA COMMS LON .... DCSA COMMS LON
DCSA NORTHWOOD .... DCSA NSTN/DIMHS BU HQ AND DCSA COMMCEN NORTHWOOD
DCSA PLYMOUTH .... Defence Communications Services Agency Plymouth
DCSA RADIO FAS .... DCSA RADIO ENGINEERING - SYSTEM CONTROL POINT FASLANE
DCSA RADIO HQ .... DCSA RADIO HEADQUARTERS
DCSA RADIO PLY .... DCSA RADIO ENGINEERING - SYSTEM CONTROL POINT PLYMOUTH
DCTA .... Defence Clothing and Textile Agency
DDA HALTON .... Defence Dental Agency Halton
DDA PLYMOUTH .... Defence Dental Agency Plymouth
DDA PORTSMOUTH .... Defence Dental Agency Portsmouth
DDA TE .... Defence Dental Agency Training Establishment
DEF DIVING SCHL .... Defence Diving School
DEF EX SVCS .... Defence Export Services
DEF MED TRG CTR .... Defence Medical Services Training Centre
DEF SCH OF LANG .... Defence School of Languages
DGA(N)SU BATH .... Director General Aircraft (Navy) Strategy Unit, Bath
DGCC .... Director General of Corporate Communications
DGCIS BRISTOL .... Director General Command and Information Systems
DGIA .... Defence Geographic and Imagery Intelligence Agency
DGICS .... Director General Information and Communication Services
DGMO .... Director General Manpower Audit
DGSPPOL .... Assistant Under Secretary (Service Personnel Policy)
DGSS BARROW .... Director General Surface Ships (Barrow)
DGSS BRISTOL .... Director General Surface Ships
DGSWS BARROW .... Director General Strategic Weapons Systems (Barrow)
DHFS .... Defence Helicopter Flying School

DHP BRISTOL .... Directorate of Helicopter Projects
DHSA .... Defence Helicopter Support Authority
DIS .... Defence Intelligence Staff
DISC .... Defence Intelligence & Security Centre
DITMTC SHRIVNHAM .... Defence Information Technology and Management Training CentreShrivenham
DLO CIS .... Defence Logistics Organisation Communication Information Systems
DLO DG FBP .... Defence Logistics Organisation Finance & Business Planning
DLO DG OBD .... Defence Logistics Organisation (Operations/Business Development)
DLO HR .... Defence Logistics Organisation Human Resources
DLO LONDON .... Defence Logistics Organisation London
DMCS .... Directorate of Management & Consultancy Services
DMO .... Director of Military Operations
DMOS ST GILES CT .... Tri-Service Resettlement Organisation
DMTO HQ .... Defence Medical Training Organisation Head Quarters
DNLP BATH .... Directorate of Naval Logistic Policy (Operations & Plans) (Bath)
DNO .... Director Naval Operations
DNR DISP TEAM .... DIRECTOR OF NAVAL RECRUITING DISPLAY TEAM
DNR E MIDLANDS .... Directorate of Naval Recruiting East Midlands
DNR EAST ANGLIA .... Directorate of Naval Recruiting East Anglia
DNR EMR .... Directorate of Naval Recruiting Ethnic Minortites Recruiting
DNR GMSY .... Directorate of Naval Recruiting Greater Manchester and South Yorkshire
DNR LONDON .... Directorate Of Naval Recruiting London & Home Counties
DNR MANW .... Directorate of Naval Recruiting Merseyside and North Wales
DNR N SCOTLAND .... Directorate of Naval Recruiting Northern Scotland
DNR NE ENGLAND .... Directorate of Naval Recruiting North East England
DNR NWENI .... Directorate of Naval Recruiting, North West England and Northern Ireland
DNR PRES TEAMS .... DIRECTOR OF NAVAL RECRUITING PRESENTATION TEAMS
DNR RCHQ NORTH .... DIRECTOR OF NAVAL RECRUITING REGIONAL HEADQUARTERS (NORTH)
DNR RCHQ SOUTH .... Director of Naval Recruiting Regional Careers Headquarters (South)
DNR S SCOTLAND .... Directorate Of Naval Recruiting Southern Scotland
DNR SOUTH EAST .... Directorate of Naval Recruiting South East England
DNR SOUTH WEST .... Directorate of Naval Recruiting South West England
DNR STH CENTRAL .... Directorate of Naval Recruiting South Central England
DNR WEST & WALES .... DIRECTORATE OF NAVAL RECRUITING WEST ENGLAND & WALES
DNR WROUGHTON .... Director of Naval Recruiting, Wroughton
DNR YORKSHIRE .... Directorate of Naval Recruiting, Yorkshire
DNSOM .... The Director of Naval Surveying Oceanography and Meteorology
DOC .... Directorate of Operational Capability
DOLPHIN SM SCHL .... Royal Naval Submarine School
DOMA .... Directorate of Overseas Military Activity
DPA BRISTOL .... Defence Procurement Agency Bristol
DRAKE CBP(CNH) .... Commander Base Personnel Drake
DRAKE DPM .... DRAKE DIRECTOR PORT MANAGEMENT
DRFC .... Director Reserve Forces & Cadets
DS SEC .... Defence Services Secretary
DSCA HQ .... Defence Secondary Care Agency Headquarters
DSQ ROSYTH .... Director Safety & Quality - ROSYTH

DSWS BRISTOL .... Director Strategic Weapons Systems
DSYPOL .... Directorate of Security (Policy)
EAGLET .... Royal Naval Reserve Mersey (RN Staff)
ELANT/NAVNORTH .... CinC Eastern Atlantic Area and Commander Naval Forces Northern Europe
ES AIR BRISTOL .... Equipment Support (Air) Bristol
ES AIR MASU .... Equipment Support (Air) MASU
ES AIR NAML .... Equipment Support (Air) Naval Aircraft Materials Laboratory
ES AIR USA .... Equipment Support (Air) USA
ES AIR WYTON .... Equipment Support (Air) Wyton
ES AIR YEO .... Equipment Support (Air) Yeovilton
EXCH ARMY SC(G) .... Exchange Service British Army On the Rhine
EXCHANGE ARMY UK .... Exchange Service UK Army Units
EXCHANGE AUSTLIA .... Exchange Service Australian Navy
EXCHANGE BELGIUM .... Exchange Service Belgium
EXCHANGE BRAZIL .... Exchange Service Brazilian Navy
EXCHANGE CANADA .... Exchange Service Canadian Armed Forces
EXCHANGE DENMARK .... Exchange Service Denmark
EXCHANGE DGST(N) .... Service with Director General Supply & Transport (Navy)
EXCHANGE FRANCE .... Exchange Service France
EXCHANGE GERMANY .... Exchange Service German Navy
EXCHANGE ITALY .... Exchange Italian Navy
EXCHANGE N ZLAND .... Exchange New Zealand
EXCHANGE NLANDS .... Exchange Service Netherlands Forces
EXCHANGE NORWAY .... Exchange Service Norway
EXCHANGE RAF GER .... Exchange Service Royal Air Force Germany
EXCHANGE RAF UK .... Exchange Service with the Royal Air Force
EXCHANGE SPAIN .... EXCHANGE SPAIN
EXCHANGE USA .... Exchange Service United States
FAAIT MAN ORG VL .... Fleet Air Arm Information Technology Management Organisation (Yeovilton)
FASM IPT .... Future Attack Submarine Integrated Project Team
FCBA IPT .... Future Carrier Borne Aircraft Integrated Project Team
FDG .... Fleet Diving Group
FDU1 .... Fleet Diving Unit (1)
FDU2 .... Fleet Diving Unit (2)
FDU3 .... Fleet Diving Unit (3)
FLYING FOX .... HMS FLYING FOX
FONA COLLINGWOOD .... Flag Officer Naval Aviation (HMS Collingwood)
FONA CRANWELL .... Flag Officer Naval Aviation (RAF Cranwell)
FONA DARTMOUTH .... Flag Officer Naval Aviation (BRNC Dartmouth)
FONA LINTON/OUSE .... Flag Officer Naval Aviation (Linton On Ouse)
FONA NORTHWOOD .... Flag Officer Naval Aviation (Northwood)
FONA SEAHAWK .... Flag Officer Naval Aviation (HMS Seahawk)
FONA VALLEY .... Flag Officer Naval Aviation (RAF Valley)
FONA .... Flag Officer Naval Aviation
FORWARD .... RNR Communications Training Centre (Birmingham) (RN Staff)
FOSF ENG DEVPT .... Flag Officer Surface Flotilla Engineering Staff (Devonport)
FOSF NORTHWOOD .... Flag Officer Surface Flotilla (Northwood)

FOSF PHOT UNIT .... Flag Officer Surface Flotilla (Photographic Unit)
FOSF ROSYTH .... Flag Officer Surface Flotilla (Rosyth)
FOSF .... Flag Officer Surface Flotilla
FOSM FASLANE .... Flag Officer Submarines (Faslane)
FOSM GOSPORT .... Flag Officer Submarines (Gosport)
FOSM NWOOD HQ .... Flag Officer Submarines (Northwood) Headquarters
FOSM NWOOD OPS .... Flag Officer Submarines (Northwood)
FOSNNI OPS CFS .... FOSNNI/Commander Clyde Operations Department
FOSNNI/NBC CLYDE .... Flag Officer Scotland & Northern Ireland/Naval Base Commander - Clyde
FOST DPORT SHORE .... Flag Officer Sea Training (Devonport)
FOST FLT TGT GRP .... Fleet Target Group
HARRIER IPT .... Harrier Intergrated Projects Team
HJPO LONDON .... Project Horizon Joint Project Office
HQ ARRC .... HQ Ace Rapid Reaction Corps
HQ BAND SERVICE .... Headquarters Band Service
HQ DCSA .... HQ Defence Fixed Telecommunications System
HQ DSF .... Headquarters Training Special Forces
HQ FIRE SVCS .... Headquarters MOD Fire Services
HQ NORTH .... Headquarters North
HQ 3 CDO BDE RM .... 3 Commando Brigade Royal Marines
HQAFNORTHWEST .... Headquarters Allied Forces North West Europe
HQBF CYPRUS .... Headquarters British Forces Cyprus
HQMATO UXBRIDGE .... Headquarters Military Air Traffic Operations Uxbridge
HQRM .... Headquarters Royal Marines
HQ3GP HQSTC .... Headquarters 3 Group
HU DERRIFORD .... Ministry of Defence Hospital Unit (Derriford)
HU FRIMLEY .... Ministry of Defence Hospital Unit Frimley Park
HU PORTSMOUTH .... Ministry of Defence Hospital Unit (Portsmouth)
IMS BRUSSELS .... International Military Staff, Brussels
INM ALVERSTOKE .... Institute of Naval Medicine
JACIG .... Joint Arms Control Implementation Group
JARIC .... Joint Air Reconnaissance and Intelligence Centre
JATEBRIZENORTON .... Joint Air Transport Establishment - Brize Norton
JDCC .... Joint Doctrine and Concepts Centre
JF HARROLE OFF .... Joint Force Harrier Role Office
JHCHQ .... JOINT HELICOPTER COMMAND HEADQUARTERS
JHQ NORTHEAST .... Baltic Approaches
JHQ SOUTHCENT .... JOINT HEADQUARTERS SOUTHCENT
JHQSW MADRID .... JHQ SOUTHWEST MADRID
JMOTS NORTHWOOD .... Joint Maritime Operational Training Staff (Northwood)
JPS UK .... Joint Planning Staff UK
JS PHOT SCHOOL .... Joint Services Photographic School
JSCSC .... Joint Services Command and Staff College
JSCSCPT .... Joint Service Command and Staff College Project Team
JSSU DIGBY .... Joint Service Signal Unit - Digby
JSSU OAKLEY .... Joint Service Signal Unit - Oakley
JSU NORTHWOOD .... Joint Support Unit Northwood

LANG TRNG(UK) .... Language Training (UK)
LARO WYTON ....
LARONE IPT .... Larone integrated Project Group
LN BANGLADESH .... Loan Bangladesh
LN BMATT (CEE) .... Loan BMATT (CEE) (Vyskov)
LN BMATT SAFRICA .... British Military Advisory and Training Team (South Africa)
LN DERA BEDFORD .... Defence Research Agency (Bedford)
LN DERA CDA HLS .... Loan Centre for Defence Analysis (HLS)
LN DERA CDA PMTH .... Centre for Defence Analysis Naval Analysis Group
LN DERA FARN .... Defence Research Agency (Farnborough)
LN DERA FRT HAL .... Defence Research Agency (Fort Halstead)
LN DERA HASLAR .... Defence Research Agency (Haslar)
LN DERA MALVERN .... Defence Research Agency (Malvern)
LN DERA PORTN DN .... Loan DERA Porton Down
LN DERA PRTSDWN .... Defence Research Agency
LN DERA WNFRITH .... Defence Research Agency (Winfrith)
LOAN ABU DHABI .... Loan Service in Abu Dhabi
LOAN ARMY ....
LOAN BALBAT .... Loan Service Baltic States
LOAN BMATT GHANA .... Bmatt West Africa
LOAN BMATT(EC) .... British Military Advisory Training Team (Eastern Caribbean)
LOAN BRUNEI .... Loan Service in Brunei
LOAN DERA ADAC .... Centre for Defence Analysis Farnborough
LOAN DERA BSC DN .... Defence Test & Evaluation Organisation (Boscombe Down)
LOAN DERA KYLE .... Defence Test & Evaluation Organisation (Kyle)
LOAN DERA PYSTCK .... Defence Test & Evaluation Organisation (Pyestock)
LOAN HYDROG .... Loan Hydrographer
LOAN INDUSTRY .... LOAN INDUSTRY
LOAN KUWAIT .... Loan Service Kuwait
LOAN MALAYSIA .... Loan Malaysia
LOAN OMAN .... Loan Service Oman
LOAN SAUDI ARAB .... Loan Service Saudi Arabia
LPD(R) IPT .... Landing Platform Dock (Replacement) Integrated Project Team
MAS BRUSSELS .... Military Agency For Standardisation (Brussels)
MCTC .... Military Corrective Training Centre
MERLIN IPT .... Merlin Integrated Project Team
MSA .... Medical Supply Agency
MWC PORTSDOWN .... Maritime Warfare Centre (Portsdown)
MWC SOUTHWICK .... Maritime Warfare Centre
NAIC NORTHOLT .... Naval Aeronautical Information Cell
NARO GOSPORT .... Naval Aircraft Repair Organisation Gosport
NATO DEF COL .... Nato Defence College
NATO MEWSG VL .... NATO Multi-Service Electronic Warfare Support Group Yeovilton
NBC PORTSMOUTH .... Naval Base Commander (Portsmouth)
NBSA HO .... NAVAL BASE SUPPORT AGENCY HEAD OFFICE
NC3 AGENCY .... NATO C3 Agency
NELSON RNSETT .... The Royal Naval School of Educational and Training Technology (RNSETT)

NEPG .... NATO & European Policy Group
NEPTUNE DSQ .... HMS Neptune - Department of Safety and Quality
NEPTUNE FD .... FACILITIES DEPARTMENT
NEPTUNE SM1 SEA .... NEPTUNE SM1 SEA
NEPTUNE SM1 .... Captain First Submarine Squadron
NEPTUNE 2SL/CNH .... HMS Neptune (NSC)
NMA GOSPORT .... Commodore Naval Drafting
NMA PORTSMOUTH .... Naval Manning Agency - Portsmouth
NMA WHALE ISLAND .... Naval Manning Agency - Whale Island
NORTH DIVING GRP .... Northern Diving Group
NP BRISTOL .... Nuclear Propulsion Bristol
NP DERBY .... Nuclear Propulsion Derby
NP DNREAY .... Nuclear Propulsion Dounreay
NP 1002 DIEGOGA .... Naval Party 1002 Diego Garcia
NP 1061 .... Naval Party 1061 - Royal Naval Liaison Officer - Split
NP 1064 .... Naval Party 1064
NP 1066 .... Naval Party 1066
NP 1067 KOSOVO .... Naval Party 1067 KOSOVO
NRO EE .... Naval Regional Officer Eastern England
NS OBERAMMERGAU .... NATO School (SHAPE) Oberammergau
NSD .... Naval Staff Directorate
NW IPT .... Nuclear Weapons Integrated Project Team
OCLC BIRM .... Officer Careers Liaison Centre, Birmingham
OCLC BRISTOL .... OFFICER CAREERS LIAISON CENTRE,BRISTOL
OCLC LONDON .... Officer Careers Liaison Centre,London
OCLC MANCH .... Officer Careers Liaison Centre, Manchester
OCLC ROSYTH .... Officer Careers Liaison Centre, Rosyth
OSG BRISTOL .... Director General Technical Services and President of the Ordnance Board
PAAMS PARIS .... Principal Anti Air Missile System Paris
PE USA .... Ministry of Defence PE USA
PJHQ OSISOSEAS .... Permanent Joint Headquarters Ocean Surveillance Information System (O/Seas)
PJHQ .... Permanent Joint Headquarters (Northwood)
PRESIDENT .... Royal Naval Reserve London (RN Staff)
PRESTWICK .... Royal Naval Air Station Prestwick
PROTOCOLOFF .... Ministry of Defence Protocol Office
PSYOPS TEAM .... Psychological Operations Team
RAF AWC .... Central Tactics and Trial Organisation Boscombe Down
RAF BENTLEY PRIY .... Royal Air Force Bentley Priory
RAF CRANWELL EFS .... Royal Air Force College Cranwell (Joint Elementary Flying Training School)
RAF HANDLING SQN .... Royal Air Force Handling Squadron
RAF SHAWBURY .... Royal Air Force Shawbury
RAF WEST DRAYTON .... Royal Air Force West Drayton
RAF WYTON .... Royal Air Force Wyton
RCDS .... Royal College of Defence Studies
RDMC BLOCKHOUSE .... Royal Defence Medical College
RH HASLAR .... The Royal Hospital Haslar
RHQ AFNORTH .... Regional Headquarters Allied Forces North

RHQ SOUTHLANT .... Regional Headquarters Southern Atlantic
RM BAND PLYMOUTH .... Band of HM Royal Marines Plymouth
RM BAND PTSMTH .... Band of HM Royal Marines Portsmouth
RM BAND SCOTLAND .... Band of HM Royal Marines Scotland
RM BICKLEIGH ....
Royal Marines Bickleigh Barracks
RM CHIVENOR .... RM Chivenor
RM NORTON MANOR .... Royal Marines Norton Manor
RM POOLE .... Royal Marines Poole
RM SCHOOL MUSIC .... Royal Marines School of Music
RM WARMINSTER .... Royal Marines Warminster
RMB STONEHOUSE .... Royal Marine Barracks Stonehouse
RMC OF SCIENCE .... Royal Military College of Science Shrivenham
RMCS SHRIVENHAM .... Royal Military College of Science
RMDIV LECONFIELD .... Royal Marines Division Army School of Mechanical Transport
RMR BRISTOL .... Royal Marines Reserve Bristol
RMR LONDON .... Royal Marines Reserve London
RMR MERSEYSIDE .... Royal Marines Reserve Merseyside
RMR SCOTLAND .... Royal Marines Reserve Scotland
RMR TYNE .... Royal Marines Reserve Tyne
RN GIBRALTAR .... Royal Navy Gibraltar
RN HYDROG SCHL .... Royal Naval Hydrographic School
RNAS CULDROSE .... Royal Naval Air Station Culdrose
RNAS YEOVILTON .... Royal Naval Air Station Yeovilton
RNEAWC .... Royal Naval Element Air Warfare Centre
RNLO GULF .... Royal Naval Liaison Officer (Gulf)
RNLO JTF4 .... Royal Naval Liaison Officer for Commander Joint Task Force 4,USN
RNSOMO .... Royal Naval School of Meteorology & Oceanography
RNSR BOVINGTON .... Royal Naval School of Recruiting, Bovington
RNU RAF DIGBY .... Royal Naval Unit RAF DIGBY
RNU ST MAWGAN .... Royal Naval Unit St Mawgan
ROCLANT PORTUGAL .... Regional Operating Centre Atlantic
ROCNORTHWEST .... Regional Operating Centre North West
ROSYTH SOSM(R) .... Senior Officer Submarine Refitting, Rosyth
ROYAL HOUSEHOLD .... Royal Household
SA ANKARA .... Service Attache Ankara
SA ATHENS .... Service Attache Athens
SA BERLIN .... Service Attache BERLIN
SA BRAZIL .... Service Attache Brazil
SA CAIRO .... Service Attache Cairo
SA CARACAS .... Service Attache Caracas
SA COPENHAGEN .... Service Attache Copenhagen
SA ISLAMABAD .... Service Attache Islamabad
SA LISBON .... Service Attache Lisbon
SA MADRID .... Service Attache Madrid
SA MALAYSIA .... Service Attache Malaysia
SA MOSCOW .... Service Attache Moscow

SA MUSCAT .... Service Attache Muscat
SA OSLO .... Service Attache Oslo
SA PARIS .... Service Attache Paris
SA PRETORIA .... Service Attache Pretoria
SA RIYADH .... Service Attache Riyadh
SA ROME .... Service Attache Rome
SA SANTIAGO .... Service Attache Santiago
SA SEOUL .... Service Attache Seoul
SA STOCKHOLM .... Service Attache Stockholm
SA THE HAGUE .... Service Attache the Hague
SA TOKYO .... Service Attache Tokyo
SACLANT BELGIUM .... Supreme Allied Commander Atlantic, Belgium
SACLANT ITALY .... Supreme Allied Commander Atlantic, Italy
SACLANT USA .... Supreme Allied Commander Atlantic, USA
SAUDI AFPS SAUDI .... Saudi Armed Forces Project Sales Saudi
SAUDI AFPS UK .... Saudi Armed Forces Project Sales UK
SCU LEYDENE ACNS .... SCU Leydene ACNS
SDG PLYMOUTH .... Southern Diving Unit (Plymouth)
SDG PORTSMOUTH .... Southern Diving Unit 2 (Portsmouth)
SEA CADET CORPS .... Sea Cadet Corps
SGD .... Defence Medical Services Directorate
SHAPE BELGIUM .... Supreme Headquarters Allied Powers In Europe (Belgium)
SHERWOOD .... RNR Communications Training Centre (Nottingham) (RN Staff)
SSA BATH .... Ships Support Agency
SSA BRISTOL .... Ship Support Agency - Bristol
SSA DEVONPORT .... Ships Support Agency Devonport
SSA PORTSMOUTH .... Director General Ships Portsmouth
SSA ROSYTH .... Director General Ships Rosyth
SSA/CWTA PORTS .... Captain Weapon Trials and Assessment (Portsmouth)
SSIP IPT .... SSIP Integrated Project Team
SSPAG .... Strategic Systems Performance Analysis Group
STG BRISTOL .... Sea Technology Group Bristol
SULTAN AIB .... Admiralty Interview Board
SUP SHIPS PTSMTH .... Superintendent Ships (Portsmouth)
SUPT OF DIVING .... Superintendent of Diving
TCM IPT .... Torpedo Counter Measures Integrated Project Team
TLAM IPT .... TLAM Integrated Project Team
TORPEDO IPT .... Torpedo Integrated Project Team
TRAINTEAM BRUNEI .... Training Team Brunei
T45 IPT .... TYPE 45 DESTROYER INTEGRATED PROJECT TEAM
UKMILREP BRUSS .... United Kingdom Military Representative Brussels
UKNMR SHAPE .... United Kingdom Military Representative SHAPE
UKNSE AFNORTH NY .... United Kingdom National Support Element Allied Forces Northern Europe
UKSU AFSOUTH .... United Kingdom Support Unit Allied Forces Southern Europe
UKSU IBERLANT .... United Kingdom Support Unit Iberlant
UNIKOM .... United Nations IRAQ KUWAIT Observation Mission
UNOMIG .... UN MONITORING IN GEORGIA

UNTAT WARMINSTER .... United Nations Training Advisory Team
URNU BIRMINGHAM .... University Royal Naval Unit (Birmingham)
URNU LIVERPOOL .... University Royal Naval Unit (Liverpool)
URNU SUSSEX .... University Royal Naval Unit (Sussex)
WEU .... Western European Union
2SL/CNH FOTR .... Flag Officer Training and Recruiting Headquarters
2SL/CNH .... Second Sea Lord/Commander-in-Chief Naval Home Command
32(THE ROYAL)SQN .... Royal Air Force Northolt - 32 The(The Royal) Squadron
40 CDO RM .... 40 Commando Royal Marines
42 CDO RM .... 42 Commando Royal Marines
45 CDO RM .... 45 Commando Royal Marines
539 ASLT SQN RM .... 539 Assault Squadron Royal Marines
702 SQN HERON .... 702 Naval Air Squadron Her Majesty's Ship Heron
750 SQN (HERON) .... Heron Flight
750 SQN OBS SCH .... 750 Naval Air Squadron/ Observers School
771 SK5 SAR .... 771 Naval Air Squadron (Sea King Mk5) Search & Rescue
815 SQN HQ .... 815 Headquarters Naval Air Squadron, Her Majesty's Ship Heron
824 NAS .... 824 Naval Air Station
848 SQN HERON .... 848 Naval Air Squadron
849 SQN HQ .... 849 Naval Air Squadron Headquarters
899 SQN HERON .... 899 Naval Air Squadron Her Majesty's Ship Heron

PRIZES, TESTIMONIALS, Etc.

(Until further notice silver-gilt medals will be substituted for gold medals)
*Subject to revision consequent upon change in training pattern for Junior Officers.

THE GEDGE MEDAL, THE CHARLES DARGAVILLE BALLARD PRIZE, THE PAYMASTER-IN-CHIEF EDWARD ROBINSON MEMORIAL PRIZE

These prize funds have had their incomes combined, under a scheme approved by the Charity Commissioners, so that the Managing Trustees may award a medal and a suitable prize annually to the outstanding officer undergoing training on the Junior Officers' Course.

The Gedge Medal was instituted when the members of the Royal Naval Accountant Officers' Dining Club subscribed the sum of £260 to institute a prize for Junior Supply Officers. The Gedge Medal is named in commemoration of Staff Paymaster Joseph T. Gedge, RN, who was killed of the 6th August 1914 when HMS Amphion was sunk by a mine and who was the first British Officer of all the fighting service to be killed during the 1914-18 war.

The Charles Dargaville Ballard Prize was founded in 1954 under the will of the late Captain G. N. Ballard, RN, in memory of his son, Acting Paymaster Sub-Lieutenant Charles Dargaville Ballard, RN, who was killed in action when HMS Manchester was torpedoed by aircraft on 23rd July 1941, while escorting a Malta convoy south of Sardinia.

The Paymaster-in-Chief Edward Robinson Memorial Prize was founded, also in 1954, under the terms of the will of the late Commander A.A.E. Robinson, OBE, RN, in memory of his father, Paymaster-in-Chief Edward Robinson, RN.

The Managing Trustee of these combined prize funds is the Commander, Royal Naval Supply School, HMS Raleigh.

The name of the recipient will be published annually in a DCI.

*THE HUGH CHEETHAM-HILL MEMORIAL TRUST FUND

This fund was established in 1958 by Dr. and Mrs. H.C. Hill, in memory of their son, Lieutenant Commander Hugh Cheetham-Hill, RN, an officer of the Navigation and Direction Branch of the Royal Navy, who died on the 5th October, 1957.

The annual income derived from the Fund's holding in the United Service Trustee Combined Charitable Fund is used to provide a prize to be known as the "Hugh Cheetham-Hill Prize" awarded annually on the recommendation of the Commodore, School of Maritime Operations, to the Officer of the Royal Navy who achieves the best results of the year on the 'n'/SM(n) Course.

The prize will consist of a cheque for the purchase of books or instruments relating to the Science of Navigation, subject to the discretion of the Commodore, School of Maritime Operations.

When two officers are judged to be of equal merit the prize money is shared.

THE ADMIRAL SIR RICHARD CLAYTON MEMORIAL SWORD

The annual award of a presentation sword to the Senior Upper Yardman Warfare Branch Officer who achieves the highest overall marks in the year through initial training at BRNC Dartmouth and the Junior

Warfare Officers' Course. The sword is donated by BAE Systems. The Commodore SMOPS approves the award.

The prize winner's name will be published annually in a DCI.

THE CARL ZEISS PRIZE

The annual award of a pair of binoculars, donated by Carl Zeiss, to the Warfare Branch Officer (Naval College Entry or Direct Graduate Entry) who obtains the highest overall marks on the Junior Warfare Officers' Course. Commodore SMOPS approves the award.

The prize winner's name is published annually in a DCI.

THE MARTIN BONIWELL MEMORIAL CUP

This trophy was instituted in 1994 in memory of Lt. Cdr. Martin Boniwell, RN, who died on 20th January 1994 whilst serving in HMS Dryad. The cup is awarded to the top student of each PWO course. Commodore SMOPS approves the award.

THE CUNNINGHAM INITIATIVE AWARDS FUND

In response to an appeal in 1965, a memorial was erected in Trafalgar Square and a plaque in St. Paul's Cathedral to commemorate the life and work of Admiral of the Fleet Viscount Cunningham of Hyndhope. After defraying the costs, there remained a sum of approximately £2,803, and in accordance with the wishes of the donors, the Cunningham Memorial committee set up the Cunningham Initiative Awards Fund.

The object of this Fund is to assist young Royal Naval Officers and Ratings, young Women Naval Service Officers and Ratings, young Royal Marines Officers and other ranks, and QARNNS Officers and Ratings, in defraying the cost of schemes of an adventurous or unconventional nature planned on their own initiative and which will result in the recipients of the awards being more useful members of their Service.

Applications should be forwarded to the Ministry of Defence in accordance with instructions contained in current Defence Council Instructions (Royal Navy).

DARTMOUTH PRIZE (1) FOR OFFICERS ON THEIR INITIAL COMMISSION

This prize is awarded termly to the Officer serving on his Initial Commission in either the Warfare or Supply Specialisations, who obtains the highest marks in the Naval Studies Course examinations in his final term at the Britannia Royal College, Dartmouth.

The prize uses income derived from holdings in the United Service Trustee Combined Charitable Fund attributed to:

a) The Geoffrey Gore-Brown, Midshipman RN, Memorial Scholarship which was founded under the terms of the will of the late Mrs. D.A. Gore-Brown in memory of her son Geoffrey.

b) The Robert Roxburgh Memorial Prize which was founded in 1917, by Mrs. J.B. Roxburgh in memory of her son, Midshipman Robert Roxburgh RN, of HMS Indefatigable, who was killed in action in the Battle of Jutland on the 31st May 1916.

c) The Ryder Memorial Fund was founded in memory of Admiral of the Fleet Sir Alfred Phillips Ryder, KCB, who died on the 30th April 1888.

d) The Wemyss prize which was founded in 1946 by the Hon. Alice Wemyss in memory of her father, Admiral of the Fleet Lord Wester Wemyss, who had been the first Captain of the Royal Naval College at Osborne

DARTMOUTH PRIZE (2) FOR AIRCREW OFFICERS

This prize is awarded termly to the officer of the Aircrew Specialisation who obtains the highest marks in the Naval Studies Course examinations in his final term at the Britannia Royal Naval College, Dartmouth.

The prize uses the income derived from holdings in the United Service Trustee Combined charitable Fund attributed to:

a) The Hickes Memorial Prize, which was founded in 1906 by Miss E.K.T. Hickes in memory of her brother, Cadet Charles Meyrick Hickes, who died in 1862 while under training in HMS Britannia at Portland.

b) The Harold Tennyson Memorial Prize, which was founded in 1917 by Lord Tennyson in memory of his son, Acting Sub-Lieutenant The Hon. Harold Courtenay Tennyson, RN, of HMS Viking, who was killed in action on the 29th January 1916.

THE HEWLETT-PACKARD SWORD

The Hewlett-Packard Company instituted in 1939 the award of a sword to the student who is adjudged to have achieved the best results during the Junior Supply officers course during that year.

The name of the recipient will be published annually in a DCI.

THE WORSHIPFUL COMPANY OF CHARTERED SECRETARIES AND ADMINISTRATORS MEDAL (OFFICER)

This prize is awarded to the Officer on the Junior Supply Officers' Course with the highest examination results in the Secretarial and Law examinations, combined with performance in the Secretarial simulator.

The medal is awarded on the recommendation of the Commander Royal Naval Supply School.

The Officer's name will be published annually in a DCI.

THE COMMANDER EGERTON PRIZE

This Prize was founded in 1901 in memory of Commander Frederick Grenville Egerton, Royal Navy, who was mortally wounded on the 2nd November 1899, in the defence of Ladysmith, whilst acting in the execution of his duty.

The dividends arising from a sum of £500 given by the relatives and invested in Government securities will be employed in providing the prize, to be called "The Commander Egerton Prize", which will be awarded annually at the discretion of the Admiralty Board to the Seaman Officer who achieves the best results of the year in the Above Water Warfare stream of the Principal Warfare Officer Course. Should there be no Officer of sufficient merit, the prize may be withheld at the discretion of the Commodore, School of Maritime Operations.

COMMANDER F.G. EMLEY MEMORIAL FUND

This prize was founded in 1972 in memory of Commander Frank Gordon Emley, RN, who died on the 17th November, 1971.

The annual income derived from the Fund's holding in the United Services Trustee Combined Charitable Fund is employed to provide a prize known as the Commander Emley Prize, in the form of an inscribed silver "Armada" Dish, to be awarded annually to the Naval Officer who gains the highest marks out of the three Nuclear General Courses held each year.

CAPTAIN FARMER MEMORIAL PRIZES

The Captain Farmer Memorial Prizes were founded by the will of Captain Donald William Farmer, RN, who died on the 4th January 1982. The annual income derived from the Charity's holding in the United Services Trustee Combined Charities Fund will be employed to provide five cash prizes annually to Royal Navy Officers as follows:

Officers Under Training *Per cent of annual income*

a) The RN Officer in his Initial Commission who gains the highest mark in examinations in professional subjects at Britannia Royal Naval College Dartmouth. 17.5

b) The RN Officer in his Initial Commission who gains the highest aggregate marks at the Fleet Board Examinations 17.5

c) The RN Officer in his Initial Commission of RN or Commonwealth Navies who gains the highest marks on the Principal Warfare Officers Course. 15

Navigation Specialists

a) The Officer who gains the highest marks on Specialist Navigation Officers Course 25

b) The RN Submarine Service officer who gains the highest marks on Specialist Navigating Officers Course 25

THE GOODENOUGH MEDAL AND FUND

This Prize was founded in memory of Captain James G. Goodenough, CB, CMG, who died on 20th August 1875, while serving as Commodore on the Australian Station, from wounds inflicted with poisoned arrows in an unprovoked attack by natives of Santa Cruz.

The annual income from the fund was formerly used to purchase a gold medal. Now its provides a cash prize awarded annually to the Warfare Branch Officer (Naval College Entry or Direct Graduate Entry) who, having achieved a first class pass at Fleetboard, attains the highest mark in the Warfare Module of the Junior Warfare Officers Course.

Commodore SMOPS approves the award and the prize winner's name is published annually in a DCI.

THE GRAHAM NAVAL HISTORY PRIZE

This Prize was founded in 1909 by Lady Graham in memory of her husband, Admiral Sir William Graham, GCB, formerly Captain HMS Britannia Training Ship.

The annual income, comprising dividends from the Fund's holding in the United Services Trustee Combined Charitable Fund, is employed in providing prizes to be awarded at the Britannia Royal Naval College, Dartmouth, to the Officers of the Seaman or Supply Specialisations for work undertaken in connection with the subject of defence.

Officers of Foreign and Commonwealth navies are eligible to receive this prize.

THE ADMIRAL SIR MAX HORTON PRIZE

The late Admiral Sir Max Horton, GCB, DSO, who served with great distinction in command of submarines during World War 1, and as Flag Officer Submarines from January 1940 to November 1942, left to the Admiralty in his Will, the sum of £500, to be applied for the benefit of Officers of the submarine service of the Royal Navy.

This sum has been invested and the interest is used, in accordance with the Admiral's wishes, to provide a prize annually to the officer of the seaman specialisation of the Royal Navy who achieves the best overall standard on his training course for submarine officer, taking into consideration the results of the examination at the ends of Parts I and II training in the Submarine School and Part III Sea Continuation Training as well as the Commanding Officers' reports from Sea.

The prize will be awarded by the Admiralty Board each year, on the recommendation of the Flag Officer Submarines.

The prize will consist of a tankard bearing a set of dolphins and inscribed with the name of the recipient and the date and nature of the award.

JACKSON-EVERETT PRIZE

In 1927, Signal Officers, past and present, on the Active List, subscribed a sum of approximately £280 to institute a prize for officers qualifying as Signal Specialists, to be known as the "Jackson-Everett Prize".

The Prize is awarded annually to the Warfare Officer who achieves the best results of the year in the Communications and Electronic Warfare Stream of the PWO Course. The prize may not be awarded in any year in which the standard of results obtained by the Officer passing the best examinations is not considered to be of sufficient merit to warrant the award at the discretion of the Commodore SMOPS.

The Prize consists of a sum of money (the income available) for the purchase of books and/or instruments.

The Officer's name will be published annually in a DCI.

THE INSTITUTE OF ADMINISTRATIVE MANAGEMENT (IAM) PRIZE

The IAM Prize was first awarded in 1999. It takes the form of a piece of engraved crystal and a cash award of £100 to the officer achieving the highest overall average examination results on the Junior Supply Officers' Course (JSOC).

THE QUEEN'S GOLD MEDAL

Awarded to the sponsored officer (Naval College Entry, University Cadet Entry or Engineering Sponsorship Scheme) of the Engineering Specialisation achieving the best academic results on degree course. Subject in the case of ESS Officers to subsequent entry to BRNC.

Officers who graduate at Cambridge University are eligible for the award.

THE QUEEN'S SWORD

A sword is awarded each year by Her Majesty the Queen, to the Initial Commission Officer Under Training of either the Warfare or Supply Branch, who achieves the highest overall performance in Naval General Training (and Naval Studies when appropriate) at the Britannia Royal Naval College, Dartmouth, in the preceding year.

A sword is also awarded each year, by Her Majesty the Queen, to the Full Career Commission Officer of the Engineering Specialisation who, on completion of the three/four year degree course and the HMS Collingwood/HMS Sultan phase of SEMC, is adjudged to have achieved the best overall results.

THE QUEEN'S BINOCULARS

Six pairs of binoculars are awarded each year at the Britannia Royal Naval College, Dartmouth, by Her Majesty the Queen, to the Officers Under Training who, on passing out, have obtained the highest score in Naval General Training in the preceding calendar year.

ADMIRALTY PRIZE

A pair of binoculars to be awarded to the best young officer on the Royal Navy Young Officers' Course in the preceding calendar year.

KING GEORGE V PRIZE SCHOLARSHIPS

In accordance with the wishes of His Majesty King George V, that the greater part of the Fund, subscribed for the purpose of commemorating His Majesty's Coronation by subjects of His Majesty bearing the Christian name 'George' in all parts of the Empire, should be utilised for the benefit of junior Officers of the Royal Marines who may find difficulty in meeting the cost of the final stage of their military training, the sum available was invested and the arising income was devoted to the institution of Scholarships termed the 'King George V Prize Scholarships'. Scholarships are awarded each year to the Officers in the Royal Marines who, after passing the Annual Competitive examination, are selected by the Commandant General to attend a British or Commonwealth Staff College.

The annual net income from the Fund will be divided equally between all those awarded a Scholarship in that year.

The first Scholarship was awarded in 1914.

THE MANTLE TROPHY

The Mantle Trophy was presented in 1984 by the Directors of the British Manufacture and Research Company Limited for competition by the Royal Navy in close range gunnery.

The trophy, in the form of a sterling silver cup and cover, is dedicated to the memory of Acting Leading Seaman Jack Mantle who won the Victoria Cross on 4 July 1940, while serving in HMS Foylebank at Portland.

The trophy is awarded every six months to the warship or Royal Fleet Auxiliary which has demonstrated the highest standard or greatest improvement in close range weapon effectiveness. The winners are nominated by the Flag Officer Sea Training.

RONALD MEGAW MEMORIAL PRIZE

This Prize, founded in 1906, is in memory of Midshipman Ronald Megaw, who was killed accidentally while at General Quarters on board HMS Montagu.

The annual income from the memorial fund provides a cash prize awarded annually to the Warfare Branch Officer (Naval College Entry) who obtains the highest aggregate of examination marks in the year. The aggregate total is a summation of the BRNC Professional, BRNC Academic, Fleetboard and Junior Warfare Officers Course marks. Commodore SMOPS approves the award and the prize winner's name is published annually in a DCI

HARWOOD PRIZE

This Prize was founded in 1946 by Sir Eugene Millington-Drake for the purpose of promoting knowledge of Hispanic culture. The annual income derived from the Fund's holding in the United Services Trustee Combined Charitable Fund is used in the provision of prizes to be awarded to the RN General List Officers from the Britannia Royal Naval College, Dartmouth, who demonstrate the highest level of excellence on the Naval Studies Course.

THE HAROLD HUDSON PLATE

The Harold Hudson Plate was donated by Mr. Hudson, a former Deputy Director of MW projects at AUWE Portland, on 15 November 1983. It is a silver plate suitably inscribed which is lodged with the Mine Warfare and Clearance Diving School.

The plate will be awarded to the Royal Naval Officer who gains the highest marks in passing the Mine Warfare Career Training Course, at present the Minewarfare module of the Long MCDO Course.

THE OGILVY MEDAL

This Medal was instituted in 1912 in memory of Captain Frederick Charles Ashley Ogilvy, RN, who died on the 18th December 1909, from typhoid fever, while in command of HMS Natal.

The dividends, arising from a sum of about £240 given by Officers of the Royal Navy and by certain friends and relatives, are employed in providing a medal to be called "The Ogilvy Medal", which is awarded annually, at the discretion of the Admiralty Board, to the Officer who achieves the best results of the year in the Underwater Warfare stream of the Principal Warfare Officer course. Should there be no Officer of sufficient merit the prize may be withheld at the discretion of the Commodore SMOPS.

THE PRENDERGAST PRIZE

It was the wish of Admiral Sir Robert Prendergast, KCB, Commander of HMS Excellent from December, 1901, to December, 1903, to arrange something to further the interest of HMS Excellent but due to ill-health and conditions he was unable to do so during his lifetime.

While it is not possible to achieve Admiral Prendergast's wishes by linking prizes with HMS Excellent, two annual prizes have been instituted as a memorial to him. Both prizes are of equal value and the money available for each will not exceed £100. The two annual prizes are awarded to:

a) The Royal Navy Officer of the WE specialisation who obtained the highest marks in the Weapon Engineering Qualification Oral Board of all the Weapons Engineering Career Courses held at HMS Collingwood in that year.

b) The rating who obtains the highest assessment of the Charge Chief, Weapon Engineering Artificer Qualifying Courses at HMS Collingwood in that year.

SHADWELL TESTIMONIAL PRIZE

The Shadwell Testimonial Prize, founded in 1888 in memory of Admiral Sir Charles F. A. Shadwell KCB, who died 1 March 1886, takes the form of a sum of money (about £100) and a certificate. The first award was made on the plans received during 1899.

The award will be made to Officers who have submitted to the Hydrographer of the Navy through their Commanding Officer or Master the most credible plans of anchorage, harbours, small boat landings or seabed features. Submissions may also include reports and/or data associated with other marine soundings such as passage soundings, amendments to sailing directions or other hydrographic officer publications, or any other form of work in support of the broad aims of improving navigational safety.

It may be awarded to the following:

1) Officers and Warrant Officers of the Royal Navy, Royal Marines or a Commonwealth Navy, of a rank not higher than Lieutenant Commander Royal Navy, Captain Royal Marines, or equivalent,

2) Officers and Warrant Officers of the Royal Naval Reserve (any list) and Royal Fleet Auxiliary, of a rank not higher than Lieutenant Commander or First Officer, serving in one of Her Majesty's Ships or Establishments, Royal Fleet Auxiliaries, or a British-registered ship or vessel,

3) Officers of the Mercantile Marine serving in a British registered ship or vessel, Who are not qualified or appointed as Hydrographic Surveyors.

The award will be made on the plans and data received at the Hydrographic Office, Taunton (UKHO), during each calendar year, by a committee consisting of the Hydrographer of the Navy, the Director of Defence Requirements and the Director of Nautical Chartering. No prize will be awarded in any year in which no work of sufficient merit is brought to the notice of the Award Committee.

In the case of cooperation in the production of a plan, a junior officer who has assisted materially in its construction may participate in the award, should the funds be sufficient.

For further information readers are advised to consult DCI RN 198/99.

THE BOYLE SOMERVILLE MEMORIAL PRIZE

A fund has been established in memory of Rear-Admiral Boyle Somerville, for the purpose of awarding a prize which will be known as the 'Boyle Somerville Memorial Prize', and has as its object the encouragement of research or development work in connection with the sciences of meteorology and oceanography.

The prize may be awarded annually to any Officer in the Royal Navy, or one of the Commonwealth navies, whose work during the period under review is adjudged to be of particular merit in connection with the development of meteorology or oceanography and their application to naval operations. Special consideration will be given to any original papers indicating a voluntary effort additional to the author's normal duties.

No prize will be awarded in any year in which no work of sufficient merit is brought to the notice of the Admiralty Board.

The amount of prize is expected to be not less than £100 in any one year and shall be expended in the purchase of books and/or instruments and/or other articles as approved by the Ministry of Defence.

The prize shall not be awarded more than once to the same Officer.

The award will be made on the material received at the Ministry in each calendar year at the sole discretion of the Director of Naval Surveying, Oceanography and Meteorology.

In case of cooperation, an Officer who has assisted in the production of material may participate in the award, should the fund be sufficient.

THE GILBERT BLANE MEDAL

In 1830, Sir Gilbert Blane, Baronet, formerly a member of the Board for Sick and Wounded Seamen, established, with the sanction of the Board of Admiralty, a fund for the encouragement of Naval Medical Science, which is vested in the Corporation of the Royal College of Surgeons of London, in trust.

This fund is employed for the purpose of conferring a Gold Medal annually on the Medical Officer of the Royal Navy who, to a degree which is considered worthy of recognition, has brought about an advance in any branch of Medical Science in its application to Naval Service, or has contributed to an improvement on any matter affecting the health or living conditions of Naval personnel.

Consideration is given to achievements on research, in original articles and reports, criticisms of a constructive character of existing conditions; and information which is brought to notice of meritorious work performed, or suggestions made, by Medical Officers within the scope of the Regulations governing the award of the Medal as stated above.

Special consideration will be given to a specific original work, which should be suitably bound, which has not previously been acknowledged by an award or academic distinction.

The Medal is awarded annually unless no Officer is considered to have qualified, in which event the Medal is held over until the following year or any subsequent year, when, if considered justifiable to do so, it is given as an additional award.

Medical Officers of all ranks are eligible for the award, and an Officer is not restricted to receiving the Medal on one occasion only during his career.

If the un-awarded Medals exceed four, their value is given to the Naval Medical Compassionate Fund.

Nominations for award should be forwarded to the Medical Director General (Navy).

CHADWICK NAVAL PRIZE

Sir Edwin Chadwick KGB, who died in 1890 aged 90, and who devoted his life to Sanitary Science, created in his Will a trust to continue his life's work. Chadwick's wishes, as expressed in the Trust scheme, embrace the promotion of sanitary science, the promotion of health, the prevention of disease and the physical training of the population. The Chadwick Trust supports research and teaching in Public Health Engineering at University College, London. It awards certificates and prizes to students at UCL and the School of Hygiene and Tropical Medicine who have shown merit in subjects within the Trust Scheme. Once in five years, the Trust may make an award to an officer of the Navy, Army or Air Force Medical Services, who has specially assisted in the promotion of the health of the Armed Forces. Nominations for awards are initiated by the Trust in conjunction with the individual Medical Directors-General.

ERROLL-ELDRIDGE FUND

This Fund was formed in June 1910 by a Trust Deed under bequest from Anne Louisa Russel Waldo-Sibthorp (in memory of her husband Commander George Harry Richard Erroll, RN, who lost his life serving his country), and William Yates Eldridge, whereby the income from, or if required, the capital of £1,500, was to be applied in carrying on at the Royal Naval Hospital at Haslar, original medical research into matters affecting the health of the Navy, especially tuberculosis, and providing and maintaining plant and other requisites for that purpose.

Owing to changed circumstances, the Fund was reconstructed in 1989 as the Erroll-Eldridge Fund to form a prize, the income being devoted to annual "Erroll Prizes" to be awarded to personnel of the Royal Naval Medical Service who have made notable contribution to, or who have carried out useful research on the improvement of the health of Royal Naval personnel.

If, in any year, nobody is nominated whose work is considered to be of specific merit, the income may be applied for any educational charitable purpose for Royal Naval Medical personnel, or it may be re-invested thereby enhancing the value of the prize(s) subsequently awarded.

Medical personnel of all ranks are eligible for the prize; an Officer is not restricted to receiving the prize on one occasion only during his career, nor precluded from receiving the prize in addition to the Gilbert Blane Medal.

THE HARVEY-FLETCHER PRIZE FOR DENTAL OFFICERS

In 1973, a Trust Fund was founded by subscription amongst serving and retired officers of the Naval Dental Services and well-wishers, to provide a prize for award to a Dental Officer of the Active List who is adjudged to have brought about an advance in dental science or the associated sciences in their application to the Naval Service which is worthy of recognition. Under the Trust Deed, any contribution to the greater efficiency of the Naval Dental Service and improvement of the health of the Fleet may be considered. The title of the Prize, which may be awarded not more than once in three years, commemorates both a medical and a dental officer. Fleet Surgeon Christopher Harvey between 1880 and 1890 made the first recorded survey of Naval dental health and urged the need for qualified dentists in Naval Hospitals; Surgeon Rear Admiral (D) E. E. Fletcher, CBE, was the head of the Naval Dental Services from their formation in 1920 until his retirement in 1946.

THE HERBERT LOTT NAVAL TRUST FUND

Mr. Herbert Lott was a member of the London Stock Exchange and was extremely interested in the Royal Navy and the part it played in the defence of the Commonwealth. In 1928 he opened negotiations with the Admiralty for the creation of a Trust Fund and made an initial donation of £20,000, which he increased shortly after by another £5,000. The Herbert Lott Naval Trust Fund was instituted in 1930 to make awards to "those who shall show marked efficiency or shall contribute in signal degree to the improvement of the appliances of the Naval and Marine Forces". When Mr. Lott died in 1948 he left the whole of the residue of his estate (over £100,000) to the Trust Fund that bears his name.

Today, the Herbert Lott Fund is run as six separate Funds, each with its own trustee. Five of these funds make awards on a Command basis to personnel for marked efficiency in their duties or to students of courses and examinations.

The sixth fund makes awards for suggestions or inventions which improve the efficiency of the Naval Service

NORTH PERSIAN FORCES PRIZE

The North Persian Forces Memorial Prize, consisting of a silver medal and a purse, will be awarded for the best paper, published in any journal during the year on tropical medicine or tropical hygiene. Tropical hygiene will be interpreted in its widest sense to include any activity logically classifiable under the heading of tropical, preventative medicine.

Medical Officers of under 12 years' service of the Royal Navy, Royal Army Medical Corps, Royal Air Force and Ministry of Overseas Development are eligible to compete. If no suitable paper is published during the year by an officer of under 12 years service, papers by officers of over 12 years service may be considered. The Award is made by the RAMC Prize Committee.

PARKE'S MEMORIAL PRIZE

The Parke's Memorial Prize, consisting of approximately £50, a silver gilt medal and a purse, may be awarded annually to the Officer who has done most by professional work of outstanding merit, to promote the study of Naval Hygiene or Army Health. This includes any activity logically classifiable under the heading of preventive medicine. First consideration is given to original articles or reports on investigations published in a medical journal.

All regular officers of the Royal Navy or Army, except those on the Staffs of the Institute of Naval Medicine and the Royal Army Medical College, are eligible for this Prize, the award of which is made by the RAMC Prize Committee.

THE SUPERINTENDENT OF DIVING'S TROPHY

This trophy was presented in 1959 by Commander J. R. Carr, OBE, RN, for use as an award for MCD Officers.

The trophy consists of a silver cup, nine inches high, mounted on a plinth, which shows the names of the winners. It will be lodged with the Mine Warfare and Clearance Diving School.

The trophy will be awarded to the Officer gaining the highest marks in the Diving Phase of the Long MCDO Course. The Commodore SMOPS approves the award.

Officers of the Commonwealth navies will be eligible to receive this trophy.

A small sum of money has been invested in trustee stock for the maintenance of the trophy.

THE BEAUFORT-WHARTON TESTIMONIAL

This prize is an amalgamation of two testimonials set up to commemorate Rear Admirals Beaufort and Wharton, both former Hydrographers of the Navy.

The annual income from the memorial fund provides a cash prize awarded annually to the Warfare Branch Officer (Naval College Entry or Direct Graduate Entry) who obtains the highest aggregate marks in the year for Navigation. The aggregate total is a summation of BRNC, Fleetboard and Junior Warfare Officers Course Navigation marks.

Commodore SMOPS approves the award and the prize winner's name will be published annually in a DCI.

THE WILKINSON SWORD OF HONOUR AWARD

An annual award, instituted in 1986 by Wilkinson Sword Limited, to be presented to the Principal Warfare Officer who achieved the best overall results in the year on course. The Commodore SMOPS approves the award. Officers of the Commonwealth are eligible to receive this prize.

The prize winner's name will be published annually in a DCI.

THE WILKINSON SWORD OF PEACE AWARD

The Wilkinson Sword of Peace Award was instituted in 1966 to be presented annually by Wilkinson Sword Limited to the RN or RM unit, establishment or ship, which is judged to have made the most valuable contribution towards establishing good and friendly relations with the inhabitants of any territory within or without the United Kingdom.

Any ship, establishment or unit (including RM Commandos serving under the operational command of the Army) is eligible for this sword.

Nominations for the award are invited annually by DCI.

SIR JAMES MARTIN AWARD

The Sir James Martin Award is presented annually by the Guild of Air Pilots and Air Navigators, to a person who has made an outstanding and practical contribution leading to the safer operation of aircraft or space vehicles, or the enhanced survival of aircrews or passengers. It may also be awarded to a person who has performed an outstanding act in the air or on the ground connected with the survival of aerospace crews, passengers or aircraft, and which can be supported by some positive follow up action leading to the safer operation of aircraft or space vehicles, or the enhanced survival of aircrews or passengers.

Nominations for the award are invited annually by DCI.

DEFENCE SURVEYORS' ASSOCIATION ANNUAL PRIZE

A prize of £150 and a certificate may be awarded to the person who, in the opinion of the Council, has made a significant contribution to the advancement of the technology associated with mapping, data acquisition and management of spatial data. Consideration will also be given to those who have made a contribution to raising the profile of the Defence Geographic Community in general.

Nominations, with supporting written recommendations by Commanding Officers, are to sent to the Captain Hydrographic Surveying Squadron. The Captain will then make his proposal to the Board for the most deserving candidate. This is then considered by the Defence Surveyors' Association at their AGM, which is usually held in June.

ROYAL INSTITUTION OF CHARTERED SURVEYORS HYDROGRAPHIC SURVEY PRIZE

The Land and Hydrographic Survey Division of the RICS will award a prize of a £40 book token to the Officer gaining the highest marks on the Long Hydrographic Course held at the Royal Naval Hydrographic School, HMS Drake each year. The Commander RNHS will forward a nomination to the RICS in October.

ROYAL MARINES SWORD OF HONOUR

The Royal Marines' Sword of Honour is awarded to the Young Officer who is placed first overall in the order of merit on completion of basic training. The Sword is suitably engraved to commemorate the occasion. There is also a Sword of Honour awarded to the Officer placed first in the Special Duties Course order of merit.

ANNUAL COMPETITION FOR NAVAL HISTORY PRIZES

The aim of this competition is to encourage naval personnel to take an greater interest in naval history.

The competition is open to all officers and ratings serving in the RN, RM or QARNNS, officers and ratings of Commonwealth navies who are serving on exchange or loan service in the RN, RM or QARNNS, and officers and ratings of Commonwealth or foreign navies undergoing training with the RN, RM or QARNNS.

Prizes will be awarded in two sections as follows:

Officers First Prize £500

Second Prize	£250
Third Prize	£150
Ratings First Prize	£500
Second Prize	£250
Third Prize	£150

All competitors submitting essays of sufficient merit will be awarded certificates. The Directorate of Naval Service Conditions, sponsors of this competition, reserves the right to increase the value and number of the prizes, to withhold the award of some or all of the prizes if essays of insufficient merit are submitted, and to combine prizes and divide them equally where prizewinning essays are of equal merit.

Essays are to be on one of the stipulated subjects and are to be in English, typed and of not more than 12,000 words.

Authorship of essays must be strictly anonymous. Each competitor is to use a 'nom de plume' which is to appear on the title page of the essay. The author's name must not appear on the essay.

Each essay is to be accompanied by a sealed envelope with the author's 'nom de plume' typed on the outside. The envelope is to contain a declaration signed by the author, that the essay is his/her unassisted work: this is to be countersigned by the author's Commanding Officer. The envelope should also contain a sheet of paper on which the competitor's 'nom de plume', name, rank/rate, official number and address have been typed.

Essays are to be sent to: Naval History Prize, Defence Studies Department, Joint Services Command and Staff College, Bracknell, Berks RG12 9DD, to arrive by 31st December of the year of the competition.

The subject for the essay for each year and the titles of the book recommended for study will be published in Defence Council Instructions (RN).

Competitors are advised to consult the note 'Naval History Prize - Advice for Competitors' which may be obtained from the Defence Studies Department, Joint Services Command and Staff College, Bracknell, Berks RG12 9DD.

Provision of Books. Authority cannot be given for the provision at official expense of books recommended for study in prize competitions. Full use should be made of the facilities afforded by the public library system, Admiralty Library, 3-5, Great Scotland Yard, London SW1A 2HW (which lends books of reference on a limited scale), and the Central Library, Drake Circus, Plymouth PL4 8AL (which lends Naval History Prize essays from previous competitions).

THE HOWARD-JOHNSTON SWORD

A Fund was established in 1985 by Rear Admiral C. D. Howard-Johnston, CB, DSC in memory of his son, Sub Lieutenant Richard Howard-Johnston who was lost at sea in HMS Affray in 1952.

The purpose of the fund is to present a sword annually to the best overall student on the Submarine Advance Warfare Course held at the Royal Naval Submarine School. The Managing Trustees have the discretion to award the prize in cash if there is insufficient income to purchase a sword.

The prize may not be awarded in any year in which the standard of results obtained by the best overall student is not considered to be of sufficient merit to warrant the award. The prize is awarded on the recommendation of the Commander, Royal Naval Submarine School, HMS Raleigh.

THE LORD FIELDHOUSE MEMORIAL PRIZE

Established by term mates of the Admiral of the Fleet the late Lord Fieldhouse, GCB, GBE, the prize will be awarded annually to the top student on the Submarine Intermediate Warfare Course on the recommendation of the Commander, Royal Naval Submarine School,. The prize takes the form of books to the value of £50.00.

SUBMARINE OFFICERS LIFE MEMBERS COMMITTEE FIELDHOUSE PRIZE

Established by the Submarine Officers Life Members Committee to commemorate Admiral of the Fleet the late Lord Fieldhouse, GCB, GBE, two prizes are awarded annually on the recommendation of the Commander, Royal Naval Submarine School, to the top student of the following courses:

a. Deputy Weapons Engineering Officer (SM) Course

b. Weapon Engineering Rating (SM) Courses for OM(WSM), OM(SSM), OM(TSM)

The prize takes the form of books to the value of £100 for officers and £50 for ratings.

THE COMMODORE'S WARFARE PRIZE

An annual award, instituted in 1984 by Ferranti Computer Systems Limited, to the Principal Warfare Officer who demonstrated outstanding achievement on course. Commodore SMOPS approves the award. Officers of the Commonwealth are eligible to receive this prize.

The prize winner's name will be published annually in a DCI

THE MARY TALBOT PRIZE

A book prize is awarded termly to the officer who demonstrates the best overall performance in leadership exercises during Terms 1 and 2 at the Royal Naval College, Dartmouth.

THE DORIS GRAHAM PRIZE

A book prize is awarded termly to the officer who achieves the highest aggregate score in the Assessed Command Exercise during Term 1 Leadership training at the Royal Naval College, Dartmouth.

ROYAL INSTITUTE OF NAVIGATION PRIZE

The Royal Institute of Navigation Prize is a silver salver which is presented annually by a representative of the Royal Institute of Navigation to the best Student on each SPEC(N) Course.

The following prizes are administered by the Officers' Training Centre at HMS SULTAN:

INSTITUTE OF MARINE ENGINEERING SILVER JUBILEE MEDAL

The Institute of Marine Engineering Silver Jubilee Medal is awarded annually to the graduate Marine Engineer Officer, of either the surface or sub-surface specialisation, who achieves the best overall results from initial and professional training.

BAE SYSTEMS SWORD

The BAE Systems Sword is awarded annually to the Senior Upper Yardman of the Engineering Specialisation who, on completion of the Britannia Royal Naval College and specialist school phases of post promotion courses, is judged to have achieved the best overall academic and professional results.

WESTLAND HELICOPTERS SWORD

The Westland Helicopters Sword was founded in 1994. The prize is awarded annually to a graduate Air Engineer Officer who, on completion of the Britannia Royal Naval College and professional courses, is judged to have achieved the best overall academic and professional results.

A W FORMAN BOOK PRIZE

The A W Forman Book Prize was founded by the Institution of Mechanical Engineers in 1982. The prize is awarded annually to the group of graduate Marine Engineer Officers, of either the surface or sub-surface specialisation, who achieves the best overall results for their Design, Make and Evaluate project during the Systems Engineering and Management Course.

ROYAL NAVAL ENGINEERS' BENEVOLENT SOCIETY CHATHAM MEMORIAL PRIZE FUND

The Chatham Memorial Fund was founded soon after World War II from the voluntary subscriptions of the Chatham Branch members of the Royal Naval Engineers' Benevolent Society. The annual income derived from the Fund's holdings is employed to provide a cash prize to the group of Senior Upper Yardman Marine Engineer Officers who achieve the best overall results for their Design and Evaluate project during the Systems Engineering and Management Course.

THE YARD PRIZE

The YARD Prize Fund was founded in 1987 by Yarrow Admiralty Research Development Limited with the object of promoting excellence in project work. The annual income derived from the Fund's holdings is employed in providing a cash prize to a graduate Marine Engineer Officer who, on completion of the Masters of Science program at University College London, is judged to have achieved the best post-graduate project.

FLEET AIR ARM PRIZES AND AWARDS

Note:

1. Nominations for prizes will be based on courses qualifying in a calendar year.

2. Should nominees not achieve a sufficiently high standard the respective trophy will not be awarded.

3. Details of Trophies and Awards are contained in Naval Air Command General Orders - Chapter 13.

4. Administration of a particular award is indicated by brackets after the award title.

THE ARMSTRONG-WHITWORTH TROPHY (RNAS Culdrose)

Originally presented by Armstrong Whitworth in 1956. It is awarded to the student obtaining best air mark on the Basic Observer Course.

THE AUSTRALIA SHIELD (COMNA)

The Australia Shield was bought from trust monies originally donated by the people of Australia and is awarded annually by the FOMA to the Front Line Squadron achieving the highest degree of operational capability over the year 1st December to 30th November.

The Silver Challenge Shield is retained in the ship or establishment having the winners on its strength. The Commanding Officer of the winning squadron has authority to spend a cash prize of £500 on amenities for the benefit of the squadron as a whole.

THE BAMBARA FLIGHT SAFETY TROPHY (COMNA)

The Bambara Flight Safety trophy, a silver cup, was allocated to the Naval Air Command in 1959 from funds made available from the paying off of HMS BAMBARA in Sri Lanka.

The trophy, and a shield for the runner-up, is awarded annually by FOMA to the unit with the best flight safety record.

THE BOYD TROPHY (COMNA)

The Boyd trophy, a silver model of a Swordfish, was presented to the Naval Air Command in 1946 by the Fairey Aviation Company Limited in commemoration of Vice Admiral Sir Dennis Boyd, KCB, CBE, DSC.

It is awarded annually to the Naval pilot(s) or aircrew(s) who, in the opinion of FOMA, has achieved the finest feat of aviation during the previous year. It is retained by the unit in which the winner was serving at the time the winning feat was achieved.

THE HENRY LEIGH CARSLAKE PRIZE (COMNA)

This is awarded annually for the best article on the subject of the work and development of the FAA. It is open to RN and RNR personnel of any specialisation who have completed their training and are currently serving in the Naval Air Command.

DAEDALUS TROPHY (RNAS Culdrose)

Originally presented by HMS Daedalus in 1956, it is awarded to the student gaining the best overall mark on each Basic Observer Course.

THE FAIRCHILD HILLER TROPHY (COMNA)

A silver "Comyns Cup" inscribed "Helicopter Ground School Trophy" presented in 1967 to the RNHGS by the Fairchild Hiller Corporation to mark the long association between the School and the Corporation.

The trophy is awarded annually to the student pilot who gains the highest marks in ground subjects on the previous years Basic Flying Training Course at DHFS.

THE FULMAR TROPHY (RNAS Culdrose)

The trophy consists of a silver, two-handled cup approximately 11 inches high on a plinth. It is awarded to the best observer completing AEW OFT.

THE PHILIP HALLAM TROPHY ((RNAS Yeovilton)

The Hallam Trophy, consisting of a silver model of a Hunter aircraft, was presented to the Fleet Air Arm in 1964 by Mr. V. Hallam in memory of his son Lieutenant P. C. G. Hallam who was killed in a flying accident at Lossiemouth in 1960. It is awarded annually to the best pilot completing Harrier OFT.

THE HARGREAVES TROPHY (RAF Cranwell)

This is a silver cup presented by Commander C. F. Hargreaves in 1968. It is awarded at the end of each course to the student pilot who obtains the best results in flying at the RNEFTS.

THE KELLY MEMORIAL PRIZE (COMNA)

The prize was founded in 1958 from the residue of donations given to erect a memorial plaque in the Chapel at BRNC Dartmouth to the late Lieutenant Commander (P) D. P. W. Kelly, Royal Navy.

The Prize consists of a silver model of a Sea Hawk mounted on a plinth carrying plaques to be inscribed with the winners' names, and is awarded annually to the best Aviator qualifying for the award of "wings".

THE KELMSLEY TROPHY (RNAS Culdrose)

This trophy was presented by the FAA Officers' Association. It is to be held at RNAS Culdrose and awarded to the best pilot completing ASW AFT.

THE MIDSHIPMAN M SIMON TROPHY (RAF Cranwell)

This trophy was presented to the RNEFTS in 1979 by Mr. and Mrs. Simon in memory of their son, Midshipman M. Simon, RN, who was killed in a flying accident at RAF Leeming in 1978. It is awarded at the end of each course to the student pilot who obtains the best results in ground school.

THE 141 NAVIGATION TROPHY (RAF Cranwell)

A wooden shield, approximately 12 inches high with a silver scroll and silver nameplates surrounding it. It was presented by the RAF Officers of 141 HSP Course in November 1968, and is awarded to the student who achieves the best overall marks in Navigation including the Final Navigation Test at the end of each course at RNEFTS.

THE LOUIS NEWMARK FLYING TROPHY (COMNA)

A silver salver presented to the Royal Naval Helicopter School in 1967 by Louis Newmark Limited in recognition of the close ties over several years between RN Helicopter Squadrons and the Company. It is awarded annually to the student pilot who achieves the highest mark in flying on the previous years' Basic Flying Training Course at DFHS.

THE ADMIRAL SIR DUDLEY POUND PRIZE FUND (COMNA)

This prize fund was established in 1955 out of monies from the Admiral Pound Memorial Fund.

Seven prizes annually are awarded to the four pilots and three observers who achieve the greatest success at an Operational Flying School in each of the following groupings:

1)	SK6/Merlin	(O)
2)	SK6/Merlin	(P)
3)	AEW	(O)
4)	Lynx	(O)
5)	Lynx	(P)
6)	SK 4	(P)
7)	FA 2	(P)

The selection of Officers is made at the end of each calendar year, and award is restricted to ab-initio students.

The prize money, currently £75, is made available for the purchase of books or instruments (including such things as watches), the choice being subject to Ministry of Defence approval.

THE ROBERT SANDISON TROPHY (COMNA)

The trophy, a silver model of a Wyvern aircraft, was presented to the Fleet Air Arm by Mr. P. Sandison in memory of his son, Lieutenant R. E. Sandison, RN, who was killed in a flying accident in September 1956. It is awarded by FOMA to the aircrew making the most valuable contribution to the development of weapons, weapon tactics or methods of delivery.

THE WALLROCK TROPHY (BRNC Dartmouth)

This trophy was presented in 1949 by Mr. Samuel Wallrock on the institution of the Short Service Commission (Aircrew) entry.

The trophy consists of a bronze plaque on an oak background and is awarded to the Supplementary List midshipman obtaining the highest marks in passing out examination for each course of general naval and air training at BRNC Dartmouth. The recipient also receives a WALLROCK tankard by British Aerospace.

THE SOPWITH PUP TROPHY (COMNA)

The Sopwith Pup trophy is a silver model of a Sopwith Pup Aircraft, which was presented to the Flag Officer Carriers and Amphibious Ships by Hawker Siddley Aviation (now British Aerospace) to mark the firm's long association with the Fleet Air Arm.

The trophy is awarded annually by COMNA to the ship whose flight achieves and maintains the highest degree of Operational Capability over the year from 1st December to 30th November. The trophy is normally to be retained in the ship, but may be transferred to the flight's parent air station at the discretion of the Commanding Officer.

THE WESTLAND PRIZE (RNAS Culdrose/RNAS Yeovilton)

The trophies are a Silver Cup, which was first awarded in 1965 by the then Westland Aircraft Company, and a Silver Salver, which was presented in 1997 by GKN Westland Helicopters Limited. Both trophies mark the company's long and close association with the rotary wing aviation in the Fleet Air Arm. They are awarded annually at RNAS Culdrose and RNAS Yeovilton, to the aircrew officer or rating who has achieved the best all-round results in Operational Flying Training on Helicopters. A prize tankard is presented to the individuals to mark the award.

THE FERRANTI BLUE FOX RADAR TROPHY (RNAS Yeovilton)

This trophy, a table model of the Blue Fox radar approximately 8.5 inches high, was presented to the Fleet Air Arm in 1982 by Ferranti Limited (Radar Systems Department) The trophy is awarded annually to the officer or rating judged to have made the most valuable engineering contribution to the Sea Harrier Weapon System.

Recipients also receive a cash award of £25.

THE ROBIN BOSTOCK TROPHY RNAS Culdrose)

A silver salver presented in 1987 by Mrs. F. J. H. Rathbone in memory of her brother-in-law who was killed in action while attacking German warships at Trondheim in 1940. It is awarded to the observer who achieves the best overall flying marks on each OFT course.

THE ROLLS ROYCE ENGINEERING EFFICIENCY TROPHY (COMNA)

The directors of Rolls Royce presented a silver trophy to be awarded annually by FOMA to the Squadron or Ship's Flight judged to have achieved the best overall standards of engineering efficiency and effectiveness. The award takes into account all aspects of engineering activities and covers the period 1 Dec to 30 Nov.

THE RACAL ORANGE CROP TROPHY (COMNA)

The Racal Orange Crop Trophy, a silver model of the Orange Crop control indicator, was presented to the Royal Navy by Racal Defence Electronics (Radar). It is awarded annually by COMNA to the front line helicopter crew who have contributed most to the Orange Crop database or tactical progression, in the year from 1 Feb to 31 Jan. The trophy is normally to be retained in the parent ship or squadron of the current holder.

THE THORN EMI TROPHY (RNAS Culdrose)

Awarded annually to the individual within 849 Naval Air Squadron contributing most to the development of the AEW Sea King or its tactical employment during the previous year.

THE REAL TIME TROPHY (RNAS Yeovilton)

A meridian clock mounted upon a mahogany base plate and covered by a glass dome. The Real Time Trophy was presented by Singer Link-Miles and is to be awarded to the Officer or Rating who has made the most outstanding contribution to the development, improvement or use of the Sea Harrier Simulator.

THE RACAL CTS TROPHY (RNAS Yeovilton)

The Trophy, a silver salver, was presented by Racal Avionics in 1990 on the commissioning of 700L Squadron. It is awarded annually to the aircrew(s) or maintainer(s) who have contributed most to the development or tactical exploitation of the Lynx Central Tactical System Software improvements.

TRENCHARD MEMORIAL TROPHY (COMNA)

The trophy is a silver model of three pilots, on a suitable base, with an inscribed plaque. The trophy was entrusted to the Central Flying School in memory of Lord Trenchard in 1959. It lay dormant until 1978 when it was first awarded on a three-yearly basis (last awarded 1993) for "outstanding written contributions to the art of flying instruction". The criteria are deliberately very broad to cast the net as wide as possible. Previous entries have included entries on "Helicopter Flight Simulation in the RN", "Economy in Flying Training", and "Teaching the Art of VSTOL Flying".

THE LEWIS TROPHY (RNAS Culdrose)

The trophy, an 18-inch silver salver, was presented to the Fleet Air Arm in November 1980 by Mr & Mrs H A Lewis in memory of their son, Lieutenant Greg Lewis who was killed in a Wessex HAS Mk3 flying accident in June 1980. It is to be retained by 810 Squadron and awarded at the end of AFT to the student Maritime Helicopter Observer who achieves the best flying pass in the Advanced Flying Training Course.

THE DOLPHIN TROPHY (RNAS Culdrose)

Sponsored by Ferranti-Thompson, the trophy is a piece of engraved glass depicting a dolphin. It is awarded, at Wings Parade, to the student showing most improvement during ASW Operational Flying Training.

THE GEOFFREY TURNER TROPHY (RNAS Culdrose)

The prize commemorates a pilot lost with his Gannet aircraft on a night sortie over the sea in 1957 and is awarded, at Wings Parade, to the best pilot completing ASW OFT.

THE PILKINGTON DAW TROPHY (RNAS Culdrose)

Presented in memory of Lt James Daw and Sub Lt David Pilkington who were killed in a car accident in 1992. The Pilkington Daw Trophy is awarded, at Wings Parade, to the student achieving best marks for character and leadership during ASW AFT/OFT.

THE ROUE TROPHY (RNAS Culdrose)

The Roue Trophy, a Caithness Glass bowl, was presented by Mrs Gill Roue in memory of her husband, Lieutenant Commander D Roue, who was killed in a flying accident in 1981. It is awarded annually to the best observer completing AEW OFT.

THE ROB MORRIS TROPHY (RNAS Culdrose)

The Rob Morris Trophy was presented to commemorate Lt Rob Morris (pilot) who died in a canoeing accident in Jan 92 whilst serving in 814 Squadron. It is awarded to the aircrew member of 814 Squadron achieving the highest mark at their Certificate of Competence Board.

THE FERGUSON SHIELD (RNAS Yeovilton)

The Ferguson Shield is a wood/silver shield and was originally presented in 1958 by the widow of Lt Cdr W A M Ferguson RN. It is presented annually to the best qualifying AWI of the year.

THE BRITISH AEROSPACE SEA SKUA TROPHY (RNAS Yeovilton)

This trophy was presented by British Aerospace Air Weapons Division in 1986. It is a silver model of a Skua and is presented annually to the best qualifying HWI of the year.

THE ADAM CAWTHORNE TROPHY (RNAS Yeovilton)

The trophy was presented by the parents of Sub Lt Adam Cawthorne (Observer) who was killed in a Lynx accident in 1985. It is awarded annually to the best ab-initio Observer gaining wings.

THE RICHARD HARPER MEMORIAL TROPHY (RNAS Yeovilton)

Awarded (on a course basis) to the 702 Squadron student who in the opinion of the staff is considered to have "worked the hardest" to pass the course.

BRITISH AEROSPACE TROPHY

Presented in 1986 by Lieutenant Commander Dave Eagles, then Chief Test Pilot with BAe Warton. Awarded to the best overall student groundschool and flying.

THE KELVIN HUGHES VECTAC TROPHY (COMNA)

The "Little Admiral" trophy, awarded annually to the ship, squadron or ship's flight which has been the most efficient in the conduct and assessment of VECTACs.

THE RENWICK SWORD (FOMA)

Presented by Mrs Renwick to FONAC in 1983. The sword, belonging to the late Captain Renwick, is awarded to the most promising Sea Harrier pilot passing through flying training. It is retained by the winner until he leaves the Service at which time it is returned to FOMA for subsequent presentation to another Sea Harrier pilot.

SOCIETIES, INSTITUTIONS AND CHARITIES

THE ROYAL NAVAL ASSOCIATION

Headquarters: 82 Chelsea Manor Street, LONDON SW3 5QJ
(Tel: 020 7352 6764. Fax: 020 7352 7385)
e-mail: rna@netcomuk.co.uk
Patron: Her Majesty the Queen

The Royal Naval Association was formed in 1950 from the Royal Naval Old Comrades Association and other naval organisations, to be the principal recognised Association of serving, and ex-serving officers, ratings and other ranks of the RN, RM, WRNS, QARNNS and all Reservists who have served for six months. A Royal Charter was granted in 1954. In 1974 the Association became a Registered Charity.

The aims of the Association are to further the efficiency of the Service in which members of the Association have served or are still serving; to perpetuate comradeship by bringing together the greatest possible number of Naval people, in Branches at home and Overseas; and to relieve members of the Association who are in conditions of need, hardship or distress.

There are currently over 38,000 members in over 490 Branches, providing focal points for the preservation of the traditions of the Service, and to perpetuate the memory of members of Her Majesty's Naval Forces who have died in the service of our Country. Many Branches run Clubs: money is raised for service charities, and members and their families in need of help receive not only financial support but continuing practical friendship. For those unable to join a Branch but who wish to demonstrate their support, a Headquarters Roll is available. Associate Membership may also be available to those who do not qualify for Full Membership but are in sympathy with the aims of the Association.

Application for Membership should be made initially to the General Secretary at the above address. The basic subscription is £6.00 per annum, but money should not accompany the initial application.

KING GEORGE'S FUND FOR SAILORS (KGFS)

8 Hatherley Street, LONDON, SW1P 2YY
(Tel: 020 7932 0000 Fax: 0120 7932 0095)

KGFS - the seafarers' charity - was founded by King George V in 1917. KGFS is the only central fund making grants to nautical charities which look after the welfare needs of seafarers and their dependants in the Royal Navy, Merchant Navy and the Fishing Fleets. Help ranges from care of elderly seafarers to financial help for those still serving who hit problems brought on by ill-health, disability, homelessness, unemployment, broken homes or bereavement. Seafarers' children also benefit with help in education.

Applications for grants are received each year from the nautical charities. Grants now being made total almost £3 million annually and are made to over 80 charities.
KGFS receives income from three sources:-

1. Voluntary contributions to fund-raising events, flagdays, donations and annual appeals.

2. Legacies.

3. Interest on Investments.

Help is always needed to raise voluntary contributions in order to meet the ever increasing amounts required to take care of the elderly seafaring veterans and those who serve today and who require help with the complex problems that beset our society. If you can help please telephone on 020 7932 0000. The Fund does not make grants to individuals but if help is needed the Fund can direct an individual to the appropriate charity through its Nautical Welfare Guide.

ROYAL NAVAL BENEVOLENT SOCIETY FOR OFFICERS

1, Fleet Street, London, EC4Y 1BD
(Tel: 020 7427 7471)

Object: To afford financial assistance to officers of the Royal Navy, Royal Marines, QARNNS and their respective reserves and their dependants when they are in need. The Executive Committee of the Society meets quarterly and can normally make grants, at the moment, of up to £1,950 for members and £650 for non-members, many of which are repeated at six-monthly intervals. Additional grants may be made for each dependent member of the family.

Membership and Subscription: All commissioned officers on the active list of the Royal Navy, Royal Marines and QARNNS and all officers on the retired list, who held such rank whilst still serving on the active list, are eligible for membership, which is available on payment of a single life subscription of £50. For those who might find it hard to pay £50 the subscription may be paid in two instalments of £25.

For the individual, membership of the Society is in the nature of an insurance against unforeseen misfortunes that may happen to officers or their dependants as a result of illness, accident, old age or other causes. At the same time, it is a practical means of supporting brother or sister officers and their families in times of need.

Further information can be obtained from the Secretary at the above address.

NAVY SPECIAL FUND
Room 49, Old Naval Academy, HM Naval Base, Portsmouth, Hampshire, PO1 3LS

The Navy Special Fund is a small charitable fund, which was formed and maintained by gifts from various non-public sources, including a grant from the Naval Prize Fund. Its primary object is the temporary relief of need, hardship or distress arising amongst persons who are serving or who have served in the Royal Navy, the Royal Marines, the Women's Royal Naval Service or Queen Alexandra's Royal Naval Nursing Service, and their dependants. Assistance takes the form of single grants or, exceptionally, loans; the latter to serving personnel only. The fund does not conflict with the functions of the Royal Naval Benevolent Trust and applications for ratings should be made to the Trust in the first place. The Navy Special Fund may be able to supplement any assistance given by the Trust or may be able to assist when the Trust has been precluded by its rules from doing so.

Applications for assistance, giving full particulars supported by any available evidence and stating, in the case of ratings, whether application has been made to the Royal Naval Benevolent Trust, should be forwarded by Commanding Officers or the Naval Personal Family Service to The Secretary.

WRNS BENEVOLENT TRUST
311 Twyford Avenue, Portsmouth PO2 8PE
(Tel: 023 9265 5301)

The object of the trust is to provide financial relief in cases of necessity or distress amongst ex-serving or serving female officers and ratings who joined the WRNS or Royal Navy between 1 September 1939 and 1 November 1993.

The Trust is managed by the Central Committee whose members are elected at each Annual General Meeting. With the exception of Honorary legal and financial advisors, all members are either serving or ex female members of the service. The Trust is reliant on grants and donations for its existence.

Applications for assistance should be forwarded in writing to the General Secretary.

QUEEN ALEXANDRA'S ROYAL NAVAL NURSING SERVICE - TRUST FUND
c/o DNS Room 133, Victory Building, HM Naval Base, Portsmouth PO1 3LS.

Object: To promote efficiency and relieve hardship amongst serving or former members of QARNNS or their dependants.

Membership: Serving or former members of QARNNS or those who have been recalled for service in war or emergency.

Management: Two Managing Trustees, namely Matron in Chief QARNNS and the Medical Director General (Naval), and the Hon. Secretary.

Custodian of the Fund: The United Services Trustee.

Assistance: The Managing Trustees will approve grants at their discretion to eligible applicants.

Further information can be obtained from the Hon. Secretary, at the above address.

NAVAL MEDICAL COMPASSIONATE FUND
c/o Sec MDG(N), Room 114, Victory Building, HM Naval Base, Portsmouth PO1 3LS

The Naval Medical Compassionate Fund was founded by Order in Council in 1915 to help the widows and orphans of Medical Officers of the Royal Navy, active or retired, who were subscribers to the Fund at the time of their death, or were not more than nine months in arrears with the subscriptions.

In addition to a grant payable on the death of the subscriber, the Directors have powers to grant relief to widows and orphans of dependants who find themselves in necessitous circumstances.

Medical Officers on the Active List of the Royal Navy, including those holding Short Service Commissions, who have not yet subscribed, are invited to do so.
All correspondence regarding the NMCF should be addressed to the Assistant Secretary NMCF at the above address.

ROYAL MARINES CHARITIES
CORPS SECRETARY HEADQUARTERS ROYAL MARINES
HMS EXCELLENT WHALE ISLAND PORTSMOUTH PO2 8ER
(Tel: 023 9254 7214. Fax: 023 9254 7207)
E-mail: royalmarines.charities@charity.vfree.com

The Royal Marines Corps Secretariat centrally administers Royal Marines Charities and prize funds, the main charities are listed below. Full details of all funds are listed in Royal Marines Instructions (BR 1283).

THE ROYAL MARINES BENEVOLENT FUND. The principal purpose of the Fund is to benefit persons who are serving or who have served in the Royal Marines, or their dependants, to relieve need, hardship or distress. The Fund was formed in 1997 and subsumed the following funds and their purposes:

The Upton Kelly Memorial Fund. The aim of this fund is to relieve distress or necessity amongst retired officers and officers' widows and their dependants.

Royal Marines Tercentenary Relief Fund. The purpose of this fund is to provide widows, or next of kin, with a sum of money on death. This is applicable to serving Royal Marines or reservists on duty.

Royal Marines Welfare Fund. The income to this fund may be used to relieve distress among serving and retired Warrant Officers, non-commissioned officers and men of the Royal Marines, their widows and dependants.

Royal Marines Band Benevolent Fund. The fund is used to relieve need or distress for serving and retired RM Band Service ranks or their dependants by making grants.
Contact: Officers - The Corps Secretary, Tel: 023 9254 7214

SNCOs, Cpls and Marines - HQRM Welfare SNCO, Tel 023 9254 7544

1939 WAR FUND. The deed of trust allows this fund to be used for maintaining and increasing the efficiency and *esprit de corps* of the Royal Marines. It may also assist in the relief of distress for past and present members of the Corps and their relatives and dependants and for making grants to other charities which may directly or indirectly assist members of the Corps.

ROYAL MARINES RESERVE 50th ANNIVERSARY RELIEF FUND. This Fund was formed in 1998 with an initial grant from the Royal Marines Benevolent Fund. Its object is to relieve the need, distress or hardship of serving or retired members of the RMR, or their widows, dependants or immediate close family, as a result of death, disability or other tragic circumstances; these circumstances will normally be in part or wholly attributable to Crown Service.

Contact: HQRM SO2 Reserves, Tel 023 9254 7655

ROYAL MARINES' ASSOCIATION. The object of the RMA is to maintain and promote fellowship and *esprit de corps* among Royal Marines, serving and retired. The Association keeps members in touch with each other through world wide branches and assists in the investigation of cases of hardship and distress. Further information on membership and subscriptions can be obtained from The General Secretary, RMA Central Office, Eastney Esplanade, Southsea, Hants, PO4 9PX - Tel: 023 9273 1978, Fax: 023 9229 6945.

THE OFFICERS' ASSOCIATION
PATRON: HER MAJESTY THE QUEEN
48 Pall Mall, London, SW1Y 5JY (Tel 020 7389 5204)

The Officers' Association provides services which are available to ex-officers of the Royal Navy (including Royal Marines), the Army and the Royal Air Force, and their widows and dependants including those who held commissions in the Women's Services.

Services include:

Employment - an efficient Employment Department to assist ex-officers of all ages and ranks to find suitable employment, both those just leaving the Services and those who are changing their civilian jobs. Many hundreds of ex-officers are found jobs every year over a wide salary range.

Benevolence - financial assistance is given in a number of ways such as cash grants and allowances for the elderly in Residential or Nursing Home Care and towards shortfalls in Home fees.

Homes advice - advice and information on independent sector Homes and Homes run by service charities and other voluntary organisations; sheltered accommodation for the elderly; convalescence homes; advice on financial assistance toward Home fees.

A Country Home - running "Huntly", a delightful country home at Bishopsteignton, South Devon, which affords comfort and security for ex-officers at or over the age of 65, both male and female, who do not need special nursing care. Selection is made with due regard to need.

Bungalows - running a 12-bungalow estate at Leavesden, Herts, for disabled ex-officers and their families.

The Association has offices in London and Dublin; the Officers' Association (Scotland) has offices in Glasgow and Edinburgh.
All enquiries should be made to: The General Secretary at the above address

SSAFA FORCES HELP (THE SOLDIERS, SAILORS, AIRMEN AND FAMILIES ASSOCIATION - FORCES HELP)
19 Queen Elizabeth Street, LONDON, SE1 2LP
(Tel: 020 7403 8783 Fax: 020 7403 8815)
E-mail: public-awareness@ssafa-forces-help.org.uk
Website: www.ssafa-forces-help.org.uk
Registered Charity Number 210760. Est 1885

Object: The national charity helping serving and ex-Service men, women and their families, in need. SSAFA Forces Help is not primarily a grant making organisation but all Branches have funds always available for emergency issue. Where there is a financial need, SSAFA Forces Help first ensures that a family is getting all they are entitled to from statutory sources and then puts up the case to the appropriate Service or Regimental benevolent funds. The Royal Navy Benevolent Trust and other Service charities use SSAFA Forces Help's nation-wide network of voluntary workers to visit their family cases and carry their generosity over the doorstep.

To carry out this work SSAFA Forces Help has a network of volunteers at home and abroad. SSAFA Forces Help provides both professional and voluntary support to Service personnel and their families in the UK and overseas. In the UK, SSAFA Forces Help supplies a social work advisory service to the Army and Royal Air Force. *All enquiries and applications to the Welfare Department at the above address.*

THE ROYAL HOMES FOR OFFICERS' WIDOWS AND DAUGHTERS
Queen Alexandra's Court, St. Mary's Road, Wimbledon
LONDON, SW19 7DE
(Tel 020 8946 5182)

Queen Alexandra's Court is managed by a Committee responsible to SSAFA Forces Help Council.

The accommodation comprises unfurnished self-contained flats for widows, divorcees or unmarried daughters of deceased officers or warrant officers, or women who are retired officers or warrant officers, of all three Services.

For full particulars application should be made to the Manager at the above address.

CHARITY OF WILLIAM KINLOCH
(The Kinloch Bequest)
(Tel: 020 7240 3718)

The Charity is administered by the Royal Scottish Corporation.

Candidates for the benefits of the Charity must be Scotsmen or women who have served in the Royal Navy, Army or Air Force who have become disabled through no fault of their own, who are in need and deserving. Preference will be given to those who have been maimed or wounded in the service of their country.

Application for the benefits must be made in the first place in writing to the **Secretary,** *Royal Scottish Corporation, 37 King Street, Covent Garden, London WC2E 8JS.* Every applicant must state his name, address, age and occupation, and the date of his entry into the Navy, Army or Air Force and the date and cause of his discharge therefrom, and must produce evidence of his qualification for the appointment.

QUEEN ADELAIDE NAVAL FUND

Guildford Cathedral Office
GUILDFORD
GU2 5UP

The objects of the Fund are the provision of help by financial grants to needy serving or retired Officers of the Royal Navy, Royal Marines, Women's Royal Naval Service and Queen Alexandra Royal Naval Nursing Service and of the Reserves of those forces and their spouses, former spouses, families and dependants.

Applications for help, preferably by letter, should be made to the Secretary at the above address.

THE MARINE SOCIETY

202 Lambeth Road, LONDON SE1 7JW
Tel: 020 7261 9535 Fax: 020 7401 2537
e-mail: enq@marine-society.org

THE MARINE SOCIETY was founded in 1756 to encourage poor men and boys to join the Royal Navy at the start of the Seven Years War. Today it is the oldest public maritime charity in the world. It is dedicated to the education, training, and well-being of professional British seafarers from all the sea services. It operates a 154 grt power-driven training ship ts Earl of Romney (formerly HMS Echo); provides tuition to Royal Navy personnel through the Forces Distance Learning Scheme; operates a free and impartial educational advice service; provides books and videos on loan or for sale at discount prices; offers financial assistance for vocational development and scholarships for academic studies in pursuit of professional goals.

For further information contact the Director or visit its website at **www.marine-society.org**

ARGYLL NAVAL FUND

Royal Highland and Agricultural Society of Scotland, Ingliston
NEWBRIDGE, Midlothian, EH28 8NF

Grants of up to £150 per annum may be made at the discretion of the Directors of the Royal Highland and Agricultural Society of Scotland, as Trustees of the above fund, to the parents or guardians of young men from the Highlands of Scotland or with Highland connections, who are successful in applying for Royal Naval Reserved Cadetships.

Application for a grant may be made to the Treasurer, after applying for a Royal Naval Reserved Cadetship. A grant will be conditional upon award of a Royal Naval Reserved Cadetship and will be entirely at the discretion of the Trustees.

KING WILLIAM IV NAVAL FOUNDATION.
Royal Naval Cottages, SOUTHWICK, Hants, PO17 6HE

Situated on the approach road to HMS DRYAD, the foundation comprises twelve cottages, for widows and orphan daughters, over the age of 40, of officers of the Royal Navy, Royal Marines and their Reserves. Lady residents are elected by the Governors as vacancies occur. Applicants, who must be in good health and capable of looking after themselves, should apply to the Resident Secretary at the above address.

THE ROYAL STAR AND GARTER HOME FOR DISABLED SAILORS, SOLDIERS AND AIRMEN
RICHMOND, Surrey, TW10 6RR
(Tel: 020 8940-3314)
REGISTERED CHARITY NO: 210119

The Royal Star and Garter Home was founded in 1916 as an independent charity to care for servicemen disabled in the Great War. Today the Home cares for up to 200 disabled ex-service men and women of all ranks and from all parts of the country, whose disability may be the result of active service, chronic illness or serious accident, providing the very best in medical and nursing care as well as being a **true** home in every sense of the word.

The Home also offers short term respite care or a period in the excellent rehabilitation unit which includes physiotherapy, hydrotherapy, speech and occupational therapy.

The Home urgently needs funds to maintain the high standards of care and facilities and to replace and update equipment. Please help us to continue this good work either by donation, or a covenant, or by a bequest in your will. All donations will be gratefully received by the Director of Fundraising, Patsy Willis, The Royal Star & Garter Home, Richmond, Surrey, TW10 6RR.

ERSKINE HOSPITAL

BISHOPTON, Renfrewshire PA7 5PU
(Tel: 0141 812 1100, Fax: 0141 812 3733
Web: www.erskine.org

For eight decades, through two World wars and the conflicts of the twentieth century, Erskine Hospital, a registered charity, has cared for more than 60,000 sailors, soldiers and airmen.

The Hospital is situated on the south bank of the River Clyde, near Bishopton in Renfrewshire and some 12 miles west of Glasgow.

As the foremost ex-Service care facility in the United Kingdom, it provides unique medical, nursing and residential and respite care for more than 500 men and women each year. Ex-Service personnel, who are war pensioners, and their families also enjoy independent living in 56 cottages within the Hospital grounds and the Erskine Workshops provide rewarding employment for those able to work. In addition there are two fully equipped holiday flats for couples (one to be ex-Service) available throughout the year for short holiday lets at modest cost.

Dignity, Privacy and respect are of paramount importance in delivering Eskine Care for both young and old ex-service personnel. As a registered charity (SC006609) outwith the NHS, Eskine needs more than £2 million in donations each year to continue its work.

In recent years, a strategic review determined that the old buildings no longer met modern care regulations and that there was no alternative but to rebuild. A £16 million 180-bed centre of nursing care excellence opening in July 2000 will replace the outdated original buildings in the estate close to the current location with a 30-bed unit a few miles away in the Erskine New Town. In addition, Erskine care will be taken to other areas of Scotland to enable ex-Service personnel to be cared for in a facility closer to their own community, family and friends. The first of these is scheduled to open in Edinburgh at the end of the year 2000.

Applications for admission and enquiries about all facilities should be addressed to the Admissions Coordinator and donations to the Director of Finance both at the above address.

THE SIR OSWALD STOLL FOUNDATION

446 Fulham Road, LONDON, SW6 1DT
(Tel. 020 7385 2110)

The Foundation consists of 138 flats, some designed for wheelchairs, with supporting services for disabled ex-servicemen and women.

For full particulars apply to the Housing Manager.

WILLIAM SIMPSON'S HOME
Main Street, Old Plean, STIRLING FK7 8BQ
(Tel: 01786 812421; Fax: 01786 815970

This Residential Home caters for the Social needs of men, irrespective of colour, creed, religion or age. It is situated in pleasant country surroundings between Stirling and Falkirk. The Home is registered with Central Regional Social Work Dept., and is subject to the Quality Assurance Inspection and Guidelines. Clients unable to meet the charges from their own resources will be able to apply for DSS and Social Work funding.

Applications for admission or for further particulars should be made to Miss J P A Lyon BA., Chief Executive, at above address.

LADY GROVER'S HOSPITAL FUND FOR OFFICERS' FAMILIES
48 Pall Mall, LONDON, SW1Y 5JY
(Tel. 020 7925 0539)

The object of the Fund is to help Officers defray expenses incurred by the illness of their dependants. Officer subscribers are NOT THEMSELVES eligible for benefit.

Membership is open to: Any Officer, male or female, of the three Services, who holds or has held a regular commission for a minimum of five years.

Membership is also open to: Widows or widowers of Officers, divorced wives or husbands of Officers, for their own benefit or that of their own children, and for descendant carers of Officers (all within certain criteria).

Annual Subscription: £30.00 per annum.

Grants: The amount of each grant is assessed on the basis of the actual expenses incurred with maximum rates as follows:-

Temporary Hospital or Nursing Home accommodation - up to £1,050.00 per week.

Temporary employment at home of a qualified nurse - up to £280.00 per week.

Convalescence away from home - up to £280.00 per week.

Temporary employment of a Home Help - up to £140.00 per week.

Ex gratia grants at the discretion of the Committee. The maximum period for which benefit is payable in a period of twelve months is eight weeks, except in the case of Home Help, when the maximum period is twelve weeks.

Applications for membership should be made to the Secretary at the above address.

THE ROYAL NAVAL AND ROYAL MARINES CHILDREN'S FUND

RN & RM Children's Fund, Swiftsure Block, HMS NELSON, Portsmouth, PO1 3HH. (Tel and Fax: 023 9281 7435)

This Fund was formed on 1st April 1999 from the former charities known as The RN & RM Children's Trust and The RN & RM Children's Home.

The object of the charity is the relief of Beneficiaries who are in need, hardship or distress. The Trustees may relieve Beneficiaries by:

a. Making grants of money to them.

b. Providing or paying for goods, services or facilities for them.

c. Making grants of money to other persons or bodies who provide goods, services or facilities to those in need.

Beneficiaries must be sons or daughters under the age of 25 of serving or former serving members of the Royal Navy, Royal Marines, Queen Alexandra's Royal Navy Nursing Service, the former Women's Royal Naval Service and the Reserves of those forces.

The majority of children are maintained at boarding schools, but some attend local schools. Subject to the financial circumstances of the family, fees and uniform expenses are met by the Trust.

Subscriptions, donations and applications should be addressed to *The Administrator at the above address.*

SAILORS' FAMILIES' SOCIETY

NEWLAND, Hull, HU6 7RJ (Tel: 01482-342331)

Patron: Her Majesty Queen Elizabeth The Queen Mother

The Society's work for seafarers' children throughout the British Isles extends to those who remain in the care of a widowed parent or other relations. Apart from financial assistance, the Seafarers' Families Support Scheme assists with gifts of clothing and the provision of holidays at seaside resorts.

As well as its work for children, the Society provides homes for elderly seafarers or their widows in Hull.

Enquiries and applications for help should be addressed to the Chief Executive, Graham J Powell.

ALEXANDRA HOUSE

(Royal United Services Short Stay Residence for Service Children)
6-8 Berthon Road, Bull Point, St. Budeaux, PLYMOUTH PL5 1EX
(Tel: 01752 365203)
Patron: H.R.H. Princess Alexandra, The Hon. Lady Ogilvy GCVO
President: Naval Base Commander, HM Naval Base Devonport

The Foundation (formerly at Newquay) has since 1839 looked after children of men and women in the Armed Services. Its short stay home is now established in a modern house to meet the immediate temporary need that arises when a family crisis occurs, such as injury to the father serving abroad, sudden departure of the mother to join him, and lack of relatives or friends to care for the children. The problem is met AT ONCE, at any hour of day or night, and the children are cared for, placed in schools and, by arrangement, given whatever special instruction, treatment or maintenance they need for up to three months, while family affairs are settled.

The House is run as a family home, not as an Institution, and the Housemother-in-Charge has long experience in schools, nursing and catering in UK. It is supported by voluntary contributions and by a modest scale of payments by the parents. Financial help can sometimes be given or lent by the Foundation.

Urgent and emergency inquiries should be made by telephone as above. Routine correspondence should be addressed to the Comptroller, Alexandra House.

Grants, covenants, donations and legacies are especially valuable to the Foundation as a Charity under current law, and an outline of the tax advantages to the donor or his estate may be obtained from the Comptroller.

It is hoped to occupy new and better premises in Autumn 2000. The telephone number will remain unchanged.

ROYAL CALEDONIAN SCHOOLS TRUST

80A High Street
BUSHEY, Herts WD2 3DE
(Tel/Fax: 020 8421 8845)
E-mail: RCST@caleybushey.demon.co.uk

The Royal Caledonian Schools Trust is able to consider applications from the children of Scottish Service men and women and from children of needy Scots currently resident in London. Grants have to be for educational purposes and range from school fees to book allowances. Enquiries should be made to the Chief Executive at the above address.

QUEEN VICTORIA SCHOOL

DUNBLANE, Perthshire FK15 OJY
Telephone:01786 822288 (Exchange)
0131-310-2901 (Direct Line to Headmaster's Secretary)
Fax No:0131-310-2926
Email address:enquiries@qvs.pkc.sch.uk
Web Address:www.qvs.pkc.sch.uk
Patron: HRH The Duke of Edinburgh KG, KT, OM, GBE

The School, which is set in 45 acres of beautiful Perthshire countryside, provides boarding school education for the children of Scottish servicemen and women and those who have served in Scotland. It is easily accessible by road, rail or air.

Quality education is provided at a low cost of £167 per term.

Pupils may be registered for entry from the age of seven and normally admitted to Primary 7 (i.e. age 10.5/11 years). Applications must reach the School by 31 December so that they may be considered for the Admissions Board which convenes in February. However, consideration will also be given, in particular circumstances, to applications made after these dates.

The School offers a wide curriculum following the Scottish educational system and includes courses at Standard and Higher grade as well as Certificate of Sixth Year Studies and SCOTVEC modules. Increasingly pupils move on to Higher and Further Education but career links with the Services remain strong. Pastoral care is afforded a very high priority along with careers guidance and personal and social education. In addition, there is a very full programme of sporting, cultural and spiritual development.

Queen Victoria School is a unique boarding school which seeks to achieve the best that is possible academically for all its pupils. The School prides itself also on developing the pupil in the widest possible sense and aims to achieve success academically, in sport, music, drama and many other extra-curricular areas. A very special and unique dimension of Queen Victoria

School is the ceremonial side which preserves the very best of the School's traditions.

For futher information write to theHeadmaster at the above address.

THE ROYAL SCHOOL, HASELMERE (formerly The Royal Naval School)
For girls aged between 4 and 18 Years
Farnham Lane, HASELMERE, Surrey GU27 1HQ
(TEL: 01428 605407)

One of the objects of the school, which was founded in 1840, is to provide a good education for the daughters and granddaughters of officers of the Royal Navy and Royal Marines. The daughters of officers of the Royal Naval Reserve, the former Royal Naval Volunteer Reserve, Royal Marines Reserve, the Women's Royal Naval Service, the Queen Alexandra's Royal Naval Nursing Service and others with naval connections may also be admitted. Daughters with connections to other of Her Majesty's Services and civilians are also admitted, but certain benefits are open to naval children only.

As at September 1999 the termly fees were: Boarders £3165- 4020 and Day Girls £1497-2562. Reduced fees are allowed as far as possible in cases of need, in particular for orphaned daughters of naval officers.

For entry into the school at LIV (Year 7) there is one foundation scholarship for 20% of tuition fees; two major academic scholarships of 30% of tuition fees; two exhibition scholarships of 15% of tuition fees as well as scholarships in Art, Music, Dance and Drama.

For further information contact the Admissions Registrar at the above address.

GREENWICH HOSPITAL
40, Queen Anne's Gate, London, SW1H 9AP
(Tel: 020 7396 0140/0150; Fax 020 7396 0149)Patron:
HRH The Duke of York

Greenwich Hospital is a Crown Charity founded in 1694 for the benefit of seafarers and their dependants. It is managed by the Admiralty Board, on behalf of the Secretary of State for Defence, who is the sole trustee. The following is a summary of the main benefits provided by Greenwich Hospital. Further information about the benefits and Greenwich Hospital's other activities may be obtained from the Director of Greenwich Hospital, D C R Heyhoe CB.

a) **The Royal Hospital School, Holbrook, Suffolk** (Headmaster N K D Ward BSc)

RHS is a thriving, independent HMC co-educational boarding school maintained by Greenwich Hospital primarily for the benefit of children or grandchildren of seafarers. The School is proud of its Royal connections and celebrates its naval heritage. Today there are some 700 pupils aged from 11 to 18 and entry is normally dependent on success in the school's entrance examination. Fees for serving members of the Royal Navy and Royal Marines are closely related to the level of parental contribution for those qualifying for the Services Boarding School Allowance. Fees for the children and grandchildren of ex-seafarers are assessed on the parents' ability to pay. This can allow for a continuity of education when parents leave the Services which might not otherwise be possible.

The School offers a wide curriculum to A level and has excellent modern teaching, boarding and recreational facilities on a 200-acre site overlooking the River Stour.

b) **Education grants**. Grants are available towards the maintenance and education of the children of deceased or distressed officers and ratings of the Royal Navy and Royal Marines and of members of their Reserve Forces who died in service.

c) **Officers' pensions**. These are means-tested pensions which may be awarded to retired permanent officers of the Royal Navy and Royal Marines in cases of need.

d) **Special pensions**. These are means-tested pensions for certain seamen and marines who are in poor health or otherwise unable to support themselves.

e) **Widows' pensions**. These are means-tested pensions for the widows of seamen and marines, and are normally restricted to widows over 65 years of men who gave long service, or who died in service or who were invalided.

f) **Jellicoe Annuities**. These annuities, funded by Greenwich Hospital, are paid by the Royal Naval Benevolent Trust to ratings and ratings' widows who are ineligible for the pensions outlined above. Further details may be obtained from; the Secretary of RNBT, 311 Twyford Avenue, Portsmouth, Hampshire PO2 8PE (Tel 023 9269 0112)

THE ROYAL NAVAL AND ROYAL MARINES DEPENDANTS' FUND

RNDF, Centurion Building, Grange Road, GOSPORT
Hants, PO13 9XA
(Tel. 023 9270 2101)

Objects: To make an immediate and substantial grant to the widow, widower or dependant of RN, RM and QARNNS personnel, who die while serving, on the active list/on regular engagements. Subscriptions: £1.80 per year payable in advance on 1st August. Subscriptions are deducted from service pay.

Further information may be obtained from BR 8588, UPOs or from the Secretary at the above address.

THE ASSOCIATION OF ROYAL NAVY OFFICERS
70 Portchester Terrace, Bayswater,
LONDON, W2 3TP

Aims: To provide all possible and speedy help to members, their wives and dependants who may be in financial or other distress.

To give financial assistance in the form of grants where there is essential expenditure beyond the member's means, and bursaries to enable children to continue their planned education where there has been a change in circumstances. To offer financial assistance to members themselves towards further education and re-training after they have left the Service.

To assist members, their wives and dependants by arranging medical, legal and financial consultations.

To keep members in touch with one another socially, and to keep the Secretary informed in cases where fellow members, their widows and dependants are in distress of any kind.

Membership: Open to serving and retired Commissioned Officers of the RN, RM, QARNNS, WRNS and their respective Reserves. Widows and Widowers of members become Honorary Members without the need to subscribe.

Subscription: £10 per annum. Life Membership £150.

Full information can be obtained from the Secretary. Tel: 020 7402 5231, Fax: 020 7402 5533.

ASSOCIATION OF WRENS
8 Hatherley Street, LONDON, SW1P 2YY
(Tel: 020 7932 0111)
Patron: HRH The Princess Royal

The Association, founded in 1920 (celebrating its 80th Anniversary in 2000), is open to all ex-members of the WRNS, WRNR, WRNVR, QARNNS, former Naval VADs, Commonwealth and South African Women's Naval Services and serving female members of the Royal Navy. The aim of the Association is to perpetuate comradeship by bringing together the greatest possible number of Wrens and Ex-Wrens at home and overseas and to help former members of the said services by bringing to the notice of Service charities persons who are in conditions of need, hardship or distress.

Applications for membership should be made to the Secretary at the above address.

ROYAL UNITED SERVICES INSTITUTE FOR DEFENCE STUDIES

Whitehall, LONDON SW1A 2ET
(Tel: 020 7930 5854 Fax: 020 7321 0943)
e-mail: defence@rusids.demon.co.uk. Web site: www.rusi.org

An independent centre free of political ties, the RUSI is the professional association of the armed forces. It is dedicated to the study, and debate of issues affecting defence, technology, the military sciences and regional and international security. The RUSI arranges lectures, conferences, public and private seminars and has a wide range of publications. When in London members may have access to the reading room and library and are able to attend the Institute's programme of events.

Subscriptions Rates: Basic Membership £48.00. (Receipt of Journal, use of library and attendance at lectures). Members may choose from a wide range of publications and membership options to suit their needs.

For further information please contact the Membership Secretary.

ROYAL NAVAL LAY READERS' SOCIETY

Royal Naval Lay Readers' Society, Room 203, Victory Building,
HM Naval Base, Portsmouth, Hants PO1 3LS.
(Tel: 023 9272 7902. Fax Number: 023 9272 7112)

Licensed Readers assist in the work of the Anglican Church amongst men and women of the Royal Navy and their families. In ships at sea and in naval establishments ashore, they work alongside Naval Chaplains in the furtherance of the Christian Faith and the welfare of the Navy's people.

The Society is dependent financially on voluntary contributions for the maintenance of its work.

Subscriptions and donations may be sent to the Treasurer at the above address

THE WHITE ENSIGN ASSOCIATION LIMITED
(President Captain Sir Donald Gosling, RNR)
(Chairman Admiral Sir Michael Bett CBE)
HMS BELFAST, Tooley Street, London SE1 2JH.
(Tel: 020 7407 8658, MOD Main Building 81945, FAX: 020 7357 6298)

The White Ensign Association formed in 1958 with Admiralty Board endorsement is a registered charity. The activities of the Association are supervised by a Council of Management, representing a distinguished body drawn from the City of London, Commerce, Industry and the Royal Navy.

Its functions are to provide independent and unbiased help on all matters of personal finance including investment and financial planning for resettlement. Also to give assistance on all matters of civilian employment including job search.

This is available to all serving and retired officers, men and women of the Royal Navy, Royal Marines, QARNNS or any of the Naval Services and their respective Reserves. It is also available to dependants of natural beneficiaries.

The White Ensign Association maintains links with the City of London, Industry and Commerce through its White Ensign Association Membership Scheme.

Enquiries to: Captain D G Wixon Royal Navy, Chief Executive, The White Ensign Association Ltd., HMS BELFAST, Tooley Street, London SE1 2JH. Tel: 020 7407 8658, MOD Main Building 81945, FAX: 020 7357 6298

THE QARNNS ASSOCIATION
2 Longwater Drive, Alverstoke, GOSPORT, Hants PO12 2UP.

Objects: The objects of the Association shall be to further the efficiency of the Queen Alexandra's Royal Naval Nursing Service for the public benefit by fostering esprit de corps amongst its members and by providing relief for past and present members and their dependants who are in conditions of need, hardship and distress.

Administration: President: A senior retired Matron-in-Chief QARNNS is invited to assume the office of President and she is given Honorary Life Membership of the Association: The Committee of the Association consists of eight Association members, the Matron-in-Chief, QARNNS, four members elected by members of the Association, and ex-officio officers appointed by the Committee to act as Chairman, Secretary and Treasurer. The organisation of subsidiary Branches will follow the same general pattern as that of the Main Association.

Membership: Open to all serving and former Nursing Officers, QARNNS and QARNNS(R)

Subscriptions: £5.00 Payable annually on 1st January.
Further information can be obtained from the Secretary, Lieutenant Commander S. Clements ARRC, at the above address.

FLEET AIR ARM OFFICERS' ASSOCIATION
FAAOA, 4 St. James' Square, LONDON SW1Y 4JU.

Full Membership is open to all Officers (Male and Female) of all Specialisations who are serving, or have served, in the Fleet Air Arm or the Royal Naval Air Service. Officers of all other UK armed services who have had, or still have, connections with the Fleet Air Arm are also eligible to join. Associate Membership is available to such persons, including Officers of foreign armed services, who are, or were, attached to, or had a close connection with, the Fleet Air Arm.

The Association originally came into being in 1957 and is a means of keeping in touch, not only for all former Naval aviators but also for serving officers. The name of the Association was given official Admiralty approval and there are now almost 3,000 members representing the entire spectrum of naval aviation from the early days of the RNAS to the present day.

The Fleet Air Arm Officers' Association exists as a focal point for all who are professionally and socially bound together by their common interest and vocation in Naval Aviation. It provides a link of friendship between the serving and the retired, the young and the old, not provided in any other form.

We keep a keen interest in Naval Air Power and can advise at high level if their is any sign of degradation or denigration to our national defence interests.

Considerable sums have been regularly donated to both Service and Maritime Charities, including the FAA Benevolent Trust, the FAA Museum, St. Bartholomew's Church, Yeovilton, the RNLI and other smaller Charities. The Association also has a substantial involvement with youth training and development such as the Sail Training Association and the Ocean Youth Club. The FAAOA Aviation Scholarship Trust, Registered Charity No. 298817, was established in 1986 to fund the Association Gliding Scholarship Scheme, which provides gliding courses for young people between 16 and 20 years of age who have a wish to join the RN as a career.

The annual subscription entitles members to receive a "FLY NAVY" Journal issued annually, News Sheets twice yearly and a Membership Book every three years. Local First of the Month Meetings are held and Association representatives can be found all over the world.

For Further information apply to the Admin. Director,

THE MISSIONS TO SEAMEN

ST. Michael Paternoster Royal, College Hill, LONDON EC4R 2RL
(Tel: 020 7248 5202 ; Fax: 020 7248 4761)
Welfare officer: Canon Ken Peters

The Missions to Seamen is a voluntary society of the Anglican Church which cares for the welfare of navy and merchant navy seafarers of all races and creeds in over 300 ports worldwide.

Working through an international network of chaplains and staff, it makes some 90,000 ship visits a year to offer friendship, practical and spiritual support, and help in emergencies.

BRITISH LIMBLESS EX-SERVICE MEN'S ASSOCIATION (BLESMA)

Frankland Moore House,
185-187 High Road,
Chadwell Heath,
Romford,
Essex RM6 6NA
Telephone: ***020 8590 1124*** ***Fax:*** **020 8599 2932**
e-mail: blemsa@btconnect.com
Patron: HRH PRINCES ALICE, Duchess of Gloucester
General Secretary R R Holland MBE, BEM, MBIM

BLESMA is a national charity catering specifically for Serving and Ex-Service limbless men and women. The Association also accepts responsibility for the dependants of its Membership and in particular their widows.

The objects of the Association are to promote the welfare of all those of either sex who have lost a limb or limbs or one or both eyes as a result of Service in any branch of Her Majesty's Forces or Auxiliary Forces and to assist their dependants.

The Association:

a) Through its Branches spread over the country, operates a Welfare Visiting Service to its Members and Widows.

b) Provides permanent residential and convalescent holiday accommodation through its two Nursing and Residential care homes at Blackpool and Crieff in Perthshire.

c) Provides a counselling service to individuals pre and post amputation.

d) Furnishes advice on pensions, allowances and, where necessary, represents

Members and their dependants at Pension Appeal Tribunals.

e) Provides financial assistance to Members and Widows in the form of grants.

f) Plans and organises rehabilitation programmes for amputees.

g) Assists in finding suitable employment for amputees.

h) Provides limited funding for research and development into artificial limbs and in the training of Prosthetists and Orthotists.

i) Acts as Consumer Watchdog in respect of the provision of artificial limbs, wheelchairs and appliances.

NAUTICAL INSTITUTE
202 Lambeth Road, LONDON SE1 7LQ or phone 020 7928-1351.

The Nautical Institute is an independent professional body for qualified mariners which is directed by a Council of whom the majority must be actively employed at sea. The Institute is recognised as an authoritative body for consultation on matters concerning the Nautical Profession; its aims are to encourage high standards of competence and knowledge and facilitate the exchange and publication of information. The Institute publishes a monthly journal.

Further details may be obtained from The Secretary, The Nautical Institute at the above address.

NAVY RECORDS SOCIETY
Department of War Studies, Kings College, LONDON WC2R 2LS.

This Society was founded to combine the practical interests of the service with the academic rigour of historians in a mutually beneficial synthesis. Since then it has published over one hundred and forty volumes dealing with all aspects of naval service over the last five hundred years. Recent volumes have covered the careers of Admirals Beatty, Cunningham and Somerville, together with the Battle of the Atlantic, Signals Intelligence and the development of shipboard organisation. Forthcoming volumes address the development of the submarine service, Henry VIII's Navy and a variety of 20th century subjects.

The Annual Subscription is £30.00, which entitles members to receive copies of all volumes published in that year, on average one or two appear each year, and to purchase copies of volumes already in print at special rates.

Those interested are invited to apply to the Hon. Secretary, Professor A. D. Lambert at the above address.